Controllership

SUBSCRIPTION NOTICE

This Wiley product is updated on a periodic basis with supplements to reflect important changes in the subject matter. If you purchased this product directly from John Wiley & Sons, Inc., we have already recorded your subscription for this update service.

If, however, you purchased this product from a bookstore and wish to receive (1) the current update at no additional charge, and (2) future updates and revised or related volumes billed separately with a 30-day examination review, please send your name, company name (if applicable), address, and the title of the product to:

Supplement Department
John Wiley & Sons, Inc.
One Wiley Drive
Somerset, NJ 08875
1-800-225-5945

For customers outside the United States, please contact the Wiley office nearest you:

Professional & Reference Division
John Wiley & Sons Canada, Ltd.
22 Worcester Road
Rexdale, Ontario M9W 1L1
CANADA
(416) 675-3580
1-800-567-4797
FAX (416) 675-6599

John Wiley & Sons, Ltd.
Baffins Lane
Chichester
West Sussex, PO19 1UD
UNITED KINGDOM
(44) (243) 779777

Jacaranda Wiley Ltd.
PRT Division
P.O. Box 174
North Ryde, NSW 2113
AUSTRALIA
(02) 805-1100
FAX (02) 805-1597

John Wiley & Sons (SEA) Pte. Ltd.
37 Jalan Pemimpin
Block B #05-04
Union Industrial Building
SINGAPORE 2057
(65) 258-1157

Controllership
The Work of the Managerial Accountant

Fifth Edition

JAMES D. WILLSON

Senior Vice-President-Finance (Retired)
Northrop Corporation

JANICE M. ROEHL-ANDERSON

Principal
Ernst & Young LLP, Denver, CO

STEVEN M. BRAGG

Director of Finance and Administration
Isolation Technologies

JOHN WILEY & SONS, INC.
New York • Chichester • Brisbane • Toronto • Singapore

Copyright © 1995 by John Wiley & Sons, Inc.

Library of Congress Cataloging-in-Publication Data:
Willson, James D.
    Controllership, the work of the managerial accountant / James D. Willson,
    Janice M. Roehl-Anderson, Steven M. Bragg — 5th ed.
            p.   cm.
    Rev. ed. of: Controllership, the work of the managerial
    accountant. 4th ed. 1990.
        Includes index.
        ISBN 0-471-11735-8 (cloth : alk. paper)
        1. Controllership. 2. Managerial accounting.   I. Roehl-Anderson,
    Janice M.   II. Bragg, Steven M.   III. Willson, James D.
    Controllership, the work of the managerial accountant. IV. Title.
        HG4026.H43   1995
        658.15′ 11—dc20   95-20426

Printed in the United States of America

10 9 8 7 6 5 4 3 2 1

PREFACE

During the last 40 plus years (i.e., the time when the first edition of *Controllership* was published in 1952 until now) there has been a significant transformation in the role of the controller. In the 1950s, the controller was the person who was primarily concerned with the proper recording of financial transactions and the preparation of publicly issued financial statements. Now, the controller must be a skilled business executive who knows how financial data should be employed in the management of the business, and who communicates relevant financial information to other executives in a format that they can understand and use in making business decisions in their area of expertise.

This evolution in the role of the controller—and indeed in the perception of the financial function—came about as a result of many influences. One of these was the pressure from demanding CEOs who expected timely and creative solutions to financial problems. Another was the growth of a large body of financial executives who were familiar with the emerging numerous, sophisticated, and complex financial and statistical techniques that could be advantageously employed in the business. Other factors included the increased competition from local and international businesses, new products, and the trend to globalization with its risks and opportunities. Yet another influence was the need for knowledgeable financial executives who, as skilled communicators, properly and honestly interpreted business trends and relationships, and financial prospects, with the expectation of securing needed funds from the public or from knowledgeable commercial sources or investment bankers.

Additionally, the timely and economical application of this financial knowledge and methodology in the new environment was assisted by the increased use of the computer and the related technologies.

To provide information in a logical manner about the controllership function, this volume is divided into seven parts:

- Part I   The Broad Management Aspects of Controllership

This segment provides basic background on the controllership function. It ranges from subjects such as the relationship of accounting and management to a brief review of accounting principles and the rule makers. It further discusses the importance of the internal audit function and internal controls, and important trends and relationships that need to be planned and monitored.

Part I also reviews, among many other topics, the importance of proper costing practices, and the impact of globalization on the duties of the controller.

Finally, because the controller can be, perhaps should be, a key executive in the interpretation of financial data to the financial community, the role of investor relations is discussed.

- Part II   The Planning Function of Controllership

This key segment explains the role of the controller in the financial planning function. It discusses strategic planning, the long-term financial plan, and the annual business plan, together with related supporting analysis. Before effective financial controls and measures are put in place, the overall basic plans first must be developed.

- Part III   Planning and Controlling Operations

This section reviews how detailed departmental plans, which serve as the foundation for the overall plan, and the control techniques, are developed—the latter to assist the cognizant executive in attaining the plan performance for those *operations* under his or her supervision. Included in this review is the impact of the newer manufacturing technologies.

While traditional, and necessary, financial measures or controls are discussed, the need for *nonfinancial* controls or standards are reviewed, including subjects such as cycle time for developing new products, measurement of on-time product deliveries, and overall manufacturing cycle time. Further, the important subject of benchmarking is reviewed.

- Part IV   Planning and Accounting Control of Assets, Liabilities, and Equity Interests

When financial planning in a business was first introduced, emphasis often was placed solely on operations. Then, as management recognized the need to plan and attain certain rates of return on assets and equity interests, and to control levels of indebtedness, planning expanded to the balance sheet.

Among other topics, this section discusses how computer technology may impact and assist in the planning and control of the level of various assets.

- Part V   Financial and Related Reports

This section begins with a discussion of the current need to greatly improve external financial reporting to provide adequate disclosure, and permit more meaningful comparisons between companies and industries. Areas of apparent weakness are highlighted.

This review is then followed by comments about most areas of financial (and closely related) matters and other reporting which is largely the responsibility of the controller. Emphasis is placed on external financial reporting as well as the content of relevant and effective internal management reports.

- Part VI   Computer Systems and Related Technology

Although *Controllership, Fourth Edition,* published in 1990, reviewed some of the basic aspects of computer use in business, the improvements in hardware and software have been unrelenting in the past five years. The rapidly changing technological aspects in financial information systems have been reviewed in the cumulative supplements.

But more recent subjects have been added in this edition, and older subject matter has been updated. Although the controller may not be in charge of financial information systems implementations, especially if the company has the position of chief information officer, certainly he or she should be informed about the function in general, and the new developments in particular. Some of the more recent relevant developments are discussed in chapters on groupware, electronic data interchange, and client/server computing. Additionally, this section contains an overview of organizational change management issues, which affect all change initiatives.

- Part VII   Some Administrative and Special Aspects of the Controller's Department

Finally, Part VII reviews some topics with which the controller will be directly concerned and usually involved, including financial planning and analysis for acquisitions and mergers, reengineering, closing procedures, and tax records and procedures. In other instances, he or she may not have direct responsibility, but should be aware of major developments and requirements as to records and procedures, for example, insurance exposures and coverages, manuals, and record retention.

We have attempted to include in this volume *practical* commentary on the various aspects of controllership. Given the growth in complexity and the rapid changes taking place in the many functions, we have secured assistance from a number of knowledgeable practitioners and writers in the relevant fields of endeavor. These contributing authors are identified in the Acknowledgments section.

Any ideas expressed herein are those of the authors and not necessarily of the entities with which they have been or are related.

JAMES D. WILLSON
JANICE M. ROEHL-ANDERSON
STEVEN M. BRAGG

Los Angeles, California
Denver, Colorado
August 1995

ACKNOWLEDGMENTS

With the rapidly changing business environment, it was essential that the material contained in this volume be accurate, up-to-date, and relevant. Accordingly, in addition to the chapters written or revised by the three co-authors, these contributing authors, listed alphabetically, wrote or revised the chapters indicated:

David M. Bassett, Senior Consultant
Ernst & Young LLP, Denver Office
> Chapter 41 (updated), Role of the Computer in Accounting and Financial Analysis
> Chapter 42, Computer Hardware Trends
> Chapter 43, Introduction to Client/Server Computing

Sandra Borchardt, Senior Manager
Ernst & Young LLP, Boston Office
> Chapter 44, Automated Financial Accounting Systems
> Chapter 46, Software Package Integration

Melissa W. Breeze, Manager
Ernst & Young LLP, Denver Office
> Chapter 48, Graphics in Business

Martin D. Gold, Senior Manager
Ernst & Young LLP, Denver Office
> Chapter 18, Tax Planning: A Strategic Analysis
> Chapter 59 (updated), Tax Records and Procedures

Hans Hultgren, President
Integrated Systems Group, Denver
> Chapter 49, Groupware

Sara Moulton, Senior Manager
Ernst & Young LLP, Denver Office
> Chapter 52, Change Management

Terry M. Palmer, Partner
Ernst & Young LLP, Denver Office

> Chapter 39 (updated), Interface with the SEC: Reports to Governmental
> Agencies and Stock Exchanges

Jeffrey L. Sturrock, Account Executive
Texas Instruments, Dallas

> Chapter 47, Electronic Data Interchange (EDI)

Jan Roehl-Anderson would like to thank God for His unending blessings. In addition, she would like to thank Nelma Mannes for her outstanding administrative skills and June Moyer for her superb editing talents, which they have demonstrated in preparing this edition. Additionally, and most important, thanks should be given to Fritz Anderson for his unending patience and moral support.

We are indebted to the Wiley editorial and production staff, especially our editor, Sheck Cho, for their assistance in guiding this new edition through the publishing process. We would also like to thank Nancy Marcus Land of Publications Development Company of Texas for her outstanding editing services.

CONTENTS

PART ONE

THE BROAD MANAGEMENT
ASPECTS OF CONTROLLERSHIP

CHAPTER 1

Accounting and Its Relation to Management

1-1 THE BUSINESS OBJECTIVE

The objective of business under the competitive "private enterprise" American economy has been characterized as the earning of maximum profit consistent with the longer-term growth of the company. In a broader sense, a business organization is an economic institution. It is created principally to provide the public with those goods or services that are needed or desired and are compatible with the social attitudes of the nation. In the eyes of the customers there is no reason for the existence of the business except the service it renders. If this service objective is not attained, then the organization ultimately will wither away and die.

There usually exist other collateral objectives that have social implications. For example, employers may seek to provide employees with the best possible working conditions or job security, consistent with the longer-term well-being of the business; or management may seek for itself the highest possible remuneration for guiding the business; or employees may attempt to secure the highest possible wages. But any such objectives are still dependent on and successfully supported only by effectively meeting the principal business objective—the satisfaction of customer needs or desires.

1-2 THE MANAGEMENT TASK

If the business objective is known, then the question arises about what function management is expected to perform in reaching the goal. It is the task of management to determine the needs and desires of consumers for goods and services, to assemble and organize the agencies of production and distribution for the satisfaction of these desires, and to direct and coordinate these agencies efficiently. This is no easy assignment. Success does not just happen. The exact goal must be intelligently conceived, and the method of accomplishment must be planned and properly executed. Moreover, this task is continuous. Needs and desires are changing constantly; new products and services that will add to the consumers' well-being and enjoyment must be continuously developed and perfected; new agencies of research, production, and distribution must be developed to accomplish the desired results most efficiently.

1-3 AN ENLIGHTENED PHILOSOPHY OF MANAGEMENT

The philosophy and the practice of business management are being subjected to a most critical analysis, an analysis directed to both the scientific aspect of business practice and the ethical basis on which such practice rests. Business management is presently contemplated both as a productive enterprise and as a social trust. Much study is being directed to an understanding of the responsibility of the business executive; it is recognized that business executives have become a most important "agency" in the guidance of our economic activity. If the march of industrial progress is to continue uninterrupted, business leaders must be skillful, intelligent, and motivated by a social responsibility. Unless they possess these qualities, there are serious questions about whether our present economic institutions can be maintained.

1-4 COMPLEXITIES OF MANAGEMENT GREATLY INCREASED

Our economic structure is tremendously complex, and its complexities continue to increase. A manager taking command of a modern business craft must direct its course through social and political currents, the courses of which are constantly changing and increasing in swiftness. The economic storms appear to be no less severe. The manager's own craft is one of extremely sensitive direction and technical complexity. The instruments of direction and control are vastly improved, and the personnel at this executive's command are more highly skilled. The seas are somewhat better charted, but the commander still has the responsibility of selecting the course, equipping the vessel, and organizing the crew, coordinating and inspiring its effort to see the voyage through. If the manager lacks skill, disaster is certain. If the manager possesses skill but is motivated only by selfish ends, he or she will become an economic pirate and a menace to all legitimate commerce. Only as the ranks of business leaders are freed of both the unskilled and the greedy can the ships of commerce make their full speed toward the ports of economic well-being.

1-5 MANAGERIAL SKILL ESSENTIAL

A management job well done involves the application of sound management principles carried out by competent and experienced personnel. Sound management principles encompass many factors relating to all leadership activity from initial planning to attainment of the goal. It involves such action as establishing both short- and long-range plans; defining specific corporate objectives; developing basic policies; building a sound organizational structure, including the establishment of definite lines of authority and responsibility; setting performance standards; creating and maintaining good communication methods and channels within the company; measuring performance; and maintaining proper human relations with employees, shareholders, the public, and customers.

There must be continuous refinement in the science of management—more intelligent planning, better coordination and facilitation, more effective direction and control of effort, more accurate measurement of and reward for performance, and greater security for workers and investors. Wastefulness and inefficiency of management are no more to be condoned than greed. In brief, there must be a high degree of managerial skill and intelligence as well as honesty of purpose. What role can and should accounting play in developing or maintaining an effective effort?

1-6 ACCOUNTING AS AN AID TO MANAGEMENT

One of the chief aids to management in making its efforts fully productive is modern accounting. It is to the chief accounting officer, the controller, more than to any other official, that the business executive often must turn for guidance in the direction, control, and protection of the business. To extend the maritime analogy, the controller is not the commander of the ship—that is the task of the chief executive—but he or she may be likened to the navigator, the one who keeps the charts. The controller must keep the commander informed about how far the company has come, where it is, what speed it is making, resistance encountered, variations from the course, dangerous reefs that lie ahead, and where the charts indicate he should go next to reach the port in safety.

There is no place for the rabbit's-foot executive in business. The successful manager must know and use the instruments of guidance and control at his command. The use of modern accounting and statistical data is the means by which the business executive is able to plan, direct, and control operations that reach beyond the range of his or her own personal observation and supervision. There is no question that the executive who is best informed about the company's operations is in the best position to take those positive actions that help to manage the business profitably.

(a) BUSINESS AND NATIONAL ECONOMIC GOALS

The predominant view of this book is that as seen from within the business. Businesses operate in a complex and changing economic, political, and social environment. Whereas national issues involving the environment will not be dealt with per se, the successful business manager must bring to the task a realization that the essential purpose or mission of the business enterprise, and the means of accomplishing this objective, must be consistent with the social and economic goals of the society of which the business is a part. For this reason, mention is made of some of the national goals and factors to be monitored to provide the necessary breadth of view in carrying out the controllership function.

The basic purposes of an economic system, applied to our "mixed economy" in the United States, may be said to include these specific national goals:

1. The preservation of our economic system in competition against other systems or ideologies existent in the world.
2. An increasingly higher standard of living with respect to goods and services, including both public and private sectors.
3. A high rate of employment to maximize the utilization of human resources.
4. Free and unfettered competition, subject, however, to such constraints as may be necessary to preserve the effectiveness of the economy.
5. A suitably high and continuous rate of economic growth.
6. The maintenance of fiscal soundness.
7. Minimizing of cyclical fluctuations in economic activity.

The proper integration of these national goals, or whatever other national goals might come to be, will require an improved understanding and the provision of required information for monitoring such matters as (not necessarily in order of importance) those listed here:

1. The impact of monetary and fiscal policy.
2. The world political and economic status.
3. The role of labor, capital, technological change, and management in fostering economic growth.
4. The nature and function of profits.
5. The interaction of costs and prices.
6. The nature, function, and strategy of competition.
7. The interacting role of governments, labor, and business.
8. The direction and degree of technological and social change.

In the broadest sense, the successful financial or accounting executive must be aware of the information needs in these areas to properly integrate relevant data into the financial reports.

(b) THE MANAGEMENT PROCESS

A good accounting system must recognize the elements of the management process if it is to assist in effective communication. This overview may prove helpful.

The work of a professional business manager may be segregated into four distinct functions or grouping of activities:

1. Planning.
2. Organizing (including proper staffing).

3. Directing.

4. Measuring.

These operations are interrelated and are not necessarily completely separated in time sequence. They are part of the whole process of managing, and in a practical working environment cannot be clearly separated from each other, any more than the stem of a plant may be separated from the leaves and roots and still grow. But classification helps us understand the more complete whole. Comments on each function follow.

Planning, in its simplest form, might be described as determining what to do, when to do it, and how to do it. Yet it involves a great many assumptions. This definition of planning might be expanded thus: *Planning is a continuous process of determining the events and activities essential to the attainment of stated goals.* Thus certain factors are necessary:

1. The goal, or desired state of affairs, some time in the future.

2. A recognition or belief that the desired goal is reasonably attainable in the light of probable external future conditions, i.e., the economic-political-social environment expected to exist.

3. A belief that the goal is within the available resources of the business.

4. The conviction that it is possible to direct or organize or implement future actions designed to achieve the objectives (or avoid conditions that would preclude achievement).

5. An understanding or recognition that the continual change, and development of unexpected conditions, will require a continual reappraisal of goals, constraints, resources, opportunities, and action plans.

Recognition of the continuous nature of planning will assist in providing the necessary flexibility in a good financial information system.

Organizing may be simply defined as securing the necessary personnel, facilities, equipment, and material. But in a broader sense, reflection will lead to the conclusion that organizing is fundamentally one of establishing basic relationships of one person to another and, of course, to the organization as a whole. An *organization* has been defined as a system of consciously coordinated activities, relationships, and responsibilities of people. In this, the business manager is the instrument for establishing and maintaining a changing or dynamic system of activities and relationships to permit the optimum utilization of talents, or skills, and resources to achieve the business objectives.

Hence the information system ought to recognize these concepts as common characteristics of an effective organization:

1. A desire or willingness to achieve a common objective that the individuals alone cannot attain.

2. The segregation or classification of the elements of the total task according to knowledge, skill, and equipment or facilities needed.

3. The assignment of responsibility of completing the task to individuals or groups.

4. The coordination of the personnel, resources, equipment, schedules, and procedures in such a way that the parts fit together smoothly, efficiently, economically.

5. The recognition of the concept of change in managing the organization.

Thus the optimum utilization of the business resources requires adequate channels and systems of communication—and continual adjustment to change.

The third basic management process, *directing,* relates to the effecting or functioning or carrying out of the activities of the organization—the doing. Whereas organizing provided the framework, the directing carries out the function. This directing involves the efficient and purposeful integration of the relationships in achieving the business task. Sometimes this function is described as "integrating," or forming into a whole, or coordinating behavior with the environment. It involves accomplishment under time and usually cost limitations.

It can be seen that directing, and integration, call for a system of communication throughout the organization—formal and informal, laterally, and upward and downward.

The last business management function has been described as *measurement.* Often this is thought of as "control," or "evaluation." In its broadest context, this activity has to do with the measurement of the efficiency or effectiveness in the movement of the material and human and financial resources toward an objective. In involves the comparison with a standard of some sort, whether it be quantity, quality, time, or value. And it implicitly involves taking necessary action where off-target conditions exist; otherwise, why measure at all? In summary, the whole process of measurement would involve these steps:

1. Establishing objectives in the light of opportunities or expected conditions.

2. Establishing a system of measure. This involves determining what to measure as well as how to measure it, and the development of an integrated system.

3. Developing selected or specific measures for each task. For example, it might be one machine hour per price of X, or a growth rate of 15% per year in sales, or one year to bring a new product to market.

4. Measurement and interpretation of actual results against the standard or objective.

Because human motivation is so basic, and because future growth or effectiveness of the business depends on how an individual is measured, this step is crucial.

5. Finally, with intelligent interpretation, taking necessary corrective action—either to get "on course" or to change an improper standard.

This measurement, of course, can apply at every people level in the company—from worker to president, indeed to total management itself. Furthermore, measurement must be considered against not merely short-term results but also long-term goals. In summary, this whole management process may be graphically depicted in Figure 1-1.

In each step of the management process, the cognizant management official or managers should be seeking continuous improvement (also called total quality management (TQM), or sometimes reengineering). (See Chapters 19 and 54.)

Figure 1-1   The Management Process.

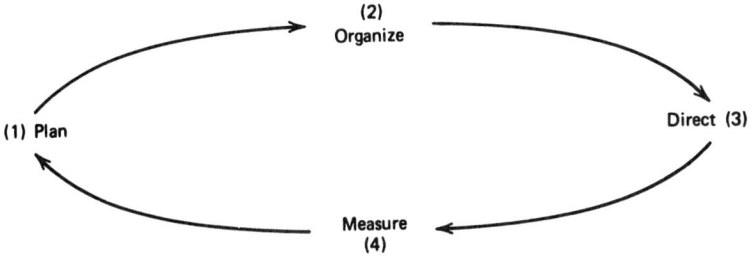

(c) MEASURING BUSINESS MANAGEMENT

Knowing that a business must be measured, a question might arise: "Measured in the eyes of whom, or by what criteria?" Also, since business management may be one of several echelons, the matter of measuring each level of responsibility should be considered. Although this latter phase is reviewed in a later chapter, since we are considering business management as a whole, it might be well to pose the question: "In a private enterprise economy such as exists in the United States, how should the overall effectiveness of business management be measured?" And business management itself ought to consider how it should be judged, and, indeed, how it ought to judge itself.

There are many measures of an enterprise, but a fourfold classification, and some specific units of measurement for each, is suggested as background in the development of a management information system:

1. *Measures of Profitability*
    a. Percent return on net sales.
    b. Percent return on assets (or capital in the economic sense).
    c. Percent return on owner equity.
    d. Percent return on capitalization (equity, plus long-term debt).
2. *Measures of Growth*
    a. Percent increase in net sales.
    b. Percent increase in aggregate net profit.
    c. Percent increase in earnings per share.
3. *Cash Flow Measures*
    a. Cash flow sufficiency.
    b. Cash flow efficiency.
4. *Other Measures*
    a. Sales per employee.
    b. Productivity—units of production per employee hour, etc.
    c. Community image.
    d. Image as seen by the employees.
    e. Share of market.

Each of these measures has value. But, finally, the consideration in developing a financial information system might be the attitude of the chief executive in terms of what he or she thinks are important criteria.

These measures ordinarily would relate to the entire business, but they can apply also to major segments, such as a division or profit center. Other yardsticks, many of a more detailed nature, may be used to gauge the effectiveness of specific or detailed functions or activities or conditions. These are reviewed in the appropriate chapter.

1-7 IDENTIFYING WEAKNESSES IN ACCOUNTING PRESENTATIONS

Most experienced controllers, and especially those who possess a professional background in public accounting, are personally aware of poor applications in the presentations and use of accounting data in the management of a business. It was often commonplace in some companies for financial data to be presented:

- In excessive detail.
- In accounting terminology versus that of the user.
- Too late to be useful.
- With inexcusable errors.
- With segregations or break-outs not germane to the problem.

In fact, one of the reasons for the publication of the first edition of *Controllership* in 1952 was to encourage a more intelligent presentation and use of accounting information.

There have been vast improvements in procedures, but there is much more to be done. In the 1990s, we are entering an era in which both the public accounting profession, and those in industry who guide management accounting, are faced with an important challenge in strengthening public confidence in, and business management regard for, the effectiveness of the accounting discipline. (See the Selected References.)

1-8 FORCES OF CHANGE

In this period of self-appraisal, pressures are converging to force changes in the nature of accounting information used or available for decision making. Some of these influences, in addition to the always present impact of government actions (such as taxes and other regulatory changes), are:

1. *External-Technological*
   a. *Computerization.* Much of the routine record keeping and related account analysis may now be done by computer. Real-time data also are available in a number of applications.
   b. *Improved networking and related communication devices.* Direct link-up between the corporate office and factory or branch sales office, and between large mainframe computers and microcomputer workstations is changing both the procedure for handling transactions and the method and time of reporting.

2. *Environmental.* This category includes economic as well as social factors. Some changes are:

a. *Economic*

- *Changes in the capital markets both as to sources and terms for obtaining needed funds.* These changes place increased analytical demand on the financial executive to know about the necessary financial impact of the proposed action, together with the need for up-to-date knowledge on the alternative possibilities, as well as innovative financial ideas.

- *Greater internationalism and increased competition.* Very often this produces demands for quicker information about the marketplace and faster response as to products or services. Financial markets as well as products are involved. These pressures have become even greater with the entrance of products from newly developing countries into the U.S. market.

- *Increased volatility.* Rather quick changes in economic conditions, inflation rates, political sentiment, currency exchange rates, to name a few, create a need to secure information quickly, to sense threats and opportunities sooner, and to attempt to peer further into the future.

b. *Social.* To a limited degree, social changes are causing business management to weigh the speed and effect of social changes through impact studies and other information sources, namely, flexible working hours, disease trends, ethnic markets, and so on.

3. *Internal Business Changes.* The forces or influences just mentioned are external to the business. But in recent years changes have come about in the type of financial/accounting data needed to make business decisions, and this situation is continuing to evolve as a result of factors internal to the business itself, including:

a. *Broadened focus of the chief executive officer.* Today's successful chief executive officers, buffeted by strong competitive pressures, both foreign and domestic, and pushed by rapidly changing market and product demands, are necessarily taking a much broader view of their responsibilities. While their personal strengths may rest in marketing or engineering, for example, they are increasingly aware of the need to focus on long-term strategy and short-term tactics for the survival and growth of the enterprise. They are now more conscious both of the need for sound financial advice, and of just what type of information reasonably should be available. They are therefore more demanding of their financial executives, including the controller, for better information, for more analytical data, and for earlier data. Their needs are another major force changing the character or nature of information to be furnished by the financial arm of the business.

b. *Changes in organization structure and style of management.* The trend to decentralized management, the establishment of profit center responsibility, and perhaps the use of a more permissive type of management, all tend to change the kind of financial data needed by the responsible managers. A profit center executive, for example, will want information quite different from that needed by a manager whose sole concern is keeping overhead within acceptable parameters.

c. *Heightened sophistication of the financial executive.* Typical controllers in a medium-sized to large concern now probably have a professional degree in business administration or accounting, perhaps have an M.B.A., and often hold a certificate as a certified public accountant. With such a background, they tend to be aware of the more advanced methods and analytical tools available, and encourage their use. For example, they know the advantages of the internal rate of return, or discounted cash flow technique, in measuring capital expenditures as compared to other methods. They may employ probability or sensitivity analysis in evaluating projects. Their higher level of knowledge tends to encourage the use of the broader and improved financial techniques.

d. *Impact of corporate reorganization.* Common terms for corporate reorganization in today's world are "restructuring" or "downsizing." Whatever the description, the drive to increase profitability, the selling of unprofitable segments, or segments with lower-than-acceptable profit rates, finally impact the financial function, whether in terms of required analysis or the need to function with less staff, or simply put, to operate more efficiently. This forces a "down-to-basics" approach in what and how various controller/financial functions are carried out.

1-9 INFORMATION NEEDS OF MANAGEMENT

A management information system (MIS) encompasses the entire spectrum of information used by management in planning, organizing, directing, and controlling the activities of a business entity. For the purposes of this book, we are focusing on the financial information system—an organized method of securing and providing business managers (from foreman to chief executive officer) with the financial data they need to make those business decisions for which they are responsible and providing this information in a timely manner, in a format they will quickly comprehend, to the end that they will understand the situation and take any actions called for.

The preceding discussion of the business objective, the nature of the management process, some of the forces of change, and the role of financial-accounting information in the management of a business necessarily has been quite general. Why? Because the authors wished to provide an overview of business management. We believe that adequate detail will be disclosed as each specific business activity is reviewed, and as each principal line in a statement of income or expense or statement of financial position, or other financial statement is considered in subsequent chapters.

It is not always practical, without talking to a particular manager, to identify the kinds or forms of financial information that would be most useful to him or her. Based on the individual manager's background, interests, experience, and style of management, he or she may find one type of data more helpful than another, such as graphs over tabulation, relative as well as absolute, or extensive detail instead of highly summarized data.

While such matters as these are discussed in later chapters in the context of specific applications, some helpful and valid general comments can be made concerning the financial data needed by a business manager. Some examples are:

1. *Key Properties of Data*
   a. *Relevance.* Relating to, or bearing upon, the matter under review.
   b. *Timeliness.* This has to do with (i) the frequency with which the information is issued, and (ii) the delay between the occurrence and when the manager receives the information.
   c. *Quantifiability.* The ability to assign numeric values—obviously important with respect to much financial data.
   d. *Accuracy.* Freedom from *significant* error.
   e. *Conciseness.* Possessing an acceptable degree of combining (not always desired).

2. *Recognition of the Managerial Level.* Executives at differing managerial levels will have differing information needs. Thus, top-level executives usually will be concerned with strategy and long-term trends as well as overall current conditions. They will deal with external as well as internal information. In contrast, foremen may be concerned only with internal data as to how each person under their supervision performed for the past eight hours or the past week.

3. *The Importance of Organization Structure.* Organization structure and the related assignment of responsibility and authority will be a factor in information needs. Thus, a middle-line executive in a decentralized structure may have profit-and-loss responsibility for a segment, and will need relevant data. In a centralized organization, a middle-line sales executive may have sales responsibility only, and would need volume and price data—quite in contrast to the manager with gross-profit responsibility. If the position description emphasizes planning responsibilities as distinguished from control duties, then the information needs will be correspondingly different.

4. *The Nature of the Functional Activity as an Important Determinant of Information Needs.* A research director, for example, will be interested in the cost to complete each project for which he or she is responsible, and how such total cost compares with the original plan or commitment. Before requesting approval of a development project, a director will want to have an estimated comparison of expected benefits and expected costs. A production manager may want to know how the actual unit cost of production, by element, compares with competition and with the estimate or standard. A credit manager may want to know how the experienced bad debt ratio compares with the estimate or with industry levels. The financial vice-president may wish to compare the terms of a proposed bank loan with other known borrowings in the industry. So each function has its own unique information needs.

1-10 STANDARDS OF ETHICAL CONDUCT FOR MANAGEMENT ACCOUNTANTS

The first two sentences in Chapter 1 of the first edition of *Controllership,* by Heckert and Willson, published in 1952, are as follows: "The philosophy and the practice of business management are being subjected to a most critical analysis. This analysis is being directed to both the scientific aspect of business practice and the ethical basis upon which such practice rests." This is essentially the same statement contained in section 1-3 of this fifth edition entitled, "An Enlightened Philosophy of Management."

The authors have long espoused ethical conduct in business and in the practice of accounting. But it seems as if business as an institution, and some managers who lead the enterprises, have come under heavy attack recently in view of a seeming increase in white-collar crime: bribes, kickbacks, and fraudulent financial reporting, to mention three types. Such improper acts, among others, have been a force in the enactment of national legislation, including the Foreign Corrupt Practices Act and the issuance of guidelines by the National Commission on Fraudulent Financial Reporting, also known as the Treadway Commission. These pronouncements and derivative or relevant actions are reviewed in Chapters 9 and 10 on Internal Control, and the Internal Audit Function, respectively.

Suffice it to say here that, in clarification of what constitutes acceptable business conduct, corporations have issued codes of ethics and other instructions dealing with the matter. Moreover, in an action more closely relating to accounting, the Institute of Management Accountants, formerly the National Association of Accountants, published an authoritative statement, "The Standards of Ethical Conduct for Management Accountants" in 1983. A copy of this Statement on Management Accounting 1B, as republished in *Management Accounting,* August 1994, is shown in Figure 1-2. Presumably we accountants have learned at home, and at school, the difference between right and wrong. However, the guidelines in Figure 1-2 may be helpful reminders for management accountants as to their preferred professional conduct in problem situations that are sometimes quite frequent.

The subsequent chapters in this volume deal with the nature of the planning and control functions as related to specific segments of income and expense, or assets, liabilities, and net worth, and with the associated financial information needs.

1-11 ETHICS IN BUSINESS MANAGEMENT

In section 1-10, we discuss standards of ethical conduct for management accountants, but the interest of the controller, as a member of top management, in ethical conduct should extend to the entire business and not merely to the accounting function. He or she would want to *know* that his or her company is doing business in a highly ethical manner. Just as the mission statement of an entity explains what the company intends to achieve, and the annual business plan describes how the annual objectives will be attained, so also the ethics statement—if one exists—indicates the kind of ethics acceptable in accomplishing the mission.

But why is more attention now being paid to business ethics? Is the moral basis on which business is conducted any less acceptable than, say, five years ago? There are several answers to these questions. An increasing number of public reports describe fraudulent acts on Wall Street, or in government contracts, and elsewhere. Moreover, with the globalization of business, competition has become more intense and the ethical basis of meeting it may have deteriorated. Some managers may feel under increased pressure to achieve the annual business plan or to meet other short-term business objectives. Also, attempts at corporate takeovers, downsizing, and the sale of entire segments of divisions have exerted an influence on executives to "look good."

Before discussing what steps are desirable to maintain an acceptable level of ethical conduct, it may be helpful to look at some typical questions that might arise in a

Figure 1-2   Standards of Ethical Conduct for Management Accounting.

Management accountants have an obligation to the organizations they serve, their profession, the public, and themselves to maintain the highest standards of ethical conduct. In recognition of this obligation, the Institute of Management Accountants has promulgated the following standards of ethical conduct for management accountants. Adherence to these standards is integral to achieving the *Objectives of Management Accounting.*[1] Management accountants shall not commit acts contrary to these standards nor shall they condone the commission of such acts by others within their organizations.

COMPETENCE
Management accountants have a responsibility to:

■ Maintain an appropriate level of professional competence by ongoing development of their knowledge and skills.
■ Perform their professional duties in accordance with relevant laws, regulations, and technical standards.
■ Prepare complete and clear reports and recommendations after appropriate analyses of relevant and reliable information.

CONFIDENTIALITY
Management accountants have a responsibility to:

■ Refrain from disclosing confidential information acquired in the course of their work except when authorized, unless legally obligated to do so.
■ Inform subordinates as appropriate regarding the confidentiality of information acquired in the course of their work and monitor their activities to assure the maintenance of that confidentiality.
■ Refrain from using or appearing to use confidential information acquired in the course of their work for unethical or illegal advantage either personally or through third parties.

INTEGRITY
Management accountants have a responsibility to:

■ Avoid actual or apparent conflicts of interest and advise all appropriate parties of any potential conflict.
■ Refrain from engaging in any activity that would prejudice their ability to carry out their duties ethically.
■ Refuse any gift, favor, or hospitality that would influence or would appear to influence their actions.
■ Refrain from either actively or passively subverting the attainment of the organization's legitimate and ethical objectives.
■ Recognize and communicate professional limitations or other constraints that would preclude responsible judgment or successful performance of an activity.
■ Communicate unfavorable as well as favorable information and professional judgments or opinions.

■ Refrain from engaging in or supporting any activity that would discredit the profession.

OBJECTIVITY
Management accountants have a responsibility to:

■ Communicate information fairly and objectively.
■ Disclose fully all relevant information that could reasonably be expected to influence an intended user's understanding of the reports, comments, and recommendations presented.

RESOLUTION OF ETHICAL CONFLICT

In applying the standards of ethical conduct, management accountants may encounter problems in identifying unethical behavior or in resolving an ethical conflict. When faced with significant ethical issues, management accountants should follow the established policies of the organization bearing on the resolution of such conflict. If these policies do not resolve the ethical conflict, management accountants should consider the following course of action:

■ Discuss such problems with the immediate superior except when it appears that the superior is involved, in which case the problem should be presented initially to the next higher managerial level. If satisfactory resolution cannot be achieved when the problem is initially presented, submit the issues to the next higher managerial level.
  If the immediate superior is the chief executive officer, or equivalent, the acceptable reviewing authority may be a group such as the audit committee, executive committee, board of directors, board of trustees, or owners. Contact with levels above the immediate superior should be initiated only with the superior's knowledge, assuming the superior is not involved.
■ Clarify relevant concepts by confidential discussion with an objective advisor to obtain an understanding of possible courses of action.
■ If the ethical conflict still exists after exhausting all levels of internal review, the management accountant may have no other recourse on significant matters than to resign from the organization and to submit an informative memorandum to an appropriate representative of the organization.

Except where legally prescribed, communication of such problems to authorities or individuals not employed or engaged by the organization is not considered appropriate. ■

[1] Institute of Management Accountants, *Statements on Management Accounting: Objectives of Management Accounting*, Statement No. 1B, June 17, 1982.

Source: Management Accounting, August 1994, p. 24. Used by permission of *Management Accounting.*

business. These are not the more easily answered questions of whether something is black or white, or whether it is clearly honest or dishonest. Further, the answers relate in large part to the integrity of the individual employee, and to a desire to be guided by a high level of values.

(a) THE MORALITY OF "MANAGING" EARNINGS

Businesspeople from the CEO down to the department managers typically are under pressure to meet the monthly budget, or to achieve the planned sales, or reach the net income target for the year.

Here are some representative actions that *operating* managers might consider in an attempt to reach an operating plan result or a net income goal for the month, quarter, or year:

- Grant special discounts at year end to stimulate sales.
- Offer special credit terms of deferred payments until the next calendar year in an effort to increase yearend sales.
- Sell surplus plant and equipment, at a profit, in order to increase the quarterly net income.
- Sell unwanted or surplus inventory to secure cash, and to increase net income to the planned level.
- Defer needed, but not essential, repairs and maintenance until the next fiscal year to stay within the budget level of expenses.
- Accelerate year end shipments through the use of overtime.
- Record as a shipment on December 31, a load of material that did not leave the factory until January 2. (The fiscal year ends December 31.)

Are these unethical actions? In the normal sales cut-off procedures, the accountants would identify the improper dating on the advanced shipment mentioned in the last item above. But if the controller knew of the impending operating decision on the other transactions, should he or she have taken any action? Is there anything wrong with decisions made to achieve plan if the action was not illegal or dishonest, or if human life was not at stake? There are some who might consider many of the above actions unethical.

A survey concerning the acceptability of some selected business practices, both operating and accounting, resulted in these generalizations.[1]

- The respondents generally viewed the management of short-term earnings by *accounting* methods as significantly less acceptable than attaining the same ends by changing *operating* decisions or procedures.
- Materiality was a factor in the decision. Short-term earnings management was judged less acceptable if the earnings impact of the action was large rather than small.

---

[1] William J. Bruns, Jr., and Kenneth A. Merchant, "The Dangerous Morality of Managing Earnings," *Management Accounting,* Aug. 1990, p. 23. The William Taylor article mentioned in the Selected Reference (*Harvard Business Review,* March/April 1989) contains a copy of the ethics test.

- The direction of the effect on earnings makes a difference. *Increasing* earnings was judged less acceptable than reducing profits.
- The time period of the impact may influence ethical judgments. Managing the short-term earnings at the end of an interim quarterly reporting period was viewed as somewhat more acceptable than taking comparable action at the end of an annual reporting period.
- Finally, the *method* of managing earnings influenced the test response. Thus, increasing profits through the use of extended credit terms was seen as less acceptable than accomplishing the same results by selling excess assets, or using overtime to accelerate the shipment.

Most of the decisions listed earlier in this segment (except that involving the sales cut-off) would have been regarded as acceptable. The ethics test results indicate that there are greatly varying opinions among operating managers as to what constitutes unacceptable ethical conduct. It can be understood, therefore, that any attempt to develop a written code of ethics to deal with such specific and detailed transactions, would require careful thought.

(b) DEFINING UNETHICAL BEHAVIOR

Deciding what is proper conduct is rather straightforward when the acts are unlawful or illegal, or when the choice is moral versus immoral, and when the important relevant facts are known. But in many cases all the facts are not known and/or we operate in grey areas. Moreover, with the passage of time, what was once considered unacceptable behavior becomes acceptable. How, then, should the top management of a company determine what is acceptable or unacceptable conduct? Some suggested steps in such a procedure might include:

- Hold discussions among the higher levels of management to identify various points of view.
- Clearly recognize the implications of any ethical decision of an action on the employees, investors, the public, and the competition.
- Balance any tentative ethical decision against the company's self interest versus some of the broader interests.
- Finally, weigh the ethical decisions against what is perceived as the traditional values espoused by the company.

If the above procedures do not result in more or less generally accepted decisions as to ethical conduct, then the chief executive will need to make the choices, based on his or her training and judgment.

(c) PROMOTING AND ENFORCING ETHICAL BEHAVIOR

Assuming the management has reached general agreement about what constitutes ethical business conduct, how are these decisions made known and enforced? Any such program probably would encompass these three steps:

1. *A code of ethics and standards of conduct should be developed and reduced to writing.*

The code should explain the basic viewpoint of top management about unethical conduct. It should also define those actions that are expected to occur, and should be equally explicit about unacceptable conduct. It should not consist of general platitudes, which merely sound good.

Guidance about types of conduct should be subdivided according to the important kinds of activities. Some illustrative topics included in some codes contain such matters as:

- Code of ethics.
- Standards of conduct.
- Conflicts of interest.
- Bidding, negotiating, and performing under U.S. government contract.
- Meals and entertainment.
- Use of company car (and other assets).
- Gifts and payments of money.
- Complete and accurate books, records, and communications.
- Preservation of assets.
- Compliance with anti-trust laws.
- Political contributions.
- Year-end and accounting adjustments.
- Year-end operating activities.
- Attaining annual business plan objectives.
- Cost consciousness.
- Workplace safety.
- Product safety.
- Employee discrimination (religion, race, sex, nationality, etc.).
- Hazardous waste disposal.
- Political activities.
- Compliance with SEC and other securities laws and regulations.
- Restrictive trade practices.
- International boycotts.
- Leave for military or other federal service.
- Corporate ethics office (ombudsman).

2. *The code of ethics and standards of conduct must be communicated to all employees.*

The employees should understand the attitude of management about unethical conduct and have clear knowledge about specific acts. The means of communicating with employees could include group meetings, training and development programs, newly hired employee orientation sessions, videotapes, and employee handbooks.

3. *The code must be enforced and monitored.*

In many cases, relevant procedures may be reviewed by the internal auditors, independent accountants, or the staff of corporate counsel. The corporate ethics office (the ombudsman) may be the device to receive complaints of alleged violations and investigate them. One rule is paramount: Uniform enforcement is essential. If employees perceive that executives are dealt with leniently, and lower level employees harshly, then code enforcement becomes difficult.

One available guideline for monitoring the business ethics and conduct of almost any company is the Defense Industry Questionnaire on Business Ethics and Conduct developed by a group of defense contractors.[2]

Another enforcement technique is to require all managers and certain key professionals to affirm annually in writing (a standard form) that each (1) is aware of the company code of conduct and (2) has adhered to it.

1-12 SELECTED REFERENCES

Andrews, Kenneth R., "Ethics in Practice," *Harvard Business Review,* Sept.–Oct. 1989, pp. 99–104.

Bhide, Amar, and Howard H. Stevenson, "Why Be Honest if Honesty Doesn't Pay?" *Harvard Business Review,* Sept.–Oct. 1990, pp. 121–129.

Bialkin, Kenneth J., "Business Ethics: Optional or Mandatory?" *Management Accounting,* April 1993, pp. 54–56.

Bruns, William J., Jr., and Kenneth A. Merchant, "The Dangerous Morality of Managing Earnings," *Management Accounting,* Aug. 1990, pp. 22–25.

Cohen, Jeffrey R., "Ethics and Budgeting," *Management Accounting,* Aug. 1988, pp. 29–31.

Gellerman, Saul W., "Why 'Good' Managers Make Bad Ethical Choices," *Harvard Business Review,* July/Aug. 1986, pp. 85–90.

Hennessy, Edward L., Jr., "Business Ethics—Is It a Priority for Corporate America?" *Financial Executive,* Oct. 1986, pp. 14–19.

Lander, Gerald H., Michael T. Cronin, and Alan Reinstein, "In Defense of the Management Accountant," *Management Accounting,* May 1990, pp. 54–57.

Rich, Anne J., Carl S. Smith, and Paul H. Mihalek, "Are Corporate Codes of Conduct Effective?" *Management Accounting,* Sept. 1990, pp. 34–35.

Rosenzweig, Kenneth, and Marilyn Fischer, "Is Managing Earnings Ethically Acceptable?" *Management Accounting,* March 1994, pp. 31–34.

Skeddle, Ronald W., "Business Ethics: Dealing in the Gray Areas," *Financial Executive,* May–June 1990, pp. 9–13.

Sweeny, Robert B., and Howard L. Siers, "Survey: Ethics in Corporate America," *Management Accounting,* June 1990, pp. 34–40.

Taylor, William, ed., "The Gray Area—Ethics Test for Everyday Managers," *Harvard Business Review,* March–April 1989, pp. 220–221.

Tucker, Francis Gaither, Seymour M. Zivan, and Robert C. Camp, "How to Measure Yourself Against the Best," *Harvard Business Review,* Jan.–Feb. 1987, pp. 8–10.

Verschoor, Curtis C., "Readers Respond to Accounting Ethics Case Study," *Management Accounting,* July 1990, pp. 53–55.

---

[2] See Official Releases, *Journal of Accountancy,* Aug. 1987, pp. 152–162 for the Questionnaire and selected questions and interpretations about it.

CHAPTER 2

The Controllership Function

2-1 EVOLUTION IN DUTIES OF FINANCIAL EXECUTIVES

Since the turn of the twentieth century at least four factors have had a significant effect on the status of the financial executive in American business. The increased size and complexity of the industrial organization, globalization, growing governmental relationships with company affairs, and more numerous sources of capital have, among other things, made financial accountability an increasingly important consideration in the conduct of business. Consequently, the functions and responsibilities of the individual financial executive have changed.

In this period, the birth and development of the separate controllership function occurred. Noticeably increased financial activities forced a wider delegation of authority and responsibility in many companies. Moreover, greater size has required more checks and balances and better internal control within the business. But perhaps most important, a demand for better management practices has brought with it the necessity for more adequate accounting and more effective management control information. Thus, for the reasons stated, the separation of the accounting function from other financial functions was a logical growth.

In this evolution of the controllership function, it is understandable that much diversity between companies would appear. In most organizations, the certificate of incorporation, or bylaws, or resolutions by the board of directors, set forth the general financial duties to be performed. However, that share of the total duties assigned to the controller had no generally accepted precedent and was influenced by such forces as the size and complexity of the company, industry practice, increase in government regulations, personality and ability of the controller, and prevailing opinion on the part of the chief executive and his associates about just what should constitute the job.

2-2 AN ESSENTIAL TO THE FUNCTION

Although the scope of the position varies from company to company, one concept is common. In the representative company, the controller is thought of simply as the chief accountant who supervises and maintains the formal corporate financial records. He is regarded as the executive who concerns himself with general accounting, cost accounting, auditing, taxes, and perhaps insurance and statistics. Such a viewpoint is backward looking.

It is true that the controller must engage in accounting activities; yet he must not restrict his role to the recording function. More properly, he is expected to extend his accounting function to its management applications. Essential to the proper fulfillment of the controllership function is an attitude of mind that energizes and vitalizes the financial data by applying it to future company activities. It is a forward-looking concept—a trained analytical approach that brings balance to the management planning and control system. The controller's viewpoint should be the management viewpoint—one that guides management's thinking to the most profitable combination of operations.

This modern concept of controllership is the one stressed in this book and is more fully described in this chapter.

2-3 VARIOUS TITLES APPLIED TO POSITION

Numerous titles are applied to the position of chief accounting officer; however, the most common and representative title used is controller. The duties are sometimes assumed by a chief accountant, office manager, comptroller, treasurer, assistant treasurer, or secretary. However, with the increasing emphasis on accounting control, and with management's need for additional statistical and financial decision-making information, the term "controllership" has gained deserved recognition. This is particularly true in the larger, more complex and better organized companies. The term "controller" is more descriptive of the expanded responsibilities of the function. In this book, controller is the title used to signify the position of the chief accounting officer responsible for financial statistics and control.

There have been some indications that the use of the title controller is not appropriate in that this person does not control the business. The management individuals responsible for operations actually do the controlling. However, they can only accomplish their objectives based on reports, analyses, recommendations, advice, and provision of control mechanisms as provided by the controller. Controlling expenses and costs of operations at all levels need a well thought-out plan with periodic reports measuring performance. A more appropriate title may be "Manager of Planning and Controls," which is somewhat descriptive of the management functions.

2-4 CONTROLLERSHIP PRINCIPLES APPLICABLE TO ALL TYPES AND SIZES OF CONCERNS

One of the obstacles to the development of the controllership function is the feeling on the part of executives that their particular business is different and does not lend itself to modern control methods.

Basically, the problems of management cannot vary much between industries and concerns. There are always the problems of determining policies, planning for future action, organization, direction of sales effort and control sales of cost, and control of production and production costs. Workers must be employed in competition with other firms; they must be trained and supervised, and their performance closely checked; materials must be purchased in proper quantities, at proper times, and investment in inventories must be closely controlled; suitable physical equipment must be selected, maintained, and replaced; finances must be arranged and kept in proper balance with regard to fixed and working funds; and, finally, all factors must be properly coordinated. Such problems are not peculiar to any business; they are common problems that form the basis of the management task. Few businesses have "peculiar" problems of accounting procedure and control.

It is true that certain peculiarities do exist in the detailed operations of certain type of businesses and with regard to the economic and political restrictions surrounding them. Utilities, insurance companies, brokerage houses, hotels, amusement concerns, financial institutions, department stores, and chain organizations present examples of certain peculiarities of organization and procedure, but here again the basic problems are similar. The controller who understands thoroughly the basic problems of accounting control can readily apply them to his industry and concern.

Moreover, the controllership function is not restricted to large companies. A business need not reach any considerable size before a qualified controller can find ample opportunity to establish his usefulness and value to his company. There are still thousands of small concerns that need the services of an accountant who envisions the full opportunity of the task.

With this general background relating to controllership, a discussion of specific functions is in order.

2-5 BASIC CONTROLLERSHIP FUNCTIONS

There have been many comprehensive definitions of the controllership function developed over the years. A review of the various position descriptions indicates that the basic functional responsibilities and activities may be categorized as follows:

1. *Planning.* Establish and maintain an integrated plan of operation consistent with the company's goals and objectives, both short and long term, analyzed and revised as required, communicated to all levels of management, with appropriate systems and procedures installed.

2. *Control.* Develop and revise standards against which to measure performance and provide guidance and assistance to other members of management in insuring

conformance of actual results to standards—some of which are financial in nature, and some are not.

3. *Reporting.* Prepare, analyze, and interpret financial results for utilization by management in the decision-making process, evaluate the data with reference to company and unit objectives; prepare and file external reports as required to satisfy government regulatory bodies, shareholders, financial institutions, customers, and the general public.

4. *Accounting.* Design, establish, and maintain general and cost accounting systems at all company levels, including corporate, divisional, plant, and unit to properly record all financial transactions in the books of accounts and records in accordance with sound accounting principles with adequate internal control—and with sufficient flexibility, to provide essential information needed by management to properly plan and control the business.

5. *Other Primary Responsibilities.* Manage and supervise such functions as federal, state, local, and international taxes, including interface with the respective taxing authorities and agents; maintain appropriate relationships with internal and external auditors; institute insurance programs, coverage, records and provision; develop and maintain systems and procedures; develop record retention programs; supervise assigned treasury functions; institute investor and financial public relations programs; office management; and direct other assigned functions.

As circumstances warrant, there are many deviations from the basic functions just described. We would like to point out that the controller's efforts should not be diluted and render him less effective by assigning to him unrelated functions of an operational nature. The financial planning and control functions are too important to the success of the business enterprise to burden the controller with activities that others can perform.

2-6 THE PLANNING FUNCTION

The establishment and maintenance of an integrated plan of operation have been described as a major function of the controller. The business objective is profit, and planning is necessary to fulfill it, for profits do not "just happen." Visualize, then, the role of the modern controller in business planning.

First, he has a responsibility to see that a plan exists and that it is supported by all levels of management. The implication of an integrated plan is that all parts will mesh together and support the business objective. For this reason, all members of management must participate willingly. It must be the company plan and not the controller's plan. He will act as coordinator in the various stages, in translating the base to monetary terms, and in putting the plan together in financial terms—finally expressed as a statement of forecast income and expense and a statement of estimated financial condition, together with supporting schedules.

Assuming the recognition of the need for a plan, and the desire by all management to participate, then the controller has a responsibility to determine that the parts in and of themselves are sound and that they fit together. For example, he should, as a staff executive, ascertain that:

1. The sales plan or forecast supports known corporate policies and objectives (market areas, types of product, etc.).

2. The sale plan appears realistic.
3. The production plan or schedule supports the sales program.
4. The production plan is within facility capabilities.
5. The cost and expense levels and relationships are proper.
6. The entire business plan is within the financial capacity of the enterprise.

When the total plan is put together, the controller should test or appraise its adequacy and report to the chief executive on his findings. It must be judged on an overall basis in terms of these concerns:

1. In the light of past experience, is it realistic?
2. Does it reflect economic conditions that are expected to prevail in the period of the plan?
3. In terms of management policy, have lines designated to be discontinued been discontinued on a practical basis with regard to inventory disposal considerations, etc.?
4. Does it meet requirements of return on investment and such other broad tests as may be applicable?

Some of the testing and analysis will be accomplished as preliminary plans are formulated, and the rest will await the total picture. But, however and whenever it is done, the controller is counselor and coordinator. He advises and suggests. Final responsibility for the overall program must rest with the chief executive; and responsibility for each operating function must be that of the applicable officer. Thus the vice-president for sales is responsible for the sales program. But this staff relationship should not deter the controller from making his considered observations.

2-7 THE CONTROL FUNCTION

The management function of control is the measurement and correction of performance so that business objectives and plans are accomplished. Management control seeks to compel conformance to plan or standard. In this function, also, the controller assists. He does not enforce control, except in his own department, but he provides information the functional executive is expected to use to achieve the required performance.

Activities in this control area absorb a great deal of time of the controller's staff. Some information is provided from hour to hour or from day to day; other data are prepared from week to week or from month to month, as circumstances require. For example, in larger companies, hourly or daily information on labor performance may be helpful, or weekly manufacturing expense figures may be needed.

In approaching problems relative to the control function, a broad view usually is helpful. The end result of the control function is not merely a report on performance. Rather it should involve concern for these considerations:

1. Assistance in setting standards for control.
2. Evaluation of standards, including related analysis.
3. Reporting short-term actual and standard performance.

4. Developing trends and relationships to assist the operating executives.

5. Ascertaining that the systems and procedures, through constant review, are providing the required, most helpful data, on the most practical and economic basis.

A little reflection will indicate that a manager cannot control the past. He may study past action to determine the place and cause of deviation. But here, as in planning, the best kind of control is forward looking. This the controller must keep in mind as he participates in the control function, giving constant thought to steps that might be taken before the operating action to assure "on-standard" or "desired" performance. This might be called preventive control.

2-8 THE REPORTING FUNCTION

Insofar as it concerns internal management, the reporting function is closely related to both the planning and the control functions. Reporting is essential to make planning and control effective. Yet the reporting function is not merely one of presentation of tabulations and is not wholly routine, although some phases become routinized. Moreover, the management that makes decisions often cannot be kept adequately informed solely from periodic statements regardless of how well designed they may be. The reporting function encompasses the interpretation of the figures, and the controller's duty is not discharged until management actually understands the facts.

The reporting function with the requisite interpretation is an opportunity to bring life and meaning to the figures.

Prior comments have related to management reporting, and this is perhaps the most interesting area. Yet information must be provided to a rather wide field. The controller will be called on to furnish data of a financial or statistical nature to such other groups as those listed here:

Shareholders of the company (annual and quarterly reports).

Creditors—banks, suppliers, other financing institutions.

Stock exchanges.

Employees and the general public.

Customers.

U.S. Government and agencies thereof:

Securities and Exchange Commission (SEC).

Internal Revenue service (IRS).

Department of Commerce.

Department of Labor.

Federal Trade Commission (FTC).

State and local governments and agencies.

2-9 THE ACCOUNTING FUNCTION

The systematic recording of financial transactions is often regarded as the principal function of the controller. Important as this is, the authors stress in this text the management aspects of accounting. In fact, within the limits explained in Chapter 1, the controller may well take the viewpoint of the businessman first and then that of the accountant.

Because the strictly accounting considerations are well known, little additional comment is necessary. The controller is expected to apply, in a practical manner, sound accounting principles and practices within his company. He is expected to keep abreast of technology so that he can provide management with needed information on the most economical and feasible basis. He is also expected to develop and maintain records and procedures, including adequate internal control, so that reports properly reflect the financial condition of the company and the operating results.

In many companies the accounting function includes maintenance of the property, plant, and equipment records.

2-10 OTHER PRIMARY RESPONSIBILITIES

In addition to planning, control, reporting, and accounting, the other primary responsibilities represent a typical grouping, some or all of which may be assigned to the controller. Factors that ordinarily influence the assignment include the size of the business entity, competence and personality of the controller, time demands of the four principal duties (planning, control, reporting, and accounting), personal interests of the controller, availability of other knowledgeable executives to supervise the duties, and the opinions of the chief executive and the chief financial officer (if the latter position exists), as to the preferred placement of the function.

As to the activities listed in section 2-5, these comments may be helpful: Because of the close relationship with the accounting records, among other reasons, the tax function usually is under the cognizance of the controller. With respect to audit activities, he must maintain an appropriate relationship with the independent auditors; but sometimes the internal auditor may report to the chief financial officer or the chief executive, although there will be rather frequent contact between the controller and the internal auditor. Comments on the internal audit function are made in Chapter 10. Ordinarily the controller is responsible for record retention and, to a greater degree than before, may participate in activities associated with investor relations or financial public relations. (See Chapter 13.) In the smaller business entities the chief accounting officer often has the responsibility for risk management (insurance) and perhaps the remaining enumerated functions.

Finally, it is about the matter of business systems and procedures and related activities that a few remarks are in order. What was once called "business systems" is now often designated as "information systems." What was formerly called "data processing" might now be entitled "information services." Because the controller, or the accounting department, was often the largest user of computer output, he often assumed responsibility for this function. However, with the tremendous changes in information technology, and the realization by senior management that it must remain competitive in this field to stay ahead of competitors in the marketplace for the company's own chief products, increasing attention often is being given to the management of information resources. This has resulted in three organizational structures:

1. In those instances where the need for improved information technology is not perceived by top management, there is no change in organization. Very often the

information executive reports to the controller or the chief financial officer, and supervises business systems development and data processing.

2. In other circumstances, senior management may attempt to serve its information needs by securing a "hybrid" executive combining the talents of the controller, or chief financial officer, and the information systems officer. Such results are often unsatisfactory in the larger companies because the financial knowledge of the information officer is not sufficiently sophisticated, or the financial executive has a superficial or shallow knowledge of information technology.

3. At least in those areas where up-to-date information technology is essential, senior management has established the post of chief information officer (CIO) who reports at a very high level—perhaps on a par with the CFO. Such a person should be knowledgeable in information technology, including computer networking (telecommunications), office automation, and data processing. Some accounting-oriented executives think this organization set-up will not stand the test of time.

When the position of chief information officer, reporting at a high level, is established, some controllers or financial executives may feel this is an infringement of the financial area (business systems and financial reporting responsibilities). However, it seems to the authors that, with the rapid changes in information technology, the controller and other financial executives should:

1. Welcome a highly qualified CIO who would provide access to proven practical, competitive telecommunications systems, compatible and suitable computer hardware and software, and economical office automation.

2. Recognize that most position descriptions of the CIO do *not* include prescribing the information needs of the controller (or other functional executives). This must be left to the operating executive *himself.* The CIO merely develops the system for production of the data.

3. Appreciate that being a *user* of information technology (data processing, networking, etc.) instead of a *provider,* releases time and effort that can be better used in the development of competitive, sophisticated *financial* techniques such as models for capital expenditures or acquisitions, improved and attractive financial reports, and enhanced techniques for preparing and/or testing short-term or long-range financial plans, including "what if" analyses.

2-11 A MORE DETAILED LIST OF FUNCTIONS

In the preceding sections, the authors have attempted to outline and explain the general functional areas of the controller. With this background, the following listing of detailed controllership functions takes on added meaning:

1. The installation and supervision of all accounting records of the corporation.

2. The preparation and interpretation of the financial statements and reports of the corporation.

3. The continuous audit of all accounts and records of the corporation wherever located.

4. The compilation of production costs.

5. The compilation of costs of distribution.

6. The taking and costing of all physical inventories.

7. The preparation and filing of tax returns and the supervision of all matters relating to taxes.

8. The preparation and interpretation of all statistical records and reports of the corporation.

9. The preparation, as budget director, in conjunction with other officers and department heads, of an annual plan covering all activities of the corporation, for submission to the board of directors prior to the beginning of the fiscal year.

10. The ascertainment currently that the properties of the corporation are properly and adequately accounted for, and insured.

11. The initiation, preparation, and issuance of standard practices relating to all accounting matters and procedures and the coordination of systems throughout the corporation, including clerical and office methods, records, reports, and procedures.

12. The maintenance of adequate records of authorized appropriations and the determination that all sums expended pursuant thereto are properly accounted for.

13. The ascertainment currently that financial transactions covered by minutes of the board of directors and/or the executive committee are properly executed and recorded.

14. The maintenance of adequate records of all contracts and leases.

15. The approval for payment (and/or countersigning) of all checks, promissory notes, and other negotiable instruments of the corporation that have been signed by the treasurer or such other officers as shall have been authorized by the bylaws of the corporation or from time to time designated by the board of directors.

16. The examination of all warrants for the withdrawal of securities from the vaults of the corporation and the determination that such withdrawals are made in conformity with the bylaws and/or regulations established from time to time by the board of directors.

17. The preparation or approval of the regulations or standard practices required to assure compliance with orders or regulations issued by duly constituted governmental agencies.

2-12 A CONTINUING EVOLUTION

For the most part, the basic functions described in the preceding sections of this chapter have been exercised by controllers for the past three or four decades. To be sure, some financial executives have been so involved in number crunching, or have been categorized as so inflexible, that they have not been asked to participate in many major business decisions. But as the controller has become aware of, and adept at using, the more sophisticated financial techniques, as business has become more global in nature with heavy knowledge requirements in such matters as taxation and foreign exchange, as information technology has changed, and as the chief executive better understands what a good controller can do, the scope of the financial executives' duties continues to evolve. For example, the question no longer is, "Should the controller participate in planning?" but rather extends to, "Where can the controller be most helpful in the *strategic* planning process?" (See Chapters 14 and 15 on strategic and long-range planning.) Or, with many managers attempting to develop their own computer-oriented information systems, the question might be, "How can the controller make certain those information systems all reflect accurate, compatible, up-to-date numbers?" Yet, another question is posed quite often: "What is the most tax-advantaged procedure for making this acquisition?"

With the right repertoire of skills for a changing environment, the controller has an important role to play in business management.

2-13   ORGANIZATIONAL STATUS

The review of the controllership responsibilities indicates the broad scope of the function. As in all management positions, the proper environment must be present if the company is to achieve planned growth and profitability. The status of the controller—regardless of his title—must be such that his function is given full expression. There is a real need in every business for a fact-finding function with the capability to analyze the facts and make appropriate recommendations. This function could be performed by others, but the controller is better equipped to gather the needed information with his broad perspective and knowledge of the business. To accomplish the task effectively, the controller should have a peer relationship to all other major functional executives. The fully qualified controller will have no difficulty maintaining the proper relationship with other executives and indeed may enjoy a position of importance second only to that of the chief executive officer. This is evidenced by the increasing number of controllers who in recent years have been promoted to positions of increasing responsibilities, including chief executive.

Although all these things are true, the evolution of the separate controllership function is relatively new compared to the secretarial or treasury functions. In view of this, among other things, the Financial Executives Institute felt that a statement about the organizational status of the controller might prove a useful guide. Accordingly, the Institute's Board of Directors accepted the codification:

1. The controller should be an executive officer at the policy-making level responsible directly to the chief executive officer of the business. His appointment or removal should require the approval of the board of directors.

2. The controller should be required by the board of directors to present directly periodic reports covering the operating results and financial conditions of the business, together with such information as it may request.

3. The controller should preferably be a member of the board of directors and all other top policy-making groups. At a minimum he should be invited to attend all meetings of such groups with the right to be heard.

It is hoped and expected that proficiency and salesmanship gradually will cause some of these concepts to be widely accepted, giving appropriate recognition to the duties of the chief financial officer.

2-14 SOURCE OF CONTROLLER'S AUTHORITY

A clear definition of duties, authority, and responsibility is generally regarded as a prerequisite to good performance. Certainly in large companies, and perhaps in smaller ones, the scope of the controller's authority and responsibility can be established in one of three ways: (1) in accordance with the bylaws of the corporation, (2) by resolution of the executive committee, or (3) by general order of the president.

Bylaw provisions vary considerably in length and content in dealing with the controllership function. In essence, however, most state that "the controller shall be the principal officer in charge of the accounts of the company." Further, most provisions also contain the statement that "he shall have such other powers and duties as may be assigned to him by the Board of Directors, or by the Executive Committee, or by the President."

(a) SPECIFIC RESPONSIBILITIES

The following specific duties and responsibilities of a controller may have been assigned by any of the aforementioned alternatives:

1. Develop and publish through authorized management, policies and procedures on accounting, budgets, taxes, business planning and forecasting, and financial reporting and performance measurement.

2. Provide policy guidance and representation for all contacts with government and industry organizations in his area of responsibility. Represent the company in establishing and maintaining contacts with and reporting to regulative government agencies relative to accounting and financial data.

3. Conduct an effective tax management program that includes and is applicable to all segments of the company. Insure that policies and procedures provide for compliance with all applicable laws, rules, and regulations pertaining to taxes.

4. Control, coordinate, and integrate the annual and long-range financial business plans related to overall corporate objectives, including projections of sales, costs, net income, cash position, facility, and capital requirements. Analyze the plans and make recommendations for executive action to insure a realistic viable business plan from a financial viewpoint.

5. Develop and implement a comprehensive system of financial reports to provide corporate management with pertinent information concerning operating results of each segment of the company.

6. Review for concurrence the financial aspects of the acquisition or disposal of property or investments.

7. Consolidate and review long-range plans for concurrence from a financial viewpoint.

8. Review the financial progress of the company, comparing results with approved plans. Submit reports and recommendations for corrective action to appropriate executives.

9. Direct the maintenance of the formal corporate financial records and books of accounts, and prepare appropriate financial statements for use of management and presentation to shareholders, financial institutions, the government, and others.

10. Direct the preparation, reporting, and analysis of the corporate operating budgets.

11. Review for concurrence the organization of segment financial groups and the selection, transfer, or termination of key financial personnel.

12. Maintain relations with professional organizations related to reporting financial results to investors and government agencies.

13. Direct, coordinate, and monitor the activities of the company's independent accountants.

2-15 CHARACTERISTICS OF THE CONTROLLERSHIP TASK

The controllership task is not an easy one; there are certain characteristics and requirements that the controller must be aware of at all times, including:

1. The controller is chiefly a staff executive whose primary function is to develop an organization and a system of accounts, policies, records, and procedures which will provide data that can be analyzed and interpreted for the benefit of other functional executives in making decisions to achieve the goals and objectives of the company. He must demonstrate a high degree of initiative as is the case with most effective staff functions. The controller must anticipate and determine the informational needs of other executives. However, he must also be responsive in a timely manner to the specific requests made for data. In addition, it is important that he be resourceful and flexible in meeting changed conditions and requirements. He must anticipate what information and facts will be required for the decision-making process.

2. Although responsibility for directing operations is assigned to other functional executives, the controller must be able to relate to and understand their problems if he is to be effective and assist in the resolution. It is important that he understand what kinds of data and reports the other executives need to manage their functions in accordance with plans. The controller should provide analyses and make recommendations from his viewpoint with a thorough understanding of the methods, procedures, and objectives of the various functional executives. It is a serious mistake for the controller not to get involved in the day-to-day issues and problems of the operating functions or units. In all businesses there are many problems to be solved in a timely manner, and most executives are confident of solutions if the necessary facts are presented and analyzed. The controller is in a unique position to anticipate these needs and gain the confidence of the other executives.

3. To be useful, the information, facts, and data must be communicated in an easily understood manner by those for which it is intended. It is not important how the

material is provided, as long as it is understood and used. In some cases charts or graphs are preferable to narrative statements, whereas in other situations an oral report will suffice. In all cases the rule should be simplicity. Data or reports should not be provided unless the purpose is clearly understood by all parties. The controller should understand the real need, develop the necessary facts and data, analyze and provide necessary interpretations to minimize the task of other executives.

4. The controller must have the ability to translate facts and statistics into trends and relationships. It is imperative in the present business environment that trends and relationships be spotted early and action considered. A comparative sales analysis to prior periods is not sufficient to redirect salespersons or other efforts. The trends and particularly the future must be understood to maximize the utilization of resources and improve profitability.

5. The controller must be accurate in his findings and reporting; however, he must also have the ability to be forward looking and be able to assess the future. He can use past performance to assist him to chart the course for the future, but caution must be exercised to properly evaluate any changed conditions.

6. Most companies have the ability to isolate their major problems; however, successful companies take positive action in a timely manner. Therefore, the controller must of necessity develop and provide information as quickly as possible. Business is dynamic, and conditions are always changing, so it is imperative that quick analyses be made. Voluminous data and details are of little value a day late. Facts are perishable and if provided too late are useless.

7. The controller should follow up his studies and interpretations. Executives are busy and inclined to delay matters not requiring immediate attention. If the records clearly reveal unsatisfactory results or adverse trends, even though of minor consequence, they should be followed through until executive action results. It is not what the controller sees in his study of the organization but what executives act on that eventually reduces cost, improves operations, and increases profits. The controller cannot force action, but he can usually secure it by keeping important matters before the executives until satisfactory action is taken.

8. The controller must gain the confidence of the other executives by providing accurate and timely information with an attitude of wanting to help. If he is dictatorial or critical, he soon will have lost his value to the decision-making process. The mark of success for the controller is when other executives seek him out for guidance and counseling. It is important that he accept this role, and it will allow him to exercise his full potential and carry out his responsibilities.

9. The controller must be fair and impartial. It is necessary that he report all the relevant facts, even when he may be giving adverse reports on a function, executive, or employee. The controllership function has the task of measuring performance of all units of the company and must report accurately. The integrity of the function must be preserved to be useful.

10. The controller must be able to market or sell his ideas and analytical ability as well as his total function. Therefore, it is important that all output be provided in a form that can be easily used. In most cases, executives like to know immediately when

they can achieve significant savings or are about to lose all their profit earned to date; don't wait for a month-end report to bury the significant facts in reams of detail. The controller must use imagination and skill in insuring that his product is accepted and used.

11. Although realizing the full purpose of his task, the controller must also realize the limitations. Statistical information, no matter how accurately collected, analyzed, and interpreted is not a substitute for executive ability. It is of tremendous value in business, and, other things being the same, the company with the best-informed executives will outstrip its rivals. There are, however, many questions on which the controller can make little contribution. The success or failure of the business may hinge on shrewdness of investments, engineering ingenuity, matters of style, etc., concerning which the controller may be able to make only a small contribution.

    Moreover, the value of accounting and statistical data must be weighed against the cost. It may be interesting to know how much of each of 10 major products is sold to a particular customer or by a particular salesman every month, but unless these data can be used definitely to further the sales program to an extent that justifies the cost of securing them, the effort results in a loss. Or if the same results could have been obtained by an occasional test rather than by a continuous analysis, the accounting task is inefficiently performed.

2-16 QUALIFICATIONS OF THE CONTROLLER

The qualifications of an effective controller would include:

1. An excellent technical foundation in accounting and finance with an understanding and thorough knowledge of accounting principles.

2. An understanding of the principles of planning, organizing, and control.

3. A general understanding of the industry in which the company competes and the social, economic, and political forces involved.

4. A thorough understanding of the company, including its technologies, products, policies, objectives, history, organization, and environment.

5. The ability to communicate with all levels of management and a basic understanding of the other functional problems related to engineering, production, procurement, industrial relations, and marketing.

6. The ability to express ideas clearly in writing or in making informative presentations.

7. The ability to motivate others to achieve positive action and results.

Compare the listed qualifications of the controller with the skills needed to be a successful CFO as revealed in a survey of CFOs.[1]

---

[1] Lawrence S. Maisel, "Proactive and Powerful—The New CFO," *Financial Executive,* July/Aug., 1990, p. 14.

	Affirmative Response (%)
Business sense/understanding of operations	84
Problem-solving ability	50
Integrity	49
Innovativeness	43
Vision of the "big picture"	43

Percentages do not total 100 due to multiple responses. As noted, more than half rated a business sense and understanding of operations, problem-solving ability, or integrity as a needed skill. But innovativeness and having a vision of the "big picture" were not far behind. Essentially, the CFO and other major executives must view the CFO as a business person (and not just a figure person) and part of the business management group before the financial executive can be effective in helping to shape the strategy and direction of the business. Mr. Controller, prepare for the future!

A controller may have the technical capability and be able to lay out the assigned tasks as well as supervise and direct his personnel, but he must also have integrity and the ability to communicate if he is to succeed. He must be fair, reasonable, and sincere with all concerned if he is to be recognized for the importance of the controllership function.

As in any executive position, the controller must be able to work with people at all levels, have respect for the ideas and opinions of others, and have the resourcefulness to meet all challenges.

The dynamic business world of today makes it essential that the controller keep current on all aspects of the business. This can be accomplished through refresher courses at various colleges and universities and membership in trade associations or professional societies. Most of the organizations provide literature analyzing the issues and problems currently confronting business. In addition, for those problems requiring more in-depth review, the professional groups provide seminars for a broader understanding. In any event, it is mandatory that the controller keep involved with the issues of the day by association with other members of the profession.

2-17 THE NEW TYPE OF MANAGER

Competition is becoming more brutal. As a result, customers are more demanding, investors expect better performance, and even corporate directors are becoming more independent and are asking tougher questions. The World War II type of manager, perhaps one of the most successful and powerful business groups ever, is passing from the scene. Witness what has happened recently at IBM, General Motors, Westinghouse Electric, and American Express. Today's chief executive simply can't be wedded to the past. Times often call for a shake-up.

The old-time autocratic manager very often told people what to do, when to do it, and how to do it. But a new type of manager and a new organizational structure are coming onto the scene, and this scene includes the controller's department. Some of the trends include flattened hierarchies, self-managed teams, and pay-for-performance systems. These new managers want to be seen as leaders, sponsors, and facilitators—anything but managers. They seek to *empower* their people—to ask questions that will help the staff solve the problems and make decisions on their own. Under the old system, decisions were perhaps made faster; under the new system, where "the team" shares in the decision, the inclination is to get the decision into operation faster. However, occasions will still arise when the leader must direct a decision.

The two types of managers can be illustrated by the following comparison:

Old-Type Manager	New-Type Manager
Follows the chain of command	Deals with whoever is necessary to get a job done
Thinks of self as manager or boss	Thinks of self as a team leader, an internal consultant, or a teacher
Makes most of the decisions alone	Invites the other members of the group to share in decision making
Keeps information to self	Shares information
Tries to master a single discipline, such as accounting or marketing	Seeks to master a broad band of managerial disciplines
Demands long hours	Demands results most of all

This new type of business executive must provide a new style of leadership which has been found very effective—one which motivates people and assists them in solving problems. Moreover, skilled financial analysis of the line items in the statements of income and expense, cash flows, and financial condition, and supporting records still will be central to the controllership efforts. However, a greater emphasis than formerly must be placed on the intangible non-financial factors essential to the success of the business. Attention to, and monitoring of, such things as customer satisfaction, development time of new products, flow time of products through the factory, quality and experience of personnel, new technology developments (including information systems), management compensation, corporate culture, and external relations, is the concern of the controller as well as the other executives. A person in this position should have valuable contributions to make. The financial executive must not be seen simply as a number cruncher.

2-18 SELECTED REFERENCES

Allen, David, "Financial Management: The Leading Edge of Management Accountancy," *Management Accounting,* June, 1992, pp. 53–54.

Byrne, John S., "Requiem for Yesterday's CEO," *Business Week,* Feb. 15, 1993, pp. 32–33.

Crescenzi, Adam D., and Jerry Kocher, "Management Support Systems: Opportunity for Controllers," *Management Accounting,* March 1984, pp. 34–37.

Dumaine, Brian, "The New Non-Manager Managers," *Fortune,* Feb. 22, 1993, pp. 80–91.

Fern, Richard H., and Manuel A. Tipgos, "Controllers as Business Strategists: A Progress Report," *Management Accounting,* March 1988, pp. 25–34.

Frishkoff, Patricia A., "Is Your Controllership Function Out of Control?" *Management Accounting,* March 1986, pp. 45–47.

Lusch, Robert F., and Michael G. Harvey, "The Case for an Off-Balance Sheet Controller," *Sloan Management Review,* Winter 1994, pp. 101–105.

Means, Grady, "The New CFO: Walking Today's Financial Tightrope," *Financial Executive,* Nov. 1984, pp. 10–16.

Pipkin, Al, "The 21st Century Controller," *Management Accounting,* Feb. 1989, pp. 21–25.

Walker, John P., and John J. Surdick, "Controllers vs. MIS Managers: Who Should Control Corporate Information Systems?" *Management Accounting,* May 1988, pp. 22–25.

CHAPTER 3

Organizational Structure for Effective Controllership

The organizational structure of a company must provide for a coordinated effort by all units and levels to take actions that will achieve a common objective. Each unit of the organization must understand its responsibilities, how each unit relates to another, and precisely what authorities have been delegated to each unit.

There are many theories on organizational structure; however, in observing well-managed companies it will be noted that the organization plan focuses on the coordination of group effort—not an individual. Through a sound organization, the tasks are grouped in such a manner that they can be accomplished effectively, the performance directed and supervised, and the results controlled. It is essential that the chief executive develop a plan of organization that will group the activities and reporting relationship to maximize the capabilities of the company.

Any organization plan must be flexible so it can be changed to meet the needs of the changing environment in which the company operates. As the business expands, as technology and products change, and as the availability of executive or managerial talent changes, the organization structure must be reevaluated and modified accordingly. A decentralized company will probably experience more difficult communication and administrative problems than a centralized company. New technologies may change the need for a different organizational concept for product development, quality control, and the accumulation and processing of data for management purposes. There are many excellent books and publications on organizations and principles, and in this chapter we highlight some of the issues that the controller should consider in organizing for the execution of the assigned tasks.

3-1 ORGANIZING FOR CONTROL

Controllership is a basic function of the enterprise that has grown in recognition and must be properly organized if the accounting controls are to function and the statistical data are to be utilized effectively. The proper procedures, methods, and records are not sufficient; the tasks must be accomplished on a well-coordinated basis, and the results communicated to those concerned. The basic principles of organization apply to the accounting function as well as to the other functions of the business. There are many factors that have enlarged the scope and recognition of the controller's function, such as increased regulatory requirements for accounting or financial reports, more data available and required for management decisions, broader public ownership of companies, and a more complex operating environment, including multinational operations with related problems. The particular organizational structure must consider the overall company organization, the size of the business, anticipated growth, nature of the business, kinds of operations, locations, degree of decentralization, extent of vertical integration that may exist, long-range plans, and the management style or personal characteristics of the executive group as a whole. There is no standard organization that can be used in all cases; the peculiarities of each company must be considered. However, there are certain basic principles that should be applied in view of the overall organizational structure of the company.

An *effective organization* may be defined as a group of individuals cooperating on taking actions successfully toward a common objective. In building an accounting team that will be responsive to management's needs in a timely manner, the controller must consider at least three factors:

1. The organizational structure—a proper grouping of functions to most effectively accomplish the assigned tasks, determine the proper relationships within the group and the company as a whole, and insure that proper elements of control exist.

2. The proper delegation of responsibility and authority to each level of the organization and each unit.

3. The selection of the right individual for each job.

The serious consideration and evaluation of these factors will determine to a great extent how well the controller's function will succeed in providing the company with a cost-effective and responsive accounting capability. How effective the organization is will depend on the following:

1. Providing management and external agencies with accurate reports, data, and information on a scheduled and timely basis.

2. Providing such information on a cost-effective basis—minimum costs for results obtained.

3. Staffing the organization with competent personnel and development of an adequate training program.

3-2 TYPICAL ORGANIZATIONAL PROBLEMS FOR THE CONTROLLER

As an enterprise grows or expands and the environment changes, the controller will be faced with issues, problems, and decisions related to the organizational structure:

1. The organizational structure, which must be continually reviewed considering the changing technologies, new requirements, different responsibilities, and the total environment in which the company operates.

2. The centralization or decentralization of the company and the problems related to the accounting function that can be performed more effectively at headquarters, division offices, plant or factory offices, branch offices, sales offices, etc.

3. The relationship of the company or corporate controller to each division or plant controller—on a direct reporting line, or through the head of the operating unit, or on a dual reporting basis.

4. Evaluation of functions performed at headquarters and at the division or plant level and redelegation of responsibilities as appropriate.

5. Proper segregation of duties within the controller's department.

6. Evaluation of the delegation of authority and related responsibilities.

3-3 TYPICAL ORGANIZATIONAL STRUCTURE FOR CONTROLLER'S DEPARTMENT

No one organizational structure fits all needs; no one plan is ideal. Certain functional groupings have been found to be practical and workable. The basic problem is to decide how the functions can be grouped for the most effective results in the particular environment. As previously discussed, other factors must be considered such as the size and nature of the business, experience of the executives and staff, personnel, physical locations, management philosophy, and business objectives. For discussion purposes a typical functional organization chart for the controller's department in a medium-sized to large company, which has as financial officers both a controller and a treasurer, is illustrated in Figure 3-1. Some comments relative to such a structure are noted here:

1. The general accounting and cost accounting groups are primarily concerned with the recording of transactions and reporting historical results. Depending on the

Figure 3-1 Typical Functional Organization Chart for Controller's Department.

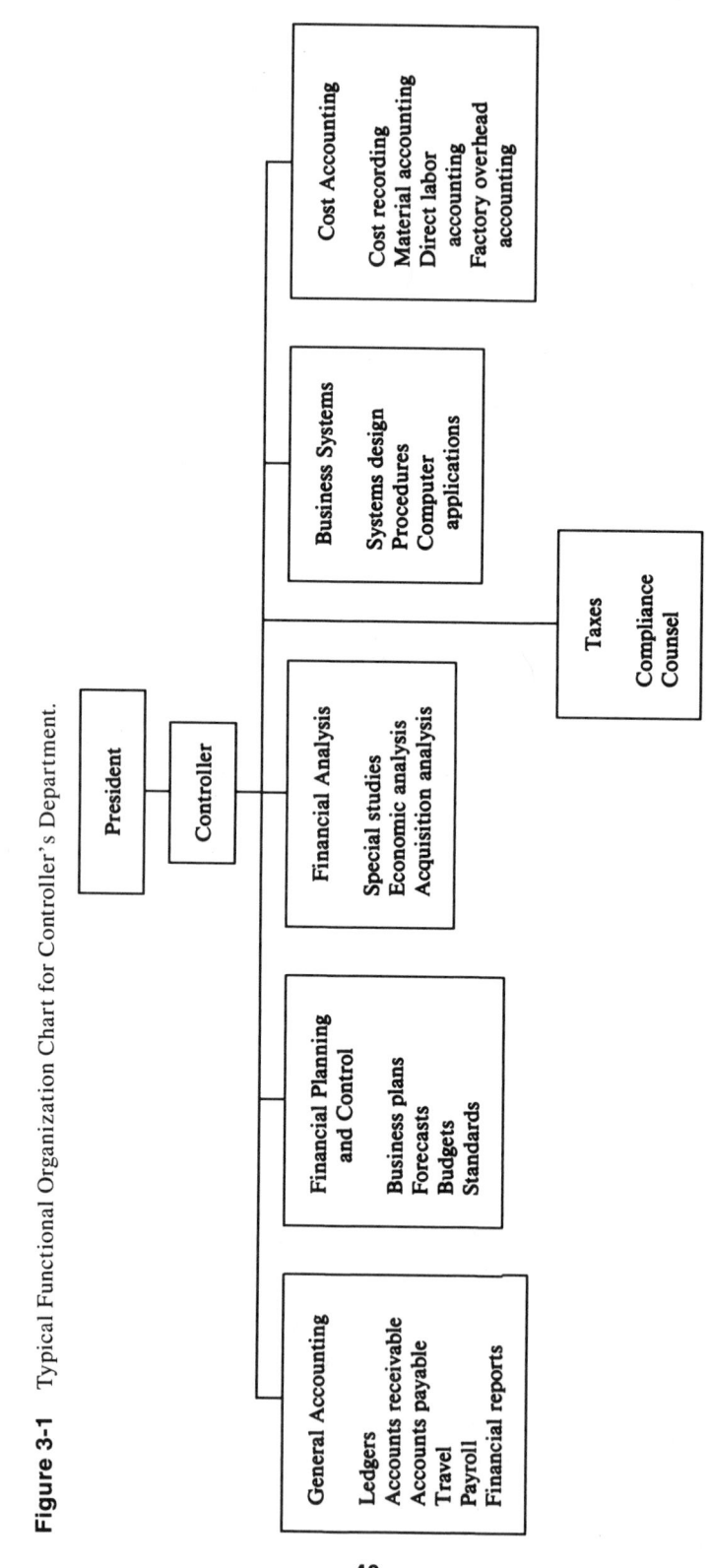

volume of transactions and the level of activity, these functions could be included in one group.

2. The financial planning and control functions are segregated from recording activities. This allows the staff to concentrate on excess costs, performance measurement, variance analysis, and recommended corrective actions. In most cases, the personnel will be more analytical and will relate to factory or operating personnel to fully understand the significance of deviations from plan.

3. In larger companies, there is a need for personnel capable of making special studies related to particular problems, plant relocation, make-or-buy decisions, and economic analyses and financial analyses of the possible acquisition of other companies.

4. A separate department should be created to have sufficient resources available for the design of accounting systems, development of implementing procedures, and coordination with the computer center personnel for those systems that have computer applications. In addition, it should insure that the systems are properly integrated.

5. In some companies, taxes and insurance are the responsibility of the controller. The functions should be segregated because of the specialization of the functions and the need for different skills.

6. Depending on the size of the company, a separate department may be established for internal auditing reporting to the controller. To achieve appropriate segregation of duties, the internal audit function should be completely segregated from other accounting responsibilities and probably should report to an executive other than the controller, such as the senior vice-president-finance or an internal audit committee that is a subset of a board of directors.

7. Where the company is small or medium sized, office-management-type functions such as communications, office services, mail, files, and reproduction services report to the controller. These are general services usually requiring very little accounting knowledge or skill. As the company grows, the controller should completely delegate these tasks or have them reassigned so that the efforts can be better directed to the main functions of controllership.

As a summary of the company finance function, the typical division of responsibility between controller and treasurer in a medium-sized to large company, as illustrated and described above, is as follows:

Treasury Responsibility	Controllership Responsibility
Control of cash and bank balances	General accounting
Bank relations	Cost accounting
Financing	Budgeting and financial planning
Credit management	Analysis of business operations
Risk (insurance) management	Financial analysis (acquisitions, etc.)
Supervision of pension funds	Federal, state, and local taxes
	Business systems

3-4 LEVELS OF CONTROLLERSHIP

Commentary in the preceding section implicitly refers to the company controller—that financial officer, operating at the top management level, responsible for the company accounting, budgeting, controls, taxes, etc. But in the real world there may be three levels of controllership, depending on the size of the company, the physical location of the facilities, and the philosophy of organization:

- The *company controller* operating at the home office or top management center.
- In an entity that is divisionally organized by product or geography, a division manager charged with carrying out the controllership activities of a division through the *division controller*.
- At the top level of management in each plant, an executive responsible for carrying out the controllership functions through the *plant controller*.

These three levels of controllership are illustrated in Figure 3-2. The exhibit reflects the decentralized style of organization discussed in the next several sections. In a functionally organized company, the division and plant controllers would report to the corporate controller.

Figure 3-2   Levels of Controllership.

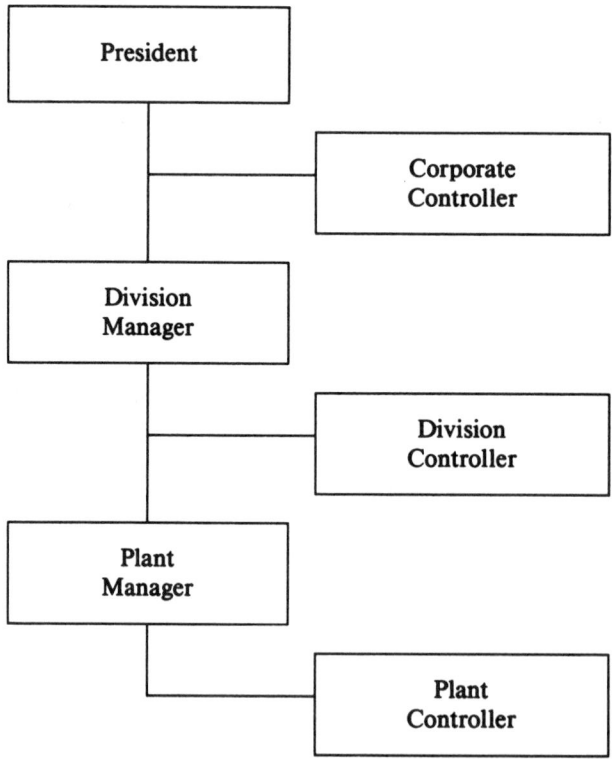

Finally, as to the three levels of controllership, each has many of the same functional responsibilities, as applied to his or her organization, that the corporate controller has company-wide. Thus, the division controller has responsibility for the division accounting, division financial planning, etc. And the plant controller has responsibility for the plant accounting, plant financial plans, and plant financial report preparation, etc.

3-5 A CENTRALIZED VS. DECENTRALIZED ACCOUNTING ORGANIZATION

Companies with divisions, subsidiaries, or branch plants are among those chiefly concerned with the problem of decentralization. Decentralization as here used relates to the trend to increased delegation of authority to subordinate operating officials at remote locations. Centralization, of course, relates to the trend toward increased executive control from the home office. Quite clearly, the matter may transcend merely the accounting organization and extend to the entire company, through every major function.

There are an infinite number of possibilities about the centralization or decentralization of accounting functions. On the one extreme is the highly centralized organization in which all records are maintained in the home office. The control and subsidiary ledgers are kept there. The sole accounting function at the factory or branch is an accumulation of the documents of original entry—the production lot sheets, material requisitions, time cards, and perhaps invoices and receiving reports. These are summarized and transmitted monthly, or on some other periodic basis, to the general offices. At the other extreme is the completely decentralized operation. Each plant or each warehouse may operate as though it were an independent company. A complete set of books is maintained; monthly statements are prepared at the branch and sent to the home office for consolidation. In between these extremes are a great number of combinations. Thus there may be a decentralized billing procedure with centralized accounts receivable records. Or there may be a centralized disbursements department with decentralized account distribution. Similarly, there are wide differences in the treatment of payrolls. As a matter of fact, with the use of factory ledger accounts and the complementary general and factory ledger control accounts, a great number of choices can be made about accounts to be centralized and those to be decentralized. Each method has its advantages as well as its problems.

There are probably five basic considerations that influence the decision about the degree of centralized accounting structure:

1. The management philosophy concerning divisional responsibility.
2. The availability of operating data.
3. The size of operating divisions or units.
4. The geographic location of the operating units.
5. The economies of the situation.

These major factors are briefly reviewed.

(a) MANAGEMENT PHILOSOPHY

As business expands to embrace several plants, each of which produces several distinct products or is a step in a complete integration, the philosophy may develop that the best operating results are obtained by creating an autonomous unit. Under this management theory, each divisional manager has complete authority over all matters affecting his operation, and this includes the accounting function. On such a basis, each division is generally complete in all respects, and the division's management is judged on the overall profit results of the operation. The home office or administrative staff deals only with overall policy or matters of company-wide application. Such a philosophy might apply, for example, to the divisions of The Ford Motor Company but might not extend to the separate plants within each division.

This same accounting concept has considerable appeal and has been applied even where the management is not judged on the overall profit results and where the home office takes a more active part in the local operations. Thus sales methods, purchasing policies, credit extension, inventory policies, and other matters may be directed or modified by top management. Moreover, the detailed expenses and income may be subject to close scrutiny through the means of periodic reports. Clearly, the same management philosophy does not apply here, although the accounting may be decentralized to give the divisional manager a certain control over the activity. Undoubtedly, there are instances where the divisional manager would be glad to be relieved of the accounting responsibility if the needed information were forthcoming. Undoubtedly, also, the practice of decentralization has been applied on this managerial concept when not warranted.

(b) AVAILABILITY OF OPERATING INFORMATION

Whether the local management is independent or not, it may need accounting information to control the business adequately. This matter involves two separate questions: (1) What information must be available on a division or plant basis? (2) Where should such information be prepared? These two questions have to be dealt with since it does not follow that, because data are required at the division level, they must be prepared at this same level.

In judging what information should be segregated by division, an important consideration is the placement of responsibility. Just who is responsible for the particular items—plant management or home office? For example, whether accounts receivable should be recorded on a divisional basis would depend on who is responsible for credit extension. If credit approval and follow-up is a divisional matter, then records should be segregated accordingly. If it is a home office charge, then a divisional classification would seem unnecessary. Fixed-asset data perhaps need to be made available only periodically, and divisional management could be advised through reports prepared either at the home office or at the division level.

There is, of course, a definite need for operating data. Here timing is an important factor. Whether the needs can be met by a centralized accounting organization will depend on the circumstances. Perhaps the factory data for labor, material, and expense control must be prepared locally, whereas selling and administrative costs are centralized. In any event, the home office must thoroughly know the operations, and the degree of coordination between branch and general office must be great, if the latter organization is to do the accounting and reporting.

(c) SIZE OF OPERATING UNIT

In some cases, the operating unit will be large enough so that all or most of the accounting functions can be carried out efficiently on a decentralized basis. Factors to be weighed include the degree of internal control that can be achieved, availability of competent personnel, degree of utilization of mechanical or electronic equipment, availability of office space, and the nature and number of accounting decisions to be resolved.

(d) GEOGRAPHICAL LOCATION

As a generalization, the farther away an operation is from the home office, the smaller the unit that would justify decentralization on the basis of geography only—to avoid or minimize delays and other complications. If a unit is only overnight mail service away, centralization of items might be more desirable than if the plants were on opposite coasts. If closeness of customer contact is important and the sales are largely restricted to the local area, perhaps decentralization of accounts receivable or billings might be desirable. Again, closeness of contact with suppliers might be a controlling factor in the decentralization of the purchasing function and accounts payable.

(e) ECONOMY OF OPERATION

If there is no compelling need for decentralization, then the matter may be resolved on an economy basis. Under these circumstances the tendency of the local unit to maintain records rather than rely on general office reports should not be overlooked. This duplication of effort should be avoided. In approaching the problem of economy, the controller will, of course, probably need an objective survey of accounting methods. The survey should emphasize the activity by accounts rather than merely the nature of the accounting function. In considering economy, the extent of machine accounting can be an important factor.

3-6 REPORTING RELATIONSHIP—CONTROLLER AND DIVISION CONTROLLER

One of the typical organizational problems faced by the corporate controller in many of the larger companies is his or her relationship to the division controller and the plant controller.

In the typical decentralized company, the division controller reports to the chief line executive of the division, and the plant controller reports directly to the plant manager. "Reports" is herein used in the *administrative* sense, i.e., a "superior-subordinate" relationship. If the division and plant controllers are administratively responsible to their respective division and plant manager, what is their relationship to the corporate controller? After all, this latter officer is responsible on a company-wide basis for all the accounting, budgeting, tax and controls, including internal controls, of the entity. The answer is that the division/plant controller is *functionally* responsible to the corporate controller for effectively carrying out his basic controllership tasks, including:

- Carrying out the corporate financial and accounting policies and procedures within his or her division/plant.
- Providing the corporate controller with timely and accurate reports on accounting/financial/control matters pertaining to the division/plant, that the corporate executive needs for the internal and external reporting requirements.

Additionally, of course, the division/plant controller has the responsibility of providing line management with the accounting/financial services needed for proper execution of their tasks.

A typical reporting relationship in a decentralized organization is illustrated in Figure 3-3. There is a "dotted line" relationship to the corporate controller and a "solid line" relationship to the division/plant manager.

In those cases where it appears the division financial executive reports solely to a corporate financial executive (in a centralized organization structure) or to a

Figure 3-3 Typical Reporting Relationships in a Decentralized Organization.

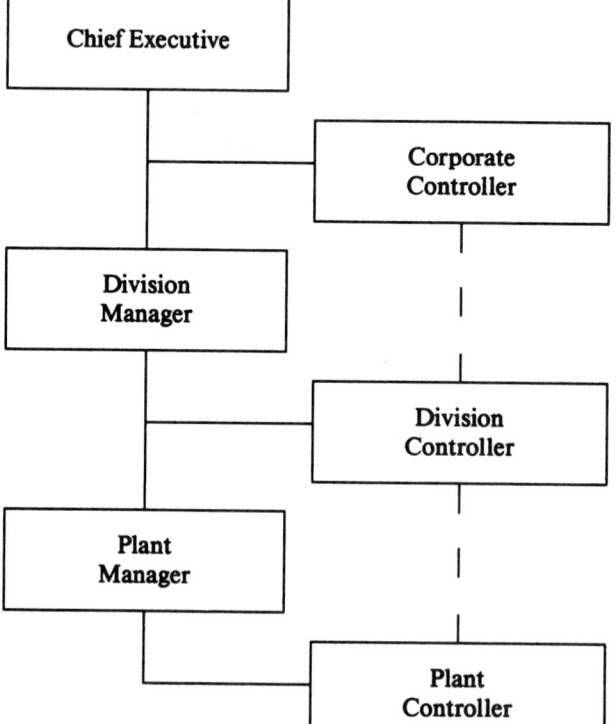

division/plant manager (a decentralized organization structure), he must satisfy both executives. Thus, he or she is subject to conflicting demands.

3-7 ADVANTAGES OF DECENTRALIZATION—A SUMMARY

Many controllers tend to favor a centralized organization if at all practical, because they feel better enabled to control accounting activities. There have been, however, some sad experiences with centralization; furthermore, the theoretical savings have not been realized or have been offset by other costs not quite as readily apparent. It is felt desirable, therefore, to emphasize the advantages of decentralization, recognizing, however, that decentralization is not always the best form of operation.

The advantages of decentralization may be noted as follows:

1. From a psychological viewpoint, decentralization tends to increase the initiative of local management. The control responsibilities are more keenly felt.

2. Local organization of data avoids some excuses for inactivity or poor performance because "the report was too late" or "the report was wrong." This factor is partly psychological in regard to its benefits.

3. Duplication can be eliminated—particularly where the branch or plant retains records so as to have current information or to "check up" on the home office report. Of course, if the records are maintained to have current data available, this may be some indication that the wrong record was centralized.

4. Under ordinary circumstances, speedier results can be attained. When the entire operation is under local control, every effort will be made to secure timely data. This should contribute to closer cost control.

5. Wider accounting responsibility in the field is a means of training field personnel for promotions and generally results in a sounder organization.

6. Competent personnel can as readily prepare data for home office use as can the central organization. With an objective accountant on the job, perhaps even a better reporting of facts can be secured. Decentralization need not be a means of denying the necessary data for executive control. For example, copies of the same reports going to divisional management could go also to home office management.

7. Decentralization is not in opposition to uniformity. It adds some flexibility and still permits the application of accounting policies and practices through the use of standard forms and standard practice manuals.

8. Any concerns regarding poor controls at off-site locations can be overcome by a competent internal audit department that is centrally located and visits each plant location in turn.

The advantages of decentralization, in a general way, are the disadvantages of centralization. However, some advantages of a centralized organization may be emphasized:

1. Permits greater flexibility in the utilization of existing personnel and facilities, including the ability to meet peak loads.

2. Frequently permits the utilization of mechanical equipment that might not be justified in a decentralized situation.

3. May permit the utilization of more qualified personnel, particularly in the higher executive echelon, because of increased responsibilities.

The extent to which these advantages may *not* be realized in a decentralized organization depends in large part on the size of the local unit.

3-8 DELEGATION OF RESPONSIBILITY AND AUTHORITY

A difficult problem confronting every controller, indeed any executive, relates to the extent to which he or she can delegate responsibility and authority. He is charged with the responsibility for a large number of duties to which he cannot give his personal attention. He *must* therefore pass on authority to accomplish certain tasks and place the responsibility for execution—although in the final analysis the controller is still responsible. Only by such delegation can he free himself to devote his time and energy to those matters that will best serve the interests of management.

What duties, then, should be delegated? As a general statement, the controller should reserve for himself the broader duties, those of wide application, such as decisions relating to accounting policy and practice. He should assign to others those matters that are smaller in scope. Moreover, he must delegate sufficient duties so that he is not burdened with details. Such delegation of authority, incidentally, has the advantage of developing the confidence and judgment of junior executives. On the other extreme, the controller should not get so far away that he loses touch with significant developments.

Because of the nature of his duties, the controller has a great personal responsibility to the management, shareholders, and government for the facts and figures issued by the accounting division. No delegation of authority can pass on this responsibility to others. However, it is suggested that any delegation of duties be accompanied by a thorough explanation of the accounting philosophy and business objectives to be followed. This practice should assist the controller in better securing the type of accomplishment desired.

Some examples may assist in clarifying what type of work may and should be delegated. All matters relating to routine operation of the accounting departments may be delegated to the department heads; only matters not covered by procedures or established policy need be referred to the controller. Again, with regard to accounting departments, all changes in budget structures, salaries, additional personnel, new procedures, accounting policy, or basic changes in reports should be reviewed by the controller; and all other aspects of operations might be delegated. As another more specific illustration, all special cost studies involving large expenditures or matters of basic management policy—such as purchase of a new production site or change in major product emphasis—should be handled by the controller. In contrast, routine cost determinations, such as formulation costs or parts costs for limited application, might be delegated to the cost accountant. As another general rule, cost studies requested by top-level management should be channeled through the controller's department. Although the details may be worked out by others, the controller should at least thoroughly review the interpretation.

3-9 THE CONTROLLER'S AUTHORITY OVER ACCOUNTING AND STATISTICAL ACTIVITIES

An organization problem to be clearly resolved involves the controller's authority in a twofold manner: (1) where the branch offices or plants are on a decentralized accounting basis, what should be the authority of the corporate controller as related to the divisional manager and the divisional controller, and (2) what should be the authority of the controller (central office or divisional) about accounting, statistical, or other office activities not under his department? The general answer to both questions is that the controller should have *functional* control and responsibility for *all* such records. Whereas the divisional controller may report to the divisional manager, for example, the corporate controller should have the right to prescribe methods and procedures if the need should arise. Also, records kept by the factory or sales staff should be subjected to the same functional control.

While the records can be physically located in the departments with which associated—in the sales department for sales statistics and in the factory for production records—there are definite advantages to be gained by placing all accounting, statistical, and office procedures under one chief accounting officer. If the job is well done, the following benefits should be realized:

1. Duplication of effort can be avoided.
2. Clerical expense can be reduced as the result of centralized and more efficient supervision.
3. All records and statistical data can be made available to all departments.
4. Accounting and statistical data will be interpreted better, and figure-facts will be more objectively presented.

3-10 ORGANIZATIONAL TRENDS

There are several management trends occurring that will impact the structure of the controller's department. These changes are occurring because of both technological improvements and corporate efforts to cut overhead in order to meet increasingly competitive pricing from overseas companies. We will briefly cover the changes caused by outsourcing, electronic data interchange (EDI), flat management structures, activity-based costing (ABC), and corporate downsizing.

(a) OUTSOURCING

Many companies have outsourced some of their functions to outside service firms. The theory behind this activity is that outside firms can specialize in an activity that the company cannot do as well, and may provide the service for less money than it originally cost the company. Outsourcing can apply to an accounting department. Very small firms can outsource the bulk of the department to a bookkeeping firm. However, larger companies may want to retain greater control over key accounting functions, and only outsource a few specialized areas. Any area that is very specialized, is not a full-time position, or involves skills that must be updated constantly is ripe for outsourcing. The three most popular areas to be outsourced are:

1. *Payroll.* Payroll information is frequently mailed or called in to a service bureau, which calculates pay and taxes, stores the information for year-end reporting, prints checks (or just remittance advices, in the case of direct deposit accounts), and issues periodic reports to management. The service bureaus keep up-to-date tax tables for deduction calculations, which the company's accounting department no longer has to do.

2. *Taxation.* Smaller firms cannot afford or have trouble retaining expert taxation personnel. In addition, regional CPA firms regularly update their tax specialists with the latest tax law changes, something the controller may not be able to do for in-house staff. As a result, outside tax people are frequently better trained than in-house staff and can generate savings greater than their (considerable) cost. Since tax consultants are expensive, any routine tax filing work that is largely clerical in nature should be retained in-house.

3. *Collections.* Though not as frequently outsourced as the above items, collections can be shifted to a collection agency, either in part or in total. Also, if the company has a factoring arrangement with an outside party, the arrangement may state that the outside party is responsible for all collections. Collection work is usually charged as a percentage of the overdue invoice, so fees can be considerable, depending on the size of the overdue balances.

(b) ELECTRONIC DATA INTERCHANGE (EDI)

If EDI is fully implemented, it will have a radical impact on the accounting department. The intent of EDI is to speed up transactions by converting paperflow to electronic data flow. If that occurs for all payables, receivables, payments, and orders, then the general accounting function (see Figure 3-1) will cease to exist except for special functions, such as processing expense reports and miscellaneous journal entries.

The EDI-based accounting department will replace its accounting clerks with systems analysts and internal auditors. Since there will be no paper flowing through the system, a new kind of audit trail will have to be created by systems analysts and internal auditors. Because a paperless system would have different risks of fraud from computer "hackers" and company insiders, a new set of fraud prevention controls would have to be created and implemented. These systems would need to be created in consultation with the company's external auditors, who would need new methods for assuring themselves of the accuracy of the company's financial information.

The advent of EDI will not necessarily reduce the cost of the accounting department. It will replace a large number of low-paid accounting clerks with a small number of well-paid analysts and auditors, so the department's payroll level may not change significantly.

(c) FLAT MANAGEMENT STRUCTURES

There is a growing trend toward eliminating layers of management in order to achieve a cheaper corporate overhead structure. The controller can implement the following items in order to reduce the number of accounting managers:

1. *High-Level Training.* The accounting staff must be very well trained. The training should not be theoretical accounting as taught in school. Instead, it should be

detailed training in all accounting procedures, and in any special situations that may arise. Extensive written procedures are helpful.

2. *Low Headcount.* Because a well-trained, well-motivated staff needs less management intervention, fewer managers will be needed. To shrink the staff, the controller should eliminate process duplication, eliminate unneeded reports, outsource applications like payroll and taxation, and automate functions wherever possible.

3. *Empowered Staff.* Allow the staff to make all but the most crucial decisions. A careful review of approvals will reveal that the risk associated with eliminating approvals is minimal in many cases. The staff's morale will improve as it is allowed to perform nearly all accounting tasks without intervention, and fewer managers will be needed.

The role of the manager changes as the above items are implemented. Training staff to perform functions previously handled by managers will be a crucial function. In addition, the manager must work closely with the accounting staff to reduce bureaucracy and improve processes. Because of this change in roles, the ideal accounting manager must be a "people" person who interacts with the staff constantly, and who is well trained in simplifying accounting processes.

(d) ACTIVITY-BASED COSTING

The advent of activity-based costing (ABC) may require a larger financial analysis group (see Figure 3-1). There are two ways to implement ABC: either alter the base-level transaction recording systems and reports so that ABC replaces the current systems, or install it on a project basis. If the project basis is used, then ABC will be used infrequently, and ABC costs will be compared to the previous ABC project results to determine cost changes.

No matter which approach is used, a well-trained group of hands-on accounting staff should be used to implement ABC. A good source of that type of person is the financial analysis group. The reason for using this group is that it has the greatest need for ABC output, and therefore should be heavily involved in the system design and implementation. Even after the ABC systems or projects are completed, there will still be a greater need for financial analysis personnel, for they will use the ABC output to recommend process changes in those areas covered by the ABC studies. Because of the increased number of recommendations coming from the financial analysis group, the skill level to be hired into it may become closer to an in-house consultant than an analyst, since presentation skills will be important, and the recommendations may not be entirely financial in nature. For example, an ABC finding might be that the cost per salesperson to sell a product is too high; an in-house consultant could work with the sales department to develop alternative selling techniques, whereas an analyst would only report the ABC finding without coming up with lower-cost alternatives.

(e) CORPORATE DOWNSIZING

An increasing number of controllers are being told to cut back on the size of their staffs in order to save costs. The following points may assist in determining which positions can safely be eliminated without harming the company:

1. *Risk.* If the company has significant risk of loss due to lawsuits, then retaining someone who is familiar with the company's insurance policies is a good idea. Similarly, if the company is deeply involved in derivatives, then eliminating the position that tracks them could lead to corporate bankruptcy if significant losses are sustained as a result.

2. *Cost Structure.* If the company has a high cost of goods sold or operates as a job shop, then cost accounting becomes more important than for a services firm.

3. *Outsourcing.* If technically competent personnel are available outside the firm to fulfill certain functions (e.g., payroll and taxes), then those internal positions could be safely eliminated.

4. *Reporting.* If the corporate staff consolidates and redistributes information that has already been summarized at the plant level, then the corporate staff could be reduced in favor of using the plant-level reports as the final reports.

5. *Financial Analysis.* If accounts are being reviewed in detail that do not involve excessive costs or risk of large fluctuations, then the analysis of those accounts could be stopped and additional staff eliminated.

6. *Automation.* If areas such as time card review can be automated by using bar coded time clocks, then such equipment could allow staff levels to be reduced.

7. *Cross-checking.* If staff are reviewing each other's work, then this is a non-value added activity. The controller should review each situation and determine the risk of error if such cross-checks can be eliminated, thereby reducing work hours.

3-11 SELECTED REFERENCES

Boyatzis, Richard A., *The Competent Manager.* New York: John Wiley & Sons, 1982.

Hickman, Craig R., *Mind of a Manager, Soul of a Leader.* New York: John Wiley & Sons, 1992.

Studies in Business Policy, published by the Conference Board: No. 56—The Duties of Financial Executives, No. 101—Divisional Financial Executives.

Vroom, Victor H., and Arthur G. Jago, *The New Leadership: Managing Participation in Organizations.* Englewood Cliffs, NJ: Prentice Hall, 1988.

CHAPTER 4

Accounting Principles and Standards—The Rule Makers

4-1 INTRODUCTION

As the chief accounting officer of the company, the controller has responsibility for the many accounting decisions involving the entity. While the emphasis of this book is on the *managerial* aspects of accounting, it may be helpful to review briefly the many types of accounting, and the impact that generally accepted accounting principles and practices has on each.

Accordingly, this chapter provides some background on the chief organizations involved in the development and monitoring of accounting principles or standards, as well as a brief review of matters related to the principles themselves. Further information can be gained from the Selected References, from independent accountants, or other individuals employed in accounting functions or tax activities.

4-2 TYPES OF ACCOUNTING AND FINANCIAL REPORTING

The Inventory of Generally Accepted Accounting Principles for Business Enterprises, Accounting Research Study No. 7, defines accounting as:

> Accounting is the body of knowledge and functions concerned with systematic originating, authenticating, recording, classifying, processing, summarizing, analyzing, interpreting and supplying of dependable and significant information covering transactions and events which are, in part at least, of a financial character, required for the management and operation of an entity and for the reports that have to be submitted thereon to meet fiduciary and other responsibilities.

This broad field of accounting may be subdivided any number of ways, but for our purposes these segments seem relevant:

(a) Financial accounting and reporting, or more descriptively, "general purpose external financial accounting and reporting."

(b) Managerial accounting and reporting.

(c) Tax accounting and reporting.

(d) Not-for-profit accounting and reporting.

(e) Accounting for certain specialized fields of business, such as:
 (1) Financial institutions.
 (2) Construction.
 (3) Real estate.
 (4) Oil, gas, and other natural resources extractive activities.
 (5) Regulated utilities, including electric utilities, gas companies, and telephone companies.

(f) International accounting, which involves the harmonizing of financial standards and reporting practices or requirements developed by authoritative bodies in countries other than the United States, in what can be called foreign or global multinational companies.

(g) National income accounting, which is not identified with a single private activity, but instead relates to the entire U.S. economic system and the related reporting requirements. This segment produces various reports of the Department of Commerce.

Some detailed comments are made about the three categories which involve most controllers:

(a) FINANCIAL ACCOUNTING AND REPORTING

This branch of accounting may be described as primarily concerned with the general purpose financial statements of business entities and not-for-profit organizations in which several groups have common financial informational needs: shareholders, creditors, other resource providers, and financial analysts.

It is this type of accounting that is the primary concern of the Financial Accounting Standards Board (FASB) in its effort, along with selected other organizations (described later) to encourage the development of generally accepted accounting principles to promote standards for accounting, and the related access to improved financial data, as well as increased comparability.

The system that used the principles or standards developed for this accounting classification and incorporated in the general purpose financial statements also, generally speaking, has been incorporated to a great extent in the financial reports used for the other groups enumerated above.

(b) MANAGEMENT ACCOUNTING AND REPORTING

This is an internally oriented activity that attempts to meet the information needs of the executives or managers responsible for the planning and control functions and decisions of the business entity or the not-for-profit organization. It is this field of accounting that requires most of the time and attention of the controller, and the one with which this volume is primarily concerned.

It will bear repeating that the accounting system that accumulates the financial data for external general purposes usually is the same system which also assembles the data needed for management purposes. The management information will be modified and supplemented, to the extent necessary, to serve management requirements. Further, the data will be in much more detail and will be prepared more frequently than general purpose financial information.

Most of the accounting data assembled for management purposes will not be disseminated outside the organization.

(c) TAX ACCOUNTING AND REPORTING

This facet of accounting has to do with the accumulating and reporting of financial data needed to properly prepare the tax returns and other reports required by the Internal Revenue Service as well as state and local taxing authorities, together, if relevant, with information needed by taxing bodies in any non-U.S. area in which the entity operates.

Again, financial data required for tax purposes in many ways is the same as for financial accounting, but there are significant differences. For example, some costs incurred in business are not allowable deductions under tax law; or amortization or depreciation periods may differ or other restrictions may apply.

In any event, it usually is the responsibility of the controller to ascertain that data needed for various tax returns or reports are accumulated accurately, and made available timely, and in proper form.

4-3 ACCOUNTING STANDARDS—THE RULE MAKERS

One objective of financial reporting should be to provide information that is useful to present and potential investors, creditors, and other users in making sound and rational investment, credit, and other decisions. Thus, accounting is an important factor in establishing effective capital markets that provide the financial resources needed to manufacture and distribute goods and services to customers.

But the capital market participants (which include business management) must have reliable information, otherwise their ability to reach sound decisions is impaired. This means that information must not be false or misleading. Moreover, it should permit comparability among investment choices, and it must be relevant and timely.

Historically, preparers of financial data sometimes used abusive tactics to gain an unfair advantage. Moreover, absent any rules, the diverse preparers would tend to define or value assets, liabilities, and shareholder equity, as well as income and expense items quite differently. Hence, financial accounting is regulated or influenced to a significant degree by certain government agencies and by professional organizations. These rule makers influence financial accounting itself in varying degree, and thus their impact extends to management accounting and tax accounting (as well as the other types of accounting discussed earlier).

The controller, as a professional accountant, should be aware, in a general way, of the nature of the standards, and of the various agencies and organizations involved with them.

Financial accounting regulations relate to (1) standards for *practice*—what are known as generally accepted accounting principles (GAAP), (2) standards for *competence,* and (3) standards for *behavior.*

This chapter will discuss primarily the standards of accounting practice—generally accepted accounting principles (GAAP). The controller and his staff should be reasonably familiar with them. The standards for competence and behavior, though not reviewed here, were developed primarily to apply to the independent public accountant, to assure that financial statements are reliable. A controller would also want to know the substance of these standards, so that they can be applied, to the extent deemed reasonable to key staff members.

The origins of the generally accepted accounting principles may seem confusing because of (a) the many organizations which were and are involved, and the predecessor units which were discontinued; (b) the role and interaction of each; (c) the innumerable topics discussed; and (d) the vast array of publications which disseminate the opinions, rules, postulates, or principles.

The remaining sections in this chapter will restrict comments to (1) identifying the groups that presently take an active role in developing the standards and regulations, (2) providing some limited details on the categories and sources concerning GAAP, (3) reviewing the present interrelationship of the groups most active in establishing accounting standards, and (4) describing the FASB and its publications.

The agencies and organizations currently involved with accounting regulations and standards include:

(a) *Government Agencies*

    (1) Securities and Exchange Commission

        Division of Corporation Finance

        Office of the Chief Accountant

        Division of Enforcement

    (2) State Boards of Accounting

(b) *Standards Setting Organizations*

    (1) Financial Accounting Standards Board (FASB)

    (2) Governmental Accounting Standards Board (GASB)

(c) *Professional Organizations*

   (1) American Institute of Certified Public Accountants (AICPA)

   (2) State societies, associations and institutes

   (3) International Accounting Standards Committee

   (4) Institute of Management Accountants (IMA) formerly the National Association of Accountants

   (5) Financial Executives Institute (FEI)

   (6) American Accounting Association (AAA)

   Some of the Selected References provide detail on the nature and functions of these organizations.

4-4 GAAP—CATEGORIES AND SOURCES

An overview of the four categories into which the American Institute of Certified Public Accountants (AICPA) has grouped the GAAP (for the U.S.) and some of the sources or publications in which the principles can be found are outlined in Figure 4-1.[1] Some brief comments on each category are as follows:

- *Category a.* As noted in Figure 4-1, Category a is comprised of pronouncements by an authoritative body that has been designated by the AICPA to establish accounting principles under Rule 203 of the AICPA Code of Professional Ethics. This rule provides that an accountant may not state that financial statements conform with GAAP if they contain a material departure from the pronouncements in Category a—unless adhering to them would cause the financial statements to be misleading.

- *Category b.* This category consists of pronouncements by groups of knowledgeable accountants which have followed due process procedures for the purpose of either establishing accounting principles or describing existing practices that are generally accepted.

   If the accounting treatment for a specific transaction is not specified in a pronouncement in Category a, then the accountant should refer to the designated authorities as listed for either Categories b or c.

- *Category c.* Category c comprises those practices or pronouncements that are widely recognized as being generally accepted because they represent the prevalent practices in a particular industry or the knowledgeable application to specific circumstances of pronouncements that are generally accepted and have been cleared by a body referred to in Category a, but have not been exposed for public comment.

- *Category d.* If the accounting treatment is not specified in the sources listed in Categories a, b, or c, then the accountant may consider the sources listed in Category d.

---

[1] For extensive details, see *AICPA Professional Standards, Vol 1, U.S. Auditing Standards Attestation Standards,* AU Section 411, AICPA, Commerce Clearing House, as of June 1, 1993.

Figure 4-1   Summary of GAAP Categories and Sources.

Category	Brief Description	Sources*	Rule 203 Governs
a	Officially established accounting principles	FASB SFASs	Yes
		FASB Interpretations	Yes
		APB Opinions	Yes
		AICPA Accounting Research Bulletins	
b	Pronouncements of bodies of expert accountants who deliberate accounting issues in public forums for the purpose of establishing accounting principles, or describing existing accounting practices that are generally accepted—if they have been exposed for public comment and have been cleared by a body referred to in Category a above.	FASB Technical Bulletins	No
		AICPA Industry Audit and Accounting Guides	No
		AICPA Statements of Position (SOP)	No
c	Pronouncements of bodies, organized by a body referred to in Category a, composed of expert accountants, that deliberate accounting issues in public forums for the purpose of interpreting or establishing accounting principles or describing existing accounting practices that are generally accepted, or pronouncements referred to in Category b that have been cleared by a body referred to in Category a but have not been exposed for public comment.	AICPA Accounting Standards Executive Committee (AcSEC)	No
		Practice Bulletins cleared by the FASB	No
		Consensus positions of FASB Emerging Issues Task Force (EITF)	No
d	Practices of pronouncements widely recognized as being generally accepted because they represent prevalent practice in a particular industry, or the knowledgeable application to specific circumstances of pronouncements that are generally accepted.	AICPA accounting interpretations and guides published by the FASB staff	No
		Practices that are widely recognized and prevalent either generally or in the industry	No
		Other accounting literature	No

*For Nongovernmental Entities

4-5 STANDARDS SETTING BODIES

As outlined in section 4-3, there are two standards setting bodies. Because the pronouncements of the Governmental Accounting Standards Board (GASB) only rarely will impact the activities of a business organization or a not-for-profit entity, this group will be discussed only briefly.

(a) GOVERNMENT ACCOUNTING STANDARDS BOARD

In response to the needs expressed by several groups, a study was initiated in the 1980s to consider how accounting standards should be established for state and local government units. While standards were being developed by professional organizations composed of government accountants, they had not been endorsed by the AICPA. Consequently there was concern whether or not they in fact constituted GAAP. As a result, the study group recommended the creation of the Government Accounting Standards Board (GASB) under the administration of the Financial Accounting Foundation (FAF). It began operations in 1984. The relationship of the GASB and the FASB is illustrated in Figure 4-2. Generally, the preparers and users of the governmental financial accounting reports will not be the same as those of business organizations under the review of the FASB. The preparers of the governmental accounting reports usually are elected or appointed government officials accountable to the voting public. The auditor constituency would be the same as for the FASB, but because of specialization the specific individuals are likely to be different.

The GASB issues *Statements, Interpretations, and Technical Bulletins* as well as exposure drafts of intended directives (Figure 4-3). It has also issued *GASB Codification* (in 1993). Activity of the GASB also receives attention through releases to *The CPA Letter* of the AICPA, and by way of other media, such as the *Journal of Accountancy*.

Data in the Selected References indicates the source of information about GASB Statements.

(b) FINANCIAL ACCOUNTING STANDARDS BOARD (FASB)

The financial accounting standards setting organization of most interest to a majority of controllers is the Financial Accounting Standards Board (FASB). In 1938, through

Figure 4-2   Structure of the Financial Accounting Foundation (FAF) and the two Standards Boards.

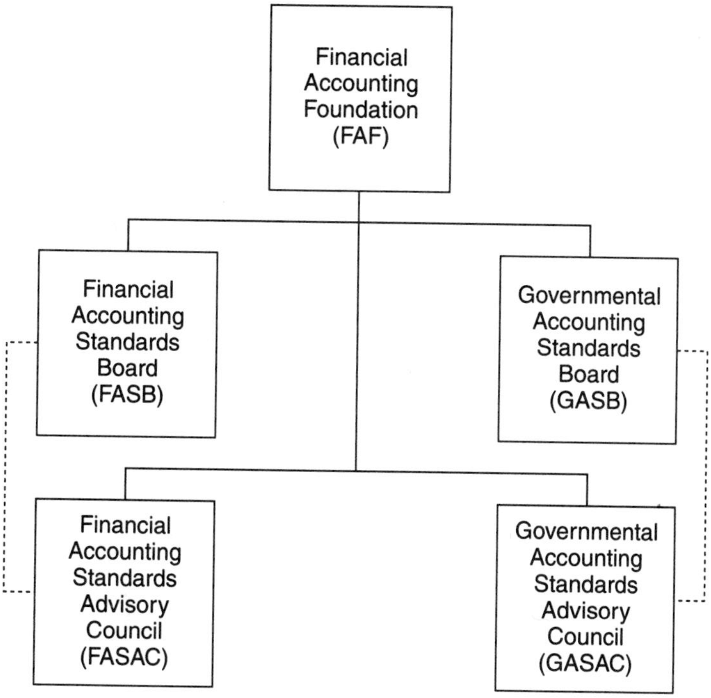

Figure 4-3   GASB Statements.

No.	Title	Issue Date
4	"Applicability of FASB Statement No. 87, *Employers Accounting for Pensions,* to State and Local Governmental Employers"	9/86
6	"Accounting and Financial Reporting for Special Assessments"	1/87
8	"Applicability of FASB Statement No. 93, *Recognition of Depreciation by Not-for-Profit Organizations,* to Certain State and Local Governmental Entities"	1/88
20	"Accounting and Financial Reporting for Proprietary Funds and Other Governmental Entities that Use Proprietary Fund Accounting"	2/94
23	"Accounting and Financial Reporting for Refundings of Debt Reported by Proprietary Activities"	3/94

the issuance of Accounting Series Release (ASR) No. 4, the Securities and Exchange Commission gave to the accounting profession a loose permission to establish GAAP. After many arguments, disagreements, and much discussion, the vehicle evolved to be the FASB. This is a unique entity in that it is a private organization charged with protecting the public interest. Although several private bodies, including the AICPA, the FEI, and the IMA, endorse and finance the FASB, it is independent of such organizations and of the major public accounting firms. The continued endorsement of the GAAP by the SEC is contingent upon the FASB remaining independent of these groups, as well as the continued protection of the public interest by the FASB.

Given the several sources of GAAP as shown in Figure 4-1, some brief comments on groups preceding the FASB may be useful. After the release of ASR No. 4 in 1938, the American Institute of Accountants (AIA), predecessor of the AICPA, used its *Committee on Accounting Procedures (CAP)* to develop some GAAP. Over roughly a 20-year period this group published more than 50 *Accounting Research Bulletins (ARBs).* But because the CAP had never been given the authority to establish binding standards, and because it was perceived to serve the auditors and their clients more than public interest, it was discontinued. Then the AICPA formed the *Accounting Principles Board (APB).* Over a 15-year period this group issued *Opinions* and *Standards.* Again, because the APB was perceived as giving preference to the interests of the auditors and their clients, as a result of the recommendations of the Wheat Study Group, an autonomous standards setting body, the FASB was established and began operating.

Political factors affect financial accounting standards. Because the interests of preparers, users, auditors, regulators, and the public can be in serious conflict, many efforts to create or change standards cause disagreement, controversy, and dissatisfaction. This problem is excerbated by the numerous detailed standards, as well as the many complex standards that are difficult to implement, especially by smaller nonpublic companies. Figure 4-4 shows the interaction between several groups. It shows that the FASB is the custodian of power from the SEC to establish GAAP for use by public companies while it has also received authority from state boards and the AICPA to establish GAAP for use by private companies.

Figure 4-4 Interrelationship of Entities.

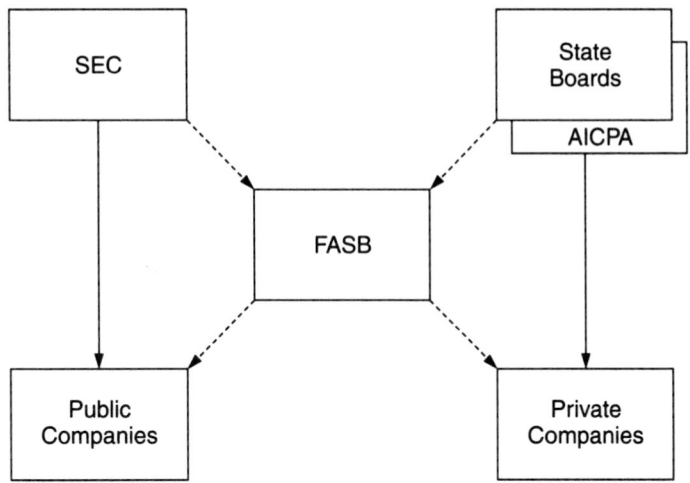

Source: Accountants' Handbook, Seventh Edition, 1991, p. 2-25, John Wiley & Sons, New York. Reprinted by permission.

4-6 FASB PUBLICATIONS

As well as primarily developing financial accounting standards, FASB also interprets standards in those instances where they are not entirely clear. Additionally, the Board was given the assignment of developing broad theoretical concepts of financial accounting. As might be expected, the publications of the FASB reflect all of these standards-related tasks.

The principal category of FASB publications is the *Statement of Financial Accounting Standards* (SFAS). By 1995, more than 100 had been promulgated. *Accounting Series Release (ASR) No. 150,* issued by the SEC in the year the FASB was created, recognizes the authority of these pronouncements. They are regarded by the council of the AICPA as the generally accepted principles for the membership of the Institute. Financial statements must be prepared in accordance with these standards if they are to receive an unqualified audit opinion.

Another category of Board publications is the *Statement of Financial Accounting Concepts* (SFACs). These statements do not constitute GAAP; but they describe the broader underlying concepts that the FASB used in developing the standards. The predecessor CAP and APB had been criticized for not developing a unified theoretical basis for resolving specific issues. Accordingly, the concepts were identified for use in setting specific standards. Six concept statements were issued by the Board and they are listed in Figure 4-5. A knowledge of the contents of the concept statements is helpful in understanding the standards.

A third category of FASB publications is the *Interpretations* (FINs) which assist in establishing GAAP. Thirty-eight Interpretations have been issued to provide guidance to the GAAP, but none have been issued since 1984. In large part this is because other media have been used to give the information that the Interpretations were intended to provide.

Figure 4-5 Financial Accounting Standards Board Statements of Concepts.

No.	Issue Date	Title
1	Nov. 1978	Objectives of Financial Reporting by Business Enterprises
2	May 1980	Qualitative Characteristics of Accounting Information
3	Dec. 1980	Elements of Financial Statement of Business Enterprises (Superseded by Concepts Statement No. 6)
4	Dec. 1980	Objectives of Financial Reporting by Nonbusiness Organization
5	Dec. 1984	Recognition and Measurement in Financial Statements of Business Enterprises
6	Dec. 1985	Elements of Financial Statements—a Replacement of Concepts Statements No. 3 (Incorporating and amendment of FASB Concepts Statement No. 2)

A fourth category of FASB publications are the *Technical Bulletins* (FTBs) issued by the Research and Technical Activities (RTA) staff. By design they are narrow in scope and interpret the existing authoritative literature such as the aforementioned ABPOs, ARBs, SFASs, and FINs.

To provide a quick response to new problems, the *Emerging Issues Task Force* (EITF) was created in 1984. It issues some highly condensed summaries of matters with which it has dealt, including the *EITF Consensuses.* Additionally, *Research Reports, Discussion Memorandums* and *Invitations to Comment* are other publications of the FASB. Finally, three news letters advise the public of the FASB activities: *Action Alert, Status Report,* and *Highlights.*

There are other pronouncements by the FASB. (See, for example, *Original Pronouncements,* Vols. I and II, P.O. Box 516, Norwalk, CT, FASB, 1993.) It is not expected that the financial officers who are not responsible for the applications of the GAAP will study the many news items and pronouncements. It is hoped that, over a period of time, they will become familiar, in a general way, with the more important of the generally accepted accounting principles—particularly through a perusal of the relevant SFASs and information in the *Journal of Accountancy,* as well as discussions with knowledgeable accountants, including the independent auditors.

4-7 ILLUSTRATIVE EXAMPLE OF GAAP AND TITLES OF SFAS

Despite the vast number of accounting principles discussed in the over 100 SFASs, as well as the APBs and other authoritative sources, it is not expected that most financial executives (other than those most directly concerned with accounting applications) will be knowledgeable about all the generally accepted accounting principles. However, we provide some short examples of GAAPs issued, as well as the titles of some SFASs. A committee of the Institute in 1932 recommended to the New York Stock Exchange a set of six financial reporting rules, being the first which the Exchange agreed to impose on listed companies. These rules, in abbreviated form, represent some of the earliest GAAPs.[2]

1. Unrealized profit should not be credited to the income account of the corporation, either directly or indirectly, through the medium of charging against such unrealized profits amounts which would ordinarily fail to be charged against the income account. Profit is deemed to be realized when a sale in the ordinary course of business is effected, unless the circumstances are such that the collector of the sales price is not reasonably assured.

2. Capital surplus, however created, should not be used to relieve the income account of the current or future years charges which would otherwise fail to be made thereagainst.

3. Earned surplus of a subsidiary company created prior to acquisition does not form a part of the consolidated earned surplus of the parent company and subsidiaries; nor can any dividend declared out of such surplus properly be credited to the income account of the parent company.

4. While it is perhaps in some circumstances permissible to show stock of a corporation held in its own treasury as an asset, if adequately disclosed, the dividends on stock so held should not be treated as a credit to the income account of the company.

5. Notes or accounts receivable due from officers, employees, or affiliated companies must be shown separately and not included under a general heading such as notes receivable or accounts receivable.

6. If capital stock is issued nominally for the acquisition of property and it appears that at about the same time, and pursuant to a previous agreement or understanding, some portion of the stock so issued is donated to the corporation, it is not permissible to treat the par value of the stock nominally issued for the property as the cost of that property. If stock so donated is subsequently sold, it is not permissible to treat the proceeds as a credit to surplus of the corporation.

Some indication of subject matter included in the SFASs can be seen in Figure 4-6.

4-8 OTHER ACCOUNTING RULE MAKERS

Comments have been made in the preceding sections about the two principal standard setting organizations—the GASB and the FASB. Other entities who might be regarded as active in regard to developing generally accepted accounting standards are discussed in this section. The entities listed earlier as having an interest in GAAP have all made helpful contributions even though their efforts, because of space limitations, are not detailed herein.

---

[2] For the complete rules, see "Restatement and Revision of Accounting Research Bulletins," *Accounting Research Bulletin No. 43*, Committee on Accounting Procedures, AICPA, NY, 1953.

Figure 4-6   Selected SFAS.

SFAS No.	Date Issued	Title
2	10/74	Accounting for Research and Development Costs
4	3/75	Reporting Gains and Losses from Extinguishment of Debt—an amendment of APB Opinion No. 30
66	10/82	Accounting for Sales of Real Estate
87	12/85	Employers' Accounting for Pensions
104	12/89	Statement of Cash Flows—Net Reporting of Certain Cash Receipts and Cash Payments and Classification of Cash Flows from Hedging Transactions—an amendment of FASB Statement No. 95
117	12/93	Financial Statements of Not-for-Profit Organizations

(a) SECURITIES AND EXCHANGE COMMISSION (SEC)

The Securities Exchange Act of 1934 created the SEC to regulate securities and to ensure adequate disclosure of financial information supplied by publicly held companies as required of them under that Act and under the Securities Act of 1933. While the Act gave the SEC statutory authority to establish uniform accounting principles and auditing practices for such companies, its role has been primarily that of oversight. The accounting profession and the SEC have cooperated with each other in developing GAAPs. Through its ASRs (Accounting Series Releases)—the predecessor to the FRRs (Financial Reporting Releases) and SABs (Staff Accounting Bulletins), among other avenues, the SEC has and does inform the accounting profession of its opinions on accounting and reporting. Also, the SEC has issued Regulations SK and SX, which together with the FRRs specify form and content of the financial statements.

The SEC has more than 2,000 employees located in its Washington, DC headquarters and its numerous regional offices. The three with which the independent accountants and the company controller and legal staff are likely to come in contact are:

- Division of Corporation Finance.
- Office of the Chief Accountant.
- Division of Enforcement.

The written documents which the accounting and legal professionals are likely to encounter include four levels for the two relevant Acts as shown in Figure 4-7.

Chapter 39 deals with the interface between accountants and the SEC.

(b) AMERICAN INSTITUTE OF CERTIFIED PUBLIC ACCOUNTANTS (AICPA)

The AICPA ceded its financial accounting standard-setting responsibility to the FASB in 1973. However, it continues to participate in influencing both the development and

Figure 4-7 Documentation of Compliance for the Securities Acts.

	Securities Act of 1933	Securities Exchange Act of 1934
Regulations and Forms	(1) Regulation SX 17CFR210 (2) Regulations 17CFR230 (3) Forms 17CFR239	(1) Regulation S-K 17CFR229 (2) Regulations 17CFR240 (3) Forms 17CFR249
Commission Releases	(1) Securities Releases (2) Financial Reporting Releases	(1) Accounting and Auditing Enforcement Releases (2) Exchange Act Releases
Staff Advice	(1) Securities Act Industry Guides (2) Staff Accounting Bulletins	(1) Exchange Act Industry Guides (2) Staff Accounting Bulletins

application of GAAP through its Accounting Standards Executive Committee (AcSEC). One of this committee's duties is to prepare letters of comment on significant accounting proposals issued by the FASB. The AcSEC also issues *Industry Audit and Accounting Guides, Statements of Position* (SOPs), *Issues Papers,* and *Practice Bulletins* to make its views known on financial and reporting matters.

(c) INTERNATIONAL ACCOUNTING STANDARDS COMMITTEE

The IASC was established in 1973 to harmonize accounting principles throughout the world. While most U.S. GAAP are the same as, or close to, the IASC standards, those of many other countries are not, in that they reflect indigenous statutory requirements or tax laws.

Various state societies of CPAs, and several national societies (FEI, IMA, AAA, etc.) make their views known on financial accounting and reporting matters.

4-9 SUMMARY

This chapter contains brief comments on the nature, need, and sources for GAAP to the extent considered important and relevant to the duties of the controller. The authors have attempted to explain how standards are set, and briefly discussed the bodies who set them, and those who influence them. In many instances, the controller will rely on the chief accountant of the company and the independent public accountants for guidance concerning current application of any GAAP. The Selected References provide sources of information concerning the standards, and indicate the addresses of some of the important players.

There will be many standards which will have no significant effect on the company operations or financial results, but some will. With respect to those having a major impact, the controller and his management may wish to influence the standard setting proposal, and further, may want to plan as far ahead as is practical on how to best deal with the relevant matter, such as reducing, capping or otherwise controlling the cost, or changing the nature of the related transaction.

Because most controllers are too busy to handle this work themselves, a knowledgeable professional can be assigned the responsibility to establish liaison with the standard-setting bodies. This person would know what subjects were being considered by each of the regulators, what Discussion Memorandums and Exposure drafts were released, what changes they included, and what schedule the program was on. He or she would keep the controller informed of these developments and have any dollar impact sized. In addition, he or she would develop a company position on each matter, using knowledgeable accounting and operating managers as needed, and present it to the controller. Approved company analyses can then be transmitted to the regulators at all stages of the standards development process, providing important input and helping influence the final product. The controller should also make higher management aware of possible changes and the estimated impact or range of impact on future financial statements of the company. Such regular briefings keep top management from having to deal with unpleasant surprises when new standards must be implemented.

4-10 SELECTED REFERENCES

Accountants' Handbook, 7th Ed. New York: John Wiley & Sons, 1991.
>Storey, Reed K., Chapter 1, "The Framework of Financial Accounting Concepts and Standards."
>Miller, Paul B. W., Chapter 2, "Financial Accounting Regulation and Organization."
>Larkin, Sherwood P., Chapter 3, "SEC Reporting Requirements."

Accounting Principles Board, "Basic Concepts and Accounting Principles Underlying Financial Statements of Business Enterprises," *APB Statement No. 4,* AICPA, New York, 1970.

American Institute of Certified Public Accountants, *Preferred Standards,* Section AU411, Chicago, IL: Commerce Clearing House, Inc., 1993.

Financial Accounting Standards Board, "Objectives of Financial Reporting by Business Enterprises," *Statement of Financial Accounting Concepts No. 1,* FASB, Stamford, CT, 1978.

Copies of relevant documents issued by the stated organizations may be obtained from these addresses:

American Institute of Certified
  Public Accountants
Harborside Financial Center
201 Plaza III
Jersey City, NJ 07311-3811

Emerging Issues Task Force
401 Merritt 7
P.O. Box 5116
Norwalk, CT 06856-5116

Financial Accounting Standards Board
401 Merritt 7
P.O. Box 5116
Norwalk, CT 06856-5116

Governmental Accounting Standards Board
401 Merritt 7
P.O. Box 5116
Norwalk, CT 06856-5116

International Accounting Standards Committee
41 Kingsway
London WC 2B 6YU
ENGLAND

United States Securities and Exchange Commission
450 5th Street, N.W.
Washington, DC 20549

CHAPTER 5

Some Key Tools Useful in Financial Planning and Control

5-1 INTRODUCTION

The increased sophistication of both chief executive officers and financial officers, coupled with competitive pressures and new technologies, has catapulted controllers from the typical role of historians or record keepers to that of broad-gauge business executives, skilled in the interpretation of financial data, with an eye on future trends and relationships. Their responsibilities extend over a vast range of activities, and therefore any number of subjects could be selected as critical to their success. For example, essential topics with which they should be conversant might include:

- Application of sound accounting principles and practices.
- Effective internal control.
- Proper organization structure of the controller's department.
- Tax planning.
- Evaluation of capital asset projects.
- Investor relations.

These are all important matters with which the controller ordinarily must deal in one way or another. Yet, if we were to be limited to four topics crucial to the performance of that financial officer in the planning and control area, they would be:

- Responsibility accounting.
- Cost behavior.

- Exception reporting.
- Interpretive reporting.

Proper handling of these matters would have the greatest impact on how the controller's role is perceived by many of the operating executives, and how he or she can be most effective with peers.

In making this selection, it is assumed that most modern controllers are well grounded in financial accounting.

One of these four topics, cost behavior, involves technical accounting knowledge. The other three deal largely with how accounting data should be treated so as to be effective in motivating or influencing people. The three are desirable ingredients in improving *communication* about the message contained in the financial information. All of the topics are interrelated.

5-2 RESPONSIBILITY ACCOUNTING

Viewed broadly, accounting might be seen as serving three different purposes:

Financial reporting.

Inventory valuation.

Performance evaluation.

The first is concerned principally with reporting the overall results of operations and the financial condition of the enterprise to the management and to the financial community: shareholders, security analysts, bondholders, banks, and so on. The second application permits the proper allocation and assignment of costs and expenses to inventory and to cost of goods sold or other current costs. The third purpose permits the measurement of individual or group performance against predetermined goals. It facilitates the measurement of actual results against plan or another selected standard, and may apply to revenues, costs, margins, or any particular combination of these. It involves the segregation of the data according to the segment being reported on. It implies accountability by the segment; hence the accounting process must identify those items, revenues, or costs that are considered "controllable" by the center.

These responsibility centers may be of three types. First, a responsibility center may be a "cost center" if the supervisor is held responsible for costs only, i.e., the expenses of his department or the direct material or direct labor costs incurred. Second, a responsibility center may broaden into a "profit center" if the supervisor is held accountable for a stipulated profit contribution. Thus a given sales office or subsidiary or division might be a profit center. And, finally, if a manager is held responsible not only for profit results but also for the investment required to produce the margin or profit, then the responsibility center is an "investment center."

It follows that the accounting accumulation and related reporting must follow the organization structure and the related functional responsibilities. It should encompass the revenues and/or costs and/or investments for which the manager reported on is responsible; that is, under most circumstances it should avoid arbitrary allocations. A simplified manufacturing company organization structure is shown in Figure 5-1, and

Figure 5-1   Typical Organization Chart—Manufacturing Company.

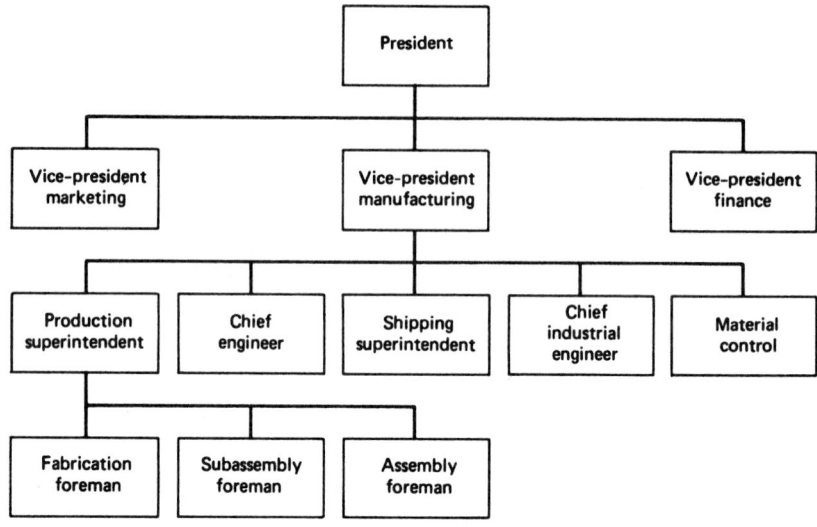

the related segregation of manufacturing expenses by echelon of management responsibility is illustrated in Figure 5-2.

Another summary report embodying the principle of responsibility accounting is that displayed in Figure 5-3, in which "total" manufacturing costs are segregated by responsibility and controllability.

5-3 COST BEHAVIOR

Rather fundamental to the entire process of planning and control, or "profit planning" as it is sometimes called, or even "management by objectives," is a clear understanding of how costs, particularly manufacturing overhead expenses or other expenses should vary as related to business volume. These principles must be known in the application of responsibility accounting, just discussed.

The detailed techniques concerning a separation of costs into the correct "blocks" for planning or control purposes is discussed in the chapter related to the type of cost involved. Suffice it to say that distinction between the types of costs are basic to a proper exercise of the controllership function. Thus, for *planning* purposes, costs may be classified as shown in Figure 5-4. In this figure, costs are identified with regard to behavior in relationship to activity or volume and, depending on the financial analysis being performed, may be segregated into total or "full" costs as contrasted to "marginal costs"—those incurred solely by the activity under study. For control purposes, costs may be segregated into those that are controllable by the executive under measurement (whether fixed or variable) or not controllable, illustrated in Figure 5-5. The costs are further classified, with regard to behavior in relationship to activity, whether fixed, variable, or semivariable, as described in Figure 5-6.

In the late 1980s and early 1990s, some financial managers came under general criticism for a less-than-acceptable analysis of costs. If costs are to be planned and controlled properly, their true nature must be understood. What makes a cost increase

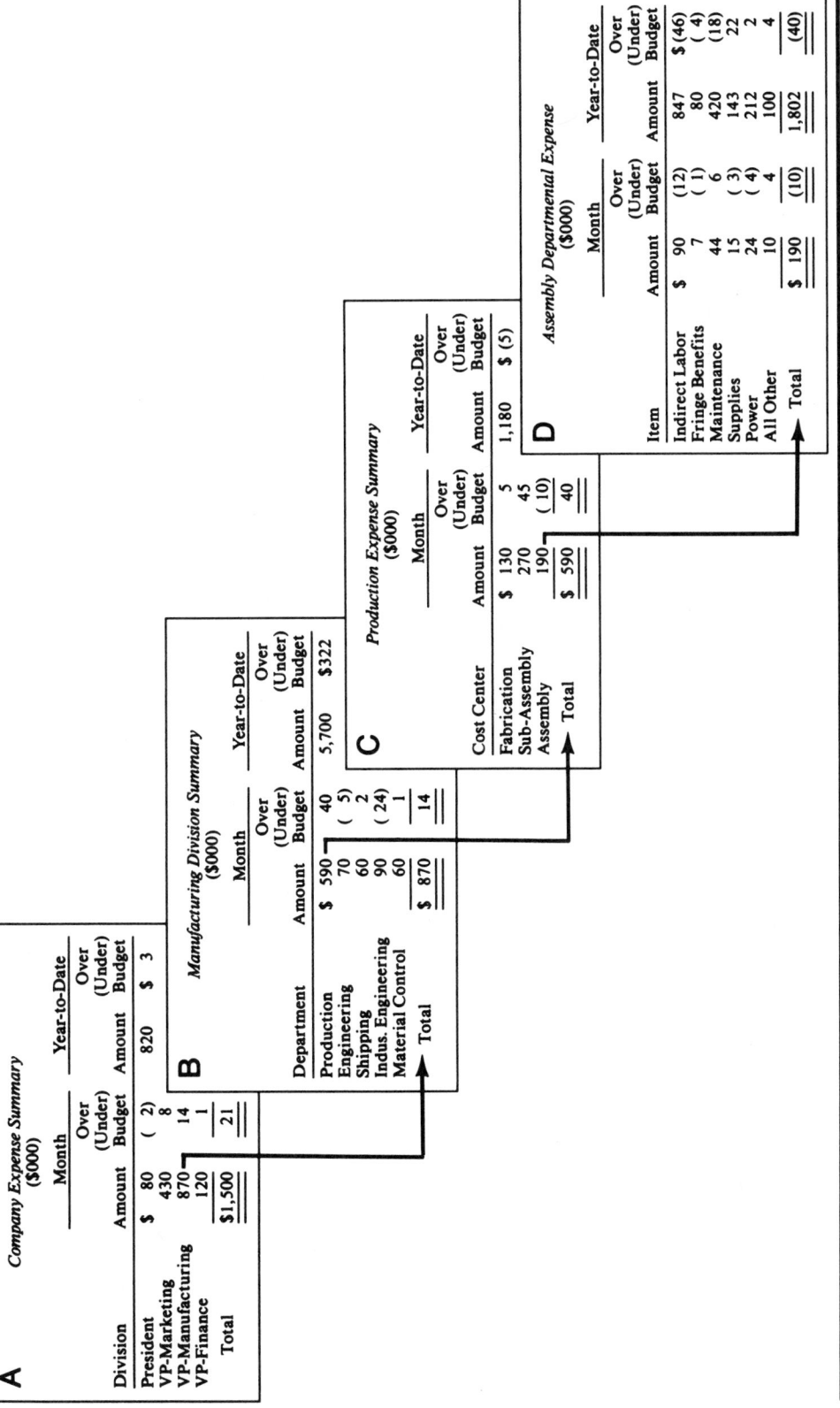

Figure 5-2 Reporting by Area of Responsibility.

The Manufacturing Company Flow of Responsibility Reporting

A

Company Expense Summary
($000)

Division	Month Amount	Over (Under) Budget	Year-to-Date Amount	Over (Under) Budget
President				
VP-Marketing	$ 80	(2)		
VP-Manufacturing	430	8	820	$ 3
VP-Finance	870	14		
	120	1		
Total	$1,500	21		

B

Manufacturing Division Summary
($000)

Department	Month Amount	Over (Under) Budget	Year-to-Date Amount	Over (Under) Budget
Production	$ 590	40	5,700	$322
Engineering	70	(5)		
Shipping	60	2		
Indus. Engineering	90	(24)		
Material Control	60	1		
Total	$ 870	14		

C

Production Expense Summary
($000)

Cost Center	Month Amount	Over (Under) Budget	Year-to-Date Amount	Over (Under) Budget
Fabrication	$ 130	5	1,180	$ (5)
Sub-Assembly	270	45		
Assembly	190	(10)		
Total	$ 590	40		

D

Assembly Departmental Expense
($000)

Item	Month Amount	Over (Under) Budget	Year-to-Date Amount	Over (Under) Budget
Indirect Labor	$ 90	(12)	847	$ (46)
Fringe Benefits	7	(1)	80	(4)
Maintenance	44	6	420	(18)
Supplies	15	(3)	143	22
Power	24	(4)	212	2
All Other	10	4	100	4
Total	$ 190	(10)	1,802	(40)

Figure 5-3   Summary of Manufacturing Costs Over (or Under) Standard by Responsibility.

The Appliance Corporation
SUMMARY OF MANUFACTURING COSTS OVER (OR UNDER)
STANDARD BY RESPONSIBILITY

Description	Total All Products	PLANT Refrig- erators	Stoves	Small Appli- ances
CONTROLLABLE COSTS				
Manufacturing Division—				
Plant Superintendent's Level				
Direct Labor—Per Budget Report	$17,277	$ 8,540	$ 6,322	$2,415
Direct Material—Per Budget Report	9,795	7,980	1,310	505
Variable Manufacturing Expense—				
Per Budget Report	7,883	4,395	2,478	1,010
Total Plant Superintendent's Responsibility	34,955	20,915	10,110	3,930
General Manufacturing Expense Over or (Under) Budget	5,260	3,110	2,070	80
Total Manufacturing Division	40,215	24,025	12,180	4,010
Purchasing Division—				
Prices Paid for Raw Materials	1,020	2,390	(910)	(460)
Sales Division—				
Idle Time—No orders (5-day cap.)	12,307	9,100	3,207	—
Special Handling	2,190	870	1,320	—
Total Sales Division	14,497	9,970	4,527	—
Financial Division—				
Cost Department Over or (Under) Budget	160	110	40	10
Payroll Department Over or (Under) Budget	(70)	(30)	(30)	(10)
Total Financial Division	90	80	10	—
TOTAL CONTROLLABLE COSTS	55,822	36,465	15,807	3,550
NONCONTROLLABLE COSTS AND STANDARD APPLICATIONS, ETC.				
Fixed Expenses—Depreciation, Taxes, Insurance	7,900	4,390	2,760	750
Fixes Expenses—General Manufac- turing, etc.	4,640	3,100	890	640
Standard Applications	935	125	770	40
Interplant Transfers	1,020	670	340	10
Total Noncontrollable Costs and Standard Applications, etc.	14,495	8,295	4,760	1,440
Total Excess Costs per Income and Expense Statement	$70,317	$44,760	$20,567	$4,990

Issued by Accounting Department—March 5, 19XX

Figure 5-4   Cost Classifications for Planning Purposes.

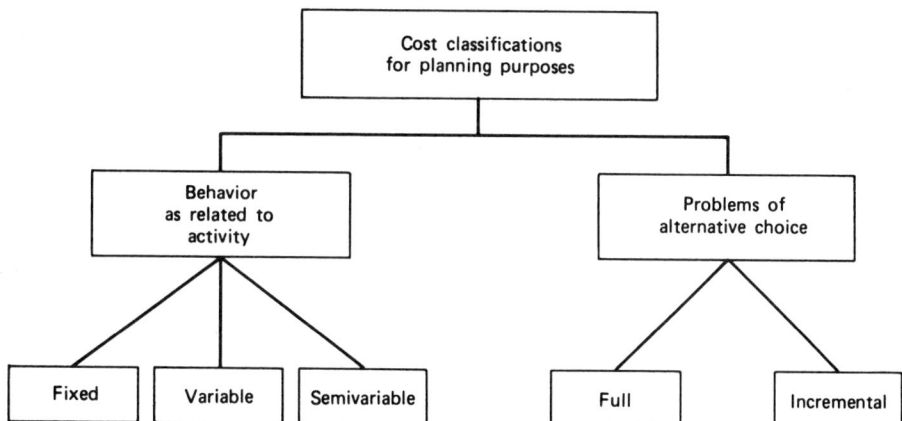

Figure 5-5   Cost Classifications for Control Purposes.

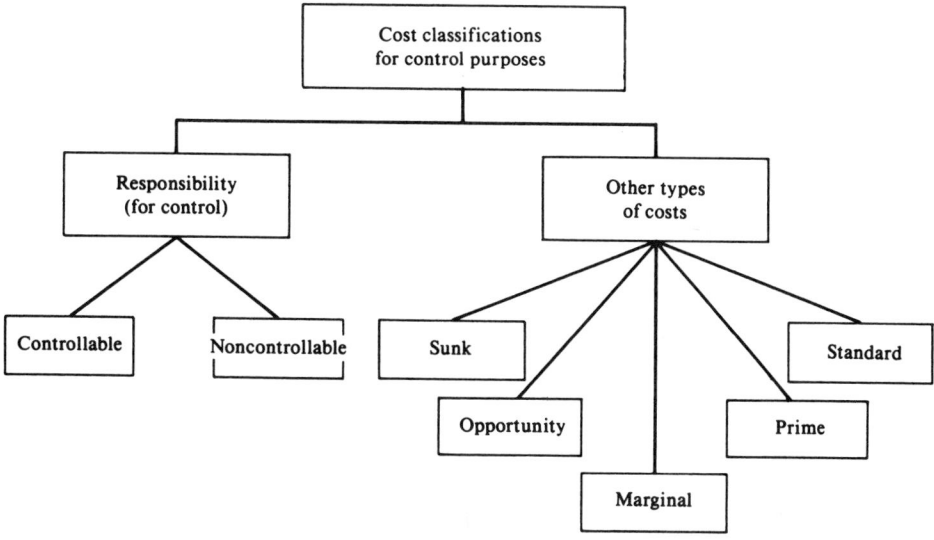

or decrease with changes in volume? What are the true drivers of cost? How should costs be assigned to processes and to product? Proper answers are vital to proper product pricing—hence to business development, competitiveness, and profitability. The current questioning of proper costing is embodied in the "activity based costing" concept. This aspect of cost management is a key factor in proper business/management, and is reviewed extensively in Chapter 6.

5-4 EXCEPTION REPORTING

The controllership function might be said to be effective to the extent it identifies, for operating management, performance that departs from an acceptable objective—

Figure 5-6 Cost Segregation Related to Activity Level.

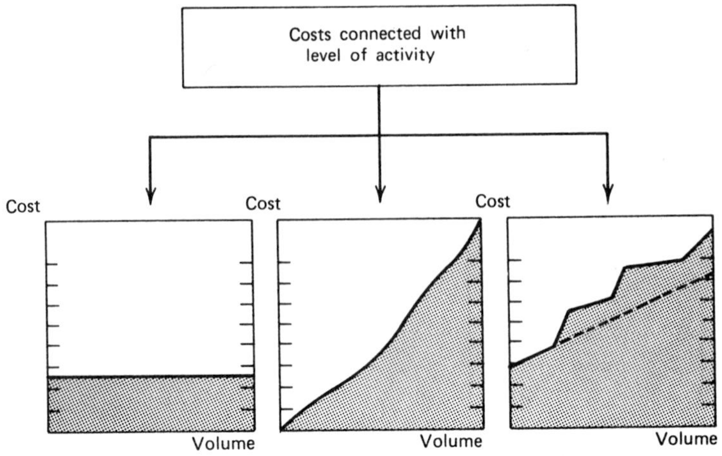

Designation	Fixed	Variable	Semivariable or semifixed
Characteristics	Does not vary at all with level of activity	Varies directly and proportionately with level of activity	Varies directly but less than proportionately with level of activity
Examples	Depreciation— amortization	Raw materials	Repairs and maintenance

whether plan or standard or past achievement. And from the accounting control viewpoint, perhaps there is nothing more wasteful than reports containing massive details that, because of this fact, are simply not used. One of the functions of the controller is to organize the information so that the facts are understood and acted on. It should be the exceptions or variances from the norm or standard that ought to be signaled. Elimination of the "cause" of the unfavorable variance, not the variance itself is the objective. Hence the report should concentrate on significant departures from standard and generally eliminate the clutter of on-standard performance. An exception report is illustrated in Figure 5-7.

5-5 INTERPRETIVE REPORTING

In general, a report is intended to communicate an idea to the user. While an accountant may be accustomed to reading figures and understanding them, others not schooled in this discipline may lack this facility. Therefore, it behooves the financial officer to either make each report self-explanatory or include interpretive commentary so that the message gets across and is clearly understood. The exception report shown in Figure 5-7 not only reveals the better-or-worse-than-budget performance, but it also contains an explanation of the reasons for such a condition and/or the corrective action taking place. It thus tends to ensure that the reader knows about substandard budget results and the effort to get the cost levels in line with plan or budget. Another preliminary report of the month and year-to-date financial operating results, as shown in Figure 5-8, for a medium-sized company tells not only *what* happened, but *why*. The

Figure 5-7   The Exception Report.

The XYZ Company
BUDGET REPORT
MONTH OF DECEMBER 19XX

			Dept. 112 Dept. Manager	Milling John Jones
	Month		Year to Date	
Description	Actual	Over/(Under) Budget	Actual	Over/(Under) Budget
Better than Budget *				
Indirect labor ...	$ 15,900	$(1,310)	$ 186,100	$(8,900)
Supplies	6,420	(220)	74,800	(1,050)
Power	17,800	(540)	201,300	(3,700)
Subtotal	40,120	(2,070)	462,200	(13,650)
Worse than Budget *				
Direct materials .	286,300	8,360	3,617,000	82,100
Maintenance	33,100	3,190	304,100	21,800
Subtotal	319,400	11,550	3,921,100	103,900
All Other	611,310	200	12,143,620	700
Total costs and expenses	$970,830	$ 9,680	$16,526,920	$ 90,950

* By 2% or $2000 or more, whichever is lower.

Comments

Accounting: Expenses were overbudget by 1.00%, which is slightly higher than the .55% overrun for the year to date.

Although severe operating problems occurred on the Nos. 9 and 10 mills, good scheduling of indirect labor, particularly the cleaners, by John Jones has saved $1310 for the month and $8900 for the year to date.

Operating: Impurities in the melamine were responsible for a 2.9% loss of material over the budget of a total loss of 3.01%. This same condition also resulted in heavy scoring of the No. 10 mill. Of the total excess costs of $11,550, it is expected that $10,000 can be recovered from the supplier.

Institution of the new screens is expected to be complete by December 8, and the resulting material savings should approximate $200,000 annually at the present rate of operations.

A change in source of felts is expected to reduce maintenance expense to budget.

chief executive officer therefore has a better sense of how the business is progressing than by simply looking at the numbers.

5-6 SUMMARY

Recognition of the four factors reviewed in this chapter translate the usual financial accounting, which most controllers understand, into useful information for the management. The principles are incorporated into the remaining discussions as applicable.

Figure 5-8 Report with Interpretive Commentary.

The Toy Importing Company
PRELIMINARY OPERATING RESULTS
(dollars in thousands except per share)
APRIL 19XX

	Year-to-Date			Total Year Outlook	
	Actual	Over/(Under) Plan	Prior Year	Estimated This Year	Over/(Under) Plan
New orders received	$71,819	(181)	92,120	122,500	$(2,500)
Net sales	42,390	390	90,615	96,300	1,300
Net income	2,501	(19)	5,165	5,778	278
% Sales	5.9	.1	5.7	6.0	—
EPS	1.25	(.01)	2.58	2.89	.14
Cash flow	2,601	(19)	5,565	6,228	328

Comments: An *order* for $200,000 from Toys-R-Us, which was expected in April, will now be received in May. However, it now appears the Big Five order of $2,400,000 included in the plan has been lost to San Francisco.

Net sales for the year to date and expected for the year are better than plan since we captured the Henderson Hobby account.

Net income is less than plan because of remodeling expenses of $45,000 in the Riverside store. With the recent closing of the San Diego warehouse, and expected sales over plan, net income for the year should exceed plan.

5-7 SELECTED REFERENCES

Estrin, T. L., Jeffrey Kantor, and David Albers, "Is ABC Suitable for Your Company?" *Management Accounting,* April 1994, pp. 40–45.

Lesser, Frederic E., "Will the Real Cost Please Stand Up?" *Management Accounting,* Nov. 1986, pp. 29–31.

CHAPTER 6

Effective Costing Practices: The Cost System

The controller, as the chief accounting executive of the company, has the responsibility to design, install, and maintain the general and cost accounting systems for the entity— at all levels, including corporate, divisional, plant, department, or unit. This is in addition to other major responsibilities related to financial planning, control, and reporting.

Sections 3 and 5 in this chapter have been adapted and reprinted with the permission of Warren, Gorham, and Lamont, Inc., from Chapter 38B, Cost Systems vs. Effective Cost Determination in *Budgeting and Profit Planning Manual,* 2nd edition, 1991 Cumulative Supplement, by James D. Willson. Copyright 1984, 1990, 1991 by Warren, Gorham, and Lamont, Inc.

The accounting principles and practices, and the related standards, which are critical to the proper operation of the general accounting system in an entity are reviewed in a general way in Chapter 4. The chief movers in developing the accounting principles and the sources for the information on the subject are discussed. Similarly, this chapter reviews some of the current issues concerning cost accounting systems and cost determination, without delving into the complex details of various costing systems. Several excellent texts and the Selected References provide useful information on the design complexities and operation of the various existent cost systems. The authors focus on those areas needing current attention, without getting involved in long discourses on costing principles.

6-1   INTRODUCTION

This is a period of change and stress for many U.S. manufacturers as they strive to compete in a global market plan. Among other things, customers are demanding improved quality, faster delivery, and perhaps a greater variety of product. Then, too, competitors are adjusting quickly to marketplace changes, are finding improved material and supply sources, relocating factories and distribution centers to secure the benefits of lower labor costs and permissible working conditions, changing manufacturing methods to reduce costs, and taking advantage of U.S. trade policies and loopholes. Service companies face many of the same problems in both United States and foreign markets. Inflation can make the problem even more difficult. This competitive pressure increases the need for good cost information. Business managers must know the cost of each product so it can be properly and competitively priced, to produce a profit. Moreover, the management must have timely and accurate data for cost planning and cost control.

In such a competitive environment cost control and cost determination have been impacted in these ways:

- In this age of advanced technologies, *manufacturing* methods and processes have changed, and proper costing procedures should reflect these changes.
- In many businesses, the *nonmanufacturing expenses* have significantly increased, so that greater care must be exercised in the application of these expenses—research and development, advertising, selling, and general and administrative expenses—to each product or product line.
- In general, the cost accountants are being forced to take a more analytical or questioning viewpoint in examining the applicability of costs to products, functions, organizational subdivisions, or other cost objects.

In this chapter, we examine some of the costing practices and the need, as well as the ways and means, to make them more specific. This background should be helpful to the reader when examining the planning and control functions in his or her company as related to each type of cost or expense, or asset, as discussed in later chapters of this book.

Another reason for writing this chapter is to place before the reader some of the alleged weaknesses outlined in recent critical articles about the "obsolete cost systems" being employed in U.S. industry. He might test the cost systems and cost determination methods under his cognizance against the criticisms. Most of us are aware that the quality of the cost systems or management accounting systems, or cost determination methods—call them what you will—usually depends on the professional astuteness of the CFO, or controller, or chief accountant, and the accounting staff. Today's alert management accountant seeks to provide management with timely and relevant planning and control information. And in our more aggressive and more competitive larger companies, he usually succeeds.

Finally, much of the controversy about cost accounting relates to the method of allocating either indirect manufacturing expenses or service and general and administrative expenses to cost objects. These are extensively discussed, along with the excellent and relevant Statements of Management Accounting (SMA) in Chapters 23 and 26. The review in this earlier chapter will make you more alert to costing implications as you read the many later sections on sales, expense, and cost planning and control.

These subjects are discussed in the balance of this chapter:

- Uses of the "cost accounting" system.
- Changes in the manufacturing environment.
- A few stated weaknesses in some cost systems.
- Activity-based costing.
- Selecting the proper cost system.

6-2 USES OF THE COST ACCOUNTING SYSTEM

In exploring just how cost accounting systems, (or management accounting systems) in some U.S. companies might be improved, it may be helpful to review typical uses of such cost accumulation methods. But even in defining a cost accounting system there is a certain looseness of terms. To many accountants, a cost accounting system refers only to those accounts and accounting functions in which are recorded the outlays and usage of assets pertaining to *manufacturing* operations, that is, to costs related to the movement of products between the raw material stage and the finished goods status. In a broader sense, the term "cost accounts" applies to that group of accounts in which are assembled the expenditures related to either manufacturing, or engineering, or research and development, or selling and distribution, or general and administrative activities, in such a manner that the costs of these separate activities are revealed in terms of some unit that has been selected as a yardstick.

Applying the broader concept of costs, most knowledgeable individuals would agree that cost systems are employed principally for these three purposes:

- Inventory valuation.
- Product cost determination.
- Cost and expense management and control.

Some persons might make a finer distinction in applications and add these uses:

- Short-term and long-term (strategic) planning.
- Justifying capital expenditures.
- Motivating and measuring managers.

A few comments are made on each of these purposes.

(a) INVENTORY VALUATION

One widely used purpose of a cost system is to value inventories. Using generally accepted accounting principles, current period production or manufacturing costs must be allocated to current production. Then, the costs of current production must be segregated between those products sold and those products in inventory. Typically, manufacturing costs are accumulated in three primary classes: direct material, direct labor, and manufacturing overhead. A discussion about the proper cost allocation of these three categories is contained in Chapters 22 and 23, and the valuation of inventories is reviewed in Chapter 30. Suffice it to say here that such valuations and allocations are used by most public companies, in conjunction with generally accepted accounting principles, for the determination of monthly, quarterly, and annual operating results as well as the periodic financial position.

   With respect to the use of the cost system for determining inventory values, these additional comments may be useful:

1. Under generally accepted accounting principles, the full production cost base may be adjusted to the lower of cost or market.

2. Quite often, the emphasis on inventory valuation is on the *aggregate* value for profit or loss determination purposes—and not necessarily on the specific value for each product.

3. Originally, when direct labor content was a major cost element, manufacturing overhead was allocated on this basis. Now, with increased automation, and so on, direct labor typically represents perhaps 15% or less of total production cost. Under such circumstances, another allocation basis may be more applicable.

4. Quite often, in the context of controlling manufacturing labor or overhead, changes are made in manufacturing method. While appropriate adjustments may be made in departmental operating budgets for such changes, because of their individual small size, often no change is made in the costing base used for inventory valuation. Accordingly, some cost differences arise, but are treated as "accounting adjustments" and create no significant problem. When *major* changes occur in manufacturing processes, or when the individually small changes become important in the aggregate, then the cost basis for inventory valuation should be adjusted.

5. Only manufacturing costs normally are used as the base for product inventory valuation. R&D, selling and general and administrative expenses, and so on are excluded.

6. With the trend to just-in-time (JIT) techniques, and resulting lower or nonexistent inventories, the inventory valuation application has lost some of its importance.

(b) PRODUCT COST DETERMINATION

Correct product costs are a critical element in the survival and growth of an enterprise. Why? Among other reasons, they very often are the basis for setting the selling price of products in general, and for proper tactical business decisions in particular. Prices are a major determinant of profitability.

   The manufactured cost of a product as developed by the cost system (employed for inventory valuation) often is the *starting point* used by the sales or manufacturing staff in making product pricing decisions—often the wrong decision. Why? Many times those who use such costs do not understand the basis of calculation or the limitations in usefulness. Some of the reasons why such a cost should not be used for marketing decisions without adjustments are these:

1. The manufactured cost of a product usually represents historical costs, and it may not be indicative of future costs.

2. The manufacturing cost typically contains a significant element of indirect or allocated costs. If the basis of manufacturing cost allocation is too general, that is, is not product specific, then the resultant cost is simply wrong or inaccurate.

3. For many pricing and marketing decisions, the *total* cost of the product, including engineering, research and development, advertising and sales promotion, selling, and general and administrative expense, are the relevant costs. (See Chapter 20.)

4. For a great number of tactical business decisions, *total* costs, including full manufacturing costs, as well as all other costs, may not be the relevant or applicable cost base. As an example, for some short-term decisions (such as securing the initial sale) perhaps the direct or variable out-of-pocket costs, plus a small margin, is the proper cost basis. (See Chapter 20.) As a general statement, for different purposes or applications a different type of cost may be needed.

5. In those instances, where total real costs are applicable, using average percentages of manufacturing costs or of the selling price for some of the indirect expenses may be improper. A particular product or product line may have its unique specific functional cost, for example, selling or advertising, which should be recovered, and which must be reflected in the cost basis used for setting the selling price.

In general then, the type of cost used should be relevant to the decision to be made. Such product manufacturing cost, or total product cost, need not be calculated every month—but only as required for a particular answer. And the costing systems should provide the basis for rather quickly determining the proper relevant cost. This is a field in which use of the combined talents and experience of the management accountant and the marketing representative, as well as the manufacturing executive, is highly desirable.

(c) COST AND EXPENSE MANAGEMENT AND CONTROL

The third purpose for which the output of the "cost system" is employed is the management and control of both costs and expenses. To be sure the same "system" that accumulates actual costs for inventory valuation also may be used for cost planning and control. But the application is quite different. For control purposes, actual costs or expenses are compared with a budget or other standard, and corrective action is taken to bring the expenditures in line with what is expected.

But these differences in the control application should be noted as compared to the once-a-month cost accumulation for inventory valuation purposes:

- *Timely* data are needed for control purposes. Accordingly, some real-time costs may be reported as incurred using a computer. In other instances, after-the-fact costs are adequate, some being provided on an hourly, daily, weekly, or monthly basis. (This contrasts with the monthly accumulation and reporting for financial purposes.)

- In the context of *control,* a manager cannot, or should not, be held accountable for those costs he cannot control. Hence, arbitrary allocations are to be avoided. If service costs are charged to the using departments, the charge should be based on actual usage at a standard rate. For inventory valuation, manufacturing costs are accumulated in the service department then allocated to the using department, and then to the product.

- Expense behavior under conditions of varying business volume is treated differently for inventory valuation purposes as contrasted to cost management. Thus, for inventory valuation, the concept of normal capacity—(see Chapter 23)—is used. Under this basis, the fixed standard manufacturing expenses are divided by the units or productive hours for the average volume over the period of the business cycle, to secure the average unit fixed manufacturing expense for inventory valuation. In contrast, for planning and control purposes, costs and expenses may be viewed as either variable, semi-variable, or fixed, (see Chapter 5) and measured for the specific applicable time horizon. And while some costs, for example, direct labor, may be viewed over the very short term as variable, for planning purposes it may be regarded as semi-variable. Or supervisory costs may be regarded as fixed over the short term, but for planning purposes may be regarded as managed (semi-variable).

- Finally, where unexpected events occur beyond the control of the department manager, for example, a hurricane work stoppage, and damage, special adjustments may be made to the departmental budget so that the department manager is not penalized in his monthly or weekly budget performance report. Such events basically may be disregarded in inventory valuation.

(d) SHORT- AND LONG-TERM (STRATEGIC) PLANNING

For the preparation of the short-term or annual business plan, the existing cost level of every department, function, activity, or product usually is the starting point in calculating cost or expense levels. These costs are then adjusted for any expected change in such matters as: volume of business activity, organization structure, functions, and such related subjects as inflation rates, price changes, raw material costs, salary and wage increases, process changes and product mix. (See Chapter 16.) In this way, the final business plan is a realistic view of what is expected to happen. Every opportunity is provided for the necessary adjustment to realistic cost levels. The managers typically prepare their own departmental plans, using guidelines approved by the CEO and CFO (with the assistance of the controller). The controller's department furnishes him or her with the historical cost or expense data on which the plan is constructed.

With respect to the strategic plan, which deals with broad classes of data, and is less detailed than the annual plan, while the "cost systems" provide much of the basic information, this is substantially adjusted to reflect expected revenue or cost levels five or ten years or more in the future. (See Chapters 14 and 15.)

In the context of business planning, ample opportunity is given to adjust revenues and cost data, as well as asset, liability and net worth data, to fit realistic expectations or alternative scenarios. The cost system output, or historical cost accumulation, is only a starting point.

(e) JUSTIFYING CAPITAL EXPENDITURES

In most businesses, capital investments in plant and equipment usually must be justified by the expected rate of return. Often, this is measured by the estimated cash flow produced by the investment over its expected life. (See Chapter 32.) If it meets a minimum rate, if funds are available, and if it is consistent with the strategic plan, the proposal usually is approved. In this application also, the starting point may be the output of the cost systems. Cost estimates for determining profitability (cash flow) must be relevant to the specific products to be produced. This is another instance where averages simply may not be applicable. The data collected in the "cost systems" usually are adjusted, as in the planning application discussed earlier, to reflect expected operating/financial conditions and, hence, the anticipated profit or return on the investment.

(f) MOTIVATING AND MEASURING MANAGEMENT

Another stated application of cost system output is to motivate and judge performance of the various segments of business management. A very common measure is comparison of actual cost or expense levels with a plan or budget or standard. Another often used measure is the return on assets or return on equity achieved by the entity, or division. The net income or operating income used as the numerator, and the related investment (inventories and fixed assets, etc.) used for the denominator is that produced directly or indirectly by the cost system. In some instances, these latter general (book accounting) measures of entity performance may be adjusted for inflation or other factors. Moreover, to financial performance factors may be added other noncosts, nonfinancial factors (for example, market share, quality standards, share of on-time deliveries). In any event, the institution of suitable or appropriate measures requires study. A measure wrongly applied, such as volume growth or departmental throughput, can cause a manager to take actions not in the best interest of the company. See the later discussion in this chapter.

6-3 CHANGES IN THE MANUFACTURING ENVIRONMENT

One important impetus for examining cost systems and cost determination methodology is the major changes which are, and have been, taking place in the manufacturing environment. To some, the advent of the advanced manufacturing technologies are a cause for concern as to the degree that management accountants are and should be assisting U.S. manufacturers become and stay competitive in the world economy. A good understanding as to just how the factory is changing is an important first step in evaluating the reliability of manufacturing cost systems in the United States generally, and in any one entity in particular.

Two knowledgeable writers have classified the changes being made in manufacturing in this fashion.[1]

---

[1] Robert A. Howell and Stephen R. Soucy, "The New Manufacturing Environment: Major Trends for Manufacturing Accounting," *Management Accounting,* July 1987, pp. 13–19.

- Higher quality.
- Lower inventories.
- Flexible flow lines.
- Automation.
- Product line organization.
- Effective use of information.

These six major changes are indicative of a commitment to produce high quality at the lowest practical cost with on-time delivery. These developments are also signs of a different management philosophy from that which prevailed in the 1960s and 1970s. High quality is no longer viewed as an alternative to lower costs; rather, it is seen as consistent with such a condition. Further, high labor utilization and its related overhead absorption is no longer, alone, necessarily considered an indication of efficiency. Such a manufacturing level might be counterproductive in that it could be the cause of overproduction as well as excess inventories and attendant write-offs.

A few expanded comments on the six areas of manufacturing change follow.

(a) HIGHER QUALITY

Attention has focused on quality for two reasons: (1) U.S. manufacturers recognized that if they did not improve quality, then foreign competitors in many instances simply would drive them out of the marketplace. (2) Business managers began to realize that poor quality was a significant cost driver. It was recognized that improved quality, secured through the use of good materials, with a highly trained labor force, together with well-maintained equipment simply reduces the costs of nonquality: scrap, rework, equipment breakdowns, higher field service, and greater warranty failures.

(b) LOWER INVENTORIES

Many managements are reducing company inventories while still maintaining delivery schedules and satisfactory customer service. They have begun to realize that:

1. The carrying of inventories requires added capital; and that the cost of such capital is much higher than it was in the recent past.

2. Aside from the interest on capital, these costs related inventories can be substantially reduced: the higher moving and handling costs; a higher level of spares, increased obsolescence, as well as the higher insurance and tax expenses on inventories.

3. Finally, management has come to recognize that many Japanese businesses have become eminently successful in meeting customer needs despite increased inventory turns and the reduced inventory levels.

(c) FLEXIBLE FLOW LINES

A substantial number of manufacturers are redesigning the factory flow lines in order to shorten the product cycle time and to permit an increase in the variety of product.

Under the flexible flow line concept the various pieces of equipment needed in the product manufacturing process are brought together in one location. Accordingly large groups of identical pieces of equipment are split up, and multiple "mini" produc lines are formed. The results are: less material handling, reduced inventory, shorte cycle time, and the ability to manufacture more than one product on the production line

(d) AUTOMATION

In the minds of many, automation may be the most visible change in the manufacturin, environment. When the management has redesigned the factory layout and has intro duced flexible flow lines, together with other operational improvements, then it ca leverage these moves through the introduction of automation.

Automation can be at any one of three levels: (1) a stand-alone piece of equip ment, such as a computer-controlled lathe; (2) a production cell, such as a flexible flov line; or (3) a fully automated factory.

In justifying such capital investments, formerly only the savings in direct labo and the related fringe benefits, together with economies of smaller inventories, wer considered. Now, the justification process also includes estimates of the benefits aris ing from improved quality, quicker delivery, and, in general, a higher level of custome satisfaction.

(e) INCREASED EMPHASIS ON PRODUCT LINE ORGANIZATION

In general, the typical manufacturing organization structure was characterized by a larg number of central service departments such as: quality control, maintenance, productio control, inspection, and engineering. This structure was based on the theory that the scal of operations would justify the economics. Very often this result did not happen.

The product line organization resulted in a reassignment of specialized servic skills to the product lines and the consequent reduction of the service organizations Among other benefits, this structure identified the resource with the using product The result was better product costing and improved pricing.

(f) IMPROVED INFORMATION TECHNOLOGY

When the new information technology is adopted, combining electronic mail, fax ma chines, and personal computers in a thoroughly integrated information system, the usual result is faster and better communication, including real-time data. As a conse quence, manufacturing control is improved: the factory manager can observe perfor mance via computer as it is happening. For example, he need not wait for a month-end scrap report, comparing actual and standard scrap generation. He can discern rathe quickly the exact status of raw material or work-in-process inventories. In some appli cations, computers can monitor and control operations—often with better results an less expense. (Machines don't get tired and need not be paid overtime.)

(g) THE IMPACT ON COSTS

So what is the impact of these, and the many other changes in the manufacturing envi ronment, on manufacturing costs and cost management? Here are a few of them:

- Increased attention being paid to engineering and product design since product cost of manufacturing often is largely determined in this early stage.
- A decrease in the direct labor cost component.
- An increase in equipment-related costs, such as depreciation, power, and equipment repair.
- A change in manufacturing costs structure, for example, use of units of production depreciation rather than straight line (or accelerated) depreciation.
- Recognition of the need to re-examine the method of allocating manufacturing overhead to departments and products.
- A decrease in some service department personnel costs, such as repair and maintenance costs.
- An increased need for real-time performance information or computer-generated data, instead of long after the fact manual data.
- An increase in the information cost component of the business.
- The need for more nonfinancial performance measures, such as the number of customer complaints, number of on-time deliveries, relative share of defect-free units—all of which are critical to quality control and customer service.

6-4 SOME VIEWS ON WEAKNESSES IN "COST SYSTEMS"

In the last five years or so, not only has there been a number of significant changes in manufacturing methods as well as costing practices, but also an increase in the number of articles in business periodicals that are highly critical of existing cost systems or costing practices. Some of these criticisms, in no particular order, and from various sources, include:

- Existing cost systems were meant primarily to value inventories and provide data for the statements of income and expense. They really were never designed to discriminate between product lines or products within those lines.
- Most cost management systems are historical financial reporting oriented and do not adequately measure operational performance.
- Traditional accounting systems fail to provide proper information for strategic decisions.
- The internal management accounting function has now become subservient to the external reporting function in U.S. firms. Contemporary U.S. practice is characterized by the internal use of accounting conventions that have been developed or mandated by external reporting authorities; and management accounting practices are now driven by an external reporting mentality.
- Management accounting reports are of little help to operating managers attempting to reduce costs and improve productivity.
- The management accounting system fails to provide accurate product costs.
- Today's cost systems measure the segment of a product's life that begins at the time it enters production.

- We are not capturing and allocating research and development costs so that management can determine the true profitability of a product over its lifetime.

- Unfortunately, managers' horizons contract to the short-term cycle of their monthly profit or loss statements.

- The control emphasis differs as between advanced manufacturing technologies (AMTs) on the one hand and accounting systems on the other. Accounting systems are basically feedback arrangements, and the expectation is that corrective action will be taken after the reporting period—a day, week, month, or year. In contrast, most AMT systems are designed to function in an opposite manner. Basically, they are primarily preventive in nature, with on-line, real-time responses often required.

- The majority of cost accounting systems are work-order oriented and do not adequately identify the impact of cost drivers (those conditions, activities, or factors that cause costs to change) on the manufacturing cost of specific operations or products.

- The new management methods stress the need for focusing on not only costs, but also on quality and flexibility. Management accounting, therefore, must look beyond transaction-based cost information to know if decisions will deliver increased profits.

Consider whether there is a weakness which should be corrected in your company. Do any of these opinions echo ones expressed by your management? Some of the opinions expressed are correct, and others are only partially correct. Some fail to distinguish between the cost accumulations for inventory valuation only, and the cost determinations individually made for specific purposes, for example, product pricing. Some focus on the manufacturing accounting system for accumulating costs and ignore the integrated management reporting practice which compares actual cost performance with a budget or standard, developed with the assistance of the operating department manager, specifically designed to measure departmental performance (regardless of the treatment of costs for inventory valuation).

6-5 ACTIVITY-BASED COSTING (ABC)

The Computer Aided Manufacturing—International (CAM-I), a nonprofit industry sponsored consortium that deals with contemporary industry problems, defines activity-based costing as "the collection of financial and operation performance information tracing the significant activities of the firm to product costs."[2] The significance of this definition will become clear as you read the following sections on activity-based costing.

But ponder, as a starting point, how important perception and the degree of analysis is to properly solving a problem—the allocation of expenses to a product.

For example, look at receiving, handling, and storage costs in a representative factory. It is a relatively simple matter to accumulate the departmental costs under the control of the foreman. These expenses are routinely gathered for planning and control

---

[2] Norm Raffish, "How Much Does That Product Really Cost? Finding Out May Be as Easy as ABC," *Management Accounting,* March 1991, p. 37.

purposes. But what about assigning such costs to a product? Very often a single basis, such as weight or value, might be used to allocate expenses to a product or component. But more in-depth analysis might reveal that different product groups required varying times and volume in storage. Hence, it is prudent to segregate storage and handling costs into those that were *transaction-related* and those that were *storage time* related. Consequently, the transaction related expenses may be assigned to parts based on the frequency of handling (received, counted, moved, and issued). The time related expenses (utilities, taxes, insurance) each being governed by actual time stored, should be charged to products accordingly.

This analysis of storage costs is an example of the need to sometimes refine the costing method to reflect the value consumed at differing rates by different parts or components. And this same principle may be what is at the heart of many differences of opinion as to how activities and costs must be managed.

Costs are caused by activities. If these activities can be reduced, then the related costs also should be lowered. Those involved with activity-based costing soon realize that most nonmaterial costs do not vary directly with labor volume, but rather, vary with product diversity and operational complexity.

Any attempt to develop activity-based product costs and to manage all costs properly, should include attention to these various steps:

- Analysis of the processes involved (Process Value Analysis-PVA).
- Development of activity-based process costing.
- Development of activity-based product costing.
- Analysis to assure that responsibility accounting is being followed.
- Re-examination of desirable performance measures, including some nonfinancial components.
- Relate investment decisions to improved efficiency and value-added activities, together with profitability.

Brief comments on each of these steps follow.

(a) PROCESS VALUE ANALYSIS (PVA)

Total cost management (TCM) is a business philosophy of managing all company resources as well as the activities that consume those resources. Managing costs in a TCM environment means focusing on the factors that cause or "drive" these cost consuming activities. The initial step in the entire procedure is process value analysis (PVA) which method defines each process, examines the need for the activity, determines the cost "drivers," and isolates those that do or do not add value; and plans corrective action. One set of suggested steps for the entire review is this:

1. *Define the process*
   - Document the process flow.
   - Define the input requirements for each process step.
   - Define the output of each step.

- Identify customer (both internal and external) requirements.
- Compare customer requirements with the input/output requirements.
- Identify or define the required (full-time equivalent) staff level for each process.

2. *Analyze the activities*

- Identify each activity within each process.
- Using customer requirements, identify each activity as value adding or nonvalue adding.
- Determine the cycle time for each activity.
- Calculate for each process the cycle efficiency—the value-added time as related to total time.
- Cumulate the efficiency through the entire business chain.

3. *Analyze the cost drivers*

- Identify the cost drivers—the cause and the effect.
- Analyze the effect of eliminating the nonvalue adding drivers.

4. *Plan improvements*

- Determine, by activity, the costs of both the value-adding and nonvalue-adding activities.
- Select methods to eliminate any nonvalue factors and optimize the value-adding ones.
- Chart performance and progress by appropriate performance measures.

Aside from the detailed analytical study necessary in PVA, these few remarks are made about the key functions or segments in a fully integrated ABC system that relates product costs to performance measurement and to asset investment.

(b) ACTIVITY-BASED PROCESS COSTING

First comes activity-based *process* costing, and after that comes activity-based *product* costing. This is to say that, according to sound costing methodology, most nonmaterial costs are first accumulated by department, which essentially is by process or activity. These activity-based process costs are next identified by product. Logically, it follows that if business management is to secure accurate product costs, it must first develop reliable *process* costs. Moreover, any reliable process costs should be related to activities. They should not be based on a somewhat arbitrary allocation of expenses which originated, for example, in some service department. Each departmental manager should be held accountable only for those costs he can control. Thus, a charge from one department to another should be based on a level of activity. For example, the power charge should be based on the amount of electricity used (at standard or predetermined rates) and not on some allocation based on arbitrary assumptions.

It should be recognized that if the units of activity can be reduced, then the departmental processing costs should be lower. But this condition will not be realized unless the excess resources at the originating spot (services) are either reduced or rerouted to more productive areas.

(c) ACTIVITY-BASED PRODUCT COSTING

For the optimum profitability of the business, accurate product costs are mandatory, whether for long-term strategy determination, or the annual business plan, or tactical decisions, or day-to-day product pricing. The preferred priority of product cost determination is that shown in Figure 6-1. The first choice is to identify costs, such as material or labor costs, by direct attribution. If this is possible, there can be little argument about the relevance of the cost. The second preferred avenue is through cost assignment which is based on the use of cost drivers. If a product can be charged for the resources it consumes, then, if the bases are correct, the costs should be regarded as acceptable. Finally, to the extent these two relationships are unknown, then the third and least desired cost assignment technique is used—cost allocation.

An excellent illustration of a matrix of costs for a computer manufacturer is reflected in Figure 6-2. This illustration shows not only production costs, but also engineering, research and development, marketing, and other expenses. Sound activity-based costing would attempt to relate these latter functional costs to specific products, and not rely solely on arbitrary allocations. One product, for example, may require substantially more sales effort than another, and such activity requirement should be reflected in the selling price.

Much of the discussion about proper product costing relates to the treatment of the indirect costs—whether manufacturing or service, or general and administrative.

Figure 6-1   Preferred Assignment of Costs.

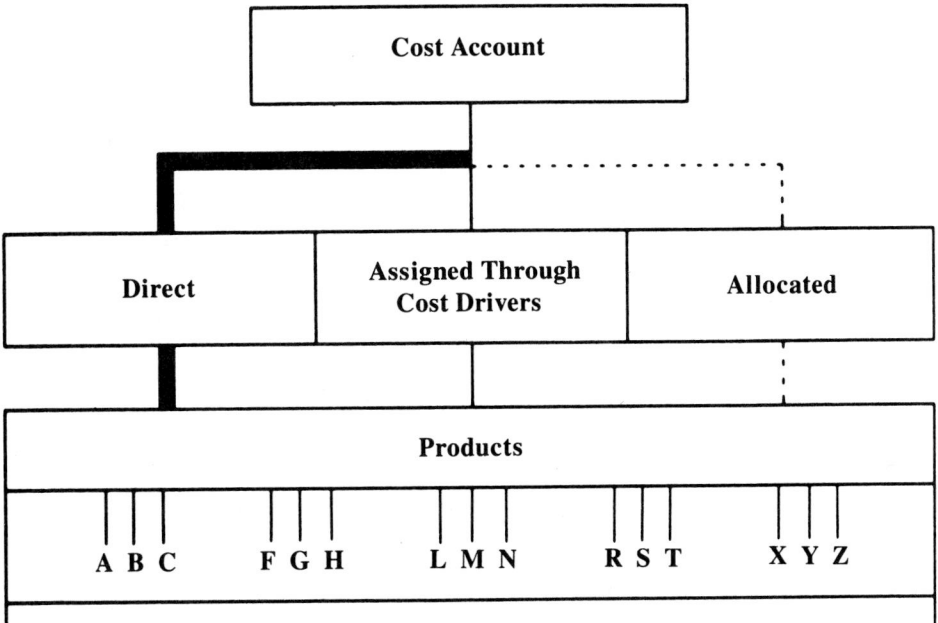

Figure 6-2   Input-Output Cost Matrix.

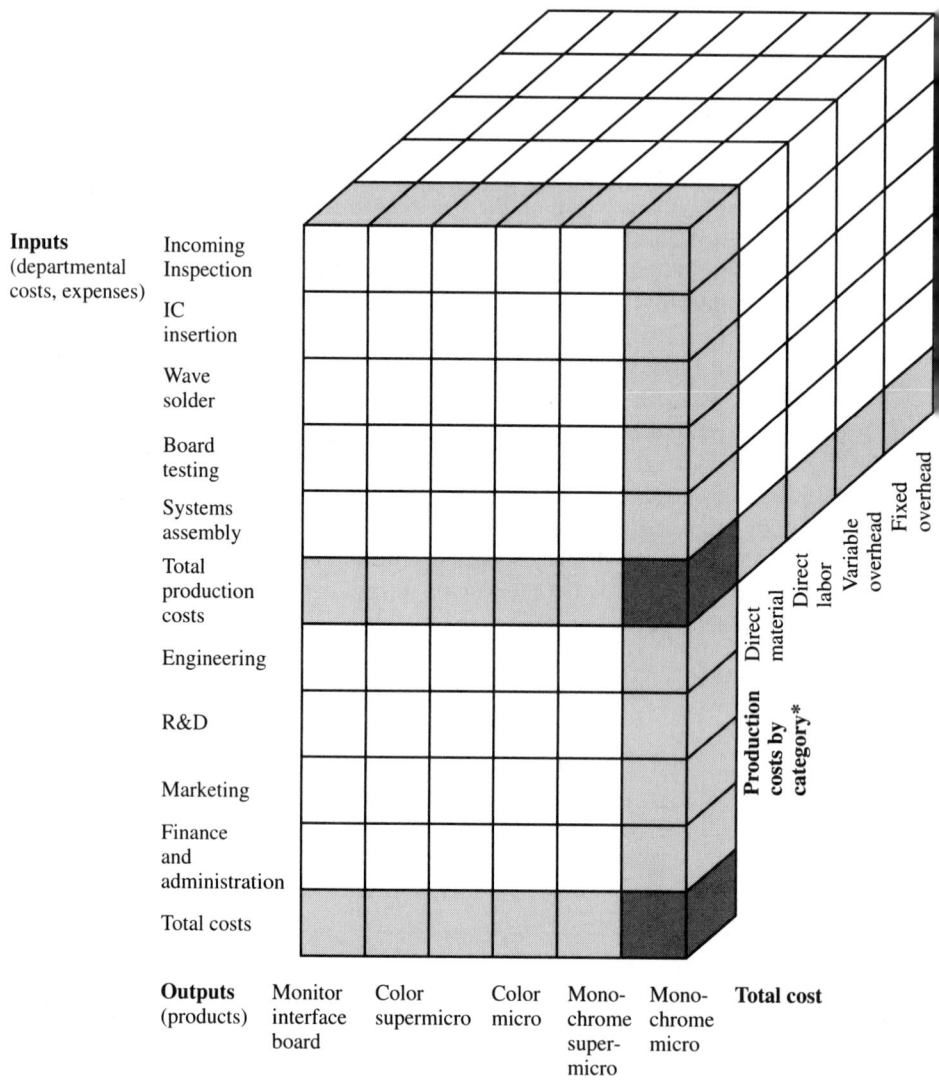

*These categories can be shown in considerably more detail, such as machine overhead, labor overhead, or material overhead.

Source: Reprinted by permission of *Harvard Business Review.* An exhibit from "What Kind of Cost System Do You Need?" by Michael J. Sandretto, Jan.–Feb. 1984. Copyright 1984 by the President and Fellows of Harvard College; all rights reserved.

As previously commented, the Statements of Management Accounting (SMA) No. 4G contained in Chapter 23, and No. 4B included in Chapter 26, can be valuable guides on the subject.

(d) RESPONSIBILITY ACCOUNTING

Another basic element related to proper costing and cost control is responsibility accounting. This key tool, one of several in sound financial planning and control, is discussed and illustrated in Chapter 5. Suffice it to state here that the concept requires that the revenues, or costs, or transactions should be recorded in such a fashion that they are identified with the supervisor or manager in the organization who controls the activity and can be held accountable for it.

To highlight the problem, a concrete example can be given. There is a tendency in some companies to charge using departments or process groups for some service costs, such as heat and power, maintenance, or computer department services, or accounting services, and so on through *general* allocations based on area, payroll, or head count. Such arbitrary allocations usually do not reflect actual consumption of the service. Hence, both process costs and product costs are distorted. In the review of activity-based costing, the objective should be to ascertain if a true activity-based method of making charges exists, and if not, can it be installed. Again, a producing department should be charged only for the activity requested or received so that the entity has true responsibility costing.

(e) PERFORMANCE MEASURES

In any well-managed company, performance measures can be one element of a sound planning and control system. Basically, performance measures should represent the mix of financial and nonfinancial operating measures that advance the business objectives, and are consistent with the level of business responsibility to which they are applied. These clarifying comments are made:

1. Chapter 7 discusses measures of *overall* business performance, including Statement on Management Accounting (SMA) 4D, entitled, "Measuring Equity Performance."

2. In the middle management area, current wisdom is to focus on nonfinancial measures, such as quality, customer satisfaction, on-time deliveries, and so on, as well as the usual financial yardsticks. Such measures, and related financial gauges, should be such that they do not maximize the performance of the individual area, department, or function, at the expense or injury of the total entity—building excess inventory to decrease unit production costs, but creating added costs elsewhere in the value chain (through faulty product), placing responsibility elsewhere.

3. The performance measures should be consistent with the process value analysis just discussed in (a) providing visibility to progress in elimination of nonvalue adding activity, and optimizing value adding activity; (b) assisting in cost reduction by measuring the real driver of activity; and (c) measuring in an appropriate way the reduction in product unit costs (not merely functional costs).

(f) INVESTMENT MANAGEMENT

The final segment of this circle of business decisions based on activity management is that related to investments. Chapter 32 reviews the fundamentals of making sound judgments regarding capital investments (and related project or working capital investments) in some detail.

Here are three pertinent observations:

1. A preferred way of evaluating a capital investment is by the discounted cash flow method. It should be obvious that if activity-based costing is desirable for product pricing and strategy planning, then this same methodology should be employed in calculating the true net cash inflow from any proposed capital investment. This requires recognizing the cash flow from each product or product line which benefits from the expenditure, and not a cash flow based on broadbrush averages.

2. Aside from net cash flow calculations based on product costs, the examination of the real cost drivers may focus attention on potential competitive activity as it may impinge on these factors.

3. In today's environment, the attention being directed to the many nonfinancial factors that influence the customer—quality, on-time delivery, and so on—should encourage estimates of their impact on the return on assets.

6-6 ACTIVITY-BASED NONMANUFACTURING COSTS

Many articles have been written about traditional cost systems. There are at least two common themes prevalent in a great number of the writings: (1) they tend to be critical of costing practices because a proper "cost driver" is not used to assign costs to a cost object; and (2) the focus seems to be on manufacturing costs to the exclusion of other functional costs.

We wish to make a couple of simple observations on these two subjects before proceeding to the main thrust of this section—attention to costing for nonmanufacturing functions. In the first instance, many articles stress that the "cost driver"—the force that should regulate the costs to be incurred—must be discovered, much as though it were a new thought. Yet, the term "cost driver" may be viewed as a modern word for "measure of activity," or "factor of variability" for the function under discussion. In some instances, as manufacturing methods changed, little attention was directed by the controller or others to the need for a new base against which a variable cost should be measured. But a great deal of accounting literature stressed the proper concept—the need for an activity base that would be a fair indicator of how the cost should vary. In discussing the relationship of costs to volume, a key step is "the selection of the activity measure or factor of variability for each function and/or cost."[3]

The second common characteristic—emphasis on manufacturing or production costs—may be explained on the basis that formerly a large share of the costs of a product were related to the cost to manufacture, and that perhaps more analysis was done

---

[3] J. Brooks Heckert and James D. Willson, *Business Budgeting and Control,* 2nd ed., New York: The Ronald Press Company, 1955, p. 57.

on manufacturing costs than, say, marketing costs. Yet, some authors stressed the need for proper analysis of distribution costs in view of the relatively high proportion of costs of this function in some companies, for example, "Yet it is sometimes forgotten that distribution costs are probably just as important as production costs in determining what price the consumer must pay for an article."[4] In the 1990s, distribution costs, which include marketing expenses as well as physical distribution costs, have assumed an even greater significance.[5] Proper analysis of distribution costs, as well as any other significant nonmanufacturing costs, is essential to assist management in making informed decisions which affect profitability. Included would be such matters as product pricing, adding or dropping production product lines, terms of sales in different territories, quantity discounts, size-of-order pricing, and many more similar decisions.

On the subject of proper costing practices, we will identify the steps in a cost and profit analysis which extends to all functions of a business. First, the general procedure is outlined, followed by specific illustrative analyses relating to products and territories. This analysis identifies several significant profit subtotals for arriving at different types of decisions. Similar steps would be required in making any of the distribution cost analyses outlined in Chapter 21. The degree in which the elements of each major functional cost (manufacturing, engineering, marketing, research and development, financial, and general administrative) are variable, and the factors of variability may differ by industry and company.

The general procedure for a meaningful analysis of costs or expenses would be as follows:

1. Determine the activities performed under each major function, for which costs or expenses should be identified or segregated, based on responsibility reporting principles, and identifiable activity measures.

   Thus, for the marketing function, the identified activities might be:

   Advertising.

   Sales promotion.

   Direct selling.

   Warehousing.

   Packing and shipping.

   Order handling.

   Marketing administration.

2. Accumulate the direct costs for each activity, by type of cost (hourly labor, fringe benefits, supplies, travel expenses, depreciation, etc.) and tentatively segregate each into the fixed, programmed, or variable cost components. (See Chapter 5.) Which costs are direct may depend on the type of analysis to be made. Thus, in a territorial analysis, the costs of territory A would be direct as to that territory; warehousing could be assigned by a cost driver; but district supervisory expense would be indirect.

---

[4] *Ibid.,* p. 232.

[5] See Sections 21-3 and 21-8. In the suggested analyses, the term "semi-direct" costs has the same meaning as costs assigned through cost drivers.

3. Select the appropriate cost drivers for the activity. Often a single basis will suffice, such as weight might apply to storage costs, for example; but a time factor also may be appropriate for those time-related costs such as depreciation or property taxes. (See section 6-5 earlier in this chapter.) For direct selling costs, gross sales may be an appropriate base, or number of sales calls might apply. Order handling could relate to number of orders.

4. Calculate the unit cost for each activity. Basically, this will represent the total cost of the activity divided by the quantity of the cost driver selected. Where no specific cost driver can be determined, then some general allocation basis, such as gross sales, must be selected. In some instances, it may be more practical to calculate the percentage distribution of the cost driver—say percentage of engineering manhours for allocation to product lines, in lieu of the unit cost for the cost driver.

5. Where no suitable cost driver can be found, then a less desirable basis must be used for cost allocation purposes. (See Figures 6-1 and 6-3.)

6. Perform the contribution margin and total margin analysis when direct costs, costs assigned through cost drivers, and the residual allocation costs can be determined through application of the appropriate base. (See Chapter 21.) Thus, these different margin levels might be calculated:

   - Contribution margin after direct variable costs.
   - Contribution margin after variable costs assigned by cost drivers.
   - Contribution margin after allocated variable costs.
   - Margin after programmed costs.
   - Margin after direct fixed costs.
   - Margin after allocated fixed costs.
   - Net income after taxes on income.

In making the contribution margin analysis, one key objective is to identify those costs that would discontinue if the product were discontinued, from those continuing fixed costs which would be a burden until the causative factor (such as a building) was either written off or was devoted to other uses and products.

The profitability analyses are reflected in Figures 6-5 and 6-6—one by product line and one by sales territory. By use of direct assignment of certain costs, and by application of the proper cost driver, management has a great deal of confidence in the costs and expenses applicable to each product (and thence to territory). It also is of the opinion that were a product (or territory) to be discontinued, the variable costs assigned to that product or cost object would cease. Further, although the programmed costs are fixed by management decision, that share applicable to a particular product could be eliminated. As a result of the product analysis, management can understand that product Y is unprofitable, but does provide enough profit margin to cover all but $14,000 of the fixed costs assigned to the product. A review probably should be made for possible sales price adjustments or the lowering of variable costs, and the impact on other products of dropping the line, before deciding to discontinue the product. The management is also made aware of the high profitability of product Z and the relatively low profit contribution by product X.

Figure 6-3 Product Line Data.

The Johnson Company
SELECTED PRODUCT LINE DATA
FOR THE YEAR 19XX

	Product Line		
Description	X	Y	Z
Unit selling price (gross)	$75	$20	$100
Unit manufacturing cost			
Direct material (variable)	$15	2	$ 1
Assigned through cost drivers (variable)	5	3	1
Allocated (fixed) based on square footage of manufacturing area	1.50	.90	.33
	$21.50	$ 5.90	$ 2.33
Quantity of units sold (net)	100,000	50,000	30,000
Unit weight of product (lbs.)	5	2	1
No. of orders handled	400	200	500

The income and expense analysis by territory reveals that the company, although located in the southwest of the United States earns 60% of its net income in the northwest, among other reasons, because of the high proportion of product Z sales in that area. Perhaps a further subanalysis of product profitability by territory, and an examination of detailed costs, can provide further useful information for the management.

Profitability analysis requires a great variety of detailed calculations. Some of supporting data for the product line and territorial analysis are shown in Figures 6-3 and 6-4. The computer can be of great assistance in gathering, as well as sorting and re-sorting, the data into various desired subcategories.

6-7 SELECTING THE PROPER COST SYSTEM

As stated earlier, the controller has a major responsibility for the design, installation, and maintenance of the cost systems of the entity. Among the reasons for providing a background on the uses of a cost system, some of the environmental changes which impact the cost system, some of the actual or alleged weaknesses in many cost systems, and commentary on activity-based costing is to motivate you to think about answers to such questions as these:

- Does the cost system or costing practices in my company have the weaknesses described?
- Does the management really know the true total unit cost for each of our major products (research and development, engineering, manufacturing, selling, advertising, distribution, and general and administrative expenses) and its real margin (over the probable life cycle as well as at the present time)?
- Is the economic justification for the company capital expenditures based on product-specific costs, or merely on averages for the nonmanufacturing elements?

Figure 6-4   Territory and Product Data.

The Johnson Company
SELECTED DATA BY TERRITORY AND PRODUCT
FOR THE YEAR 19XX

Description		Total	Territory Northwest	Southwest
Unit Sales				
Product				
X		100,000	30,000	70,000
Y		50,000	25,000	25,000
Z		30,000	20,000	10,000
Orders Handled				
Product				
X		400	120	280
Y		200	100	100
Z		500	333	167
Pounds Shipped	Unit Weight			
Product				
X	5	500,000	150,000	350,000
Y	2	100,000	50,000	50,000
Z	1	30,000	20,000	10,000
Engineering Hours & Cost	% Total	($000)		
Product				
X	65	$101	$ 30	$ 71
Y	3	4	2	2
Z	32	50	33	17
Total	100	$155	$ 65	$ 90
Research and Development	% Professional Hours	Cost ($000)		
Product				
X	39	$199	$ 60	$139
Y	2	10	5	5
Z	59	301	199	102
Total	100	$510	$264	$246

Figure 6-5 Statement of Income and Expense by Product.

The Johnson Company

STATEMENT OF INCOME AND EXPENSE FOR THE YEAR 19XX BY PRODUCT LINE ($ IN 000)

Description	Total	Product Line X	Product Line Y	Product Line Z	Assigned Cost Driver or Allocation Base
Gross Sales	$11,600	$7,600	$1,000	$3,000	
Less:					
Returns and Allowances	120	110	10	—	Direct as to product
Freight—Out	150	—	—	150	Direct as to product
Total	270	110	10	150	
Net Sales	11,330	7,490	990	2,850	
Cost of Sales					
Direct—Variable	1,630	1,500	100	30	Direct as to product
Assigned thru Cost Drivers (Variable)	680	500	150	30	(Various cost drivers determined by manufacturing process or department)
Total	2,310	2,000	250	60	
Gross Margin After Variable Manufacturing Costs	9,020	5,490	740	2,790	
Other Costs and Expenses—Variable					
Marketing					
Selling	1,160	760	100	300	10% of gross sales
Advertising	700	500	50	150	Units sold
Warehousing	630	500	100	30	$1 per lbs. shipped
Packing and Shipping	180	100	50	30	$1 per unit sold
Order Handling	55	20	10	25	$50 per order handled
Total	2,725	1,880	310	535	
Engineering					
Research and Development	462	400	50	12	20% of variable manufacturing expense
General and Administrative	1,133	749	99	285	10% of net sales
	1,133	749	99	285	10% of net sales
Total Variable	5,453	3,778	588	1,117	

(continued)

Figure 6-5 *(continued)*

Description	Total	Product Line			Assigned Cost Driver or Allocation Base
		X	Y	Z	
Margin After Variable Costs	3,567	1,712	182	1,673	
Programmed Costs (Fixed)					
Engineering	155	100	5	50	Engineering manhours—direct as to product
Research and Development	510	200	10	300	Manhours on each project—product oriented
Total Programmed Costs	665	300	15	350	
Margin After Programmed Costs	2,902	1,412	167	1,323	
Fixed Expenses					
Manufacturing	205	150	45	10	Square footage
Marketing	260	180	30	50	% of variable marketing expense
Engineering	31	20	1	10	20% programmed engineering costs
Research and Development	105	40	5	60	20% programmed research and dev. costs
General and Administrative	1,160	760	100	300	10% of gross sales
Total Fixed Costs	1,761	1,150	181	430	
Margin (Loss) After Fixed Costs	1,141	262	(14)	893	
Taxes Based on Income (38%)	434	100	(5)	339	
Net Income (Loss)	$ 707	162	(9)	$ 554	
% Net Sales	6.2%	2.2%	(.1%)	19.4%	

Figure 6-6 Statement of Income and Expense by Territory.

The Johnson Company
STATEMENT OF INCOME AND EXPENSE BY TERRITORY FOR THE YEAR 19XX ($ IN 000)

Description	Total	Territory Northwest	Southwest	Assigned Cost Driver or Allocation Base, etc.
Gross Sales	$11,600	$4,825	$6,775	
Less:				
Return and Allowances	120	38	82	
Freight-out	150	150	—	
Total	$ 270	$ 188	$ 82	
Net Sales	11,330	4,637	6,693	
Cost of Sales				
Direct (material)—Variable	1,630	520	1,110	Direct as to product; by product to territory
Assigned Through Cost Drivers—Variable	680	245	435	Various cost drivers determined by process and department
Total	$ 2,310	$ 765	$1,545	
Gross Margin After Variable Manufacturing Expenses	9,020	3,872	5,148	
Other Costs and Expenses—Variable				
Marketing				
Selling (Direct)	1,160	483	677	Direct as to territory
Advertising	700	275	425	Units sold
Warehousing	630	220	410	Lbs. shipped
Packing and Shipping	180	75	105	Units sold
Order Handling	55	28	27	Cost per order handled
Total	$ 2,725	$1,081	$1,644	
Engineering	462	153	309	20% of variable manufacturing costs
Research and Development	1,133	464	669	10% of net sales
General and Administrative	1,133	464	669	10% of net sales
Total Variable	5,453	2,162	3,291	

(continued)

Figure 6-6 *(continued)*

Description	Total	Territory Northwest	Territory Southwest	Assigned Cost Driver or Allocation Base, etc.
Margin After Variable Costs	3,567	1,710	1,857	
Programmed Costs (Fixed)				
Engineering	155	65	90	Engineering hours direct as to product
Research and Development	$ 510	$ 264	$ 246	Manhours on each project—product oriented
Total Programmed Costs	$ 665	$ 329	$ 336	
Margin After Programmed Costs	$ 2,902	$1,381	$1,521	
Fixed Costs—Allocated				
Manufacturing	205	74	131	Square footage
Marketing	260	104	156	% of variable marketing expense
Engineering	31	10	21	20% of programmed engineering costs
Research and Development	105	43	62	20% of programmed research and development costs
General and Administrative	$ 1,160	$482	$ 678	10% of gross sales
Total Fixed Costs	$ 1,761	$ 713	$1,048	
Margin After Fixed Costs	1,141	668	473	
Taxes Based on Income (38%)	$ 434	$ 254	$ 180	
Net Income	$ 707	$ 414	$ 285	
% Net Sales	6.2%	8.9%	4.3%	

The survival and long-term growth of the company may depend on positive responses to these questions. This should bring the controller and the chief cost accountant to ask themselves, "Just what kind of cost system or cost determination procedure is proper for my company?" We are not concerned solely with the cost system for inventory valuation, but with the broader task of proper cost determination including the relevant costs of all functions—not just manufacturing.

A number of factors need to be considered when designing or selecting (or updating) a cost system. These include:

- Nature of the product.
- Competitive posture of the company or product.
- Type of manufacturing process.
- Extent to which costs are needed for planning purposes.
- Degree of control desired by management.
- Size of the company.
- Nature and demands of the distribution system (for nonmanufacturing cost determination).
- Nature of analyses required by management.

The cost matrix shown in Figure 6-2 provides an indication of both the input (departmental expenses, labor and material) and the output (product costs and functional costs) possibilities of a total cost system. Typically, management wants to know costs by type of cost, by department, and by product, for each activity and type of input and for a designated time period. Where the product has only a single or few material components and is made in a high-volume automated process, the cost system can be simple. Where there are many components of material (each important) and many operations, the cost system is much more complex. However, computers make a detailed, complex cost system economically feasible.

Some managements may need little *control* information in a continuous standardized process. They can see the waste or slippage, and can check the speed of machinery, as a result, little cost control information may be needed. Or, in a small plant, the manager may be so knowledgeable about the product and process that by observation he can see if costs are in line. For *planning* purposes, the scope of cost determination or analysis and the availability of alternative scenarios probably will be the feature getting most management attention when selecting the system.

There are practical limits to the amount of data that can be accumulated or calculated under a cost system. In a high volume simple product environment, such as petroleum refining, it is relatively easy and unobtrusive to collect cost data. At the other extreme, consider a low volume multifunctional job such as that of a doctor or nurse in a general hospital. Can anyone imagine a system wherein the doctor or nurse records the time spent with each patient—perhaps 3 or 4 minutes for each event, and perhaps 30 events per day? Patients would be annoyed; and the service staff would need to be expanded substantially. It logically follows that in any cost system, installation and operating costs must be considered, as well as interruption of the basic process.

It is generally known that a number of types of cost systems are in use. Some provide detailed and accurate costs; others may provide only estimated or average costs.

Some may produce actual or historical costs; in other cases, a predetermined cost plus variances may be the output. For the manufacturing function, cost systems may be classified as follows:

A. *Actual costs*
   (1) Job order costs
   (2) Process costs
B. *Predetermined costs*
   (1) Standard costs
      (a) Job order
      (b) Process
   (2) Estimated costs
      (a) Job order
      (b) Process

A job order system is one which collects separately each element of cost for each job or order on which work is being done. Hence, the ability to identify or segregate quantities of product going through the plant is a requisite. This system will be found in plants manufacturing to customer order or doing special jobs.

A process cost system is one which accumulates costs for continuous or mass production, wherein the output consists of like units with each unit being processed in a similar manner. This system would be applicable where the product is manufactured in bulk or as a homogeneous total, making a differentiation of articles difficult. Thus, process costs are applicable where there is:

1. A continuous or mass production.
2. A loss of identity of individual items or lots.
3. A complete standardization of product and process exists.

A process cost system is based on average costs and can be applied on an actual cost or standard cost basis.

Predetermined costs are costs calculated in advance of manufacture, based on specified future conditions. They may be standard costs or estimated costs. Management is interested in what the costs should be. Actual costs are accumulated for comparison with the predetermined costs, and the *variances* are reported.

In a standard cost system, scientific estimates are made of the quantity as well as the cost of material, labor, and manufacturing expenses which should be incurred in making the article. Analyses of variations from standard are made as they occur.

Estimated costs are, as the name indicates, mere estimates of what the costs should be. They are less accurate than standard costs. This method may supplement the financial accounting in firms that have incomplete or inadequate cost systems. Again, as in a standard cost system, actual costs may be compared with the estimated cost, and the variances reported for investigation.

The previous discussion of cost systems has been limited to *manufacturing* cost systems. In addition to a manufacturing cost system, provision needs to be made to accumulate and properly classify the nonmanufacturing expenses (research and development, advertising, selling, distribution, as well as general and administrative). Such expenses probably need to be segregated and identified:

1. By nature of expense (salaries and wages, fringe benefits, supplies, travel, and so on).
2. By function or department (selling, etc.).
3. By expense behavior, that is, fixed, variable, or semi-variable.

The proper cost identification facilitates a grouping of the relevant costs for the decision under consideration.

These cost systems have been described only in a very general way. While many managers may think a cost system is very simple in nature, in actuality it may be very complex. To become familiar with the many complications and variations, the reader may wish to review some of the excellent texts on cost systems and costing techniques as well as the Selected References.

The nature of the product and the manufacturing process are the important determinants in selecting a manufacturing cost system. These two factors often will influence management as to the amount of planning or control data required. Figure 6-7 identifies eight groups of products and companies, classified according to input and operating characteristics, by the type of cost system probably most applicable.

The purpose for which the costs are used will be a factor in the *manner of cost segregation* required, and the frequency needed. Thus, for *planning* purposes it may be desirable to segregate costs into their variable, semi-variable and fixed components, and perhaps to distinguish incremental costs from full costs. Moreover, such data will be needed only when a planning exercise is underway—perhaps once a year or once a quarter—and not every month.

In contrast, for *control* purposes, costs and expenses should be classified as controllable or uncontrollable (for certain short-term decisions). The nature of the product and process and the relative importance of each cost element will largely determine which detailed cost elements need to be monitored, and the frequency of review. Here are some examples:

*   A low-margin, high-volume product where price is the primary factor for customer selection, probably will require a detailed and precise cost system. In contrast, it may not be as critical for a high-margin unique product of low volume.
*   The cost structure of the product may dictate what cost elements must be closely controlled. If material costs are 95% of the cost, then little attention need be directed to labor or overhead.
*   The size of the producing company will influence the cost system design. When it is small, perhaps personal observation is sufficient. When it grows, and must rely on reporting methods, a formal cost system may be required—especially if the product or process is complex.
*   The product cycle is a consideration. In the early product life, the article may be unique and command such a high margin that cost control is not important. When the product matures and margins become smaller, then cost control may be the center of attention.

Figure 6-7   A Framework for Cost Systems.

	Job-order process	Batch process	Assembly process	Continuous process
Discrete-part products, many materials inputs	Machine shop Construction Shipbuilding Oil well drilling	General purpose machine tools Medium-volume industrial products	Automobiles Electronics Household appliances	
Single or few materials inputs	Printing	Utility poles Bakery goods Cutting tools— drill bits, grinding wheels, etc.	Canned goods Household utensils Simple tools	Paint Glass Simple chemicals
Services		Department store Large daily newspaper General hospital Electronics repair	Fast-food restaurant Tabloid newspaper Dialysis clinic Muffler repair	
Joint products		◄——— Meat packer Sawmill	Integrated circuits manufacturer* ———►	
		◄——— Integrated wood products company	Chemical plant† ———► Oil refinery	

*Few products, little choice of output.
†Many products, wide choice of output.

Source: Reprinted by permission of *Harvard Business Review*. An Exhibit from "What Kind of Cost System Do You Need?" by Michael J. Sandretto, Jan.–Feb. 1984. Copyright 1984 by the President and Fellows of Harvard College; all rights reserved.

- Market position may be the key factor in selecting the degree of cost control. If one company dominates a market where volume is crucial, then a detailed cost system may be necessary to control costs and be more reliable when changing prices.

Often the unique qualities of the product, and related demand, will set the price—not costs. But in those instances where costs are the determinant of market strategy and price, then accurate product cost determination is critical.

6-8 SOFTWARE FOR ACTIVITY-BASED COST MANAGEMENT

There are any number of software packages presently available for use in activity-based costing and activity-based cost management. And there are continually new developments for use on a personal computer. A few of the existing packages and the developers or sources of information are given in Figure 6-8. Available software for ABC management is continually changing and improving. The numerous publications on computer technology, such as *PC Computing,* and others, as well as dealers in computer software may be helpful in explaining the new developments.

Figure 6-8   Software for Activity-Based Cost Management.

Software Packages	Developer or Sponsor
(1) AB Cost Manager	Coopers & Lybrand 203 N. LaSalle St. Chicago, IL 60601 (312) 701-5783
(2) ACTIVA	Price Waterhouse 1 Boatman's Plaza St. Louis, MO 63101 (314) 425-0500
(3) CASSO (Cost Accounting System for Service Organizations)	Automation Consulting 11500 Hyne Rd., Brighton, MI 48116 (313) 229-2099
(4) Power ABC	Genesis Consulting Group, Inc. 111 Shores Acre Drive Box 085486 Racine, WI 53408-5486 (414) 639-1084
(5) Profit Manager	KPMG Peat Marwick, Suite 1200 150 West Jefferson Detroit, MI 48226 (800) 537-0047
(6) Quote-A-Profit	Manufacturing Management Systems, Inc. P.O. Box 686 355 Hyder Drive Madison, OH 44057 (216) 428-4068
(7) TR/ACM	Deloitte & Touche 125 Summer Street Boston, MA 02110 (617) 261-8505; or (617) 261-8623

6-9 SUMMARY

The controller has the basic responsibility for the proper design, installation, and operation (and revision when required) of the basic cost determination methods of his or her company. The term "cost determination methods" encompasses the costs or expenses of every department, function, activity, or product of the entity. This expression is intended to be all inclusive, and not restricted to the "cost system," which may be interpreted by many as only the manufacturing cost system.

While the controller has responsibility for the methods used to accumulate costs, to be effective he or she must take into account the information needs of all members of management. The "system" should be composed of the proper building blocks (see, for example, Figure 6-2) so that the management can be provided with most of the required financial and related data on an economical basis. Properly done, especially in this age of computers, the need for many exhaustive and lengthy manual cost studies, or the tendency of the engineers to develop their own systems, should be held to a minimum.

Such information systems envision the following:

1. Provision of cost data for *planning* purposes, including information for alternative scenarios, on a timely basis and in a usable format. Recognition would be given to cost behavior—whether fixed, variable, or semi-variable—and to the costs *relevant* for the decision. These cost segregations would apply, as may be applicable, to each department or organizational unit or product or other cost object.

2. Provision for *control* purposes, on a timely basis and in usable format, embodying the principle of responsibility accounting, the required monetary data and other quantified data (manhours, machine hours, scrap generation percentages, on-time deliveries, etc.). Much control data may be furnished on a repetitive basis, but provision should be made for a reasonable amount of special analyses.

3. Provision for required inventory valuation data and other financial information for monthly (or sometimes more frequently) income and expense and financial position determination.

4. As may be appropriate, the cost data should be compiled to recognize the impact of the cost drivers and other appropriate measures of cost activity.

5. The various segments should be regularly audited or monitored so that they reflect existent operating procedures.

The excellence or suitability of the cost accumulation procedures and reports will depend in large part on the astuteness of the controller and the staff who deal with the cost accounting practices.

6-10 SELECTED REFERENCES

Ames, B. Charles, and James D. Hlavacek, "Vital Truths About Managing Your Costs," *Harvard Business Review*, Jan.–Feb. 1990, pp. 140–147 (HBR Reprint No. 90102).

Brimson, James A., "How Advanced Manufacturing Technologies Are Reshaping Cost Management," *Management Accounting*, Mar. 1986, pp. 25–29.

Cheatham, Carole, "Updating Standard Cost Systems; Making Them Better Tools for Today's Manufacturing Environment," *Journal of Accountancy,* Dec. 1990, pp. 57–60.

Cooper, Robin, "You Need a New Cost System When . . . ," *Harvard Business Review,* Jan.–Feb. 1989, pp. 77–82 (HBR Reprint No. 89102).

Cooper, Robin, and Robert S. Kaplan, "Measure Costs Right: Make the Right Decisions," *Harvard Business Review,* Sept.–Oct. 1988, pp. 96–103 (HBR Reprint No. 88503).

————, "How Cost Accounting Distorts Product Costs," *Management Accounting,* April 1988, pp. 20–27.

Dearden, John, "Measuring Profit Center Managers," *Harvard Business Review,* Sept.–Oct. 1987, pp. 84–88 (HBR Reprint No. 87503).

Dilts, David M., and Grant W. Russell, "Accounting for the Factory of the Future," *Management Accounting,* April 1985, pp. 34–40.

Dudick, Thomas S., "Why SG&A Doesn't Always Work," *Harvard Business Review,* Jan.–Feb. 1987, pp. 4–7 (HBR Reprint No. 87106).

Estrin, T. L., Jeffrey Kantor, and David Albers, "Is ABC Suitable for Your Company?" *Management Accounting,* April 1994, pp. 40–45.

Ferrara, William L., "More Questions than Answers. Is the Management Accounting System as Hopeless as the Critics Say?" *Management Accounting,* Oct. 1990, pp. 48–52.

Foster, George, and Charles T. Horngren, "JIT: Cost Accounting and Cost Management Issues," *Management Accounting,* June 1987, pp. 19–25.

Howell, Robert A., and Stephen R. Soucy, "Cost Accounting in the New Manufacturing Environment," *Management Accounting,* Aug. 1987, pp. 42–48.

————, "Operating Controls in the New Manufacturing Environment," *Management Accounting,* Oct. 1987, pp. 25–31.

Johnson, H. Thomas, "A Blueprint for World Class Management Accounting," *Management Accounting,* June 1988, pp. 23–30.

Kaplan, Robert S., "One Cost System Isn't Enough," *Harvard Business Review,* Jan.–Feb. 1988, pp. 61–66 (HBR Reprint No. 88106).

Lewis, Ronald J., "Activity-Based Costing for Marketing," *Management Accounting,* Nov. 1991, pp. 33–38.

McIlhattan, Robert D., "How Cost Management Can Support the JIT Philosophy," *Management Accounting,* Sept. 1987, pp. 20–26.

McNair, C. J., and William Mosconi, "Measuring Performance in an Advanced Manufacturing Environment," *Management Accounting,* July 1987, pp. 28–31.

O'Guin, Michael, "Focus the Factory with Activity-Based Costing," *Management Accounting,* Feb. 1990, pp. 36–41.

Ostrenga, Michael R., "Activities: The Focal Point of Total Cost Management," *Management Accounting,* Feb. 1990, pp. 42–49.

Pattison, Diane D., and Carrie Gavan Arendt, "Activity-Based Costing: It Doesn't Work All the Time," *Management Accounting,* April 1994, pp. 55–61.

Raffish, Norm, "How Much Does That Product Really Cost?" *Management Accounting,* March 1991, pp. 36–39.

Sandretto, Michael J., "What Kind of Cost System Do You Need?" *Harvard Business Review,* Jan.–Feb. 1985, pp. 110–118 (HBR Reprint No. 85113).

Smith, Malcolm, "Managing Your ABC System," *Management Accounting,* April 1994, pp. 46–47.

CHAPTER 7

An Overall Appraisal of the Business: Some Yardsticks of Overall Performance

7-1 A BROAD MANAGEMENT VIEWPOINT

The first part of this volume is devoted to the broad management aspects of controllership. If controllers are to be management oriented, if, indeed, they are to best serve *all* management, then obviously they must be able objectively to take an overall look at the business. They must be familiar with its strengths and weaknesses. They must understand the interrelationship of the functions of the organization. Just as any prudent buyer of a business must appraise it carefully in all its important aspects, so also controllers lay the best foundation for doing an effective job by having a broad understanding of the business of which they are a part.

In such a review, controllers are in a somewhat enviable position, for they are part of the management and usually will have an opportunity to get at the facts and opinions that will enable them to draw the correct conclusions. In contrast, many of the outside financial interests—security analysts, shareholders, commercial bankers, long-term lenders, and investment brokers—will be searching for this same information. It is one of the responsibilities of the financial officers to become knowledgeable about the business ingredients and convey such information, when appropriate and when not beneficial to competition, to the financial community.

In a volume such as this, addressed largely to a financial audience, it is understandable that emphasis would be placed on financial yardsticks. Yet, there are a great many nonfinancial factors that bulk large in business success. The financial executive should be sensitive to these other operating measures that ultimately impact on financial performance. This phase of measurement is reviewed at some length in section 7-20.

7-2 THE BUSINESS INGREDIENTS

This matter of reviewing or appraising a business from the overall vantage point may be approached in any one of several ways. However, the following factors or ingredients should be evaluated during the process of analysis:

1. *The Objectives and Policies.* These factors have to do with the purpose of the business and its parts and the guiding principles or rules of action to be followed in achieving that purpose.

2. *The Organization.* This element is concerned with the employees, including the organizational structure, that is, the relationship to one another, and the duties, authorities, and responsibilities of each.

3. *The Products.* These are the means of satisfying customer demands. Many of the other factors are heavily influenced by them.

4. *The Market.* This factor has to do with the customers, their location, and the extent and nature of their wants.

5. *The Distribution Program.* This element relates to ways and means of getting the products to market.

6. *The Production Plan.* This factor relates to the all-inclusive segment of the facilities in which the product is manufactured and the techniques that are used in the process.

7. *The Research and Development Program.* This has reference to the efforts and effectiveness in creating new products or improving existing products or product applications.

8. *The Financial Structure, Accounting Policies and Practices, and Financial Trends and Relationships.* This is a broad category in which the controller should be especially knowledgeable.

9. *The Control System.* This element includes the methods or techniques used in developing and guiding the functions to achieve the business objective.

An understanding of the nature, importance, interrelationship, and effectiveness of each of these factors in his company should facilitate the more useful functioning of the controller.

When seeking to understand each of these business ingredients, the reader should identify the "critical success factors," if any, that are contained in each. The critical success factors are those attributes which are essential to (1) a company's success and (2) sound strategic planning. They are discussed in more detail in Chapter 14.

7-3 BUSINESS OBJECTIVES AND POLICIES

In the controller's review of his company, he should be concerned not with a general business objective, but with the more specific objectives of his company and the policies of operation. A company must know what it wants to accomplish. The controller should attempt to seek out management's real goals. Are they in writing? Not only should the company objective be known but also there should exist specific objectives for each operating division, such as marketing, production, research, engineering, and finance. If the company is organized on a decentralized basis, each operating group ought to have goals. Further, the objectives of each group should be in tune with the overall company objectives.

An example of an overall company goal might be "An intelligent, well-established industrial enterprise, organized to return continual maximum benefits, in the light-metal fabrication field, to customers, employees, and shareholders." A subsidiary goal might include the attainment of X dollars of sales by the year 19XX. The specific goal of each sales function in the autonomous divisions should support these objectives. If the company objectives are not in writing, then the controller should encourage such action.

Company policies should support the company objectives. Business policies may be classified as general, major, or minor. General policies govern the conduct of the business as a whole; they are the basic principles the company proposes to follow. As an example, a general policy might be expressed in these words: "The company will confine its business to the continental United States." General policies will relate to both internal and external matters.

Major policies govern performance and control of the principal functions of the business. Thus, for an ultimately successful operation there must be a sales policy, purchasing policy, engineering policy, and so on. An example of a purchasing policy may be, "No division must necessarily purchase parts from other divisions of the company."

Finally, minor policies will relate to the activities of a department or segment of a major division. For example, the policy of a division credit department may be, "The maximum credit extension, without home office approval, to a C class appliance dealer, will be $25,000."

In his or her review, the controller should be aware of the existence or absence of written policies of the company and should attempt to conduct planning and control, or other controllership functions, within the confines of sound policy.

7-4 THE ORGANIZATION

Many of the problems of business relate to organization—or lack of it. The ability to stand away from the trees and study the forest of organization—its strong and weak points—should be valuable in effective planning and control work. The interrelationship of the various groups and the duties and responsibilities of each position are important considerations in the effectiveness of planning and control systems.

An *organization* may be defined as a group of individuals, under leadership, working toward a common goal. This is the dynamic, the vital part of the business, upon which all else chiefly depends. Andrew Carnegie is reported to have said, "Take away my mills, but leave me my organization and I will be back in business in a year." Some of the basic problems of business arise by reason of organizational troubles. The business functions must be properly segregated, and the relationship between functions and organizational groups must be clearly defined. Some of the specific points bearing on the subject are:

1. *The Management*
   a. The track record of the management—perhaps as measured in financial terms.
   b. The environment the management attempts to promote—one of creativity, permissiveness, or working cooperatively?
   c. Character of the management. Is it highly ethical? Does it condone any practices to secure business? Does it honor its commitments?
   d. The internally perceived effectiveness of the management process. Does it identify the essential strategies? Does it set realistic (but sometimes difficult) objectives or goals, and does it follow through to see that they are attained?

2. *Organization Chart*
   a. Has an organization chart been prepared?
   b. Are the line and staff relationships evident?

3. *Manual of Organization.* Is a manual in existence that, in detail, outlines for supervisory personnel at least the following:
   a. Title of position?
   b. Position to which responsible?
   c. General functions, together with authority and responsibility?
   d. Detailed duties and responsibilities?

4. *Competitive Posture.* Is provision made for some of the more recent concepts for improving the competitive posture of the company, such as reengineering, or benchmarking, or work groups and outsourcing?

5. *Standard Practice Instructions.* Are such aids available about the repetitive and routine functions, indicating (a) the responsibility of the several departments and (b) the procedure to be followed?

6. *Compliance with Applicable Labor Laws.* Is the company complying with equal opportunity laws or regulations?

7. *Labor Relations.* Can the company be considered farsighted or enlightened in this field? What is the evidence? Is the company competitive in its practices?

8. *Selection of Personnel.* What basis is used?

9. *Training of Personnel.* Has any program been established for either formal or informal training?

10. *Coordination of Functions.* How is coordination attained?

7-5 THE PRODUCTS

The management audit or review can very logically begin with the product line. The most effective selling force, a skillfully developed advertising program, an efficient production group, the best-equipped plant, and an excellent organization in general will be unable to secure a satisfactory return on investment if the product line is basically one that cannot secure customer acceptance under such circumstances that it returns a proper share of profits. The analysis of the product line or lines must include several phases:

1. *Trends in Sales Volume.* These should be known and explained and not merely as an overall sales pattern. Rather in each territory and for each product the trend should be determined and analyzed as to cause.

2. *Competitive Advantages.* Such a comparison should reveal the weak and strong points of each product. The advantages may not necessarily be restricted to the product itself but may relate to customer service, etc. Knowledge of these points may disclose sales arguments that may be used more effectively.

3. *Gross Margins and/or Contribution Margins.* An analysis of gross margins or contribution margins will reveal the more important products from a profit contribution viewpoint.

4. *Completeness of Line.* Consideration of these phases may reveal deficiencies and the cause of wasted sales effort. However, smart merchandising does not necessarily require that all sizes, colors, etc., be handled.

5. *Prices.* This phase of the audit should cover three avenues:

   a. Does the price provide the necessary margin?

   b. Is the price competitive?

   c. Is the price such as to secure the greatest profit? The turnover as well as individual unit margin must be considered.

6. *Product Diversification.* Is only one industry served, and is the consumption seasonal? Can other products be fitted into the line to promote stability of employment and operations?

7. *Quality.* What is the trade opinion on this factor? Does analysis of returns and allowances support the results of field reports?

8. *Design and Styling.* What are the prevailing opinions on this point? Should a market study be made on this aspect?

9. *Identification.* Through the use of brand names, trademarks, method of packaging, and similar devices, is the company securing the maximum transfer of goodwill between products?

Answers to these product considerations will provide a sound basis for business planning. Moreover, such a review can be instrumental in changing the objective of the company regarding the area of activity.

7-6 THE MARKET

After a thorough understanding of the product has been secured, the next logical spot for study is the market in which it must be sold. Successful marketing of a product requires a good product, properly priced, and an effective method of selling and distribution. Market knowledge is thus seen to be essential in any business planning.

Information about the market may be secured from two sources: (1) a study of the internal records of the company and (2) the analysis of data from external sources. Both the qualitative considerations of the market—information about customer characteristics, such as who buys what and how—as well as the quantitative phases—how much of and where the product is to be sold—must be critically studied. Suggestive of the market information a company should possess are the following:

1. *Data on Present Customers.* These may be secured through an analysis of internal records:

    a. Who buys?

    b. Location.

    c. Volume of sales for each.

    d. Profitability.

    e. Size of orders.

    f. Method of delivery.

2. *Seasonal or Cyclical Characteristics.* Secured from industry sales data as well as company records.

3. *Market Potentials.* A determination of reasonably expected sales volume by products, territory, industry, and customers is essential to the intelligent direction of the selling effort. Such data may be developed from government and industry information in conjunction with internal records.

4. *Customer Purchasing Habits, Buying Preference.* May be secured through field surveys.

5. *Competitive Activity.* Usually secured through sales channels, trade paper reports, and similar sources.

6. *Technical Advances.* Such developments may affect the demand for the product, whether in the same line or in competitive product types.

This information is fundamental to the development of a sound marketing plan.

7-7 THE DISTRIBUTION PROGRAM

With a knowledge of the product and the market, the effectiveness of reaching that market must then be examined. This sphere of activity is generally known as sales management and involves a great many considerations. Suggestive of the subjects to be covered in the review or audit are these:

1. *Selection and Training of Salespersons.* What is the program? Its cost? How does it compare with competitive practice?

2. *Selection of Channels of Distribution and Methods of Sale.* Are the methods as effective as those used by the competition? Are the number and types of outlets adequate? What is the relative profitability of the various channels or methods of sale employed?

3. *Determination of Sales Quotas.* Are they related to market potentials? On what basis are they changed?

4. *Sales Territories.* Is full coverage provided? Is the company selling in territories too far from home—uneconomical territories?

5. *Routing of Salespersons.* Are the salespeople economically routed? Does a supervisor aid them? How are calls planned?

6. *Advertising and Sales Promotion Aids.* Are the programs correlated with the sales effort? Is the coverage adequate? Is there coverage where no sales outlets are available?

7. *Salespeople's Compensation.* Does the basis of compensation provide incentive? Does the method secure the type of salesman the company wants? Is there a definite relationship between such compensation and desired sales volume?

8. *Price Policies.* How are prices set? Is provision made for an adequate margin? How is price competition met? On what basis are prices set when business volume is low? How are differing costs of production recognized in quantity brackets?

9. *Other Sales Policies*
   a. On returns and allowances.
   b. On entertainment.
   c. Use of company cars.
   d. Terms of sale.

10. *Distribution Costs.* Are the following costs known?
    a. Distribution costs by territories, salespeople, product, or such segment as may be applicable.
    b. Costs per dollars of sales, per call.
    c. Freight equalization by areas.
    d. By functions, such as warehouse handling, credits and collections, packaging, order handling.

Such information will reveal the strong and weak points of the company from the marketing viewpoint.

7-8 THE PRODUCTION PLAN

When the major characteristics of the product, its market, and the program for reaching that market are known, the next logical area of study is the plan for manufacturing the product. There are three major subdivisions:

1. Materials, parts, and supplies.
2. Plant and facilities.
3. Production process.

Among the topics that need to be considered are the following:

1. *Materials, Parts, and Supplies*
   a. Relative share of cost represented by raw materials or purchased parts.
   b. Sources of raw material and their adequacy.
   c. Program of reviewing materials and searching for cheaper substitutes.
   d. Competitive position in regard to raw materials.
   e. Method of inventory control. Are just-in-time (JIT) techniques used?
2. *Plant and Facilities*
   a. Location
      1. Location of manufacturing facility in relation to major market. Are freight costs, including freight equalization, high?
      2. Location in relation to raw materials. Again, the problem of freight costs arises.
      3. Location of warehouse facilities in relation to market.
   b. Layout and Adequacy.
      1. Layout of equipment. Is the plant layout such that it helps to avoid or minimize back-handling of material in the manufacturing process?
      2. Adequacy of space. Is there adequate space for the storage of raw materials and finished goods? Or must expensive public warehousing be used? Is sufficient space made available for the service departments?
      3. Plant capacity. What is normal capacity? Maximum? In relation to market?
3. *Production Process*
   a. Extent of time and methods study. Is there a planned program for cost reduction?
   b. Method of determining and revising bill of material.
   c. Existence of incentive plan for hourly labor as well as supervision.
   d. Production control system.
   e. Labor rates in relation to market.
   f. Inspection and quality control methods.
   g. Maintenance program—existence of preventive maintenance program, knowledge of maintenance cost by piece of equipment, etc.
   h. Relative production costs as compared to competitors.

Such a review should reveal the strength and weakness of the production facilities and methods.

7-9 RESEARCH AND DEVELOPMENT PROGRAM

To an increasing degree the life of a business enterprise is dependent on an adequate program for the development and improvement of the company's products. Whereas the chemical or drug industry is often given as a prime example, the principle is applicable to most industries. These points will provide a background for appraisal of this function:

1. What new or improved products have been developed in the past five years? What share of total sales do they represent?

2. What is the nature of the research program? Are specific projects assigned for research purposes and periodically reviewed regarding progress? Are probable benefits measured against cost?

3. What is the extent of correlation between the research department and the sales department about new products? Is there a smooth transfer from a laboratory product status to a commercial status?

4. How do the expenditures for research and development compare with industry or competition regarding the total amount or a percentage of the sales dollar?

5. To what extent are independent laboratories used to add flexibility to the research staff?

6. Is the time cycle for introducing new or improved products competitive?

7-10 FINANCIAL STRENGTH AND ORGANIZATION

Financial or accounting controls are reviewed in succeeding chapters. Discussion here relates to the noncontrol phases. In brief, sufficient financial strength must be available to carry out the sales, production, and research programs. As a general survey of this aspect, the following matters should be checked:

1. *Soundness of Financial Structure*
   a. Sources of working capital.
   b. Analysis by use of ratios.
   c. Nature of indebtedness.
   d. General credit standing.
   e. Relationship of debt to equity.

2. *Operating Trends*
   a. Operating margins by division, segment, or product line.
   b. Trend of expenses by function or organizational segment.
   c. Ratios of overhead to production labor.
   d. Trend of headcounts.

3. *The Financial Organization and Functions*
   a. Structure.
   b. Relationship of functions, one to the other.
   c. Relationship of group or division controllers to the corporate controller.
   d. Segregation of duties of the financial function among financial vice-president, treasurer, and controller.
   e. Competence of staff.

    f. Accounting policies and practices—conservative? Applicable in a changing environment?

    g. Adequacy of internal controls.

  4. *Profitability and Cash Generation*

    a. Return on shareholders' equity—trends and relationship to competition and cost of capital.

    b. Return on assets employed—in the aggregate—by division or product line.

    c. Free cash flow.

7-11 THE CONTROL SYSTEM

The last important business factor to be considered in a management audit is the control system. Preceding sections have dealt with a review of the specialized functions of the enterprise—distribution, manufacturing, research, and finance. Yet it is not enough that each of these activities be seemingly well performed in and of itself. Management must *know* that these tasks are being efficiently executed; there must be little guesswork. Furthermore, each activity must be kept in balance with the related activity. For example, the production program must keep step with the sales program. Inventories must be kept ample to meet customer needs but should not become unduly high. How are these things accomplished? Just as the mortar binds the bricks in a building, so also the accounting control system provides the information and procedures for the proper guidance of the business and the coordination and proper integration.

Why is such a system necessary? When the enterprise is small, direct or "personal," observation and control may be exercised by the owner or manager. However, as the size of the organization grows, this high degree of personal contact between each individual employee and the manager is largely lost. Another means of control becomes necessary, and this means is an adequate reporting system. Fundamentally, the process becomes one of the following:

  1. Setting a standard of measurement.

  2. Comparing actual and standard performance.

  3. Ferreting out the cause of variance.

  4. Taking the necessary corrective action.

The standards must be set by those best qualified by experience to judge exactly what constitutes good, acceptable performance. Actual results must be reported by an independent and unbiased agency—the accounting department—and compared with the standard. From appropriately designed reports, those whose performance is being measured must be advised of their progress. Similarly, management is advised of the degree of performance, trends, and relationships. Through the use of such reports, management is enabled to plan, supervise, evaluate, and coordinate the activities of the various departments or divisions.

Accounting control of operations is the use of accounting and statistical reports as part of a well-conceived plan to maintain the pressures necessary for efficiency and to expose unfavorable trends or variations. Thus it can be seen that such control is a necessary ingredient in modern business management. But while adequate control is essential, every controller should recognize that management emphasis must *first* be on the proper strategy and on efficient operations, and so on, so that the controls are monitoring the correct factors.

The business factors discussed in the preceding sections are, in the opinion of the authors, fundamental. An understanding of each of these, as practiced in his company, would give each accounting executive or controller a sound foundation on which to build his contribution as part of a sound management team. Without this perspective his efforts must indeed be relegated to a narrower, more specialized, and less fruitful area of activity.

7-12 YARDSTICKS OF OVERALL FINANCIAL PERFORMANCE

(a) THE NEED FOR SOME OVERALL TESTS

Much of the discussion in this book is devoted to planning and control of specific parts of the business enterprise. Yet each of these areas is but a segment of the business. Although the controller necessarily must consider each function in the business, it is still desirable that overall tests or measurements be used. The fact that each individual area might appear to be satisfactory does not necessarily warrant the conclusion that the entire business is moving properly toward its objective. Further, if management is to do a good job, it must have readily available ways and means of judging its overall performance. Then, too, the financial community rather continuously attempts to judge the financial capabilities of those companies in which it has an interest. These same groups seek techniques of making their determinations simply and quickly, without the necessity of reviewing a mass of detail.

Under the circumstances, the need for simple overall yardsticks is understandable. It is expected that the controller will be an influential voice in selecting the ones most suitable for the company.

Some of the measurements in rather common use are reviewed here, and the authors indicate certain of those that may be more applicable than others in judging financial progress. Suffice it to say that certain measures are suitable for certain purposes, and probably several will be found helpful.

(b) AN OUTLINE OF SOME GENERAL YARDSTICKS

Under private enterprise capitalism, and within the scope of the social objectives of the business enterprise, management is expected to make a profit. One might say that management is expected to make the optimum *money* on *money* over a period of time. This goal serves as the underlying clue to the more important overall tests of financial performance.

Some suggested broad yardsticks that company management may utilize in judging its performance, whether by itself or in relationship to competitors, other companies, or other industries, are as follows:

1. *Measures of Profitability*
   a. Percent return on net sales.
   b. Percent operating margin as related to sales.

   c. Percent return on assets employed.

   d. Percent return on shareholder equity (ROE).

   e. Percent return on total capital employed.

2. *Measures of Growth*

   a. Percent increase in sales.

   b. Percent increase in net income.

   c. Percent increase in the EPS.

   d. Increase in cash flow or free cash flow.

3. *Other Nonfinancial Measures*

   a. Sales per employee.

   b. Productivity improvement—unit output per employee hour, etc.

   c. Market share.

   d. Customer service.

- Number or percent of on-time deliveries.
- Response time to customer queries.
- Delivery response time.
- Number of customer complaints.
- Quoted lead time for:
  —repairs.
  —product delivery.
  —shipment of spare parts.

   e. New product development.

- Time required from inception of idea to marketing of product.
- Percent of sales from products developed in past X years.
- Number of new products introduced to market in X time period.

   f. Make-up of workforce.

- Share of minorities.
- Share of females.

   g. General acceptance in the community.

Although emphasis in this chapter is on the total business picture, these same controls or tests may be effectively applied to individual segments of the business, such as divisions or product groups or subsidiaries.

These ratios apply to actual results that may be compared readily with actual results of other business concerns. They are in addition to the forecasting or budget comparisons described in Part II that provide another type of overall business control principally for internal applications.

Comments on these and related measures, and potential refinements, are contained in the remainder of this chapter.

7-13 MEASURES OF PROFITABILITY

(a) PERCENT RETURN ON NET SALES

One of the most commonly encountered measures of profitability is the relationship of net income to net sales. The ratio, usually expressed as a percentage, indicates what share of the sales dollar is translated into profit. The trend of this relationship is important and should be watched by management.

The widespread use of the income-to-sales ratio permits easy comparison with other companies or with industry performance. The interim and annual reports to shareholders of publicly held corporations facilitate measurement against individual business concerns. In addition, the FTC and the SEC are important sources for broad industry averages. Among private groups that also supply useful information are Dun & Bradstreet, Inc., the National Industrial Conference Board, the U.S. Chamber of Commerce, trade associations, and other credit agencies.

Profit as a percent of net sales has much value, but alone it is an insufficient measure of profitability. That business producing the highest percent of net profit to sales (or profit before income taxes to net sales) may not be giving the best financial performance. After all, the measurement of net income against net sales is but one yardstick of profitability.

(b) PERCENT OPERATING MARGIN AS RELATED TO SALES

This measures relates the operating margin or gross profit of the business to net sales. It attempts to identify the trend in profitability unmarred by changes in income tax rates or other income and other expense. To some it is a measure of trends regarding manufacturing or operating efficiency of the business.

For the outside world, such as security analysts, the data by each business area or product line may be deemed significant.

(c) PERCENT RETURN ON ASSETS EMPLOYED

In a certain sense, management is a steward of the assets used in the business and is charged with optimizing net income on all the assets employed, regardless of how the concern is financed. The percent of return on assets employed is often used as an internal measure, both for the company as a whole and by product line or organization segment. It might be argued that additional resources should be allotted to that segment producing the highest return on assets—not in a single year but over a period of time.

But the return on assets in reality is composed of two elements as shown in Figure 7-1: (1) net earnings as related to net sales and (2) the utilization of the assets in relationship to the sales volume, otherwise known as "turnover." Why consider each element separately? Why not simply divide net income by the cost of the assets employed to determine the rate of return? The answer is that a change in the rate of return may be accomplished by a change in the asset base involved or in the rate of profitability or both. Each factor, therefore, must be analyzed.

If there has been no change in selling price, then any improvement in the profit-sales ratio indicates cost reduction. If, on the other hand, there is no change in the selling price or in total investment, then an improvement in turnover indicates that capital is being utilized more effectively, that management is securing more sales volume

Figure 7-1   The Relationship of Major Factors Influencing Return on Assets.

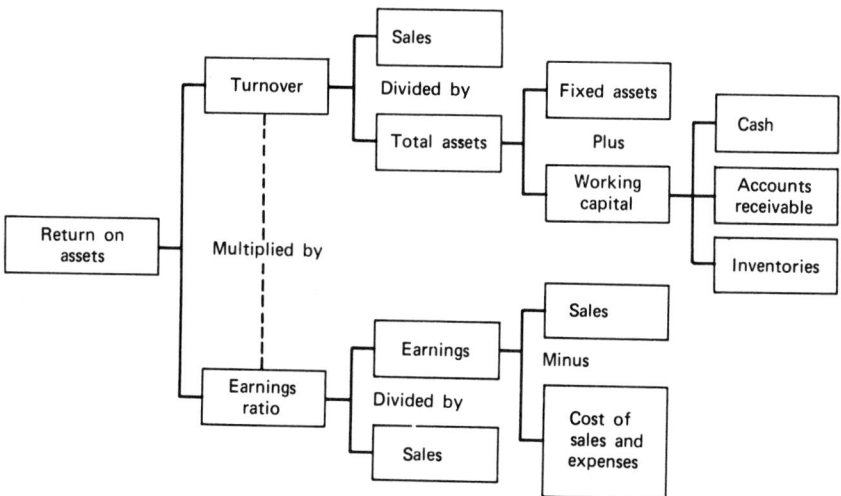

from the same working capital and plant. The management that can control both of these relationships has done much to control overall corporate financial performance.

The use of two factors has sometimes been a source of confusion. Let us review the formula in algebraic form and then follow it through in two examples. The formula might be set forth in this manner:

$$\frac{sales}{assets} \times \frac{profit}{sales} = \text{return on assets}$$

or cancel out sales:

$$\frac{\cancel{sales}}{assets} \times \frac{profit}{\cancel{sales}} = \frac{profit}{assets} = \text{return on assets}$$

Now assume a company with these results:

Net sales	$2,000,000
Assets employed	1,000,000
Net income	200,000

Applying the formula, it can be determined not only that the return is 20% but also that the turnover was 2 and earnings on sales was 10%.

$$\frac{sales}{assets} = \text{turnover} = \frac{\$2,000,000}{\$1,000,000} = 2$$

$$\frac{net\ income}{sales} = \%\ \text{profit on sales} = \frac{\$200,000}{\$2,000,000} = 10\%$$

Turnover $\times$ earnings as a % of sales = return on assets

$$2 \times 10\% = 20\%$$

Now assume the company is able to accomplish these results:

Net sales	$3,000,000
Assets employed	1,250,000
Net income	270,000

Then what is the return on assets employed? Has the company improved its use of assets, and why?

Turnover is calculated:

$$\frac{\$3,000,000}{\$1,250,000} = 2.4 \text{ times}$$

% Return on net sales is determined:

$$\frac{\$270,000}{\$3,000,000} = 9\%$$

Consequently, the return on assets is 2.4 × 9% or 21.6%.

This was achieved through a 20% higher turnover rate and a 10% drop in rate of net income to sales.

It would be logical to review competitive results to form an opinion about the optimum or most desirable turnover rates and the optimum profit percent of net sales. The next step would be to determine what improvement this management should make, longer-term results considered.

It might be well to keep a chart showing trends as in Figure 7-2. If month-to-month results are plotted, it is desirable to average the capital employed at the beginning and end of the period and to annualize the earnings.

Figure 7-2   Comparative Return on Assets Employed (Income as a Percentage of Assets Used).

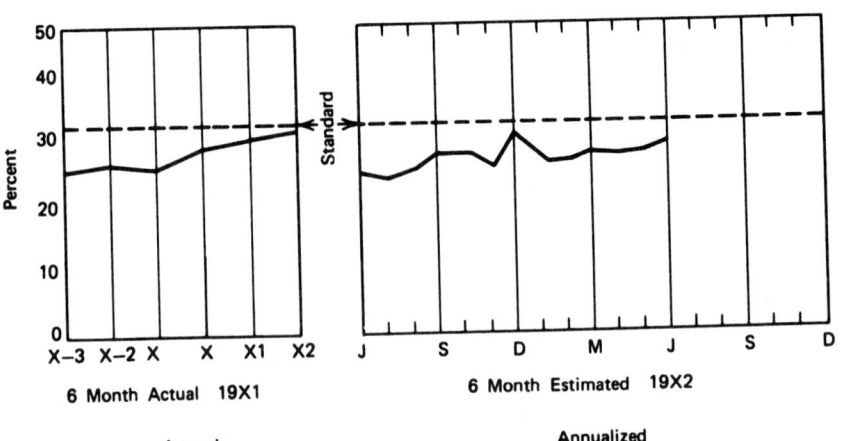

(d) LIMITATIONS IN THE USE OF RETURN ON ASSETS (ROA)

The use of return on assets is a convenient means of measuring the historical performance of companies in the same industry. It provides a means to measure management performance against competitors. It has limited value in comparisons between companies in different industries. Thus, some companies may have a low return on assets—banks and insurance companies—but a high return on shareholder equity. Accordingly, from a security analyst's viewpoint, a comparison of ROA for different industries would have little value. Return on assets, independent of risk, must be properly interpreted.

In a given company, the controller has the advantage of looking at "projections" of earnings and cash flow (net income, plus depreciation). For purpose of investment decisions, what is significant is the present value of the future cash flow or cash payout of the expenditure.[1]

(e) RETURN ON SHAREHOLDERS' EQUITY

Although corporate management has a responsibility to provide an acceptable rate of return on the assets employed in the business, certain schools will hold that the principal duty of management is to optimize or maximize the return to the shareholders. This return to shareholders, consisting of both the dividend yield and appreciation in the value of the shares, will grow in relationship to the return on equity. Hence, in the opinion of many, including the authors, the return on shareholders' equity is one of the *best* measures of performance. It seeks to reflect not only operating efficiency but also the impact of the means of financing or "leverage." The return on shareholders' equity simply adds to the return on assets formula the factor of the percentage of assets in relationship to shareholders' equity.

We have stated that return on assets may be represented by these factors:

$$\text{Return on assets} = \frac{\text{sales}}{\text{assets}} \times \frac{\text{net income}}{\text{sales}}$$

Cancel out sales

$$= \frac{\cancel{\text{sales}}}{\text{assets}} \times \frac{\text{net income}}{\cancel{\text{sales}}}$$

$$= \frac{\text{net income}}{\text{assets}}$$

Calculation of return on shareholders' equity adds one further step:

$$\text{Return on shareholders' equity} = \frac{\text{sales}}{\text{assets}} \times \frac{\text{net income}}{\text{sales}} \times \frac{\text{assets}}{\text{shareholders' equity}}$$

Cancel sales and assets

$$\frac{\cancel{\text{sales}}}{\cancel{\text{assets}}} \times \frac{\text{net income}}{\cancel{\text{sales}}} \times \frac{\cancel{\text{assets}}}{\text{shareholders' equity}} = \frac{\text{net income}}{\text{shareholders' equity}}$$

---

[1] See Chapter 32.

Assume these facts for company A:

Net sales	$20,000,000
Net income	1,000,000
Assets employed	10,000,000
Shareholder equity	5,000,000

What is the return on assets and return on equity?
Substituting in the formula,

$$\text{return on assets} = \frac{\text{sales } (\$20,000,000)}{\text{assets } (\$10,000,000)} \times \frac{\text{net income } (\$1,000,000)}{\text{sales } (\$20,000,000)}$$

$$= 10\%$$

Continuing the calculation of return on shareholders' equity:

$$\text{Return on shareholder equity} = \text{turnover} \times \text{profit rate} \times \frac{\text{assets}}{\text{shareholders' equity}}$$

$$= 2 \times .05 \times \frac{\$10,000,000}{5,000,000}$$

$$= 2 \times .05 \times 2$$

$$= 20\%$$

Proper financing can have a multiplier effect and increase the return on shareholders' equity.

(f) RETURN ON TOTAL CAPITAL

Another measure of performance relates to the total capital investment, meaning long-term debt and shareholders' equity. This is sometimes called "return on investment" (ROI) or return on capital employed and seeks to measure the return on the long-term funds invested in the business. It does not distinguish between long-term debt and equity. In effect it evaluates the return on working capital, plus noncurrent assets. In the formula, total capitalization is substituted for assets and/or equity.

7-14 MEASURES OF GROWTH

(a) PERCENT INCREASE IN SALES

In addition to the profitability indexes discussed, consideration might well be given to the growth picture. One measure of growth is in net sales. Many business executives want to know how the sales volume has changed in each of the past five years. This rate of increase can be measured against competition and industry to judge relative performance.

Within the controller's own company some more useful refinements may be developed, for example:

1. The share of sales gains because of higher prices vs. movement of more units.
2. The share caused by abnormal or "windfall" conditions.

An illustration of a simple worksheet form the controller can prepare is shown in Figure 7-3. Mere sales volume is not sufficient; consideration must be given to the quality of sales as reflected in the profits earned.

(b) PERCENT INCREASE IN NET INCOME

Net income is calculated in accordance with generally accepted accounting principles (GAAP), and may be expressed in aggregate monetary units or as related to the number of common shares outstanding (discussed in the next section). Many managements measure themselves by the change in aggregate net income from year to year for the company, as well as with the percent change in net income reported by other competitors or selected entities. It is an attempt to measure value creation for a period of time based on the accounting transactions that took place. Some managements set as a goal for the annual plan a given percent increase in net income for the plan year as compared with the prior year.

While this measure has some merit, it suffers in that it does not consider the assets or equity used to achieve the stated level. Also, by itself it does not deal with the impact of inflation or to value-creating management decisions that may relate to the longer term earnings.

(c) PERCENT INCREASE IN EARNINGS PER SHARE (EPS)

Earnings per share (EPS) represents the net income available for common stock divided by the number of common shares outstanding. It can be modulated by either a change in earnings or in the number of shares outstanding. Hence the more significant facet is the "change" in earnings, not necessarily the EPS in and of itself. For this reason, many managements view the change in the EPS as an indicator of growth or lack of it. And the financial community places a great deal of stress on growth in the EPS.

Earnings are relative and must therefore be judged against competitive or industry performance. Moreover, in an age of expansion by acquisition, sometimes a percentage change from year to year does not take into account earnings from acquired companies purchased through exchange of stock. Hence some thought should be given to this growth as reflected in per share earnings. Other things being equal, a large share of aggregate net income brought down to "per share" net income indicates either avoidance of dilution, or the wise use of borrowed capital, or the intelligent employment of plowed-back earnings.

Therefore, not only should net income in the absolute and its year-to-year change be considered, but also the changes per share of common stock outstanding.

A variation of the EPS, useful to the financial group, is the change in cash flow per common share from year to year.

7-15   EPS VS. ROI

Very often management is singularly concerned with the EPS because of the importance attributed to the trend of this figure by the financial community. Certainly, it is a convenient figure to calculate. In this chapter, we comment on yardsticks of overall performance, and the controller should be aware of this one and its strengths and weaknesses.

Figure 7-3 Summary Sales Analysis.

The Manhattan Company
ANALYSIS OF SALES INCREASES
($ in thousands)

Description	Current Year Annualized		Prior Year	2 Years Ago	3 Years Ago	4 Years Ago	5 Years Ago
	Actual	Plan					
Net sales	$37,896	$37,000	$35,011	$34,260	$33,190	$31,010	$29,660
Deduct:							
Nonrecurring special adjustments	(560)	—	(211)	(40)	—	—	—
Price increases	(70)	(70)	(300)	(260)	(300)	(100)	(100)
Net sales as adjusted ...	$37,266	$36,930	$34,500	$33,960	$32,890	$30,910	$29,560
Increase (decrease) from prior year	$2,766		540	1,070	1,980	1,350	
% Change	8.1		1.6	3.3	6.4	4.6	

Evaluation of this measure should give weight to why the EPS changes and the trend in other measures as well.

These comments may be helpful:

1. The EPS can be influenced, among other things, by the following:

   a. Normal plowback of earnings.

   b. Retirement of common stock through the use of surplus cash.

   c. Increasing leverage in the company through use of long-term debt.

   d. Acquisition of a company with a lower price earning (P/E) ratio.

   Therefore, these matters should be examined to see if the change in the EPS is from significant causes or share manipulation.

2. An increase in the EPS does *not* signify an increasing rate of return on either shareholders' equity (ROE) or total long-term capital employed (ROI).

In fact, even if the rate of return on equity is constant, the EPS will increase from the plowback of earnings. This is illustrated in Figure 7-4. Whereas the return on shareholder's equity is 10%, the plowback of 60% of the earnings results in a per share earnings growth rate of 6%: 60% (100% − 40%) × 10% = 6%. If the rate of return on the "old" capital remains constant, and *something* is earned on the "new" capital, the retained earnings, then earnings per share *must* increase. The rate of growth in the EPS, as a result of plowback of earnings, is a function of the earnings retained and the return on shareholder equity. Mathematically, it is derived by multiplying the percent of earnings retained [total earnings (100%), less dividends paid out (40% in the example)] by the rate of return on the common equity (10%).

A company can show an increase in EPS despite a decline in the return on shareholder equity or total long-term capitalization.

3. Over the long term, the return on equity is the moving or leading function, with the EPS following this—barring the operation of other factors.

In summary, then, although the trend of the EPS should be observed and considered, basic management decisions and financing strategy must consider the return on capital employed. Lack of concern with cash flow and its timing and the productivity of capital employed finally can be fatal.

7-16 CASH FLOW MEASURES

Recent years have seen an increase in published articles on the subject of "cash flow." In fact a number of financial writers, security analysts, and company executives have accepted the view that cash flow yields a better measure of operating performance than does the statement of income and expense and statement of financial position. Whether or not this is true may be a matter of opinion. However, the reader should be aware of its use as an overall measurement. Discussion of statement formats is contained in Chapter 27 on cash planning and control. This review addresses solely the use of cash flow for broad measurement purposes.

Figure 7-4 Increase in the EPS with Constant Return on Equity.

The Illustrative Company
GROWTH IN EPS VS. RETURN ON EQUITY (ROE)
($ in thousands, except per share)

Year	Beginning Shareholder Equity	Net Earnings	Dividends Paid	Ending Shareholder Equity	Return on Equity (percentage)	Dividend Payout Ratio (percentage)	Dividends per Share	Earnings per Share	EPS Growth Rate (percentage)
19X1	$10,000.0	$1,000.0	$400.0	$10,600.0	10	40	$4.00	$10.00	—
19X2	10,600.0	1,060.0	424.0	11,236.0	10	40	4.24	10.60	6
19X3	11,236.0	1,123.6	449.6	11,910.0	10	40	4.50	11.24	6
19X4	11,910.0	1,191.0	476.4	12,624.6	10	40	4.76	11.91	6
19X5	12,624.6	1,262.5	505.0	13,382.1	10	40	5.05	12.63	6

130

"Cash flow" traditionally has been defined as net income plus the noncash charges to net income, such as depreciation, amortization, and deferred items. Cash flow, adjusted for revenues not affecting working capital, plus changes in working capital (accounts receivable inventories, accounts payable, and accrued liabilities), produces "Operating Cash Flow" (OCF). This normally reflects more accurately the rise or fall in cash resulting from operations. The typical statement of cash flows adds the changes in cash resulting from (1) operations, (2) financing activities (sale of stock, proceeds from long-term debt, changes in short-term debt, and dividend payments, etc.), (3) investing activities, such as purchase of plant and equipment, or acquisitions, collection of long-term notes, etc., and (4) other extraordinary items, to arrive at the net change in the cash balance for the year.

Another concept involving cash flow is "free cash flow." This is defined as net operating profit (which excludes financing costs) after taxes paid (i.e., deferred income taxes are ignored), less net new capital investment. Net capital investment consists of capital expenditures on fixed assets, plus other long-term investments, and minus depreciation and other noncash expenses, for example depreciation, depletion, and amortization. Free cash flow may be calculated also as:

Net operating profit after taxes,

Plus depreciation and other noncash expenses,

Minus additions to working capital (current assets minus non-interest-bearing current liabilities) plus additions of gross capital expenditures.[2]

Some financial executives also deduct cash dividends on stock in arriving at free cash flow.

Internally generated cash long has been a gauge to measure a company's ability to service its debt and its dividend-paying ability. Some executives have concluded that net income, as defined, often has been misleading and have turned to operating cash flow as the "real thing" in evaluating the performance of the entity and that of its competitors.

The various measures of cash flows used by some managements include:

1. Aggregate operating cash flow.
2. Changes in cash flow.
3. Cash flow related to net assets employed.
4. Free cash flow.

In summary, cash flows may be used to measure ability to service debt, pay dividends, provide for growth and remain solvent, and to judge cash management performance. Because they are less influenced by accounting estimates or adjustment they may aid in understanding the workings of the company. However, the reasons for the cash flows must be understood. Thus, a young entity may have excellent prospects but reflect a negative cash flow, whereas a mature or declining company may reflect a high

---

[2] See the Joel M. Stern article in Selected References.

cash flow relationship but have a questionable long-term future. Thus, mere cash flow is not a judge of the quality of management.

7-17 REFINING FINANCIAL MEASURES OF PERFORMANCE

The yardsticks discussed just before this cash flow section might best be described as historical accounting measures that are more or less traditional. And, when attempts are made to judge overall entity performance against competitors or other companies, much of the data base is available in published form for the publicly owned companies (though not necessarily for segments of the business). The ease of comparison is a factor in favor of their use.

But occasionally attempts are made to secure a better reading through either adjusting the historical data or using some less traditional and more subjective measure.

Typical adjustments to historical data include (1) eliminating *known* unusual or special conditions, e.g., impact of prolonged drought or market segments not relevant or effects of extended strikes or embargoes, etc.; and (2) correcting for the impact of inflation. Even so-called mild inflation can have cumulative significant effects. Of course, in different time periods and different locations the monetary unit has differing values. Inflation-adjusted performance measures attempt to more accurately gauge the replacement value of assets and resources used in the creation of wealth. Often this type of inflation accounting is more subjective and more prone to manipulation.

Some of the least known, and perhaps somewhat more controversial measures, include:

1. *Economic Income.* Economic income is sometimes defined as the change in present value of future cash flows expected to accrue to the owners (the net investment).

   Just as discounted cash flow can be used to judge the worth of acquisitions or capital expenditures, so also it could measure entity performance by reason of efficiencies achieved, products developed, strategies implemented, etc., during the measurement period. Yet the discount rate may be subject to debate; the amount and timing of the cash flow may be highly uncertain. In practice, these measures may be imprecise.

2. *Market Value.* Some believe that in an efficient stock market, the changes in expectation about future cash flows are reflected in the market price of the stock. To the extent that the estimate of stock appreciation and dividend yield are based on realism, perhaps market price is an indicator of overall performance.

3. *Residual Income.* Residual income represents adjusted net income (accounting net income plus after-tax interest) less the cost of capital. Accordingly, if the residual income is positive, the return exceeds the cost of capital used in the computation.

   Some firms employ this concept in measuring the profitability of segments. The rate used for cost of capital may be varied according to the perceived risks.

   The ability to compare business entities or segments may be questionable because the cost of capital may vary considerably by reason of size, geographic location, the content of the investment base, etc.

   This concept is not widely used.

7-18 LIMITS TO THE USE OF OVERALL TESTS

Useful though they are, statistical guides are not the ultimate measures of management ability. Mere figures cannot tell the entire story, and those who use them should be aware of their limitations. For example, these percentages cannot take into account the relative difficulties of the task; the possibility that the management with the best ratios is also the management with the easiest job. Further, a wise management may be laying the groundwork for sound growth.

Although alluded to earlier, it will bear repeating that the primary financial measures of performance tend to reflect patterns that are associated with stages of the entity's growth. These stages may be characterized as (1) the start-up or entrepreneurial stage, (2) the period of rapid growth, (3) the maturity stage when growth slows or flattens (and cash flow increases rapidly), and (4) a period of decline.

Consequently, a company may not be shown at its best in statistical compilations over a short-term period. In the reverse situation, a firm showing good performance in these measurements may be omitting some function, such as research and development, that is essential to its long-term growth.

In some companies, there may be a tendency to emphasize short-term performance, especially when such performance is rewarded by financial incentives.

Finally, to the extent that foreign subsidiaries in a multinational environment are gauged by the same measures used in U.S. domestic operations, care must be taken in isolating those elements (such as exchange losses, in some instances) not controlled by the subsidiary. (See Chapter 11.)

Concisely stated, it is important that the figures be properly interpreted and that they be regarded as measures of "financial" performance and not of the entire gamut of the management field. In most entities, experience will often lead to certain factors that can be important gauges or precursors of developing trends.

7-19 RECOMMENDATIONS OF THE INSTITUTE OF MANAGEMENT ACCOUNTANTS (IMA)

The Institute of Management Accountants (formerly known as the National Association of Accountants), through its Management Accounting Practices (MAP) Committee has developed Statements on Management Accounting (SMA) to serve as guides on various accounting subjects. One such guideline is the Statement on Management Accounting 4D, Measuring Entity Performance. While the reader may wish to review the entire statement, a three-paragraph Summary of IMA Recommendations follows:

45. This Statement summarizes current practices in the measurement of entity performance and suggests that:

    a. Many measurement practices are incomplete or too narrow; that is, they focus principally on one or a few measures rather than on a more comprehensive set of measures.

    b. Some measures rely too heavily on historical-cost-based calculations rather than on making appropriate adjustments to compensate for real economic changes.

c. Performance evaluation that utilizes only financial measures may tend to focus too narrowly on the short term. Including some broader, nonfinancial measures provides a more comprehensive picture of the entity's performance.

46. Therefore, the IMA makes the following recommendations:

a. Financial measures of entity performance should be comprehensive and should include aspects of growth, income, cash flows, and return on investment simultaneously.

b. At each stage of growth in an entity's life cycle, different measures of financial performance take on varying degrees of importance. Therefore, neither growth nor net income nor cash flows nor return on investment should be emphasized to the exclusion of other meaningful measures.

c. The measurement of performance by a multiple set of financial measures should be enhanced by the development and use of a budgeted set of expectations against which actual results are compared.

d. Historical-cost-based accounting calculations, especially in times of significant inflation, should not be relied upon exclusively in entities that are affected by inflation.

e. An entity also should consider appropriate nonfinancial, longer-term measurements pertaining to such facets of the business as market, product, operations, new product development, and human resources rather than strictly short-term financial measures of performance.

47. An important objective of a business entity is to improve its long-term value to shareholders as well as its utility to employees and to society at large. A number of performance measures should be used to keep management on the track of reaching this objective. These measures should include revenues, net income, return on assets employed, and cash flows as the principal measures of financial performance and should include such nonfinancial measures as market share, quality and service, productivity, and innovation.[3]

7-20 A BALANCED MEASURING SYSTEM— NONFINANCIAL PERFORMANCE MEASURES

It will be observed that the IMA, in paragraph 46e of its Statement on Management Accounting 4D, issued in 1986, recommends that an entity should consider, in addition to financial measures, appropriate nonfinancial longer term measurements. In the past decade, there has been increased attention given to a balanced measuring system which includes (1) relevant financial measures that reflect the results of actions already taken, and (2) operational measures of nonfinancial factors which are the drivers of future financial performance. Presumably these nonfinancial measures would include the critical success factors identified by the management. While the areas of attention may differ by company and industry, some of the fields monitored by nonfinancial measures include these:

---

[3] From Institute of Management Accountants, "Statement on Management Accounting 4D, Measuring Entity Performance," *Management Accounting,* March 1986, p. 58. Used by permission of *Management Accounting.*

- Customer satisfaction.
- Creativity or innovation progress.
- Selective internal efficiency factors.

For each of these groups, a few of the measures that are in current use in some entities are identified. However, which of these measurement factors are of sufficient importance to merit continuous attention at the top management level (or are only semi-important) is a call to be made by the management itself.

[ ]   *Measures of Customer Satisfaction*

- Number or percentage of on time deliveries (as defined by customers).
- Delivery response time (hours).
- Number of (major) accounts for which the entity is a preferred supplier.
- Number of customer complaints.
- Share of sales represented by new products introduced in one year or in X years.
- Return as % of sales.

[ ]   *Creativity or Innovation Indicators*

- Time from idea to market (months).
- Number of products reaching market before competitor.
- Time to develop next generation product (months).
- Percent of sales generated by new products introduced within past two years.
- Reduction in manufacturing time for selected products (%).

[ ]   *Selected Internal Efficiency Measures*

- Cycle time.
- % acceptable product or yield (vs. rejects).
- Unit cost vs. prior period, or competitor, etc.
- Value added per factory hour.
- Sales per employee.
- Productivity per employee.

To repeat, which of such operating measures are useful must be decided by management. Which deserve the same attention as these financial measures (or any used by top management) is a matter to be settled by the company executives.

- Return on shareholders' equity.
- Return on assets.
- Percent return on sales.
- Percentage operating margin by product.
- % increase in sales.
- % increase in net income.

- % of plan attained (sales, operating income, net income, etc.).
- Earnings per share.

7-21 SUMMARY

In this chapter the authors have attempted to briefly explain some of the commonly used measures of profitability and growth—measures usually available in the public press for comparative purposes (especially within the industry). Some of the leading business publications such as *Business Week, Forbes,* and *Fortune,* annually and periodically publish the financial performance results reflected by measures discussed in this chapter, as well as other common yardsticks, for most of the Fortune 500 companies.

Although several yardsticks have been discussed, including the related components, it has been stressed that perhaps the fundamental measures probably relate to return on shareholders' equity and return on total long-term capital. Other supplementary ratios have been suggested as guides in shedding some light on a particular item. Additionally, comments have been made about the need for a balanced measuring system, which includes the essential operating measures which lead or cause the financial results which management monitors closely.

The use of a *few* sound relationships has much to recommend it, in contrast to the deluging of top management with many ratios and trends. The controller, indeed, may maintain a chart book that is exhaustive in its scope and that is primarily an analytical tool for *his own use,* to' better explain to management the background and reasons for the conditions. Perhaps periodically he may discuss more detailed trends with top management or with the second echelon of management. In general, emphasis should be on *analysis* by the controller to the degree he feels necessary but *simplicity* in what is presented to management.

The value of some of the more detailed relationships as a means of comparing performance or condition and as applied to certain segments of the business is explained in the next chapter.

7-22 SELECTED REFERENCES

Casey, Cornelius J., and Norman J. Bartczak, "Cash Flow—It's Not the Bottom Line," *Harvard Business Review,* July–Aug. 1984, pp. 61–66.

Hovey, Dann F., "Memo to FASB: A Cash Flow Statement Suggestion," *Management Accounting,* Nov. 1986, pp. 63–67.

Kaplan, Robert S., and David P. Norton, "The Balanced Scorecard—Measures that Drive Performance," *Harvard Business Review,* Jan.–Feb. 1992, pp. 71–79.

Knight, Charles F., "Emerson Electric: Consistent Profits, Consistently," *Harvard Business Review,* Jan.–Feb. 1992, pp. 57–70.

National Association of Accountants, "Statement on Management Accounting 4D, Measuring Entity Performance," *Management Accounting,* March 1986, pp. 53–58.

Reece, James S., and William R. Cool, "ROI Is Still Viewed as the Most Useful Measure of a Division's Performance," *Harvard Business Review,* May–June 1978.

Stern, Joel M., "Free Cash Flow as a Measure of Corporate Performance," in *The Modern Accountant's Handbook,* ed. James Don Edwards and Homer A. Black. Homewood, IL: Dow Jones-Irwin, 1976.

CHAPTER 8

Financial and Operating Ratios, Trends, and Relationships

8-1 OVERVIEW

To know relative progress or relative condition, it is necessary to have some measures of comparison. And what is more natural than for business management to want to compare itself with competition—either individual companies or industry averages? Some of these comparisons will be used only by financial management, and others will be valuable to overall and functional executives in other fields.

Almost anyone with some knowledge and experience in financial matters can review one or more of a series of statements and arrive at some logical conclusions about the business. However, the use of dollar figures by themselves is very often misleading. For example, an annual net income of $5,000,000 may sound quite large. Yet if one is given further information that such net income is but $\frac{1}{4}\%$ of sales or $\frac{1}{8}\%$ of net worth, then a better perspective is secured.

This difficulty in using absolute amounts has led to the adoption of ratios as a more understandable means of measuring trends and relationships. A ratio, simply defined, is one number expressed in terms of another. It is calculated by dividing one number, the base, into the other. Thus, a ratio of $265,800 to a base of $112,500 is 2.36 to 1. A percentage is simply a ratio in which the base equals 100%, and the quotient is expressed as a percent of the base. In the example just given, if the base of $112,500 is considered 100%, then the quotient is 236% of the base.

A great number of ratios can be calculated by or for those who use them. Some of the more commonly used are discussed in this chapter. However, it is not expected that every analyst will compute every, or even most, of the possible relationships. Rather, only those applicable to the problem at hand need be determined. For example, if liquidity is the focus of attention, then ratios measuring profitability may be irrelevant. Or if leverage or use of debt is the primary target, then measures of cost control or asset activity may be disregarded for such a review.

Generally speaking, each industry has certain key figures that are relevant to successful operations. These are the ones that should be monitored by the controller for the guidance of management. Thus, turnover of inventory might be a significant ratio—aside from those relating to a specific problem.

Experience has shown that trends and relationships may be just as significant, and perhaps easier to recognize, than the absolute figures. The use of ratios may make the financial statements more useful and meaningful to the reader.

A knowledge of the significant ratios, and their status and trends, may assist in ferreting out weaknesses that need correction. But the important thing is not solely such relationships, but a management that understands the meaning of figures and has sufficient determination and power to take corrective action where needed. The controller can be an important force in seeing that the information is understood.

8-2 WHO SHOULD USE RATIO ANALYSIS?

Before discussing ratios in detail, it may be worthwhile to comment on the four principal groups of people who would be interested, in varying degrees, in the traditional or classic financial ratios—each group having a somewhat different use for the data. These four are:

- The board of directors of the company—to provide overall visibility or a closer look at troublesome spots.

- The company management—in terms of planning or control or other operational review of the company, and perhaps in much more detail than a perusal by the board of directors. Additionally, management may want ratio analysis for potential acquisition targets.
- The commercial bank lending officer and his or her associates, as well as long-term lenders—from the standpoint of granting credit and related liquidity.
- Other outside investors, potential investors, suppliers, or security analysts—whose view might relate to only the more public data (and perhaps in much less detail).

In most instances, the controller will prepare the data for the first two groups. He will need to know what trends and relationships are important and properly should be brought to the attention of this audience. Of course, their particular interests or focus also will be an important factor in selecting the data.

The controller may or may not provide the ratios to the commercial bankers or long-term lenders, but certainly he would be responsible for seeing that the basic relevant data is made available. Even if he does not calculate the ratios, he should be aware, to the extent that he can be, of the types of ratios determined by them, and the use to which they are put. This will enable him to monitor these facets and keep them in line, or at least to be prepared to comment upon and answer questions about favorable or unfavorable trends and relationships. Moreover, he may be able to guide the users in the proper interpretation of the relationships and expected future trends.

While perhaps of lesser importance, the controller can present and interpret ratios to the security analysts or other investors, if he knows their interests and the use to be made of the data.

8-3 RATIOS AVAILABLE

Some overall measures of performance were discussed in Chapter 7. In addition, a sizable number of ratios have been developed for analyzing financial statements with particular reference to a specific segment of a business. Some of the more common ones are explained in the following paragraphs.

For discussion purposes, three main groups of ratios may be distinguished: (1) financial ratios, (2) financial-operating ratios, and (3) operating ratios. In addition, there are numerous miscellaneous ratios.

1. *Financial ratios,* as here used, are those expressing a relationship between the various items on the same balance sheet. Some of the more commonly used financial ratios are these:
   a. Current assets to current liabilities.
   b. Cash, temporary investments, and receivables to current liabilities.
   c. Long-term debt to tangible shareholders' equity.
   d. Total liabilities to tangible shareholders' equity.
   e. Fixed assets to tangible shareholders' equity.
2. *Financial-operating ratios* express a relationship between items in the statement of income and expense and the balance sheet. A few of the more widely used relationships are as follows:

a. Net sales to receivables.

b. Cost of goods sold to inventory.

c. Net sales to current assets.

d. Net sales to working capital.

e. Net sales to fixed assets.

f. Net sales to total assets.

g. Repairs and maintenance expense to fixed assets.

h. Depreciation to fixed assets.

i. Net income to shareholders' equity.

3. *Operating ratios* express a relationship between different items in the statement of income and expense. Included in this category are the following:

a. Sales deductions to gross sales.

b. Gross profit to net sales.

c. Cost of goods sold to net sales.

d. Operating expenses to net sales.

e. Net income to net sales.

f. Salaries and wages to net sales.

g. Sales discounts to net sales.

h. Purchase discounts to purchases.

i. Indirect labor expense to direct labor.

4. Finally, *miscellaneous ratios* permit useful comparisons:

a. Number of times fixed charges are earned.

b. Dividends to net profit (payout ratio).

c. EPS of common stock.

d. Book value per common share.

e. Average amount of fixed assets per employee.

f. Average shareholder investment per employee.

g. Average hourly wage rate.

h. Average yearly wage per employee.

8-4 ANOTHER CATEGORIZATION OF RATIOS

The preceding classification of ratios is based on the type of financial statement or statements used in their calculations, such as the statement of financial condition, statement of income and expense, or a combination of both. Another categorization could be by the basic purpose of the relationship. Neither grouping is all-inclusive, but another useful description is (1) liquidity ratios, (2) debt ratios, (3) activity ratios, and (4) profitability ratios.

1. *Liquidity* ratios relate to a firm's ability to meet its short-term obligations as they become due. Some of the more useful measures under this classification would be:

   a. Current ratio.

   b. Quick ratio.

   c. Amount of net working capital.

   d. Fixed assets to the shareholders' equity ratio.

2. Some of the more common *debt* ratios include:

   a. Long-term debt to equity ratio.

   b. Debt ratio (total debt to total assets).

   c. Total interest coverage ratio.

   d. Fixed payment coverage ratio.

3. *Activity* ratios basically measure how intensively certain assets are used or, as sometimes expressed, how quickly the asset is converted into sales or cash. Some of the gauges of asset usage (or liability) are these:

   a. Accounts receivable turnover.

   b. Average collection period.

   c. Aging of accounts receivable.

   d. Inventory turnover.

   e. Net sales to working capital.

   f. Fixed asset turnover.

   g. Total asset turnover.

   h. Accounts payable turnover.

   i. Average age of accounts payable.

4. A key set of relationships are *profitability* measures, which seek to relate some profit factor (such as gross margin or profit, operating margin or net income) to a significant base. Some profit ratios are as follows:

   a. Gross margin to net sales.

   b. Operating margin to net sales.

   c. Net income to net sales.

   d. Return on assets (or assets employed).

   e. Return on total capital (long-term debt plus shareholders' equity).

   f. Return on shareholders' equity.

   g. Earnings per share of common stock (EPS).

   h. Price/earnings ratio (P/E).

Another category of ratios gaining in popularity is cash flow ratios. Increasing use of these ratios began especially after the Financial Accounting Standards Board (FASB) required the preparation of a statement of cash flows—the successor statement to the statement of sources and uses of cash.

Cash flow ratios may be classified as: (a) sufficiency ratios and (b) efficiency ratios. Sufficiency ratio describes the adequacy of the cash flows in meeting the needs of the entity. The efficiency ratio indicates how well a company generates cash relative to selected measures. The ratios can be compared to other companies and to successive years in the same entity.

The *sufficiency ratios* are outlined as follows:

Ratio	Derivation
Cash flow adequacy	$$\dfrac{\text{Cash from operations}}{\text{Long-term debt paid + funds from assets purchased + dividends paid}}$$
Long-term debt repayment	$$\dfrac{\text{Long-term debt payments}}{\text{Cash from operations}}$$
Dividend payout	$$\dfrac{\text{Dividends}}{\text{Cash from operations}}$$
Reinvestment	$$\dfrac{\text{Purchase of assets}}{\text{Cash from operations}}$$
Debt coverage	$$\dfrac{\text{Total debt}}{\text{Cash from operations}}$$
Depreciation— Amortizaion relationship	$$\dfrac{\text{Depreciation + amortization}}{\text{Cash from operations}}$$

1. The *cash flow adequacy ratio* measures the ability of the entity to generate sufficient cash to pay its debts, reinvest in its operations and pay dividends to the
owners. A value in excess of 1 over a period of years reflects an ability to satisfactorily cover these principal cash requirements.

2. The next three ratios of *long-term debt repayment, dividend payout,* and *reinvestment* reflect the sufficiency of cash to meet each of these purposes. When added,
and expressed as a ratio, a percentage of the resulting number shows the share of
cash required for these three purposes combined, without the need to borrow or
use other sources of funds.

3. The *debt coverage ratio* reflects how many years, at the current level of cash generation, is needed to retire all existing debt.

4. The *depreciation—amortization relationship* reflects how much of the cash flow
from operations is due to the impact of the depreciation and amortization
charges, and the ability of the entity to maintain its asset base.

The three *efficiency ratios* growing in use are:

Ratio	Derivation
Cash flow to sales	$$\dfrac{\text{Cash flow from operations}}{\text{Sales}}$$
Operations index	$$\dfrac{\text{Cash flow from operations}}{\text{Income from continuing operations}}$$
Cash flow return on assets	$$\dfrac{\text{Cash flow from operations}}{\text{Total assets (or total assets employed)}}$$

The cash efficiency ratios reflect the effectiveness or efficiency by which cash is generated from either operations or assets. Specifically:

1. The *cash flow to sales ratio* reflects the percentage of each sales dollar realized as cash.

2. The *operations index* reflects the ratio of cash generated to the income from continuing operations.

3. The *cash flow return on assets* reflects the relative amount of cash which the assets (or assets employed) are able to generate.

These cash flow ratios permit company management to compare its performance with specific competition or the industry results.

Many of these relationships are discussed later in this chapter.

8-5 NEED FOR STANDARD RATIOS

An important factor in planning and in the control of performance is comparison with an appropriate measuring stick. So also in analyzing financial and operating relationships and in judging the significance of trends much the same need exists. Ratio and trend analyses tend to lose a great deal of their significance except when judged by proper standards—standard ratios.

A number of standards of comparison may be available to the controller. Because each industry has its own characteristics that influence the operating and financial relationships, it is more desirable to use measures of the particular industry than those of business generally. The standards of comparison may include any or all of the following:

1. Ratios of the individual industry of which the company is a member.

2. Ratios of competing companies, particularly the more progressive ones.

3. Past experience of the company itself.

4. General relationships developed by the controller or others, based on observation and past experience.

Such standards as these do not have the exactness of factory standards set by time and motion studies and should be considered in this light when evaluating a company's position. Although a ratio may depart substantially from the standard, the first impression of a weak position may not be supported. Differences in accounting policy, geographic location, depreciation or amortization policy, credit policy, ownership versus leasing of properties, or integration versus buying of many processed materials—all these may substantially affect the ratios. The specific condition of the business may result in very different ratios. Such factors must be properly weighed in comparing a single company's position with ratios that usually are averages.

When a comparison is made of selected ratios of the company with those of particular competitors, much of the data base can be secured from the annual report to shareholders or the SEC 10K report, if the measurement is against a public company. Industry averages also may prove useful. Figures for this type of comparison can be secured from a number of sources, including *Almanac of Business and Industrial*

Financial Ratios, Business Month, Dun & Bradstreet's Key Business Ratios, Federal Trade Commission *Quarterly Reports, Robert Morris Associates Statement Studies,* as well as SEC publications, and industry association releases.

(a) STATISTICAL REFINEMENT OF RATIOS

Many of the published ratios are averages and, accordingly, are greatly influenced by either extremely high or extremely low figures. For this reason, it is desirable to secure more refined ratios, if at all possible. It may be helpful to know the "median" figure—that occurring most frequently—or the "upper quartile"—that figure between the top of the series and the median—or the "lower quartile." The Business Economics Division of Dun & Bradstreet, Inc., publishes this segregation in its "Key Business Ratios" release for 125 lines in retailing, wholesaling, manufacturing, and construction.

The advent of electronic data interchange (EDI) may have a significant impact on the acceptability of certain ratios. If a company were to use EDI for all transactions, the turnover of inventories, receivables, and payables would greatly accelerate, resulting in minimal amounts of all three items on the balance sheet. As a result, the following ratios that include inventories, receivables, and/or payables would be highly skewed:

- Current ratio.
- Quick ratio.
- Ratio of net sales to receivables.
- Average collection period.
- Turnover of inventories.
- Turnover of current assets.
- Ratio of net sales to working capital.

The changes imposed by EDI will render industry comparisons useless, unless the entire industry converts to EDI at the same time, allowing all companies to report the new ratio levels.

8-6 TRENDS EXPRESSED BY PERCENTAGES

Before reviewing in detail some of the ratios commonly employed in evaluating financial statements, it may be well to consider some of the simpler and more effective tools available for use. Financial statements can be studied in several different ways—in addition to a review of the absolute data. One already mentioned is the relationship between figures in the same statement or in the related operating statement. Another is the compilation of trends by means of percentages. Still a third method is the preparation of percentage statements.

Controllers are often so deeply engrossed in current problems that they fail to watch trends. The use of trend percentages is similar to that used in calculating index numbers. A base period is selected and given a weighting of 100. Each similar item in other periods is related to the comparable value of the base period. It is a simple division problem. An increase will result in a percentage greater than 100, and a decrease, in a percentage less than 100. Selection of the base period is important, for it must be typical or representative. Otherwise, comparisons will give evidence of extreme conditions when such are not the case.

As a practical matter, it may not be desirable or necessary to apply such a technique to all the items in a statement but rather only to those values that should bear some relationship to each other. Thus the cost of goods sold should show a certain relationship to sales, or accounts receivable should increase somewhat in proportion to an increase in sales. Further, in planning the use of trend statements, the absolute data are not to be ignored. A major increase percentagewise may be insignificant from a dollar standpoint, and little time should be wasted in considering such an item.

The raw data from which trends may be determined, and which usually should be a part of any interpretive report, are illustrated in Figures 8-1 and 8-2. The trend statement is developed simply by dividing each yearly value by that of the base year (or multiplying by the reciprocal), and results in data similar to Figure 8-3. In this example, 19XX has been selected as a normal business year.

8-7 ILLUSTRATIVE INTERPRETATION OF TRENDS

The financial statements of the Plastic Corporation show, for example, the growth in current assets, current liabilities, and net worth. But it is not easy to determine whether the inventories and receivables have increased unduly. Figure 8-3, the trend percentages, facilitates a quick comparison, when used in conjunction with Figures 8-1 and 8-2.

For the period 19XX through 19X3, the company experienced a gradual growth in net sales so that sales in the year 19X3 were 107% of 19XX. Cost of goods sold also increased some but at a slower rate. Consequently, the gross profit margin was more favorable—109% of the 19XX base year. This condition was not unreasonable because of the fixed element in the cost of sales. A further analysis would reveal how important a role the volume increase played. Operating expenses increased somewhat but the corporation also experienced a growth at a slower rate than net sales. The combined effect of these favorable factors was a rise in operating profit to 134% in 19X1 to 120% in 19X3, as compared with the base year.

This growth was also evidenced in the balance sheet. The total net worth, all of it in the retained earnings section, gradually grew larger so that in 19X3 it was 113% of the 19XX level. The current assets were in relatively good shape in that the rate of increase in receivables and inventories was less than that of net sales or cost of sales, thus evidencing a faster turnover. There was a tendency to allow current liabilities to increase at a faster rate than sales, but this was largely the result of increasing state income taxes. Further than that, the current ratio was well over 2 to 1. The mortgage payable was reduced until 19X2, when an expansion began.

This expansion made itself felt in 19X4 through 19X6. Beginning in 19X4 several unfavorable trends developed. Net sales increased tremendously, but the cost of sales climbed at an even higher rate so that the gross profit suffered correspondingly. Here, again, further analysis would provide information about the effect of volume. Operating expenses were not well controlled in that they kept pace with the rate of sales increase in 19X5 and surpassed it in 19X6. These factors, together with heavier

Figure 8-1 Comparative Statement of Financial Condition.

The Plastic Company
CONDENSED COMPARATIVE STATEMENT OF FINANCIAL CONDITION
AS OF DECEMBER 31, 19XX THROUGH 19X6
($ in thousands)

Description	19XX	19X1	19X2	19X3	19X4	19X5	19X6
ASSETS							
Current Assets							
Cash	$ 20,000	$ 25,000	$ 25,000	$ 50,000	$ 40,000	$ 30,000	$ 35,000
Receivables, Net	80,000	83,000	83,000	84,000	117,000	134,000	137,000
Marketable Securities	10,000	10,000	10,000	—	—	—	—
Inventories	90,000	92,000	93,000	92,000	128,000	145,000	151,000
Total Current Assets	200,000	210,000	211,000	226,000	285,000	309,000	323,000
Fixed Assets							
Land and Buildings, Net	20,000	20,000	19,000	20,000	25,000	24,000	24,000
Machinery and Equipment, Net	80,000	81,000	81,000	103,000	142,000	146,000	160,000
Total Fixed Assets	100,000	101,000	100,000	123,000	167,000	170,000	184,000
Total Assets	$300,000	$311,000	$311,000	$349,000	$452,000	$479,000	$507,000
LIABILITIES AND NET WORTH							
Liabilities							
Current Liabilities							
Accounts Payable	$ 40,000	$ 41,000	$ 43,000	$ 42,000	$ 82,000	$110,000	$120,000
Accrued Salaries and Wages	5,000	6,000	3,000	7,000	10,000	12,000	10,000
Accrued Taxes	15,000	16,000	19,000	22,000	13,000	17,000	18,000
Total Current Liabilities	60,000	63,000	65,000	71,000	105,000	139,000	148,000
Mortgage Payable	30,000	25,000	20,000	40,000	45,000	45,000	65,000
Total Liabilities	90,000	88,000	85,000	111,000	150,000	184,000	213,000
Net Worth							
Capital Stock	100,000	100,000	100,000	100,000	170,000	170,000	180,000
Retained Earnings	110,000	123,000	126,000	138,000	132,000	125,000	114,000
Total Net Worth	210,000	223,000	226,000	238,000	302,000	295,000	294,000
Total Liabilities and Net Worth	$300,000	$311,000	$311,000	$349,000	$452,000	$479,000	$507,000

Figure 8-2 Comparative Statement of Income and Expense.

The Plastic Corporation
CONDENSED COMPARATIVE STATEMENT OF INCOME AND EXPENSE
FOR THE YEARS ENDED DECEMBER 31, 19XX THROUGH 19X6
($ in thousands)

Description	19XX	19X1	19X2	19X3	19X4	19X5	19X6
Net Sales	$400,000	$420,000	$422,000	$428,000	$510,000	$590,000	$620,000
Cost of Goods Sold	265,000	270,000	275,000	281,000	368,000	421,000	437,000
Gross Profit	135,000	150,000	147,000	147,000	142,000	169,000	183,000
Operating Expenses	100,000	103,000	104,000	105,000	125,000	147,000	159,000
Operating Profit	35,000	47,000	43,000	42,000	17,000	22,000	24,000
Other Income and Expenses	5,000	4,000	6,000	3,000	4,000	3,000	4,000
Profit Before Taxes	40,000	51,000	49,000	45,000	21,000	25,000	28,000
Federal Income Taxes	8,000	10,000	12,000	13,000	6,000	10,000	11,000
Net Profit	$ 32,000	$ 41,000	$ 37,000	$ 32,000	$ 15,000	$ 15,000	$ 17,000

Figure 8-3 Trend Statement, Using Percentages.

The Plastic Corporation
SELECTED COMPARATIVE PERCENTAGES
FOR THE PERIOD 19XX THROUGH 19X6
(19XX = 100%)

	19XX	19X1	19X2	19X3	19X4	19X5	19X6
FINANCIAL CONDITION (As of 12/31)							
Cash	100	125	125	250	200	150	175
Receivables, Net	100	104	104	105	146	167	171
Inventories	100	102	103	102	142	161	168
Total Current Assets	100	105	106	113	143	155	162
Fixed Assets	100	101	100	123	167	170	184
Total Assets	100	104	104	116	151	160	169
Current Liabilities	100	105	108	118	175	232	247
Long-Term Debt	100	83	67	133	150	150	217
Capital Stock	100	100	100	100	170	170	180
Retained Earnings	100	112	115	125	120	114	104
Total Net Worth	100	106	108	113	144	140	140
STATEMENT OF INCOME AND EXPENSE							
Net Sales	100	105	106	107	127	147	155
Cost of Goods Sold	100	102	104	106	139	159	165
Gross Profit	100	111	109	109	105	125	136
Operating Expenses	100	103	104	105	125	147	159
Operating Profit	100	134	123	120	49	63	69
Net Profit	100	128	116	100	47	47	53

taxes, reduced net profit to 53% of the 19XX level, despite sales in 19X6 or 155% of the 19XX level. To compound errors, as it were, the company continued dividend payments at a rate higher than net profit. The effect was to permit a reduction of retained earnings from 125% in 19X3 to only 104% in 19X6.

The sales expansion was accompanied by, or resulted from, the physical plant growth. Although some funds were secured through the issuance of additional capital stock, an increase in long-term debt was permitted. Current liabilities grew at a more rapid rate than sales or current assets with a result that in 19X6 they were 247% of the 19XX level, whereas current assets were only 162% of this same base period. Although the current ratio was not as favorable in the latter years, the cash and receivables were more than adequate to cover the current liabilities. This is some indication that the best use of funds was not made in the early period. However, the rate of increase in receivables and inventories is substantially greater than the corresponding increase in net sales. A net sales percentage of 155 in 19X6 compares to 171 and 168 for receivables and inventories, respectively, for the same period. This indicates a tendency toward a slower turnover in these categories. Further analysis is desirable to determine the cause.

This illustrates the use of trend percentages to help interpret financial statements.

8-8   PERCENTAGE STATEMENTS

The controller may often be interested in comparing the financial statements of different companies in the same industry and in checking the distribution of expenses in the income and expense statement or assets and liabilities in the balance sheet. This is accomplished more readily by using percentages instead of the actual dollars. Such a method is another approach in analyzing statements—the use of percentage components, often called "common-size statements."

Most companies employ this analysis in some degree for the income and expense statement for internal management purposes and usually include percentages relating all costs, expenses, and income to the net sales. The use of percentages on the balance sheet is less extensive. The technique is merely that of considering the total assets, and total liabilities and net worth in the balance sheet, and the net sales in the statement of income and expense as each equal to 100%. All other items in the statement are related, as percentages, to the base. The same approach may be used for subsections of a statement. Such a device will indicate the distribution of the items but will not give evidence of growth or decline. Thus cash may be 2% of the total assets in one year and only 1% in another year. It cannot be concluded that less cash is available, because the total assets may have expanded considerably while the cash remained about the same.

8-9   PERCENTAGE STATEMENTS ILLUSTRATED

Common-size statements may be prepared for a company and comparisons made from month to month and from year to year. Another application is the comparison with competing companies. Such statements are illustrated in Figures 8-4 and 8-5. Some of

Figure 8-4   Comparative Statement of Financial Condition—Amounts and Percentages.

Selected Chemical Companies
COMPARATIVE STATEMENT OF FINANCIAL CONDITION
AS OF DECEMBER 31, 19XX
(*$ in thousands*)

	The Dow Company		The Santo Company		Cyanamid, Inc.	
	Amount	%	Amount	%	Amount	%
ASSETS						
Current Assets						
Cash	$ 150,000	2.45	$ 300,000	3.68	$ 410,000	6.90
Receivables	900,000	14.71	1,665,000	20.44	930,000	15.66
Inventories	750,000	12.26	1,105,000	13.57	775,000	13.05
Other	100,000	1.63	10,000	.12	5,000	.08
Total Current Assets	1,900,000	31.05	3,080,000	37.81	2,120,000	35.69
Fixed Assets						
Land and Buildings, Net	120,000	1.96	175,000	2.15	200,000	3.37
Machinery and Equipment, Net	4,100,000	66.99	4,890,000	60.04	3,620,000	60.94
Total Fixed Assets	4,220,000	68.95	5,065,000	62.19	3,820,000	64.31
Total Assets	$6,120,000	100.00	$8,145,000	100.00	$5,940,000	100.00

		%		%		%
Current Liabilities						
Accounts Payable	$ 205,000	3.35	$ 410,000	5.03	$ 507,000	8.54
Accrued Salaries and Wages	42,000	.69	89,000	1.09	92,000	1.55
Accrued Taxes	575,000	9.39	865,000	10.62	705,000	11.87
Total Current Liabilities	822,000	13.43	1,364,000	16.74	1,304,000	21.96
Long-Term Liabilities	—	—	120,000	1.48	400,000	6.73
Total Liabilities	822,000	13.43	1,484,000	18.22	1,704,000	28.69
Net Worth						
Capital Stock	$3,500,000	57.19	3,000,000	36.83	2,750,000	46.30
Paid-in Capital	500,000	8.17	—	—	—	—
Retained Earnings	1,298,000	21.21	3,661,000	44.95	1,486,000	25.01
Total Net Worth	5,298,000	86.57	6,661,000	81.78	4,236,000	71.31
Total Liabilities and Net Worth	$6,120,000	100.00	$8,145,000	100.00	$5,940,000	100.00

151

Figure 8-5 Comparative Statement of Income and Expense—Amounts and Percentages.

Selected Chemical Companies
COMPARATIVE STATEMENT OF INCOME AND EXPENSE
FOR THE YEAR ENDED DECEMBER 31, 19XX

	The Dow Company		The Santo Company		Cyanamid, Inc.	
	Amount	%	Amount	%	Amount	%
Net sales	$4,300,000	100.00	$7,100,000	100.00	$5,900,000	100.00
Cost of goods sold	3,010,000	70.00	5,360,500	75.50	4,307,000	73.00
Gross margin	1,290,000	30.00	1,739,500	24.50	1,593,000	27.00
Operating expenses						
Administrative and general	86,000	2.00	177,500	2.50	118,000	2.00
Selling and advertising	172,000	4.00	248,500	3.50	177,000	3.00
Research and development	172,000	4.00	71,000	1.00	177,000	3.00
Total operating expenses	430,000	10.00	497,000	7.00	472,000	8.00
Operating profit	860,000	20.00	1,242,500	17.50	1,212,000	19.00
Other income (net)	4,300	.10	35,500	.50	5,900	.10
Profit before federal income taxes	864,300	20.10	1,278,000	18.00	1,126,900	19.10
Provision for federal income taxes	516,000	12.00	766,800	10.80	672,600	11.40
Net profit	$ 348,300	8.10	$ 511,200	7.20	$ 454,300	7.70

the significant features in evaluating the comparative strength of the companies that are revealed more clearly by the use of percentages are these:

Statement of Financial Condition

1. The Dow Company has only 2.45% of its assets in cash, whereas Cyanamid, Inc., has 6.90%. The former may have too small a cash balance to operate most effectively. Reference to other years' experience will indicate the trend. Further analysis may be necessary to determine a reasonable amount.

2. The Santo Company has a much heavier proportion of its property in the form of receivables—20.44% as compared with only 14.71% for the Dow Company and 15.66% for Cyanamid. The trend of receivables and sales may be compared for several years to determine whether this particular year is out of line. The turnover of receivables is about 4.25 for Santo and 4.8 for Dow. This can be some indication that the credit and collection policy of the latter is more efficient.

3. The investment in inventories is proportionately much the same for each of the companies. In fact, Dow would appear in a slightly more favorable position in that it has the smallest share of assets in inventories. However, a comparison of turnover rates indicates a "turn" of only 4 times for Dow; 4.85 times for Santo; and 5.56 times for Cyanamid. If these inventories are representative for the year, then Dow appears to have an overinvestment in this category. Further analysis is desirable.

4. A relatively larger share of Dow properties is in the form of fixed assets— 68.95%, contrasted to 62.19% for Santo and 64.31% for Cyanamid. Further analysis of turnover as measured by the relationship of cost to sales to plant investment reveals a serious overinvestment in fixed assets. Trends should be studied. Further analysis is indicated.

5. The Dow Company is the most conservatively financed corporation of the three. Whereas 86.57% of its capital is furnished by the owners, only 71.31% of Cyanamid capital is from stockholders.

6. The current liabilities of Cyanamid, Inc., are 21.96% of total liabilities and net worth; but only 13.43% and 16.74%, respectively, of the capital for Dow and Santo is furnished by current creditors.

Statement of Income and Expense

1. From the standpoint of gross margin, Dow is in the most favorable position. The average gross margin was 30% of sales, but Santo secured a gross of only 24.5% of net sales. Cyanamid was somewhat better with a margin of 27%. Trends should be analyzed.

However, 10% of every sales dollar of Dow is used for operating expenses. This offsets some of the advantages of the higher gross, for operating expenses of Santo were only 7% of net sales, and those of Cyanamid were 8% of net sales.

It will be observed that 4% of net sales is spent by Dow for research and development activity—much more than Santo, which spent only 1%—and more than the 3%

expended by Cyanamid. This may be the reason for the higher gross margin. Also, it may indicate a forward-looking management.

8-10 FINANCIAL RATIOS

(a) CURRENT RATIO

One of the most widely used ratios, particularly among credit people, to assess liquidity is the current ratio. It is calculated by dividing the total current assets of a company by the total current liabilities. In this fashion:

$$\frac{\text{current assets (\$290,000)}}{\text{current liabilities (\$110,000)}} = \text{current ratio} = 2.64$$

In this example, a firm having current assets of $290,000 and current liabilities of $110,000 is said to have a current ratio of 2.64 to 1. Expressed in another manner, the current ratio is 264%, or the current assets are 264% of current liabilities.

A ratio of 2 to 1 has long been considered as reflecting a satisfactory condition. The ratio is presumed to measure in some degree the liquidity of the business or the ability of the concern to meet its current obligations.

With the advent of the computer and improved receivable and inventory control procedures, some reduction in this relationship may be found possible and acceptable. It must be realized, also, that the type of business as well as the seasonal characteristics may affect the current ratio. Therefore, it would be unwise to conclude, without further review, that a current ratio of less than 2 to 1 was unsatisfactory. Again, it can be seen that the ratio is only one indicator. A company might have a very high current ratio and be in a poor liquid condition in that a heavy inventory might make up most of the current assets. Further, the accounts receivable might be questionable. The controller will realize that (1) other relationships in the current asset group must be considered and (2) in his own company current assets should be properly valued.

(b) QUICK RATIO

A supplemental ratio to the current ratio is known variously as the "quick" ratio or "acid test." This is the relationship of cash, plus receivables, plus temporary investments to the current liabilities.

$$\frac{\text{cash + receivables + temporary investments (\$300,000)}}{\text{current liabilities (\$250,000)}} = \text{quick ratio} = 1.2$$

The "quick" assets are 120% of the current liabilities. Such a relationship permits a better estimate than the current ratio of the immediate ability of the business to meet its current obligations. Inventories are not included because it would take time to sell and/or convert the materials into finished goods for sale.

A quick ratio of 100% is usually considered a satisfactory current financial condition. Trends are important, however, and any evidence of a decline should be checked thoroughly.

(c) DISTRIBUTION OF CURRENT ASSETS

Component percentages may be used in evaluating current assets. Favorable or unfavorable trends can be readily detected through the use of a common-size statement. The following tabulation of the current assets of a business points out tendencies that need to be checked:

	Percentage				
Description	19X5	19X6	19X7	19X8	19X9
Cash	3.6	3.4	3.0	2.7	2.6
Accounts receivable, net ..	34.2	35.3	35.7	36.0	37.1
Notes receivable	4.1	4.0	4.3	4.0	2.0
Temporary investments ..	3.9	2.7	2.0	—	—
Inventories	54.2	54.6	55.0	57.3	58.3
Total	100.0	100.0	100.0	100.0	100.0

(d) RATIO OF LONG-TERM DEBT TO TANGIBLE SHAREHOLDERS' EQUITY

This ratio expresses the relationship of long-term debt to shareholders' equity, less any intangibles (such as goodwill) on the balance sheet. It is calculated as follows:

$$\frac{\text{long-term debt}}{\text{shareholders' equity, less intangibles}} = \frac{\$20,800,000}{\$46,320,000 \text{ minus } \$3,210,000}$$

$$= \frac{\$20,800,000}{\$43,110,000} = 0.48 = 48\%$$

The relationship is an expression of the capitalization of the company. Long-term investors, as well as commercial bankers, compare this ratio of the company with acceptable norms for the industry. An excessive amount of long-term debt financing as related to net worth—for example, over 80%—raises questions of solvency in adverse times and usually heightens the cost of debt financing.

Many times the ratio is calculated simply as the relationship of long-term debt to shareholders' equity, without any adjustment for intangibles. If the intangibles are significant, then the relationship to tangible net worth is the important one.

(e) RATIO OF TOTAL LIABILITIES TO TANGIBLE SHAREHOLDERS' EQUITY

This ratio measures the total liabilities of the company against the shareholders' equity, net of intangibles. Here, again, too much debt of whatever nature, as related to net worth, raises questions about the financial viability of the concern in difficult times, such as business slowdowns. Usually, credit agreements set an overall limit of total debt to tangible equity—such as 200% or 250%.

(f) RATIO OF FIXED ASSETS TO SHAREHOLDERS' EQUITY

The relationship is calculated in this fashion:

$$\frac{\text{fixed assets}}{\text{shareholders' equity}} = \frac{\$6,800,000}{\$12,200,000} = 0.56$$

This ratio may be determined on a year-end basis, on a yearly average basis, or even on a monthly average basis.

A ratio wherein the relationship of fixed assets to shareholders' equity is less than one indicates that the shareholders are supplying some of the working capital. And this is probably as it should be. Also, too high a relationship of fixed assets to shareholder equity may signify an overinvestment in plant and equipment.

8-11 FINANCIAL AND OPERATING RELATIONSHIPS

Financial ratios are useful in evaluating the security of investment, perhaps more from the quantitative standpoint. Financial and operating relationships bring more qualitative factors into play and provide the management with valuable guides about actual conditions. Some of the more commonly used ones are discussed here.

(a) RATIO OF NET SALES TO RECEIVABLES

The investment in customers' accounts and notes receivable should bear a reasonable relationship to net sales. This factor, often called the "turnover of receivables," is measured by dividing the net sales (or net credit sales, where data are available and credit sales do not account for most of the sales) by the receivables at the end of the period. For example,

$$\frac{\text{net sales}}{\text{customers' accounts and notes receivable}} = \frac{\$1,100,000}{\$200,000} = 5.5$$

The reserve for bad debts is not deducted, since this would understate the investment in receivables.

This calculation may be interpreted somewhat as follows: receivables have been "turned over" or collected 5.5 times during the year. If the industry standard turnover ratio is eight, then the company has too low a turnover. Such a condition may be the result, among other things, of overextension of credit, ineffective collection policies, too liberal a credit policy, or ineffective credit investigation. Further analysis should be made of the trend within the business.

This same ratio may be calculated by using a shorter period than one year, such as three months, and restricting the divisor to trade receivables:

$$\frac{\text{net sales (last three months annualized)}}{\text{average trade receivables (last three months)}}$$

The foregoing ratio may also be stated as indicating that (1) net sales are 550% of customers' accounts and notes receivable and (2) for every $5.50 of net sales during the year, $1.00 is still uncollected.

(b) AVERAGE COLLECTION PERIOD

Another ratio used to monitor accounts receivable is the average collection period. It may be calculated for a yearly period as:

$$\frac{\text{total trade receivables}}{\text{net sales}} \times 360 \text{ (days in a year)}$$

It also might be determined for a three-month period as follows:

$$\frac{\text{average trade receivables (last three months)}}{\text{average sales per day (last three months)}}$$

The denominator is determined by dividing the net sales for the last three months by the number of selling days in the same period. Such ratios could be compared to the normal sales terms.

(c) TURNOVER OF INVENTORIES

This relationship reveals how many times during the period the inventories are sold or used and replaced. The turnover of finished goods would be measured:

$$\frac{\text{cost of goods sold}}{\text{average finished inventory}} = \frac{\$290,000}{\$40,000} = \text{turnover of 7.25 times}$$

The turnover of raw materials would be calculated thus:

$$\frac{\text{raw material issues}}{\text{average raw material inventory}} = \frac{\$120,000}{\$14,000} = \text{turnover of 8.57 times}$$

These ratios may be divided into the numbers of business days per year to determine the number of days of inventory on hand.

Use of average inventories may be misleading if the business is seasonal. Under such circumstances, it might be desirable to check the monthly turnover rates, for considerable fluctuation may be revealed. Further, some interesting questions of inventory control will arise. For example, if a beginning inventory of $30,000 was adequate to provide for sales of $40,000 in January, then why is a beginning inventory of $60,000 needed to provide for sales of only $50,000 in July?

All of the facts must be secured by the controller before drawing conclusions about inventories. Higher inventories may be secured in anticipation of a price rise or in view of increased sales in the following period. Also, turnover rate cannot be considered by itself. A high turnover could be secured by lowering prices or by a disproportionate increase in selling and advertising expense. Too low an inventory turnover rate might prompt a detailed analysis of inventories to find the types of goods that are slow moving, and corrective action could then be suggested.

(d) TURNOVER OF CURRENT ASSETS

A general indication of the efficiency and profitability of the use of current assets can be secured by three relationships. The turnover of current assets can be measured by dividing the sum of the cost of goods sold and operating expenses (less depreciation and amortization charges, for more accuracy) by the average of the total current assets at the beginning and end of the accounting period. Closely related to turnover is the profitability that can be calculated by dividing the net income by the average current assets. From these, the profitability per turn can be determined. Trends are important in measuring a company by this means. This method is illustrated by the figures shown below.

The company achieved an increased turnover of current assets and, because of a tremendously higher volume and greater markup, was able to report a much higher profitability in the use of current assets.

		19X5	19X6	19X7
Net sales		$300,000	$350,000	$450,000
Cost of sales and operating expenses (exclusive of depreciation)	(a)	250,000	287,500	367,500
Depreciation		22,000	22,500	22,500
Total costs and expenses		272,000	310,000	390,000
Net income	(b)	28,000	40,000	60,000
Current assets				
Beginning of year		88,000	92,000	87,700
End of year		92,000	87,700	106,160
Average	(c)	$ 90,000	$ 89,850	$ 96,430
Turnover of current assets (a ÷ c)	(d)	2.78	3.20	3.81
Profitability of current asset turnover (b ÷ c)	(e)	31.11%	44.52%	66.22%
Rate of profit per turn (e ÷ d)		11.19%	13.91%	16.33%

(e) RATIO OF NET SALES TO WORKING CAPITAL

An increase in sales volume is usually accompanied by an increase in receivables and inventories. Because of this relationship, analysts have developed the ratio of net sales to working capital as a measure of the efficiency in the use of working capital.

Such a ratio has limited use because of the many factors influencing working capital. A low turnover may result from heavy inventories or receivables. But it might be the effect of a large cash balance. A high ratio could be the result of favorable turnovers of receivables and inventories. But it might also reflect inadequate working capital—current assets kept high through a substantial increase in current liabilities that may mature before the inventories can be converted into cash.

(f) RATIO OF NET SALES TO PLANT INVESTMENT

Another guide often used to measure investment in fixed assets is the turnover rate, calculated on an annual basis as follows:

$$\frac{\text{annual sales}}{\text{monthly average fixed assets}}$$

Too low a ratio might indicate an overinvestment in plant and equipment. This same ratio could be calculated using a shorter time span, such as three-month annualized sales, and a corresponding average of three months' fixed assets.

It is probably desirable to determine the trend of the relationship of net sales to plant investment, particularly when there can be significant shifts in sales or net investment as is reflected in these three annual periods:

		19X5	19X6	19X7
Net sales	(a)	$900,000	$950,000	$1,000,000
Fixed assets (net)	(b)	$325,000	$320,000	$ 380,000
Ratio of sales to fixed assets (a + b)		2.77	2.97	2.63

Since sales are influenced by markups, it is desirable to use the cost of goods manufactured if the information is available.

This ratio should be considered with the operating profit in determining the effect of investment in plant and equipment.

(g) RATIO OF NET SALES TO TOTAL ASSETS

A general gauge of management efficiency is the relationship of net sales to total assets used in the business. Presumably, the greater the volume of business done, the greater the efficiency in the use of the assets. However, this condition should be considered in relation to profits. High volume does not necessarily mean high profits.

See Chapter 7 for a rather complete discussion of return on assets and the influence of the turnover factor.

(h) RETURN ON ASSETS

The relationship of net income to the total assets (or assets employed in the business—if a significant value is not currently used, e.g., idle land) is one measure of the management's ability to generate income on the assets of the business. It is calculated as:

$$\frac{\text{net income}}{\text{total assets}} = \frac{\$10,260,000}{\$82,100,000} = 12\%$$

The calculation may be made on year-end assets, or average annual assets, or average assets over a period of years. The measure reflects both the turnover of total assets as well as the profitability on net sales. Chapter 7 discusses each of these factors in the context of improving return on assets and return on equity.

(i) RATIO OF REPAIRS AND MAINTENANCE TO FIXED ASSETS

Maintenance expense is a major item in most companies and increases in importance as the investment in machinery and equipment grows. The ratio of repairs and maintenance expense to fixed assets is a valuable guide in checking maintenance policy. In periods of low profits, some managements tend to defer maintenance, allowing the equipment to get into a state of disrepair, in an effort to continue reporting profits. This policy tends to increase long-run maintenance expense and probably property losses. For external analysis, such information often is not available.

(j) RATIO OF DEPRECIATION TO FIXED ASSETS

This ratio is a rough check on the adequacy of the depreciation policy. It furnishes a simple means of comparison with other companies. Differences in accounting policy, maintenance policy, and the share of fixed assets owned have their effect on the ratio.

(k) RATIO OF NET INCOME TO SHAREHOLDERS' EQUITY

To the owners of a business, one of the most important general measures is the relationship of net income to the shareholders' equity. Since one objective of business is net income, this ratio is one measure of achievement. It is calculated in this manner:

$$\frac{\text{net income}}{\text{shareholders' equity}} = \frac{\$6,348,000}{\$42,315,000} = 0.15 = 15\%$$

The base may be year-end equity, or average annual equity, or some other basis— preferably consistent with the method used in the comparison. Well-operated companies typically earn above 15% per annum on shareholders' equity. A high ratio may be the result of any one of several factors: efficient management, good general business conditions, and advantageous use of creditors' funds (trading on the equity).

    Chapter 7 reviews in detail the importance of this ratio and the elements of the calculation.

8-12 OPERATING RATIOS AND TRENDS

The controller is concerned with the financial ratios for credit and investment purposes, and he must watch the utilization of capital and assets as measured by financial and operating relationships. However, a much greater share of his time and energy will be devoted to a study of operating ratios and the concomitant analysis that will be found necessary. Analysis of operating data gets into the very bowels of the business. Some of the more common ratios are described here.

(a) RATIO OF SALES RETURNS AND ALLOWANCES TO GROSS SALES

The ratio returns and allowances to gross sales is of value in accounting for variations in net profit because it reflects a cause of change in gross margin through reducing the sales income. The relationship is an indication of the pressure on the sales force for price concessions and a weathervane of customer satisfaction. Increases in this ratio usually signify not only lost sales but also higher freight costs because of returns and increased expense in adjusting and handling such matters.

(b) RATIO OF GROSS PROFIT TO NET SALES

The ratio of gross profit to net sales is usually expressed as a percentage of net sales. Most controllers find it a very pertinent ratio and analyze it each month. The business must secure a gross profit high enough to cover operating expenses and return a normal profit. Where significant changes occur, they must be analyzed in terms of cause and corrective action recommended. Changes in the volume of sales, manufacturing costs, and the mixture of products sold will affect this ratio.

It may be found desirable to calculate for the monthly statements the standard gross margin percentage by major product groups as well as the actual margin.

A low gross margin may be evidence, among other things, of intense price competition, poor pricing policies, or insufficient volume to cover fixed manufacturing costs adequately.

In analyzing statements, the trend of the gross margin should be watched. The determination of the gross margin percentage, illustrated in Figure 8-6, is but a step in analyzing the reason for changes.

Reference to the dollar amounts in Figure 8-6 indicates a gradual increase in sales volume and margins and a decrease in variances until 19XY. But the basic weakness is better illustrated in a review of the margin in relation to net sales and the trend percentages. From 19XX through 19X9, there was a rather general decline in both standard margin and actual gross profit as related to net sales. Some of the decline in standard gross was offset by increased efficiencies. However, in 19XY the situation permitted a restoration of the standard gross margin of 32% of net sales and an actual manufacturing profit of 30.5% of net sales. The lowered margins are also reflected in the trend percentages in that the manufacturing profit, as related to 19XX, lagged behind the sales growth until 19XY, when it ran ahead. The two rates of growth were identical in 19XZ.

(c) RATIO OF OPERATING EXPENSES TO NET SALES

A widely used device for internal management purposes, as well as external analysis, is the measurement of operating expenses against net sales. This review can be made by individual types of expenses, groups of expenses, or total functional expense in relation to net sales. The resulting percentages indicate in part the ability of the management to adjust expenses to varying sales volumes.

Merely measuring such expenses in relation to net sales can be extremely misleading in that sales volume may account for the lower ratio, and management might interpret the results as stemming from increased efficiency. It therefore becomes important that the controller compare trend percentages and absolute data as well as the percentage of expense to net sales. One such analysis is illustrated in Figure 8-7.

The illustration can be interpreted somewhat as follows: overall selling expenses increased from $256,000 in 19XX to $310,000 in 19X4, an increase of $54,000. The direct selling expense increased by $36,000, whereas advertising and sales promotion

Figure 8-6 Statement of Comparative Gross Profit, including Trend Percentages.

The Jones Company
STATEMENT OF COMPARATIVE GROSS PROFIT
FOR THE YEARS 19XX–19XZ

Year	Net Sales	Standard Cost of Sales	Standard Gross Margin	Variances	Manufacturing Profit	Percentage of Net Sales — Standard Gross Margin	Percentage of Net Sales — Manufacturing Profit	Trend Percentages — Net Sales (19XX = 100%)	Trend Percentages — Manufacturing Profit
19XX	$ 322,000	$218,960	$103,040	$ 6,440	$ 96,600	32.00%	30.00%	100.00	100.00
19X1	310,000	211,575	98,425	5,425	93,000	31.75	30.00	96.27	96.27
19X2	300,000	207,000	93,000	6,000	87,000	31.00	29.00	93.17	90.06
19X3	327,000	222,360	104,640	9,810	94,830	32.00	29.00	101.55	98.17
19X4	330,000	227,700	102,300	8,250	94,050	31.00	28.50	102.48	97.36
19X5	350,000	243,250	106,750	5,250	101,500	30.50	29.00	108.70	105.07
19X6	396,000	277,200	118,800	3,960	114,840	30.00	29.00	122.98	118.89
19X7	522,000	370,620	151,380	2,610	148,770	29.00	28.50	162.11	154.01
19X8	687,000	496,700	190,300	6,870	183,430	27.70	26.70	213.35	189.89
19X9	993,000	714,960	278,040	4,965	273,075	28.00	27.50	308.39	282.69
19XY	1,029,000	699,720	329,280	15,435	313,845	32.00	30.50	319.57	324.89
19XZ	1,222,000	837,070	384,930	18,330	366,600	31.50	30.00	379.50	379.50

Figure 8-7 Comparative Statement of Selling Expense—Percent of Sales and Trend Percentages.

The Distributing Company, Inc.
COMPARATIVE STATEMENT OF SELLING EXPENSE
FOR THE YEARS 19XX THROUGH 19X4

	19XX Amount	%	19X1 Amount	%	19X2 Amount	%	19X3 Amount	%	19X4 Amount	%
NET SALES	$820,000		$870,000		$960,000		$910,000		$1,030,000	
SELLING EXPENSES										
Direct Selling Expense										
Salaries—Supervisory	$ 25,000	3.05	$ 26,000	2.99	$ 28,000	2.92	$ 30,000	3.30	$ 33,000	3.20
Salaries—Salesmen	48,000	5.86	47,500	5.46	48,000	5.00	50,000	5.49	48,000	4.66
Salaries—Clerical	14,000	1.70	14,500	1.67	15,000	1.56	15,000	1.65	17,000	1.65
Commissions	20,000	2.44	26,000	2.99	32,000	3.33	27,000	2.97	28,000	2.72
Traveling	35,000	4.27	37,000	4.25	40,200	4.20	40,000	4.40	39,500	3.84
Rent	12,000	1.46	15,000	1.72	15,000	1.56	15,000	1.65	18,000	1.75
Office Supplies	7,000	.85	6,000	.69	6,500	.68	6,000	.66	6,500	.63
Samples	4,000	.49	4,500	.52	6,000	.62	6,500	.71	9,000	.87
Telephone and Telegraph	6,000	.73	6,800	.78	7,900	.82	7,500	.82	8,000	.78
Depreciation	3,000	.37	3,000	.34	3,000	.31	3,000	.33	3,000	.29
Total Direct Selling Expense	174,000	21.22	186,300	21.41	201,600	21.00	200,000	21.98	210,000	20.39
Advertising and Sales Promotion										
Salaries	15,000	1.83	16,500	1.90	16,500	1.72	16,500	1.81	17,500	1.70
Traveling	9,000	1.10	8,000	.92	10,000	1.04	9,000	.99	10,000	.97
Supplies	6,000	.73	6,500	.75	7,500	.78	8,500	.93	9,000	.87
Newspaper Advertising	15,000	1.83	15,000	1.72	17,500	1.82	16,000	1.76	15,000	1.46
Magazine Advertising	35,000	4.27	38,000	4.37	36,500	3.80	38,000	4.18	47,500	4.61
Miscellaneous Advertising	2,000	.24	3,000	.34	2,000	.21	2,000	.22	1,000	.10
Total Advertising and Sales Promotion	82,000	10.00	87,000	10.00	90,000	9.37	90,000	9.89	100,000	9.71
Total Selling Expense	$256,000	31.22	$273,300	31.41	$291,600	30.37	$290,000	31.87	$ 310,000	30.10

(continued)

Figure 8-7 (continued)

	19XX		19X1		19X2		19X3		19X4	
	Amount	%	Amount	%	Amount	%	Amount	%	Amount	%
		%		%		%		%		%
TREND PERCENTAGES										
Direct Selling Expense										
Salaries—Supervisory		100.00		104.00		112.00		120.00		132.00
Salaries—Salesmen		100.00		98.96		100.00		104.17		100.00
Salaries—Clerical		100.00		103.57		107.14		107.14		121.43
Commissions		100.00		130.00		160.00		135.00		140.00
Traveling		100.00		105.71		114.86		114.29		112.86
Rent		100.00		125.00		125.00		125.00		150.00
Office Supplies		100.00		85.71		92.86		85.71		92.86
Samples		100.00		112.50		150.00		162.50		225.00
Telephone and Telegraph		100.00		113.33		131.67		125.00		133.33
Depreciation		100.00		100.00		100.00		100.00		100.00
Total Direct Selling Expense		100.00		107.07		115.86		114.94		120.69
Advertising and Sales Promotion										
Salaries		100.00		110.00		110.00		110.00		116.67
Traveling		100.00		88.89		111.11		100.00		111.11
Supplies		100.00		108.33		125.00		141.67		150.00
Newspaper Advertising		100.00		100.00		116.67		106.67		100.00
Magazine Advertising		100.00		108.57		104.29		108.57		135.71
Miscellaneous Advertising		100.00		150.00		100.00		100.00		50.00
Total Advertising and Sales Promotion		100.00		106.10		109.76		109.76		121.95
Total Selling Expense		100.00		106.76		113.91		113.28		121.09
Net Sales		100.00		106.10		117.07		110.98		125.61

expenses were \$18,000 higher in 19X4 compared to 19XX. However, such expenses did not increase in direct proportion to sales. Although total selling expense was 31.22% of net sales in 19XX, four years later such expense was only 30.10% of net sales. This is not necessarily an indication of efficiency, because certain expenses are largely fixed in nature and should not increase as sales become higher.

Reference to the percentage of net sales will indicate that the following expenses took a larger share of the sales dollar in 19X4 than in 19XX:

	% Net Sales	
	19XX	19X4
DIRECT SELLING EXPENSE		
Salaries—supervisory	3.05	3.20
Commissions	2.44	2.72
Rent	1.46	1.75
Samples	.49	.87
Telephone and telegraph	.73	.78
ADVERTISING AND SALES PROMOTION EXPENSE		
Supplies	.73	.87
Magazine advertising	4.27	4.61

These expenses, which increased at a rate faster than net sales, were offset by other expenses that actually decreased or increased at a slower rate than net sales.

The rate of growth is also indicated by the trend percentages. Whereas net sales in 19X4 were 125.61% of 19XX sales, total selling expenses were only 121.09% of the base period. The largest increase, 225%, occurred in sample expense, which, from a dollars-of-expenditures viewpoint is not as significant as the 132% increase in supervisory salaries. Rent expense is 150% of the 19XX level.

From a control standpoint, those expenses that increased at a relatively high rate should be analyzed to determine what reductions can be effected—or whether the company is receiving full value for monies paid out. Standard ratios and individual expense standards are useful in evaluating the results of such analysis.

(d) RATIO OF NET INCOME TO NET SALES

A business should earn a reasonable net profit in relation to sales as well as capital invested. This ratio is valuable for overall control purposes and is usually incorporated in the periodic internal statements. It is discussed in Chapter 7.

8-13 MISCELLANEOUS RATIOS

(a) NUMBER OF TIMES FIXED CHARGES ARE EARNED

The ratio of the number of times fixed charges are earned is used to indicate the margin of safety for the bondholder. It is determined by dividing the net profit after taxes by the interest on fixed indebtedness, including discount amortization. When more than one issue of bonds is to be considered, the margin on each can be determined separately. The method of calculating the margin is as follows:

		19XX	19X1	19X2 (Estimated)
Net income before fixed changes ...	(a)	$62,000	$79,000	$110,000
Interest on first mortgage bonds ...	(b)	5,000	5,000	7,000
Balance	(c)	57,000	74,000	103,000
Interest on debentures	(d)	7,000	7,000	6,000
Balance	(e)	$50,000	$67,000	$ 97,000
Number of times charges are earned				
First mortgage bonds $(c + b)$		11.40	14.80	14.71
Debentures $[e + (b + d)]$		4.17	5.58	7.46

Some analysts do not deduct the interest charges before making the calculation. When so determined, one time must be omitted when measuring the real margin.

(b) EPS OF COMMON STOCK

A common ratio in financial circles is the EPS of common stock. Essentially, this is calculated by deducting from the net income any dividends for preferred stock and dividing the result by the number of shares of common stock outstanding at the end of the period. The EPS of common stock can be expressed also as a percentage of the par value or market value of the stock.

(c) BOOK VALUE OF COMMON STOCK

The book value of common stock is determined by dividing the total net worth of the corporation by the number of outstanding shares of common stock, provided there is no preferred stock issued and outstanding. If more than one class of stock is outstanding, it is necessary to segregate the capital according to the respective rights of each and then divide each equity by the outstanding shares to arrive at the book value.

8-14 JIT RATIOS

The controller needs to use a different set of ratios when evaluating the performance of a just-in-time (JIT) manufacturing system. A JIT system operates on the principle that the facility should receive only enough supplier components to build parts, produce only enough parts to build the desired number of products, and produce only enough products to meet demand. In order to do this, the receipts must be delivered to the company on time, in the right quantities, and with perfect quality (no defective components). In order to produce only enough parts to build the desired number of products, setup times must be minimized, work-in-process (WIP) must be drastically reduced, and scrap must be carefully tracked. In short, the controller must devise data collection procedures for information that does not appear on the balance sheet or income statement. The only ratio related to JIT that can be derived from the balance sheet is inventory turnover.

Appropriate JIT measurements are:

Ratio	Derivation
On-time part delivery	$\dfrac{\text{Number of parts delivered on-time}}{\text{Number of parts ordered for delivery date}}$
Part delivery in correct quantities	$\dfrac{\text{Quantity of parts delivered}}{\text{Quantity of parts ordered}}$
Quality of delivered parts	$\dfrac{(\text{Total number of parts}) - (\text{Number of defective parts})}{\text{Total number of parts}}$
Average setup time	Time from end of previous production run to start of next production run
Inventory turnover	$\dfrac{\text{Cost of goods sold}}{\text{Average inventory}}$
Amount of scrap	$\dfrac{\text{Dollar value of scrap}}{\text{Dollar value of production}}$

1. The *on-time part delivery* measure should be tracked by supplier. The performance measure should then be graphed on a trend line and shared with the supplier, so that worsening trends can be discussed and corrected. The definition of "on-time" will vary by company, since some must have the product within a specified hour, while others can wait a day or more. Also, excessively early deliveries should not be considered "on-time," for the company must then store the materials longer than it should.

2. The *part delivery in correct quantities* measure should be tracked by supplier. Again, the measure should be graphed on a trend line, and the information shared with the supplier. Excessive amounts of delivered quantities should be considered incorrect quantities, since the company must then store and track the excess items.

3. The *quality of delivered parts* measure should be tracked by supplier. Again, the measure should be graphed on a trend line, and the information shared with the supplier. The allowable tolerance limits used to define an item as being "within specifications" should be continually narrowed as the more generous tolerance goals are attained by the supplier, so that quality levels constantly improve.

4. The *average setup time* measure should be tracked by machine, and plotted on a trend line. Management should closely follow the setup times of machines that cause bottlenecks, and prioritize setup reduction analyses on those machines.

5. The *inventory turnover* measure should be broken down into raw materials, work in process, and finished goods, so that slow turnover areas can be more easily highlighted.

6. The *scrap* measure should be broken down into many categories, such as losses due to obsolescence, damage caused by material movement, and pilferage. Using such a detailed analysis, management can quickly focus on the most significant scrap problems.

8-15 THE INTERRELATIONSHIP OF RATIOS

Focusing on a "problem" ratio and fixing the underlying issues can create problems with other related ratios. For example, a company's debt covenant may specify a current ratio of 2:1. If the ratio is 1.5:1, the controller can borrow money and retain the cash to improve the current ratio. However, the controller's action also worsened the company's ratio of long-term debt to shareholders' equity. The table on page 169 shows examples of the impact on related ratios of efforts by management to alter 10 key ratios.

8-16 PRESENTING THE ANALYSIS

The only purpose in making a ratio analysis is to point out significant trends and secure corrective action, if in order. Although particular situations may demand a different approach, the normal line of procedure would be somewhat as follows:

1. Determine what ratios should be presented. The significant ratios should be selected that will serve to point out all aspects of the particular weakness to be corrected.

2. Determine the trend of the selected ratios over a reasonable period of time.

3. To the extent possible, secure ratios for comparative purposes. These may include similar ratios of competing companies or industry ratios.

4. Present the ratios in suitable form.

5. Interpret the data in an accompanying report, pointing out unusual features and suggesting corrective action.

A number of means are available for presenting the information in an interesting and attention-getting form. Since the data lend themselves to interpretation, it is desirable that the controller include a brief narrative. However, ratios can be presented: (1) in narrative form only, (2) in tabular form, (3) in graphic form, or (4) in supplementary tables and graphs as part of a narrative report.

Pie charts and percentage bar charts are very suitable for graphically presenting component percentages. Trends can be shown by simple straight-line graphs or bar charts. A simple line chart graphing the trend of monthly operating profit, compared to plan and the same period of the prior year, is shown in Figure 8-8. A simple vertical bar chart, as illustrated in Figure 8-9, depicts working capital turns compared to plan and prior year, in a company where the financing of working capital was critical.

A Change in this Ratio	Impacts These Ratios
Current ratio	Management improves the ratio by borrowing money and retaining the cash; the *ratio of long-term debt to shareholders' equity* worsens because debt has increased.
Ratio of long-term debt to shareholders' equity	Management improves the ratio by liquidating short-term investments to pay down the long-term debt; the *current ratio* worsens because investments have been reduced.
Ratio of net sales to receivables	Management improves the ratio by factoring receivables; the *ratio of net profits to net sales* worsens because there is a service charge associated with factoring the receivables.
Turnover of inventories	Management improves the ratio by selling off inventories; the *ratio of gross profit to net sales* worsens because management must pay premium prices to buy raw materials on short notice and ship it to the company by express freight.
Ratio of net sales to working capital	Management improves the ratio by extending payables; the *ratio of gross profit to net sales* worsens because suppliers will not ship additional raw materials, so management must pay premium prices to buy raw materials on short notice and ship it to the company by express freight.
Ratio of repairs and maintenance to fixed assets	Management improves the ratio by cutting the amount of maintenance work on equipment; *the ratio of net income to net sales* worsens because production capacity drops when equipment breaks down.
Number of times fixed charges are earned	Management improves the ratio by using cash on hand to pay down debt; the *current ratio* worsens because the cash is used.
Ratio of gross profit to net sales	Management improves the ratio by increasing prices; the *ratio of net income to net sales* worsens because fewer people buy the product at the higher price.
Ratio of operating expenses to net sales	Management improves the ratio by reducing the accounting department's payroll; the *ratio of gross profit to net sales* worsens because there is no cost accountant to review increased product costs.
Ratio of net income to net sales	Management improves the ratio by selling manufacturing equipment and recording a gain on the sale; *the ratio of gross profit to net sales* worsens because production capacity is reduced, and production must be given to subcontractors at a higher cost.

Figure 8-8   Operating Profit as Percent of Sales.

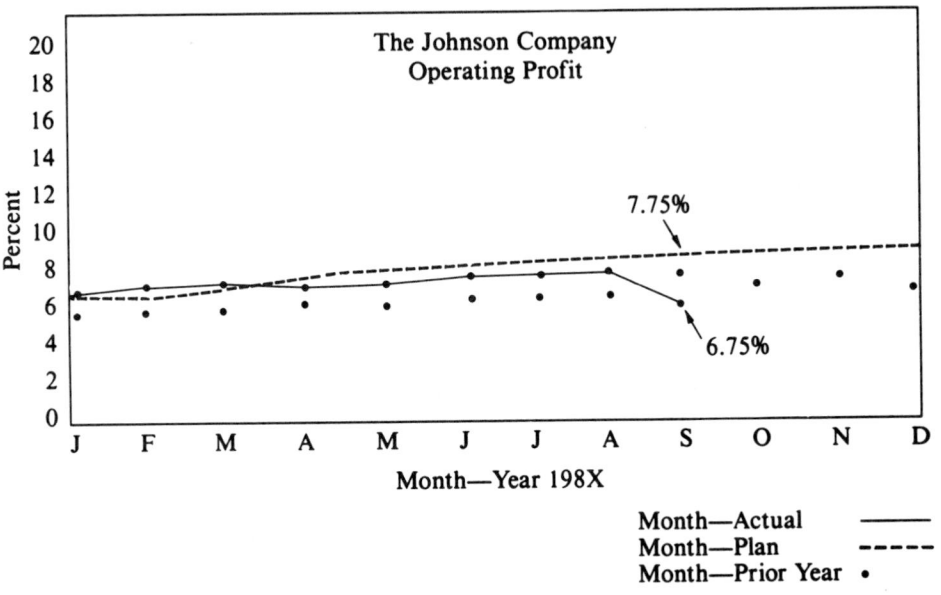

Figure 8-9   Working Capital Turns.

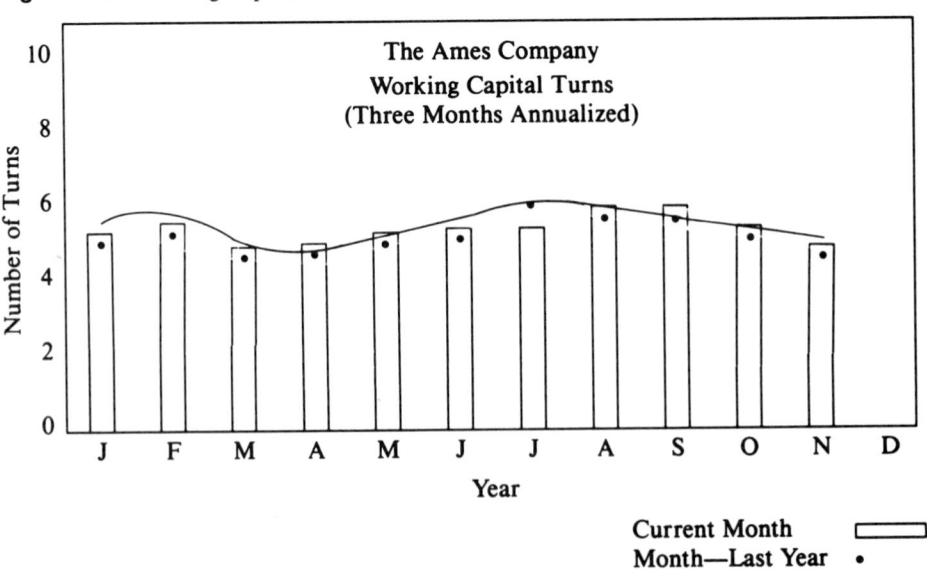

Some companies maintain a "war room" or chart room on the walls of which is maintained a series of various critical graphs used in monitoring company performance or condition.

8-17 SELECTED REFERENCES

Berton, Lee, "Investors Have a New Tool for Judging Issues' Health: 'Cash Flow Adequacy,'" *The Wall Street Journal,* Jan. 10, 1994, pp. C1, C1 1.

Faulke, Roy A., *Practical Financial Statement Analysis* (6th ed.). New York: McGraw-Hill, 1968.

Giacomino, Don E., and David E. Mielke, "Cash Flows: Another Approach to Ratio Analysis," *Journal of Accountancy,* March 1993, pp. 55–58.

Gitman, Lawrence J., *Principles of Managerial Finance* (4th ed.). New York: Harper & Row, 1985, Chap. 4.

CHAPTER 9

Internal Control—A Change in Emphasis: Prevention of Significant Errors and Fraud

9-1 MANAGEMENT CONCERN WITH INTERNAL CONTROL

Business managers have an interest in earning a profit. The business objective has been to maximize the return on shareholder equity or "to enhance shareholder value." By implication, therefore, the businessperson has a corollary interest in the practices or procedures including controls, used to reach the goal of the enterprise.

The focus of attention on business principles, practices, and procedures has been heightened by the publicity given white-collar crime, some with management involvement, such as issuance of fraudulent financial statements, and acts of bribery and kickbacks. The result has been, among other things, (a) legislation, including the Foreign Corrupt Practices Act of 1977, (b) recommendations from quasi-legal entities, such as those contained in the Report of the National Commission on Fraudulent Financial Reporting, as well as (c) the new and revised Statements on Auditing Standards issued by the Auditing Standards Board of the American Institute of Certified Public Accountants.

All of these matters are addressed in this chapter primarily from the viewpoint of the corporate financial officers, and especially the controller. In most enterprises, this official has a basic responsibility for the internal controls and the validity of the published financial statements. Other members of management, as well as the independent auditor, have stated responsibilities. But in the view of the authors, a major share will fall on the controller as the chief accounting officer of the company.

9-2 BASIC ELEMENTS OF AN INTERNAL CONTROL STRUCTURE

As used herein, there is a host of policies and procedures that have been established to provide reasonable assurance that the specific objectives of the entity will be achieved. It is this grouping that is referred to as the internal control structure. Technically, appropriate control procedures apply to every function, to every activity of the enterprise. The emphasis in this chapter is on those controls relevant to a proper recording of transactions (income, expenses, assets, liabilities, and net worth), and the proper reporting thereof, together with safeguarding the assets of the entity. The applicable control objectives, discussed later in this chapter, are a basic concern of the controller.

Until the issuance of Statement on Auditing Standards No. 55 by the Auditing Standards Board of the AICPA, in April 1988, much of the discussion focused on three types of controls. The Committee on Auditing Procedure of the Institute, in Statement of Auditing Standards No. 1, defined internal control in the broad sense as including either accounting or administrative control. *Accounting controls* were defined as the plan of organization and all methods and procedures that are concerned mainly with, and relate directly to, the safeguarding of assets and the reliability of the financial records. They generally included such controls as the systems of authorization and approval; separation of duties concerned with record keeping and accounting reports from those concerned with operations or asset custody; physical controls over assets; and internal auditing. It was these controls with which the independent accountant was primarily concerned.

Administrative controls were defined as comprising the plan of organization and all methods and procedures that relate mainly to operational efficiency and adherence to managerial policies, and usually were only indirectly concerned with the financial records. Included would be such controls as statistical analyses, time and motion studies, performance reports, employee training programs, and quality control. The Committee did state that the independent auditor should consider evaluating the administrative controls if they had an important bearing on the reliability of the financial records. Aside from these distinctions the practicing controller will recognize that in running a business the principal direction and guidance on major policy matters comes from the chief executive and his top management. This control, which may be described as *primary operational control* relates to the establishment of policy and basic guidelines by which an enterprise will be directed as a means of achieving the business objectives. Practically speaking, all three types of control must be evaluated in reaching conclusions about the effectiveness of the enterprise.

Given the recent broadening in the traditional definition of controls, and the various pronouncements or statements on the subject, it facilitates discussion if the internal control structure of an entity is viewed in these segments:

- Control environment.
- Accounting systems.
- Control procedures.

(a) THE CONTROL ENVIRONMENT

A company's control environment is the corporate atmosphere in which the accounting (and other) controls exist and in which the financial statements are prepared. It may be said to reflect management's commitment to an effective system of internal control. This is the phase that recently has been given increased importance when dealing with controls. It represents the collective effect of many factors, including:

1. *Management Philosophy and Operating Style.* This factor relates to "the tone at the top" and includes a broad range of topics that influence the control environment, including:

   a. Emphasis on meeting profit goals, or targets, or budgets.

   b. Basic attitude about risk taking.

   c. Attitude about need for controls.

   d. Attitude about the importance and sanctity of the financial statements, both internal and published.

2. *Organization Structure.* How is the organizing, planning, directing and controlling of operations handled? On a decentralized basis? Does strong central control exist? Does one or a few individuals dominate the company?

3. *Functioning of the Board of Directors and the Board Committees.* Does the board exert influence or largely follow the dictates of the CEO? Does it examine or discuss important policies and procedures? Does an audit committee composed of outside directors exist? Does it oversee accounting policies and procedures, including controls? Does it meet independently with the outside auditors, and with internal auditors?

4. *Methods of Assigning Authority and Responsibility.* Are policy matters such as ethical standards, conflicts of interest, competitive response discussed?

5. *Management Control Methods.* This category relates to the heart of operational control—how management delegates authority to others and effectively supervises all company activities. Included would be a consideration of:

    a. The planning system—both short- and long-term.

    b. The measurement system, comparing actual with planned performance, and communication of the results to appropriate individuals.

    c. The methods of taking timely and corrective action to bring actual performance at least to plan.

    d. The methods of developing procedures, modifying systems, and monitoring systems and procedures.

6. *The Existence and Effectiveness of an Internal Audit Function.* Included are the proper authority, organization structure and status, properly qualified personnel, and adequate resources. (This subject is discussed in Chapter 10.)

7. *Personnel Policies and Procedures.* This category includes adequate policies and procedures as to hiring, training, evaluating, promoting, and compensating personnel so that a proper and adequate core of employees is available and permitted to carry out their assigned responsibilities.

8. *Influence of External Factors.* While external influences are largely outside the control of an entity, how the management monitors and deals with outside influences such as legislative and regulatory bodies, international events, economic trends, and how it complies with the requirements, is germane to accomplishing the entity's objectives.

How the management copes with these factors reveals the overall attitude of the board of directors and top management concerning the importance attached to ethics and the significance of proper controls. Anyone searching for a fraud situation could use these elements of the control environment to narrow the search area; for example, if a department had a poor attitude toward controls, then an auditor might consider that department to be a high risk area.

The controller, as the chief accounting officer, should understand how these various factors operate *in fact* as to his or her areas of responsibility; that is, it is one thing to have written policies and procedures, but another concern to be certain that they are followed. Management may give lip service to certain policies, but act in ways that condone departures from the standard. In a sense as to the control environment, attention should be on the same matters that would warrant examination by the independent auditor.

(b) MANAGEMENT PHILOSOPHY AND OPERATING STYLE

As experience is gained in the operation of control systems, and especially with the increased attention to business ethics, changes in organization structure, downsizing, and changes in manufacturing and information technologies, new facets will be emphasized in developing and maintaining an effective control system. One such change is in the management philosophy and operating style of many companies—an important element of the control environment.

Many operating managers regarded the internal control structure as primarily a financial or accounting concern. In part this may have been due to the evaluations that were made as a result of audits by either the internal auditors or the independent accountants. There was no direct tie-in to corporate governance and the achievement of the corporate objectives, such as profitability, growth, and adherence to ethical standards. What was needed, and what is occurring in many companies, is the education of operating management about their role in the control system.

One company, in an effort to educate all of their management, held a series of one-day seminars for the professional and management staff of the organization. In these meetings, the business objectives for each department were stated by the departmental vice president and supplemented by group discussion. Basically the "control mechanisms" or actions required to accomplish each department's objectives were reviewed for their effectiveness. The relationship of the elements of internal control to attaining the departmental objectives were appraised.

While the elements may differ by entity, these were the control segments covered by this company as meaningful to its operating management:[1]

- Organization controls: Personnel standards, a plan of organization, and the corporate culture.
- System development and change controls.
- Authorization and reporting controls; planning and budgeting; accountability.
- Accounting system controls.
- Safeguarding controls: Protection of assets and avoidance of unintentional risks.
- Management supervisory controls: Supervision and management information.
- Documentation controls: Formal policies and procedures; systems documentation.

The objective was to involve all of management in the educational process and make use of the informal mechanisms of the company.

(c) INFLUENCE OF EXTERNAL FACTORS

The other aspect of the control environment now receiving greater recognition is the influence of external factors. These outside influences are largely beyond the control of the entity; but how management deals with them may be relevant to how it attains its objectives. Until recently, external factors received scant attention in evaluating control systems. The Auditing Standards Board (ASB) in an internal control risk assessment pronouncement stated merely that there are various "external influences that affect an entity's operations and practices, such as examinations by bank regulatory agencies."[2]

When external factors are mentioned, often it is legislatures and regulatory bodies and their laws or pronouncements that first come to mind. In a report prepared for the Treadway Commission relating to fraudulent financial reporting, its authors stated that "The scope of internal auditing responsibilities for examining and evaluating control should extend to every point affected by the organization—even to certain external entities."[3]

---

[1] Paul G. Makosz, and Bruce W. McCuaig, Gulf Canada Resources, "Is Everything under Control? A New Approach to Corporate Governance," *Financial Executive,* Jan./Feb. 1990, p. 26.

[2] Auditing Standards Board, "Consideration of the Internal Control Structure in a Financial Statement Audit," SAS No. 55 (AICPA, April 1988), paragraph 9.

[3] Michael J. Barrett, and R. N. Carolus, "Control and Internal Auditing," *The Institute of Internal Auditors Report on Fraud,* Institute of Internal Auditors, Sept. 1986, p. 65.

The report grouped the external entities into these three general classes: regulators, customers, and suppliers. Our concern in this segment is with significant suppliers and customers.

Consider, first, the recent trend to just-in-time manufacturing. A successful JIT system depends on a close buyer-vendor relationship, with a limited number of dependable suppliers who will deliver materials on time. Moreover, the supplier will deliver in smaller lot sizes, using statistical quality control to maintain a high-quality, defect-free product, and thus reduce or avoid the cost of inspecting the incoming units. In effect, the input inspection is transferred to the supplier organization, and an important control point is moved to an external location. When such a transfer happens, the internal auditors of the manufacturer, in conjunction with the purchasing and manufacturing staff, must at least consider the need to review the adequacy and effectiveness of the external inspection system.

Similarly, with the expansion of electronic data interchange between large suppliers, as well as large customers, the concept of external control becomes relevant. If, for example, certain predetermined conditions automatically trigger large buy or sell orders, some of the traditional control mechanisms disappear, and new concerns must be addressed. Thus, as between a manufacturer and a large retailer, who has the right or authority to structure a transaction, place it in the electronic envelope, send it, and to receive the message? Under such circumstances, transaction control becomes the responsibility of the seller-buyer partnership and not that of a single party.

There are now many circumstances where new technologies are making it desirable to examine external control points. Sometimes this examination may be part of a JIT agreement. In other instances, no legal agreement may exist, but the buying and selling parties establish close working relationships that facilitate internal auditor access to selected external control points.

(d) THE ACCOUNTING SYSTEM

The second element composing the internal control structure is the accounting system. This is defined by the Auditing Standards Board of the AICPA as "The methods and records established to identify, assemble, analyze, classify, record and report an entity's transactions and to maintain accountability for the related assets and liabilities."[4]

The proper direction of the accounting system is one of the principal responsibilities of the controller. An effective accounting system encompasses those principles, methods, and procedures, as well as records that will:

1. Identify properly and record all valid transactions.

2. Describe the transactions on a timely basis and in sufficient detail to permit proper classification of transactions for financial reporting.

3. Determine the time period in which the transactions occurred so as to permit recording in the proper accounting period.

4. Measure the value of the transaction in a manner that permits their recording in their proper monetary value in the financial statements.

5. Permit proper presentation of the transactions and related required disclosures in the financial statements.

---

[4] Statement on Auditing Standards, No. 55, April 1988, p. 28.

It is probably clear that the independent auditor, as well as the chief financial officer and controller, will have an interest in seeing that these objectives are met.

(e) THE CONTROL PROCEDURES

Finally, the third arm of the triad composing the internal control structure is the control procedures. These may be defined as[5] "The policies and procedures in addition to the control environment and accounting system that management has established to provide reasonable assurance that specific entity objectives will be achieved." In most companies, the official most likely to be held responsible for adequate control procedures, and probably with justification, is the controller. Accordingly the elements generally regarded as essential to a proper control system are discussed in some detail later in this chapter. Suffice it to state here that the procedures include adequate segregation of duties, adequate records, and proper procedures for authorization of transactions.

9-3 VARIABILITY OF CONTROL PROCEDURES

Having discussed the basic elements of an internal control structure, it may be helpful to review some of the influences that shape the system.

The importance and content of specific segments of the control environment, the accounting systems, and the control procedures will vary considerably from company to company depending on many factors. Among these are:

1. Overall size of the entity.
2. Nature of the business.
3. Geographic dispersion of operating units.
4. Degree of centralization or decentralization.
5. Management philosophy.
6. Data processing methods, including telecommunication and networking facilities.
7. Applicable regulatory or legal requirements.
8. Management style.

Reflection about each of these items will bring to mind how they influence the environment, the accounting system, and the control procedures. Thus, in a small company of perhaps 10 people, the owners or managers will supervise all activities. They ordinarily will know if accounts receivable are being collected, if inventories are too high, if product quality is satisfactory. As the business grows and is decentralized, this personal contact may be lost, and other means of monitoring activity must be employed—written reports, comparison with standards or plan, use of auditors, etc. Or, in another company, manual records may be employed while another communicates through computer networks. Again, each entity has key success factors that will be monitored by a prudent management, and these differ from industry to industry. So the impact of all these factors must be weighed in understanding the operations.

---

[5] *Ibid.*

9-4 STANDARDS AND OTHER GUIDELINES FOR CONTROL PROCEDURES

Before presenting an example of an approach to examining controls and discussing in a limited way some of the basics, the reader should be aware of some of the authoritative sources about control systems.

Guidance on methods of evaluating control systems can be found in literature published by the following:

- The American Institute of Certified Public Accountants.
- The Institute of Internal Auditors.
- The U.S. General Accounting Office.

The *American Institute of Certified Public Accountants, Inc.* (1211 Avenue of the Americas, New York, NY 10036-8775) may be contacted about its many publications. But some Statements on Auditing Standards include:

- Statement of Auditing Standards No. 53, "The Auditor's Responsibility to Detect and Report Errors and Irregularities," April 1988.
- Statement on Auditing Standards No. 54, "Illegal Acts by Clients," April 1988.
- Statement on Auditing Standards No. 55, "Consideration of the Internal Control Structure in a Financial Statement Audit," April 1988.

The *Institute of Internal Auditors, Inc.* (294 Maitland Avenue, Altamonte Springs, FL 32701) through its Professional Standards and Responsibilities Committee, has issued Statements on Internal Auditing Standards, including S/AS No. 1—Control: Concepts and Responsibilities.

In 1983, the *Comptroller General of the United States* (Washington, DC, U.S. General Accounting Office) issued Standards for Internal Controls in the Federal Government. Additionally, these groups and select commissions publish other relevant data.

Rather than discuss internal controls in too much detail in this text, we refer the reader to these other publications.

9-5 AN OVERVIEW OF THE APPRAISAL OF THE CONTROL SYSTEM

With the apparent rise in inappropriate activity by some businesspersons, such as issuance of fraudulent financial statements, kickbacks, and bribery, the adequacy of the control systems takes on increased importance. Yet such a determination usually cannot be done quickly or easily. An analytical and detailed approach probably is desirable. Some representative actions in the procedure, some essential elements in the control system, and a suggested assignment of responsibility for different phases of control are discussed in the next few sections.

The prevailing literature indicates that there are perhaps three fundamental steps to be taken by appropriate management levels in evaluating the internal controls. In summary, what the system is supposed to do should be defined before attempting to determine how well the system is operating, by these three steps:

1. Identify the principal activities, risks, and exposures in each operating component of the business and define the control objectives related to those activities.

2. Describe, perhaps by flowcharts, and understand the various systems used to process transactions, safeguard assets, and prepare the financial-accounting reports.

3. Finally, evaluate the system, giving particular attention to possible significant weaknesses, to ascertain that the system provides reasonable assurance that the control objective probably is achieved.

(a) IDENTIFYING THE ACTIVITIES, RISKS, AND CONTROL OBJECTIVES

In identifying the principal activities and control objectives, several approaches may be taken, depending on the nature of the business. One suggestion is to segregate the typical commercial company into four basic operating components and define the typical control objectives of the various activities in each function. Suggested components are sales, production or service, finance, and administration. The detailed functions to be considered in the viewpoint of a major public accounting firm are shown in Figure 9-1. Then the control objectives are defined, for example in sales, as follows:[6]

Sales

Customer orders require approval of credit and terms before acceptance.

Uncollectible amounts are promptly identified and provided for.

Products shipped or services rendered are billed.

Billings are for the correct amount.

Revenues are recorded correctly regarding account, amount, and period.

Recorded billings are valid transactions.

Customer returns and other allowances are approved and recorded correctly regarding account, amount, and period.

The same approach regarding functions and specific control objectives would be used to cover all significant functions.

Another approach is to identify types of transactions common to most businesses. Each transaction flow is a grouping of related events, and the focus is on whether appropriate control exists over each step in the transaction through the processing system. Some suggested transaction cycles are these:

Revenue cycle.

Production cycle.

Payments cycle.

Time cycle (economic events caused by time, i.e., interest accrual).

---

[6] "A Guide for Management and Directors," *Evaluating Internal Controls* (Cleveland, OH: Ernst & Young), p. 8.

Figure 9-1   Operating Components of a Typical Commercial Business.

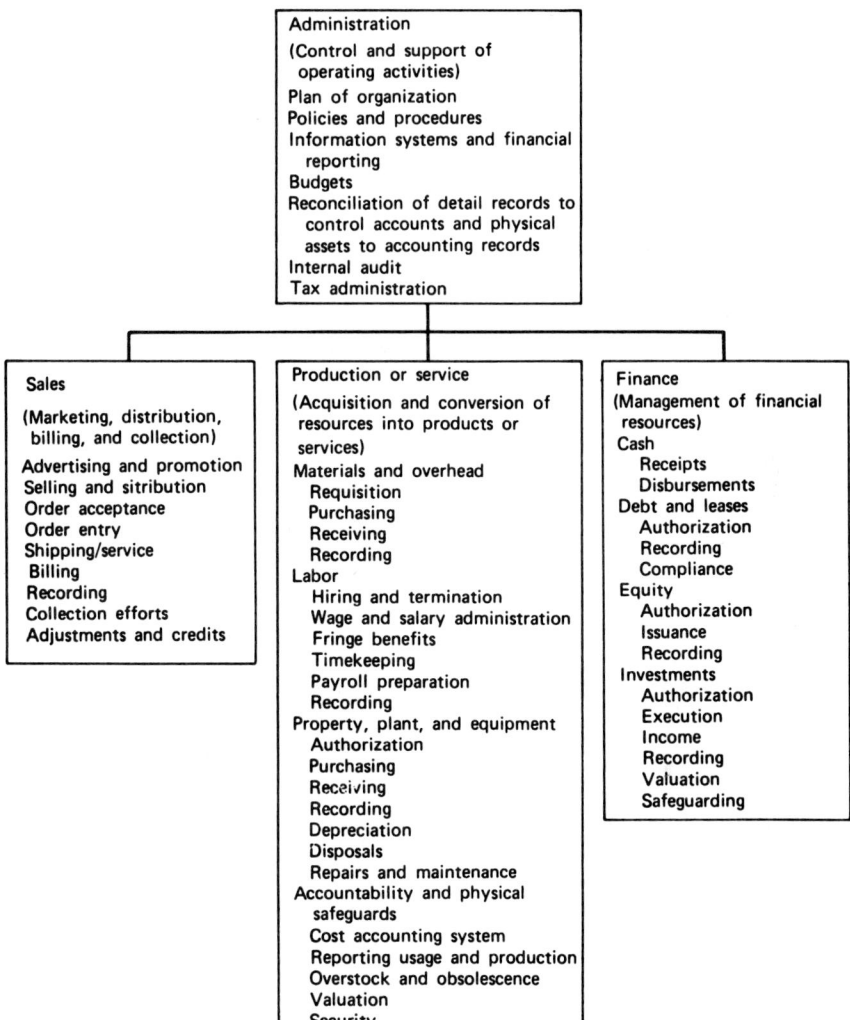

Whatever approach is used results in the identification of major functions and the control objectives for each.

In reviewing the operations, transactions, or cycles, the possibility of loss or risk (or error about the financial statements) should be considered in an effort to minimize intentional losses, for example, and provide for early warning of other potential loss, including, but not limited to, those arising by reason of such matters as those listed here:

Loss or destruction of assets.

Fraud or embezzlement.

Statutory sanctions or violations.

Excessive costs or insufficient revenues.

Unacceptable accounting.

Erroneous recording.

Expropriation.

It is a matter of being sensitive to "what can go wrong."

(b) DESCRIBING THE SYSTEM

Knowing the principal activities, related risks, and control objectives in the operating components of the business, the next step is to understand in detail the various accounting systems used to process transactions. These transaction cycles or groupings, as previously discussed, should be clearly described, perhaps flowcharted, so that they are understood and can be studied for possible weaknesses. An illustrative flowchart of a customer order and daily sales system is shown in Figure 9-2.

Figure 9-2   Customer Order and Daily Sales System.

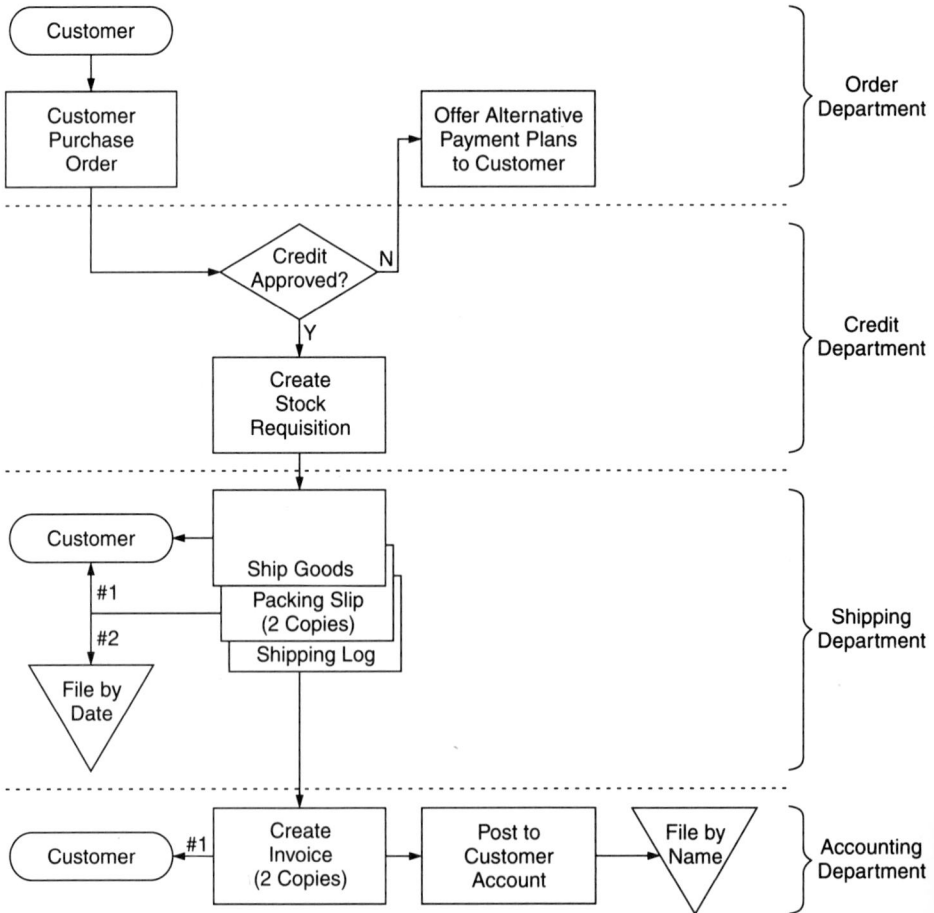

(c) EVALUATING THE SYSTEM

When the system has been documented, and understood, it should be evaluated, perhaps by members of the controller's staff, to see that it meets the control purposes intended. It involves a businessman's perspective on what should be done, a consideration of the things that could go wrong, and recognition of the accounts which would be affected. An example of a guide for evaluation of the first control objective under the "sales" function, described in section 9-5(a), is illustrated in Figure 9-3.

9-6 CONTROL OBJECTIVES

A review of the Accounting Standards Provision of the Foreign Corrupt Practices Act of 1977, and mature reflection about the basic elements of control, will suggest perhaps five general control objectives that should apply to transactions:

1. *Authorization.* Was the transaction authorized by management? This could be evidenced in a general way by establishing related policies, contract authorization limits, investment limits, standard price lists, etc. Or, in a given situation, a specific authorization may be needed.

2. *Recording.* Transactions should be recorded—in the proper account, at the proper time (proper cutoff), with the proper description. No fictitious transactions should be recorded, and erroneous material or incomplete descriptions should be avoided.

3. *Safeguarding.* Physical assets should not be under the physical custody of those responsible for related record-keeping functions. Access to the assets should be restricted to certain designated individuals.

4. *Reconciliation.* Periodic reconciliations of physical assets to records, or control accounts, should be made—e.g., bank reconciliations, securities inventories and

---

Figure 9-3   Guides for Evaluation of Control Objectives—The Sales Function.

Possible procedures to use for credit authorizations:
- New customers researched for credit risk prior to sales efforts being undertaken
- Salesmen required to assist in collecting from customers
- Signed purchase orders required from customers
- Approved list of credit and discount terms for customers
- Formal internal audit reviews of sales processes
- Formal management approval of new customers
- Regular review of customer credit reports (such as those produced by Dun & Bradstreet), with credit limit changes based on those reports

System deviations that can occur:
- Products shipped to customers on credit hold
- Orders accepted from high-risk customers
- Non-standard credit terms extended to customers

---

physical inventories of raw material, and work in process and finished goods to control accounts.

5. *Valuation.* Provision should be made for assurances that the assets are properly valued in accordance with generally accepted accounting principles—and that the adjustments are valid.

These five control objectives relate to the "prevention" of errors and to the "detection" of any errors or irregularities. As the evaluation of the internal control system is made, these objectives must be considered.

9-7 ELEMENTS OF INTERNAL ACCOUNTING CONTROL

To meet the broad objectives of good internal accounting control—safeguarding the assets against loss arising from intentional (fraud) or unintentional errors and producing reliable financial records of internal use and for external reporting purposes—there are seven basic required elements:

1. *Competent and Trustworthy Personnel, with Clearly Defined Lines of Authority and Responsibility.* People are probably the most important ingredient in a control system. If employees are competent and trustworthy, then reliable financial statements can result, even though other control elements are missing. Incompetent and dishonest personnel, given a theoretically good system of controls, can result in worthless statements.

   A proper evaluation of employees is paramount.

2. *Adequate Segregation of Duties.* To prevent intentional or unintentional errors, several segregations are desirable:

   a. *Segregation of operating responsibility from financial record keeping.* In those instances where an operating department maintains its own records and prepares its own financial reports, there is a temptation to biased data to report improved performance. Segregation of the financial records under a controller is desirable.

   b. *Separation of custody of the assets from the accounting records.* Separation of the accounting from custody is to protect the company against defalcation. Thus the segregation of custody of cash from maintenance of the accounts receivable is desirable to reduce the possibility of converting cash to personal use and adjusting the customer account by a fictitious credit.

   c. *Segregation of the authorization of transactions from the custody of any related assets.* For example, the person authorizing the payment of an invoice should not sign the check that pays the bill.

   d. *Separation of duties within the accounting function.* As an example, segregation of those maintaining the general ledger should be made from those handling the subsidiary ledger, or those handling cash journals should be separated from those handling sales journals.

3. *Proper Procedures for Authorization of Transactions.* Such authorizations may be general or specific, depending on management desires. Thus management may give general approval for sales to customers, given a certain credit approval. Or

management may desire to approve each contract above a given amount, say, $10 million.

4. *Existence of Adequate Records and Documents.* The documents must provide reasonable assurance that the transaction is properly recorded and that the asset is controlled. Thus purchase orders, receiving reports, and vendor invoices should exist.

5. *Existence of Proper Physical Control over Both Assets and Records.* Properly controlled warehouses, safety deposit vaults, or fireproof safes are examples of physical control. Proper safeguard of records against destruction or other loss is necessary.

6. *Proper Procedures for Adequate Record Keeping.* Procedures to assure the proper recording of all transactions—such as procedure manuals—may be desirable.

7. *Existence of a System for Independent Verifications.* The existence of an internal audit staff, or other means of checking, may be helpful.

The controller must continuously evaluate the existence of these conditions or devices to assure the adequacy of proper internal accounting controls.

9-8 LEVEL OF CONTROLS

In reviewing internal controls, the greatest amount of time is usually spent in analyzing and evaluating the very detailed controls that exist. And perhaps this is the way it should be. However, given the responsibilities of the board of directors and top management, the ultimate purpose of the system is to aid in meeting the business goals and objectives. Hence the control system to be reviewed should include *all* levels of planning and related control. These might be divided into these three groups:

1. *Strategic—Board of Directors and Top Management*
   Organization structure.
   Corporate goals and objectives.
   Long-range planning procedures.
   Marketing policy decision making.
   Management policy decision making.
   Financial policy decision making.

2. *Tactical—Board of Directors and Senior Management*
   Annual profit plans.
   Executive—personnel policies (inventories, replacement).
   Capital expenditures.
   Annual research and development plan.

3. *Operational*
   Credit approval practices.
   Treatment of uncollectible accounts.
   Billing procedure.

Purchasing procedure.

Salary and wage authorization.

Pension plan performance.

Consideration has to be given to which of the controls in a company should be handled at each level and, further, which should require corporate level review and approval versus divisional.

9-9 RESPONSIBILITY FOR PROPER INTERNAL CONTROLS

Given the recent emphasis on internal controls, the passage of the Foreign Corrupt Practices Act and the Report of the National Commission on Fraudulent Financial Reporting, also known as the Treadway Commission, who should be responsible for the existence of proper controls? It probably will develop that several groups will have specific responsibilities. Some suggested perimeters of responsibility for several management levels, and the independent public accountants, are outlined next:

1. *Role of the Board of Directors.* The board of directors probably is finally responsible for general oversight and the monitoring of management, without getting too involved in details. These specifics may be of assistance. The board of directors must do the following:

   a. Understand in a general way how the financial-accounting recording system works.

   b. Satisfy itself, perhaps through the audit committee, that an adequate system of internal control exists.

   c. Ascertain that the system is effective and sufficient to the proper safeguarding of assets, and issuance of correct financial reports—as well as achieving compliance with federal or state regulation.

   d. Determine that a carefully prepared code of ethics exists to govern the conduct of the corporate employees.

   e. Assume ultimate responsibility for monitoring compliance of management and other employees with rules of corporate governance and the Act and for taking appropriate action for violations.

2. *Role of Senior Corporate Management.* Although the board of directors may have an oversight responsibility, it is the management of the company that must assume primary responsibility—a responsibility it had even before passage of the Act—for the proper company environment and for an adequate and effective system that allows for internal control, correct financial statements, and safeguarding of assets. It is this management group that is responsible for detailed implementation and enforcement of the systems.

   In another sense, senior corporate management must do the following:

   a. Identify the risks inherent in the business venture and the potential for errors and irregularities.

b. Provide the proper environment, including policies, directives, and other communications, to enforce the necessary controls.

c. Direct those responsible for the business decisions and those who technically must be involved to do the following:

  (i) Create and maintain a documented internal control system.

  (ii) Employ appropriate legal review of the system.

d. Assume responsibility to shareholders, etc., for the financial statements.

These responsibilities likewise are largely imposed on the operating management in all profit centers, as well as that of the entire corporation.

3. *Role of Financial Management.* The senior financial management and the other financial management have the responsibilities for internal controls that the other senior and operating management have. But in another sense, the financial officers, and especially the controller, have a greater responsibility for effective internal accounting controls, given their presumed professionalism and experience in the controls area. It is in the accounting area that the bulk of the checks and balances will come to bear.

Specifically, with regard to internal accounting controls, the controller should have these obligations:

a. Know the technical requirements of a sound and adequate internal accounting control system. Install and maintain an effective system.

b. Ascertain that the system exists and operates.

c. Enforce conformance to policy and procedure.

d. Assume responsibility to the chief executive officer (CEO) and senior financial management for accuracy and reliability of the financial statements.

4. *Role of the Internal Auditor.* The existence of a qualified internal audit department, in a medium to large company, at least, is an important element of the system of internal control. The internal auditor of such a department is the eyes and ears of management to ascertain the status of the internal control system—and especially the internal accounting controls.

The chief internal auditor is responsible to assure senior management and financial management, on a review basis, of the following:

a. That an adequate system exists in each profit center.

b. That the systems are effective for the purposes intended.

c. That any deficiencies are brought to the attention of appropriate parties for corrective actions—an evaluation of the system.

5. *Role of the Independent Auditor.* The independent auditor is not, of course, a part of the company's internal accounting control system. However, he must evaluate the system to ascertain its reliability as a basis for planning the extent of audit necessary to render an opinion on the financial statements. Further, he is in a unique position to advise the board of directors on an independent and objective basis concerning the adequacy of the internal accounting controls—grounded on the firm's experience and association with the systems of other companies, etc.

Accordingly, the duties of the independent auditor may be summarized as here:

1. Review system of internal control to do the following:
   a. Determine the degree of reliance to be placed thereon in forming the nature and extent of audit tests to be performed on financial statements.
   b. Communicate material findings to the appropriate level of management—audit committee, senior management, and financial management at various levels.
2. Provide instructional manuals on methods and techniques for reviewing, testing, and evaluating internal controls.
3. Conduct training programs for company personnel selected to review and modify internal controls.

Aside from these responsibilities, the independent auditor, given present SEC proclivities, may be required to concur in the management representations about the adequacy of the internal accounting controls.

9-10 FRAUD AND ERROR DEFINED

One clearly stated definition of fraud is as follows: "Fraud may be defined as an intentional deception, misappropriation of a company's assets or the manipulation of its financial data to the advantage of the perpetrator."[7] Another description is, "Fraud encompasses an array of irregularities and illegal acts characterized by intentional deception."[8] The word has been used rather synonymously with such related terms as "defalcation," "embezzlement," "irregularity," and "swindle."

The term "errors" usually refers to unintentional mistakes or omissions or misstatements. Thus, errors in financial statements may involve:[9]

- Mistakes in gathering or processing accounting data from which financial statements are prepared.
- Incorrect accounting estimates arising from oversight or misinterpretation of facts.
- Mistakes in the application of accounting principles relating to amount, classification, manner of presentation, or disclosure.

This same source defines "irregularities" as *intentional* misstatements or omissions of amounts or disclosures in financial statements. Hence, the primary distinction between "errors" and "irregularities" is intent—but this may be difficult to determine,

---

[7] Marvin M. Levy, "Financial Fraud: Schemes and Indicia," *Journal of Accountancy,* Aug. 1985, p. 78.

[8] Definition of 11A in S/AS No. 3, "Standards for the Deterrent, Detection, Investigation and Reporting of Fraud," para 1.

[9] From Statement on Auditing Standards No. 53, "The Auditor's Responsibility to Detect and Report Errors and Irregularities," para. 2, April 1988.

especially in matters involving accounting estimates or application of accounting principles.

One purpose of a good system of internal control is to reduce or eliminate errors or irregularities.

(a) COMMON TYPES OF FRAUD

Fraud is a complex subject and is not fully discussed in this chapter. Different types of individuals and different vehicles or activities may be involved. Some of the different types of fraud are variously described as:

- Management fraud.
- Employee (nonmanagement) fraud.
- Computer fraud.
- Procurement fraud (as in government contracts.)
- Financial reporting fraud.

While the controller has an interest in preventing any type of fraud, this chapter discusses the two kinds with which he should be especially concerned: management fraud and financial reporting fraud. As to the other common types, the reader is referred to the many books and articles on the subject, some of which are listed in the Selected References.

(b) SOME CAUSES OF FRAUD

If a controller is aware of the circumstances that encourage fraud or of the causes of fraud, he may be more sensitive to signs that it has occurred. In most circumstances, and certainly when collusion is involved, there is no way to guarantee the absence of fraud. But there is reason to conclude that fraud results from a combination of pressures on the individual officer or employee and the circumstances that allow the act to occur. Some of the conditions that lay the foundation include these:

1. *Poor Internal Controls or a Poor Internal Control Environment*
   - Management does not punish or prosecute offenders.
   - Management does not set an example of high ethical standards.
   - Management does not stress the need for strong controls.
   - Management has not published rules governing ethical conduct.
   - Highly placed executives are seen as lavish spenders on business trips.
   - The CEO approves heavy business expenditures by his staff despite restrictive policies and procedures.
2. *Existence of Heavy Financial Pressures on Individuals*
   - Heavy personal indebtedness, such as for mortgages, household furnishings, etc.

- Socially unacceptable behavior (heavy gambling, use of drugs, drinking, extramarital affairs).
- Extravagant means of living.
- High inflation rates not accompanied by adequate adjustment in compensation.

3. *Other Sources of Pressure*

- Unreasonable profit goals for the company, or for a division or subsidiary.
- High rate of management personnel turnover.
- Management operating and financial decisions dominated by a very aggressive individual.
- A declining industry of which the company is a part.

4. *Contributing Conditions*

- Inadequate hiring practices (e.g., lack of reference checks).
- Deteriorating living environment.
- Undesirable personal traits.
- Unsatisfactory home life.

Some of the signs are difficult to detect.

(c) MANAGEMENT OVERRIDE

The responsibility for an effective internal control system rests with management. Yet some of the most widely publicized cases of improper activity are those that were carried on by a limited number of business managers themselves. It is these cases that are among the most difficult to detect.

Quite often the effort by senior management to commit fraud is more subtle than the "ordinary ways." It involves management override. This condition occurs when executives with sufficient real or apparent authority cause subordinates to improperly conceal or record transactions, or cause documents to be processed outside of the established procedure. These executives are in a position to override or circumvent the controls. Such actions may result in a material misstatement of financial results or condition, and/or a defrauding of the company. The controller, along with the independent accountants and internal auditors, should be alert to, or assess the risks of, such a possibility. The condition could occur in the divisions or subsidiaries, as well as at the corporate headquarters level. Management override probably would not occur under normal circumstances. But these conditions might tempt some (in a division or subsidiary, or even at the corporate level):

- Management compensation is directly affected, in a substantial way by operating results, and oftentimes such results tend to be erratic.
- The management of the segment or entity is under extreme pressure to achieve specified earnings.
- The operating entity is in an industry experiencing a large number of business failures.

- The entity has been sold and the management will benefit from the price—which is related to operating results and financial condition.

Some of the areas where management override is more common include:

- *Reserve Estimates.* Inventory reserves, reserves for doubtful accounts, tax accruals, litigation reserves, among others, may be understated so as to increase profits.
- *Depreciation Allowances.* Depreciation rates on machinery and equipment might be changed.
- *Sales.* Advance sales may be billed, or shipments may be made ahead of schedule.
- *Cost of Sales.* Cost of sales may be understated, thus providing higher margins (and possibly later inventory losses).
- *Deferring Expenses.* Current expenses may be capitalized on one pretext or another, to be written off over a period of time.

These are examples where management override might be involved. The controller should be alert to the need to scrutinize the accounting when the pressures on the operating executives seem great. Such reviews sometimes require great discretion.

9-11 AUDITING FOR FRAUD

Auditing for fraud, especially for small-scale fraud, is like looking for the proverbial needle in the haystack. There are several reasons why it is so difficult to find:

1. *Too Many Transactions*—The auditor typically reviews only a small number of transactions. If fraud is only being committed with one transaction out of many, the odds of finding the fraud are slim.
2. *Ineffective Use of Audit Time*—Looking for fraud is very time consuming. There are hundreds if not thousands of ways to illegally remove company assets, and tracking down all possibilities will fill the work schedule of any internal audit staff.
3. *Audits Have Time Limits*—Like all well-run projects, fraud audits have specific time boundaries; once the completion date is reached, the audit team moves on to another audit. Since fraud audits can take considerable periods of time to uncover issues, there may not be time available to detect a suspected fraud situation.
4. *Trend Analysis Is Not Sufficient*—Smaller cases of fraud will not be highlighted by analyzing expense levels over time, because the small expense surges will not appear significant.
5. *Perpetrators Know the Procedures*—Those who are conducting frauds may not only know the procedures being circumvented, but also may be in charge of the procedures. If so, then frauds may be cleverly concealed, since the criminal parties are experts in the control procedures. The auditor, on the other hand, is not primarily trained in fraud detection, but in evaluating overall systems of controls and reporting. Thus, in terms of training or ability, the perpetrator may outclass the auditor.

6. *Fraud Is Hard to Recognize*—Fraud is difficult to detect even when you are look-ing for it. The perpetrator has probably taken a great deal of time to conduct the fraud, and has either eliminated or reduced all traces of the crime. For example, when conducting an audit, how many auditors will follow up on missing documentation? The reason for the missing documentation may be simple misfiling, but it may also be deliberate misplacement to cover a fraud situation.

The points are not designed to make the auditor despair of ever uncovering a fraud; doing so is difficult, but *not* impossible. The problem is, what tools can you use to quickly hone in on likely fraud situations? The following suggestions may help:

1. *Watch the Environment*—As stated several times, the environment is a key factor. If the management has a low regard for controls, then the attitude may "rub off" on their employees. If management uses the company for personal gain, then other employees may feel that it is acceptable for them to do so as well. The environment may be worse in one area; if so, then the auditor's fraud search should narrow to that area.

2. *Watch the Controls*—If control over an area is concentrated into one person's job, then the opportunity for fraud has been presented to the employee. The auditor should not only review such situations, but also recommend splitting responsibilities in order to remove any temptation from the employee.

3. *Watch Employee Lifestyles*—Some perpetrators flaunt their wealth and bring their gains back to the workplace in the form of fancy automobiles or new clothes. We are not suggesting that the auditor review the parking lot each day, but an inquiring person might want to know why an accounting clerk is driving a Porsche.

4. *Be Available*—Fraud can be surprisingly well-known among employees. For the auditor to be told about such situations by employees, availability is crucial. Consequently, the successful fraud auditor is one who talks to auditees frequently, is available at audit sites, and is known for protecting sources.

A few of the more common kinds of fraud are listed below. This list should not be considered complete, since the types of fraud are limited only by the imagination of the perpetrator. For an ongoing listing of fraud cases, please refer to the "Round Table" department of the *Internal Auditor,* the journal of the Institute of Internal Auditors.

- *Bills from Nonexistent Companies*—Employees can bill the company for services from a nonexistent company. This is easy if the accounts payable staff does not review services for completion or materials for receipt. The fraud is detected by auditing billing approvals. Also, the auditor can review the numerical sequence of invoices received from the supplier to see if most of the supplier's invoices are going to the company.

- *Use Telephones*—Employees can use company's phone lines for personal calls. The fraud is detected by reviewing the phone bills for numbers called.

- *Pay Personal Bills*—Employees can have the company pay their own bills for them, or have the company pay for items that were ordered for the employees through the company. The fraud is detected by auditing bills received, and can only be prevented by rigorous approvals of all expenses.

- *Alter Approved Expense Amounts*—Employees can alter expense reports after supervisors have approved the reports. The fraud is difficult to detect, but auditors may be able to find altered or erased numbers on the reports. Prevention is by routing expense reports directly to the accounts payable department after the supervisors approve the reports, so that the employees who originally submitted the reports do not have further access to the documents.

- *Rig Bids Between Purchasers and Suppliers*—Buyers can be influenced to accept high bids in exchange for kickbacks from suppliers. The fraud is detected by comparing winning bid amounts to market rates, and by reviewing the number of rejected bids due to spurious causes. For example, cheaper bids can be thrown out by marking the bid receipt date as being later than the posted due date (and can be audited by comparing the bidder sign-in date in the visitor log to the date posted on the bid by the purchasing department).

- *Submit Multiple Expense Receipts*—Employees can submit credit card receipts in one month for reimbursement and then submit the actual receipt for reimbursement in a different month. The fraud is detected by comparing expense reports that were submitted over a period of several months.

- *Cancel Reimbursed Education*—Employees can cancel classes that are paid for by the company and pocket the proceeds (or have the classes paid for by a second party, such as the Veteran's Administration, and keep the overpayment). The fraud is detected by getting permission to review the college's financial records for each employee. The fraud can still occur if the company only pays on proof of completion of a class, since a second party can still pay for the class.

- *Sell Company Assets*—Employees can sell company assets right off the company premises and have the check made out to and delivered to them. The fraud is detected by frequent reviews of fixed assets records to actual assets. Prevention can be difficult if a high-level person is the perpetrator.

9-12 FRAUDULENT FINANCIAL REPORTING

Another area of fraud with particular interest for the controller is that involving fraudulent financial reporting. The possibility of fraudulent financial reporting was a consideration in the passage of legislation such as:

- The Securities Act of 1933.
- The Securities and Exchange Act of 1934.
- More recently, the Foreign Corrupt Practices Act of 1977 (FCPA), as well as the related regulations issued by the SEC.

In October 1985, the National Commission on Fraudulent Financial Reporting (NCFFR), also known as the Treadway Commission, was formed as a private sector initiative, sponsored and funded by the prominent associations concerned with the subject (AICPA, AAA, FEI, IIA, and the NAA) to delve into the matter. It focused on publicly owned companies, and was directed to examine three principal areas:

1. The extent to which fraudulent financial reporting undermines the integrity of financial reporting, including the environment; forces contributing to the fraudulent acts; and, among other things, the extent to which it can be detected and prevented.

2. The role of the independent public accountant in detecting fraud.

3. Those attributes of the corporate structure that may contribute to acts of fraudulent financial reporting, or to the failure to promptly detect such acts.

The scope of the study was broad, extending from the complex aspects of the corporate study itself, to the independent public accountants who opined about the financial statements, through the regulatory bodies and legal environment, to the education of those participants who might become involved in the financial reporting process.

(a) RECOMMENDATIONS OF THE TREADWAY COMMISSION

In October 1987, the Commission issued its final report. The recommendations provide an insight into the problem. However, it should be recognized that, while many of the public companies were already doing largely (but not wholly) what was recommended, many were not and have since complied to a large degree. Moreover, with some of its recommendations, the Commission is extending somewhat the edges of the act on science in detecting fraudulent actions.

While it is suggested the reader examine the report itself, a summary of the recommendations follows:[10]

1. Recommendations for the Public Company

- **The Tone at the Top**

    Recommendation: For the top management of a public company to discharge its obligation to oversee the financial reporting process, it must identify, understand, and assess the factors that may cause the company's financial statements to be fraudulently misstated.

    Recommendation: Public companies should maintain internal controls that are adequate to prevent and detect fraudulent financial reporting.

    Recommendation: Public companies should develop and enforce written codes of corporate conduct. Codes of conduct should foster a strong ethical climate and open channels of communication to help protect against fraudulent financial reporting. As a part of its ongoing oversight of the effectiveness of internal controls, a company's audit committee should review annually the program that management establishes to monitor compliance with the code.

- **Accounting Function and Chief Accounting Officer**

    Recommendation: Public companies should maintain accounting functions that are designed to meet their financial reporting obligations.

---

[10] Originally published in *Internal Auditing Manual, Second Edition,* James D. Willson and Steven J. Root. Reprinted with the permission of Warren, Gorham & Lamont, Inc. Copyright © 1989, Warren, Gorham & Lamont, Inc.

- **Internal Audit Function and Chief Internal Auditor**

  Recommendation: Public companies should maintain an effective internal audit function staffed with an adequate number of qualified personnel appropriate to the size and the nature of the company.

  Recommendation: Public companies should ensure that their internal audit functions are objective.

  Recommendation: Internal auditors should consider the implications of their nonfinancial audit findings for the company's financial statements.

  Recommendation: Management and the audit committee should ensure that the internal auditors' involvement in the audit of the entire financial reporting process is appropriate and properly coordinated with the independent public accountant.

- **Mandatory Independent Audit Committee**

  Recommendation: The board of directors of all public companies should be required by SEC rule to establish audit committees comprised solely of independent directors.

  Recommendation: Audit committees should be informed, vigilant, and effective overseers of the financial reporting process and the company's internal controls.

  Recommendation: All public companies should develop a written charter setting forth the duties and responsibilities of the audit committee. The board of directors should approve the charter, review it periodically, and modify it as necessary.

  Recommendation: Audit committees should have adequate resources and authority to discharge their responsibilities.

  Recommendation: The audit committee should review management's evaluation of factors related to the independence of the company's public accountant. Both the audit committee and management should assist the public accountant in preserving his independence.

  Recommendation: Before the beginning of each year, the audit committee should review management's plans for engaging the company's independent public accountant to perform management advisory services during the coming year, considering both the types of services that may be rendered and the projected fees.

- **Reporting on Responsibilities in the Annual Report to Stockholders**

  Recommendation: All public companies should be required by SEC rule to include in their annual reports to stockholders management reports signed by the chief executive officer and chief accounting officer. The management report should acknowledge management's responsibilities for the financial statements and internal control, discuss how these responsibilities were fulfilled, and provide management's assessment of the effectiveness of the company's internal controls.

  Recommendation: All public companies should be required by SEC rule to include in their annual reports to stockholders a letter signed by the chairman of the audit committee describing the committee's responsibilities and activities during the year.

• **Seeking a Second Opinion**

Recommendation: Management should advise the audit committee when it seeks a second opinion on a significant accounting issue.

Recommendation: When a public company changes independent public accountants, it should be required by SEC rule to disclose publicly the nature of any material accounting or auditing issue discussed with both its old and new auditor during the three-year period preceding the change.

• **Quarterly Reporting**

Recommendation: Audit committees should oversee the quarterly reporting process. This oversight should include approving financial results prior to public release.

• **Guidance on Internal Control**

Recommendation: The Commission's sponsoring organizations should cooperate in developing additional, integrated guidance on internal control.

2.   Recommendations for the Independent Public Accountant

• **Recognizing Responsibility for Detecting Fraudulent Financial Reporting**

Recommendation: The Auditing Standards Board should revise standards to restate the independent public accountant's responsibility for detection of fraudulent financial reporting, requiring the independent public accountant to (1) take affirmative steps in each audit to assess the potential for such reporting and (2) design tests to provide reasonable assurance of detection. Revised standards should include guidance for assessing risks and pursuing detection when risks are identified.

• **Improving Detection Capabilities**

Recommendation: The Auditing Standards Board should establish standards to require independent public accountants to perform analytical review procedures in all audit engagements and should provide improved guidance on the appropriate use of these procedures.

Recommendation: The SEC should require independent public accountants to review quarterly financial data of public companies before release to the public.

• **Improving Audit Quality**

Recommendation: The AICPA's SEC Practices Section should strengthen its peer review program by increasing review of audit engagements involving public company clients new to a firm. For each office selected for peer review, the first audit of all such new clients should be reviewed.

Recommendation: The AICPA's SEC Practices Section requirement for a concurring, or second partner, review of the audit report should be revised as part of an ongoing process of review of this requirement. Standards for the concurring review should, among other things, (1) require concurring review partner involvement in the planning stage of the audit in addition to the final review stage, (2) specify qualifications of the concurring review partner to require prior experience with audits of SEC registrants and familiarity with the client's industry, and (3) require the concurring review partner to consider himself a peer of the engagement partner for purposes of the review.

Recommendation: Public accounting firms should recognize and control the organizational and individual pressures that potentially reduce audit quality.

- **Communicating the Auditor's Role**

Recommendation: The Auditing Standards Board should revise the auditor's standard report to state that the audit provides reasonable but not absolute assurance that the audited financial statements are free from material misstatements as a result of fraud or error.

Recommendation: The Auditing Standards Board should revise the auditor's standard report to describe the extent to which the independent public accountant has reviewed and evaluated the system of internal accounting control. The Auditing Standards Board also should provide explicit guidance to address the situation where, as a result of his knowledge of the company's internal accounting controls, the independent public accountant disagrees with management's assessment as stated in the proposed management's report.

- **Reorganization of the Auditing Standards Board**

Recommendation: The AICPA should reorganize the Auditing Standards Board to afford a full participatory role in the standard-setting process to knowledgeable persons who are affected by and interested in auditing standards but who either are not CPAs or are CPAs no longer in public practice.

3. **Recommendations for the SEC and Others to Improve the Regulatory and Legal Environment**

- **Additional SEC Enforcement Remedies**

Recommendation: The SEC should have the authority to impose civil money penalties in administrative proceedings [including Rule 2(e) proceedings] and to seek civil money penalties from a court directly in an injunctive proceeding.

Recommendation: The SEC should have the authority to issue a cease and desist order when it finds a securities law violation.

Recommendation: The SEC should seek explicit statutory authority to bar or suspend corporate officers and directors involved in fraudulent financial reporting from future service in that capacity in a public company.

- **Increased Criminal Prosecution**

Recommendation: Criminal prosecution of fraudulent financial reporting cases should become a higher priority. The SEC should conduct an affirmative program to promote increased criminal prosecution of fraudulent financial reporting cases by educating and assisting government officials with criminal prosecution powers.

- **Improved Regulation of the Public Accounting Profession**

Recommendation: The SEC should require all public accounting firms that audit public companies to be members of a professional organization that has peer review and independent oversight functions and is approved by the SEC, such as that specified by the SECPS of the AICPA's Division for CPA Firms.

Recommendation: The SEC should take enforcement action when a public accounting firm fails to remedy deficiencies cited in the public accounting profession's quality assurance program.

- **SEC Resources**

Recommendation: The SEC must be given adequate resources to perform existing and additional functions that help prevent, detect, and deter fraudulent financial reporting.

- **Financial Institution Regulatory Agencies**

Recommendation: The Office of the Comptroller of the Currency, the Federal Reserve Board, the Federal Deposit Insurance Corporation, and the Federal Home Loan Bank Board (including the Federal Savings and Loan Insurance Corporation) should adopt measures patterned on the Commission's recommendations directed to the SEC to carry out their own regulatory responsibility relating to financial reporting under the federal securities laws.

Recommendation: The financial institution regulatory agencies and the public accounting profession should provide for the regulatory examiner and the independent public accountant to have mutual access to information they develop about examined financial institutions.

- **Enhanced Enforcement by State Boards of Accountancy**

Recommendation: State boards of accountancy should implement positive enforcement programs that periodically would review the quality of services that the independent public accountants they license render.

- **Considering the Implications of Liability on Audit Quality**

Recommendation: Parties charged with responding to various tort reform initiatives should consider the implications that the perceived liability crisis holds for long-term audit quality and the independent public accountant's detection of fraudulent financial reporting.

- **Reconsidering Corporate Indemnification**

Recommendation: The SEC should reconsider its long-standing position, insofar as it applies to independent directors, that the corporate indemnification of officers and directors for liabilities that arise under the Securities Act of 1933 is against public policy and therefore unenforceable.

4. Recommendations for Education

- **Business and Accounting Curricula**

Recommendation: Throughout the business and accounting curricula, educators should foster knowledge and understanding of the factors that may cause fraudulent financial reporting and the strategies that can lead to a reduction in its incidence.

Recommendation: The business and accounting curricula should promote a better understanding of the function and the importance of internal controls, including the control environment, in preventing, detecting, and deterring fraudulent financial reporting.

Recommendation: Business and accounting students should be well-informed about the regulation and enforcement activities by which government and private bodies safeguard the financial reporting system and thereby protect the public interest.

Recommendation: The business and accounting curricula should help students develop stronger analytical, problem solving, and judgment skills to help prevent, detect, and deter fraudulent financial reporting when they become participants in the financial reporting process.

Recommendation: The business and accounting curricula should emphasize ethical values by integrating their development with the acquisition of knowledge and skills to help prevent, detect, and deter fraudulent financial reporting.

Recommendation: Business schools should encourage business and accounting faculty to develop their own personal competence as well as classroom materials for conveying information, skills, and ethical values that can help prevent, detect, and deter fraudulent financial reporting. Business school faculty reward systems should recognize and reward the contributions of faculty who develop such competence and materials.

- **Professional Certification Examinations**

  Recommendation: Professional certification examinations should test students on the information, skills, and ethnical values that further the understanding of fraudulent financial reporting and that promote its reduction.

- **Continuing Professional Education**

  Recommendation: As part of their continuing professional education, independent public accountants, internal auditors, and corporate accountants should study the forces and opportunities that contribute to fraudulent financial reporting, the risk factors that may indicate its occurrence, and the relevant ethical and technical standards.

(b) MANAGEMENT REPRESENTATIONS IN THE ANNUAL REPORT

One of the recommendations of the NCFFR is that by SEC rule all public companies should be required to include in their annual report to stockholders a management report signed by the CEO and the chief accounting officer. It should acknowledge management's responsibilities for the financial statements and internal control, discuss how these responsibilities were fulfilled, and provide management's assessment of the effectiveness of the company's internal controls.

For some years now the larger public companies, and many others, have included a statement on management's responsibility for the financial statements included in the annual report to shareholders. One such statement, which deals at more length with the subjects referred to in the Treadway Commission report, is shown in Figure 9-4.

Figure 9-4   Management's Discussion of Financial Responsibility.

The financial data in this report, including the audited financial statements, have been prepared by management using the best available information and applying judgment. Accounting principles used in preparing the financial statements are those that are generally accepted in the United States.

Management believes that a sound, dynamic system of internal financial controls that balances benefits and costs provides the best safeguard for Company assets. Professional financial managers are responsible for implementing and overseeing the financial control system, reporting on management's stewardship of the assets entrusted to it by share owners and maintaining accurate records.

GE is dedicated to the highest standards of integrity, ethics and social responsibility. This dedication is reflected in written policy statements covering, among other subjects, environmental protection, potentially conflicting outside interests of employees, compliance with antitrust laws, proper business practices, and adherence to the highest standards of conduct and practices in transactions with the U.S. government. Management continually emphasizes to all employees that even the appearance of impropriety can erode public confidence in the Company.

Ongoing education and communication programs and review activities such as those conducted by the Company's Policy Compliance Review Board are designed to create a strong compliance culture — one that encourages employees to raise their policy questions and concerns and prohibits retribution for doing so.

KPMG Peat Marwick provide an objective, independent review of management's discharge of its obligations relating to the fairness of reporting operating results and financial condition. Their report for 1993 appears below.

The Audit Committee of the Board (consisting solely of Directors from outside GE) maintains an ongoing appraisal — on behalf of share owners — of the activities and independence of the Company's independent auditors, the activities of its internal audit staff, financial reporting process, internal financial controls and compliance with key Company policies.

John F. Welch, Jr.
Chairman of the Board and
Chief Executive Officer

Dennis D. Dammerman
Senior Vice President
Finance

February 11, 1994

Source: From General Electric Corporation *Annual Report,* 1994, p. 44. Used by permission of General Electric.

(c) SUGGESTIONS FOR THE CONTROLLER

The NCFFR has provided yardsticks by which companies, public accountants, higher education institutions, and others may measure themselves. Many companies have performed a self-evaluation review and others should. Moreover, the various professional accounting associations have reexamined their positions. It is probable that the Treadway Commission report was a factor in the issuance of Statements on Auditing Standards Nos. 53, 54, and 55 referred to previously.

In any event, if the controller has not already done so, it is suggested he consider the following:

1. Study the entire NCFFR report, and especially review the 20 recommendations for the public company to evaluate the ease with which fraudulent financial reporting could occur in his company. Also, read the Report of the Committee of Sponsoring Organizations (COSO),[11] which is summarized later in this section. This report is a sequel to the Treadway Commission report, which suggested that its sponsoring organizations work together in an effort to integrate the various internal control concepts and definitions, and develop a commonly accepted reference point regarding internal control concepts and definitions. This suggestion was made because the various groups (independent accountants, managements of public companies, the SEC and other regulatory bodies, and academia) each

---

[11] Issued in 1992. See selected references.

emphasized somewhat different aspects of internal control, depending on their particular interests.

2. Suggest to the CEO that all senior officers review the Treadway Commission and COSO reports and consider what their responsibilities are, and where special problems could arise.

3. Arrange for the internal audit department, on a timely basis, to evaluate and report on the internal controls.

4. Examine and make recommendations to appropriate authority (CEO, Audit Committee, etc.) whether the actions of top management match the Code of Conduct and the spoken words.

5. Be quite certain that the controller and appropriate staff members understand the interrelationship of the financial statements, and the possible impact of alternative acceptable accounting principles.

6. Encourage the development of qualified professional personnel in the accounting function, as well as in internal auditing. (This does not mean that all such staff members need be CPAs, or CMAs, or CIAs, although an adequate number is considered desirable.) Encourage professional development.

7. Encourage objectivity by the internal auditor, whether he reports to the CEO, the CFO, or the CAO, and see that he has direct access to the CEO and Audit Committee.

Since the controller is primarily responsible for the issuance of proper financial statements, he should support the above suggestions even though he may not have direct responsibility for some of the activities.

(d) REPORT OF THE COMMITTEE OF SPONSORING ORGANIZATIONS (COSO)

The COSO report, previously mentioned, entitled *Internal Control—Integrated Framework,* consists of four volumes:

- *Executive Summary*—A top-level overview directed to the CEO, other senior executives, and the board of directors, as well as to legislators, regulators, professional organizations, and academics.

- *Framework*—A definition of internal control together with its components and provides criteria against which managements, boards of directors, and others can assess a relevant control system.

- *Reporting to External Parties*—A guide to entities that report publicly on internal control regarding the preparation of relevant published financial statements.

- *Evaluation Tools*—A set of illustrations of material that could be useful in conducting an evaluation of an internal control system.

The following comments show how the COSO report has expanded on the concept of internal control from that reflected in earlier writings and reviews some of the subject matter stressed in this report.

(e) EVOLUTION OF THE INTERNAL CONTROL CONCEPT

The concept of internal control has been expanded from that contained in earlier accounting literature. In the 1930s and 1940s, internal control concentrated on accounting controls and administrative controls so as to safeguard the assets of the corporation by reducing theft as well as internal fraud. Later, attention focused on compliance with laws and regulations because of illegal payments to foreign representatives, bribery, or similar practices. Finally, in the 1980s, attention was further expanded to encompass fraudulent financial reporting. Now, according to the COSO report, a review of internal control should extend to the entire range of business activities that have to do with achieving various business objectives (such as meeting the annual business plan) and to the related tasks inherent in the process. To many, it has seemed that the review of internal controls does not significantly distinguish between such processes and the other aspects of the business management function. In fairness, however, it should be stated that the COSO report attempts to make clear that management activities such as establishing objectives, reaching business decisions, and carrying out management plans are activities that should be integrated with, but not made a part of, the internal control system. In today's competitive world, the existence of effective and efficient operations is germane to the survival of the business and the enhancement of shareholder value.

(f) REVISED AND ENLARGED DEFINITION OF INTERNAL CONTROL

Internal control is broadly defined as a process or group of processes, effected by an entity's board of directors, management, and other personnel, designed to provide reasonable assurance regarding the achievement of objectives in each of the following three categories:

1. Effectiveness and efficiency of operations.
2. Reliability of financial reporting.
3. Compliance with applicable laws and regulations.

Several concepts are inherent in this definition. First, internal control is not just a single event, but rather a series of actions that permeate an entity's activities. Internal control is intertwined with a business's operating activities and exists for fundamental reasons.

Second, the system provides only reasonable, not absolute, assurance to management and the board of directors that the specified objectives are being achieved. It cannot provide absolute assurance because systems do break down, and controls can be circumvented by the collusion of two or more individuals. Moreover, management has the ability to override the internal control system.

Third, internal control is accomplished or effected by people—whether the board of directors, or management, or other personnel in the entity. People establish the objectives and put the controls into operation. By the same token, internal controls affect the actions of the people involved, and these people may fail to understand, to communicate properly, or to perform consistently.

Fourth, internal controls are objective-oriented and relate to many categories. The three categories mentioned in the above definition concern (1) the effective and efficient use of resources, including safeguarding assets or meeting the business plan; (2) the preparation of reliable published financial statements; and (3) the tracking and enforcement of compliance with applicable laws and regulations.

The definition of internal controls is broad. This phrasing facilitates the use of subsets of internal control definitions and activities so that those concerned with special aspects (such as accounting control or budgetary control) can focus on those concerns and establish consistent subdefinitions. The system of controls in particular business units or activities of the entity can be accommodated. The definition is broad, also, because this is the manner in which top management often views the subject of controls.

(g) THE COMPONENTS OF INTERNAL CONTROL

The COSO report identified a fivefold segregation of the components of internal control, all of which are interrelated and all of which must exist to a sufficient degree if the internal control system is to function properly and if the business objectives are to be achieved. These components are described next.

(i) Control Environment.

The control environment sets the "tone" of the entity and influences the control consciousness of all members of the organization. Because it provides both structure and discipline, it is the very foundation of the other four components of internal control. The factors in the control environment include:

1. The integrity, ethical values, and competence of the people.
2. The philosophy and operating style of the management.
3. The manner in which management assigns authority, responsibility, and accountability.
4. The ways in which management organizes and develops its people.
5. The direction provided by the board of directors and its various committees.

(ii) Risk Assessment.

Risk assessment is the identification and analysis of relevant risks to achieving certain stated objectives. It forms the basis for determining how risk should be managed. Thus, objective setting—which is not an internal control function—is a precondition to risk assessment, and risk assessment *is* an internal control function.

Given the definition of internal control, three broad categories can be established:

1. Operations objectives, which pertain to the effectiveness and efficiency of the entity's operations. Operations objectives may range from profitability goals or objectives down to division objectives, department objectives, and even activity objectives such as processing sales orders or handling customer invoices.
2. Financial reporting objectives, which relate to the preparation of reliable published financial statements and the prevention of fraudulent public financial reporting.

3. Compliance objectives, which relate to the adherence to laws and regulations with which the entity must comply.

When the objectives are set, procedures must be established to track performance in meeting the objectives and keeping the identified risk within acceptable bounds.

As to risk assessment, when internal controls were more restricted to safeguarding assets and similar concerns, the relevant objectives seem to have had a narrower nature (such as seeing that all sales invoices were recorded in the accounts receivable), rather than the present broad management objectives, such as profit goals.

(iii) Control Activities.   Control activities are the policies and procedures that help ensure that the necessary actions are taken to address the risks involved in achieving the objectives of the entity. Control activities occur throughout the entire organization—at all levels and for all activities and conditions. In addition to a top-management review of entity performance, they include a vast range of actions: reviewing unit and departmental performance, requiring certain authorizations or approvals, performing reconciliations, verifying certain conditions, segregating duties, restricting access to certain areas or assets, and so on.

(iv) Information and Communication.   For management to be effective, it is essential that all relevant and pertinent information be identified, secured, or captured, and communicated in a proper format and within a suitable time period so that people may carry out their responsibilities. It should be relevant, timely, and accurate, and should be prepared in a format that is usable, comparable, and accessible. It may be financial or nonfinancial, and it may relate to some standard or objective, to internal or external operations, or to specific conditions. In short, the information to be made available should be that which facilitates decision making and related reporting.

Not only must the information itself be available, but it must also be communicated in a manner that secures attention and gets it used. It may be necessary to communicate the data to more than one individual—to higher and lower echelons; to those in charge of related functions; and to creditors, suppliers, regulatory agencies, owners, and other outside parties.

(v) Monitoring.   The final component of an effective control system consists of monitoring. This process of watching, observing, or checking the internal control system permits an assessment of the quality of the system's performance. Monitoring may be performed in an ongoing fashion by observing the findings or results of each regular, periodic review of each element—for example, each day, each month, or each quarter. Or, it may be accomplished as a separate evaluation. Whether a special evaluation is necessary will depend on the extent and nature of occurring changes, the extent of risks, the competence of the people who implement the controls, and what developments are disclosed by the ongoing monitoring. Perhaps both types of monitoring will be necessary.

Monitoring should extend, as circumstances demand, to every element of the internal control system (control environment, risk assessment, control activities, information and communication). Important deficiencies or violations should be reported to either senior management or the board of directors.

(h) EFFECTIVENESS OF INTERNAL CONTROL

The controller, and indeed the management of a public company or any other entity, often must ask, "How can we judge that the internal control system of our organization is effective?" Because the internal control system is defined as a threefold objective-oriented process, the COSO report and other writings, perhaps influenced by the COSO report, have provided the following standard:

Internal control can be judged effective in each of the three categories, respectively, if the board of directors and management have reasonable assurance that:

1. They understand the extent to which the entity's operational objectives are being achieved.
2. Published financial statements are being prepared reliably.
3. Applicable laws and regulations are being complied with.

Conclusions regarding the effectiveness of the control system can be reached for each of the three objectives only when the five components (control environment, risk assessment, control activities, information and communication, and monitoring) are present and are functioning properly. In each entity, each component may function somewhat differently. Further, components may complement each other in differing degrees, or may differ in how they address a particular risk. Determining whether a particular internal control system is effective is, therefore, a subjective judgment and must include a review of the components as well as the objectives. A member of management may know that risks have been evaluated, but may not realize that an important risk has been overlooked. Continuing periodic monitoring and evaluation are necessary.

In the fourth volume, *Evaluation Tools,* the COSO report contains a good discussion of the effectiveness of the internal control system and includes an excellent guide to assist the cognizant executive and others in appraising the internal control system and its various components. The coverage is specifically stated to be illustrative only, and not indicative of all matters that need to be considered in a particular situation. The listings of points of focus, objectives, and risks should prove useful.

Other topics that the COSO report addresses include: responsibility for internal control by the various members of management, by external auditors, and by other interested groups reporting to external parties: and limitations on internal control. These subjects and others are reviewed earlier in this chapter.

For a more thorough review of the subject, the reader should secure a copy of *Internal Control—Integrated Framework.* Orders are processed by the AICPA and the Institute of Management Accountants.

9-13 THE FOREIGN CORRUPT PRACTICES ACT (FCPA)

As stated earlier in this chapter, responsible business management long has had an interest in the proper operation of internal controls of the entity. In 1977, after disclosure by the Office of the Watergate Special Prosecutor and the SEC of the use of U.S. corporate resources for domestic political contributions and for the bribery of foreign government officials, Congress enacted the Foreign Corrupt Practices Act (FCPA). Commentary on some events indicated that some of the payments were illegal and others were questionable. A few were achieved through the use of "off-the-books" funds as well as methods that circumvented the internal accounting control systems. The effect of the Act was to set certain accounting standards for a company subject to the Securities Exchange Act of 1934 (a company with publicly traded stock). Basically, the Accounting Standards Provision of the Act, which is the segment in which the controller should be particularly interested if his employer is subject to the law, requires that the company keep in reasonable detail "books, records and accounts" that accurately and fairly reflect the company's transactions and disposition of assets, and maintain an adequate system of internal controls. More specifically, the words of the Act are that every issuer covered by the law shall:

(A) make and keep books, records, and accounts, which, in reasonable detail, accurately and fairly reflect the transactions and dispositions of the assets of the issuer; and

(B) devise and maintain a system of internal accounting controls sufficient to provide reasonable assurances that—

   (i)   transactions are executed in accordance with management's general or specific authorization;

   (ii)   transactions are recorded as necessary (I) to permit preparation of financial statements in comformity with generally accepted accounting principles or any other criteria applicable to such statements, and (II) to maintain accountability for assets;

   (iii) access to assets is permitted only in accordance with management's general or specific authorization; and

   (iv)   the recorded accountability for assets is compared with the existing assets at reasonable intervals and appropriate action is taken with respect to any differences.[12]

While little is heard in the current business publications about this section of the Act, it continues in effect, and the controller, especially of a multinational entity (although the law is applied much broader than merely to multinationals) should be aware of its existence and comply with the terms. It is suggested that the controller keep in mind continually that financial record keeping is not in fact separable from the internal accounting systems that generate the records, and that the operation of the entire internal control system should be consistently monitored. A minority of skillful executives might sometimes be tempted to override or bypass the system, and cause records to be created that look entirely proper to even a trained person who is not suspicious and who is not aware of the deviation from the usual routine.

9-14 REVISION IN GOVERNMENT AUDITING STANDARDS

Just as the report of the Committee of Sponsoring Organizations (COSO) has influenced the enlarged concept of internal control as applied to public companies, so also it appears to be having an impact on government auditing standards. The U.S. General

---

[12] Currently codified as Title 15, United States Code, Section 78M(b)(2)(1988).

Accounting Office (GAO) is now seeking comments on an exposure draft of *Government Auditing Standards,* also known as the "yellow book."

The current yellow book reflects the views of Statement on Auditing Standards No. 53, *Consideration of the Internal Control Structure in a Financial Statement Audit.* But research performance by the GAO staff and the experience of the members of the Government Auditing Standards Advisory Council concluded that the SAS No. 55 minimum requirements were no longer adequate.

Among other things, the exposure draft proposes to expand the auditor's responsibilities in two areas: the control environment and the safeguarding of assets. Under current requirements, auditors need not specifically assess the control environment. The exposure draft requires that auditors specifically assess whether or not the control environment enhances or undermines the effectiveness of control procedures. Additionally, auditors will be given the responsibility for considering how management safeguards assets. They must identify potentially vulnerable assets and search for a link between such assets and possible material misstatements of financial statement assertions. If a link could exist, the auditors must determine what controls management has in place to safeguard the assets.

9-15 SELECTED REFERENCES

Akst, Daniel, "How Barry Minkow Fooled the Auditors," *Forbes* (Oct. 2, 1989).

Albrecht, W. Steve, Keith R. Howe, and Marshall B. Romney, *Deterring Fraud: The Internal Auditor's Perspective.* Altamonte Springs, FL: The Institute of Internal Auditors, 1984.

Bull, Ivan, and Florence Cowan Sharp, "Advising Clients on Treadway Audit Committee Recommendations," *Journal of Accountancy,* Feb. 1989, pp. 46–52.

Carmichael, D. R., "The Auditor's New Guide to Errors, Irregularities and Illegal Acts," *Journal of Accountancy,* Sept. 1988, pp. 40–48.

Chrysler, Earl, and Donald E. Keller, "Preventing Computer Fraud," *Management Accounting,* April 1988, pp. 28–32.

"CPAs May Soon Have to Report Fraud Earlier," *The Wall Street Journal,* Jan. 22, 1989.

Crosby, Philip, "Employee Theft," *INC Magazine,* Feb. 1988.

Harrison, Steven R., "South Central Bell and the Treadway Commission Report," *Management Accounting,* Aug. 1988, pp. 21–27.

The Institute of Internal Auditors Reports on Fraud. Altamonte Springs, FL: The Institute of Internal Auditors, Sept. 1986.

Internal Control—Integrated Framework, Committee of Sponsoring Organizations of the Treadway Commission (COSO), 1992. (Orders processed by Order Department, American Institute of Certified Public Accountants, Harborside Financial Center, 201 Plaza III, Jersey City, NJ 07311-3881.)

Jacobson, Alan, *How to Detect Fraud Through Auditing,* Altamonte Springs, FL: The Institute of Internal Auditors Research Foundation, 1990.

Kelley, Thomas P., "The COSO Report: Challenge and Counterchallenge," *Journal of Accountancy,* Feb. 1993, pp. 10–18.

Keys, E. Theodore, *How to Save Millions,* Altamonte Springs, FL: The Institute of Internal Auditors, 1988.

Marsh, Hugh L., and Thomas E. Powell, "The Audit Committee Charter: Rx for Fraud Prevention," *Journal of Accountancy,* Feb. 1989, pp. 55–57.

McNamie, Patrick, "The New Yellow Book: Focus on Internal Controls," *Journal of Accountancy,* Oct. 1993, pp. 83–86.

Report of the National Commission on Fraudulent Financial Reporting, Washington, DC: National Commission on Fraudulent Financial Reporting, 1987.

Rezaee, Zabihollah, "Implementing the COSO Report," *Management Accounting,* July 1994, pp. 35–37.

Statement on Auditing Standards No. 53, "The Auditor's Responsibility to Detect and Report Errors and Irregularities," April 1988. New York: Auditing Standards Board, American Institute of Certified Public Accountants.

Statement on Auditing Standards No. 54, "Illegal Acts by Clients," April 1988. New York: Auditing Standards Board, American Institute of Certified Public Accountants.

Statement on Auditing Standards No. 55, "Consideration of the Internal Control Structure in a Financial Statement Audit," April 1988. New York: Auditing Standards Board, American Institute of Certified Public Accountants.

Sweeny, Robert B., "Executive Summary: The Report of the National Commission on Fraudulent Financial Reporting," *Management Accounting,* March 1989, pp. 17–26.

Willson, James D., and Steven J. Root, *Internal Auditing Manual* (2nd ed.). Boston: Warren, Gorham & Lamont, 1989. Chaps. 17, 22, 23, 24, and 25.

CHAPTER 10

The Internal Audit Function

10-1 INTRODUCTION

The question might well be asked, "Why should the controller have an interest in the internal audit function?" There are several reasons. First, in many companies, especially the smaller ones, the chief internal auditor often reports to the chief accounting official. Under these circumstances, the controller should have a good understanding of the basics of internal auditing. Second, as mentioned in Chapter 9 on internal controls, the controller is probably the executive most likely to be held responsible for the adequacy of the systems of internal control, and internal auditing is an important element of such a system. He should therefore have a good knowledge of what an internal auditor ought to do in regard to examining the control system, among other duties, and how to judge the effectiveness of the job being done. Additionally, the internal audit function, through its operational auditing activity, can suggest improvements in departmental practices or procedures so as to increase efficiency. The controller should be interested in improved productivity not only in the departments reporting to him, but also in all financial and operating departments.

Consequently, this chapter attempts to review some of the important organizational and operational aspects of the internal auditing function. More detailed information may be gleaned from the many books and periodicals covering the subject, including the Selected References.

10-2 INTERNAL AUDITING DEFINED

Internal auditing has been variously defined in professional literature. Each definition differs in some connotation or point of emphasis, for example:

1. Internal auditing is an independent appraisal function established within an organization to examine and evaluate its activities as a service to the organization.[1]

2. Internal auditing, which is ultimately responsible to the owners of the enterprise, is a service to senior management and other enterprise interests that includes (1) monitoring management controls; (2) anticipating, identifying, and assessing risks to enterprise assets and activities; (3) investigating actual and potential lapses of control and incidents of risk; and (4) making recommendations for improvement of control, the response to risk, and the attainment of enterprise objectives.[2]

3. Internal auditing is an independent appraisal of the diverse operations and controls within an organization to determine whether risks are identified and reduced, acceptable policies and procedures are followed, established standards are met, resources are used efficiently and economically, and the organization's objectives are achieved.[3]

4. Internal auditing . . . is organized and operated primarily for the purpose of conducting audits, in accordance with professional standards, of systems of internal control, including operational controls and information systems processing applications and techniques. The evidential matter gathered from these audits forms the basis for furnishing opinions and other relevant information to affected members of management and the board of directors, or audit committees thereof, as is necessary in the opinion of the chief auditor and performing members of the audit team . . .[4]

While readers may differ with some aspect of each of these above statements and their connotations, the first definition is the authoritative voice of The Institute of Internal Auditors. Some significant points derived from the four statements include:

1. The function is an internal and independent appraisal one.

2. The reviews should be conducted in accordance with professional standards.

3. The principal subject of the appraisal or review is the operations and controls of the entity.

---

[1] The Institute of Internal Auditors, Inc., *Standards for Professional Practice of Internal Auditing* (Altamonte Springs, FL: The Institute of Internal Auditors, 1981).

[2] Robert K. Mautz, Ph.D., Peter Tiessen, Ph.D., and Robert H. Colson, Ph.D., *Internal Auditing: Directions and Opportunities* (Altamonte Springs, FL: The Institute of Internal Auditors, 1984), pp. 6–7.

[3] Larry B. Sawyer in "Letters to the Editor," *The Internal Auditor*, Aug. 1984, p. 6.

[4] James D. Willson, and Steven J. Root, *Internal Auditing Manual*, 2nd ed. (Boston: Warren, Gorham & Lamont, 1989), pp. 1–4 and 1–5.

4. The objective of the appraisal is to form an opinion as to:

- Adequacy of internal controls.
- Degree of compliance with standards or established policies and procedures.
- Efficiency and effectiveness of the policies and procedures.
- The extent to which organizational objectives are achieved.

5. The work product is opinions and related findings and recommendations.

If the appraisal or audit is objective, then questions such as to whom the function is ultimately responsible, whether the auditors monitor or test-check controls, and such matters are perhaps of more academic interest than of practical concern to the management of a private enterprise.

A new term that arisen that may eventually become a function of the internal auditor—*forensic accounting*. We define forensic accounting as collecting financial evidence in cases of misuse of corporate assets that may have legal implications for those involved. Forensic accounting has been performed for many years, but usually by external consultants. Those conducting such analyses must be informed about what financial evidence will be admissible in court, and know how to properly interview any witnesses. These are not skills normally needed for internal auditing. Consequently, we will only lightly touch upon forensic accounting issues in this chapter, and recommend that management continue to bring in forensic experts when they choose to prosecute illegal activities.

10-3 SOURCE OF AUTHORITY FOR THE FUNCTION

With the recent increased attention being given to internal controls, including the recommendation of The Treadway Commission that "Public companies should maintain an effective internal audit function staffed with an adequate number of qualified personnel appropriate to the size and the nature of the company" (see Chapter 9), the authority for the function should be substantive. A clear definition of duties, responsibilities, and authority coming from a top-level source in the entity, is highly desirable.

The source of authority for the audit function often is now established in one of four ways: (1) in accordance with the bylaws of the corporation, (2) by resolution of the board of directors, (3) by general order of the chief executive officer, or (4) as published as a Corporate Policy Directive approved by the CEO.

The Policy Directive or other document establishing the function presumably would include the following:

- Company policy clearly establishing the function.
- Reason or purpose in establishing the function.
- Organizational reporting relationship.
- Responsibilities of the function head.
- Responsibilities of other operating managers as regards the function.

One such directive for a decentralized manufacturing company is shown in Figure 10-1. The related functional outline or position description of the chief internal auditor is illustrated in Figure 10-2.

Figure 10-1   Audit Charter for a Large Manufacturing Company.

I. **Policy.** It is the policy of the company to maintain a comprehensive program of internal auditing as an overall control measure and as a service to the organization. Its purpose is to aid corporate management and management at operational levels in achieving business goals without undue risk.

II. **Responsibilities:**

A. The Senior Vice-President–Finance is responsible for providing direction to the Corporate Director–Internal Audit in carrying out company policy in regard to the corporate audit function.

B. The Corporate Director–Internal Audit is responsible for the following:

   1. Designing and implementing procedural guidelines to assure that

      a. Internal controls of reporting entities achieve the objectives thereof and adequately safeguard the assets of the company.

      b. Financial statements of reporting entities are complete and accurate and comply with corporate policy, generally accepted accounting principles, requirements of government agencies such as the Securities and Exchange Commission and the Cost Accounting Standards Board, etc.

      c. Reporting entities are in compliance with operational policies and standards of ethical business practices that promote the well-being of the company.

      d. Controls over the development, maintenance, and operation of electronic data processing systems are sufficient to result in the processing of accurate and complete data.

   2. Coordinating coverage with independent outside auditors, division and subsidiary auditors, and others.

   3. Designing an annual plan for audit coverage that fulfills the responsibility of the department.

   4. Performing supervisory functions and staff training and development activities.

   5. Providing written reports of audit findings to such levels of management as may be necessary to effect remedial action.

   6. Performing and reporting on special reviews as may be required by the Audit Committee of the Board of Directors, the Senior Vice-President–Finance, or others.

C. The manager of each operating element is responsible for:

   1. Providing the Corporate Internal Audit Department sufficient access to records, documents, personnel, and facilities to enable the department to carry out its function.

   2. Providing timely written responses to the Corporate Internal Audit Department indicating actions taken or planned regarding the recommendations set forth in the audit report.

Figure 10-2 Position Description of Chief Internal Auditor.

Corporate Functional Outline

No.:	CFO No. 316
Page:	1 of 2
Date:	12 October 1994
Supermodel:	CPD No. 212
	dtd. 4 June 1982

CHIEF INTERNAL AUDITOR

SUMMARY

The Chief Internal Auditor reports to the Senior Vice President-Finance and is responsible for directing a comprehensive program of internal auditing as an overall internal control measure to aid management at the Corporate Office and at operating elements in achieving business goals in accordance with established policies and procedures and without undue business risk.

SPECIFIC RESPONSIBILITIES

1. Develops and maintains the auditing standards, the approach, and the techniques by which all internal auditing at _____ is to be performed and publishes this information in the Corporate Auditing Manual.

2. Devises annual plans of audit coverage that will result in a reasonable sampling of relevant business transactions, cycles, functions, and operations and provides a basis for forming opinions and reporting other information with respect to:

   • the adequacy of the company's total internal accounting controls systems for achieving stated objectives

   • compliance by company elements with Corporate Policy Directives, with emphasis on those pertaining to standards of business conduct

   • the efficiency and effectiveness of functions and techniques used by company elements for achieving operational objectives

   • the adequacy of security, control, and operational efficiency present in the company's various electronic data processing installations.

(continued)

Figure 10-2 *(continued)*

3. Coordinates audit coverage with independent outside auditors and operating element internal audit organizations to ensure reasonable coverage and to avoid unnecessary duplications of effort.

4. Provides advice and counsel to operating element management and chief auditors in organizing and staffing internal auditing organizations.

5. Reviews the performance of company element internal auditing functions for compliance with the requirements of the Corporate Auditing Manual.

6. Collects evidential matter when the company takes legal action against employees or other entities involving misappropriation of company assets.

7. Where appropriate, coordinates assignments with subsidiary and division management to facilitate efficient completion.

8. Develops the professional capability of the internal audit staff by on-the-job training, staff meetings, seminars, and other forms of professional training.

9. Ensures that evidential matter contained in work papers adequately documents works performed and supports conclusions contained in reports.

10. Reviews audit report drafts to ensure their high quality and to ensure that matters requiring management action are brought to its attention in a timely fashion.

11. Follows up audit recommendations to determine that they are implemented by affected management.

12. Directs the performance of such other special reviews as many be requested by the Audit Committee of the Board of Directors, the Senior Vice President-Finance, or others.

13. Reports to the Audit Committee of the Board of Directors the opinions and other information developed from the program of audit coverage.

* * * *

10-4 THE BASIC ACTIVITIES

Having defined internal auditing, and having examined the source of authority for the function, it may be useful to discuss some of the essential activities. These basic functions perhaps can be gleaned from the audit charter (Figure 10-1) as well as the functional outline for the chief internal auditor (Figure 10-2). However, the following brief summary may be helpful. These basic functions or activities might be described as the various kinds of auditing usually performed. Any such classifications would usually be based on the audit objectives or purposes, or the area to be examined, perhaps combined with the related technical skills found necessary. Any number of audit objectives could be devised; but a practical segregation, recognizing current general practices, is:

- Financial.
- Operational.
- Information systems (electronic data processing).
- Ethical business practices.

A brief commentary on each category follows.

(a) FINANCIAL AUDITS

A financial audit could be described as the traditional type of internal audit. It basically describes examinations relating to the reliability of the accounting records and the financial statements, including internal controls.

An expanded statement of the principal audit objective might be the following:

- To determine the reliability and accuracy of the financial reporting system, including:
    a. The financial records.
    b. The financial statements.
    c. The related management reports.
    d. The consistency of interim financial statements with the GAAP used in the published financial statements or appropriate reconciliation with them.
- To ascertain the sufficiency of the system of internal control so as to assure that the internal control objectives pertaining to authorization, recording, and reporting of business activities are attained, and that the related safeguarding of assets is achieved. (See Chapter 9.)

External Factors. The audit program necessary to achieve the financial audit objective—ascertaining the sufficiency of the internal control system—may require modification as the method of conducting business changes. While a review of internal control long has related to matters within the company and under the control of the management, now the control environment must recognize the impact of external factors—especially the newer and closer relationship between the company and its important customers and/or suppliers.

Two examples will illustrate the new conditions. With the development of extensive electronic transmission, a large retail customer may bypass the sales department of the manufacturer, avoid the extensive paperwork and control points of its own order department, and send the purchase request directly to the factory. Therefore, the internal audit department may need to review the control procedures for the buyers department of the retailer. Or with the just-in-time (JIT) manufacturing system, inspection of the raw materials or purchased parts may in fact be performed by the supplier instead of the receiving department of the manufacturer. Again, the internal auditors may have reason to review the external quality control system and control over defective units.

Adequacy of the internal control system, and other required procedures, may extend to an examination or consideration of external influences, including required procedures of regulatory agencies.

(b) OPERATIONAL AUDITS

In recent years, operational auditing increasingly has become an important responsibility of the internal auditing department. Operational auditing is a sort of generic term, which is also described as systems auditing, efficiency auditing, functional auditing, management auditing, expanded scope auditing, or organizational auditing. An operational audit may be defined as a systematic review and evaluation of an organizational unit (or even an entire organization) for the purpose of determining its effectiveness and efficiency. (Such audits may be made of government units as well as organizations in the private sector.)

Just what areas in a particular company might be selected for these non-financial audits varies from entity to entity. One factor in determining the scope of operational reviews is the attitude of management. For example, some managements might be of the opinion that the auditor could review procedures and controls to determine their adequacy. But this same management could be reluctant to have the internal auditors evaluate operating performance of, say, an engineering department. Then, at the other extreme are those managements that expect the largely accounting-trained staff to judge performance of functions where the auditors usually are not qualified to reach such conclusions without assistance of members of the discipline involved. So what may be realistically examined will depend also on the type of industry, the capability of the audit staff, and available human resources to draw on as to certain activities. It should be mentioned in passing that the audit staff may permanently or temporarily add persons knowledgeable in other disciplines: design, industrial engineering, manufacturing, marketing, computer application, and research, and so on.

Recognizing that there may be limited segments in each function either that the internal auditors cannot evaluate or about which they must be exceedingly careful in reaching conclusions (more so than usual), some activities typically considered for operational audits include:

- Financial management.
- Credit and collections.
- Inventory management.
- Facilities management.
- Marketing management.
- Program management.
- Retirement plan.

- R&D management.
- Personnel policies.
- Purchasing policies and procedures.
- Risk management (insurance).
- Quality control.
- Critical success factors.

At a minimum, the internal auditor should assist in measuring the company's critical success factors (CSFs). These are the issues that management feels are key to the success of the company. For example, a CSF for customer service might be defined as the number of times a phone rings before being answered by the customer service staff. As another example, a CSF might be filling 99% of all orders within one day of order receipt. The internal audit staff can measure both of these CSFs. Also, for an MRP system, the audit staff can conduct ongoing audits of the three CSFs related to MRP—accurate inventories, bills of material, and labor routings.

(c) INFORMATION SYSTEMS AUDITING (EDP)

The third classification of internal auditing listed earlier is information systems auditing, also called EDP auditing. This category is separate, probably because of the technical knowledge required about computer applications, especially in a rapidly changing environment.

With the growth in the dependence of companies on computers, for both operations and information, with a rapidly evolving and changing technology, with evidence that insufficient attention was directed to adequate control in many original installations, and with a trend to decentralized organizations, business management has become increasingly wary about the dependability of computer operations. Responding to this concern has been a growth in the number of auditors skilled in EDP audits and the increasing competence of such auditors, as well as new powerful software programs and other tools to assist in the examination.

Suffice it to say that the objectives of I/S auditing include:

- Accurate and complete processing of data.
- Adequate internal controls to safeguard data and assets.
- Efficient and effective EDP operations.
- Development and maintenance of information systems that satisfy user requirements.

Four basic types of I/S auditing have been developed.[5] These are:

1. Detailed functional auditing.
2. Installation reviews.
3. Applications auditing.
4. Developing systems auditing.

---

[5] James D. Willson, and Steven J. Root, *Internal Auditing Manual,* 2nd ed. (Boston: Warren, Gorham & Lamont, 1989), pp. 27–5 to 27–23.

The reader may wish to check the references for distinctions as to scope of auditing, and the facets of I/S that are reviewed. Basically all are post-implementation audits except the latter. In this instance the high cost of making changes once the system is designed has caused the auditor to be involved during the system development rather than afterward.

A new concern for internal auditors is the control risk associated with electronic data interchange (EDI) systems. These systems create transactions with suppliers and customers without any paper at all (indeed, that is one of the reasons for having EDI). The lack of paper creates internal control concerns, since, without proper planning, there may be no audit trail for EDI transactions. For example, if a customer generates an order on EDI, it usually flows through a third-party processor (known as a value-added network, or VAN), and is electronically pulled from a VAN mailbox by the EDI software of the company without a paper or electronic record being kept anywhere.

To ensure an EDI audit trail, the internal auditor must be included in the EDI installation phase, and review the adequacy of the audit trail. The audit trail should include systems to authorize users, record transactions, and reconcile transactions with other internal systems (only useful if transactions are generated by the company and not with a trading partner). Let's look at these items in more detail:

1. *Authorize Users*—EDI empowers a user to order products from suppliers as well as pay them; this concentrates great responsibility in the EDI user. The internal auditor should rigorously test the authorization approval and deletion procedure as well as access procedures. Access procedures involve authenticating the person requesting access to the system as the same person for whom access has been authorized; many new authentication systems are now available, and the internal auditor should therefore review biometric systems (e.g., automated fingerprinting, retina vascularization, keyboard latencies, dynamics of the signature, voice recognition, and geometry of the hand).

2. *Record Transactions*—EDI systems generally do not retain transaction records for very long. However, the internal auditor can recommend the need for an EDI add-on transaction storage facility, and then test the effectiveness of such a system. In addition, the auditor can send confirmations to VANs and trading partners regarding the authenticity of EDI transactions. However, once again, these external entities may not record transactions for long periods, rendering confirmations useless.

3. *Reconcile Transactions*—EDI systems are frequently linked to MRP systems to automatically generate EDI ordering transactions. Alternatively, orders may be manually input into the EDI system. In either case, the internal auditor should either manually reconcile EDI transactions to internally generated requirements, or review the output of an automatic reconciling system. Without such a transaction crosscheck, the company may suffer from inadequate parts orders or so many that it cannot use all of the parts received.

The problem with the above controls is that only one, user authorization, protects the company from loss. The other controls inform the company of losses after the fact. In order to keep corporate losses at a minimum, the internal auditor must recommend the creation of and then review on-line auditing modules that flag EDI control problems as they occur. For example, an on-line authorization module would not just record an attempt at unauthorized access, but also would notify company personnel of the transgression immediately.

A final issue regarding EDI is that the internal auditor must test EDI backup systems. The problem with EDI is that it increases the company's dependence on computers. If the EDI hardware or software crashes, then the company must have off-site backup storage, hot sites, and well-tested backup and recovery procedures. The internal auditor should closely review such backup systems to ensure that the company will suffer minimal "down time" if its EDI systems fail.

(d) ETHICAL BUSINESS PRACTICE AUDITING

The last category of internal auditing has been described as ethical business practice auditing. Originally internal auditing was focused mainly on financial audits, with some reviews being made for fraud. Then the points of emphasis expanded to operational auditing, and I/S examinations. Now, with an apparent growth in white-collar crime, including management involvement, increased attention is being paid to ethical business practice auditing. This has been designated in some current literature as a separate type of examination.

In 1985, the Institute of Internal Auditors issued Statement of Internal Auditing (S/AS) No. 3 entitled, "Deterrence, Detection, Investigation, and Reporting of Fraud."[6] In this abbreviated review of the standard, it should be mentioned that the guidance statement, while providing no specific audit procedures, does say this: "Internal auditors should maintain sufficient knowledge of fraud patterns to enable them to be reasonably effective in identifying opportunities for potential perpetrators to commit fraud. They should be alert to such opportunities and evidence that indicates fraud might have been committed." Then later in the section, dealing with detection of fraud, the statement is made that, "Internal auditors cannot be expected to have knowledge equivalent to a person whose sole responsibility is detecting fraud and other irregularities."

This is a difficult area for audit. Those responsible for such a review must be aware of the care that must be exercised in reaching conclusions. If a decision is made to investigate for possible fraud, steps must be taken to ensure that the review is conducted by persons, known as forensic accountants, who have the appropriate type and level of technical expertise. Forensic accountants usually have considerable accounting experience; they can effectively interview witnesses and reconstruct financial information that will be admissible in court. Most internal auditors do not possess this kind of training, so specialists are normally hired to deal with fraud situations.

Some CEOs may think that their internal audit staffs can deal with data collection to prove that a fraud was committed. If so, how would an internal auditor prove that a warehouse manager was stealing inventory if the manager had burned down the warehouse? Alternatively, how would an internal auditor prove that a company trucker was stealing excess fuel from the company's fuel depot? The construction of a plausible case against either person in these scenarios is clearly outside of the scope of an internal auditor. If the CEO is still determined to use internal staff to investigate such situations, then, at a minimum, legal advice should be sought.

See Chapter 9 for commentary on types of fraud, on circumstances that encourage fraud, and on warning signals or red flags that might indicate fraudulent activity.

---

[6] See *Ibid.*, Chapter 22, for a detailed statement of the standard and for a lengthy discussion of business ethics and fraud.

10-5 SOME ORGANIZATIONAL MATTERS

A few comments are in order about the organizational status of the internal audit function, some reporting/access relationships, and the departmental structure. When establishing the internal audit function or examining the best arrangements, some commonplace questions such as these arise:

- To whom should the chief internal auditor report?
- What is the most suitable departmental structure for the auditing activities?
- When the basic structure of the operational elements is decentralized, what is the best organizational pattern for internal auditing?
- What should be the relationship of the internal audit function to the audit committee of the board of directors?
- What is the relationship of the internal auditing function to the independent accountants?

The suggestions made in the following few paragraphs reflect the practical experience of the authors. The circumstances of each situation ultimately must govern decisions.

(a) REPORTING LEVEL

Most experienced business executives know that the amount of "clout" exercised by managers and how well they are listened to, initially at least, depend on where they stand in the management structure. Moreover, the CFOs, as well as some other executives, know that to be effective the internal audit function should report at a high level. But how high? The recent Treadway Commission report (see Chapter 9) includes this statement in its recommendations for the public company: ". . . The internal auditor's qualifications, staff, status within the company, reporting lines, and relationship with the audit committee of the board of directors must be adequate to ensure the internal audit function's effectiveness and objectivity." A "sort of" organization chart included in the Treadway Report and intended to depict the corporate culture, seems to show the internal audit function as reporting to the CEO. Possibilities include reporting to:

- The chief executive officer.
- The audit committee.
- A high level (nonfinancial) senior operating executive.
- The controller.
- The chief financial officer.

Following are some summary comments on each of these alternatives:
- *The Chief Executive Officer.* While such a reporting level would be high, indeed:
    a. In many instances the CEO has neither the time nor the inclination to supervise an internal audit function.

b. Frankly speaking, usually the CEO does not have the financial background or expertise to be very helpful in providing adequate guidance.

c. The CEO's time probably can be used more productively in dealing with strategic planning or other major policy matters.

- *The Audit Committee.* The relationship with the audit committee certainly must be close. However, probably no outside director or board committee should assume responsibility for direction of an ongoing, normal company function on a day to day basis. Such actions might be viewed as interfering with the management of the enterprise. Additionally, many audit committee members have neither the time nor background.

- *A High Level (Nonfinancial) Executive.* Generally the same comments apply to such a reporting status as to the CEO alternative discussed above.

- *The Controller.* Selection of the controller as the reporting level certainly has much to support it. This executive:

a. Has an immediate interest in the effectiveness of the internal controls as well as the internal audit function.

b. Usually possesses the requisite accounting/financial background.

c. Operates at a high management level.

d. Usually has the time and inclination to supervise a function such as internal auditing.

e. Usually is much aware of the importance of the internal audit function.

f. Has a good sense of the areas of greatest risk as to controls.

In those circumstances where the controller is in fact the chief financial officer, probably the chief internal auditor should report at this level. However, objectively speaking, much of the activity of the audit function will involve an appraisal of the accounting principles, systems and practices for which the controller is responsible. Further, any examination of the internal control system again is a review of a largely controller-responsibility area. It may be argued therefore that much of the review would be regarded as the controller "auditing himself." So, especially in larger companies, probably the CIA should *not* report to the controller.

- *Chief Financial Officer.* When the financial function is segregated or departmentalized as among financial vice-president, treasurer, controller, and possibly others, the chief internal auditor should report to the CFO. This provides the advantages similar to those of reporting to the controller, together with a possibly desirable segregation of responsibility for this audit function from responsibility for the accounting systems and procedures, and so on.

The six most often designated titles to whom the chief internal auditor reports functionally for U.S./Canada medium and large companies include:[7]

- Audit or Executive Committee.
- Vice-President-Finance.

---

[7] *Ibid.*, pp. 7–26.

- Vice President and/or Chief Financial Officer.
- Controller or assistant.
- President.
- Chairman of the Board and CEO.

Again, the totality of the circumstances must be weighed. Arguments could be made, in particular cases, for a reporting relationship to any one of the several enumerated above. In any event, the chief internal auditor, regardless of reporting level, must be assured of unimpeded access to appropriate levels of management, including the CEO, the Audit Committee, and the independent accountants.

(b) DEPARTMENTAL STRUCTURE OF INTERNAL AUDITING

Another frequently raised question concerns the most appropriate departmental organization structure for the internal audit function. Again, some of the usual common-sense factors must be considered in selecting a suitable framework:

- Size of company.
- Dominant management philosophy (centralized or decentralized organization).
- Management regard for financial/accounting functions.
- Types of audits required (financial, operational, internal control, information systems, special, etc.).
- Physical location of units.
- Qualifications of staff.
- Industry practice.

A typical departmental structure in a centralized status, with sophisticated electronic information systems, and a desire for operational audits as well as financial audits, and a "project" approach[8] to many special audits is shown in Figure 10-3.

(c) CENTRALIZED VS. DECENTRALIZED STRUCTURE

Another typical structure question relates to the centralized vs. decentralized problem. In a company with a predominantly decentralized structure—each division or subsidiary has a profit responsibility and is semiautonomous, how should the internal audit department be organized? Should the audit unit of the division or subsidiary report to the corporate chief internal auditor or to the general manager of the division?

The most effective structure is a decentralized one, as illustrated in Figure 10-4. Note that the unit audit chief has a "dotted line" relationship to the corporate chief internal auditor. On such a basis:

1. The unit audit chief reports to the general manager of the division and is on a boss-subordinate relationship, i.e., an *administrative* reporting status. In this

---

[8] On a project basis, different audit skills may be grouped for a particular audit project. During an extended period, a particular auditor may report to differing audit managers for each separate audit project.

Figure 10-3   Organization Chart—Centralized Internal Audit Operation.

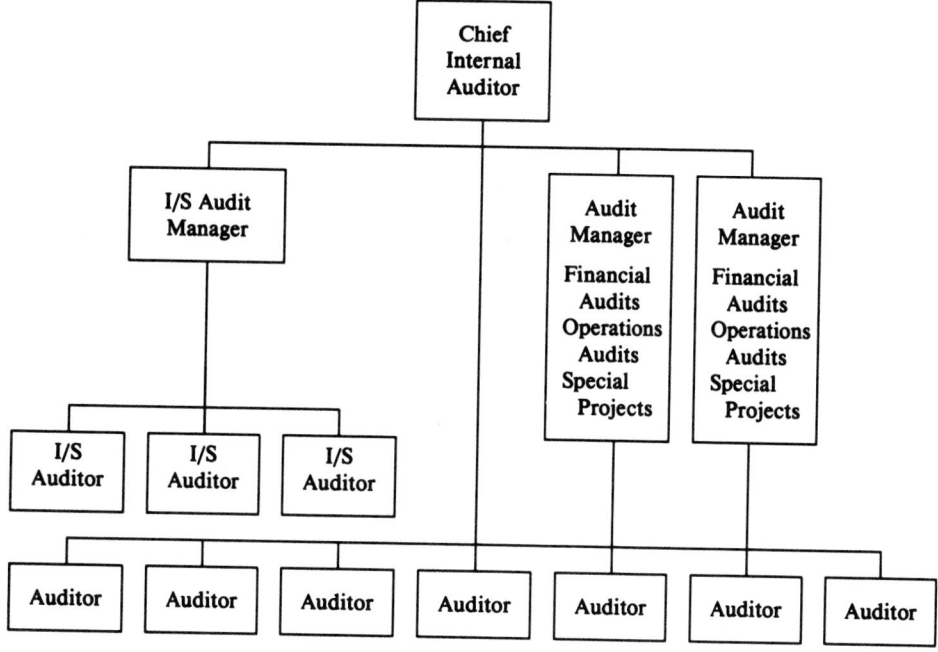

way, the division has its own audit group to assist in the necessary appraisal activity of financial systems, internal control, and operating efficiency.

2. The unit audit chief has a *functional* reporting responsibility to the chief internal auditor as to how technically and professionally the audit performs—and often as to the subject to be audited.

Under such an arrangement, the chief internal auditor has a voice in the *technical* aspects of unit auditing, without such unit being regarded as a "snooping" operation of the corporate office. The corporate audit group occasionally could be assigned special duties in a unit audit.

(d) RELATIONSHIP TO THE AUDIT COMMITTEE

Increased attention has focused on the need for an audit committee of the board of directors, composed of outside or independent members of the board. Among other duties most arrangements provide for this committee to oversee the company's financial reporting process and internal controls, and to monitor in a general way some of the activities of the internal audit department.

The chief internal auditor should be prepared, probably annually, for an exchange of information or response to these matters:

1. A review of the proposed program of audit coverage for the upcoming year, including man-hours, areas of interest, and total budget.

Figure 10-4 Internal Audit Department Structure in a Decentralized Environment.

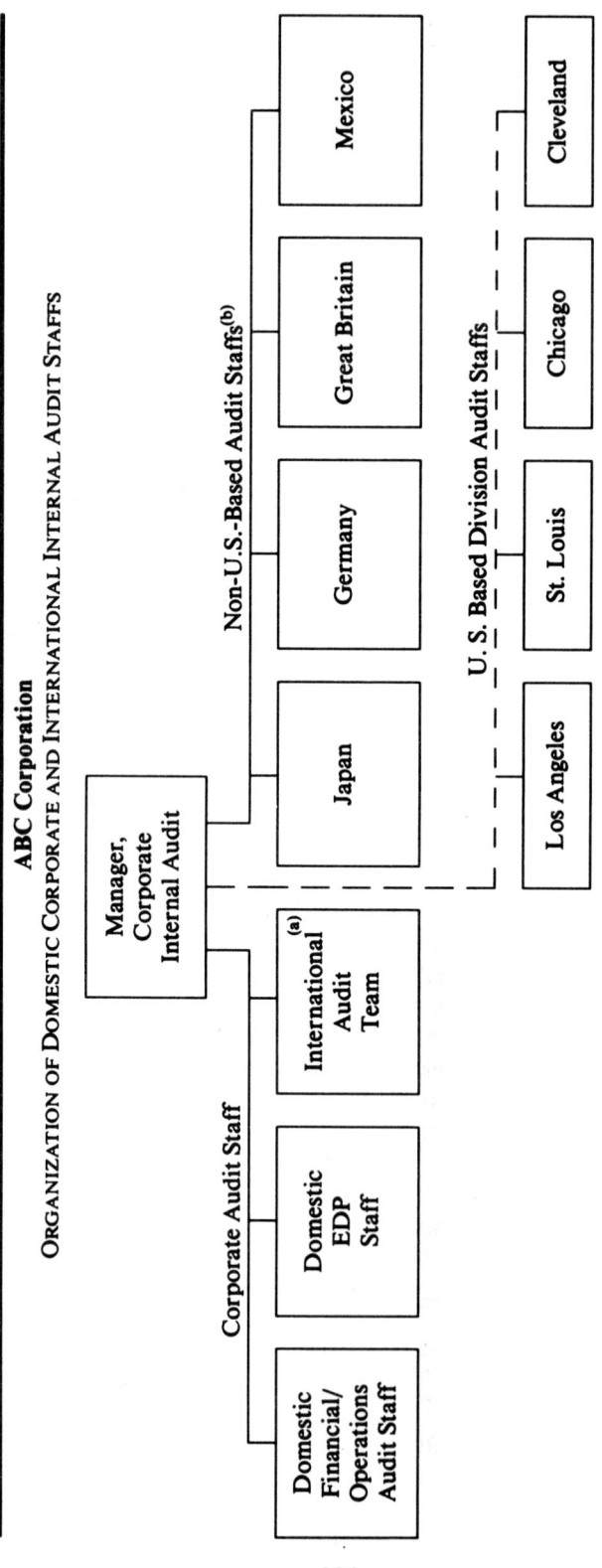

ABC Corporation

ORGANIZATION OF DOMESTIC CORPORATE AND INTERNATIONAL INTERNAL AUDIT STAFFS

(a) All international EDP auditing is performed by the domestic corporate I/S staff who coordinates and integrates its work with the international staff.
(b) Each of the audit staffs reports to a Director of Finance or General Manager of the subsidiary or division. Audit plans and activities are reported to and coordinated with the Manager, Corporate Internal Audit.

2. A review of the internal audit activities of the past year, including comparison of planned and actual man-hours on the regular or special examinations and a general summary of findings.

3. A special report on any significant and troubling findings on a particular major audit, and corrective action taken.

4. A review of the internal control systems with discussion of significant weaknesses found and corrective action taken.

5. The results of any special examination requested by the audit committee.

6. Personnel information so that the audit committee may evaluate the internal audit staff as to professional background, experience, effectiveness, and the program for professional development.

This listing comprises the more important subjects for exchange between the chief internal auditor and the audit committee. It should be repeated that in this period of increased concern with corporate governance, the CIA should have unimpeded access to the audit committee (and CEO), regardless of the organizational reporting structure.

(e) RELATIONSHIP TO THE INDEPENDENT ACCOUNTANTS

Another "organizational matter" discussed in this chapter is the relationship between the internal auditor and the independent accountant, also called the independent or external auditor.

Both groups of auditors, external and internal, are usually strong in the accounting discipline and have a common interest in certain areas—although the emphasis may differ. These points of shared interest include:

- The accounting system.
- The system of internal controls.
- Financial reporting.
- Business ethics and conduct.
- Compliance with statutes and other legal requirements.

Since each group performs investigations in these areas, among others, each may benefit through the work efforts of the other. Not only can audits be more effective, but also external audit fees may be reduced. However, close coordination is a must, and this is the responsibility principally of either the chief financial officer or the controller.

Business management looks to the independent auditor to provide an opinion on the fairness of operating results and financial condition as reflected in the annual financial statements. Additionally the external accountants may perform interim financial statement reviews, provide tax advice, and other management advisory services. Management expects the internal auditor to provide a continuing review of the internal control system, the correctness of accounting records and internal reports, conformance to established policies and procedures, and to perform efficiency audits and reviews of business conduct. But, despite the differences in services provided, instances of specific interdependency and cooperation can occur in these areas:

- *Review of Internal Control System.* When the work of the internal auditor is deemed satisfactory in a professional sense, it may be considered by the independent auditor in determining the nature and timing of his own audit procedures. (Of course, it may be helpful if the work to be done by the internal auditor is discussed in advance with the independent accountant.)

- *Transaction Tests.* Where substantial transaction tests are made by the internal auditor, these may influence the audit procedures of the independent accountant (subject to the conditions mentioned above).

- *Access to Working Papers.* Sharing of working papers may avoid redundant effort.

- *Sharing of Audit Tools.* Each group often has developed generalized software, time-sharing programs, checklists, and audit questionnaires. The sharing or joint use of such tools can be mutually helpful.

- *Direct Assistance.* Often arrangements can be made for the internal auditors to directly assist the independent auditor during the course of his examination. If the internal audit staff is properly qualified (e.g., are CPAs, CMAs, CIAs, etc.), it is hoped they will perform audit procedures suitable to their professional experience (i.e., not "dog work").

    Conversely, the internal auditor may seek the assistance of the independent accountants. Examples could be on limited financial reviews, compliance checking, computer-aided audit procedures.

- *Training.* Some of the larger public accounting firms direct training programs for their own staff. Under appropriate circumstances, some internal auditors may attend such classes.

- *Technical Assistance.* Most of the major public accounting firms have developed copyrighted material, e.g., on income taxes, EDP, financial reporting. This often is made available to client company personnel, including the internal auditor.

The above discussed areas provide some examples where the efforts of any one group may be helpful to the other.

(f) INTERNAL VS. EXTERNAL AUDITORS: REDUCING THE TENSION

As indicated in the section on the relationship of the internal auditors to the independent accountants, there are several points of shared interest between the two organizations. Yet the cooperation between the two groups, especially at year-end, often is accomplished with some strain on both sides, and might be viewed as an uneasy alliance. It is the controller who is the principal interface of company management with those partners or managers conducting the independent audit and who, at the same time, must rely on the chief internal auditor's reviews to help maintain a strong system of internal controls, proper financial reporting, and a high ethical level of business conduct. Given the controller's interface role with both groups, he may be in a position to improve the working relationship between the two functions.

The extent and cause of the uneasy relationship differs from organization to organization, but these generalizations probably are valid: The outward strains between the two audit groups probably are more evident at the staff level rather than at the partner/chief internal auditor level. In some situations, the internal auditors are well-qualified CPAs with prior public experience, but in others, they do not have the advantage of the professional education and training, with the natural result that the public accountants sometimes regard the internal auditors as second-class citizens—mere accounting clerks. Moreover, the two audit groups have differing audit objectives; and the year-end audit by the independent accountants is more financially oriented than are the reviews by the internal auditors with his greater concern about efficiency and effectiveness of operations, compliance with policies and procedures, and internal controls. Further, there may exist a difference in emphasis, with the independent auditor concerned with the materiality threshold, but the internal auditor concentrating on correcting the procedure. Moreover, requirements as to working paper documentation, or methods of reviewing working papers, or clearing of review notes may differ. However, the external audit staff may have only a limited understanding of the function of the internal auditor and the business environment in a particular entity. On the other hand, the internal auditor may not appreciate the need for some of the independent auditor procedures. Then, too, the independent audit staff tends to be quite young, while the internal auditors tend to be older, and often with long business experience. So each side shares in the cause of the problem.

What can the controller do to improve the relationship? The principals in each of the two audit groups should enlighten their staffs on the role of the other organization, and about the objectives, problems, and environments, and so on. It is also worthwhile for the controller to chair a joint one-day meeting with each group (or combined groups in some cases) to describe the functions and viewpoint of the other organization—from the perspective of the chief accounting officer of the entity. Each of the groups can benefit from a better understanding of the of the audit assignments of the other.

10-6 THE HUMAN RESOURCE FACTOR

Prior sections of this chapter have briefly discussed the nature of internal auditing, the source of authority for the function, and some basic organizational matters. But the key to a successful, effective internal audit department lies largely in the capabilities and motivation of the audit staff, together with proper management direction. It is true that in the past many internal auditors were glorified clerks whose principal duties consisted of checking the mathematical accuracy of invoices, or tabulations of inventory, and similar routine operations. But in most companies those days are long gone. Now, as likely as not, the internal audit staff consists of professional accountants, many having the B.S., B.A., or M.B.A. degree, and perhaps holding the CPA or CMA certificate. Additionally, some may be proficient in computers or be professional engineers. So a few comments are in order about personnel management in the internal auditing department.

The same principles that apply to sound personnel management, more recently also called human resource management, in any function apply equally to the internal audit function. A few observations, with some specificity as to the auditing activity, and applying to all but the smallest of companies, are as follows:

- *Job Descriptions.* Written job descriptions probably should be developed for each audit level. They may follow the format illustrated in Figure 10-2, indicating

(a) the general responsibility and (b) specific responsibilities. Some also provide the expected job qualifications (primarily education preferred, experience required, etc.).

- *Recruiting.* Job candidates to be screened, interviewed, and evaluated, etc. tend to be located by three means: (a) direct advertising (*The Wall Street Journal,* business section of local newspapers, *Journal of Accountancy, Management Accounting,* etc.); (b) informal checks with associates, either within or from without the company; and (c) inquiries of the several professional societies—Institute of Internal Auditors (IIA), American Institute of CPAs (AICPA), etc.

  These searches may be handled directly by the Personnel Department of the company or a professional recruiter or the chief internal auditor and perhaps the audit managers. Sources of the candidates include:

  a. Universities and colleges (business schools). A great many of the candidates have either a bachelor's degree or an M.B.A. Many with good accounting backgrounds are attracted into public accounting firms, or private industry (accounting department) to the exclusion of internal auditing. However, some will consider a good spot in the internal auditing department.

  b. Professional firms. When a promotion, or good compensation, including fringe benefits, is offered, some will leave professional practice (travel disadvantage, etc.) and enter internal auditing—as a chance to move higher in a particular company.

  c. Other private companies. Again, the opportunity for a higher-level job will cause some experienced internal auditors to relocate to other companies.

  d. Internal sources. Finally, some entities feel that knowledge of the company is an important factor in good audit performance and encourage internal transfers. Some managements believe auditing is useful experience in moving up the management chain.

- *Performance Measurement.* Performance measurement of the individual, usually annually in connection with a salary increase, is highly desirable as a motivational factor. The process may be somewhat subjective but could include a quality evaluation of each phase of the job, e.g., planning an audit, development of a good testing program, quality of documentation, perception of important audit points or findings, quantitative factor (speed, etc.), and audit follow-up. An evaluation of the auditor's communication ability also might be desirable.

- *Continual Professional Development.* Finally, given the rapid changes occurring in information technology, in available software for audits, and in management needs, based on improved analytical techniques, most auditors probably would find professional development most helpful. Such actions as the following might be considered:

  a. Outside training at company expense—university attendance, looking to an M.B.A. degree; seminars; conferences, etc.

  b. On-the-job training.

  c. Maintenance of an information distribution network—publications, including daily and weekly business papers; professional literature (IIA, AICPA, etc.);

trade association data; government literature; CPA firms' publications; and textbooks.

d. In-house staff training—perhaps one afternoon a month.

e. Maintenance of a library.

10-7 OTHER INTERNAL AUDIT ACTIVITIES

All of the commentary in the preceding sections has been intended to provide an overview of the internal audit function: what it is, the basic segments, organization structure and some limited words about administrative matters. A great many subjects have not been discussed, including:

* Auditing standards.
* Planning and management of audits.
* "How-to" aspects of the audit function.
* Preparing effective audit reports.
* Some of the very technical audit procedures phases including sampling and specialized audit techniques using computers.
* Commentary on specialized audit subjects.

In a book on controllership it was considered best to take a broad viewpoint. If the controller is interested in these more detailed aspects, a great deal has been written, and some good reading material is included in the Selected References listing.

10-8 HOW SHOULD INTERNAL AUDITING BE EVALUATED?

Finally, of interest to the controller might be commentary on how internal auditing should be evaluated—whether by a special management task force or in the executive suite, or otherwise. This section may provide valuable clues on how he or she should measure the effectiveness of the internal auditing performed in his company.

To begin with, there are several sources of information that can be utilized in arriving at a decision as to the capability and effectiveness of the internal audit department. These include many of these:

* *Written Data*
  —Reports on specific audits.
  —Periodic activity reports (e.g., for the supervisors, CFO, or audit committee).
  —Summary audit plans.
  —Budget reports.
  —Comparison of audit plans and audits completed.
  —Organization charts.
  —Position descriptions.
  —Audit manual (policies and procedures).

- *Oral Data* (from)

  —Auditees.

  —Independent accountants of the company (who presumably have made internal audits, have dealt with the chief and his staff, and have read many audit reports).

  —Chief internal auditor and staff.

  —Executive to whom the department reports.

  —Audit committee (who has heard oral reports, answers to questions, etc.).

  —Others who have had contact with the department (CEO, top executives, etc.).

So there are numerous sources of information.

Given the growing importance of the internal audit function and greater expectations from the activities, the accounting firm of Price Waterhouse published an excellent guide, "Does Your Internal Audit Department Measure Up?,"[9] with a foreword by The Institute of Internal Auditors, for reading by internal auditors, management, and audit committee members.

It is suggested that a small task force of senior management, with staff assistance for gathering material, and using a common-sense approach to recognized management concepts and a review of demonstrated results of the department's work, should be able to reach a conclusion on the department's capabilities and effectiveness.[10] The approach is to ask some basic questions, and then make comments about what reasonably might be expected, for these important topics:

- The internal audit department—role and scope of activities.
- The effect of organizational status on independence.
- Personnel—a critical factor.
- Internal audit department management.
- Demonstrated performance.
- External quality assurance reviews.

The questions on each segment are well conceived and are republished here with the permission of Price Waterhouse.[11]

The Internal Audit Department—Role and Scope of Activities

Questions:

- Is there a policy statement defining the department's purpose, responsibilities and authority?

---

[9] New York, 1985.

[10] *Ibid.*, p. 1.

[11] Reprinted with permission of Price Waterhouse from "Does Your Internal Audit Department Measure Up?" pp. 1–15. © 1985 Price Waterhouse. All rights reserved.

- Has the policy statement been approved by the Board of Directors, the Audit Committee or an appropriate level of executive management?
- Does the policy statement provide for a scope of audit work which encompasses all of the organization's activities?
- Is the primary thrust of the department's activities in line with management expectations and principal needs?
- Is there an appropriate emphasis on the system of internal control, including relevant computer-based and administrative controls?
- Is the extent of the department's involvement with operational auditing consistent with management's objectives and the policy statement defining the department's activities?
- Has the internal audit department been assigned a role in reviewing and testing computer-based systems, EDP departmental organization, data security and disaster recovery procedures?
- Is the internal audit department actively involved in reviewing new computer-based systems during the development stage for the purpose of recommending controls necessary to minimize computer-related risks?
- Has the internal audit department been assigned a role in monitoring codes of employee conduct?
- Have reporting relationships with and access to the organization's audit committee been considered and specified?
- Do the internal auditors meet regularly with the Audit Committee?
- Are the scale and nature of any nonaudit projects assigned to the department such that (a) the audit schedule is not unduly disrupted, and (2) the objectivity of future audits is preserved?
- Have internal audit responsibilities for coordination of work with that of the external auditors been defined?
- In smaller organizations, is a special effort made to maintain internal audit priorities.

The Effect of Organizational Status on Independence

Questions:

- Is the department's organizational status consistent with the importance of its assigned responsibilities?
- Is the organizational level sufficient to ensure unrestricted audit coverage and appropriate action in response to audit findings?
- Does the corporate director of internal audit have functional responsibility for all internal audit activities?
- Does the form of departmental organization—i.e., centralized vs. decentralized promote audit independence and the effective management and supervision of day-to-day department activities?
- Does the internal audit department report to a level of management that will ensure that audit findings and recommendations will receive appropriate attention?

Personnel—a Critical Factor

Questions:

- Is the audit director a capable, articulate executive with a strong technical background?
- Do staff members have an appropriate educational background and is appropriate emphasis placed on professional certification, especially for department supervisors?
- Is there a proper mix of experience within the department to ensure adequate supervision and development of personnel?
- Does the staff include the necessary number of individuals with the specialized skills and level of experience needed for the department's work?
- Does the department have a staff development plan that is responsive to both organizational and individual needs and is continuing education an integral part of the plan?
- Is the department staffed and administered with a view toward providing adequate opportunities for career advancement?
- Is the staff large enough to achieve the department's goals?
- Is staff morale generally high and turnover at an acceptable level?
- Does the department have the respect and cooperation of others in the organization?

Internal Audit Department Management

Questions:

- Is there a comprehensive audit plan which provides for coverage within a reasonable time frame of all audit areas for which the department is responsible?
- Is there reasonable correlation between work completed during the past year and the audit plan and between actual and budgeted costs?
- Is all audit work required to be planned, programmed in advance of the field visit and documented in working paper files?
- Is adequate provision made for supervision and review of all audit work?
- Where warranted by the size of the department, is there a current audit manual containing departmental policies and procedures?
- Are the audit working papers neatly filed, legible and logically arranged?
- Is staff development through continuing education encouraged?
- Is there an in-house quality assurance review program?

Demonstrated Performance

Questions:

- Do audit recommendations receive prompt consideration and result in prompt remedial action or sound reasons for rejection?

- Has the organization been relatively free of control failures that, if recurring on other than an isolated basis, an alert internal auditing department might have discovered or prevented?
- Is a report summarizing the department's activities prepared at least annually for submission to management and the audit committee?
- Are the reports prepared on individual examinations timely, concise and understandable?
- Do the reports contain constructive recommendations about substantive matters?
- Is the internal audit effort coordinated with that of the external auditors to an extent that appears desirable?

External Quality Assurance Reviews

Question:

- Should an external quality assurance review of the internal audit department be considered at this time?

The commentary on what should be expected is also excellent. It is suggested the references be obtained and read.

The controller may wish to suggest a management task force review of the internal audit function. In the absence of such an activity, how can he, or any other interested executive, get an evaluation of internal auditing in the company? He may form an opinion based on such evidence as this:

- *The Nature of the Recommendations in the Audit Reports.* Are they significant, dealing with important items, helpful, positive in nature? Or do they represent the sometimes typical "nit-picking," negative comments of some accountants?
- *The Image Created by the Chief Internal Auditor and Staff.* How do they make presentations to the audit committee, or answer questions concerning audits, programs, findings, etc.? Are they concise, complete, objective, and responsive?
- *The Opinion of the Independent Accountant.* He should be in a position to offer objective comment.
- *The Reaction of the Auditee.* Did he feel the audit was helpful, timely, etc.?
- *Character of Audit Planning and Execution.* Do audits seem well planned? Are they completed as scheduled? Do they delve into areas of probable risk? By and large, are they so well planned as to subject that unpleasant surprises are avoided?
- *The Reaction of the Audit Committee Members and Top Management.* Is it favorable?
- *Personnel Practices.* Do they seem sound? Are qualified, professional people hired? Are there development programs to encourage promotions and an even higher grade/quality of work? Is provision made for examining and/or using the proven new technological tools?

These items may tend to be somewhat subjective (except perhaps to a skilled accountant/auditor). But the proper answer probably gives the proper signal.

And there are other quantitative measures that may be considered:

- Savings suggested vs. the cost of the examination.
- Number of audits scheduled vs. completed.
- Budgeted costs vs. actual costs.
- Number of requests for a review.
- Number of recommendations made.

While these quantitative measures may be of some value, perhaps the qualitative factors listed above are more significant.

10-9 SELECTED REFERENCES

Albrecht, W. Steve, Keith R. Howe, Kevin D. Stocks, and Dennis Schueler, "How Successful Internal Audit Departments Are Evaluated," *Financial Executive,* May/June, 1989, pp. 39–42.

Audit, Control, and Security of Paperless Systems. Altamonte Springs, FL: The Institute of Internal Auditors Research Foundation, 1990.

Bull, Ivan, and Florence Cowan Sharp, "Advising Clients on Treadway Audit Committee Recommendations," *Journal of Accountancy,* Feb. 1989, pp. 46–52.

Maher, Michael W., and Ramachandran Ramanan, "Does Internal Auditing Improve Managerial Performance?" *Management Accounting,* March 1988, pp. 54–58.

Price Waterhouse, *"Does Your Internal Audit Department Measure Up?"* 1985.

Report of the National Commission on Fraudulent Financial Reporting. Washington, DC: National Commission on Fraudulent Financial Reporting, 1987.

Standards for the Professional Practice of Internal Auditing. Altamonte Springs, FL: The Institute of Internal Auditors, 1978.

Statement on Auditing Standards No. 9, Dec. 1975. New York: American Institute of Certified Public Accountants.

Weisberg, Ellen M., "The Rise of the Internal Auditors," *Financial Executive,* Feb. 1983, pp. 33–34.

Willson, James D., and Steven J. Root, *Internal Auditing Manual* (2nd ed.). Boston: Warren, Gorham & Lamont, 1989.

CHAPTER 11

Globalization: Complexities and Opportunities

11-1 INTRODUCTION: PERVASIVE NATURE OF GLOBALIZATION

Those active in business know that change is constant. It seems some subjects are emphasized, then de-emphasized and later emphasized again, for example, benchmarking, re-engineering, empowered workteams, leveraged buyouts, mergers and acquisitions, explosion of new technologies, the changing nature of capital markets. And now we have globalization.

The recent changes in international trade practices and investment possibilities complicate the tasks. This chapter discusses how globalization is impacting U.S. economy and U.S. business.

In the 1970s and 1980s, international trade, in the eyes of many, focused on North America, Europe, and Japan—the most developed markets. Now vast new markets are opening for Western goods in Asia, South America, and Eastern Europe. It is these developing areas, which include the Pacific Rim, India, Latin America, China, and Africa, that need attention. This is where the largest growth will be.

With the greatly expanded global horizon, the financial executive should be aware of these aspects:

1. The expanded markets for U.S. goods and services, and the related impact on specific industries, required changes in packaging and product design, and distributions to meet local tastes.

2. Potential changes in sources for raw materials and supplies.

3. Widened financial investment opportunities, with differing rates of return and diversification possibilities in foreign stocks (including ADRs—American Depositary Receipts), bonds, and global mutual funds specific to a particular county or region.

4. Possible impact on organization structure, including top management structure and related local management chain of command and financial management structure.

    While the subject of globalization is currently popular, it bears mentioning that though many managements may attempt to do business globally, a very large number do not. Converting a local business to a global basis is difficult. The differences in style of management required, in control and lack thereof, and in business practices, causes some management to shy away from globalization. (See section 11-7.) But the rewards, if successful, are great—shared resources, shared management talent, broadened markets, lessened impact of a local economy downtrend. Globalization under the proper conditions can open up a world of opportunity.

5. Possible changes in corporate or entity relationships, including the virtual corporation.

6. Changes in policies and procedures relating to planning and control responsibilities or other activities required by U.S., or foreign national, or local, laws and regulations—as well as transfer pricing guidelines.

Most of these subjects are discussed in this chapter. Additionally, the Selected References provide sources of further information.

11-2 THE CHANGING NATURE OF INTERNATIONAL TRADE

U.S. companies have engaged in international trade for many years by (a) exporting U.S. produced goods or services, (b) importing selected foreign products, and (c) utilizing factories in foreign countries to assemble products for sale in the United States. With the emergence of huge trading blocs in North America (including the implementation of the North American Free Trade Agreement (NAFTA), Europe (the European Union), and East Asia (the Pacific Rim)) and the growth in other areas, major changes are taking place as to the manner in which global or multinational organizations are doing business. Cross-border trade and investments are both rising dramatically.

These specific developments illustrate the trend:

• Many U.S. companies are increasing their foreign capital investments in plant and equipment.

- U.S. investors are putting record funds into foreign investment—ADRs, some stocks, bonds, and mutual funds.
- Some U.S. corporations are engaging in sophisticated or advanced research and development (R&D) in foreign laboratories instead of the United States.
- U.S. owned companies are beginning to employ large numbers of foreign workers relative to the number of U.S. employees.
- Many U.S. owned corporations are exporting foreign produced goods to the United States. Conversely, some foreign-owned companies are establishing manufacturing plants and distribution facilities in the United States for the sale of their U.S. produced goods.
- Many non-U.S. companies with facilities in the United States are exporting a significant value of U.S. produced goods to foreign markets.

For many years, U.S. global companies regarded foreign plants as appendages for the manufacture and sale of products designed or engineered in the United States. But, given competitive pressures, the superior knowledge that foreign nationals have about local practices or customs in their country, and perhaps a less dominant position of some U.S. products and services, there is now more of a cross flow of technology, capital, and talents in many directions. In reality, the nationality of a company is not as clear as it once was; and the chain of command may include many U.S. citizens as well as foreign nationals.

All these developments add to the complexities of doing business on a global basis.

11-3 THE IMPACT OF GLOBAL TRADE ON SEGMENTS OF THE U.S. ECONOMY

It should be of general interest to know how global trade affects different segments of the U.S. economy. How does it impact a particular industry or company? Because U.S. government statistics do not provide much assistance, *Business Week* made its own review after dividing the U.S. economy into three segments: (1) exporting trade, (2) import-competing trade, and (3) domestic trade.[1] The make-up of the sectors and the general conclusions are as follows:

1. *Exporting Trade.* The exporting sector consists of industries that are competing effectively in markets at home and abroad. To be included, the industry group must export at least 10 percent of its output. The exporting sector includes industries such as:

Aircraft	Chemicals
Business services (e.g., consulting and accounting)	Computers
	Drugs

---

[1] Michael J. Mandel, and Aaron Bernstein, "Dispelling the Myths That Are Holding Us Back," *Business Week,* Dec. 17, 1990, p. 67.

Electronic equipment and components	International communications and transportation
Financial services	Lumber and paper products
Higher education	Moviemaking and other entertainment
Instruments	

The *Business Week* report indicates that workers in the exporting sector are winners in the trend toward a global economy. Exporters have expanded output and sales, and they also have boosted productivity by reducing jobs and substituting capital for labor. Although employment was flat, average real wages increased by 5.2 percent since 1980. As one economist stated, "Export success means rising wages."

2. *Import-Competing Trade.* Industries in the import-competing category import no more than 10 percent of foreign goods into the U.S. market. This sector includes the following categories of industry:

Automobiles and motorcycles	Most industrial machinery
Cement	Screws, nuts, and other small
Clothing	hardware
Consumer electronics	Shoes and luggage
Furniture	Steel, aluminum, and other metals
Machine tools	Tires
Mining	Toys

Employees in this segment have been hurt by the direct and indirect effects of foreign competition. Jobs have become scarce, and wages, once good, have fallen.

3. *Domestic.* This category includes industries that do little importing or exporting. Most are service industries, although some manufacturing is included (e.g., concrete blocks) when local tastes, standards, or economics limit international trade. The domestic sector includes these industries:

Business services	Food processing
Commercial printing	Health services
Concrete products	Personal services (e.g., hair
Construction	dressing and automobile repair)
Domestic transportation and communications	Publishing
	Rubber and plastic products
Education (primary and secondary)	Wholesale and retail trade
Financial services, real estate, and insurance	

Global competition has pushed down wages in the domestic sector. While it may be relatively easy to find work, pay has decreased and is getting lower. Moreover, as imports or increasing productivity reduce the number of jobs in other categories, many employees have migrated to the service sector, making competition a more important factor.

Global trade can affect just about everyone in every sector of the economy.

11-4 HELPING U.S. MANUFACTURERS COMPETE GLOBALLY

From 1945 to the late 1960s, the United States had an unusual advantage in the global business competition: It possessed a very large home market that had not been damaged by the war; and the country benefited from the surge in technology that grew out of the war. But the position of dominance was not a normal one. The United States has lost such a preferred status and is now in a global market where it is merely one of several competitors. The reasons for this change in position are as follows:

- U.S. merchandise imports grew more rapidly than exports.
- Growth in productivity has lagged behind that of both Germany and Japan.
- During the 1980s, the United States lost technical leadership in some important areas, such as computer chips and machine tools.
- Civilian investment in R&D is a lower percentage of GNP in the United States than it is in Germany and Japan.
- The national savings rate is below that of many industrialized countries.

Given the circumstances, what changes must take place so that U.S. companies can secure an increased share of the global market? H. A. Hammerly, Executive Vice President of 3M Company, discussed this subject at some length in one of his articles.[2] Summarized below are his recommendations on what must be done:

Actions required on the part of U.S. companies

- Make the acquisition of global markets a higher national priority.
- Establish a commitment to quality of manufacturing.
- Focus on customer satisfaction in the local market, and not on what the customer should want as determined from a nationwide perspective—as 3M says, "Think global and act local."
- Make the required investments in individual foreign markets.
- Emphasize innovation in products as well as services.
- Stress to both the U.S. government and the public the need to improve the nation's position among global competitors.

Actions required on the part of the U.S. government

- Put the U.S. financial house in order by reducing the national deficit and encouraging investment rather than consumption (e.g., through consumption taxes and discontinuation of entitlement increases).
- Ensure access to foreign markets by means of tough U.S. government demands (such as renewing executive order Super 301).

---

[2] See H. A. Hammerly, "Can American Manufacturers Compete Outside the U.S.?" *Financial Executive*, Sept.–Oct. 1990, pp. 27–31.

- Correct the tax structure by eliminating (1) the tax on foreign profits that are earned overseas, taxed by foreign government, and never brought back to the United States; (2) the double taxation of dividends; and (3) the advantage of debt financing over equity financing.
- Use the Export Control Act realistically, and not so as to restrict trade (as in the case of grain embargoes), thus risking loss of the market.
- Adopt realistic environmental regulations. Some regulations may be so unreasonable as to restrict trade.
- Attain realistic currency values.
- Adopt a stronger national technology policy to support the U.S. position in manufacturing.
- Encourage industrial research by committing government funds to this purpose.
- Remove antitrust barriers to joint manufacturing efforts.
- Provide stronger support to education.

It is Hammerly's belief that U.S. manufacturers can compete in global markets. However, industry and government must work together more effectively, and U.S. society must be committed to competitiveness in the global marketplace.

Other actions also may be taken, such as the use of the *virtual corporation,* to assemble the needed core competencies—as discussed in section 11-7, or acquiring significant minority interests in foreign corporations.

11-5 DETERMINING AND IMPLEMENTING SUCCESSFUL GLOBAL STRATEGIES

A great many factors influence whether a particular entity will be successful in the global marketplace. Perhaps no factor is more important than the selection of the proper strategies; and this includes determining the strategy decided upon in the proper manner. It is a reflection of the "NIH" syndrome—not invented here.

A key player in carrying out global strategies is the subsidiary top manager. Some research into the viewpoints of these managers revealed these conclusions as to the process by which strategies should be determined:[3]

1. *It is important that the head office executives become familiar with local conditions.* Only where the subsidiary managers believe the head office executives understand how the local market operates do they respect the decisions reached, and make a greater effort to follow them.

2. *Two-way communication is essential.* Subsidiary top managers value the ability to voice their opinions and exchange ideas with the home office in reaching a strategic decision.

3. *Subsidiary managers must regard the decision-making practices as consistent.* In other words, strategic decision making is a *political* process as well as any

---

[3] W. Chan Kim, and Renee A. Mauborgne, "Making Global Strategies Work," *Sloan Management Review,* Spring 1993, pp. 11–26.

economic and *competitive* process. Subsidiary managers must not conclude that those on the "inside track" will be heard, but that all others will be overlooked.

4. *Subsidiary managers must believe they have the ability to reflect or openly challenge the head office decision.* In such an environment, the subsidiary managers think the head office may better recognize that strategic decisions will be of a higher quality, and will be made in the overall economic interest—not primarily a political interest.

5. *Subsidiary top managers think it is only fair that the head office explain the reasons for the final global strategic decisions.* When such a procedure is followed, many subsidiary managers tend to believe that the head office at least considered the subsidiary position, and that they thereby acted in a fair and impartial manner.

The existence of a fair *process* of establishing global strategies is key to making the strategy successful. It tends to cause subsidiary managers to pursue *voluntary* execution—doing more than is required—rather than *compulsory* execution—meeting minimum requirements. The traditional mechanism for strategy enforcement—incentive compensation, auditing or monitoring systems, heavy-handed disciplining by the head office, and other rewards or punishments—are of some worth. But these mechanisms are of declining value by reason of such trends or factors as these, among others:

- Increasing size of subsidiary units.
- A growth in unique or distinctive skills in the subsidiaries.
- Growing and extensive communication between the subsidiaries in comparing ideas (and excluding the home office).
- Growing importance of subcultures.
- Increasing difficulty in monitoring efforts in enforcing the prescribed strategy— due to an inability to distinguish the cause of failure—whether the result of factors beyond the control of the manager, or poor implementation that he or she *can* control.
- Growing loss of control by the central office.

The growing complexities in the global marketplace make a participative management approach, perceived as fair and equitable, increasingly important. Aside from the psychological environment, the most important factor is the actual strategy adopted. The predominant philosophy or type of strategy will depend, among other things, upon the product, the industry, the specific market, and the nature of the competition. A study of styles of competition in the semi-conductor business made by a Fordham University Graduate School of Business professor concluded that, in this instance, U.S. firms tended to develop a unique strategy while the effective Japanese competitors tended to win by implementing in a superior manner a not-so-unique strategy.[4] A comparative summary of different competitive actions in this specific market are shown in Figure 11-1.

---

[4] See William G. Egelhoff, "Great Strategy or Great Strategy Implementation—Two Ways of Competing in Global Markets," *Sloan Management Review,* Winter 1993, pp. 37–50.

Figure 11-1   Comparative Competitive Styles.

	Dominant Competitive Style	
Action	U.S. Company	Japanese Company
Securing unique product-market advantage.	Attempts to develop unique advantage for each product line.	Does not seek unique product-market advantage; relies on low cost and high quality.
Role of process technology (which transfers a product design into marketable products).	Great variance from company to company. Large firms may attempt to stay in the forefront of process technology, whereas firms that rely most heavily on product-market differentiation may consider process technology less important.	Emphasizes staying at the forefront of technology—both for product development and for capital improvement.
Sources of process technology know-how.	Often depends on external sources—e.g., by engaging in collaborative research, by outright purchase, or by seeking assistance from equipment manufacturers.	Tending to favor internal development.
Withdrawal from the market.	Tends to withdraw from product-market segment when clear advantage cannot be gained, often after competitive pressures make segment unprofitable.	Seldom withdraws from market; tends to remain in product segment and to strive for profitability through efficiency.
Status of vertical integration.	Generally values such integration only when related products contribute uniqueness.	Highly values vertical integration as part of drive to self-sufficiency.

As might be expected, the dominant competitive style influences any industry structure, which in turn influences the industry's member firms, their suppliers, and their customers. Figure 11-2 compares the impact of the two competitive styles on some important industry factors and characteristics. Note that the impact could be either an advantage or a disadvantage for any given particular firm.

11-6 ORGANIZATION STRUCTURE IN A GLOBAL ENTERPRISE

The removal of trade barriers and the trend toward a global economy is changing the manner in which companies do business and, as a consequence, often also causes a change in some organizational arrangements. As entities become global, new threats appear in the home market as well as the foreign market. New products enter the marketplace, and competition increases for existing as well as new customers. These competitive forces are causing these changes:

- *Increased Customer Demands.* Customers tend to require faster deliveries, improved quality, and more numerous other related services.

Figure 11-2 "Superior Strategy" vs. More Effective Implementation of a Non-Unique Strategy.

Distinguishing Characteristics	Competing Style	
	"Superior" Strategy	More Effective Implementation
Impact on Factor		
Strategic variety.	Greater variety of strategies results in greater range of products as well as greater segmentation of markets.	Fewer strategies, resulting in more direct competition between products and product substitutes, with emphasis on quality and cost.
Industry concentration.	Many successful competitors and low industry concentration.	Only a few successful competitors and high industry concentration.
Industry survival pattern.	Innovative competitors survive and dominate industry, with high turnover among leaders.	Efficient competitors survive and dominate industry, with lower turnover among leaders.
Industry Characteristics		
Product life cycle.	Strategy is most effective in early stage of product life cycle, when technological and/or environmental change is rapid and a variety of feasible product designs exist.	Strategy works best in later stages of product life cycle, when technological and/or environmental change is slow and the basic designs have evolved.
Risk of Technological or environmental change.	Entity risks losing competitive advantage when there are fewer such changes and when imitators enter market.	Entity risks losing competitive advantage when technological and/or environmental change dominates market.
Profit margins.	Less direct competition, resulting in higher profit margins.	More direct competition, resulting in lower profit margins.

- *Quicker Responses.* It becomes increasingly necessary to react quickly to competitive actions, as well as changing market conditions, and to shorten the time for development of new products and services.

- *Improved Outsourcing or Subcontracting.* Another frequent requirement is the developing of closer relations with key suppliers so as to facilitate just-in-time delivery of materials or parts or other fast response needs.

- *Strengthening Core Competencies.* With the need to assemble and strengthen core competencies, some entities are forming flexible partnerships—as discussed in section 11-7. These business adaptations, coupled with the changes in information technology and the inflexibility of traditional, cumbersome, and bureaucratic structures, excessive management layers, and onerous procedures, are resulting in some new organization structures. Some may be recognized in a realigned organization, and others are reflected in "new organizations" that are not usually a part of the typical organization chart. A few of these new relationships are reflected in the phenomena listed next.

- *High Performance Teams.* This is a group of individuals with differing skills brought together to function as a team and to completely re-engineer a process—such as filling customer orders or a manufacturing sequence. The team works as a group using shared information and groupware—especially designed software to support collaborative effort.

- *Integrated Organization.* In reality this is a change in the access and flow of information. Instead of, for example, three separate resource areas (a) financial, (b) physical assets, and (c) human resources, a new integrated information system lets executives directly access the required data. This new information system removes layers of management and modifying influences.

- *The Extended Business.* With the help of industry standards, computer systems are extending outward and linking with both customers and suppliers. In a sense, a change is taking place from a vertical organization to a horizontal entity. Again, some of this change is seen in the virtual corporation.

We see the impetus of international competition forcing the elimination of layers of management, and effective working groups built around key processes instead of single functions or departments. Moreover, knowledge of local markets and important customers argues for a great deal of decentralization.

In the context of organization structure, two other changes are occurring:

1. *Unit Headquarters.* In this increasingly global economy, many U.S. companies are transferring abroad the world headquarters of important business units. Astute managements are recognizing that they must operate near key customers and closer to competitors—not in a far away location. Many large businesses are finding that a company cannot be run from a single location; several different headquarters may be required for different product lines or competitive postures. With such changes, some loss of control may result. Hence, the controller must be sensitive to these developments.

2. *The Finance Organization.* Just as the principle of decentralization applies to the marketing function, it could be advantageous in the finance organization. The chief financial planning and control office of the subsidiary unit should report *administratively* to the local unit manager. This structure tends to make the financial executive a member of the local management, and not be perceived as the eyes and ears of the corporate office. Also, it should make the local financial manager more responsive to the needs of local management. The corporate controller could then provide *functional* guidance, such as the financial procedures to be used, internal control procedures, and report requirements for the home office.

The staff relationship of the unit controllers to the corporate controller is illustrated in Figure 11-3.

11-7 THE VIRTUAL CORPORATION

In the context of meeting global competition, a new form of organization—the virtual corporation—is emerging to more quickly take advantage of new economic opportunities.

Figure 11-3   Global Organization Structure (with Emphasis on the Financial Organization).

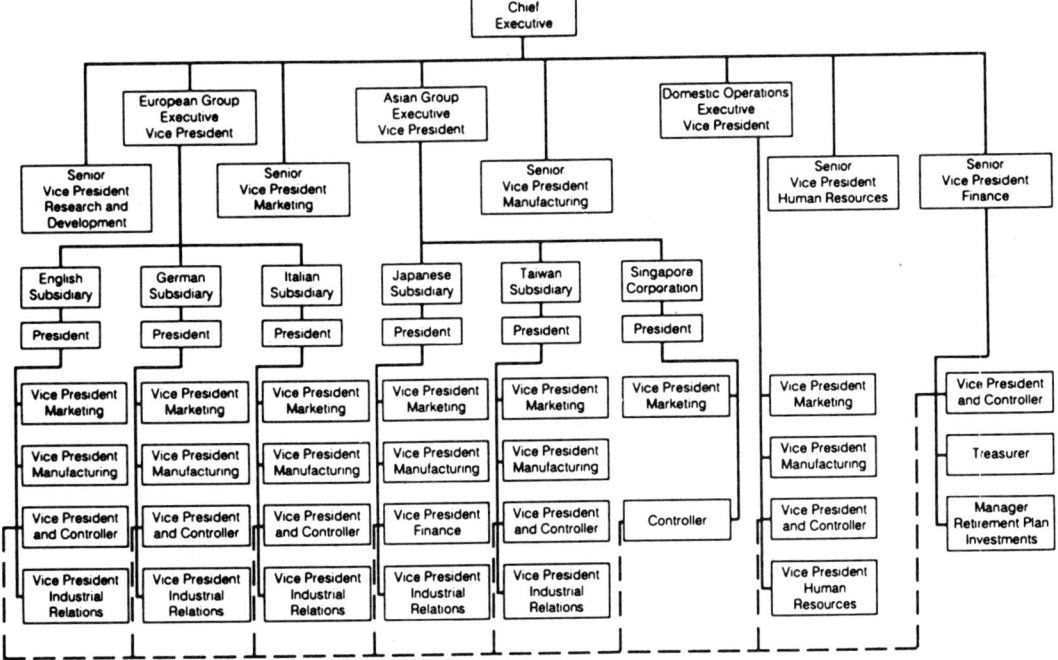

Global Enterprise, Inc.
MASTER ORGANIZATION CHART

This development in organization structure warrants discussion in a separate section. While often used in connection with outsourcing, the concept may spread to other functions.

Webster's Ninth New Collegiate Dictionary defines "virtual" as "being such in essence or effect though not formally recognized or admitted." By this definition, a virtual corporation is an entity that, although not formally recognized or admitted as a corporation, is such in effect. As typically described, it is a temporary, flexible network of independent organizations linked by information technology for the purpose of sharing skills, costs, and access to one another's markets. It is a means of quickly meeting competitive pressures. The principal characteristics of this form of organization are these:

1. *Excellence.* Each participant in the organization commits its "core competence" to the joint effort—with the result that each function or process can be world class in a faster time than other methods. A single corporation only rarely can achieve world class status in most of its functions.

2. *Opportunistic and Temporary.* The association is less likely to be either permanent or formal than other arrangements. The entities band together to meet a particular need or to take advantage of a particular opportunity. When the need no longer exists, or the benefits have been realized, then the organizations disband. But benefits have accrued for each member.

3. *Existence of Indeterminate Borders.* With the many contacts among suppliers, customers, and perhaps competitors, the corporate boundaries often become blurred.

4. *Technology Dependent.* The new information technology enables the widely dispersed entities to communicate and work cooperatively. The electronics interchange reduces greatly the time required for legal decisions, or link-ups, or making changes.

5. *Co-Dependence.* The nature of the new relationship makes each participant quite dependent on the other members of the group.

6. *Loss of Control.* The various characteristics listed above results in some loss of control over some operations, with possible related difficulties.

This form of organization should be considered by some global entities.

11-8 TECHNICAL ASPECTS OF THE CONTROLLERSHIP FUNCTION UNDER GLOBALIZATION

The bulk of the preceding discussion in this chpater has related to those *general* aspects of globalization or international trade of which the controller should be aware. Additionally, in properly carrying out the duties of a controller in a situation involving multicountry operations, as contrasted with single country activities, these subjects are germane and specific to the task—and they are all interrelated:

a. Open communications.

b. Need for uniformity in data definition.

c. Complying with international accounting requirements.

d. Measuring foreign operations.

e. Translating financial statements.

f. Evaluating foreign investments—capital expenditures, R&D projects, operating programs (such as designing and constructing an aircraft), etc.

g. Transfer pricing.

h. Taxation.

i. Import/export regulations.

j. Managing currency risk.

k. The Foreign Corrupt Practices Act.

(a) OPEN COMMUNICATIONS

Two factors contribute to communication problems in an international operation. They are language and distance. It is important for a controller to address these problems and develop a satisfactory solution.

The most obvious way to handle the language problem is to ensure that someone with good bilingual skills is representing the controller in the overseas operation. This individual must be able to deal effectively with the local country officials and employees and then communicate important and necessary information back to the parent.

The communication can be in person, by phone, by letter, and by data transmission. In larger operations, private communications systems will allow easy teleprocessing and telecommunications. In smaller organizations, careful planning of when calls and data are transmitted will result in good communications.

However, even after placing a qualified representative in the foreign operation, the controller must remain aware of the importance of clear information exchange. The need becomes even greater as the company expands into more countries and as the foreign operations become a bigger part of the business.

One technique that has proved effective is to issue written instructions on important matters such as:

- Planning assumptions.
- Accounting and reporting requirements.
- Control assessments.
- Disbursement practices.

The instructions should be formal notification to the subsidiaries as to what is required of them. The letters or instructions should be controlled, e.g., a sequential number assigned to each one so that all recipients are aware of all communiques. It is helpful to the subsidiaries if the parent periodically issues a summary of all such instructions that are still in force.

A second, and probably invaluable, communication technique is the one-on-one meeting. It is here that all the nuances of operation are really covered. These meetings of key people (controller to controller) should take place at least once a year and probably more often if there are difficult issues to be resolved.

Another effective communication vehicle is the use of group meetings, seminars, and classes wherein the controller sponsors a meeting of international people perhaps from several countries at which specific items of mutual interest are discussed. This also allows people with the same problems to come together and informally talk about problems. There has proved to be a continuing benefit in this approach in that the people stay in touch with one another to discuss ongoing and future problems and share solutions.

New developments in groupware, as discussed in Chapter 49, to provide meeting support can assist in keeping the communication lines open.

(b) UNIFORM DATA REQUIREMENTS

When operating internationally it is essential that there be worldwide uniformity in data definitions for three reasons:

- It simplifies consolidation of financial statements and reports.
- It allows for comparability of results.
- It permits timely release of reports.

The use of a standard schedule of accounts, developed and maintained centrally but responsive to country needs, is the most obvious way to achieve uniformity or reporting. It becomes simple then to define the aggregation of data in order to achieve usable reports. This results in one scorecard that is then used by all parts of the organizations within the company. To be effective, use of a standard reporting chart of accounts requires that headquarters have a knowledge of the out-of-country business and how it is to be recorded and summarized. It also requires an interpretation of U.S. accounting standards, which must be articulated and promulgated to all subsidiaries so that financial reports have a uniformity of structure and content.

To sum up, a world-class accounting operation would be organized to:

- Keep responsibility for recording at the country level.
- Provide clear instructions to the countries as to how transactions would be summarized and reported.
- Have each country prepare statements in the parent-company currency using U.S. GAAP.

This structure will result in uniform accounting reports to allow comparison between units. It will also permit tighter closing schedules and the resultant earlier release of information both within the company and externally.

(c) INTERNATIONAL ACCOUNTING REQUIREMENTS

In putting together a world-class accounting operation the controller must address the following:

- Records of a subsidiary must be kept in the *local* currency and language and must meet local fiscal, professional, and tax requirements.
- The records must then (a) be adjusted to "generally accepted accounting principles" of the parent, (b) be translated into the currency of the parent. (Less commonly, a second ledger may be maintained in the currency of the parent and in accordance with GAAP of the parent.)

The record keeping of the subsidiary is generally done locally. The day-to-day transactions covering payment of salaries, purchasing of goods and services, billings to customers, and collecting cash, as well as maintaining and controlling assets and liabilities all take place locally and in local currency. The accounting for these transactions is most effectively done where and when they transpire.

The accounting records must be constructed so as to provide adequate information to prepare tax returns and produce local financial statements for regulators, creditors, unions, and other interested parties, and to facilitate reporting to the parent company. The accounting standards to be followed must be those of the host country so the record keeping must be done using those standards or easily convertible to them. This conversion is necessary if the accounting standards used are not local standards but rather are those of the parent company's country.

It should be noted that the accounting standards required by the authorities vary from country to country. The International Accounting Standards Committee (IASC) is attempting to minimize alternatives by issuing international standards, but all such standards must then be adopted by the appropriate authorities in each of the countries before they become official. This could be a long and tedious process. In the meantime a broad knowledge of each country's generally accepted accounting policies must be developed and maintained by the controller of a multinational company. A listing of International Accounting Standards as issued by the IASC is available, but the acceptance by each country must be determined individually.

The translation and remeasurement of local results can be done by either the local country or the parent. If done in-house by local personnel, there will be a need for each country controller to understand U.S. GAAP. This can be accomplished in several ways: through a program of individual education, through in-house seminars and workshops, and through centrally developed and issued accounting instructions, all of which must be directed by the corporate controller. The latter provides the best opportunity for uniformity in recording and reporting and probably will be necessary even if local finance people become knowledgeable about parent-company GAAP.

If the translation and adjustments are done at the parent-company headquarters, there are several areas of concern. First, country management will not have an opportunity to review the dollar results before they are put into the consolidation process, and valuable insight into cause and effects of current operations will be missing. Second, higher management at the parent headquarters will be viewing reports that have not yet been seen at the operating level. Communications could easily become confused and important decisions delayed.

It is the authors' observation that having the translation and remeasurement work done at the country level is the more effective approach.

(d) MEASURING FOREIGN OPERATIONS

In most organizations, the primary control and measurement techniques are:

- Define key objectives.
- Prepare a financial plan, compare actual results to it, and take corrective action.
- Compare actual results to a prior period.

The multinational company generally uses these techniques to measure the translated results of its foreign subsidiaries. The technique is effective if the variable of currency fluctuation is recognized and adjusted for. As mentioned elsewhere in this chapter, translated results can present a very different picture of operations and financial condition than local currency results reflect. The controller should be familiar with both sets of data and the analysis supporting them. However, it is the parent-company currency that is used for external reporting; therefore the use and understanding of translated financial statements will remain a key part of the controller's work.

As an overall summary of this task of measuring the financial performance of a global unit manager, the reports should reflect these objectives:

1. To reflect the *financial* plan for all activities under the control or responsibility of the local manager.
2. To measure *actual results* against plan for those matters under the control of the local manager.
3. To reflect the planned results *translated* into the parent company currency; and to identify planned vs. actual results segregated between (a) those reflecting the entity manager's performance and (b) those which are due to the impact of currency fluctuations.

(i) Comparisons with Budget or Plan.   The biggest unique planning and control problem facing the controller of an international business is that of fluctuations in the currency exchange rate. When plans or budgets are established an estimated exchange rate must be used to express in the parent's currency the budget amounts developed in local currency. The "actuals" from the accounting records are translated at the current rate, which is usually different from the rate used for the plan, for example:

CURRENCY EXCHANGE RATES	
Plan assumptions	4 local currency (L/C) = $1
Actual	5 local currency (L/C) = $1

STATEMENT OF OPERATIONS			
	Actual	Budget	Variance (Unfavorable)
Sales (L/C) . . .	1,000,000	1,000,000	-0-
Rate	5:1	4:1	
Sales ($)	200,000	250,000	(50,000)

In this example the parent-company currency, the U.S. dollar, has strengthened, and it now takes more local currency units to equal one dollar than was planned. The effect is that, when viewed from a local perspective sales are on plan, but when viewed from a parent company perspective, i.e., the dollar, the subsidiary is under plan and substantially so, requiring analysis and explanation. One way to give a better view of what is happening is to add two more columns to the report, showing the effect of currency. The report now tells the reader that the unfavorable variance is all due to a currency exchange movement.

STATEMENT OF OPERATIONS					
				Amount Due to	
	Actual	Budget	Variance (Unfavorable)	Currency Translation	Business Performance
Sales $	200,000	250,000	(50,000)	(50,000)	-0-

If the example was changed to include a modest over-budget situation in local currency, it would be reported as follows:

	Actual	Budget	Variance (Unfavorable)
Sales (L/C)	1,100,000	1,000,000	100,000
Exchange rate . . .	5:1	4:1	
Sales ($)	220,000	250,000	(30,000)

In this example the results shown in dollars portray a misleading result, but when the currency effect is shown separately, a much clearer picture emerges.

	Actual	Budget	Variance (Unfavorable)	Amount Due to Currency Translation	Amount Due to Business Performance
Sales $	220,000	250,000	(30,000)	(55,000)	25,000

The amount of variance due to business is calculated by either: (1) taking the variance in local currency and translating it at the current rate, or (2) more commonly since local currency results are not usually transmitted early, having the countries calculate the actual results translated at the plan rates. In the examples, both budget and actual would be translated into dollars using the plan rate of 4 L/C = $1.

The analyst would keep the budget amount constant at a 4:1 translation rate and prepare an "actual" using the same translation rate to produce the following result:

	Actual	Budget	Variance (Unfavorable)
Sales (L/C)	1,100,000	1,000,000	100,000
Exchange rate . . .	4:1	4:1	
Sales ($)	275,000	250,000	25,000

The above variance is attributed to sales being higher than plan and is therefore the variance due to business operations. The difference between the total variance in translated amounts and the business variance determined above is attributed to the effect of currency changes.

(ii) Comparisons with Prior Year.   A similar problem in plan/actual comparisons occurs when current actual results are compared to the actual results of prior periods. If the exchange rates used for the two periods are different, then the results are clouded by the change. For example, if

	Current Year	Prior Year	Increase/ (Decrease)
Sales (L/C)	1,100,000	900,000	200,000
Exchange rate . .	5:1	4:1	
Sales ($)	220,000	225,000	(5,000)

However, if the exchange rates are normalized by translating the current period using the same exchange as the period being compared to, the following picture results:

	Actual	Budget	Variance (Unfavorable)	Amount Due to Currency Translation	Amount Due to Business Performance
Sales $	220,000	225,000	(5,000)	(55,000)	50,000

As in the plan/actual analysis, the "actual" results in both periods would be translated at the same exchange rate to produce the following result:

	Current Year	Prior Year	Increase/ (Decrease)
Sales (L/C)	1,100,000	900,000	200,000
Exchange rate . .	4:1	4:1	
Sales ($)	275,000	225,000	50,000

By isolating the currency exchange effect, we can see that there was a growth in the business of $50,000 or 22%, rather than a 2% decline. We can also see that the currency effect was to reduce sales, in dollars, by 25%, wiping out the operating growth and resulting in a decline in reported sales compared to the prior year.

(iii) Inflation. In a multinational company, the impact of inflation on the business results is not different from a national company; usually it is just more volatile. The same analyses and actions taken in regard to home-country inflation generally apply to translated results. However, there are many less developed nations that experience hyperinflation (i.e., annual inflation in the hundreds or thousands of percent). For these situations, some special analysis of local currency results must be made to normalize for inflation.

Establishing a base year for currency value and then adjusting subsequent years results to that value presents a more accurate picture of growth or decline. For example, hyperinflationary country A experiences a 100% inflation rate in the current year. Its sales results for this year and last year are:

Current year	L/C	1,000,000
Prior year	L/C	750,000
Increase	L/C	250,000
Percentage		33%

However using the prior years' currency value as 1, the current year value is 0.5 after adjusting for 100% inflation ($1/+100\%$ 1). The current year sales value when compared to last year is L/C 500,000 (1,000,000 × 0.5). So instead of a 33% gain in sales, there has been a 33% decrease—a very different result and one requiring further analysis and action. This is called constant currency and the results are:

Current year	L/C	500,000
Prior year	L/C	750,000
Decrease	L/C	(250,000)
Percentage		33%

As indicated above, this inflation move is reflected in currency translation rates and translated results therefore have only the parent-company inflation rate included.

(e) TRANSLATION OF FINANCIAL STATEMENTS

In order to prepare consolidated statements all results recorded in foreign currency must be translated or remeasured into the parent company's currency. In the United States the procedures directing how this translation is to be done are detailed in Statement of Financial Accounting Standards No. 52 (FAS 52).

Since foreign results are often analyzed and assessed in the parent currency, it is important to understand how such results are developed.

(i) History of Translation Methods. Prior to the adoption of FAS 52 in 1982, the accounting convention used to report foreign operations was to both "measure" and express the financial results in U.S. dollars. This required that monetary assets, and liabilities (e.g., cash and debt) be translated into U.S. dollars using the rate in effect on the date of the financial statement. Nonmonetary assets and liabilities, e.g., inventories and fixed assets, were translated using a "historical" rate, i.e., the rate in effect when the asset was originally recorded. The income and expense statement was translated at the average rate for the period, except that depreciation and cost of inventory were translated at the historical rate used to record the asset. Any gain or loss arising from translating net assets or liabilities at different rates from period to period was recognized in the income statement for the period.

This translation method was required by Financial Accounting Standard No. 8, issued in 1976. Prior to 1976 a method was used based on a concept of translating current assets and liabilities at a current rate and noncurrent assets and liabilities at a historical rate.

These translation methods are summarized in Figures 11-4 and 11-5.

From the time FAS 8 was issued there were continuing criticisms of its effect. Some said the results it produced were incompatible with economic events; others, that

Figure 11-4 History of Foreign Currency Translation Methods.

PRINCIPLE PRIOR TO 1976

- Current assets and liabilities translated at current rate.
- Noncurrent—capital assets & long-term liabilities—at historical rate.
- Income and expense average rate for period except depreciation—historical rate.
- Translations gain or loss includable in income (losses were recognized; gains deferred to offset future losses)

1976—FAS 8 ADOPTED

- Monetary assets and liabilities translated at current rate.
- Long-term debt now at current rate.
- Nonmonetary assets and liabilities translated at historical rate.
- Inventories now at historical rates.
- Income and expense average rate for period except depreciation and cost of inventory—historical.
- Translation gain or loss recognized in income immediately.

Figure 11-5   Translation Rates.

	PRE-FAS 8	FAS 8
BALANCE SHEET		
Assets		
Cash and receivables	Current	Current
Inventories	Current	Historical
Fixed assets	Historical	Historical
Liabilities		
Current	Current	Current
Long-term debt	Historical	Current
INCOME AND EXPENSE STATEMENT		
Sales	Current average	Current average
Cost of sales	Current average	Historical
Depreciation	Historical	Historical
Operating Expense	Current average	Current average
Translation G/L	Gain deferrable	In profit
Transaction G/L	In profit	In profit

it distorted profit margins; and almost all said that it produced an unwanted volatility in earnings from period to period.

(ii) Financial Accounting Standard No. 52.   The board reconsidered the basic objectives of translation and concluded that foreign operations should be "measured" in the *functional* currency of the foreign entity and provide information that is compatible with expected cash flows. Those results would then be expressed in U.S. dollars, but maintaining each foreign entities' financial relationships in consolidation.

This new view had three key concepts:

- Functional currency.
- Translation.
- Remeasurement.

Functional Currency.   The functional currency concept recognized that an enterprise can operate in a number of separate economic environments. Each subsidiary should be "measured" in the currency of the economic environment in which it operates. If it operates in U.S. dollars, it should be measured in U.S. dollars. If it operates in a local currency, it should be measured in that local currency. Factors to be considered in determining functional currency included:[5]

- National sovereignty.
- Inflation.

---

[5] For a complete listing of criteria see Financial Accounting Standard No. 52 issued by the Financial Accounting Standards Board, Dec. 1981.

- Degree of integration with parent operation.
- Long-term vs. short-term commitment of parent to the foreign enterprise.

The most important factor in weighing the facts to determine functional currency was indicated to be management judgment.

The benefits of using local currency as the functional currency are:

- Profit margins are no longer affected by changes in exchange rates.
- Translation gains and losses will not affect earnings.
- Greater income and expense stability is provided in periods of changing exchange rates; however, it results in some balance sheet instability.

Translation. The new concept of translation was that it arises only out of the need to restate financial statements from "functional currency" into "reporting currency." Therefore:

- The entire balance sheet would be translated at the current rate (in effect at date of statement).
- The entire income statement would be translated at the average rate for the period.
- Adjustments arising from the translation process are not to be included in income but are to be recorded in a new section of stockholders' equity.

Remeasurement. Remeasurement was the third new concept. It required that operations denominated in a currency other than functional currency must be restated into the functional currency. This meant that foreign entities whose functional currency would be the U.S. dollar, but whose records were in local currency, must be remeasured. The remeasurement is similar to translation under FAS 8.

A comparison of translation rates is shown in Figure 11-6.

FAS 52 is a complex and lengthy document. Its implementation has reduced the dissatisfaction that accompanied FAS 8 but the use of the "functional currency" concept does result in noncomparable subsidiary financial reports for countries where local currency is the functional currency vs. those where the U.S. dollar is the functional currency.

The following key items are affected by this anomaly:

- Cost of goods sold (inventory and depreciation effect).
- Gross profit.
  Gross profit margins.
- Expenses (depreciation effect).
- Net earnings.
  Net profit margins.
- Statement of financial position.
  Inventory.
  Fixed assets.
  New component of stockholder equity.

Figure 11-6 Comparison of Translation Rates.

	PRE-FAS 8	FAS 8 and FAS 52 $ Countries	FAS 52 L/C Countries
BALANCE SHEET			
Assets			
Cash and receivables ..	Current	Current	Current
Inventories	Current	Historical	Current
Fixed assets	Historical	Historical	Current
Liabilities			
Current	Current	Current	Current
Long-term debt	Historical	Current	Current
Income and Expense			
Sales	Current average	Current average	Current average
Cost of sales	Current average	Historical	Current average
Depreciation	Historical	Historical	Current average
Operating expense	Current average	Current average	Current average
Operating profit			Current average
Translation G/L	Gain deferrable	In profit	In equity
Transaction G/L	In profit	In profit	In profit

- Other.

  Return on investment.

  Return on assets.

  Statement of cash flows.

It is interesting to note that the International Accounting Standards Committee (IASC) in its standard on translation of foreign results does not require the use of functional currency/remeasurement concepts. Perhaps the FASB will reconsider this requirement in the interest of simplicity.

Finally, since many companies use translated statements in controlling and measuring the foreign subsidiaries, it is important to keep in mind that the translated results do not necessarily reflect the same story as is seen when viewing the same results in the local currency.

(f) EVALUATING CAPITAL EXPENDITURES

When the question "Should we invest overseas?" is raised, all the analyses used in making capital investment decisions in the home country will have to be made. Additionally the new risks of exchange rate fluctuations and political uncertainty must be considered.

Unless there are unusual circumstances (e.g., a need to maintain special know-how available in a specific location), the key consideration in the investment discussion is the return on assets or return on equity that relates to "cash flow to the parent."

(i) Exchange Rate Fluctuations. The impact of currency movements on financial statements and the analysis of them is discussed in detail in the section of this

chapter titled "Measuring Foreign Operations." Exchange rate fluctuations will also have a significant effect on the cash flow to the parent of an investment in a foreign country and so must be recognized in the planning and assessment of investment alternatives. It should be noted that the analysis of investment returns when calculated in the currency of the country where the investment will be made results in a different answer than when it is done in the currency of the parent.

For example, using a "net present value" analysis to determine the return in both currencies shows the comparison illustrated in Figure 11-7.

A rule of thumb is that if this investment does not yield a positive cash flow in the parent's currency then it should not be made.

If the return is positive then the required internal rate of return and/or the hurdle rate of return must be met. Another good rule of thumb is that the rate of return should at least exceed the expected interest rate of government securities in that country.

In estimating the value in the parents' currency of future cash flows it is necessary to forecast for each of the years included in the analysis:

- Exchange rates.
- Withholding taxes.
- Currency restrictions.
- Political risks.

A difficult but doable effort.

(ii) Exchange Rates. In considering the economic exposure to future foreign exchange risk, both the cash flows in foreign currency and the value of dividends in the

Figure 11-7 Calculation of Net Present Value in Two Currencies.

	Subsidiary Currency	Parent Currency
Present value of cash inflows over the life of the project	Net profit before depreciation	After-tax value of dividends, interest, and royalties remitted by the subsidiary
Plus		
Present value of terminal value (liquidation value)	After-tax recoverable amount	After-tax amount remitted to parent
Equals		
Total present value of cash inflows	Estimated amount	Translated value of remitted amounts
Minus		
Original investment (plant and working capital)	Translated amount	Established amount in parent currency
Equals		
Net present value		

parent currency must be considered. For example, a devaluation of the foreign currency will result in a decrease in the value of foreign currency dividends in the parent currency. But, it may also lead to an increase in foreign currency profit as a result of increased sales volume or sales price on exports. The net impact on the cash flow to the parent is the sum of both effects.

The analysis should begin with an assessment of the most likely exchange rates anticipated by year. Then simulate what would happen to cash flows under a variety of "what if" scenarios. For example, if it is decided that the most likely case is a 5% devaluation of the foreign currency each year, a cash flow plan using that premise should be prepared. It can then be varied by asking "what if" it is less or more than 5% and the same plan and assessment done at 3% and 4%, or 6%, 7%, 10%, etc. Another scenario that should be performed is "what if" there is appreciation rather than devaluation and the plan is assembled using +2% or +5%, etc. The relevant range of possible changes depends upon the foreign currency under consideration. Brazil can be safely expected to have its currency continually devalue, and only devalue. The range, however, is very wide and volatile, perhaps 100% to 200% per year. The Netherlands on the other hand could have its currency move in either direction but probably no more than 10% each way.

After the economic analysis is finished then a probability-of-occurrence analysis should be performed and a weighting given to the results. For example, if there are two probable scenarios—a 5% devaluation and an 8% devaluation—and the probability is judged to be 80% for the 5% case and 20% for the 8% case then the following cost estimate can be made and incorporated into the estimated results:

$$5\% \text{ devaluation} = \text{NPV} \times 0.80 = \text{A}$$
$$8\% \text{ devaluation} = \text{NPV} \times 0.20 = \underline{\text{B}}$$
$$\text{Expected value of exchange movement} = \text{A} + \text{B}$$

(iii) Political Risks. It is necessary to estimate the costs associated with the political risk of investing in a particular country. This risk can be defined as the risk that the foreign government intervenes in some unexpected way that affects cash flow to the parent. There are several exposures in this area:

- Unexpected change in repatriation restrictions. In order to force reinvestment in its country, a government may forbid any funds from leaving the country or it might severely limit the amount or percent. For example, in India the amount "repatriable" is negotiable but must be approved by the authorities.
- An unexpected change in withholding taxes on remittances.
- An unexpected change in import duties.
- An unexpected change in labor and wage laws.
- Devaluation of currency.
- Expropriation of assets.

In this latter extreme situation there are two effects on the cash flow to the parent:

a. The assets are not paid for by the expropriating government, or the payment is less than fair market value.

b. Future cash flows from operations are lost.

Insurance against expropriation can be purchased in the United States through the Overseas Private Investment Corporation (OPIC), but there is a premium to be paid that represents immediate cash outflow that must be weighed against the present value of the possible future loss.

There are sources of information on each of the political risks. For example, in the United States there is Frost and Sullivan's *World Political Risk Forecasts.* This publication summarizes the expert opinions of individuals knowledgeable about each country relative to three kinds of investments:

- Financial—loans to the country.
- Investment—direct investment in the country.
- Exporting—exports to the country.

It assesses the political stability of the country, government restrictions (duties, tariffs, control of natural resources), and economic policies that affect inflation and exchange fluctuations.

This information and data like it make it possible to establish ranges of probability in estimating factors over many future years that will affect cash flows of foreign subsidiaries. It is the controller's responsibility to ensure that this analysis is done as best it can be and not ignored because it is too difficult or includes too much "soft" data.

(g) TRANSFER PRICING

A international transfer price is the value given to goods or services produced or performed in one country for the benefit or use by a related company in another country. For example, the ABC Company, and American Company has subsidiaries in Germany and France. It has a manufacturing plant in Germany that supplies products to both France and the United States. It has a computer center in France that services France and Germany. Its headquarters and research and development facilities are in the United States. Transfer prices have to be developed for:

- Products shipped from Germany to France and to the United Stats.
- Information services performed by France for Germany.
- A share of research and development expense to be paid by France and Germany.
- A management fee assessed by the U.S. parent on its subsidiaries.

We will now examine how each transfer price could be determined.

(i) Development of the Transfer Price.   It is usually the responsibility of the corporate controller to develop the transfer prices that will be used in dealings between subsidiaries or between parent and subsidiaries. The price used will result in a profit or loss for the exporting country and will directly influence the profit or loss ultimately realized in the importing country. Such a situation has led some multinationals to develop transfer prices that are very subjective and result in the lowest profit (or even losses) being reported in the highest tax rate countries and conversely the highest profit being realized in the lowest tax rate countries. While this approach seems logical and defensible at first glance, it is unfair and has resulted in more laws and restrictions by the countries that believe they are being taken advantage of. Furthermore, in recent years the IRS has taken a more aggressive stance in its search for transfer pricing abuses. The use of subjectively developed transfer prices also complicates the measurement system and frustrates local management because it cannot control or influence a significant item of cost.

A more businesslike approach is for the controller to establish a uniform, objective system of transfer pricing that is:

- Simple and inexpensive to administer,
- Understandable to the users, and
- Fair in its effect on measurements.

An arm's length, objective system can take two forms:

- Cost based.
- Market based.

(ii) Cost-Based System.   A cost-based system, the one usually favored by American companies, uses the output of the company's cost accounting systems and adds a markup for profit to it. This profit factor is usually established for the long term and not changed unless it becomes unrealistic. One approach to establishing the profit factor for a country that manufactures a product is to use a long-term (e.g., 10-year) average of the consolidated company's net-income-before-taxes margin. Other objective and fair methods can be identified by each company. Once established, the estimated transfer price should be published and used in the preparation of financial plans by the various units.

The markup on the transfer of services performed by one unit for another is more subjective and a flat percentage is usually established and not changed. For example, computer services could be marked up 10%, treasury services 5%, etc. The important factor is that after a reasonable decision is made as to amount, then it should not be changed and it should be applied uniformly in all countries. If products are marked up 15% and services 10%, there should be no exceptions made based on unique facts and circumstances. To allow deviations introduces complexity and confusion into the internal system and causes consternation and distrust on the part of country regulators and tax authorities.

(iii) Market-Based System.   A market-based system, the one usually favored by many European countries, starts with the expected selling price in the importing countries and reduces it by estimated locally incurred cost, expenses, and profit, to arrive at a transfer price that is affordable to the importer. This price is then used by the exporter in billing the related company and should recover the actual costs incurred in the production of the goods and services along with a reasonable profit. In order to make a market-based transfer-pricing system effective, the transfer price must be accurately developed and then published and used until it is revised.

(iv) Royalties.   Whether a cost-based transfer price system or a market-based transfer price system is used by a multinational company it will probably also employ a "royalty" system in addition. The transfer price system is used to move goods and services between related companies. A royalty system is used to recover, from the subsidiaries, compensation for "know-how," the use of brand names, company logos, etc. The two most common royalties charged to subsidiaries are for:

- Research and development.
- Parent-company management.

The royalty for R&D is traditionally a percentage of sales. It can be based on the ratio of R&D expense of the consolidated company to total sales of the consolidated company applied to the total sales of the subsidiary company. The resultant amount, less any locally incurred R&D, would be the R&D royalty due to the parent company.

A parent-company management royalty is usually not based on a ratio but is rather an apportionment of the total parent-company staff and general expense based on a relationship of the subsidiaries. One method is the percent each subsidiary contributes to gross income applied to the total parent-headquarters expense pool. Another is a negotiated fee based on number of employees, profit margin, growth, etc., but which recovers all parent-headquarters expenses.

In applying these approaches to the example given at the beginning of this section, the transfer prices shown in Figures 11-8 through 11-11 would be developed.

(h) TAXATION

Tax laws in each country are extensive, complex, and changeable. Since the impact of the laws is to share a significant percentage of the company's profit (on average, 30% to 60%) with the various governments of the countries in which the firm does business, it is essential that local tax experts be available to the company. These local tax professionals have the responsibility to understand local tax law, interpret the laws as it applies to the company business, advise local management how to minimize taxes, and handle the filing and reporting of local tax returns. The local tax expert should also be aware of possible tax changes and assess the effect of such changes on the local business. He would then keep the parent's tax executive (e.g., controller), informed of important matters.

While it is essential to have local tax experts it is also important to have a coordinated tax operation. This will require an expertise that is broader but perhaps not as

Figure 11-8   Development of Transfer Price for Products.

a. Product manufactured in Germany at a cost of 1,000 DM

b. ABC Company NEBT margin = 12% (for last 15 years)

c. Transfer price = 1,000 + 12%
(12% × 1,000)   120

     Total = 1,120 DM

Figure 11-9   Development of Transfer Price for Nonproduct Services.

a. Computer center work done in France at a cost of 100 FF

b. Uniform markup for all nonproduct goods and services = 10%

c. Transfer price = 100 + 10%
(10% × 100)   10

     Total   = 110 FF

Figure 11-10 Development of Royalty for Research and Development.

---

a. R&D expense for consolidated ABC Company = $10,000 (average 10 years)

b. Total gross income for Consolidated ABC Company = $200,000 (average 10 years)

c. Royalty for R&D

$$\frac{\text{R\&D Expense}}{\text{Gross Income}} = \frac{\$\ 10,000}{\$200,000}$$

= 5% of Gross Income

d. Germany current year gross
income	80,000 DM
Royalty at	5%
Total	4,000 DM
at 2 DM = $1 =	$ 2,000

France current year gross
income	100,000 FF
Royalty at	5%
Total	5,000 FF
at 4 FF = $1 =	$ 1,000

Figure 11-11 Development of Royalty for Parent-Company Management.

---

a. The parent-company corporate expense for current year = $20,000

b. Gross income by unit

	$	%
U.S.	100,000	63
France	20,000	12
Germany	40,000	25
Total	$160,000	100%

Management fee $20,000 ×

	%	$
U.S.	63	12,600
France	12	2,400
Germany	25	5,000
Total	100%	$20,000

deep as the local requirements. It is this centralized organization that develops tax planning and strategies and thereby contributes to the overall financial plan of the company. The senior tax executive has the responsibility of:

- Estimating taxes to be paid by period.
- Negotiating disputes with authorities.
- Providing advice and counsel to local experts.

He should also have the authority to resolve disputes and disagreements.

Aside from the complications of foreign taxes, the controller must be sensitive to the U.S. tax laws and regulations. The IRS carefully checks transfer prices. New tax laws are being enacted to eliminate loopholes. In 1993, a law was passed to eliminate "earnings stripping" by foreign companies. This occurs when a foreign entity uses large loans instead of direct equity investment to fund its U.S. activities. The interest payments on the loans become a tax deduction, thus "stripping" away U.S. tax exposure.

The controller and tax executives minimize taxes in all legal ways; therefore, they must be continually aware of any relevant changes in U.S. tax laws.

(i) IMPORT/EXPORT REGULATIONS

At one time, up until the early part of this century, the primary source of income for the various governments was from tariffs on imports. The regulations covering the tariffs are lengthy and complex. They represent an accumulation of many years of continual tinkering with the rules and laws. It is therefore of real importance that the controller have an understanding of these regulations so that he can organize and operate in the most effective manner and in the best interest of the company. Very often the import/export department does not report to the controller, but the controller must be knowledgeable about the operation and be involved in negotiations, procedural controls, and so on.

Duties are usually assessed on imports not on exports. However, it is the exporter who must prepare documentation in accordance with the regulations of the country of import so that the goods delivered into the country are clearly labeled and identified. This facilitates customs clearance and should result in earlier delivery of products or services to customers and earlier receipt of payment by the exporter.

There are many import/export brokers who are invaluable in helping firms find their way through this most complex operation, worldwide. Their services should be utilized. The parent company working with subsidiary company management should identify and engage the broker best qualified to handle the kind of business in which the company is engaged.

(j) MANAGING CURRENCY RISK

A controller can take some steps to lessen the impact of wildly fluctuating currency on the operation of the business, insofar as imports and exports are concerned. If, for example, the parent currency is stable and strong, then billing and requiring payment in the parent's currency will eliminate losses due to the decline in value of a foreign currency. Assume the following wherein the foreign currency has an inflation rate of 10% with a corresponding loss in value of its currency.

	May 1	June 1
U.S. dollar	1	1
= Foreign currency	1	0.9

The U.S. company sells 1,000 units at $1.00 each on May 1 and bills the customer $1,000 to be paid in 30 days. On June 1, $1,000 is received from the customer and deposited in the bank. There is no gain or loss on the transaction.

However, what happens if the U.S. company sells 1,000 units at 1 foreign currency each on May 1 and bills the customer 1,000 foreign currency. On June 1, 1,000 foreign currency is received from the customer but when converted into dollars at the bank only $900.00 is deposited. There is a $100.00 loss due to changes in exchange rates (inflation).

What can the U.S. company do to protect itself against such a loss? There are several actions available.

1. Do business only in the parent company's currency.

2. Require cash payment on delivery if business is done in foreign currency.

3. Buy a forward exchange contract if business is done in foreign currency and credit terms are offered.

(i) Currency Hedging. The first two items need little elaboration. If the transaction is made in the seller's currency then all risk of loss is transferred to the buyer. If cash is paid on delivery there is no risk of exchange loss.

However, in many instances, those two options are not available and the seller must do business in foreign currency and offer credit terms. In these instances, in order to mitigate the exchange loss the seller can buy a contract from a bank to sell foreign currency 30 days after the transaction. In the example, the contract would be bought on May 1 to deliver 1,000 foreign currency on June 1. The price is established by the bank (which is also entering contracts to deliver foreign currency to other customers) and might be for $950 for each 1,000 foreign currency delivered. The amount of loss is therefore known at the time the contract is entered into. This is called hedging and while it takes uncertainty out of the transaction, it will still produce some loss to the company, since the bank will charge a fee for handling the exchange contract in addition to reflecting an estimate in the movement of the currency.

If the company is purchasing from a foreign business, similar dynamics are at work. If you buy in foreign currency you stand the risk of inflation impacts. If the foreign currency declines faster than the buyer's currency there will be a gain; if slower, there will be a loss. The loss can be hedged by buying a contract to purchase foreign currency at a set price at some time in the future. Again, this will not usually eliminate the exchange loss, but it will eliminate uncertainty as to how much it will be.

Hedging can be used in connection with the payment of dividends, interest, and royalties, and can also be extended further into the future to cover probable purchases (e.g., where there is a single foreign supplier) and sales in an ongoing operation.

(k) FOREIGN CORRUPT PRACTICES ACT

No discussion of the controller's role in international operations would be complete without addressing the Foreign Corrupt Practices Act (FCPA). In the 1960s and 1970s, some multinationals had been involved in bribing foreign officials in order to get or keep business in their countries. It was a serious problem that had to be resolved. In December 1977, the U.S. Congress passed an act making it illegal for an issuer of securities in the United States to make certain payments to foreign officials. It also required such issuers to maintain accurate records. Following is a summary of the act's key requirements:

1. *Payments to Officials.* The act made it unlawful for American companies to offer money or gifts to any foreign official, political party, or political candidate in order to influence that person in his official capacity. Influence meant having the person fail to perform his official duties or having the person use his influence with others in order for the company to obtain or retain business in the foreign country.

   The penalties for violation of this act are fines of up to $1,000,000 for any concern convicted of the violation. In addition, individuals involved in such illegal payoffs are subject personally to fines up to $10,000 and prison for up to five years.

2. *Accounting and Control Requirements.* The act also requires that issuers of securities make and keep books, records and accounts in reasonable detail, that accurately and fairly reflect the transactions and dispositions of assets.

Devise and maintain a system of internal accounting controls that is sufficient to provide reasonable assurances that:

a. The transactions are executed in accordance with management's general or specific authorization.

b. Transactions are recorded as necessary to permit preparation of financial statements in conformity with GAAP.

c. Transactions are recorded to maintain accountability for assets.

d. Access to assets is permitted only in accordance with management's authorization.

e. Asset records are verified with physical assets periodically and appropriate action taken with respect to any differences.

The controller has a basic responsibility to comply with the requirements of the FCPA and any related legislation and amendments which pertain to maintaining an adequate system of internal control. (See Chapter 9.)

11-9 THE GLOBAL INVESTOR

The bulk of this chapter relates to global trade and the impact of such growth on business management or operations including organization, especially the financial organization, and financial procedures. We would be remiss, however, if we did not comment on global financial investments.

Suffice it to say that many portfolio managers recommend some investment, whether for diversification or otherwise, in foreign funds or stocks or other investment vehicles. This is an area where recent growth in value has been greater than in U.S. financial investments. The opportunities and vehicles are much greater than a decade ago. The U.S. now accounts for less than 40% of the world equity market. As Nicholas Bratt, president of the Scudder International Fund, states: "Why not buy the best companies in the world?"[6]

There are great risks in some foreign investments, and there is a lack of adequate information on many. Accounting methods differ sharply from country to country so that comparisons of price/earning ratios and book value can be frustrating. Choice of vehicles for foreign investment have been growing, and include:

• Global U.S. mutual funds.

• Area or country-specific mutual funds.

• Specific stock or ADRs registered on the New York stock exchange.

• Listings on foreign bourses.

As a further example, investors in London can even buy into a developing markets index fund, called Emerging Markets Index Tracker Funds with stocks from Greece to Brazil to Thailand. When discussing the global economy, the possibility of investment in foreign instruments sometimes could prove to be worthwhile. The financial executive can seek guidance from those knowledgeable in this field.

---

[6] William Glasgall et al., "The Global Investor," *Business Week*, Oct. 11, 1993, p. 121.

11-10 SELECTED REFERENCES

Abdullah, Wagdy M., and Donald E. Keller, "Measuring the Multinational's Performance," *Management Accounting,* Oct. 1985, pp. 26–30.

Allio, Robert J., "Formulating Global Strategy." *Planning Review,* Mar.–Apr. 1989, pp. 22–28.

Anderson, Nancy, "The Globalization Gap," *Management Accounting,* Aug. 1993, pp. 52–54.

Bartlett, Christopher A., and Sumantra Ghoskal, "What Is a Global Manager?" *Harvard Business Review,* Sept./Oct. 1992, pp. 124–132.

Byrne, John A., Richard Brandt, and Otis Port, "The Virtual Corporation," *Business Week,* Feb. 8, 1993, pp. 98–102.

Egelhoff, William G., "Great Strategy or Great Strategy Implementation—Two Ways of Competing in Global Markets," *Sloan Management Review,* Winter 1993, pp. 37–50.

Farnham, Alan, "Global or Just Globaloney?" *Fortune,* June 27, 1994, pp. 97–100.

Farrell, Christopher, and Michael Mandel, "Why Are We So Afraid of Growth?" *Business Week,* May 16, 1994, pp. 62–72.

Garsombke, Diane J., "International Competitor Analysis," *Planning Review,* May–June 1989, pp. 42–47.

Gibson, Richard, "Growth Formula. Gerber Missed the Boat in Quest to Go Global, So It Turned to Sandoz," *The Wall Street Journal,* May 24, 1994, pp. A1, A4.

Glasgall, William et al., "The Global Investor," *Business Week,* Oct. 11, 1993, pp. 120–126.

Hale, David D., "Global Finance and the Retreat to Managed Trade," *Harvard Business Review,* Jan.–Feb. 1990, pp. 150–162.

Hammerly, H. A., "Can American Manufacturers Compete Outside the U.S.?" *Financial Executive,* Sept.–Oct. 1990, pp. 24–31.

Hirschhorn, Larry, and Thomas Gilmore, "The New Boundaries of the 'Boundaryless' Company," *Harvard Business Review,* May–June 1992, pp. 104–115.

Keefe, Gary L., "Helping Clients Prepare for Global Markets," *Journal of Accountancy,* July 1989, pp. 54–65.

Kim, Chan W., and Renee A. Mauborgne, "Making Global Strategies Work," *Sloan Management Review,* Spring 1993, pp. 11–26.

Kupfer, Andrew, "How to Be a Global Manager." *Fortune,* Mar. 14, 1988, pp. 52–58.

Mannino, Paul V., and Ken Milani, "Budgeting for an International Business," *Management Accounting,* Feb. 1992, pp. 36–41.

Menssen, Merle D., "A Contract Price Policy for Multinationals," *Management Accounting,* Oct. 1988, 27–31.

Porter, Michael E., "The Competitive Advantage of Nations," *Harvard Business Review,* Mar.–Apr. 1990, pp. 73–93.

Prahalad, C. K., and Gary Hamel, "The Core Competence of the Corporation," *Harvard Business Review,* May–June 1990, pp. 79–91.

Reich, Robert B., "Who Is Us?" *Harvard Business Review,* Jan.–Feb. 1990, pp. 53–64.

Sookdeo, Ricardo, "The New Global Consumer," *Fortune,* Autumn/Winter 1993, pp. 68–77.

Wright, Deloris R., "Play-It-Safe Transfer Pricing," *Financial Executive,* Nov./Dec., 1992, pp. 51–55.

CHAPTER 12

Recruiting, Training, and Supervision for the Controllership Function

12-1 THE IMPORTANCE OF THE HIRING DECISION

There is probably no management responsibility more important than the hiring of people. An effective and efficient controller's operation is dependent upon the work of the professional staff and the professional quality of that work is directly related to the abilities of the individuals doing it. Therefore, hiring effectiveness is fundamental in assuring a creative and effective work group.

The hiring of the nonprofessional staff is an important aspect of the controller's people-management responsibilities, but since there are many tests and techniques that have proved effective in identifying people who will do a good job in routine or clerical tasks, this chapter focuses its attention on the recruiting, training, and supervising of accounting and other financial professionals in the controller's organization.

(a) RECRUITING PROFESSIONAL STAFF

Each professional brings with himself a personal style and approach to work. How problems are identified, what considerations are brought to a solution, the interaction with the rest of the group in developing the answer, all represent a unique contribution. It is therefore of great importance that the individuals brought into an organization are the best that can be found. Ambitious, self-motivated, knowledgeable employees are the ingredients needed to make a high-quality financial function.

Most experienced managers of professionals will agree that a person who is a high performer will continue to be a high performer over the course of his work life. Conversely, someone who is a poor performer generally cannot be motivated into becoming a high performer. The hiring decision is absolutely key to the long-term performance of the group, and as much information, skill, and time as can be brought to the task must be dedicated to it, so that the high performers are identified through the hiring process.

12-2 EXPERIENCED PROFESSIONAL OR NEW COLLEGE GRADUATE

(a) PROMOTION FROM WITHIN

In the hiring process, the controller must decide what kind of applicant he wants to bring aboard: an experienced professional or a new college graduate. Some controllers have a policy that they will hire only new college graduates who will be trained in-house and prepared for promotions. Almost all job openings above the entry level will be filled by people already in the organization, the policy of promotion from within. This approach has proved successful in many large corporations and in large public accounting firms where there are many people hired each year, some of whom prove capable of continual advancement within the organization.

Other companies use a more pragmatic approach to hiring. Senior job openings are filled both by people onboard and by new, experienced professionals depending on the job requirements. This practice sometimes results in dissatisfaction on the part of existing employees who feel they were qualified for the job and should have gotten it since they were already in the organization. It requires good management skills to keep employees informed and motivated when they think they should have gotten a position filled by an experienced outsider. The new employee must clearly have skills needed by the company and not available in the existing staff. Some examples are SEC filings experience, an extensive knowledge of taxes, broad auditing background, well-grounded information systems knowledge, etc. This latter hiring practice of bringing in skills needed, if done judiciously, acknowledges the benefits of promoting from within while accepting the idea that exceptions must sometimes be made. It also has proved to be a successful approach.

Smaller companies, wherein there are very few professional or management positions, may have to hire from the outside for each opening that occurs since there is such a limited group to choose from.

However, job security and opportunity for advancement are both important factors in retaining high-performing professionals. All companies, large and small, should demonstrate that they acknowledge this fact by considering existing employees for all job openings before they turn to the outside. Such policies are recognized and appreciated by the professional staff.

(b) DIFFICULTIES IN ASSESSING CANDIDATES

The qualities that an interviewer focuses on in determining the fitness of an applicant are difficult to assess in an experienced professional and extremely difficult with a new college graduate. Most of the judgments made will be from a negative viewpoint. That is, the candidate will show more evidence that he does not have some quality or qualities that the company wants rather than that he has all the outstanding qualifications being looked for. For example, it is far easier to say that a new graduate who is a liberal arts major does not have the technical capability to be an accountant than it is to assess the relative level of technical capability between new graduates that have majored in accounting. Grades are often used to make such a distinction, but there is no evidence to correlate grades received in college with excellent performance in the workplace.

Similarly, a judgment is frequently made that certain colleges produce more technically qualified people than do others. This also can be questioned. It is observable that the difference in professional knowledge is greater between the best student in a class and the worst student in the same class than between the best students at different institutions. However, all graduates of accredited colleges who majored in finance/accounting should have adequate technical knowledge.

Assessing new college graduates is a harder job than assessing experienced professionals. It is almost impossible to make a reliable judgment because there just is not enough information available about their professional competence and potential. There are several things that a controller can do to help the process. Several interviewers (at least three) can be used and a unanimous assessment of excellence required. The candidates can be observed in a work situation through the use of co-op or intern programs or summer employment. If these part-time or temporary employment activities are used, the students should be given challenging work and managed and assessed closely. If they are just put into routine clerical assignments or are assigned to watch what a financial executive does, for example, as an administrative assistant, they are likely to be turned off and the company will never see them again. The manager responsible for such part-time employees should give them assignments that are challenging and from which he can develop an accurate assessment of their ability and potential.

It is somewhat easier to assess an experienced professional with a track record that shows:

- Years of experience.
- Kinds of experience/advancement.

- Salary progression and level.
- Evidence of creativity.

Using this information along with informal recommendations from prior managers and colleagues should allow a reasonably accurate assessment of the applicant's qualifications.

If there is doubt about any candidate, then that candidate should not be hired.

12-3 QUALITIES TO LOOK FOR IN AN APPLICANT

While any list of criteria for hiring professionals will vary based on the experiences of the person who compiles the list, the following qualities seem to be mentioned most often:

- Technical capability.
- Mental discipline and agility.
- Integrity.
- Communication skills.
- Ability to contribute to the quality of the group.
- Good mental and physical health.
- Probability of staying with the company.
- Creativity.

(a) TECHNICAL CAPABILITY

In a controller's organization the knowledge that is acquired through the courses normally required for a bachelor's degree with an accounting or finance major or in the concentrated focus of an M.B.A. is the basic technical know-how that a new professional employee should have. If a person has one of these degrees from an accredited college or university he should be considered technically qualified. If he does not have the academic credentials, then further evaluation is necessary to ensure that he has acquired the necessary knowledge. To bring unqualified persons into a professional environment is not fair to them; they cannot compete with others for better jobs and may even have difficulty in handling their assigned responsibilities. It is also not fair to the staff who will be depending on the new employee to pull his weight. Bringing an incapable individual into a professional job, no matter how good the other qualifications, almost always results in that person becoming dissatisfied and discouraged and eventually leaving the company or requiring unusual amounts of management attention.

(b) MENTAL DISCIPLINE AND AGILITY

Unlike in school, the business problems in the real world are never tidy, usually have more than one facet, and change constantly. To be effective, a professional must be able to deal with such complexities. He or she must also have good analytical skills. This requires an ability to stay with a problem, to determine necessary facts, and to integrate them into a conclusion. It requires a good attention span and a willingness (if not an inclination) to deal in details. One of the myths of corporate America is that top management does not deal in detail. In a new and complex situation, the only way to understand a problem is through dealing with a limited amount of detail and executives do so as needed. The candidate's broadness of interests, his view of social conditions, his affiliations and hobbies, all give some indication of mental capacity and should be explored.

(c) INTEGRITY

While ethical behavior is needed throughout the company, professionals in the controller's organization must be especially trustworthy since they have more opportunities than most to go astray. Much of the white-collar crime of the 1980s—insider trading, bribes, kickbacks and defense contract padding—may all relate to or result from activities in the controller's function or from the absence of controls that were the controller's responsibility. These were illegal actions that went far beyond ethics and integrity but happened because individuals were not concerned about doing the right thing. A lack of personal integrity was the necessary predisposition to dishonesty. Financial people must care about their reputation for honesty and objectivity. They must be willing to point out unethical considerations or actions to higher management even if such things are not illegal but perhaps only misleading or unfair. This is not usually easy and at times very difficult, but the long-term payback to the company is invaluable. (See standards of ethical conduct for management accountants in Chapter 1.)

The job candidate must understand what will be expected, and his or her response to this requirement has to be carefully assessed by the interviewers.

(d) COMMUNICATION SKILLS

Being a good communicator does not just mean having a big vocabulary, excellent sentence structure, and fine enunciation. It also means:

- Participating in discussions with colleagues and contributing to meetings.
- An ability to summarize information and present it so that the listener clearly understands what is being communicated.
- Knowing *when* something should be reported and to whom.
- Producing understandable, concise reports and clear, effective letters and reports.
- Reaching one other person in a one-on-one meeting or 50 or 500 at a conference or seminar.
- Understanding what media is available and appropriate for the occasion.

It ultimately means having others understand what you want to tell them. This is sometimes difficult when financial people communicate with nonfinancial people, especially executives. The complexity and jargon of the profession must be replaced with simple business language.

In a large company, strong communication skills on the part of the professional in the controller's department are essential to the effective operation of the function and also to the career advancement of the individual. This quality can be evaluated by an interview and should be a key focus item during the hiring process.

(e) ABILITY TO INTEGRATE INTO THE GROUP

This assessment has to do with how well the applicant will function with the rest of the group. Again, it is easier to identify characteristics that will inhibit integration rather than those that will guarantee it. If a candidate, who should be on his best behavior, comes across as crude, insulting, or otherwise abrasive, you can be reasonably sure that he will be a negative influence on the work group. He will probably turn off his fellow workers and require inordinately large amounts of his manager's attention. Both results will detract from the quality of performance of the work group as a whole.

In professional organizations, an important factor for success is the willingness of the members to initiate action and act independently. It is important to try to assess if the new candidate has this same orientation. In looking at a new college graduate the only evidence, and it is not strong, is the kind of work done while in college, the activities involved in, and the leadership roles taken. A new graduate who earned college expenses through unusual or creative efforts, for example, designing and selling tee shirts, has shown signs of initiative. Someone who was elected to officer roles in clubs usually is a self-starter as well as self-motivated. An experienced professional can be questioned about work, accomplishments and honors and other involvements, and this history used to develop a picture of the candidate's initiative-taking ability.

(f) GOOD MENTAL AND PHYSICAL HEALTH

The physical demands of professional financial positions vary. Almost all, however, require some extraordinary activity from time to time—having to work all night to meet a deadline, long trips, or back-to-back trips sandwiched between meetings—these are physically demanding and an applicant must be able to handle them. An examination by a physician representing the company is the most satisfactory way to make this assessment, but a discussion with the applicant is also revealing.

Most financial positions require a high tolerance for stress. The nature of the work makes it important for an applicant to have the ability to deal with pressure questions. Things that require quick turnaround, and/or have lot of uncertainty because they are new, are not unusual in a controller's function. A financial professional must also be able to deal with contention since financial people must often use that technique to identify issues and escalate problems. All these things require an individual with good mental health and an ability to manage stress. It is very difficult to assess this characteristic in an applicant. One way that has been found useful is to describe some situations that have occurred and ask the candidate if he would be disposed to function in such an environment.

(g) PROBABILITY OF STAYING WITH THE COMPANY

Since it is a time-consuming and expensive process to hire a professional, it follows that the people who are hired should have a high probability of staying with the company. There are many considerations in trying to assess a candidate's "staying" potential. Some of them are:

From the Candidate's Perspective:

- Will he be satisfied with his professional responsibilities?
- Will he be satisfied with his advancement?
- Will he be comfortable in the culture of the organization?

From the Company's Perspective:

- Will he be able to handle changing environments?
- Will he accept retraining and updating of capabilities?
- Will he relocate if needed?

This may be the most difficult assessment of all for a recruiter to make. There are no guarantees. Each of the above subjects should be discussed in depth and the candidate's views and preferences carefully considered.

(h) CREATIVITY

No list of qualifications for a professional job would ever leave out creativity, and so it is on the list of controller's requirements. The danger in seeking this qualification is that a truly creative person probably would not be at home in the financial organization of a corporation. But since there are very few such people around and they usually find their right niche it is not a great concern in assessing new applicants that a candidate will be too creative.

What a controller's operation does need are people who can see and anticipate what should be changed and how, what new things are needed, and what old things should be eliminated. No geniuses are needed. Just people who are open-minded and willing to abandon the status quo when it is appropriate to do so. It is not easy to find creative people and there are no litmus tests to identify them. They appear in all organizations, and in fact, in most organizations each member of a professional team will show some creativity over the course of his or her career. The best thing that can be done is to hire the best people and then create an environment for them where creative thinking is encouraged and rewarded.

12-4 SOURCES OF INFORMATION FOR APPLICANT ASSESSMENT

Several things are used to assess an applicant:

- Personal interviews.
- Resume/application.
- References/personal recommendations.

(a) PERSONAL INTERVIEWS

The interview is very important in the hiring process, but to be valuable there must be several (probably at least three) interviewers who unanimously agree on a candidate's excellence. The interview process is an artificial environment and in order to be a reliable indicator of the applicant's future work performance, it must be conducted carefully and intelligently. The candidate is on his best behavior, he knows what will probably be asked, and has rehearsed his answers. Questions like "What are your career goals?" "What subjects did you enjoy in college and why?" "Why did you leave your last job?" have become commonplace and almost trite. In addition, the applicant will have thought about the kinds of questions interviewers like to hear, e.g., "What are the advancement probabilities?" "Is superior performance rewarded?" In an interview that usually lasts no more than one hour, it is very difficult to gain insights into the individual being interviewed unless the interviewer has a very clear idea of what qualities he is looking for and how to elicit information that will allow a good judgment to be made about them. A carelessly prepared-for and conducted interview is a waste of time and squanders an important source of information.

(b) RESUME/APPLICATION

The resume and application are more objective pieces of input to the decision process. They will show work experience, salary progression, and other accomplishments. Some of the information may be exaggerated and perhaps some important information is not included, but in most cases what is shown on these documents can be accepted as accurate and realistic.

The interviewer will be able to discuss very specific items especially with an experienced professional. For example, salary progression seems accelerated (or slow), areas of responsibility expanded rapidly (or very little). Each of these matters can be examined with the applicant to determine which of the characteristics the company is looking for are present.

(c) REFERENCES/RECOMMENDATIONS

Accepting written references and recommendations usually does not accomplish very much, if not followed up via a personal visit or phone call. These documents are carefully sanitized and reveal very little more about the candidate than does the resume or application. But, it is the spoken references that may be helpful in assessing qualifications. Nuances of speech, emphasis, choice of specific words, are all indications and clues that can be pursued with people who are being used as references. It is from these discussions that subtleties of ability and character may appear that will give an interviewer additional insight to an applicant.

It is time consuming to personally call references, but it will prove valuable in making an informed decision.

12-5 SOURCES OF APPLICANTS

Candidates for job openings can be identified through the following sources:

1. Colleagues of present employees.
2. Unsolicited applications.
3. Employment agencies.

4. Newspaper/magazine advertisements.

5. College placement offices/campus recruiting efforts.

Women, blacks, hispanics, and other minorities are important resources and any hiring development and training program must consider them an integral part of the overall strategy. There may be special actions needed to identify and recruit them—for example, recruiting at minority and women's colleges, advertising in publications that are aimed at these groups, liaisoning with organizations that include a high percentage of women and minorities. The additional effort required to provide equal opportunities to this group can result in reaching excellent candidates who may otherwise have been missed.

(a) COLLEAGUES

Most professional people have a wide range of colleagues and associates in the same field. Some are known from college days, others from prior jobs, still others from professional associations and even some from social contacts. These people represent a very wide and deep pool of talent that should be investigated whenever there is a need for an experienced new employee.

There are several benefits to asking an exiting employee to recommend someone for a job. If an employee recommends someone for a position in the same function and perhaps even department or group, he will not make the recommendation frivolously. The employee has made his own assessment of how well the colleague will fit into the organization and has concluded that the person being recommended has the ability and makeup to be an effective member of the group. This judgment will generally be based on a longtime relationship wherein the employee has assessed technical ability, communication skills, integrity, health, general intelligence, and the ability to integrate well into the organization. He would not want to recommend someone who will fail since it would be a reflection on his own judgment. In addition, the employee has probably discussed the company with the colleague who has made a judgment that it is the kind of organization he wants to join. Such a candidate is about the best kind one can hope for.

When there are job openings, be sure to ask your staff if they can recommend someone; there is no better source of experienced people.

(b) UNSOLICITED APPLICATIONS

All good companies receive resumes from people who want to work for the company. When these come from professionals, the person sending it has probably done some homework on the company. If qualified technically, the candidate is worth pursuing since he presumably has made an informed decision on wanting to join the company and will therefore be available if the company decides that he has all the necessary qualifications to be offered a job (this is not true of solicited applicants; even if the company decides it wants to hire one, there could be a decline by the applicant).

(c) EMPLOYMENT AGENCIES

If there are large numbers of applicants and few jobs a good employment agency can be helpful in weeding out those candidates who do not have the knowledge or experience required for the opening. If there are few applicants and many jobs in the area, using a well-known employment agency may provide candidates that the company would not otherwise see. Agencies can be a helpful recruiting tool, but they are more expensive than the other alternatives and should be used in conjunction with other actions.

(d) NEWSPAPER/MAGAZINE ADVERTISEMENTS

This source will reach people who may not be actively seeking a new job but become interested because of the opportunity described in the ad or the reputation of the company. The makeup and composition of the ad is very important and should be carefully developed.

After the ad is prepared, it must be placed in media that will bring a good response. Trade and professional publications like the NAA's *Management Accounting* and the AICPA's *Journal of Accountancy* should be used along with key metropolitan and local newspapers. The well-designed ad campaign will produce many qualified applicants for consideration.

(e) COLLEGE RECRUITING

New college graduates generally represent the largest source of professional hires. Even though it is difficult to assess their potential, almost all companies recruit new graduates, and so it is important to approach the job in a serious and organized way. Step one is to decide at which school(s) the company wants to recruit. Having made that decision, step two is to establish contact with the school: meet the deans and the department heads of the disciplines that are of interest (accounting, finance, computer science, etc.). There should be a frank discussion about the company's plans relative to recruiting. It should cover how often the company plans to recruit and approximately how many candidates will be hired. It should also include an assessment of whether there might be years when no recruiting at all will take place. The school will then have an idea of how important the company will be in the placement process of each year's graduates.

As part of the relationship, the company should consider entering into school activities. It can provide technical speakers for business school programs. It can provide counsel in interviewing, resume preparation, and other hiring activities. It can provide financial support. The relationship that is developed can also help the company in its identification of good candidates. Being on campus will allow the company's representatives to meet and get to know the students during the year. From this contact a better assessment of potential can be made at interview time.

Finally, and very important if the company plans to do a lot of new college hiring, arrangements can be made with the school for co-op and/or intern programs and for summer employees. In a co-op or intern program, students are brought into the company during the school year, and the students work rather than attend class. The length of the program varies but is typically one semester of work, one semester of school. As mentioned earlier in this chapter, if the co-op student is given a challenging assignment and is closely managed and appraised on performance, the arrangement will provide excellent evidence of how well the student will perform if given a permanent position. If the school does not have intern/co-op programs, arrangements can usually be made to hire students for the summer. Again if they are challenged, a good assessment can be made of their performance and potential as permanent employees.

12-6 EMPLOYEE DEVELOPMENT

Once a person is hired, the job of influencing him/her to achieve the maximum development of potential and the highest degree of satisfaction begins.

(a) FIRST ASSIGNMENT

The first assignment an employee receives is a very important one. It introduces him or her to the company's culture and to the professional style of the controller's organization. If the group joined is a dissatisfied one or has sloppy work habits, this environment will strongly influence the new employee to also become dissatisfied and careless. On the other hand if a new employee becomes part of a highly motivated group that strives for excellence, then he will pattern his performance the same way. He will most likely become an excellent employee, and that superiority will continue during his career with the company. The person whose initial job is in a mediocre operation will probably become a mediocre performer, and it will be very difficult to change him. It is important, therefore, to bring new people into the best functions and not the poorer ones. There is a tendency to want to get "new blood" into an area that is not performing well, but a change in this situation should be implemented within the company, not in the form of new employees.

(b) PERFORMANCE PLANNING AND EVALUATION

Since it is sometimes difficult to define professional performance in terms of objective criteria, most performance evaluations of professional people are quite subjective. It is essential therefore that the manager and employee discuss what is expected of the job, and, as importantly, what distinguishes excellent performance from poor performance. The manager should subsequently recognize both excellent and poor performance as it occurs and discuss the situations with the employee. Even if the company has a formal program of performance evaluation, which requires annual documentation and discussion of each employee's performance for the preceding year, the informal planning and ad hoc evaluations made during the year have proved to be a more effective way to manage professionals and should be used.

In discussing an employee's performance it is helpful to focus on what the review is about. It is the person's work that is being evaluated and not the individual. At times people are told by a manager that they are below average. The manager means their work is below average. The employee takes it to mean they themselves, not their work output. There is then an immediate defensive response and not much more communication takes place. The manager must establish early in the discussion that the review is about work performance: weaknesses and strengths, achievements and failures, and quality of output. As the interview progresses, the employee's feelings about job satisfaction, development needs, and career plans should be covered.

(c) CAREER PLANNING

Related to job performance evaluation is the question of what happens next in the employee's career. The responsibility for a career and career planning is each individual's, but an experienced and thoughtful manager can and should work with employees to define career goals and prepare a plan of how to achieve them, with milestones and a timetable included. For example, a career plan with the controller's position as the goal might be:

Responsibility	Year
General accounting	—
Manufacturing/cost accounting	2
Budgeting	4
Manager	6
Assistant controller	8
Controller	11

If the goal was higher, additional experience would be:

Responsibility	Year
Assistant general manager—operations	14
General manager—operations	16
Chief financial officer	19
President	23

The goals timetable and milestones can be changed as well as the specific experience needed, but each time a change is made it should be the result of a serious assessment. The goals may be judged to be too lofty or too low as the individual matures and changes. The timetable can be accelerated or delayed as the environment or personal ambitions dictate. But the principle remains: A plan should be prepared and developments assessed against it periodically.

Most careers hit a plateau from time to time during which advancement is stopped. A manager must understand when this has happened to one of the employees and discuss the situation honestly. If the individual still has higher aspirations and management does not agree, the employee should be told so that he can either accept the situation or change his performance or look for another job. Dissatisfaction and subsequent poor performance usually result when an ambitious employee plateaus and does not understand why, and no one talks about it with him.

(d) CONTINUING EDUCATION

Truly professional people want to stay current on developments in their field. They are usually interested in expanding their personal and professional knowledge. Both of these things are also valuable to the employer and are necessary in order to have a dynamic and responsive work group. The company therefore should encourage ongoing education through both company-run programs and outside courses, seminars, etc. paid for by the company and attended on company time. It takes a lot of work to put together company-sponsored courses, but they are usually extremely beneficial because they can be developed to address a specific need and within the company context. If there is in-house education for the controller's staff, a knowledgeable manager should be appointed as "course sponsor" for each course and be responsible for the content and frequency of the offering. If in-house education is not affordable, then the professional staff should be encouraged to attend specifically authorized outside programs.

(e) CERTIFICATIONS

Another development technique is to encourage your staff to study for and pass any of the professional certifications that are available. The traditional accounting certification is the Certified Public Accountant (CPA), but there are many other certifications that are of value to accounting personnel, including the Certified Management Accountant (CMA) and Certified Internal Auditor (CIA), which test one's knowledge of reporting, controls, organizational behavior, ethics, and decision analysis. The examinations are similar in difficulty to the CPA examination.

There are other related certifications that the controller should present to the accounting staff as worthwhile study options. For example, the information systems function is sometimes supervised by the controller. If so, the controller could take any of the three computer certifications supervised by the Institute for Certification of Computer Professionals (ICCP), thereby gaining a general understanding of computer systems. Also, some controllers supervise the materials function. If so, then the knowledge derived from studying for the Certified Purchasing Manager (C.P.M.) and the Certified Production and Inventory Manager (CPIM) examinations can be very useful. The accounting staff frequently interacts with these other company functions in either designing systems, understanding interactions with the accounting department, or conducting internal audits. Consequently, it is useful for these personnel to take the examinations. Finally, a staff person's career can be enhanced by having multiple certifications, since it implies extensive knowledge and the willingness to expand beyond the boundaries of the accounting field.

Contact information is listed below for some of the major certifications, including the address and phone number of the sponsoring organization. Also, Continuing Professional Education (CPE) hour requirements are listed for each certification. Please note that some certifications require more than passing grades on the examination to be certified. Since these additional requirements are both complicated, change constantly, and may vary by state, they are not listed. Please contact the sponsoring organizations for more details.

Certified Public Accountant (CPA)

> The examination is standardized, but the additional certification requirements vary greatly by state. Contact your state's Department of Regulatory Agencies (or such similar organization) for more details.

Certified Management Accountant (CMA)

> Institute of Certified Management Accountants
> 10 Paragon Drive
> Montvale, New Jersey 07645-1759
> (201) 573-6300
>
> Requires 90 hours of CPE every three years.

Certified Internal Auditor (CIA)

> Institute of Internal Auditors
> 249 Maitland Avenue
> Altamonte Springs, FL 32701-4201
> (407) 830-7600

> Requires 100 hours of CPE every three years.

Certified Production and Inventory Manager (CPIM)

> American Production & Inventory Control Society
> 500 W. Annandale Rd.
> Falls Church, VA 22046
> (800) 444-2742

> Requires no CPE.

Certified Purchasing Manager (C.P.M.)

> National Association of Purchasing Management
> P.O. Box 22160
> Tempe, AZ 85285-2160
> (602) 752-6276

> Requires recertification every five years based on a complicated points-earned system that equates to about 96 hours of CPE.

Certified Data Processor (CDP)
Certified Systems Professional (CSP)
Certified Computer Programmer (CCP)

> Institute for Certification of Computer Professionals
> 2200 E. Devon Avenue, Suite 268
> Des Plaines, IL 60018
> (708) 299-4227

> Requires 120 hours of CPE to recertify every three years. The CPE credit applies to all three certifications, not to each one individually.

12-7 MANAGEMENT AND MOTIVATION OF PROFESSIONAL STAFFS

Much has been written on motivation and management of professionals. There are several references at the end of the chapter and most libraries will reveal many others. This section does not enter into a detailed exposition of motivation theory that is readily available elsewhere and in great detail; rather, it addresses several observations the author has made during his corporate career.

Most financial professionals assume that what the well-known motivational expert Frederick Herzberg called "hygienic factors" will be in place in a well-run company. These include: a safe and clean workplace, adequate and competitive salary, fair and reasonable promotion and increase programs, and sound and unobtrusive administrative policies. If these fundamental things are not present, the professional employee will be diverted from work and focus an inordinate amount of attention on them. They are motivational "dissatisfiers," in Herzberg's terms, and will cause people to be unhappy and often leave the organization. While most of these influences are outside the control of the controller, they are important to the effective and efficient operation of his function. As an executive of the company, the controller must ensure that there are few or no dissatisfiers influencing his group.

With the hygienic factors in place, the manager can turn attention to how to influence the professional staff to do tasks in an excellent way in order to benefit the company. The things that most professionals look for in their work are:

- A challenging assignment.
- The authority to do the job.
- Recognition of their contribution.

It is up to managers to provide these elements to their staff.

Challenges can take many forms. Some are complex intellectual problems. Others require extensive coordination efforts for success. Still others need fast decisions with close-in completion dates. Many have elements of all three situations. The professional should have the problem described and the due date established and then be given the backing and resources needed to finish the job. They should be allowed to make decisions, use other staff members, and have access to information systems.

Their work should be evaluated when completed, and an evaluation made as to the success and quality of it. If the job was done in an excellent way, recognition should be expressed both privately by the manager to the employee, and publicly by a bonus or award that should be presented in front of the work group.

The key ingredient in motivating a professional staff is the manager and how well he understands and communicates with the people. He has to be a good listener in order to understand the needs of the people and also must be able to have the employees understand what is being told to them. Frequent (weekly) meetings of the whole work group, wherein each person updates the group on current activities is an effective means of developing team involvement. Members of the group should feel free to comment and offer suggestions or criticisms of anyone else's work efforts. The one-on-one meeting should happen routinely, but certainly no less than once a month. If a manager is an effective communicator, no employee will ever be uncertain about what is expected of him and will always have a good understanding of how his work is perceived and what management sees as his future in the company.

What the manager must remember is that each person is different and has different expectations and needs. What stimulates one (e.g., praise) may make another complacent. The effective manager's job is to understand each of the people in the organization and permit and encourage each to grow and achieve in his or her own best interests and those of the company.

12-8 SELECTED REFERENCES

Cribben, James J., *Effective Management Leadership.* New York: American Management Association, 1972.

Herzberg, F., B. Mausner, and B. Snyderman, *The Motivation to Work.* New York: Wiley, 1959.

Reddin, W. J., *Effective Management by Objectives.* New York: McGraw-Hill, 1971.

Rogers, R. E., and R. H. McIntire, *Organization and Management Theory.* New York: Wiley, 1983.

Sargent, Alice G., *The Androgynous Manager.* New York: American Management Association, 1981.

Schiff, Jonathan B., and Claire May, "Finance Training and Development for the Competitive Edge," *Management Accounting,* April 1993, pp. 43–46.

Welsh, A. N., *The Skills of Management.* New York: American Management Association, 1981.

CHAPTER 13

The Controller's Role in Investor Relations

13-1 INTRODUCTION

Very little has been written about the controller's role in investor relations (IR). This is partially because many controllers, by all outward signs, are not actively engaged in this function—at least as far as the public is concerned. In Chapter 2 of this text, investor relations activities of the controller are included in the last category of "Other Primary Duties." To many outsiders with an interest in investments, the controller is variously regarded as the "inside man," the number cruncher, the figure man, or the introverted accountant. To be sure, many of these same representatives do not have a real understanding of what the controller should do or can do.

In contrast to this view of the controller, in discussions with security analysts, they have expressed opinions to the authors concerning a preference for talking about financial matters with the controller because "he has the facts" (while many of the non-accounting-trained public relations persons do not). Certainly if the chief accounting officer wishes to climb the financial ladder or aspire to a broader executive career, experience in the investor relations arena may be very useful.

In reaching some conclusion concerning those duties the controller might perform in this interesting investor relations function, a review of the following facets may help in ferreting out those activities for which he might be suited, and which he might enjoy:

- The objectives or purpose of the investor relations function.
- The nature of the function.
- The principal vehicles used to convey financial information.
- The nature of the "customer."
- What type of information is desired and limits on its disclosure.
- Some brief observations about organization structure in this field.

13-2 OBJECTIVES OF THE INVESTOR RELATIONS FUNCTION

In a general sense, it may be said that the principal purpose of the investor relations function, regardless of who performs it, is the enhancement of shareholder value. Isn't this a familiar term? The stated purpose by the perpetrators of some hostile takeovers is "to enhance shareholder value"; the defense against such actions, as voiced by some CFOs of the targets, is an effort "to enhance shareholder values by increasing the price of the common stock." As a matter of fact, one of the purposes of sound financial policy is to enable the company to raise funds, on an acceptable basis, to meet its needs, so as to enhance the long-term interests of the shareholder; and a related corollary is to cause the entity to be so well regarded in the financial marketplace that its stock will command an acceptable price/earnings ratio.

Some CEOs might still regard the IR function as a simple financial reporting activity, with no intent to affect the stock price. But many chief financial officers will bluntly state that the objective is to maximize the market price so as to minimize the cost of equity capital. Executives of brokerage houses will acknowledge that a continuing investor relations program helps prepare the market for a public offering, and influences the credit ratings of fixed-income securities. Certainly the importance of the stock price is not lost on those CEOs engaged in sell-offs, or acquisitions, or other restructuring. In the view of the authors, these enumerated purposes, however described, translate into an objective of enhancing shareholder value.

In today's environment, companies must compete for investment capital—whether in the bond market or the equity market. But to secure recognition, the story of the enterprise must be told. Just as the advantages and uses of a company's service or product must be described and marketed, so also information about the value of an entity's securities and its financial prospects must be disseminated, understood, and accepted.

13-3 EVOLVING NATURE OF THE FUNCTION

Investor relations has been, and probably still is, an evolving activity. About 30 years ago, it often was a part of the public relations department, perhaps viewed as a somewhat specialized communication function. In the 1950s through the 1960s and into the early 1970s, with the rapid growth of employee retirement funds, many blue-chip companies including General Electric, used skilled communicators to "educate" portfolio managers and brokerage intermediaries about the investment merits of the company's stock. By the mid-1970s, when many individual investors abandoned the stock market, when the market was dominated by large institutions, when many less-than-blue-chip companies felt they were neglected by the brokers and investing institutions, and when the need for more capital intensified, many managements became more aggressive, and began directly contacting potential investors, both institutional and individual, who were willing to take more risks and were often receptive to growth situations and better-than-average returns. The individuals representing these companies were variously communication specialists and security analysts. In this time frame, with the growth of dividend reinvestment plans, self registration, and an increased recognition of the need to plan and sell new security issues, the IR function became more marketing oriented.

These changes also induced changes in the nature of the IR specialist. While communicators (public relations) and security analysts had predominated, gradually more and more individuals well acquainted with finance assumed a greater role. The customers became far more sophisticated about what they needed. So the IR function more and more evolved into a combination of two disciplines—communications and finance.

Accordingly, in the 1990s, the investor relations function must not only communicate effectively about past performance, but it must more closely align itself with the strategic plans of management and tell its customers more about corporate goals and the entity's strengths and weaknesses.

13-4 COMMUNICATION VEHICLES FOR INVESTOR RELATIONS

At this point, perhaps a recap of the several vehicles now commonly used to communicate with "investor relations customers" may be helpful. Each is directed to a somewhat different audience, and each typically conveys a disparate or varied message—but always with an investor-related aspect. They are distinct in words and tone from the typical product or service advertising originating with the advertising or marketing department. The methods used to communicate investor-related messages, in no special order, include:

- Annual report to shareholders.
- Quarterly reports to shareholders (and the financial community).
- Annual meeting with shareholders.
- Reports to the SEC:
  a. Annual Report Form 10-K.
  b. Quarterly Report Form 10-Q.
  c. Current Report Form 8-K.
- Regular or special meetings with security analysts, institutional investors, brokers, and large individual investors—often arranged in cooperation with one of the several associations or societies for analysts.
- Institutional advertising in newspapers or periodicals (financial or general interest).

- Dividend stuffers.
- Corporate announcements of special interest to investors or potential investors:
  a. New products or services.
  b. Management changes.
  c. Acquisitions and/or divestments.
  d. Reorganization attempts, etc.: restructuring, unfriendly takeovers.
- Videocassettes dealing with financial matters.
- Use of toll-free telephone numbers.
- Individual meetings with government representatives and the stock exchanges concerned with financial matters (IRS, SEC, etc.).

13-5 INVESTOR RELATIONS MESSAGE RECIPIENTS

Broadly and technically speaking, the IR function must service an unusually complex and diverse audience. For example, here is a typical listing (with some overlapping) of the vast potential "customers":

- Investors and potential stock investors (small).
- Large institutional stock investors and potential investors.
- Security analysts.
- Credit-rating agencies.
- Financial advisory services.
- Brokerage firms.
- Bond-rating agencies.
- Bank loan officers.
- Bondholders.
- Financial press.
- Portfolio managers.
- European/Japanese investors.
- Acquisition candidates.
- Government agencies dealing with financial matters (federal, state, and local).
- Employees.

Having said this, it should be realized that three broad groups with which the IR activity is *primarily* and continuously directed are (a) security analysts, (b) stockbrokers, and (c) large institutional investors. Practically speaking, and as discussed later, some of these information-seeking persons would deal directly with the chief financial officer—that is, the bank loan officer handling most of the company's current bank borrowings, the bond-rating agency, or credit-rating agency—in some kind of one-on-one desired meeting that is heavily and technically financial in nature.

Many of the members of the three principal groups mentioned—security analysts, stockbrokers, or institutional or other large investors (or their representatives)—are quite sophisticated financially. Each of the three groups may, and usually does, have different information needs; and each may be motivated, for different reasons, to discuss the financial affairs of the entity.

13-6 INFORMATION NEEDS OF THE FINANCIAL ANALYST

The management of a company usually desires that it be perceived in its most favorable light—hopefully without exaggeration, and as objectively determined. While communication with all segments of the IR audience on this matter is important, perhaps the key person is the financial analyst, also called the security analyst. He is in a position to influence a large cross-section of investors. It therefore especially behooves the IR executives to know what information the analyst needs and how he will probably use it. It is imperative that the financial executive involved (CFO or controller) properly interpret the information for this analyst and not merely infer certain conclusions. In most instances, the analyst desires information so that he can reasonably predict earnings (and hence market price, potential of the stock dividend rate, etc.).

A most important source of information for the security analyst is management presentations generally made to large institutional investors, and brokers, or investment bankers, as well as the analysts themselves. The information gained from such meetings, plus that distilled from annual and quarterly reports, or Form 10-Ks, etc., together with discussions among other analysts, and other articles about the company and the industry, enable the analyst to reach certain conclusions about the entity, and aid in helping him predict financial performance.

These analyst meetings present an unusual opportunity for the company to portray itself in its best light. They not only permit the company to make *factual* presentations, but also to subjectively influence the analyst about the depth of management and long-term objectives of the company. Moreover, they enable management to directly answer the questions of the group and fully explain troublesome events, such as complicated footnotes to the annual report, etc.

Each industry and each company has certain factors that are important to its well-being and growth. For example, in the aerospace business, the order backlog is of significance, as well as the status of various contracts or programs. In other companies, product development might be of major interest. Facts and opinions should be divulged within the limits of prudent disclosure. Such meetings with analysts are not just public relations events. Solid and specific information is needed.

While each entity has its own requirements, here are some suggestions about presentation content to analysts for a well-established, reputable company.

1. To give a sense of an experienced, in-depth, and well-qualified management:
   a. The CEO should be present and give the principal talk—about prospects, style of management, management development programs, market position, etc.
   b. The key executives should be introduced, and usually should make some short comments about their areas of responsibility.
   c. Perhaps the organization structure and incentive system, etc., should be discussed.
2. To provide an insight into the long-term prospects of the entity, the following subjects might be covered by a knowledgeable executive (CEO, executive vice-president, senior vice-president of Finance or controller)

    a. The system or method of strategic planning.

    b. The short-term or annual plan process, and the related control system.

    c. Some examples of long-range objectives that have been achieved (and perhaps some that were not).

    d. The long-range outlook for the industry or selected products or markets.

    e. The status of market penetration or dominance for some key products.

    f. Important research and development programs underway. (Whether or not specific quantified projections or plans should be divulged may depend on the individual circumstances.)

3. To provide a broad financial picture, including the financial strength of the company, perhaps a slide presentation (graphs and charts) could be given that would identify:

    a. Status of orders on hand.

    b. Trend of sales, by product line.

    c. Margins by product line, or organizational units, and trends thereof.

    d. Financial position through comments about a condensed balance sheet, with emphasis on key ratios or relationships.

    e. The trend of long-term indebtedness, times debt service is covered; debt capacity, etc.

    f. The trend of cash flow by important segments: from operations, investing activities, and financing activities, and perhaps cash flow per share from operations.

    g. Trends on equity and earnings:

      • Growth in equity.

      • Equity relationships (ROE).

      • Earnings per share.

      • Return on assets.

    h. By simple explanation and illustration, any aspect of the financial statements that often causes confusion (inventory, valuation method, tax accruals, reserves, etc.).

    i. Perhaps some comparative ratios with industry or selected competitors.

    j. Company posture regarding acquisitions or diversification.

4. The chief marketing executive probably should make a presentation that would describe and illustrate major new products, or major revenue procedures, and the sales prospects for the next year or two.

5. Other executives, as appropriate, might discuss any timely topics, such as:

    a. Employee relations.

    b. Cost reduction programs.

    c. Process improvements, including use of computers.

    d. Information resource management.

    e. Quality control changes.

    f. Any major troublesome contracts or publicity items, etc.

The objective should include a demonstration of financial conservatism, stability, and ability to raise capital when needed. Interpretation of what the figures mean should be given; it should not be left to the unaided judgment of the analyst.

In fact, the executives deeply involved in the process should know their audiences and determine what they need to know, so that the analysts (and others) may make a proper evaluation of the entity.

These are some key points that should be covered. Experience at meetings with analysts, including their questions, will provide guidance as to other subjects of interest.

The data presented to the analysts might serve as a point of departure for responding to the information needs of other groups.

Above all, the presentations by management, and the responses to questions raised by the analysts, must be open, frank, and responsive to the information needs. Any sense that management is not forthright and will not truthfully answer reasonable questions will cause analysts to choose not to follow the company's progress.

13-7 INFORMATION NEEDS OF OTHER GROUPS

The financial analysts and large investors of all groups, as might be expected, do the most probing. Their approach is highly analytical. Usually, when a company can adequately communicate with this group, it can deal effectively with most others.

These other players have varying interests, some of which involve answers to the items raised in the preceding sections. Perhaps the typical individual shareholder is most concerned with the general progress of the company and the prospect of continued and increasing dividend payments. A highly skilled financial background is not required to meet his inquiries. At the other extreme, a bank loan officer will be interested in the prospects of repaying the loan on time; and it might be proper to make available to him the annual plan or budget for the next year or two, and perhaps the long-range financial plan. His relationship is more confidential than the general public, and he is entitled to such knowledge. Bond-rating agencies may be exposed to past and prospective debt service coverage and related matters. Credit agencies, who have the published annual report available, may direct their questions to the content of the balance sheet items, and prospective earnings. Many other investors may be interested in the significance of certain litigation, or product development. The required financial knowledge of the IR interface person will depend on the types of questions and the inquisitor's knowledge and interest.

13-8 DISCLOSURE POLICY

In providing information to or communicating with analysts, brokers, investors, or others, a matter to be resolved is: What constitutes proper and adequate disclosure? Typically management is concerned about excessive disclosure that may harm the company. On the other side of the question, there should be sufficient disclosure to enable the analysts and others to discern shareholder value. Hence, the problem is one of weighing the benefits versus the costs.

On the one hand, the dangers of excessive disclosure include these:

- Loss of competitive advantage through early disclosure of new products or marketing strategy or other strategic information.

- Exposing the entity to litigation by reason of allegedly providing insider information, or attempting to foreclose competition or otherwise violate antitrust laws.
- Generating earlier competitive reaction, or even new competitors, than would otherwise be the case.
- Revealing strengths or weaknesses that might invite an unfriendly takeover attempt.

Most analysts would prefer to get information first, or early, but normally there is no benefit to them in causing long-term share decline. And most appreciate the need to protect competitive information.

While there is a danger in excessive disclosure, there are sometimes unrecognized costs of insufficient disclosure. Some of these are the following, resulting in a share price lower than normally might be the case:

- Failure to provide adequate data may encourage analysts and others to avoid the company and fail to follow its progress.
- Lack of information may cause unpleasant or unexpected surprises—something the financial community abhors.
- If the management does not maintain good relations with analysts and investors, it usually takes much longer for positive developments to become known and reflected in the stock price.
- Most importantly, lack of firsthand knowledge, such as that secured through personal contact, prevents analysts and other interested parties from "kicking the tires"—from assessing the depth and quality of management, the adequacy of the company's controls, its ability to cope with change, as well as the quality of the product and services.

The IR group and management must thoroughly weigh what constitutes a proper balance in its disclosure policy.

13-9 ORGANIZATION STRUCTURE FOR INVESTOR RELATIONS

A successful IR program must, as previously mentioned, permit the exercise of two skills by company executives: the ability to (a) communicate effectively and (b) ferret out and comprehend the financial significance of operating trends and relationships, together with the composition of the various elements in the financial statements and their significance or impact. Company representatives must clearly, and often in sophisticated or knowledgeable financial terms, discuss highly technical financial issues with a great many types of investors or potential investors. What organizational structure best fills or facilitates this execution?

Several structures may be observed in operation, but one truth is paramount: There must be a coordinated approach; the company must speak with one voice. Thus, confusion is created if the vice-president of sales discusses the potential financial impact of a new product to a group of distributors as having certain results, and the financial vice-president describes a quite different financial impact with a group of financial analysts.

Assuming adequate and effective coordination among the company's spokespersons, as to the presentation of financial data, what organizational structure is desirable? One answer is, "The one that is effective."

The external or investing public of a company is viewed by many top executives as consisting of several parts of the whole. The result is a dichotomy of views about proper organization:

1. In some companies there is no single executive who is responsible for the external investor relations (as distinguished from employee relations). Basically, each major executive meets with his audience, e.g., a research audience, a marketing audience, a manufacturing group, a financial group. However, whenever financial content is involved, it would be cleared with the proper financial executive.

2. In other entities, a single executive is held accountable for the IR function.

   Under this latter scenario, the IR activities might be a segment of the public relations department (renamed an investor relations department). Also, under such a plan the finance department, including the controller, would be considered an internal function—a resource to be made available to those responsible for the IR activities.

3. Some other organizational structures divide the responsibility into two segments: (a) The activity relating to preparation of the annual and quarterly reports to shareholders, institutional or financial advertisement, and small shareholder inquiries, etc., is handled by the public relations department (and coordinated with finance)—the so-called mass media facet; (b) The unit relating principally to contacts with security analysts, large institutional or individual investors, investment bankers, rating agencies, etc.—that audience assumed to possess considerable financial know-how—is handled by an investor relations unit reporting to the CFO or a financial officer. Presumably the members of this unit have a financial background (CPAs, accounting, investment banking) but have also been trained in communication skills.

The type of "customer" determines the unit most likely assigned the task. There must be coordination with the public relations segment or unit.

Finally, one other factor should be mentioned as a possible participant in the IR activity, and that is a professional IR agency. While such a firm often may be used by small companies, sometimes they can also be helpful consultants to medium-sized and larger entities in properly organizing the IR function. The authors should point out, however, that most investor/analyst types prefer to deal with a member of management, and not an outsider, in seeking financial information about a company.

The proper organizational structure for a specific company will depend, again, on the interests, ability, and personality (and perhaps financial interest) of the officers and executives who are actual or potential participants—consistent with management philosophy, style of management, available time, etc.

13-10 ROLE OF THE CONTROLLER AND OTHER PRINCIPALS

Having provided only a very general background on the sources of financial information about the company, the type of inquirers, and suggestions about management presentations to the security analysts in particular, the basic question is, "What should be the role of the controller?"

As is often true, what functions an officer performs depends on several factors, including his or her ability, personality and interests, along with the interest and capabilities of the other officers, as well as the size of the company, management organization structure, management style, etc. If there is a chief financial officer as well as a controller, the duties will be shared. And in those instances where the CEO feels he himself should play a major role in IR, that will further divide the effort. If the controller is a good financial analyst, certain activities will tend to be assigned to this position; and if the chief accounting officer is, in addition, a good presenter or communicator, then still other duties are likely to fall in this direction.

For the typical medium-sized to large company, where the CEO is somewhat active in IR, and where the CFO tends to spend some time with IR activities, a likely split of functions might be listed as follows:

Controller

1. An *information resource* or source for any *financial* data, for those officers and executives who need it for IR purposes including:

   a. Financial statements reflecting actual results and/or condition of the entity and/or any segments, such as

      (i)   Statement of income and expense.

      (ii) Statement of cash flows.

      (iii) Statement of financial condition.

   b. Relevant financial *analyses* of actual data and trends of these statements, as required for IR purposes, such as

      (i)   Inventories.

      (ii) Accounts receivable.

      (iii) Long-term debt, by category of debt.

      (iv) Plant and equipment, by location.

      (v)   Relevant ratios, including comparisons with industry and competitors.

      (vi) Detail and type of revenue and expenses by appropriate segment.

   c. Financial statements and related analyses representing *planned* or *forecasted* results or condition, both the annual plan and long-range plan, for the consolidated entity and any segment. (This data should be available, but often should not be disclosed to the analyst groups, etc.)

   d. Relevant *graphs* and tabulations, showing financial trends and relationships, actual and projected. Basically, all financial data (whether to be presented to outsiders, or simply used as background or a reference source) should be prepared under the supervision of, or by, the controller, subject to appropriate suggestions or constraints by the CFO or CEO.

2. As required, an *interpreter* of the financial data, when asked to do so by other major officers or executives present, to the appropriate IR audience (groups, individuals—analysts, investors, financial information sources such as Dun & Bradstreet, TRW, bank loan officers, etc.).

3. A *communicator* of financial information to individuals and groups entitled to receive it, under the applicable working rules. This would include presentations to groups or individual analysts, investors, or brokers, etc., as well as the answering of their questions. It might be that the controller would (1) make presentations in the absence of the CFO, (2) give talks to small groups regularly, with the CFO (or even the CEO) handling the larger or more important meetings. Certainly, if the controller is a good communicator he should be trained to be the alter ego of the CFO.

4. Either prepares, or reviews for accuracy and completeness, any financial commentary in such financial documents as the annual report to shareholders, quarterly report to shareholders, Form 10-K, or 10-Q, etc.

5. A *reviewer* for content and accuracy all news releases, special announcements, and publications of the investor relations activity (and those of other executives) dealing with *financial/accounting* matters. As applicable, he would make his recommendations or comments to the CFO, unless he is authorized to make the final decision in the event of disagreement or needed major changes.

When the controller is de facto the chief financial officer, he would exercise the duties listed above, plus those of the CFO enumerated next.

Chief Financial Officer

1. Should be the principal communicator of financial policy, and the reasons therefor, financial status and operating trends and relationships to major groups, including the leading security analysts of the industry, major brokerage houses, and large investors—actual or potential—whether institutional or individual.

2. Should be the principal spokesman or negotiator, subject to approval of the CEO and/or board of directors, as may be applicable, in connection with the actual and imminent raising of capital—whether equity or indebtedness. Thus, he or she would be the principal contact with investment bankers, large commercial bankers, lessors, and institutions, using such advice and assistance deemed necessary.

3. Should delegate to the controller any of the above duties, and any lesser ones, relative to investor relations when deemed to be in the interest of the company, and assuming the controller is experienced and capable.

4. Should review all major published financial documents (annual report to shareholders, quarterly reports, financial news releases), and receive comments from controller, for accuracy, completeness, adequate disclosure, etc.

5. If the IR department is a part of the financial organization, should direct its activities, establish appropriate disclosure policies, and develop a competent and professional IR staff to handle those functions not assigned to the CEO or the controller or himself.

 If the IR activities are under the cognizance of the CEO or a public relations officer, the CFO should make appropriate recommendations on suggested improvements.

Chief Executive Officer

1. Preside over major meetings with security analysts, large investors, and the like and present the background and related information on such important matters as:

   a. Company mission, purpose, goals and objectives, etc.

   b. Competitive position of the company.

   c. Major operating accomplishments in recent periods.

   d. Direction company is headed.

   e. Any forthcoming major events that can be announced (management changes, acquisitions, divestments, etc.).

   Additionally, he should answer the questions of the audience on major public matters, etc. By bearing and knowledge he should demonstrate that he is, indeed, the CEO.

2. Meet, on a one-to-one basis or with a few individuals only, any major investor, opinion makers, banker, etc., who wish to see him. Discuss major points as in 1 above.

3. As appropriate in IR meetings, refer financial questions to the vice-president of finance or controller, and certain operating questions to the operating executive present.

4. As to important financing matters, meet with other major players, as deemed proper: commercial bankers, investment bankers, rating agencies, institutional investors, etc. He should lend support to the proposed transactions, provide relevant background about the company, and answer questions directed to him.

5. Ascertain that the messages in any important public statements, e.g., the annual report, quarterly financial reports, financial-type news releases are as he thinks they should be, or understand why not.

6. Address important company matters and the annual meeting of shareholders.

13-11 CHANGES IN THE CAPITAL MARKETS

Among other objectives, a purpose of the IR function is to enable the company to raise funds to meet its needs, on an acceptable economic basis, so as to enhance the long-term interests of the shareholders. But the financial environment changes, among other things, as the business cycle changes, or the perceived relative status of the company or industry changes, or, indeed, as the moods of the investor vacillates. Some recent developments include demands by some pension funds that they have a greater voice in certain company policy decisions; increased agitation by unhappy shareholders about exorbitant levels of executive compensation or perquisites; pressures by some institutional investors to make the board of directors more independent of the CEO; proposals by company management for the "protection of shareholders" in the event of an unsolicited bid for the corporation; and vastly increased volatility in the stock market. While circumstances will differ company by company, there will be instances wherein the CFO, probably assisted by the controller, will find it necessary to become more aggressive in cultivating the financial market, and take these actions: (1) Establish *specific* financial market related objectives, which will be in the shareholders' interest, and (2) Develop some methods of helping to reach these (new) objectives. All of this is to say that the investor relations function is not merely a passive communication caper.

(a) SOME SUGGESTED FINANCIAL MARKET OBJECTIVES

The objectives of the company, with respect to financial markets will depend on what condition appears to need improvement or change. In the experience of the authors, here are some typical objectives, one or more of which might apply to a particular entity:

- Increase the P/E ratio to X, or to the S&P 500 level, or to the best in the industry.
- Lengthen the average stock holding period by attracting more long-term investors.
- Reacquire 25% of the present outstanding shares through stock repurchase programs.
- Increase the average daily share sales volume—to, say, 100,000 (so that institutions can buy or sell in a given day without significantly moving the stock price).
- Reduce volatility by expanding the shareholder base.
- Build shareholder demand (by diversifying the shareholder base).
- Create a greater demand for company bonds or other debt securities.
- Reduce the proportion of shares held by institutional investors.

While consistent earnings growth, based on good products and capable marketing, and a sound financial position, are fundamental in attaining and maintaining many of these objectives, another aid is to target particular markets and properly communicate relevant financial information. Which targets need to be reached will require an analysis of the present shareholder types, etc. A few comments on this phase follow.

(b) SOME SUGGESTED METHODS

A successful investor relations program involves providing reliable, consistent, timely, and truthful information about the company on such matters as depth of management, developments as to products and markets, probable trend of sales and earnings, and some guidance on company financial objectives—not only to the usual array of stock brokers, security analysts, and individuals, but more especially to carefully selected institutions that probably would be a desirable type of shareholder—who could aid in meeting the objectives set out in the investor relations agenda. Some suggestions include:

1. *Maintain a current, well-documented background book which is available to all key executives, and for all key contacts with the investing groups.*
   Such an information source would provide these benefits:
   (a) The reader will have a better idea of what subjects are matters of concern to an investor or potential investor.
   (b) The executives will have a consistent and uniform response to the queries.
   (c) The reader will be up-dated on the current developments in his company which should be communicated to the investing public.

   In terms of content, aside from the financially relevant information on the company itself, the data book might contain information about potential investor contacts: location, position, investment patterns, availability for conference calls, and so on.
2. *Be certain that all key internal officers are current on new and important developments and that the investor significance is understood.*

With such a background, the likelihood is reduced of making offhand comments which can be misinterpreted.

3. *Establish close one-on-one relationships with selected institutional investors where particular investor relations objectives can be furthered.*

It already has been mentioned that increasing the investor base by the addition of long-term investors will lengthen the average holding period. Creating closer relations with institutional investors also may reduce volatility. Volatility occurs or increases because large segments of the shareholder population decide to take the same action at the same time, for example, sell the shares. If large shareholders are kept informed about the company, this may decrease the tendency to follow the actions of other investors. These long-term investors may buy more shares while the short-horizon investors may be selling—thus creating a balance in the marketplace, and maintaining the price.

The program for contacting large institutional investors or potential investors can include periodically scheduled visits (once or twice a year) to the financial centers (New York, Boston, Chicago, San Francisco, etc.) to meet particular institutional investors and security analysts.

4. *Consider the possibility of conference calls to selected investors or security analysts.*

This has the advantages of (a) making one call instead of numerous ones, (b) releasing the data to many sources at the same time, and (c) tends to keep the message more consistent. A disadvantage arises of making it more difficult to answer all the questions of every analyst, and so on.

5. *In some circumstances, increase the contacts with non-institutional investors.*

Some corporate financial executives have felt their company might be vulnerable to extend pressures when too large a portion—say 75 to 80%—of the shares were in the hands of institutional investors. For example, the entity might become a target for a hostile take-over. Hence, there could be merit in expanding the ownership base through appropriate and frequent contacts with buy-side security analysts, brokers, and so on.

So there is much to be said for considering certain *specific* investor relations objectives and developing a specific program to meet them.

13-12 SELECTED REFERENCES

Abrahamson, Carol, and Joe Rodgers, "The New Investor Relations Game," *Financial Executive,* March–April, 1992, pp. 18–21.

Appleman, Mark J., "Rediscovering Investor Relations," *Financial Executive,* Sept. 1984, pp. 10–14.

Chugh, Lal C., and Joseph W. Meador, "Break the Barrier Between You and Your Analysts," *Financial Executive,* Sept. 1984, pp. 16–21.

Graves, Joseph J., Jr., "A Recipe for Investor Relations Success," *Financial Executive,* Sept. 1984, pp. 22–30.

Groves, Ray J., "Financial Disclosure: When More Is Not Better," *Financial Executive,* May–June, 1994, pp. 11–14.

Weaver, Constance K., "Lessons in Courting Overseas Investors," *Financial Executive,* March–April, 1994, pp. 52–54.

PART TWO

THE PLANNING FUNCTION OF CONTROLLERSHIP

CHAPTER 14

Business Plans and Planning: The Interrelationship of Plans, Strategic Planning

14-1 INTRODUCTION

Business planning, when properly done, is a complicated but fascinating procedure, intertwined with all the functions or departments of the entity.

This chapter discusses how the various elements of the strategic plan are interrelated and provides an overview of the planning process. It seeks to review some of the basic questions raised in the planning process and to consider in some detail the elements of strategic planning.

Chapter 15 further shows how the elements of the strategic plan are combined into an integrated plan, expressed in financial terms, covering a span of several years—a task of particular importance to the chief financial executive and the controller.

Chapter 16 then provides an overview of the short-term planning process and how the parts are combined into the annual business plan.

14-2 BUSINESS PLANNING DEFINED

The concept of business planning is not new. Many companies have utilized formal or organized plans for years. What is different, however, is the emergence of comprehensive planning systems and a new sense of urgency about the need to plan—whether it be because of the disastrous inflation of the late 1970s and early 1980s, the heightened foreign competition, the increased social responsibilities of business, or the speed of the technological changes. Be that as it may, the financial aspects of planning are important to business survival and growth; and the financial officers of the corporation should be aware of the interrelationship of plans, methods of planning, problem areas, and the concomitant financial implications of each.

Given the need for sound planning, what, then, is a plan? It is a predetermined course of action. The process of thinking ahead, of making a judgment on a course of action for which consideration has been given to the many feasible alternatives available, is the planning process. A plan, accordingly, must recognize three factors.

1. It must involve the future.
2. It must involve action.
3. It should give recognition to the organizational structure of responsibility, authority, and accountability by which action takes place in a given business.

A plan is the predetermination to take action; that characterizes planning from other thinking about the future—which distinguishes it, for example, from mere daydreaming or forecasting. Forecasting may involve predicting the future to some degree, but it does not necessarily involve future action by the planner or his company. It often involves future action by someone else. Hence forecasting may be used to predict future conditions or action by other forces, such as governments, competitors, and environment. But the planner, using such knowledge, determines a course of action to reach his objective.

Such planning may be done only in the mind of the chief executive or may involve a well-organized effort by many individuals. The problems of what, why, and how will be discussed.

14-3 FRAMEWORK FOR BUSINESS PLANNING

Perhaps the best way to understand what constitutes good business planning is to recognize three separate and related elements:

1. The system of plans that should comprise the whole—for *all* activities of the business and for *all* planning periods—and the relationship of each to the other.

2. The orderly process by which each plan is formulated.

3. The basic elements that should be inherent in any sound plan of action.

But before the planning system and process is discussed, it may be desirable to review the "time factor."

14-4 TIME AS RELATED TO PLANNING

In a sense, planning may be described as an opportunity to consider and experiment with the valuable assets (including both men and materials) of a company before committing them to risk. The future period for which different industries must commit these resources varies greatly as, for example, from the season-oriented women's apparel business to the decade-oriented orchard or ranch operations.

It is obvious in the planting of citrus groves or the building of a butadiene plant that a period beyond the immediate future must be considered. This properly should involve "long-range planning." This difference in period for which planning must be undertaken can be better viewed in the light of "generations" of product and market. A company has existing products that are being sold in present-day markets and may be described as current generation products and markets. But at an unknown time in the future these existing products and markets will be superseded and replaced by new products and/or new markets, and so on ad infinitum.

The same business judgment that recognizes the inevitability of the change or evolution of things also understands the need for a complete planning process. This continual change in business environment as related to the potential of the company is best illustrated in Figure 14-1.

The profile of projected earnings indicates a downward trend in earnings from existing products or situations. Development projects now underway will slow the

Figure 14-1   Source of a Company's Net Income—
The "Gap."

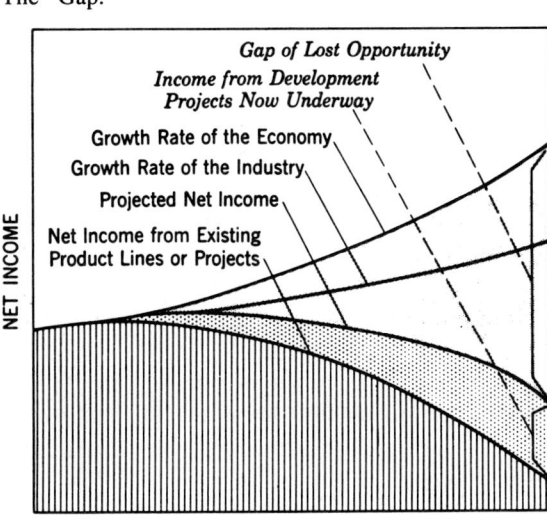

deterioration. However, it may be inferred from the diagram that this company must attain at least the growth rate of the industry—through new developments, including a reevaluation of the existing business and present research and development projects, to avoid the "gap" of lost opportunity. And this process, if carried out properly, will involve all phases of business planning.

14-5 THE PLANNING PERIOD—HOW LONG IS "LONG RANGE"?

Strategic planning sometimes is referred to as "long-range planning." But just how far ahead should a company plan? What are some of the factors to be considered in selecting the proper period for which to plan?

Each business has characteristics that need to be identified in determining the time period of planning. A company should plan ahead only so far as it is useful. Surveys on this subject indicate that among companies that do long-range planning, the most common period is five years, although the trend is toward a greater distance into the future.

Some of the factors that serve as a guide in selecting the proper planning time span are these:

1. *Lead Time for Product Development.* This includes the length of time from the idea of a new product until the design, manufacture, and distribution are completed. One company may take three months, whereas another may require several years.

2. *Length of Life of the Product.* The probable period before a product is considered obsolete clearly will be a factor.

3. *Market Development Time.* This period can vary tremendously—from several years for a complicated industrial product to perhaps only several weeks for women's fashions.

4. *Development Time for Raw Materials and Components.* Some extractive industries such as iron ore mining or oil drilling may require a decade of advance planning. Wood products companies may consider a period beyond the life expectancy of their present management.

5. *Time for Construction of Physical Facilities.* For many plants a minimum of two years for design and construction of a plant and its equipment is needed.

6. *Payout Period for Capital Investment.* Obviously, the period over which the investment in capital equipment will be recovered must be weighed. Payoff may vary from several months in a highly speculative and profitable field such as certain chemicals to perhaps more than a decade for some utilities. Thought must be given to conditions that will prevail during this payout period to focus on the probability of recovering the investment and earning an adequate return on it.

Consideration of these factors, plus any other pertinent ones, will give some indication of the minimum period for strategic planning.

14-6 THE SYSTEM OF PLANS

One of the best diagrammatic explanations of the structure of business plans, and the interrelationship of each, is that published by the Business Intelligence Program of SRI

Figure 14-2   The System of Plans.

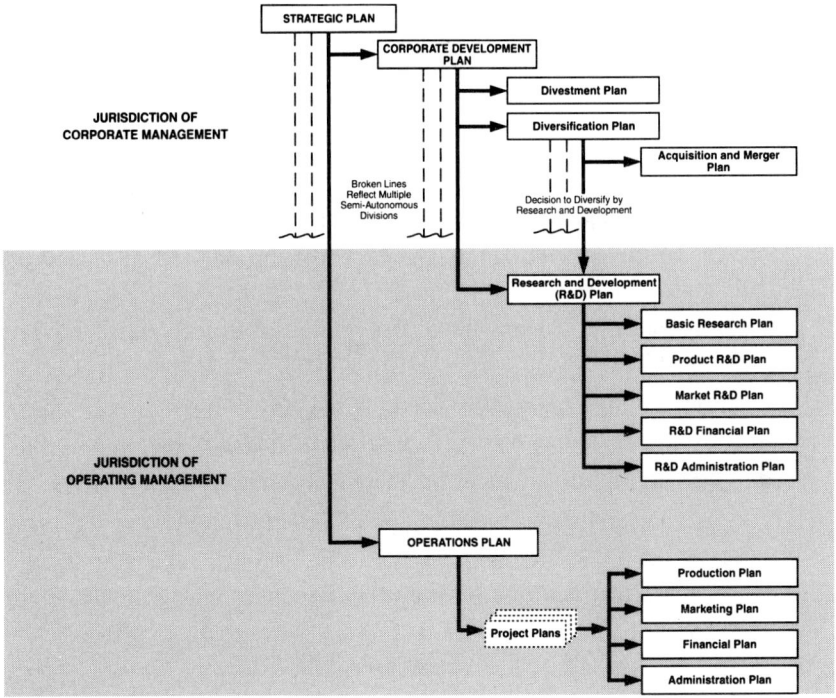

Source: Used with permission. Robert F. Stewart, *Report* No. 162, A Framework for Business Planning. © 1963 by SRI International, Business Intelligence Program.

International, as shown in Figure 14-2. As can be seen, there are three major components in an integrated planning structure:

1. At the summit or vertex is the "strategic plan." It seeks to outline in general terms the characteristics and objectives of the firm.
2. Stemming from the strategic plan is the corporate "development plan" that concerns itself with the development of "new" products and markets.
3. Also deriving from the strategic plan is the "operations plan" that focuses largely on the existing generation of products and existing markets.

Each is discussed subsequently.

14-7 THE STRATEGIC PLAN—AN OVERVIEW

Strategic planning begins with the present and extends to the most remote period selected as useful for planning purposes and therefore should be included in the planning cycle. The purpose of strategic planning is to set the guidelines and policies of the company that serve as the basis for the next echelon of plans—the development plan and the operations plan. The strategic plan focuses attention on the needs, dangers, and opportunities facing the company. It identifies the key decisions that must be made and usually sets guidelines and deadlines for making them. The process guides the company in decisions about the current generation of products as well as the next and succeeding generations of products and markets. Through this thinking and communicating process it helps assure that the plans and decisions of the various units are moving the company to the same agreed-on objectives.

A strategic plan generally involves the following components:

1. A clear and understandable statement of the company's basic purpose. Examples of such statements are these: to maintain the existing share of market; to maintain financial performance at not less than current levels; to develop new business capabilities that will enable the company to have a faster rate of growth than the industry.

2. A carefully thought-out strategy or means to accomplish this basic purpose. This should include certain specific actions, such as these:

   a. Eliminate Division E and market area R.

   b. Accelerate advertising program in Territory B.

   c. Build Research and Development competence in X product line.

   d. Diversify by acquisition into S product line.

3. A statement of specific goals to be achieved under the strategy and means of measuring progress toward each. Examples include financially expressed goals, such as the following:

	By the Year	
	199X	200X
a. Sales		
1. Dollars	$160MM	$350MM
2. Percent of present product total	75%	55%
b. Rate of return on investment		
1. On assets employed	12%	15%
2. On common shareholder equity	17%	23%
3. On net sales	5%	7%
c. Per share earnings	$2.50	$3.40

4. A statement of the assumptions or conditions used or needed to achieve the goals. These may include the following:

   a. Continued guarantees of foreign investments.

   b. Favorable decisions by the U.S. Department of Justice on pending cases.

   c. Increase in the GNP by at least 3.5% annually.

   d. Availability of suitable financing at a cost of less than 11% per annum.

   e. Establishment of a computer center for scientific applications.

   f. Inflation rates: 1996–1999, inclusive, 5%; 2000–2005, 7%

14-8 THE CORPORATE DEVELOPMENT PLAN

Auxiliary to the strategic plan—and in the second echelon of plans as outlined in Figure 14-2—is the corporate development plan. It may be said to relate principally to the new product and market activities, to the actions or methods by which the new generations of products and/or markets will join existing ones.

This product- and market-oriented development activity will concern itself largely with the following:

1. The establishment of those conditions or business climate that foster and encourage the creation or discovery of new products and markets.

2. The gathering together of pertinent data to identify those fields with the highest potential return on the corporate resources. A corollary to this effort, of course, is the establishment of the necessary procedures to identify areas of less desirable growth (including existing products, etc.).

3. The determination of resource requirements and the scheduling needed to implement the program as it passes into normal operations.

The corporate development plan has several segments: first, the Divestment Plan, which relates to the sale or merger or shutting down of major parts or divisions of the business; second, the Diversification Plan, which relates to the development of new products for new markets and also considers whether entry into the markets should be by acquisition or merger on the one hand or by internal development of these new products on the other; third, the Research and Development Plan, which involves the many aspects of research and development as illustrated in Figure 14-2.

14-9 OPERATIONS PLAN

The remaining indicated second echelon of planning is what is termed the "operations plan," since it is concerned principally with current business actions. Essentially, it covers the near-term activities and extends to every function of the firm. It deals with and influences the functions directly and indirectly involved in distributing the present generation of products to existing markets.

Basically, it relates to the development of the plan of operations for the next year or two. It is essentially detailed in nature and specifies plans by individual function, the whole of which becomes the "annual plan" or some such designation.

14-10 BASIC ELEMENTS IN ANY PLAN

The strategic plan is broad and general in nature. Conversely, the annual operations plan is quite detailed and specific—and becomes the budget or control tool for the near term.

Plans may differ in the time period covered or in subject matter. But mature consideration will indicate that *each sound plan* must contain these basic qualities, some of which have been implied in the preceding discussion:

1. *A Statement of Purpose.* Identifying the purpose of the plan gives the reader the reason for the action required. It answers the "why" part of the question. It sets forth the objective. The purpose of the strategic plan may be broad and general. But as the plans become more detailed, so also must the reasons for proposed action become more specific, more refined, more detailed.

2. *The Identification of Action to Be Taken.* Obviously, the purpose of formulating a plan is to take action, and the plan must stipulate what kind of action need be taken. Again, the more detailed the purpose, the more specific or concrete must be the action—from broad general terms in the strategic plan to minute details in a segment of an operating plan.

3. *The Specification of the Resources to Be Used.* The basic task of management is to use all resources wisely. A firm's resources include not only funds but also people, plant and equipment, technical know-how, and other proprietary knowledge. Plans must indicate which resources are needed—and whether they are on hand or must be acquired—to avoid a conflicting assignment of their sources or *a less* than optimal use.

4. *The Identification of Goals.* The goals define the level of accomplishment expected from the action taken. Stated otherwise, goals answer the question of what is to result from the activity.

5. *Establishment of Definite Time Schedules and Adherence Thereto.* Progress toward the goals must be measured not only in degree of achievement but also in time.

6. *Identification of Conditions to Be Met or Assumptions Made.* Generally, the important underlying conditions on which the plan depends must be made known to those who must approve the recommendations. If these conditions do not come to pass, then the responsible executive must be made aware of this situation at definite checkpoints so that corrective action, including changes in plans if necessary may be made.

14-11 THE PLANNING PROCESS

With the various segments or elements in a strategic plan identified, as in Figure 14-2, it is probably easier to focus now on the planning process itself.

Assume a decentralized management-type company, wherein each division management must consider the environment in which it operates, and reach conclusions about its product lines, etc. The planning cycle at the division may be as illustrated in Figure 14-3—an iterative process. A brief description of the steps is as follows:

1. The management sets certain tentative goals and objectives, based in part on guidelines developed by the corporate office.

2. An analysis is made of the expected internal and external environment in which it expects to operate for the planning period.

3-4. Basic assumptions are made about this environment and the division's current posture.

5. A market analysis is made to determine or confirm the most effective marketing method.

6. A marketing plan is devised (taking into account the new products and markets, and status of existing markets and products) for each year of the planning cycle.

7. The market support plan by years is made (sales strategy, required staff, advertising and sales promotion, etc.).

8. Using the factors determined from steps 6 and 7, the sales estimate by years, by product, by territory, and by salesperson is developed.

Figure 14-3 Division Strategic Plan Cycle.

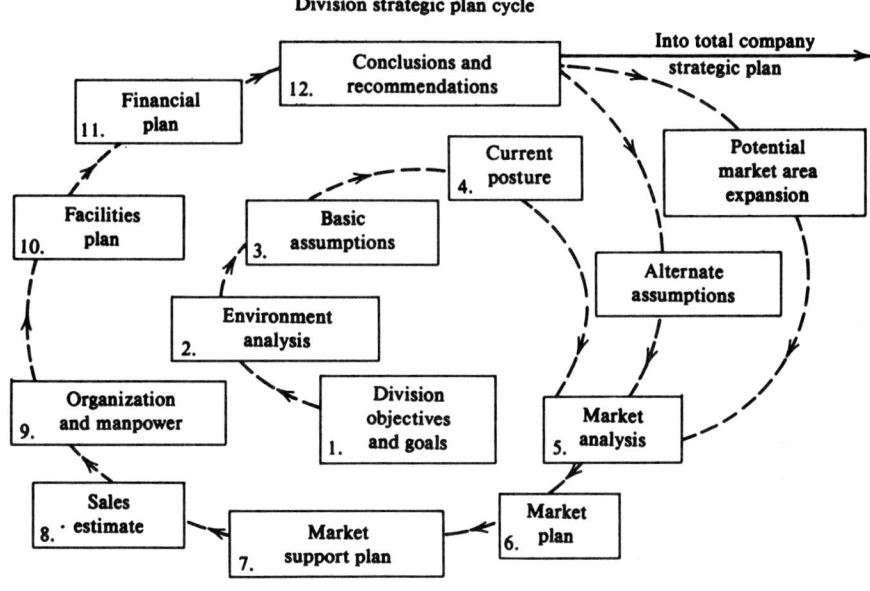

Division strategic plan cycle

9. Based on the sales estimate, the related organization and manpower needs throughout the rest of the division (production, research, services, etc.) are completed and costed on a time-phased basis.

10. Fixed asset (facilities) plans are developed by year of need and amount of expenditure.

11. The financial plan (cash, cash generation, income and financial condition, time-phased) is developed.

12. Conclusions are reached as to whether or not the plan is satisfactory. If not, the iterative process may begin again until an acceptable plan is developed. This plan, with assumptions and recommendations, is presented to the corporate management and, if approved, is incorporated into the total company plan.

Meanwhile, at the corporate office, comparable analyses and studies have been taking place, giving consideration to the thinking of the CEO and other corporate executives. These reviews are intended to facilitate an independent judgment on suitable corporate objectives, as well as to provide guidance, where appropriate, to the divisions and subsidiaries.

The planning cycle, including the relationship of the strategic plan to the annual operating plan of the corporate office, is illustrated in Figure 14-4. The basic steps are as follows:

1. Selected strategic studies are made, perhaps covering a period of 30 years, and on some phases, as appropriate, in cooperation with the division having fundamental knowledge of products and markets.

2. An environmental analysis (discussed later in this chapter) is made and tentative conclusions reached.

Figure 14-4   Aerospace Company Overall Planning and Review System.

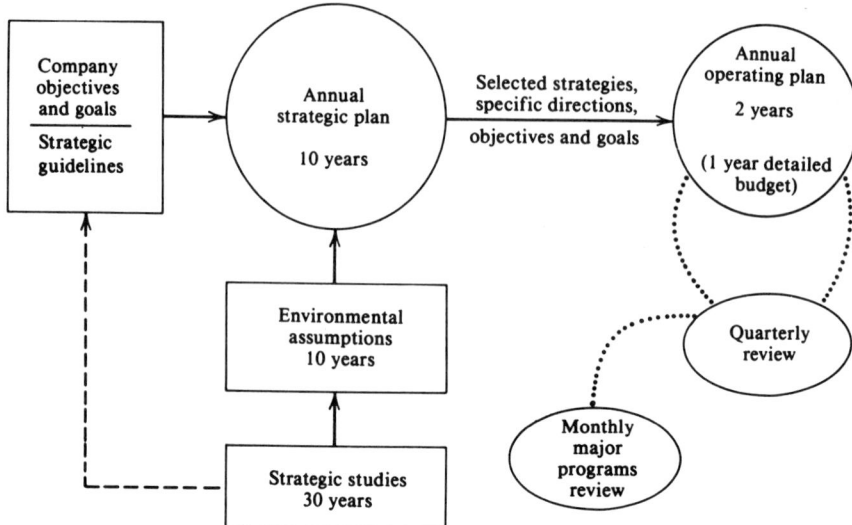

3. Based on the studies in steps 1 and 2, strategic guidelines are developed for the divisions, as well as the corporate functions. Company objectives and goals (tentative) are established.

4. With the corporate input as well as the division/subsidiary data, the strategic plan (for 10 years) is developed. If it is not satisfactory, adjustments are made, through an iterative process, until it is deemed acceptable.

5. When the strategic plan is approved, the appropriate sections serve as the basis for developing a detailed annual plan for the first one or two years.

The approved annual plan becomes a commitment and a budget—perhaps monthly for major programs and at least quarterly for the total company/division performance. Corrective action is taken as warranted.

14-12 PLAN FREQUENCY

A question might be asked, "How often should the business plan be updated or revised?" In general, it might be stated that planning is a "continuous" process and that as significant developments occur, such should be inputted to the master strategic plan. Given computer technology, this task is made somewhat easier. In regard to the frequency of formal updating or revision, many companies find it practical to update the strategic plan on an annual basis. In effect, one year is dropped, and a new one is added. Each year, as new perceptions of the business or new opportunities or threats emerge, these, in effect, are studied and incorporated into the planning process and resultant plan.

The short-term business plan, of course, should be prepared each year. However, since the annual plan is not only a plan but also a control tool, it would seem prudent to review it if *major* events change. Thus, if a major contract is canceled, or a war occurs, or any important plant is destroyed, a new plan would be needed. However, changes in conditions per se should not be the excuse for revision of the plan because the operating group is not achieving the goals. The impact of the deviation, and expected year-end (or other period) result, can be identified without changing the plan, but by quantifying the indicated final results for the year, and the departure from the business budget (plan).

14-13 PLAN GUIDELINES

The heart of sound planning, as previously mentioned, is *thinking* and *communicating,* whether for the strategic plan or the short-range plan. The expectations and instructions from top management are necessary, among other reasons, to communicate concepts vital to effective planning to all participants. The attempt should be to motivate thinking and not merely provide instruction on completing a form. Furthermore, especially from the financial viewpoint, and particularly in decentralized operations, a somewhat structured system of reporting the plans is required, for without it, consolidation at the corporate level is difficult or almost impossible. What should be included in the instructions for both division and corporate must be developed by each company.

To assist division managers in communicating with top management, and top management with the board of directors, some idea of subjects covered may be gleaned from instructions in a manufacturing company regarding the content in the executive summary to be presented in the division strategic plan—with further details provided in supporting schedules and related information in the short-term plan. The contents of the executive summary are to include the following:

1. Comparison to the prior year plan.
2. The major planning assumptions (external and internal).
3. Growth strategy.
4. Business goals.
5. Perceived strengths, weaknesses, opportunities, problems, and threats.
6. Optimization of profit plans for the existing business.
7. Programs and strategy for new business development.
8. Financial summaries of major factors, trends, and return on assets.

14-14 WHO SHOULD DO THE PLANNING?

Having defined plans—and discussed the types of plans, the time covered by plans, and the planning process—then a logical question arises about who does the planning. This subject can best be discussed by differentiating between the strategic plan, discussed in this chapter, and the short-range plan, discussed in the next chapter.

There is little doubt that the CEO is responsible to the board of directors for the strategic plans of the company—the direction in which the company intends to go. Some would say he is the chief long-range planner. Certainly, the CEO's style of management will have a direct impact on the planning process. But ultimately long-range planning must involve most elements of management. Accordingly, *who* does the planning will depend on circumstances. The planning could involve the following:

1. Only the CEO.
2. The chief executive and his staff.
3. A committee, perhaps part time, composed of representatives of each major discipline, or each major operating group.
4. A separate permanent planning department that would provide leadership and coordination in the process—with adequate support from the chief line and staff executives.

Which of these structures it will be hinges on several factors, including these:

1. *The Stage of Evolution of Planning in the Company.* If the planning is informal and sporadic, the chances are that, in fact, the chief executive will be the chief planner—with limited assistance from others.
2. *The Attitude of the CEO.* This may determine the extent or depth of the planning activity. Support from this source is a "must" for effective planning.
3. *The Size of the Company.* Generally, the larger the company the more likely it is to make formal long-range plans.
4. *The Nature of the Company's Markets.* Military suppliers, for example, often do more planning than the consumer goods manufacturers.

Without getting into a prolonged discussion of organization, there are some general observations that may be helpful if a company is staffing a corporate-level planning group. First, a balanced group containing several disciplines is desirable. Several functions must be included, namely, marketing, engineering, finance, human resources, and research. Regardless of background, prime requisites of the individual are flexibility or adaptability and creativity.

Excessive formalization in planning, especially strategic planning, can destroy what it is all about—the surfacing of creativity and intuition. In developing strategies, specific procedures and analysis are required. But the real benefits of strategic thinking are the inventing of new ideas, and not just rearranging old ones. (See the article in Selected References by Henry Mintzberg.)

14-15 SUPPLEMENTAL PLANNING: ALTERNATIVE SCENARIOS

Much planning is done with the most likely set of events being used in the assumptions. Accordingly, it may be called the most probable scenario or case. Yet a company must be prepared if these events do not take place. Hence alternative plans also are necessary. Thus management must be made aware of financial results should certain possible but improbable occurrences happen. Again, financial management must have some sense of the maximum financing needs should events proceed far better than expected. Given these conditions, some managements prepare supplemental financial plans to give a sense of a reasonable range of possibilities. A summary might appear for one year in the plan as follows:

	Net Sales ($000)	Net Income ($000)	Earnings per Share
Optimistic case	$	$	$
Most probable case			
Pessimistic case			

Although the emphasis may be on the most probable case, sufficient analysis should be done on the alternate scenarios so that the full financial implications are understood.

14-16 PLANNING TIMETABLE OR SCHEDULE

To achieve a sound strategic or short-term plan on a reasonably timely basis, it will be found desirable to prepare a calendar of events. With respect to the strategic plan, this may be issued at the time of the chief executive's announcement of the annual strategic planning effort.

A short, simple calendar of events used by an aerospace company is outlined next. In this instance, the cycle for the strategic plan is separated from the short-range planning cycle, among other reasons, to distribute more evenly the time spent in the planning effort. The key plan dates are as follows:

Issuance of general guidelines (environment, etc.) by the CEO to division heads and others interested parties	April 30
Receipt of division plans by chief planning officer	July 31
Completion of review and analysis of division plans by corporate staff	September 30
Preparation of consolidated and corporate position	October 31
Review with top management and board of directors	November 30

Although the dates cited indicate the latest acceptable time for completion of the activity, in fact there is a continuous interface between the corporate and division planners, and often the financial officer will perform alternate scenarios that are needed for the long-term financial plans.

14-17 STRATEGIC PLANNING: AN IN-DEPTH REVIEW

Now that an overview of the planning process has been completed, it is perhaps in order to delve a little more deeply into strategic planning. This may provide a more in-depth background concerning some of the steps in the strategic planning cycle. In this manner, the reader gains a more detailed understanding of the strategic planning cycle, and more mature conclusions can be reached as to just what the controller's role should be.

Various names have been attached to the business planning function that encompasses a period of time beyond the next year or two. Included are these: total planning, comprehensive integrated planning, top management planning, comprehensive corporate planning, long-range planning, and strategic planning—to name a few.

14-18 STRATEGIC PLANNING CYCLE

For our purposes, an understandable, practical definition is that used by George A. Steiner:[1] "Strategic planning is the systematic and more or less formalized effort of a company to establish basic company purposes, objectives, policies, and strategies and to develop detailed plans to implement policies and strategies to achieve objectives and basic company purposes."

At the risk of repetition, the strategic planning cycle, an iterative process, may be depicted graphically as shown in Figure 14-5. Thus, most strategic planning processes encompass these steps:

1. Analysis of the industry and business environment and status.
2. Determining the corporate mission or purpose. (In some instances the sequence of these first two activities, both closely related, may be reversed.)
3. Selecting the company's long-term objectives.
4. Developing appropriate strategies.
5. Preparing the long-range plan, including the financial plan.
6. Measuring actual performance (of the milestones to be attained each year) against the plan.
7. Analyzing the reasons for departure from the plan, and taking any appropriate action.

It is to be observed (in Figure 14-5) that the authors have separated the cycle into two phases: (1) the strategic planning segment where much conceptual thinking usually takes place, with emphasis on product and marketing considerations, and (2) the long-range planning phase. This second phase often is more financially oriented in terms of considering funding sources and timing, and financial structure, etc., for the several years—a function in which the controller must play a more important role, perhaps, than in the first phase.

Some detailed comments follow on each of these steps, with the long-range financial plan being reviewed in the next chapter.

14-19 ENVIRONMENTAL ANALYSIS

Logically, in determining the steps a company should take to ensure its survival and long-term growth, it is important to understand the environment in which it probably will be operating. This has two aspects:

1. The *external* environment—those influences *outside* the company that are or will be dominant factors in its activities, and

---

[1] George A. Steiner, *Strategic Planning, What Every Manager Must Know* (New York: The Free Press, 1979), p. 15.

Figure 14-5 The Strategic Planning Cycle.

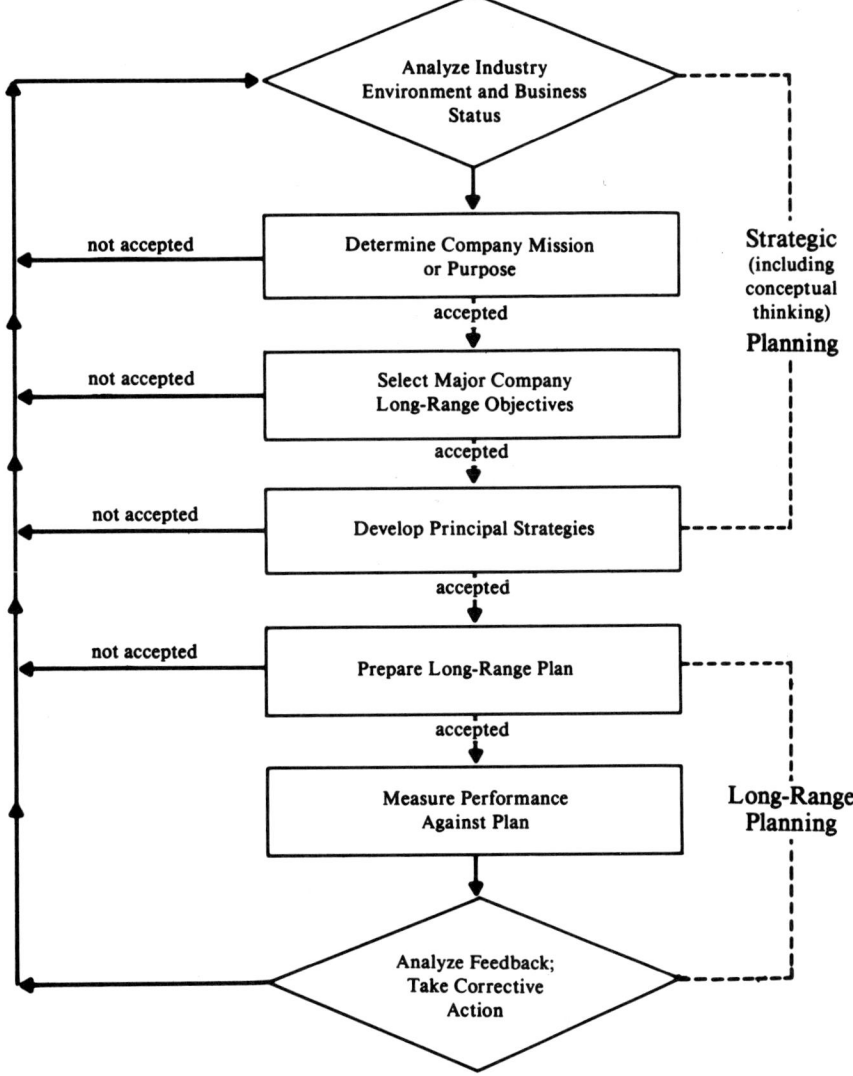

2. The *internal* environment—those forces *inside* the entity that will be significant forces in just how it will function.

The external influences may be grouped for discussion purposes into these four categories, perhaps in order of importance, for most companies:

1. Economic.
2. Technical.
3. Legal or political.
4. Social.

In deciding on certain actions, such as expanding into a new territory, or introducing a new product, or selling a segment of the business, these economic factors should be weighed:

- Level or stage of the business cycle.
- Level of general business activity.
- Entrance of competitors.[2]
- The industry cycle.
- Foreign exchange rates.

For other decisions, other economic factors might have to be considered.

A partial list of *technical* factors, which may be more important in some industries than in others, relate to the following:

- New products of the same general type.
- New products of a different kind that can serve the same need.
- New processes.
- New capital equipment (which can greatly impact unit manufacturing costs).

Legal or *political* considerations that may influence company behavior include these:

- Legislation affecting the product or activity—local, national, foreign, or domestic.
- Court decisions relating to interpretation of the laws.
- Administrative actions—local or national, that affect the enforcement of the law.

Some legal developments may aid the proposed actions; some may be discriminatory.

Finally, the *social* acceptance of the product or service sold, or the manufacturing process may be an influence. Social mores do change; and what is acceptable in one community or country may be unacceptable in another.

Each of these external factors must be considered in terms of impact on the company.

An equally key environmental factor is a proper evaluation of the business status—an *introspective* look. The management must try to objectively view itself. In looking at "what makes the company tick," these are some matters to be considered:

1. *Company Strengths and Weaknesses.* This involves (a) knowing the functions and areas in which the company performs well, (b) understanding how its strengths compare with competitors', and (c) reaching conclusions on whether or not its strong points may be improved and its weaknesses overcome. Among the many indicators to be examined are these:

---

[2] For suggestions on analyzing competitor strengths and on securing hard-to-find data on competitors' divisions, see *Planning Review,* May–June 1989.

    a. Product acceptability.

    b. Share of market.

    c. Marketing posture.

    d. Proprietary product status.

    e. Manufacturing costs.

    f. Quality control.

    g. Product deliverability (availability and speed).

    h. Patent status.

    i. Research and development success.

    j. Raw material sources.

    k. Foreign market status.

    l. Plant capacity.

    m. Financial strength.

    n. Judgment and skill of the management.

    o. Flexibility and capacity to change.

2. *The "Critical Success" Factors.* This refers to knowing what particular attributes are responsible for the company's success. It may be such characteristics as good quality control, quick response time to sales orders, personality of the representatives, or sound engineering, etc. (see section 14-20).

3. *Status of Each Product in Each Market Segment.* Included in this grouping might be:

    a. Understanding the life cycle stage of each product—embryonic, growth, mature, declining (see Figure 14-9).

    b. Understanding each business segment as to market share and growth rate, according to the Boston Consulting Group matrix[3] as either:

        (i) A *star*—high market share, high growth rate.

        (ii) A *cash cow*—high market share, low growth rate, significant generator of cash.

        (iii) A *wild cat*—low market share, high growth rate; probably a cash user until the product and market are more developed.

        (iv) A *dog*—low market share, low growth; a candidate for divestment.

Those who know the market and the product must be able to reach objective decisions about each. Knowledge of the preceding factors in all three categories is important in deciding on the corporate mission and the strategy to reach the corporate objectives.

---

[3] H. W. Allen Sweeny, and Robert Rachlin (eds.), *Handbook of Budgeting* (New York: John Wiley & Sons, 1981), Chap. 2.

14-20 THE CRITICAL SUCCESS FACTORS (CSFs)

The "success" factors are also called key success factors, or perhaps more popular now, in planning jargon, the *critical* success factors (CSFs). These normally would be identified in the environmental analysis. The characteristics that surround or identify the CSFs are:

- Vital or essential to achievement of the overall corporate objectives.
- Expressed as actions that must be taken, either continuously or when threats appear, or as conditions develop that must be overcome.
- Somewhat limited in number, that is, not everything that can be done is critical.
- Controllable by the entity to which they apply, or capable of being offset by other actions of the entity.
- Hierarchical by nature, that is, they may apply to the business as a whole, or for each division, or for each major function, such as marketing, manufacturing, finance, or research and development.
- Applicable to each entity that has the same objective in the industry.

While the CEO and other long-time major executives probably will have in mind some or all of the critical success factors, some logical spots to search or examine in the environmental analysis are these:

- Product or service areas where the greatest growth is expected.
- Product areas that are generating, or are expected to generate, a major portion of the sales and/or operating income.
- Functional or product/service areas where the greatest technological advances are expected.

Critical success factors may be deduced from the strategies selected by particular companies or by the major problems the management thinks it must solve. Here are some examples:

For a food products manufacturer:

- Need to improve quality control.
- Necessity of making packaging more attractive.
- Need to introduce competitive product within three months of the leader.

For a retail food chain:

- Need to increase gross margins on meats and fruits and vegetables.
- Necessity of expanding in more affluent suburbs.
- Desirability of adding a delicatessen.

For an aircraft manufacturer:

- Desirability of adding a manufacturing and repair facility in country X to better service customers in that growing market.

- Need to introduce just-in-time (JIT) inventory controls.
- Need to penetrate foreign markets of Asia to offset declining U.S. business.

14-21 THE BUSINESS MISSION OR PURPOSE

The environmental analysis discussed in the preceding section is intended to provide the background for the early step of determining the corporate mission or purpose. Of course, management may decide to tentatively establish the business purpose or mission and then see if the environmental analysis seems to indicate that conditions will reasonably permit its achievement.

One of the principal tasks of top management is to formulate the basic purposes and missions of the company. As Peter Drucker has said, management must decide, "What is our business and what should it be?"[4]

This requires a great deal of conceptual thinking as to what the business is all about. It is this mission statement that serves as the guideline for strategic planning.

How should the mission statement be formulated? In smaller companies it tends to depend largely on the thinking and values of the CEO. But in larger companies it is done more effectively by consultation and exchange of ideas among the management—albeit that the CEO has an important voice. Why? Because any basic change in the nature of the business can have major ramifications for the operating methods, the interrelationship of people, and use of skills, etc. One source suggests an offsite planning meeting of the key management. A questionnaire, such as the one illustrated in Figure 14-6, is provided to each participant, perhaps ahead of the meeting, and answers are prepared. Such answers may be tabulated and each discussed separately. Item by item, there is a thorough review and a consensus is reached. To repeat, good conceptual thinking, based on experience and knowledge of the business, is essential.

There is no uniform content of mission statement. They vary from lofty statements of principle, representing the values of the CEO, to very detailed and concrete guidelines. Excess detail may be counterproductive, and vague general statements may not be useful in formulating objectives and strategies. Perhaps a middle ground may best serve the purpose. Suffice it to repeat a comment by George A. Steiner, "Carefully prepared missions have been the source of success of companies. Revised missions have turned companies around. On the other hand, poorly formulated missions have brought disaster to some companies."[5]

The list of questions contained in Figure 14-6 may be helpful in probing subjects that are to be contained in a mission statement, and that give recognition to the unique business. For example, if the marketing channel of a pharmaceutical company is through doctors of medicine to the ultimate patient, then some statement concerning the doctors may be germane.

So what factors are important to the survival and growth of the entity—in the eyes of management? Perhaps these subjects, which can be identified and/or refined by

---

[4] Peter Drucker, *Management: Tasks, Responsibilities, Practices* (New York: Harper & Row, 1974), p. 75.

[5] George A. Steiner, *Strategic Planning, What Every Planner Must Know* (New York: The Free Press, 1979), p. 162.

Figure 14-6   Clarifying an Organization's Mission.

1. What business should we be in?
2. Why do we exist (what is our basic purpose)?
3. What is unique or distinctive about our organization?
4. Who are our principal customers, clients, or users?
5. What are our principal products/services, present and future?
6. What are our principal market segments, present and future?
7. What are our principal outlets/distribution channels, present and future?
8. What is different about our business from what it was between three and five years ago?
9. What is likely to be different about our business three to five years in the future?
10. What are our principal economic concerns, and how are they measured?
11. What philosophical issues are important to our organizations's future?
12. What special considerations do we have in regard to the following stakeholders (as applicable)?
    —Owner/stockholders/investors/constituents
    —Board of directors
    —Parent organization
    —Legislative bodies
    —Employees
    —Customers, clients, or users
    —Suppliers
    —General public
    —Others (specify)

Source From *The Executive Guide to Strategic Planning* by Patrick J. Below, George L. Morrisey, and Betty L. Acomb. San Francisco: Jossey-Bass. Copyright © 1987. Permission to reproduce hereby granted.

the planning meetings, should be a part of the mission statement. Some suggested items for inclusion are:

- Product or product line.
- Market and market share.
- Profitability on
    —sales, and/or
    —assets, and/or
    —shareholders' equity.
- Growth in (select some)
    —sales,
    —market share,
    —specific product lines,

—earnings,

—earnings per share,

—jobs, and/or

—markets served.

- Research and development.
- Productivity or efficiency.
- Flexibility in

—Manufacturing process

—R&D methods and technology,

—Meeting customer delivery needs,

—Responding to competitive actions,

—Meeting changing societal needs.

- Company image.
- Observing code of conduct.
- Developing managerial pool.

It should be mentioned that the preceding items may be in response to these basic subject categories:

- Survival or continuance.
- Profitability.
- Growth.
- Flexibility.

Having covered some possible subjects, what are some illustrative examples of company statements of purpose? Here are some concise mission statements from company policy manuals.

- To be the predominant supplier of electronics countermeasures to the U.S. Air Force.
- The primary mission of the (XYZ corporation) is to assist our clients in achieving cost-effective employee benefit plans through the effective marketing of innovative and especially designed concepts intended to reflect the strengths of the client company.
- The mission of the [Custom Engineering Corporation] is to maintain a viable growing business by designing, developing, manufacturing, and marketing custom engineered products and services to meet the needs of selected utility and construction companies.

Some practical observations about mission statements are these:

1. *The principal application of a mission statement is to serve as a guide to policy decisions, to provide direction.* Accordingly, it should be quite specific, and not a lofty statement of admirable purpose.

2. *As to products or product lines, careful designation may be important—whether the product/service is defined in broad terms or more narrowly described.* The wording can be significant. Thus, a statement that company Y is in the communication business might have quite a different impact than to specify narrower business lines, such as newspapers, television, and/or radio.

3. *The mission generally should include the scope of operations.* While the mission will identify the line of business, the *scope* will delineate the market, e.g., U.S. rather than worldwide.

4. *A realistic statement of purpose probably will be influenced by these three factors:*

   • The basic competence and characteristics of the entity itself, e.g., skill of the management, capital resources, operational capabilities, physical assets, geographical location, availability of skilled personnel, raw materials sources, etc.

   • The expectations of the stakeholders—those who have something at stake within the firm: the management, shareholders, creditors, employees, suppliers, customers. The relative weight of each faction's influence will help shape the relative importance of different elements of the mission.

   • The nature of the expected future external environment, e.g., regulation, social trends, inflation rates, the stage of the business cycle, etc.

14-22 LONG-RANGE BUSINESS PLANNING OBJECTIVES

Some managements use the terms *purpose, objective,* and *goal* interchangeably. For our discussion, the term *objective* shall refer to a desired result or condition to be achieved by a stated time. By some definitions, a quantified objective is a *goal.*

As shown in Figure 14-5, once the business purposes or missions have been determined, then the long-term objectives may be established. It should be realized, of course, that the establishment of objectives is an iterative process, closely coupled with the determination of strategies. One influences the other. In any event, experience shows that the criteria for satisfactory long-term objectives include these characteristics:

   • *Suitable.* Quite logically, an objective should support the basic purposes and missions of the entity. Achieving the objective should move the enterprise in the direction of meeting its purpose.

   • *Feasible.* Objectives should be achievable. It serves no useful purpose to set an unrealistic objective or goal. Any objective should be established giving recognition to the expected environment: competitive actions, technical achievements, political feasibility, social acquiescence, etc.

   • *Compatible.* Each objective should be compatible with the other objectives. For example, the objective for Product A or strategic business unit X (SBU) should be in harmony with, or certainly not in conflict with, the objectives for the overall entity.

   • *Measurable.* Actual results should be measurable against planned results over a specified time span. Thus, if the objective is "To attain a sales level of $100 million by the year 1999," then attainment is readily identifiable. Objectives may be quantified in any one of several ways: monetary units, unit quantity, cost, rate, percentage. Only when the objective is stated in concrete terms and for specified periods of time can their attainment be measured reasonably objectively.

- *Flexible.* Objectives should not be easily changed; nor should they be immovable. When major unforeseen contingencies occur, they should be changeable to be more realistic.

- *Motivating.* Another important characteristic of a proper objective is its motivating power. An objective should not be so easily achieved that it is certain of attainment. Nor should it be too difficult to accomplish. It should be at such an effort level that those to be judged by it generally agree it can be reached. This implies that those who are to meet an objective should have a voice in setting it. The management members involved should regard it as a commitment to be met with adequate effort.

(a) ILLUSTRATIVE LONG-RANGE OBJECTIVES

In practice, most enterprises have only a few long-term planning objectives. In theory, however, goals or objectives could be set for every function and every department in the business. Typically, many of the objectives are financially expressed and relate to sales volume, profitability, and market share. But measures may be developed for any number of factors that need change: labor content, share of minorities in the work force, skill diversification in the engineering or research staff, labor turnover rates, productivity, R&D expenditures, share of sales from nearly developed products (over a five-year span), and ad infinitum.

Planning objectives should be set for those critical factors essential to the success of the enterprise.

Objective	Achieve by Year	
	1999	2005
Aggregate sales volume (millions)	$560	$1,200
Percent of non-U.S. sales	20%	25%
Percent of new products	15%	30%
Operating profit (% of sales)	17%	22%
Rate of return:		
On total assets	10%	12%
On net worth	19%	25%
Earnings per share	$2.50	$4.25
Price/earnings ratio	11X	15X
Labor content in products	25%	22%
Minorities as % of work force	15%	20%

(b) LINKING OBJECTIVES

Those involved in setting overall company objectives, or, indeed objectives for each SBU, should realize that major objectives are closely related to subobjectives. Thus, the return on shareholders' equity must be supported by a proper gross margin objective (translated to a percent of net income to sales objective) and asset turnover objective, and a satisfactory leverage factor (see Chapter 7). The margin objective in turn could relate to a product mix objective, a sales volume objective and, perhaps, a productivity increase goal. Some sense of this interrelationship or linking of objectives and subobjectives may be gleaned from the tree shown in Figure 14-7.

(c) SETTING THE LONG-RANGE OBJECTIVES

When a decision is to be made about the major long-range objectives, two questions may come to mind: (1) *Who* should set the objectives? (2) *How* should the objectives be established?

Figure 14-7   Linking Objectives and Subobjectives.

Long-Range Objective	Subobjectives (To Be Specified by Year)	Sub-Subobjectives (Most to Be Achieved by 1999)
Earn 25% on average shareholders' equity by 1999 (Specify objective for each year)	Attain a net sales volume of $990 million by 1999	Increase market share per year for these products: X-12% Y- 5% Z- 9% Introduce new products that will provide 25% of sales volume by 1999 Acquire *K* company or equivalent in *S* product area
	Earn a net profit to sales ratio of 10% by 1999	Reduce material costs by: 25% in 1997 10% in 1998 Increase high margin product share by 40% by 1999 Reduce overhead content by 20% by 1999
	Achieve a capital structure by 1998 of: Debt 30% Equity 70%	Purchase common stock aggregating $250 million by 1998 Issue senior debt of $800 million (assuming proper market environment) by 1998
	Attain a productivity increase of 5% per year	Change to process *N* in Los Angeles Robotize 10% of operations Introduce team concept in four plants by 1998
	Double manufacturing capacity by 1999	Lease space in Pacific Southwest Expand training programs in Arizona and New Mexico

(i) Who Should Set the Objectives? On the matter of who should set the objectives, several factors will be at play. These include the size of the company; the style of management; the organization structure; the personality and interests of the CEO; the capabilities of, knowledge of the business by, and interests of, the top management. Recognizing these elements, the following comments are made:

- The CEO might establish the major long-range planning objectives—provided he is knowledgeable and has a good sense of the business.

   But while this procedure may be satisfactory in a small company, as the company gets larger this is less than desirable because (a) the typical subsidiary president usually resents being given a goal without any voice in setting it; and (b) the CEO often does not have the requisite product and market knowledge.

- Top management might dictate the objectives. While such a base is broader than the CEO alone, it can suffer the same deficiencies as mentioned above.

- In those instances where the business is larger, and is basically on a decentralized style of organization, the objectives may be negotiated between the head of the SBU and the top management. Usually it is not satisfactory for the unit heads to establish the objectives because few top managements are willing to have targets set without their review and approval.

- Finally, in the larger companies, where the SBU has its planners and the central management has its corporate planner or planning coordinator, through the iterative process of discussing alternative strategies, objectives, and the corporate mission—agreement often can be reached on what constitutes an acceptable objective. Such a base, of course, is much broader than merely the top management and the head of the SBU.

(ii) Methods of Setting the Long-Term Objectives. Setting realistic long-term objectives is not quite as simple as just having one executive, the CEO, or a group, dictate a figure or goal. To be sure, the process might commence with suggestions from those sources; but it is infinitely more satisfactory to have some identifiable points of reference recognizable by those who must meet the objective. What are these? How can they be determined? Some of the methods employed in business, depending on circumstances, are these:

1. *Past performance—with some type of trend extrapolation—might be used.* In some instances, to use last year's performance and to adjust for experienced improvement or some arbitrary factor is not using the available tools, and it may be downright naive, by letting poor performance continue.

2. *Past performance adjusted for the estimated impact of expected forces might be a basis.* Recognition is given to the result of expected changes, both internal and external, such as: product obsolescence, government regulations, new product developments, competitive actions, industry sales forecasts, etc.

3. *Competitive analysis could be useful.* With the availability of the 10-K reports of competitors, analyses could be made of competitive performance. Return on assets, gross margin percentage, sales volume trends, funds spent on R&D, selling expenses, individual competitor data or group data can be used as a basis for

calculating desired performance on some item. (See Selected References on competitor intelligence.)

4. *Environmental analysis, situation analysis, or strategic analysis—all these various analytical studies probably will provide useful data.* In the analytical study of the operations, certain comparative relationships will become evident—some good and some poor. The impact of expanding the more productive or effective ones can be judged or calculated on such matters as sales volume (impact of advertising, or using a certain channel of distribution, changing prices, or using a given source of raw material, etc.). The best methods used in one area might be applied to other areas, etc. In turn, these actions could impact the objective.

5. *Strategy iteration may provide guidelines.* This is similar in principle to the preceding situation analysis. New strategies may be developed and the impact could be estimated as to certain objectives.

There are several bases and supporting statistical analyses of various types that can aid in the selection of suitable long-term planning objectives.

14-23 DEVELOPING STRATEGIES

The final function mentioned in Figure 14-5 as requiring a great deal of conceptual thinking is that of developing the appropriate strategies to achieve the business objectives. After the basic mission or purpose and long-range planning objectives have been determined, then the next step is to search out those strategies best able to achieve the objectives. As used herein, "strategy" means the way, or means, or path, or program by which the entity deploys its human and financial resources and its physical assets to achieve the business purpose.

A great deal has been written about identifying and evaluating strategies. Yet the fact remains that the process is largely an art, and developing a successful strategy often involves a great deal of luck. As previously mentioned, in strategic planning the emphasis usually is on products, market, and marketing. In developing successful strategies, it is probably desirable that the company's creative talents be energized into suggesting the most ingenious and comprehensive methods or paths as possible. This development task may be assigned to gifted individuals or groups in marketing, planning, or other departments who have a reasonable knowledge of the operations—with the evaluation and selection assigned possibly to other groups. Sources that might provide clues for potential alternative strategies include these:

- A review of company reports and records.
- Observation and discussion of the operations, including the known or alleged strengths and weaknesses.
- Review of competitive or somewhat comparable activities.
- Discussion of the situation and alternatives with persons familiar with the industry and the company, and similar problems—consultants, educators, board of director members, think tanks, etc.

In any event, when t1he list of alternative strategies has been developed, they should be screened by knowledgeable people (perhaps the CEO and other top management) to eliminate the impractical. Then, the remaining strategies should be evaluated on both a qualitative and quantitative basis. Qualitative factors might involve the impact on other product lines or organizational units, on the corporate image, etc. Quantitative measures could include contribution margin, cost effectiveness, return on assets, market share, and operating profit.

In connection with evaluating alternative strategies, George A. Steiner has said,[6] " . . . The most effective universal approach to decision making is to ask the right question at the right time." To identify and evaluate strategies, he has devised a list of 38 questions that may help ensure a decision with the odds of being correct—if asked at the right time and given proper weight.[7] These are listed in Figure 14-8.

This art of strategy determination seems to involve a good insight into the company's strengths and weaknesses, the problem, combined with good judgment and intuition, and a willingness to examine some new ideas.

A summary of the facets of strategy development includes these elements:

1. Comprehending the current status of the business and where continuance of the same policies and strategies will take it. This involves identifying such factors as these:
   - Major products.
   - Major markets.
   - Important strengths and weaknesses of the entity as compared to competition.
   - Present major strategies in the several fields.
   - Knowing the economic contribution (cash flow, operating profit, asset usage) of the various segments (product, market, profit center, etc.).

2. Understanding the company objectives and how they differ from results of continuing the present activity—the gap. (See Figure 14-1.)

3. Recognizing some of the strategies that may or could be involved in the strategic planning, and selecting the practical ones for study.
   - *Product strategies.* Product design, new product development, adding new products by purchase or acquisition, product obsolescence, life cycle of products—that will influence strategy. (See Figure 14-9.)
   - *Market strategies.* Adding or dropping markets; changing distribution channels, methods of sale, prices, terms of sale, delivery methods, advertising media, promotional methods.
   - *Manufacturing strategies.* Plant locations, subcontracting, foreign sources, manufacturing techniques, material content, quality control.
   - *R&D strategies.* University affiliations, joint ventures, licensing, purchase of rights.
   - *Financial strategies.* Inventory financing, credit terms, debt structure, ESOPs, stock issues, control systems, planning system, inflation hedging, foreign exchange practices, leasing instead of purchasing fixed assets, etc.

---

[6] *Ibid.,* p. 192.

[7] *Ibid.,* pp. 194–195.

Figure 14-8   Major Tests for Evaluating Strategies.

A. Is the Strategy Consistent with Environment?
   1. Is your strategy consistent with the environment of your company?
   2. Is your strategy acceptable to the major constituents of your company?
   3. Do you really have an honest and accurate appraisal of your competition? Are you underestimating your competition?
   4. Does your strategy leave you vulnerable to the power of one major customer?
   5. Have you fallen prey to the hockeystick project syndrome?
   6. Does your strategy follow that of a strong competitor?
   7. Does your strategy pit you against a powerful competitor?
   8. Is your market share (present and/or prospective) sufficient to be competitive and make an acceptable profit?
   9. If your strategy seeks an enlarged market share is it likely to be stopped by the Antitrust Division of the Department of Justice?
   10. Is it possible that other federal government agencies will prevent your achieving the objectives sought by your strategy?
   11. Is your strategy legal and in conformance with moral and ethical codes of conduct applicable to your company?

B. Is the Strategy Consistent with Your Internal Policies, Styles of Management, Philosophy, and Operating Procedures?
   12. Is your strategy identifiable and understood by all those in the company with a need to know?
   13. Has the strategy been tested by developing subplans for an extended period of time in the future which appear to be acceptable and doable?
   14. Is your strategy consistent with the internal strengths, objectives, and policies of your organization?
   15. Is the strategy under evaluation divided into substrategies that interrelate properly?
   16. Does the strategy under review conflict with other strategies in your company?
   17. Does the strategy exploit your strengths and avoid your major weaknesses?
   18. Is your organizational structure consistent with your strategy?
   19. Is the strategy consistent with the values of top management and other key people in the organization?

C. Is the Strategy Appropriate in Light of Your Resources?
   Money
   20. Do you have sufficient capital, or can you get it, to see the strategy through to successful implementation?
   21. What will be the financial consequences associated with the allocation of capital to this strategy? What other projects may be denied funding? Are the financial substrategies associated with this funding acceptable?
   Physical Plant
   22. Is your strategy appropriate with respect to existing and prospective physical plants?
   Managerial Resources
   23. Are there identifiable available and committed managers to implement the strategy?

Figure 14-8 *(continued)*

D. Are the Risks in Pursuing the Strategy Acceptable?

24. Has the strategy been tested with appropriate risk analysis, such as return on investment, sensitivity analysis, the firm's ability and willingness to bear specific risks, etc.?
25. Does your strategy balance the acceptance of minimum risk with the maximum profit potential consistent with your company's resources and prospects?
26. Do you have too much capital and management tied into this strategy?
27. Is the payback period acceptable in light of potential environmental change?
28. Does the strategy take you too far from your current products and markets?

E. Does the Strategy Fit Product Life Cycle and Market Strength/Market Attractiveness Situation?

29. Is the strategy appropriate for the present and prospective position in the market strength/attractiveness matrix?
30. Does the strategy fit the life cycle of the product(s) involved?
31. Are you rushing a revolutionary product to market?
32. Does your strategy involve the production of a new product for a new market? If so, have you really assessed the requirements to implement successfully?
33. Does your strategy fit a niche in the market that is not now filled by others? Is this niche likely to remain open to you for a long enough time to return your capital investment plus a required profit?

F. Is the Timing of Proposed Implementation Correct?

34. Is the timing of implementation appropriate in light of what is known about market conditions, competition, etc.?

G. Are There Other Important Considerations?

35. Overall, can the strategy be implemented in an efficient and effective fashion?
36. Have you tried to identify the major forces inside and outside the organization that will be most influential in insuring the success of the strategy and/or in raising problems of implementation? Have you given them the proper evaluation?
37. Are the assumptions realistic upon which your strategy is based?
38. Aside from the above questions, are there any other that are pertinent to an evaluation of this strategy?

Source: George A. Steiner, *Strategic Managerial Planning* (Planning Executive Institute, 1977), pp. 22–23. Used by permission of The Planning Forum.

Figure 14-9   Product Life Cycle—An Influence on Strategy Selection.

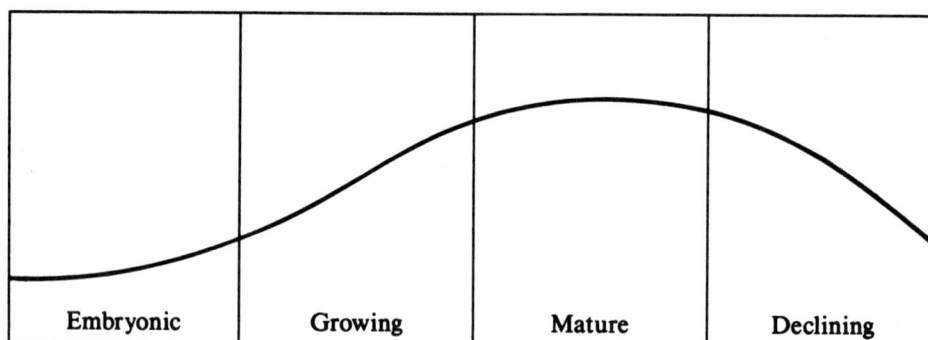

Product Life Cycle

- *Human resource strategies.* Organization structure, style of management, de-centralization, downsizing, recruitment programs, training programs, wage and salary levels, executive replacement.

4. Evaluating the proposed individual strategies and judging how they will assist in meeting the business objective.

(a) APPRAISING ALTERNATIVE STRATEGIES

As the strategic planning cycle illustration in Figure 14-5 reflects, the last step before preparing the long-range plan is to develop the principal strategies by which the company objectives and basic purposes will be achieved. But as also stated, the process of selecting the proper strategies involves a great deal of art as well as science.

Presumably, after much discussion between the principal functional officers and the CEO, the most appropriate strategies will be tentatively selected. If the process is done properly, the chosen means will be evaluated both qualitatively and quantitatively. It is in the realm of quantitative analysis that the controller can bring to bear his expertise in marshalling the financial facts in order to present the financial effect on the company of the strategy. Depending on the subject matter, the strategy may impact on:

- Net revenues.
- Manufacturing costs.
- Selling expense, and distribution costs.
- Research and development.
- General and administrative expense.
- Assets or investment required.
- Liabilities assumed.
- Return on assets and equity.
- Earnings per share.

But evaluating the one strategy may not be enough. Business decisions usually involve the selection of alternatives. Therefore, a good financial job would include evaluating one or two *practical* alternatives. And the most favorable, after full review by the management, would be that included in the formal strategic plan.

In presenting the formal strategic plan to top management, or the board of directors, it may be desirable to advise the audience of the impact of the other feasible, practical, or considered likely, scenarios. The impact on earnings per share of the alternative strategies is shown in Figure 15-11.

Should some of those more drastic, but *unlikely,* events be appraised, even if not formally incorporated in the plan presentation? For example, should the impact of war, or a major earthquake, or loss of a major customer (if the strategy fails) be evaluated? We believe that the answer is "yes," *within reason.* By such appraisals, management will gain insight as to the effect (both cost and duration) of major unlikely events. This type of information would be restricted to the top management of the entity.

(b) SOME ILLUSTRATIVE STRATEGIES

From the listing of the basic types of strategies, some alternative strategies may be deduced. However, listed below are a few specific illustrations of strategies undertaken. What strategies must be employed or changed obviously depends on the problems to be overcome. The strategies have been grouped into typical groupings of product strategies, market strategies, and operating efficiency:

Products

1. Change the style of packaging to appeal to the middle-aged group.
2. Change packaging to smaller quantities to attract the elderly singles.
3. Add a related product that would use the same distribution channel and methods as the other products.
4. Drop line Y, which provides no contribution margin.
5. Modify product so it will serve a function not now recognized.
6. Consider private brands in the Southeast.

Markets and Marketing

1. Enter growing European market through a joint venture.
2. Change prices to meet competition of "R" chain.
3. Increase local advertising to cover TV in markets W, X, and Y.
4. Change from sales representatives to agents in the Northwest territory.
5. Reduce promotional effort on product "T" in marketplace because of its declining stage in the life cycle.

Operating Efficiency

1. Switch to "just-in-time" inventory control method in Los Angeles and San Francisco.

2. Establish warehouse in Denver.

3. Enforce terms of sales so as to increase receivables turnover.

4. Dispose of Kansas City subsidiary in view of losses and lack of growth prospects.

5. Sell Chicago office building, in present inflated market, reduce space requirements, and move to less expensive location.

14-24 STRATEGIES AND THE PLANNING PERIOD

In discussing strategic planning, one more important subject relates to timing. When should a particular strategy start? Different strategies often must start at different time periods. In the context of strategic planning, it is important that the proper plan—the annual plan or the strategic plan—provide for implementation of the strategy. This is best illustrated in Figure 14-10. Some strategies must commence during the short-term or annual plan so as to be fully effective at a stipulated time in the strategic plan. Thus, strategies 1, 2, and 4 start in the indicated quarter of the annual plan. The others begin in another planning period. The annual plan, discussed in Chapter 16, must provide for those strategies which need to start in that time frame, so as to be fully effective by a specified date in the strategic plan.

Figure 14-10 Relationship of Strategies to the Planning Periods.

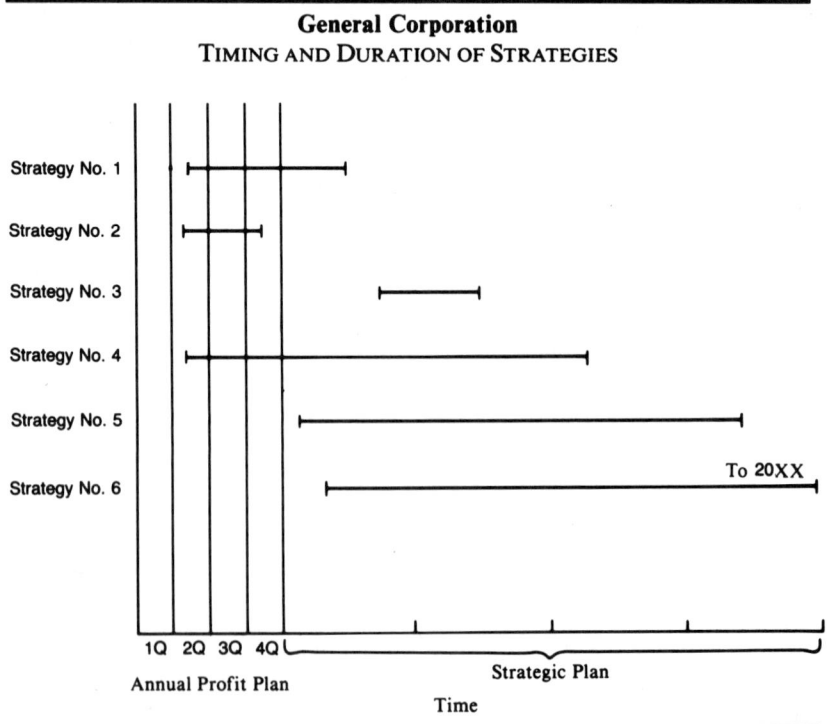

General Corporation
TIMING AND DURATION OF STRATEGIES

14-25 ROLE OF THE CONTROLLER

It may be taken for granted that when the selected strategies and plans are combined and consolidated into financial terms for the planning period (discussed in the next chapter), the controller and his staff will be heavily involved. But what is his role in those earlier phases of strategic planning that require a great deal of conceptual thinking, such as the following:

- Determining the corporate mission.
- Selecting company long-range objectives.
- Developing strategies.

It is precisely these areas that call for an extensive knowledge of the products and markets, and external environment, as well as the internal influences. It is also an area where a great deal of subjective judgment takes place in an unstructured setting. Many of the factors are not subject to measurement; and much guessing takes place. According to a survey of controllers, a usable sample of 92 responses,[8] a great number of controllers desired to participate more fully in the entire strategic planning process. In a 17% response rate to a similar questionnaire to CEOs, the chief executives were stated as not being enthusiastic about expanding the controllers' participation in the three phases mentioned above. So what can we conclude?

Obviously, the degree to which a controller should be involved depends in part on his ability to contribute something of value to the process. This, in turn, may depend on his knowledge of the business—especially the markets and products—as compared to the other functional executives. Moreover, technically speaking, involvement could mean either giving informal advice, providing data or analyses, or actually making decisions, e.g., choosing alternatives. In the typical enterprise, with a highly competent managerial staff, the authors make these observations in the context of their own knowledge of controller capabilities and performance, excluding the informal advice role, and recognizing that the controllers are or should be the skilled financial analysts and interpreters of the figures:

1. *General.* In those areas susceptible to financial or economic analyses, whether based on internal and/or external data, where the controller is knowledgeable, he should prepare the analysis and present recommendations. This can be done based on a request or at his own instigation.

   Additionally, if he has significant information, is reasonably knowledgeable, and believes conclusions reached are based on erroneous assumptions or information, he should make his own observations known (at his own risk if he doesn't have the correct facts or doesn't really comprehend the picture).

2. *The Company Mission.* The company mission or purpose will be determined based on a thorough knowledge of the entity's strengths and weaknesses and a host of subjective opinions. If he is aware of erroneous financial or economic assumptions used (which he should disclose) in reaching the decisions, then he can

---

[8] Richard H. Fern, and Manuel A. Tipgos, "Controllers as Business Strategists: A Progress Report," *Management Accounting,* March 1988, pp. 25–29.

and should provide alternative suggestions. Otherwise, this area should be left to the decisions of the other officers.

3. *Long-Range Objectives.* As to those long-range objectives that involve conclusions based on financial facts or calculations (such as return on shareholders' equity), he should make or assist in making the necessary analysis. If the conclusions reached are erroneous or not realistic, he has an obligation to bring this to the attention of the appropriate executive and to demonstrate in what way the objective is unrealistic (or too easy of attainment) and what might be more appropriate.

It would seem that there are a great many areas relating to long-range planning objectives where the expertise of the controller should be useful—but not all.

4. *Developing Strategies.* In this phase, also, financial analysis probably could be applied to some of the strategies. Suggestions would be those relative to profit impact of alternative choices, or relative to cost/effectiveness, or unrealistic earnings estimates of proposed acquisitions, or unduly optimistic economic assumptions, or too high an inflation rate, or cost estimates that are too low, etc.

Of course, the controller (or his superior, or the CEO), has the task of selling to top management, or the planning group, the usefulness of his capabilities in financial analysis; and if he desires to work in the unstructured environment and more subjective arena he has to demonstrate just how he can be helpful.

14-26 IMPROVING THE STRATEGIC PLANNING PROCESS

We have attempted to explain the desired procedures to make strategic planning a success, but weaknesses do creep into procedures. Here is a summary of comments which express the thoughts of many experienced strategic planners:

- In too many companies, strategic planning has become overly bureaucratic, absurdly quantitative, and largely irrelevant (because of the changing environment).

- Companies must think and act strategically every day—not just in the annual planning (once a year) cycle.

- Key words are "focus" and "flexibility." Focus refers to the need to figure out what the company does best, and build on it. It means developing the "core competence" to meet customer needs. Flexibility means sketching rough scenarios of the future—the "bands of possibilities"—and being ready to use them when the opportunities arise.

- The basic function of the "corporate planner" is to coordinate and advise the line managers. It is the latter who have prime responsibility for formulating and implementing the planning.

- Because many companies reward short-term results, such as increasing sales or reducing costs, it is difficult to encourage truly long-term, far-sighted planning.

- Strategic planning still largely involves unquantifiable factors such as experience, instinct, guesswork, and just pure luck.

14-27 SUMMARY

This somewhat detailed review of strategic planning is not intended to make the reader an "immediate expert" on the subject. There are many facets not touched upon in this chapter, and the topic is highly complex. It is intended, however, to provide the reader with a greater appreciation of the complicated process and the many talents required to do a reasonably acceptable job in strategic planning.

14-28 SELECTED REFERENCES

Below, Patrick J., George L. Morrisey, and Betty L. Acomb, *The Executive Guide to Strategic Planning*. San Francisco: Jossey-Bass, 1987.

Cvitkovic, Emilio, "Profiling Your Competitors," *Planning Review,* May–June 1988, pp. 28–30.

Fern, Richard H., and Manual A. Tipgos, "Controllers as Business Strategists: A Progress Report," *Management Accounting,* March 1988, pp. 25–29.

Fisher, Anne B., "Is Long-Range Planning Worth It?" *Fortune,* April 23, 1990, pp. 281–284.

Granger, Charles H., "The Hierarchy of Objectives," *Harvard Business Review,* May–June 1964.

Henkoff, Ronald, "How to Plan for 1995," *Fortune,* Dec. 31, 1990, pp. 70–79.

Kight, Leila K., "The Search for Intelligence on Divisions and Subsidiaries," *Planning Review,* May–June 1989, pp. 40–41.

Knight, Ray A., and Lee G. Knight, "Planning: The Key to Small Business Survival," *Management Accounting,* Feb. 1993, pp. 33–34.

Mintzberg, Henry, "The Rise and Fall of Strategic Planning," *Harvard Business Review,* Jan./Feb. 1994, pp. 107–114.

Norman, Richard, and Rafael Ramirez, "From Value Chain to Value Constellation: Designing Interactive Strategy," *Harvard Business Review,* July/Aug. 1993, pp. 65–77.

O'Connor, Rochelle, *The Corporate Planning Department: Responsibilities and Staffing,* Conference Board Report No. 806. New York: The Conference Board, Inc., 1981.

O'Connor, Rochelle, *Facing Strategic Issues: New Planning Guides and Practices,* Conference Board Report No. 867. New York: The Conference Board, Inc., 1985.

Steiner, George A., *Strategic Planning, What Every Manager Must Know.* New York: The Free Press, 1979.

Steiner, George A., *Top Management Planning.* London: Macmillan, 1969.

Stewart, Robert F., *A Framework for Business Planning,* a research report by the Long Range Planning Service, Stanford Research Institute (SRI), Menlo Park, California, Feb. 1963.

Stewart, Robert F., J. Knight Allen, and J. Morse Cavender, *The Strategic Plan,* a confidential report by the Long Range Planning Service, Stanford Research Institute (SRI), Menlo Park, California, April 1963.

Willson, James D., *Budgeting and Profit Planning Manual (1994 ed.).* Boston: Warren, Gorham & Lamont, Chap. 3.

CHAPTER 15

Financial Impact of the Strategic Plan: The Long-Range Financial Plan

15-1 INTRODUCTION

Chapter 14 dealt with the system of business plans, the essential components of each, and the general relationship of the strategic plan to the short-term annual plan. It also discussed the development of appropriate strategies for each function of the business: marketing, manufacturing, R&D, human resources, and financial. The concepts were introduced without attaching numbers.

This chapter addresses the *communication* of the business plans to top management and the board of directors. It identifies the key elements of the strategic plan that should be discussed between the board of directors and top operating management as well as between corporate management and the heads of the strategic business unit (where applicable). And most important, the strategic plan is quantified in the format of the long-range financial plan. This chapter also defines the objectives of the long-range financial plan presentation. To further clarify the strategic planning process, the strategic plan is contrasted with the annual plan, business risks are discussed, and the concept of capital investment is introduced. The content of the long-range financial plan presentation is illustrated with a complete sequence of financial exhibits.

15-2 KEY ELEMENTS OF A STRATEGIC PLAN

This discussion assumes a decentralized organization with several strategic business units. It is necessary to present the relevant data on each. If a business is not decentralized or is composed of basically one area, the same key elements discussed herein should be presented for the business as a whole.

In the review of a strategic business plan, very often emphasis is first on the basic issues without an excessive amount of quantified data. The purpose is to provide insight about the operating center, or SBU. While the specific content will depend on the individual circumstances, these elements probably should be included in the plan presentation:

1. A basic statement by the division general manager or subsidiary president about:
   a. The mission of the center or SBU,
   b. The key issues and opportunities critical to its future,
   c. The long-range objectives, and
   d. The basic strategies.

2. The long-range plan for each business area, including:
   a. A definition of the products and services to be provided.
   b. Principal markets served and the primary customers.
   c. Principal competitors in each market, their primary characteristics, strengths, and weaknesses, the anticipated strategies of the competitor, and how the operating center expects to compete with them.
   d. Key issues of each business area, including the threats and opportunities.
   e. Objectives for the business area.
   f. Strategies to be pursued.
   g. Milestones for each business area that will describe the key steps to be reached, on a scheduled basis, as an indication of progress toward carrying out the strategy and reaching the objective.
   h. The most vulnerable or weakest strategies or objectives in the strategic plan, and reasons for this judgment.

3. Summarized financial schedules for the SBU or business area, and operating center (discussed later).

4. Human resources overview of the operating center—a summary of the plans for growth, retention, productivity improvement, upgrading quality of management, or other key factors, external or internal, relating to this subject.

5. Perhaps an information resource management overview of the data processing function for the operating center, including major systems to be acquired, renovated, or developed.

6. A facilities overview of the operating center, including the impact of any changing technology, or major subcontract plans, and other significant factors that would impact such matters as sales per square foot of covered area, or square foot of covered area per employee.

7. An overview of productivity improvement plan for the operating center.

8. An overview of any other functional area, such as research and development activity, that is crucial to the success of the SBU or operating center. Such narrative would relate to programs, strategies, and objectives, each time-phased.

This listing provides some sense of the scope of the strategic plan review, above and beyond the financial aspects.

15-3 CONTRAST OF STRATEGIC PLAN (FINANCIAL ASPECTS) WITH THE ANNUAL PLAN

The business strategic plan is discussed in Chapter 14 and this chapter; and the annual business plan is discussed in Chapter 16. As explained in section 14-5, the strategic plan relates to many years and is concerned with basic strategies, and the mission of the business entity. The annual plan deals with a much shorter time period—only a year or two—is concerned primarily with current operations; it includes much more detail. It is the supporting or supplementing phase of the first year of the strategic plan.

Figure 15-1 differentiates between the financial accumulations or groupings of the two plans. The strategic plan emphasizes the corporate mission, strategies, and key relationships; and does not deal with the very detailed expenses of each department. The strategic plan may involve substantial analyses of alternative scenarios.

15-4 CAPITAL INVESTMENTS

Both long-term and short-term financial plans identify the planned investment in assets, both working capital and plant and equipment, required during the planning period, in order to achieve the planned profit objectives.

For plant and equipment planned expenditures, the annual plan usually includes a section on the capital budget—as explained in Chapter 32. The required facilities and purpose are described in some detail and a specific cost or expenditure for each identified. The board of directors is advised of the required cost for each significant item, a well as the expected rate of return on the investment. In some instances, the board will grant specific authorization at the time the annual plan is approved. In other cases, when the time for making the commitment is near, the board may require a further detailed review, and then approve an acceptable appropriation.

Figure 15-1   Long-Range versus Annual Plan.

Accounting Focus	Long-Range Financial Plan	Annual Plan
Details costs by individual account (type of cost, e.g., labor)	No	Yes
Includes departmental budgets (purchasing, receiving, etc.)	No	Yes
Used for monthly comparison of planned with actual results	No	Yes
Includes cash budget	Yes	Yes
Includes income and expense plans	Yes	Yes
Includes plan for financial condition	Yes	Yes

As a contrast, in the long-range planning cycle, each strategic plan usually contains only a highly condensed summary of expected plant and equipment expenditures. A plan may identify the estimated expenditure in one of these ways, depending on the relative amount of financial resources needed, and the extent of the analysis or study undertaken to quantify the planned cost:

1. By a single one figure item for each year of the strategic plan. (See Figure 15-3.)
2. By identifying by plan year the amount of the planned expenditure as to *purpose,* such as:

    Expansion (higher sales volume).

    Diversification (new products).

    Increased efficiency (e.g., reducing manufacturing costs).

    Replacement (e.g., worn out or obsolete equipment).

3. By identifying the expenditures by product line or business unit, such as electronics, telecommunications, or aircraft assemblies, for each of the plan years.

Use of any such highly condensed presentation or disclosure in the strategic plan approval process by the board of directors, or top management, is usually only an approval "in principle." It does not constitute authority to make commitments for the expenditures. Approval of a specific appropriation for the specific asset or group project is still generally required.

As to the capital requirements for current assets for both the strategic plan and the annual plan, these are determined based on experienced or planned turnover rates, the expected sales volume, the expected inflation rate, and other factors affecting the asset investment. In the strategic or long-range plan, the estimate is general and usually is related to *total* product sales. In contrast, in the more detailed annual plan, the receivable investment may be calculated based on expected specific product sales to specific large volume buyers or groups, the terms of sales, and the expected turnover rates. Planned inventory investment in the strategic plan is based on general turnover rates. In contrast, the annual plan investment in inventories may be based on specific monthly production plans by product, by plant, and so on.

With the growing trend to a reduced investment in receivables and inventories, through the use of computer technology, just-in-time techniques, and new group manufacturing methods, lower receivable and inventory levels should be planned.

The rate of return on assets employed in the business is one test of the competence of management. (See section 15-6 on key relationships.) Hence, the level of capital investment is critical.

15-5 RISK ANALYSIS

Engaging in business involves the assumption of risks. The proper assessment of risks that may occur and their probability is important in both plans, but it is especially significant in strategic planning. To the extent practical, the possible impact of major risks should be incorporated in the financial statements, and alternate scenarios suggested. Some of the risks that might need consideration include:

1. *Competitive Response*—Competitors will have a response to any new product introduction or expansion into a new geographical area. The response may be price cuts, lawsuits, lobbying for government regulation, or other possibilities.

2. *Capital Cost Overruns*—Construction projects have been known to exceed budgets. A worst-case scenario could help management anticipate funding requirements.

3. *Nationalization of Facilities*—Some countries have a history of nationalizing certain industries with little or no compensation to the previous owners of expropriated facilities. If management becomes aware of such a problem, then it may wish to relocate its new facilities.

4. *Ecological costs*—Some companies, for example, Manville Corporation, the tobacco industry, and pharmaceutical companies, have been targets of lawsuits due to products that were later found to be unsafe. In addition, any product or process that has significant chemical waste byproducts should be brought to the attention of management, since resulting lawsuits or government fines could destroy any profits from sale of the product.

5. *Sales Fluctuations*—Sales projections are sometimes inaccurate. Management should be aware of the worst and best case scenarios. The worst case may result in significant losses to the company, and the best case (as recently experienced by several personal computer manufacturers) may require construction of additional production facilities.

6. *Raw Material Scarcity*—Some raw materials are in short supply (computer chips) or are tightly controlled by the producer (oil by OPEC in the 1970s). If so, sales projections may fall short due to the inability of the company to produce enough of the product to meet demand.

7. *Deterioration of Margins*—Competing products may come onto the market that will force margins to deteriorate due to price cuts. The company should make some attempt to identify this risk from both national and international competitors and derive a likely range of margin percentage reductions to factor into the long-range plan.

8. *Technological Advances*—Advances in technology may make a product obsolete (e.g., calculators versus slide rules). Though these advances may be hard to predict, some rudimentary technology can be found in trade literature that will allow the company to forecast a decline in its market. For example, the movie video rental market is projected to decline as on-demand movie rentals become available through cable television companies.

Proper risk assessment is essential in business planning. Consideration of such exposures can help in building a plan that keeps such risks within an acceptable level.

15-6 KEY RELATIONSHIPS

Key relationships are important guides in any business planning, and they are particularly valuable in constructing the long-range financial plan. Ratio analysis is discussed in Chapter 8, and the importance of selected ratios is reviewed in the relevant chapters of this book (see chapters on liabilities and shareholders' equity). Some especially significant ratios to consider in long-range planning are:

- Percentage return on assets (see Figure 15-16).
- Percentage return on shareholders' equity (see Figure 15-17).
- Turnover of assets.
- Operating margin as a percent of sales.
- Net income as a percent of sales (see Figure 15-3).
- Earnings per share (see Figure 15-11).
- Book value per share (see Figure 15-3).
- Ratios of long-term debt to net worth (see Figure 15-18).
- Current ratio (see Figure 15-19).
- Times fixed charges are earned.

The importance of each of these relationships or ratios is explained in Chapter 8, as well as in other subject-related chapters.

15-7 OBJECTIVES OF THE LONG-RANGE FINANCIAL PLAN

Having briefly reviewed the subjects that the line officer of the SBU and/or the company planning officer would discuss in a top-side review of the strategic plan, the remainder of this chapter will dwell on the long-range *financial* plan.

The preceding chapter deals largely with establishing the mission or purpose of the entity, then deciding *what* steps must be taken (objectives), and *how* they will be carried out (strategies) to reach the planned mission. In a sense, these constitute a series of actions for which the individual costs and results (income) must be determined. It is somewhat akin to locating a piece of a puzzle. But these pieces or segments then must be fitted together, and it must be determined that the resulting total picture is what was expected or desired.

The chief financial officer, usually working through the controller and his staff, must analyze each new segment or action in terms of costs and revenue, add it to the other continuing planned functions of the business, provide additional financial input where appropriate, consider the financial policy implications of each, and summarize or consolidate the various segments, on a time-phased basis, to the end that the chief executive officer, the other top executives, and the board of directors will:

1. Comprehend the results of the strategic planning, in financial terms, as to all important factors, including:
   a. Income and expense,
   b. Cash sources and uses,
   c. Capital (fixed assets) commitments and expenditures, and
   d. Financial position.
2. Be aware of the significant financial risks or exposures, if any.

3. Be assured that all reasonable financial resources probably will be available as needed, on an acceptable basis, to meet the needs of the company.

4. Recognize that the planned financial position or health of the entity must be continuously maintained in an acceptable manner so as to command respect from investors of all types (shareholders, institutional investors, commercial bankers, and others) over the longer term.

5. Have confidence that the terms of any existing or potential credit agreements— bond indentures, commercial bank lending agreements, long-term loan contracts—can be met without endangering the company.

6. Understand that shareholders' value probably will increase.

7. Expect that the various approved financial goals can be met, e.g., increasing the return on shareholders' equity, the return on assets, increasing earnings per share, etc.

15-8 THE CONSOLIDATION AND TESTING PROCESS

In many companies, the focus of the management, as far as the strategic plan is concerned, often is on the income statement, and perhaps the statement of cash flows. But an astute management, and especially the chief financial officer, knows that attention must be given to the financial position as well as to operating results. The entity must maintain adequate financial health to attract capital when needed, to pay dividends on a competitive basis, and otherwise enhance shareholder value.

So how can the accounting process of summarizing the long-range financial plan be described? In principle, the process of preparing the financial statements for the strategic plan will be substantially the same as preparing the statements of actual results for each monthly closing, with these differences:

1. Essentially the same type of entries will be prepared for the *planned* figures as is done for the actual figures; i.e., there will be an entry to charge accounts receivable and credit sales for the planned sales; another to charge inventory, with a credit to the various liability accounts for the cost of material, labor, and manufacturing overhead for the manufacturing activity. The entries for the long-range plan will parallel those for the regular monthly closing. However, in most instances, the entries will be made on an *annual basis* so that annual financial statements can be prepared. (Thus, if it is expected that events *during* a given year will cause a failure to meet credit agreement standards, then—and only then—need interim statements be generated.)

2. Detail costs by each department and/or cost center probably need not be determined for the annual data, but only for the total function. Thus, manufacturing costs in total should be known in order to arrive at the inventory valuation, etc.

3. The year-end financial position should be checked at each year end to see that it meets acceptable financial standards. Thus, if cash is inadequate at year-end, then borrowings must be assumed or planned so that adequate cash is available, and plans for its repayment must be incorporated in other future years. Or, if receivables appear too low, the cash collections and/or terms of sales need to be reviewed; or, if dividends on common stock appear low in relation to earnings, the assumption about payout should be checked, etc.

4. Naturally, the cost or financial impact of any proposed or planned strategy must be reflected in the annual accounting entries, e.g., the added expense of new salespersons or a new sales promotion program—just as in the short-term plan. The impact on income and expense, cash, and balance sheet of any planned acquisition; the result of any assumed new stock issue, etc., must be reflected in the statements.

Computer programs are available to assist in translating plans to financial terms. Most of the above comments are precautionary because some financial staff in the past have prepared financial statements with excessive or unnecessary detail—which often clouds the issues. In other instances, the financial plan entries have not been checked to ascertain that the cost/revenues, etc. impact of a proposed strategy has not been overlooked.

15-9 REPRESENTATIVE FINANCIAL CONTENT OF A LONG-RANGE PLAN

What information should be included in the financial commentary and related exhibits of the long-range plan, expressed in financial terms? The intent is to communicate the important points or facts of the plan. Accordingly, it should be tailored to fit the audience (executive management and the board of directors), and excessive detail should be avoided. Some relevant comments on a suitable financial plan presentation are as follows:

1. The subjects addressed should be these:

- Those that the CEO and the CFO think are essential to a full disclosure of any significant financial aspects of the strategic plan and to the direction in which the company is moving.
- Those that are essential to convey a full appreciation of the financial risks to be taken, and the potential rewards.
- Those in which the board (or executive management) has shown particular interest—as judged by past comments or questions in previous board meetings.
- Finally, if not contained in the above, the underlying financial or economic assumptions—even though the CEO and/or the CFO might regard them as implied or understood.

2. The method of presentation should invite attention and be easy to understand. It could be a written report, but an oral presentation with visual aids might be more effective. This latter technique usually permits the immediate answering of any questions that might arise. While the usual rules for effective presentations apply, here are some reminders:

- Keep it simple and not in financial jargon (if the board is not composed of experienced financial people).
- Use a largely graphic presentation in color. New computer software facilitates this.
- Have only a relatively few lines or figures on each chart.

- Show relationships, not just absolute data.
- Keep the monetary units large—thousands or millions, not individual units.
- Present the data in a logical order so that each financial statement can be followed and the relationship to other financials can be comprehended.

15-10 ILLUSTRATIVE FINANCIAL EXHIBITS IN THE PLAN PRESENTATION

The actual exhibits to be presented to the executives will vary from industry to industry and from company to company, depending on, among other things, the critical success factors (discussed earlier), past problem areas, and those facets of particular interest to the audience. Some of the exhibits of an actual strategic plan presentation for an electronics company have been used (all figures are fictitious), as being representative of a decentralized management, with several strategic business units, and a history of excessive debt load when viewed against a probable cyclical downturn and the management's conservative standards.

A brief commentary on each exhibit is as follows:

Figure 15-2: Basic Financial/Economic Assumptions. In any plan, the assumptions often are critical and the management should be advised of the important ones.

Figure 15-3: Financial Highlights. The exhibit shows the trend of those factors that the management (and the industry) regard as key to progress. The format is highly condensed as each item later will be discussed in detail by the use of a supporting slide.

Figure 15-4: Statement of Consolidated Earnings. The exhibit presents a traditional income and expense statement showing net sales and the related major functional costs and can indicate the percent of sales operating margin and net income ratios.

Figure 15-2   Basic Financial/Economic Assumptions.

THE HI-TECH CORPORATION BASIC FINANCIAL/ECONOMIC ASSUMPTIONS 1997–2001 STRATEGIC PLAN	
Inflation rate (average)	5%
Interest rates (average)	
Prime rate	10%–13%
Long-term (30 years).	9%–12%
Capital expenditures	$670 million
Research and development expenditures	$320 million
Major acquisitions	Not in planning period
No change in income tax rates or base No recession Defense expenditures drastically reducing	

Figure 15-3 Financial Highlights.

THE HI-TECH CORPORATION
FINANCIAL HIGHLIGHTS
1997–2001 STRATEGIC PLAN
(dollars in millions except per share)

| Item | Actual | | | | Plan Year | | |
	Past Year	This Year (Indicated Final)	1997	1998	1999	2000	2001
New Orders	$ 3,800	3,600	2,500	8,470	6,400	7,500	$ 8,200
Sales Backlog (year end)	5,650	3,750	250	3,020	3,020	3,520	3,720
Net Sales (consolidated)	5,052	5,500	6,000	5,700	6,400	7,000	8,000
Net Earnings							
Amount	96	176	212	163	318	445	627
Percent of Sales	1.9%	3.2%	3.5%	2.9%	5.0%	6.4%	7.8%
Per Share	3.09	5.66	6.79	5.22	10.16	14.22	20.00
Capital Expenditures	115	115	420	100	50	50	50
Research and Development Expense	50	55	60	57	64	69	70
Book Value per Share (year end)	$ 43.03	46.93	51.87	55.38	63.57	75.91	$ 93.78
Return on Average Equity – %	7.45%	12.59%	13.78%	9.74%	17.11%	20.39%	23.59%
No. Common Shares Outstanding (thousands) – year end	31,050	31,110	31,210	31,220	31,290	31,300	31,350

Figure 15-4 Statement of Consolidated Earnings.

THE HI-TECH CORPORATION
STATEMENT OF CONSOLIDATED EARNINGS
1997–2001 STRATEGIC PLAN
(dollars in millions)

Item	Actual Past Year	This Year (Indicated Final)	Plan Year 1997	1998	1999	2000	2001
Net Sales	$5,052	5,500	6,000	5,700	6,400	7,000	$8,000
Operating Costs							
Manufacturing	$4,461	4,815	5,204	4,995	5,420	5,791	$6,544
Marketing	40	41	39	40	42	46	52
Research and Development	50	55	120	114	128	140	160
General and Administrative	41	39	37	38	42	43	44
Total	$4,592	4,950	5,400	5,187	5,632	6,020	$6,800
Operating Margin	$ 460	550	600	513	768	980	$1,200
Other Expenses							
Interest Expense	$ 181	223	200	190	180	100	$ 50
Other (Net)	111	15	15	(10)	10	10	10
Total	$ 292	238	215	180	190	110	$ 60
Earnings Before Income Taxes	$ 168	312	385	333	578	870	$1,140
Income Taxes	72	136	173	170	260	425	513
Net Earnings	$ 96	176	212	163	318	445	$ 627

Figure 15-5: Consolidated Net Sales. The trend of planned sales for five years, compared with the actual company sales of the past year and estimated sales for the current year is illustrated.

Figure 15-6: Net Sales by Strategic Business Unit. In addition to consolidated sales, the sales by strategic business unit are shown. Presumably each SBU has been discussed by the general manager. This exhibit relates the individual sales to each other and to the whole.

Figure 15-7: Percentage of Net Sales to U.S. Department of Defense. The management does not wish to remain highly dependent on sales to the Department of Defense and carefully monitors the trend in the volume of such business.

Figure 15-8: Consolidated Sales Backlog—By Strategic Business Unit. In the high-technology area, the orders on hand, the sales backlog, is an important gauge of the business trend. This exhibit reveals how much firm business has already been contracted for several years in the future, and the relative share of each SBU.

Figures 15-9 and 15-10: Consolidated Net Income (in total and by strategic business unit). These exhibits reflect the trend of consolidated net income, together with the net income of each SBU. They are supported by a condensed traditional statement of income and expense for each SBU, showing the percent operating profit and percent net income to sales—important signals in the business—as well as the absolute figures.

Figure 15-5   Consolidated Net Sales.

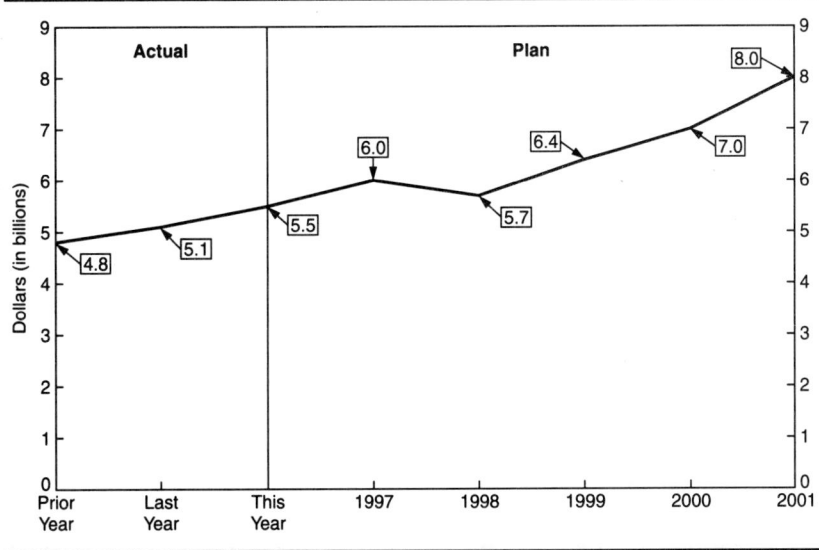

THE HI-TECH CORPORATION
CONSOLIDATED NET SALES
1997–2001 STRATEGIC PLAN
(dollars in billions)

Figure 15-6   Net Sales by Strategic Business Unit.

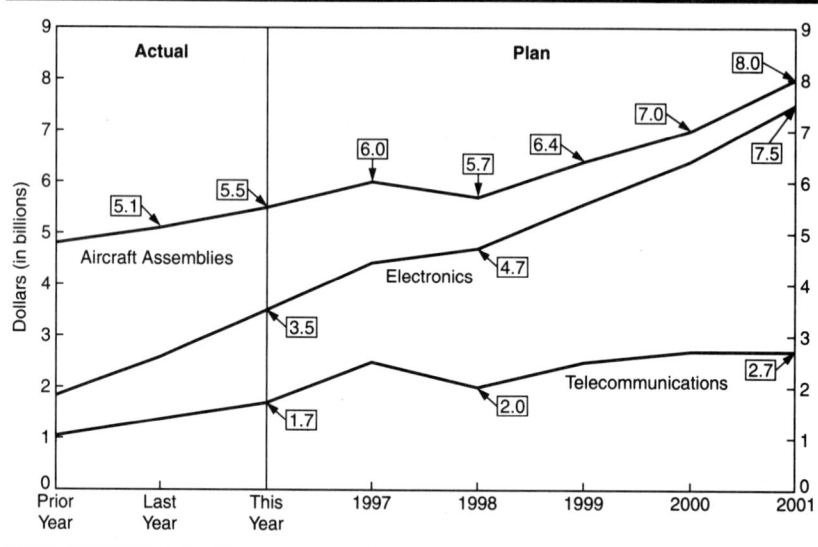

THE HI-TECH CORPORATION
NET SALES BY STRATEGIC BUSINESS UNIT
1997–2001 STRATEGIC PLAN
(dollars in billions)

Figure 15-7   Net Sales—Percentage to U.S. Department of Defense.

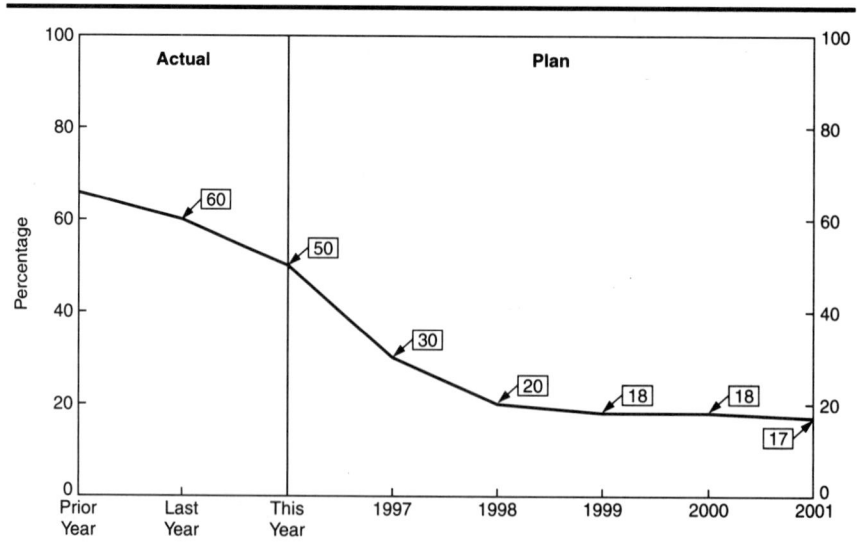

THE HI-TECH CORPORATION
NET SALES—PERCENTAGE TO U.S. DEPARTMENT OF DEFENSE
1997–2001 STRATEGIC PLAN

Figure 15-8 Sales Backlog by Strategic Business Unit.

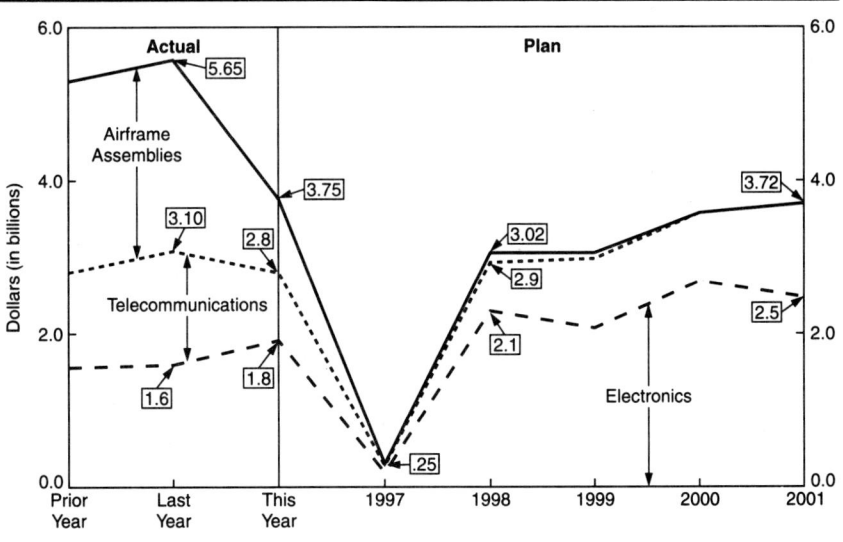

Figure 15-9 Consolidated Net Earnings.

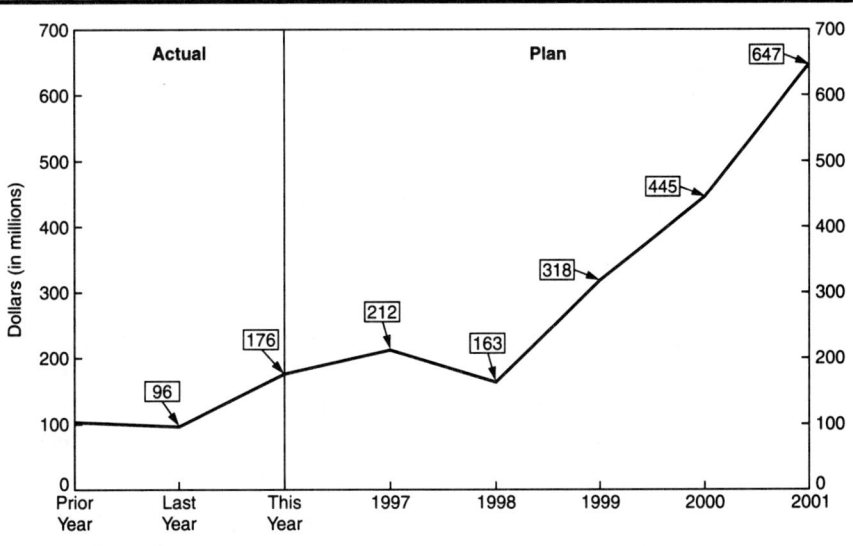

Figure 15-10   Consolidated Net Income—By Strategic Business Unit.

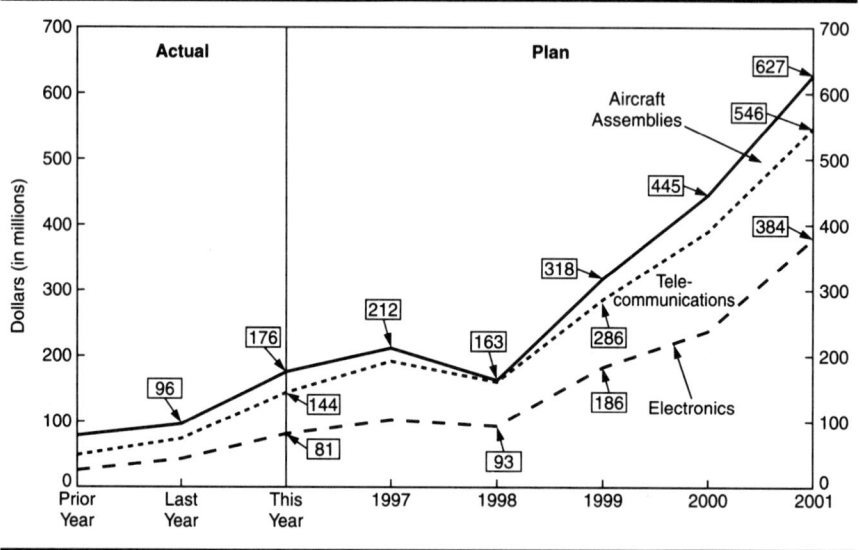

THE HI-TECH CORPORATION
CONSOLIDATED NET INCOME BY STRATEGIC BUSINESS UNIT
1997–2001 STRATEGIC PLAN
(dollars in millions)

Figure 15-11: Earnings per Share. The board of directors and the management, as expected, are interested in the earnings per share and the growth rate. Incentive compensation depends on (a) achieving plan, and (b) the percent increase from the preceding year. This chart is supplemented by one showing the growth rate imputed to each SBU.

Figure 15-12: Earnings per Share—Three Scenarios. Since plan achievement is never certain, the impact of selected other strategies is quantified. The reason for selecting the particular strategies in the plan was discussed at the operating center level and is repeated in condensed terms at the top management/board level. Comparable charts are prepared for cash flow, return on assets, return on shareholders' equity, etc.

Figure 15-13: Statement of Consolidated Cash Flows. The sources and uses of cash are identified in this highly condensed statement—with no detail by working capital items. Supporting this statement is a similar one for each SBU.

Figures 15-14 and 15-15: Consolidated Financial Position. A condensed statement of planned financial position is presented, and points of compliance (or noncompliance) with the bond indenture requirements or important contracts, or management standards are identified. Additionally, the aging of accounts receivable, composition of inventory, make-up of accounts payable and accruals, and paydown of senior debt (before due date) may be discussed.

Figure 15-16: Return on Assets Employed. Return on assets is an important measure of the management's use of assets, particularly at the SBU level. The trend in total is

Figure 15-11   Earnings per Share.

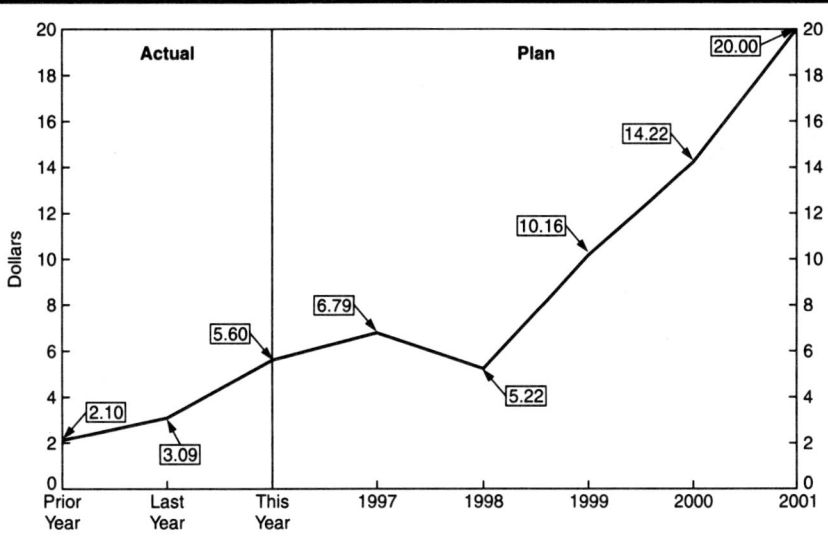

THE HI-TECH CORPORATION
EARNINGS PER SHARE
1997–2001 STRATEGIC PLAN

Figure 15-12   Earnings per Share—Three Scenarios.

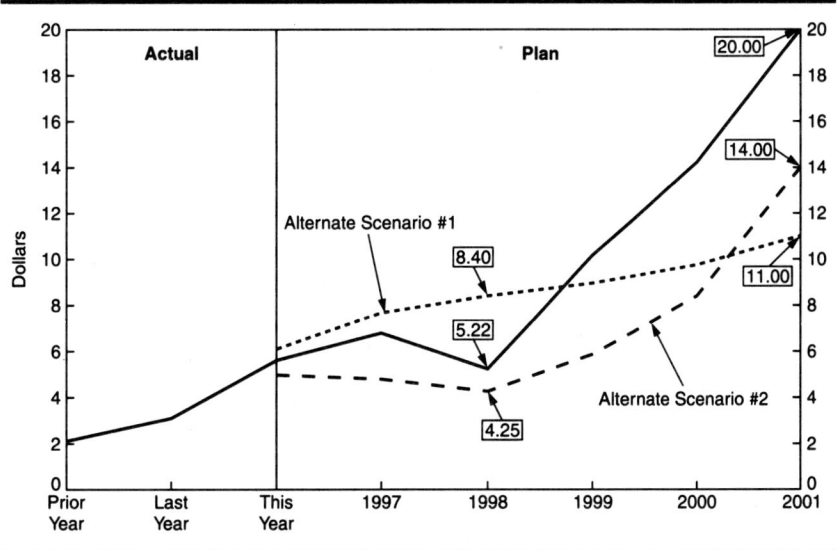

THE HI-TECH CORPORATION
EARNINGS PER SHARE—THREE SCENARIOS
1997–2001 STRATEGIC PLAN

Figure 15-13 Statement of Consolidated Cash Flows.

THE HI-TECH CORPORATION
STATEMENT OF CONSOLIDATED CASH FLOWS
1997–2001 STRATEGIC PLAN
(dollars in millions)

	Present Year (Indicated Final)	1997	Plan Year			
			1998	1999	2000	2001
Cash Flows from Operating Activities						
Net Earnings	$176	212	163	318	445	$627
Depreciation and Amortization	174	214	244	240	250	200
Deferred Taxes, etc.	4	4	—	—	—	—
Working Capital Provided by Operations	354	430	407	558	695	827
Increase (decrease) in Operating Related Working Capital Items	255	149	(221)	(7)	(55)	(45)
Net Cash Flows from Operating Activities	99	281	628	551	640	872
Cash Flows from (Used by) Investing Activities						
Equity Interest – Corp. X	—	—	—	—	—	(800)
Capital Expenditures	(118)	(420)	(100)	(50)	(50)	(50)
Proceeds from Asset Sales and Retirements	1	—	20	—	—	—
Net Cash Flows Used in Investing Activities	(117)	(420)	(80)	(50)	(50)	(850)
Cash Flows from (Used by) Financing Activities						
Dividends to Shareholders	(52)	(53)	(53)	(58)	(58)	(63)
Change (reduction) in Short-Term Bank Debt	116	(135)	(200)	(150)	—	—
Additions to Long-Term Debt	—	500	—	—	—	—
Reduction in Long-Term Debt	(21)	(42)	(50)	(250)	(240)	(350)
Net Cash Flows from (used by) Financing Activities	43	270	(303)	(458)	(298)	(413)
Increase (decrease) in cash and cash equivalents	25	131	245	43	292	(391)
Cash and Equivalents at Beginning of Year	172	197	328	573	616	908
Cash and Equivalents at End of Year	$197	328	573	616	908	$517

Figure 15-14 Statement of Consolidated Financial Position (Assets).

THE HI-TECH CORPORATION
STATEMENT OF CONSOLIDATED FINANCIAL POSITION AT YEAR END
1997–2001 STRATEGIC PLAN
(dollars in millions)

Assets	Actual 12/31/95	Actual 12/31/96 (Indicated Final)	At Plan Year End 1997	1998	1999	2000	2001
Current Assets							
Cash and Equivalents	$ 172	197	328	573	616	908	$ 517
Receivables	576	614	640	510	550	650	600
Inventories	1,037	1,320	1,400	1,200	1,300	1,200	1,200
Prepaid Items	46	44	40	40	40	40	40
Total	1,831	2,175	2,408	2,323	2,506	2,798	2,357
Long-Term Assets							
Minority Interests (Corp. X)	—		—	—		—	800
Property, Plant and Equipment	2,407	2,522	2,942	3,022	3,072	3,122	3,172
Less: Accumulated Depreciation and Amortization	792	966	1,180	1,404	1,644	1,894	2,094
Net	1,615	1,556	1,762	1,618	1,428	1,228	1,078
Other Assets	75	80	80	80	80	80	80
Total	1,690	1,636	1,842	1,698	1,508	1,308	1,958
Total Assets	$3,521	3,811	4,250	4,021	4,014	4,106	$4,315

Figure 15-15 Statement of Consolidated Financial Position (Liabilities and Equity).

THE HI-TECH CORPORATION
STATEMENT OF CONSOLIDATED FINANCIAL POSITION AT YEAR END
1997–2001 STRATEGIC PLAN
(dollars in millions)

Liabilities and Equity	Actual 12/31/95	Actual 12/31/96 (Indicated Final)	At Plan Year End 1997	1998	1999	2000	2001
Current Liabilities							
Notes Payable to Banks	$ 319	435	300	100	—	—	$ —
Current Portion of Long-Term Debt	21	21	—	50	50	50	50
Accounts Payable	563	590	610	540	590	500	500
Accrued Items	187	212	200	160	170	190	170
Income Tax Payable	17	34	43	37	65	90	100
Other Current Liabilities	26	27	28	15	20	20	25
Total	$1,133	1,319	1,181	902	895	850	$ 845
Long-Term Obligations							
Senior Debt – Existing	$ 863	842	800	750	500	300	$ —
Senior Debt – New	—	—	500	500	500	450	400
Other Long-Term Obligations	142	140	110	110	110	120	120
Total	$1,005	982	1,410	1,360	1,110	870	$ 520
Deferred Income Taxes	$ 47	50	40	30	20	10	$ 10
Shareholders' Equity							
Paid-in Capital	$ 310	310	310	310	310	310	310
Retained Earnings	1,026	1,150	1,309	1,419	1,679	2,066	2,630
Total Equity	$1,336	1,460	1,619	1,729	1,989	2,376	$2,940
Total Liabilities and Equity	$3,521	3,811	4,250	4,021	4,014	4,106	$4,315

Figure 15-16 Percentage Return on Average Assets.

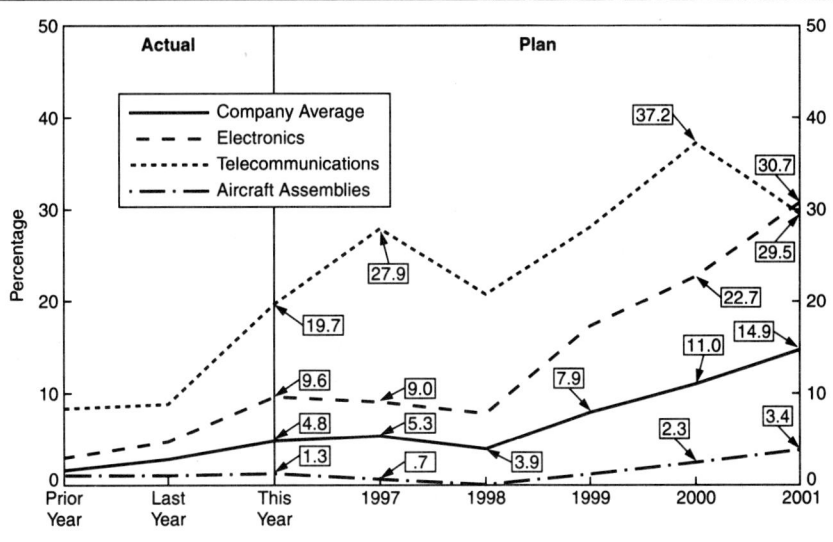

THE HI-TECH CORPORATION
PERCENTAGE RETURN ON AVERAGE ASSETS
1997–2001 STRATEGIC PLAN

discussed, and performance by each SBU is reviewed, showing the analysis by the two relevant factors: turnover and percent return on sales.

Figure 15-17: Percent Return on Average Shareholders' Equity. A key measure of this management is return on shareholders' equity—the trend as well as the entity's performance vs. competitors.

Figures 15-18 and 15-19: Ratio of Long-Term Debt to Net Worth, and Current Ratio. Given the preoccupation with debt, and the covenants of the indenture, the long-term debt to net worth ratio especially is reviewed, as is the current ratio.

Figure 15-20: Beyond the Five Years. Given some far-reaching changes in technology—the "supertechnology"—and the perceived opportunity for an advantageous acquisition, the technical staff briefly touched on this subject during the long-range technical activity overview. Because the data are not yet firm enough to quantify, but because the opportunity may develop in about three years, the CEO wanted the board of directors to be made aware of a possible major use of cash—including related debt and equity sources, and possible diversion of research talent. An estimate of the needs in a three-year time frame, beyond the long-range planning period, is shown in Figure 15-20.

15-11 ROLE OF THE CONTROLLER

For the early phases of the strategic planning process—developing the company mission, objectives, and strategies—the controller generally provides financial data

Figure 15-17   Percentage Return on Average Shareholders' Equity.

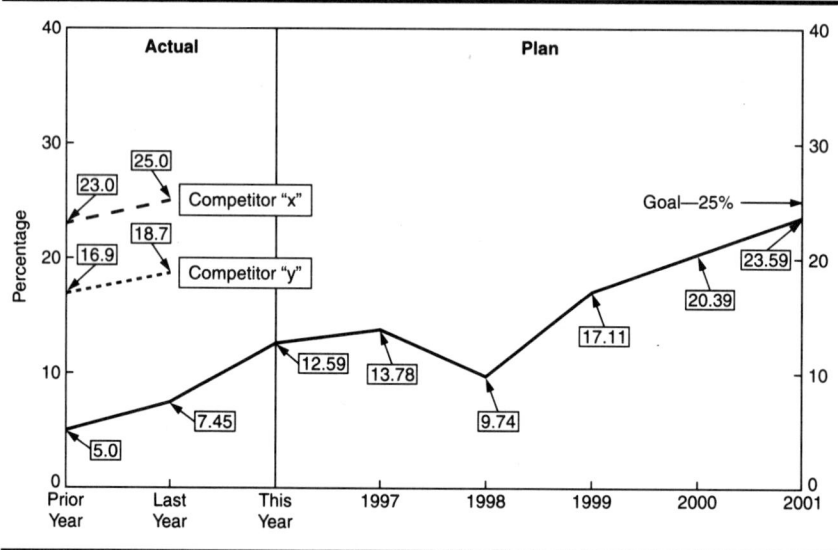

Figure 15-18   Ratio of Long-Term Debt to Net Worth.

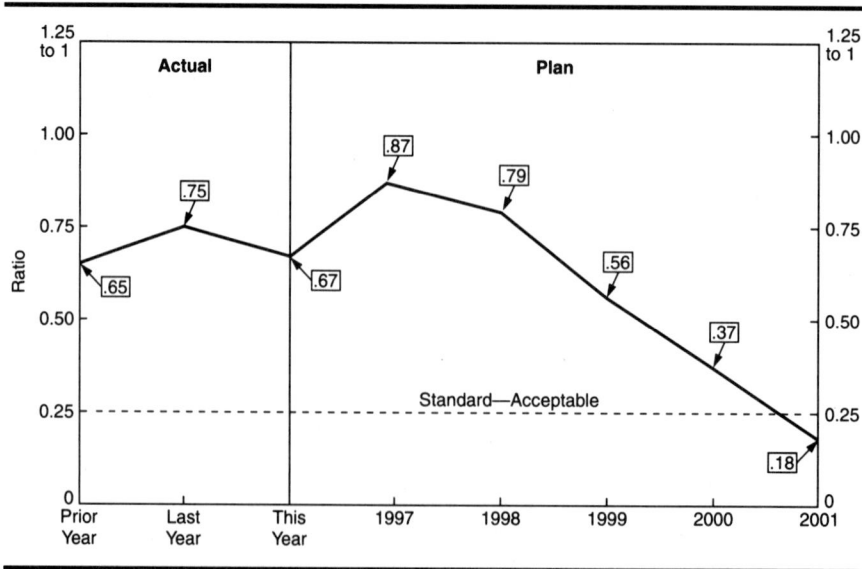

Figure 15-19   Current Ratio.

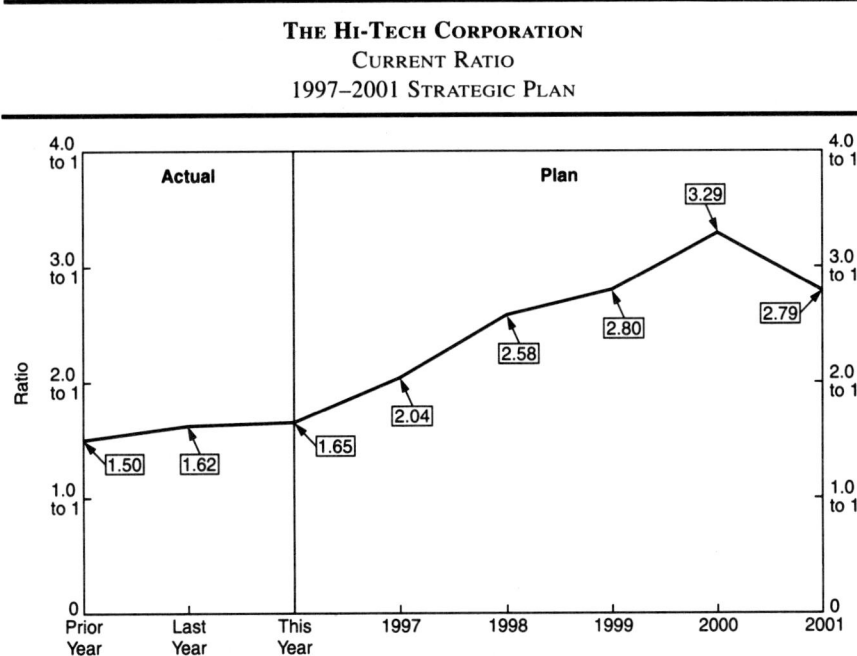

Figure 15-20   "Beyond the Five Years."

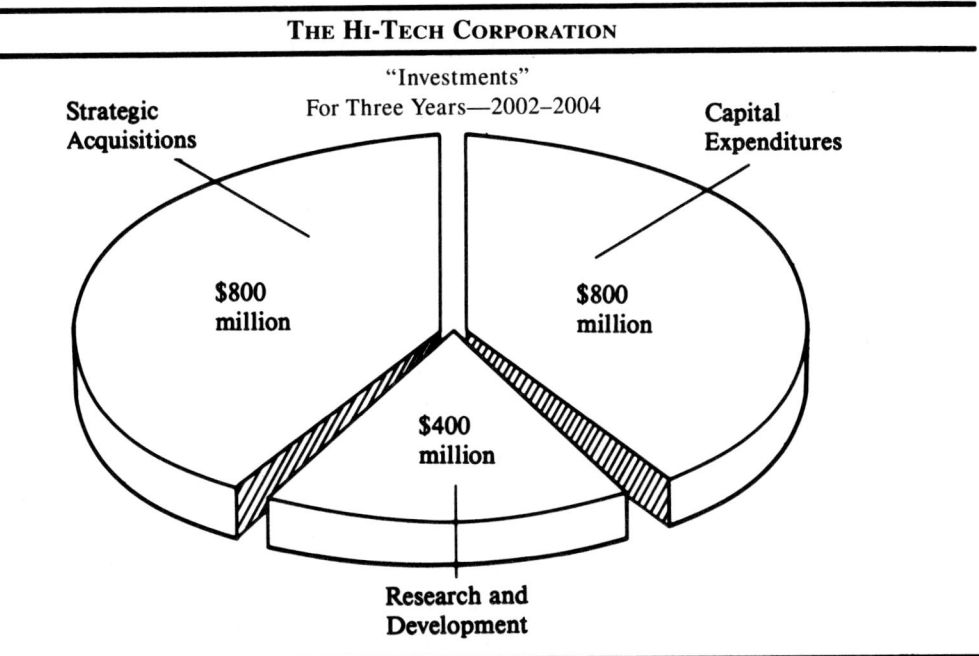

needed by other executives and makes financial analyses for them, to assist in setting appropriate objectives and testing the alternative strategies. But what are his functions when the task is to translate all operations and financial conditions into a time-phase plan expressed in financial terms? While we term the plan, "the long-range financial plan," it is not the plan of the financial executives, but rather the plan of each major executive, integrated into a single plan, expressed in financial terms. Since the chief sales executive will be responsible for meeting the sales plan and its related milestones, year by year, the controller must make quite certain that the sales segment, and marketing segment, the combining of continuing strategies or plans with the newly determined strategies, translates into a plan suitable to, or agreed to, by the sales executive. Comparable assistance must be given to all other nonfinancial executives. In the financial area itself, in conjunction with the chief financial executive, the financial operations and financing activities must be translated into realistic plans on a year-to-year basis. Then the consolidated plan must be tested against prudent standards and the objectives set by company management.

Accordingly, the responsibilities of the controller might be grouped into (a) supportive facilitating functions, and (b) exercise of the primarily financial functions in consolidating and testing the plan from a financial standpoint. A more detailed listing of his suggested responsibilities is as follows:

1. *Supportive.* In general to provide financial-type data, together with requested analyses, to the other executives involved in developing the plan, including:

   a. Provision of analytical data.

      (i)   Sales, in units and value, as appropriate, by year, by requested breakdown: products, territories, channels of distribution.

      (ii) Profit margin analyses; operating margin, contribution margin by sectors: products, territories, etc.

      (iii) Costs and expenses by functions, or appropriate organizational segment, type of expense, and/or other break-outs: marketing, research and development, engineering, administrative.

      (iv) Data regarding asset utilization and/or investment.

   b. Assistance in organizing financial data, as needed, for the use of the other executives in their plan presentations.

   c. Assistance in goal setting such as:

      (i)   Return on sales (or operating margin),

      (ii) Return on assets,

      (iii) Return on shareholders' equity, and

      (iv) Turnover on assets

      on an overall basis and/or by segment of the organization (division, subsidiary, etc.).

2. *Directly Financial*

   a. Consolidate all plans in financial terms, by year or other appropriate time segment (two years, or quarters, in some instances) for the planning period. The primary financial statements produced would include:

(i) Statement of Planned Income and Expense.

(ii) Statement of Planned Cash Flows.

(iii) Statement of Planned Financial Position.

(iv) Statement of Planned Capital (Fixed Assets), both Commitments and Expenditures.

b. Evaluate or appraise the strategic plans as an overall management device against such standards as:

(i) Corporate goals.

(ii) Past performance or condition.

(iii) Selected competitors.

(iv) Industry performance.

These tests could relate to:

(i) Profitability—on sales, assets, or net worth.

(ii) Growth rates—sales, aggregate earnings, earnings per share.

c. Judge the planned financial condition including that of any segments against such requirements as credit agreements, merger or acquisition contracts, indentures, or against selected ratios: debt to equity, current ratio, working capital, etc. These calculations can be made to test yearly operating results or year-end condition.

d. Measure dividend policy, stock purchase plans, or other financial policies against perceived needs, and market requirements, as related to future capital requirements.

e. Evaluate the plan, or any segments, as to reasonableness, weaknesses, attainability, undue optimism, etc.

f. Finally, assuming the plan will be met each year, evaluate it in the context of market expectation (analysts), P/E ratio, etc.

The consolidation of the strategic plan is not a simple routine matter of adding some numbers: It involves a complete appraisal or judging of results in the eyes not only of management, but also the financial community. The company must be kept on a path that will enable it to secure the needed capital for growth or expansion, even under somewhat adverse economic conditions.

15-12 SELECTED REFERENCES

Below, Patrick J., George L. Morrisey, and Betty L. Acomb, *The Executive Guide to Strategic Planning*. San Francisco: Jossey-Bass, 1987, Chap. 8.

Steiner, George A., *Strategic Planning, What Every Manager Must Know*. New York: The Free Press, 1979.

CHAPTER 16

Profit-Planning: The Annual Plan

16-1 INTRODUCTION

This chapter explains in some detail the short-term profit planning or budgeting procedures. Long-range or strategic planning is a management process that focuses on the corporate objectives and the means of accomplishing them. As previously explained, it usually covers a period of several years, perhaps 5 or 10.

Supportive of the long-range plan is short-range or short-term planning that usually concerns itself with the next year or two. It is the detailed planning that involves the development of operating programs which works to assure the effective implementation of the long-range profit goals but recognizes the limitations and opportunities of the present and near-term resources and business environment. *Profit planning* has been defined by several authorities as the process of developing detailed plans for a specified near-term period in the future, and integrating these plans into a comprehensive whole.[1]

---

[1] See, for example, Robert Beyer and Donald J. Trawicki, *Profitability Accounting* (New York: Ronald Press, 1972), p. 17.

In this profit-planning process, expected revenues, costs, levels of operation, facilities, financial resources, and personnel are all considered and interrelated. The appropriateness of levels and types of costs and expenses are analyzed and interrelated by techniques discussed in the next chapter. Modeling techniques may be involved in this profit-planning process to provide management with (1) a quantitative analysis of the probable effects on operating results, (2) the financial condition of alternative decisions, and (3) alternative uses of resources to optimize the return to the shareholders. Thus profit planning is an iterative process that aids the manager in revising and modifying plans until an acceptable one is reached.

This entire short-term profit planning and control process may be summarized as including these elements:

1. Arriving at an acceptable plan or program.
2. Measuring actual performance against the plan (and against other related standards).
3. Deciding on, and implementing, corrective action.

The detailed planning and control process of Emerson Electric[2] is a classic of its kind and has been the subject of many schools of business case studies and involves the above three segments. It seeks to identify problems before they start and commence corrective action. For an extended period the planning sessions focused on costs, margins, and profits. As a result, the managers had little incentive to emphasize growth or risky new products that would reduce near-term profits. But that is changing because a primary need of the company now is growth—whether by going global or by acquiring new companies or by participating in joint ventures. The annual plan should seek to address the perceived needs of the business.

This chapter describes the short-term planning process, including a simplified illustrative plan; and the role of the controller as a chief player. The next chapter discusses some related financial analysis techniques that assist the company in developing an acceptable annual or short-range business plan.

But, first, what is the need for and what are the advantages of this business planning and budgeting?

16-2 PURPOSE OF BUDGETING

A fundamental purpose of business budgeting is to find the most profitable course through which the efforts of the business may be directed in meeting its primary service objective. Another purpose is to assist management in holding the business as nearly as possible on that charted course. In most business concerns there are numerous decisions to be made about the policies to be followed and the methods to be used. Decisions must be made, for example, about the choice of goods and services to be made and sold; the selection of customers; the level of prices; the methods of production, distribution, and financing; credit terms; the degree of integration of operating

---

[2] See the Seth Lubove article in *Forbes* as mentioned in the Selected References regarding the task of annual planning.

units; and so on, almost without limit. Which selection of policies and methods will be most profitable? Can any combination be found that gives reasonable promise of an adequate return on the investment? If none can, the venture should be stopped, the business merged with another, or the capital shifted to other channels, before further losses result. If profitable courses are open, each should be examined and translated into its profit possibilities.

Although it is easy to speak in general terms of the desirability of budgeting, the practical advantages in an actual case are not always so apparent. Conditions change rapidly in business; the actions of customers and competitors cannot be entirely controlled, and after they become known a business must, to a degree, govern itself accordingly, regardless of any previously developed program. Plans, when made intelligently, require exhaustive study and research, and this constitutes an expensive procedure. What, then, are the specific advantages to be gained?

The benefits of budgeting lie in three primary fields of business activity: first, directly in the *planning;* second, in the *coordinating* phase; and, third, in the *control* area. These activities are each very wide in scope and contain within themselves several supplemental or detailed advantages. A somewhat more concrete outline of the reasons for budgeting follows.

16-3 PLANNING

1. *To Base Action upon Thorough Investigation, Study, and Research.* Perhaps the cardinal advantage of systematic budgeting is that it tends to bring the executives to an early study of their problems and instills into the organization the habit of careful study before a decision about action is made. This is not easy to achieve. Intensive study is to many a distasteful exercise. Most of us prefer to postpone difficult decisions until necessity compels us to act. Businesses, like individuals, tend to become opportunists; they wait until a decision is forced, then turn quickly, often without time for careful study of the problems, in the direction offering the easiest immediate escape from their troubles.

   If the executives, from general manager to foremen, know that their plans are to be formally expressed and that they will be charged with responsibility for their execution, they can be brought to an earlier and more intensive study of the problems at hand.

   This habit of making plans will benefit every activity. Specifically, it will relate to financial requirements, inventory levels, production facilities, production, purchasing, advertising, selling, sales promotion, product development, organization growth or expansion, labor relations—in short, the advantages can accrue to every function.

2. *To Enlist the Assistance of the Entire Organization in Determining the Most Profitable Course.* When budgeting is undertaken in ample time and on a regular schedule, there is full opportunity to enlist the assistance of foremen, salespeople, branch managers, department heads, and all operating officials—major and minor. In some lines of business the suggestions and counsel from such sources are essential to the development of the best operating plans, and in most lines of business such assistance is highly desirable. The final plans should be expressive of the combined judgment of the entire organization, thereby eliminating such bias or prejudice as frequently affects the judgment of individual groups.

3. *To Serve as a Declaration of Policies.* Nothing so restrains the enthusiasm and energy of an organization as uncertainty. The budget procedure provides a vehicle through which basic policies are periodically reexamined, restated, and set forth as guiding principles for the organization at large. Basic policies, not temporary expediency, should be the guiding factors of a business, and the organization should be schooled in such policies.

4. *To Define Objectives.* The successful manager must surround himself with capable associates who will accept his leadership and execute his program. But he must demonstrate his ability to lead. Men will follow a leader when they realize that he has a sensible plan of action and definite objectives in mind. Such objectives should be clearly expressed and, to a certain degree, should stand as goals of attainment for the entire organization. Objectives, however, must not be the product of hope but rather the logical consequence of carefully laid plans. The executive who can clearly define his objectives and delineate a program that can logically be expected to reach such objectives can command the cooperation and loyalty of his associates.

5. *To Stabilize Employment.* No employer of labor, regardless of his social or economic philosophy, can longer disregard the welfare of his employees. We have passed the time when workers can be laid aside at will when not needed, like flasks or patterns in the foundry. To be sure, the responsibility to workers must be balanced with the responsibility to investors, and the welfare of both must be considered, but the business program must consider stability of employment. Intelligent business budgeting rather than governmental regulation offers the greatest hope for providing stability of employment.

6. *To Make More Effective Use of Physical Equipment.* During the course of planning, the excess cost of idle capacity will be revealed. Moreover, in considering those plans that offer the greatest profit, the maximum use of available facilities will inevitably be a factor. The result normally would be the elimination of some of the social wastes related to the uneconomical use of physical facilities.

16-4 COORDINATION

1. *To Coordinate and Correlate Human Effort within the Business Structure.* In some respects this is the most important purpose of budgeting. In many concerns there is a definite lack of coordination of effort. This is a restraining factor. Full steam cannot be applied in some divisions of the business because of uncertainty about the program in other divisions. Only when the effort of all divisions is properly timed and coordinated can the full power of united action be secured.

This, however, emphasizes another important element of budgeting and that is the necessity of constant review and revision of the plans. If unforeseen and uncontrollable situations arise (and in many industries this is certain to happen) that materially alter the operations of one division, the machinery must be available for quick readjustment of the program in other divisions affected thereby. Wars, floods, droughts, strikes, price wars, political changes, collapse of foreign markets, etc., give rise to such situations.

The success of business budgeting should be measured not so much by the nearness of the ultimate results to the original plans as by the extent to which all executives—major and minor—know at all times just what is the immediate program and what are their respective parts therein. There must be no restraint or uncertainty if the organization is to function with full power.

The chief executive is the financial coordinating official, but the complexities of the modern business are such that he cannot exercise this function without the assistance and guidance of clearly defined objectives and detailed plans that are projected throughout the entire organization.

2. *To Relate the Activities of the Business to the Expected General Trend of Business Conditions.* Numerous studies have been made which would seem to indicate that profits are full as much (if not more) the result of changes in fundamental conditions as of competitive efficiency. This emphasizes the importance of coordinating the plans of the business with the general trend of economic conditions. The failure of economists to agree on the causes of the business cycle and the frequent differences of opinion among business analysts about future trends have led many executives to the point of skepticism regarding the whole matter of forecasting; however, the fact remains that business moves through periods of high and low activity and that there are frequently signals of the movements as related to a particular business. These signals must be watched and the plans of the business must reflect courage or caution, depending on the expected trend.

3. *To Direct Capital and Effort into the Most Profitable Channels by Means of a Balanced and Unified Program.* Before spending money, serious study should be given to the amount that can be profitably spent, where it is to come from, just how it should be spent, and what results may be reasonably expected. A certain amount of funds must be directed toward equipment and inventories and a certain amount to the promotion of sales, but these amounts must be kept in proper balance. No more ambitious project should be attempted than that for which there is available capital, no more production should be made than that which can be profitably sold, and no sales program should be developed beyond that needed for the planned production. Such a balance of factors directed toward a definite objective represents the ideal and, although it can seldom be fully achieved in practice, its attainment will be more likely as a result of careful advance planning. Without such planning, inventories are likely to be out of proportion to sales and production requirements, customers may be excessively financed, and irregularity is likely to arise in the use of production facilities.

Where plans and decisions are made from day to day, the program frequently becomes unconsciously warped. Executives are often, through previous training or experience, biased in the direction of sales, engineering, or finance, with the result that one factor receives a disproportionate emphasis. A well-balanced program set up in advance and based on careful study will help to avoid this danger.

4. *To Reveal Weakness in Organization.* As plans are made and the responsibility for their execution delegated, weaknesses in organization will be revealed. Executives will not accept responsibility unless lines of authority are so delineated that they will be unhampered in the execution of their tasks. Where joint responsibilities are necessary, provision must be made in advance for an orderly procedure of joint action. No management activity so quickly reveals weakness in organization as the procedure of systematic budgeting.

16-5 CONTROL

1. *To Control Specific Operations or Expenditures.* Although the primary purpose of budgeting is to ascertain the most profitable course for the business to follow and to develop a balanced and coordinated program which will hold the company to that course, the budget also provides a valuable tool of control over certain business operations.

   Some operations and expenditures are subject to very definite control. It may be decided, for example, that $200,000 should be invested in plant expansion, that $100,000 should be appropriated for various sales promotion projects related to a new product, that 1000 units of the new product should be sold during the period under consideration, and that these units should be manufactured at a cost of $200 each. Assuming that the plans have been predicated on careful study and the considered judgment of the entire organization, the foundation has been laid for a certain degree of control. The investment in the plant can be rigidly held to the prescribed limits in spite of the enthusiasm of production officials to be beyond. Likewise, the expenditure for sales promotion can be definitely held to the predetermined plan. The orders for 1000 units may not be realized. This might result from the fact (1) that external conditions have changed rapidly and that such changes could not be foreseen, or (2) that the production of the units—either in quantity or cost—has not met expectations. In such cases the budget provides a certain degree of control. Expenditures are limited and directed into the channels that offered most promise. If external conditions beyond the control of management change, the program must be promptly revised. If such conditions do not change and failure of execution lies within the organization, the budget serves as a very definite tool of control. The failure of sales and production performance to meet expectation provides the signal for corrective action.

2. *Generally to Prevent Waste.* This is a more general aspect of control. A searching inquiry into every contemplated expenditure and the reason therefor—an analytical approach extending to every function and every department of the business—will constitute an effective preventive of waste.

   It can be seen that many of these specific advantages are very closely related to all three primary reasons for budgeting. However, the segregation should assist in a better understanding of the advantages of business planning and budgeting.

16-6 THE ANNUAL PLANNING CYCLE—ILLUSTRATIVE

Given the desirability of an annual plan, what are the basic steps involved? Assuming a company with several operating divisions, whose managers are held responsible for operating results, an overview of the process of developing a plan and budget is shown in Figure 16-1.

The steps may be described briefly as follows:

1. Very specific guidelines concerning the plan are issued by the company management to the operating divisions and the corporate executives involved. Such constraints are intended to assure the following:

   a. Actions taken during the year will be consistent with corporate policy and strategy as decided in the strategic plan.

Figure 16-1   The Company Annual Operation Plan Process.

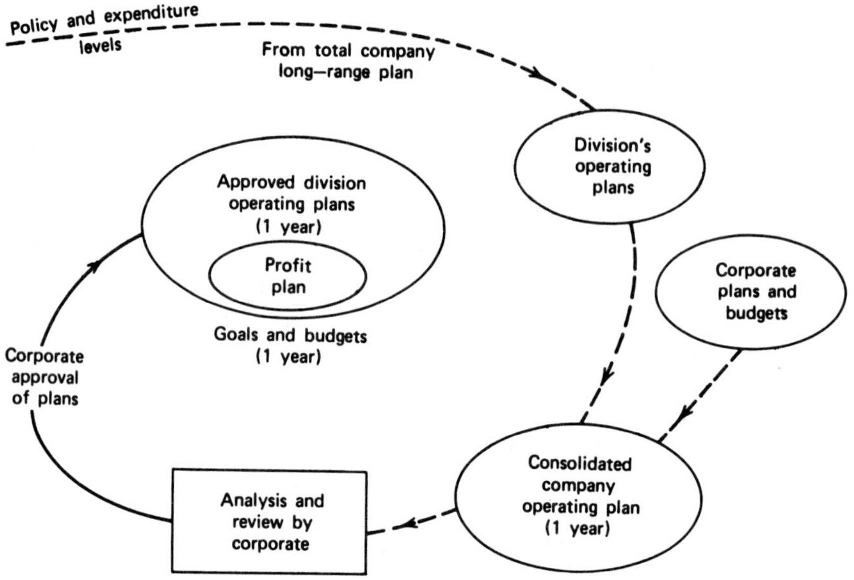

b. The financial assumptions will be consistent (where applicable) and realistic, i.e., federal and state income tax rates, inflation rates, capital expenditure limits, Social Security tax rate, independent research and development expense levels, etc.

c. Sufficient detail is forthcoming to permit an evaluation of the division plan.

2. When received, the division plans, along with other related plans (corporate organization, special departments, etc.), are consolidated to secure the total company picture. The division plans are prepared by functional segments, as may be deduced from Figure 16-2.

3. The consolidated plan, and that of each operating unit, etc., is evaluated in the corporate office (marketing, technical, financial, and general management). Some reiteration may be necessary to arrive at an acceptable plan (adequate profit rate, etc.).

4. When the overall picture is judged satisfactory at top management and board of director levels, the division is notified of the approved plan.

16-7 SUPPORTIVE FINANCIAL STATEMENTS AND BUDGETS

Finally, a business plan is expressed in financial terms. The plan should be summarized in these basic financial statements:

Statement of Planned Income and Expense.

Statement of Planned Sources and Uses of Cash (or Statement of Planned Cash Flows).

Statement of Planned Financial Position.

Figure 16-2   The Division Operating Plan.

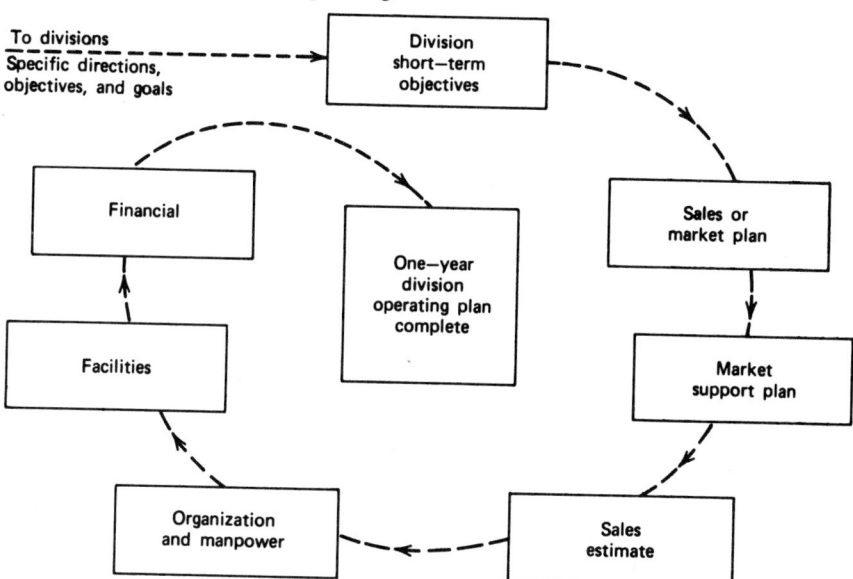

Such summaries should be supported by appropriate detailed plans or budgets on an organizational basis—showing in summary and by operational element, according to responsibility, these detailed plans—that become budgets or standards on final approval:

The Operational Budgets

1. Sales budget.
2. Production budget.
3. Materials units budget.
4. Purchases budget.
5. Labor budget.
6. Manufacturing expense budget.
7. Cost of goods sold budget.
8. Administrative and general expense budget.
9. Selling expense budget.
10. Advertising budget.
11. Research and development expense budget.
12. Other income and expense budgets.

Capital Assets Budget (including commitments)
Cash Budget
Other Working Capital Budgets

1. Receivables.
2. Inventories.

3. Short-term liabilities.

4. Prepaid items.

Other Long-Term Budgets

1. Investments.

2. Liabilities.

3. Shareholder equity.

All these budgets or plans are interrelated. Changes in the capital asset budget can affect the operational budgets and vice versa. The same can be said for the cash budget and the plans for long-term liabilities or shareholders' equity.

An overly simplified summary of these budgets that nevertheless illustrates the relationship of one to the other and the extent of planning involved is shown in the following segments. The complicated nature of each of the above-mentioned budgets, and the detailed analysis necessary for the preparation of a realistic budget or plan for each department and function, are described in the relevant chapters of this volume.

Given the complicated nature of this planning and control process, the specific functions and the key role of the controller are reviewed in some detail in section 16-22.

16-8 SALES BUDGET

Usually, the sales forecast is the starting point in budget preparation. The Illustrative Company manufactures and sells only four products. Based on the estimate of units received from the sales manager, and the expected unit prices, the sales budget is constructed as shown in Figure 16-3.

16-9 PRODUCTION BUDGET

Once the tentative estimate of sales has been agreed on, the usual next step is a determination of the quantities of finished goods that must be produced to meet both the sales and inventory requirements. This calculation of units to be produced is illustrated in Figure 16-4.

Figure 16-3 Sales Budget.

The Illustrative Company
PRELIMINARY SALES BUDGET
FOR THE YEAR ENDING DECEMBER 31, 19X2

Product	No. of Units	Unit Selling Price	Total Sales
R	20,000	$33.00	$ 660,000
S	30,000	54.50	1,635,000
T	50,000	21.25	1,062,500
U	5,000	78.50	392,500
Total	105,000		$3,750,000

Figure 16-4   Production Budget.

The Illustrative Company
TENTATIVE PRODUCTION BUDGET (UNITS)
FOR THE YEAR ENDING DECEMBER 31, 19X2

Description	Products			
	R	S	T	U
Quantity required for sale	20,000	30,000	50,000	5,000
Desired ending inventory	5,000	5,000	10,000	500
Total requirements	25,000	35,000	60,000	5,500
Less:				
Beginning inventory	3,000	2,000	8,000	1,000
Required production	22,000	33,000	52,000	4,500

16-10 PURCHASES BUDGET

After the levels of production have been set, the next job to be undertaken is the some-times laborious task of determining the quantities of raw material needed to meet the production and inventory requirements—a function made much easier by the personal computer. This function is, first, a matter of extending the units of production times the units of each raw material needed:

COMPUTATION OF UNITS OF RAW MATERIAL

Raw Material	Finished Product				Total Unit Requirements
	R	S	T	U	
AA	11,000	33,000	—	9,000	53,000
BB	22,000	—	52,000	9,000	83,000
CC	11,000	66,000	104,000	4,500	185,500

Then, after usage has been calculated, the value of purchases can be set, giving con-sideration to inventories. The dollar value is determined on the basis of expected unit cost prices that may be furnished by the purchasing department. The purchases budget is constructed basically in the manner of Figure 16-5.

Very often it is necessary to group purchases by class of material rather than to enumerate each individual type of material. This practice is often used where unit prices are small.

16-11 DIRECT LABOR BUDGET

Another budget dependent on the production budget is that relating to direct labor. This cost is computed as shown in Figure 16-6.

Figure 16-5 Purchases Budget.

The Illustrative Company
TENTATIVE PURCHASES BUDGET
FOR THE YEAR ENDING DECEMBER 31, 19X2

Raw Material	Produc- tion	Requirements Ending Inven- tory	Total	Less: Beginning Inventory	Quantity to Be Purchased	Unit Price	Purchases Budget
AA	53,000	2,000	55,000	3,000	52,000	$4.00	$208,000
BB	83,000	5,000	88,000	10,000	78,000	2.00	156,000
CC	185,500	20,000	205,500	20,000	185,500	1.00	185,500
Total							$549,500

Figure 16-6 Direct Labor Budget.

The Illustrative Company
TENTATIVE DIRECT LABOR BUDGET
FOR THE YEAR ENDING DECEMBER 31, 19X2

Product	Quantity	Standard Labor Hours per Unit	Total Standard Labor Hours	Direct Labor Budget (At $6.00 per Std. Labor Hour)
R	22,000	1.0	22,000	$132,000
S	33,000	2.5	82,500	495,000
T	52,000	.5	26,000	156,000
U	4,500	2.5	11,250	67,500
Total			141,750	$850,500

16-12 MANUFACTURING EXPENSE BUDGET

Total manufacturing expenses for the expected production level must be ascertained on the basis of the activity of each type of expense and/or each department or cost center. The final estimate, arbitrarily assumed to be 50% of direct labor for this overly simplified illustration, is summarized in Figure 16-7.

16-13 INVENTORY BUDGET

All information necessary to calculate the investment in inventories is now available. The value of the finished inventory would be computed as demonstrated in Figure 16-8.

A similar procedure would be followed with respect to raw materials, supplies, and work in process. The total value of inventories might then be summarized as in Figure 16-9.

Figure 16-7   Budget of Manufacturing Expenses.

The Illustrative Company
TENTATIVE BUDGET OF MANUFACTURING EXPENSES
FOR THE YEAR ENDING DECEMBER 31, 19X2

Description	Amount
Indirect labor	$125,000
Payroll taxes and insurance (40%)	50,000
Provision for vacation wages	43,250
Power	52,000
Supplies	25,000
Repairs and maintenance	67,000
Depreciation	47,000
Property taxes	10,000
Property insurance	6,000
Total	$425,250

Figure 16-8   Computation of Finished Goods Inventory.

The Illustrative Company
COMPUTATION OF ESTIMATED ENDING
INVENTORY OF FINISHED GOODS
AS OF DECEMBER 31, 19X2

Product	Quantity	Unit Cost	Total Sales
R	5,000	$14.00	$ 70,000
S	5,000	28.50	142,500
T	10,000	8.50	85,000
U	500	35.50	17,750
Total			$315,250

Figure 16-9   The Inventory Budget.

The Illustrative Company
STATEMENT OF ESTIMATED ENDING INVENTORIES
AS OF DECEMBER 31, 19X2

Raw materials	$ 38,000
Supplies and parts	4,000
Work in process	97,500
Finished goods	315,250
Total	$454,750

In actual practice, these summaries would be supported by supplemental de╵ These data would permit both testing and checking of turnover rates, and so on.

16-14 OPERATING EXPENSE BUDGET

Through detailed budgeting and summary by individual departments, the other ╵ penses of the business are estimated. They are summarized in Figure 16-10.

It is assumed that the only item of nonoperating income is discount on purcha╵ estimated to be $5,000.

16-15 CAPITAL EXPENDITURES BUDGET

Based on a detailed review of facility requirements and the availability of cash, a ╵ get for capital expenditures is prepared as in Figure 16-11.

Figure 16-10   Budgeted Operating and Other Expenses.

The Illustrative Company
STATEMENT OF BUDGETED OPERATING EXPENSES
FOR THE YEAR ENDING DECEMBER 31, 19X2

Items	Selling Expense	General and Administrative Expense	Finan╵ Expe╵
Salaries—executives	$ 74,000	$ 90,000	$ —
Salaries—salesmen	198,00	—	—
Commissions—agents	17,500	—	—
Fringe benefits	108,800	36,000	—
Advertising space	50,000	—	—
Bad debts	—	10,000	—
Traveling expenses	220,000	9,500	—
Rent	12,000	3,000	—
Supplies	21,000	7,000	—
Interest expense	—	—	1,╵
Discount on sales	—	—	18,╵
Total	$701,300	$155,500	$19,╵

Figure 16-11   Budget for Capital Expenditures.

The Illustrative Company
BUDGET FOR CAPITAL EXPENDITURES
FOR THE YEAR ENDING DECEMBER 31, 19X2

Buildings	$120,000
Machinery and equipment	132,500
Total	$252,500

16-16 COST OF GOODS SOLD

The requisite information is now available to prepare a tentative statement of income and expense. First, the statement of estimated cost of goods sold is computed. (See Figure 16-12.)

16-17 STATEMENT OF ESTIMATED INCOME AND EXPENSE

The next logical step is the preparation of the Statement of Estimated Income and Expense. (See Figure 16-13.)

In practice, the Statement of Estimated Income and Expense might be detailed by product lines, territories, or channels of distribution. Also, other significant relationships would be calculated for discussion purposes.

16-18 CASH BUDGET

Another important budget statement relates to estimated cash receipts and disbursements. The summary of the *cash* transactions for the year is shown in the tabulation of Figure 16-14.

In actual practice, the cash budget statement may simply summarize the cash receipts and cash disbursements, each separately. Or, the source or use of cash generation

Figure 16-12   Statement of Estimated Cost of Goods Sold.

The Illustrative Company STATEMENT OF ESTIMATED COST OF GOODS SOLD FOR THE YEAR ENDING DECEMBER 31, 19X2	
Raw Materials	
Inventory, January 1, 19X2	$ 52,000
Add: Purchases (Figure 16-5)	549,500
Total available	601,500
Less: Inventory, December 31, 19X2	38,000
Transfer to work in process	563,500
Direct Labor (Figure 16-6)	850,500
Manufacturing Expense (Figure 16-7)	425,250
Total charges to cost of production	1,839,250
Add: Work in process, January 1, 19X2	97,500
Total	1,936,750
Less: Work in process, December 31, 19X2	97,500
Transfer to finished goods	1,839,250
Add: Finished goods inventory, January 1, 19X2	202,500
Total	2,041,750
Less: Finished goods inventory, December 31, 19X2 (Figure 16-8)	315,250
Estimated cost of goods sold	$1,726,500

Figure 16-13   Statement of Estimated Income and Expense.

The Illustrative Company
STATEMENT OF ESTIMATED INCOME AND EXPENSE
FOR THE YEAR ENDING DECEMBER 31, 19X2

	Amount	% to Sales
Net sales (Figure 16–3)	$3,750,000	100
Cost of goods sold (Figure 16–12)	1,726,500	46
Gross profit	2,023,500	54
Operating expenses:		
Advertising and selling (Figure 16–10)	701,300	19
General and administrative (Figure 16–10)	155,500	4
Total operating expenses	856,800	23
Operating profit	1,166,700	31
Other income—discount on purchases	5,000	
	1,171,700	31
Other expenses:		
Interest expense (Figure 16–10)	1,900	
Discount on sales (Figure 16–10)	18,000	
	19,900	
Profit before income taxes	1,151,800	30
Income taxes (40%)	460,720	12
Net income	$ 691,080	18

may be grouped as from operations, investing activity, and financing activity. An ample of this format, although not using figures from The Illustrative Company shown in Figure 16-15. It has the advantage of reconciling planned net income with cash budget, but has the disadvantage of not identifying the specific details of planned cash receipts and planned cash disbursements.

16-19 STATEMENT OF ESTIMATED FINANCIAL CONDITION

The final effect of all the planning is reflected in the statement of estimated financial condition at the close of the budget period. Usually, such a statement is prepared in comparative form with the actual or expected condition at the beginning of budget period as well as at the close. The concluding budget statement of estimated financial condition and the related statement of retained earnings are illustrated Figures 16-16 and 16-17.

16-20 APPROVAL OF THE BUDGET

This comprehensive review of budget preparation has progressed from one step mediately to the next. In actual practice, the path is not as smooth or well defined

Figure 16-14 Statement of Estimated Cash Receipts and Disbursements.

The Illustrative Company		
STATEMENT OF ESTIMATED CASH RECEIPTS AND DISBURSEMENTS		
FOR THE YEAR ENDING DECEMBER 31, 19X2		
Cash balance, December 31, 19X1		$ 460,000
Estimated cash receipts:		
Collections on accounts receivable	$3,672,500	
Proceeds from sale of common stock	500,000	
Proceeds from notes payable	50,000	
Total estimated receipts		4,222,500
Total cash available		$4,682,500
Estimated cash disbursements:		
Accounts payable—materials and supplies	$ 580,600	
Accounts payable—other	428,000	
Notes payable	300,000	
Salaries and wages	1,330,000	
Accrued income taxes	785,050	
Items—other	202,050	
Interest expense	1,900	
Dividends	210,000	
Capital assets	252,500	
Total estimated disbursements		4,090,100
Estimated cash balance, December 31, 19X2		$ 592,400

Usually, after each of the detailed budgets is prepared by the accounting staff, the figures are compared with past experience and tested by checking significant relationships. Discussions are held with the functional supervisors or department heads to clarify or correct any seemingly out-of-line condition. Such a process can well require several revisions.

When agreement has been reached on the detailed budgets, then the pieces are put together; the master budget is prepared. This overall budget is presented to the president and/or budget committee for analysis and review. If the management is not satisfied with the operating results or the expected financial condition, or if these executives are not convinced that the best possible program is reflected in the plan, then the alternative plans must be introduced and expressed in monetary terms. When the principals are in accord, the budget for the coming period may be submitted for approval to the board of directors.

16-21 THE CONTROL FUNCTION

Up to the stage of top-side approval, the planning function has predominated. Presumably, the best possible course of action was selected and every member of the organization was assisting with the expression of such a plan. However, once the budget is approved, the business enters a new phase. The budget must be attained, the ship must

Figure 16-15   Statement of Estimated Cash Flows.

The Global Company
STATEMENT OF ESTIMATED CASH FLOWS
FOR THE YEAR ENDING DECEMBER 31, 19XX
(dollars in thousands)

Cash Flows from Operating Activities

Net income	$12,7
Adjustments to reconcile net income to net cash provided	
by operating activities:	
Depreciation	1,0
Amortization	4
Deferred income taxes	(1
Accounts receivable	4
Inventories	(2
Other working capital changes	1
Net cash provided by operating activities	14,4

Cash Flows from Investing Activities

Capital expenditures	(4,2
Disposals of plant and equipment	8
Acquisitions and other investments	2
Proceeds from divestitures	1
Net cash used in investing activities	(2,8

Cash Flows from Financing Activities

Proceeds from long-term debt	8
Repayment of long-term debt	(6
Purchases of treasury stock	(4
Payment of dividends	(1,0
Net cash used in financing activities	(1,3
Effect of exchange rates on cash	1
Net increase in cash and equivalents	10,4
Cash and equivalents at beginning of year	5,4
Cash and equivalents at end of year	$15,9

be kept on course. So the budget becomes a control tool. For this purpose, actual operating results of the day, or week, or month are compared with the budget. Variances are analyzed, and corrective action is taken wherever necessary. Quite often, strong winds force the ship off its course, so a new one must be charted; the plan budget must be revised.

16-22 ROLE OF THE CONTROLLER—A KEY PLAYER

The annual business plan, or budget, is the plan of all members of *management,* as company moves toward its long-range objectives and goals. While it is expressed in nancial terms for many phases, it is not the plan of the CFO or the controller. But

Figure 16-16   Comparative Statement of Financial Condition.

The Illustrative Company
COMPARATIVE STATEMENT OF FINANCIAL CONDITION
ACTUAL AS OF DECEMBER 31, 19X1, AND ESTIMATED AS OF DECEMBER 31, 19X2

	Assets				
	Actual December 31, 19X1		Estimated December 31, 19X2		Increase or (Decrease)
Current Assets					
Cash		$ 460,000		$ 592,400	$132,400
Accounts receivable .	$ 250,000		$ 322,500		
Less: Reserve for					
doubtful accounts .	15,000	235,000	20,000	302,500	67,500
Inventories:					
Raw material	$ 52,000		$ 38,000		
Supplies	4,000		4,000		
Work in process ..	97,500		97,500		
Finished goods ...	202,500	356,000	315,250	454,750	98,750
Prepaid items		3,000		3,000	—
Total current					
assets		$1,054,000		$1,352,650	$298,650
Fixed Assets					
Land and land					
improvements ...	$ 25,000		$ 25,000		
Buildings	375,000		495,000		
Machinery and					
equipment	625,000		757,500		
Total	$1,025,000		$1,277,500		
Less: Reserve for					
depreciation	210,000	815,000	257,000	1,020,500	205,500
Total assets		$1,869,000		$2,373,150	$504,150

(continued)

financial executives, and especially the controller, usually play a key role in the planning *process*. Since the annual plan is quite detailed in nature—for example, by type of expense, by department, by function, by month or quarter—and because the plans of one function must be consistent and properly relate to each affected function, and must be tested or evaluated against selected criteria, either by department function, or overall, it is essential that necessary data be made available in the proper *format*, based on the proper *assumptions*, and contained within a given timeframe. This section details many of the actions a controller might take in a typical entity.

The financial arm of the company, whether the CFO or budget director, but most likely the controller in most instances, should assure that these steps take place:

1. *Designate in detail the data to be supplied by the departmental or function executive, through appropriate channels, to the controller.*

Figure 16-16   *(continued)*

	Liabilities and Shareholders' Equity		
	Actual December 31, 19X1	Estimated December 31, 19X2	Increase or (Decrease)
Current Liabilities			
Accounts payable	$ 60,000	$ 80,400	$ 20,400
Notes payable	300,000	50,000	(250,000)
Accrued salaries and wages	30,000	55,000	25,000
Accrued income taxes	370,400	46,070	(324,330)
Accrued items—other	28,000	80,000	52,000
Total current liabilities	$ 788,400	$ 311,470	$(476,930)
Ownership Equity			
Common stock, $5 par value, authorized 100,000 shares; outstanding, 50,000 shares in 19X1, & 70,000 in 19X2	$ 250,000	$ 350,000	$ 100,000
Capital contributed for common stock in excess of par value ...	500,000	900,000	400,000
Retained earnings	330,600	811,680	481,080
Total ownership equity	$1,080,600	$2,061,680	$ 981,080
Total liabilities and shareholders' equity	$1,869,000	$2,373,150	$ 504,150

Figure 16-17   Statement of Estimated Retained Earnings.

The Illustrative Company
STATEMENT OF ESTIMATED RETAINED EARNINGS
AS OF DECEMBER 31, 19X2

Balance, December 31, 19X1	$ 330,600
Add: Estimated net income for the year 19X2	691,080
Total	$1,021,680
Less: Dividends to be paid in 19X2	210,000
Estimated balance, December 31, 19X2	$ 811,680

For example, as to the *sales* function, it might include unit and dollar sales for the planning period;

by product

by sales person

by territory, and

by month

compared with prior performance at certain levels.

As to *expenses,* it could include the amount of expense by department, by type of expense, and by month, for the planning period, compared with the prior period. These expenses in total, or individually, for the period also might be compared with sales, or factory output (or selected competitors, if known).

Much of this same data will be used later to compare actual performance with plan—another reason for the great detail.

2. *Provide the format in which the data should be presented.*

The format should fit the needs not only of the controller but especially also those of the cognizant operating executives.

Instructions as to both content and format are necessary to permit analysis and comparisons, and to facilitate consolidation of the financial data.

3. *Provide historical financial data, or other related data, which the operating executives may use for comparable purposes in preparing the plan year data.* Examples could include:

(a) Prior year comparative company data.

(b) Historical company trends and relationships.

(c) Industry comparative data, or selected competitor figures.

4. *Provide underlying guidelines to be used in preparing the data for the planning year.* Information such as this might be needed:

(a) Probable tax rates and data—federal, state, and local—including:

(1) Payroll tax rates.

(2) Property tax rates.

(3) Income tax rates.

(4) Social security tax rates.

(b) Selected economic data, such as:

(1) Inflation rates—in general or on specific products.

(2) Gross domestic product.

(3) Selected regional economic growth rate, unemployment rate, etc.

(c) Interest rates, where applicable.

(d) Goals or constraints set by top management, e.g.:

(1) Return on assets—in total and for each division.

(2) Expected rate of sales increase—in total and/or for selected products.

(3) Expected gross margin percent.

(4) Advertising expenditures.

(e) Capital asset expenditure limits.

5. *Set forth the time schedule of the due date for the relevant segment or phase of the annual plan.*

   This may be a simple due date schedule each year of important steps as authorized by the CEO. An example could be a simple letter from the controller to each division executive and the corporate functional executive (in a decentralized organization) outlining the dates:

Steps	Completion Date
1. Submission of complete business plan (including monthly and other supporting detail) to corporate controller	September 15, 19xx
2. Review and analysis of division plans by corporate staff of finance, marketing, manufacturing, and R&D, etc.	October 31, 19xx
3. Consolidation of division plans and corporate operations, and overall financial appraisal by the finance department	November 25, 19xx
4. Review (and revise if necessary) of final plan by CEO and senior management	December 10, 19xx
5. Review and approval by board of directors	December 22, 19xx

   In larger companies, where more follow-up might be necessary, and when the sequence is critical, a Gantt chart might be useful. See Figure 16-18 which indicates both the plan and the present status.

6. *Review and analyze all segments of the plan for completeness, reliability and reasonableness.*

7. *If applicable, make suggestions for improved productivity or profitability as the subplans are being prepared.*

8. *Consolidate the financial statements to determine the overall company picture: earnings, cash, capital expenditures, financial position, etc.*

9. *Evaluate the plan, and the important segments by reference to such measures as:*

   (a) Conformance to CEO or board of director goals, constraints, etc.

   (b) Commonly used comparisons, such as:

       (1) Return on equity.

       (2) Return on assets.

       (3) Earnings per share.

       (4) Net Income as percent of sales.

       (5) Turnover ratios:

           Receivables.

           Inventory.

           Fixed assets.

       (6) Working capital.

Figure 16-18   Gantt Chart for Subsidiary Annual Planning Cycle.

THE 19XX ANNUAL PLAN
GLOBAL COMPANY (AUSTRALIA) INC.
(STATUS AS OF 10/15/19xx)

THE 19XX ANNUAL PLAN
GLOBAL COMPANY (AUSTRALIA) INC.
(Status as of 10/15/19xx)

Plan Step	Description of Task	September	October	November	December
1	Receipt of goals and objectives from corporate office				
2	Review threats and opportunities and develop tactics				
3	Develop marketing plan				
4	Establish sales volume plan				
5	Develop production plan				
6	Determine departmental budgets				
	General administration				
	Marketing				
	Manufacturing				
	Research				
	Finance				
7	Set the capital asset budget				
8	Consolidate the plans and budgets				
9	Review and revise plans				
10	Review and approval of final division plan				
11	Present plan, with supporting data, to corporate office				

Schedule
Completed
Today's date ◆

(7) Competitive or industry performance.

(8) Financial market expectations.

(c) Conformance to major credit agreements terms.

(d) Identification of possible weak spots; effect of not meeting the plan, etc.

(e) Use some alternative scenarios (20% less than plan, 20% more than plan) to show financial impact, effect on working capital, etc.

10. *Summarize the plan in a form which communicates to the management and the board of directors the significant aspects.* (See the next section.)

The detailed instructions on data content and format for the annual plan often are included as part of a finance manual (or planning manual) as they are often quite voluminous. It is desirable that the instructions be precise and in non-accounting terms, so that the operating staff understands them. Those aspects being handled by the finance staff should be explicit. A section from a planning manual that describes

Figure 16-19   Budget Responsibilities of Vice President of Sales.

SECTION FROM A PLANNING MANUAL—BUDGET RESPONSIBILITIES
OF THE VICE PRESIDENT–SALES

Type of Budget	Action to Be Taken	Schedule Annually	Schedule Monthly
Sales Budget	1. Provides product sales managers with sales history, and related data, and requests sales estimates in physical quantities by product line, and by territory from product sales managers (in format denoted in this manual).	3 months before start of budget period.	2 weeks before budget period.
	2. Requests unit price data.	"	"
	3. Reviews sales estimates of product sales managers for reasonableness and unfavorable trends. Gives consideration to past sales experience, price policies, advertising and sales promotion policy, general business conditions, competitive situation, etc.	2 months before start of budget period.	6 business days before budget period.
	4. Submits tentative sales budget to Budget Director for review as to completeness and format.	6 weeks before start of budget period.	4 business days before budget period.
	5. Accepts approved sales budget from Planning Group and transmits to product sales managers.	2 weeks before start of budget period.	2 days before budget period.
	6. Receives comparison of actual and budgeted sales performance from Budget Director.		4th working day of next month.
	7. Explains reasons for variances and corrective action taken.		9th working day of following period.
Advertising Expense Budget	1. Requests advertising manager to prepare overall estimate of advertising expenditures, including detailed projects.	3 months before start of budget period.	
	2. Receives proposal and reviews.	2 months before start of budget period.	
	3. Transmits tentative budget to Budget Director for review in prescribed format.	6 weeks before start of budget period.	
	4. Receives approved advertising budget.	1 month before start of budget period.	
	5. Advises Advertising Manager of program.	"	

Figure 16-19   *(continued)*

Type of Budget	Action to Be Taken	Schedule Annually	Schedule Monthly
	6. Receives reports on budget and actual expenditures.		5th working day of following month.
	7. Submits comments and corrective action statement on any significant departures from budget.		10th working day of following month.
	8. Requests budget revision.	As needed.	
Selling Expense Budget	1. Provides department managers with history of cost experience, plans for next year, etc.	2 months before start of budget period.	
	2. Requests selling expense budgets in approved format.	"	
	3. Reviews subject budgets, checks reasonableness of expense, correlation with sales program, etc.	6 weeks before start of budget period.	
	4. Passes expense budgets to Budget Director for review.	6 weeks before start of budget period.	
	5. Receives approved budgets and advises department managers of results.	2 weeks before start of budget period.	
	6. Receives comparison of departmental budget performance with actual.		5th day after month end.
	7. Secures comments from managers and reports on variances.		10th day after month end.
	8. Requests budget adjustments when applicable.	As needed.	

the duties of the vice president of sales for the three annual plan segments for which he is responsible is shown in Figure 16-19. (See also Chapter 56.)

The controller must be sensitive to relevant analysis and effective communication techniques.

16-23 MANAGEMENT APPROVAL OF THE PLAN

When the annual operating plan is approved by the board of directors, the plan, in effect, becomes a commitment and budget from the corporate management to the board and by appropriate organizational segment, from the managers of the segment to the top management of the company. The plan becomes the basic control tool against which actual performance is measured.

Figure 16-20 Highlights of the Annual Plan.

Aerospace Industry Inc.
19X2 ANNUAL PLAN HIGHLIGHTS
(*dollars in millions, except per share*)

	Plan	19X1 Estimated	Increase (Decrease) Dollars	Perce
Contract acquisitions	1,100.0	1,106.8	(6.8)	(.6
Backlog	1,293.7	1,863.7	(570.0)	(30.6
Sales	1,670.0	1,594.3	75.7	4.7
Net income				
Amount	71.4	65.7	5.7	8.7
Percent of sales	4.3	4.1		
Earnings per share	5.03	4.77	.26	5.5
Cash flow from operations . .	95.4	88.5	6.9	7.7
Capital expenditures	42.0	33.0	9.0	27.3
Percent return				
Assets	9.3	10.1		
Equity	22.9	25.8		

Mindful that planning is a communicating process, when approval of the shoꞏ
term plan—the profit plan—is sought, the authors wish to stress these points:

1. The financial officers should ascertain that all *significant* factors be brought
   the attention of the approving authorities in a timely manner and that appropriaꞏ
   recommendations are made. Perhaps the highlights summary should identiꞏ
   whatever the crucial or significant matters for the company or industry are—
   viewed by management or the board of directors. An illustrative summary prꞏ
   sentation is shown in Figure 16-20. This is supported by detailed schedules ꞏ
   all important elements.

2. The board of directors and top management should be made aware of the undeꞏ
   lying major assumptions used in constructing the plan.

3. The higher levels of management should not be inundated with excessive aꞏ
   counting details. Only major or important data should be presented.

4. The probabilities of attaining the plan—or the degree of difficulty in achieviꞏ
   it—should be conveyed to the management.

16-24 SELECTED REFERENCES

Dethomas, Arthur D., William B. Fredenberger, and Monojit Ghosal, "Turnarounds: Lessoꞏ
for the Management Accountants," *Management Accounting,* July 1994, pp. 23–25.

Knight, Ray A., and Lee G. Knight, "Planning: The Key to Small Business Survival," *Managꞏ
ment Accounting,* Feb. 1993, pp. 33–34.

Lubove, Seth, "It Ain't Broke, but Fix It Anyway," *Forbes,* Aug. 1, 1994, pp. 56–60.

CHAPTER 17

Profit-Planning: Supporting Financial Analysis for the Annual Plan

17-1 BASIC APPROACH IN PROFIT PLANNING

A fundamental objective of business management is to find the most profitable course to which effort should be directed and to hold the enterprise to that course. This, indeed, is planning and control of profits. Thus the term "profit planning" has become associated with the flexible budget technique of planning and controlling operations. This involves, basically, a recognition of the fact that some costs or expenses vary with production or sales volume, whereas others are "time" costs and are more or less independent of volume. Changes in "time" or fixed costs are accomplished generally by management action. In terms of application, the utilization of cost and income data in determining what to produce and at what price to sell is all embodied in profit planning. Moreover, it involves the concept of variable costs and marginal income as contrasted with the use of conventional total costs.

It is not our purpose, in this chapter, to review budgetary procedures but rather to point out applications or problems associated with the cost-volume-profit relationship in business. Profit planning is here being restricted to special phases or applications of planning and control and does not involve the detailed techniques concerned with cost segregation. The matter of cost segregation as between fixed, semivariable and variable costs is discussed in Chapters 5, 6, and 23. However, it should be emphasized that any valid cost-volume-profit studies reflect the true cost drivers—as in activity-based costing (ABC). The cost-volume-profit analyses reviewed in this chapter illustrate how the methodology may be used to answer questions that may arise in specific applications regarding alternative actions during the annual planning process.

17-2 GENERAL COMMENTS ON THE COST-VOLUME-PROFIT RELATIONSHIP

Most business decisions involve the selection of alternatives—whether to accept certain business at a specified price or not, whether to sell aggressively products A or B, whether to expand in territory X or Y. In all these decisions, as well as in many others, three factors must be considered: volume, costs, and profit. An understanding of the relationship among these three forces, and of the probable effect that any change in sales volume would have on the business, should be extremely helpful to management in a broad variety of problems involving planning and control. The interrelationship of cost, volume, and profit makes up what may be described as the profit structure of a company. Through the knowledge and intelligent use of such information, it is possible to predict the effect of any number of contemplated actions.

The data used in a review of this relationship may come from several channels and may differ considerably in adaptability or usefulness. In companies where a rather complete sales analysis is made, and where flexible budgets and standard costs are available, the records will provide the necessary information in readily usable form. Costs in all probability will have been segregated into the fixed and variable elements. If such sources are not available, then the conventional historical records might be utilized. Much analysis may be necessary to isolate the effect of changes in volume, selling prices, and variable costs. Moreover, if cost control has been poor, then the relationship between volume and costs will be difficult to detect and the margin of error will depend greatly on the reliability of the data and the validity of the assumptions.

Very often, for investment or credit purposes, published financial statements are used as source data in studying the effect of volume on the business. It should be kept in mind that such statements are usually highly condensed and give little indication of the factors that may greatly influence the results—such as change in product mixture. Consequently, the extent of reliability is very limited.

17-3 THE BREAK-EVEN CHART

The profit structure of a company is often presented in the familiar break-even chart form. By such a presentation, management can understand the interrelationship of

Figure 17-1 Break-Even Chart Illustrating the Interrelationship of Costs, Volume, and Profit.

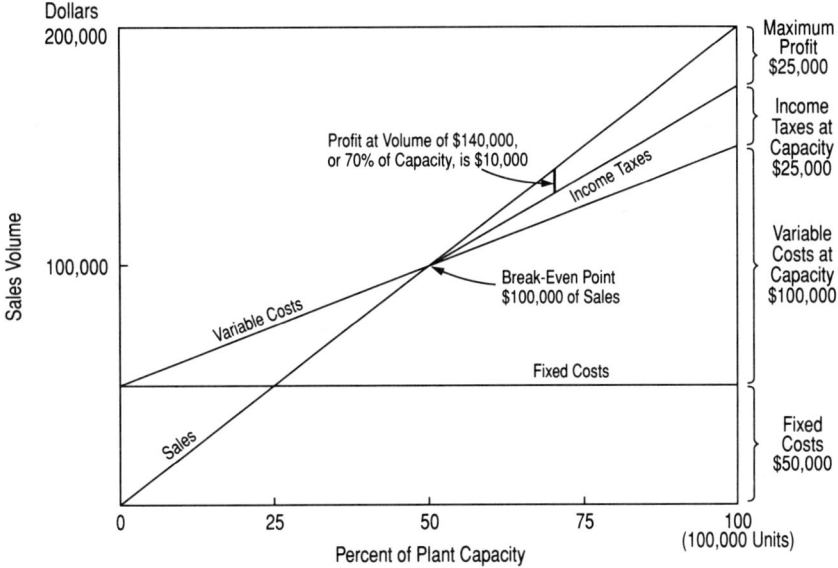

cost, profit, and volume much more readily than by tables. The simple chart illustrated in Figure 17-1 is based on the following assumptions:

1. That prices will remain unchanged.
2. That fixed costs will remain the same up to the maximum capacity of the plant.
3. That variable costs will vary in direct ratio to volume.
4. That income taxes will be 50% of all income before taxes.

Figure 17-1 clearly presents the following information for management:

1. Fixed costs of the business are $50,000 monthly.
2. Under present tax laws, and with present facilities, the maximum net profit is $25,000 per month or $300,000 per year.
3. At present prices, a monthly sales volume of $100,000 or 50,000 units is required to break even. This makes no provision for dividends to the stockholders.
4. To realize a net profit of $10,000 per month will require a sales volume of $140,000 per month.
5. Plant capacity expressed in sales dollars under existing prices and processes is $200,000 per month.

It may be observed that the net profit is measured by the vertical line between sales income and income taxes. Income taxes have been figured only from the break-even point.

Figure 17-2   Graphic Presentation of Relationships between Sales Volume and Profit or Loss.

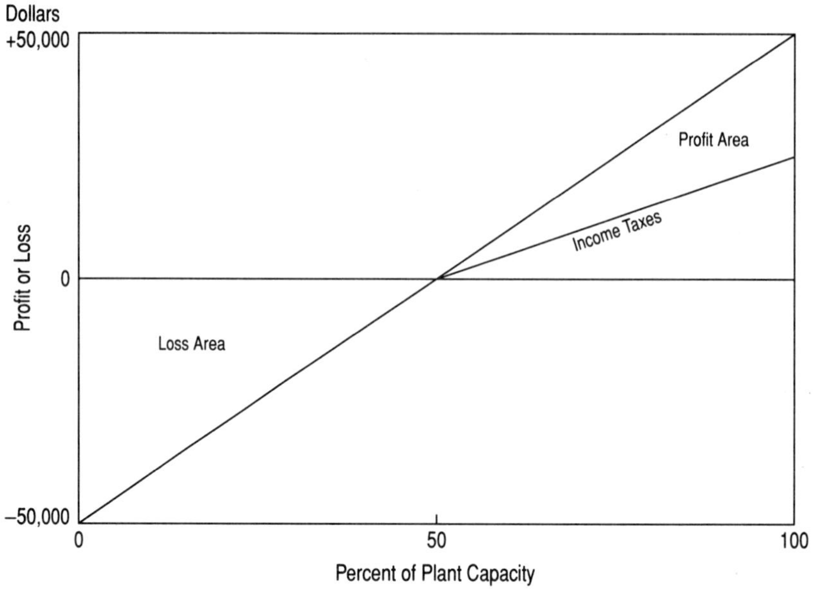

Another means of showing the relationship between net profit and sales volume is illustrated in Figure 17-2. It can be seen that some of the essential cost factors are not disclosed.

A break-even chart that illustrates not only the operating factors but also the dividend requirements is shown in Figure 17-3.

Needless to say, in most businesses the cost-volume-profit relationship is more complex than can be shown in any single break-even chart. This is discussed later. Moreover, it is not necessary to draw a chart to find the break-even point of a business. This can always be done by a simple calculation:

$$\text{break-even point} = \frac{\text{aggregate fixed expense}}{\text{ratio of variable income to sales}^1}$$

17-4 CHANGES IN SALES REVENUE

In analyzing the revenue factor, the controller may find it necessary to consider three aspects of the problem:

1. Treatment of difference between sales and production volume.
2. Changes in the composition of sales.
3. Changes in sales prices.

---

[1] Variable income represents sales income less the variable expense applicable to such sales.

Figure 17-3 Break-Even Chart Illustrating Sales Income and Its Disposition.

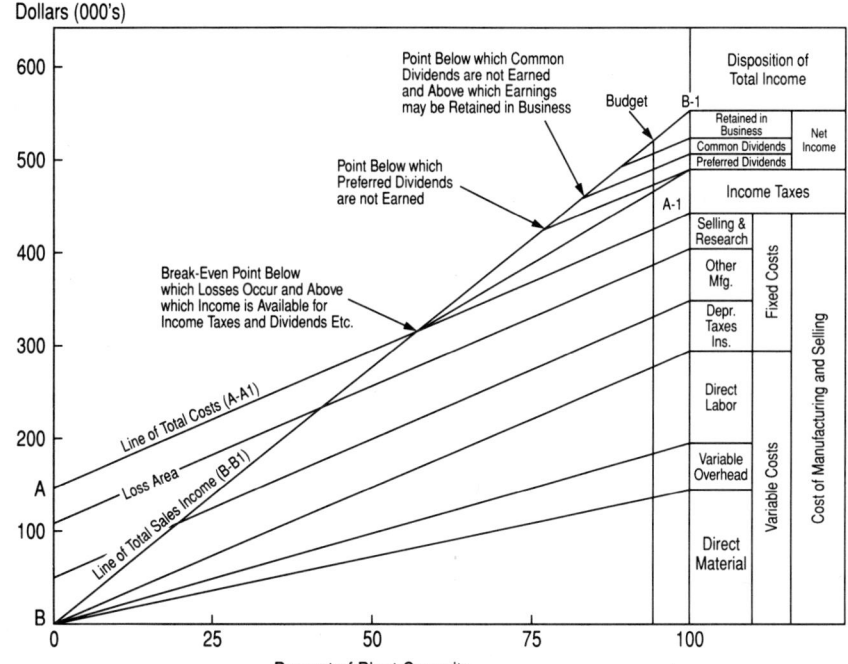

When past experience is being analyzed, a problem is presented where the sales volume is greatly different from the production volume, with a corresponding change taking place in the finished goods inventory. An adjustment must be made because two different indexes of activity are being used—the production volume for variable manufacturing costs and sales volume for certain selling and other expenses. The solution lies in converting to a common basis, namely, the sales dollar. First, manufacturing costs must be analyzed or compared to physical production converted to a sales basis—the sales value of production. Next, the nonmanufacturing costs are measured against the sales value. The costs can then be superimposed on each other at the respective levels, and the total costs for various levels of activity can be determined.

17-5 CHANGES IN SALES MIXTURE

Most companies have a variety of product lines, each making a different contribution toward fixed expenses. Changes in the break-even point as well as the operating profit can result from shifts in the mixture of products sold, even though the sales prices are unchanged and the total dollar sales volume meets expectancy. Such results can occur also from changes in distribution channels or sales to different classes of customers if the rearrangement affects the contribution of the product over and above variable costs. Actually, when a break-even chart is used, an underlying assumption is that the proportion of each product sold, or sales through each channel of distribution, is un-changed. Very often this does not happen; the proportionate drop is not the same for all products. The higher-priced lines, for example, may decline much more rapidly than others. Such changes must be recognized in evaluating the data.

The effect of a change in sales mixture can be illustrated by the following calcu-lations. Assume the following proportion of sales among three products, the indicated variable costs, fixed costs, and profit:

Product	Sales %	Sales Amount	Variable Costs	Marginal Income over Variable Costs Amount	Marginal Income over Variable Costs % of Net Sales
A	40.00	$ 4,000.00	$2,600.00	$1,400.00	35.00
B	50.00	5,000.00	4,000.00	1,000.00	20.00
C	10.00	1,000.00	875.00	125.00	12.50
Total ...	100.00	$10,000.00	$7,475.00	2,525.00	25.25
Fixed costs				1,200.00	
Operating profit				$1,325.00	

The break-even point can be calculated as follows:

$$\frac{\$1,200}{.2525} = \$4,752$$

If, however, sales increase on the higher-margin items, the break-even point would nat-urally decrease. Such a change is illustrated as follows:

Product	Sales %	Sales Amount	Variable Costs	Marginal Income over Variable Costs Amount	Marginal Income over Variable Costs % of Net Sales
A	60.00	$ 6,000.00	$3,900.00	$2,100.00	35.00
B	35.00	3,500.00	2,800.00	700.00	20.00
C	5.00	500.00	437.50	62.50	12.50
Total ...	100.00	$10,000.00	$7,137.50	2,862.50	28.625
Fixed costs				1,200.00	
Operating profit				$1,662.50	

The break-even point would be:

$$\frac{\$1,200}{.28625} = \$4,192$$

This break-even point has dropped by $560 only as a result of the changes in sales mixture.

17-6 CHANGES IN SALES PRICE

On the typical break-even chart the sales value is represented by a line that starts at zero and proceeds upward as the volume increases. Sales value equals unit selling price times number of units. It can be understood that the slope of the line changes if the unit sales price changes. The effect of a 10% increase in selling prices is illustrated in Figure 17-4 (on page 390).

Quite often some of the variable costs—commissions or royalties, for example—are related to the sales price. Consequently, the variable cost line as well as the sales value line might change as a result of selling price changes. In Figure 17-4 it has been assumed that variable costs relate only to units sold and not to value. As a direct result of the increase in selling price, the break-even point has dropped from $100,000 to $91,650, or by 8.35%.

It should be clear that a change in selling price affects the break-even point and the relationship between income and variable costs. The controller should also be aware that a change in selling price may have an even greater effect on marginal income than a corresponding percentage increase in variable costs. For example, in the following illustration, a 10% drop in selling prices is equivalent to an 11.1% increase in variable costs as regards the break-even point and marginal income:

	At Present Selling Prices		With a 10% Reduction in Sales Price		Equivalent Increase in Variable Costs	
	Amount	% of Net Sales	Amount	% of Net Sales	Amount	% of Net Sales
Sales	$50,000	100.00	$45,000	100.00	$50,000	100.00
Variable costs	20,000	40.00	20,000	44.44	22,222	44.44
Marginal income ..	30,000	60.00	25,000	55.56	27,778	55.56
Fixed costs	15,000	30.00	15,000	33.33	15,000	30.00
Operating profit ..	15,000	30.00	10,000	22.23	12,778	25.56
Break-even volume	$25,000		$27,000		$27,000	

Sales were reduced by 10% of $50,000 to a level of $45,000. As variable costs were not changed, these costs as a percent of sales are 44.44% or an increase of 11.1% (44.44 − 40 = 4.44; 4.44 + 40 = 11.1%). Relating the revised variable cost as a percent of net sales to the original $50,000 of sales produces a variable cost of $22,222. This is 11.1% higher than the original variable cost.

17-7 CHANGES IN COSTS

Interpretation of the effect of changes in the cost level presents some interesting problems as well as opportunities for the controller.

Figure 17-4   Graphic Illustration Effect of Sales Price Change on Net Income.

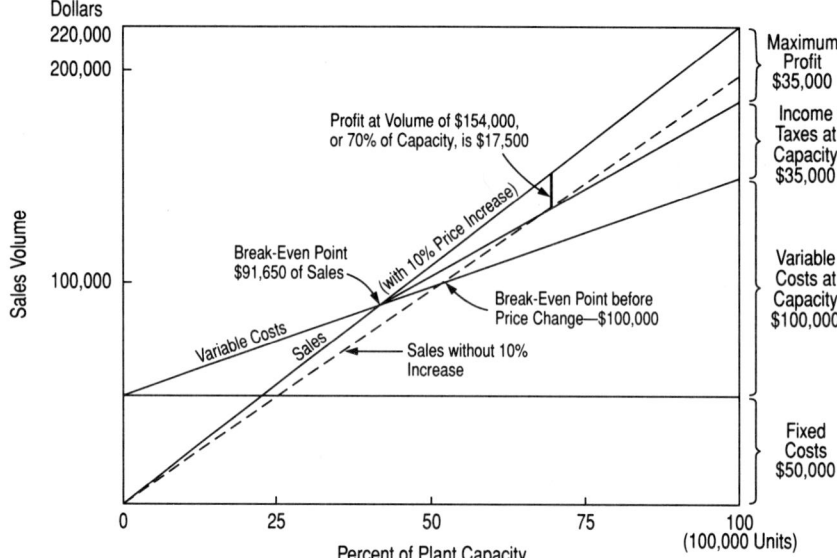

An increase or decrease in the amount of fixed cost has a twofold effect: (1) the operating profit is changed by a like *amount,* and (2) the break-even point is changed by a like *percentage.* To illustrate, assume a case where fixed costs are reduced by $10,000 or 33⅓%. The operating profit and break-even points would be thus:

	Present		Fixed Costs Reduced by $10,000	
	Amount	% of Net Sales	Amount	% of Net Sales
Net sales	$200,000	100	$200,000	100
Variable costs	120,000	60	120,000	60
Marginal income	80,000	40	80,000	40
Fixed costs	30,000	15	20,000	10
Operating profit	50,000	25	60,000	30
Break-even point sales	$ 75,000		$ 50,000	

With a reduction of $10,000 in fixed costs, the operating profit naturally increased by a like amount. Moreover, fixed costs were reduced 33⅓%, and so the break-even point also declined by 33⅓% or from a $75,000 sales volume to $50,000.

This calculation assumes that no change would take place in variable costs, but in practice a change in fixed costs may be accompanied by a change in the variable. For example, installation of a labor-saving device may increase depreciation and maintenance charges and decrease direct labor costs and related payroll charges. Such possibilities must be considered. Needless to say, if an increase in fixed costs is being discussed, the probability of an increased sales volume should be reviewed. Furthermore, it would be well to examine possible alternatives, such as subcontracting or renting of space and equipment in lieu of purchasing. Acquisition of permanent assets will decrease the concern's ability to adjust its costs to lower levels should a reduced sales volume ever necessitate such action. Opportunities for the reduction of fixed expenses should not be overlooked in any attempt to reduce costs. A lowering of fixed costs increases the margin at any sales level and, by reducing the break-even point, enables the company to withstand a greater drop in income before losses appear.

Changes in unit variable costs or expenses, of course, also affect the break-even point as well as the "marginal income" factor (discussed in the next section). Perhaps most cost reduction programs center about this category. A great many possibilities are open. For example, changes in the type of material used, or the purchase price of material, or the amount of scrap or waste can affect variable costs. Changes in manufacturing processes, hourly labor rates, plant layout, or employee training methods or the introduction of incentive payments can all affect the labor costs. General economic conditions may influence the ability of a firm to reduce variable costs. Very often the reduced sales volume permits more effective maintenance of equipment in the shutdown periods. Then, too, in such periods the labor turnover rate and material prices are usually reduced. Of course, such conditions may force sales price reductions on the company's own products.

The effect of reduced fixed and variable costs is graphically illustrated in Figure 17-5.

Figure 17-5   Chart Illustrating Effect on Profit of Reduction in Variable and Fixed Costs.

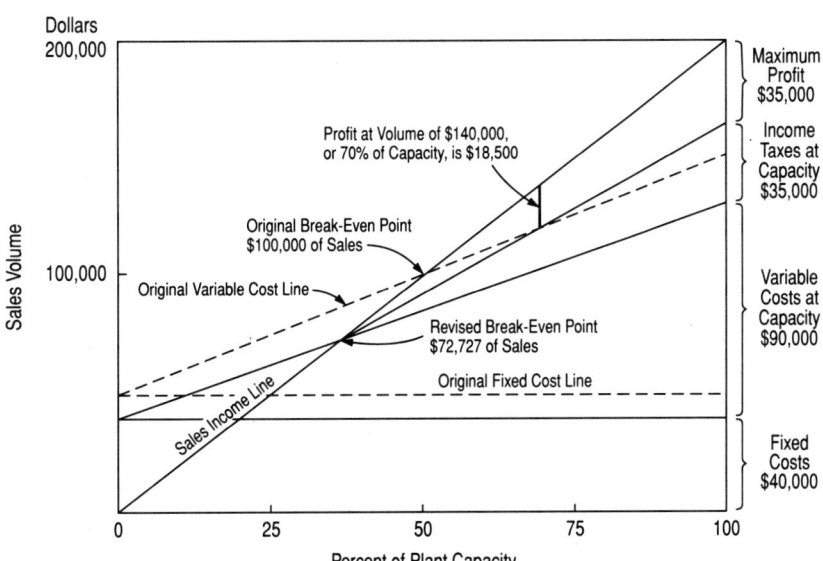

17-8 MARGINAL INCOME RATIO AND MARGIN OF SAFETY

In any review of the interrelationship of cost and volume, one of the most significant figures is the marginal income ratio. This may be defined as the residual value after deducting the variable cost from net sales, expressed as a percentage of the net sales. The marginal income ratio represents the share of the sales dollars remaining to cover fixed expenses, income taxes, and net profit. It is indeed a highly useful figure, for it can be employed to determine readily the break-even point or the added income resulting from increased sales volume. To illustrate, if sales are to be increased by $30,000 and the marginal income ratio is 40%, then such sales should result in additional income before taxes, all other factors unchanged, of $12,000 (40% of $30,000). To determine the break-even sales volume, it is necessary merely to divide total fixed costs by the marginal income ratio, as mentioned earlier. The marginal income ratio is useful, also, in determining how low a price may be quoted or what sales volume is required to support a salesperson in a territory. It is probably a much more useful figure than the break-even point. Where the marginal income ratio is high, a change in sales volume has a tremendous effect on profit. Thus an increase of $100,000 in sales will increase operating profit by $60,000 for a company with a 60% marginal income ratio but only $20,000 for a firm with a 20% marginal income ratio. A high ratio, of course, may carry with it high fixed charges. Incidentally, if the controller can prepare the income and expense statements to indicate the marginal income, the use of such statements will be greatly enhanced.

Another figure often used in conjunction with cost-volume-profit analyses is the "margin of safety." It is defined as the excess of actual or budgeted sales over the break-even sales volume and is a measure of the extent to which sales may drop before losses appear. The profit strength of a business might be said to be proportionate to the distance between its existing sales volume and its break-even point. Over the period of a business cycle, as between any two companies of the same size with the same percentage of net profit on present sales volume, the one with the greater margin of safety may have the greater earning power.

17-9 ANALYSIS BY PRODUCT

Since most companies have more than one product or product line, a large number of business decisions relate to *individual* product lines. For this reason, it is desirable to apply the cost-volume-profit analysis to specific product lines so that management can better understand the effect on profits of changes in volume of selected products or of the relative proportion of products sold.

The same technique applied to overall operations can be applied to individual product lines. Decisions reached from such studies should be a guide in determining which products should be sold aggressively (or emphasized because of profits or sold through a particular channel of distribution); which products should be continued but not promoted, merely because of some contribution toward fixed expense; and which lines or commodities should be discontinued or replaced by more profitable lines. Obviously, general economic conditions, relative supply and demand, and the long-range effect on customer relationships are some noncost factors that must be weighed.

In making any profit analyses the reliability of the results depends in part on the organizational structure and the extent or type of analysis made. To illustrate, a product manufactured in one plant and requiring all the plant's facilities, that is then marketed through its own separate sales organization, presents few cost allocation problems. Only part of the general administrative expenses need be allocated to the line. Quite in contrast to such a situation is a product whose production and distribution facilities are shared by many other items. In such a case the allocation of fixed and indirect costs requires careful attention, for the reliability of break-even points is greatly dependent on the manner in which such common costs or expenses are distributed to product lines. If, on the other hand, the objective is not the determination of break-even points but rather a knowledge of marginal income by products, then no allocation of fixed costs would be necessary. The development of variable costs, depending on usage, would be relatively simple. And many companies predicate important decisions on the relative contribution of each line to fixed costs and profit.

Any controller who has had the task of determining an overall break-even point for his company and then has determined the break-even point by product lines has perhaps been confused by the fact that the sum of the individual break-even points usually did not equal the overall break-even point—unless the sales figures for each break-even point bore the same relationship to total sales as the individual break-even points bore to the overall break-even point. Such a condition is well explained as follows:[2]

A business with three products has calculated break-even points for the individual products as follows:

| | Product | | | |
	A	B	C	Totals
Sales	$30	$25	$80	$135
Variable costs	12	10	60	82
Fixed costs	6	30	10	42
Break-even sales	10	50	40	100 (by cross-footing)
				117 (by computation from totals above)

The break-even point calculated on an overall basis is found to exceed the break-even point obtained by summing individual product break-even points. However, if sales of each product have been at the break-even volume for that product, individual break-even points could be cross-footed to obtain the break-even point based on total sales of the three products combined as illustrated below:

| | Product | | | |
	A	B	C	Totals
Sales	$10	$50	$40	$100
Variable costs	4	20	30	54
Fixed costs	6	30	10	46
Sales to break-even	10	50	40	100

[2] "The Analysis of Cost-Volume-Profit Relationships," *NACA Bulletin*, Dec. 1949, pp. 539–40.

The reason for the difference between the two sets of figures lies in the fact that the sales mix is not the same. Thus, in the first example, the products are sold in proportions of 22%, 19%, and 59%, whereas in the second they are sold in proportions of 10%, 50%, and 40%; the individual product break-even points add up to the overall break-even point as shown below:

	Product			
	A	B	C	Totals
Sales	$20	$100	$80	$200
Variable costs	8	40	60	108
Fixed costs	6	30	10	46
Sales to break-even	10	50	40	100

The effect of such changes in mix is exerted on the break-even point through changes in the overall marginal income ratio. Unless individual product marginal ratios are weighted by sales figures in the ratio of the individual product break-even volumes, a different overall marginal income ratio and hence a different overall break-even point results.

Where several product lines are being analyzed, the controller may find it advantageous to prepare break-even charts for each product if they are useful to the executives in profit planning. The relative profitability can be determined by observing the slope of the profit line, assuming the same relative scale is used. It is rather difficult to construct a break-even chart for all products combined that would be of much practical significance. Some companies have used charts similar to Figure 17-6. Obviously, all the factors cannot be presented.

17-10 APPLICATION OF COST-VOLUME-PROFIT ANALYSIS

Even if the controller is fully aware of all the ramifications of the cost, volume, and profit relationship, the question arises about how he can best put this information to work for management. The principal use of the data, of course, is in planning and policy-making decisions. The chief value of the data lies in the facility with which volume can be treated as a variable factor. Through applying such information, it is fairly simple to determine at various ranges of volume exactly what the effect on profits will be of contemplated changes. The traditional income and expense statement simply does not permit this.

A great variety of questions are asked in the management of a business, such as these:

1. What will be the profit or loss at *x* sales level?
2. What additional sales volume will be needed to meet the fixed charges arising from the proposed plant expansion program?
3. What is the possibility of earning a profit on *x* product?
4. What sales volume is required to earn a certain designated profit?
5. At a sales level of *x* per month, what reduction in fixed and variable costs must be made to earn a profit, before taxes, of some designated amount?

Figure 17-6   Profitability of Products in Relation to Break-Even Point.

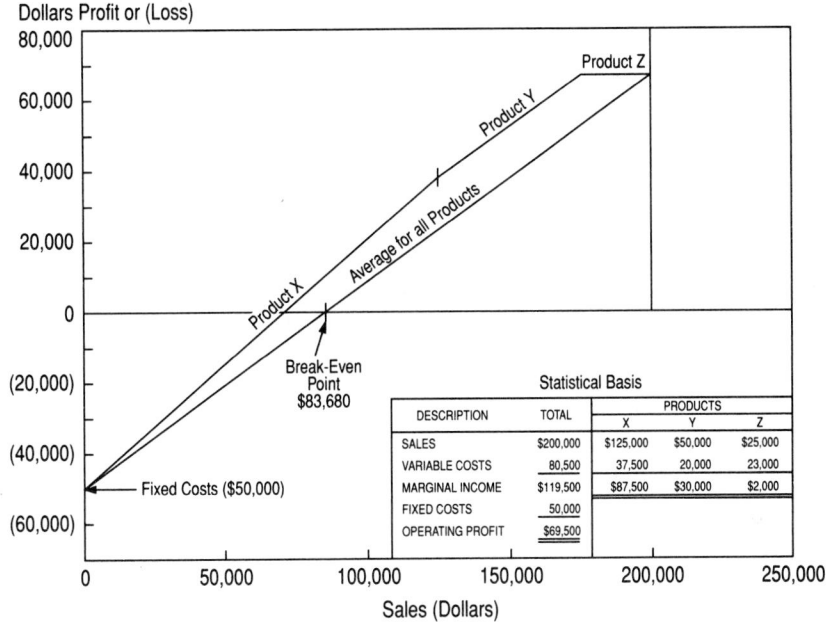

DESCRIPTION	TOTAL	PRODUCTS		
		X	Y	Z
SALES	$200,000	$125,000	$50,000	$25,000
VARIABLE COSTS	80,500	37,500	20,000	23,000
MARGINAL INCOME	$119,500	$87,500	$30,000	$2,000
FIXED COSTS	50,000			
OPERATING PROFIT	$69,500			

6. What will be the effect of adding a second shift operation?

7. What effect will a 15% increase in sales volume have on profits?

For questions such as these, the controller should find the answers very easily through the analyses just described. Stated positively, a thorough understanding and analysis of cost-volume-profit data can provide information for such uses as the following:

1. Sales and pricing policies.

    a. Determination of profit that will result from any given volume of sales.

    b. Analysis of the effect of changes in selling prices.

    c. Effect of change in product mixture.

    d. Additional sales volume needed to support a salesperson in a territory, a warehouse, etc.

    e. Lowest prices at which business may be accepted to utilize facilities and contribute something toward net profit.

    f. The particular products to be emphasized to reflect the greatest net profit.

2. Financial and production problems.

    a. Interpretation of proposed or alternative budgets and the effect of suggested cost and other changes—when the goals are not satisfactory to management.

    b. Determination of unit costs at various volume levels.

    c. Determination of the probable effect of investment in new plant and equipment.

    d. Determination of most profitable use of scarce materials.

    e. Assistance in choice between subcontracting work or manufacturing certa
articles.

  3. General.

    a. General understanding of profit structure of the business and effect of volum
changes—for the major executives.

    b. General educational purposes for plant supervision.

Some of these applications are discussed in the following pages.

17-11 SELECTING THE MOST PROFITABLE PRODUCTS

When all the productive facilities of a company are fully occupied, and when the de
mand is much greater than supply, a decision must be reached about the products to b
manufactured. The long-term customer reactions, the availability of material, and th
probable continued price differential between different products must be weighed. B
relative costs and profit should be important factors in the decision. Whether one e
many products are manufactured, the principle is valid. Of course, where several proc
ucts are manufactured by different processes and in different departments, the bottle
neck department should be considered separately.

    In earlier sections the importance of marginal income was emphasized, and th
greatest marginal income is desirable because it usually results in the highest ne
profit. However, when considering marginal income, the greatest income per piece e
per pound is not the sole factor, for the effect of the rate of production must be reck
oned with. To be specific, refer to Figure 17-7. The greatest marginal profit per unit e
sale, per hundredweight, is realized on product A. Product B returns only $6.67 ma
ginal income per unit. If only this "unit" marginal contribution were considered, th
business would not be making the best use of the facilities. When the operating hour
taken into account, product B returns 11.12% more than A—$100.05 per machine hou
as compared with $90 for product A.

    In making decisions of this nature, other cost factors must be kept in mind—e.g
(1) cost of carrying inventories and receivables, and (2) changes in the relationship c
fixed and variable expense.

17-12 THE MINIMUM SELLING PRICE

In theory, perhaps, each product should yield a net profit. However, under our compe
itive economy this does not usually happen. Some products bear their own direct costs
a full share of indirect expenses, and return a net profit. Others may carry only a pa
tial share of their indirect costs. In any event, the objective is to secure the greates
overall profit. When all the available capacity is not being utilized, the problem arise
about the lowest price to be charged that will still contribute something to the overa
profit. The obvious answer is recovery of variable costs, taking into account any addi
tional maintenance or other costs. Such costs set the floor, and anything above this i
making a contribution toward fixed expenses. The concept of fixed and variable cost
is necessary to such a determination. Obviously, the controller should be realistic e
conservative in the segregation of costs. Further, any legal implications—e.g., the pos
sibility of violating the Robinson-Patman Act—must be reviewed.

Figure 17-7 Computation of Marginal Profit per Unit of Product and per Machine.

	Product	
Description	A	B
Per Hundred Pounds		
Selling price	$35.00	$ 28.00
Costs		
Variable:		
Material	18.00	16.00
Labor and overhead	8.00	5.33
Total variable	26.00	21.33
Fixed	5.00	3.33
Total cost	31.00	24.66
Operating profit	4.00	3.34
Marginal profit	$ 9.00	$ 6.67
Per Machine Hour		
Rate of production (cwt.)	10	15
Operating profit ($4.00 times 10; and $3.34 times 15)	$40.00	$ 50.10
Marginal profit ($9.00 times 10; and $6.67 times 15)	$90.00	$100.05

17-13 UNIT COSTS AT DIFFERENT VOLUME LEVELS

Another application of the cost-volume-profit relationship is in the determination of unit costs. Suppose, for example, that management desires to know what the unit cost would be at various sales volume levels, with prices remaining fixed. It may be assumed that, in the illustration at hand, the selling price is $2 per unit. What would be the unit cost were the sales to be increased to $240,000? It is assumed that the present sales consist of 50,000 units and that the present unit cost is $2.40, consisting of $.80 of fixed costs and $1.60 of variable costs.

The proposed volume is 120,000 units ($240,000 ÷ $2). The new unit cost would then be as follows:

$$= \frac{\text{fixed costs}}{\text{proposed unit volume}} + \text{present variable unit cost}$$

$$= \frac{\$40,000}{120,000} + \$1.60$$

$$= \$.333 + \$1.60$$

$$= \$1.933$$

At a sales volume of $240,000, the unit cost is $1.933.

17-14 INCREASED SALES VOLUME TO OFFSET REDUCED SELLING PRICES

In the same illustration, let it be assumed that the sales department insists that the present low volume is due to the fact that the company's prices are out of line with those of competing concerns or with competing products. A reduction of 10% in selling prices is advised. What percentage increase in volume will be necessary to yield a profit of $5,000 if selling prices are reduced 10%?

The assumptions are the same as those mentioned previously, except for the change in prices. In this case, the solution is as follows:

increased sales volume required to offset reduced selling price

$$
= \cfrac{\text{profit desired plus fixed costs}}{1 - \left(\cfrac{\text{present variable ratio}}{1 - \text{proposed percentage reduction in selling price}}\right)}
$$

$$
= \cfrac{\cfrac{\$5,000 + \$40,000}{\$80,000}}{1 - \cfrac{\$100,000}{1 - .10}} = \cfrac{\$45,000}{1 - \cfrac{.8}{.9}}
$$

$$
= \frac{\$45,000}{.111111} = \$405,000
$$

Therefore, a sales volume of $405,000 or 225,000 units must be secured to produce a profit of $5,000 if prices are reduced by 10%. If this goes beyond the capacity of the plant, such a program is impossible without further increase in fixed costs.

17-15 MOST PROFITABLE USE OF SCARCE MATERIALS

Another interesting application of the cost and profit relationship is the determination of the best use of restricted or scarce materials. Assume, for example, that only partial requirements are available of a chemical common to five products. How should the ingredient "X" be distributed, considering only the greatest net profit to the company? It is assumed that rates of production are about the same and that all products are manufactured with the same facilities. The solution is evident from the following example:

Product	Unit Selling Price	Unit Variable Cost	Unit Marginal Income Contribution	Pounds of "X" per Lb. of Product	Marginal Profit per Lb. of "X"
1	$2.00	$1.00	$1.00	.5	$2.00
2	2.50	1.50	1.00	.3	3.33
3	4.00	2.50	1.50	.5	3.00
4	3.00	1.00	2.00	1.5	1.33
5	5.00	2.50	2.50	2.0	1.25

Product 2 yields the greatest profit per pound of "X" and these requirements should be met first, all other factors being equal.

17-16 ADVISABILITY OF PLANT EXPANSION

Break-even and related data are helpful when considering plant expansion. The following information would be useful in arriving at a decision:

1. The relative break-even points.
2. The sales volume required to earn existing profits.
3. The sales volume required to net a fair return on the investment.
4. The maximum profit.

Assume the following present average earnings statement (monthly) of the company:

Net sales	$500,000
Costs and expenses	
Variable (60% net sales)	300,000
Fixed	100,000
Total	400,000
Net profit before taxes	100,000
Income taxes (50%)	50,000
Net profit	$ 50,000

Increased fixed costs with plant expansion—$50,000
Additional income desired on investment—$5,000
Maximum production in new plant—$300,000

Using the available data, these determinations can be made:

1. *Break-Even Points.*

   Present facilities:

   $$\frac{\text{fixed costs}}{\text{marginal income ratio}} = \frac{\$100,000}{.40} = \$250,000 \text{ sales volume}$$

   Proposed:

   $$\frac{\text{present + additional fixed costs}}{\text{marginal income ratio}} = \frac{\$150,000}{.40} = \$375,000 \text{ sales volume}$$

2. *Sales Volume Required to Earn Existing Profit.*

   $$= \frac{\text{present fixed costs + additional fixed costs + existing profit}}{\text{marginal income ratio}}$$

   $$= \frac{\$100,000 + \$50,000 + \$100,000}{.40}$$

   $$= \frac{\$250,000}{.40}$$

   $$= \$625,000 \text{ sales volume}$$

3. *Sales Volume to Net a Fair Return on Added Investment.*

Assume a fair return on the added investment to be $500 (monthly) after income taxes or $10,000 before.

Then a fair return equals at least existing profit, plus the above return.

$$= \frac{\text{present fixed costs} + \text{additional fixed costs} + \text{existing profit} + \text{return on added investment}}{\text{marginal income ratio}}$$

$$= \frac{\$260,000}{.40}$$

$$= \$650,000 \text{ sales volume}$$

4. *Maximum Earnings with New Plant.*

Net sales ($500,000 + $300,000)	$800,000
Costs and expenses	
Variable (60% of net sales)	480,000
Fixed	150,000
Total	630,000
Net profit before taxes	170,000
Income taxes (50%)	85,000
Net profit	$ 85,000

These computations may be summarized as follows:

Item	Present	Prospective	Increase
Break-even sales volume (monthly)	$250,000	$375,000	$125,000
Sales volume to earn existing profit	500,000	625,000	125,000
Sales volume to earn 6% on new plant cost ..	—	650,000	—
Maximum profit	50,000	85,000	35,000
Sales volume to earn maximum profit	500,000	800,000	300,000

The management must consider the possibility of increasing sales by $125,000 monthly to maintain existing profits. It must also weigh the probability of sales remaining at least $125,000 higher, for profits before income taxes will be reduced by $50,000 per month if the expansion is made but sales continue at the present level. Sales must be increased by $125,000 just to retain existing profits, but this disadvantage may be offset by the higher potential earnings of $35,000 per month.

Incidentally, these calculations illustrate the variety of simple arithmetical formulas that may be helpful in profit planning and control.

17-17 BREAK-EVEN ANALYSIS TO EVALUATE A FORECAST

The discussion of the cost-volume-profit technique[3] has been applied in large part to segments of the business—to individual products, or areas, or projects such as a new

---

[3] Adapted in part from James D. Willson, "Practical Applications of Cost-Volume-Profit Analysis," *NACA Bulletin,* March 1960, pp. 5–18.

plant. Yet the same approach can be useful in judging the business plans of a division or a company. Typically, a projection is compared with some past year, usually the immediately preceding year, to determine whether it appears satisfactory. Such a comparison has value. It may be a gauge of the adequacy of the sales volume, and, in a general way, it may raise questions about cost or expense levels. However, such a comparison is not as sharp a tool as is available. Most of the time, the sales level and product mix in the forecast year will not be identical with that of the past year. Therefore, it may be difficult to measure more precisely the propriety of the costs and expenses in relationship to sales volume. To further complicate the problem, management, when looking at a higher sales volume and a net income that appears more favorable, tends to be less critical. In most instances, if net income expressed as a percent of sales is greater than the preceding year, the forecast is gleefully pronounced satisfactory.

Why not use a superior tool that permits a more effective evaluation of the volume factor? Once management has agreed on a reasonable sales objective, a volume for the year under forecast, then it becomes practical to measure the proposed forecast against the break-even structure, i.e., to apply the break-even economic structure of the company to the projected sales volume. Essentially, this means that management should decide on a reasonable cost-profit-volume relationship and that this standard should be used as a measure of the forecast. The results of the application of the break-even factors, as shown in Figure 17-8, to a projected sales volume (standard profit structure) and the comparison of such results with the aggregate costs and expenses as set forth in an illustrative forecast, are shown in Figure 17-9. It is to be noted that percentage relationships are developed to aid in detecting out-of-line conditions. The exhibit portrays one of the basic considerations in the preparation of forecasts, i.e., that the company must not be allowed to develop or assume a less favorable cost structure.

Figure 17-8   Standard Profit Structure.

The Sample Company
PROFIT STRUCTURE

Description	Fixed Costs	Variable Costs Total	Variable Costs % Net Sales	Combined
Net sales				$10,000,000
Cost and expenses				
Direct material		$4,000,000	40.00%	
Direct labor		1,000,000	10.00	
Manufacturing expenses ...	$ 500,000	1,000,000	10.00	
Selling expenses	400,000	100,000	1.00	
Research and development				
expenses	250,000	50,000	.50	
General and administrative				
expenses	150,000	50,000	.50	
	$1,300,000	$6,200,000	62.00%	7,500,000
Profit before income taxes ...				$ 2,500,000

Figure 17-9 Comparison of Standard and Forecast Profit Structure.

The Sample Company
BREAK-EVEN ANALYSIS OF FORECAST
FISCAL YEAR 19XX

Description	Application of Standard Profit Structure	Tentative Forecast	Forecast Over (Under) Standard	
			Amount	%
Net sales	$12,500,000	$12,500,000		
Cost of sales				
Direct material	5,000,000	5,250,000	$250,000	5.00%
Direct labor	1,250,000	1,310,000	60,000	4.80
Manufacturing expenses ...	1,750,000	1,820,000	70,000	4.00
Total	8,000,000	8,380,000	380,000	4.75
Gross margin	4,500,000	4,120,000	(380,000)	(8.44)
Operating expenses				
Selling	525,000	540,000	15,000	2.86
Research and development ..	312,500	310,000	(2,500)	(.80)
General and administrative .	212,500	190,000	(22,500)	(10.59)
Total	1,050,000	1,040,000	(10,000)	(.95)
Profit before taxes	$ 3,450,000	$ 3,080,000	$370,000	(10.72%)
Other data				
Break-even point	$ 3,421,050	$ 3,714,290	$293,240	8.6%
Marginal income ratio	.38	.35		

Hence it is necessary to apply some overall tests quite distinct, for example, from individual departmental budget performance.

The greatest dollar increase and relative increase is in prime material costs. This 5% or $250,000 increase must be analyzed to determine whether the cost increase results from changes in product mix or from cost increases in any given product line. The initial break-even application has isolated this apparently excessive cost relationship. Now it should be analyzed in more depth and a decision made about an acceptable plan. Perhaps the product mix is not the optimum believed to be attainable in the forecast year. Perhaps action can be taken on cost increases to reduce or eliminate them.

Second, the next largest *relative* increase, amounting to $60,000, is in direct labor. A similar analysis should be made to localize the cause and seek an improvement in the plan.

Next, manufacturing expenses have increased by 4% or $70,000. Departmental budgets should be reviewed to determine the areas of greatest increase and their causes. Management must then decide what corrective action must be taken. If, for example, the increase is in maintenance expense, is it sound to defer projects? What is the best approach when considering the longer-term interests of the business? Similar analyses should be made of the other expense areas. If expenses are *under* the standard, the accountant should ascertain that no omissions have been made erroneously.

It is to be observed that the break-even point has risen by 8.6% to $3,714,290. Perhaps a better way to state the case is that the forecast is based on a somewhat changed cost structure. This change may be shown graphically as in Figure 17-10. The solid lines indicate the acceptable cost-volume-profit structure, and the dotted lines reveal the condition as planned in the forecast. Incidentally, any change in this relationship can be readily shown on the graph, whether in sales, variable costs, or fixed expense.

In poor economic weather, a reasonable margin of safety is necessary. Accordingly, in the Sample Company, if management agrees that the standard profit structure must be maintained, every element should be analyzed and explored by the accountant so that the final business plan for the ensuing year retains the characteristics of this structure. As an alternative, once the most satisfactory cost-volume-profit relationship is determined, including the proper product mix, then the possibility of securing additional sales volume to offset cost increases is to be considered.

Figure 17-10   Profit Graph Comparing Standard and Forecast Performance.

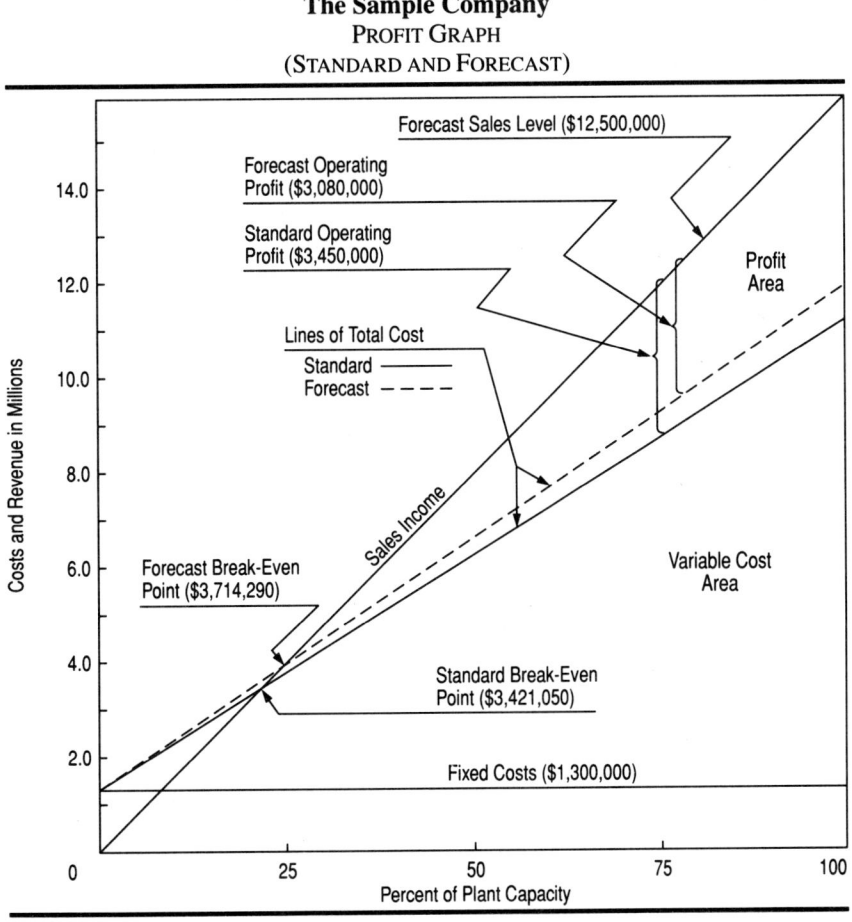

The Sample Company
PROFIT GRAPH
(STANDARD AND FORECAST)

17-18 A WORKABLE STATEMENT OF INCOME AND EXPENSE

The conventional statement of income and expense can be quite misleading. In practice, managements have been known to take action on the basis of such statements, when the action was unwarranted on the basis of actual facts. Companies have discontinued products that showed losses on the conventional statements only to find that the loss increased as a result of the discontinuance. Further, goods have been sold at prices below cost in the belief that added volume would reduce the costs and result in a profit. Of course, the controller may explain that action should not be taken on the strength of a monthly statement of income and expense, which is very true. He may emphasize that all the facts should be marshaled in making a decision—which means a detailed analysis. But the fact remains that some executives may take corrective action, however ill-advised, after seeing the monthly statement. The chief accounting official should devise a form of statement that may be a little more informative or helpful in giving some clues and will give a better perspective of the situation. Basically, of course, this merely means making a distinction between fixed and variable costs or expenses. One such statement for internal management purposes is illustrated in Figure 17-11. The contribution of each product line toward fixed expenses and profits is shown, and a great deal of information can be gleaned from the supplementary data shown thereon. Such a statement may be supported by other schedules giving the details of actual and standard manufacturing expenses, as in Figure 17-12. Where desirable, a statement of cost of goods manufactured can be prepared using the same principle of segregating fixed and variable costs.

17-19 SOME PRACTICAL GENERALIZATIONS

The primary purpose in any analysis of the cost-volume-profit relationship is to permit the planning of larger profits in the future. Such reviews may disclose basic weaknesses in the profit structure and assist in suggesting remedies. Because the field is so broad, it is felt desirable to summarize some generalizations that should be clearly understood by the controller and by other members of management as well. These general comments are as follows:

1. A change in the *amount* of *fixed* costs changes the break-even point by a similar percentage and the operating profit by a like amount but does not affect the marginal income ratio.

2. A change in the selling price changes the break-even point and marginal income ratio. Such a change, percentage-wise, may be quite different in the effect on the marginal income ratio than a similar percentage change in variable costs.

3. A change in variable costs, likewise, changes the break-even point and marginal income ratio.

4. When the marginal income ratio is high, large profits may result from comparatively small increases in sales volume above the break-even point. For the same reason, small declines in revenue will cut sharply into profits. By like token, a low marginal income ratio requires considerable change in sales volume to reflect any significant change in profits.

5. A high margin of safety indicates that a substantial drop in sales volume can take place before losses develop.

Figure 17-11 Statement of Income and Expenses with Segregation of Fixed and Variable Manufacturing Costs.

The Toledo Manufacturing Company
Statement of Income and Expense by Product Lines
For the Month Ended November 30, 19XX

	ALL PRODUCTS		PLASTIC MOLDINGS			PAINTS			DISHWARE		
	Amount	% of Net Sales	Amount	% of Net Sales	Per Cwt.	Amount	% of Net Sales	Per Cwt.	Amount	% of Net Sales	Per Cwt.
SALES											
Gross Sales	$146,835		$143,575			$1,210			$2,050		
Less: Returns and Allowances	7,750		7,742			4			4		
Net Sales	139,085	100.0	135,833	100.0	$20.65	1,206	100.0	$10.26	2,046	100.0	$62.00
COST OF SALES											
At Standard											
Variable											
Material	62,792	45.1	60,913	44.8	9.26	539	44.7	4.58	1,340	65.5	40.61
Manufacturing Expense	16,145	11.6	15,977	11.8	2.43	105	8.7	.89	63	3.1	1.91
Royalties	69	—	—	—	—	—	—	—	69	3.4	2.09
Total Variable Cost	79,006	56.7	76,890	56.6	11.69	644	53.4	5.47	1,472	72.0	44.61
Fixed	8,245	6.0	8,169	6.0	1.24	45	3.8	.40	31	1.4	.94
Total	87,251	62.7	85,059	62.6	12.93	689	57.2	5.87	1,503	73.4	45.55
Standard Manufacturing Profit	51,834	37.3	50,774	37.4	7.72	517	42.8	4.39	543	26.6	16.45

(continued)

Figure 17-11 (continued)

	ALL PRODUCTS		PLASTIC MOLDINGS			PAINTS			DISHWARE		
	Amount	% of Net Sales	Amount	% of Net Sales	Per Cwt.	Amount	% of Net Sales	Per Cwt.	Amount	% of Net Sales	Per Cwt.
OVER (OR UNDER) STANDARD											
Material and Freight—Price	(137)	(.1)	(133)	(.1)	—	(3)	(.3)	(.03)	(1)	—	(.03)
Material Usage	3,215	2.3	3,186	2.3	.48	4	.4	.03	25	1.2	.76
Variable Labor and Manufacturing Expense	14,112	10.2	13,833	10.2	2.10	269	22.3	2.29	10	.5	.30
Subtotal	17,190	12.4	16,886	12.4	2.58	270	22.4	2.29	34	1.7	1.03
Fixed Manufacturing Expense	5,023	3.6	4,977	3.7	.77	27	2.2	.22	19	.9	.58
Total	22,213	16.0	21,863*	16.1	3.35	297	24.6	2.51	53	2.6	1.61
MANUFACTURING PROFIT	29,621	21.3	28,911	21.3	4.37	220	18.2	1.88	490	24.0	14.84
OPERATING EXPENSE											
Administrative	3,107	2.2	3,034	2.3	.45	27	2.2	.23	46	2.2	1.38
Selling and Advertising	17,484	12.6	17,075	12.5	2.59	151	12.5	1.29	258	12.6	7.80
Research and Development	6,761	4.9	6,603	4.9	1.00	59	5.0	.50	99	4.9	3.00
Total	27,352	19.7	26,712	19.7	4.04	237	19.7	2.02	403	19.7	12.18
Operating Profit (or Loss)	2,269	1.6	$ 2,199	1.6	$ .33	$(16)	(1.5)	$(.14)	$ 87	4.3	$ 2.66
Other Income (net)	6,205	4.4									
Profit Before Federal Income Taxes	8,474	6.0									
Federal Income Taxes	3,389	2.4									
Net Profit	$ 5,085	3.6									
Net Shipments—Pounds	673,835		657,775			11,760			3,300		
Production—Pounds	688,800		654,244			34,563			1,000		

* See Figure 17-12 for details.

Figure 17-12 Comparison of Actual and Standard Manufacturing Costs.

The Toledo Manufacturing Company
COMPARISON OF ACTUAL AND STANDARD MANUFACTURING COSTS
OF PLASTIC MOLDINGS
FOR THE MONTH ENDED NOVEMBER 30, 19X1

Description	Actual	Standard	Actual (Over) or Under Standard
PRICE			
Material	$ 41,277	$41,370	$ 93
Freight	3,061	3,101	40
Total	44,338	44,471	133
MATERIAL USAGE			
Yield	2,730	—	(2,730)
Containers	3,519	3,292	(227)
Inventory shortages	229	—	(229)
Total material usage	6,478	3,292	(3,186)
DIRECT LABOR AND MANUFACTURING EXPENSE			
Variable			
Direct labor			
Preforming	2,174	2,001	(173)
Molding	16,861	10,179	(6,682)
Polishing	2,941	2,147	(794)
Packing	6,987	2,830	(4,157)
Total direct labor	28,963	17,157	(11,806)
Manufacturing expense			
Preforming	873	862	(11)
Molding	2,016	1,698	(318)
Polishing	910	920	10
Packing	2,110	1,742	(368)
Receiving	1,847	1,074	(773)
Shipping	1,994	1,427	(567)
Total manufacturing expense	9,750	7,723	(2,027)
Total variable direct labor and manufacturing expense	38,713	24,880	(13,833)
Fixed Expense			
Direct overhead	1,204	1,016	(188)
General manufacturing overhead	677	623	(54)
Depreciation*	11,806	7,118	(4,688)
Property taxes and insurance	850	803	(47)
Total fixed expense	14,537	9,560	(4,977)
Total direct labor and manufacturing expense	53,250	34,440	(18,810)
Total	$104,066	$82,203	$(21,863)

*Includes $4,123 applicable to prior months.

6. When certain conditions exist, some general conclusions about points of attack can be suggested. Consider, for example, these two points.

    a. A high marginal income ratio with a low margin of safety probably indicates an excess of fixed costs for the sales volume. The remedy lies in either reducing such fixed costs or increasing the sales volume.

    b. A low marginal income ratio and a low margin of safety may indicate that selling prices are too low or variable costs are too high. If prices are as high as competition will allow, then variable costs should be combed for possible reductions.

17-20 STATISTICAL TECHNIQUES FOR PLANNING

Business is complex, and the decisions faced by management become increasingly difficult as more alternatives need to be considered. The many products, the many processes, the constant change simply accentuate the pressure for the most modern techniques in the planning and forecasting area. Speed is necessary if adequate attention is to be paid to the various possible courses of action. Moreover, once a business plan has been conceived, a review every three months may be too infrequent. As one month closes, and as more information about probable conditions in the following 30 days is available, management wants to know the outlook for the succeeding period.

An analysis of such alternatives and the need for constant projections into the future places a tremendous burden on the accounting staff unless statistical techniques are utilized. The break-even analysis approach must be combined with linear programming, statistical decision theory, and the use of electronic computers if a satisfactory planning job is to be done. The controller must add these latest mathematical techniques to his know-how.

17-21 PROGRAM EVALUATION USING DISCOUNTED CASH FLOW

Given the fact that short-term plans will provide for the start of new programs or projects, often it will be found desirable to know the financial impact in detail and to determine the expected return on assets employed and after leverage or borrowings. Assume plans to facilitate and commence the manufacture of a new electronic device. Management should know the probable rate of return and financial requirements before authorizing the project and approving the plan.

If the cutoff rate of return on assets employed is 9.5% per year, a determination is made, as illustrated in Figure 17-13, about what rate reasonably may be expected and whether it satisfied the criterion. Detailed techniques are discussed in Chapter 32. In this project evaluation, an initial capital expenditure of $10,000,000 is required, together with $2,000,000 for working capital. Additional needs are projected in later years. The investment outflow by years and cash flow are shown. The return on gross investment calculates to be 9.9% per annum (assuming sale of the business after six years). With borrowing capacity, the return on "equity equivalent" is 41.9% per annum as shown in Figure 17-14.

Since time value of cash received is very important, the discounted cash flow technique should be considered in planning.

Figure 17-13   Discounted Cash Flow on Total Investment.

DISCOUNTED CASH FLOW
GROSS INVESTMENT
(dollars in thousands)

Year	Investment Permanent	Investment Working Capital	Profit after Taxes and Depreciation	Depreciation (DDB)	Cash Flow	Cash Generation (Requirement)	Discounted at 9% Factor	Discounted at 9% Amount	Discounted at 10% Factor	Discounted at 10% Amount
0	$(10,000)	(2,000)				$(12,000)	1.000	$(12,000)	1.000	$(12,000)
1	(1,500)		460	490	950	950	.917	871	.909	864
2		(400)	890	610	1,500	—	.842	—	.826	—
3		(300)	1,340	540	1,880	1,480	.772	1,142	.751	1,111
4		(300)	1,460	470	1,930	1,630	.708	1,154	.683	1,113
5			1,510	420	1,930	1,630	.650	1,060	.620	1,011
6			1,670	400	2,070	2,070	.596	1,224	.564	1,167
Subtotal			7,330	2,930	10,260	11,850		7,063		6,683
Salvage (net of tax)		(3,000)				(4,240)	.596		.564	
Total	$(11,500)	(3,000)				7,610		514		(51)

Discounted Rate of Return: $9\% + 1\% \left[\dfrac{514}{514 - (-51)} \right] = 9.9\%$

409

Figure 17-14 Discounted Cash Flow, Net of Borrowing.

DISCOUNTED CASH FLOW
INVESTMENT NET OF BORROWINGS
(dollars in thousands)

Year	Gross Investment	Profit After Taxes and Depreciation	Depreciation (Double Declining Balance)	Cash Flow	Interest Expense (Net)	Gross Cash Generation (Requirement)	Borrowings	Net Cash Generation (Requirement)	Discounted Cash Flow Discounted at 41% Factor	Amount	Discounted at 42% Factor	Amount
0	$(12,000)	—				(12,000)	9,600	(2,400)	1.000	(2,400)	1.000	$(2,400)
1	—	460	490	950	(288)	662	—	662	.709	469	.704	466
2	(1,500)	890	610	1,500	(303)	(303)	1,350	1,047	.503	527	.496	519
3	(400)	1,340	540	1,880	(328)	1,152	360	1,512	.357	540	.349	528
4	(300)	1,460	470	1,930	(344)	1,286	270	1,556	.253	394	.246	383
5	(300)	1,510	420	1,930	(352)	1,278	270	1,548	.179	277	.173	268
6	—	1,670	400	2,070	(178)	1,892	—	1,892	.127	240	.122	231
Subtotal							11,850	5,817		47		(5)
Loan Repayment (Net)							(11,850)	(11,850)				
Salvage (Net)								11,850				
Total	$(14,500)	7,330	2,930	10,260	(1,793)	(6,033)		5,817		47		$(5)

Discounted rate of return: $41\% + 1\% \left[\dfrac{47}{47 - (-5)} \right] = 41.9\%$

410

17-22 FINANCIAL ANALYSIS OF UNACCEPTABLE OPERATING RESULTS

Given an unacceptable segment of an annual plan, or actual operating results that depart significantly from plan, or loss operations, the financial staff often will be called on to make an in-depth review. Assuming the proper working relations with the operating staff, joint efforts, or at least cooperation, may provide information to correct unsatisfactory financial results.

Illustrated in this section is an analysis prepared as the basis for executive discussion by the officers of an integrated chemical company. In this case, it is assumed that the company has operated heavily in the red in one of three divisions, and the management can see no immediate prospects of improving the condition.

The general steps in the analysis, although partially evident from accompanying figures, are outlined as follows:

1. The operations for the past year were reviewed to secure some indication of the nature of the costs and the points of apparent waste or excessive costs.

2. Unit standard costs, budgets, and variances were analyzed and segregated into their fixed and variable elements.

3. Sales were analyzed to determine a representative product mixture by certain commodity groups.

4. With known product mixture, total costs and income at capacity were determined.

5. On the basis of information determined in step 4, profit graphs were prepared.

6. Within each product group, marginal income for each product was determined to suggest a more profitable sales mixture.

7. The data were interpreted in a narrative report containing recommendations for improvement.

The remainder of this chapter reproduces in full the report prepared by the controller.

Chemical Manufacturing Corporation
Chicago Division
Report on Profit Potential and Break-Even Points

General Comments

Operations at the Chicago Division for the year ended December 31, 19X resulted in a net loss of $730,142.

It may be taken for granted that the past year was one of experimentation a inefficiency which might be expected normally as a part of the start-up cost o new plant. However, the question which now can be asked is: "What is the norn profit expectancy, now that operating experience has been gained?" Other qu tions frequently posed include these:

1. Would the company as a whole have lost less if the Chicago Division h not operated?
2. What are the earning possibilities of the Division?
3. What are the break-even points of the three major product lines?
4. What action can be taken to minimize losses or increase profits?

It is hoped that some of the facts and opinions expressed in this report will sti ulate thinking as to possible corrective action.

Figure 17-15   Statement of Income and Expense.

Chemical Manufacturing Corporation—Chicago Division
STATEMENT OF INCOME AND EXPENSE
FOR THE YEAR ENDED DECEMBER 31, 19XX

		Amount	% o Sal
Net sales		$2,030,958	100.
Cost of sales			
At standard:			
Material	$1,515,062		
Variable expense	82,705		
Fixed expense	164,022	1,761,789	86.
Standard gross margin		269,169	13.
Over standard:			
Material	168,305		
Variable expense	135,182		
Fixed expense	268,082	571,569	28.
Manufacturing loss		302,400	14.
Operating expenses		441,639	21.
Operating loss		744,039	36.
Other income (net)		13,897	.
Loss before-income-tax impact		$ 730,142	35.

Operations for the Year 19XX

A summary of operating results is presented in Figure 17-15. The loss of $730,142 represents 35.95% of net sales. It will be observed that the standard gross margin is only 13.25% of net sales, and that it was insufficient to cover the operating expenses. If the plant had operated close to capacity the excess fixed costs of $268,082 would have largely disappeared. Furthermore, the additional income, even at a low margin rate, probably would have been sufficient to offset a major share of the excess manufacturing costs and operating expenses. Even at the higher volume level, the results would have been disappointing.

However, the overall company losses for the year would have been greater if the Chicago Division had not operated. This results from the fact that the sales income was greater than the direct out-of-pocket charges. A balance was available to cover either a share of the general office expenses, or Illinois Division expenses, or the depreciation and insurance costs which would have continued. The net advantage of operating the Chicago Division was $185,646, calculated as follows:

Net sales		$2,030,958
Other income (net)		13,897
Total		2,044,855
Deduct:		
Direct out-of-pocket costs		
Material	$1,683,367	
Expenses	175,842	1,859,209
Income in excess of out-of-pocket costs		$ 185,646

This gain is reconciled with the net loss in this manner:

Allocated expenses	
Illinois Division expenses	$510,859
General offices expenses	214,114
Total allocated expenses	724,973
Continung fixed charges—depreciation, etc.	190,815
Total costs	915,788
Deduct:	
Income in excess of out-of-pocket costs	185,646
Net loss	$730,142

It is to be observed that the fixed charges of $190,815 would not have been incurred if the Chicago Division properties had not been purchased, and that they will continue until the property is either fully depreciated or disposed of. Moreover, the income in excess of out-of-pocket expenses, an amount of $185,646, was almost enough to cover the continuing fixed charges.

Prospects for the Future

The severe losses of last year have prompted a thorough review of future po sibilities. After extensive discussions with the General Sales Manager and Wor Manager, together with a critical analysis of present sales trends and expect cost levels, it appears that present plans would result in an operating profit, plant capacity, of $28,727 per month or $344,724 per year. While this is more e couraging than a loss of $730,142, yet overall profit is only 5.97% of net sal. The condensed statement by product lines is shown in Figure 17-16. A most se ous aspect is the almost total lack of profit, even at capacity levels, on our mo voluminous product—paints. Quite in contrast, the coke by-products show a po sible operating profit of 19.31% of net sales at capacity.

The Chicago Division, of course, has not yet attained 100% of plant capaci sales volume.

Profit Potentials at Various Volume Levels

Because the Division may experience several different monthly sales and pr duction levels, it has been felt desirable to construct profit graphs so that the o erating profit on any of the three product lines may be anticipated with reasonable degree of accuracy. These are illustrated in Figures 17-17, 17-18, a 17-19. The probable profit or loss at any selected volume level is measured by t vertical difference between the sales income line and total cost line at that lev For example, at a 50% plant capacity level, the operating profit or loss would about as follows:

Product	Sales Volume at 50% Level	Monthly Operating Profit (or Loss)
Paints	$141,025	$(17,687)
Ammonia derivatives	51,810	(5,423)
Coke by-products	59,410	73
Total	$252,245	$(23,037)

These figures have been calculated, but a close approximation can be read on t graphs.

These charts also indicate the break-even points at which income balances e pense. The break-even points are quite dissimilar:

	Break-Even Point		
		Sales per Month	
Product	% of Five-Day Capacity	Pounds	Dollar
Paints	98.7	1,415,161	$278,4:
Ammonia derivatives	73.4	383,148	76,0
Coke by-products	49.9	228,043	59,2

Figure 17-16 Statement of Estimated Income and Expense by Product Line.

Chemical Manufacturing Corporation—Chicago Division
STATEMENT OF ESTIMATED INCOME AND EXPENSE
AT PLANT CAPACITY (5-DAY WEEK) FOR ONE MONTH

Description	Paints			Ammonia Derivatives			Coke By-Products			Total		
	Amount	Per Cwt.	% Net Sales	Amount	Per Cwt.	% Net Sales	Amount	Per Cwt.	% Net Sales	Amount	Per Cwt.	% Net Sales
Net sales before freight allowance	$282,050	$19.6742	105.26	$103,617	$19.8500	104.81	$118,820	$26.0000	103.96	$504,487	$20.9105	104.86
Less: Freight allowance	14,099	.9835	5.26	4,754	.9107	4.81	4,521	.9893	3.96	23,374	.9688	4.86
Net sales	267,951	18.6907	100.00	98,863	18.9393	100.00	114,299	25.0107	100.00	481,113	19.9417	100.00
Cost of sales												
Variable	231,657	16.1591	86.45	75,621	14.4868	76.49	70,308	15.3847	61.51	377,586	15.6506	78.48
Fixed	16,010	1.1168	5.98	9,442	1.8088	9.55	13,554	2.9659	11.86	39,006	1.6168	8.11
Total cost of sales	247,667	17.2759	92.43	85,063	16.2956	86.04	83,862	18.3506	73.37	416,592	17.2674	86.59
Manufacturing profit	20,284	1.4149	7.57	13,800	2.6437	13.96	30,437	6.6602	26.63	64,521	2.6743	13.41
Operating expenses	19,823	1.3827	7.40	7,603	1.4565	7.69	8,368	1.8311	7.32	35,794	1.4836	7.44
Operating profit	$ 461	$ .0322	.17	$ 6,197	$ 1.1872	6.27	$ 22,069	$ 4.8291	19.31	$ 28,727	$ 1.1907	5.97
Pounds manufactured and sold	1,433,600			522,000			457,000			2,412,600		

Notes:
(1) Variable expenses shown above are those indicated in Fig. 17-20, except that freight costs have been deducted from sales (and not included in cost of sales) to arrive at a net sales figure consistent with the usual statement presentation.
(2) Reference is made to the appended comments which are an integral part of this report.

Figure 17-17   Break-Even Chart—Paint Works.

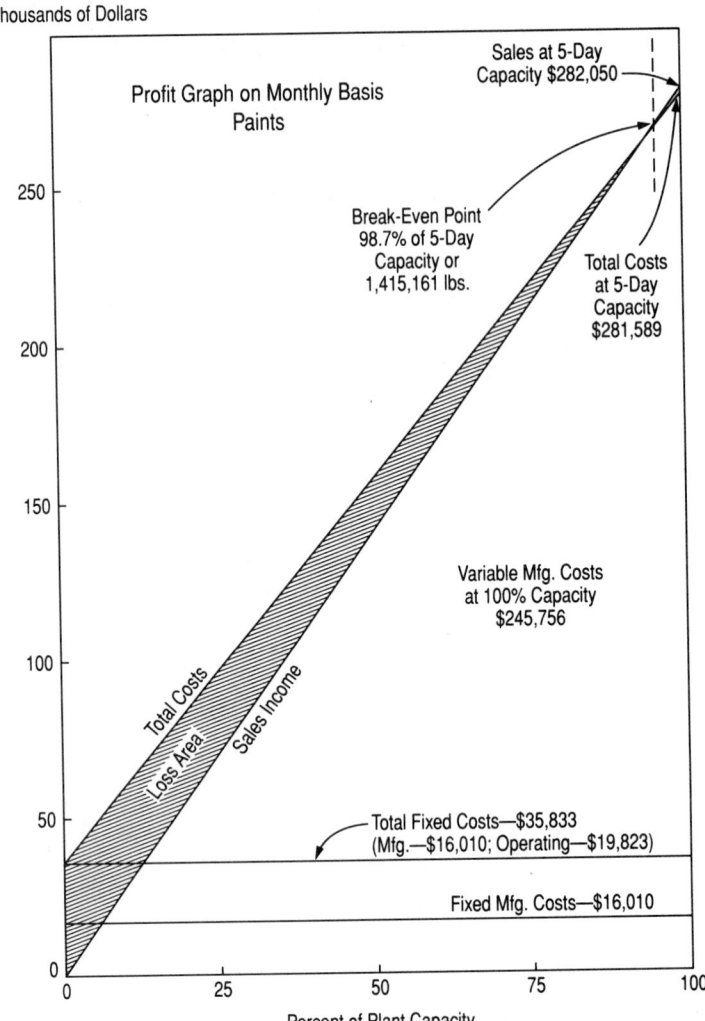

Thousands of Dollars

Profit Graph on Monthly Basis
Paints

Sales at 5-Day
Capacity $282,050

Break-Even Point
98.7% of 5-Day
Capacity or
1,415,161 lbs.

Total Costs
at 5-Day
Capacity
$281,589

Variable Mfg. Costs
at 100% Capacity
$245,756

Total Costs

Loss Area

Sales Income

Total Fixed Costs—$35,833
(Mfg.—$16,010; Operating—$19,823)

Fixed Mfg. Costs—$16,010

Percent of Plant Capacity

The details of costs and income on which these break-even points are predicate
are set forth in Figures 17-20, 17-21, and 17-22.

The chief problem of the Chicago Division centers about the paint line, wher
a plant capacity operation is required in order to avoid a loss. This is, indeed,
disturbing condition; and the remaining comments relate chiefly to this produc
line.

Paints—Recommendations

In reviewing the profit structure, a detailed analysis was made of each of th
more popular items in each product group. The total income and standar

Figure 17-18 Break-Even Chart—Ammonia Plant.

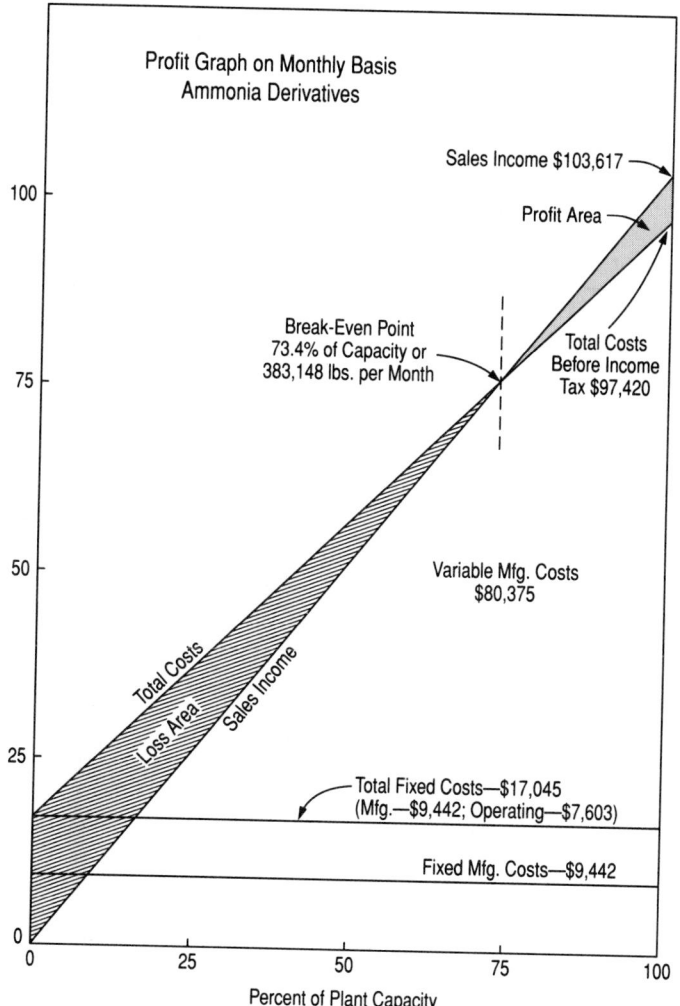

Thousands of Dollars

Profit Graph on Monthly Basis
Ammonia Derivatives

Sales Income $103,617

Profit Area

100

Break-Even Point
73.4% of Capacity or
383,148 lbs. per Month

Total Costs
Before Income
Tax $97,420

75

Variable Mfg. Costs
$80,375

50

Total Costs

Loss Area

Sales Income

25

Total Fixed Costs—$17,045
(Mfg.—$9,442; Operating—$7,603)

Fixed Mfg. Costs—$9,442

0

0   25   50   75   100

Percent of Plant Capacity

variable costs are outlined in Figure 17-20. The hundredweight data and marginal income per machine or kettle hour are shown in Figure 17-23. It will be observed that items 103 and 105 contribute the greatest income over variable expense, per machine hour, to help meet the fixed expenses, income taxes, and profit. It would seem desirable, and is possible in the opinion of the General Sales Manager, to increase the proportion of sales of these two items. As items 102 and 104 contribute the lowest marginal income, these should not be promoted. Of course, until the system is at capacity, every drum of paint sold helps reduce losses or increase profits.

A review of sales indicates that 85% of the volume is secured from 15% of the customers. Furthermore, from what information we piece together it appears our

Figure 17-19 Break-Even Chart—Coke By-Products Plant.

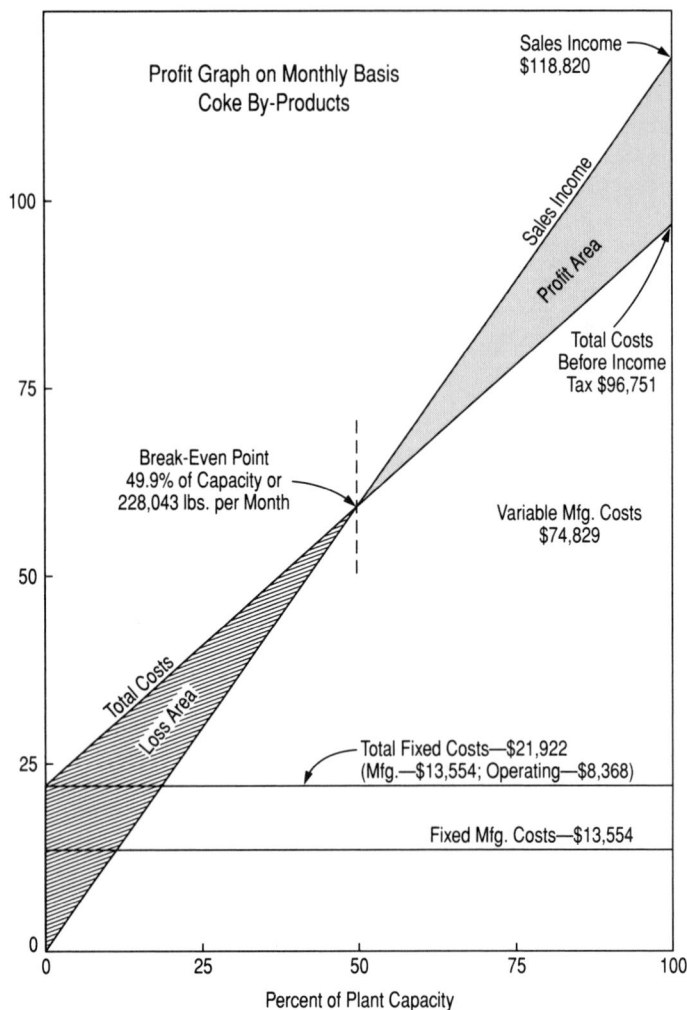

Thousands of Dollars

Profit Graph on Monthly Basis
Coke By-Products

Sales Income
$118,820

Sales Income

Profit Area

Total Costs
Before Income
Tax $96,751

Break-Even Point
49.9% of Capacity or
228,043 lbs. per Month

Variable Mfg. Costs
$74,829

Total Costs

Loss Area

Total Fixed Costs—$21,922
(Mfg.—$13,554; Operating—$8,368)

Fixed Mfg. Costs—$13,554

Percent of Plant Capacity

operating expenses are out of line with our competitors. There is some indication also, that the cycle time in production is on the high side. The Works Manager is of the opinion that reductions can be made in production time. Such improvement would, of course, reduce the variable cost per hundredweight and increase the plant capacity and therefore the potential marginal income.

On the basis of available information, it is recommended that immediate step be taken to:

1. Reduce selling expenses (fixed costs) by $3,300 per month through the re lease of three salesmen. The remaining staff can readily cover our larg volume customers and contact other possible users.

Chemical Manufacturing Corporation—Chicago Division
BREAKDOWN BY PRODUCT OF VARIABLE INCOME AND COSTS
USED IN DEVELOPMENT OF PROFIT GRAPH

Product	SALES		VARIABLE COSTS (STANDARD)								Marginal Income
	Pounds	Value	Freight	Material	Shipping	Drums	Processing	Material Handling	Royalties	Total	
PAINTS											
101	235,200	$ 47,040.00	$ 2,312.73	$ 34,958.48	$ 141.12	$ 2,373.87	$ 924.81	$ 367.85	$ —	$ 41,078.86	$ 5,961.14
102	235,200	47,040.00	2,312.73	37,600.48	141.12	2,373.87	928.81	489.92	—	43,846.69	3,193.31
103	336,000	67,200.00	3,303.89	46,783.97	201.60	3,391.25	1,501.58	593.38	—	55,775.67	11,424.33
104	156,800	34,496.00	1,541.81	27,408.48	94.08	1,582.58	653.86	190.04	—	31,470.85	3,025.15
105	313,800	53,346.00	3,085.60	35,005.65	188.28	3,167.18	1,264.30	560.45	—	43,271.46	10,074.54
106	156,800	32,928.00	1,541.81	23,697.81	94.08	1,582.58	568.09	266.87	14.11	27,765.35	5,162.65
Total Paints ...	1,433,800	282,050.00	14,098.57	205,454.87	860.28	14,471.33	5,841.21	2,468.51	14.11	243,208.88	38,841.12
AMMONIA DERIVATIVES											
205	78,300	14,877.00	713.16	9,703.41	46.98	341.70	541.84	80.34	—	11,427.43	3,449.57
206	208,800	41,760.00	1,901.75	26,307.76	125.28	911.20	1,426.10	152.84	—	30,824.93	10,935.07
207	156,000	31,320.00	1,426.31	20,492.83	93.96	683.40	1,027.45	158.48	—	23,882.43	7,437.57
208	78,300	15,660.00	713.16	11,708.67	46.98	341.70	485.15	58.96	113.61	13,468.23	2,191.77
Total Ammonia Derivatives ...	522,000	103,617.00	4,754.38	68,212.67	313.20	2,278.00	3,480.54	450.62	113.61	79,603.02	24,013.98

(continued)

Figure 17-20 *(continued)*

VARIABLE COSTS (STANDARD)

Product	SALES Pounds	SALES Value	Freight	Material	Shipping	Drums	Processing	Material Handling	Royalties	Total	Marginal Income
COKE BY-PRODUCTS											
301	343,000	89,180.00	3,393.30	42,062.78	205.80	4,372.91	3,352.48	1,919.43	—	55,306.70	33,873.30
302	114,000	29,640.00	1,127.80	12,536.92	68.40	1,453.39	1,290.94	621.19	—	17,098.64	12,541.36
Total Coke By-Products ..	457,000	118,820.00	4,521.10	54,599.70	274.20	5,826.30	4,643.42	2,540.62	—	72,405.34	46,414.66
Total Variable Income and Costs —All Products ..	2,412,800	$504,487.00	$23,374.05	$328,267.24	$1,447.68	$22,575.63	$13,965.17	$5,459.75	$127.72	$395,217.24	$109,269.76

COST DATA USED IN PROFIT GRAPH

	Paints	Ammonia Derivatives	Coke By-Products	Total
Variable Costs, as above	$243,209	$79,603	$72,405	$395,217
Deduct:				
Costs Assumed to Be Fixed in Nature	1,168	696	929	2,793
Net	242,041	78,907	71,476	392,424
Add:				
Assumed Material Losses—1%	2,055	682	546	3,283
Assumed Overrun on Standards (20% of Processing and Handling)	1,660	786	1,436	3,882
Assumed Short-Term Excess Costs	—	—	1,371	1,371
Total Variable Costs	$245,756	$80,375	$74,829	$400,960

Figure 17-21 Detail of Monthly Fixed Costs for Use in Profit Graph.

Chemical Manufacturing Corporation—Chicago Division
DETAIL OF MONTHLY FIXED COSTS
USED IN DEVELOPMENT OF PROFIT GRAPH

Item	Product			Total	Comments
	Paints	Ammonia Derivatives	Coke By-Products		
MANUFACTURING					
DIRECT					
Depreciation—Buildings	$ 1,408	$ 537	$ 710	$ 2,655	Actual Expense—19XX
Depreciation—Machinery and Equipment	4,818	2,363	2,783	9,964	Actual Expense—19XX
Property Insurance	62	23	31	116	Actual Expense—19XX
Real and Personal Property Taxes	815	306	386	1,507	Actual Expense—19XX
Building Costs (Heat, Lighting, Janitor Service, etc.)	2,184	833	1,100	4,117	Average Budgeted Cost—19X1; allocated to products on cubic ft. basis
General Plant Costs	826	1,116	1,530	3,472	Average Budgeted Cost—19X1; allocated to products on forecasted conversion cost basis
Control Laboratory	952	1,287	1,765	4,004	Average Budgeted Cost—19X1; allocated to products on forecasted conversion cost basis

(continued)

Figure 17-21 *(continued)*

Item	Product			Total	Comments
	Paints	Ammonia Derivatives	Coke By-Products		
Vacuum Boilers (Labor and Related Costs)	624	208	—	832	Actual Expense—19XX
Total Direct Manufacturing Expense	11,689	6,673	8,305	26,667	
ALLOCATED					
General Works Cost	2,106	1,591	2,499	6,196	Budgeted Cost—19X1
Boiler House Fixed Costs	47	82	1,221	1,350	Budgeted Cost—19X1
Total Allocated Costs	2,153	1,673	3,720	7,546	
Total Fixed Manufacturing Expenses Before Adjustments	13,842	8,346	12,025	34,213	
Add:					
Share of Undistributed Water and Steam Costs	1,000	400	600	2,000	Expected Experience—19X1 budget
20% of Processing Costs Assumed to Be Fixed	1,168	696	929	2,793	
Total Fixed Manufacturing Costs for Construction of Profit Graph	16,010	9,442	13,554	39,006	
OPERATING EXPENSES					
Administrative, Selling, and Advertising, Technical, etc., per Figure 17-22	19,823	7,603	8,368	35,794	
Total Fixed Expense for Construction of Profit Graph	$35,833	$17,045	$21,922	$74,800	

Figure 17-22 Detail of Monthly Operating Expenses for Use in Profit Graph.

Chemical Manufacturing Corporation—Chicago Division
DETAIL OF MONTHLY OPERATING EXPENSES
USED IN DEVELOPMENT OF PROFIT GRAPH

Item	Product				Comments
	Paints	Ammonia Derivatives	Coke By-Products	Total	
DIRECT					
Advertising and Sales Promotion	$ 1,587	$1,146	$ 975	$ 3,708	Budget—19X1
Selling	7,743	2,717	3,124	13,584	
Technical Service	1,126	395	456	1,977	
Research	1,701	597	686	2,984	
Total Direct Operating Expense	12,157	4,855	5,241	22,253	
ALLOCATED					
Administrative	840	295	338	1,473	Based on Budget—19X1; allocated to Chicago Division on forecasted net sales for 19X1
Advertising and Sales Promotion	412	144	166	722	
Selling	1,097	385	442	1,924	
Technical Service	1,653	580	667	2,900	
Research	858	301	347	1,506	
Engineering	565	198	229	992	
Patents	439	154	177	770	
Total Allocated Operating Expense	5,864	2,057	2,366	10,287	
Total Operating Expense Before Adjustment	18,021	6,912	7,607	32,540	
Add:					
Assumed 10% Overrun on Budget	1,802	691	761	3,254	
Total Operating Expense for Construction of Profit Graph	$19,823	$7,603	$8,368	$35,794	

Figure 17-23 Comparative Unit Costs and Income.

Chemical Manufacturing Corporation—Chicago Division
COMPARATIVE UNIT COSTS AND INCOME

	Sales Price	Variable Costs				Marginal Income	Fixed Costs and Expenses	Operating Profit or (Loss)	Per Machine Hour	
		Material	Container	Other	Total				Production (lbs.)	Marginal Income
PAINTS										
101	$20.00	$14.8633	$1.0093	$1.5929	$17.4655	$2.5345	$4.2681	$(1.7336)	1,032	$26.16
102	20.00	15.9866	1.0093	1.6464	18.6423	1.3577	3.5458	(2.1881)	884	12.00
103	20.00	13.9238	1.0093	1.6668	16.5999	3.4001	3.5666	(.1665)	943	32.06
104	22.00	17.4799	1.0093	1.5815	20.0707	1.9293	3.6981	(1.7688)	775	14.95
105	17.00	11.1554	1.0093	1.6248	13.7895	3.2105	3.1721	.0384	852	27.35
106	21.00	15.1134	1.0093	1.5848	17.7075	3.2925	3.5831	(.2906)	774	25.48
AMMONIA DERIVATIVES										
205	19.00	12.3926	.4364	1.7654	14.5944	4.4056	3.8752	.5304	963	42.43
206	20.00	12.5995	.4364	1.7270	14.7629	5.2371	3.7995	1.4376	947	49.60
207	20.00	13.0861	.4364	1.7281	15.2506	4.7494	3.7313	1.0181	985	46.78
208	20.00	14.9536	.4364	1.8108	17.2008	2.7992	3.5728	(.7736)	1,032	30.40
COKE BY-PRODUCTS										
301	26.00	12.2632	1.2749	2.5863	16.1244	9.8756	4.7988	5.0768	895	88.39
302	26.00	10.9973	1.2749	2.7266	14.9988	11.0012	3.9772	7.0240	831	91.42

2. Emphasize the more profitable products, increasing the proportion of 103 and 105.
3. Concentrate on a reduction of cycle times by 10%.

The effect of each successive action, detailed in Figure 17-24 as to marginal income, would be as follows:

Action		Break-Even Sales Volume (Monthly)	Monthly Operating Profit at Capacity
Present plans	(a)	$278,400	$ 461
Reduce fixed expenses by $3,330 per month	(b)	252,800	3,761
Change sales mixture to higher proportion of profitable items, plus (b)	(c)	214,000	9,131
Reduce cycle time by 10%, plus (b) and (c)		210,770	15,561

The accomplishment of these objectives would result in a net profit of 5.0% of sales at capacity.

The profit graph on paints, with these changes incorporated, would appear as in Figure 17-25. As a long-range program, research should be intensified on material costs so as to increase the margin of selling price over such costs. Since the net profit as a percentage of investment, even with the improved results, would not be satisfactory, perhaps consideration can be given to new product lines with higher margins that could advantageously be manufactured in the paint facilities.

Further details can be made available as requested.

CONTROLLER

Figure 17-24 Statement of Standard Marginal Income Giving Effect to Changes in Products Sold and Manufacturing Efficiency.

Chemical Manufacturing Corporation—Chicago Division Paints
DETERMINATION OF STANDARD MARGINAL INCOME AT CAPACITY

Product	Present Sales Mixture			Change in Sales Mixture			10% Reduction in Cycle Time		
	(000's) Pounds	% Total	Marginal Income	(000's) Pounds	% Total	Marginal Income	(000's) Pounds	% Total	Marginal Income
101	235.2	16.4	$ 5,961.14	235.2	16.6	$ 5,961.14	261.3	16.3	$ 6,725.34
102	235.2	16.4	3,193.31	117.0	8.3	1,588.51	130.4	8.1	1,821.95
103	336.0	23.5	11,424.33	461.0	32.6	15,674.47	512.0	31.8	17,637.38
104	156.8	10.9	3,025.15	77.5	5.4	1,495.21	86.0	5.4	1,695.06
105	313.8	21.9	10,074.54	400.0	28.3	12,842.00	444.6	27.6	14,453.06
106	156.8	10.9	5,162.65	124.6	8.8	4,102.46	173.1	10.8	5,761.98
Total	1,433.8	100.0	$38,841.12	1,415.3	100.0	$41,663.79	1,607.4	100.0	$48,094.77

Figure 17-25   Profit Graph Giving Effect to Changes in Income and Costs—Paint Works.

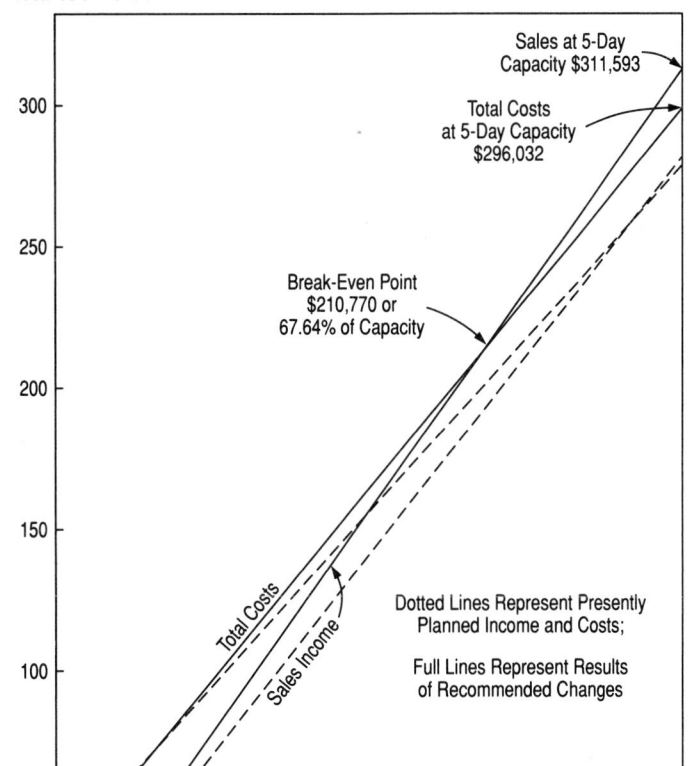

Thousands of Dollars

Sales at 5-Day
Capacity $311,593

Total Costs
at 5-Day Capacity
$296,032

Break-Even Point
$210,770 or
67.64% of Capacity

Total Costs

Sales Income

Dotted Lines Represent Presently
Planned Income and Costs;

Full Lines Represent Results
of Recommended Changes

Present Fixed Costs—$35,833

Assumed Fixed Costs—$32,533

Percent of Plant Capacity

17-23 MORE SOPHISTICATED ANALYSES

The illustrations presented in this chapter have been some of the more simple applications of the cost-volume-profit relationship. They deal with the more frequently asked questions relating to near-term applications where, for the volume range under discussion, the cost behavior of the elements is largely determinable; that is, the techniques for determining whether a cost is fixed or variable, or for what proportion of a mixed cost is fixed (see Chapter 23), are valid over a shorter period for the range in volume levels. Of course, over a longer period additions often must be made to fixed costs (e.g., depreciation) to provide for greater capacity. Some would say this illustrates that fixed costs are often variable. While the techniques used are deemed valid by the

authors for most uses, those who want to probe for, or speculate on, possible answe
to other longer term or more sophisticated applications, the references may provi
some interesting analyses. Thus, there is a discussion of break-even analysis wh
cost behavior is unknown, also identified as break-even analysis under conditions
uncertainty. Break-even points are calculated under alternative assumptions of fix
or variable cost behavior to see if a product's profitability is very sensitive to cost I
havior. Another reference (Howard Martin, "Breaking Through the Break-Even B.
riers") deals with the impact of inflation over the longer term, and also incorpora
the cost of capital.

17-24 SELECTED REFERENCES

Frank, Gary B., Steven A. Fisher, and Allen R. Wilkie, "Linking Cost to Price and Profi
    Management Accounting, June 1989, pp. 22–26.

Martin, Howard, "Breaking Through the Break-Even Barriers," *Management Accounting,* M
    1985, pp. 31–34.

Mazhin, Reza, "CVP Analysis with an Electronic Spreadsheet," *Journal of Accountancy,* J.
    1987, pp. 110–116.

Montgomery, Douglas C., and Elizabeth A. Peak, *Introduction to Linear Regression Analy.*
    New York: John Wiley & Sons, 1982.

Sinclair, Kenneth P., and James A. Talbott, Jr., "Using Breakeven Analysis When Cost Beh.
    ior Is Unknown," *Management Accounting,* July 1986, pp. 52–55.

CHAPTER 18

Tax Planning: A Strategic Analysis

This chapter was written by Marty Gold, Senior Manager, Ernst & Young LLP, Denver, Colorado.

18-1 INTRODUCTION

Taxes—it's one of the certainties of life . . . it's a necessity of modern society . . . and it is a true headache to cash flow planning. Taxes are a challenge that every profitable company must live with. The controller *is not* fulfilling his or her responsibilities if these taxes are passively accepted. Tax planning provides dynamic ways that a company can improve its cash flow, including strategies for maximizing tax deferrals, accelerating tax deductions, and reducing the overall tax rate by taking advantage of whatever tax credits are available. Although this book is not intended to be a technical tax treatise, this chapter will explore some opportunities for the prudent controller to improve tax flow.

18-2 OBJECTIVES OF TAX PLANNING

Tax planning in general may not be something that is intuitive to many controllers. Its objectives are different from GAAP and financial accounting in a number of significant ways.

Unlike GAAP and financial accounting, tax accounting is primarily income statement based. The balance sheet (other than how it may be used relative to FASB Statement No. 109 discussed later) plays a subsidiary role to the income statement. Unlike in financial accounting where the goal for many corporations may be to maximize income, the objective for tax accounting is to minimize current income.

These differences in philosophies, however, are not unreconcilable and do not require the keeping of two sets of books. There are no requirements that tax accounting be the same as book accounting. As discussed in Chapter 59, book/tax differences must be documented and adequate records must be kept. It is these book tax differences that foster tax savings and cash flow planning.

Please keep in mind that tax laws are constantly changing and that each business entity has its own set of facts and circumstances. The planning ideas presented here are meant as starting points for controllers. We will not be giving tax advice. Controllers should consult with their internal or external tax consultants for specific applicability of these planning ideas and issues.

(a) MAXIMIZING TAX DEFERRALS

Maximizing tax deferrals generally means finding ways of recognizing income for tax purposes later, rather than sooner. Although various tax legislation has made this task more difficult, it is still possible to defer income that would otherwise be recognizable. For example, corporate consolidations and reorganizations can be structured to be tax free. Gain can also be deferred through the use of like-kind exchanges. Certain service revenue received in advance can also be deferred. The prudent controller, through his or her knowledge of the company and using tax consultants, when necessary, should constantly be challenging the company's transactions for tax deferral issues.

(b) ACCELERATING DEDUCTIONS

The corollary to maximizing income deferrals is to accelerate the recognition of expenses, where possible. Examples of accelerating deductions include choosing accelerated methods of depreciation, adopting a LIFO inventory method, and donating inventory instead of cash as a charitable contribution.

As with deferring income, accelerating deductions defers, but does not eliminate tax. However, this deferral increases cash flow and is, in effect, like an interest-free loan from the government.

(c) TAX CREDITS

Unlike deferring income and accelerating expenses, tax credits are permanent reductions in tax. Prior to 1986, the most prevalent of these credits was the investment tax credit (ITC), which allowed a specified percent of the purchase price of certain fixed assets as a direct reduction of the tax liability. Since the repeal of this credit, the most prevalent credits are the research and experimental tax credit and the foreign tax credit.

(d) AVOIDING TAX PITFALLS

Congress has not been generous with tax breaks; however, tax pitfalls or traps remain numerous in the tax code (The Internal Revenue Code of 1986, as amended). Congress has limited or eliminated many tax opportunities that used to exist; they have limited deductions for meals and entertainment, net operating loss deductions, and implemented a parallel tax system called the alternative minimum tax.

The following sections will discuss specific areas of the tax code that provide both opportunities and pitfalls for the controller, and through him or her, the company.

18-3 DEPRECIATION

For tax purposes, as for financial reporting purposes, depreciation represents a large deduction, especially in capital intensive businesses. Internal Revenue Code (IRC) §§ 167 and 168 are the tax law provisions that permit deductions to systematically recover the cost of a capital asset over its useful life. For tax purposes, the depreciation methods and lives available are very specific. For most assets placed in service, the company must use the Modified Accelerated Cost Recovery System (MACRS). This system assigns specific lives, methods, and conventions to specific types of assets.

(a) ASSET LIVES

Under MACRS, asset lives are broken up into eight categories. These are three-year property, five-year property, seven-year property, ten-year property, fifteen-year property, twenty-year property, nonresidential real property, and residential rental property. The IRS has published a list through Revenue Procedure 87-56 that states what property fits in what category. The company has the choice of depreciating the property over the corresponding life, also known as the general depreciation system (e.g., 7 years for 7-year property or 5 years for 5-year property) or a longer life known as the alternative depreciation system (see Figure 18-1 for an example from Revenue Procedure 87-56).

Figure 18-1   Revenue Procedure 87–56.

Asset class	Description of assets included	Class Life (in years)	General Depreciation System	Alternative Depreciation System
			Recovery Periods (in years)	

SPECIFIC DEPRECIABLE ASSETS USED IN ALL BUSINESS ACTIVITIES, EXCEPT AS NOTED:

00.11 **Office Furniture, Fixtures, and Equipment:**

Includes furniture and fixtures that are not a structural component of a building. Includes such assets as desks, files, safes, and communications equipment. Does not include communications equipment that is included in other classes.   10   7   10

00.12 **Information Systems:**

Includes computers and their peripheral equipment used in administering normal business transactions and the maintenance of business records, their retrieval and analysis. Information systems are defined as:

1) Computers: A computer is a programmable electronically activated device capable of accepting information, applying prescribed processes to the information, and supplying the results of these processes with or without human intervention. It usually consists of a central processing unit containing extensive storage, logic, arithmetic, and control capabilities. Excluded from this category are adding machines, electronic desk calculators, etc., and other equipment described in class 00.13.

2) Peripheral equipment consists of the auxiliary machines which are designed to be placed under control of the central processing unit. Nonlimiting examples are: Card readers, card punches, magnetic tape feeds, high speed printers, optical character readers, tape cassettes, mass storage units, paper tape equipment, keypunches, data entry devices, teleprinters, terminals, tape drives, disc drives, disc files, disc packs, visual image projector tubes, card sorters, plotters, and collators. Peripheral equipment may be used on-line or off-line.

Does not include equipment that is an integral part of other capital equipment that is included in other classes of economic activity, i.e., computers used primarily for process or production control, switching, channeling, and automating distributive trades and services such as point of sale (POS) computer systems. Also, does not include equipment of a kind used primarily for amusement or entertainment of the user.   6   5*   5*

00.13 **Data Handling Equipment, except Computers:**

Includes only typewriters, calculators, adding and accounting machines, copiers, and duplicating equipment.   6   5   6

00.21 **Airplanes** (airframes and engines), except those used in commercial or contract carrying of passengers or freight, and all helicopters (airframes and engines).   6   5   6

00.22 **Automobiles, Taxis.**   3   5   5

00.23 **Buses.**   9   5   9

00.241 **Light General Purpose Trucks:**

Includes trucks for use over the road (actual unloaded weight less than 13,000 pounds).   4   5   5

00.242 **Heavy General Purpose Trucks:**

Includes heavy general purpose trucks, concrete ready mix-truckers, and ore trucks, for use over the road (actual unloaded weight 13,000 pounds or more).   6   5   6

*Property described in asset class 00.12 which is qualified technological equipment as defined in section 168(i)(2) is assigned a recovery period of 5 years notwithstanding its class life. See section 3 of the revenue procedure.

Figure 18-1 *(continued)*

Asset class	Description of assets included	Class Life (in years)	General Depreciation System	Alternative Depreciation System
			Recovery Periods (in years)	
00.25	**Railroad Cars and Locomotives, except those owned by railroad transportation companies.**	15	7	15
00.26	**Tractor Units For Use Over-The-Road.**	4	3	4
00.27	**Trailers and Trailer-Mounted Containers.**	6	5	6
00.28	**Vessels, Barges, Tugs, and Similar Water Transportation Equipment, except those used in marine construction.**	18	10	18
00.3	**Land Improvements:** Includes improvements directly to or added to land, whether such improvements are section 1245 property or section 1250 property, provided such improvements are depreciable. Examples of such assets might include sidewalks, roads, canals, waterways, drainage facilities, sewers (not including municipal sewers in Class 51), wharves and docks, bridges, fences, landscaping, shubbery, or radio and television transmitting towers. Does not include land improvements that are explicitly included in any other class, and buildings and structural components as defined in section 1.48–1(e) of the regulations. Excludes public utility initial clearing and grading land improvements as specified in Rev. Rul. 72–403, 1972–2 C.B. 102.	20	15	20
00.4	**Industrial Steam and Electric Generation and/or Distribution Systems:** Includes assets, whether such assets are section 1245 property or 1250 property, providing such assets are depreciable, used in the production and/or distribution of electricity with rated total capacity in excess of 500 Kilowatts and/or assets used in the production and/or distribution of steam with rated total capacity in excess of 12,500 pounds per hour for use by the taxpayer in its industrial manufacturing process or plant activity and not ordinarily available for sale to others. Does not include buildings and structural components as defined in section 1.48–1(e) of the regulations. Assets used to generate and/or distribute electricity or steam of the type described above but of lesser rated capacity are not included, but are included in the appropriate manufacturing equipment classes elsewhere specified. Also includes electric generating and steam distribution assets, which may utilize steam produced by a waste reduction and resource recovery plant, used by the taxpayer in its industrial manufacturing process or plant activity. Steam and chemical recovery boiler systems used for the recovery and regeneration of chemicals used in manufacturing, with rated capacity in excess of that described above, with specifically related distribution and return systems are not included but are included in appropriate manufacturing equipment classes elsewhere specified. An example of an excluded steam and chemical recovery boiler system is that used in the pulp and paper manufacturing industry.	22	15	22

DEPRECIABLE ASSETS USED IN THE FOLLOWING ACTIVITIES:

Asset class	Description of assets included	Class Life (in years)	General Depreciation System	Alternative Depreciation System
01.1	**Agriculture:** Includes machinery and equipment, grain bins, and fences but no other land improvements, that are used in the production of crops or plants, vines, and trees; livestock; the operation of farm dairies, nurseries, greenhouses, sod farms, mushroom cellars, cranberry bogs, apiaries, and fur farms; the performance of agriculture, animal husbandry, and horticultural services.	10	7	10
01.11	**Cotton Ginning Assets.**	12	7	12

(continued)

Figure 18-1 (*continued*)

Asset class	Description of assets included	Class Life (in years)	Recovery Periods (in years) General Depreciation System	Recovery Periods (in years) Alternative Depreciation System
01.21	**Cattle, Breeding or Dairy.**	7	5	7
01.221	**Any breeding or work horse that is 12 years old or less at the time it is placed in service.****	10	7	10
01.222	**Any breeding or work horse that is more than 12 years old at the time it is placed in service.****	10	3	10
01.223	**Any race horse that is more than 2 years old at the time it is placed in service.****	*	3	12
01.224	**Any horse that is more than 12 years old at the time it is placed in service and that is neither a race horse nor a horse described in class 01.222.****	*	3	12
01.225	**Any horse not described in classes 01.221, 01.222, 01.223, or 01.224.**	*	7	12
01.23	**Hogs, Breeding.**	3	3	3
01.24	**Sheep and Goats, Breeding.**	5	5	5
01.3	**Farm buildings except structures included in Class 01.4.**	25	20	25
01.4	**Single purpose agricultural or horticultural structures** (within the meaning of section 48(p) of the Code).	15	7	15
10.0	**Mining:** Includes assets used in the mining and quarrying of metallic and nonmetallic minerals (including sand, gravel, stone, and clay) and the milling, beneficiation and other primary preparation of such materials.	10	7	10

*Property described in asset classes 01.223, 01.224, and 01.225 are assigned recovery periods under either section 168(e)(3)(A) or section 168(g)(2)(C) but have no class lives.
**A horse is more than 2 (or 12) years old after the day that is 24 (or 144) months after its actual birthdate.

(b) DEPRECIATION METHOD

Generally, there are three methods for depreciating property. For three-year property through 10-year property, the general depreciation system method for depreciation is the 200% declining balance method, switching to the straight-line method when that would yield a greater amount of depreciation. For 15-year and 20-year property, the general depreciation system method for depreciation is the 150% declining balance method, switching to the straight-line method when that would yield a greater amount of depreciation. The straight-line method is generally used for real property and railroad grading or tunnel bores. For all of these methods, the IRC allows the company to elect a slower method (i.e., 150% declining balance or straight line for 200% declining balance property, or straight line for 150% declining balance property).

(c) APPLICABLE CONVENTION

For property other than real property, the half-year convention is generally used. This means that all property placed in service during the year is treated as though it was placed in service at the midpoint of the year. However, if greater than 40% of the property normally subject to the half-year convention is placed in service in the last quarter of the year, then the half-year convention will not apply to all this property, but rather, the mid-quarter convention will apply. The mid-quarter convention assumes that all property placed in service in that quarter is treated as though it was placed in service at the midpoint of that quarter.

For real property, the mid-month convention is used. This means that real property placed in service during the month is treated as though it was placed in service at the midpoint of that month.

(d) APPLICATION

The controller, with assistance from the internal or external tax consultants (if necessary), should evaluate all of the tax depreciation options and choose the option that most benefits the company. For example, if the company will be in a sustained tax loss position, it may be more beneficial to use a slower depreciation method and a longer life. Conversely, a profitable company would probably want to use the shortest lives and the most generous depreciation method.

18-4 THE ALTERNATIVE MINIMUM TAX

The alternative minimum tax (AMT) is parallel and separate from the regular tax system. It was enacted by Congress to ensure that taxpayers would not be able to escape taxation entirely by utilizing certain tax deductions, losses, and exemptions (also known as tax preference items). The system recalculates taxable income (called alternative minimum taxable income or AMTI) and calculates a 20% tax (for corporations) against this income. This tax is then compared to the regular tax, and the greater of the two is owed. The amount that the total tax liability exceeds the regular tax liability is the AMT.

Taxable income is the starting point for calculating AMT. Mechanically, the calculation for a corporation is as follows:

Taxable Income

+/− Adjustments

+   Tax Preference Items

+/− ACE Adjustments

−   AMT Net Operating Loss Deduction

=   AMTI

−   Exemption

×   20%

−   AMT Foreign Tax Credit

=   Tentative Minimum Tax

−   Regular Tax Liability

=   Alternative Minimum Tax

(a) ADJUSTMENTS

Adjustments can be either positive or negative in calculating AMTI. They represent different accounting methods that must be used for this alternative tax purpose. By far the most common adjustment is the depreciation adjustment.

For AMT purposes, depreciation must be recalculated using the Alternative Depreciation System lives (see Figure 18-1) and using a slower depreciation method. In general, assets that used the 200% declining balance method for regular tax purposes must use the 150% declining balance for AMT purposes. For any given asset, this adjustment is usually positive (increasing AMTI) for the early years of depreciation, and negative for the latter years of depreciation.

Other adjustments include longer amortization lives for certain mining costs, different accounting for long-term contracts and installment sales of certain property, and basis adjustments on the sale or exchange of property (related to the differences in basis due to different depreciation methods).

(b) TAX PREFERENCE ITEMS

Tax preference items—items that can only increase (but not decrease) AMTI—include percentage depletion in excess of basis, tax-exempt interest from private activity bonds issued after August 7, 1986, certain charitable contributions, certain intangible drilling costs, certain reserves for losses on bad debts on financial institutions, pre-1987 accelerated depreciation on real property (over straight line), and certain accelerated depreciation over straight line on leased personal property placed in service before 1987.

(c) ACE ADJUSTMENTS

The Adjusted Current Earnings (ACE) adjustment is designed to increase AMTI by narrowing the differences between taxable income and earnings and profits. Earnings and profits, is a tax term that relates loosely (but not very closely) to the economic income of the company. It is generally used (among other things) to determine for tax purposes what part of a corporate distribution would be considered a dividend, and what part of a corporate distribution would be a return of capital.

For AMT purposes, certain adjustments are made to pre-ACE AMTI to come up with ACE. ACE is then compared to pre-ACE AMTI and 75% of the amount by which ACE exceeds pre-ACE AMTI is added to AMTI as an ACE adjustment.

The dominant component in calculating ACE is depreciation. This third iteration of depreciation required for tax purposes starts with AMT depreciation, and requires all assets to be depreciated over the alternative depreciation life using only the straight line method. Thankfully, the ACE depreciation adjustment has been repealed for assets placed in service after December 31, 1993. So its future impact is limited primarily to MACRS assets placed in service before 1994.

Other income items of significance that need to be added back for ACE purposes include the receipt of life insurance proceeds and interest income from tax exempt obligations. Additionally, certain deductions are not allowed, or must be adjusted for ACE purposes. These include intangible drilling costs, organizational expenditures, LIFO adjustments, and all depletion except cost depletion. Additionally, the basis of property sold or exchanged must be adjusted to it's ACE basis to calculate ACE gain or loss.

(d) OTHER AMT ITEMS

The net operating loss for AMT purposes (ATNOL) is calculated using AMTI instead of regular taxable income or loss. Further, the utilization of an ATNOL is limited to 90% of AMTI. This is very important. This means that the controller cannot assume that just because a company has a large net operating loss, it will have no tax. Typically, if current AMTI is greater than $400,000, no matter how large an ATNOL is, that company will pay at least some AMT. The first $400,000 will usually not trigger any AMT (assuming adequate ATNOLs), since the 10% of this amount that is not eliminated by utilizing the ATNOL will be eliminated by the $40,000 AMT exemption. This $40,000 exemption begins to be phased out as AMTI (after ATNOL) reaches $150,000 and is completely phased out when AMTI (after ATNOL) reaches $310,000.

AMT is also reduced by the AMT foreign tax credit (AMTFTC). This foreign tax credit is similar to the regular tax foreign tax credit, except it is calculated using AMTI and AMT adjustments. As with the ATNOL, the AMTFTC (combined with the ATNOL) cannot eliminate more than 90% of the AMT that would otherwise be calculated without those items.

(e) PLANNING IDEA

Companies that are in AMT that are planning to purchase assets may want to consider leasing. If the economics permit, leasing allows the company deductible expenses for the lease payments without causing an AMT adjustment.

18-5 UNIFORM CAPITALIZATION

The Tax Reform Act of 1986 radically changed how a company accounts for produced goods and goods acquired for resale. Congress came up with a methodology that increased the scope of costs that must be capitalized, as opposed to being directly expensed.

Typically, the uniform capitalization rules, or unicap rules, use a theory of absorption that goes beyond that which is typically required for financial accounting purposes. See Figure 18-2 for a list of costs that are subject to capitalization. Figure 18-2 also lists costs not subject to capitalization and noncapitalizable service costs.

Unicap is a very complex yet important area, especially for manufacturing, wholesaling, and retailing companies. The controller should seek assistance from competent tax consultants in order to minimize capitalization and maximize deductible expenses.

18-6 RESEARCH AND EXPERIMENTAL CREDIT

Since the demise of the Investment Tax Credit, one of the few remaining significant credits is the research and experimental tax credit. This credit is potentially available to any company that is attempting to eliminate uncertainty in product or process

Figure 18-2   Costs Subject to Capitalization.

I. DIRECT PRODUCTION COSTS SUBJECT TO CAPITALIZATION

Direct materials   ❑
Direct labor   ❑

II. INDIRECT PRODUCTION COSTS SUBJECT TO CAPITALIZATION

Indirect labor (including unclassified time)   ❑
Officers' compensation   ❑
Pension and other related costs   ❑
Employee benefit expenses   ❑
Indirect material costs   ❑
Purchasing costs (see also III below)   ❑
Handling costs (excluding "pick and pack" activities)   ❑
Storage costs   ❑
Depreciation and other cost recovery allowances   ❑
Depletion   ❑
Rent   ❑
Taxes (other than state, local, foreign, and franchise taxes assessed on the basis of income) ❑
Insurance   ❑
Utilities   ❑
Repairs and maintenance   ❑
Engineering and design costs   ❑
Spoilage   ❑
Tools and equipment   ❑
Quality control   ❑
Successful bidding costs   ❑
Licensing and franchise costs   ❑
Interest[1]   ❑

III. CAPITALIZABLE SERVICE COSTS
(G&A COSTS BENEFITING PRODUCTION)

Administration and coordination of production   ❑
Personnel operations   ❑
Purchasing operations   ❑
Materials handling and warehousing and storage operations   ❑
Accounting and data services operations   ❑
Data processing   ❑
Security services   ❑
Legal services   ❑

IV. COSTS NOT SUBJECT TO CAPITALIZATION
(Other Than Non-Capitalizable Service Costs)

Selling and *distribution costs (including "pick and pack" activities)*   ❑
Research and experimental expenditures   ❑
Section 179 costs   ❑

[1]Most manufacturers are not required to capitalize interest to inventory because the threshold tests under §263A(f)(1) and Notice 88-99 are not met. Under these rules, a taxpayer must capitalize interest incurred during the production period if the property being produced is (1) real property, (2) personal property with a class life of 20 years or more, or (3) personal property with an estimated production period exceeding two years or (4) personal property with an estimated production period exceeding one year and an estimated cost of production exceeding $1 million.

Figure 18-2   *(continued)*

Section 165 losses	❏
Cost recovery allowances on temporarily idle equipment and facilities	❏
Taxes assessed on the basis of income (including income based franchise taxes)	❏
Strike expenses	❏
Warranty and product liability costs	❏
On-site storage costs	❏
Unsuccessful bidding expenses	❏

V. NON-CAPITALIZABLE SERVICE COSTS

Departments or functions responsible for overall management or for overall policy	❏
Strategic business planning	❏
General financial accounting	❏
General financial planning and financial management	❏
Personnel policy	❏
Quality control policy	❏
Safety engineering policy	❏
Insurance or risk management policy	❏
Environmental management policy	❏
General economic analysis and forecasting	❏
Internal audit	❏
Shareholder, public, and industrial relations	❏
Tax services	❏
Marketing, selling, or advertising	❏

development through use of physical or biological sciences, engineering, or computer science activities. The credit is also available, in certain circumstances, for the development of internal use software.

(a) CALCULATION OF THE CREDIT

Through the wisdom of Congress, the calculation of the credit follows a rather peculiar logic. The amount of current year credit is equal to 20% of the amount by which the current year's qualified research expenses exceed a base amount.

The base amount is equal to the fixed base percentage multiplied by the average annual gross receipts (net of returns and allowances) of the company for the previous four tax years before the current tax year. However, the base amount is never less than 50% of the current year qualified research expenses.

The fixed base percentage is the lesser of the aggregate qualified research expenses for the taxable years beginning after December 31, 1983, and beginning before January 1, 1989, divided by the aggregate gross receipts (net of returns and allowances) for those same years, or 16%. Companies that have fewer than three taxable years in the above period with both gross receipts and qualified research expenses are considered "start-up" companies and must use a fixed base percentage of 3%.

(b) QUALIFIED RESEARCH EXPENSES

Only specific kinds of research expenses qualify for the credit, as calculated above. They include wages paid or incurred for qualified research and experimental services, supplies (excluding depreciable property) used in the conduct of qualified research, payment to another person for the use of computer time in qualified research, and 65% of any amount paid to a nonemployee for qualified research (contract research expenses).

(c) QUALIFIED RESEARCH ACTIVITIES

As mentioned above, qualified research activities primarily involve eliminating uncertainty as to if or how a business component can be developed through the use of the "hard" or computer sciences. Business components include products, processes, computer software, techniques, formulas, and inventions, whether held for sale or lease by the taxpayer or used in the tax payer's trade or business.

Due to the broad definition of qualified research expenses, many companies that are not the typical "white coat" research company may qualify for this credit. The controller should take a close look at the company's activities to ascertain if this credit is applicable.

To reiterate, a tax credit is a true reduction of taxes, not a deferral. If a company discovers that it can utilize this credit, it will immediately reduce its overall tax rate, reduce its tax provision, and increase its cash flow.

18-7 INTERNATIONAL TAX ISSUES

Companies with multinational operations face the daunting task of tax planning with far more complexities than a company with only domestic operations. In addition to all the U.S. tax issues, the company may encounter, among other things, foreign income taxes, value-added taxes, customs taxes, income sourcing issues, and various income tax treaties.

However, with complexity comes opportunity. This is another place where tax consultants may be useful. The task of the controller in an international tax situation is no different than in the domestic situation: to reduce the overall tax burden of the company.

Congress has focused much time and attention on taxation of multinational companies. As a result, the body of U.S. tax law related to international issues is enormously complex. This section will discuss in very general terms some issues that the controller should be aware of as well as potential opportunities.

(a) THE FOREIGN TAX CREDIT

Under U.S. tax law, domestic corporations are taxed on their worldwide income, regardless of source. This would seem to subject a company to double taxation—in the United States and in the country whose source the income came from. To eliminate this double taxation, Congress created the foreign tax credit (FTC). Simply put, the credit is the lesser of foreign source taxable income divided by total taxable income multiplied by the U.S. tax liability, or the amount of foreign income tax paid. There are, however, many complex rules related to implementation of the credit. These include rules on how to source income and expenses, how to segregate income into different baskets, what constitutes a foreign income tax, what items are deemed foreign source or domestic, and so on. A thorough discussion of the FTC could be the subject of an entire book and is beyond the scope of this chapter.

Within the rules and regulations that a controller must deal with in this area, there is some room for planning. A nightmare tax situation (with regard to FTC) is one in which the company has domestic source losses with foreign source income. This can have a negative impact on the companies' ability to utilize FTCs since U.S. source losses reduce foreign source income. If a company finds itself in this situation, it should consider (if possible):

- Deferring foreign source income such as dividends from foreign subsidiaries.
- Accelerate U.S. source income or defer U.S. source deductions.

(b) EARNINGS STRIPPING

Another provision to be wary of is the so-called earnings stripping provisions. These provisions limit interest deductions of U.S. companies (1) whose debt-equity ratio exceeds 1.5 to 1, (2) that pay or accrue interest to a related party that is wholly or partially exempt from U.S. tax (this would include most foreign affiliates or parents), and (3) that have "excess interest expense" (i.e., net interest expense that exceeds 50% of "adjusted taxable income" plus excess limitation carryforwards).

Controllers should be wary of these provisions, especially if debt servicing is a significant amount.

(c) RECORDKEEPING AND REPORTING REQUIREMENTS

Domestic companies that are at least 25% foreign-owned or are a U.S. branch of a foreign corporation have additional and more stringent reporting requirements. These companies must report certain transactions with foreign-related parties and provide information with respect to related parties to the IRS. Additionally, these companies and the foreign-related parties must maintain prescribed records to the extent relevant to the company's U.S. income tax return. The tax law imposes severe penalties for noncompliance with these provisions.

(d) TRANSFER PRICING

Transfer pricing has become a very "hot" issue for the IRS of late. The issue revolves around the pricing of intercompany transactions between a domestic company and foreign-related party. The concern is that the U.S. company will sell goods or services at a reduced price, or buy goods or services at an inflated price to or from the foreign-related party.

Extremely complex regulations have recently been issued. The purpose of the regulations are to ensure that the U.S. and foreign-related party are dealing with each other at "arm's length," or put another way, are dealing with each other as they would if they were not related parties.

It is incumbent upon a controller to make sure that transfer pricing issues are dealt with. This is another area where it may be prudent to gain assistance from tax consultants, as it is very complex, confusing, and could have costly ramifications.

(e) CUSTOMS AND VAT

Another area of taxation that relates particularly to multinational companies is custom duties, value-added tax (VAT), and goods and services taxes (GST). These taxes vary from country to country. It is important that the controller stay on top of these tax requirements, as he or she normally would in a state tax situation.

18-8 MERGERS, ACQUISITIONS, REORGANIZATIONS, EXCHANGES AND LOSSES

Doing justice to the tax issues involved with mergers, acquisitions, reorganizations, exchanges, and losses would take many volumes. The purpose here is to point out various areas that could be helpful or may be troublesome.

(a) MERGERS, ACQUISITIONS, AND REORGANIZATIONS

This is an area where GAAP and tax law differ greatly. Many mergers, acquisitions, and reorganizations occur where the participant's tax basis is far less than the fair market value based on current markets. Without good tax planning in transactions such as these, companies and individuals could have a much higher tax cost than anticipated.

Under the tax code, there are very specific ways that mergers and acquisitions can be tax free. These include statutory mergers, certain stock for stock, and stock for assets transactions. The controller should be aware and should also make his or her tax consultants aware of these transactions before they occur if the structure of the transactions will have the intended results without adverse tax consequences.

IRC § 368 defines the types of reorganizations that typically will not result in taxation of the transaction. Other than like-kind exchanges (discussed next) and § 368, exchanges are generally taxable transactions. In other words, the tax basis of the assets are compared with the fair market value of the assets received, and the difference is either recognized gain or loss. IRC § 368 defines the different tax-free reorganizations as:

(A) A statutory merger or consolidation;

(B) The acquisition by one corporation, in exchange solely for all or a part of its voting stock (or in exchange solely for all or a part of the voting stock of a corporation which is in control of the acquiring corporation), of stock of another corporation if, immediately after the acquisition, the acquiring corporation has control [80%] of such other corporation (whether or not such acquiring corporation had control immediately before the acquisition);

(C) The acquisition by one corporation, in exchange solely for all or a part of its voting stock (or in exchange solely for all or a part of the voting stock of a corporation which is in control of the acquiring corporation), of substantially all of the properties of another corporation, but in determining whether the exchange is solely for stock the assumption by the acquiring corporation of a liability of the other, or the fact that property acquired is subject to a liability, shall be disregarded;

(D) A transfer by a corporation of all or a part of its assets to another corporation if immediately after the transfer, the transferor, or one or more of its shareholders (including persons who were shareholders immediately before the transfer), or any combination thereof, is in control of the corporation to which the assets are transferred; but only if, in pursuance of the plan, stock, or securities of the corporation to which the assets are transferred, are distributed in a transaction which qualifies under §§ 354, 355, or 356. [Section 354 discusses certain exchanges of stock that are parties to the plan of reorganization; § 355 discusses certain distributions of stock; and § 356 discusses receipt of other property besides stock.]

(E) A recapitalization;

(F) A mere change in identity, form, or place of organization of one corporation, however effected; or

(G) A transfer by a corporation of all or part of its assets to another corporation in a title 11 or similar case, but only if, in pursuance of the plan, stock, or securities of the corporation to which the assets are transferred, are distributed in a transaction that qualifies under §§ 354, 355, and 356.

As one can probably tell from this excerpt of the Internal Revenue Code, the tax-free reorganization provisions are highly complex and require very specialized expertise to interpret correctly.

To reiterate, without careful consideration of the above, the controller may face unintended and unfavorable tax consequences.

(b) EXCHANGES

Most exchanges (one party gives up cash, securities, or other property in exchange for cash, securities, or other property) are taxed on the difference between the basis given up and the fair market value of the property received. Aside from reorganizations, certain exchanges of similar kinds of property may also be made without tax recognition of gains or losses. These "like-kind exchanges" are defined in § 1031 of the Internal Revenue Code.

Congress has defined "like-kind" very broadly. Basically, if investment property is exchanged for investment property, or trade or business property is exchanged for other trade or business property, the exchange is considered to be "like-kind." There are notable exceptions (as always) to what can be exchanged tax-free. Section 1031 defines the following property as exempt from the "like-kind" exchange rules:

(A) Stock in trade or other property held for sale [inventory],

(B) Stocks, bonds, or notes,

(C) Other securities, or evidence of indebtedness or interest,

(D) Interests in partnerships,

(E) Certificates of trust or beneficial interests or

(F) Choices in action.

If cash or debt is involved in the exchange, then it is possible that a portion of the realized gain can be recognized at the time of the exchange. Otherwise, the gain on the exchange will be deferred effectively through retaining the basis of the property given up. The provisions also allows (in certain circumstances) 3-party exchange transactions.

(c) LOSSES

In general terms, when a corporation incurs a net operating loss (NOL) during a year, it can take this loss and apply it to income of other years. Specifically, it can "carry-back" the loss for three years, and if not utilized, then "carryforward" the loss for 15 years.

To prevent abuse (real or perceived), Congress has implemented certain rules that limit the use of NOLs after certain transactions. The two most common limitations are the separate return limitation year (SRLY) and the loss limitation from a 50% change of ownership (§ 382 limitation).

(d) SRLYs

In general, SRLY rules apply when a company that has NOLs is acquired by another company, and then files a consolidated return with that other company. Typically in a consolidated return situation, all of the consolidated companies combine their income and losses (including NOLs) to determine the net income or loss of the consolidated group. When there is a company with a SRLY, that company's NOL can only be offset by that same company's taxable income. In other words, the SRLY company's NOL cannot be utilized by any other member of the consolidated group.

The controller must be wary of this. In many acquisition situations, the purchase price may include the value of NOLs. It is important that the controller be aware of any limitation on a NOL, so that the value of the NOL is calculated with the ultimate chance of its utilization in mind.

(e) § 382 LIMITATION

Under the provisions of § 382, if during what is typically a 3-year period (the testing period), the percentage of stock owned by 1 or more 5% shareholders (or groups of shareholders considered to be a "5% shareholder") has increased by more than 50 percentage points over the lowest percentage of stock owned by those same 5% shareholders, there is considered to be a change of ownership of the corporation, if that corporation at the time has NOLs.

If this occurs, the value of the stock of the corporation (immediately before the ownership change) is multiplied by the federal long-term tax-exempt rate to come up with the amount of NOL of that company that is allowed to be utilized each year. Any of the limited loss not utilized in a given year can carry forward to the next year. Also, if the corporation, at the time of the ownership change, had net unrecognized built in gains or losses, at the point they are recognized, these gains or losses will increase or decrease the amount of limited losses that can be utilized.

The rules regarding changes of ownership are highly complex, and like many other areas of the tax code, require expertise to properly interpret. As with SRLYs, the controller or other company personnel should evaluate the potential for utilizing § 382 losses before assessing or accepting a purchase value for them.

18-9 STATE AND LOCAL TAX ISSUES

As federal budget deficits put more pressure on the federal government, it is likely that more and more governmental responsibilities will become the domain of state and local government. This will put more pressure on state and local governments to either increase taxes or be more efficient in collecting the taxes already on the books.

Since state and local taxes involve the laws of literally hundreds of jurisdictions, it is impossible to list specific issues and planning ideas that would be universally effective. However, there are certain state and local tax considerations that multistate companies can employ that will help keep state and local taxes to a minimum. These considerations relate to state and local income taxes, sales and use taxes, property taxes, and employment taxes.

(a) STATE AND LOCAL INCOME TAX CONSIDERATIONS

The first duty of the controller, in state and local income tax planning is to determine those jurisdictions (states and, as appropriate, cities) where the company has activities (e.g., sales, property, and/or wages) sufficient to render it subject to income tax filing and payment requirements. This is the concept of *nexus*.

Every state (and some localities) has a slightly different definition of nexus, and it is important to determine if the company meets that threshold. In general, merely shipping sales into a state is not enough to establish nexus. On the other extreme, if a company has property, payroll, and sales in a state, it is likely that it does have nexus.

If the controller (or tax executive) incorrectly determines nexus, the company will not be filing tax returns where it is subject to tax and later potentially be subject to back taxes and penalties. Alternately, if it is determined incorrectly that a company has nexus in a state or locality, the company needlessly subjects itself to taxes that it shouldn't be paying.

Once it is determined that the company does have nexus in a state or locality, the controller or tax executive should analyze the rules for computing the tax base (e.g., modifications from federal taxable income, characterization of income as business or nonbusiness, rules for allocating and apportioning income). Every state and locality may have a different method of calculating what base of income that it taxes.

Typically a state will apportion income based on three factors:

1. Where property is located (the property factor). Sometimes this includes the rental expense of property for the year multiplied by a numerical factor such as 7 or 8.

2. Sales (the sales factor). This is typically the state where title passes for the goods sold.

3. Payroll (the payroll factor). This is determined by where the employee carries out his employment function.

These factors vary from state to state and are weighted differently in their application. A common apportionment calculation would take the federal taxable income adjusted by state factors, and multiply it by a sum of three factors—the property factor, the sales factor, and the payroll factor. These factors are usually calculated with the state portion of the factor as the numerator, and the total (national or worldwide) factor as the denominator. For example, if Company A had $100,000 of payroll in state A, and had a total payroll of $500,000, its payroll factor for state A would be 20%. If Company A had a sales factor of 15% in state A and a property factor of 55% in state A, and federal taxable income adjusted for state items of $1,000,000, its state taxable income would be $300,000. This is calculated by taking the sum of the 3 factors (20% + 15% + 55%) or 90% and dividing this by 3 to get an average of 30%. The 30% would then be multiplied by the $1 million of state-adjusted taxable income to arrive at a state taxable income of $300,000.

With consolidated or affiliated groups, the controller or tax executive should review the available filing options (e.g., separate returns, consolidated returns, combined returns), if any, that are available and choose the most advantageous filing option. For example, if Companies A and B file a consolidated return where A has separate taxable income and B has a separate taxable loss, it may be helpful to file separately (if allowed) in states that B has nexus and A does not. This would keep A's income from being taxed in states where it has no nexus.

Some states require combined filing where related companies have sufficiently integrated operations (unitary companies). If the companies or a related company engages in business in a state that applies this unitary concept, the controller should determine whether combined returns are required or available and whether unitary status affects the treatment of intercompany payments. This could have an impact on the total state tax liability.

(b) STATE AND LOCAL SALES/USE TAX CONSIDERATIONS

Sales and use taxes are the taxes that states and localities charge when a company sells an item at retail, or internally uses an item that it purchases. These taxes can be significant. Complying with all applicable tax laws can also be very cumbersome, since in many states, sales and use taxes are legislated and administered by localities.

The controller should determine those jurisdictions (states and, as appropriate, cities, counties, districts, etc.) where the company has activities (e.g., sales, property, and/or wages) sufficient to render it subject to sales/use tax collection or payment and filing obligations. If a company's multijurisdictional sales are significant, it may warrant the use of experts in this area.

Once jurisdiction and sales/use tax nexus is determined, the company should inventory those items sold by the corporation that are subject to sales tax in the jurisdictions where there is a collection/filing requirement. The company should also inventory those items for which the company is subject to sales or use tax when it makes purchases. The company should also properly document any exemptions from the sales/use tax that are available to the company.

As with income taxes, failure to get a good handle on the jurisdictional filing requirements can mean either too much tax can be paid, or back taxes and penalties can be owed.

(c) PROPERTY TAX CONSIDERATIONS

In addition to taxing income, sales, and use of property, states, counties, cities, and districts impose property taxes—taxes for owning property, both real and personal.

Typically, property taxes are assessed based on a determined value by the state or local taxing authority. The controller or tax executive should review, and if appropriate, challenge property tax assessments. In many taxing jurisdictions, there are very short periods during which the taxpayer must act in the process of challenging an assessment. Challenging assessments can often be successful, and hence save the company significant amounts of taxes.

The controller should also determine those jurisdictions where the company is required to file personal property tax returns. Failure to accurately complete these returns can lead to fines, penalties, and back taxes.

(d) EMPLOYMENT TAX CONSIDERATIONS

Since every state and many localities can have different withholding requirements, it is important to determine the appropriate state and local withholding from employee compensation (e.g., the correct state of withholding, the amount of withholding for income tax and unemployment tax, any local withholdings). The controller or tax executive should also periodically review state unemployment withholding for possible reduction opportunities through experience methods, or other methods.

State and local taxes can be extremely burdensome. However, they make up a significant percent of a company's tax expense, and they are ignored at the controller's and the company's peril.

18-10 FASB STATEMENT NO. 109

In February 1992, the Financial Accounting Standards Board issued FASB Statement No. 109. This new and hopefully final statement supersedes both FASB Statement No. 96 and APB Opinion No. 11. Adoption of FASB 109 was effective for fiscal years beginning after December 15, 1992. It adopts the liability method of income tax accounting. What follows is a brief summary of the provisions of FASB 109.

(a) RECOGNITION

FASB 109 allows for the recognition of deferred tax assets and liabilities for the expected future tax consequences of events that have already been recognized either in the financial statements or the income tax returns. Deferred tax liabilities are recognized for temporary differences (items in which the timing of book and tax recognition of income or expense differs) that will result in increased tax liability (taxable amounts) in future years. Deferred tax assets are recognized for deductible temporary differences, future utilization of NOLs, and future utilization of tax credits that will result in decreased tax liability in future years. However, recognition of deferred tax assets are subject to certain measurement requirements.

(b) MEASUREMENT

FASB 109 generally tries to apply a logical, yet conservative, approach to measuring liabilities and assets. The deferred tax assets and liabilities are generally measured using tax rates that are expected to apply to the tax year in which the deferred tax asset or liability is expected to be utilized. The tax rate used should realistically take into consideration any graduated rates plus a state tax rate to come up with an average or effective tax rate.

The recognition of a net deferred tax asset, however, is not always a given. The company must evaluate whether or not it's "more likely than not" that some or all of the deferred tax asset will or will not be realized. To the extent that it is "more likely than not" that the asset will not be realized, the company must book a valuation allowance against that portion of the deferred tax asset. "More likely than not" means that the realization likelihood is greater than 50%. With these new measurement standards, the company can incorporate expectations as to future operations of the company—a major departure from the philosophy of FASB Statement 96. However, the corollary is not true for deferred tax liabilities. Future losses cannot be anticipated for minimizing deferred tax liabilities.

(c) BUSINESS COMBINATIONS

In business combinations, FASB 109 requires a deferred tax asset or liability be recognized for differences between the assigned book value and the tax bases of assets acquired and liabilities assumed. This would not include goodwill that is not deductible. However, since goodwill can be amortizable over 15 years under § 197, the basis of tax-amortizable goodwill would be included. Pre-FASB 109 business combinations would be remeasured on this basis if prior financial statements are restated. If there is no restatement, the remaining balances of assets (excluding nontax-amortizable goodwill) and liabilities should be adjusted to their pretax amounts from their net-of-tax amounts. Any differences between the adjusted amounts and their respective tax bases would be considered temporary differences. For transition purposes, the tax benefit related to the acquired deductible temporary differences, NOLs, and tax credit carryforwards are first applied to reduce any acquired goodwill to zero. If any benefit remains, it is then applied to reduce acquired noncurrent intangible assets to zero. If benefits still remain, they are used to credit the excess, if any, to the cumulative effect adjustment relating to the accounting change. Any deferred tax liability relating to acquired taxable temporary differences would be included in the accounting change cumulative effect adjustment.

If the above procedure for accounting for pre-FASB 109 business combinations would prove to be too onerous, the Statement allows for a short-cut method. Instead of adjusting net-of-tax balances, the difference between those unadjusted balances and the tax bases of those assets would be considered temporary differences and a deferred tax asset or liability would be recognized for those temporary differences at the transition date.

(d) APB OPINION 23 TEMPORARY DIFFERENCES

For domestic subsidiaries, corporate joint ventures, or U.S. steamship enterprises, undistributed earnings would trigger the recognition of a deferred tax liability on a prospective basis (post implementation). Generally, no deferred tax liability is required for differences arising before the implementation of FASB 109.

APB Opinion 23 allowed companies with foreign subsidiaries to escape the requirement for providing tax on those foreign earnings if those companies permanently reinvested those earnings in the foreign subsidiaries. Under FASB 109, this exception remains in effect.

(e) TAX PLANNING STRATEGIES

When evaluating the need for and amount of a valuation allowance, it is permissible to consider tax planning strategies. However, this tax benefit must be tempered by the additional tax losses that these strategies might create through additional expense or loss recognition. However, it is not permissible to use tax planning strategies to reduce a deferred tax liability.

(f) INTERCORPORATE TAX ALLOCATIONS

If a company or group of companies files a consolidated return, yet has separate financial reporting requirements, there could be issues as to who gets allocated what portion of the income tax. Under FASB 109, income tax allocation must follow the broader principles of the Statement. Say, for example, that Company A and Company B file a consolidated tax return. Company A has taxable income of $50,000, and Company B has a loss of $100,000. Combined, they have a NOL for the year of $50,000 and, hence, no income tax. Under the Statement, it would not be permissible to allocate a zero tax to both companies. This is because on a separate company basis, Company A would be liable for tax. It would be proper to allocate a tax to each on a separate company basis. Perhaps an intercompany receivable account would be set up for B (and a payable account for A) for A's use of B's loss. This would be an intuitive way of reconciling the logic of no consolidated tax, with the separate reporting requirements.

(g) FINANCIAL STATEMENT DISCLOSURE

For the most part, the disclosures required under FASB 109 are similar to those required under FASB 96 and APB 11. There are, however, some differences. The components of the net deferred tax liability or asset must be disclosed. The disclosure would include total deferred tax liabilities, total deferred tax assets, and the amount of any valuation allowance. If there is a valuation allowance, this can be disclosed either on the face of the balance sheet, or in the accompanying notes to the financial statements. Additionally, changes in the valuation allowance must also be disclosed. The company must also disclose the tax effect of carryforwards and temporary differences that create significant amounts of deferred tax assets and liabilities.

(h) FINANCIAL STATEMENT PRESENTATION

As a point of simplification from FASB 96, current and noncurrent classifications of deferred tax assets and liabilities are characterized based on the nature of the related asset or liability; not based on when the difference is expected to turn or reverse. If there is a valuation allowance, it would be allocated pro-rata between current and noncurrent. For presentation purposes, there is an offset between current tax assets and liabilities to come to one net number for each tax paying component and tax jurisdiction. The same is true for noncurrent assets.

18-11 SELECTED REFERENCES

Internal Revenue Code, Chicago, IL: Commerce Clearing House, 1993.

Implementing the New Rules on Accounting for Income Taxes, FASB Statement 109, Ernst & Young LLP, 1992.

Income Tax Regulations, Chicago, IL: Commerce Clearing House, 1994.

The Ernst & Young Tax-Saving Strategies Guide 1995, New York: John Wiley & Sons, 1995.

Ernst & Young's Guide to the New Tax Law, New York: John Wiley & Sons, 1993.

PART THREE

PLANNING AND CONTROLLING OPERATIONS

CHAPTER 19

General Discussion of Accounting/Statistical Standards: Benchmarking

19-1 MEANING OF ACCOUNTING/STATISTICAL CONTROL

Control by definition assumes that a plan of action or a standard has been established against which performance can be measured. To achieve the objectives that have been set forth for the business enterprise, controls must be developed so that decisions can be made in conformance with the plan.

In small plants or organizations, the manager or owner personally can observe and control all operations. He or she normally knows all the factory workers and by daily observation of the work flow can determine the efficiency of operations. It is easy to observe the production effort of each employee as well as the level of raw materials and work-in-process inventory. In most cases, by the observation of the factory operation, he can detect inefficient or improper methods and correct such conditions on the spot. The sales orders can be reviewed and determination made about whether shipments are being made promptly. Through intimate knowledge of the total business—communicating on a daily basis with most employees, including salesmen, as well as customers—the owner is able to discern the effectiveness of sales effort and customer satisfaction with the products.

However, as the organization grows, this close contact or direct supervision by the owner or manager is necessarily diminished. Other means of control are required to manage effectively—accounting controls and statistical reports. By the use of reports, management is enabled to plan, supervise, direct, evaluate, and coordinate the activities of the various functions, departments, and operating units. Accounting controls and reports of operations are part of a well-integrated plan to maintain efficiency and determine unfavorable variances or trends. The use of the accounting structure allows for the control of costs and expenses and comparison of such expenditures to some predetermined plan of action. Through the measurement of performance by means of accounting and statistical records and reports, management can provide appropriate guidance and direct the business activities. The effective application of accounting controls must be fully integrated into the company plans and provide a degree of before-the-fact control. The accounting/statistical control system must include records that establish accountability and responsibility reporting to really be effective.

19-2 EXTENT OF ACCOUNTING/STATISTICAL CONTROL

Effective control extends to every operation of the business, including every unit, every function, every department, every territory or area, and every individual. Accounting control encompasses all aspects of financial transactions such as cash disbursements, cash receipts, funds flow, judicious investment of cash, and protection of the funds from unauthorized use. It includes control of receivables, avoidance of losses through inappropriate credit and collection procedures. Accounting control includes planning and controlling inventories to prevent disruption of production schedules and shipments or losses from scrap and obsolescence. It involves generating all the necessary facts on the performance of all functions such as manufacturing, research, engineering, marketing, and financial activities. It is mandatory that management be informed about the utilization of labor and material against a plan in producing the finished goods. The effectiveness of the sales effort in each territory or for each product must be subjected to review by management. Control relates to every classification in the balance sheet or statement of financial position and to each item in the statement of income and expense. In short, accounting/statistical control extends to all activities of the business. The accounting system that includes the accounting controls when integrated with the operating controls provides a powerful tool for management to plan and direct the performance of the business enterprise.

Statistical control also may relate to the nonfinancial quantitative measurement of any business functions and their effect, for example, customer satisfaction, development time for new products, cycle time from receipt of customer order to delivery of product.

19-3   NEED FOR STANDARDS

As industry has developed, grown, and become more complex, the need for increased efficiency and productivity has become more imperative. The successful executives developed more effective means of regulating and controlling the activities. It is no longer sufficient just to know the cost to manufacture or sell. There is a real need to know if we are using the most economical manufacturing techniques and processes. The distribution and selling costs must be evaluated and measured against some predetermined factors. Performance measurement should be applied to all activities. It is essential that a yardstick of desirable or planned results be established against which actual results may be compared if the performance measurement is to be effective. It is natural to compare current performance with historical performance such as last month, last quarter, or last year. Such a comparison points out trends, but it also serves to perpetuate inefficiencies. This comparison only serves a useful purpose if the measuring stick or past performance represents effective and efficient performance. Furthermore, changes in technologies, price levels, manufacturing processes, and the relative volume of production tend to limit the value of historical costs in determining what current costs should be.

There certainly is a compelling need for something other than historical costs for the standard of performance. Aside from cost control, for planning and pricing, management needs cost information that is not distorted by defective material, poor worker performance, or other unusual characteristics. Scientific management recognizes the value and need for some kind of engineering standards to plan manufacturing operations and evaluate the effectiveness with which the objectives are being accomplished. Engineering standards, expressed in financial terms, become cost standards; these standards, based on careful study and analysis about what it should cost to perform the operations by the best methods, become a much more reliable yardstick with which to measure and control costs.

Standards are the foundation and basis of effective accounting control. Standards provide the management tools with which to measure and judge performance. The use of standards is as adaptable to the control of income or expense as to the control of assets or liabilities. Standards are applicable to all phases of business and are an extremely important management tool.

19-4   DEFINITION OF STANDARDS

A standard of any type is a measuring stick or the means by which something else is judged. The standard method of doing anything can usually be described as the best method devised, as far as humanly possible, at the time the standard is set. It follows that the standard cost is the amount that should be expended under normal operating conditions. It is a predetermined cost scientifically determined in advance, in contrast to an actual or historical cost. It is not an actual or average cost, although past experience may be a factor in setting the standard.

Since a standard has been defined as a scientifically developed measure of performance, it follows that at least two conditions are implied in setting the standard:

1. *Standards are the result of careful investigation or analysis of past performance and take into consideration expected future conditions.* They are not mere guesses; they are the opinions, based on available facts, of the men best qualified to judge what performance should be.

2. *Standards may need review and revision from time to time.* A standard is set on the basis of certain conditions. As these conditions change, the standard must change; otherwise, it would not be a true measuring stick. Where there is really effective teamwork, and particularly, where standards are related to incentive payments, the probability of change is great.

Most of the foregoing comments on standards relate to that phase of the definition on which there is general agreement. There are, however, differences of opinion that seem to relate principally to the following points:

1. Whether a standard should be (a) a *current standard,* that is, one that reflects what performance should be in the period for which the standard is to be used, or (b) a *basic standard,* which serves merely as a point of reference.

2. The level at which a standard should be set—an *ideal* level of accomplishment, a *normal* level, or the *expected* level.

Where standard costs are carried into the formal records and financial statements, the current standard is generally the one used. Reference to the variances immediately indicates the extent to which actual costs departed from what they should have been in the period. A basic standard, on the other hand, does not indicate what performance should have been. Instead, it is somewhat like the base on which a price index is figured. Basic standards are usually based on prices and production levels prevailing when the standards are set. When once established, they are permanent and remain unchanged until the manufacturing processes change. Thus they are a stationary basis of measurement. Improvement or lack of improvement involves the comparison of ratios or percentages of actual to the base standard.

The level at which standards should be set is discussed later in this chapter under the subject of standards for cost control.

19-5 ADVANTAGES OF STANDARDS

It has already been mentioned that standards arose, as part of the scientific management movement, from the necessity of better control of manufacturing costs. The relationship between this need and the advantages of standards is close. However, the benefits from the use of standards extend beyond the relationship with cost control to all the other applications, such as price setting or inventory valuation. Therefore, it may be well to summarize the principal advantages of standards, and the related scientific methods, by the four primary functions in which they are used:

1. *In Controlling Costs.*

    a. *Standards provide a better measuring stick of performance.* The use of standards sets out the area of excessive cost that otherwise might not be known or realized. Without scientifically set standards, cost comparison is limited to other periods that in themselves may contain inefficiencies.

    b. *Use of the "principle of exception" is permitted, with the consequent saving of much time.* It is not necessary to review and report on all operations but only those that depart significantly from standard. The attention of management may be focused on those spots requiring corrective action.

    c. *Economies in accounting costs are possible.* Clerical costs may be reduced because fewer records are necessary and simplified procedures may be adopted. Many of the detailed subsidiary records, such as production orders or time reports, are not necessary. Again, if inventories are carried as a standard value, there is no need to calculate actual costs each time new lots are made or received. Still further, much of the data for month-end closing can be set up in advance with a reduction in peak load work.

    d. *A prompter reporting of cost control information is possible.* Through the use of simplified records and procedures and the application of the exception principle, less time is required to secure the necessary information.

    e. *Standards serve as incentives to personnel.* If an employee has a fair goal, he will tend to work more efficiently with the consequent reduction in cost. This applies to executives, supervisors, and workers alike.

2. *In Setting Selling Prices.*

    a. *Better cost information is available as a basis for setting prices.* Through the use of predetermined standards, costs are secured that are free from abnormal distortions caused by excess spoilage and other unusual conditions. Furthermore, the use of standard overhead rates eliminates the influence of current activity. A means is provided to secure, over the long run, a full recovery of overhead expenses, including marketing, administrative, and research expense.

    b. *Flexibility is added to selling price data.* Through the use of predetermined rates, changes in the product or processes can be quickly reflected in the cost. Furthermore, adjustments to material prices or labor rates are easily made. Again, the use of standards requires a distinction between fixed and variable costs. This cost information permits cost calculations on different bases. Since pricing is sometimes a matter of selection of alternatives, this flexibility is essential.

    c. *Prompter pricing data can be furnished.* Again, the use of predetermined rates permits the securing of information more quickly.

3. *In Valuing Inventories.*

    a. *A "better" cost is secured.* Here, too, as in pricing applications, a more reliable cost is secured. The effect of idle capacity, or of abnormal wastes or inefficiencies, is eliminated.

    b. *Simplicity in valuing inventories is obtained.* All like products are valued a
the same cost. This not only assists in the recurring monthly closings but als
is an added advantage in pricing the annual physical inventory.

4. *In Budgetary Planning.*

    a. *Determination of total standard costs is facilitated.* The standard unit cost
provide the basic data for converting the sales and production schedules int
total costs. The unit costs can readily be translated into total costs for any vol
ume or mixture of product by simple multiplication. Without standards, ex
tensive analysis is necessary to secure the required information because o
the inclusion of nonrecurring costs.

    b. *The means is provided for setting out anticipated substandard performance.* A
history of the variances is available, together with the causes. Since actua
costs cannot be kept exactly in line with standard costs, this record provide
the basis for forecasting the variances that can reasonably be expected in th
budget period under discussion. This segregation permits a determination o
realistic operating results without losing sight of unfavorable expected costs

19-6 RELATIONSHIP OF ENTITY GOALS TO PERFORMANCE STANDARDS

Much of the discussion in this chapter relates to detailed performance measures o
standards. However, prior to any review of such standards, a key relationship to certai
company goals or broad financial standards should be emphasized.

Some of the overall *financial* goals for a business, as outlined in Chapter 7, in
clude (1) measures of *profitability,* such as return on shareholder equity, return on as
sets, return on sales, (2) measures of *growth,* such as increase in sales, increase in ne
income, and increase in earnings per share, and (3) *cash flow* measures, including ag
gregate operating cash flow or free cash flow. But is there, or should there be, any re
lationship between such overall goals, which are a type of standard, and more specifi
performance measures, such as the direct labor hour standard in cost center 21 fo
manufacturing product A? A business usually has goals or objectives as well as strate
gies for reaching them. It is only logical, therefore, that the goals or standards of a cos
center, or factory, or function or division, support the entity goals. The hierarchy o
goals, or performance measures or standards, may be pictured as a pyramid. (See Fig
ure 19-1.)

In examining performance measures, beginning at the top of the pyramid (com
pany goals) and moving down the structure, these characteristics exist (although no
all are identified):

- Performance measures usually become narrower and more specific.
- The planning horizon becomes shorter.
- In the lower levels, cost factors tend to dominate more; and the measurement o
activity period shortens considerably from years to months, days, or even hours

Performance measures at the lower levels should be expressed in terms of wha
an individual employee can do. For example, an accounts payable clerk might have as a

Figure 19-1   The Hierarchy of Performance Measures.

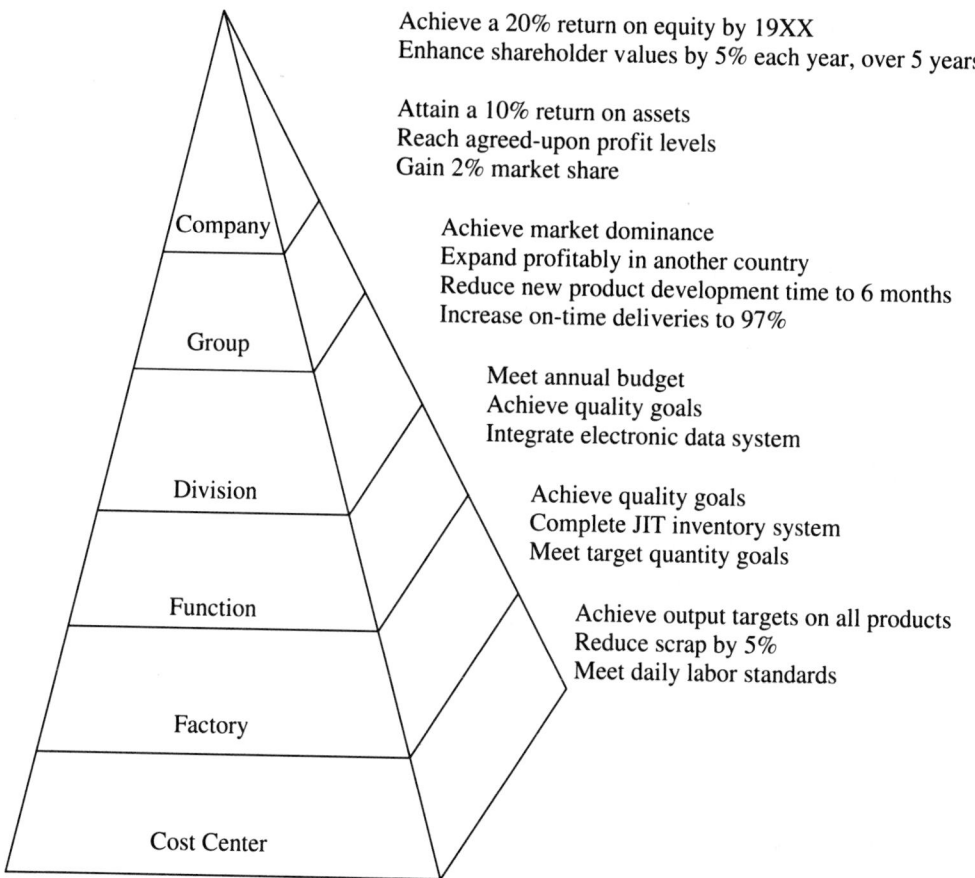

standard the number of invoices processed per day, or the number of cash discounts taken (or lost). This activity level performance cannot be directly measured against a percent return on assets goal.

As the standards are expressed in terms of smaller, specific tasks, the time span between assigning the task, accomplishing the task and rewarding the employee should grow shorter.

Care should be taken that objectives at the lower levels are not contradictory. For example, encouraging higher throughput should not be at the expense of causing excess inventories in another department. A given individual, cost center, or department should not be overpowered by having to meet too many different standards. Standards should be current, that is, they should relate to the processes or methods in use—not obsolete ones. They should be updated minimally each year, ideally, each quarter.

Formulating consistent standards that move the company objective forward takes a great deal of thought and time and is a management task of great importance.

19-7 TYPES OF STANDARDS NEEDED

(a) STANDARDS FOR ALL BUSINESS ACTIVITY

Managerial control extends to all business functions—selling, production, finance, and research. It would appear highly desirable, therefore, to have available standards for measuring effort and results in all these activities. The word *standard* in much of the accounting literature applies to manufacturing costs. But the fact remains that the principles underlying the development of standards can and should be applied to many nonmanufacturing functions. Business executives generally do not question the need or desirability of standards for the control of administrative, distribution, and financial activities; they do, however, recognize the difficulties involved. Some activities are more susceptible to measurement than others, but application of some standard is generally possible. Moreover, as business processes change, some performance standards will increase in importance, while others will decrease, for example, the use of a labor standard in which "direct" labor is less crucial and will be combined with related service support labor standards such as inspection or quality control.

(b) STANDARDS FOR INDIVIDUAL PERFORMANCE

Costs are controlled by people. It is through the action of an individual or group of individuals that costs are corrected or reduced to an acceptable level. It is by the efforts of the individual salesman that the necessary sales volume is secured. It is largely through the operational control of the departmental foreman that labor efficiency is maintained. As a result, any standards, to be most effective, must relate to specific phases of performance rather than merely general results. In a manufacturing operation, for example, standards should relate to the quantity of labor, material, or overhead in the execution of a particular operation—rather than the complete product cost standard. In the selling field, a sales quota must be set for the individual salesman, perhaps by product, and not just for the branch or territory.

Thus the setting of standards and measurement of performance against such yeardsticks fit into the scheme of "responsibility accounting."

Keeping in mind these general comments, specific types of standards can now be examined. In addition to the remarks in this chapter, further observations are made in some of the chapters in which the relevant function is reviewed.

(c) MATERIAL QUANTITY STANDARDS

In producing an article, one of the most obvious cost factors is the quantity of material used. Quantitative standards, based on engineering specifications, outline the kind and quantity of material that should be used to make the product. This measuring stick is the primary basis for material cost control. This quantity standard, when multiplied by the unit material price standard, results in the cost standard. When more than one type of material is involved, the sum of the individual material cost standards equals the total standard material cost of the product.

(d) MATERIAL PRICE STANDARDS

To isolate cost variances arising out of excess material usage from those arising because of price changes, it is necessary to establish a material price standard. Usually, this price standard represents the expected cost instead of a desired or "efficient" cost. In many companies, this price is set for a period of a year, and, although actual cost may fluctuate, these changes are not reflected in the standard unit cost of material used. In other words, every piece of material used is charged with this predetermined cost.

(e) LABOR QUANTITY STANDARDS

The labor content of many products is the most costly element. But whether it is the most costly or not, it is usually important. And because we are dealing with the human element, the labor cost is one of the most variable. It is indeed a fertile field for cost reduction and cost control.

For these reasons it is necessary to know the amount of labor needed to produce the article. The technique is that of determining the time needed to complete each operation when working under standard conditions; hence time and motion study is involved.

(f) LABOR RATE STANDARDS

The price of labor is generally determined by factors outside the complete control of the individual business, perhaps as a result of union negotiations or the prevailing rate in the area. In any event, it is desirable to have a fixed labor rate on each operation to be able to isolate high costs resulting from the use of an excess quantity of labor. Also, the utilization of labor within a plant is within the control of management, and some rate variances arise of actions controllable by it. Examples are the assignment of the wrong men (too high a rate) to the job or the use of overtime.

The standard time required, when multiplied by the standard rate, gives the standard labor cost of the operation.

(g) MANUFACTURING OVERHEAD EXPENSE STANDARDS

One of the many problems most controllers must resolve is that of determining standards for the control of manufacturing overhead as well as absorption into inventory. The determination of these standards is somewhat more complicated than in the development of material or labor standards. Several conditions are responsible:

1. Manufacturing overhead consists of a great variety of expenses, each of which reacts in a different fashion at varying levels of plant activity. Some costs, such as depreciation, remain largely independent of plant activity; others vary with changes in production, but not in direct proportion. Examples are supervisory labor, maintenance, and clerical expense. Still other overhead expense varies directly with, and proportionately to, plant volume. This may include certain supplies, indirect labor, and fuel expense.

2. Control of overhead expenses rests with a large number of individuals in the organization. For example, the chief maintenance engineer may be responsible for maintenance costs; the factory accountant, for factory clerical costs; foremen in productive departments, for indirect labor.

3. The proper estimate of the rate and amount of production must be made to serve as the basis of setting standard rates. An improper level of activity not

only affects the statement of income and expense but also gives management an erroneous picture of the cost of an insufficient volume of business and distorts inventory values.

Overhead expenses are best controlled through the use of a flexible budget. It requires a segregation of fixed and variable expenses, and proper analysis and control permit a realistic look at overhead variances in terms of cause: (1) volume, (2) rate of expenditure, and (3) efficiency.

Standards for manufacturing overhead can be expressed in the total amount budgeted by each type of expense as well as unit standards for each item, such as power cost per operating hour or supplies per man-hour. Such standards should reflect the impact of JIT production techniques as well as the "cost drivers" (see Chapter 23).

(h) SALES STANDARDS

Sales standards may be set for the purpose of controlling and measuring the effectiveness of the sales or marketing operations. They also may be used for incentive awards, stimulating sales efforts or the reallocation of sales resources. The most common form of standard for a territory, branch, or salesman is the sales quota, usually expressed as a dollar of physical volume. Other types of standards found useful in managing and directing sales effort are these:

Number of total customers to be retained.

Number of new customers to be secured.

Number of personal calls to be made per period.

Number of telephone contacts to be made per period.

Average size of order to be secured.

Amount of gross profit to be obtained.

(i) DISTRIBUTION COST STANDARDS

Just as production standards have been found useful in controlling manufacturing costs, so an increasing number of companies are finding that distribution cost standards are a valuable aid in properly directing the selling effort. The extent of application and degree of completeness of distribution cost standards will differ from production standards, but the potential benefits from the use of such standards are equally important.

Some general standards can be used in measuring the distribution effort and results; however, more effective standards are those measuring individual performance. Some illustrative standards are listed here:

Selling expense per unit sold.

Selling expense as a percent of net sales.

Cost per account sold.

Cost per call.

Cost per day.

Cost per mile of travel.

Cost per sales order.

In addition to individual performance standards, another type of control relates to budgets for selling expenses. The procedure for setting budgets is similar to that used for manufacturing operations.

(j) ADMINISTRATIVE EXPENSE STANDARDS

As business expands and volume increases, there is a tendency for administrative expenses to increase proportionately and get out of line. The same need for control exists for these types of expenses as for manufacturing or production costs. Control can be exercised through departmental or responsibility budgets as well as through unit or individual performance standards. The general approach to control administrative expenses is essentially the same as for control of selling and manufacturing expenses. It is necessary to develop an appropriate standard for each function or operation to be measured.

Examples of types of standards to be considered are as follows:

Function	Standard Unit of Measurement
Purchasing	Cost per purchase order
Billing	Cost per invoice rendered
Personnel	Cost per employee hired
Traffic	Cost per shipment
Payroll	Cost per employee
Clerical	Cost per item handled (filed)

(k) FINANCIAL RATIOS

The types of standards discussed to this point relate primarily to human performance associated with elements of the statement of income and expense—sales revenues, cost factors, and expense categories of several types. Yet another category of standards deals with the utilization of assets or shareholders' equity, or the liquidity of the entity. These measures relating to financial condition and profitability rates are of special interest to the financial executives in testing business plans and the financial health of the enterprise.

Chapters 7 and 8 dealt in some detail with many financial and operating ratios, but a short list of some of the more important measures includes:

1. Current ratio.
2. Quick ratio.
3. Ratio of net sales to receivables.
4. Turnover of inventory.
5. Turnover of current assets.
6. Ratio of net sales to working capital.
7. Ratio of net sales to assets.

8. Return on assets.
9. Return on shareholders' equity.
10. Other profitability ratios:

    —Ratio of net income to sales

    —Gross margin percentage.

Generally speaking, the standards for these financial ratios may be developed from several sources:

- Ratios accepted by the industry of which the company is a member—perhaps developed by the industry association.
- Ratios ascertained from the published financial statements of the principal competitors of the entity, or industry leaders.
- Ratios developed by computer modeling.
- Ratios based on the past (and best) experience of the company or on the opinion of its officers.

19-8 TREND TO MORE COMPREHENSIVE PERFORMANCE MEASURES

The majority of the standards described relate to very specific activities and are largely *cost* standards (labor cost per unit). Additionally, some relate to number or size of functions performed (number of sales calls made), or financial relationships. It is common practice in U.S. companies to compare hourly, daily, weekly, or monthly actual performance with such a standard, or a budget, or prior experience. Such comparisons with the relevant internal activity of a prior period or calculated proper measure are useful.

But managements are discovering that other types of measures may be helpful for a number of reasons:

- Some *noncost-related* measures can highlight functional areas that need improvement, for example, number of new customers, number of customer complaints, product development time.
- For some activities, comparisons with an *external* standard, such as industry average, or performance of a principal competitor may provide useful guidelines. Examples include inventory turnover, research and development expenditures.
- Quantified standards may cause supervisors to focus attention on the wrong objective. For instance, attention to the average size of sales orders may take attention away from the need for a profitable product mix.
- On occasion, emphasis on output can create problems in, or transfer problems to, other departments (defects, excessive inventory, or wrong mix of parts).
- Some standards may conflict with other management efforts, such as attempting to reduce indirect manufacturing expense as related to direct labor, when the overall trend is to automation.

In this search for a possible broader base—broader than accounting or financial standards—to check or measure company performance, the controller or his representatives, perhaps in collaboration with other functional executives, could take these actions:

- Discuss with management members the critical success factors of the company, suspected areas of weaker performance, and what changes might be examined.
- Review existing performance measures and try to ascertain if they are relevant to the newer techniques or processes (JIT purchasing, delivery and manufacturing).
- Seek to determine if the measures relate to the true cost drivers of the function under review.
- Update practices, using the current literature or periodicals for possible leads to examine.
- Talk with controllers, line managers, or workers, in other companies about the performance measures and other guides they use.
- Consider hiring outside consultants to review areas of suspected weaknesses and to make recommendations. Such a review might lead to a starting list of (1) cost measures and (2) noncost performance measures for important internal activity checking (based on trends and relative *internal* importance, and relative cost and noncost measures when examined or compared to *external* factors).

From a review of the *internal* activities or functions, the impact of these factors, and the importance of trends, could be weighed:

(A) Internal Factors

Cost Measures

Direct labor costs

Direct material costs

Manufacturing expense

Marketing expense

Research and development costs

Delivery costs

Inventory carrying costs

Accounts receivable carrying costs

Noncost Measures

Length of design cycle

Number of engineering changes

Number of new products

Manufacturing cycle time

Number of parts/raw material deliveries

Number of on-time customer deliveries

Number of suppliers

Number of parts

(B) External Factors (Relative Measurement)

Cost Measures

> Relative R&D expense
>
> Relative material content cost
>
> Relative labor cost content
>
> Relative delivery expense
>
> Relative selling expenses

(a) TIME-BASED STANDARDS

One group of standards receiving attention are time-based measures. Those managements which use these diagnostic tools believe that time analysis is more useful than simply cost analysis because activity review identifies exactly what occurs every hour of the working day. It seems to encourage such time-oriented questions as: Why are the two tasks done serially and not in parallel? Why is the process speeded up in some departments only to then let the product lie idle? When points of time are identified, the related cost reduction possibilities can be examined.

Examples of time-based standards that have been found useful in some key functions include:

1. *Decision-making process:* Time lost in waiting for a decision
   —product development
   —manufacturing
   —marketing
   —finance—accounting

2. *New product development*
   • Total time required from inception of idea to marketing of product
   • Number of times (or percent) company has beat a competitor to market
   • Number of new products marketed in a given time period

3. *Manufacturing or processing*
   • Cycle time from commencement of manufacture through billing process
   • Inventory turnover
   • Total elapsed time from product development to first time acceptable output
   • Value added per factory hour
   • Credit approval time
   • Billing cycle time—from receipt of shipping notice to completion of invoice preparation
   • Collection time—from mailing of invoice to receipt of payment

4. *Customer service*
   • Number (or percent) of on-time deliveries
   • Response time to customer questions

- Quoted lead time for
  - —shipment of spare parts
  - —repairs
  - —product delivery
- Delivery response time.

See the Selected References for additional sources of information on time-based management.

19-9 BENCHMARKING

The practice by a company of measuring products, services, and business practices against the toughest competitor or those companies best in its class, or against other measures, has been named "benchmarking." Technically, those who consult about the process differentiate between three kinds, depending on the consultant. Distinctions are made about these three types:

- Competitive benchmarking.
- Noncompetitive benchmarking.
- Internal benchmarking.

Competitive benchmarking studies compare a company's performance with respect to customer-determined notions of quality against direct competitors.

Noncompetitive benchmarking refers to studying the "best-in-class" in a specific business function. For example, it might encompass the billing practices of a company in a completely different industry.

Internal benchmarking can refer to comparisons between plants, or departments, or product lines within the same organization. The benchmarking studies involve steps such as:

- Determining which functions within the company to benchmark.
- Selecting or identifing the key performance variables which should be measured.
- Determining which companies are the best-in-class for the function under review.
- Measuring the performance of the best-in-class companies.
- Measuring the performance of your company as to the function under study.
- Determining those actions necessary to meet and surpass the best-in-class company.
- Implementing and monitoring the improvement program.

Several companies have successfully implemented a program for benchmarking, including Xerox, Hughes Aircraft Company, Consolidated Rail Corp., Douglas Aircraft Company, Hewlett-Packard, and Digital Equipment Corporation. Guidance from some consultants experienced in the benchmarking process may be helpful.

Although benchmarking has produced some legendary corporate successes, often has not produced an improvement on the net income line. In part, this reflects the fact that it is a complicated process and does not consist merely of some random observations of different methods used by some businesses, or some short field trips. A successful benchmarking effort must be undertaken in a clearly defined and systematic manner. A benchmarking study wherein the only product or result is a report to management, with no modification of a substandard activity, could be regarded as a failure.

To put the topic of benchmarking in the proper perspective, it should be recognized that successful benchmarking efforts have addressed a wide variety of issues, including:

- Increased market share.
- Improved corporate strategy.
- Increased profitability.
- Streamlined processes.
- Reduced costs.
- More effective research and development activities.
- Improved quality.
- Higher levels of customer satisfaction.

In those instances when benchmarking activity has not met expectations, some of the reasons include:

1. Top management did not comprehend the full potential of the proposed change and consequently did not push aggressively for their adoption.
2. The functions or activities selected for improvement may in fact have been improved, but the greater efficiency was too small to have a meaningful impact on overall business performance.
3. The study team made observations but failed to develop an actionable plan.
4. In some instances, the analysis was incomplete: the study team learned *what* the best-in-class companies were doing, but it did not learn *how* the actions were implemented.

One other facet of benchmarking should be noted: The makeup of the study team is important. It should include persons in the company who have been performing the function. Those selected should be highly knowledgeable about the function, should be good communicators, and should be curious and highly analytical. It probably is preferable to have consultants, and not company employees, make contacts with competitors. In some circumstances, the presence of a member of the board of directors might be the means of better communicating to the board the complexities and potential impact of the study.

In summary, benchmarking is a complicated process, and full preparation should be made. The subject cannot be adequately discussed in this volume; but some of the Selected References may be useful.

19-10 A BALANCED SYSTEM OF PERFORMANCE MEASURES

Performance measures range from broad company standards to *detailed* functional standards applied to a daily departmental manufacturing activity. Moreover, many of these standards are used for both planning and control purposes. Then, too, some are cost-related and others are noncost measures; some address the important subject of customer satisfaction, and others simple efficiency; and finally, some deal with innovation while others emphasize routine operations.

Many years ago, the use of standards for control purposes was the point of emphasis—and they generally were of a cost type. But management long has recognized that it cannot rely on one set of measures to the exclusion of all others. Rather, a combination of measures are necessary; moreover they must properly relate to each other, and must take into account the critical success factors of the enterprise. This is to say that management needs a balanced set of performance measures.

The article by Kaplan and Norton, which is included in the Selected References, mentions a company that grouped its performance measures into four types, each with separate measures of performance, and each critical to the future success of the entity.

The four measurement groups discussed, together with some added goals and measures of individual performance mentioned earlier in this chapter follow.

Financial Perspective		Customer Perspective	
Goals	Measures	Goals	Measures
Survive	Cash flow	New products	% of sales from new products
Succeed	Sales & income growth	Customer supply	Number of on-time deliveries
Prosper	Return on equity	Preferred supplier	Share of key account purchases

Internal Business Perspective		Innovation Perspective	
Goals	Measures	Goals	Measures
Manufacturing excellence	Unit cost cycle time	Time to market	Vs. competition
New product introduction	Actual vs. planned introduction schedule	Technology leadership	Time to develop new process

19-11 SETTING THE STANDARDS

(a) WHO SHOULD SET THE STANDARDS?

Standards should be set by those who are best qualified by training and experience to judge what good performance should be. It is often a joint process requiring cooperation between the staffs of two or more divisions of the business. Fundamentally, the setting of standards requires careful study and analysis. The controller and his staff, trained in analysis and possessing essential records on the various activities, are in an excellent position to play an important part in the establishment of yardsticks of performance.

Since standards are yardsticks of performance, they should not be set by those whose performance is to be measured. Sufficient independence of thought should exist. The standards should be reviewed with those who will be judged by them and any suggestions considered. However, final authority in establishing the standard should be placed in other hands.

Exactly which staff members cooperate in setting standards depends on the standards under consideration. Material quantity standards, for example, are generally determined by the engineers who are familiar with the operation methods employed as well as the product design. Assisting the engineers may be the production staff and the accounting staff. The production men can make valuable contributions because of their knowledge of the process. Furthermore, permitting the production staff to assist usually enlists their cooperation in making the standards effective. The accounting department assists by providing necessary information on past experience.

The determination of material price standards is usually the responsibility of both the purchasing and accounting departments. The purchasing department may indicate what expected prices are. These should then be challenged by the accounting department, taking into account current prices and reasonably expected changes. In other instances the accounting department sets the standards, based again on current prices, but takes into consideration the opinion of the purchasing department about future trends.

Quantitative labor standards are usually set by industrial engineers through the use of time and motion study. This is properly an engineering function in that a thorough background of the processes is necessary. On occasion, the accounting department furnishes information of past performance as a guide. Standard labor rates are set by the department having available the detailed job rates and other necessary information—typically the cost department. The cost department must also translate the physical standards into cost standards.

Manufacturing overhead standards, too, are often a matter of cooperation between the accounting and engineering departments. Engineers may be called on to furnish technical data, such as power consumption in a particular department, or maintenance required, or type of supplies necessary. However, this is then costed by the accounting staff. In other instances, the unit standards or budgets may be set in large part on past experience. The role played by the accountant tends to be much greater in the establishment of overhead standards since he is familiar with the techniques of organizing the data into their most useful form for cost and budget reporting. Setting the standards for distribution activities is best done through the cooperation of sales, sales research, and accounting executives. Reliance is placed on the sales staff for the supplying of information pertaining to market potentials and sales methods. The accountant contributes the analysis and interpretation of past performance, trends, and relationships. The sales and accounting executives jointly must interpret the available data as applied to future activity.

Unit standards for the measurement of administrative expenses are usually determined on the basis of time and motion study by industrial engineers, observation of the functions, or a detailed analysis of past performance to insure that standards reflect the norm. In many instances, the accountant is involved in either costing the data or analyzing past experience.

Financial and operating ratios should be set by the controller based on the objectives for the company, experience in the particular company or industry, and special analysis or consideration of factors that have a significant influence on the ratio or external sources.

In many instances, it may be desirable to have the assistance of independent consultants. For example, when sources outside the company are to be contacted, as in "benchmarking," these noncompany personnel may be especially helpful.

(b) METHOD OF SETTING STANDARDS

Those aspects of setting standards that are beyond the sphere of accounting responsibility are adequately covered in various management and engineering literature. Only the general steps taken in the establishment of standards will be considered here. Any outline of procedure regarding standards is basically only the application of logic and prudent judgment to the problem. The various phases involved in the setting of standards may be summarized as follows:

1. *Recognition of the Need for a Standard in the Particular Application.* Obviously, before action is taken, the need should exist. This need must be acknowledged so that the problem can be attacked.

2. *Preliminary Observation and Analysis.* This involves "getting the feel" of the subject, recognizing the scope of the problem, and securing a general understanding of the factors involved.

3. *Segregation of the Function, or Activity, and/or Costs in Terms of Individual Responsibility.* Since standards are to control individual actions, the outer limits of the responsibility of each individual must be ascertained in the particular application.

4. *Determination of the Unit of Measurement in Which the Standard Should Be Expressed.* To arrive at the quotient, the divisor is necessary. And in many applications, the base selected can be one of many.

5. *Determination of the Best Method.* This may involve time and motion study, a thorough review of possible materials, or an analysis of past experience. It must also involve consideration of possible changes in conditions.

6. *Statement or Expression of the Standard.* When the best method and the unit of measurement have been determined, the tentative standard can be set.

7. *Testing of the Standard.* After analysis and synthesis and preliminary determination, the standard must be tested to see that it meets the requirements.

8. *Final Application of the Standard.* The testing of a standard will often result in certain compromises or changes. When this has been effected, when the best judgment of all the executives concerned has been secured, then and only then can the standard be considered set and ready to be applied.

19-12 USE OF STANDARDS FOR CONTROL

The fact that management has set standards for cost control by no means assures control of costs. It takes positive action by individuals to keep costs within some predetermined limits. It is a management challenge to communicate the value of standards to all concerned and convince them how the yardsticks can be utilized in accomplishing the goals and objectives. To be effective it must be demonstrated that the standards are fair and reasonable.

The controller must have sufficient facts to illustrate the reasonableness of the standards when questions arise or the yardsticks are considered unfair.

When standards are shown clearly to be unreasonable, the controller must be prepared to gather new data and make appropriate adjustments.

(a) TECHNIQUE OF COST CONTROL

In the final analysis, the objective of cost control is to secure the greatest amount of production or results of a desired quality from a given amount of material, manpower effort, or facilities. It is the securing of the best result at the lowest possible cost under existing conditions. In this control of performance, the first step is the setting of standards of comparison; the next step is the recording of actual performance, and the third step is the comparing of actual and standard costs as the work progresses. This last step involves the following:

1. Determining the variance between standard and actual.
2. Analyzing the cause of the variance.
3. Taking remedial action to bring unfavorable actual costs in line with the predetermined standards.

Control is established through prompt follow-up, before the unfavorable trends or tendencies develop into large losses. It is important that any variances be determined quickly, and it is equally important that the unfavorable variance be stated in terms that those responsible will understand. The speed and method of presentation have a profound bearing on the corrective action that will be taken and, hence, on the effectiveness of control.

(b) ROLE OF STATISTICAL PROCESS CONTROL (SPC)

One approach to cost control is to determine the variance between a standard and actual performance, seek out the cause of the variance, and take remedial action. Yet global competition is causing management to adopt more sophisticated strategies to remain or become competitive. Among these devices are automatic JIT (just-in-time practices), TQM (total quality management), and SPC (statistical process control). This latter technique can assist in properly setting standards and in better evaluating or interpreting variances. SPC is based on the assumption that process performance is dynamic, that variation is the rule. Consequently, proper assessment of performance requires correct interpretation of the variation over a period of time. Charts or graphic aids are used in SPC to understand and reduce the fluctuations in processes until they are considered stable (under control). A stable process would have only the normal variances. On the other hand, an unstable process is subject to uncommon fluctuation, resulting from special causes. The performance of a stable process can be improved only by making fundamental changes in the process itself, while an unstable production process can be stabilized only by locating and eliminating the special causes. The statistical approach assists in identifying the character of the variance. An incorrect decision that a process is operating in an unstable manner may result in costs of searching for special causes of process variation that do not exist. An incorrect decision that a process is operating in a stable manner will result in failure to search for special causes that do exist.

Suffice it to say that SPC is a complex subject that seeks to provide long-term solutions. Someone with a high level of statistical knowledge ordinarily will be needed to assist in implementing the strategy. Management accountants should understand the SPC approach. (See Selected References.)

(c) WHO SHOULD CONTROL COSTS?

Costs must be controlled by individuals, and the question is raised about who should control costs—the controller, as representing accounting personnel; or the operating executive in charge of the activity—manufacturing sales, or research—to be cost controlled. It has already been explained that operational control preceded accounting control. And in many thousands of small businesses, operating control is the only type used. Cost control is not primarily an accounting process, although accounting plays an important part. Control of costs is an operating function. The controller, in the capacity of an operating executive, may control costs within the accounting department. Beyond this, the function of the controller is to report the facts on other activities of the business so that corrective action may be taken and to inform management of its effectiveness in cost control. The part played by the controller is advisory or facilitative in nature.

In many instances, the development of the standards to be used in measuring performance is largely the work of nonaccountants—whether product specifications, operational methods, time requirements, or other factors. Likewise, decision about the corrective action to be taken is generally up to the operating personnel. However, the controller is in an excellent position to stimulate and guide the interest of management in the control of costs through the means of reports analyzing out-of-line conditions. The controller's work is usually confined to summarizing basic information, analyzing results, and preparing intelligently conceived reports. It follows that the controller must produce reports that a non-accounting-trained executive or operator can understand and will act on. To do this, he must be thoroughly conversant with the operating problems and viewpoints. The effectiveness of any cost control system depends on the degree of coordination between the accounting control personnel and the operating personnel. One presents the facts in an understandable manner; the other takes the remedial action.

Cooperation at *all* levels is essential in the control of costs. Cooperation is secured, in part, through the application of correct management policies. The use of standards, when fully understood, should be of great assistance in securing this cooperation, for the measuring stick is based on careful analysis and not preconceived ideas or rule-of-thumb methods.

(d) THE LEVEL OF THE STANDARD

Since one of the primary purposes of a standard is as a control tool—to see that performance is held to what it should be—it is necessary to determine at what level the standard should be set. Just how "tight" should a standard be? Although there is no clear-cut line of demarcation among them, the three following levels may be distinguished:

1. The ideal standard.
2. The average of past performance.
3. The attainable good performance standard.

The ideal standard is the one representing the best performance that can be attained under the most favorable conditions possible. It is not a standard that is expected to be attained but rather a goal toward which to strive in an attempt to improve efficiency. Hence variances are always unfavorable and represent the inability to reach the ideal level of efficiency. The use of an unattainably tight standard confuses the objectives of cost reduction and cost control. Cost reduction involves the finding of ways and means to achieve a given result through improved design, better methods, new layouts, new equipment, better plant layout, etc., and therefore results in the establishment of new standards. If the standards set are more restrictive than currently attainable performance, the lower cost will not necessarily result until cost reduction has found the means by which the standard may be attained. Ideal standards, then, are not highly desirable as a means of cost control.

Standards are frequently set on the basis of what was done in the past, without adjustments to reflect improved methods or elimination of wastes. A standard set on this basis is likewise a poor measuring stick in that it can be met by poor performance. Hence the very inefficiencies that standards should disclose are obscured by the loose standard.

A third level at which a standard may be set is the attainable level of good performance. This standard includes waste or spoilage, lost time, and other inefficiencies only to the extent that they are considered impractical of elimination. This type of standard can be met or bettered by efficient performance. It is a standard set at a high level but is attainable with reasonably diligent effort. Such a standard would seem to be the most effective for cost control purposes.

(e) THE POINT OF CONTROL

Since costs are controlled by individuals, it follows that the accounting classifications must reflect both standard and actual performance in such a manner that individual performance can be measured. As stated previously, "responsibility accounting" must be adopted. Provision must be made for the accumulation of costs by cost centers or cost pools or departments that follows organizational structure. Furthermore, this cost accumulation must reflect, first, only those costs that are direct as to the specific function being measured. Allocations and reallocations may be made for product cost *determination* and for certain other *planning* applications, but this is not desirable for cost *control*. If a great many prorations are made, it is often difficult to determine where the inefficiency exists or the extent of it. Therefore, it is desirable from a cost control standpoint to collect the costs at the point of incurrence.

If, as in some companies, allocated costs are reflected in control reports, it is desirable to separate them from direct expenses or costs. Some companies show allocated costs so that the department manager will be aware of the cost of the facilities or services they use.

Discussion of the point of control of costs involves, in addition to placement of responsibility, the matter of timing. Costs must be controlled not only at the point of incurrence but also, preferably, at or before the time of incurrence. Thus, if a department on a budget basis processes a purchase requisition and is advised at that time of the excess cost over budget, perhaps action can be taken then—either delaying the expenditure until the following month or getting a less expensive yet satisfactory substitute. Again, material control is best exercised at the point of issuance. Only the standard quantity should be issued. Or, in the case of purchases, the price and type are best controlled at the time of purchase.

(f) WHAT COSTS SHOULD HAVE STANDARDS?

From the viewpoint of standards for cost control, a question may be raised about the extent to which attempts should be made to set standards. Factors to be considered include the relative amount of cost and the degree of control possible over the cost.

It may be stated that standards should be set for all cost items of a significant or material amount. In many cases, the more important the cost, the greater is the opportunity or need for cost control. With such items as overhead, it may be necessary to combine certain elements, but so far as practicable a standard should be set to measure performance.

Another factor to be considered is the degree of control possible or needed or desired over the cost. At first blush, it might appear that little control can be exercised over some types of cost, such as depreciation, salaries of key personnel, or personal property taxes. However, the fact is that most costs can be controlled by someone. The time and place and method of control of costs generally considered as "fixed" may differ from the control of material, direct labor, or variable overhead expense, but a certain degree of control is possible. Control of the fixed charges may be exercised in at least two ways:

1. *By Limiting the Expenditure to a Predetermined Amount.* For example, depreciation charges are controlled through the acquisition of plant and equipment. Any control must be exercised at the time of purchase or construction of the asset. This is usually done by means of an appropriation budget, which is a type of standard. A similar plan can be applied to the group of salaried personnel generally considered as a part of the fixed charges. In many instances, control of this type of expense or expenditure is a top-management decision. It may be observed, however, that control at this high level does exist.

2. *By Securing the Proper Utilization of the Facilities and Organization Represented by the Fixed Charges.* The controller can assist in this task by properly isolating the volume costs or cost of idle equipment. An acceptable standard might be the percent of plant utilization as related to "normal." In the monthly statement of income and expense, the lack of volume costs should be set out as part of the effort to direct management's attention to the excess costs and to a consideration of ways and means of reducing personnel, if necessary, or increasing volume through other products, intensified sales activity, etc.

19-13 PROCEDURE FOR REVISING STANDARDS

(a) REVISION OF STANDARDS

Whether standards are used for cost control or the related function of budgetary planning or whether standards are for the purpose of price setting or inventory valuation, they must be kept up to date to be most useful. Revision appears desirable when important changes are made in material specifications or prices, methods of production, or labor efficiency or price—from the viewpoint of manufacturing operations. Changes in the methods or channels of distribution, or basic organizational or functional changes, would necessitate standard changes in the selling, research, or administrative activities. Stated in other terms, current standards must be revised when conditions have changed to such an extent that the standard no longer represents a realistic or fair measure of performance.

It is obvious that standard revisions should not be made for every change—only the important ones. However, the constant search for better methods and for better measurements of performance subjects every standard to possible revision. The controller constantly must be on the alert about the desirability of adjusting standards to prevent the furnishing of misleading information to management.

(b) A PROGRAM FOR STANDARD REVISION

The changing of standards is time consuming and may be expensive. For this reason, it should not be treated in a haphazard manner. It is desirable to plan in advance the steps to be taken in revising standards. Through the use of an orderly program for constant review and revision of standards, the time and money spent on standard changes can be less and the effort more productive.

In planning the program of standard revision, the ramifications of any changes should be considered. For example, changes in manufacturing standards usually necessitate changes in inventory values. Accordingly, it may appear desirable to review the standards at the end of each fiscal year and make the necessary changes. In a chemical plant with which the authors are familiar, a review of material price standards is made every quarter. In this instance, the selling price of the finished product is sympathetic to changes in commodity prices. This more frequent revision results in cost information that is more useful to the sales department. In some companies, a general practice is to change standards whenever basic selling price changes occur. This results in a more constant standard gross profit figure by which to judge sales performance. In considering frequent changes, however, the expense should be weighed against the benefits, in this connection, the value for cost control should be matched against the lessened degree of comparability of the variances from period to period.

Judgment should be exercised about the necessity for, and extent of, changes in the records. For example, general changes in labor rates, raw material costs, standard overhead rates, or product design may dictate a complete revision of product and departmental costs, extending through every stage of manufacture. On the other hand, a change in one department, or in one part, or in a small assembly might necessitate the change of only one standard for control purposes. The difference between old and new, with respect to other stages of manufacture, or the finished product cost, could be temporarily written off as a variance until the time is ripe for a complete product standard revision.

19-14 RECORDING STANDARDS

(a) IMPORTANCE OF ADEQUATE RECORDS

If the controller is to serve management most effectively and if the business is to have the advantage of accurate, reliable, and prompt cost information, then an adequate recording of the facts is necessary. This principle is as applicable to recording standards and standard costs as it is to actual costs—perhaps even more so. The degree of intelligence applied to the form and method of recording determines in large measure that (1) the data underlying the development and revision of standards will be available as needed, (2) the facts relating to operating efficiency will be ascertainable and accurately analyzed, (3) the information will be made available on an economical basis, and (4) the records will have the necessary flexibility to meet promptly the needs of the various applications of the standards.

(b) TYPES OF RECORDS NECESSARY

In the manufacturing function, the records incident to the establishment and use of standards may be classified into four basic groups:

1. Physical specifications that outline the required material and the sequence of manufacturing operations which must be performed.
2. Details of standard or budgeted overhead based on normal capacity.
3. Standard cost sheets for each product and component part; these sheets indicate standard cost by elements.
4. Variance accounts that indicate the type of departure from standard.

The extent and form of these records depend on the size and characteristics of the business. In an assembly-type operation, for example, there would be a product specification for each part. These, in turn, would form the basis for cost sheets on subassemblies and assemblies. In most cases this data would be recorded, accumulated, stored, and reported through the integrated computer processing system. This would include information from the production order, standard labor hours for each operation, and the ability to calculate the standard cost of each part and assembly. With the details of standards available, changes are easily made for substitution of parts in determining the standard cost of modifications of a basic product. Standards are equally applicable to processing operations like the chemical industry—the key is setting fair and reasonable standards for each operation or process and making adjustments for changed conditions.

(c) ADMINISTRATIVE CONTROLS

Although the use of standards is not as well developed for administrative functions as for manufacturing operations, yardsticks can be established for such usage in most cases. Some companies collect and analyze statistical data from which some performance measurements can be made. The controller should continue to evaluate these functions to determine the best method or standard against which actual performance can be compared.

(d) INCORPORATION OF STANDARD COSTS IN ACCOUNTS

Historically, some companies use standard costs for statistical comparisons only and do not incorporate them into the accounting record system. This is probably more true for administrative-type expenses than for direct manufacturing costs. With the data storage and processing capabilities of computers, it appears essential that the standard cost records be integrated into the accounting system. This will result in better cost control, inventory valuation, budgeting, and pricing.

19-15 APPLICATION OF STANDARD COSTS

Even though standard costs are incorporated in the accounts, there is considerable difference about the period in the accounting cycle when the standards should be recorded. Whereas there are several variations in accounting treatment, the distinction may be twofold:

1. Recognition of the standard cost at the time of cost incurrence.
2. Recognition of the standard cost at the time of cost completion.

The first method charges work in progress at standard cost, whereas the second method develops the standard cost at the time of transfer to the finished goods account. Recognition of costs at incurrence would imply a recording of material price variance at the time of purchase and material usage variance at the time of usage or transfer to work in process. However, many firms record material at actual cost and recognize price variances only as the material is used. This practice permits a write-off of excess costs proportionate to usage so that unit costs tend to approximate the actual cost each month.

19-16 MANAGEMENT USE OF STANDARD COSTS

Extensive use of standard cost data can be made by management in directing the activities of the company. Some areas to be considered are as follows:

1. Planning and forecasting.
2. Motivation of employees.
3. Rewarding employees.
4. Performance measurement.
5. Analyzing alternative courses of action—new products.
6. Pricing decisions.
7. Inventory valuation.
8. Make or buy decisions.
9. Control and cost reduction.

19-17 SELECTED REFERENCES

Bogan, Christopher E., and Michael J. English, "Benchmarking: A Wakeup Call for Board Members (and CEOs Too)," *Planning Review,* Jan./Feb. 1993, pp. 28–33.

Calvasina, Richard V., and Eugene J. Calvasina, "Standard Costing Games That Managers Play," *Management Accounting,* March 1984, pp. 49–51.

Camp, Robert C., "A Bible for Benchmarking, by Xerox," *Financial Executive,* July/Aug. 1993, pp. 23–27.

Jaouen, Pauline R., and Bruce R. Neumann, "Variance Analysis, Konban and JIT: A Further Study," *Journal of Accountancy,* June 1987, pp. 164–173.

Kaplan, Robert S., "One Cost System Isn't Enough," *Harvard Business Review,* Jan./Feb. 1988, pp. 61–66.

Kaplan, Robert S., and David P. Norton, "The Balanced Scorecard—Measures That Drive Performance," *Harvard Business Review,* Jan.–Feb. 1992, pp. 71–79.

Keys, David E., and Kurt F. Reding, "Statistical Process Control: What Management Accountants Need to Know," *Management Accounting,* Jan. 1992, pp. 26–30.

Krause, Irv, and John Liu, "Benchmarking R&D Productivity," *Planning Review,* Jan./Feb. 1993, pp. 16–21, 52.

Maturi, Richard J., "Benchmarking: The Search for Quality," *The Financial Manager,* Mar./April 1990, pp. 26–31.

Pryor, Laurence S., and Steven J. Katz, "How Benchmarking Goes Wrong (and How to Do It Right)," *Planning Review,* Jan./Feb. 1993, pp. 6–11, 53.

Ransley, Derek L., "Training Managers to Benchmark," *Planning Review,* Jan./Feb. 1993, pp. 32–36.

Stalk, George, Jr., and Thomas M. Hout, *Competing Against Time: How Time-Based Competition Is Reshaping Global Markets,* New York: The Free Press, 1990.

Tucker, Frances Gaither, Seymour M. Ziven, and Robert C. Camp, "How to Measure Yourself Against the Best," *Harvard Business Review,* Jan./Feb. 1987, pp. 8–10.

Turney, Peter B. B., "Beyond TQM with Workforce Activity Based Management," *Management Accounting,* Sept. 1993, pp. 28–31.

Verschoor, Curtis C., "Benchmarking the Audit Committee," *Journal of Accountancy,* Sept. 1993, pp. 59–64.

Watson, Gregory H., "How Process Benchmarking Supports Corporate Strategy," *Planning Review,* Jan./Feb. 1993, pp. 12–15.

CHAPTER 20

Planning and Control of Sales

20-1 INTRODUCTION

Primary responsibility for the planning and control of sales, of course, rests with the chief sales or marketing executive of the company or the business segment. However, the chief accounting officer, with his knowledge of costs and cost behavior as well as his familiarity with sales accounting and analysis, is in a position to use these skills to assist the various marketing executives. Some of the areas where he might be helpful include these:

- Selection and application of mathematical/statistical methods to develop or verify sales level trends and relationships.
- Analysis of internal sales data to reveal trends and relationships.
- Analysis and assembling of the proposed sales plan/budget.
- Development and application of sales standards for use by the marketing executive, if applicable.
- Application of the relevant costs as a factor in setting product sales prices.

While the controller has a supporting role to the chief sales executive with respect to sales planning and control, he also has some basic independent responsibilities, as a member of the financial staff, to see that adequate procedures are followed and that the sales planning and control is sound from a financial or economic viewpoint.

These subjects and others are discussed in this chapter. First, however, to provide background for the controller or for other readers, a brief review is made of the sales management function and some of its concerns.

20-2 SALES MANAGEMENT CONCERNS

The tasks of any management function are many and are varied and complex. Sales management is certainly confronted with a broad range of problems. It is a dynamic area, with changing conditions, constantly resulting in new and different problems. The controller can be an important influence on the resolution of these problems and decisions. An extensive and objective analysis of sales and distribution costs can assist sales executives in making prudent decisions consistent with the short- and long-range goals of the company.

One problem area that has a significant impact on the planning process of the company is sales forecasting. The accuracy of the sales forecast is essential to good planning. The controller can work with sales management to realistically evaluate the degree to which the actual sales will relate to sales budget or forecast. There are many mathematical techniques available to establish standard deviations or variations that can be expected.

Significant progress has been made in developing more sophisticated management tools for sales executives. With the utilization of personal computers, management can have available summarized information on sales activity allowing it to make effective decisions in a timely manner. The controller should be an active participant in the development of these information systems and reports.

Although there are many types of problems encountered in the sales management function, there may be some that are found in most companies. The following is representative of some of the fundamental questions that are constantly raised:

1. *Product.* What product is to be sold and in what quantity? Is it to be the highest quality in its field or lower? Is the product to be a specialty or a staple?

2. *Pricing.* At what price is the article to be sold? Shall the company follow a policy of meeting any and all price competition? What are the terms of sale to be granted?

3. *Distribution.* To whom shall the product be sold, i.e., shall the firm sell directly to the ultimate consumer or through others, such as wholesalers? What channels of distribution should be used?

4. *Method of Sale.* How shall the goods be sold? Is it to be by personal solicitation, advertising, or direct mail? What sales promotion means shall be used?

5. *Organization.* How shall salespersons be selected, and how shall they be trained? What is to be the basic organizational setup? Are there to be branch offices? Will sales supervisors handle all lines of product, or will each specialize? Into what departments shall the sales organization be divided? How many salespersons should be employed?

6. *Planning and Control.* How are sales territories to be set up? Shall sales standards be used as measuring sticks of performance? How will salespersons be compensated—salary, commission, bonus? What controls will be employed?

Questions relating to these six categories are found in every company, regardless of size. The answers to many depend, in large part, on the facts available within each organization.

20-3 THE CONTROLLER'S ASSISTIVE ROLE IN SALES MANAGEMENT PROBLEMS

As stated earlier, the final solution to sales management concerns must, of course, rest largely with the chief sales executive. However, an intelligent executive will always seek any assistance available. In this respect, the controller can help by bringing to bear a scientific, analytical approach. While doing this, he is expected to use judgment as well as imagination. It should be realized that the solution in one firm may not be the solution in another. It should be realized further that the answers to today's problems may not be the answer tomorrow—for industry is dynamic. The controller is of value primarily in getting the facts—he is the fact finder. In presenting the facts, though, he will have to merchandise or sell his product; the controller's approach must be one that invites reception.

The degree of assistance the controller can render in solving the previously mentioned sales problems is indicated in the following outline.

1. *Problems of Product.* The initial selection of the product or consideration of changes in the line, sizes, and colors should generally be based on the collective judgment of the marketing considerations by the sales manager, of production problems by the manufacturing executive, and of cost considerations by the controller. Costs are not the only factor in the decision, but they are an important factor. The chief accounting official should be able to indicate the probable margin on the product, as well as the margins on alternative choices. He should also be able to indicate the probable effect of volume on the margin or the effect of changes in quality, composition, and manufacturing processes on the cost to make or sell.

    In the continuous reviews of sales trends, the controller may be able to identify unfavorable trends that might call for redirection of the sales effort or a change in product.

2. *Problems of Price.* In many companies, pricing procedures are not reviewed on a periodic or methodical basis. The pricing procedure may not be responsive to increased costs. Although cost is not the only determining factor, it must be considered in maximizing the return on investment. The controller must be able to provide all the available information. Total costs, marginal or differential costs, out-of-pocket costs, or cost differences must be considered in developing the price structure. This is true for competitive bids or establishing price lists for the usual type of sale.

    In an analysis of sales volume and related prices, it may be revealed that unfavorable variances often have resulted from salespersons or sales managers having too much authority in setting a selling price. As production costs change, the information should be communicated to the sales executives for consideration of appropriate price changes. Also, assistance should be provided in setting volume price breaks for different sizes of orders.

3. *Problems of Distribution.* Toward the solution of these problems, too, the controller contributes the cost analysis necessary, as well as a review of statistics for unfavorable trends. He is able to provide indications of the selling cost through the various channels of distribution. He should be on the alert for major changes in sales trends through particular channels or margins thereon. He frequently has a chance to show ingenuity in analysis regarding types and sizes of accounts and orders to be sought. Questions of policy on which he should provide many of the facts, for example, relate to the following:

    a. The minimum order to be accepted.

    b. Restriction of the sales effort on large volume accounts that purchase only low-margin products or are unprofitable because of special laboratory service.

    c. Desirability of servicing particular types of accounts through jobbers, telephone, mail order, etc.

    d. Discontinuance of aggressive sales effort on accounts where annual sales volume is too low.

    e. Best location for branch warehouses.

4. *Problems Relating to the Method of Sale.* Many factors will determine the method of sale, and the sales management must make this determination in view of the long-term goals and objectives. The controller can assist by providing information on historical costs and preparing alternative cost estimates for various methods. For example, analyses could be made related to the distribution of samples and the impact on costs and sales trends. Cost data related to advertising programs are useful in making decisions for future media communications. Special cost structures can be developed for market-test situations to determine the cost effectiveness. In the long run, of course, the best method should result in achieving the greatest sales volume with the best return on investment.

5. *Problems of Organization.* Because the sales management function is dynamic, organizational changes are necessary to satisfy the new requirements. In making these changes, information related to potential sales by product or territory may assist in reassigning or hiring new salespersons. Also, comparative cost data on different organizational structures are useful in determining the change.

6. *Problems of Planning and Control.* So numerous are the applications where the controller can be of assistance in planning and controlling the sales effort that only a few can be indicated. The controller is able to aid the sales executive in solving some of the previously mentioned problems through special studies, yet in the planning and control fields many of his functions are repetitive. Suggestive of the contributions by the accounting official are the following:

a. *Sales budgets and quotas.* Detailed records and knowledge about the distribution of sales by territory, product, and customer, coupled with the knowledge of the sales manager on product changes and trends, provide basic information necessary in an intelligent setting of sales budgets, quotas, and standards. The controller also may provide services in connection with forecasting and market studies.

b. *Distribution expense budgets and standards.* A history of past expenses as recorded in the accounting department provides much needed data in setting budgets and standards for the measurement and control of selling effort.

c. *Monthly or periodic income and expense statements:*
   (i)   By territories.
   (ii) By commodities.
   (iii) By methods of sale.
   (iv) By customers.
   (v)   By salespersons.
   (vi) By organization or operating divisions.

   These and other analytical statements can provide a vast amount of useful information. The disclosure of the contribution to the net profit of each territory or some other factor analyzed, over and above the direct expense, may reveal spots of weakness.

d. *Special analyses to reveal conditions needing correction or as an audit of performance:*
   (i)   Sales incentive plans. The probable cost of various plans as applied to the business and degree to which they are mutually profitable for the

company and salesman. A determination about whether they direct salesmen's efforts toward the most profitable products.

(ii) Branch office and warehouse expense. Periodic reviews of expense, in relationship to sales, growth, and earnings of the activity.

(iii) Customer development expense. Analysis of entertainment expense or other business development expense by customer, salesman, or territory, with emphasis on necessity and possible alternatives—all with reference to the related margin or profit.

(iv) Salespersons' compensation and expenses. Review and analysis of salespersons' salaries, bonuses, and expenses related to budgets, salary structure, and industry.

20-4 CONTROLLER'S INDEPENDENT ROLE IN THE PLANNING AND CONTROL OF SALES

As previously stated, the primary responsibility for the development of the sales plan and its subsequent implementation is that of the chief sales executive. But, as just commented on in the preceding section, the controller can be of substantial assistance to the sales executive in supplying analytical and historical data for use in planning and control decisions. However, it should not be assumed that the controller will provide only the data the sales executive wants and that the controllership role is by and large a passive one as to sales activity. Given the analytical background of controllers and their knowledge of the financial data concerning the company, they have a series of independent functions to perform in furtherance of a sound business plan and prudent control procedures. Some of their conclusions might not be in agreement with the initial thinking of the sales executive; and some of the procedures they develop might appear redundant to some salespersons. Yet to one sensitive to the need for financially sound policies and procedures, and the desirability of proper checks and balances, the role of the controller is indispensable. For most companies, the responsibility of the controller and his or her staff extends to these functions in the development of a sound annual sales plan (as well as the entire annual business plan) and the related implementation:

1. *The Planning Phase.*
   a. Development, and revision when required, of a practical set of systems and procedures for arriving at a suitable sales plan (and the entire financial aspects of the annual plan). This would include:
   - Outlining the steps in the planning procedure.
   - Assigning responsibility for each specific procedure to specific executive positions (with the concurrence of executive management).
   - Providing the format in which the sales plan (quantified data) must be presented.
   - Examining the economic justification for certain decisions.
   - Providing the schedule when the data are to be submitted.
   - Assuring that the cognizant sales executives have the necessary statistical and historical internal sales data required to develop a sound sales plan.

    b. Supplying the relevant analyses of past sales performance, including the significant trends and relationships, for the appropriate executives sales management.

    c. Providing for an in-depth financial analysis and evaluation of the tentative sales plan, when completed by the marketing executives. The analysis should bring to the attention of the appropriate executive any inconsistencies, questionable assumptions, reasonableness tests, or other matters that warrant discussion. These could include adequacy of margins, comparisons with competitive prices, questions about market growth, economic comparisons of different product sales mixes, etc.

    d. When the iteration is complete, preparing the consolidated sales plan, with related supplemental adjustments for such matters as returns and allowances, and other sales deductions.

    e. Incorporating the sales plan into the total business plan for the period involved, including comparative profit data.

2. *The Control Phase.*

    a. Develop, and revise, when necessary, appropriate financial control systems for the use of the cognizant executive.

    b. Provide the useful and timely comparisons of budget and actual sales performance for the sales executive, by appropriate segment, and in a form he understands (i.e., by product, by territory, by salesperson, etc.).

    c. Provide useful supplemental analytical data such as sales trends, gross margin trends and relationships, market share information, sales effectiveness, etc., and other control type information. These data can be furnished on a regular basis or when an observed unfavorable condition seems to be arising.

These are some of the basic functions performed by many controllers. In each situation, accounting executives will find ways in which their analytical capability and business acumen may be put to use.

20-5 CONTROL OF SALES

Sales must be controlled to achieve the best or expected return on investment. The optimum net income is realized only when a proper relationship exists among these four factors: (1) investment in working capital and facilities, (2) volume of sales, (3) operating expenses, and (4) gross margins. The accounting control of sales, therefore, relates to the reports analyzing sales activity that bring to light undesirable trends and relationships or departures from goals, budgets, or standards in the manner best calculated to secure corrective action.

20-6 SALES ANALYSIS

(a) GETTING AT THE FACTS

The stress sometimes placed on sales volume can be misleading. If a business were to ignore the profit factor, it could probably secure any desired volume. Through the cutting of prices, through the spending of huge amounts on direct selling expense or sales promotion or advertising, volume itself could be secured. Yet what good would result? It is obvious that the implied factor is *profitable* sales volume.

If business is to achieve profitable sales, it must know where the areas of greatest profit are. This means both sales analysis and cost analysis. There is little doubt that the analysis of sales has reached different peaks of achievement in different firms and industries. Many large companies devote a great deal of time to this phase of marketing control and have well-developed programs. A large number of medium-sized or small firms have little or none. It is also probably true that the sales executive in consumer goods lines has many more facts than the industrial marketing executive.

The evidence is unmistakably clear in any business that overall or average figures are not sufficient. Such general information is of little value in making key marketing decisions and directing sales efforts. The data must be specific and related directly to the problem on which a resolution must be achieved.

(b) USE OF THE COMPUTER

This chapter deals with the many types of sales analysis found useful in guiding the sales direction and the marketing effort. The emphasis is on the analysis of the internal company records. Such studies are made even more complex when sales and marketing effort (discussed in Chapter 21) are joined in the same review. However, these analyses are made more feasible and cost-effective with the use of powerful computers and related software. The role of the computer in business is discussed in Chapter 41.

Computers permit the introduction of a new sales tool by analyzing a mass of data about customer preferences and buying practices. Questionnaires that accompany credit card applications, or coupons, or warranty cards, and a host of other sources, provide a vast amount of information about the customer. Such data are combined with other information from public records. Using sophisticated statistical techniques, data from these various sources are combined, consolidated, and analyzed in numerous ways. The end result is a market effort directed to specific users. This database marketing is another powerful technique to assist the selling effort.

(c) TYPES OF SALES ANALYSES NEEDED

What is needed, then, is detailed analysis to guide sales effort. Some required analysis relates solely to past sales performance as such. Other studies involve the determination of trends by comparison with previous periods. Still other reviews show the relationship to budget or standard, to gross profit, selling expense, or net profit. Analyses may be expressed in physical units, or dollar volume, or both.

The types of analyses frequently used are as follows:

1. *Product*—type of product sold, colors, sizes, price lines, style, quality (reclaimed material, odd lot, first quality).
2. *Territory*—area used for sales direction—states, cities, counties, other marketing areas.
3. *Channel of distribution*—wholesalers, retailers, brokers, agents.
4. *Method of sale*—direct mail, house call, ad or coupon, delivered vs. non-delivered.

5. *Customer*—domestic vs. foreign, industrial vs. ultimate consumer, private vs. governmental, tabulated according to volume of purchases.

6. *Size of order*—average size of individual purchase.

7. *Terms of sale*—cash, cash on delivery (C.O.D.), regular charge account, installment, lay-away.

8. *Organization*—branches, departments.

9. *Salesperson*—either individual or groups.

These analyses may be developed, not merely with regard to sales but through gross profit to profit after direct selling expense or ultimately to the net profit of the segment being measured.

Other analyses relating to unrealized sales may also be useful, for example:

1. Orders received.

2. Unfilled orders.

3. Cancellations.

4. Lost sales.

These studies may be used as an integral part of sales planning or to eliminate reasons for ineffective effort. Analysis of orders may be important where production is made to order. For example, all sales of a given size or type may be summarized to necessitate only one production run in the period.

Many subanalyses can be prepared. Thus management may want to know not merely the overall sales by product but the product sales in each territory.

The controller may find that the sales manager can use certain of these analyses monthly or periodically—for example, sales by territory, by product lines, or by salesperson. Other analyses may be made only as a special investigation, when it is expected the tabulation will reveal out-of-line conditions. In any event, it is the controller's responsibility to design and install procedures and records in such a fashion that the maximum information is made available with the minimum of time and effort, both clerical and analytical. It is axiomatic that in many situations the company getting the information most quickly is in a better competitive position.

This information will answer the typical questions of an analytical sales executive: What was sold? Where was it sold? Who sold it? What was the profit?

(d) DEDUCTIONS FROM SALES

In any analysis of sales the importance of sales deductions should not be overlooked. Although reviews may relate to net sales, the clue to substandard profits may lie in the deductions—high freight cost, special allowances, or discounts. These factors may reveal why unit prices appear low.

Useful analyses and reports on sales deductions can be prepared. For example, an informative summary may be compiled to indicate the general types and amounts of sales deductions, namely, returns, freight allowances, price adjustments, or customer sales policy adjustments. It may be helpful, also, to prepare an analysis of deductions by responsibility—the manufacturing division for defective product, the traffic department for erroneous freight allowances, the sales division for allowances to retain customer goodwill.

(e) TYPICAL CONDITIONS FOUND BY SALES ANALYSIS

In many businesses, a large proportion of the sales volume is done in a small share of the product line. Likewise, a relatively small proportion of customers will provide the bulk of the volume. Such conditions reflect the fact that only a very small part of the selling effort is responsible for most of the business. This information should prove useful to the sales executive. It might permit the concentration of sales effort and the consequent reduction in selling expense. Again, it might mean a change in territorial assignments of sales staff. Where product analysis reveals unsatisfactory conditions, a simplification of the product line may be indicated. Although the line may not be limited to only volume items, many sales managers are beginning to realize that not all sizes, all colors, and all varieties need be carried. Smart executives will let their competitors have the odd sizes or odd colors and concentrate on the more profitable articles. After all, the economies of production also must be considered in developing the product line.

(f) ILLUSTRATIVE USE OF SALES ANALYSIS— CONTROL APPLICATION

Some examples will help in illustrating certain of the benefits to be gained from sales analysis. Assume a case where the sales executive has just been advised by the accountant that sales for the month then ended total $125,000. Assume further that this is $15,000 lower than the preceding month and that the aggregate volume failed by $25,000 to meet the commitment to the chief executive. What can the sales manager do with merely the information that sales were $125,000? The answer, of course, is that he cannot do very much. He is in the position of a hunter who has a shotgun but needs a high-powered rifle. This sales manager's controller has done a poor job.

Now assume that an analysis of sales by territories is made available. The results might be as shown in the following set of figures. This analysis gives the sales executive some useful information. Instead of prodding the managers of all territories, he can concentrate his efforts on the poor performers—B, D, and C, probably in just that order.

Territory	Total Sales		Over (or Under) Budget	
	Actual	Budget	Value	%
A	$ 15,000	$ 12,500	$ 2,500	20.00
B	50,000	70,000	(20,000)	(28.56)
C	10,000	12,500	(2,500)	(20.00)
D	25,000	37,500	(12,500)	(33.33)
E	13,000	8,500	4,500	52.94
F	12,000	9,000	3,000	33.33
Total	$125,000	$150,000	$(25,000)	(16.67)

If more than one salesperson is assigned to a territory, a further analysis of the substandard territories could prove useful. Although territory B, for example, was badly under budget, it could well be that some of the salespersons did a good job. The picture might appear thus:

| | Total Sales | | Over (or Under) Budget | |
Salesperson	Actual	Budget	Value	%
Knight	$17,000	$14,000	$ 3,000	21.43
Black	11,500	15,000	(3,500)	(23.33)
Smith	8,500	20,500	(12,000)	(58.54)
Jones	8,000	16,000	(8,000)	(50.00)
Nesser	5,000	4,500	500	11.11
Total	$50,000	$70,000	$(20,000)	(28.56)

Territory B—Analysis by Salesperson

It is evident that something went wrong in the areas covered by Smith, Jones, and Black. Where did they fall down? A subanalysis of the sales by Smith might reveal the following:

| | Sales | | | Over (or Under) Budget | |
Product	Potential	Actual	Budget	Value	%
Urea molding compound ...	$20,000	$2,500	$12,000	$(9,500)	(79.17)
Alkyd molding compound ..	4,000	500	3,600	(3,100)	(86.11)
Hard resins	1,000	1,000	900	100	11.11
Powdered glue	6,000	4,500	4,000	500	12.50
Total	$31,000	$8,500	$20,500	$(12,000)	(58.54)

Now we are beginning to get at the root of the trouble! Smith has done much better than expected on hard resins and glue. He is getting what sales management feels is his maximum share of hard resin sales in the territory. Whereas he can get still a greater share of the potential sales, he actually exceeded his budget. However, Smith has performed very poorly on molding compound. A review of Smith's call reports indicates that he is not calling on the important users of molding compound. For example, he is completely overlooking the molders of electrical fixtures, yet this is where the greatest potential lies. His sales, as an analysis by customers shows, have been only to molders of bottle caps and the like. Now the sales manager has the facts and can take corrective action, and the controller can feel that his analysis has been useful.

(g) OTHER USES OF SALES ANALYSIS

In many businesses, particularly small concerns, budget applications are neither well developed nor applied. Budget information by product or by salesperson is not available. In some instances, the cost of maintaining an elaborate budget system is not cost effective. Sales analyses may be made that are useful but not related to a budget. An analysis by customer by commodity class, indicating sales this month, sales same month last year, sales year to date, and sales last year to date will provide some comparative data as well as trends. If the sales executive has detailed knowledge of each territory and general level of activity by customer, the report can be of use in directing the sales effort. Observations can be made about which customers are growing or declining in sales volume. With knowledge of the margin by commodity class, it can be determined if growth is in the profitable lines or on the low margin products; this may indicate that prices should be reviewed.

There are many simple analyses that can be made to guide the sales effort. The controller should continuously work with sales executives to develop those reports that are most useful—in some instances special or one-time reports. The information developed should be interpreted and the important trends or measures should be highlighted.

Other uses of sales analyses that may be considered are as follows:

1. *For Sales Planning and Setting of Quotas.* Past experience is a factor.
2. *For Inventory Control.* To properly plan inventories, a business should be familiar with past sales and probable future trends in terms of seasonal fluctuations and type of product.
3. *For the Setting of Certain Sales Standards.* Here, also, past experience is a factor.
4. *For the Better Distribution of Sales Effort in Territories.* It may well prove that the business is concentrating its effort in too restrictive an area. Consideration of potential sales, competitive conditions, and cost factors may dictate a wider coverage. Again, analysis might reveal that the territory is not being fully covered.
5. *For Better Direction of Sales Effort on Products.* A study of sales and the potentials may reveal the restriction of sales effort to certain products to the neglect of other and more profitable ones. Also, a comparison of sales by product with previous periods will reveal trends. If the trends are away from the more profitable lines, corrective action may be necessary.
6. *For Better Direction of Sales Effort in Terms of Customers.* Analysis by customers should reveal trends about the types of merchandise purchased by each customer. Also, comparison with the sales of a similar period for the previous year will reveal facts on whether the company is making headway in securing the maximum amount of profitable business from the customer. Analysis by customer account, coupled with other information and discussions with the sales manager, will show certain accounts that cannot possibly provide a profitable volume, even if developed. This, too, may permit greater utilization of sales effort elsewhere.

(h) SALES AND GROSS PROFIT ANALYSIS

Sales efforts, as previously stated, should be directed and focused on *profitable* volume. To accomplish this, sales executives must be provided with all the facts related to profit. Therefore, analysis of sales must include a detailed analysis of contribution margin and/or gross profit. For example, a sales report by a salesperson should indicate the comparative gross profit by periods as well as sales. Although high gross profit does not necessarily signify a high net profit, since the selling costs may be excessive, it is an indicator. It certainly serves as a guide, however, in determining areas for concentration of the sales effort.

One other aspect of gross profit deserves comment. Variations in gross profit may result from changes in the selling price, product sales mixture, returns, or volume—largely controlled by the sales executive—or from changes in manufacturing efficiency—controlled by the production executive. These facts should be recognized when reviewing changes in gross profit. The causes should be isolated. If a standard cost system is in operation, this process is simplified somewhat. In this case, the best measure of sales performance will be standard gross profit. When the standard eliminates the manufacturing efficiency factor, then the sales department is generally responsible for the result, as well as the volume variance.

(i) LIMITATIONS OF SALES ANALYSIS

Sales analysis is only one management tool used by the sales executive. Such analysis, however, is no substitute for the professional leadership needed to properly direct and manage the sales function. It is obvious that analysis of the actual sales volume must be used in conjunction with other factors—sales potential, plans, budgets, standards, historical performance, industry comparisons, manufacturing costs, and operating expenses. Most important, the sales executive must use the data to make effective decisions.

Although sales volume analyses can be used extensively in measuring or studying sales performance, those using the data must recognize that high volume does not mean high profits. Profits will certainly vary, and a business does not earn the same rate of profit on all products. An analysis of sales volume alone will not provide sufficient information to maximize the return on investment on any given product. Many other factors must be considered. Even with some limitations, the analysis of sales is an integral part of any well managed sales function.

20-7 SALES PLANNING: THE BASIS OF ALL BUSINESS PLANS

Sales analysis is a useful function. As mentioned in the prior section, it may be applied to better direct and control sales effort, and for other related sales *control* activities. Yet, one of the other principal applications is to sales *planning;* that is, in helping to determine a proper sales level (by product or territory or salesperson, etc.) for the annual business plan—the next year or two; and in selecting the more profitable sales potential areas for the strategic, or long-range, plan.

It will bear mentioning that the sales plan is the foundation for the entire system of plans (see Chapters 14 and 16): for the production plan, the marketing plan, the research and development plan, the administrative expense plan, to say nothing of the facilities plan, the working capital plan, and the financing plan. Thus, the sales plan is so pervasive and fundamental that it is in the interest of the company to develop the best possible plan, using all fairly available information—both internal and external.

A reasonable amount of time will be spent in developing the short-term sales plan or budget for the next year in considerable detail. But the chief sales executive has to keep in perspective the relationship of the immediate short-term or tactical plan to the strategic longer term plan. The flow of products and services in these two plans may be as illustrated in Figure 20-1. As a practical matter, the sales manager often will view the marketing task as threefold:

- Sales of existing products and/or services to existing customers;
- Sales of existing products/services to new customers; and
- Sales of new products to existing, as well as new customers.

Sales often may be estimated by these segments.

Figure 20-1   Strategic and Tactical Sales Plan.

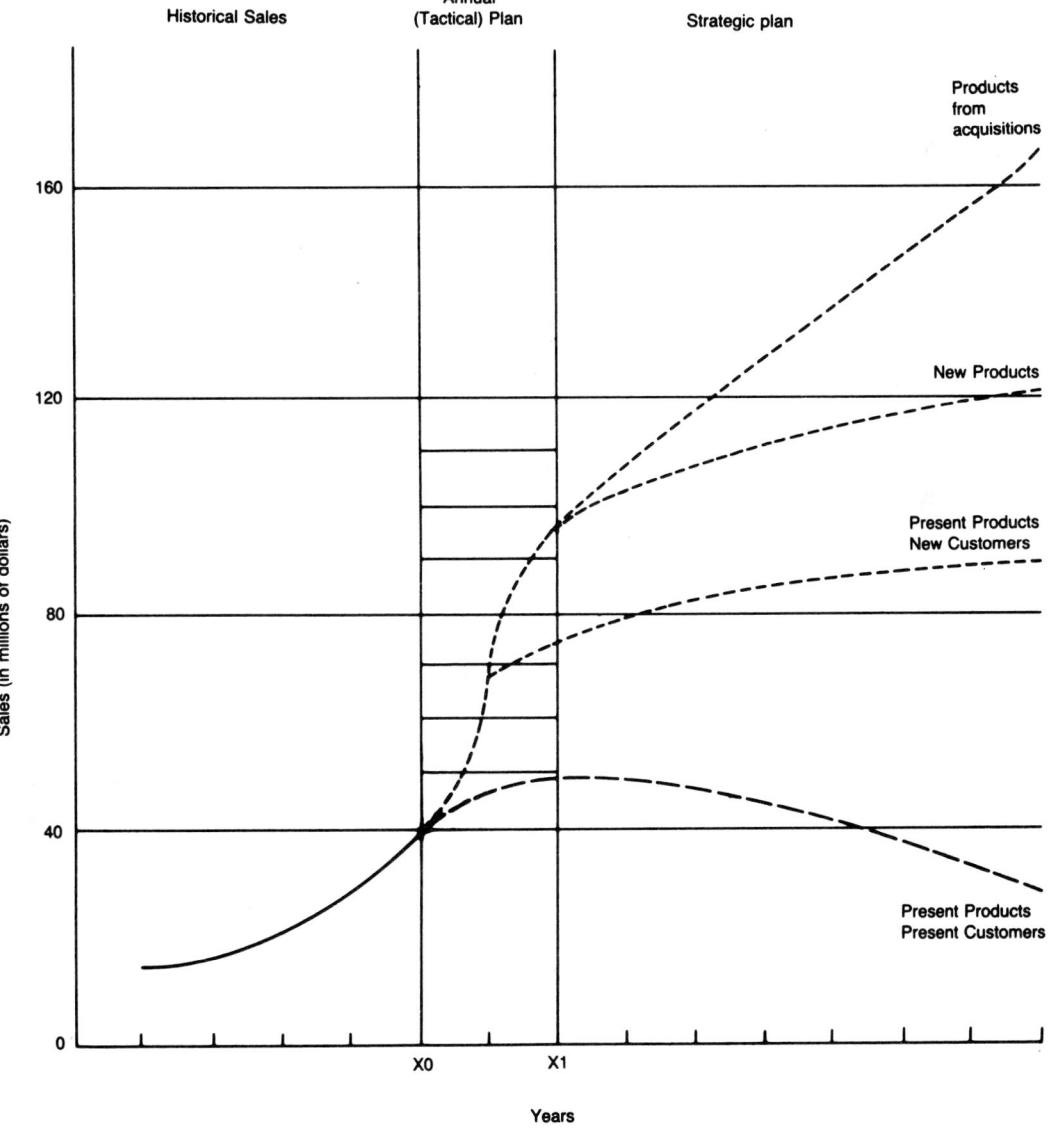

These facets of the near- and long-term sales plans, as well as the increase in sales from acquisitions (newly acquired companies or products), are shown in Figure 20-1. All these sales targets may be necessary to avoid the natural decline in sales over a period of time, and to reach the long-term corporate sales objective.

20-8 STEPS IN DEVELOPING THE NEAR-TERM SALES PLAN/BUDGET

Each company has its own way of developing the sales plan or budget, and providing such information to those executives, who, in turn, use it for developing their segment of the total business plan.

The planning steps listed next are somewhat typical when industry estimates of future sales levels are available, or when some useful external data may be secure, and when the involved executives are accustomed to being provided with relevant sales and gross profit analyses.

1. The chief sales executive who is responsible for preparing the sales plan, also called the sales budget, and meeting it, is given some or all of the following data:

    a. Computer sheets or other worksheets in proper format for providing the sales estimate, by month, and by product or salesperson, for the planning year.

    b. Sales performance for the last year (estimated for the balance of current year) or two by salesperson, and perhaps subanalyzed by territory or customer—in monetary or physical units.

    c. Industry data on expected next-year total sales.

    d. Any other analyses based on external information, developed by the market research department or economist or perhaps the controller, giving a clue as to expected sales (correlation techniques, etc., U.S. government statistics) or business conditions for the coming plan year.

    e. Any other data the sales manager or salespersons reasonably request as helpful in developing sales estimates.

    f. Analyses, if available, giving the estimated sales impact of planned sales promotions, and reasons for the cause or precise location of below-plan performance in the sales area (current year).

    g. Any guidance, or expected sales levels that the CEO or other influential executives (e.g., manufacturing executives as to new production capacity) may wish to, or can provide.

2. The sales executive provides an estimate of sales for the planning year in appropriate detail (by product, salesperson, or territory). He may prepare such an estimate unaided. Preferably, however, he will ask each salesperson (through appropriate organization channels) to make an estimate of sales for that person's assigned area or product, in appropriate detail, by month or other time period, for the coming year. The chief sales executive, directly or acting through territorial or product sales managers, will provide guidance to the sales staff on such subjects as these:

    Percent sales increase expected.

    Estimated impact of planned promotional programs.

    Competitive actions, etc.

(The various methods of estimating sales level are discussed in the next section.) Assuming each salesperson prepares his own estimate (by customer, or product, etc.), as the plan is forwarded up the organization structure to the chief sales executive, it may be modified by the intervening sales executives—each giving reasons for the changes.

3. Finally, at the top executive level, the estimates are consolidated (probably by the controller's staff) and company totals determined.

    The summarized sales plan, following the territorial organization structure is illustrated in Figure 20-2. Supporting territorial budgets for each territory sales manager, by salesperson, would be available from the data base. Other analyses, such as by product, could be prepared.

4. Each proposed sales level is discussed by executive management as to acceptability, reasonableness, etc.

5. When the sales budget is tentatively approved (an iterative process) then other functional executives who need the data are provided with it so they can develop their segments of the annual plan—the marketing plan, production plan, research and development plan. Several iterations can take place (adjusting for capacity, competitive actions, probable lack of raw material, etc.) until an operating plan is agreed upon.

6. The operating budget and capital budget, together with the related financial statements, are consolidated and tested for financial acceptability, and so on. Through iteration a final plan is arrived at.

7. When the board of directors approves the plan, each segment becomes a commitment for the plan period by the relevant or responsible executive.

Figure 20-2   Sales Plan by Territory.

The Illustrative Company
SALES PLAN BY TERRITORY
FOR THE YEAR 199X
(dollars in thousands)

| | Sales This Year | | Plan | | | |
| | | | | Quarter | | |
Territory		Total	1	2	3	4
West	$212,400	$230,000	$ 46,000	$ 63,720	$ 79,040	$ 41,240
Rockies	75,000	78,750	15,750	23,620	31,500	7,880
Southwest	134,600	150,750	37,690	45,200	45,200	22,660
Central Plains ...	53,400	56,100	14,000	16,900	16,900	8,300
Middle West	171,300	186,700	33,600	65,300	50,000	37,800
Southeast	91,400	95,100	19,000	28,500	21,000	26,600
Total	$738,100	$797,400	$166,040	$243,240	$243,640	$144,480

20-9 THE CONTROL PHASE

In the context of the budgeting process—a two-pronged device consisting of (a) the planning phase and (b) the control phase—the above steps complete the *planning* phase when the sales plan is approved by the board of directors. Then, the task consists of, among other things, monitoring actual sales results and directing the sales effort so that the plan is achieved. This is generally identified as the *control* phase. The implementing steps are essentially as follows:

- Actual performance is compared with plan (or quota), for each salesperson involved in the sales effort, for the appropriate time period, which may be the day (cumulative), week, or month.
- The data are analyzed, much as described earlier, to determine the cause of the subperformance.
- Corrective action, if needed, is taken by the sales executive to get sales "on plan." This might include special sales promotion, etc., especially if the cause of under-plan sales is a general condition, i.e., not one induced by the lack of effort of a salesperson.
- Aside from analysis of actual and planned sales, a review of some selected statistical performance measures may provide clues on how sales could be improved, e.g., conversion rate of prospects to customers. See the sections on standards and benchmarking.

20-10 METHODS OF DETERMINING THE SALES LEVEL

The development of a sound sales plan, together with the program for directing the sales effort, ultimately must rest largely on the judgment of the cognizant sales executive. The means he uses to arrive at his decision obviously may influence its quality. Ordinarily, weight must be given to both external and internal factors. External factors—which include such elements as general economic conditions, industry trends, total market potential, and competitive actions or reactions—are beyond the control of the individual company, but nevertheless may largely prescribe the sales potential. Internal factors relate to conditions within the entity and are composed of matters such as production capacity, product quality, sales experience and history, special advertising and sales promotion programs, pricing policy, sales method changes.

In this section, some of the more commonly used methods of estimating sales levels, to help the sales executive reach decisions or judgments, are discussed. What system will be used may depend on several related attributes:

1. *Time.* The time span available, the frequency of the data.
2. *Resources Needed or Available.* Manpower, computers, financial sophistication, cost.
3. *Data Input.* What is needed, consistency, availability, variability.
4. *Output.* Reliability, extent of detail, capability of detecting trend changes, capability of revealing direction changes that have taken place.

For the knowledge of the controller, the more or less proven techniques of forecasting sales demand may be categorized in these three groups:

1. *Mathematical/Statistical Methods.*

   - Time series analysis.
   - Correlation.

2. *Judgmental Methods (Nonstatistical).*

   - Estimates of salespersons.
   - Customer surveys.
   - Executive opinion composites.

3. *Other Methods.*

   - Share of market.
   - End-use analysis.
   - Product line analysis.
   - Market simulation.
   - Combinations of methods.

Brief comments are made on each of these procedures. However, the Selected References include several useful publications on the various techniques.

(a) MATHEMATICAL/STATISTICAL METHODS

The various mathematical/statistical methods usually require the services of a person or persons skilled in the techniques: statisticians, economists, or perhaps accountants. Basically, a statistical technique is applied to a series of relevant numbers to arrive at a *forecast* of sales for the industry or company. Then, this *forecast* is modified by the expected impact of sales efforts, promotional campaigns, etc., to arrive at a sales *plan* for the company. Two types of mathematical applications are addressed here.

(i) Time Series Analysis.   With the use of a model already programmed in the computer, or by the application of the well-known least squares method, an existing series of values is converted into a trend, and extrapolated for a future time period. Basically, the existing series of values is isolated into its statistical components:

- Secular or long-term trend.
- Cyclical movements.
- Seasonal patterns.
- The remaining random fluctuations.

The long-term trend is projected, to estimate the future sales for the planning periods.

(ii) Correlation Analysis.   As the name implies, a series is located with which the company sales, or sales of a particular product line, seem to correlate or move sympathetically. Presumably, the data are readily and timely available, are reliable, and are those that lead the company sales. The annual product sales are plotted against the index and, based on the leading factor, calculated for the planning period. Some illustrative correlation bases could be the U.S. Department of Commerce composite index of leading indicators (discussed later) or Series No. 20, contracts and orders for plant and equipment, also issued by the U.S. Department of Commerce, or the Federal Reserve Index of Industrial Production.

Other statistical methods, such as the Box-Jenkins computer-based iterative procedure, or use of moving averages, can be employed.

See the Selected References for an excellent summary of the various methods of sales forecasting by Georgoff and Murdick.

(b) JUDGMENTAL METHODS

Another popular method is the gathering of opinions or estimates from several groups. Some common variations of this method are discussed.

(c) ESTIMATES OF SALESPERSONS

In using the estimates of salespeople, one method involves securing the estimates of the sales staff itself. Each salesperson is provided with a record of his/her sales, by month, for the past year or two. With this data and that person's knowledge of the sales territory and customer, an estimate by product and/or customer is obtained from the person who will be responsible for securing the sale.

A variation of this procedure is to have the sales manager to whom the salesperson reports and the salesperson jointly arrive at a sales estimate.

Another procedure involving the sales department personnel is to secure the opinions of the various sales managers—the product sales managers, division sales managers, or territory sales managers, together with the general sales manager. Through discussions and cross-checking, and considering the impact of sales programs, many believe a reliable estimate can be secured. Of course, the extent of knowledge of the sales-manager level must be considered. Hopefully, they are close enough to the firing line to know the sales conditions, products, and customers.

The use of only sales department personnel has both advantages and disadvantages:

1. *Advantages.*
   - The knowledge of the persons closest to the sales picture is used.
   - Those who must meet plan have a voice in setting it.

2. *Disadvantages.*
   - The level may be biased in that sales personnel often tend to provide optimistic estimates when the business level is high, and too-low estimates when the level is poor.
   - The participants may not give proper weight to broad economic trends that the sales force or managers either do not recognize or fail to properly evaluate.
   - If compensation levels depend on meeting the sales plan, a deliberate effort might be made to keep the estimate on the low side so that enhanced remuneration is more likely.

Care must be taken (by the CEO, other top executives, or the controller) in weighing the sales personnel opinions.

(d) CUSTOMER SURVEYS

The practice of asking customers for their estimate of purchases for the coming year often is used when there is no other source of reliable and specific data to make a sales estimate. It may be employed when there is a good relationship between the salesperson and the customer, and when the customers tend to be very large and limited in number. An example is the glass companies who make the windshields and glass windows used by the automobile manufacturers.

The disadvantages include the facts that:

- The user may be ill-informed or uncooperative in such sensitive matters.
- It is time consuming if many customers must be contacted.

On the other hand:

- It may be the only suitable manner of preparing a sales plan.
- It gives the questioner an opportunity to delve into the thinking of the customers about the business outlook.
- It is an opportunity to secure information directly from those who will be using the product.

(e) EXECUTIVE OPINION COMPOSITES

Another commonly used and convenient method of estimating future sales volume is by securing opinions from a group of top and middle management executives who have reason to be familiar with the industry and company sales picture. The method involves simply securing the estimates from a group of executives, perhaps weighting them, and then combining the opinions. Thus, the CEO and sales, production, research, and financial executives may be contacted, and weightings given to their opinions, depending on their knowledge of the market and perhaps on the accuracy of their past estimates. Each executive may determine his expectation based on his own methods; and the groups may meet to discuss the levels and the basis for the opinion.

While this method may provide a broader base than from sales personnel only, and be more convenient, if the executives don't really know the market, then the opinion may be one big guess, based on few facts.

(f) OTHER METHODS

There are numerous other methods for developing sales forecasts or plans, some of which may be used alone or in combination with other procedures. A few brief comments follow.

(i) Share of Market. For some types of products the total market is well known. In addition to the industry total unit volume and/or dollar volume, the rate of growth has been calculated, and often the estimated sales for the next year or two have been determined—perhaps by the industry association. In any event, the planner knows what share of the market his company has secured in the past. This market share, say 27%, adjusted for the estimated impact of special sales promotions, or guessed competitive activity is applied to the projected total market to arrive at the company segment of, say, 29% of the estimated industry sales for the coming year. Some expanded comments on this increasingly popular forecasting method, including some of its complications, are provided in section 20-11.

(ii) End-Use Analysis.   This technique depends on having a sound estimate of the total end-use market for which products the company's articles serve as component parts or elements. Again, to use the automotive industry as an example, if the expected unit sales of automobiles are known or have been estimated, then the supplier company can estimate its probable sales for the planning period for its product, for the new car business. This market, plus the estimated replacement business, or other business, can be combined to arrive at sales expectations. This method bears a close relationship, in some cases, to the customer survey procedure.

(iii) Product Line Analysis.   Quite often major products are sold through different channels of distribution or methods of sales than other products, and the sales and sales effort may be managed by product line. Under these circumstances, a company's internal sales (and gross profit) analyses by product, subanalyzed by territory, etc. (as discussed earlier in this chapter) may be the starting point of determining the sales estimate, supplemented by some of the other techniques to arrive at the sales plan.

(iv) Market Simulation.   This technique ordinarily involves the use of a computer, and the construction of a mathematical model of the market. Modifying input for the different factors that influence the market, permits the calculation of various sales estimates. This is another helpful tool, often developed by the market research organization, that can assist in arriving at a realistic sales plan.

It should be understood that, whatever estimating technique is used:

- Even a good forecast reduces only *some* of the risk that confronts sales management.
- It is often helpful to compare the results of several forecasting methods.
- Some of the simplest methods work best, because they are more easily understood; and the heart of good forecasting probably often is intelligently based intuition on the part of sales management.

20-11 MORE ABOUT SHARE OF MARKET

To the sales manager inexperienced in estimating future sales, it might seem a relatively easy task to plan company sales if industry demand forecasts are available. Yet, there are at least two hazards: (1) Industry-wide forecasts can be grossly inaccurate; and (2) many times an individual company may not be selling in the entire industry market, but only in a single segment—for which special information is required. Here are two illustrations of both cases. In 1974, U.S. electric utilities made plans to double generating capacity by the mid-1980s, based on an annual growth demand of 7% per year. In fact, during the 1975–1985 decade, load grew at only 2% per year. So the excess capacity has hurt the industry for years. As to market segments, if a gas water heater manufacturer services only the replacement market, and not the new construction market, then total industry estimates of demand would be of little value.

William Barrett[1] has suggested that there are four necessary steps in developing a useful total market forecast:

1. Define the market.
2. Divide total industry demand into its main components or markets.
3. Forecast the drivers of demand in each of the segments and project how each is likely to change.
4. Conduct sensitivity analyses in an effort to understand the most critical assumptions and to judge risks to the baseline forecast.

In defining the market, it probably is prudent to describe it so broadly as to include *all* potential users, and thus identify the demand drivers as well as any potential surprise product substitutes. The factors that drive the total market may not be those that determine a particular market share or product category share (as in the gas water heater example). By careful study of customer usage patterns, the probability of future product switching can often be detected; and the review of relevant technologies possibly can uncover potential product threats.

The second step of dividing total demand into its principal components is for the purpose of making the necessary analysis. Those responsible for the study must decide whether existing data on segment size appears adequate and reliable. Some large industries may have adequate data, whether from industry associations, or the federal government, or private sources. For others, an independent study by a knowledgeable group may be desirable. It should be mentioned, also, that the segment size should be small enough that the demand drivers will apply to most of the segment constituency, but large enough to make the analysis worthwhile. Further, a "tree" approach may be useful in identifying the various end-use categories, and then dividing each limb (end use category) into branches, each of which represents a cost driver. The objective is to accurately identify the demand drivers for each end use category, and then to develop forecasts of demand. Both facets, identifying the real demand drivers, and predicting demand can be difficult. As each driver, and the rate of growth/nongrowth is determined, the analysis must consider what could make the estimated future level go wrong, and how much each driver would influence the market. Good analysis should identify the potential risks, including competing technologies, the industry competitive status, and supplier changes. Use of sensitivity analysis should reveal which assumptions or factors are most critical.

20-12 USEFUL SOURCES OF FORECASTING INFORMATION

Business executives long have been intrigued by the promise of a practical indicator of business trends that could be useful in their business forecasting. Some have found broad economic measures helpful, such as gross national product (GNP), or new car sales in a given territory, etc. But for many, no practical guide has been located—not for the business as a whole, not for major lines. Many of the broad indicators have suffered from late availability, significant revisions, inaccuracies in compilation,

---

[1] F. William Barrett, "Four Steps to Forecast Total Market Demand," *Harvard Business Review,* July–Aug. 1988, p. 3 (HBR reprint No. 88401).

components out of touch with the market—to name a few. These executives, therefore, have encouraged their staffs to develop in-house models, perhaps based on some readily available indicators. Sometimes these models have been built from data furnished by commercial banks, or in other instances developed from a factor, such as regional car sales, that an executive has noticed appears to correlate quite closely with the company's sales experience on certain products.

Given the conflicting or indecisive signals put out by some indicators and the inability to find a suitable one—to repeat—sometimes the intuition of the chief executive or chief sales executive is one of the best guides.

But the controller should be aware of external sources of sales forecasting data just in case the present sales estimating techniques could stand some testing or improvement.

(a) SOME SPECIFIC SOURCES

There are numerous sources, ranging from the federal government to selected financial services, such as Standard & Poor's and Moody's, that supply information which may be useful in sales forecasting. Market planners, market research analysts, and many financial executives often are familiar with them. Of course, libraries may provide assistance on this subject. The secret is to find an index or economic data that are useful in a particular business. A partial listing of some sources follows:

1. *U.S. Government Sources.*
   a. Department of Commerce.
      (i)   Bureau of Economic Analysis (BEA).
            Includes cyclical indicators and economic measures published in the *Survey of Current Business.*[2]
      (ii) Department of Labor.
            Bureau of Labor Statistics.
      (iii) Department of Agriculture.
      (iv) Bureau of Mines.
      (v)   U.S. Government Printing Office.
2. *Commercial Banks.*[3]
   Examples: The Morgan Guaranty Survey published periodically by Morgan Guaranty Trust Company of New York, containing projections. Wells Fargo Bank (NA), Economics Department, *Business Review,* which publishes annually a Special Outlook issue providing forecast data on the U.S. economy as well as that of California.

---

[2] This is discussed later.

[3] The controller can check through the appropriate company channel or directly from its commercial bankers as to data available.

3. *Other Sources.*

    a. Trade associations.

    b. State governments.

    c. Federal Reserve Board.

    d. Universities (economics departments and schools of business, etc.).

    e. Financial services providing economic data for pay.

    f. Numerous business magazines, such as:

        (i) *Survey of Current Business.*

        (ii) *Business Week* with its weekly Business Week Leading Index.

        (iii) *Fortune* Magazine (its Forecast).

    g. Libraries.

(b) CYCLICAL INDICATORS; LEADING INDICATORS

The Bureau of Economic Analyses of the U.S. Department of Commerce periodically publishes (in addition to other data) certain economic indicators (including graphs and charts) that are helpful in sales planning.

    Of particular value are these three groups of indicators:

1. *Leading indicators,* or series that usually reach peaks or troughs before general economic activity.

2. *Roughly coincident indicators,* or series that tend to move with aggregate economic activity (more or less).

3. *Lagging indicators,* or series that usually reach turning points after the aggregate economic activity has.

    And especially useful to some companies, despite the revisions and occasional delays in publication, are the above listed "leading indicators."

    The makeup of these three groups of indicators is as follows:[4]

LEADING INDICATORS AND RELATED INDEXES

Series No.	Title (and Unit of Measure)
1.	Average weekly hours in manufacturing (hours)
5.	Average weekly initial claims for unemployment insurance, state programs (thous.)
8.	Mfrs. new orders in 1987 dollars, consumer goods and materials industries (bil.dol.)
19.	Stock prices, 500 common stocks (index: $1941 - 43 = 10$)
20.	Contracts and orders for plant and equipment in 1987 dollars (bil. dol.)
29.	New private housing units authorized by local building permits (index: $1967 = 100$)
32.	Vendor performance, percent of companies receiving slower deliveries (percent)
36.	Change in inventories on hand and on order in 1982 dol., smoothed (ann. rate, bil. dol.)
83.	Index of consumer expectations, U. of Michigan, $1966 = 100$

[4] From *Survey of Current Business,* March, 1994, p. C-1.

Series No.	Title (and Unit of Measure)
92.	Change in mfgrs. unfilled orders, durable goods bil $1987, smoothed
99.	Change in sensitive materials prices, smoothed (percent)
106.	Money supply M2 in 1987 dollars (bil. dol.)
910.	Composite index of leading indicators (index: 1987 = 100)
950.	Diffusion index of 11 leading indicator components

ROUGHLY COINCIDENT INDICATORS AND RELATED INDEXES

Series No.	Title (and Unit of Measure)
41.	Employees on nonagricultural payrolls (thous.)
47.	Industrial production (index: 1987 = 100)
51.	Personal, income less transfer payments in 1987 dollars (ann. rate, bil. dol.)
57.	Manufacturing and trade sales in 1987 dollars (mil. dol.)
920.	Composite index of roughly coincident indicators (index: 1987 = 100)
951.	Diffusion index of 4 coincident indicator components

LAGGING INDICATORS AND RELATED INDEXES

Series No.	Title (and Unit of Measure)
62.	Labor cost per unit of output, manufacturing—actual data as a percent of trend (percent)
77.	Ratio, manufacturing and trade inventories to sales in 1987 dollars (ratio)
91.	Average duration of unemployment (weeks)
95.	Ratio, consumer installment credit outstanding to personal income (percent)
101.	Commercial and industrial loans outstanding in 1982 dollars (mil. dol.)
109.	Average prime rate charged by banks (percent)
930.	Composite index of lagging indicators (index: 1967 = 100)
940.	Ratio, coincident index to lagging index (1987 = 100)
952.	Diffusion index of 7 lagging indicator components

The leading indicators previously listed are called leading indicators because each has shown a tendency to change before the economy itself made a major turn. Comments on each component are as follows (the number refers to the series number):

1. *Average Weekly Hours in Manufacturing.* By and large, employers find it more economical to increase the number of hours worked each week before hiring additional employees. These longer work weeks may lead an upturn by one or more months, or they may coincide with the change.

5. *Average Weekly Initial Claims for Unemployment Insurance.* Generally, the number of persons who sign up for jobless benefits reflects the change in present or anticipated business activity. Obviously the fewer who sign up, the better. This index has turned up—sometimes before, sometimes after—a turning point in economic activity.

8. *Manufacturers' New Orders for Consumer Goods and Materials.* When new orders are received, materials and supplies are purchased, workers are hired, and

output increases. Recoveries in general have occurred as much as four months after gains in new orders.

19. *Stock Prices.* A rise in the Standard & Poor's Corporation index of 500 companies usually indicates higher actual and expected profits (or lower interest rates, or changes in other concerns). Advances in the stock market have preceded improvements in business activity by three to eight months.

20. *Contracts and Orders for Plant and Equipment.* When such orders are received, construction and manufacturing activity increases. These signals have preceded economic upturns by as much as six months, but also have trailed such change by up to nine months.

29. *New Private Housing Units Authorized.* From the time a building permit is issued until commencement of construction, several months pass. Thus, the trend may be designated a leading indicator. Gains in building permits issued have led business upturns by zero to 10 months.

32. *Vendor Performance.* This is measured by the percentage of companies receiving slower deliveries of product. As business increases, companies simply cannot deliver product as soon after the order as they did at one time. Factories are filling up and working closer to capacity. This index has foreshadowed increased economic activity from a one-month lag to an 11-month forerunner.

83. *Index of Consumer Expectations.* This index was added in 1989, based on a monthly telephone survey, it measures consumer confidence.

92. *Change in Mfgrs. Unfilled Orders.* The data shown on *changes* from the preceding month. Positive values reflect an increase. The series gives an indication of durable goods "backlogs." An increasing backlog signals increased demands before it is met. Declining backlogs signal that production in the future will be lower.

99. *Changes in Sensitive Materials Prices.* Generally, a rise in the price of selected raw materials, such as iron and steel scrap, foreshadows a rise in factory demand. The nation's plants are being readied for a step-up in production. In recent times, economic recoveries have followed price rises by one to 10 months.

106. *Money Supply—M2.* Presumably an increase in the money supply indicates that funds are available to finance heightened economic activity. This series has foretold rising economic activity by two to 14 months. It can be seen that the indicators vary from cycle to cycle in the lead time identified. Moreover, not all indicators rise at the same time; nor do they indicate the magnitude of the swing, only the direction (if that).

The above 11 components permit the calculation of the *Index.*

910. *Composite Index of Leading Indicators.* This is an index of the above leading indicators with a detailed weighting based upon: economic significance; statistical adequacy; consistency of timing at business cycle peaks and troughs; conformity to business expansions and contractions; and prompt availability.

The makeup of the components of each index, as well as its weighting, occasionally are changed by the Bureau of Economic Analyses. Data on the changes and the current composition now is published in the *Survey of Current Business.*

(c) VALIDITY OF ECONOMIC INDICATORS

While the wealth of economic data provided by Washington is useful, the data need careful interpretation by those who know what to look for.

20-13 SALES STANDARDS

(a) DEFINITION OF SALES STANDARDS

A *standard* has been defined as a scientifically developed measure of performance. It was further noted that standards can be adapted to the measurement of sales performance in somewhat the same way they have been used to judge performance in the factory. The primary requirements in developing tools for the sales executive are threefold:

1. *Sales standards are the result of careful investigation and analysis of past performance, taking into consideration expected future conditions.* Sales standards represent the opinion of those best qualified to judge what constitutes satisfactory performance. Judgment about detailed operations must rest largely with the sales executives. Opinions about expected general business conditions and market potentials should represent the combined judgment of the executive staff, including the chief executive, the sales manager, and the controller.

2. *Sales standards must be fair and reasonable measures of performance.* Nothing will be so destructive of morale as a sales quota, or any other standard, set much too high. Experience shows that such standards will be ignored. The standards must be attainable by the caliber of salesman the company expects to be representative of its selling staff.

3. *Sales standards will need review and revision from time to time.* As sales conditions change frequently, so the measuring stick must change.

(b) PURPOSE OF SALES STANDARDS

Sales managers are sometimes of the opinion that sales standards are not welcome. Some sales executives feel that sales standards are an attempt to substitute impersonal statistics for sales leadership. There is no substitute for dynamic and farsighted sales executives; there is no intent that sales standards in any way replace personal guidance. But sales standards do provide management with an important tool of sales control, a basis for fairly rewarding merit, and a stimulating device under many circumstances, but not all. As a tool of control they reveal weaknesses in performance that, if properly analyzed in terms of causes, open the way for correction and strengthening. As a basis for rewarding merit they result in a fairer and more accurate relationship between compensation and performance. As a stimulating device they provide each salesperson and executive with a goal of accomplishment and with assurance of fair reward.

(c) NATURE OF SALES STANDARDS

The sales standards may be expressed in terms of effort, results, or the relation of effort to result. For example, a salesman may be required to make 3 calls a day or 15 calls per week. If he makes this number of calls, he meets this particular standard of effort. Again, he may, as a result of these calls, be expected to secure 10 orders for every 15 calls or a certain dollar volume per call. If he does this, he meets this particular relationship standard. Or he may simply be asked to secure a certain dollar volume from a given territory, regardless of the number of calls made or the orders and sales per call. If he does this, he meets this particular standard of results.

Again, the standards may involve a relationship between selling cost and sales results. For example, in a retail furniture store, the standard may require that one prospective customer be attracted to the store for every $2 expended in advertising or that $1 of sales be secured for every $0.07 expended for advertising. If these goals are achieved, those responsible for the advertising expenditures are meeting the standards of advertising results.

(d) ILLUSTRATIONS OF SALES STANDARDS

Although the applicability of sales standards to various industries and types of trading concerns may differ, suggestive standards the controller may consider discussing with the sales manager are outlined here:

Standards of Effort

Number of calls to be made per period.

Number of calls to be made on prospective customers.

Number of dealers and agencies to be established.

Number of units of sales promotional effort to be used, e.g., demonstrations or pieces of direct mail sent.

Standards of Results

Percentage of prospects to whom sales are to be made.

Number of customers to whom new articles are to be introduced or sold.

Number of new customers to be secured.

Amount of dollar volume to be secured.

Number of physical units to be sold.

Amount of gross profit to be secured.

Amount of profit to be secured (here profit is frequently considered as the excess of gross profit over the expenses that are subject to the control of the salesperson or executive to whom the standard is to apply).

Amounts to be sold to individual customers (especially larger customers).

Dollar or physical volume of individual products or product classes to be sold.

Percentage of gross profit to be returned (where there is a varied line or where the salesman has price latitude).

Average size of order to be secured.

Relation of sales deductions to gross sales.

Standards Expressing Relationship of Effort and Result

Number of orders to be received per call made.

Number of new customers to be secured per call made on prospects.

Number of inquiries or orders to be received per unit or per dollar of sales promotional effort expended.

Relation of individual direct selling expense items to volume or gross profit.

Relation of sales administration or supervision costs to volume or gross profit.

(e) DEVELOPING SALES STANDARDS—BENCHMARKING

Now that sales standards have been defined, their purpose and nature explained, and illustrations provided, the question arises as to *how* sales standards are and should be developed.

To be effective, the standards must be accepted by those who use them as fair and reasonable—not the product of the whim of some over-zealous bean counter. Benchmarking is used by a company to measure its products, services, and business practices against the toughest competitor, or those companies best in its class, or other comparisons. Brief commentary on this process and results are presented in section 19-9.

(f) REVISION OF SALES STANDARDS

Some standards of sales performance can be set with a high degree of exactness. The number of calls a salesperson should make, the percentage of prospects to whom sales should be made, and the physical units that should be sold to each customer are illustrative of performances that frequently lend themselves to accurate measurements. On the other hand, there are many factors in sales performance that are so governed by conditions beyond the control of the salespeople that the standards must be promptly revised to meet important changes in such conditions. Where a salesperson is given some latitude in price setting, his gross profit percentage may vary with competitive conditions beyond his control. Strikes, droughts, and floods may suddenly affect the sales possibilities in a particular territory. If the sales standards are to be effective measures of sales performance, they must be promptly revised as conditions change. Careless measurement of performance soon leads to discouragement, resentment, and disinterest in the task.

(g) USE OF SALES STANDARDS

As stated previously, the purposes of sales standards are to control sales operations, to reward merit, and to stimulate sales effort. The standards in themselves are of limited value, except as they are made effective in the accomplishment of such purposes. To make the standards so effective requires the following be done:

The variations between actual and standard performance be promptly determined.

The causes of such variations be investigated and explained.

The responsibility for the variations be definitely fixed.

The individuals held responsible be given full opportunity to present their explanations.

Prompt action be taken to correct any weaknesses revealed.

The method of compensation shall provide a fair and accurate reward for performance.

(h) SALES QUOTAS AS STANDARDS

The most widely used sales standard is the sales quota. As usually constituted, the sales quota is the amount of dollar of physical volume of sales assigned to a particular salesman, department, branch, territory, or other division as a measure of satisfactory performance. The quota may, however, involve other considerations, such as gross profit, new customers, collections, or traveling expense, thereby representing something of a composite or collective standard of performance.

The quota does not differ in its purpose and use from other sales standards as discussed earlier. The applicability of the quota to various types of concerns depends largely on the extent to which sales and other results are actually affected by the direct efforts of the salespeople involved and the extent to which such results are affected by other factors, such as expenditures for advertising, special sales promotion, styles, and acceptability of products. Where the former is the dominant factor, sales quotas constitute a valuable type of sales standard.

(i) BASIS OF SALES QUOTAS

Generally speaking, sales quotas are of value only to the extent that they are based on known facts relative to sales possibilities. They must not be based on the greed of the company or fanciful ideas of what might be done but on actual facts relating to past sales, sales in allied industries, population, buying power, or territorial conditions. The sales representative should be thoroughly informed about the method of arriving at his quota and convinced that the amount of sales assigned to him is entirely justified according to the existing conditions. Then, and only then, will he exert his full effort to meet his quota.

The quota should not be thought of primarily as a basis for contests. The salesperson should consider his quota as representing a careful measurement of his task rather than a temporary target at which to shoot.

Actual experience with sales quotas, as with all standards, will reveal that sales representatives react to them somewhat differently, particularly at first. Some are stimulated to their highest efficiency, whereas others are discouraged. Some sales executives place considerable emphasis on this human element in setting their quotas. In general, however, good salespeople will, in the long run, respond favorably to intelligently devised quotas, particularly when compensation is fairly adjusted to performance.

The objection sometimes raised, that efforts are lessened after quotas are reached, is seldom valid if performance is properly rewarded. The chief difficulty arises when quotas are exceeded as a result of some fortuitous circumstance in which the sales representative has had no part or for which his share of the credit is uncertain. The solution here usually rests with extreme fairness in handling individual cases and with the development of confidence in the knowledge and integrity of sales executives.

The method of establishing sales quotas is still unsatisfactory in many concerns. The matter is frequently given insufficient study, and the results are ineffective. There has, however, been a vast improvement in such methods in recent years, and alert controllers have made a substantial contribution to this improvement.

Past performance is greatly influenced by conditions beyond the control of the individual salesperson. Hence a quota set when business is poor is likely to result in undue reward to the salesman. Conversely, one set when business is good is likely to prove too high to serve as an effective incentive, or even provide fair compensation.

(j) METHOD OF EXPRESSING QUOTAS

Insofar as practicable, quotas should be broken down into their detailed elements. This helps to show the sales representative where, how, and to whom the goods should be sold. To illustrate, a certain company gives each of its sales representatives the following details relative to his sales quota:

1. The proportion of the quota assigned to each product line.
2. The part of the quota that represents an expected increase in business from new customers.
3. The part of the quota that represents an expected increase in business among old customers.
4. The part of the quota to be secured in cities of various sizes.
5. The part of the quota assigned to particular kinds of outlets or classes of customers.
6. The part of the quota to be secured from special or exceptional sources.
7. The distribution of the quota by months.

Although such a plan entails considerable work, it tends to balance the sales effort and to assist the sales representative in directing his work most effectively.

It should be realized that such details require the necessary detailed analysis of past performance by the controller's staff. Furthermore, such detail is indicative of a well-developed program. Many firms, particularly the small and medium sized, will express quotas in general terms only—so many dollars of sales or so many overall units. Where quotas are relatively new, the controller should proceed cautiously and develop the details gradually so that the sales executives can be guided step by step. Only when the data are available and the sales staff realizes the advantages of detailed planning can the quota type of standard serve most usefully.

It frequently happens that the quota cannot be fairly expressed directly in money or physical volume. For example, a sale of $100 of class A goods may deserve more credit than a like amount of class B goods, or a sale to a new customer may deserve more credit than a similar sale to an old customer. In such cases, the quota may be expressed in points that give effect to a weighting for different types of sales performance. Thus a sale of $100 class A goods may be counted as 10 points, whereas $100 of class B goods would be counted as only 5 points. The "point" system may likewise be extended to include other types of service, such as calls on new prospects, demonstrations, or collections.

The final requirement for effective standards is an adequate method of compensation as a reward for good performance.

20-14 SALES REPORTS

(a) EFFECTING SALES CONTROL

Fundamentally, control is the prompt follow-up of unfavorable trends or conditions before they develop into large losses. In the small business, the owners or manager can exercise current control of sales through a review of orders received, etc. In the larger businesses, however, such personal contact must be supplemented by reports that indicate current conditions and trends as well as current performance.

It is the function of the controller, of course, to furnish the sales executives with the sales facts. However, it is one thing to furnish the information; it is quite another thing to see that it is understood and acted on. To assure the necessary understanding, the controller must adapt the report to his reader. Information for the needs of the chief executive will be different from that for the sales manager, and reports for subordinate sales executives will differ even more. The extent of the information required and the form of presentation will depend on the capabilities of the individual, the type of organization, the responsibilities of the man, and the philosophy of sales management.

(b) NATURE OF SALES REPORTS

Sales executives have many management styles and backgrounds. Some sales managers can effectively use vast amount of statistical data, whereas others prefer summarizations. Accordingly, the controller should offer to develop reports to meet the requirement. The use of charts, graphs, and summaries will greatly enhance the communication of the sales data to sales management. In many instances, a narrative report citing the significant issues or problems is the most effective tool. Depending on the seriousness of the problem, or where major actions are being recommended, a meeting may be in order. It is up to the controller to insure that the information provided is understood and can be properly used.

(c) CONTENT OF SALES REPORTS

The matters that may be included in a sales report cover a broad front. Such reports might contain the following:

1. Actual sales performance, with month or year-to-date figures.
2. Budgeted sales for both the period and year to date.
3. Comparison of actual sales by firm with industry figures, including percentages of total.
4. Analysis of variances between budgeted and actual sales and reasons for differences.
5. Sale-cost relationships, such as cost per order received.
6. Sales standards—comparison of actual and quota sales by salesman.
7. Unit sales price data.
8. Gross profit data.

These data often may be expressed in physical units or in dollars. Aside from actual or standard sales performance, some may relate to orders, cancellations, returns or allowances, or lost sales.

(d) ILLUSTRATIVE FEATURES IN SALES REPORTS

As stated previously, the content of sales reports must be varied to suit the needs and personality of the user. Reports to the chief executive and top sales executive, for example, should present the overall view in summary fashion. A simple comparison of actual and planned sales by major product line or territory, as shown in Figure 20-3, summarizes the sales in a brief but informative manner. Summary information is also presented comparing the company performance against industry by months (or years) in Figure 20-4. A graphic comparison of actual with planned sales as illustrated in Figure 20-5 is also useful.

Sales executives also find trend reports on product lines to be of value. A percentage bar chart, illustrated in Figure 20-6, would be particularly significant if the profit by product group is greatly different. Trends in sales volume are easily shown by vertical bar charts similar to that pictured in Figure 20-6. Sales managers typically need information on the probable future course of sales. For this purpose, timely reports summarizing the orders-on-hand picture are helpful. Such a report—which may be desired daily, weekly, or monthly—is illustrated in Figure 20-7.

The graphs and reports presented thus far have been rather simple in nature. Whereas reports always should be understood, in many cases, particularly in larger companies, they must be more analytical or detailed in nature. Moreover, for control purposes and adopting the concept of "responsibility reporting," the performance of each segment of the sales organization should be made known to the supervisor responsible. It follows, therefore, that reporting must be available for each division, district, area, branch, or salesperson. A typical branch report is illustrated in Figure 20-8 and is very brief. However, as reports relate to increasingly lower levels of management, such information can become massive in extent. Therefore, although data may be periodically prepared on each segment of the organization, it has been found practical to apply the "exceptional principle" in a great many cases. This method eliminates data where performance was satisfactory and details only that which did not reach acceptable levels. An example is Figure 20-9, indicating only those salespersons who were 5% or more under budget. Another report prepared on only out-of-line performance is that shown in Figure 20-10. Only customers on which a loss was realized are listed. It is to be noted that two profit or loss computations are made: (1) actual out-of-pocket losses, using the direct costing concept, and (2) gross loss, wherein all fixed and allocated charges are considered.

(e) IMPACT OF PC HARDWARE AND SOFTWARE

The continuous improvements in computer hardware and software, and related technology, greatly facilitate the scope of reports and improve the timeliness of data presentation. The various chapters in Part Six on Computer Systems and Related Technology provide more details on the reporting possibilities.

Figure 20-3 Comparison of Actual to Planned Sales.

ABC Manufacturing Company
COMPARATIVE STATEMENT OF SALES
MONTH OF ———— 19XX

Product or Territory	Month				Year to Date				Total Year		
	Actual	Plan	Over (under) Plan	Last Year Actual	Actual	Plan	Over (under) Plan	Last Year Actual	Indi-cated Final	Plan	Over (under) Plan
Product line "A"											
Item 1											
Item 2											
Item 3											
Item 4											
Total											
Product line "B"											
Item 1											
Item 2											
Item 3											
Item 4											
Total											
Total											

Comments (to be coded
   to figures)
* Significance variance.
(1) Action assigned to.
(2) Strike.
(3) Other—(explain).

Figure 20-4 Graphic Comparison of Company vs. Industry Sales.

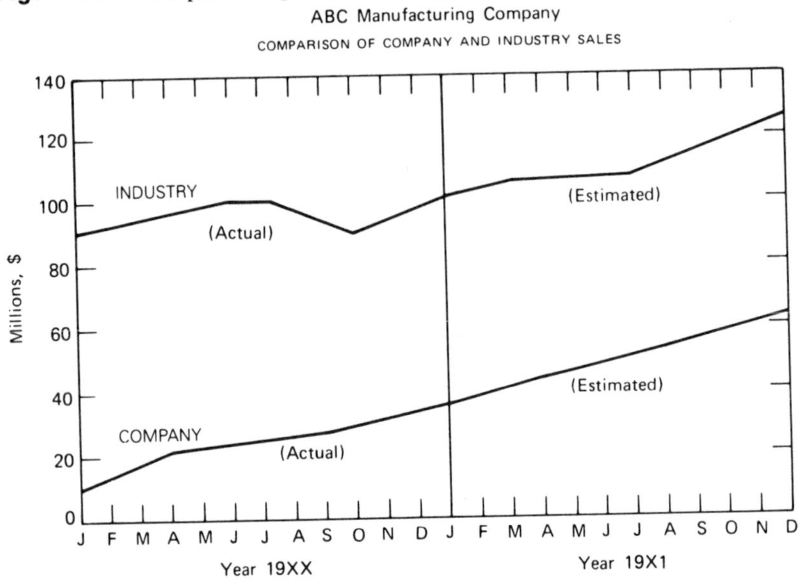

ABC Manufacturing Company

COMPARISON OF COMPANY AND INDUSTRY SALES

Figure 20-5 Actual and Planned Sales; Sales Trend.

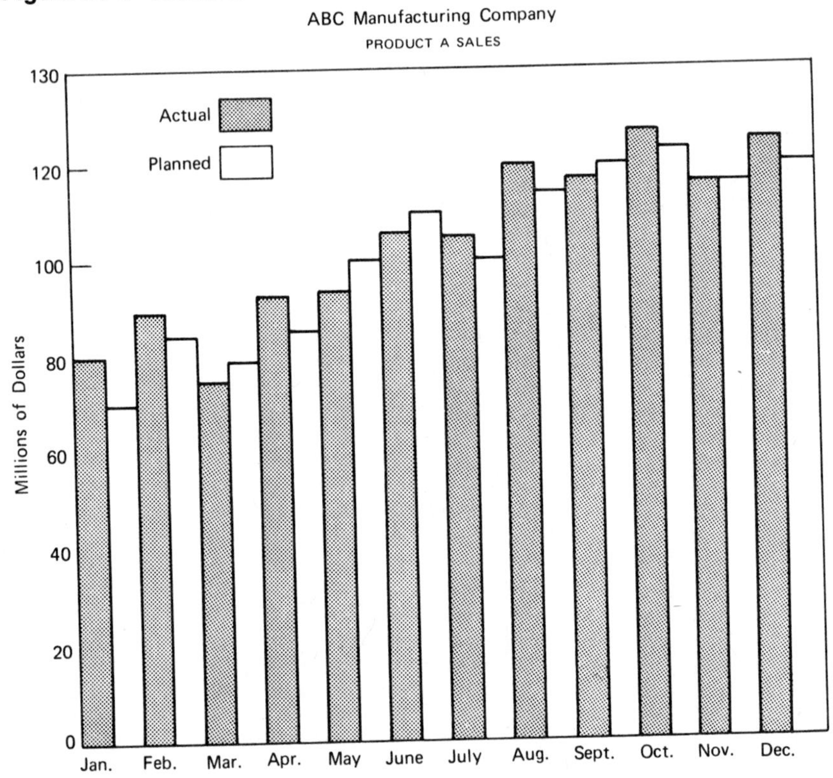

ABC Manufacturing Company

PRODUCT A SALES

Figure 20-6 Percentage of Sales by Product Lines.

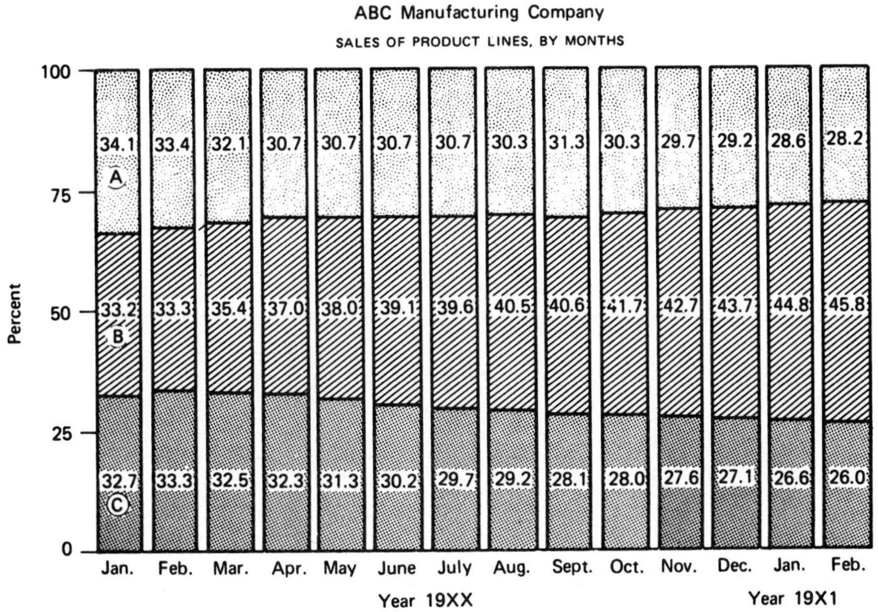

ABC Manufacturing Company

SALES OF PRODUCT LINES, BY MONTHS

(f) FREQUENCY OF REPORTS

The frequency of any report will depend on the individual requirements of each executive or staff member—whether daily, weekly, monthly, or quarterly. For example, the top executive and general sales manager may want a daily report on sales, orders received, and orders on hand; or a weekly report may suffice; or a report may be wanted daily during a critical period and less frequently thereafter.

In those cases where sales data are collected by use of data input devices from remote locations and stored in the computer, reports and data can be provided on a visual display unit on a real-time basis.

Figure 20-7 Report on Sales Order Activity.

					Orders on Hand July 31, 19XX	
Description	Orders on Hand June 30, 19XX	Orders Received	Orders Canceled	Orders Delivered	Units	Sales Value ($ in thousands)
ABC Manufacturing Company SUMMARY OF ORDERS ON HAND						
Vehicles						
Type A ...	50	25	5	10	60	120.0
Type B ...	100	—	5	20	75	262.5
Type C ...	150	50	—	5	195	838.5
Type D ...	60	10	—	5	65	97.5

Figure 20-8 Comparison of Budgeted and Actual Sales by Branch.

GENERAL MANUFACTURING COMPANY

REPORT No. 7

DATE December

COMPARISON OF BUDGETED AND ACTUAL SALES BY BRANCH

DESCRIPTION	BRANCH NUMBER	NET SALES THIS MONTH	SALES BUDGET THIS MONTH	VARIANCE THIS MONTH	NET SALES YEAR TO DATE	SALES BUDGET YEAR TO DATE	VARIANCE YEAR TO DATE
BOSTON	1	1 443 564	1 500 000	56 436 CR	19 056 325	18 000 000	1 056 325
CHICAGO	4	2 348 217	2 000 000	348 217	25 637 940	24 000 000	1 637 940
CLEVELAND	7	2 607 686	2 500 000	107 686	32 642 950	30 000 000	2 642 950
DETROIT	10	1 112 667	1 000 000	112 667	10 912 624	12 000 000	1 087 376 CR
BALTIMORE	12	425 835	500 000	74 165 CR	7 316 940	6 000 000	1 316 940
HOUSTON	13	495 133	500 000	4 867 CR	6 923 423	6 000 000	923 423
LOS ANGELES	16	592 329	500 000	92 329	5 730 916	6 000 000	269 084 CR
NEW ORLEANS	19	442 174	500 000	57 826 CR	6 612 213	6 000 000	612 213
NEW YORK	22	4 094 685	4 000 000	94 685	50 364 912	48 000 000	2 364 912
PHILADELPHIA	25	1 007 489	1 000 000	7 489	13 064 175	12 000 000	1 064 175
PITTSBURGH	28	935 731	1 000 000	64 269 CR	10 316 942	12 000 000	1 683 058 BCR
SAN FRANCISCO	31	913 875	1 000 000	86 125 CR	12 316 431	12 000 000	316 431
ST. LOUIS	34	662 284	500 000	162 284	6 014 314	6 000 000	14 314
FACTORY	58	279 504		279 504	1 210 640		1 210 640
		17 361 173	16 500 000	861 173	208 120 745		10 120 745

Figure 20-9 Exception Reporting—Salesperson Performance.

ABC Manufacturing Company
SALES ANALYSIS BY SALESPERSON—UNDER BUDGET 5% OR MORE—YEAR TO DATE
DISTRICT PITTSBURGH
APRIL 19XX AND YEAR TO DATE

Description	Salesperson No.	Current Month			Year to Date			"Lost Gross"
		Actual Sales	Under Budget Amount	%	Actual Sales	Under Budget Amount	%	
PERFORMANCE SATISFACTORY:		$ 827,432	$112,610 *	15.8 *	$4,623,096	$497,830 *	12.1 *	
UNDER BUDGET PERFORMANCE:								
Abernathy	2609	32,016	1,760	5.2	102,600	6,300	5.8	$ 1,520
Bristol	2671	17,433	1,390	7.4	61,080	4,270	6.5	1,080
Caldwell	2685	19,811	1,320	6.2	70,100	4,600	6.2	1,150
Fischer	2716	24,033	1,470	5.8	84,390	5,090	5.7	1,270
Gordon	2804	8,995	480	5.1	31,600	1,810	5.4	450
Inch	2827	27,666	1,820	6.2	97,010	5,930	5.8	1,480
Long	2982	4,277	600	12.3	15,020	900	5.7	230
Mather	3007	39,474	3,800	8.8	138,400	8,540	5.8	2,150
Owens	5066	43,189	4,400	9.6	151,800	9,080	5.6	2,270
Subtotal		216,894	17,040	7.3	752,000	46,520	5.8	
District Total		$1,044,326	$ 95,570 *	10.1 *	$5,375,096	$451,310 *	9.2 *	$11,600

* Better than budget.

Figure 20-10 Sales Analysis by Customers—Exception Basis.

ABC Manufacturing Company
SALES ANALYSIS BY CUSTOMER—GROSS LOSSES ONLY
DISTRICT CALIFORNIA
YEAR TO DATE THROUGH JUNE 30, 19XX
(*dollars in thousands*)

Customer	Customer No.	Net Sales	Direct Costs	Gain or Loss over Direct Costs		Gross Margin or Loss	
				Amount	% Net Sales	Amount	% Net Sales
Margins satisfactory		$224,390	$156,430	$67,960	30.3	$37,301	16.6
Gross losses year to date:							
American Steel Co. ...	839	127	94	33	25.9	13	10.2
Barrett Machine Corp.	876	243	246	3	1.2	62	25.5
Benson Mfg. Co. ...	11314	182	189	7	3.8	23	12.6
Central Heating Co. ...	207	24	20	4	16.7	12	50.0
Fagan Steel, Inc. ...	436	281	307	26	9.3	56	19.9
Jones Iron Co. ...	920	19	22	3	15.8	9	47.4
Luckey Bridge Corp. ...	800	76	70	6	7.9	6	7.9
Oppowa Metals Co. ...	392	32	43	11	34.4	20	62.5
Subtotal		984	991	7	.7	201	20.4
District total		$225,374	$157,421	$67,953	30.2	$37,100	16.5

20-15 PRODUCT PRICING—POLICY AND PROCEDURE

(a) PRICES IN A COMPETITIVE ECONOMY

From the economic viewpoint, prices are the regulator of our economy in that they determine the distribution of goods and services. Over the long run, when prices in a given industry are insufficient to provide an adequate return, capital and labor tend to shift to more attractive fields. In the individual business, also, skill in setting prices has a tremendous impact on the profitability of the operation and therefore on its economic life.

Product pricing is a difficult area in which to make decisions because of the many forces at play. It is so complex a subject that it is not ordinarily a one-man job or one-activity job. Rather the combined talents of marketer, accountant, engineer, and economist may be needed. It might be said that pricing is one-third computation and two-thirds judgment. From the accounting viewpoint, however, the one-third computation is an essential aid to the judgment factor. Factors that influence prices include market conditions, costs of manufacturing and distribution, plant capacity, competitive activity, capital investments, financial liquidity, government pressures, and a multitude of others. It is therefore understandable that there exists a diversity of approaches to the problem. But this situation presents an equally valid reason to attempt to set out some guiding principles.

(b) PRICES AND THE CONTROLLER

The accountant's contribution to the accounting control of sales is in most cases largely after the fact. That is, comparisons of actual performance are made with budget, forecast, or standard; or sales data are analyzed to reveal unfavorable trends and relationships. In the field of product pricing, however, the controller may be able to exert "preventive" accounting control—before the occurrence. He may bring facts to bear on the problem before unwise decisions are made. This activity is closely related to profit planning as well as control. The influence of prices on company profits is obvious, and the finest controls on costs and expenses will not succeed in producing a profit if selling prices are incorrectly set. If the controller is charged with a responsibility for protecting the assets of the company, or of exercising the control function on costs and expenses, or on capital expenditures, then he should also play an important role in price determination.

And just what should his function be in price determination and related accounting control? It is hoped that he will not be merely a source of information, providing data only when requested, and even then in the form and of the content specified. In many companies, it is questionable whether the pricing officials are fully aware of the kinds of facts required. Therefore, the controller should be expected to show some initiative and supply intelligent information from his legitimate sphere of activity. More specifically, the chief accounting official ordinarily can be of assistance by performing the following functions:

1. Help establish a pricing policy that will be consistent with the corporate objectives—for example, earning the desired return on investment.
2. Provide unit cost analysis, in proper form, as one factor in price setting.

3. Project the effect on earnings of proposed price changes and alternatives.

4. To the extent necessary or practicable, gather pertinent information on competitive price activity (this may be the function of the market research group or economics department in some companies).

5. Analyze the historical data on prices and volumes to substantiate probable trends as they may influence proposed price changes.

6. Determine for management, on a regular basis—such as the monthly operations report—the influence on profit of changes in price, product mix, sales volume, etc.; in other words, focus attention on the price problem where such action may bring about intelligent direction.

Some of these procedures are reviewed in the sections that follow.

(c) COST BASIS FOR PRICING

There is a great tendency to either underrate or overrate costs as a factor in setting prices. Frequently, the statement is heard that "prices are based on competition." Less often the statement is made that "prices are based on costs." There are certainly circumstances where these comments apply. Rarely, however, can costs be ignored entirely.

Over any extended period, no business can consistently sell all or most products at less than cost—cost that results from production and distribution functions and the related service activities. It is further recognized as a highly desirable condition that a profit be made on every product, in every territory, with every customer. Although this may not always be practicable, the closer such conditions are approached, the more certain or assured is the net profit. Hence it is apparent that adequate cost information is absolutely indispensable.

In summary, costs may be viewed as the point of departure or starting place in product pricing. And the role to be played by the cost factor depends on the circumstances. If the product is built to customer order, and is not a stock item, costs will be more important. Further, if competition is weak or if the company is a price leader, cost information will play a larger part than if the opposite situations exist. Also, elasticity of demand influences the weighting of costs in that (1) an inelastic demand probably will cause costs to be a greater factor and (2) costs at various volume levels must be studied to maximize earnings.

The question then arises, "What kinds of costs are required?" For different purposes, different types of costs may be desirable. One type of cost may be suitable for a short-range decision and quite another type for longer term purposes. Moreover, for pricing, the usual historical cost approach may not meet the requirement. In summary, then, the controller is expected to be aware of the several costing methods and the limitations of each and to select that concept most suited to the purpose at hand.

Before reviewing several alternative costing techniques, some general observations are desirable. First, prices relate to the future. Therefore, costs to be used in determining prices must be prospective. Recognition should be given to cost levels expected to prevail in the period under review. Probable raw material and labor costs should be considered. Prospective changes in process ought to be reflected in the cost estimates.

Inflation must be considered, and the best available information should be obtained to recognize what future rates of inflation can be expected. In this forecasting or projecting, the modern scientific tools should be utilized to the extent practicable, such as statistical sampling, sound economic principles, simulation methods, decision analysis techniques, price level analysis. Consideration should also be given to replacement cost of the productive capacity or capital assets. Prices must provide for the future replacement of these productive assets at the projected costs.

Finally, it should be obvious that *all* costs related to a product should be considered and not merely the cost to manufacture. It defeats the purpose if manufacturing costs are carefully calculated but selling or other expenses are applied as an overall percent without regard to the direct expense and effort specifically applicable to the product.

Although many costing methods or variations are in use, there are three basic approaches that warrant discussion:

1. Total cost method.
2. Marginal or direct cost method.
3. Return on assets method.

As a prelude to reviewing costing methods, it seems desirable first to review an example of the influence of costs on profit at differing volume levels. Further, the role of competitive conditions and demand in relation to costs needs to be understood.

(d) ELASTICITY OF DEMAND

In exercising judgment on prices, elasticity of demand should be given proper weighting in any cost-profit-volume calculations. Normally the pricing executives will have some general knowledge of the extent to which demand will react to changes in price. However, to provide supplemental assurance, perhaps controlled experimentation will be helpful in gauging this factor. If demand is relatively inelastic, and competitive conditions permit, then it may be possible to pass cost increases on to the customers. Under such circumstances, the controller can show the effect of cost changes on profits and the desirability of effecting price changes. If demand is highly elastic, and the market is somewhat noncompetitive, unit costs can be employed to determine the optimum price with which to produce the optimum profit.

Under such circumstances, it is desirable to determine the sales price that will produce the greatest net profit over a long period of time. Too high a profit over a short term might invite competition or governmental regulation.

Where conditions approach monopoly, it is perhaps of interest to review a typical procedure in setting selling prices. Basically, an estimate is secured from the sales manager about the probable number of units that can be sold at various price levels. Then the unit cost and total cost at the corresponding production level are calculated. That volume at which the greatest total profit is secured can then be determined.

Figure 20-11 illustrates the application of this procedure. Here it is suggested that the unit selling price may be set at $12, $10, $8, $6, $4, or $2. Estimates are then made about the number of units that can be sold at each price. These are indicated by

Figure 20-11   Methods of Setting Selling Price in a Controlled Market.

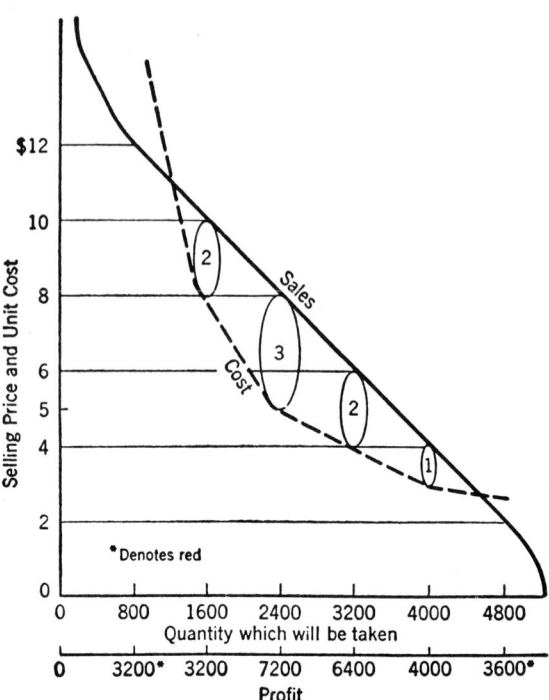

the *sales* line. Thus it is estimated that 1600 units can be sold at a price of $10 per unit, whereas 4000 units can be sold at a price of $4. Likewise, the *cost* line shows the estimated total unit cost (including interest on investment) at each volume level. Thus it is estimated that the unit cost will be $5 when volume reaches 2400 units. The spread between selling price and costs constitutes the unit profit that, multiplied by the number of units, gives the total profit at various price levels. At a price of $10, the profit will be $2 per unit, the volume 1600 units, and the total profit $3200. At a price of $8, the total profit will be $7200. At a price of $6, the total profit will be $6400. It is apparent here that the greatest profit will be made at a unit price of $8.

(e) TOTAL COST METHOD

Now let us consider the three important costing techniques, the first of which is the "total cost" or "full cost" method. Under this concept the cost of the individual product is determined, and to this figure is added the desired profit margin. Such a margin is usually expressed as a percentage of either cost or the selling price. As an example, the proposed selling price might be calculated as shown here:

	Unit Cost and Selling Price	
	Product A	Product B
Cost and expenses		
Raw material (quantity × expected purchase cost)	$10.00	$ 3.00
Direct labor (hours × expected hourly rate)	4.00	8.00
Manufacturing overhead (150% of direct labor)	6.00	12.00
Total manufacturing cost	20.00	23.00
Research and development expense (10% of manufacturing cost)	2.00	2.30
Selling and advertising expense (20% of manufacturing cost)	4.00	4.60
General and administrative expense (10% of manufacturing overhead)	.60	1.20
Total cost	26.60	31.10
Desired profit margin (25% of total cost)	6.65	7.78
Proposed selling price	$33.25	$38.88

In this illustration, costs were used as the basis for determination of the markup, as well as the charge for each of the nonmanufacturing expense levels. As an alternative, each cost element could have been calculated in relation to the proposed selling price. Thus the profit margin might have been expressed in the formulas as 20% of the selling price, and expenses might have been treated in the same manner.

Such a method has at least two advantages: (1) it is simple in application, and (2) it bases selling prices on all costs expected to be incurred—thus tending to assure full cost recovery, if the product sells and if the costs are generally as estimated. Over the longer run, all costs must be recovered.

From the cost viewpoint at least four disadvantages exist in using such a method exclusively:

1. It fails to distinguish between out-of-pocket costs and total costs. In the short run and with available plant capacity, there will be circumstances when business should be accepted on something less than a total cost basis.

2. It does not recognize the inability of all products to return the same rate of profit. Moreover, it fails to distinguish the elements of cost creating the profit, some of which cannot be expected logically to generate the same rate of income. For example, a product that is largely purchased materials may not reasonably return the same percentage of profit on total cost as one constituted mainly of labor and a consequent higher relative share of factory overhead and management talent.

3. The method does not recognize the optimum profit potential. The effect of elasticity in demand and the consequent point of greatest return are ignored.

4. This method of calculating tends to encourage a constant overhead application percent to the exclusion of volume factor likely to be applicable.

The cost calculations can be modified to overcome the second objection. Then, too, several computations can be made to compensate partially for differing volumes.

(f) THE MARGINAL COST METHOD

The marginal cost approach to prices gives recognition to the "incremental" or "marginal" costs of the product. These are costs directly associated with the product that would not be incurred if the product were not manufactured or sold. Any selling price received above this floor represents a contribution to fixed expenses and/or profit.

The application of this principle to products A and B described in the full cost method might produce a picture as follows:

	Unit Cost	
	Product A	Product B
Raw materials	$10.00	$ 3.00
Direct labor	4.00	8.00
Variable manufacturing expense	1.50	2.00
Variable selling expense	1.50	1.90
Variable administrative expense	.30	.40
Total variable or incremental cost	17.30	15.30
Fixed expense directly applicable to product	2.50	3.10
Total direct costs	$19.80	$18.40

In this tabulation, incremental costs have been segregated from direct expenses of a fixed nature applicable to the product, and these direct costs have been identified separately from the allocated costs of a fixed nature.

If the product must be sold for the incremental costs or less, then the company would earn no less a profit, or possibly even a higher profit, by *not* manufacturing and selling such product. Full consideration must be given, of course, to related profit results, namely, sales of other products to the customers, and so on, if the withdrawal of a given product would in fact cause loss of the other business. From the longer-range viewpoint, the minimum price to be charged would be that covering all direct costs, and for the company to continue in business over the longer term, all costs must be recouped.

It can be appreciated that marginal and direct cost data—before allocated continuing costs—are of value in any one of several situations:

1. Where additional sales may be made at reduced prices, over and above direct costs, to another class of customer, namely, private brand business, or under another trade name, etc.

2. Where idle plant capacity can be utilized only at reduced prices and in other than regular sales outlets.

3. Under circumstances where these added sales at reduced prices do not create problems in the regular market place.

The use of marginal costs is for short-term decisions only. The great danger is the tendency to secure a larger and larger volume of sales on an incremental basis, with an ultimate deteriorating effect in the market and a large share of business that does not return its full and proper share of all costs. Furthermore, under such conditions there is no return on assets employed from the products priced at not more than total costs.

(g) RETURN-ON-ASSETS-EMPLOYED METHOD

From the profit viewpoint, the most desirable costing method is that which maximizes the return on total assets employed. This is the approach that has been given more attention in recent years. It is to be noted that under the two costing procedures just reviewed, no consideration has been given, for example, to the capital invested in manufacturing or sales facilities or in working capital. Yet, as discussed in Chapter 7, the real test of business efficiency is the rate of return on total assets employed. Growth generally takes place only when the product yields a reasonable return on the funds devoted to it. If the business objective is to maximize return on capital, then, as a starting point at least, the price of each product required to achieve the desired rate of return should be known.

This method of determining markup over total costs for the desired percent return on assets rather than markup for a percent return on costs (or percent of net sales) has considerable merit in the opinion of the authors. Some of the assets employed are fixed in nature, such as plant and equipment. But a share of the investment—primarily current assets—is a variable of volume and prices. For example, accounts receivable will be higher as sales volume and sales prices are higher. Investment in inventory will increase or decrease as volume changes and as manufacturing costs and raw material prices fluctuate. In view of the variables, a formula may be employed to calculate the sales price required to produce a planned return on assets employed:

$$\text{unit price} = \frac{\dfrac{\text{cost} + (\text{desired \% return} \times \text{fixed assets})}{\text{annual sales volume in units}}}{1 - \left(\dfrac{\text{desired \%}}{\text{return}}\right)\left(\begin{array}{c}\text{variable assets expressed}\\ \text{as \% of sales volume}\end{array}\right)}$$

In the formula:

Cost represents total cost of manufacturing, selling, administrative, research, etc.

% return represents that rate desired on assets employed (before income taxes).

The fixed assets represents plant and equipment, although some of the current assets might be placed in this category.

The variable assets represents the current assets that are a function of volume and prices.

Applying some assumptions, a unit price on product A may be calculated as follows:

$$= \frac{\dfrac{\$2,660,000 + (.20 \times \$300,000)}{100,000}}{1 - (.20 \times .30)}$$

$$= \frac{\$2,720,000/100,000 \text{ units}}{1 - .06}$$

$$= \frac{27.20}{.94} = \$28.936$$

The proof is computed in this manner:

Income and costs	
Sales (100,000 units at $28.936)	$2,893,600
Costs	2,660,000
Income before taxes	$ 233,600
Assets employed	
Variable (30% of $2,893,600)	$ 868,080
Fixed	300,000
Total assets employed	$1,168,080
20% Return on assets employed of $1,168,080 (fractions ignored)	$ 233,600

The foregoing is intended to show the method of determining unit sales prices to provide a target or planned return on investment. Although applied to a single product, the percentages used were those of the product class or group of which product A is one segment.

(h) APPLYING THE RETURN-ON-ASSETS-EMPLOYED CONCEPT

The simple example just cited purposely avoided some of the controversial or problem areas in using the return-on-assets-employed concept. Some brief observations on the subject may prove helpful.

Under this procedure, total assets employed is considered to include all assets used in manufacturing and selling the product (including related services). It is immaterial how the funds were provided—whether by debt or equity. The management of a company should effectively use all assets, whether owner supplied or creditor supplied.

Another question often raised is the basis of valuation of assets. Should replacement value be considered? Should fixed assets be included on a gross or depreciated basis? Essentially, policies of valuation will have no appreciable effect on price determination. Recognition can be provided directly or indirectly in the rate of return objective. Consistency is the important consideration.

In a multiproduct company, a problem to be solved is the allocation of capital employed to the various product lines. On reflection, this need not be a major stumbling block. Just as controllers have been allocating costs to products for years, so also they can allocate assets on a reasonable basis consistent with the facts of the particular business. Some suggested methods of prorating assets to product lines are these:

Item	Possible Bases
Cash	In ratio to total product cost
Accounts receivable	In ratio to sales, adjusted for significant differences in terms of sale
Raw material	In ratio to actual or expected usage
Work in process	In ratio to actual or expected usage
Finished goods	In ratio to cost of manufacture
Fixed assets	In ratio to conversion costs (labor and variable manufacturing overhead) or labor hours—either actual, normal, or standard

(i) CONVERSION COSTS FOR PRICING PURPOSES

Still another economic concept useful in pricing is termed the "conversion cost theory of value." In essence, this view holds that profits are, or should be, earned commensurate with the effort and risk inherent in converting raw materials into finished products. This approach has merit, particularly in situations where relative material content varies widely by product. For example, if one product is largely an assembly of purchased parts and another requires extensive processing in expensive facilities, application of the same markup to each probably would result in a price too high on the assembly item and too low on the fabricated product. Differences in types of costs may therefore need to be recognized. A combined use of the return-on-assets concept and direct costs may be illustrative.

Assume the following is a typical pricing and profit-planning problem:

1. A given product line R is made up of products of varying material content.
2. $24,000,000 are the gross assets employed for the line.
3. Management desires a 20% return (before taxes) on the assets employed.
4. The pertinent profit data are as follows:
   a. Period (fixed or continuing) expenses are $6,000,000.
   b. The profit to volume or contribution margin (P/V) ratio is 30%.
   c. Direct materials and conversion expenses are, on the average, in a 4 to 3 ratio.
   d. Material turnover is twice a year.

With these premises it is necessary to calculate the following:

1. The sales volume needed to produce the desired rate of return.
2. The markup to be applied on each of the direct cost factors in the product line.

Net sales and aggregate costs by element may be determined in this manner:

Required operating profit (20% of $24,000,000)		$ 4,800,000
Add: Continuing or period expenses		6,000,000
Required margin over direct costs		10,800,000
Required sales [$10,800,000 ÷ 30% (P/V ratio)]		36,000,000
Deduct: Margin		10,800,000
Direct costs		25,200,000
Segregated on a 4 to 3 ratio as follows:		
Direct material	$14,400,000	
Conversion	10,800,000	$25,200,000

Inasmuch as the material turnover is two times per year, the investment is $7,200,000 ($14,400,000 ÷ 2). Twenty percent of this figure is $1,440,000. Consequently, the additive factor is 10% ($1,440,000 ÷ $14,400,000), and the portion of sales revenue needed to provide a 20% return is $15,840,000 ($14,400,000 + $1,440,000).

The additive factor on conversion costs may be determined by the difference method as follows:

Total required income (sales)	$36,000,000
Less: Direct material and related profit additive	15,840,000
Balance attributable to conversion factor	$20,160,000

Thus the conversion markup is 1.867 ($20,160,000 ÷ $10,800,000).

If the direct costs of product R162 in the line are known, the target or "ideal" selling price is then determined in this fashion:

	Unit Direct Cost	Factor	Unit Selling Price
Direct material	$16.10	1.100	$17.71
Conversion	20.30	2.867	58.20
Total	$36.40		$75.91

Such proposed prices are a starting point only—they must be considered in relationship to competitive prices.

The setting of product prices is complex and includes the evaluation of many variables. It is the task of the controller to provide for management's judgment all pertinent facts. The various costing methods must be considered and the most appropriate applied in the particular company set of circumstances. In addition to the applicable costs, other factors in setting product prices to be summarized for management's review are these:

1. Return on invested capital or assets employed.
2. Assets employed and turnover.

3. Percent of plant capacity utilized.
4. Percent of product line for each product.
5. Percent of market.
6. Competition pricing and percent of market.
7. Margin over direct costs.

Recognizing the numerous "what-if" situations in setting prices, the controller should be familiar with the many computer models available for evaluating such business decision as price formulation. The variable inputs can be provided to the system, and when combined with the stored data, the alternatives can be quickly and easily evaluated. From a control viewpoint, a key responsibility for the controller is to participate actively in the costing and pricing function.

20-16 IMPACT OF GLOBALIZATION

A few words are in order about globalization and its impact on sales planning. Current business literature is replete with the successes of globalization, but the failures are seldom mentioned. Undoubtedly, many sales executives are fully aware of the complexities and risks, and reflect these in the sales plans for the company. The controller must also be sensitive to the possible greater exposure as the entity increases its efforts in the global marketplace. Some of the reasons for less than sensational sales results include these factors:

- *Inadequate or insufficient market research.* Some marketing executives sometimes think that the experience in one market is automatically transferable to others.

- *Tendency to overstandardization.* Instead of encouraging some local innovation, some salespersons think the same product or same packaging applies to all markets. "Be reasonable; accept the U.S. product." This logic often does not apply.

- *Inflexibility in the entire marketing program.* The same programs are forced on every unit. Yet experience has shown that some facets are unacceptable in local markets. While some central guidance is desirable, forced adoption, without listening to local arguments, destroys local enthusiasm.

- *Lack of adequate follow-up.* While there may be impressive kickoff programs, momentum is lost because local progress is not monitored.

If a company is alert to the advantages of globalization and is desirous of taking advantage of the economics of scale in marketing, manufacturing, R&D, distribution and purchasing, then it needs to avoid the deficiencies mentioned above. And the controller should be aware that progress is being made by monitoring results, and seeing that the weaknesses are not developing.

As stated at the beginning of this section, these comments relate to the impact of globalization on sales planning and control. Business management obviously must be aware of, and plan for, the exposures on foreign operations—currency risks, taxation, transfer prices and cash flow from—and capital expenditures, as discussed in Chapters 11 and 53.

(a) TRANSFER PRICING

The prior discussion on product pricing in section 20-16 has to do principally with establishing prices for unrelated customers under competitive conditions. A special aspect of product pricing relates to international transfer prices—the value assigned to goods or services produced in one country for the use or benefit of a *related* company in another country. This topic is of particular interest in that the IRS regulations are now being changed, and such prices are under special scrutiny with the objective of increasing U.S. tax revenues.

Transfer prices, which should be reflected in the sales plans and planned net income of both the producing and receiving companies, probably should be established through the joint efforts of the sales executive and a member of the controller's department. Why? Simply because precise and complicated IRS regulations, which must be followed carefully, relate to actual or expected costs, capital employed, functions performed by each party, and the risks involved. Proper cost accounting is essential.

20-17 SELECTED REFERENCES

Allio, Robert J., "Formulating Global Strategy," *Planning Review,* March/April, 1989, pp. 22–28.

Barnett, F. William, "Four Steps to Forecast Total Market Demand," *Harvard Business Review,* July–Aug. 1988, pp. 25–30, 34–38.

Berry, Jonathan, et al., "A Potent New Tool for Selling—Database Marketing," *Business Week,* Sept. 5, 1994, pp. 56–62.

Croxton, Frederick E., Dudley J. Cowden, and Ben W. Bolch, *Practical Business Statistics* (4th ed.). Englewood Cliffs, NJ: Prentice-Hall, 1969.

Davis, Stanley M., "From 'Future Perfect' Mass Customizing," *Planning Review,* March/April, 1989, pp. 16–21.

Downing, Douglas, and Jeffrey Clark, *Business Statistics.* New York: Barron's, 1985.

Farrell, Christopher, "The Economic Outlook Is Perfect—or Lousy. How Do You Tell?" *Business Week,* Oct. 2, 1989, pp. 84–85.

Frank, Gary B., Steven A. Fisher, and Allen R. Wilkie, "Linking Cost to Price and Profit," *Management Accounting,* June 1989, pp. 22–26.

Gangloff, John J., "Providing Real-World Financial Support to Sales," *Management Accounting,* Jan. 1989, pp. 41–44.

Georgoff, David M., and Robert G. Murdick, "Manager's Guide to Forecasting," *Harvard Business Review,* Jan.–Feb. 1986, pp. 110–120.

Kashani, Kamran, "Beware the Pitfalls of Global Marketing," *Harvard Business Review,* Sept.–Oct. 1989, pp. 91–95.

Olsen, Richard J., "Niche Shock: And How to Survive It," *Planning Review,* July/Aug. 1988, pp. 6–13.

Pine, B. Joseph, II, "Mass Customizing Products and Services," *Planning Review,* July/Aug. 1993, pp. 6–13, 55.

Pryor, Lawrence S., and Steven J. Katz, "How Benchmarking Goes Wrong (and How to Do It Right)," *Planning Review,* Jan./Feb., 1993, pp. 6–15.

Ranck, J. Harold, Jr., "Avoiding the Pitfalls in Sales Forecasting," *Management Accounting,* Sept. 1986, pp. 51–55.

Robertson, Thomas S., and Hubert Gatignon, "How Innovators Thwart New Entrants into Their Market," *Planning Review,* Sept./Oct. 1991, pp. 4–11, 48.

Roth, Harold P., and Thomas L. Albright, "What Are the Costs of Variability?" *Management Accounting,* Jan. 1994, pp. 51–55.

Wheelwright, Steven C., and Spyros Makridokis, *Forecasting Methods for Management.* New York: John Wiley & Sons, 1985.

CHAPTER 21

Planning and Control of Marketing Expenses

21-1 INTRODUCTION

The planning and control of sales are discussed in the preceding chapter. But the relationship between sales and the effort—the marketing effort—to achieve the sales plan is so close, that it is practical to now review the planning and control of marketing expenses.

21-2 DEFINITION OF MARKETING EXPENSES

In a broad sense, *marketing expenses* may be defined as the costs relative to all activities from the time goods are produced/manufactured or from the time of purchase in a nonmanufacturing company until the products reach the customer—the cost of marketing or selling. This would include the applicable portion of all costs, including general, administrative, and financial expenses. For our purposes here, however, the discussion is limited to those expenses, exclusive of general, administrative and financial expenses, that are normally under the control of the marketing or sales executive. They may include, but are not limited to, the following general classifications:

1. *Direct Selling Expense.* All the direct expense of order-getting costs, including direct expenses of salespersons, sales management and supervision, branch sales offices, and sales service—the expenses generally incident to the solicitation of orders.

2. *Advertising and Sales Promotion Expense.* All media advertising expenditures, expenses relating to various types of sales promotions, market development, and publicity.

3. *Transportation Expense.* All transportation charges on outbound goods to customers and returned sales and costs of managing and maintaining the operation of outbound transportation facilities.

4. *Warehousing and Storage Expense.* Includes all costs of warehousing, storing, inventory handling, order-filling, and packaging and preparation for shipment.

5. *Market Research Expense.* The expenses of the various project studies, including the expenses of administering the department activity, undertaken to test or obtain information on the various products, markets, channels of distribution, or other distribution segments.

6. *General Distribution Expense.* All other expenses related to distribution functions under sales management that are not included in the foregoing items. They may include general sales management expenses, recruitment and training, and staff functions such as accounting, if applicable.

21-3 SIGNIFICANCE OF MARKETING EXPENSES

The costs of getting the manufactured products to the customer, consumer, or user have become increasingly more significant in recent years. In fact, for many companies the total costs of distribution of the products are in excess of the production or procurement costs. In general, it may be stated that the manufacturing costs have been decreasing, whereas the costs of selling and distributing the product have been increasing. To some degree, the increase in selling expense that results in increased sales volume has enabled companies to achieve greater efficiency in the manufacturing process.

In most companies, more effort has been directed toward analysis and control of production costs, and the costs of marketing have either not been available in usable form or not communicated to responsible marketing management for decision making. Executives responsible for the selling and distribution of the products must be made aware of the cost components to effectively plan and carry out a proper distribution system effort. The controller must develop the control mechanisms, secure the facts and interpret them, and communicate the information to the marketing executives. To be effective, the marketing executive must understand the accounting control information and use it in developing his marketing plans and resolving any problems that may develop. The increasing costs of marketing can be effectively controlled and even reduced if the controller works with the sales and marketing management to develop the necessary control techniques and thus obviously have a positive impact on the bottom line—net profit.

21-4 FACTORS INCREASING THE DIFFICULTY OF COST CONTROL

Any controller who tackles the matter of marketing expenses control will find that the problems usually are much more complex than those relating to production costs. First, the psychological factors require more consideration. In selling, the attitude of the buyer as well as the salesman is variable, and competitive reaction cannot be overlooked. This is in sharp contrast to production where the worker is generally the only human element. Moreover, in marketing activities the methods are more flexible and more numerous than in production, and several agencies or channels of distribution may be used. Such conditions make the activities more difficult to standardize than production activities. Also, the constant changes or switches in method of sale or channel of distribution are factors that make it harder to secure basic information. Even when the information is secured great care must be used in interpretation. Finally, the nature of the activities requires different types of costs than might be needed in production. Where the indirect or allocated costs are significant, the analyses may require a more relative marginal or incremental cost approach under various circumstances.

Such conditions create problems that may test the ingenuity of the controller.

21-5 THE SALES MANAGER AND MARKETING EXPENSES

The sales manager is responsible for two primary functions in a business: (1) the requisite sales volume of the right products, and (2) the planning and control of marketing expenses. These may seem like two diametrically opposed objectives. However, the situation may be described as a problem of balance: if more money is spent for the distribution effort, what does the business receive in return? Usually, the sales manager will be under continuous pressure to increase sales and yet reduce selling expenses. It is obvious, then, that he must be in a position to know whether marketing expenses really are too high, and if they are too high, just where—what salesman? what territory? what expense? The sales effort must be wisely guided, and if this is to be done the controller must provide the necessary financial facts. The sales manager must have an intelligent analysis of distribution costs as a basis on which to work. Marketing decisions must be based on adequate knowledge.

21-6 BASIC APPROACH IN THE PLANNING AND CONTROL OF MARKETING EXPENSES

The many variables already mentioned in connection with marketing costs should make it fairly obvious that the problem of control is complex and difficult. In production cost control, a usual procedure is to compare actual and standard or budgeted expenses and exert continuous pressure on actual expenses until they are brought in line with the standard or budget. To an extent this can be done with respect to marketing costs, particularly those of a routine, repetitive, and nonselling nature, such as order handling or warehousing. But by and large, a more positive approach is necessary to avoid an injurious curtailment of necessary distribution services. That approach consists in securing the greatest possible effectiveness in the selling or marketing operations.

As a matter of experience, any controller will find many occasions when suggestions that selling costs be reduced will arouse resentment on the part of the sales force. But almost any sales manager will listen when the approach is that of getting more distribution effort and results for the same money. Unit selling costs can be effectively reduced by getting greater volume from the same sales force, whether by securing larger orders, more customers, or otherwise. This does not obviate the fact that there will be many instances where costs must and will be reduced, but it does emphasize the consideration necessary about the effect on sales volume of reduced marketing expenses.

Since emphasis in the marketing operations is in large measure directed to securing more effective results—that is, more earnings per dollar of distribution cost—it can be seen that much of the study and effort will be applied in a preventive way. Comparative margins and distribution costs may be used in setting *future* action, in changing plans to secure improved results.

21-7 MARKETING EXPENSE ANALYSIS

(a) WHY ANALYZE MARKETING EXPENSE?

Marketing costs are analyzed for three primary purposes: (1) cost determination, (2) cost control, and (3) the planning and direction of the selling and distribution effort. Perhaps the least important of these is cost determination. Yet costs must be ascertained to establish selling prices, formulate distribution policies, and prepare various operating statements. However, the most important purpose is to supply the marketing executives with the necessary information in the planning, direction, and control of the marketing effort. Sales plans must be developed on the basis of those programs or projects that seem to offer a reasonable return. The sales effort must be directed along the most profitable channels, and inefficiencies eliminated. The what, when, and where questions of sales direction must be answered. An analysis of marketing expenses will not provide all the answers to all the sales manager's problems, but it can play an important part in making decisions. Therefore, since marketing cost analysis is useful in the early stages of both the planning and control of costs, it seems logical to review this function before proceeding to the detailed planning and control procedures.

21-8 TYPES OF ANALYSES

There are three basic methods of analyzing marketing expenses:

1. By nature of the expense or object of expenditure.
2. By functions or functional operations performed.
3. By the manner of application of the distribution effort.

The effective direction and control of sales effort usually require all these various types of analyses if the sales manager is to be furnished with the necessary information.

(a) ANALYSIS BY NATURE OF EXPENSE

Generally, the ledger accounts in even the smallest companies provide for a recording of marketing expenses by nature of expense or object of expenditure. For example, salaries, payroll taxes, supplies, rent, traveling expense, and advertising space are usually set out in separate accounts. This is often the first, and sometimes the only, analysis made of marketing expenses.

Such an analysis does provide some information for cost control purposes, general though it may be. With the type of expense segregated month by month, it is possible to follow trends and compare the expense with the previous month and with the same month last year. The ratio of the expense to net sales can also be determined. But a comparison with other periods serves to perpetuate inefficiency, and weaknesses will be revealed only in extreme instances.

It should be clear that an analysis by nature of the expense is of limited value only. The cost of marketing *generally* is known. Yet the controller cannot tell the sales manager his traveling expense is too high or that too much is being spent on advertising. He must be told whose selling expenses are too high and how it is known they are too high. The points of high cost must be clearly defined and responsibility placed, and possibly even the solution suggested. The controller cannot expect cooperation from the sales manager or chief executive on the basis of generalities. The excess cost of specific operations or the excess cost of securing particular results must be set out if an intelligent effort is to be made in reducing the cost or improving the effectiveness of the effort.

The limitation of analysis by the nature of the expense, from a control standpoint, is obvious. And since the information provided is very general, it serves little useful purpose for the direction of the sales effort.

(b) ANALYSIS BY FUNCTIONAL OPERATIONS

An analysis that has been found useful, particularly for the *control* of marketing expenses, is that by functions or functional operations. It is of assistance in measuring the performance by individual responsibility, especially in those applications where the organization is complex or large.

The approach is substantially similar to that used in analyzing production costs and may be outlined as follows:

1. Establish the functional operations to be measured, taking care to see that the functions are properly segregated in terms of individual responsibility. Some illustrative functional operations are these:
   a. Salesperson's calls on prospects or customers.
   b. Shipments from warehouse.
   c. Circular mailing.
2. Provide for a cost segregation of these functions. In this connection the classification should provide for those costs that are direct in regard to the function. For

cost determination, perhaps cost allocations should be made. Generally, however, for *cost control,* emphasis must be on the direct expenses only. Thus in a small branch warehouse such expenses as the indirect labor, supervisory salaries, and fuel should be known, but these costs should be distinct from the allocated share of the regional sales office expense.

3. Establish units of measurement of functional service to the extent practicable. For example, the pounds of shipments might be the measure of the shipping expense, or the number of salesmen's calls might serve as one measurement of direct field selling expense.

4. Calculate a unit cost of operation by dividing the total controllable functional cost by the number of units.

5. Take corrective action if out-of-line conditions appear. This situation may become more readily apparent if standards are established and actual performance is measured against them.

It will be appreciated that this method cannot be applied to all marketing costs, but it may extend to a considerable portion.

The functional approach is useful in control and also in analysis by manner of application. For example, if an analysis is being made by territories, it is necessary to record the number of functional units of the particular activity used in that territory and then simply multiply this number by the unit cost to arrive at a fair cost of the function for each territory.

A specific application of the functional analysis in controlling costs is discussed in the section of this chapter dealing with standards.

(c) ANALYSIS BY MANNER OF APPLICATION

It is one thing to have an efficient organization from the standpoint of performance of the individual functions and quite another thing to see that the performance is so directed and coordinated that it is productive of the most fruitful results. For example, the controller might well show the sales manager that the cost per call is very reasonable or that the cost per hundredweight of handling material in the New York warehouse is below standard. Yet he must go much further in his analysis. It is as important, perhaps even more important, that the controller provide information about income or results achieved in relation to the effort or cost expended. Sales effort must relate to sales possibilities, and these factors must be brought into proper balance. Analysis by manner of application is primarily for the purpose of providing information in the direction of sales effort. The income from a particular factor is being measured against the cost applied against the factor. This type of analysis indicates the distribution cost of different territories, products, customers, channels of distribution, methods of sale, or salespeople. Depending on the problem, the controller must counsel with the sales manager and decide which ones are most useful. These analyses probably will extend to various subanalyses. For example, the breakdown of territorial costs among different products distributed or expected to be distributed might be necessary.

In making any analysis by manner of application, an important consideration is the proper segregation of costs. The value of the cost study will depend in large part on this factor. For this type of analysis, marketing expenses may be divided into three main groups: direct costs, semidirect costs, and indirect costs. As the name implies, direct costs are those immediately identified with a segment and need no allocation. For example, in an analysis by salesperson, the field expense of salary, traveling expense, and entertainment incurred by that salesperson is direct. However, in an analysis by product these expenses might be semidirect or indirect. Expenses that are direct in one application are usually not in another. Ordinarily, the classification of accounts is such that one application is direct for many of the expenses.

Semidirect costs are those related in some measurable way with the particular segments under study. The variability factor responsible for the amount of the expense is known and recorded quantitatively, and the costs may be distributed in accordance with the service required. Thus the cost factor of the warehousing function might be pounds handled. The order-handling costs might relate to the number of item-lines. Stated in other terms, the basis of allocation is less arbitrary than a basis selected at random, such as net sales; and the cost results are therefore of more significance. This might be said to be the distinction between the semidirect costs and those other common or joint costs here designated as indirect.

Indirect expenses are a general charge against the business and must be allocated on a more or less arbitrary basis. No simple measure is available to identify the expense with one territory or product, as distinguished from any other. In practice this may be found to be due as much to records kept as to the nature of the expense. Common examples are institutional advertising or the salaries of general sales executives. There perhaps is little relationship between institutional advertising and the sales in the Western territory as contrasted with the Middle Atlantic territory. There might be little relationship between the costs of general sales administration and sales of product X as compared with product Y. Where it is practical for the general sales executive to keep a time record, the allocation of the expense may be less arbitrary and of more significance.

For marketing expense analysis, as for any intelligent analysis, the type of costs most suitable will depend on the purpose of the study. For long-term decisions, total costs should be known; hence allocated costs need to be identified. If, on the other hand, decisions are of limited scope and for a short period, such as the sale to a private brand customer for the next year, then perhaps only direct expenses ought to be considered. The advisability of making arbitrary allocations of indirect costs may be questioned. It is most important, however, that those who use the figures are knowledgeable about limitations.

(d) THE CONTRIBUTION MARGIN APPROACH

In making a choice between alternative business decisions, usually some costs are unaffected regardless of the conclusions reached. For this reason, among others, it has been found practical to isolate and identify those costs that do change to the exclusion of those costs that do not. The contribution margin approach adopts this concept, although such a segregation may be made in a total cost study as well.

The "contribution margin" is calculated by deducting from sales income those costs incurred in obtaining that segment of the sales income being analyzed. It may be the sales and costs of a given territory or product or customer and need not relate to the company's entire sales of the period. These costs may be described as those costs that would not be incurred if the segment being reported on were not present. Such costs are sometimes known also as "variable costs" or as "direct costs." As costs are defined in the preceding section, the costs deducted would include all direct costs, plus, in some instances, the semidirect costs. The inclusion of the latter would depend on the extent to which some of the content is fixed or continuing in nature. As an example, if the bulk of warehousing expense is variable, the period expense content, such as the foreman's salary, might be ignored. In such a case, the entire semidirect costs for the warehousing function might be included. (As a practical matter, the authors assume in all illustrations of semidirect costs that such costs relate basically to an activity factor and would be reduced generally in proportion to volume.)

The costs and expenses not deducted from sales income in computing contribution margins are those not changed in the total amount by the decision under review. The contribution margin, therefore, is the contribution that the activity under question makes toward meeting the fixed or continuing expenses and profit. The use of such an approach does not ignore the period costs. Rather it recognizes that (1) the separation of the common expenses in relation to the business decision at hand serves little useful purpose and (2) emphasis should be placed on the "contribution" or provision made by the segment toward the joint expenses and profit.

The contribution margin approach and the related "direct costing" have these several advantages:

1. Measurement of the immediate gain to the company's overall profit by the transaction or segment under review.
2. Facilitation of management's decision because those costs to be changed are already separated from costs not affected.
3. Avoidance of errors and controversy that arise by reason of cost allocations and allocation methods.
4. Simplicity of application, since direct costs usually are identifiable more readily than total costs, including the necessary allocations.
5. Data can be secured much more quickly and with less effort.

In practice, marginal costs are used for short-term tactical decisions—and their value can be appreciated. However, over the longer term, a business must recover total costs and a reasonable profit if it is to survive. Under the circumstances, there is no good reason why the total cost method and contribution margin approach cannot be used jointly. Such a statement would indicate the immediate profit effect of the business decision and, by inclusion of the joint or pooled costs, can reveal the operating income picture.

Management's needs and the judgment of the controller will ordinarily dictate the type of costing most adaptable. For reasons of prudence, sometimes distribution costs will be segregated on a contribution basis, whereas manufacturing costs will be shown in total. An example of such a situation would be in circumstances where top management adopts the viewpoint that a sale must always recoup all manufacturing expenses, plus, at a minimum, the direct selling expenses.

Some illustrations of the marginal cost approach are presented later in this chapter.

(e) TECHNIQUE OF ANALYSIS BY MANNER OF APPLICATION

There has been sufficient experience with marketing expense analysis by manner of application to prove the value of the technique. Although the degree of refinement may vary in different companies, the general approach may be outlined as follows:

1. Determine which analysis (or analyses) needs to be made. Determine which might be required in a particular application, such as an analysis by method of delivery. Again, some may be recurring and others may be made only as weaknesses are indicated.

2. Classify marketing expense according to those that are direct, semidirect, and indirect.

3. Select and apply the allocation bases to the semidirect and indirect expenses. This includes a segregation and proper treatment of variable, as contrasted with fixed, costs where such a segregation is a factor.

4. Prepare the analysis and commentary for the use of the proper executive. This will involve the following steps in arriving at significant cost and profit relationships:

   a. Determine the gross profit by segment (e.g., territory, product, size of order).

   b. Accumulate the direct expense by segment, and deduct this from gross profit to arrive at *profit after direct expense.*

   c. Distribute the semidirect expenses, and deduct these to arrive at *profit after semidirect expense.*

   d. Prorate the indirect expense to arrive at the final net profit (in some instances steps c and d will be combined).

   e. Prepare the necessary subanalyses to pinpoint the conditions needing correction.

These comments should indicate the principles and technique involved so that any controller can proceed to prepare the facts necessary in his particular situation.

Comments on the need and use of certain analyses by manner of application are made hereafter.

(f) ANALYSIS BY TERRITORY

A *territory* may be defined, for this purpose, as any geographical area, whether city, trading area, county, state, or sales district, used by a company for sales planning, direction, or analysis. Where, or in which territory, goods are sold has a great effect on the net profit. There are striking variations between territories in terms of sales potentials, net profit, and gross margins. If goods are sold free on board (f.o.b.) a central point and at the same price, the gross profit, of course, is unchanged. But if the product is sold on a delivered price basis, the gross margin is different because of transportation charges. In different areas the consumers' wants and needs are different, and this factor affects the total gross margins. Even aside from these considerations, experience has shown that the costs to sell and distribute are different in different territories. The cost to sell in densely populated New York is much different from the cost to sell in western Texas. Because of all these dissimilar conditions, executives must have an analysis of distribution costs by territory. Such information permits the sales manager to rearrange sales effort where necessary and direct sales effort into the most profitable areas. Control of marketing costs is facilitated through this same analysis, perhaps with the aid of cost standards. Sales planning, of course, with respect to new territories and new markets is affected by distribution cost considerations.

Not every concern will find analysis by territory necessary. Such an analysis applies largely in those instances where a large geographical area is covered. Thus a manufacturer covering a national market would greatly benefit from such an analysis, whereas a retail store probably would not. Exactly what type of territorial analysis needs to be made depends on the problem and type of organization. If a territorial sales executive is largely responsible for costs and results, a complete analysis by this responsibility area is desirable. Or if the problem is one of costs to sell in small towns vs. cities, such a segregation is to be made.

A statement of income and expense by territory is shown in Figure 21-1.

Once the points of weakness are discovered through analysis, corrective action needs to be taken. Some of the possibilities for such are as follows:

1. Reorganization of territories to permit effort more nearly in line with potentials.
2. Rearrangement of territorial boundaries to reduce selling expense, secure better coverage, etc.
3. Shifting of salespersons.
4. Increased emphasis on neglected lines or customers in territory.
5. Change in method of sale or channel of distribution (shift from salesperson to agent, etc.).
6. Changes in physical facilities (warehouses, etc.) in territory.
7. Elimination of unprofitable territories (potentials of area and out-of-pocket costs vs. allocated costs considered).
8. Change in advertising policy or expenditure in territory.

(g) ANALYSIS BY PRODUCT

In our dynamic and competitive economy, the design or style or type of product a firm sells may change constantly. The tremendous strides of research, among other factors, are repeatedly bringing new products into the market. Hence every company is sooner or later faced with the problem of what products it should sell. Will the firm sell the best or the cheapest line? Will it promote the use of a new plastic? Should it introduce a silent airplane motor? The answer to questions like these are twofold. First, through market analysis a determination must be made about what the consumers want and what price they will pay. Then, through cost analysis it must be determined whether the company can make and sell the article at a profit. Therefore, an analysis by products is desirable.

Many firms, in their urge to increase sales volume to better utilize facilities and personnel, often add new products to the line. Sometimes these new products "fit" into the line and permit certain economies. Often, however, the different products require services in varying degree. For this reason, too, an analysis by product is necessary to determine the cost to sell, as well as the net profit.

Figure 21-1 Statement of Income and Expense by Territory.

The P Company
STATEMENT OF INCOME AND EXPENSE BY TERRITORY
FOR THE MONTH ENDED JANUARY 31, 19XX

	Total		West		Middle West		Middle Atlantic		New England	
		Territory								
Description	Amount	% of Net Sales	Amount	% of Net Sales	Amount	%of Net Sales	Amount	% of Net Sales	Amount	% of Net Sales
Gross sales	$840,000		$50,000		$390,000		$240,000		$160,000	
Less:										
Freight	35,359		4,200		13,500		10,750		6,909	
Returns	5,000		750		1,050		1,840		1,360	
Allowances	10,650		670		3,890		3,750		2,340	
Total sales deductions	51,009		5,620		18,440		16,340		10,609	
Net sales	788,991	100.00	44,380	100.00	371,560	100.00	223,660	100.00	149,391	100.00
Cost of sales	550,127	69.73	31,066	70.00	241,514	65.00	167,745	75.00	109,802	73.50
Gross profit	238,864	30.27	13,314	30.00	130,046	35.00	55,915	25.00	39,589	26.50
Direct selling expenses	45,568	5.78	2,219	5.00	16,720	4.50	20,129	9.00	6,500	4.35
Profit after direct selling expenses	193,296	24.49	11,095	25.00	113,326	30.50	35,786	16.00	33,089	22.15
Semidirect expenses	17,854	2.26	1,000	2.25	7,800	2.10	6,330	2.83	2,724	1.82
Profit after semidirect expenses	175,442	22.23	10,095	22.75	105,526	28.40	29,456	13.17	30,365	20.33
Allocated share of general expenses	15,780	2.00	888	2.00	7,431	2.00	4,473	2.00	2,988	2.00
Profit before income taxes	$159,662	20.23	$ 9,207	20.75	$ 98,095	26.40	$ 24,983	11.17	$ 27,377	18.33
Other Data										
Units sold	36,692		2,000		17,333		10,550		6,809	
Sales potential	$850,000		$85,000		$400,000		$225,000		$140,000	
% of potential	92.8		52.2		92.9		99.4		106.7	

542

Generally speaking, sales effort should be directed toward those products with the greatest net profit possibilities, and cost analysis is necessary to know just which products these are. This is not to say that a company should drop a low-margin item; it may be contributing more than out-of-pocket costs, or it may be necessary for customer convenience. Furthermore, there may be little possibility of selling a high-margin item to a customer. For example, there may be no chance of selling to a paint manufacturer any quantity of a high-profit glue instead of a low-margin paint vehicle. There are more factors than merely cost considerations in selling. But such conditions must be watched and held within reasonable limits. Marketing expense analyses by commodity, then, are of use in the direction of the sales effort.

Many controllers may find, in making product cost analyses, that the net profit on an entire line of products is not great enough or even that losses are being sustained. When such conditions are revealed, steps are usually taken to increase that margin because the firm may not be in a position to drop an entire line. This is but another way of saying that analysis is a means of controlling costs, because the manufacturing costs or marketing costs may be too high.

Finally, product cost analyses are helpful in setting selling prices when the company is in a position to use costs as a major guide. Such analyses are desirable in conjunction with determining maximum price differentials to particular customers.

It is probably self-evident to most controllers or accountants that a product analysis of distribution costs should be made when the characteristics of the commodity or their methods of marketing are such that a uniform basis of allocation is not indicative of the effort or cost to sell. Thus pounds or units of sale or sales dollars may be a fair measure of selling expense. But there are numerous circumstances when such an apportionment is inaccurate or misleading:

1. *If there are differences in the time or amount of sales effort required.* Thus product A that sells at $0.60 each may require about three times the effort of product V which sells at $0.30 each. Neither sales dollar nor units would be a fair basis. Perhaps one product would require a high degree of technical assistance with frequent callbacks as compared with another. Again, specialty salespeople may merchandise one product, and a general-line salesperson may handle another. All such circumstances result in different costs to sell, and should be so reflected in the analyses.

2. *If there are differences in the method of sale.* Obviously, if one product is sold exclusively by mail order and another by salespeople, the selling cost cannot be prorated on a sales dollar or unit basis.

3. *If there are differences in the size of the order.* When one product is sold in 10-pound lots and another is sold in tank cars, many of the distribution costs can be different.

4. *If there are differences in channels of distribution.* One product may be sold directly to retailers, whereas another is distributed through wholesalers. Here, also, there is a difference in distribution cost.

The analysis by product ordinarily will reveal areas of weakness about which corrective action can be taken in some degree, such as the following:

1. Shifting emphasis of the sales effort to more profitable lines or bringing effort in line with sales potential.
2. Adjusting sales prices.
3. Eliminating certain unprofitable lines, package sizes, colors, etc.
4. Adding product lines related to the "family," with consequent sharing of fixed distribution expense.
5. Changing the method of sale or channel of distribution.
6. Changing the type, amount, and emphasis of advertising.
7. Revising packages, design, quality, etc.

A statement of income and expense that incorporates the contribution margin concept by products is shown in Figure 21-2.

(h) ANALYSIS BY CUSTOMER

It is no secret that many manufacturers or distributors carry unprofitable accounts or customers. Such a condition may result from a philosophy of "get the volume," or from insufficient effort to do something about the status quo, or probably because the sales executive just does not have sufficient knowledge about his marketing costs.

Yet it costs more to sell to some types of customers than to others and more to one customer within a type than another. Some customers require more services than others, such as warehousing, delivery, or financing. Some customers insist on different prices, particularly where different size orders or annual purchases are factors. Again, the types of products sold to some classes differ from others. All these are reasons why analyses by customers are necessary to measure the difference in net profit. Aside from use in the direction of sales effort, these analyses serve in setting prices and controlling distribution costs.

In most firms, the analyses by customers will not be continuous. Perhaps the sales manager will be interested in whether money is being made on a particular account, or changes may be contemplated only on certain groups of accounts. On these occasions special analyses can be made.

Although analyses may be made by individual customers, particularly when there are a few high-volume accounts, by and large the analyses will relate to certain groups or categories. The two basic factors in selecting the classification to be used are the amount of marketing services required, for this is the primary reason for differences in marketing costs, and the practicability of segregating the marketing costs. Classifications that have proved useful are these:

1. Amount of annual purchases.
2. Size of orders.
3. Location.
4. Frequency of salespersons' calls.
5. Type of agent (retailer, wholesaler, or jobber).
6. Credit rating of customers.

Figure 21-2 Statement of Income and Expense by Product.

The Best Company
STATEMENT OF INCOME AND EXPENSE BY PRODUCT
FOR THE MONTH ENDED JUNE 30, 19XX

	All Products		Product A		Product B		Product C		Product D	
Description	Amount	% of Net Sales	Amount	Per Cwt.	Amount	Per Cwt.	Amount	Per Cwt.	Amount	Per Cwt.
GROSS SALES	$27,890		$14,600	$14.60	$620	$12.40	$11,040	$13.80	$1,630	$16.30
Less: Sales Deductions	1,295		600	.60	25	.50	640	.80	30	.30
Net Sales	26,595	100.0	14,000	14.00	595	11.90	10,400	13.00	1,600	16.00
Variable Cost of Sales	8,100	30.5	5,000	5.00	300	6.00	2,400	3.00	400	4.00
Profit After Direct Mfg. Costs	18,495	69.5	9,000	9.00	295	5.90	8,000	10.00	1,200	12.00
Direct Marketing Expense	1,255	4.7	500	.50	25	.50	640	.80	90	.90
Semidirect Distribution Expense (Variable)	3,355	12.6	800	.80	185	3.70	1,840	2.30	530	5.30
Contribution Margin	13,885	52.2	7,700	7.70	85	1.70	5,520	6.90	580	5.80
Fixed Expenses										
Manufacturing	4,900	18.4	3,000	3.00	100	2.00	1,600	2.00	200	2.00
Marketing	1,170	4.4	600	.60	30	.60	480	.60	60	.60
Total	6,070	22.8	3,600	3.60	130	2.60	2,080	2.60	260	2.60
Profit or (Loss) Before Income Tax	$ 7,815	29.4	$ 4,100	$ 4.10	$(45)	$(.90)	$ 3,440	$ 4.30	$ 320	$ 3.20
OTHER DATA										
Hundredweight Sold	1,950		1,000		50		800		100	
Average Sale per Call (when sold)	$348.63		$486.67		$124.00		$736.00		$54.33	
Number of "No Sale" Calls	20		10		3		4		3	
Lack of Volume Manufacturing Costs	$2,800		$ 600		$ 500		$ 1,400		$ 300	

In making an analysis by classification of customer, one approach is to segregate all customers in the applicable group and determine total costs for each group. This may often be time consuming. Another method involves a sampling procedure, wherein representative customers in each category are selected and the cost of servicing them is determined. A modification of this approach is to make a thoroughly detailed analysis in some areas and a sample run in other areas.

It will be appreciated that relatively few marketing expense items can be charged directly to customers and that allocations must be made. Statistical data from various reports will be found necessary, namely, the number of calls made to customers or customer classes and the time spent with customers or the number of orders.

Presentation of the analysis by customers may take the form of an income and expense statement as shown in Figure 21-3. This example classifies customers according to type, but a similar analysis could be made by annual volume of sales.

Occasions will arise when a decision must be made about whether the business with a specific customer should be continued or whether the method of sale to him ought to be changed. The use of unit analysis of individual customers, the contribution margin concept, and an alternative method of sale for small customers are illustrated in Figure 21-4. In this instance, changing the selling method from field calls to a phone basis resulted in the retention of valuable business and securing a contribution margin in line with normal operating requirements. Other data may be presented in graphic form, as in Figure 21-5.

An analysis by customers will provide information of great value to the sales manager. It will give a clear view of the number of accounts in various volume brackets and the average value of orders. In using this information for corrective action, consideration must be given to potential volume and the absorption of fixed production costs. But it will furnish facts for executive discussion regarding the following:

1. Discontinuance of certain customer groups.
2. Price adjustments.
3. Need for higher margin for certain groups.
4. Change in method of sale.

(i) ANALYSIS BY SIZE OF ORDER

Another analysis that may be made advantageously in many business concerns is that by size of orders. It has been recognized for some time that one of the causes of both high marketing expense and unprofitable sales is the small order—generally not because it is small in itself but because the prices are not high enough to cover the costs and leave a profit. There are many instances where small orders cannot be discontinued. But again, the problem can be solved. Corrective action can be taken; it can be brought under control. Obviously, the first step a controller must take is to get the facts through an analysis of marketing costs by size of order.

The problem is naturally more important in some concerns than in others, particularly where the order-handling costs are relatively large or fixed.

By and large, the procedure for analyzing marketing expense by size of order is similar to that for other analyses. It involves segregating costs by factor of variability and applying the factors. In this case, certain costs will be recognized as fixed for all

Figure 21-3 Statement of Income and Expense by Customer Class.

The Best Company
STATEMENT OF INCOME AND EXPENSE BY CUSTOMER CLASS
FOR THE MONTH ENDED APRIL 30, 19XX

Description	Total		Retailers		Jobbers		Mail Order Houses	
	Amount	% of Net Sales	Amount	% of Net Sales	Amount	% of Net Sales	Amount	% of Net Sales
Gross Sales	$1,220,000		$690,000		$220,000		$310,000	
Less: Sales deductions	33,000		20,000		3,000		10,000	
Net sales	1,187,000	100.0	670,000	100.0	217,000	100.0	300,000	100.0
Cost of goods sold	957,600	80.7	503,800	75.2	187,700	86.5	266,100	88.7
Gross profit	229,400	19.3	166,200	24.8	29,300	13.5	33,900	11.3
Direct customer marketing costs	108,300	9.1	82,400	12.3	20,800	9.6	5,100	1.7
Profit remaining after direct costs	121,100	10.2	83,800	12.5	8,500	3.9	28,800	9.6
Indirect customer marketing costs	53,400	4.5	40,900	6.1	8,900	4.1	3,600	1.2
Profit or (loss) after marketing costs (and before income taxes)	$ 67,700	5.7	$ 42,900	6.4	$ (400)	(.2)	$ 25,200	8.4

Figure 21-4   Customer Analysis on Contribution Margin Basis.

The Roth Company
SELECTED CUSTOMER ANALYSIS ON A SALES UNIT BASIS
FOR THE SIX MONTHS ENDED JUNE 30, 19XX

	By Calls of Field Force				Proposed Centralized Phone Order Desk
	Customer W	Customer X	Customer Y	Customer Z	Customer Z
Net sales	$10.09	$10.16	$10.13	$10.21	$10.21
Direct costs					
Manufacturing	8.07	8.09	8.08	8.08	8.08
Transportation	.11	.12	.14	.18	.18
Warehousing	.02	.02	.02	.04	.04
Selling	.09	.10	.09	.22	.09
Total	8.29	8.33	8.33	8.52	8.39
Contribution margin	$ 1.80	$ 1.83	$ 1.80	$ 1.69	$ 1.82
Units sold	1,200	1,090	800	390	390
Aggregate contribution	$2,160	$1,995	$1,440	$ 559	$ 710

sizes or orders, others will vary with the money volume, and still others will vary with physical volume. By way of general suggestion, the steps to be followed might be these:

1. Determine the size of the order groups to be studied—e.g., below $25, $25 to $50.

2. Classify the costs according to (a) those that vary with the size of the order, e.g., packing; (b) those uniform for orders of all sizes, e.g., accounts receivable bookkeeping; and (c) those that must be considered as general overhead with no direct relation to orders, e.g., certain advertising and supervision costs.

3. Identify the factors that appear to govern the amount of the variable expense (that expense which varies with the size of the order) applicable to orders of different sizes, e.g., dollar value, weight, or handling time.

4. Apply the factors of variability to the variable expenses and add the uniform costs, thereby arriving at a direct cost of orders by sizes.

5. Apply the overhead costs by some suitable factor, such as hundredweight or dollar value, to arrive at the total order cost.

Figure 21-5 Comparative Data on Profitable and Unprofitable Accounts.

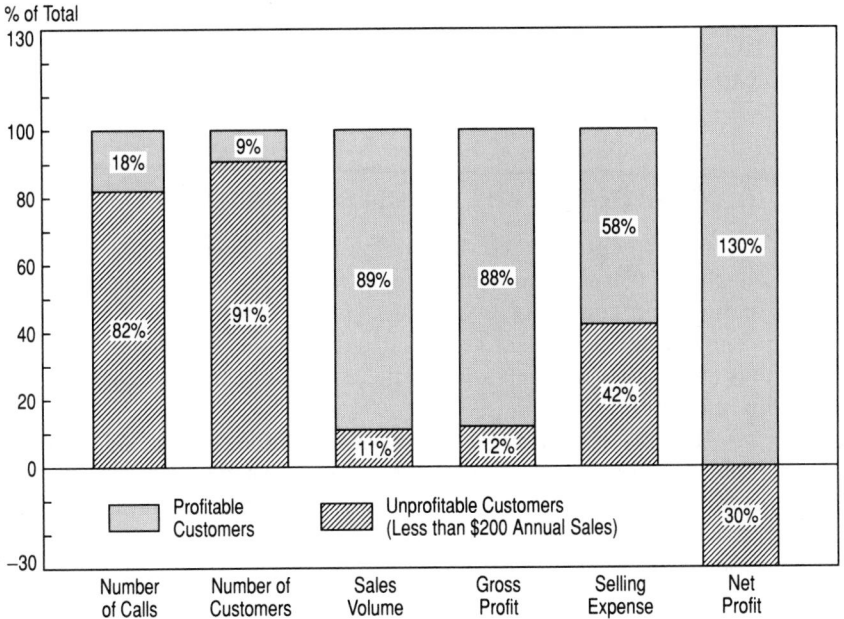

COMPARISON OF PROFITABLE AND UNPROFITABLE CUSTOMERS
NUMBER OF CASES, NUMBER OF CUSTOMERS, SALES VOLUME,
GROSS MARGIN AND SELLING EXPENSE

Based on Annual Sales Volume

(j) OTHER ANALYSES

There are other analyses that may prove useful in a particular concern, for example:

1. *By Channel of Distribution.* Useful where a choice in channel of distribution may be made in order to direct sales into the most profitable channel. The analysis needs to be made from time to time as cost trends change.

2. *By Method of Sale.* The same comments are applicable as in the case of analysis by channels of distribution.

3. *By Salesperson.* For the purpose of measuring the salesperson's performance in terms of profit and to better direct salespeople in their activity.

4. *By Organization or Operating Division.* Useful where there are separate and distinct selling division. Such an analysis is used to measure performance of the divisional executive. Examples are analyses by departments in a department store, by stores in a retail chain store company, or by branches in a manufacturing organization.

(k) USING MATHEMATICAL TECHNIQUES

The analyses indicated herein are only illustrative. The many variables and alternatives in the distribution or marketing function can indeed make the task of analyzing seem overwhelming. Problems to be solved include warehouse locations, transportation routes, most economical shipment patterns, and a host of others. To perform the needed review, and to effect economies in these functions, use of mathematical formulas or "models" in conjunction with a personal computer can be most helpful. By using mathematical symbolization and techniques, the many relationships and quantities can be expressed and dealt with. (See Chapter 5.)

(l) INTERPRETING THE RESULTS OF ANALYSIS

It has already been stated that the primary purpose of distribution cost analysis is to supply the marketing executives with the necessary information for the planning, direction, and control of marketing effort. The preceding section has suggested the technique and purpose or use of various analyses. It is clear, however, that these methods and studies will be varied as the controller finds necessary to fit the purposes he has in mind.

He must be alert to the pitfalls or limitations of any figures prepared. Perhaps the problem will be attacked from several sides. In some cases only the variable marketing expenses (or even production costs) will be used, whereas in others both the fixed and variable will be included. Again, in making recommendations based on the marketing expense analysis, the decisions reached must consider every possible effect on every activity of the business. For example, the conclusion that a certain territory must be dropped must consider the net effect on profit—the change in factory volume with the same fixed expense and resulting differences in unit costs.

21-9 PLANNING MARKETING EXPENSES

Just as sales must be planned in attempting to reach the annual profit objective, so also must marketing expenses. It is usually the task of the controller or the budget director to develop the procedures for estimating the expense levels, and to provide the proper format and supporting data so that the chief marketing executive can furnish the financial data for consolidating the annual business plan.

But marketing costs differ in nature—especially as to how the costs vary, or should vary, with volume and how they are best planned and controlled. Depending on industry practice and company experience, budgetary control of distribution costs may be achieved through one of these types of budgets:

- Administrative.
- Project.
- Volume—variable.
- Competitive service.

Each of these types is described and illustrated in the following sections.

(a) ADMINISTRATIVE-TYPE BUDGET

Probably the most commonly used budget for planning and controlling marketing expenses is what is described here as an "administrative-type" budget. The circumstances when this kind of planning and control device is most applicable include these:

- The expense level is not, and should not be, influenced by the day-to-day variations in the sales level. To be sure, expenses must bear a certain relationship to sales, but this is accomplished over a longer time span, say from year to year.
- The output is not necessarily or easily quantified over very short periods, but rather over months—if then. Moreover, often the function is subjective in nature and relates to planning and controlling sales or to some other distribution effort.
- The number of routine and recurring functions is limited.
- Most of the expense is in the form of "people costs," represented largely by the expense of salaries, fringe benefits, occupancy, and travel and entertainment.
- The function is such that it cannot be planned and controlled on a project or program basis—as discussed in the next section.

Typical departments whose expenses usually are managed by an administrative budget include direct selling, field sales offices, general and territorial or product sales management units, and possibly the order department.

A typical procedure for developing an administrative-type planning budget is as follows (see also Chapter 26):

1. The controller or budget administrator provides each marketing department manager (who will use this kind of budget) with last year's budget, and with the current head count and year-to-date expenses (by type of expense). This may be furnished through computer access or by worksheet.
2. The department manager estimates expenses for the remaining period of the current year (as in Figure 21-6). He thus has two years of cost experience as a guide.
3. The sales executive estimates the departmental expenses, by type of expenses, and by month or quarter for the coming year. He takes into account the activity level expected, special tasks to be performed, general pay increases, and any other expected change in the function. Of course, he is provided with appropriate guidelines, such as fringe benefit rates, and other data he might need, by the controller. If traveling expenses are applicable, the marketing executive must estimate them, based on the number and types of trips to be made, etc.
4. The completed estimate is forwarded by the marketing manager through organization channels for review and approval, before reaching the financial representative.
5. The controller or budget officer reviews the departmental estimates for completeness and reasonableness. When the data seem in order, they are summarized for the marketing function. An administrative-type departmental marketing budget might appear as in Figure 21-6.

Figure 21-6 Administrative-Type Budget.

The Illustrative Company
ANNUAL BUDGET
SALES ADMINISTRATION DEPARTMENT
(dollars in thousands)

| | | Current Year | | | Plan | |
| | Prior | Actual | Estimated | | Year | Increase |
Item	Year	(9 mos)	(3 mos)	Total	Total	(Decrease)
No. of staff	6	8	8	8	10	2
Expenses						
Salaries and wages	$209	$194	$ 65	$259	$306	$47
Fringe benefit costs (40%)	84	78	26	104	123	19
Travel	110	90	32	122	133	11
Entertainment	49	40	13	53	60	7
Communication	8	7	2	9	10	1
Occupancy	25	19	7	26	28	2
Supplies	12	12	2	14	16	2
Depreciation	8	6	2	8	8	—
Insurance	6	6	1	7	8	1
Dues and subscriptions . .	5	5	—	5	6	1
Miscellaneous	1	1	—	1	1	—
Total	$517	$458	$150	$608	$699	$91

6. When the business plan is completed and approved, the departmental executive is so informed. (Of course, there may be iterative changes.)

7. After the planning period has commenced, the marketing executive is provided periodically (usually monthly) a comparison of actual and budgeted expenses for his information and for corrective action, if warranted. (See Figure 21-7.)

(b) PROJECT-TYPE BUDGET

Probably the second most widely used budget in the planning and control of marketing expenses is the project type. This is so designated because many of the cost elements are best planned on a project basis; that is, certain tasks or programs or projects are planned, then executed, and then the results are measured sometime in the future. The level of planned expense is not directly related to the *immediate* sales, but rather future sales over perhaps a year or two. The project is completed and the expense largely stops until another project is undertaken. The expense level bears a necessary relationship to sales, but only indirectly and over a period of time. Emphasis is on getting a certain task done within a certain time and within cost constraints. Typical activities handled largely on a project basis are advertising and sales promotion expense or market research.

Figure 21-7 Budget Report—A Sales Department.

The Illustrative Company
BUDGET REPORT
SALES ADMINISTRATION DEPARTMENT
(dollars in thousands)

Month: June

Item	Current Month			Year to Date		
	Actual	Budget	(Over) Under Budget	Actual	Budget	(Over) Under Budget
No. of staff	9	10	1 (a)	9	10	1
Expenses						
Salaries and wages	$23	$25	$ 2	$138	$150	$12
Fringe benefit costs (40%) .	10	10	—	55.2	60.0	4.8
Travel	14	11	(3)(b)	75	67	(8.0)(b)
Entertainment	4	5	1	29	30	1
Communications	1	1	—	5	5	—
Occupancy	3	3	—	14	14	—
Supplies	2	1	(1)	8	8	—
Depreciation	.5	.5	—	4	4	—
Insurance	.7	.7	—	4	4	—
Dues and subscriptions ...	.5	.5	—	3	3	—
Miscellaneous	.1	.1	—	.5	.5	—
Total	$58.8	$57.8	$(1)	$335.7	$345.5	$ 9.8

Commentary: (a) Market analyst not yet located.
(b) No provision made for London trips.

The budgetary procedure for a project type budget is essentially as follows:

1. The marketing executives agree or decide what projects of a given departmental type are necessary to attain the planned sales objective or are otherwise desirable.

2. The department manager (e.g., advertising or market research) estimates the cost for each project by type of expense, if applicable—usually in a format suggested by the controller. In some instances, budget limits are set based on estimated unit sales, or as related to prior year expenses, e.g., advertising.

3. The various projects are summarized and included in the departmental budget for the planning period. (See Figure 21-8.)

4. After appropriate review and change, if necessary, the budget is approved as part of the annual plan. (In many companies the advertising budget is approved by the board of directors as a special budget.)

5. Periodically, perhaps monthly, the actual expenses and commitments are updated and compared with the project budget and corrective action taken if necessary or possible. (See Figure 21-9.)

Figure 21-8   Advertising and Sales Promotion Budget.

The Illustrative Company, Inc.				
ADVERTISING AND SALES PROMOTION BUDGET				
(dollars in thousands)				
Category	Current Year Project Budget	Plan Year Requested Budget	(Increase) Decrease over Current Year	Comments
Broadcast media				
Radio—local	$ 500	$ 525	$(25)	Price increase
Television				
Regional	1,300	1,400	(100)	Price increase ($65,000) Expanded coverage
Local spots	2,500	2,625	(125)	5% price increase
Total	3,800	4,025	(225)	
Total broadcast media .	4,300	4,550	(250)	
Print media				
Local newspapers	400	420	(20)	Price increase
Business publications .	700	700	—	
General public				
magazines	1,200	1,100	100	Elimination of Oregon
Subtotal	2,300	2,220	80	
Catalogs	900	900	—	
Newspaper stuffers ...	350	300	50	
Direct mail	1,900	2,000	(100)	
Total print media ..	5,450	5,420	30	
Total media	9,750	9,970	(220)	
Advertising administration				
Salaries and wages ...	400	420	(20)	General wage increase—5%
Fringe benefits	160	168	(8)	
Travel	140	120	20	No foreign trips
Communications	100	90	10	Negotiation Pac Bell and AT&T
All other	90	90	—	
Total administration	890	888	2	
Grand total	$10,640	$10,858	$(218)	
Percent of sales	8.0%	7.4%		

The Illustrative Company, Inc.
ADVERTISING AND SALES PROMOTION BUDGET
STATUS REPORT AS AT JUNE 30, 19XX
(dollars in thousands)

Category	Project Budget	Actual to 6/30/XX			Estimated Cost to Complete	Indicated Total Cost	(Over) Under Budget
		Expenditures	Commitments	Total			
Broadcast media							
Radio—local	$ 525	$ 220	$ 60	$ 280	$ 245	$ 525	$ —
Television							
Regional	1,400	600	700	1,300	200	1,500	(100)
Local spots	2,625	1,125	500	1,625	800	2,425	200
Total	4,025	1,725	1,200	2,925	1,000	3,925	100
Total broadcast media	4,550	1,945	1,260	3,205	1,245	4,450	100
Print media							
Local newspapers	420	140	60	200	200	400	20
Business publications	700	450	150	600	150	750	(50)
General public magazines	1,100	510	400	910	200	1,110	(10)
Subtotal	2,220	1,100	610	1,710	550	2,260	(40)
Catalogs	900	400	300	700	200	900	—
Newspaper stuffers	300	100	50	150	150	300	—
Direct mail	2,000	1,300	900	2,200	—	2,200	(200)
Total print media	5,420	2,900	1,860	4,760	900	5,660	(240)
Total media	9,970	4,845	3,120	7,965	2,145	10,110	(140)
Advertising administration							
Salaries and wages	420	210	—	210	210	420	—
Fringe benefits	168	84	—	84	84	168	—
Travel	120	50	—	50	60	110	10
Communications	90	40	—	40	50	90	—
All other costs	90	50	—	50	40	90	—
Total administration	888	434	—	434	444	878	10
Grand total	$10,858	$5,279	$3,120	$8,399	$2,589	$10,988	$(130)
Percent of sales	7.4%					7.5%	

555

(c) VARIABLE VOLUME BUDGET

A limited number of distribution activities are high-volume repetitive tasks that probably can be directly related to the immediate physical volume handled. The loading and unloading of trucks, freight cars, or packaging products are examples. Giving recognition to the need to have an adequate number of workers available, even when the volume fluctuates greatly, these activities can be planned, measured, and controlled much like some factory operations.

The steps involved in this type of variable budget are as follows (see also Chapter 23):

1. For each department or activity grouping, expenses are identified by type (salaries and wages, fringe benefits, supplies, etc.).

2. Such expenses are segregated into their fixed and variable components for the planning period. Recognition must be given to the true cost drivers, as in activity-based costing. (See Chapters 6 and 23.)

3. For the *planning* budget, the estimated expenses are determined for each applicable time period (monthly or quarterly) by applying the estimated units to be handled to the unit variable expense rate, and adding the fixed components. (See Figure 21-10, which is expanded to show budget structure.) This planning budget is approved by the supervisor, when in order, and consolidated with the other distribution cost budgets to arrive at the total marketing department budget.

4. When approved, and when the year is underway, actual costs are measured monthly against the budgeted expense (fixed costs plus unit variable expense multiplied by the units handled) and corrective action taken if necessary. (See Figure 21-11.)

(d) COMPETITIVE SERVICE BUDGET

In a limited number of cases, the competitive service-type budget, or profit or loss-type budget, may be useful. Basically, it can be applied when the costs of a distribution operation can be readily compared with an independent and similar service activity. Examples include building maintenance or warehousing activities.

The procedure is closely related to the variable budget system just reviewed, combined with an in-house billing rate based on competitive prices. Steps in the process are these:

1. The competitive price to be charged for each type of service is determined based on the area prevailing practice.

2. Expenses are accumulated on a responsibility accounting basis for the department.

3. Expenses are analyzed or identified into their fixed and variable components.

4. For the planning budget, the expected unit volumes are estimated and applied to the budget structure of fixed and variable elements:

   a. To the competitive unit service prices to arrive at the net billings. (See Figure 21-12.)

Figure 21-10 Variable Volume Budget.

The Illustrative Company
LOS ANGELES TERMINAL
ANNUAL PLANNING BUDGET FOR THE YEAR 199X

Estimated Units—199W 360,000
199X 420,000

Item	Mo. Budget Structure		Est. Budget—Current Year 199W			Estimated Budget—199X		
	Fixed	Variable	Fixed	Variable	Total	Fixed	Variable	Total
Salaries	$15,000	—	$180,000	—	$ 180,000	$189,000	—	$ 189,000
Hourly wages	6,000	.70	72,000	$252,000	324,000	75,600	$323,400	399,000
Incentive pay—M.	1,500	—	18,000	—	18,000	18,900	—	18,900
—H.	600	.07	7,200	25,200	32,400	7,560	30,870	38,430
Subtotal	23,100		277,200	277,200	554,400	291,060	354,270	645,330
Fringe benefits	9,240		110,880	110,880	221,760	116,424	141,708	258,132
Supplies	1,000	.10	12,000	36,000	48,000	12,000	42,000	54,000
Gas and oil	1,000	.30	12,000	108,000	120,000	12,000	126,000	138,000
Repairs—regular	400	.10	4,800	36,000	40,800	4,800	42,000	46,800
special	500	.20	6,000	72,000	78,000	6,000	84,000	90,000
Communications	1,000	.03	12,000	10,800	22,800	12,000	12,600	24,600
Occupancy	3,000	—	36,000	—	36,000	36,000	—	36,000
Utilities	650	.15	7,800	54,000	61,800	7,800	63,000	70,800
Property taxes and insurance	700	—	8,400	—	8,400	8,400	—	8,400
Depreciation	2,500	—	30,000	—	30,000	30,000	—	30,000
Miscellaneous	100	.05	1,200	18,000	17,200	1,200	21,000	22,200
Total	$43,190		$518,280	$722,880	$1,241,160	$537,684	$886,578	$1,424,262

Notes: Increases requested: 5% on all salaries and wages and incentive pay.
No other changes.

Figure 21-11 Variable Budget Control Report.

The Illustrative Company
Los Angeles Terminal
Budget Report—Month of March

Supervisor _____ Johnsen
Units Handled _____ 36,000

Item	Budget Fixed	Budget Variable	Budget Total	March Actual	March (Over) Under Budget	Year to Date Budget	Year to Date Actual	Year to Date (Over) Under Budget
Salaries	$15,750	—	$15,750	$ 15,750	—	$ 47,250	$ 47,250	$ —
Hourly wages	6,300	$26,460	32,760	32,500	$ 260	98,280	98,000	280
Incentive pay—M.	1,575	—	1,575	1,575	—	4,725	4,725	—
—H.	630	2,646	3,276	3,250	26	9,828	9,800	28
Subtotal	24,255	29,106	53,361	53,075	286	160,083	159,775	308
Fringe benefits (40%)	9,702	11,642	21,344	21,230	114	64,032	63,910	122
Supplies	1,000	3,600	4,600	4,300	300	13,800	13,900	(100)
Gas and oil	1,000	10,800	11,800	12,120	(320)	35,400	35,000	400
Repairs—regular	400	3,600	4,000	4,600	(600)	12,000	12,000	—
special	500	7,200	7,700	7,200	500	23,100	21,100	2,000
Communications	1,000	1,080	2,080	2,000	80	6,240	6,040	200
Occupancy	3,000	—	3,000	3,000	—	9,000	9,000	—
Utilities	650	5,400	6,050	5,950	100	18,150	18,000	150
Property taxes and insurance	700	—	700	700	—	2,100	2,100	—
Depreciation	2,500	—	2,500	2,500	—	7,500	7,500	—
Miscellaneous	100	1,800	1,900	1,300	600	5,700	5,900	(200)
Total	$44,807	$74,228	$119,035	$117,975	$1,060	$357,105	$354,225	$2,880

Notes: Telephone companies have announced an 8% increase in the tariff. Since no budget was provided for such an increase, Johnsen is requesting a budget adjustment.

558

Figure 21-12 Competitive Service Budget Report.

The Illustrative Company
OREGON DISTRIBUTION CENTER
BUDGET REPORT

Month of ___January___
Units handled ___200,000___

Item	Budget	Actual	Favorable (Unfavorable) Variance
Net billings to using activities	$242,330	$201,100	$(41,230)
Operating Expenses			
Salaries and wages	162,500	164,100	(1,600)
Supplies	4,900	4,810	90
Vehicle maintenance	18,760	16,440	2,320
Repairs	5,800	5,900	(100)
Occupancy charges	25,000	25,000	—
Depreciation	10,000	10,000	—
Property taxes	3,000	3,000	—
Miscellaneous	300	310	(10)
Total	$230,260	$229,560	$ 700
Operating profit (or loss)	$ 12,070	$(28,460)	$(40,530)

b. To unit variable cost rates to arrive at the variable budget. This is added to the fixed expense budget, by type of expense, to arrive at the budget level for each type of expense.

c. As to "billings," these should be properly handled in the distribution budget consolidation (i.e., eliminated in most cases).

5. For control purposes, the unit budget times the actual volume handled, plus the budgeted fixed costs, is compared to actual expense to determine budget performance. (See Figure 21-12.)

6. Corrective action is taken as required.

(e) SUMMARIZED MARKETING EXPENSE BUDGET

When the individual department planning budgets are approved, they are summarized by the controller's staff to arrive at the tentative marketing expense budget as in Figure 21-13. For illustrative purposes only, this summary budget identifies the supporting types of budgets in the marketing function. When the complete annual plan is approved, the chief sales executive is advised by the CEO of the approved budget. This becomes a commitment by him as to expense levels for the year.

Figure 21-13 Summary Marketing Expense Budget.

The Johnson Company, Inc.
SUMMARY MARKETING DIVISION BUDGET
FOR THE PLAN YEAR ENDING DECEMBER 31, 19XX
(dollars in thousands)

Department	Type of Budget	Prior Year Actual	Plan Year Total	Quarter 1	Quarter 2	Quarter 3	Quarter 4	Annual Budget (Increase) Decrease
General and administrative								
V.P. sales	Administrative	$ 3,840	$ 3,910	$ 950	$ 990	$ 1,010	$ 960	$ 70
Customer relations	Administrative	780	820	205	205	205	205	40
Market research	Project	1,120	1,140	280	290	285	285	20
Total		5,740	5,870	1,435	1,485	1,500	1,450	130
Branch offices								
San Francisco	Administrative	410	415	104	103	105	103	5
Chicago	Administrative	620	630	158	157	159	156	10
New Orleans	Administrative	360	365	91	91	92	91	5
Total		1,390	1,410	353	351	356	350	20
Direct selling								
West	Administrative	8,310	9,120	2,270	2,290	2,310	2,250	810
Rocky Mountains	Administrative	6,120	6,230	1,550	1,570	1,590	1,520	110
Great Plains	Administrative	5,870	6,040	1,510	1,510	1,530	1,490	170
Southwest	Administrative	7,960	8,170	2,020	2,050	2,070	2,030	210
Middle West	Administrative	9,540	9,980	2,470	2,510	2,500	2,500	440
Total		37,800	39,540	9,820	9,930	10,000	9,790	1,740
Advertising and sales promotion	Project	10,470	10,560	2,220	2,610	2,140	3,590	90
Warehousing								
Portland	Variable	2,960	3,170	790	780	810	790	210
Denver	Variable	1,840	1,990	480	500	510	500	150
Chicago	Variable	3,480	3,495	860	870	865	900	15
New Orleans	Variable	1,710	1,725	420	430	460	415	15
Total		9,990	10,380	2,550	2,580	2,645	2,605	390
Grand total—division		$65,390	$67,760	$16,378	$16,956	$16,641	$17,785	$2,370
Percent of sales		12.4%	11.9%					

560

21-10 SPECIAL COMMENTS ON ADVERTISING AND SALES PROMOTION EXPENSE

In discussing marketing expenses, the example selected for a project-type budget (see Figure 21-8) was advertising and sales promotion expense. This expense, as well as market research expense, often is planned and controlled on a project basis. Planning and controlling advertising and sales promotion expense is the responsibility of the chief sales executive, and such expenses are included in the marketing expense budget for internal administration purposes. However, the approval process at the board-of-director level often considers this kind of expense in a separate budget review. For this reason, among others, some special comments appear appropriate.

First, it may be well to define advertising as any paid form of nonpersonal presentation and promotion of ideas, goods, and services by an identified sponsor. Inherent in this and similar definitions is the fact that presentations are nonpersonal, that is, there is no face-to-face personal selling to the customer. It is a controlled, paid-for service—not free publicity. Sales promotion is more difficult to describe. It may be supplementary to either advertising or personal selling. Typically, it takes the form of a special effort, usually for a limited time only, of inducements such as price reductions, cents-off coupons, cash refunds, or contests or prizes, to induce the purchase of the goods or service. The campaign may be directed to consumers, or salespeople, or other intermediaries.

Second, the reasons for often separate consideration or approval by a board of directors (or internal management) include these factors:

- For many companies, such as retail stores or consumer goods producers such as Procter & Gamble or Kimberly-Clark or Coca-Cola, Inc., it is a major expenditure.
- It is difficult to measure the effectiveness of advertising or sales promotion programs.
- Closely related to the difficulty of measurement is the fact that the results of the program may be less immediate and less direct than some other type of marketing effort, such as direct selling.
- Finally, advertising and sales promotion effort is usually organized as a separate department or as an outside agency, as compared with other selling efforts.

All of these factors are among the reasons for separate budgetary treatment.

Third, the type of expenses involved here differ somewhat from other marketing expenses. A large portion will represent media costs, whether for television or radio broadcasts, for printed media (such as newspapers and/or magazines), or for direct mail costs, or other public media costs (such as outdoor advertising). Associated with the media costs are the usual administrative expenses: salaries and wages, fringe benefits, travel, occupancy costs, automobile maintenance, etc.

Fourth, the purpose of advertising will vary in differing circumstances. While the general purpose is to support the broad marketing objectives, more specific goals may include these:

- Educate consumers in the use of the product or service.
- Reduce the cost of other selling effort.

- Increase sales.
- Establish or maintain trademarks or brand names.
- Develop new markets.
- Meet or outdo competition.
- Maintain prices.
- Introduce new products or services.
- Create favorable public opinion.
- Avoid unfavorable legislation.

Fifth, two basic ways are currently in use of establishing an advertising and sales promotion budget: (1) the lump-sum appropriation method, (2) estimating the amount required to attain certain objectives. Comments on each follow.

The simple lump-sum appropriation method consists of authorizing the expenditure for advertising and sales promotions related to some factor. Under this plan the total amount to be spent could be based on:

- A percentage of planned or budgeted sales.
- A percentage of the prior year sales or perhaps of an average of several past years.
- A fixed amount per unit of product expected to be sold (the units are obtained from the sales plan).
- An arbitrary percentage increase over the prior year's expenditure.
- A percent of gross profit on the product for the prior year or the planning year.
- A percentage of net income of the prior year or the planning year.

The advantage of the lump-sum appropriation method is sheer simplicity. Basically it seems to lack any scientific basis, although there may be a perceived long-term relationship between advertising expenditures and level of sales.

The estimated "cost of attaining the objective" procedure seems a more logical process: Objectives are set; the detailed steps to reach the objective are decided upon; the relevant costs for each such program are estimated and are summarized to arrive at the total cost for the planning year. This estimating process may be performed by the advertising department, perhaps assisted by an outside advertising agency, or sometimes it is done by the agency itself. Obviously, a skilled financial analyst should review such costs for any evidence of waste. Moreover, in some cases the marginal or gross profit from the additional units estimated to be sold can be compared with the advertising expense to determine if the project seems to make financial sense. This can be done on an incremental advertising expense and quantity basis to ascertain at which point, if any, the incremental unit advertising cost exceeds the incremental marginal profit after all direct expenses.

A simple example is shown in the matrix illustrated in Figure 21-14. If these estimates are valid, then not more than $100,000 (incremental block 5) should be spent in advertising Product 10. Financial analysis would sometimes identify some possibly uneconomic programs.

It is beyond the scope of this section to review the many facets of advertising and sales promotion that might interest the controller or staff in attempting to financially

Figure 21-14 Incremental Advertising Expense Compared to Incremental Profit Margin.

Incremental Block	Incremental Advertising Expense	Additional Units Estimated to be Sold	Estimated Marginal Unit Income*	Incremental Unit Advertising Cost	Unit Increment or (Decrement) to Profit	Total Margin
1	$ -0-	20,000	$1.00	$ —	$1.00	$20,000
2	25,000	30,000	1.20	.83	.37	11,100
3	25,000	70,000	1.30	.36	.94	65,800
4	25,000	50,000	.90	.50	.40	20,000
5	25,000	50,000	.80	.50	.30	15,000
6	25,000	30,000	.70	.83	(.13)	(3,900)
7	25,000	30,000	.60	.83	(.23)	(6,900)
8	25,000	20,000	.50	1.25	(.75)	(15,000)
9	25,000	10,000	.40	2.50	(2.10)	(21,000)

* After all direct costs and before advertising cost.

appraise the advertising and sales promotion budget. Books on advertising and sales promotion are worth perusing for more detailed information.

21-11 CONTROL OF MARKETING EXPENSES

As already explained, the budgetary control process involves comparing the actual expenses with the budgeted expenses (or the budgeted rates time the actual volume handled for variable expenses) and taking corrective action.

Where budgets are not used, actual expenses may be compared with the unit standards and actual unit volumes, as reviewed in the next section.

21-12 MARKETING EXPENSE STANDARDS

(a) STANDARDS AND CONTROL

The very foundation of marketing cost control lies in the correlation of sales effort with the potential and the use of analysis to avoid misdirection. Although this may be done, and although the income and expense statement may reveal a satisfactory result for a time, still this is not enough. We must know that the business is being operated efficiently, and this requires measuring sticks—standards.

A complete analysis of past operations must be taken as a starting point. By this we may determine that 1,000 calls have been made by salespeople in a given territory, at a cost of $5 per call, and with certain sales results. But the questions are left unanswered about how many calls should have been made by the salesmen and what the cost per call should have been. These also must be ascertained if effective control of sales effort is to be exercised. We may know that 1,000 orders have been handled at a clerical cost of $0.50 per order, but we need to know also what the cost would have been if the clerical work had been efficiently directed. In brief, we need standards by which to judge the distribution performance and signal its weaknesses. Knowing in detail what it has been is not enough; we need also to know in detail what it should be in the immediate future.

(b) CAN STANDARDS BE ESTABLISHED FOR MARKETING ACTIVITY?

It would be foolish to contend that all distribution activity can be highly standardized. In fact, it is never possible completely to standardize production activities. The answer to just exactly what results should be obtained from a dollar expended for advertising or direct sales effort when developing a new territory or a new product or just what costs will be necessary to accomplish certain definite ends pertaining to customer goodwill is frequently problematical. But it would be equally foolish, and a fatal management error, to evade the fact that standards can be successfully applied to a vast amount of the distribution activity. If no one is competent to judge what distribution effort is necessary to secure certain results and what it will cost to do it, then management must indeed be in a helpless position.

Although a new venture may be undertaken here and there on something of an experimental basis, the entire distribution effort will scarcely be directed along such lines continuously. It is hardly to be expected that an intelligent executive will direct one million dollars into the distribution effort in the vain hope that profit will result at the end of the year. Rather he may be expected to provide for the continuous measurement of individual and group performance as expressed in costs and results. He will want to know when billing clerks are wasting time, when automotive equipment is too costly, when direct mail prices fail to "pull," when bad debt losses are excessive, when warehouse labor hours are too high, when long-distance telephone costs are exorbitant, and when salespeople produce insufficient orders. If these costs and performance factors are not under constant control, the executive's profit goal is almost certain to be unmet. But such control implies standards and depends entirely on the establishment and use of standards. Warehouse labor hours never appear too high in the absolute. They become too high only when measured against what they should be under the circumstances—only when a standard is applied.

Although it must be admitted that it is difficult to establish standards for some marketing activities; that psychological factors are relatively more, and physical and mechanical factors relatively less, influential than in production; that relatively more depends on the judgment of executives and relatively less on objective measurements; and that a somewhat greater tolerance must be allowed in the consideration of variances, it should be understood that this applies only to a part of the marketing activity. Much of the marketing activity is fully as measurable as production. There is no important difference, for example, between the method of establishing standards for order handling, warehousing, shipping, delivery, and clerical work and the methods employed in production. Even those distribution activities that are largely affected by psychological factors, such as advertising and personal selling, are usually capable of reasonably accurate measurement when the activities are continuous or repetitive.

The types of standards needed, as well as the techniques used for their establishment, change as circumstances change, such as increased globalization. Whereas at one time much attention was focused on internal unit cost standards and unit revenue standards, now other facets are involved. While internal comparisons of internal trends and relationships are still made, there is a movement to measure against *external* standards. Moreover, some standards are now *time* related, such as the time required to develop a new product. Standards might relate to customer satisfaction, such as number of prospects converted to customer status. Some of the newer standards, some of which are applicable to marketing efforts, are reviewed in Chapter 19.

(c) TYPES OF MARKETING EXPENSE STANDARDS

Marketing expense standards may be either (1) of a very general nature, and applicable to distribution functions as a whole, or by major divisions, or (2) units that measure individual performance. Illustrative of the former are the following:

1. Selling cost as a percent of net sales.
2. Cost per dollar of gross profit.
3. Cost per unit sold.
4. Cost per sales transaction.
5. Cost per order received.
6. Cost per customer account.

Standards such as these are useful indicators of trends for the entire distribution effort. Furthermore, such standards can be applied to individual products, territories, branches, or departments.

However, these general standards do not necessarily indicate points of weaknesses in terms of individual responsibility. If costs are to be controlled, the performance of the individual must be measured. Hence it is necessary to set standards for controllable costs of individual cost items or functions. In warehousing, for example, standards might be set for direct labor as follows:

Cost per item handled.

Cost per pound handled.

Cost per shipment.

Cost per order filled.

Similar standards might be set for shipping supplies or delivery and truck expense. In the direct sales field, standards might be set for a salesperson's automobile expense in terms of the following:

Cost per mile traveled.

Cost per day.

Cost per month.

Again, entertainment expense standards might relate to cost per customer or cost per dollar of net sales.

(d) OTHER CONSIDERATIONS IN SETTING MARKETING EXPENSE STANDARDS

The controller has a joint responsibility with the sales executives in setting marketing expense standards. In fulfilling this responsibility, it is well that he keep in mind the complications. For example, in manufacturing there is usually only one standard cost for the product. There are, however, many standard costs for distribution of the same article. Thus the cost per call may be different in every territory or sales district. Even in the same territory the standard cost to sell to different classes of customers may vary.

By and large, the same principles applicable to manufacturing expense standards apply to distribution costs. Thus standards will require revision when operating conditions change materially. Also, where fixed elements of cost are included in the standards, the effect of volume must be recognized.

(e) HOW TO SET MARKETING EXPENSE STANDARDS—BENCHMARKING

The methods of establishing standards vary depending on whether external or only internal standards are the objective. A procedure of measuring products, or services, or business practice against the toughest competitor, or the companies best in their class, or other measures—benchmarking—is discussed in Section 19-9.

Another method that may be somewhat more internally oriented, but also involves an analytical approach is reviewed next. Finally, procedures for reviewing and improving business processes (and establishing selected standards) are discussed as reengineering and productivity improvement in Chapter 54.

When the need for standards has been agreed to with the sales executive, the detailed work of setting standards can proceed.

The first step in setting the marketing expense standards is to classify the costs according to functions and activities expressive of individual responsibility. How far such classification can and should be carried depends, of course, on the nature of the business, its size, methods of operation, and internal organization. The cost of such major functions as direct selling, advertising, transportation, warehousing, credit and collection, and financing can be separated in most businesses and subjected to individual study and control. Even such a general classification as this is not universal. For example, in a concern doing a house-to-house business, the functions of direct selling and credit and collection are merged, since the work is done by the same people under the same supervision.

The costs of the major functions should be further classified by individual activities that make up the functional service. For example, the credit and collection costs may be separated into credit approvals, posting charges, posting credits, preparing customers' monthly statements, writing collection letters, and so on.

The second step is to select units or bases of measurement through which the standards can be expressed. Such units or bases will vary with the type of measurement to be applied; thus the measurement may apply to effort used, to cost, to results achieved, or to the relationship of these factors. To illustrate, a salesperson may be expected to make a given number of calls per day. This constitutes a measure of effort used and the unit of measure is the call. The cost of writing orders in the order department may be measured in terms of the number of orders or order lines[1] written. This is a measure of costs, and the unit of measurement is the order or order line. Salespeople may each be expected to produce a certain number of orders or to secure a certain number of new accounts. This is a measure of results, and the units of measurement are orders and new accounts. Finally, salespeople may be required to hold their direct costs within 8% of their sales volume. Here the measurement is in terms of the relationship of particular costs to the results in the sales volumes and the basis of measurement is the ratio of one to the other.

Although such specific units of measurement are not available for all distribution activities, some basis must be selected before the standards can be applied. Where specific units are not available, more inclusive or composite bases must be used. For example, the entire credit and collection cost may be measured by the number of accounts carried, or the entire advertising cost may be measured by its ratio to dollar sales volume.

The third step is to analyze past experience relative to the cost of the functions and specific activities involved with a view to selecting the best experience and indications about the best procedure. This may involve intensive study of individual methods of procedure and operation similar to that employed in the development of production standards.

---

[1] *Order line* here means the writing of one line on a sales order—e.g., "200$\frac{1}{2}$" Malleable Iron Nipples No. 682 at $8.00 = $16.00.

The fourth step is to consider the effect on costs of expected changes in external conditions and of the sales program as planned. If increased sales resistance is expected, an estimate must be made about its effect on such costs as advertising and direct selling. If the program calls for a lengthening of the installment credit period, the effect on the financing cost must be estimated.

The final step is to summarize the judgment of those executives, division heads, department heads, and salespersons whose experience and training qualify them to judge the measures of satisfactory performance. The standards set must be the final expression of such judgment, based on an intelligent study of past experience and future outlook.

Standards as finally set will result in much overlapping. Thus a standard cost may be applied to the warehousing function as a whole. Within this general function, many individual cost standards may be applied that relate to specific activities such as clerical costs of order handling and physical assembling.

Finally, different standards must frequently be set for different territories, products, channels of distribution, classes of customers, departments, etc., wherein different conditions prevail.

(f) ADDITIONAL INFORMATION NEEDED

To establish and use marketing expense standards successfully, a concern must accumulate and have available a considerable amount of information relative to marketing activities and the cost factors pertaining to such activities. This includes a considerable body of information not available in the regular accounting records. Permanent records must be designed for regularly recording and accumulating these data in readily usable form. Just as it is now the custom to record regularly such production factors as labor hours, chargeable hours, idle hours, machine hours, power loads, and number of operations, records must likewise be made of the marketing factors.

Illustrative of such data are the following:

1. Analyses of sales in physical units.
2. Number of sales transactions classified in terms of size, hour of day, etc.
3. Number of quotations made.
4. Number of orders classified in terms of size, period in which received, etc.
5. Number of order lines written.
6. Average number of salespersons.
7. Number of salesperson-days.
8. Number of calls on old and new customers.
9. Number of days of salespersons' travel.
10. Number of miles of salespersons' travel.
11. Average number of customers classified with regard to location, annual volume, etc.
12. Number of labor hours of salespeople, advertising and display people, warehouse workers, truck drivers, delivery men, maintenance workers, clerical workers, etc.
13. Number of returns and allowances classified in terms of cause.

14. Number of units of advertising space or time used in the various advertising media.

15. Number of advertising pieces mailed: letters, circulars, folders, calendars, etc.

16. Number of pieces of advertising material distributed: window cards, store displays, inserts, etc.

17. Number of samples distributed.

18. Number of demonstrations made.

19. Number of inquiries received.

20. Number of new customers secured.

21. Number of shipments.

22. Analyses of shipments in physical units.

23. Dollar value of shipments.

24. Number of ton-mile units of shipping.

25. Number of deliveries.

26. Number of parcels delivered.

27. Number of miles of truck operation.

28. Number of shipping claims handled.

29. Physical volume of goods handled in warehouses.

30. Average size of physical inventory carried.

31. Rates of turnover in dollars and physical units.

32. Average number of accounts carried.

33. Number of invoices.

34. Number of invoice lines.

35. Number of remittances received.

36. Number of credit letters sent.

37. Average number of days accounts are outstanding.

38. Average amount of receivables carried.

39. Number of mail pieces handled.

40. Number of postings.

41. Number of letters written—distribution sections.

42. Number of units filed.

43. Percentage of sales from new products.

44. Percentage of on-time customer deliveries.

45. Number of customers for which company is sole supplier.

Many of the foregoing items must be further classified by territories, commodities, and departments to supply the full information needed.

Such information will be found useful for many purposes in the direction of distribution activity but is essential to a program of standards. Many concerns have in the past neglected to accumulate and use such information. It is not uncommon to find a concern that has the most exacting records of a production machine—the date of its purchase, full detail about its cost, working hours, number and cause of idle hours, and cost of maintenance—almost to the point of a complete diary of the machine's daily routine over a long period of years. During the same time, the concern may have been employing a salesperson whose total cost through the years has greatly exceeded the cost and maintenance of the machine, but little detailed record of his activities has been kept. How he has spent his time, the number of calls made, the number of prospects interviewed, orders received, gross profit, and even the type of goods sold have not always been recorded. The salesperson's activity report can provide some of these data.

With many concerns the distribution information is entirely too meager. More information must be collected if the distribution program is to be wisely directed.

(g) USE OF STANDARDS FOR CONTROL

The essence of control is the prompt follow-up of unfavorable trends before they develop into large losses. Once the standards are determined, the stage is set for action. The controller compares actual and standard performance and reports the results to the sales executive.

21-13 SELECTED REFERENCES

Bluestein, Abram I., "Leadership Practices in Marketing," *Planning Review,* Sept./Oct., 1994, pp. 35–36.

Gale, Bradley T., and Robert D. Buzzell, "Market Perceived Quality: Key Strategic Concept," *Planning Review,* March/April, 1989, pp. 6–15, 48.

Jenster, Per V., and David Hover, "How to Focus Marketing Intelligence to Serve Strategy," *Planning Review,* July/Aug., 1994, pp. 32–37.

Levitt, Theodore, "The Globalization of Markets," *Harvard Business Review,* May–June, 1983, pp. 92–102.

Pine, B. Joseph, II, "Making Mass Customization Happen: Strategies for the New Competitive Realities," *Planning Review,* Sept./Oct., 1993, pp. 23–24.

Quelch, J. A., and Kristina Cannon-Bonventre, "Better Marketing at the Point of Purchases," *Harvard Business Review,* Nov.–Dec. 1983, pp. 162–169.

Robertson, Thomas S., and Howard Barich, "A Successful Approach to Segmenting Industrial Markets," *Planning Review,* Nov./Dec. 1992, pp. 4–11, 48.

Stern, Louis W., and Frederick D. Sturdivant, "Customer-Driven Distribution Systems," *Harvard Business Review,* July–Aug. 1987, pp. 34–41.

Willigan, Geraldine E., "High-Performance Marketing: An Interview with Nike's Phil Knight," *Harvard Business Review,* July/Aug., 1992, pp. 91–101.

CHAPTER 22

Planning and Control of Manufacturing Costs: Direct Material and Direct Labor

22-1 GENERAL ASPECTS OF MANUFACTURING

(a) RESPONSIBILITIES OF THE MANUFACTURING EXECUTIVE

To those not familiar with the intricacies of the modern manufacturing processes, it might seem that once a determination has been made of the products to be manufactured and sold, and of the quantities required, then the remaining task is simple: proceed to manufacture the articles. As compared with the task of the sales executive, many of the variables in manufacturing are more subject to the control of the executive than they are in selling, many are more easily measured, and the psychological factors may be less pronounced. But the job is by no means an easy one, and many difficulties plague the manufacturing manager who is attempting to deliver a quality product, within cost, and on schedule.

Consider some of the numerous decisions the manufacturing executive is called upon to make—in many of which the controller is not involved at all, others with which he may be only tangentially concerned, and yet others where he may be, or should be, of assistance to the production executive. While any number of classifications may be used, these groupings of the duties seem practical:

Physical Facilities

- Acquisition of plant and equipment.
- Proper layout of machinery and equipment, storage facilities, etc.
- Adequate maintenance of plant and equipment.
- Proper safeguarding of the physical assets (security).

Product and Production Planning

- Product design.
- Decisions on product specifications.
- Determination of material requirements—specifications and quantities.
- Selection of manufacturing processes.
- Planning the production schedule.
- Decisions on manufacturing or purchasing the components—"make-or-buy" decisions.
- Material purchases.
- Labor requirements.
  a. Skill needs.
  b. Employment.
  c. Training.
  d. Job assignment and transfer.
- Inventory levels required.
- Preparing the production and manufacturing plans—short and long term.

The Manufacturing Process

- Planning and controlling labor.
- Receiving, handling, routing, and processing raw materials and work-in-process in an economical manner.
- Controlling quality.
- Coordinating manufacturing with sales.
- Planning and controlling all manufacturing costs—direct and indirect.

And the list could go on.

For some phases, the controller may coordinate procedures and see that adequate internal controls exist, that needed economic analysis is made, as in acquisition of plant and equipment or as part of the annual planning process. But perhaps the biggest contribution of the controller is the development and maintenance of a general accounting and cost system that will assist the manufacturing executive, and that will provide the necessary information for the planning and control of the business.

(b) OBJECTIVES OF MANUFACTURING COST ACCOUNTING

A manufacturing cost accounting system is an integral part of the total management information system. In analyzing costing systems for control, the controller must recognize the purpose of the manufacturing cost accounting system and relate it to the production or operating management problems. The objectives must be clearly defined if the system is to be effectively utilized. There are fundamental purposes of a cost system that may vary in importance from one organization to another; however, they may be summarized as follows:

1. For control of costs.
2. For planning and performance measurement.
3. For inventory valuation.
4. For deriving anticipated prices.

Control of costs is a primary use of manufacturing cost accounting and cost analysis. The major elements of costs—labor, material, and manufacturing expenses—must be segregated by product, by type of cost and by responsibility. For example, the actual number of parts used in the assembly of an airplane section, such as a wing, may be compared to the bill of materials and corrective action taken when appropriate.

Closely related to cost control is the use of cost data for effective planning and performance measurement. Some of the same information used for cost control purposes may be used for the planning of manufacturing operations. For example, the standards used for cost control of manufacturing expenses can be used to plan these expenses for future periods with due consideration to past experience relative to the established standards. Cost analysis can be utilized, as part of the planning process, to determine the probable effect of different courses of action. Again, a comparison of manufacturing costs vs. purchasing a particular part or component can be made in making the determination in make-or-buy decisions. The use of costs and analysis would extend to many facets of the total planning process.

One of the key objectives of a costing system is the determination of product unit cost and the valuation of inventories. This is also a prerequisite to an accurate determination of the cost of goods sold in the statement of income and expense. The manufacturing cost system should recognize this fact and include sufficient cost details, such as layering part costs and quantities for items in inventory, to accomplish this purpose.

A critical purpose of cost data is for establishing selling prices. The manufactured cost of a product is not necessarily the sole determinant in setting prices, since the desired gross margin and the price acceptable to the market are also significant factors. As more companies realize that direct labor and materials are relatively fixed costs, management will concentrate on designing the product to fit a specific price, cost, and gross margin; the controller should be included in this process to advise management about indirect and direct costs.

(c) THE CONTROLLER AND MANUFACTURING MANAGEMENT PROBLEMS

A fundamental responsibility of the controller is to insure that the manufacturing cost systems have been established to serve the needs and requirements of production executives. He is the fact finder regarding costs, and it is his responsibility to see that factory management is furnished with sufficient cost information on a timely basis and in a proper format to effect proper control and planning. Unfortunately, under a just-in-time (JIT) system, manufacturing managers need feedback regarding costs far more frequently than on a monthly basis. JIT products are manufactured with little or no wait time, and consequently can be produced in periods far less than was the case under the line manufacturing concept. Therefore, if a cost problem occurred, such as too many direct labor hours required to finish a part, the formal accounting system would not tell the line managers until well after the problem had happened.

Fortunately, JIT principles stress the need to shrink inventories and streamline processes, thereby making manufacturing problems highly visible *without* any product costing reports. A subset of JIT is cellular (i.e., group) manufacturing, in which equipment is generally arranged in a horseshoe shape, and one employee uses those machines to make one part, taking the piece from machine to machine. Consequently, there is little or no work-in-process (WIP) to track, and any scrapped parts are immediately visible to management. Based on this kind of manufacturing concept, line managers can do without reports, with the exception of daily production quantities versus budgeted quantities that meet quality standards.

Just-in-time manufacturing places the controller in the unique position of looking for something to report on. Since direct labor and materials costs are now largely fixed, the controller's time emphasis should switch to planning the costs of new products, and tracking planned costs versus actual costs. Since the JIT manufacturing environment tends to have small cost variances, the controller should seriously question the amount of effort to be invested in tracking direct labor and materials variances versus the benefit of collecting the data.

Another area in which the controller can profitably invest time tracking information is the number of items that increase a product's cycle time or the nonvalue-added cost of producing a product. Management can then work to reduce the frequency of these items, thereby reducing the costs associated with them. Here is a partial list of such items:

- Number of material moves.
- Number of part numbers used by the company.
- Number of set-ups required to build a product.
- Number of products sold by the company, including the number of options offered.
- Number of product distribution locations used.
- Number of engineering change notices.
- Number of parts reworked.

If a process is value-added, the controller can initiate an operational audit to find any bottlenecks in the process, thereby improving the capacity of the process. For example, engineering a custom product is clearly value-added; internal auditors could recommend new hardware or software for designing the product to allow the engineering department to design twice as many products with the same number of staff.

Under JIT, there are several traditional performance measures that the controller should be careful *not* to report:

1. If the report is on machine efficiency, then line managers will have an incentive to create an excessive amount of WIP in order to keep their machines running at maximum utilization.

2. If the report is on purchase price variances, the materials staff will have an incentive to purchase large quantities of raw materials in order to get volume discounts.

3. If the report is on headcount, the manufacturing manager will have an incentive to hire untrained contract workers, who may produce more scrap than full-time, better-trained employees.

4. If you include a scrap factor into a product's standard cost, then line managers will take no corrective action unless scrap exceeds the budgeted level, thereby incorporating scrap into the production process.

5. If the report is on labor variances, then the accountants will expend considerable labor in an area that has relatively fixed costs and not put time into areas that require more analysis.

6. If the report is on standard cost overhead absorption, then management will have an incentive to overproduce to absorb more overhead than was actually expended, thereby increasing profits, increasing inventory, and reducing available cash.

(d) TYPES OF MANUFACTURING COST ANALYSES

The question will arise often about what type of cost data should be presented. Just how should production costs be analyzed? This will depend on the purpose for which the costs are to be used, as well as the cost experience of those who use the information.

Unit costs or total costs may be accumulated in an infinite variety of ways. The primary segregation may be by any one of the following:

Product or class of product	Process
Operation	Customer order
Department	Worker responsible
Machine or machine center	Cost element

Each of the primary segregations may be subdivided a number of ways. For example, the out-of-pocket costs may be separated from the "continuing costs," those that would be incurred whether a particular order or run was made. Again, production costs might be segregated between those which are direct or indirect; that is, those attributable directly to the operation and those prorated. Thus the material used to fashion a cup might be direct, whereas the power used to operate the press would be indirect. Sometimes the analysis of costs will differentiate between those that vary with production volume and those which are constant within the range of production usually experienced. For example, the direct labor consumed may relate directly to volume, whereas depreciation remains unchanged. The controller must use his judgment and experience in deciding what type of analysis is necessary to present the essential facts.

The mix of product-cost components has shifted away from direct labor and material dominance to overhead, (such as depreciation, materials management, and engineering time) that takes up a greater proportion of a typical product's cost. Because of this change in mix, the controller will find that product cost analyses will depend heavily on how to assign overhead costs to a product. Activity-based costing (ABC) is of considerable use in this area. For more information about ABC, refer to Chapter 23.

(e) TYPES OF COST SYSTEMS

Experience in cost determination in various industries and specific companies has given rise to several types of cost systems that best suit the kinds of manufacturing activities. A traditional costing system known as a "job order cost system" is normally used for manufacturing products to a specific customer order or unique product. For example, the assembly or fabrication operations of a particular job or contract are collected in a separate job order number. Another widely used costing system is known as a "process cost system." This system assigns costs to a cost center rather than to a particular job. All the production costs of a department are collected, and the departmental cost per unit is determined by dividing the total departmental costs by the number of units processed through the department. Process cost systems are more commonly used in food processing, oil refining, flour milling, paint manufacturing, etc. No two cost accounting systems are identical. There are many factors that determine the kind of system to use, such as product mix, plant location, product diversity, number of specific customer orders, and complexity of the manufacturing process. It may be advisable to combine certain characteristics of both types of systems in certain situations. For example, in a steel mill the primary system may be a process cost system; however, minor activities such as maintenance may be on a job cost basis. The controller should thoroughly analyze all operations to determine the system that best satisfies all needs.

There are two issues currently affecting the job order and process costing systems that the controller should be aware of:

1. JIT manufacturing systems allow the controller to reduce or eliminate the recordkeeping needed for job cost reporting. Since JIT tends to eliminate variances on the shop floor by eliminating the WIP that used to mask problems, there are few cost variances for the cost accountant to accumulate in a job cost report. Therefore, the time needed to accumulate information for job costing may no longer be worth the increase in accuracy derived from it, and the controller should consider using the initial planned job cost as the actual job cost.

2. One of the primary differences between process and job-shop costing systems is the presence (job shop) or absence (process flow) of WIP. Since installing a JIT manufacturing system inherently implies reducing or eliminating WIP, a JIT job-shop costing system may not vary that much from a process costing system.

(f) FACTORY ACCOUNTS AND GENERAL ACCOUNTS

The selection of the manufacturing cost accounting system should recognize the relationship of the factory cost accounts to the general accounts. Normally, the factory accounts should be tied into the general accounts for control purposes. It should enhance the accuracy of the cost information included in the top-level manufacturing cost reports as well as the profit or loss statements and balance sheet. Periodic review and reconciliation of the accounts will also minimize unexpected or year-end adjustments. This integration of the cost accounts is extremely important as the company expands and the operations are more complex.

Although there are situations where the factory and general accounts are not coordinated, it is not recommended. If such a system is used additional effort is required to insure the accuracy and preclude misstatement of cost information. Such a procedure requires extreme care in cutoffs for liabilities and the taking of physical inventories as well as analyzing inventory differences.

22-2 DIRECT MATERIAL COSTS—PLANNING AND CONTROL

(a) SCOPE OF DIRECT MATERIAL INVOLVEMENT

Direct material, as the term is used by cost accountants, refers to material that can be definitely or specifically charged to a particular product, process, or job, and that becomes a component part of the finished product. The definition must be applied in a practical way, for if the material cannot be conveniently charged as direct or if it is an insignificant item of cost, then it would probably be classified as *indirect material* and allocated with other manufacturing expenses to the product on some logical basis. Although this section deals primarily with direct material, certain of the phases relate also to indirect material.

In its broadest phase, material planning and control is simply the providing of the required quantity and quality of material at the required time and place in the manufacturing process. By implication, the material secured must not be excessive in amount, *and* it must be fully accounted for and used as intended. The extent of material planning and control is broad and should cover many phases or areas, such as plans and specifications; purchasing; receiving and handling; inventories; usage; and scrap, waste, and salvage. In each of these phases, the controller has certain responsibilities and can make contributions toward an efficient operation.

(b) BENEFITS FROM PROPER MATERIAL PLANNING AND CONTROL

Because material is such a large cost item in most manufacturing concerns, effective utilization is an important factor in the financial success or failure of the business. Proper planning and control of materials with the related adequate accounting, has the following advantages:

1. Reduces inefficient use or waste of materials.
2. Reduces or prevents production delays by reason of lack of materials.
3. Reduces the risk from theft or fraud.
4. Reduces the investment in inventories.
5. May reduce the required investment in storage facilities.
6. Provides more accurate interim financial statements.
7. Assists buyers through a better coordinated buying program.
8. Provides a basis for proper product pricing.
9. Provides more accurate inventory values.
10. Reduces the cost of insurance for inventory.

(c) IMA STATEMENT OF MANAGEMENT ACCOUNTING NO. 4E: DEFINITION AND MEASUREMENT OF DIRECT MATERIAL COST

Before discussing in detail the planning and control of direct material costs, and the controller's role therein, it may be helpful to review the authoritative guidelines provided by the Institute of Management Accountants (IMA) in SMA No. 4E. The statement is reproduced in full as follows:[1]

Acknowledgments

The Institute of Management Accountants is grateful to the many individuals who contributed to the publication of Statement 4E, *Definition and Measurement of Direct Material Cost.* Appreciation is extended to members of the Management Accounting Practices Committee and its Subcommittee on MAP Statement Promulgation. Special thanks are extended to Michael J. Sandretto, Price Waterhouse & Co., Columbus, Ohio, for his research and writing associated with this project.

Definition and Measurement of Direct Material Cost

1. The term "direct material cost" as used in practice, in literature, and in litigation has a wide variety of meanings. Unless the intended meaning in a given context is clear, confusion and misunderstanding are likely to result. The purpose of this Statement is to provide a conceptual definition of "direct material cost" that, in the absence of a specified alternative, should be taken as the meaning of this term.

---

[1] From *Management Accounting,* Sept. 1986, pp. 65–67. Reprinted with permission.

2. This Statement makes the conceptual definition more concrete by describing how direct material costs should be measured. Measurement has two aspects:

    a. The quantity of material that is to be included as direct material, that is, the inputs that are to be counted.

    b. The unit price by which each of these quantities is multiplied to arrive at a monetary cost.

3. Many of the examples used in this Statement refer to the direct material cost of goods produced in manufacturing companies. The examples apply equally well to the same or similar transactions for projects, services, and other cost objects. The allocation of joint product or by-product costs is not addressed in this Statement.

4. In a manufacturing company, direct material cost is an element of inventory cost and of cost of sales. Differences in how companies define this term result in variations in the amount recorded as direct material cost and the amount recorded as overhead or expense. Differences in the way material costs are accounted for in cost-type contracts, in projects, and for other cost objects also lead to differences in the amounts recorded as direct material cost and the amounts recorded as overhead or expense. If users do not understand what items are included in direct material cost in such situations, their interpretation of the information may be erroneous, and they may make unsound decisions.

Definitions

5. *Direct Material Cost*—Quantities of material that can be specifically identified with a cost object in an economically feasible manner, priced at the unit price of direct material.

6. *Cost Object*—A product, contract, project, organizational subdivision, function, or other unit for which costs are measured or estimated.

7. *Direct Cost*—A cost that can be specifically identified with a cost object in an economically feasible manner.

8. *Material Quantity*—A physical amount of material, such as a pound of copper, a 50-gallon drum of a chemical, or a batch of 100 semiconductors.

9. *Scrap*—Material residue from manufacturing operations that has some value. Examples of scrap include border material from stamping operations, shavings, filings, borings, and turnings. Scrap may have relatively minor recovery value, as in the case of steel, or it may be of significant value, as in the case of gold.

10. *Waste*—Material that is lost, evaporates, or shrinks in a manufacturing process or is a residue that has no significant recovery value in excess of its disposal costs.

11. *Defective Units*—Production that does not meet quality standards. Defective units may be reworked and sold, or they may be rejected and disposed of for salvage value.

12. *Material-Related Costs*—Costs, other than direct material costs, that are incurred as a result of the acquisition, inspection, storage, or movement of direct material quantities.

13. *Cost Item*—A subdivision of cost, such as freight, duty, insurance, sales tax, or outside processing costs.

14. *Unit Price of Direct Material*—Invoice price and acquisition-related cost items that can be specifically identified with direct material quantities in an economically feasible manner and that can be measured with reasonable accuracy.

Materiality

15. If a cost item is immaterial, it should be accounted for in a manner that is economically feasible.

Material Quantities

16. If the cost object is the production of a manufactured or processed product, its direct material cost normally should include quantities of material that become a physical part of the cost object and those materials that are consumed in the manufacturing process that can be specifically identified with that cost object.

17. If the cost object is the production of a service, its direct material cost normally should include all quantities of material that can be specifically identified with producing the service.

18. If the cost object is the production of a project, its direct material cost normally should include all quantities of material that can be specifically identified with the project. For a large project, direct material cost typically includes far more categories of direct material quantities than in a product because it is relatively easy to identify quantities of material specifically with a large project. Examples include fasteners, adhesives, lubricants, and other items whose unit costs are too low to be considered direct material costs for many manufactured products. If a large project is broken down into a series of smaller projects, products, or subassemblies, the material categories listed in this paragraph typically are not included in the direct material cost of these subdivisions.

19. Costs classified as direct material costs must be excluded from costs used in calculating overhead rates. For example, if one project is large enough to include fasteners and lubricants in direct material quantities, but those items are included in overhead for other projects, the cost of fasteners and lubricants should not be included in the overhead rate applied to the first project. It follows that entities that define direct material costs differently for different cost objects will have two or more overhead rates.

20. Material quantity should include the cost of packaging material to the extent it is included in the finished product. Examples include bottles for liquor and perfume and containers for cosmetics and medical products.

21. Material quantity should include packing supplies necessary to deliver goods to customers, to the extent that the goods are packed with these supplies as part of the production process.

Material Lost in the Production Process

22. Direct material cost should include the material cost of scrap, waste, and normally anticipated defective units that occur in the ordinary course of the production process. The following examples depict situations in which such costs should be classified as direct material costs:

   a. A part is stamped from a roll of strip steel, or a finished unit is produced by turning a casting. The amount of material lost in these processes through ordinary scrap usually can be predicted with reasonable accuracy. The cost of the predicted scrap should be included in the direct material cost of the part.

   b. A quantity is lost in the production process through evaporation, dehydration, spoilage, shrinkage, or similar causes. The amount of material that is lost in these processes usually can be predicted with reasonable accuracy. The cost of the predicted amount of lost material should be included in the direct material cost.

   c. Engineering estimates are developed for the percentage of defective units expected from a given production process, and they are reasonably accurate. The cost of material in the estimated percentage of defective units should be included in the direct material cost of completed production.

   d. In most cases, the net salvage value of estimated scrap, waste, and defective units should reduce the direct material cost. However, the direct material cost should be increased if the related costs exceed the salvage value, as in the case of certain chemical or nuclear wastes.

23. Unanticipated quantities of scrap, waste, or defective units should not be included in direct material cost. These quantities should be included in manufacturing overhead or should be expensed.

Samples, Prototypes, and Initial Production Runs

24. Routine quality assurance samples that are tested to destruction should be included in direct material cost. Nonroutine quality assurance samples taken due to quality problems should not be included in direct material cost.

25. The material cost of marketing samples and prototypes should not be included in direct material cost.

Unit Price of Direct Material

26. The unit price of direct material should include the invoice price and other costs paid to vendors to deliver the material quantity to the production facility or to a point of free delivery. The following costs are included in the unit price of direct material:

   • Invoice price for direct material quantity,

   • Invoice price for outside processing,

   • Shipping costs (inward freight) paid or owed to outside vendors,

   • Sales tax,

- Duty, and
- Cost of delivery containers and pallets, net of return refunds.

27. Trade discounts, refunds, and rebates should be deducted in calculating the unit price of direct material.

28. If cash discounts offered by the vendor exceed reasonable interest rates, the price of direct material should be reduced by the excess.

29. Demurrage charges should not be included in direct material cost.

30. Royalty payments and licenses should be included in direct material cost if they are functions of direct material quantities used in producing the cost object.

Use of Estimates

31. Estimates of direct material quantities and unit prices may be used if they are sufficiently accurate to be considered "specifically identified" with a cost object. The following situations are examples of estimates that are sufficiently accurate to be considered direct material costs in most instances:

    a. A manufacturing firm establishes standard material quantities for its products, but its system does not trace variances to these products. Nevertheless, there is a reasonable expectation that variances are proportional to the standard quantities and thus that the actual material quantities are proportional to the standard quantities.

    b. A manufacturing firm uses standard purchase prices for its materials. Although standard purchase prices are not necessarily the same as actual purchase prices, the firm is able to associate major deviations from standard purchase prices with specific products or product lines.

    c. Inward freight costs are added to direct material costs by a rate that approximates the actual cost, such as a percentage of price paid to the vendor or a percentage of the weight per unit of cost.

Material-Related Costs

32. Certain costs are closely related to the quantity of material acquired or used, but they cannot be specifically identified with a cost object in an economically feasible manner. These indirect costs are material-related costs. Material-related costs should be allocated to cost objects on the basis of some measure of direct material quantity or cost rather than on direct labor hours or cost. Costs for the following functions usually are considered material-related costs:

- Purchasing,
- Receiving,
- Receiving inspection,
- Material storage costs prior to purchased material entering production, and
- Issuing costs for material initially entering the production process.

33. Certain cost items may be closely related to material quantities and may be allocated to cost objects based on direct material quantities or costs. They are, however, more closely related to the production process than to the acquisition of material and are not typically considered material-related costs. Furthermore, they may be applicable to different time periods than the period in which the direct material cost was incurred. Examples of those cost items are:

- Material storage costs subsequent to entering the production process,
- Issuing costs for material subsequent to entering the production process,
- Production planning and control costs, and
- Internal transportation costs.

Cost Systems

34. This Statement does not discuss standard cost systems in detail and does not address how standards should be determined. In most cases, cost analysis and control are improved if the standard material quantity includes normal scrap and waste as defined in this Statement but excludes all lost or defective units. Differentiating between good units and normally anticipated lost units helps focus management's attention on lost units. Additionally, including in direct material the standard material quantity of both good units and normally anticipated lost units helps focus management's attention on total material cost.

35. The cost accounting systems of some firms, particularly retail firms, include many material-related costs as direct material cost. In such systems, direct material is defined more broadly than in this Statement. Nevertheless, if the relevant material-related costs are allocated on the basis of direct material, the resulting product costs may be substantially the same under this Statement as under a broader definition of direct material cost. The broader definition is useful for certain management accounting purposes. However, it should be recognized that direct material cost as measured in such systems—and for other purposes—may be different from direct material cost as measured according to the concepts of this Statement.

36. The cost accounting systems of many firms allocate material-related costs on some measure of direct labor, as contrasted with a measure of direct material, as recommended by this Statement. Allocation based on direct labor is, in many cases, easier to compute. It is likely, however, that allocation on some measure of direct material yields a more accurate measure of both direct and total cost of a cost object.

(d) PLANNING FOR DIRECT MATERIAL

The planning aspect of direct material relates to four phases, budgets, or plans:

1. *The Material Usage Budget.* This budget involves determining the quantities and related cost of the raw materials and purchased parts needed to meet the production budget (quantities of product to be manufactured) on a time-phased basis.

Basically it is a matter of multiplying the volume of finished articles to be produced times the number of individual components needed for its manufacture. This determination is the responsibility of the manufacturing executive. However, the aggregate costs must be provided to the controller in a format he or she needs. In most instances, it will be under the direction of the controller that the planning procedure and format of exhibits required will be established. The controller requires the total cost, by time period, to provide for the charge to work-in-process inventory and for relief of raw materials and purchased parts inventory in the financial planning process of preparing the business plan for the year or for other planning periods. Obviously, the material usage budget must be known so that the required purchases can be made and the required inventory level maintained.

The determination of the material usage budget is described in more detail in Chapter 29 on inventory planning and control.

The material usage budget generally will be summarized by physical quantities of significant items for use by manufacturing personnel. A cost summary is needed by the controller for preparing the plan in monetary terms. The usage budget may be presented in any one of several ways. A time-phased summary by major category of raw material for a small aircraft manufacturer is illustrated in Figure 22-1.

2. *The Material Purchases Budget.* When the material usage budget is known, the purchases budget can be determined (by the purchasing department), taking into account the required inventory levels.

Figure 22-1   Summarized Material Usage Budget.

The Aircraft Company
SUMMARIZED MATERIAL USAGE BUDGET
FOR THE PLAN YEAR 19XX
(dollars in thousands)

			Material Category			
Month	Engine	Aluminum	Electrical	Purchased Sub-Assemblies	All Other	Total
January ...	$ 7,500	$ 1,500	$ 990	$ 790	$ 200	$ 10,980
February ..	5,500	1,000	660	530	130	7,820
March	8,000	1,600	1,050	840	210	11,700
April	8,500	1,800	1,200	960	240	12,700
May	9,000	1,800	1,200	960	240	13,200
June	10,000	2,000	1,320	1,060	260	14,640
July	9,000	1,800	1,200	960	240	13,200
August	8,000	1,600	1,050	840	210	11,700
September .	7,000	1,400	920	740	190	10,250
October ...	6,000	1,200	790	630	160	8,780
November .	5,000	1,000	660	530	130	7,320
December .	6,000	1,200	790	630	160	8,780
Total	$89,500	$17,900	$11,830	$9,470	$2,370	$131,070

The time-phased material purchases budget is provided by the purchasing director (usually reporting to the manufacturing executive) to the controller for use in planning cash disbursements, and additions to the raw materials and purchased parts inventories—as part of the annual planning process (or planning for any other period). A highly condensed raw material purchases budget for the annual plan is illustrated in Figure 22-2.

3. *The Finished Production Budget.* This represents the quantities of finished product to be manufactured in the planning period. Such estimates are provided by the manufacturing executive to the controller for determining the additions to the finished goods inventory and the relief to the work-in-process inventory.

The quantities of production usually are costed by the cost department under the supervision of the controller.

4. *The Inventories Budgets.* The three preceding budgets, plus the cost-of-goods-sold budget, determine the inventory budgets for the planning period. In the annual planning process, the inventory costs usually are determined monthly.

Inventory budgets, together with the related purchases, usage, and completed product, are shown in Chapter 29 on planning and control of inventories.

While the raw materials, purchased parts and work-in-process budgets usually are the responsibility of the manufacturing executive, and the finished goods budget is the responsibility of either the manufacturing executive or the sales executive, the controller has certain reporting functions (see Chapter 29) as to planned vs. actual inventory levels and turnover rates, as well as responsibility for the adequacy of the internal control system.

To summarize, any *planning* responsibilities for direct materials rest with other line executives, although the controller will use these related data in the financial

Figure 22-2 Summarized Raw Material Purchase Budget.

The Illustrative Company					
SUMMARIZED RAW MATERIAL PURCHASES BUDGET					
FOR THE PLAN YEAR 19XX					
(dollars in hundreds)					
	Material Category				
Quarter/Month	A	B	C	D	Total
Quarter 1					
January	$ 40,000	$ 20,000	$ 50,000	$ 10,000	$ 120,000
February	35,000	17,000	45,000	8,000	105,000
March	50,000	25,000	60,000	12,000	147,000
Subtotal	125,000	62,000	155,000	30,000	372,000
Quarter 2	150,000	70,000	165,000	40,000	425,000
Quarter 3	116,000	60,000	150,000	20,000	346,000
Quarter 4	103,000	50,000	160,000	25,000	358,000
Total	$514,000	$242,000	$630,000	$115,000	$1,501,000

Note: A 5% price increase is assumed for the last two quarters.

planning process—in preparing the statement of estimated income and expense, the statement of estimated financial condition, and statement of estimated cash flows. Also, he will often test-check or audit the information furnished by the manufacturing executive for completeness, reasonableness, and compatibility with other plans. On occasion, the chief manufacturing executive will request the controller and staff to assemble the needed figures, with the help of the production staff.

The various budgets related to materials generally will be developed following a procedure and format coordinated (and sometimes developed by) the controller.

Those interested in a more detailed explanation of developing the plans or budgets for raw material usage and purchases may wish to check some of the current literature.[2]

(e) BASIC APPROACH TO DIRECT MATERIAL COST CONTROL

With an overview of the *planning* function behind us, we can now review the *control* function. With respect to materials, as with other costs, control in its simplest form involves the comparison of actual performance with a measuring stick—standard performance—and the prompt follow-up of adverse trends. However, it is not simply a matter of saying "350 yards of material were used, and the standard quantity is only 325" or "The standard price is $10.25 but the actual cost to the company was $13.60 each." Many other refinements or applications are involved. The standards must be reviewed and better methods found. Or checks and controls must be exercised before the cost is incurred. The central theme, however, is still the use of a standard as a point of measurement.

Although the applications will vary in different concerns, some of the problems or considerations that must be handled by the controller are as follows:

1. *Purchasing and Receiving.*

   a. Establishment and maintenance of internal checks to assure that materials paid for are received and used for the purposes intended. Since some purchases are now received on a just-in-time basis, the controller may find that materials are now paid for based on the amount of product manufactured by the company in a given period, instead of on a large quantity of paperwork associated with a large number of small-quantity receipts.

   b. Audit of purchasing procedures to ascertain that bids are received where applicable. A JIT manufacturing system uses a small number of long-term suppliers, however, so the controller may find that bids are restricted to providers of services such as janitorial duties and maintenance activities.

   c. Comparative studies of prices paid for commodities with industry prices or indexes.

   d. Measurement of price trends on raw materials. Many JIT supplier contracts call for price decreases by suppliers at set intervals; the controller should be aware of the terms of these contracts and audit the timing and amount of the changes.

---

[2] For example, see James D. Willson, *Budgeting and Profit Planning Manual*, 1994 ed. (Boston: Warren, Gorham & Lamont, 1994), Chap. B4.

e. Determination of price variance on current purchases through comparison of actual and standard costs. This may relate to purchases at the time of ordering or at time of receipt. The same approach may be used in a review of current purchase orders to advise management in advance about the effect on standard costs. In a JIT environment, most part costs would be contractually set with a small number of suppliers, so the controller would examine prices charged for any variations from the agreed-upon rates.

2. *Usage.*

a. Comparison of actual and standard quantities used in production. A variance may indicate an incorrect quantity on the product's bill of materials, misplaced parts, pilferage, or incorrect part quantities recorded in inventory.

b. Preparation of standard cost formulas (to emphasize major cost items and as part of a cost reduction program).

c. Preparation of reports on spoilage, scrap, and waste as compared with standard. In a JIT environment, no scrap is allowed for and therefore is not included in the budget as a standard.

d. Calculation of costs to make vs. costs to buy.

This list only suggests some of the methods available to the controller in dealing with material cost control.

(f) SETTING MATERIAL QUANTITY STANDARDS

Because an important phase of material control is the comparison of actual usage with standard, the controller is interested in the method of setting these quantitative standards. First, he can render assistance by contributing information about past experience. Second, he should act as a check in seeing that the standards are not so loose that they bury poor performance, on the one hand, and represent realistic but attainable performance, on the other.

Standards of material usage may be established by at least three procedures:

1. By engineering studies to determine the best kind and quality of material, taking into account the product design requirements and production methods.

2. By an analysis of past experience for the same or similar operations.

3. By making test runs under controlled conditions.

Although a combination of these methods may be used, best practice usually dictates that engineering studies be made. To the theoretical loss must be added a provision for those other unavoidable losses that it is impractical to eliminate. In this decision, past experience will play a part. Past performance alone, of course, is not desirable in that certain known wastes may be perpetuated. This engineering study, combined with a few test runs, should give fairly reliable standards.

(g) REVISION OF MATERIAL QUANTITY STANDARDS

Standards are based on certain production methods and product specifications. It would be expected, therefore, that these standards should be modified as these other factors change, if such changes affect material usage. For the measuring stick to be an effective control tool, it must relate to the function being measured. However, the adjustment need not be carried through as a change in inventory value, unless it is significant.

(h) USING THE QUANTITY STANDARDS FOR COST CONTROL

The key to material quantity control is to know in advance how much material should be used on the job, frequently to secure information about how actual performance compares with standard during the progress of the work, and to take corrective action where necessary. The supervisor responsible for the use of materials, as well as his superior, should be aware of these facts. At the lowest supervisory level, details of each operation and process should be in the hands of those who can control usage. At higher levels, only overall results need be known.

The method to be used in comparing the actual and standard usage will differ in each company, depending on several conditions. Some of the more important factors that will influence the controller in applying control procedures about material usage are these:

1. The production method in use.
2. The type and value of the materials.
3. The degree to which cost reports are utilized by management for cost control purposes.

A simple excess material report that is issued daily is shown in Figure 22-3. It shows not only the type of material involved as excess usage, but also the cause of the

Figure 22-3   Daily Excess Material Usage Report.

	The Computer Chip Company DAILY EXCESS MATERIAL USAGE (DATE)					Dept. No. ___42___ Foreman: _Magraudy_	
Material Used	Amount of Finished Product	Standard Usage (Units)	Actual Usage (Units)	Excess Usage (Units)	Unit Cost	Total Excess Cost	Comments
A	3,960	3,960	4,110	150	$ 4.75	$ 712.50	(a)
B	7,920	15,840	15,960	120	2.00	240.00	(b)
C	1,980	3,960	4,000	40	21.50	860.00	(c)
D	3,960	3,960	3,970	10	65.40	654.00	(d)
E	15,840	15,840	15,920	80	3.25	260.00	(e)
Total						$2,726.50	

Comments:
(a) Parts defective (Vendor Bush).
(b) Careless workmanship.
(c) Power down.
(d) Wrong speed drilling.
(e) Handyman dropped case.

condition. This report could be available on a real-time basis, with the use of a computer, and could be summarized daily for the plant manager.

One of the most important considerations is the nature of the production process. In a job order or lot system, such as an assembly operation in an aircraft plant, where a definite quantity is to be produced, the procedure is quite simple. A production order is issued, and a bill of material or "standard requisition" states the exact quantity of material needed to complete the order. If parts are spoiled or lost, it then becomes necessary to secure replacements by means of a nonstandard or excess usage requisition. Usually, the foreman must approve this request, and, consequently, the excess usage can be identified immediately. A special color (red) requisition may be used, and a summary report issued at certain intervals for the use of the production executives responsible.

If production is on a continuous process basis, then periodically a comparison can be made of material used in relation to the finished product. Corrective action may not be as quick here, but measures can be taken to avoid future losses.

Just as the production process is a vital factor in determining the cost accounting plan, so also it is a consideration in the method of detecting material losses. If losses are to be localized, then inspections must be made at selected points in the process of manufacture. At these various stations, the rejected material can be counted or weighed and costed if necessary. When there are several distinct steps in the manufacturing process, the controller may have to persuade the production group of the need and desirability of establishing count stations for control purposes. Once these stations are established, the chief contribution of the accountant is to summarize and report the losses over standard. The process can be adopted to the use of personal computers and provision of control information on a real-time basis.

Another obvious factor in the method of reporting material usage is the type and value of the item itself. A cardinal principle in cost control is to place primary emphasis on high-value items. Hence valuable airplane motors, for example, would be identified by serial number and otherwise accurately accounted for. Items with less unit value, or not readily segregated, might be controlled through less accurate periodic reporting. An example might be lumber. The nature and value of the materials determine whether the *time* factor or the *unit* factor would be predominant in usage reporting.

Management is often not directly interested in *dollar cost* for control purposes but rather only in *units*. There is no difference in the principle involved but merely in the application. Under these conditions, the controller should see that management is informed of losses in terms of physical units—something it understands. In this case, the cost report would be merely a summary of the losses. Experience will often show, however, that as the controller gives an accounting in dollars, the other members of management will become more cost conscious.

The essence of any control program, regardless of the method of reporting, however, is to follow up on substandard performance and take corrective action.

A variation on using quantity standards and materials variation reporting is JIT variance reporting. One of the cornerstones of the JIT concept is that you order only what you need. That means you won't waste what you use and that there should be no materials variances. Of course, even at world-class JIT practitioners such as Motorola and Toyota, there is scrap; however, there is much less than will be found at a non-JIT company. Consequently, the controller must examine the cost of collecting the variance information against its value in correcting the amount of scrap accumulation. The conclusion may be that JIT does not require much materials variance reporting, if any.

(i) LIMITED USEFULNESS OF MATERIAL PRICE STANDARDS

In comparing actual and standard material costs, the use of price standards permits the segregation of variances as a result of excess usage from those incurred by reason of price changes. By and large, however, the material price standards used for inventory valuation cannot be considered as a satisfactory guide in measuring the performance of the purchasing department. Prices of materials are affected by so many factors outside the business that the standards represent merely a measure of what prices are being paid as compared with what was expected to be paid.

A review of price variances may, however, reveal some informative data. Exceedingly high prices may reveal special purchases for quick delivery because someone had not properly scheduled purchases. Or higher prices may reveal shipment via express when freight shipments would have been satisfactory. Again, the lowest cost supplier may not be utilized because of the advantages of excellent quality control methods in place at a competitive shop. The total cost of production and impact on the marketplace needs to be considered—not merely the purchase price of the specific item. To generalize, the exact cause for any price variance must be ascertained before valid conclusions can be drawn. Some companies have found it advisable to establish two standards—one for inventory valuation and quite another to be used by the purchasing department as a goal to be attained. One negative result of recording a purchase price variance is that the purchasing department may give up close supplier relationships in order to get the lowest part cost through the bidding process. Part bidding is the nemesis of close supplier parings (a cornerstone of JIT), since suppliers know they will be kicked off the supplier list, no matter how good their delivery or quality, unless they bid the lowest cost.

(j) SETTING MATERIAL PRICE STANDARDS

Practice varies somewhat about the responsibility for setting price standards. Sometimes the cost department assumes this responsibility on the basis of a review of past prices. In other cases, the purchasing staff gives its estimate of expected prices that is subject to a thorough and analytical check by the accounting staff. Probably, the most satisfactory setup is through the combined effort of these two departments.

(k) OTHER APPLICATIONS OF MATERIAL CONTROL

By using a little imagination, every controller will be able to devise simple reports that will be of great value in material control—whether in merely making the production staff aware of the high-cost items of the product or in stimulating a program of cost reduction. For example, in a chemical processing plant, a simple report detailing the material components cost of a formulation could be used to advantage. Another report is illustrated in Figure 22-4, wherein the standard material cost of an assembly-type operation, in this case a self-guided small plane, is given.

Where the products are quite costly, and relatively few in number, it may be useful to provide management periodically with the changes in contracted prices, as well

Figure 22-4 Detail of, and Changes in, Standard Material Costs.

The Small Plane Manufacturing Company
Statement on Unit Standard Material Costs
For the Month of June 19XX

Description	Standard Cost 5/31/XX	Changes Increases	Changes Decreases	Standard Cost 6/30/XX	Remarks
Power Unit	$ 820.00	$30.00	$ —	$ 850.00	Price increased by manufacturer
Raw Stock Aluminum	277.40	—	—	277.40	
Fabric	142.60	—	—	142.60	
Paint	127.54	—	22.54	105.00	Installation of electric equipment
Steel Tubing	117.50	—	—	117.50	
Stabilizer	106.22	—	—	106.22	
Instruments	93.14	—	1.14	92.00	New altimeter
Hardware	92.20	—	—	92.20	
Radio Equipment	91.20	—	—	91.20	
Exhaust Stock	34.17	—	—	34.17	
Steel Small Parts	76.16	—	—	76.16	
Synthetic Small Parts	14.20	—	—	14.20	
Plastic	19.06	—	.06	19.00	
Rubber	12.00	—	—	12.00	
Aluminum Forging	32.14	—	2.00	30.14	Substitute "R" forging
Raw Stock Steel	43.15	—	—	43.15	
Directional Control Component	39.15	—	—	39.15	
Battery	18.00	—	—	18.00	
Cushion	14.70	—	—	14.70	
Miscellaneous Trim Parts	22.13	—	—	22.13	
Total	$2,192.66	$30.00	$25.74	$2,196.92	

as an indication about the effect of price changes on the planned cost of the product. Such statements may stimulate thinking about material substitutions or changes in processes or specifications.

22-3 LABOR COSTS—PLANNING AND CONTROL

(a) LABOR ACCOUNTING UNDER PRIVATE ENTERPRISE

One of the most important factors in the success of a business is the maintenance of a satisfactory relationship between management and employees. The controller and his staff can do much to encourage and promote such a relationship, whether it is such a simple matter as seeing that the payroll checks are ready on time or whether it extends to the development of a wage system that rewards meritorious performance.

Aside from this fact, labor accounting and control are important. As automation and the use of robots and computers become even more prevalent, what was once called direct labor may not any longer increase in relative importance. But labor is still a significant cost. Likewise, those costs usually closely related to labor costs have grown by leaps and bounds—costs for longer vacations, more adequate health and welfare plans, pension plans, and increased Social Security taxes. These fringe benefit costs are 50% or more of many payrolls. For all these reasons, the cost of labor is an important cost factor.

The objectives of labor accounting may be outlined as follows:

1. A prompt and accurate determination of the amount of wages due the employee.
2. The analysis and determination of labor costs in such a manner as may be needed by management—e.g., by product, operation, department, or category of labor—for planning and control purposes.
3. The advent of JIT manufacturing systems has called into question the need for reporting the direct labor utilization variance. This variance revolves around the amount of a product that is produced with a given amount of labor; thus, a positive labor utilization variance can be achieved by producing more product than may be needed. An underlying principle of JIT is that you produce only as much as you need to produce, so JIT and labor utilization variance reporting are inherently at odds with each other. If JIT has been installed, then the controller should consider eliminating this type of variance reporting.

(b) CLASSIFICATION OF LABOR COSTS

With the increasing trends to automation, to continuous process type of manufacturing, and to integrated machine operations under which individual hand operations are replaced, the traditional accounting definition of *direct labor* must be modernized. As a practical matter, where labor is charged to a cost center and is directly related to the main function of that center, whether it is direct or indirect labor is of no consequence. Rather, attention must be directed to *labor* costs. Perhaps the primary considerations are measurability and materiality rather than physical association with the product. For planning and control purposes, any factory wages or salaries that are identifiable with a directly productive department as contrasted with a service department and are of significance in that department are defined as "manufacturing labor."

All other labor will be defined as "indirect labor," treated as overhead expense, and discussed under manufacturing expenses.

(c) IMA STATEMENT ON MANAGEMENT ACCOUNTING NO. 4C: DEFINITION AND MEASUREMENT OF DIRECT LABOR COST

The short definition of direct labor given in the preceding section will serve many purposes. However, a more expanded statement is that provided by the Institute of Management Accountants in its "Statement on Management Accounting No. 4C: Definition and Measurement of Direct Labor Cost."[3]

Definition and Measurement of Direct Labor Cost

1. The term "direct labor cost" as used in practice, in literature, and in litigation has a wide variety of meanings. Unless the meaning intended in a given context is clear, confusion and misunderstanding are likely to result. The purpose of this Statement is to provide a conceptual definition of direct labor costs that, in the absence of a specified alternative, should be taken as the meaning of this term.

2. In a manufacturing company, direct labor cost is an element of inventory cost and of cost of sales. Differences in the way companies define this term result in variations in the amount recorded as direct labor and the amount recorded as overhead. Differences in the way labor costs are accounted for in cost-type contracts and differences in the way labor costs are measured for responsibility centers, for projects, for functions (such as marketing, administration), and for other purposes also lead to differences in the distinction between direct labor costs and overhead costs and hence in differences in the amount of total costs recorded. If users do not understand what elements are included in direct labor cost in such situations, their interpretations of the numbers may be erroneous.

3. This Statement makes the conceptual definition more concrete by describing how direct labor costs should be measured. Measurement has two aspects: (a) the quantity of labor effort that is to be included as direct labor, that is, the types of hours or other units of time that are to be counted, and (b) the unit price by which each of these quantities is multiplied to arrive at a monetary cost.

Definitions

4. *Direct Labor Cost.* Labor quantities that can be specifically identified with a cost object in an economically feasible manner, priced at the unit price of direct labor.

5. *Cost Object.* A product, contract, project, organizational subdivision, function, or other unit for which costs are measured or estimated.

6. *Direct Cost.* Any cost that can be specifically identified with a cost object in an economically feasible manner.

---

[3] *Management Accounting,* Oct. 1989, pp. 67–69. Reprinted with permission.

7. *Labor Quantity.* A unit of labor time, such as a minute, hour, week, or month.

8. *Nonproductive Labor.* Labor quantities that do not contribute directly to the production of goods or services. Examples include coffee-break time, downtime, and personal time.

9. *Cost Element.* A subdivision of cost, such as basic compensation, employer's FICA tax, or health and life insurance costs.

10. *Unit Price of Direct Labor.* Compensation and compensation-related cost elements that can be specifically identified with the direct labor quantity in an economically feasible manner and that can be measured with reasonable accuracy.

Measurement

11. Estimates of direct labor quantities and unit prices may be sufficiently accurate to be considered "specifically identified" with a cost object. The following are examples of estimates that are sufficiently accurate to be considered direct labor costs in most circumstances:

    a. A manufacturing firm establishes standard labor times for its products, but its system does not trace variances from these standards to individual products. Nevertheless, there is a reasonable expectation that variances are proportional to the standard quantities and thus that the actual labor quantities are proportional to the standard quantities.

    b. A manufacturing firm uses a plant-wide predetermined labor rate in its cost system. Its average direct labor unit prices are approximately the same for all products. Wage rate variances are written off as period expenses and cannot be assigned to products.

    c. Break time and personal time relate to all productive time in a day. Nevertheless, break time and personal time are assigned to standard labor time as an average percentage of productive time.

    d. Health insurance premium is added to direct labor cost as a percentage of direct labor cost or as a fixed amount per hour of direct labor.

Labor Quantities

12. If the cost object is a manufactured or processed product, its direct labor cost normally includes all labor directly associated with transforming or adding value to the product. Such labor includes fabrication, processing, process or machine tending, assembly, packaging, and on-line inspection labor.

13. If the cost object is a service, its direct labor cost normally includes all labor that can be specifically identified with providing the service.

14. If the cost object is a project, its direct labor cost normally includes all labor that can be specifically identified with the project. For a large project, direct labor cost typically includes far more categories of direct labor because it is relatively easy to specifically identify employees with such a project. Examples include the time of janitors, material handlers, maintenance personnel, draftsmen, managers, and engineers. If a large project is broken down into a series of smaller projects, products, or subassemblies, the labor categories

listed in this paragraph typically are not included in the direct labor cost of these subdivisions.

15. Costs classified as direct labor costs must be excluded from costs used in calculating overhead rates. For example, if one project is large enough to require the full-time services of a janitor, but other projects share janitorial services, the costs of the shared janitorial services should not be included in the overhead rate applied to the first project.

Nonproductive Labor Quantities

16. Nonproductive time may be a normal and unavoidable part of total labor time. In such cases, a pro rata share of nonproductive time should be classified as direct labor time. For example, coffee breaks and personal time may be established by custom, specified in labor contracts, or legislated. An employee who works seven and one-half hours might be given an additional one-half hour of paid time for coffee breaks and for personal time. If so, and if 15 hours of productive time are associated directly with a cost object, the direct labor quantity should include one hour of nonproductive time, making a total of 16 direct labor hours for the cost object.

17. Other categories of nonproductive labor, such as downtime, clean-up, and training, are less likely to be direct labor quantities. The amount of downtime usually cannot be specifically identified with a particular cost object; it may result from a parts shortage or a broken machine. Similarly, clean-up or training may be a fill-in for a shortage of work. In these cases, nonproductive time is not a direct labor cost because it cannot be specifically identified with a cost object.

Unit Price of Labor: Cost Elements in Direct Labor Cost

18. The following cost elements should be included in the unit price of direct labor because they can be specifically identified with a quantity of labor and because they can be measured accurately for the direct labor quantity that is used on a cost object:
   - Basic compensation.
   - Individual production efficiency bonuses.
   - Group production efficiency bonuses.
   - FICA (employer's portion).
   - Cost of living allowances (COLA).

19. The following cost items usually should be included in the unit price of direct labor quantity by firms with relatively stable operations. Although the relationship between direct labor quantities and these cost elements is less certain than the relationship of the cost elements listed in paragraph 17, these costs are incurred because an organization uses a quantity of labor. These elements can be specifically identified with direct labor quantities over a period of approximately one year or less:
   - Health insurance.
   - Group life insurance.

- Holiday pay.
- Vacation pay.
- Pension costs and other post-retirement benefits.
- Workers' compensation insurance expense.
- Unemployment compensation insurance—state and federal.

20. Premium pay for overtime, holidays, and second- or third-shift work some- times is considered direct labor cost and sometimes indirect labor cost. If a premium is incurred because of a particular product or other cost object, the premium is considered a direct labor cost of the cost object causing the pre- mium to be paid, even if that cost object is not produced by premium labor time. If the premium is earned only occasionally and if it is not clear which product caused its incurrence, the premium usually should be considered an indirect labor cost. If premiums are a significant and usual part of compen- sation, they usually should be included in direct labor cost as an average cost per hour or as an average percentage of direct labor cost.

21. The following items usually are excluded from the unit price of direct labor because they cannot be identified with direct labor quantities, except over the long term:
- Wage continuation plans (for example, separation allowances).
- Contributions to Supplemental Unemployment Benefit (SUB) plans.
- Membership dues.
- Safety-related items.
- Company-sponsored cafeteria.
- Recreational facilities.

22. Some firms grant employees sick leave credit based on time worked—one day of sick leave for each two months worked, for example. That credit can be accumulated, then taken as vacation or as additional pay after a certain length of time. In such cases, the cost should be considered part of the unit price.

23. Certain activities are related to direct labor quantities. However, except in the case of large cost objects, these activities relate to more than one cost object and are not a part of direct labor cost. Examples are:
- Payroll department.
- Personnel department.

24. Some firms have profit-sharing plans or other bonus plans based on income. In many such firms, the relationship between a labor quantity and the bonus is not specific enough to have the bonus qualify as a part of the unit price of direct labor. The bonus is identified with the firm's overall profitability rather than with the direct labor cost of individual cost objects.

25. An exception to the above profit plan principle is a bonus plan that is limited to, for example, 15% of basic compensation and where profit is almost al- ways greater than needed to pay the maximum bonus. In such cases, the bonus should be considered an element of the unit price of labor.

Cost Systems

26. The cost accounting systems of many firms treat labor costs as consisting only of payroll costs and define direct labor cost as only the payroll cost associated with operations that physically transform or add value to a product. Other labor quantities and other elements of the unit price of labor are treated as overhead. In such systems, direct labor cost is defined more narrowly than in this Statement. Nevertheless, if the relevant overhead is allocated on the basis of direct labor, the resulting product costs may be substantially the same as those resulting from application of the concepts in this Statement. The identification of direct payroll costs in such systems provides information that is needed for many management accounting purposes. However, it should be recognized that direct labor cost as measured in such systems—and for other purposes—may be different from direct labor cost as measured according to the concepts of this Statement.

(d) PLANNING OF LABOR COSTS

Planning labor costs might be described as planning or estimating the required manpower and costs associated with direct manufacturing departments (not indirect) for the annual plan or some other relevant planning period. It consists of determining the labor planning budget.

The process, which is essentially the responsibility of the manufacturing executive, consists of extrapolating the planned production of units times the standard labor content, plus an allowance for variances, to arrive at the labor-hours required. This is a tedious job, but the computer as applied to the standard labor hour content of expected production makes it much easier. Essentially, this process has several purposes, such as:

- Ascertaining by department, by skill, and by time period the number and type of workers needed to carry out the production program for the planning horizon.
- Determining the labor cost for the production program, including:
  a. Labor input.
  b. Labor content of completed product.
  c. Labor content of work-in-process.
  These data may then be used by the controller for determining the transfers to/from work-in-process and finished goods—in the same manner material costs were accounted for.
- Determining the estimated cost (payroll) requirements of the time-phased manufacturing labor budget for the planning period.
- Determining the unit labor content of each product so that the inventory values, cost of manufacturer, and cost of sales can be calculated for use in the statements of planned income and expense, planned financial condition, and planned cash flows.
- Seeing that the planned funds are available to meet the payroll.

Figure 22-5 Summarized Direct Labor Budget.

The Gidget Company
SUMMARIZED DIRECT LABOR BUDGET
FOR PLAN YEAR 19XX

Month/Quarter	Direct Labor Hours			Gross Cost		
	Standard	Provision for Variances	Total	Standard	Provision for Variances	Total
First Quarter						
January	222,500	4,450	226,950	$ 3,337,500	$ 66,750	$ 3,404,250
February	204,300	4,100	208,400	3,064,500	61,500	3,126,000
March	223,400	4,500	227,900	3,351,000	67,500	3,418,500
Total	650,200	13,050	663,250	9,753,000	195,750	9,948,750
Second Quarter .	712,000	14,240	726,240	10,680,000	213,600	10,893,600
Third Quarter ..	725,700	10,890	736,590	11,429,775	171,518	11,601,293
Fourth Quarter .	719,300	11,510	730,810	11,328,975	181,283	11,510,258
Total	2,807,200	49,690	2,856,890	$43,191,750	$762,151	$43,953,901

Note: Present wage rates used through second quarter. Balance of year assumes a 5% wage increase.

A summarized direct labor budget for annual planning purposes, based on the underlying required labor-hours by department, by product and time-phased, might appear as in Figure 22-5.

A JIT manufacturing environment creates significant changes in direct labor costs that the controller should be aware of. When a manufacturing facility changes from an assembly line to manufacturing cells, the labor efficiency level drops, because machine setups become more frequent. A major JIT technique is to reduce setup times to minimal levels, but nonetheless, even the small setup times required for cellular manufacturing require more labor time than the zero setup times used in long assembly line production runs. Consequently, if management is contemplating switching to cellular manufacturing, the controller should expect an increase in the labor hours budget. Also, if the labor cost does not increase, the controller should see if the engineering staff has changed the labor routings to increase the number of expected setup times.

To the extent more information is desired on the planning aspects of direct labor, the reader may wish to consult some of the books on the subject.[4]

(e) THE CONTROLLER'S CONTRIBUTION TO CONTROL

In controlling direct labor costs, as with most manufacturing costs, the ultimate responsibility must rest with the line supervision. Yet this group must be given

---

[4] See, for example, James D. Willson, *Budgeting and Profit Planning Manual,* 3rd ed. (Boston: Warren, Gorham & Lamont, 1994). Chap. B3.

assistance in measuring performance, and certain other policing or restraining functions must be exercised. Herein lie the primary duties of the controller's organization. Among the means at the disposal of the chief accounting executive for his part in labor control are the following:[5]

1. Institute procedures to limit the number of employees placed on the payroll to that called for by the production plan.

2. Provide preplanning information for use in determining standard labor crews by calculating required standard labor-hours for the production program.

3. Report hourly, daily, or weekly standard and actual labor performance.

4. Institute procedures for accurate distribution of actual labor costs, including significant labor classifications to provide informative labor cost analyses.

5. Provide data on past experience with respect to the establishment of standards.

6. Keep adequate records on labor standards and be on the alert for necessary revisions.

7. Furnish other supplementary labor data reports, such as these:

   a. Hours and cost of overtime premium, for control of overtime.

   b. Cost of call-in pay for time not worked to measure efficiency of those responsible for call-in by union seniority.

   c. Comparative contract costs, i.e., old and new union contracts.

   d. Average hours worked per week, average take-home pay, and similar data for labor negotiations.

   e. Detailed analysis of labor costs over or under standard.

   f. Statistical data on labor turnover, length of service, training costs.

   g. Union time—cost of time spent on union business.

(f) SETTING LABOR PERFORMANCE STANDARDS

The improvement of labor performance and the parallel reduction and control of costs require labor standards—operating time standards and the related cost standards. Setting labor performance standards is a highly analytical job that requires a technical background of the production processes as well as a knowledge of time study methods. This may be the responsibility of a standards department, industrial engineering department, or cost control department. Occasionally, although rarely, it is under the jurisdiction of the controller. Establishment of the standard operation time requires a determination of the time needed to complete each operation when working under standard conditions. Hence this study embodies working conditions, including the material control plan, the production planning and scheduling procedure, and layout of equipment and facilities. After all these factors are considered, a standard can be set by the engineers.

In using time standards for measuring labor performance the accounting staff must work closely with the industrial engineers or those responsible for setting the

---

[5] In a JIT environment, this reporting would not be necessary in items 3, 4, 5, and 7e.

standards. The related cost standards must be consistent; the accumulation of cost information must consider how the standards were set and how the variances are analyzed.

The following discussion on labor standards does not apply to a JIT manufacturing environment, especially one that uses cellular (i.e., group) manufacturing layouts. Labor utilization standards can be improved by increasing the amount of production for a set level of labor, and this is considered to be good in an assembly line environment. Under JIT, however, producing large quantities of parts is not considered acceptable; under JIT, good performance is producing the exact quantity of parts that are needed, and doing so with quality that is within preset tolerance levels. Once the correct quantity of parts are produced, the direct labor staff stops production; this creates unfavorable labor utilization variances. Therefore, measuring a JIT production facility with a labor utilization variance would work against the intent of JIT, since the production manager would have an incentive to produce more parts than needed, and would not be mindful of the part quality.

(g) REVISION OF LABOR PERFORMANCE STANDARDS

Generally, performance standards are not revised until a change of method or process occurs. Since standards serve as the basis of control, the accounting staff should be on the alert for changes put into effect in the factory but not reported for standard revision. If the revised process requires more time, the production staff will usually make quite certain that their measuring stick is modified. However, if the new process requires less time, it is understandable that the change might not be reported promptly. Each supervisor naturally desires to make the best possible showing. The prompt reporting of time reductions might be stimulated through periodic review of changes in standard labor hours or costs. In other words, the current labor performance of actual hours compared to standard should be but one measure of performance; another is standard time reductions, also measured against a goal for the year.

It should be the responsibility of the controller to see that the standards are changed as the process changes to report true performance. If a wage incentive system is related to these standards, the need for adjusting process changes is emphasized. An analysis of variances, whether favorable or unfavorable, will often serve to indicate revisions not yet reported.

Although standard revisions will often be made for control purposes, it may not be practical or desirable to change product cost standards. The differences may be treated as cost variances until they are of sufficient magnitude to warrant a cost revision.

(h) OPERATING UNDER PERFORMANCE STANDARDS

Effective labor control through the use of standards requires *frequent* reporting of actual and standard performance. Furthermore, the variance report must be by *responsibility*. For this reason the report on performance is prepared for each foreman as well as the plant superintendent. The report may or may not be expressed in terms of dollars. It may compare labor-hours or units of production instead of monetary units. But it does compare actual and standard performance.

Some operations lend themselves to daily reporting. Through the use of computer equipment or other means, daily production may be evaluated and promptly reported on. A simple form of daily report, available to the plant superintendent by 8:00 AM for the preceding day's operations, is shown as follows:

_____ PLANT
DAILY LABOR REPORT
FOR DAY ENDING AT 4:00 PM ON __(DATE)__

Department	Man-Hours Actual	Man-Hours Standard	% Standard to Actual
51 Fabricating	2,322	2,360	101.6
52 Subassembly	1,846	1,821	98.6
53 Painting	492	500	101.6
54 Assembly	3,960	4,110	103.8
55 Polishing	2,120	2,060	97.2
56 Packing	970	1,320	136.1
Total	11,170	12,171	103.9

With the use of computers, this data can be made available, essentially on a real-time basis.

If required, the detail of this summary report can be made available to indicate on what classification and shift the substandard operations were performed. Another report, issued weekly, that details the general reason for excess labor hours is illustrated in Figure 22-6.

In a JIT environment, the manufacturing departments are tightly interlocked with minimal WIP between each department to cover for reduced staff problems. In other words, if an area is understaffed, then downstream work stations will quickly run short of work. Consequently, the most critical direct labor measure in a JIT environment is a report of absent personnel, delivered promptly to the production managers at the start of the work day, so they can reshuffle the staff to cover all departments, and contact the missing personnel.

(i) USE OF LABOR RATE STANDARDS

Generally speaking, labor rates paid by a company are determined by external factors. The rate standard used is usually that normally paid for the job or classification as set by collective bargaining. If standards are set under this policy, no significant variances should develop because of base rates paid. There are, however, some rate variances that may be created and are controllable by management. Some of these reasons, which should be set out for corrective action, include these:

1. Overtime in excess of that provided in the standard.
2. Use of higher-rated classifications on the job.
3. Failure to place staff on incentive.
4. Use of crew mixture different from standard (more higher classifications and fewer of the lower).

The application of the standard labor rate to the job poses no great problem. Usually, this is performed by the accounting department after securing the rates from the

Figure 22-6   Weekly Labor Report.

Johnson Manufacturing Company
WEEKLY LABOR REPORT
WEEK ENDED DECEMBER 28, 19XX

MAN–HOURS

Department	Units Reported (a)	Actual Hours	Standard Hours	(Over) or Under Standard	Training	Lack of Material	Machine Breakdown	Low Production
						(Over) or Under Standard Due to		
25 Stamping (b).............	16,320	153	194	41	–	–	–	41
26 Foundry (b).............	4,390	56	103	47	–	–	–	47
27 Paint........	12,800	30	25	(5)	–	–	(5)	–
41 Subassembly A........	18,920	366	384	18	(5)	(2)	–	25
42 Final Assembly........	17,777	106	120	14	–	(6)	–	20
44 Receiving and Shipping........	44,310	323	271	(52)	(16)	–	–	(36)
Total............		1,034	1,097	63	(21)	(8)	(5)	97
Per Cent (Over) or Under Standard........				5.7	(1.9)	(.7)	(.5)	8.8

Notes:
(a)   Equivalent units per 6/12/XX letter.
(b)   Standards for Departments 25 and 26 are in process of review.

Issued by Cost Department— December 29, 19XX

Distribution: J.R.M.
J.A.M. (2)
L.L.B. (6)
R.E.H.
File

personnel department. Where overtime is contemplated in the standard, it is necessary, of course, to consult with production to determine the probable extent of overtime for the capacity at which the standard is set.

It should be mentioned that the basic design of the product will play a part in control of costs by establishing the skill necessary and therefore the job classification required to do the work.

(j) CONTROL THROUGH PREPLANNING

The use of the control tools previously discussed serves to point out labor inefficiencies *after* they have happened. Another type of control requires a determination about what should happen and makes plans to assure, to the extent possible, that it does happen. It is forward looking and preventive. This approach embodies budgetary control and can be applied to the control of labor costs. For example, if the staff requirements for the production program one month hence can be determined, then steps can be taken to make certain that excess labor costs do not arise because too many people are on the payroll. This factor can be controlled; thus the remaining factors are rate and quality of production and overtime. Overtime costs can be held within limits through the use of authorization slips.

The degree to which this preplanning can take place depends on the industry and particular conditions within the individual business firm. Are business conditions sufficiently stable so that some reasonably accurate planning can be done? Can the sales department indicate with reasonable accuracy what the requirements will be over the short run? An application might be in a machine shop where thousands of parts are made. If production requirements are known, the standard labor-hours necessary can be calculated and converted to staff hours. The standard labor-hours may be stored in a computer by skills required and by department. After evaluating the particular production job, an experienced efficiency factor may be determined. Thus if 12,320 standard labor-hours are needed for the planned production but an efficiency rate of only 80% is expected, then 15,400 actual labor-hours must be scheduled. This requires a crew of 385 people (40 hours per week). This can be further refined by skills or an analysis made of the economics of some overtime. Steps should be taken to assure that only the required number is authorized on the payroll for this production. As the requirements change, the standard labor-hours should be reevaluated.

In an MRP II environment, labor routings must be at least 95% accurate, and the firm must strictly adhere to a master production schedule. If the controller works in such an environment, then labor requirements can easily be predicted by multiplying the related labor routings by the unit types and quantities shown on the master schedule.

There are many computer-based labor control systems available for adoption to particular or specific needs. The controller should make sure that he or his accountants are familiar with the various systems so that labor costs are controlled and performance reported in a timely and accurate manner.

(k) LABOR ACCOUNTING AND STATUTORY REQUIREMENTS

One of the functions of a controller is to insure that the company maintains the various payroll and other records required by various federal and state government agencies, including the IRS. It is mandatory that the employees' earning records be properly and accurately maintained, including all deductions from gross pay. The required reports must be submitted, and withheld amounts transmitted to the appropriate agencies. It is not the purpose of this book to discuss in detail these reporting requirements, since many publications are available to the controller on this subject.

(l) WAGE INCENTIVE PLANS: RELATIONSHIP TO COST STANDARDS

In an effort to increase efficiency, a number of companies have introduced wage incentive plans—with good results. The controller is involved through the payroll department, which must calculate the amount. His responsibilities for the system are best left to authorities on the subject. One facet, however, is germane to the costing process and should be discussed. When an incentive wage plan is introduced into an operation already on a standard cost basis, a problem arises about the relationship between the standard level at which incentive earnings commence and the standard level used for costing purposes. Moreover, what effect should the wage incentive plan have on the standard labor cost and standard manufacturing expense of the product? To cite a specific situation, a company may be willing to pay an incentive to labor for performance that is lower than that assumed in the cost standard (but much higher than actual experience). If such a bonus is excluded from the cost standard, the labor cost at the cost standard level will be *understated*. Further, there may be no offsetting savings in manufacturing expenses since the costs are incurred to secure performance at a *lower* level than the cost standard. These statements assume that the existing cost standard represents efficient performance even under incentive conditions. On the other hand, if the effect of the incentive plan is to increase sustained production levels well above those contemplated in the cost standards, it may be that the product will be *overcosted* by using present cost standards and that these standards are no longer applicable. How should the cost standards be set in relation to the incentive plan?

In reviewing the problem, several generalizations may be made. First, there is no necessary relationship between standards for incentive purposes and standards for costing purposes. The former are intended to stimulate effort, whereas the latter are used to determine what the labor cost of the product should be. One is a problem in personnel management, whereas the other is strictly an accounting problem. With such dissimilar objectives, the levels of performance could logically be quite different.

Then, too, the matter of labor costing for statement purposes should be differentiated from labor control. As we have seen, labor control may involve nonfinancial terms—pieces per hour, pounds per labor-hour, etc. Labor control can be accomplished through the use of quantitative standards. Even if costs are used, the measuring stick for control need not be the same as for product costing. Control is centered on variations from performance standards and not on product cost variations.

A thorough consideration of the problem results in the conclusion that labor standards for costing purposes should be based on normal expectations from the operation of a wage incentive system under standard operating conditions. The expected earnings under the bonus plan should be reflected in the standard unit cost of the product. It does not necessarily follow that the *product* standard cost will be higher than that used before introduction of the incentive plan. It may mean, however, that the direct labor cost will be higher by reason of bonus payments. Yet, because of increased production and material savings, the *total* unit standard manufacturing cost should be lower.

22-4 SELECTED REFERENCES

Foster, George, and Charles T. Horngren, "JIT: Cost Accounting and Cost Management Issues," *Management Accounting,* June 1987, pp. 19–25.

Howell, Robert A., and Stephen B. Soucy, "The New Manufacturing Environment: Major Trends for Management Accountants," *Management Accounting,* July 1987, pp. 21–27.

Jayson, Susan, "Goldratt and Foy: Revolutionizing the Factory Floor," *Management Accounting,* May 1987, pp. 18–22.

Johnson, H. Thomas, and Robert S. Kaplan, "The Rise and Fall of Management Accounting," *Management Accounting,* Jan. 1987, pp. 22–30.

Kaplan, Robert S., "One Cost System Isn't Enough," *Harvard Business Review,* Jan.–Feb. 1988, pp. 61–66.

Keegan, Donald P., and Robert G. Eiler, "Let's Reengineer Cost Accounting," *Management Accounting,* Aug. 1994, pp. 26–31.

Lammert, Thomas B., and Robert Ehrsam, "The Human Element: The Real Challenge in Modernizing Cost Systems," *Management Accounting,* July 1987, pp. 32–37.

Mackey, James T., "11 Key Issues in Manufacturing Accounting," *Management Accounting,* Jan. 1987, pp. 32–37.

McNair, C. J., and William Mosconi, "Measuring Performance in an Advanced Manufacturing Environment," *Management Accounting,* July 1987, pp. 28–31.

Robinson, Michael A., and John E. Timmerman, "Vendor Analysis Supports JIT Manufacturing," *Management Accounting,* Dec. 1987, pp. 20–24.

Tatikonda, Lakshmi, "Production Managers Need a Course in Cost Accounting," *Management Accounting,* June 1987, pp. 26–29.

Tully, Shawn, "Raiding a Company's Hidden Cash," *Fortune,* Aug. 22, 1994, pp. 82–88.

CHAPTER 23

Planning and Control of Manufacturing Costs: Manufacturing Expenses

23-1 NATURE OF MANUFACTURING EXPENSES

The indirect manufacturing expenses or overhead costs of a manufacturing operation
have increased significantly as business has become more complex, and the utilization

of more sophisticated machinery and equipment is more prevalent. As the investment in computer-controlled machinery has increased, improving productivity and reducing direct labor hours, the control of depreciation expense, power costs, machinery repairs and maintenance, and similar items has received a greater emphasis by management.

Manufacturing overhead has several distinguishing characteristics as compared with the direct manufacturing costs of material and labor. It includes a wide variety of expenses, such as depreciation, property taxes, insurance, fringe benefit costs, indirect labor, supplies, power and other utilities, clerical costs, maintenance and repairs, and other costs that cannot be directly identified to a product, process, or job. These types of costs behave differently from direct costs, as the volume of production varies. Some will fluctuate proportionately as production increases or decreases, and some will remain constant or fixed and will not be sensitive to the change in the number of units produced. Some costs are semivariable and for a particular volume level are fixed; however, they may vary with volume but less proportionately and probably can be segregated into their fixed and variable components.

The control of overhead costs rests with many individuals involved in the manufacturing process. Certain costs such as repairs and maintenance are controlled by the head of the maintenance department. Manufacturing supplies may be controlled by each department head who uses the supplies in carrying out his function. Other costs may be decided by management and assigned to a particular manager for control—for example, depreciation, taxes, insurance. Accounting planning and control of manufacturing indirect expenses is diverse and a challenging opportunity for the controller.

23-2 RESPONSIBILITY FOR PLANNING AND CONTROL OF MANUFACTURING EXPENSES

Responsibility for the planning and control of manufacturing expenses is clearly that of the manufacturing or production executive. However, he or she will be working through a financial information system largely designed by the chief accounting official or his staff—although there should be full participation by the production staff on many aspects of the system development.

In formulating the expense account structure under which expenses will be planned and actual expenses matched against the budget or other standards, the controller should heed these common sense suggestions to make the reports more useful to the manufacturing executive:

- The budget (or other standard) should be based on technical data that are sound from a manufacturing viewpoint.

  Among other things, this will call for cooperation with the industrial engineers or process engineers who will supply the technical data required in developing the budget and/or standards. As manufacturing processes change, the standards must change. Adoption of just-in-time (JIT) techniques may require, for example, a different alignment of cost centers. Further, with the increased use of robots or other types of mechanization, direct labor will play a less important role, while manufacturing expense (through higher depreciation charges, perhaps more indirect labor, higher repairs and maintenance, and power) will become relatively more significant. (The impact of advanced manufacturing technologies is discussed later in this chapter.)

- The manufacturing department supervisors, who will do the actual planning and control of expenses, must be given the opportunity to fully understand the system, including the manner in which the budget expense structure is developed, and to generally concur in the fairness of the system.
- The account classifications must be practical, the cost departments should follow the manufacturing organization structure (responsibility accounting and reporting), and the allocation methods must permit the proper valuation of inventories (usually under general accepted accounting principles), as well as proper control of expense.
- The manufacturing costs must be allocated as accurately as possible, so the manufacturing executive can determine the expense of various products and processes. This topic is covered in more detail later in this chapter, under activity-based costing.

Also, industrial engineers will provide the technical data required for the development of standards, such as manpower needs, power requirements, expected downtime, and maintenance requirements. Finally, if an activity-based costing system is in place, then the manufacturing executive should work with the controller to develop information collection procedures for resource drivers.

23-3 ITEMS REQUIRING SPECIAL ATTENTION

For a budgetary system or accounting control system to operate properly in the manufacturing environment, attention should be paid to these subjects, which are discussed later:

- Proper departmentalization of expense.
- Proper segregation of expenses into fixed and variable components.
- Proper determination of "normal activity" level.
- Selection of the proper activity base.
- Use of the proper expense allocation basis for (a) inventory valuation and (b) control of service costs.

For an activity-based costing system to operate correctly, the controller must have properly identified activities and output measures, accurately collected output measures, and properly formulated cost pools. (See the discussion later in this chapter.)

23-4 APPROACH IN CONTROL OF MANUFACTURING EXPENSES

The diverse types of expenses in overhead and the divided responsibility may contribute to the incurrence of excessive costs. Furthermore, the fact that many cost elements seem to be quite small and insignificant in terms of consumption or cost per unit often encourages neglect of proper control. For example, it is natural to increase clerical help as required when volume increases to higher levels, but there is a reluctance and usually a delay from a timing viewpoint in eliminating such help when no longer needed. The reduced requirement must be forecasted and anticipated and appropriate actions taken in a timely manner. There are numerous expenses of small unit-cost items that may be insignificant but in the aggregate can make the company less competitive. Some examples are excessive labor hours for maintenance, use of special forms or supplies when standard items would be sufficient, personal use of supplies, and indiscriminate use of communication and reproduction facilities. All types of overhead expenses must be evaluated and controls established to achieve cost reduction wherever possible.

Although these factors may complicate somewhat the control of manufacturing overhead, the basic approach to this control is fundamentally the same as that applying to direct costs: the setting of budgets or standards, the measurement of actual performance against these standards, and the taking of corrective action when those responsible for meeting budgets or standards repeatedly fail to reach the goal. Standards may change at different volume levels; or stated in other terms, they must have sufficient flexibility to adjust to the level of operations under which the supervisor is working. To this extent the setting and application of overhead standards may differ from the procedure used in the control of direct material and direct labor. The degree of refinement and extent of application will vary with the cost involved. The controller should make every attempt to apply fair and meaningful standards, not thinking that little is needed or that nothing can be accomplished.

Also, the controller can use activity-based costing to assign costs to products, (or other entities, such as production departments or customers). This approach is better than the traditional method of assigning a uniform overhead rate to all production, since it assigns overhead costs to specific products based on their use of various activities, resulting in more accurate product costs.

23-5 PROPER DEPARTMENTALIZATION OF EXPENSES

One of the most essential requirements for either adequate cost control or accurate cost determination is the proper classification of accounts. Control must be exercised at the source, and since costs are controlled by individuals, the primary classification of accounts must be by individual responsibility—"responsibility accounting." This generally requires a breakdown of expenses by factory departments that may be either productive departments or service departments, such as maintenance, power, or tool crib. Sometimes, however, it becomes necessary to divide the expense classification more finely to secure a proper control or costing of products—to determine actual expenses and expense standards by cost center. This decision about the degree of refinement will depend largely on whether improved product costs result or whether better expense control can be achieved.

A cost center, which is ordinarily the most minute division of costs, is determined on one of the following bases:

1. One or more similar or identical machines.
2. The performance of a single operation or group of similar or related operations in the manufacturing process.

The separation of operations or functions is essential because a foreman may have more than one type of machine or operation in his department—all of which affect costs. One product may require the use of expensive machinery in a department, and another may need only some simple hand operations. The segregation by cost center will reveal this cost difference. Different overhead rates are needed to reflect differences in services or machines required.

If the controller chooses to install an activity-based costing (ABC) system, a very different kind of cost breakdown will be required. The ABC method collects costs by activities, rather than by department; for example, information might be collected about the costs associated with engineering change orders, rather than the cost of the entire engineering department. If management decides that it wants both ABC and departmental cost information, then the controller must record the information twice—once by department and again by activity.

23-6 FIXED AND VARIABLE EXPENSES

Another important step in the control of manufacturing overhead is the segregation of costs into two groups—fixed or variable. Truly variable costs increase or decrease in direct proportion to the volume of work within the plant. Control is exercised by keeping the expense within the limits determined for the particular level of activity. Fixed costs do not vary with activity but remain much the same over a relatively short period of time. Control over this type of expense rests largely with general executives who determine policy with respect to plant investment, inventory level, and size of organization. Failure to distinguish between these two types of expenses can result in failure to control overhead. Why? Because it cannot be determined whether increased costs result from higher unit fixed costs as a result of lower volume or from failure to keep variable costs within proper bounds.

The segregation of fixed and variable expense permits the adoption of the "flexible budget"—a budget that provides allowances which vary with the activity of the department involved. Contrasted with this flexible budget is the "fixed" budget that is planned for a particular level of activity. Rarely does activity remain at one level or, indeed, at the level anticipated. Therefore, unless provision is made for the change in activity, the budget can be of little value as a control tool when volume is at another level.

Sometimes a separate classification of manufacturing expenses is recognized—semivariable expenses. These expenses vary with the volume of production but not in direct proportion. To control these expenses two techniques are available. One method is to determine for each semivariable expense in each department just what the cost should be at various operating levels. For example, if the expected range is between 60% and 90% of capacity, costs should be budgeted at every 5% level—65%, 70%, 75%, etc. The budget applicable to the actual volume level would be selected and interpolated between the 5% range if thought desirable. Then actual costs would be compared periodically with the budget and corrective action taken.

Another method of applying budgetary control to semivariable expenses is to resolve them into their fixed and variable portions and treat each accordingly. The fixed portion could be considered the necessary expense at the lower level of the expected volume, and the difference between this and the higher level could be treated as variable.

23-7 DETERMINING FIXED AND VARIABLE
EXPENSE COMPONENTS

With the knowledge that adequate control of manufacturing overhead cannot be successful without the application of a flexible standard that recognizes differences in the volume of activity, the next subject is the method or approach. The aim, of course, is to establish total fixed costs by responsibility, plus the variable unit standard cost to be applied to the level of activity reached. If both are known, the total budgeted or standard cost can be determined. A good starting point is a review of past experience. This review should encompass not only total costs but also various measures of activity. It is necessary to determine how much costs vary, as well as the best tool or factor for measuring activity. To illustrate, past activity may be related to standard direct labor hours, actual direct labor hours, standard machine hours, units of production, etc.

Another consideration is the degree of refinement necessary. If costs are properly segregated by responsibility, perhaps the review need extend only to total departmental costs and not to individual items of expense. On this basis, a fixed budget of $15,300 per month and a variable expense allowance of $12.40 per standard labor hour might be established for the fabrication department. Under this approach, the exact way in which the supervisor spends his budgeted cost is a matter for his judgment. In other cases, it may be found desirable to analyze each type of departmental expense. This will often reveal more information about the expense behavior in the department and permit the development of a better budget. All these individual costs can be totaled to arrive at an overall measuring stick of the department, or they can be applied individually.

Review of past experience must be supplemented by good judgment in applying the data to future periods. Changes in wage rates, material costs, or supervisory staff, for example, must be considered in modifying the data for standard purposes.

A simple analysis of the tabulated data on manufacturing overhead and a knowledge of operating conditions will usually permit some immediate conclusions about whether expenses are fixed or variable. The fixed costs should be classified into those fixed by general management decisions and those currently fixed as a result of decisions by the production executives. Illustrative of the twofold segregation of fixed manufacturing expenses are the following:

1. Fixed by general management decisions.
   a. Depreciation on buildings and machinery (if unit of production method is not used).
   b. Real and personal property taxes on buildings, equipment, and inventories.
   c. Insurance—property and liability.
   d. Salaries of production executives.
   e. Fringe benefit costs.
   f. Patent amortization.
2. Fixed by production executive decisions.
   a. Salaries of factory supervisory staff.
   b. Factory administrative expense.
   c. Safety expenses.

Costs may be considered fixed if the review and analysis of the expense is determined to be the same amount for each month or reporting period. Other expenses are either variable or semivariable. If the incurrence of a type of expense has a direct relationship to a factor of variability, such as the number of units produced, it is classified as variable. Typical examples of variable manufacturing indirect expenses are these:

> Royalties (on units produced).
>
> Small tool expense.
>
> Supplies.
>
> Testing expense.
>
> Salvage expense.

A large number of expenses will be found to contain both fixed and variable components—the semivariable costs. Some examples are as follows:

> Repairs and maintenance.
>
> Factory office salaries and expense.
>
> Payroll taxes and insurance.
>
> Some utilities.

(a) DETERMINATION USING TWO POINTS— THE HIGH-LOW METHOD

The illustrative separation of the fixed and variable elements of a manufacturing expense by a simple method is shown next. Assumptions for the example are as follows:

1. At a level of 50% of normal capacity, the maintenance department expense is $80,000 per month, whereas experience shows that at a level of 80% of capacity, the cost is $128,000.
2. The variable factor or measuring stick is standard labor hours of production.
3. At an 80% capacity, the standard labor hours are 160,000.

The variable costs may be considered to be $48,000, and the variable budget allowance $0.80 per standard labor hour, calculated as follows:

	Capacity	
% Normal Activity	Standard Labor Hours	Cost
80%	160,000	$128,000
50%	100,000	80,000
Variable	60,000	$ 48,000
Unit variable cost ($48,000 ÷ 60,000)		$ 0.80

On such a budget structure (assuming a portion is to be treated as fixed) the maintenance department allowance for a month of 120,000 standard labor hours of production will be the following:

Fixed portion	$80,000
Variable ($0.80 × 120,000 – 100,000)	16,000
Total	$96,000

It will be observed that the variable allowance is granted only for standard labor hours in excess of what was considered the lowest probable level of activity. However, the entire cost might be treated as variable with the same budget (120,000 × $0.80 = $96,000).

(b) GRAPHIC DETERMINATION OF FIXED AND VARIABLE COSTS

The use of only two or a few points to determine the variable expense is of limited value, since only a few levels are considered. If more accuracy is desired, another convenient approach is the use of a scatter chart. Assume, for illustrative purposes, that the following data on personnel department costs are available, adjusted for wage differences and similar factors.

Month	Reference	Factory Standard Labor Hours	Total Departmental Costs
January	(1)	20,000	12,200
February	(2)	16,000	10,600
March	(3)	13,000	9,400
April	(4)	14,000	9,800
May	(5)	17,000	10,400
June	(6)	19,000	12,000
July	(7)	21,000	12,400
August	(8)	23,000	12,600
September	(9)	25,000	13,600
October	(10)	22,000	12,200
November	(11)	18,000	11,800
December	(12)	19,000	11,600

These points are then plotted on a chart as shown in Figure 23-1, each point being numbered for reference purposes. The vertical axis represents the dollar costs, and the horizontal axis represents the factor of variability—standard labor hours in the illustration. After the points are plotted, a line of best fit may be drawn by inspection—drawn in such a manner that about one-half of the points are above it and the other half below. Any highly variant items should be disregarded. For a higher degree of refinement the method of least squares may be used instead of inspection.

The point at which the line of best fit intersects the vertical axis indicates the fixed cost that might be expected if the plant were in an operating condition but producing nothing. The total cost at any level of activity is determined by reading the chart. For example, at a level of 25,000 standard labor hours, the budgeted expense would be $13,400. This is made up of $5,500 fixed and $7,900 variable elements. The variable rate is $0.316 per standard labor hour.

Figure 23-1 Graphic Determination of Fixed and Variable Costs.

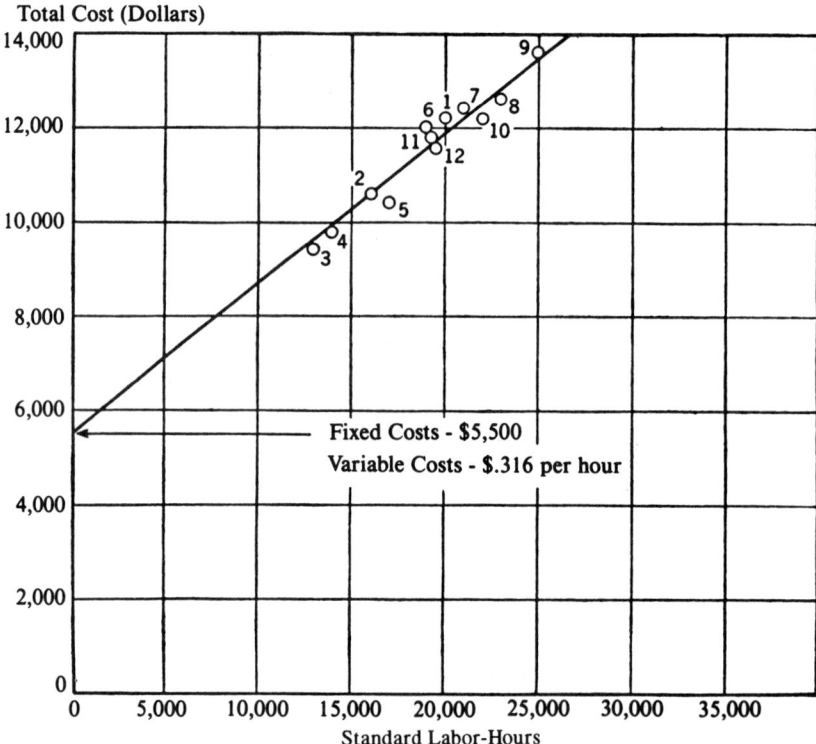

In reviewing the chart it can be seen that the slope of the line indicates the degree of variability. Thus a horizontal line would represent a fixed cost, whereas a line that goes through the point of origin indicates a completely variable cost. Sometimes in constructing a chart the points show no tendency to arrange themselves along a line. If this situation does exist, then either the control of costs has been absent or a poor choice has been made about the factor of variability. Use of another factor should be tested to ascertain the cause. Incidentally, the chart may be used as a tool in illustrating the degree of success in controlling costs, the extent of accomplishment being measured by the closeness of actual expense to the line of budgeted expenses.

23-8 NORMAL ACTIVITY

A significant consideration in the control of manufacturing overhead expense through the analysis of variances is the level of activity selected in setting the standard costs. While it has no direct bearing on the planning and control of the manufacturing expenses of each individual department, it does have an impact on the statement of income and expenses (both planned and actual) as well as on the statement of financial position. As to the income statement, it is desirable to identify the amount of manufacturing expense "absorbed" by or allocated to the manufactured product, with the excess expense identified as variance from the standard cost. This variance or excess cost ordinarily should be classified as to cause. As to the statement of financial position, the normal activity level has a direct impact on inventory valuation and, consequently, on the cost-of-goods-sold element of the income statement, in that it helps determine the standard product cost. It should be obvious that the fixed element of unit product costs is greatly influenced by the total quantity of production assumed. Of equal importance is the necessity of a clear understanding by management of the significance of the level selected, because in large part it determines the "volume" variance.

Generally speaking, there are three levels on which fixed standard manufacturing overhead may be set:

1. The expected sales volume for the year, or other period, when the standards are to be applied.
2. Practical plant capacity, representing the volume at which a plant could produce if there were no lack of orders.
3. The normal or average sales volume, here defined as normal capacity.

Some general comments may be made about each of these three levels. If expected sales volume is used, all costs are adjusted from year to year. Consequently, certain cost comparisons are difficult to make. Furthermore, the resulting statements fail to give management what may be considered the most useful information about volume costs. Standard costs would be higher in low-volume years, when lower prices might be needed to get more business, and lower in high-volume years, when the increased demand presumably would tend toward higher prices. Another weakness is that the estimate of sales used as a basis would not be too accurate in many cases.

Practical plant capacity as a basis tends to give the lowest cost. This can be misleading because sales volume will not average this level. Generally, there will always be large unfavorable variances, the unabsorbed expense.

Normal sales volume or *activity* has been defined as the utilization of the plant that is necessary to meet the average sales demand over the period of a business cycle or at least long enough to level out cyclical and seasonal influences. This base permits a certain stabilization of costs and the recognition of long-term trends in sales. Each basis has its advantages and disadvantages, but normal capacity would seem to be the most desirable under ordinary circumstances.

Where one product is manufactured, normal capacity can be stated in the quantity of this unit. In those cases where many products are made, it is usually necessary to select a common unit for the denominator. Productive hours are a practical measure. If the normal productive hours for all departments or cost centers are known, the sum of these will represent the total for the plant. The total fixed costs divided by the productive hours at normal capacity results in the standard fixed cost per productive hour.

Volume variances can also cause costing problems in an activity-based costing (ABC) environment. Activity costs are derived by dividing estimated volumes of activity drivers into activity cost pools to derive costs for individual activities. If the estimated volume of an activity driver deviates excessively from the actual amount, then the activity cost applied to a product may significantly alter the product's ABC cost. For example, there are estimated to be 1,000 material moves associated with a product in a month, and the total cost of those moves in a month is $10,000, which is $10 per move. If the actual number of moves associated with the product is 2,000, then the cost per move that is applied to product costs is off by $5 per move. However, if the ABC system collects activity driver volume information for every accounting period, then the volume variance will not occur.

23-9 COST ASSIGNMENT: ACTIVITY-BASED COSTING

The following section discusses traditional cost accounting systems, the need for activity-based costing (ABC), problems with the ABC model, and reporting ABC information to management. We also briefly outline an ABC installation, ABC software models, analyzing nonvalue-added processes, and converting indirect costs to direct costs. The ABC topic is much larger than this abbreviated discussion allows, so we recommend that a reader who wishes to implement such a system consult one of the many books available on the subject.

(a) INTRODUCTION

Traditional cost accounting systems apply overhead to products based on the amount of direct labor they use. When direct labor was a significant proportion of the value being added to a product, this did not skew product costs significantly. However, as direct labor was gradually replaced by automation, the direct labor component dropped while overhead costs increased. As a result, many businesses find that their overhead rates are at 300% or more of their direct labor. Consequently, a slight change in a product's direct labor charge yields a significant product cost variation as the applied overhead amount swings dramatically up or down.

To combat this overhead application problem, several companies began to apply overhead based on other, more relevant factors than direct labor. This resulted in multiple overhead rates being used at one time, and required additional data collection for the different overhead application bases. Eventually, activity-based costing (ABC) was invented. ABC is not a direct offshoot of the multiple overhead rate system. Instead, it assumes that costs are assigned based on resources consumed, so that resource costs are identified and then assigned to products based on their use of those resources. The ABC information is then accumulated into reports by product, customer, geographic region, or other reporting entities.

An ABC system requires a large amount of data collection. Cost data must be accumulated in ways that are usually not the same as the traditional departmental chart of accounts system. The controller must therefore re-combine costs into "cost pools." In addition, the ABC system must derive a cost for various activities, and then the use of those activities by the reporting entity (products, customers, geographic regions, etc.) must be measured. This data collection is handled on a project basis, so that ABC costs are only derived once, or it is built into a new costing system that either supersedes or exists beside the traditional costing system. Also, the ABC system must be carefully designed so that the data collection is not too burdensome. The ABC team should keep the number of cost pools and activity measures to a minimum. Once an ABC system is operational, the ABC team can analyze the model's accuracy and selectively add or delete items requiring data collection.

The information derived from an ABC model can be used to provide product cost information, inventory valuations, and control nonvalue-added costs. One of its greatest benefits is to assist management in determining the true costs of products that are otherwise buried in overhead and misapplied elsewhere. As a result, management has better gross margin information and can more intelligently add or delete products or options with that information. If the ABC information is not presented to management, then its benefits will not be significant.

The information provided by the traditional costing system may conflict with the information provided by the ABC system. If, for example, management bonuses are calculated based on the results of the traditional system, then the ABC results may be ignored. Also, if a company has several divisions and ABC is not implemented in all of them, then the corporate controller will have incomplete comparative costing information. As a result, management action based on cost comparisons would not be possible.

(b) DEVELOPING AN ABC MODEL

For the purposes of this discussion, we will assume that costs are only being accumulated to report on product costs. To develop an ABC model, the following steps must be completed:

1. *Identify Activities.* This step has the following components:

   • *Define the Boundaries of the Project.* An ABC analysis can involve all aspects of the company, but completing such a project may take too long to retain management's interest. Instead, the ABC project leader should consider a small, important target area for the initial ABC analysis, and then expand the process at a later date. For example, the initial project could include the engineering and materials departments, but exclude marketing.

   • *Document Process Flows.* List all activities within each target area. This information is usually recorded on a flowchart. Activities may cross over department boundaries. For example, the materials ordering process begins with the bill of materials in the engineering department before it moves to the materials department where the actual ordering occurs. The flowcharts should be reviewed with key personnel from the areas being studied, so that flaws in the model can be corrected.

2. *Identify All Direct Costs.* Traditional costing methods already track direct costs in some detail, so this is an easy step if there are existing costing systems in place. If not, then identify the direct labor and materials costs that are associated with individual products. Accurate labor routings and bills of material are needed for proper direct cost identification. If there is an existing Material Requirements Planning (MRP) system in place, then routings and bills of material should already be available.

3. *Assign Indirect Costs to Cost Pools.* Use the flowcharts developed during the first step to identify logical clusters of costs. This can be very time-consuming, because the costs in the general ledger are organized to support a traditional costing system, not an activity-based system that requires a different chart of accounts. As a result, many general ledger accounts will have to be subdivided into smaller pieces that are then summarized into cost pools. Here is a sample list of cost pools that a manufacturing company might use:

   • Accounts payable.

   • Depreciation.

   • Maintenance labor.

- Material movement.
- Plant management.
- Production control.
- Purchasing.
- Quality control.
- Receiving.
- Rework.
- Scrap.
- Utilities.

4. *Identify Output Measures.* Use the flowcharts developed during the first step to identify activities that consume costs. These activities measure the frequency and volume of demand placed on an activity by the product or service being produced. For example, every time a product is moved, costs are incurred for the labor of the forklift driver and depreciation expense for the forklift. Other examples of output measures are:

- Number of parts.
- Number of suppliers.
- Number of units reworked.
- Number of material moves.
- Number of purchase orders.
- Number of customer orders.
- Number of engineering change requests.

5. *Collect Output Measures.* Most companies use ABC on a project basis, so that output measures are only collected once. Those companies assume that output measures do not vary significantly in the short term, and thus rely on ABC information for which the foundation data was only collected once. The alternative, and more accurate approach, is to collect the output measure information for each reporting period. Doing so requires information collection systems for items that were not previously tracked. Some output measures are difficult to track, so management must commit in advance to the extra time and cost of doing so.

6. *Calculate Activity Costs.* Divide the output measures into the cost pools to derive activity costs. For example, an output measure may be that 210 invoices were paid by accounts payable in a period. The cost of the accounts payable labor for that period was $1,672, so the cost per accounts payable activity (paying the invoice) was $7.96.

7. *Calculate Product Costs.* There are several layers of costs to add to a product under the ABC model:

- *Add Direct Costs.* These are the direct labor and material costs that are directly attributable to a product, and are usually derived from labor routings and bills of material.
- *Add Activity Costs.* Add the costs of all costed activities to the product cost. For example, if 32 invoices were paid in order to produce a product, then the

cost of the payables activity for that product (using the $7.96 amount from the previous example) would be $7.96 multiplied 32 times, or $254.72.

- *Add Other Cost Pools.* Other costs can be added from cost pools for areas such as marketing and general and administrative expenses. For example, if costs by geographic region are desired, then advertising costs can be subdivided by region and added to the total cost of products sold into each region.

8. *Use the Information.* Review product costs based on the traditional costing system versus the new costing system. An ABC review will highlight costs that would otherwise have been lost in the total overhead cost. Typical management actions to reduce the overhead cost are:

- *Reduce the Number of Product Options.* The cost of designing, scheduling, and building product options is located in overhead and can be reduced by cutting the number of product options.

- *Reduce the Number of Parts Used.* The cost of designing, sourcing, and purchasing parts is located in overhead and can be reduced by cutting the number of product options.

- *Reduce the Number of Material Moves.* The cost of moving parts is located in the materials department part of the overhead cost and can be reduced by cutting the number of material moves (which also cuts the cycle time!).

- *Reduce the Number of Engineering Change Requests.* The cost of redesigning parts, sourcing new suppliers, and expediting purchases is located in the overhead cost and can be reduced by cutting the number of engineering change requests.

- *Reduce the Number of Suppliers.* The cost of sourcing and qualifying new suppliers is located in the materials department portion of the overhead cost and can be reduced by cutting the number of suppliers.

The list of possible management actions is identical to the activities used in the ABC model. The ABC model is designed in this manner to focus attention on activities in the production cycle. If management reduces the number of activities, then not only is the "traditional" overhead cost reduced, but also the production cycle time slashed.

(c) ADDITIONAL COMMENTS

Convert Indirect Costs to Direct Costs. If indirect costs can be converted to direct costs, then product costs will be more accurate. One area for such improvement is converting to a cellular manufacturing arrangement from an assembly line arrangement. Product costing for an assembly line can be inaccurate because many product types may pass through specific workstations or departments. As a result, costs are accumulated by workstation or department and then assigned to products based on labor hours or machine hours. In a cellular manufacturing environment, a small number of products are built by a small number of workers using a cluster of workstations that are reserved for producing that set of products. Consequently, costs are more easily assigned to products, and the costs of those grouped workstations can be considered direct instead of indirect.

Purchase an ABC Software Package. Many companies build ABC systems that are separate from their traditional accounting systems. Many ABC software packages are now available, for example:

- ABC Technologies, Inc. (Easy ABC)
  5075 S.W. Griffith Drive
  Beaverton, OR 97005
  Phone: (503) 626-4895

- Armstrong Laing, Inc. (Hyper ABC)
  7 Piedmont Center, Suite 500
  3525 Piedmont Road
  Atlanta, GA 30305
  Phone: (404) 364-1836

- Sapling, Inc. (Net Prophet II)
  1 Bridge Lane #400
  Fort Lee, NJ 07024
  Phone: (800) 335-5050

Another approach to building ABC systems is to use the alphanumeric fields sometimes provided with general ledger packages to store output measures for each reporting period.

Review Nonvalue-Added Processes. The controller can add a function to the process review phase of ABC, and review the process flowcharts for value added versus nonvalue-added activities. A value-added activity converts resources into products or services. A nonvalue-added activity can be eliminated with no reduction in a product or service's functionality or quality. This added step allows the controller to target nonvalue-added processes for elimination. The nonvalue-added processes can be ranked in importance by the time or cost required for each one. Armed with that information, management can then prioritize them for elimination or reduction. Examples of nonvalue-added activities are:

- Inspection.
- Rework.
- Moving.
- Storage.
- Queue time.

A value-added analysis also notes the company's value-added activities. The controller can highlight this information and encourage an engineering team to reduce or eliminate any bottlenecks in those operations. This action increases the company's production capacity.

Implement a Bill of Activities. To create an on-line ABC system, the company should create a bill of activities (BOA) that is similar to the bill of materials (BOM) already used for its products. The BOA lists the types and quantities of activities used during the production of a product. Management can focus on the BOA to discern the primary sources of activity-based costs, and act to reduce those costs. Also, the BOA is needed to roll up activity costs for each period's cost reports, just as the BOM is used to roll up direct costs for each product.

23-10 IMA GUIDE ON ALLOCATION OF INDIRECT PRODUCTION COSTS, SMA NO. 4G

Having given some general observations on allocation of manufacturing expenses, it may be helpful to review the authoritative comments of the Institute of Management Accountants as covered in Statement of Management Accounting 4G, Accounting for Indirect Production Costs. This statement is quoted in its entirety.[1]

Introduction

1. For many purposes management accountants find it necessary, or desirable, to allocate indirect production costs to goods, projects, services, contracts, or other cost objects. These purposes include inventory valuation and related profit measurement, contract pricing and other pricing, measurement of product or segment profitability, control of costs, and other long- and short-term management decisions. A number of different techniques may be used to allocate indirect production costs to cost objects. Some techniques are preferable to others. The purpose of this Statement is to provide guidance to management accountants in the allocation of indirect production costs to cost objects.

2. The objective of allocating indirect production costs to cost objects is to assign an appropriate share of the total costs incurred during a specified period of time to each cost object. If feasible, costs should be allocated in proportion to the amount of cost that each cost object caused. If a causal connection is not feasible, some other criterion, such as benefits received, should be used.

Statement Scope

3. Production costs incurred for a cost object are either direct costs or indirect costs of that cost object. A cost item is a direct cost if it can be identified specifically with a single cost object in an economically feasible manner. Direct production costs include direct materials, direct labor, and other directly assignable costs. A cost item is an indirect cost if it is common to two or more cost objects and cannot be identified specifically with a single cost object in an economically feasible manner. Indirect production costs may include costs such as indirect labor, repairs and maintenance, indirect materials and supplies, depreciation, insurance, and property taxes. Indirect production costs also may be referred to as production overhead.

    Indirect production costs may be divided further into categories for particular cost or profitability constructions. Examples of these categories are short-run controllable vs. long-run controllable costs and variable (with volume of production) vs. fixed costs. This Statement is concerned with the allocation of all categories of indirect production costs.

---

[1] *Management Accounting,* June 1987, pp. 43–49. Reprinted with permission.

4. This Statement describes the allocation of indirect production costs to products. Products may be either tangible goods or intangible services, such as those provided by hospitals, schools, professional firms, and hotels.

5. a. There are two types of cost allocations: (a) the allocation of costs to time periods (e.g., the allocation of the cost of depreciable assets to the time periods that represent their useful lives, via the depreciation mechanism) and (b) the allocation of all the costs of a time period to cost objects for which costs were incurred during that time period. This Statement deals only with the latter type of allocation.

   b. There are three general types of production cost construction: responsibility costs, full costs, and differential costs. Each is intended to serve a specific set of purposes, but responsibility costs, full costs, and some information useful in estimating differential costs typically are outputs of a single cost accounting system. These three types of cost construction are discussed separately because the cost allocation problem for each is somewhat different.

   c. Indirect production costs may be viewed in either a historical perspective or an estimated future perspective. This Statement is concerned with both historical costs and estimated future costs.

6. This Statement applies only to allocations of indirect production costs that are material in amount, that is, to practices that might make a significant difference in the amount of cost measured.

7. This Statement is concerned with the allocation of service and administrative costs that are associated with the production function. Other service and administrative costs are covered in Statement on Management Accounting 4B.

Definitions

8. a. *Production Costs*—Costs incurred in the production process to bring goods to the point at which they are ready for sale or costs incurred to produce services.

   b. *Direct Cost*—A cost item that can be identified specifically with a single cost object in an economically feasible manner.

   c. *Indirect Cost*—A cost item that is common to two or more cost objects and cannot be identified specifically with any one of these cost objects in an economically feasible manner; also called overhead cost.

   d. *Full Cost*—The sum of the direct costs and applicable indirect costs assigned to a cost object.

   e. *Cost Assignment*—The distribution of cost items to cost objects. A direct cost is assigned directly to a cost object. An indirect cost is allocated to cost objects.

   f. *Cost Allocation*—The distribution of indirect production costs to individual cost objects.

   g. *Cost Object*—A function, organizational subdivision, or product whose costs are measured.

h. *Final Cost Object*—In a cost accounting system, the product whose cost is measured.

i. *Intermediate Cost Object*—In a cost accounting system, a focal point for the grouping of costs prior to their assignment to final cost objects; a cost center. Intermediate cost objects may be cost responsibility centers, service cost centers, production cost centers, or production cost pools.

j. *Cost Responsibility Center*—An identifiable organization subdivision headed by a manager who is held accountable for the accomplishment of specific functions and for control of the costs of those functions.

k. *Service Cost Center*—A cost responsibility center whose functions are to provide support or service to other cost centers. Examples could be maintenance, general factory, and occupancy.

l. *Production Cost Center*—A cost responsibility center whose functions contribute directly to the production of a product.

m. *Production Cost Pool*—A grouping of indirect production costs that have a similar causal relationship to the cost objects to which they will be assigned. A production cost pool also may be a cost responsibility center. Alternatively, the cost items in several cost responsibility centers may be grouped in a single production cost pool, or the cost items in a single responsibility center may be disaggregated into several ·production cost pools. (See Figure 23-2.)

Figure 23-2 Flow of Indirect Production Costs from Incurrence to Final Cost Object.

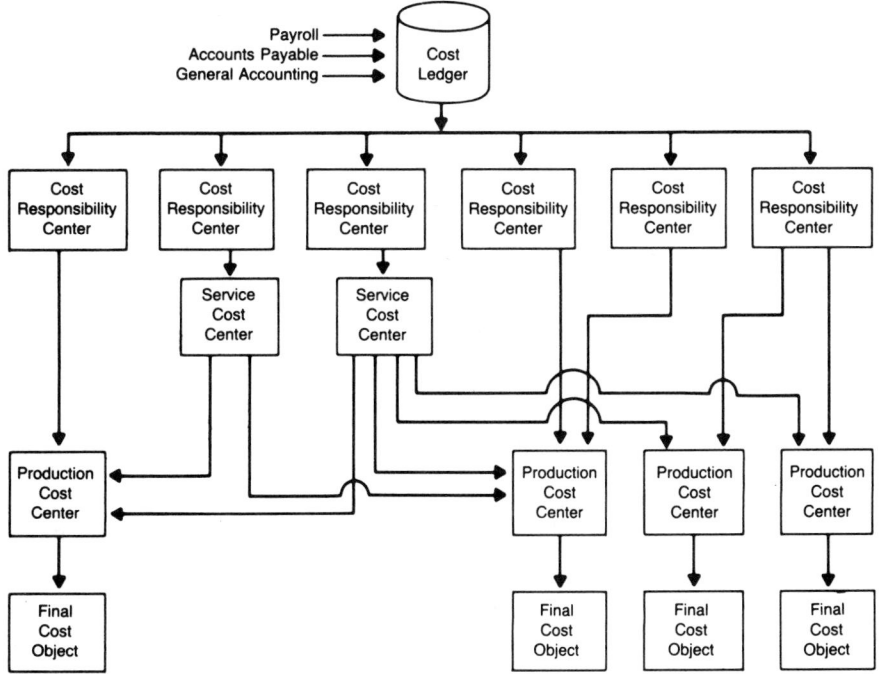

n. *Overhead Rate*—The ratio of indirect costs for a period of time to the volume of some measurable associated causal or beneficial factor in the same period of time.

o. *Variable Cost*—A cost that is expected to increase as the volume of production, sales, or some other cost-causing factor in a period increases and that is expected to decrease as the volume in a period decreases.

p. *Fixed Cost*—A cost that is expected to be at a constant amount in a given time period regardless of changes in volume in that time period.

q. *Discretionary Cost*—A cost whose amount within a time period is governed by a management decision to incur the cost. The amount is not related to the volume of production or sales or to the capacity of the organization. Most discretionary costs are fixed, but some may be variable.

r. *Contribution Margin*—The difference between revenues and total variable costs.

s. *Segment Contribution*—The difference between revenues and the total of the variable costs and the direct fixed costs assigned to a segment of the organization.

t. *Operating Income*—The difference between revenues and the total of the variable costs, the direct fixed costs, and the indirect fixed costs assigned to a segment of the organization.

u. *Cost Accounting System*—The system within an organization that provides for the collection and assignment of costs to intermediate and final cost objects.

v. *Standard Cost System*—A product costing system in which the costs assigned to individual products are the costs that should have been incurred rather than the costs that actually were incurred.

w. *Equivalent Units of Product*—A common denominator of the cost causation impact of different products produced in a product cost center.

Cost Accounting System

9. A cost accounting system collects direct and indirect costs and assigns these costs to cost objects. The cost accounting system for an organization should be designed to provide cost information that is useful to managers and cost information that is required for financial accounting purposes (inventory cost, contract cost). Such a system should identify costs initially by responsibility center (responsibility costs) and ultimately with final cost objects (full costs). See Figure 23-2. Production costs should be separated into *variable* and *fixed* components prior to assignment to final cost objects and thus provide an indication of those *differential costs* that vary with the volume of production. The data flowing through the cost accounting system should be internally consistent; that is, for each period, the total production costs incurred should be equal to the total of costs assigned to final cost objects.

Responsibility Costs

10. Responsibility costs are cost items classified in a way that aids in the *control* of costs. Usually implementation of this concept requires that each item be identified with the manager who is responsible for the control of that item.

11. Indirect production costs are difficult to control because they include a variety of different cost items with different behavioral characteristics. Some costs, such as occupancy costs and certain salaries, are expected to be the same amount per period regardless of changes in volume of production. Other items usually vary with changes in volume. Some cost items are discretionary; that is, they vary only in response to decisions of managers about the level of spending. Examples of discretionary costs are those related to research and development and management development and training.

12. *Flexible budgets* usually are the most effective tool for measuring management performance in controlling indirect production costs. A flexible budget is a plan that specifies the amount of cost for each item that should be incurred for any volume of production that might reasonably be expected to occur during a specified period of time. Differences between planned costs and actual costs are spending variances and, at least in part, are the responsibility of the manager of the responsibility center that incurs the costs. The identification of costs by responsibility should be the first step in accounting for costs because once the process of assignment of costs to intermediate and final cost objects is begun, the opportunity to measure effectiveness in controlling costs is lost.

13. The cost accounting system should identify *service cost centers* and *production cost centers* separately. A dual responsibility exists for the costs of a service cost center. The service cost center manager is responsible for the costs incurred by the service cost center in providing units of service. Managers of the cost centers served are, at least in part, responsible for the amount of the service consumed by their cost centers. Usually this dual responsibility for costs should be recognized by charging the production cost center and crediting the service cost center for actual services consumed at a predetermined rate per unit of service and by incorporating provisions for these charges and credits into the flexible budgets of the respective cost centers.

14. Responsibility cost items are identifiable directly with a responsibility center. Even though a cost item may not be controllable in the short run, such as depreciation expense on plant and equipment used by a department, the cost item nevertheless may be a responsibility cost.

Full Production Cost

15. The *full production cost* of a cost object is the sum of its direct production costs plus an appropriate share of applicable indirect production costs.

   Full production cost is the cost at which completed products should be carried in inventory or in unbilled services. It also is the cost that should be recorded as cost of sales when products are sold. In addition to these uses, the measurement of full production cost is a necessary step in the accumulation of

Figure 23-3 Profitability Model Full Costs.

	Total Company	Business Segments (Cost Objects)		
		A	B	C
REVENUES	$706	$423	$134	$149
COST OF SALES	2			
Direct production costs:				
Direct materials	$185	$107	$ 17	$ 61
Direct labor	85	57	7	21
Indirect production costs	153	58	39	56
TOTAL COST OF SALES	$423	$222	$ 63	$138
GROSS PROFIT	$283	$201	$ 71	$ 11
SELLING AND ADMINISTRATION COSTS	143	85	29	29
OPERATING INCOME BEFORE INCOME TAXES	$140	$116	$42	$(18)

full costs of the organization, including direct and indirect selling, general and administrative expenses. (See Statement on Management Accounting 4B for the usefulness of full cost constructions.) Figure 23-3 is an illustration of a profitability model that incorporates full production costs.

16. The allocation of indirect production costs to final cost objects is accomplished in a series of steps:

   a. Each indirect production cost item is assigned to a production cost center or a service cost center.

   b. The total costs of each service cost center are reassigned to production cost centers.

   c. The total indirect costs accumulated in each production cost center are allocated to products produced in the respective production cost centers.

17. Service cost centers incur costs to provide service to other cost centers or to the entire organization. The costs in service cost centers should be assigned to other cost centers in two ways:

   a. Those costs that can be identified directly with the services rendered to another cost center should be assigned directly to that cost center at predetermined rates per unit of service, as described in paragraph 13.

   b. The other costs in a service cost center should be allocated to other cost centers based on the causal relationship between the service costs and the cost center receiving the allocation.

18. Some service cost centers may receive services from other service centers. In such situations, the cost accounting system should provide for a step-down sequence of allocation of service center costs in which either the service center that provides the most service to other service centers or receives the

least service from other service centers is allocated first, then the other service centers are allocated in order according to the criteria selected. Once the costs of a service center have been allocated, no additional costs are assigned to that service center. Alternatively, service center costs may be allocated to other service centers by a system of reciprocal distribution utilizing the techniques of matrix algebra.

19. Many cost items that are indirect costs with respect to a final cost object may be direct costs with respect to an intermediate cost object and therefore are assigned directly to that cost object. Those cost items that cannot be assigned directly to a cost center and those service center costs that cannot be assigned directly to other cost centers should be allocated to cost centers based upon the causal relationship between the costs and the cost center receiving the allocation. The base for the allocation of indirect costs to cost centers should be the one that best expresses the causal relationship between the costs and the cost centers. Most of the possible allocation bases are included in the following principal categories:

   a. *People-oriented costs.* Costs that are caused primarily by the number of employees should be allocated based on the number of employees or the number of labor hours in the respective cost centers.

   b. *Payroll-oriented costs.* Costs that are related primarily to the amount that employees are paid should be allocated based on some measure of the labor costs in the respective cost centers.

   c. *Equipment-oriented costs.* Costs that are related primarily to the usage of equipment should be allocated based on a measure of equipment utilization, such as machine hours.

   d. *Materials-oriented costs.* Costs that are caused primarily by acquisition, storage, or movement of materials should be allocated based on either a physical measure or cost of direct materials used in the respective cost centers. See SMA 4E.

   e. *Space-oriented costs.* Costs that are caused primarily by the need to provide and maintain work or storage space should be allocated based on a physical measure of the space required by the respective cost centers.

   f. *Transaction-oriented costs.* Costs that are caused primarily by production transactions, such as production orders issued, engineering change orders, and scheduling and expediting activities, should be allocated according to the number of transactions generated by the respective cost centers.

   g. *Total activity-oriented costs.* Those costs that are presumed to be caused by the overall activity of an organization should be allocated according to some measure of overall activity, such as total direct costs or total full costs in the respective cost centers.

20. The basic technique for the allocation of indirect production costs of a production cost center to final cost objects involves the use of *overhead rates.* An overhead rate applies a constant amount of cost to each equivalent unit of production.

To develop an overhead rate for a production cost center, the total indirect cost for a period is divided by the total units of production passing through that cost center in that period. The result is an overhead rate stated in cost per unit of production. The cost accounting system allocates this cost to each unit passing through the production cost center. Each product is assigned the appropriate cost for each production cost center it passes through.

The selection of the unit of volume used to develop the overhead rate for a production cost center and, subsequently, to allocate costs to products is a matter of judgment. The unit selected should:

a. Be common to and measurable for all products worked on in the production cost center.

b. Have a high correlation—i.e., a high causal relationship—between the volume measure and the amount of costs in the cost center.

  The volume measures used most frequently and appropriately include direct labor hours, direct labor dollars, machine hours, production orders, engineering change orders, or some product-related physical measure such as tons, gallons, or equivalent units produced.

21. The procedures described above imply that the overhead rate is determined after the period has ended. In fact, in most situations it is desirable to estimate annually the incurrence and allocation of indirect costs and predetermine the overhead rate to be used in each production cost center for the coming year. The reasons for using predetermined overhead rates are:

a. Seasonal cost factors and monthly changes in volume of production may produce fluctuations in overhead rates that are calculated monthly. These fluctuations serve no useful purpose and often are misleading. They can be avoided by using predetermined overhead rates.

b. The use of predetermined overhead rates permits end-of-period accounting to be accomplished much more quickly.

c. Predetermining overhead rates annually requires less effort than going through the allocation process each period. An annual period is appropriate for the predetermination of overhead rates unless the production/marketing cycle of the entity is such that the use of a longer or shorter period would clearly provide more useful information.

22. Predetermined overhead rates require an estimate of the level of activity in each responsibility center and an estimate of the average production volume in each production cost center. The estimate of the average production volume for production cost centers is particularly sensitive because many items of indirect cost are fixed or discretionary and do not vary with volume changes. If the estimate of average production volume is too high, too little cost will be assigned to final cost objects. If the estimate of average production volume is too low, too much cost will be assigned to final cost objects. The flexible budgets for indirect costs are used to simulate the amount of cost to be incurred for each cost item at the anticipated level of activity. Then the allocation methodology decided upon is used to simulate the amount of cost for each production cost center. The final step is to divide the estimated amount of indirect cost in each production cost center by the estimated equivalent units of volume anticipated to pass through the product cost center to

obtain the predetermined overhead rate. Predetermined overhead rates should be revised during the year if there are significant changes in cost levels, anticipated production volumes, or the production process.

23. Actual indirect costs incurred in each period usually are greater or less than the estimated costs, and actual production volume usually differs from the estimated production volume used to calculate the predetermined overhead rate. Consequently, actual indirect costs incurred will differ from the amount of indirect costs allocated to final cost objects. When actual costs are greater than allocated costs, overhead is underabsorbed. When actual costs are less than allocated costs, overhead is overabsorbed. For management accounting purposes, overabsorbed or underabsorbed overhead should be credited or charged to earnings in the current period. For financial reporting, however, if the amounts involved are material, they should be assigned to cost of sales and inventory in the proportions in which the costs of production during the period have been assigned to cost of sales and inventory.

24. The procedures described for full costing are applicable when the primary objective of the cost accounting system is the assignment of actual costs to final cost objects. In many situations, however, management is concerned with what costs *should be incurred* for a final cost object and where in the organization and in what amount the actual costs incurred differ from the costs that should have been incurred. This kind of information is provided by a *standard cost system*. Standard costs are statements of what costs should be. Standard direct material costs and standard direct labor costs are described in Statements 4E and 4D, respectively.

A standard cost system uses predetermined overhead rates to allocate indirect production costs to final cost objects, following the procedures described in the preceding paragraphs, with two exceptions:

a. Both in the simulation described in paragraph 22 and in the actual allocation of costs to final cost objects, only the costs that should have been included. Any differences between planned costs and actual costs incurred are identified as spending variances by the flexible budgeting system. Spending variances are identified by responsibility center and are signals to management that indirect costs are not being incurred as planned in those segments of the organization. For management accounting purposes, spending variances are charged or credited to earnings in the period in which they are incurred.

b. In the production cost center, the units of volume that are the basis for the allocation of production center costs to final cost objects are stated at standard rather than actual.

Because spending variances have been identified and dealt with separately, any remaining overabsorbed or underabsorbed overhead is attributable primarily to differences between the actual volume in a period and the estimated volume that was used to calculate the predetermined overhead rate. The differences are called volume variances and for management accounting purposes are charged or credited to earnings in the current period. For financial reporting purposes, if the amounts of spending and volume variances are material, they should be assigned to cost of sales and inventory in the proportions in which the costs of production during the period have been assigned to cost of sales and inventory.

Differential Production Costs

25. Differential costs are costs that are different under one set of conditions than they would be under another set of conditions. Differential costs always relate to the future and can be defined only in the context of a specific situation. Many management decisions require estimates of differences in some or all of the following:

   a.   Revenues.

   b.   Direct production costs.

   c.   Indirect production costs.

   d.   Direct selling and administration costs.

   e.   Indirect selling and administration costs.

   Many management decisions also require the estimation of these data for individual segments of the entity rather than for the entity as a whole. The cost accounting system should be designed to provide data that will be useful in estimating the differential costs for a wide variety of management decisions.

Profitability Model

26. This Statement is concerned primarily with indirect production costs. It is useful, however, to consider all elements of cost in the profitability model shown in Figure 23-4, which is the framework for this section of the Statement.

   In this model, direct fixed costs are those costs that will exist if that business segment (cost object) continues to exist but should disappear if the business segment is discontinued. Indirect fixed costs are those overall costs of the entity that would continue if the segment were discontinued. These costs would have to be reallocated among the remaining segments. In this model, profitability is measured at three levels for each segment of the business:

   a.   Contribution margin.

   b.   Segment contribution.

   c.   Operating income.

   The measure of operating income in this profitability model is consistent with the same measure in the full cost profitability model illustrated in Figure 23-3. The classification of costs into their variable and fixed components, and the further classification of fixed costs into those that are direct to a segment of the business and those that are not, provide the necessary data from which to determine the differential costs relevant to a wide variety of management decisions. For example, if the alternatives in a decision involve operating at different volume levels, the differential costs may be equal to the variable costs. If the alternatives involve adding or dropping a segment of the business, the differential costs may include the direct fixed costs of the segment in addition to the variable costs.

Figure 23-4   Profitability Model Differential Costs.

	Total Company	Business Segments (Cost Objects)		
		A	B	C
1 REVENUES	$706	$423	$134	$149
2 VARIABLE COSTS				
3 Direct production costs:				
4 Direct materials	$185	$107	$ 17	$ 61
5 Direct labor	85	57	7	21
6 Indirect production costs	61	20	24	17
7 Selling and administration costs	21	12	4	5
8 TOTAL VARIABLE COST	$352	$196	$ 52	$104
9 CONTRIBUTION MARGIN	354	227	82	45
10 % of Revenues	50.1%	53.7%	61.2%	30.2%
11 DIRECT FIXED COSTS				
12 Production costs	51	24	9	18
13 Selling and administration costs	28	19	7	2
14 TOTAL SEGMENT DIRECT COSTS	$ 79	$ 43	$ 16	$ 20
15 SEGMENT CONTRIBUTION	$275	$184	$ 66	$ 25
16 ALLOCATED SHARE OF INDIRECT FIXED COSTS				
17 Production costs	41	14	6	21
18 Selling and administration costs	94	54	18	22
19 TOTAL SEGMENT INDIRECT COSTS	$135	$ 68	$ 24	$ 43
20 OPERATING INCOME BEFORE INCOME TAXES	$140	$116	$ 42	$(18)

27. The segregation of the fixed and variable components of indirect production costs can be accomplished by an extension of the simulation technique described in paragraphs 22–24 for the annual predetermination of overhead rates. In addition to using the flexible budgets to determine the total amount of cost for each indirect cost item each month at the anticipated level of activity, the flexible budget rates can be extended to a cost intercept at zero volume of activity. The cost at the point of intercept is deemed the *fixed component* of the cost. The fixed component is subtracted from the total cost at the anticipated level of activity, and the difference is deemed the *variable component*. The simulation then uses the allocation methodology decided upon to determine the amount of variable indirect costs for each product cost center. The final step of dividing the amount of variable indirect costs in each production cost center by the equivalent units of production anticipated to pass through the production cost center will produce a predetermined *variable overhead rate*. The fixed component of an indirect production cost

item is stated as an amount per period rather than as a rate per unit of volume. Discretionary indirect production costs also are stated as an amount per period.

28. The subsequent classification of fixed and discretionary indirect production costs into those that are direct to a segment of the business and those that are not is done by examining and classifying each cost item.

29. Many entities have more than one dimension of segmentation that they find useful for management purposes. For example, one dimension of segmentation might be by product line, another might be by channel of distribution, and still another might be by geographical region. Variable costs follow the product or service and usually require no further analysis for a different dimension of segmentation. For each dimension of segmentation, however, fixed indirect production costs and other fixed costs should be examined separately and classified as either direct to a segment or not direct.

23-11 BUDGETARY PLANNING AND CONTROL OF MANUFACTURING EXPENSES

Having discussed those special factors that are important in the proper planning and control of manufacturing expense, we will now review some of the *budgetary* methods. It should be understood that manufacturing expenses can be controlled through the use of unit standards applied to the expense type or department under consideration. But probably budgetary control is the technique more useful in the overall planning of expense levels, as well as the control phase.

Three types of budgets might be applied in the manufacturing expense area:

- A fixed or administrative type budget.
- A flexible budget, wherein certain expenses should vary with volume handled.
- A step-type budget.

(a) FIXED-TYPE BUDGET

The fixed-type budget is, as the name implies, more or less constant in the amount of budgeted or allowed expenses for each month. The permitted expense level does change somewhat to reflect a differing volume of manufacturing. Basically, the planning procedure is one wherein the department manager estimates the level of expenses, by account, for each month of the planning period, with some recognition given to expected differing amounts of production. These monthly estimates are subject to review by a superior (with the advice in some instances of the controller or budget director). The control phase consists in comparing actual expense incurred with the predetermined estimate.

An example of a summary planning budget of the fixed type for the manufacturing department is illustrated in Figure 23-5. While the budget estimate in this figure reflects only the annual and quarterly amounts, in practice the estimate is prepared on a monthly basis.

This fixed type of budget has the advantage of simplicity, and some recognition is given to the small changes in production level. Where production volume is nearly

Figure 23-5   Manufacturing Expense—Fixed-Type Budget.

The Johnson Controls Co.
MANUFACTURING DIVISION—ANNUAL BUDGET
MANUFACTURING EXPENSE

Item/Expense	Present Year Indicated Final	Plan Year Total	Quarter 1	Quarter 2	Quarter 3	Quarter 4	Increase (Decrease) over Present Year
Planned production (machine hours)	412,000	440,000	110,000	130,000	100,000	100,000	28,000
Expenses							
Supervisory salaries	$ 170,000	$ 178,500	$ 44,625	$ 44,625	$ 44,625	$ 44,625	$ 8,500
Other salaries	66,000	70,000	17,500	17,500	17,500	17,500	4,000
Indirect wages	742,000	786,500	200,000	226,520	180,000	180,000	44,520
Subtotal	978,000	1,035,020	262,125	288,645	242,125	242,125	57,020
Fringe benefits (40%)	391,200	414,000	104,850	115,450	96,850	96,850	22,800
Repairs and maintenance	243,100	267,400	67,100	82,400	60,000	57,900	24,300
Power	191,300	200,860	50,600	59,800	46,000	44,460	9,560
Supplies	71,000	72,000	18,000	18,000	18,000	18,000	1,000
Depreciation	129,500	129,500	32,375	32,375	32,375	32,375	—
Communications	62,000	63,000	15,400	18,200	15,400	14,000	1,000
Occupancy	98,700	98,700	24,675	24,675	24,675	24,675	—
Other	10,200	9,000	2,000	3,000	2,000	2,000	(1,200)
Total	$2,175,000	$2,289,480	$577,125	$642,545	$537,425	$532,385	$114,480

constant, perhaps the method is satisfactory. But if the monthly budget in the example is predicated on a volume of 43,333 machine hours ($\frac{1}{3}$ of 130,000) and the actual level turns out to be 51,000, can the resulting budget comparison be deemed a good control tool? For expenses that are truly fixed, it would be satisfactory. For expenses that should vary by production volume, the "allowed" budget may be inadequate—if such a wide variance happens frequently.

(b) FLEXIBLE BUDGET

The flexible or variable budget recognizes that some expense levels should change as the volume of production varies, and it is the type suggested for proper planning and control of manufacturing expenses in many instances. An illustrative annual planning budget is shown in Figure 23-6. And an example of a related budgetary control report is presented in Figure 23-7.

Basically, the budgetary procedure is as follows:

1. By an examination and analysis of the expenses in each department, for each type of expense the budget structure of a fixed amount and a variable rate per factor of variability is determined. For an illustrative structure, see Figure 23-6.

2. The department manager, when the planned production level is known, applies the budget structure to the planned volume level, probably by month, and arrives at the annual budget. (See Figure 23-6.)

3. The planned budget is reviewed by the manager's supervisors, etc.; after the iterative process is complete, the approved budget becomes part of the manufacturing division budget.

4. This budget is incorporated in the company/division annual plan.

5. Each month the actual expenses are compared to the flexible budget as applied to the actual volume level experienced. (See Figure 23-7.)

6. Corrective action, if necessary, is taken by the department manager.

For most applications this flexible-type budget probably is the more suitable.

(c) STEP-TYPE BUDGET

Some companies desire budgets that more or less reflect what expenses should be at particular levels, but wish to avoid a monthly calculation of the allowable budget based on the fixed amount and variable unit rate as in the flexible budget. Rather, the management prefers to establish a budget for each level of activity within a range of possible activity levels. Such a budget is illustrated in Figure 23-8.

Budgetary control consists of comparing actual expenses, by account, with the budget level closest to the activity level experienced. Some applications provide for interpolating between budget levels for the allowed budget.

(d) SUMMARIZED MANUFACTURING EXPENSE PLANNING BUDGET

In the context of planning, the annual planning budget should be prepared for each department in the manufacturing department, on a responsibility basis. Whatever type of

Figure 23-6   Manufacturing Expense—Flexible Budget.

The Adamson Controls Co.
MANUFACTURING EXPENSE—ANNUAL BUDGET
FLEXIBLE TYPE
PLANNED ACTIVITY LEVEL

Department __62__
Machine Hours __640,000__

Item/Expense	Budget Structure (a) Budget Fixed per Month	Variable Rate Per Hour	Estimated Final— Current Year	Planning Year Total	Fixed	Variable	Increase (Decrease) Annual
Machine Hours			598,000	740,000			142,000
Expenses							
Supervisory salaries	$ 7,310	$ —	$ 82,000	$ 87,720	$ 87,720	$ —	$ 5,720
Other salaries	4,340	.10	112,000	116,080	52,080	64,000	4,000
Indirect wages	24,900	.50	493,400	618,800	298,800	320,000	125,400
Subtotal	36,550	.60	687,400	822,600	438,600	384,000	135,200
Fringe benefits (40%)	14,620	.24	274,960	329,040	175,440	153,600	54,080
Repairs and maintenance	6,000	.11	142,800	142,400	72,000	70,400	(400)
Power	10,000	.23	246,100	267,200	120,000	147,200	21,100
Communications	2,000	.10	81,100	88,000	24,000	64,000	6,900
Occupancy	30,000	—	334,800	360,000	360,000	—	35,200
Supplies	3,000	.05	61,400	68,000	36,000	32,000	6,600
Depreciation	40,000	—	420,000	480,000	480,000	—	60,000
Total	$142,170	$1.33	$2,248,560	$2,557,240	$1,706,040	$851,200	$308,680

Note: (a) Adjusted to reflect new expense levels (inflation, cost reduction, and restructuring).

Figure 23-7 Departmental Budget Report.

The Adamson Controls Co.
BUDGET REPORT—DEPT. 62(b)
MONTH OF MARCH, 19XX

Activity Level   52,100 Machine Hours

Item/Expense	Month			Year to Date		
	Actual	Budget	(Over)/under Budget	Actual	Budget	(Over)/under Budget
Machine Hours	52,100			162,000		
Expenses						
Supervisory salaries	$ 7,310	$ 7,310	$ —	$ 21,930	$ 21,930	$ —
Other salaries	9,220	9,550	330	29,000	29,220	222
Indirect wages	52,100	50,950	(1,150)	156,700	155,700	(1,000)
Subtotal	68,630	67,810	(820)	207,630	206,850	(780)
Fringe benefits (40%)	27,452	27,124	(328)	83,052	82,740	(312)
Repairs and maintenance	13,401	11,731	(1,670)	33,620	35,820	2,200
Power	20,012	21,983	1,971	63,260	67,260	4,000
Communications	6,910	7,210	300	22,000	22,200	200
Occupancy	30,000	30,000	—	90,000	90,000	—
Supplies	5,600	5,605	5	16,900	17,100	200
Depreciation	40,000	40,000	—	120,000	120,000	—
Total	$212,005	$211,463(a)	$(542)	$636,462	$641,970	$ 5,508

Notes: (Over)/under Budget—not significant

(a) Budget—Fixed $142,170 $426,510
         Variable   69,293   215,460
         Total $211,463 $641,970

(b) Despite the disruptions to his operations from on-going construction, Foreman Johnson has done an excellent job controlling costs.

636

Figure 23-8 Manufacturing Expense Budget—Step Type.

The General Corporation
HEATER DIVISION
MONTHLY MANUFACTURING EXPENSE BUDGET

Department ___Fabrication___
Department Head ___Ship___

Year ___19XX___
Normal Activity (month) ___85,000___
Base ___Standard Machine Hours___

	Percent of Normal Activity (N.A.)							
	60%	70%	80%	90%	100% (N.A.)	110%	120%	130%
Salaries and wages								
General foremen	$ 8,000	$ 8,000	$ 8,000	$ 8,000	$ 8,000	$ 8,000	$ 8,000	$ 8,000
Foremen	17,000	19,000	21,000	24,000	24,000	24,000	27,000	27,000
Clerical	1,500	1,500	2,000	2,000	2,000	2,000	2,500	2,500
Indirect labor	20,000	22,000	25,000	30,000	30,000	30,000	32,000	34,000
Subtotal	46,500	50,500	56,000	64,000	64,000	64,000	69,500	71,500
Fringe benefits (40%)	18,600	20,200	22,400	25,600	25,600	25,600	27,800	28,600
Maintenance and repairs	19,000	21,000	24,000	29,000	30,000	34,000	37,000	39,000
Power	38,000	39,000	41,000	43,000	45,000	47,000	50,000	52,000
Traveling	8,000	8,000	10,000	10,000	12,000	12,000	12,000	12,000
Communications	6,000	7,000	7,000	8,000	8,000	8,000	9,000	9,000
Supplies	8,000	8,000	9,000	9,000	10,000	11,000	12,000	12,000
All other controllable	1,600	1,700	1,800	2,000	2,000	2,000	2,500	3,000
Subtotal	145,700	155,400	171,200	190,600	196,600	203,600	219,800	227,100
Depreciation	40,000	40,000	40,000	40,000	40,000	40,000	40,000	40,000
Property taxes	5,000	5,000	5,000	5,000	5,000	5,000	5,000	5,000
Insurance	3,000	3,000	3,000	3,000	3,000	3,000	3,000	3,000
Total	$193,700	$203,400	$219,200	$238,600	$244,600	$251,600	$267,800	$275,100

budget is to be used—whether fixed or variable—the department budgets for the expected production level for the plan year should be summarized as part of the annual planning process. (See Chapter 16.) A summarized manufacturing expense budget, after completion of the iterative process and approval by the chief production executive, could be in the format reflected in Figure 23-9. This planning budget is then used in the process of determining the total cost of goods manufactured. While the illustrated budget is presented on an annual basis only, in fact the budget is prepared to show monthly data.

From a control viewpoint, each month the actual departmental expenses, by type of expense, under the control of the department manager, are compared with the monthly budget, reasons for variance are established, and corrective action taken. A representative departmental control report is shown in Figure 23-7, as already commented upon.

23-12 REVISION OF MANUFACTURING EXPENSE BUDGETS

It is intended that any budget procedure be a useful function. Since the budget structure is founded on certain assumptions, standards, and criteria, these need to be periodically checked. Normally, the expense structure does not change very often, but there will be occasions when the data should be updated, such as when:

- There are major changes in the manufacturing process (e.g., introduction of JIT techniques) such as cellular manufacturing or departmental functions.
- Major changes take place in the salary, wage, or employee fringe benefits package.
- Major organizational changes take place (new departmental structure).
- Major inflationary or other external price changes occur in commodities or services purchased, etc.

Many of these adjustments can be made in connection with the annual planning cycle. During the interim period, small cost level advances probably can be ignored, but major increases need to be instituted on a timely basis.

23-13 SECURING CONTROL OF OVERHEAD

As previously stated, the basic approach in controlling factory overhead is to set standards of performance and operate within the limits of these standards. Two avenues may be followed to accomplish this objective: one involves the preplanning or preventive approach; the other, the after-the-fact approach of reporting unfavorable trends and performance.

Preplanning can be accomplished on many items of manufacturing overhead expense in somewhat the same fashion as discussed in connection with direct labor. For example, the crews for indirect labor can be planned just as well as the crews for direct labor. The preplanning approach will be found useful where a substantial dollar cost is involved for purchase of supplies or repair materials. It may be found desirable to maintain a record of purchase commitments, by responsibility, for these accounts. Each purchase requisition, for example, might require the approval of the budget department. When the budget limit is reached, then no further purchases

Figure 23-9 Summarized Manufacturing Expense Budget, by Department.

The Adamson Controls Co.
SUMMARY MANUFACTURING EXPENSE BUDGET
FOR THE PLANNING YEAR 199X
(dollars in thousands)

Department	Indicated Final Current Year	Annual Plan	Plan Year 199X Quarter			
			1	2	3	4
Standard machine hours (000)	11,780	12,500	3,125	3,500	2,700	3,175
Manufacturing administration	$ 212.1	$ 225.0	$ 56.25	$ 56.25	$ 56.25	$ 56.25
Fabrication	2,316.4	2,480.0	620.00	670.00	535.70	654.30
Sub-assembly	2,721.3	2,850.0	712.50	790.00	627.00	720.50
Final assembly	2,016.9	2,160.0	540.00	604.80	470.20	545.00
Production control	472.5	505.0	126.25	141.40	110.10	127.25
Industrial engineering	389.2	410.0	102.50	102.50	102.50	102.50
Quality control	140.0	150.0	37.50	42.50	32.50	37.50
Tooling	89.7	112.1	28.03	30.03	26.01	28.03
Purchasing	167.6	170.2	42.55	44.55	40.55	42.55
Shipping	212.4	225.3	56.00	60.10	52.50	56.70
Power	1,014.1	1,080.4	270.10	300.50	237.70	272.10
Maintenance	687.3	730.2	182.55	184.55	180.55	182.55
Less: Interdepartmental transfers(a)	(1,624.3)	(1,922.7)	(480.68)	(515.08)	(444.20)	(482.68)
Total	$8,815.2	$9,175.5	$2,293.55	$2,512.10	$2,027.30	$2,342.55

Note: (a) Represents allocation from tooling, power, and maintenance departments.

639

would be permitted except with the approval of much higher authority. Again, where stores or stock requisitions are the sources of charges, the department manager may be kept informed periodically of the cumulative monthly cost, and steps may be taken to stop further issues, except in emergencies, as the budget limit is approached. The controller will be able to find ways and means of assisting the department operating executives to keep within budget limits by providing this kind of information.

The other policing function of control is the reporting of unfavorable trends and performance. This involves an analysis of expense variances. Here the problem is somewhat different as compared with direct labor or material because of the factor of different levels of activity. Overhead variances may be grouped into the following classifications:

Controllable by departmental supervision.

Rate or spending variance.

Efficiency variance.

Responsibility of top management.

Volume variance.

It is important to recognize the cause of variances if corrective action is to be taken. For this reason, the variance due to business volume must be isolated from that controllable by the departmental supervisors.

Activity-based costing is rarely used for budgeting, but if the controller wishes to use it, then bills of activity (as described earlier in this chapter) and bills of material should be used as the foundation data for standard costs. Multiplying the planned production quantities by the activity costs found in the bills of activity and direct costs found in the bills of lading will yield the bulk of all anticipated manufacturing costs for the budget period. The appropriate management use of budgeted activity costs is to target reductions in the use of activities by various products, as well as to reduce the cost of those activities. For example, the cost of paying a supplier invoice for a part used by the company's product can be reduced by either automating the activity to reduce its cost, or to reduce the product's use of the activity, such as by reducing the number of suppliers, reducing the number of parts used in the product, or grouping invoices and only paying the supplier on a monthly basis.

(a) ANALYSIS OF EXPENSE VARIANCES

The exact method and degree of refinement in analyzing variances will depend on the desires of management and the opinion of the controller about requirements. However, the volume variance, regardless of cause, must be segregated from the controllable variances. *Volume variance* may be defined, simply, as the difference between budgeted expense for current activity and the standard cost for the same level. It arises because production is above or below normal activity and relates primarily to the fixed costs of the business. The variance can be analyzed in more detail about whether it is due to seasonal causes, the number of calendar days in the month, or other causes.

The controllable variances may be defined as the difference between the budget at the current activity level and actual expenses. They must be set out for each cost center and analyzed in such detail that the supervisor knows exactly what caused the condition. At least two general categories can be recognized. The first is the rate of spending variance. Simply stated, this variance arises because more or less than standard was spent for each machine hour, operating hour, or standard labor hour. This variance must be isolated for each cost element of production expense. An analysis of the variance on indirect labor, for example, may indicate what share of the excess cost is due to (1) overtime, (2) an excess number of workers, or (3) use of higher-rated workers than standard. The analysis may be detailed to show the excess by craft and by shift. As another example, supplies may be analyzed to show the cause of variance as (1) too large a quantity of certain items, (2) a different material or quality being used, or (3) higher prices than anticipated.

Another general type of controllable variance is the "production" or "efficiency" variance. This variance represents the difference between actual hours used in production and the standard hours allowed for the same volume. Such a loss involves all elements of overhead. Here, too, the controller should analyze the causes, usually with the assistance of production personnel. The lost production might be due to mechanical failure, poor material, inefficient labor, or lack of material. Such an analysis points out weaknesses and paves the way to corrective action by the line executives.

The accounting staff must be prepared to analyze overhead variances quickly and accurately to keep the manufacturing supervision and management informed. The variance analysis should relate to overhead losses or gains for which unit supervision is responsible and include such features as:

1. The expenditure or rate variance for each cost element as an over or under the budget condition for the reporting period and year to date. The budgeted amount for controllable expenses may be calculated by multiplying the operating hours by the standard rate per cost element and compared to actual.

2. The departmental variance related to the level of production.

3. The amount of fixed costs, even though the particular supervisor may not be responsible for the incurrence.

4. Interpretative comments as to areas for corrective action, trends and reasons for any negative variances.

It is not sufficient just to render a budget report to the manufacturing supervision; this group must be informed about the reasons for variances. The information must be communicated and a continuous follow-up must be undertaken to see that any unfavorable conditions are corrected. This may take the form of reviewing and analyzing weekly or even daily reports. Abnormal conditions such as excess training, overtime, absenteeism, and excessive usage of supplies must be isolated and brought to the attention of the responsible individuals who can take remedial action. There also may be other data available such as repair records, material and supplies usage reports, personnel statistics—including turnover and attendance records that are useful.

Responsibility must be established for all significant variances in a timely manner so that appropriate corrective action is taken.

(b) INCENTIVES TO REDUCE COSTS

It has been stated repeatedly that costs are controlled by individuals. In the control of manufacturing expenses, as in the case of direct labor and material, a most important factor is the first-line supervision. As representatives of management who are on the scene observing production the first-line supervisors can detect immediately deficient conditions and take action or influence the utilization of resources. Reports showing the performance of this group are of great assistance. However, the experience of many companies has shown that standard costs or budgets covering indirect costs are a more effective management tool when related to some type of incentive or financial reward. Usually, this incentive takes the form of a percentage of the savings or is based on achieving a performance realization above some predetermined norm. If a supervisor realizes he will participate in the savings from being under the budget it is a powerful force in obtaining maximum efficiency. Since variances will fluctuate from month to month, it is advisable to consider an incentive plan for supervision on a cumulative performance basis—a quarter or a year.

23-14 INDIRECT LABOR—A MORE PRECISE TECHNIQUE

Indirect labor often is one of the largest controllable elements of manufacturing expense and therefore may warrant a special review. In the examples provided earlier in this chapter, an acceptable cost level for this type of expense was determined by measuring the historical cost against a factor of variability such as standard machine hours or direct labor hours. Sometimes the correlation may not be as close as desired and a more analytical technique may be necessary—which involves the aid of industrial or process engineers. The method, which closely resembles the calculation of the required direct labor for any given manufacturing operation, essentially is as follows:

- The engineers study the specific function to be performed by the departmental indirect labor crew, including the exact labor hours required at differing activity levels.

- An activity base is selected, such as standard machine hours, that would be a fair and easily determinable measure of just what labor hours are needed for each function of the indirect labor crew.

- Estimates are made as to just what portion of the crew is fixed, and what portion can be treated as variable (perhaps by performing other functions), and the related labor hours are determined.

- The hours data are costed (by the cost accountants), the fixed budget allowance determined, and the variable rate calculated per unit of activity.

The process is summarized on the cost worksheet as shown in Figure 23-10. First, the technical data are summarized, and then the cost bases are calculated.

Where deemed appropriate, this more exact method can be used in arriving at the flexible budget base.

23-15 OTHER ASPECTS OF APPLYING BUDGETARY CONTROL

In applying budgetary control to manufacturing expenses, an alert controller will generate ideas of how to make the budget report more usable to those managers who use it. There are many techniques that can be found; however, in any case it takes good communication. Normally, accountants will develop budgets in terms of dollars or value. Sometimes, production managers cannot relate their operations to monetary units. In

Figure 23-10 Engineering–Based Indirect Labor Budget Structure.

Account Name	Indirect Labor		Plant	Sylvan
Account No.	6201		Dept.	Machine Shop
Length of Period	Month		Year	199X

Normal Work Week: Shifts per day **1**
Hours per shift **8**
Days per week

Operating Range **70%–100%**

Activity Base **Standard Hours**
Activity Units at Capacity **6,880**

TECHNICAL DATA
(workers per shift)

Job Code	Description	Requirement at Activity Level			Data at 100% Level	
		70%	80%	100%	Fixed	Variable
601	Janitorial	.5	.3	.5	.5	—
602	Moving	2.0	2.5	3.0	—	3.0
603	Testing	1.0	1.0	1.5	—	1.5
604	Preparation	.5	.7	1.0	.5	.5
605	Inspection	2.0	2.5	3.0	—	3.0
	Total	6.0	7.0	9.0	1.0	8.0

COST DATA

Job Code	Description	Requirement at Activity Level			Rate per Hour	100% Activity Level				Variable Rate per M Units	
						Fixed		Variable			
		70%	80%	100%		Man-hours	Amount	Man-hours	Amount	Man-hours	Amount
601	Janitorial	86	86	86	$15.00	86	$1,290	—	$ —	—	—
602	Moving	344	430	516	16.50	—	—	516	8,514	75.00	$1,237.50
603	Testing	172	172	258	18.50	—	—	258	4,773	37.50	693.75
604	Preparation	86	86	172	20.00	86	1,720	86	1,720	12.50	250.00
605	Inspection	344	430	516	22.50	—	—	516	11,610	16.15	1,687.50
485	All Other	38	40	42	17.00	30	510	12	510	.38	74.12
		1,070	1,244	1,590		202	$3,520	1,388	$27,127	141.53	$3,942.88

Supplementary Data and Comments:

1. Calculation of hours at capacity: a = 40 machines at capacity; a = 40 machines per shift, b = 8 hours per shift, c = 5 days per week, d = 4.3 weeks per month = a × b × c × d = 40 × 8 × 5 × 4.3 = 6,880 hours.
2. At a 100% operation, one tester will spend one-half of time on janitorial. At the 70% operation, preparation man will spend alternate days on janitorial.
3. Time for 80–90 codes will be offset by overtime if needed.
4. All other consists of union meetings, training, and physical inventory.

most cases they think and manage in terms of labor hours. If this is more understandable, the budget can easily be stated in terms of labor hours per standard labor hours or some other factor. The budgeted allowances of other expenses may be expressed in units of consumption-kilowatt hours of power, gallons of fuel, tons of coal, pounds of grease, and so on.

One of the purposes of budgetary control is to maintain expenses within the limits of income. To this end, common factors of variability are *standard* labor hours or *standard* machine hours—bases affected by the quantity of approved production. If manufacturing difficulties are encountered, the budget allowance of all departments on such a base would be reduced. The controller might hear many vehement arguments by the maintenance foreman, for example, that he should not be penalized in his budget because production was inefficient or that plans once set cannot be changed constantly because production does not come up to expectations. Such a situation may be resolved in one of at least two ways: (1) the forecast standard hours could be used as the basis for the variable allowance, or (2) the maintenance foreman could be informed regularly if production, and therefore the standard budget allowance, will be under that anticipated. The first suggestion departs somewhat from the income-producing sources but does permit a budget allowance within the limits of income and does not require constant changes of labor force over a very short period. The second suggestion makes for more coordination between departments although it injects the element of instability to a slight degree.

Extraordinary or unanticipated expenditures of a manufacturing expense nature must frequently be made. These may fall well without the scope of the usual budget, even when the cumulative yearly condition is considered. In such instances, and if the expenditure is considered necessary and advisable, a special budget allowance will be made over and above the usual budget—something superimposed on the regular flexible budget structure.

Another point should not be overlooked by the accounting staff: the important consideration is not *how* flexibility is introduced into the standard or budget but rather that it *is* injected. Whether charts or tables are used to determine the allowable budget on a more or less automatic basis or whether the budget is adjusted monthly or quarterly on the basis of special review in relation to business volume is not too essential, because either method can be successfully employed. The major consideration is that of securing an adequate measuring stick that also keeps expenses at the proper level in relation to activity or income.

23-16 OTHER CONTROL PROCEDURES

The budgetary process has been emphasized for control of manufacturing overhead expenses in this chapter for these reasons:

- It more closely recognizes the cost behavior of the specific types of expense through its fixed and variable expense structure determination.
- It not only addresses the *control* process, but also is a *planning* device.
- It tends to promote coordination among functions.

There will be occasions when, for whatever reason, the top management and/or functional management does not wish to adopt budgetary procedures. Under these circumstances, in some departments other standards may be employed. In other instances, selected standards may supplement the budget standards. In fact, it is in the manufacturing function that standards were first employed in the control of not only direct labor and direct material, but also many of the indirect expenses.

Such a system involves the establishment of standards (see Chapter 19) and the comparison of actual expenses—either individual accounts, or departmental totals—against such standards, and the taking of corrective action where appropriate. Many manufacturing executives in particular industries know from observation that certain expense relationships are the key to a profitable operation. Their experience has led to the use of a number of standards or standard relationships for manufacturing expenses. These ratios are usually collected and distributed by industry trade associations or magazines devoted to the affairs of specific industries. Some comparisons often used, or trends followed, are these:

Item	As Related to
Total manufacturing expenses (or selected departments)	Total direct labor costs Total direct costs
Indirect labor expense	Total standard direct labor Per direct labor hour Per actual direct labor hour Per machine hour Total manufacturing expense
Repair and maintenance expense	Per machine hour
Power	Per operating hour
Supplies	Per labor-hour
Shipping and receiving	Per ton handled
Downtime expense	Per operating hour

For any *significant* expenses, quite often trends can be observed in the absolute and in relationship to selected or total manufacturing expenses.

23-17 ROLE OF THE CONTROLLER

Much has been said about the technique of setting manufacturing expense budgets or standards, but little mention has been made about *who* prepares the budgets and applies them. This duty is usually delegated to the controller and his staff and understandably so. Past experience is an important factor in setting expense budgets. An analysis of expenses and their behavior in relation to volume is required, and the principal source of information is the accounting records. The accountants are the best qualified to make these analyses of the historical information. Then, too, the accounting staff usually possesses the necessary technical qualifications for organizing the data into the desired shape. Furthermore, the approach must be objective, and the independent position of the accounting department makes it suitable for the setting of fair standards or budgets.

Although the controller "carries the ball" in preparing the budgets, he is only part of the team. Successful control of manufacturing expenses requires the cooperation of the operating departments' supervisors who are charged with the responsibility of meeting their budgets. For this reason, among others, each supervisor should agree to his budget before it is put into effect. Moreover, each supervisor's experience and knowledge of operating conditions must be utilized in the preparation of the budget. The controller and his staff act as coordinators in seeing that the job gets done reasonably well and that it is accomplished on time.

The role of the controller and staff in the accounting for, and planning and control of, manufacturing expenses may be summarized in this fashion. The controller should:

1. Provide that expenses are accumulated in such account categories that control is reasonably simple; that is, the natural expense groupings should originate from the same sources, or a comparable method of control or time or point of control should be employed. Thus, repairs done by outside sources and controlled on a purchase order basis, perhaps should be isolated from in-house repairs that are controlled by requisition.

2. Arrange the departmental accounts on a responsibility basis, by natural expense classifications, so that costs are accumulated according to the authority delegated to plan and control the expenses. This categorization also should permit the accumulation of product costs in a suitable manner.

3. Where a budgetary process is in effect, arrange that the *procedure* facilitates the preparation of the planning budget in an effective and timely manner (by provision of adequate instructions, forms, schedules, etc.); and that the control procedure provides a timely accumulation of actual expenses, compared with budget, together with reasons for any significant departure from plan, if known.

4. Provide reasonable assistance to department managers in their preparation of the annual plan or budget (including requested analyses), and in searching out causes of standard deviation and perhaps methods of correction.

5. Where flexible budgets are in use, either identify, or assist in the identification of, the fixed and variable portions.

6. Where budget structures need revision by reason of changed expense levels (inflation, etc.) or new manufacturing processes, see that timely revisions are made to the end that the budgets are useful and not outdated.

7. Evaluate the planned level of manufacturing expenses in the process of consolidating and testing the annual plan.

8. If budgetary procedures, for whatever reason, are not used, see if some other sort of standard application may be of value in planning and controlling the manufacturing expenses.

9. Determine that the costing methods provide reliable and acceptable accumulation and allocation by cost object—product, department (as to service operations), etc.—and that variances are properly analyzed.

23-18 REPORTS FOR MANUFACTURING EXECUTIVES

(a) SCOPE OF COVERAGE

The supervisory staff of the production organization extends over several levels of authority and responsibility from the assistant foreman, foreman, general foreman, division head, plant superintendent, etc., up to the works manager. Likewise, the matters the supervisory staff controls relate to materials, labor, and overhead, and each of these subjects has special aspects to be reported on. Production reports must cover a wide field of both reader and subject matter. Effective production control is possible only when the production executives are aware of the necessary facts related to the plant operations, and the higher the executive the more he must rely on reports instead of personal contacts and observations. As a result, a system of reports has been developed in most industrial organizations for presenting the pertinent facts on the production activities.

It will bear mentioning that the recent developments in computer hardware and software (programs) permit an improved monitoring of operations. Information on some activities must be, and is, available on a real-time basis. With the advent of personal computers, interesting combination reports consisting of commentary, tabulations, and graphs in an inviting appearance are now possible.

The number of variance reports that are used by manufacturing management will decline as cellular manufacturing becomes the standard form of production. Since cellular manufacturing uses minimal work-in-process (WIP), month-end variance reports from the accounting department will arrive far too late for the information to be useful. For example, if a machine produces a part out of specification, then a cellular layout will immediately detect the problem, because the part will not be hidden in a pile of WIP. Consequently, management can detect and correct the problem immediately without the need for a report.

(b) TYPES OF REPORTS ON ACTUAL PERFORMANCE

The reports will differ from industry to industry and from company to company so that no standardized reports can be set for business generally. However, they may be divided into two general categories according to their purpose. These may be classified as (1) control reports and (2) summary reports. As the name implies, control reports are issued primarily to highlight substandard performance so that corrective action may be taken promptly. These reports deal with performance at the occurrence level and are therefore usually detailed in nature and frequent in issuance. On the other hand, summary reports show the results of performance over a longer period of time, such as a month, and are an overall recapitulation of performance. They serve to keep the general executives aware of factory performance and are, in effect, a summary of the control reports.

Indicative of the subjects the reports to production executives may cover, including direct and indirect costs for which the executive may be responsible, are the following:

Material

       Inventories.

       Spoilage and waste.

       Unit standard costs.

       Material consumed.

       Actual vs. standard usage.

Labor

> Total payroll.
>
> Unit output per labor hour.
>
> Total production in units.
>
> Average hourly labor rates.
>
> Overtime hours and costs.
>
> Bonus costs.
>
> Turnover.
>
> Relationship of supervisory personnel to direct labor.
>
> Actual and standard unit and total labor costs.

Overhead

> Actual vs. budgeted costs.
>
> Idle facilities.
>
> Maintenance costs.
>
> Supplies used.
>
> Cost of union business.
>
> Subcontracted repairs.
>
> Ratio of indirect to direct labor.

In a production environment that has adopted just-in-time (JIT) manufacturing systems, reports will no longer include standards, because JIT assumes that most cost improvements can be managed in the design phase, not in the production phase, and that collecting variance information costs more in effort than is gained in tangible results. A set of JIT reports would include the following:

- Inventory turnover.
- Unit output per labor hour.
- Total production in units.
- Staff turnover.
- Actual purchased costs versus planned costs.
- Inventory accuracy.
- Bill of material accuracy.
- Bill of activities accuracy.

(c) PRESENTATION OF DATA

It is the experience of the authors that most production executives will make good use of data bearing on their operations provided certain fundamental rules are followed:

1. The reports should be expressed in the language of the executive who is to use them and in the form preferred by him.

Figure 23-11 Labor Analysis Report.

OPERATIONS LABOR ANALYSIS
NDP1M-01

	HOURS					DOLLARS				
	WEEKLY		YEAR TO DATE			WEEKLY		YEAR TO DATE		
	PLAN	ACTUAL	PLAN	ACTUAL	VAR	PLAN	ACTUAL	PLAN	ACTUAL	VAR
OPERATIONS SECTION										
BURDEN										
SUPERVISOR	574	459	7,860	6,946	914	8,437	6,822	115,471	103,099	12,372–
CLERICAL	341	418	4,517	6,096	1,579–	2,244	2,814	29,722	41,778	12,056–
V C BURDEN	32	19	445	238	207	227	157	3,125	2,026	1,099
STAFF & TECH	463	504	6,339	6,291	48	5,651	6,017	77,352	75,040	2,312
OPS LEAD	105	105	1,442	1,566	124–	1,081	1,082	14,869	16,090	1,221–
KEY LEAD	213	159	2,931	3,084	153–	1,776	1,348	24,413	25,676	1,265–
COMM ACT										
MISCELLANEOUS	69	22	920	445	475	493	157	6,578	2,987	3,591
IDLE-EQUIP FAIL				22	22–				153	153–
CONFERENCE				16	16–				244	244
TRAINING	131	510	1,698	4,675	2,977–	1,076	3,421	13,962	32,610	18,648–
PREMIUM PAY						1,139	2,338	21,143	31,732	10,589–
TOTAL BURDEN	1,928	2,196	26,152	29,379	3,227–	22,124	24,156	306,635	331,437	24,802–
FRINGE										
VACATION TAKEN	248	409	3,423	3,152	271	2,128	3,574	29,547	26,203	3,344
HOLIDAY	263	280	3,112	2,877	235			26,898	24,573	2,325
PAID ABSENCE			3,488	3,445	43	2,262	2,026	30,096	27,812	2,286
TOTAL FRINGE	511	689	10,023	9,474	549	4,390	5,600	86,543	78,586	7,955
SUB TOTAL	2,439	2,885	36,175	38,853	2,678–	26,514	29,756	393,178	410,025	16,847–
ADJUSTMENTS										
TIME CARD VAR										
SUSPENSE/CORRECT		152		152			1,079		1,079	1,079–
VAC ADVANCES		40–		160–			402–		716–	716–
EDIT REJECTS				40			5		320	320–
TOTAL ADJUSTMENTS		112		32			682		681	681–
TOTAL OPS PAYROLL	7,965	7,958	109,363	106,055	3,308	69,671	68,640	464,202	431,627	32,575

Figure 23-12 Factory Overhead Budget Report.

REPORT NO. C24.206

SUMMARY OF ACCOUNTS

ACCOUNT		--- MONTH ---			-- YEAR TO DATE --		
		BUDGET	ACTUAL	VARIANCE	BUDGET	ACTUAL	VARIANCE
OTHER EXPENSES							
014-02	TRAINING	16642	4130	12512	30421	14420	16000
014-03	MEDICAL	333		333	999	603	396
014-07	MOVING EXP	2000	104-	2104	6000	13879	7879-
	ACCOUNT TOTAL	18975	4025	14949	37420	28902	8517
020-01	ADV PER PROC	8333	9695	1362-	24999	28723	3724-
020-02	AGENCY FEES	4167	6435	2268-	12501	15435	2934-
	ACCOUNT TOTAL	12500	16130	3630-	37500	44158	6658-
024-01	MILAGE	417	750	333-	1251	2394	1143-
024-02	CO.VEHICLES	125		125	375	338	36
	ACCOUNT TOTAL	542	750	208-	1626	2732	1106-
028-01	BUS. CONF.	25	128	128-	100	310	210-
028-02	O/T MEALS	25		25	25		25
	ACCOUNT TOTAL	25	128	103-	125	310	185-
030-01	TELEPHONE	15834	13-	15847	47502	30171	17330
033-02	DEPR OTHER	10623	10535	87	31961	31699	261
035-01	DUE NON MEMR	3750		3750	17250	17755	505-
035-02	SCI TECH	2432	270	2162	5366	3340	2026
	ACCOUNT TOTAL	6182	270	5912	22616	21095	1521
041-01	EMP REL MISC						
015-01	GEN INS	1942		1042	3126	848	2277
057-03	CONSULTANTS					1569	1569-
062-08	RENT-OFF.EQ.	1225		1225	3675	2212	1462
065-07	MAINT-OFF EQ	4708	4636	71	17624	23533	5909-

P U R C H A S E D   S E R V I C E S

OFFSITE

067-13 PUR SYSTEMS	162416	211637	49221-	488723	720935	232212-
067-14 PUR PRG LABR	4833	11541	6708-	31499	17241	14257
067-19 MISC.						
ACCOUNT TOTAL	342404	358783	16379-	1097513	1204229	106716-
SUB GROUP TOTAL	342404	358783	16379-	1097513	1204229	106716-
GROUP TOTAL	456938	421641	35296	1443864	1514544	70680-

S U P P L I E S

DP SUPPLIES

071-20 MISC.	3887	11361	7474-	9795	39188	29393-
071-21 MAG. TAPE	3100	1931	1168	9300	3863	5436
071-22 PAPER TAPE	2583	2560	22	6749	5507	1241
071-23 CARDS	3975	2954	1020	11925	11963	30-
071-24 PAPER	101529	111349	9820-	316544	321759	5215-
071-25 RIBBON	7826	15027	7201-	24322	29039	4717-
071-27 FORM PAPER	38472	87904-	126376	95380	11507-	106887
071-28 MICROFILM SU	13238	6494	6743	42910	37706	5203
071-29 FICHE SUPP.		236-	236		236-	236
ACCOUNT TOTAL	174610	63539	111070	516925	437284	79640
SUB GROUP TOTAL	174610	63539	111070	516925	437284	79640

OTHER SUPPLIES

071-01 OFFICE	3175	3087	87	9525	8375	1149
071-03 M EQ NON DP	12500	622	11877	37500	13237	24262
ACCOUNT TOTAL	15675	3709	11965	47025	21613	25411
SUB GROUP TOTAL	15675	3709	11965	47025	21613	25411
GROUP TOTAL	190285	67249	123035	563950	458897	105052

651

2. Reports should be submitted promptly enough to serve the purpose intended. Control reports are of little value if issued too late to take corrective action.

3. The form and content of the report should be in keeping with the responsibility of the executive receiving it. Minor executives are interested in details, whereas higher executives are interested in departmental summaries, trends, and relationships.

Some of the reports prepared by the accounting department will be on costs, and others will be expressed in nonfinancial terms. Some may be narrative; others will be in tabular or graphic form. But all should follow the principles just set forth.

(d) ILLUSTRATIVE REPORTS

As indicated previously, indirect manufacturing costs have increased significantly, resulting in the need for better visibility and control of these expenses. Figures 23-7 through 23-11 are examples of reports that may be adapted to a particular company or type of manufacturing operation.

Figure 23-11 provides an analysis of weekly and year-to-date hours and costs of the indirect labor and related fringe costs of a manufacturing department.

Figure 23-13   Comparative Cost History Chart.

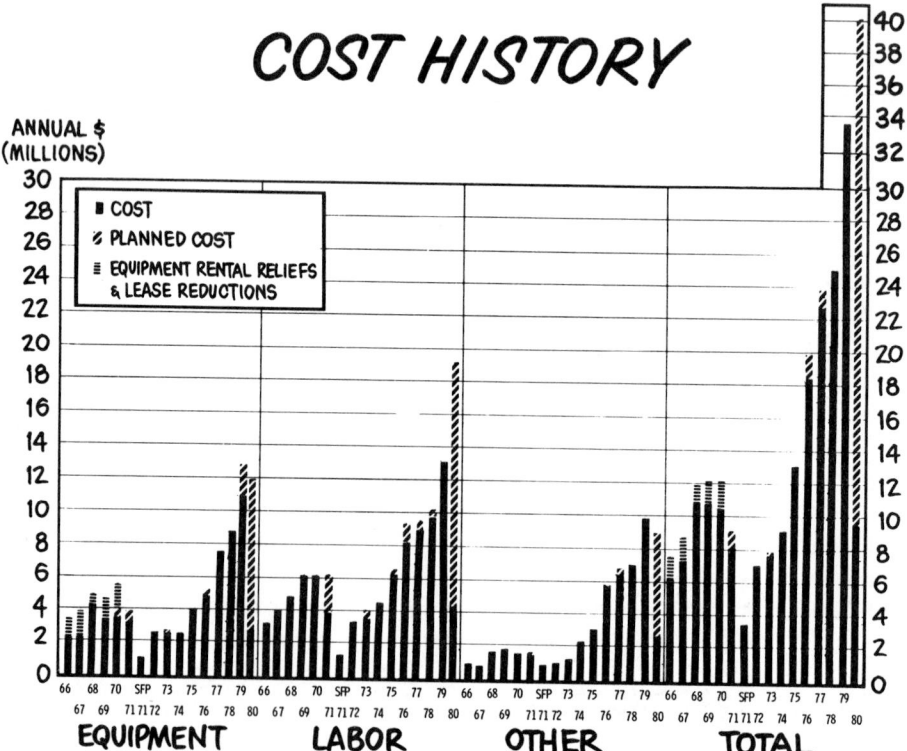

Figure 23-12 is a summary and analysis of the monthly and year-to-date expenses for the activity of three manufacturing expense accounts being monitored: supplies, purchased services, and "other" expenses.

For the manufacturing executives who watch the *trend* of manufacturing expenses in graphic form, Figures 23-13, 23-14, and 23-15 reflect the trend of selected costs.

23-19 SELECTED REFERENCES

Betts, Mitch, "As Easy as ABC?" *Computerworld,* May 23, 1994, pp. 107–108.

Brunton, Nancy M., "Evaluation of Overhead Allocations," *Management Accounting,* July 1988, pp. 23–26.

Cooper, Robin, and Robert S. Kaplan, "How Cost Accounting Distorts Product Costs," *Management Accounting,* April 1988, pp. 20–27.

Cornick, Michael, William D. Cooper, and Susan B. Wilson, "How Do Companies Analyze Overhead?" *Management Accounting,* June 1988, pp. 41–43.

Foster, George, and Charles T. Horngren, "JIT: Cost Accounting and Cost Management Issues," *Management Accounting,* June 1987, pp. 19–25.

Howell, Robert A., and Stephen R. Soucy, "The New Manufacturing Environment: Major Trends for Management Accounting," *Management Accounting,* July 1987, pp. 21–27.

Johnson, H. Thomas, and Robert S. Kaplan, "The Rise and Fall of Management Accounting," *Management Accounting,* Jan. 1987, pp. 23–30.

Lammert, Thomas B., and Robert Ehrsam, "The Human Element: The Real Challenge in Modernizing Cost Systems," *Management Accounting,* July 1987, pp. 33–37.

McIlhattan, Robert D., "How Cost Management Systems Can Support the JIT Philosophy," *Management Accounting,* Sept. 1987, pp. 20–27.

McNair, C. J., and William Mosconi, "Measuring Performance in an Advanced Manufacturing Environment," *Management Accounting,* July 1987, pp. 28–31.

Roth, Harold P., and A. Faye Borthick, "Getting Closer to *Real* Product Costs," *Management Accounting,* May 1989, pp. 28–33.

Spoede, Charlene, Emerson O. Henke, and Mike Umble, "Using Activity Analysis to Locate Profitability Drivers," *Management Accounting,* May 1994, pp. 43–48.

Figure 23-14 Trend Analysis Chart.

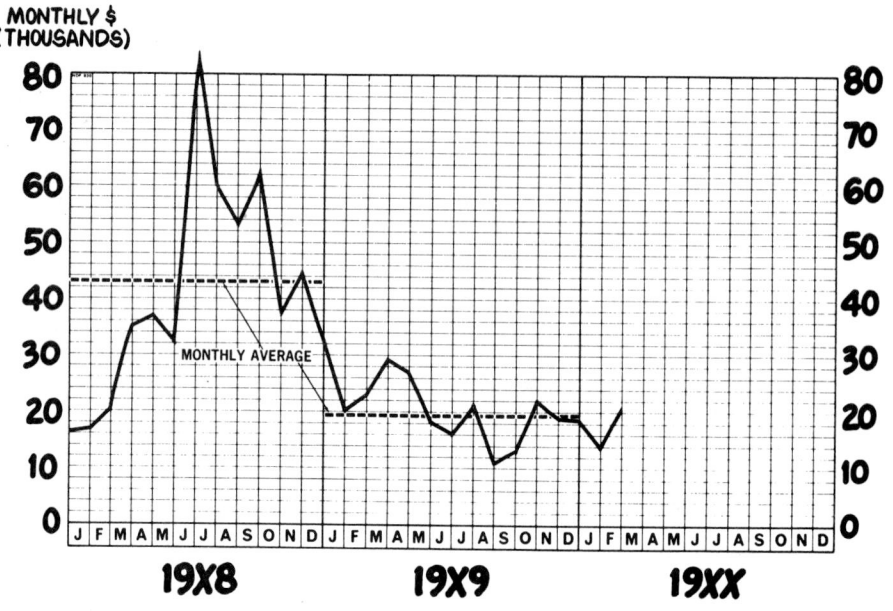

Figure 23-15 Trend Analysis Chart.

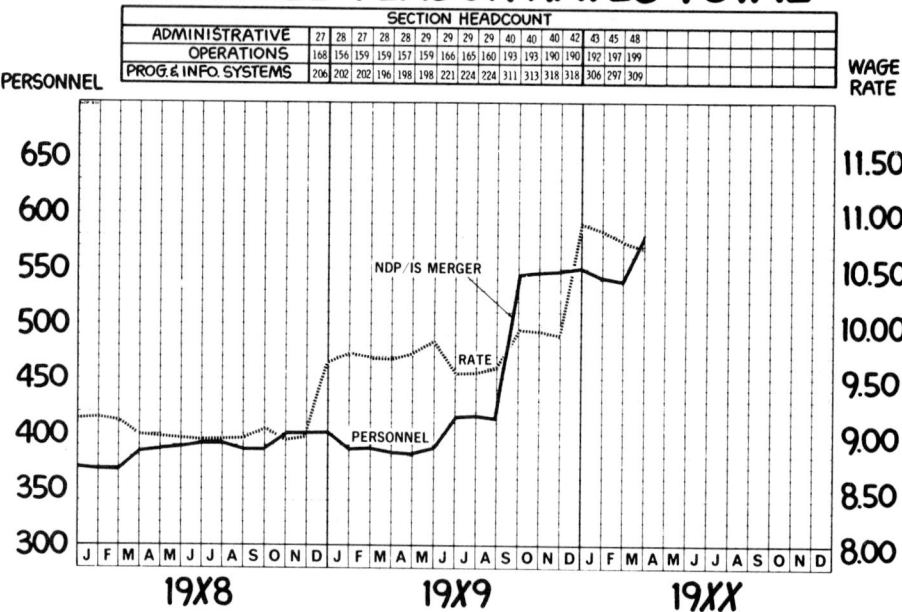

CHAPTER 24

Planning and Control of Research and Development (R&D) Expenses

24-1 RESEARCH AND DEVELOPMENT (R&D) ACTIVITIES

The terms "research" and "development" are often used imprecisely. Each may have a myriad of connotations, and even though these two words often are used together, each represents a different process with differing implications in terms of planning and control. Research as used herein relates to those activities in a business enterprise that are directed to a search for new facts, or new applications of accepted facts, or possibly new interpretations of available information, primarily as related to the physical sciences. It is the activities or functions undertaken, often in the laboratory, to discover new products or processes. *Development,* on the other hand, as discussed herein, denotes those activities that attempt to place on a commercial basis that knowledge gained from research. In another sense, the efforts discussed in this chapter are those that normally would be managed by the vice-president or director of research and development.

Although R&D activities may be grouped in any number of ways—and proper classification is important in the planning and control function—this segregation is often used internally by those entities that do extensive work in these areas:

1. *Basic or Fundamental Research.* This may be defined as investigation for the advancement of scientific knowledge that does not have any specific commercial objective. It may or may not be, in fields of present, or of possible, interest to a company or a customer.

2. *Applied Research.* Activity in this area would relate to the practical application of new scientific knowledge to products or processes in which the company has an interest.

3. *Development.* Functions under this classification would include those efforts or studies to get the product or process into full-scale commercial production.

For those financial executives who deal with budgeting efforts in the R&D area, and who are desirous of having the activity defined and having examples of research and development activities, this definition has been provided by the Financial Accounting Standards Board:[1]

a. *Research* is planned search or critical investigation aimed at discovery of new knowledge with the hope that such knowledge will be useful in developing a new product or service (hereinafter "product") or a new process or technique (hereinafter "process") or in bringing about a significant improvement to an existing product or process.

b. *Development* is the translation of research findings or other knowledge into a plan or design for a new product or process or for a significant improvement to an existing product or process whether intended for sale or use. It includes the conceptual formulation, design, and testing of product alternatives, construction of prototypes, and operation of pilot plants. It does not include routine or periodic alterations to existing products, production lines, manufacturing processes, and other ongoing operations even though those alterations may represent improvements and it does not include market research or market testing activities.

24-2 IMPACT OF R&D ACTIVITIES ON CORPORATE EARNINGS

The most effective assistance of the financial discipline in respect to the planning and control of R&D expenses probably must recognize the role these expenditures can and should play in the economy as well as in a given business.

R&D in the United States is conducted by a diverse number of institutions: the federal government and other governments; industry; universities and colleges; nonprofit types of organizations; and professional firms that conduct research for others. Although the efforts of these groups have resulted in the technological superiority of

---

[1] FASB Statement No. 2, *Accounting for Research and Development Costs,* is copyrighted by the Financial Accounting Standards Board, 401 Merritt 7, P.O. Box 5116, Norwalk, CN, 06856-5116, U.S.A. Portions are reprinted with permission. Copies of the complete document are available from the FASB.

the United States in the mid-twentieth century, now it has become evident that reduced expenditures at the federal level and a hostile climate for new ideas and products are threatening this position. Whether it be because of uncertain business conditions, shortsighted corporate management, lack of adequate incentive, unacceptable governmental regulation or procedures, the fact remains that such a trend may well have adverse implications for the U.S. economy.

There is evidence, in an aggregate sense, of the relationship between technical innovation and the stimulation of economic development. Within a given manufacturing company, in terms of a particular project or projects, perhaps no simple cause-and-effect relationship between R&D expenditures and net income can be found. However, statistical correlation suggests a tendency for earnings to increase, over a period of time, with an increase in research spending. Empirical data tend to show that under the private enterprise system, industrial firms grow and prosper by developing, or investing in new products or processes, or improving existing ones. It simply is not enough to do reasonably well that which is being done, for competitors will pass by such a business. Innovation or improvement and management of change are the intangible attributes that distinguish the progressive company from one on the road to decline. And the wise planning and control of research and development costs should recognize this relationship.

In the early to mid-1990s, R&D expenditure growth has slowed sharply. Data Resources, Inc. (DRI), a McGraw-Hill unit, attributes the ongoing slump in R&D spending to management's concern with short-term profits—a trend fostered in part by the merger and acquisition boom, rising debt burdens, and the high level of real interest rates. Yet, as economist Nigel Gault notes, research studies suggest that after a few years, R&D investment produces annual returns of about 20% for the initial investors, plus another 25% that accrues to society as a whole as new technologies and other advances spill over into the rest of the economy. Indeed, DRI's economic model suggests that a permanent 1% reduction in the growth rate of real R&D investment eventually leads to a 0.85% cut in the potential growth rate of the economy.[2]

In a very real sense, the funds spent on R&D are quite different from many other expenses. They are an investment in the regeneration, growth, and continued existence of the business and should be evaluated, insofar as possible, as an investment.

24-3 R&D ACTIVITIES IN RELATION TO CORPORATE OBJECTIVES

From the strategic and long-range viewpoint, the important corporate activities should support the corporate goals and objectives. Certainly research and development efforts should fit this category. For example, if an entity is planning substantial growth in the compact disc field, then research and development in this area should be considered. Conversely, if strategic plans call for divestiture of a television operation, then it makes little sense to expend sizable sums on R&D in this field. Moreover, R&D input regarding acquisition targets, competitive R&D activity, or the state of the art should be helpful in strategic planning. Further, strategic planning should consider

---

[2] Gene Koretz, "Business Talks a Better R&D Game Than It Plays," *Business Week*, Aug. 21, 1989, p. 20.

Figure 24-1 Interrelationship of Corporate Goals and Objectives with the R&D Plan.

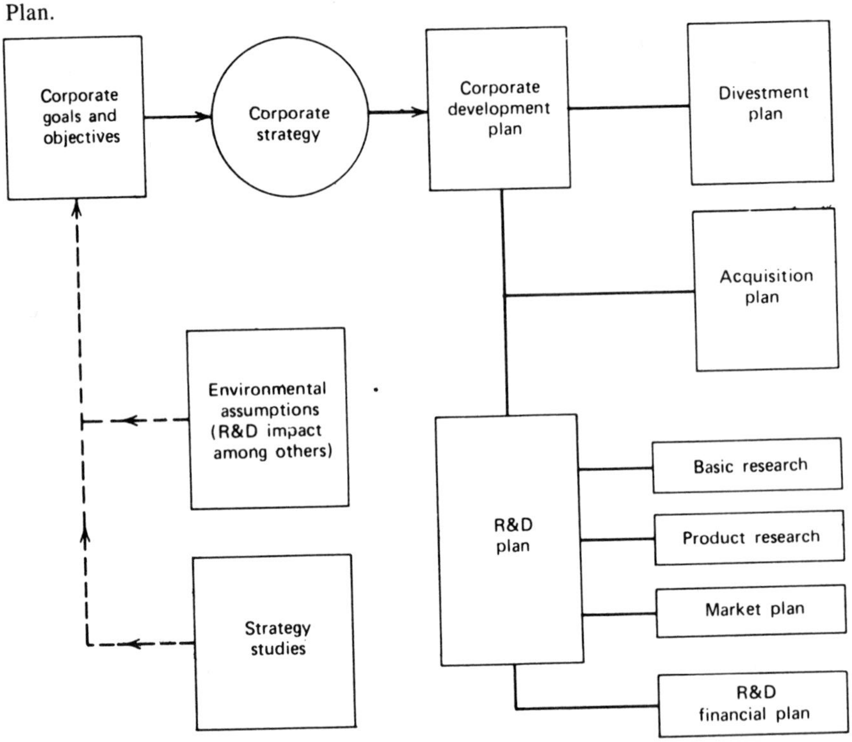

the alternative of performing research in-house or of purchasing an entity already active in the product line.

This preferred relationship between corporate objectives and the R&D plan is shown in Figure 24-1.

24-4 INTEGRATION OF R&D WITH OTHER FUNCTIONS

Aside from understanding the proper relationship of R&D to corporate objectives, the increased competition, the often critical time factor in developing new products, and perhaps greater wisdom about the nature of R&D, is forcing a new approach in many complex R&D situations. This viewpoint has been denoted as *system focus* by one author.[3]

System focus is a philosophy which emphasizes the importance of technology integration *early* in the process: the mutual adaptation of new technology, product design, the manufacturing process, and user needs.

The traditional approach to R&D might be regarded as one group of executive after another adding its contribution to the developing product and then passing the task later to others down the line—in the engineering department and then in the

---

[3] See the *Harvard Business Review* article by Marco Iansiti in the Selected References.

manufacturing process and finally in marketing. This transfer of knowledge is mostly downstream. Often there is little incentive or no mechanism for sending knowledge back upstream so it can improve the technology in the next go-around. In the systems focused organization, the goal of new product development shifts from a compartmentalized sequential approach to optimizing the whole system. Under such circumstances, the company early in the R&D process forms an *integration team* composed of a core group of managers, scientists, and engineers. This team investigates the impact of various technical choices on the design of the product and the manufacturing system.

The purpose of this brief section is to alert the controller to the time and cost savings inherent in this systems integration. He or she should be aware of the potential in any relevant discussions with the R&D manager, and in the formulation of the planning and control system.

24-5 ORGANIZATION FOR THE R&D FINANCIAL FUNCTIONS

Another relevant background matter is organization. The importance of the R&D function in many companies has led to the establishment of separate organizational units, such as a division or subsidiary. Although the size of the company, scope of the research function, management philosophy, and type of research may influence the organization structure, a pattern is discernible in a review of different corporations. A self-contained unit is illustrated in Figure 24-2. The financial officer handling the financial aspects of R&D activity reports to the vice-president, R&D, and provides the necessary financial analysis, accounting and reporting services, and coordination with the corporate finance group. In this instance, a "dotted line" relationship is maintained with the corporate vice-president and controller.

The precise manner in which the R&D function is organized directly affects the accounting for the activity. The organization responsibilities, as defined by the functional outline or charter, provide the basis for budgeting and controlling the costs. The reporting and measurement of expenses must be guided by the organization plan; it must parallel the responsibilities of each organizational unit.

24-6 ACCOUNTING TREATMENT OF R&D IN FINANCIAL STATEMENTS

In public corporations, prior to the mid-1970s, there existed a wide difference in the balance sheet treatment of R&D costs. Given the tendency or desire in some quarters to report the highest possible earnings, as well as the high degree of uncertainty about the future economic benefits of *individual* R&D projects, such variations are understandable. Therefore, because of this reason, among others, and before deciding on the preferred accounting treatment of R&D costs, the Financial Accounting Standards Board in 1973 considered four alternative methods of accounting for such costs as incurred:

a. Charge all costs to expense as incurred.

b. Capitalize all costs as incurred.

c. Capitalize costs when incurred, if specified conditions are fulfilled, and charge all other costs to expense.

Figure 24-2 Organization Chart for Research and Development Activities.

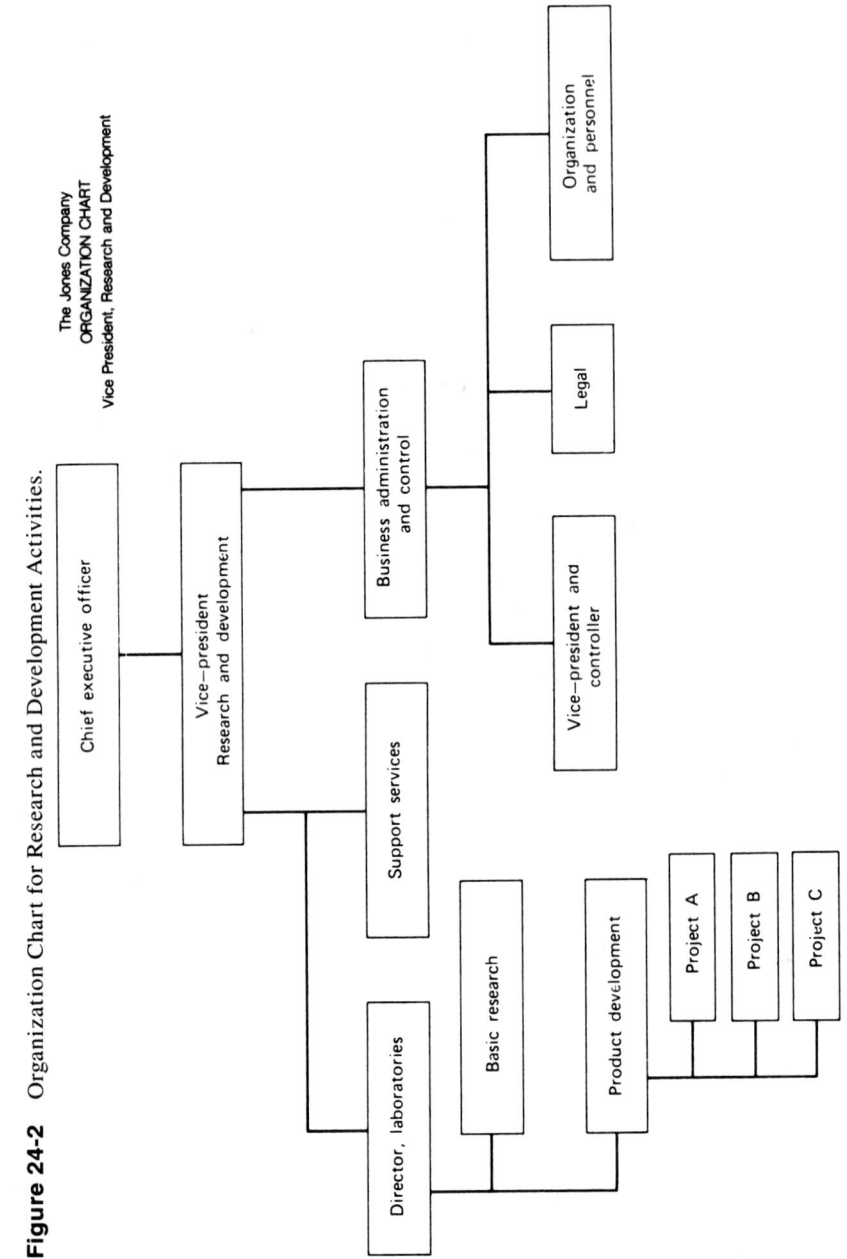

The Jones Company
ORGANIZATION CHART
Vice President, Research and Development

d. Accumulate all costs in a special category until the existence of future benefits could be determined.

Suffice it to state that the Board concluded that all R&D costs (except those covered by contract) should be charged to expense when incurred. This treatment was to be effective for fiscal years beginning on or after January 1, 1975.[4]

The above comments relate to R&D costs exclusive of costs of developing of software. Suffice it to state here that U.S. firms may account for the costs of development of similar software products in different ways. Some costs of development of software to be sold, leased, or otherwise marketed, following SFAS 86, may be capitalized. On the other hand, all the costs of development of similar software created for internal use may be expensed by some firms and capitalized by others.

There seem to be differences of opinion between the Institute of Management Accounting (IMA) and the FASB. The results of a survey by Kirsch and Sakthivel published in January 1993, covering 139 completed questionnaires mailed to 417 of the *Fortune 500* companies showed this treatment of software development costs:[5]

Systems Software		Application Software
Expense	84%	78%
Capitalize	9	10
Expense and Capitalize	7	12
	100%	100%

Readers, if interested, can keep updated on the directives concerning accounting for software development costs.

24-7 ELEMENTS OF R&D COSTS

The Statement of Financial Accounting Standards No. 2 does not apply to the costs of R&D conducted for others under a contractual arrangement; this is covered by statements relating to accounting for contracts in general. It does apply to the types of costs discussed in this chapter but not incurred under a contract to outside parties.

Elements of costs identified with R&D activities would include costs of (a) materials, equipment and special facilities, (b) personnel, (c) intangibles purchased from others, (d) contract services, and (e) indirect costs. Illustrative activities, the costs of which typically would be included in R&D and would be expensed unless conducted for others under a contractual arrangement as outlined in the FASB's Statement No. 2, include the following:[6]

---

[4] See FASB, Statement of Financial Accounting Standards No. 2, "Accounting for Research and Developments Costs," Oct. 1974, para. 15; also FASB, Statement of Accounting Standards No. 86, "Accounting for the Cost of Computer Software to Be Sold, Leased or Otherwise Marketed," Aug. 1985.

[5] See article by Kirsch and Sakthivel in *Management Accounting* noted in the Selected References.

[6] FASB Statement No. 2, *Accounting for Research and Development Costs,* is copyrighted by the Financial Accounting Standards Board, 401 Merritt 7, P.O. Box 5116, Norwalk, CN, 06856-5116, U.S.A. Portions are reprinted with permission. Copies of the complete document are available from the FASB.

a. Laboratory research aimed at the discovery of new knowledge.

b. Searching for applications of new research findings or other knowledge.

c. Conceptual foundation and design of possible product or process alternatives.

d. Testing in search for or evaluation of product or process alternatives.

e. Modification of the formulation or design of a product or process.

f. Design, construction, and testing of preproduction prototypes and models.

g. Design of tools, jigs, molds, and dies involving new technology.

h. Design, construction, and operation of a pilot plant that is not of a scale econom ically feasible to the enterprise for commercial production.

Examples of activities that typically would be excluded from R&D would include the following:

a. Engineering follow-through in an early phase of commercial production.

b. Quality control during commercial production, including routine testing of products.

c. Troubleshooting in connection with breakdowns during commercial production.

d. Routine, ongoing efforts to refine, enrich, or otherwise improve the qualities of an existing product.

e. Adaptation of an existing capability to a particular requirement or customer' need as part of a continuing commercial activity.

f. Seasonal or other periodic design changes to existing products.

g. Routine designs of tools, jigs, molds, and dies.

h. Activity, including design and construction engineering, related to the construc tion, relocation, rearrangement, or start-up of facilities or equipment other than (1) pilot plants (see paragraph 9(h)) and (2) facilities or equipment whose sole use is for a particular R&D project (see paragraph 11(a)).

i. Legal work in connection with patent applications or litigation and the sale or li censing of patents.

The accounting background of the controller should permit him to properly identify and accumulate by department, by project, and by type of cost, the necessary data for the proper planning and control of R&D expenses.

Research and development effort is an activity wherein "people" costs predomi nate. In fact, the recruitment of properly qualified professional staff and a correct bal ancing with other talents and capabilities probably is the key to a successful function.

Expenses must be accumulated by the proper staff classifications, and by (a) na ture of expense, (b) department, and (c) project. Typical categories of expense includ these:

1. *Personnel Costs.* This grouping includes the salaries and wages, by proper job category, and the related fringe benefit costs for:

   • Department managers and administrative staff.

   • Professional staff.

- • Technical staff of a nonprofessional status.
- • Clerical.
- • All other (hourly).

2. *Materials and Supplies.*
- • Chemicals and drugs.
- • Other laboratory supplies.
- • Expendable (capital) equipment with no other use.
- • Repair materials and supplies.

3. *Contract Services.*
- • Services, by category, purchased from others under contract. This could include routine testing and analysis, legal services, and security services, etc.

4. *Purchased Services.* This could include certain aspects or phases of periodically purchased research, delivery services, photographic services, and maintenance, etc.

5. *Patents.* Outside legal services and other expenses related to securing patents, purchasing patents, or litigating patent rights.

6. *Other Direct Expenses.* Included could be:
- • Computer usage fees or rental.
- • Consulting fees.
- • Subscriptions and periodicals.
- • Traveling.
- • Dues and membership costs.
- • Depreciation.
- • Communications.

7. *Allocated General Overhead.* In some instances, the R&D activity or department may be charged for a share of the home office general and administrative expense—allocated on some logical basis.

24-8   ROLE OF THE FINANCIAL EXECUTIVE IN R&D

Now that much of the background information has been briefly reviewed, it might be useful to discuss some of the areas where the knowledge of the financial executive should be helpful to the research director before talking about the technical financial aspects relating to planning and control of R&D costs.

Primary responsibility for the R&D activities rests with the officer in charge of the function. However, the corporate controller and the cognizant financial executive assigned to the R&D financial duties should be knowledgeable and exercise leadership in these areas (not necessarily in the order of importance):

- • Provide the necessary *accounting* accumulation and reporting of the costs and expenses, and assets and liabilities, of the R&D activities in an economical way, and in a manner that provides useful financial data to the R&D executives. As to expenses, this will include accumulation by type of expense, by department, and where appropriate, by project.

- Establish and maintain proper internal controls.
- In conjunction with the headquarters controller, if applicable, and the R&D executives and managers, establish and maintain an adequate budgetary planning and control system.
- Assist in developing guidelines for the *total amount* to be spent on R&D activities (for the annual plan and/or strategic planning).
- Where applicable, and where quantitative analysis may be helpful, and in those instances where an economic/business viewpoint is needed, provide data to guide in establishing budgets and cost/benefit and relative risk comparisons, for R&D projects. (See the discussion of "stage-gate systems" at the end of section 24-14 The Effectiveness of R&D Effort.)
- Assist the R&D managers in developing the *planning budgets* for which each is responsible.
- Assist in preparing the annual capital budget (discussed in Chapter 32).
- Provide acceptable, practical expense control reports—either budgetary or otherwise (standards).

The remainder of this chapter relates to specific questions or tasks in the planning and control of R&D expenses.

24-9 THE GENERAL BUDGETARY PROCEDURE

By and large the planning and control of R&D expenses in the United States are handled through a budgetary process. The principal steps are these:

1. Determine the *total* amount to be spent on R&D activities for the planning period.
2. Establish the individual project budgets and, where appropriate, provide related risks and costs/benefits information.
3. Where applicable, as in the overall administrative function, establish the individual departmental budgets.
4. After appraisal and consolidation, secure approval of the budget.
5. Provide the periodic comparisons of actual vs. planned expenses and the cost to completion of project budgets.
6. Where needed, provide data on a standards basis—actual vs. standard performance.
7. Where feasible, provide measures on the effectiveness of R&D activity.

24-10 DETERMINING THE TOTAL R&D BUDGET

"How much should the company spend on R&D this year?" A great many managements ask this question. And since expenditures should give weight to the long term the query is really a multi-year one. There are innumerable projects which innovative R&D executives can conjure up; but there are limits on what a company should spend

Many constraints must be considered, including these, in determining the total R&D budget for any given time period:

- *Funds Available.* Most entities have financial limitations; and the funds must be within reach, not merely in the one year, but perhaps extending over several years—depending on the projects.
- *Availability of Manpower.* In the United States, companies often are unable to secure the needed professional or technical talent for a given project.
- *Competitive Actions.* What the competitors are doing in R&D, or not doing, usually is a factor that management must weigh. The firm should be reasonably up to date on its R&D efforts.
- *Amount Required to Make the Effort Effective.* If the company embarks on some specific programs, sufficient amounts must be spent. It may be foolish to spend too little; better not to attempt the project.
- *The Strategic Plans.* Future needs over the longer term to meet the strategic plan may eliminate some proposed new projects.
- *General Economic and Company Outlook.* Is the company about to enter a cyclical downturn? What is the expected trend in earnings? These factors may deter new projects if the outlook seems downbeat for a time.

So, if the constraints are known, there are several guidelines in current use for determining the limits of R&D spending. Some of these measures are useful guides in determining the overall budget:

- The amount spent in the past and/or current year, perhaps adjusted by a factor for inflation as well as growth.
- A percent of planned net sales, perhaps using past experience as a guide.
- An amount per employee.
- A percent of planned operating profit.
- A percent of planned net income.
- A fixed amount per unit of product sold (experience) or estimated to be sold.
- A share of estimated cash flow from operations.

24-11 INFORMATION SOURCES ON R&D SPENDING

Aside from internal experience data developed from company records by either the R&D director or the controller, some useful information may be obtained from several external sources. Thus, trade associations may have available data on a particular industry. The Industrial Research Institute, Inc. of Washington, DC, may be another source. If a company is required to file a Form 10K with the SEC, this document may be available. Further, most of the national business publications such as *Business Week* or *Fortune* or *Planning Review* and others periodically discuss the subject. One of the best sources is the annual "R&D Scoreboard" published in June or July of each year by *Business Week.* Typical material in each annual report is similar to this:

- The amount spent on company sponsored research and development as reported by each entity to the Securities and Exchange Commission on Form 10K.

- R&D expenditures for the year, by industry, as summarized in Figure 24-3.
- Commentary on R&D's biggest U.S. spenders.
- Comparison of R&D expenditures by U.S. companies vs. those in other leading countries.
- Significant recent developments in R&D Activity.

For example, in 1994 it was reported that R&D managers were learning to "make do" in a period of difficult economic times by such actions as:

1. Discontinuing marginal projects.
2. Decentralizing R&D efforts.
3. Collaborating with outside experts such as consortiums, universities, other companies, or government laboratories.
4. Continuing internationalism in that
   (a) more research is now headquartered overseas,
   (b) research efforts are more open to foreign participation,
   (c) new technology is being shared with developing countries, and
   (d) patent rights are being shared among certain participants.

Figure 24-3   Industry Summary—Selected R&D Expenditure Data for 1993.

Industry	Total 1993 R&D Expenditures ($ Millions)	Per Employee R&D Expenditures	R&D as a % of Sales	R&D as a % of Profit
Aerospace & Defense	$ 4,210.4	$ 6,470.8	4.2%	77.7%
Automotive	13,441.4	8,975.9	4.0	115.0
Chemicals	4,993.0	6,987.4	4.1	66.3
Conglomerates	3,432.3	4,776.9	2.5	29.5
Consumer Products	2,322.9	2,294.7	1.5	16.6
Containers and Packaging	154.0	1,347.2	0.9	82.2
Electrical and Electronics	8,504.5	9,524.0	5.5	59.4
Food	640.8	1,390.8	0.8	10.7
Fuel	2,660.4	4,466.7	0.8	12.0
Health Care	13,886.9	18,247.8	10.6	72.7
Housing	494.7	2,743.6	1.8	22.3
Leisure Time Products	1,891.5	8,087.1	5.4	109.2
Manufacturing	3,931.1	4,314.7	3.0	49.8
Metals and Mining	360.6	1,541.5	0.9	neg
Office Equipment & Services	17,212.6	15,739.5	8.0	neg
Paper & Forest Products	440.6	2,051.7	1.1	27.8
Services industries	205.8	1,141.1	1.0	31.1
Telecommunications	4,240.6	7,149.1	3.7	52.5
All Industry Composite	$83,023.8	$ 7,476.4	3.8%	64.1%

Of course, any R&D statistical information must be carefully interpreted in that the start of major new projects or the cessation of completed ones can severely impact the quantified results of a company's effort.

24-12 ESTABLISHING THE R&D OPERATING BUDGETS

Determining the total amount to be spent on R&D for the planning year merely establishes a maximum limit on aggregate expenditures. In terms of effective planning and control, three related segments of the total operating expenses need to be determined:

- The R&D specific "projects" and their related costs.
- The indirect expenses associated with the departmental R&D activities, but not part of the project direct expenses.
- The departmental expenses, developed following the organization structure and "responsibility" accounting and reporting—and consisting of the project expenses for which the department manager will be held responsible, and the related (or not related) indirect expenses.

Because many departmental expenses depend on which projects will be undertaken and on the estimated cost of each, the project selection and cost estimating are discussed first.

(a) PROJECT SELECTION

The selection of the particular R&D projects is primarily the responsibility of the research director, giving weight to resources available, the amount of risk found acceptable by management, the strategic plan of the company, and a proper balance between the various types of projects.

In a practical way, a judgment will be made about the relative amount of effort to be spent on various categories of projects. A typical categorization might include these, perhaps in the order of ascending risk or cost, or reducing chance of economic return:

- Sales service (projects originated by the marketing department and involving field selling practices and delivery).
- Factory service (projects requested by the manufacturing arm and relating to manufacturing processes).
- Product improvement (includes efforts to improve appearance, or quality, or usefulness of the product).
- New product research (on products about which some facts are known, but which are not yet in the product line).
- Fundamental research (research of a fundamental or basic nature) where no foreseeable commercial application is yet envisioned, and which may or may not be in fields of interest to the company.

Numerous influences will enter into the decision of project selection. The research director, for example, probably would consider these factors, among others:

- *Availability of Qualified Professional Personnel.* In some time spans, the neces sary professional skills simply might not be available.
- *Urgency of the Project from a Marketing or Manufacturing Viewpoint.* Some matters may be so important, that further manufacturing or marketing of the product is not feasible until the problem is solved.
- *Time Required for the Research.* It may be that some significant problem proba bly can be very quickly solved, and it is considered better to resolve the matter before proceeding to other projects with a longer time span.
- *Prior Research Already Done by Others.* Clues or significant beginnings, either within or without the organization (universities, joint ventures, etc.), may have been found or achieved. It might be the judgment of the head of research that this past effort should be capitalized upon in the present time span.
- *Finally, the Prospect of Economic Gain as the Predominant Influence.* Perhaps the management may believe the possible economic returns from successful re search or development are so high that a given project should be undertaken without delay.

The projects to be initiated will depend on the judgment of the research director and other members of top management. However, these general observations are made including some comments as to how a controller or financial executive may be useful:

- Since the odds of economic benefit from an investment in pure or fundamental research is quite remote, some managements may wish to place modest limits on such expenditures.
- Development projects ordinarily should be given a high priority since successful applications would tend to be more likely.
- All development projects should be "ranked" or evaluated much as are capital budget projects (see Chapter 32). The financial discipline should be helpful, ap plying discounted cash flow techniques, or other quantitative methods, to infor mation provided by the research and/or marketing staff in determining:
  a. Total investment needed, anticipated revenue, operating expenses, and return on investment.
  b. The relative risk.
  c. Potential licensing income, etc.

(b) SOME QUANTITATIVE TECHNIQUES IN EVALUATING R&D EXPENDITURES

It is no easy task to decide on an economic basis whether R&D on a given project should be undertaken. However, there will be instances when it can be attempted.

Consider, first, return on assets, sometimes described as return on investment. The cost-volume-profit relationship (see Chapter 17) may add a dimension to the R&D investment decision:

Assume these conditions:

1. Management has set a 10% return on gross assets, net after taxes, as the mini mum acceptable rate.

2. In one or two years after development is complete, the estimated sales of the newly developed Product T ought to attain a stable level so that aggregate sales should total $100 million.

3. The typical gross margin in the business is 30%, and Product T should be no exception.

4. It is expected that, when research and development is complete, the required asset investment will be:

Working capital	$11,000,000
Plant and equipment	5,000,000
Total	$16,000,000

5. The expected income tax rate—federal, state, and local (netted) is 40%.

With this sales and gross margin expectation and a minimum 10% return on assets, how much can the company spend on research and development on Product T?

Some indication of the approximate expenditure level can be gained from this calculation:

$$\text{return on assets} = \frac{\text{net income}}{\text{assets}}$$

$$\text{net income} = \text{gross margin} - \text{R\&D} - \text{income taxes}$$

$$\text{income tax} = (\text{gross margin} - \text{R\&D}) \times 40\%$$

$$\text{gross margin} = \text{sales} \times 30\%$$

$$\text{ROA} = 10\%$$

By substitution:

$$\text{net income} = \text{gross margin} - \text{R\&D} - [(\text{gross margin} - \text{R\&D} \times 40\%)]$$

$$\text{ROA} = \frac{\text{gross margin} - \text{R\&D} - [(\text{gross margin} - \text{R\&D}) \times 40\%]}{\text{total assets}}$$

$$10\% = \frac{(\$100,000,000 \times 30\%) - \text{R\&D} - [(\$100,000,000 \times 30\% - \text{R\&D}) \times 40\%]}{\$16,000,000}$$

Simplify:

$$\$1,600,000 = \$30,000,000 - \text{R\&D} - (\$30,000,000 - \text{R\&D})0.40$$

$$\$1,600,000 = \$30,000,000 - \text{R\&D}$$

$$- \$12,000,000 - 0.40\,\text{R\&D}$$

$$1,600,000 = \$18,000,000 - \text{R\&D} - 0.40\,\text{R\&D}$$

$$- \$16,400,000 = - \text{R\&D} + 0.40\,\text{R\&D}$$

$$0.6\,\text{R\&D} = \$16,400,000$$

$$\text{R\&D} = \$27,333,333$$

Proof:

Sales	$100,000,000
Gross margin at 30%	$ 30,000,000
Less: R&D	27,333,333
Income before taxes	$ 2,666,667
Income tax at 40%	1,066,667
Net	$ 1,600,000
Assets	$ 16,000,000
ROA =	10%

The $27,333,333 permissible R&D can be converted to a budgeted amount per annum.

Another quantitative analysis related to percent return on net sales. Some managements judge the acceptability of a product by the adequacy of its percent return on sales.

Make these assumptions and then decide how much can be spent on R&D for the product:

1. The minimum acceptable net return on product sales is 10%.
2. Sales of the new product are expected to aggregate $160 million.
3. The (net) income tax rate (federal and state) is 40%.

The calculation is as follows:

$$\text{return on sales} = \frac{\text{net income}}{\text{net sales}}$$

wherein again,

$$\text{net income} = \text{gross margin} - \text{R\&D} - \text{income tax}$$

$$\text{income taxes} = (\text{gross margin} - \text{R\&D})\, 40\%$$

$$\text{gross margin} = \text{sales} \times 20\%$$

$$\text{ROS} = 10\%$$

By substitution:

$$\text{net income} = \text{gross margin} - \text{R\&D} - (\text{gross margin} - \text{R\&D}) \times 40\%$$

$$\text{ROS} = \frac{\text{gross margin} - \text{R\&D} - (\text{gross margin} - \text{R\&D}) \times 40\%}{\text{sales}}$$

$$10\% = \frac{\$32,000,000 - \text{R\&D} - (32,000,000 - \text{R\&D})\, 0.40}{\$160,000,000}$$

Simplify:

$$0.10 = \frac{\$32,000,000,000 - R\&D - \$12,800,000 + 0.40\ R\&D}{\$160,000,000}$$

$$\$16,000,000 = \$19,200,000 - 0.6\ R\&D$$

$$0.6\ R\&D = \$19,200,000 - \$16,000,000$$

$$0.6\ R\&D = \$3,200,000$$

$$R\&D = \underline{\underline{\$5,333,333}}$$

Proof:

Sales	$160,000,000
Gross margin 20%	$ 32,000,000
Less: R&D	5,333,333
Margin before income taxes	26,666,667
Income taxes 40%	10,666,667
Net income	$ 16,000,000
Sales =	$160,000,000
ROS =	10%

(c) PROJECT RISK

As previously mentioned, one factor in determining how much should be spent on a given project is the risk of that project. Although it may be difficult to calculate risk, analysis (by the controller) may provide management with some sense of the *relative* risk. One approach is based on the logical assumptions that (a) risk increases as a company ventures into new markets and new products, and (b) risks also increase with time from the completion of R&D until product sales commence.[7] The concept is illustrated by the matrix in Figure 24-4, wherein the market objective and the time span are the factors of risk. The objective of a completed matrix is to graphically illustrate how relative risk for the planning year compares with the prior year, or how risks on R&D in one division compare with another or how one project may relate to another.

The steps in identifying the *relative* risk are these:

1. The various proposed R&D projects for each division or marketing group or the entity as a whole are grouped by market objective (new product in new market or new product in existing market, etc.) in order of risk.
2. The year when the product will be initially sold is estimated.
3. The proposed spending for each product having the same market objective is tabulated, as in Figure 24-5.

---

[7] For more details, see Richard A. Hafter and Robert C. Sparks, "Can You Evaluate Your R&D Spending?" *Management Accounting,* Jan. 1986, pp. 53–55.

Figure 24-4   Market Objective and Relative R&D Risk.

Increasing Risk ⟶

	Year				
	1	2	3	Beyond	Total
New Product in New Market					
New Product in Current Market					
Replacement Product in Current Market					
Improved Product in Current Market					
Total	___	___	___	___	___

(Increasing Risk — vertical axis label)

4. The results are summarized by market objective, translated to percent as in Figure 24-6.

As illustrated in Figure 24-6, 30% of the expenditures in planning year 1 (199R) are contemplated in the area of most risk—new products in new markets, as compared with only 5% in the market area deemed least risky.

The research director must judge how prudent such risk is, together with the return on assets for completing products, the total potential return, and so on.

Figure 24-5   Illustrative R&D Expenditures for a Market Objective—New Product, Current Market.

Health Care Division
PLANNED 199R R&D EXPENDITURES
MARKET OBJECTIVE: NEW PRODUCT IN CURRENT MARKET
(dollar amounts in thousands)

Project	Year of Initial Impact				
	199R	199S	199T	Beyond	Total
1	$140				$140
2	90				90
3		$ 80	$ 50	$30	160
4		60	40	10	110
5	___	___	30	10	40
Total	$230	$140	$120	$50	$540

Figure 24-6   Distribution of 199R Planned R&D by Market Objective and Year of Initial Impact.

Johnson Company
DISTRIBUTION OF 199R R&D EXPENDITURES
BY MARKET OBJECTIVE AND YEAR OF INITIAL COMMERCIAL IMPACT

Market Objective	Effective Year (%)				
	199R	199S	199T	Beyond	Total
New products in new market	30	20	10		60
New product in current market	15	10		5	30
Replacement product in current market . .	5				5
Improved product in current market	5	—	—	–	5
Total	55	30	10	5	100

24-13 THE DETAILED BUDGETING PROCEDURE

Having reviewed how the overall expenditures for R&D for a given year might be determined, some of the influences in determining what projects might be considered, and a couple of illustrations of a possible quantitative approach to judging the desirability of a given project, it might help to summarize a typical budgeting procedure and provide budgetary examples.

These are the steps that the research director might take, with the assistance of the controller or financial executive, in some phases:

1. Determine the total budget for the planning period. This may include the comparisons with some of the measures discussed earlier.

2. Review the individual projects. Select those deemed the more suitable and determine the total cost in some reasonable degree of detail, as in Figure 24-7. Some managements may want the "other expenses" broken down into more detail.

3. Determine each departmental budget, based on the project costs determined in step 2, and the necessary indirect expenses, as in Figure 24-8. This well may involve an iterative procedure as between project costs and total departmental budgets.

4. Summarize the project and departmental budgets to arrive at the proposed total R&D planning budget, as in Figure 24-9. Supporting this summary would be the project and departmental budgets.

5. Secure necessary approval of the R&D budget (board of directors, etc.). This should be regarded as approval in principle.

6. As specific projects are to begin, prepare a project budget request, with adjusted or updated data, if applicable, and secure *specific* budget approval.

7. Provide periodic control reports, comparing, as in Figure 24-10, actual project costs to date and cost to complete, with the budget, and comparing department actual costs with budget, as in Figure 24-11. In this latter case, costs are controlled by department, but not by project.

8. Take any necessary corrective action.

Figure 24-7 Summary Project Budget.

The Plastics Company
PROJECT BUDGETS
FOR PLANNING YEAR 199X
($ in thousands)

Dept.	Project	Project No.	Prior Year(s) Professional Labor Hours (100's)	Prior Year(s) Total Costs	Planning Year Professional Labor Hours (100's)	Professional Salaries	All Other Wages	Total Salaries and Wages	All Other Expenses	Total Costs	Future Years Costs	Estimated Total Cost
New Product Research												
102	Alkyd resin "Q"	1026	—	$ —	100	$ 300	$ 76	$ 376	$ 526	$ 902	$ 90	$ 992
102	Paint thinner "S"	1029	—	—	60	150	38	188	264	452	90	542
105	Melamine "P"	1057	—	—	100	250	65	315	457	772	—	772
105	Urea surface "L"	1059	65.6	2,624	80	120	30	150	215	365	—	2,989
107	Urea mold "N"	1073	—	—	140	350	90	440	618	1,058	180	1,238
109	Urea filler "R"	1095	91.0	546	460	960	240	1,200	1,740	2,940	—	3,486
	Subtotal		156.6	3,170	940	2,130	539	2,669	3,820	6,489	360	10,019
Product Improvement												
102	Alkyd dryer "K"	1028	—	—	60	138	55	193	267	460	—	460
102	Wet agent "T"	1022	—	—	40	52	13	65	90	155	—	155
107	Urea composite "U"	1072	—	—	20	37	15	52	75	127	—	127
107	Urea fast mold "Y"	1079	—	—	480	840	294	1,134	1,587	2,721	—	2,721
109	Phenolic resin "Z"	1091	—	—	180	365	106	471	660	1,131	450	1,581
214	Adhesive "D"	2143	—	—	80	320	104	424	590	1,016	110	1,126
	Subtotal		—	—	860	1,750	587	2,339	3,271	5,610	560	6,170

Manufacturing Service

102	Anti-caker	102M	—	—	40	60	30	90	128	218	—	218
105	Solvent remover	105M	—	—	20	35	12	47	69	116	—	116
112	Anti-pollutant "K"	112M	—	—	60	120	45	165	247	412	—	412
	Subtotal		—	—	120	215	87	302	444	746	—	746
Sales Service												
216	Product storage	216S	—	—	20	30	12	42	59	101	—	101
219	Curing rate—#7	219S	—	—	60	110	40	150	221	371	—	472
	Subtotal		—	—	80	140	52	192	280	472	—	472
Fundamental Research												
301	Reflective surfaces	3012	—	—	100	200	70	270	380	650	—	650
303	Hardening compounds	3033	—	—	160	240	80	320	460	780	—	780
	Subtotal		—	—	260	440	150	590	840	1,930	—	1,430
	Grant total R&D project budget		156.6	$3,170	2260	$4,677	$1,415	$6,092	$8,655	$14,747	$920	$18,837

Figure 24-8   Departmental Planning Budget (Dept. 102).

The Plastics Company
DEPARTMENT 102—TOLEDO—R&D BUDGET
PLANNING YEAR 199X

Item	Total Professional Labor Hours (100's)	Professional Salaries	All Other(2) Costs	Budget Total
Projects				
New Project Research				
Alkyd resin "Q"	100	$300,000	$ 602,000	$ 902,000
Paint thinner "S"	60	150,000	302,000	452,000
Subtotal	160	450,000	904,000	1,354,000
Product Improvement				
Alkyd dryer "K"	60	138,000	322,000	460,000
Wet agent "T"	40	52,000	103,000	155,000
Subtotal	100	190,000	425,000	615,000
Manufacturing Service				
Anti-caker	40	60,000	158,000	218,000
Total projects	300	$700,000	$1,487,000	$2,187,000
Administrative Expenses				
General				290,000
Library				46,000
Research associates ..				12,000
Total administrative(1)				348,000
Grand total budget				$2,535,000

Notes:
(1) **Ratio of indirect to project costs**   16%
(2) **Other Costs:** Salaries and wages $ 212,000
                  Fringe benefit costs   84,800
                  Supplies   210,000
                  All others   980,200
                                            $1,487,000

24-14 OTHER CONTROL METHODS

As previously explained, the *control* phase of the budgeting process consists of comparing actual expenses and budgeted expenses for the indirect or administrative type expenses of the R&D function. Project direct expenses also could be judged in the same fashion. But it makes more sense, in this latter case, to compare estimated total expenses to complete the project—a continuous or monthly updating process—with the project budget. In this manner, if it appears that expenses are going over budget, perhaps steps can be taken to reduce some of the anticipated costs. Budgetary control

Figure 24-9 Summary R&D Budget.

The Plastics Company
SUMMARY BUDGET FOR R&D
PLANNING YEAR 199X
(dollars in thousands)

Item	Year 199X Professional Labor Hours (100's)	Professional Salaries	Total Expense	Estimated Current Year Costs
Project Costs by Category				
Fundamental research	260	$ 440	$ 1,430	$ 1,220
New-product research	940	2,130	6,489	5,200
Product improvement development	860	1,752	5,610	5,080
Manufacturing services	120	215	746	750
Sales service	80	140	472	460
Total direct project costs/hrs.	2,260	$4,677	$14,747	$12,710
Administrative				
General administration			580	520
Department administration ...			1,160	1,040
Libraries			120	110
Patent activity			240	170
Other			110	90
Total administrative			2,210	1,930
Grand total			$16,957	$14,640
Ratio indirect to project costs ...			15%	15%

probably is the most widely used method of monitoring expense trends, and correcting over-budget conditions.

In some instances, performance standards also may be used to control costs—or to supplement budgetary control. While many phases of the R&D effort are varied and not easily subject to measurement, there are circumstances where performance standards may be useful in evaluating some of the quantitative phases of the work. Some suggested performance standards for those functions that are repetitive and perhaps voluminous include:

- Number of tests per employee, per month.
- Number of formulas developed per labor-week.
- Cost per patent application.
- Cost per operating hour (pilot plant or lab).
- Number of requisitions filled per worker, per month (lab supply room).
- Number of pages of patent applications created per man-day.
- Cost per professional man-hour of total research or departmental expense.

Figure 24-10 Project Budget Status Report.

The Plastics Company
PROJECT BUDGET STATUS REPORT
FOR THE PERIOD ENDED MARCH 31, 199X
(dollars in thousands)

Project	Project No.	Current Month Labor Hours (100's)	Total Costs	Cumulative Year to Date Labor Hours (100's)	Costs	Purchase Order Commitments	Estimated Cost to Complete Labor Hours (100's)	Costs	Prior Year Labor Hours (100's)	Costs	Indicated Project Total Costs	Budget	Indicated Cost (over) Under Budget
New Product Research													
Alkyd resin "Q"	1026	8.33	$ 72	25	$ 220	$ 4	75	$ 693	—	—	$ 917	$ 992	$ 75
Paint thinner "S"	1029	5.00	4	15	112	—	45	433	—	—	545	542	(3)
Melamine "P"	1057	8.50	66	25	197	8	75	565	—	—	770	772	2
Urea surface "L"	1059	6.67	31	20	89	7	55	2,880	65.6	$2,624	5,600	5,613	13
Urea mold "N"	1073	11.67	93	35	271	12	105	932	—	—	1,215	1,238	23
Urea filler "R"	1095	38.33	245	115	742	83	350	2,808	91.0	546	4,179	4,032	(147)
Subtotal		78.50	511	235	1,631	114	705	8,311	156.6	3,170	13,226	13,189	(37)
Product Improvement													
Alkyd dryer "K"	1028	5.00	38	15	117	12	45	320	—	—	449	460	11
Wet agent "T"	1022	3.33	12	10	36	7	30	110	—	—	153	155	2
Urea composite "Z"	1072	1.67	10	5	30	2	15	98	—	—	130	127	(3)
Urea fast mold "Y"	1079	40.00	229	120	697	47	360	2,066	—	—	2,810	2,721	(89)
Phenolic resin "Z"	1091	15.00	90	45	280	31	135	1,259	—	—	1,570	1,581	—
Adhesive "O"	2143	6.67	81	20	250	14	60	862	—	—	1,126	1,126	—
Subtotal		71.67	460	215	1,410	113	645	4,715	—	—	6,238	6,170	(68)

Manufacturing Service												
Anti-caker	102M	3.33	18	10	54	2	30	154	—	—	210	218	8
Solvent remover	105M	1.67	9	5	30	1	15	85	—	—	116	116	—
Anti-pollutant "K"	112M	5.00	35	15	101	12	45	300	—	—	415	412	(3)
Subtotal		10.00	62	30	185	15	90	541	—	—	741	746	5
Sales Service												
Product storage	216S	1.67	6	5	27	2	15	71	—	—	100	101	1
Curing rate #7	219S	5.00	31	15	90	6	45	284	—	—	380	371	(9)
Subtotal		6.67	37	20	117	8	60	355	—	—	480	472	(8)
Fundamental Research												
Reflective surfaces	3012	8.33	57	25	155	7	75	491	—	—	653	650	(3)
Hardening compounds	3033	13.33	64	40	192	6	120	579	—	—	777	780	3
Subtotal		21.66	121	65	347	13	195	1,070	—	—	1,430	1,430	—
Grand total—project budgets		188.50	$1,221	565	$3,690	$263	1,695	$14,992	156.6	$3,170	$22,115	$22,007	$(108)

Figure 24-11 Summary of Actual and Budgeted Technical Division Expense by Departments.

ACE MANUFACTURING COMPANY		BUDGET REPORT					
MONTH October		DEPT. HEAD R.R. Jones DEPARTMENT TECHNICAL DIVISION NO.					

DESCRIPTION	CURRENT MONTH			YEAR TO DATE		
	BUDGET	ACTUAL	(OVER)/UNDER	BUDGET	ACTUAL	(OVER)/UNDER
SUMMARY OF TECHNICAL DIVISION EXPENSE BY DEPARTMENTS						
RESEARCH & DEVELOPMENT						
901 Aluminum	$ 5,327	$ 5,195	$ 132	$ 29,129	$ 28,073	$1,056
902 Plastic	1,959	1,752	207	11,165	10,583	583
903 Rubber	3,074	3,246	(172)	16,454	16,333	121
904 Other Metals	3,169	2,815	354	16,941	16,090	851
TECHNICAL SERVICE						
911 Automotive	870	757	113	4,800	4,510	290
913 Aircraft	1,285	1,162	123	7,196	6,718	478
914 Boats	1,120	1,257	(137)	6,870	6,675	195
917 Military	1,573	1,444	129	8,293	8,075	218
918 Appliances - Small	1,194	1,162	32	6,996	6,823	173
OTHER						
920 General	129	129	-	1,527	1,527	-
930 Pilot Plant	9,587	9,587	-	55,455	54,369	1,086
945 Patents	6,355	6,941	(586)	38,130	38,557	(427)
949 Chicago Project	21,424	20,716	708	72,198	69,621	2,577
950 Library	752	752	-	752	752	-
TOTAL DEPARTMENT PERFORMANCE	$ 57,818	$ 56,915	$ 903	$ 275,906	$ 268,706	$7,200
PER CENT (OVER)/UNDER BUDGET			1.6%			2.7%

ISSUED BY THE ACCOUNTING DEPT. November 14

- Supply cost per man-hour.
- Pounds of production per hour (pilot plant).

The knowledge of the research staff should be used in devising useful perf mance standards and in gathering relevant data. This is another chance for the joint fort of R&D staff members and accountants. Of course, just because the repetit operations are within standard, the conclusion should not be reached that the R&D tivities are well-managed—such a condition indicates only that the measured ope tions are within acceptable limits.

24-15 THE EFFECTIVENESS OF R&D EFFORT

Management has often asked, and still asks, "Are the R&D expenditures worthwhile?" or "Is the company research effective?" Questions such as these do not relate to budgetary performance or performance standard results. Rather, they go to the heart of the contribution that the R&D activity, or segments of it, makes to the economic well-being of the company.

Some research efforts, such as basic research, are difficult to measure because no specific or direct objective is discernible. But the reason for some projects is clearly economic, such as the discovery of a cheaper manufacturing process or a new product. For these, a kind of measurement is possible.

Some economic measures or indices that the accountant might suggest, or perhaps assist in developing, include these:

- *For a Lower Cost Manufacturing Process.* The savings over 1–5 years vs. the development expense.
- *For a New Product.*
  - —The operating profit of the product over X years as compared to the cost of development.
  - —Rate of return on new products (DCF).
  - —An index of market share:

$$\frac{\text{sales}}{\text{market potential}}$$

  - —An index of share of sales from new products:

$$\frac{\text{sales of new products}}{\text{total sales}}$$

- *For Improved Products.*
  - —The operating profit from the estimated additional sales over X years vs. the development cost.
  - —Some of the ratios or measures suggested above for new products can be adapted for improved products.

The effectiveness of R&D effort is principally the responsibility of the executive in charge of such activity. With the high level of foreign competition, in those instances where research and development is a critical success factor for the business, the process of benchmarking may be a means of increasing R&D productivity. Although this method has been used extensively with regard to manufacturing and marketing functions, it can be applied also to R&D activity. As discussed in Chapter 19, benchmarking is the measuring of a company's functions against those of companies considered to be the best in their class, and the initiation of actions to improve the activity under review.

In the event the controller is asked for advice regarding the application of benchmarking in R&D activities, he/she should be aware that the process has been a factor in creating (for the R&D function) the following benefits in some companies:

- Significant acceleration of the time-to-market for new products and new processes.

- Assistance in transferring technology from the R&D organization to the business unit involved (an operating division or subsidiary).

- Identification and definition of the core R&D technologies needed to support the companies' planned long-term growth.

- Help with the companies' efforts to tap global technical resources.

- Assistance in evaluating research project selection.

- Improvement in cross-functional participation in many R&D projects.

A review of the relevant articles in the Selected References may provide some useful ideas for the R&D executive as well as the controller.

Finally, in judging the effectiveness of product development, a broad business viewpoint must be considered—not merely the R&D project and/or revenue calculated for budget purposes. Management must allow for the right combination or trade-offs between cost, time, and performance requirements. This is where the financial executive, and especially the controller, can be of assistance to other management in the periodic evaluation of product development projects. Increasingly, the controller is a member of the "stage gate" group that monitors the progress of the project.[8]

The "stage-gate" system segregates a company's new-product process into a series of development stages. These stages are partitioned by a series of "gates" which are periodic check points for such matters as cost escalation, market changes, quality control, and other risks. Each project must meet certain criteria before it can pass through the gate and down the development path. The senior managers involved, as well as the financial executive, review progress as the product approaches its market launch. Typically, in the early development phase, accurate information is lacking and financial risk is low. As the project reaches a critical point, a detailed financial analysis is desirable. The controller's department, or CFO, integrates financial analysis, technical analysis, and manufacturing and marketing plans. Revealed are sales forecasts, prices, profit margins, and possibly impact of a discontinued project. The end result is said to be more efficient development operation, more new product successes, and a more flexible cost latitude (e.g., recognizing the time factor in the product success).

The stage-gate system offers a strong role for finance, but also provides sometimes beneficial cost-time trade-offs and plan changes for the product developers.

24-16 SELECTED REFERENCES

Anderson, Lane K., "Recovering the Costs of R&D," *Management Accounting,* Jan. 1994, pp. 45–48.

Anderson, Richard E., "Can Stage-Gate Systems Deliver the Goods?" *Financial Executive,* Nov./Dec. 1993, pp. 34–37.

---

[8] See the article "Can Stage-Gate Systems Deliver the Goods?" by Richard E. Anderson, as listed in the Selected References.

Chambers, John C., Robert L. Emerald, and Albert Rubenstein, "Coupling Corporate Strategy and R&D Planning," *Managerial Planning,* May–June 1985, pp. 35–37, 42–49.

Collier, Donald W., "Linking Business and Technology Strategy," *Planning Review,* Sept. 1985, pp. 28–35, 44.

Elmer-Dewitt, Philip, "Don't Tread on My Lab," *Time,* Jan. 24, 1994, pp. 44–45.

Faltermayer, Edmund, "Invest or Die," *Fortune,* Feb. 22, 1993, pp. 42–52.

Gross, Neil, John Carey, and Joseph Weber, "Who Says Science Has to Pay Off Fast?" *Business Week,* Mar. 21, 1994, pp. 110–111.

Hafter, Richard A., and Robert C. Sparks, "Can You Evaluate Your R&D Spending?" *Management Accounting,* Jan. 1986, pp. 53–55.

Iansiti, Marco, "Real-World R&D: Jumping the Product Generation Gap," *Harvard Business Review,* May/June 1993, pp. 138–147.

"Innovation in America," *Business Week,* Special 1989 Bonus Issue, June 16, 1989.

Kirsch, Robert J., and Sachi Sakthivel, "Capitalize or Expense?" *Management Accounting,* Jan. 1993, pp. 38–43.

Krause, Irv, and John Liu, "Benchmarking R&D Productivity," *Planning Review,* Jan./Feb. 1993, pp. 16–21, 52–53.

Roussel, Philip A., "Cutting Down the Guesswork in R&D," *Harvard Business Review,* Sept.–Oct. 1983, pp. 154–160.

Schmitt, Ronald W., "Successful Corporate R&D," *Harvard Business Review,* May–June 1985, pp. 124–128.

CHAPTER 25

Financial Planning and Control in a Service Company

25-1 INTRODUCTION

"Service" businesses have grown rapidly over the past 20 years and now are believed t[o] represent a greater percent of U.S. jobs and GDP than does the manufacturing sector o[f] the economy. This growth is expected to continue as more companies understand th[e] variety of services that can be provided. Some of these services are new, for exampl[e] on-line databases. Others are specialized business services that can be supplie[d] cheaper than being done in-house, for example, cleaning services, payroll processin[g,] security, travel arrangements. Finally there are the traditional service organization[s] like bankers, brokerage houses, legal firms, advertising agencies, accountants, insu[r]ance companies, etc., that have shown steady growth as the economy expanded.

Much of what exists in literature on the financial planning and control of bus[i]ness has been prepared within the context of a manufacturing organization. But muc[h] of what pertains to the nonproduction aspects of a manufacturing business is also a[p]plicable to a service business. The considerations that a controller must address rela[-]tive to the selling, development and general and administrative expenses are the sam[e] in both kinds of businesses. And while certain ratios and relationships may be diffe[r]ent, the problems related to the planning and control of cash, accounts receivable, fixe[d] assets, investments, long- and short-term debt, etc., are similar. That leaves as a majo[r] area of difference only the planning and control of the "direct" cost of providing the services and the proper assignment of costs to the cost objective—the specific type of service, the insurance policy size group, or the contract, etc.

The objective of all businesses is to grow and prosper and thus optimize or maximize, over the longer term, the economic return to the owners. To do that, and perhaps even to survive, it is necessary to have information available that will give a company the ability to analyze and understand where revenue is coming from, what costs were incurred to produce that revenue, and what other costs and expenses the business has incurred. Using this information, unsatisfactory profit performance can be identified and an analysis made to understand the reasons for poor results and what can be done to improve things. Satisfactory profit performance can also be analyzed to understand the reasons for good results and what can be done to expand those areas. Finally, trends can be monitored on a regular basis to identify emerging problems easily and quickly.

But to perform these essential analyses, the controller must define the level of detail that is to be recorded in the accounting system. Each firm will require data based on its unique circumstances including its organization structure, but at a minimum the following segregation should be made as to the elements of:

- Product/service.
- Contract/customer.

25-2 ORGANIZATIONAL CONSIDERATIONS

As the controller prepares to exercise his responsibilities in a service company he must understand the company's organization so that he can institute a system of control based on responsibility. In its simplest form, if the business is structured by office or area, then office or area should be the primary income/expense/profit/investment center. If the structure is by contract, then contract profit should be the primary control point. Figure 25-1 depicts an office-oriented organization (geographic) and Figure 25-2, a contract-oriented one (major activity).

In these examples a manager usually would be assigned responsibility for the production of income either for a geographic territory or for a major contract. There are many variations on these alternatives and each company has to make its own determination.

Figure 25-1 Organization by Office.

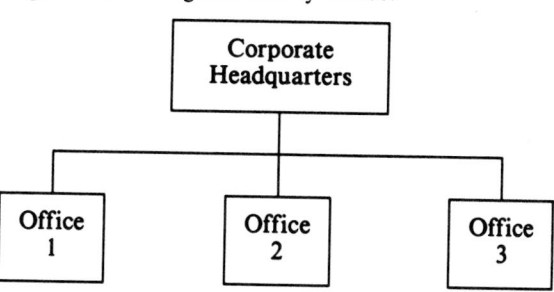

Figure 25-2   Organization by Contract.

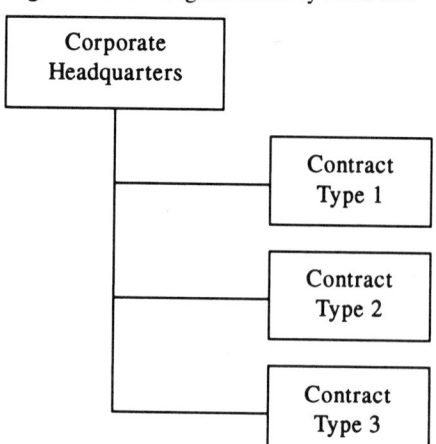

25-3 DATA CLASSIFICATION

After understanding the primary responsibility points in the company organization the controller must next oversee an intelligent series of accounts to record and control the specific aspects of the business. This account structure will become the business language of the firm and can influence employee motivation and actions, company culture, and operating results.

The first set of judgments in assembling a schedule of accounts is what revenue will be brought into the firm and what segregation of it is needed to understand and run the business. Taking a legal firm as an example, revenue might be anticipated from:

- Real estate transactions.
- Preparation of wills.
- Divorces.

All revenue would then be recorded into one of these three categories. If the firm subsequently handled other matters, then new revenue accounts would be opened up as needed.

It is also usually of interest in a law firm to know which lawyer is generating revenue for the firm and so that information would also be captured.

The final important segregation of revenue would be by client. This information is essential for billing and for client relations. Therefore in a typical law firm the recording of revenue would be:

- By office (if more than one).
- By lawyer.
- By matter (wills, etc.).
- By client.

It is easy to then summarize revenue into these four totals. It is also possible to re-sort it using any combination of these categories.

As another example, in an advertising agency the revenue is derived from individual clients' placing advertisements in various media. The first segregation of revenue then would probably be by client. Further information relative to what media is used is also considered important, so additional segregation might be required for:

- Newspaper.
- Magazine.
- Television.
- Radio.
- Billboard.
- Flyer.

The recording could be further segregated into campaigns and products if more than one of each is expected to occur. So in this example of an ad agency, revenue would be recorded:

- By client.
- By product/campaign.
- By media (magazines, etc.).

A different example of revenue segregation is that usually found in a bank operation. In this instance the organizational responsibility is usually by business area, e.g., bank credit cards, international loans, retail (branch office) operations, and investment trusts. The primary identification of revenue would be into these categories. A second segregation could be geographic, i.e., by country, by city, by office. As in the previous examples the data can be sorted into any combination to allow reporting and analysis by responsibility.

To repeat, capturing the revenue by key element or activity is essential to being able to understand what is happening in each individual business and to allow sorting and combining of data into useful information available for analysis.

25-4 COST OF SERVICES; ACTIVITY-BASED COSTING

While it is relatively easy to plan and record revenue after the appropriate categories and segregations have been determined, it is sometimes difficult to identify the costs planned and/or incurred to earn the various classifications of revenue. It is obvious that people have been paid, materials and supplies purchased, and facilities acquired and used by the employees of the company. The task of accumulating and assigning these expenditures to the revenue they generated is the responsibility of the controller and to do so, some kind of cost accounting system must be used.

Each type of service business has its own peculiarities—which the controller must learn to identify in developing the proper planning and control system. But the same basic principle applies to each—the need for an activity-based costing system.

This is discussed in Chapter 6 and can provide guidance for service as well as manufacturing businesses.

In implementing activity-based costing, a difficulty may arise in some service businesses. Most internal operating expenses are employee-related. But the nature of the job is such that the employees must work on multiple activities, so it is often difficult to isolate employee time devoted to specific activities. Moreover, activity time may vary greatly by different product and customer, and so on. Given the need for activity-based costing, and the variability of the task, it may be desirable to *test sample* the operations in arriving at the proper cost assignment.

Finally, because of the multiple tasks performed by the employees, and the changes over time in the nature of many service businesses, it may be useful to establish expense performance benchmarks so that the appropriate resources are applied to each task.

25-5 COST ACCOUNTING IN A SERVICE ORGANIZATION

In a manufacturing environment a key distinction in cost accounting is the difference between a product cost and a period cost. Product costs are defined as all those things that are necessary to produce the product and, generally speaking, they all become part of inventory value to be subsequently matched against the revenue they produce. All other items are considered period expenses and are charged against income as they are incurred. Examples of product cost are direct factory labor, direct materials, and other factory overhead costs. Examples of period expenses are research and development expense, marketing expense, and administrative and general expenses.

In a service organization, there is no product produced, all costs have the characteristics of period expenses, and no inventory is accumulated in the balance sheet as an asset. The direct work done produces revenue in the same period the work is performed, for example, legal work, cleaning services, security. Therefore, the cost of revenue becomes more a classification issue than an accumulation and/or deferral issue. However, a cost accounting system is needed to classify all appropriate activities into the correct cost of revenue accounts. Reliable cost information is used by management to:

* Plan the service areas or categories.
* Provide input for pricing purposes.
* Control cost levels.
* Analyze profitability.
* Identify cost reduction opportunities.

There is not much guidance around to help develop such a system, but many of the concepts used in manufacturing cost accounting have applicability to cost-of-service accounting.

Several exceptions to using manufacturing costing techniques are:

* Many of the costs in a service company are "fixed" over the short term. So the traditional distinction of variable costs is generally not as useful in a service business.

- Materials are not a significant item in the delivery of a service (except in businesses like retailing and restaurants), so it is not necessary to have a comprehensive procedure to identify and record their receipt and utilization.

Having eliminated materials as an important factor, we can now examine what elements should be included in a service company's cost accounting system.

(a) "DIRECT" LABOR

The primary cost of providing a service is the salary and related expenses of the people who are performing the service. These are the "direct" expenses of a service business. In order to identify the direct cost of revenue, it is necessary to capture the time worked by the "direct" people in the same classifications as revenue is recorded. This is accomplished by having the direct personnel keep track of their time and report it to the accounting department. This reporting is so fundamental to an effective information (and billing) system that many firms use the time reports to also initiate paychecks. If someone does not submit a time report, their pay is delayed. These reports generally are prepared and processed each day to ensure accuracy (and also spread processing work over a longer period, thereby eliminating or minimizing the last-minute rush often associated with such an operation).

Again, circumstances may dictate variations as to how often and even how time is to be reported. In instances where people are permanently assigned to the same contract or work effort, (e.g, an advertising campaign), then weekly reporting might be an acceptable procedure. In cases where people are usually assigned to the same effort but may occasionally be used somewhere else, then daily exception reporting could be the most effective way to report.

A system should then assign the individuals' pay rate to the hours reported by contract or matter and develop a "cost" of these items by individual. This rate can be either an actual rate by individual or a standard rate by job classification or grouping. This data would be recorded in the cost accounts using the same classification as the revenue accounts discussed earlier.

(b) OTHER DIRECT EXPENSES

In addition to keeping track of the time expended by revenue category, it is also necessary to identify other "direct" expenses by the same categories. These other direct expenses are those that are incurred for a specific client or a contract. They can be identified as ordered or incurred as pertaining to a defined accumulation point and so recorded. Examples are:

- Services procured (e.g., printing).
- Materials purchased (e.g., cleaning supplies).
- Travel expenses incurred.

As these expenses are incurred they should be recorded using the same classifications and subclassifications as the revenue that they were incurred to produce.

(c) ALLOCATED EXPENSES

While time and direct expenses are easily identified to specific revenue, there are other expenses that are incurred that, like factory overhead, are necessary to the delivery of a service but are not directly attributable to any specific contract or customer. These items must be assigned or allocated.

(i) Direct (or Proximate) Overhead.
The first segregation of these allocated expenses should be those attributable to the "direct" workers and might be called "direct" or "proximate" overhead. Such items would include:

- Employee benefits expense (of the direct workers).
- Office space (including lighting, heating, power, telephone, and mail costs).
- Use of desks and other office furniture and equipment.
- Use of a computer and other equipment, etc.
- Nonbillable time (e.g., time spent at education, meetings).

These expenses would be first attributed to each direct worker and then assigned to the project that the employee spent his/her time on in direct proportion as the time was spent. In other words, using traditional manufacturing cost accounting terminology, the first "overhead" pools to be used would be those that directly supported the direct labor of the services delivered. These pools would probably be charged to the cost of revenue based on the hours of direct labor.

(ii) Indirect (or Remote) Overhead.
This overhead pool would include all other expenses associated with the production of revenue, but not as directly as the direct pool. It would include such things as a share of secretarial expense, a share of accounting expense, a share of direct supervision expense, etc. It would not include research and development, selling, and general and administrative expenses nor would it include shares of other income and other expenses. These latter expenses may subsequently be apportioned to revenue categories or offices or contracts to develop a net profit amount, but they will not be entered into the cost accounting system nor used in determining gross profit amounts and margins.

To summarize, the cost of service revenue is to be determined using a cost accounting system that will accumulate and assign to all classes and subclasses of revenue those expenses incurred in direct performance of the service, i.e., labor, purchased services and materials and directly identifiable support activities.

The objective of the above is to produce a statement of gross income, cost and gross profit that gives management a reliable and understandable view of the business. Such a statement prepared in accordance with the above guidelines might look like that in Figures 25-3 and 25-4.

With the information developed in Figure 25-3, it is easy to then apportion the other operating expenses of the company to develop a complete statement of income and expense by primary cost objective (office, client, or service). (See Figure 25-4.)

These apportionments are usually made using very broad factors, such as percent of total revenue or percent of total direct head count. The result is that a responsible executive can see his gross and net contribution to the business and can include the

Figure 25-3   Statement of Gross Income, Cost, and Gross Profit.

Office/Product Identification	Total	Service A	Service B	Service C
Gross income				

Cost of gross income
  Direct labor
  Other direct expense
  Allocated expense—proximate pool
  Allocated expense—remote pool				

Total cost
  Gross profit
  Gross profit margin				

Figure 25-4   Example: Income and Expense Statement (Including Apportionment of General Expenses).

Office/Product Identification	Total	Service A	Service B	Service C
Total gross profit (from Statement of Gross Profit)				

Apportionments
  Selling expenses
  Development expenses
  General and administrative expenses				

Total apportioned expense				
Net income before taxes Income taxes Net income Margin				

apportioned values in the pricing algorithms. General management also can assess the relative performance of the segments of the company.

25-6 THE PLANNING SYSTEM

Having established an accounting system that will intelligently and fairly present the financial transactions of the business, the next step needed to manage and control it is an effective planning system. There seems to be more difficulty in nurturing the concepts of sound management in young service firms than in young manufacturing companies. Perhaps some of the reasons are:

- The founder is reluctant to delegate authority as the firm grows and needs decentralization.

- The creative people such as in an advertising agency, or the contentious peop[le] such as lawyers or accountants in professional organizations, have a great ind[i]viduality and like to make their own decisions in an unrestricted environment.

- The growth and success of the business in its early years resulted from the sum[?]mation of individual ideas and actions and no formal system of planning and co[n]trol was needed.

However if growth is to continue, a clearly defined and coordinated approach [?] steering the firm is required. The first logical step in this process is the preparation [of] an annual budget. The annual budget will represent a plan of action developed [?] agreed to by responsible managers. The budget should then become part of the fina[n]cial reporting system. Each month (or quarter) statements should be prepared that wi[ll] display period revenue and/or expenditures compared to budget and variances ident[i]fied as favorable or unfavorable. (See Figure 25-5.) The annual budget should also re[p]resent the tactical implementation of a long-range strategic plan.

(a) ANNUAL BUDGETS

(i) Sales Budget.

As with any other business, the sales plan in a service compan[y] is the foundation for the entire system of plans. Its preparation must be given all the a[t]tention required at all levels of the company. It will influence the human resource pla[n,] the facilities plan, the operating expenses plan, and the cash flow plan. The materi[al] covered in Chapter 20, "Planning and Control of Sales," applies, to a great deal, to [a] service business and should be helpful to a service industry controller.

The responsibility for preparing the short-term sales plan is usually assigned [to] the individual responsible for the profit contribution of an office, contrac[t,] product/service, etc., working in conjunction with the chief sales executive (if there i[s] one). It is this individual who must acquire the knowledge to estimate potential futur[e] sales. In order to do this the executive must consider both internal and external ma[t]ters. The internal considerations include:

- Company growth objectives including expansion to new customers and services[.]
- Available resources; human, physical, and financial.
- Planned advertising, promotion, and public relations campaigns.
- Pricing actions.

The external considerations include:

- Competition (including price).
- Growth potential/demographics.
- Technological changes.
- General economic trends.

Chapter 20 also lists some sources of useful economic data. The controller's contribu[?]tion to the preparation of the annual sales plan, generally involves helping the respon[?]sible executives to identify and use good sources of information, to assist in sale[s]

Figure 25-5 Statement of Gross Income, Cost, and Gross Profit.

Office/Product Identification	Current Month		Year to Date		Variance ( ) = Unfavorable		Full Year
	Actual	Plan	Actual	Plan	C/M	YTD	Plan
Gross Income							
Service A							
Service B							
Service C							
Total							
Cost of Gross Income							
Service A							
Direct labor							
Other direct expense							
Allocated expense—proximate pool							
Allocated expense—remote pool							
Total cost							
Gross profit							
Gross profit margin							
Service B							
Direct labor							
Other direct expense							
Allocated expense—proximate pool							
Allocated expense—remote pool							
Total cost							
Gross profit							
Gross profit margin							
Service C							
Direct labor							
Other direct expense							
Allocated expense—proximate pool							
Allocated expense—remote pool							
Total cost							
Gross profit							
Gross profit margin							
Total gross profit							
Margin							
Apportionments							
Selling expenses							
Development expenses							
General & admin. expense							
Total apportioned expense							
Net income before taxes							
Income taxes							
Net income							
Margin							

analysis and perhaps most importantly to manage the budget process. This latter effo
will do the following:

a. Establish timing of budget input.

b. Define data input including the details required and definitional consistency.

c. Provide the necessary forms and worksheets to be prepared.

d. Verify or test the reliability of data and the calculations applied thereto.

e. Assemble and consolidate input for promulgation to other executives to be use
as the basis for preparing their annual budgets.

When the annual sales plan, has been approved (after an interactive process
change and modification), it is then necessary to establish a control track for the pla
period by breaking it into quarters and months. This important information will I
used to help control operations by comparing actual results to planned results and ide
tifying areas or items that require analysis and action. Figure 25-6 illustrates a conso
idated sales plan broken down by quarter and month. Each of the services (A, B, C)
the example is the responsibility of a separate executive and the annual sales plan w

Figure 25-6   A Consolidated Sales Plan by Period.

The Illustrative Company
SALES PLAN
19XX
(000s omitted)

	Total	Service A	Service B	Service C
January	$ 475	$ 100	$ 125	$ 250
February	475	110	125	240
March	470	110	125	235
1st quarter	1,420	320	375	725
April	470	110	125	235
May	480	115	125	240
June	495	120	125	250
2nd quarter	1,445	345	375	725
July	495	120	125	250
August	500	125	125	250
September	515	130	125	260
3rd quarter	1,510	375	375	760
October	535	130	125	280
November	535	130	125	280
December	565	140	125	300
4th quarter	1,635	400	375	860
Full year	$6,010	$1,440	$1,500	$3,070

developed, individually, by service. A format useful in the preparation of each service sales plan is shown in Figures 25-7 and 25-8.

Figure 25-7 reflects one service (A) and shows the expected revenue from all of the contracts that provide that service. The prior year and current year actuals are included for comparative purposes.

Figure 25-8, continuing the example, reflects the lowest level of sales budgeting and therefore the basic projections and decisions. It reflects a single contract for 12 months from August of the current year through July of the next year. The manager of this contract believes that it will be renewed with an upward price adjustment of 5% and expanded to include additional coverage. This projection was supported by analyses, approved by the executive responsible for Service A and so is included in the sales plan. Each other contract manager would prepare the same kind of estimate, review it with the executive responsible for the service and, when agreed to, it becomes his plan and commitment for the next year's sales.

(ii) Direct Labor Budget.   A detailed coverage of direct labor is covered in Chapter 22, "Planning and Control of Manufacturing Costs: Direct Material and Direct Labor." While the context of Chapter 22 is a manufacturing environment, the process of preparing a direct labor budget is generally applicable to a service company. In addition, Chapter 21, "Planning and Control of Marketing Expenses," provides examples of various types of budgets that have direct applicability to service company budgeting needs. Chapter 21 also describes various analyses, that is, by nature of expense, by functional operation, by manner of application, etc., that can be helpful in analyzing service company contracts, clients, offerings, etc. The reader interested in the planning and control of a service business is encouraged to review both chapters since much of the content will be useful to him or her. A brief summary of key points relative to planning labor costs follow.

The basic question is to determine the number and skill level of workers needed to provide the services included in the sales budget. The operating executive responsible for delivering the service has the primary responsibility for developing this

Figure 25-7   An Annual Sales Plan by Contract.

The Illustrative Company
SALES PLAN—SERVICE A
BY CONTRACT
19XX
(000s omitted)

	Actual		Plan
	Prior Year	Current Year	19XX
Contract 1	$400	$400	$400
Contract 2	—	200	200
Contract 3	—	150	410
Contract 4	—	—	430
Total	$400	$750	$1,440

Figure 25-8 A Sales Plan by Month.

The Illustrative Company
SALES PLAN—SERVICE A
CONTRACT 3
19XX
(000s omitted)

	Actual		
	Prior Year	Current Year	Plan 19XX
January	$—	$—	$ 30
February	—	—	30
March	—	—	30
April	—	—	30
May	—	—	30
June	—	—	30
July	—	—	30
August	—	30	40
September	—	30	40
October	—	30	40
November	—	30	40
December	—	30	40
Total	$—	$150	$410

estimate. The labor input must be assembled with a timing plan by contract and service. The controller should test-check the information to ensure its reasonableness and compatibility with the sales plan. The controller's cost accounting people can then estimate the cost of the labor by applying estimated pay rates to the estimated labor hours by skill category.

Using the sales plan for Service A, Contract 3, shown in Figure 25-8, the direct labor budget might be summarized as in Figure 25-9.

(iii) Other Costs of Services Budget. Chapter 23, "Planning and Control of Manufacturing Costs: Factory Expenses," describes how to identify, plan, control, and allocate overhead expenses in a manufacturing environment. Chapter 24, "Planning and Control of General and Administrative Expenses" describes the techniques used for nonmanufacturing items. Both chapters, along with previously mentioned Chapter 21, will be helpful in developing the annual budget for other costs of services.

As with the direct labor budget, other direct cost-of-service estimates should be prepared by the responsible manager and, after their compilation, be approved by the senior executive. The overhead items will probably first be assembled as administrative budgets by knowledgeable, responsible executives and then allocated to the various contracts/clients, etc., using the cost accounting system described earlier. The other direct costs and overhead budgets should also be prepared by month so that complete budget actual comparisons can be made on a regular, recurring basis.

Figure 25-9 A Direct Labor Budget by Month.

The Illustrative Company
SERVICE A—CONTRACT 3
DIRECT LABOR BUDGET
19XX
(000s omitted)

	Direct Labor Hours	Gross Cost
January	2,000	$ 20,000
February	2,000	20,000
March	2,000	20,000
April	2,000	20,000
May	2,000	20,000
June	2,000	20,000
July	2,000	20,000
August	2,500	26,250
September	2,500	26,250
October	2,500	26,250
November	2,500	26,250
December	2,500	26,250
	26,500	$271,250

Note: Assumptions: 25% increase in manpower when contract is renegotiated in August.
5% salary rate increase effective August 1.

(iv) Other Plans and Budgets. Important to the good management of all businesses are annual plans for financial condition and cash flows. Some service businesses pay scant attention to their statement of financial position since very often the only significant item on it is accounts receivable. However, almost all service businesses are concerned with their cash position and cash flow. It is therefore necessary to carefully develop an effective planning system to manage this important element. Such a system must include the development of a financial condition plan for both the full year and interim months.

The elements and techniques that are useful in establishing such plans are the same in all businesses; just the emphasis changes. In a manufacturing business, inventory and property, plant and equipment, are material, and significant attention is paid to those items. In a service business, cash and accounts receivable along with short-term debt usually are the matters that are significant and require emphasis and attention.

The point is that an effective planning system will include budgets for the statement of financial position as well as for the statement of operations. These two budgets can then be used to prepare a representative and reliable budgeted cash flow statement.

25-7 STRATEGIC PLANNING

Another most important step is the initiation of strategic planning. It is this technique that will identify growth opportunities, human resources needs and resources allocation requirements. Without strategic planning the average service company will drift aimlessly from one hot opportunity to another. The controller should recognize that much of the service business is dominated by one crucial characteristic: That is, once a day's utilization is lost, it is lost forever. The service, unlike products, cannot be stored in inventory; last night's empty hotel room is a lost asset forever. Therefore, profitability is heavily dependent on how effectively the marketing efforts achieve *high utilization;* and how effectively the company communicates its particular advantages to the customer.

All the prerequisites of long-range planning discussed in other sections of this book apply to the service firm; but the most important is the commitment of top management to the concept. The decision makers must be willing to support the effort with the necessary resources and their own time or the effort will fail.

The financial history of the firm can be observed and key ratios, trends, and comparisons developed through the use of prior and current period statements:

- Financial condition.
- Income and expense.
- Cash flows.

With this data as a starting point, future activities can be projected and analyzed. The strengths and weaknesses of the firm can be reviewed and appropriate goals and directions formulated. Some of the considerations that a service company should assess are:

- Image of the firm as perceived by clients and others.
- Quality of the work, product, location, and accessibility to customers.

In addition, the following factors should be addressed in developing the strategic plan.

- Who and where are the potential new clients/customers?
- What will be the source of new hires as they are needed?
- What governmental actions will impact the firm?
- What technological improvements can be expected?

25-8 SUMMARY

To effectively assist in the planning and control of a service business, the controller needs to do the following:

- Establish an effective recording and reporting system based on responsibility accounting.
- Develop an intelligent, practical, and flexible schedule of accounts.
- Install an information system that is responsive and timely. This would include at least general ledger, costing accounting, billing, and collection applications.

With the tremendous improvement in personal computers and the related software, a cost effective information system may include useful data beyond merely the routine financial data:

(a) *Real time* operating performance information, inventory data, etc.

(b) Selected information as regards:

- Quality control.

- Customer satisfaction (e.g., on time deliveries, etc.)

- Customer marketing information, e.g., trends in the market; affluence, age, work behavior.

(c) Complex analyses of sales and marketing effort expenses. (See Chapters 20 and 21.)

See also Part Six, Computer Systems and Related Technology.

- Implement a *planning* system that includes annual plans and strategic plans expressed in financial terms.

- Periodically review the control reports comparing actual vs. planned performance to assure that the operating executives are receiving the required data and are satisfied with the reporting system.

25-9 SELECTED REFERENCES

Allen, Michael G., "Competitive Confrontation in Consumer Services," *Planning Review*, Jan./Feb. 1989, pp. 4–8, 46.

Browne, Jim, *Management and Analysis of Service Operations*, New York: North-Holland, 1984.

Crane, Michael, and John Meyer, "Focusing on True Costs in a Service Organization," *Management Accounting*, Feb. 1993, pp. 41–45.

Dearden, John, "Cost Accounting Comes to Service Industries," *Harvard Business Review*, Sept.–Oct. 1978, p. 132.

Fitzsimmons, James A., and Robert S. Sullivan, *Service Operations Management*, New York: McGraw-Hill, 1982.

Gagnan, Christopher E., and James Brian Quinn, "Will Services Follow Manufacturing into Decline?" *Harvard Business Review*, Nov.–Dec. 1986, p. 95.

Heskett, James L., *Managing In the Service Economy*, Boston: Harvard Business School Press, 1986.

Heskett, J. T., "Thank Heaven for the Service Sector," *Business Week*, Jan. 22, 1987, p. 22.

National Association of Accountants, "Statement on Management Accounting No. 4B—Allocation of Service and Administrative Costs."

Wentz, Daniel, "How We Match Costs and Revenue in a Service Business," *Management Accounting*, Oct. 1985, pp. 36–42.

CHAPTER 26

Planning and Control of General and Administrative Expenses and Financial Expenses

26-1 FUNCTIONS INVOLVED

The category of expenses known as general and administrative (G&A) expense relates primarily to the costs of the various top management functions at the headquarters level (or possibly those of a division or other large segment) having to do with overall policy determination, and direction of the entity. The typical medium-sized to large company would include these departments:

1. Office of chairman of the board.

2. Office of the president.

3. Financial organization:

  a. Office of the chief financial officer.

  b. Controller's department:

  (i)   Office of the controller.
  (ii)   Accounting department.
  (iii) Tax department.
  (iv) Financial planning and control.
  (v)   Financial information systems.
 c. Treasurer's department:
  (i)   Office of the treasurer.
  (ii)   Cash administration.
  (iii) Risk management (insurance).
  (iv) Retirement plan investments.
 d. Office of the chief internal auditor:
  (i)   Financial auditing.
  (ii)   Systems auditing.
  (iii) Special reviews.
4. Legal department:
 a. Office of vice-president-legal.
 b. Office of corporate secretary.
 c. Litigation.
 d. SEC relations.
 e. Patents and trademarks.
5. Corporate offices for the direction and control of these major functions:
 a. Marketing.
 b. Manufacturing.
 c. Research and development.
 d. Human resources.
 e. Management information systems.
 f. Public relations.
 g. Strategic planning.

To the extent that the purpose of the preceding departments or organization units have to do with the overall policy determination, planning, direction, and control, they probably would be classified as G&A in the annual report to shareholders. Comparable expenses at the division or subsidiary level might or might not be so classified (although the methods of planning and control would be similar to those for the corporate activity).

26-2 CATEGORIES OF EXPENSE

The usual departmental operating expenses would include these classifications:

- Salaries and wages.
- Fringe benefits.

- Travel and entertainment.
- Telecommunications.
- Repairs and maintenance.
- Rent.
- Dues and subscriptions.
- Utilities.
- Purchased services.
- Depreciation.
- Insurance.
- Allocated expenses.
- Other.

In addition to these "usual" expenses, there are "special" types not found in the normal operating department, but that are essential to the corporate or business existence, that are needed for control or accountability purposes:

- Incentive pay.
- Director fees and expenses.
- Outside legal fees.
- Audit fees.
- Corporate expenses (registration fees, etc.).
- Charitable contributions.
- Consultant fees.
- Gain or loss on sale of assets.
- Cash discounts.
- Provision for doubtful accounts.

The chapter title includes the phrase "financial expenses," and these are intended to be those often in the "other income and expense" section of the income statement:

- Interest expense.
- Nonrecurring gains or losses.
- Amortization of bond discount.

In some accounting systems these items may be treated as financial department expenses for the purposes of planning and control.

26-3 ACCOUNTING FOR, AND ALLOCATION OF, ADMINISTRATIVE EXPENSES

The controller is responsible for developing and maintaining an accounting system that serves, among others, the following purposes:

- Permits the reporting of expenses for external purposes in accordance with generally accepted accounting principles.

- Allows the accumulation of costs by natural expense category in such a way as to facilitate planning and control.

- Accumulates costs on a "responsibility" basis so that a specific individual may be assigned responsibility for the planning and control of the costs.

- Where appropriate, permits the allocation of expenses on some acceptable basis, such as benefits received, to cost objects—which might include divisions or cost centers or products that use the service.

- Gives due weight to internal control concerns.

Methods of allocation, and when costs should be allocated, are of special concern in the planning and control of costs. A basic tenet for responsibility accounting is that expenses should not be allocated to a department unless the supervisor can exercise control over such costs. This subject is reviewed in the next section.

26-4 IMA GUIDE ON ALLOCATION OF SERVICE AND ADMINISTRATIVE EXPENSES—SMA NO. 4B

In the context of sound planning and control, the controller, or budget director, must consider whether allocation of general and administrative expenses, or portion of them, serves any useful purpose. An authoritative statement on this subject is that published by the Institute of Management Accountants (IMA), known as Statement on Management Accounting No. 4B—Allocation of Service and Administrative Costs. In view of its importance, the statement is reproduced here in its entirety except for the annotated bibliography.[1]

Introduction

1. This Statement is intended to help management accountants deal with problems associated with the allocation of service and administrative costs. It is the position of the Institute of Management Accountants (IMA) that allocations are appropriate in certain circumstances and that some approaches to allocating these costs are superior to others. A summary of IMA recommendations may be found in paragraphs 33–37.

2. The allocation of service and administrative costs is of concern to operating executives as well as to management accountants because these costs often are substantial and have a significant impact on segment profitability, product cost finding, government contract pricing, and the valuation of assets.

3. Problems in allocating service and administrative costs have been highlighted by recent court cases, often in situations involving rate-regulated industries. The decisions of the courts are a reflection of common and case law. They lack consistency with regard to the allocation of corporate costs to cost objectives.

---

[1] As published in *Management Accounting*, Sept. 1985, pp. 55–59. Reprinted with permission.

4. Under various circumstances, some or all of the elements of service and administrative costs are allocated to cost objects. This Statement suggests the circumstances under which these costs should be allocated and the methods of allocation that are appropriate in each of these circumstances.

Statement Scope

5. Costs assigned to a given cost object are either direct costs or indirect costs of that cost object. A cost item is a direct cost if it can be identified specifically with a cost object in an economically feasible manner. A direct cost, therefore, is a cost that is assigned directly to a cost object.

   A cost item is an indirect cost if it cannot be identified specifically with a cost object in an economically feasible manner. An indirect cost is allocated to the applicable cost objects on some reasonable basis. This Statement is limited to allocated costs.

6. There are two types of cost allocations: (a) the allocation of costs to time periods (for example, the allocation of the cost of plant to the periods for which the plant is used, via the depreciation mechanism) and (b) the allocation of the costs of a time period to the cost object whose costs are measured during that period. This Statement is limited to allocations of the latter type.

7. There are three general types of cost construction: full costs, responsibility costs, and differential costs. Because the cost allocation problem for each is considerably different, the types are discussed separately.

8. The Statement applies only to allocations that are material in amount, that is, to practices that might make a difference in the actions of the person who uses the cost information.

9. This Statement relates primarily to broad cost objects such as divisions, or similar responsibility centers, and product lines within a larger entity. Service and administrative costs collected in production cost centers are assigned to products flowing through these cost centers. The allocation of such costs to products is not addressed in this Statement.

Definitions

10. Service and administrative costs are costs that are incurred by headquarters staffs or other central units, as contrasted with costs that are incurred in production, marketing, or other operating units. In general, service units exist to provide services to other units, and administrative costs are incurred for the entity as a whole. For the purpose of this Statement, there is no need to make a precise distinction between them.

    A cost object is a product, contract, project, organizational subdivision, or other unit for which costs are measured or estimated.

Full Costs

11. The full cost of a cost object is the sum of its direct costs plus a fair share of applicable indirect costs. Therefore, if the purpose of assigning costs is to

measure full costs, a fair share of service and administrative costs should be allocated to those cost objects to which they are applicable.

12. The circumstances in which the measurement of full costs may be appropriate include: (a) external reporting per Financial Accounting Standards Board (FASB) and Securities & Exchange Commission (SEC) guidelines; (b) analysis of the economic profitability of a division, or other subdivision of an entity, or product line; (c) measurement of the cost of providing a service (for example, the cost of operating a company's cafeteria); (d) calculation of a price that is based on full cost, such as the rates charged by regulated companies, the price of a cost-type contract, and prices usually charged for goods and services in many companies; and (e) allocation of state income taxes.

13. Service and administrative costs are allocated to divisions to satisfy the external reporting requirements of the Financial Accounting Standards Board and the Securities & Exchange Commission. Statement of Financial Accounting Standards (SFAS) No. 14, "Financial Reporting for Segments of a Business Enterprise," requires that operating expenses not traceable directly to an industry segment be allocated on a reasonable basis to those segments deriving benefits. (Certain expenses, however, are not to be allocated for FAS 14 purposes: general corporate expenses, interest expense, and income taxes.) For SEC purposes, in filings that for the first time include separate financial statements of a subsidiary, division, or lesser component of a corporate entity, historical income statements may have to be revised to include an allocation of corporate costs not allocated previously. Examples include cases of initial registration statements for spinoffs or significant acquisitions.

14. If the objective is to measure full costs, the preferable method of allocating service and administrative costs is based on a hierarchy of alternatives, arranged in the order of how closely they are related to the cause of the cost's incurrence:

   a. To the extent feasible, elements of these costs should be allocated by measuring the amount of resources consumed by the cost center receiving the service. For example, if a division uses a measured number of hours of the corporate legal staff for a problem that relates to that division, the legal cost should be assigned on the basis of a cost per hour used.

   b. If a direct measure of the amount of services provided to a cost center is not available or is not cost-effective to produce, the costs should be allocated on some basis that reflects the relative amount caused by the various cost centers. Examples of such bases of allocation are given in paragraph 15.

   c. If no causal connection for the amount of cost applicable to cost centers can be found, service and administrative costs should be allocated on the basis of the relative overall activity of the cost center. Activity may be measured by a single criterion, such as the total costs incurred in each cost center, or by an average of several criteria. A commonly used measure is the three-factor "Massachusetts Formula," which is a simple average of the cost center's payroll, revenue, and assets as a proportion of the company's total payroll, revenue, and assets.

15. In allocating costs on the basis of a presumed causal connection, the costs first are grouped into relatively homogeneous pools, then allocated to cost centers on bases such as the following:

   a. *Personnel-related costs.* Costs such as personnel department costs, payroll preparation costs, cafeteria losses, and medical department costs may be allocated on the basis of the relative number of employees of the cost object.

   b. *Payroll-related costs.* Costs such as pensions, other fringe benefits, and payroll taxes may be allocated on the basis of the relative labor costs of the cost object.

   c. *Material-related costs.* Costs such as purchasing, material handling, and storage may be allocated on the basis of the relative material cost of the cost object or, in some circumstances, on the basis of physical quantities.

   d. *Space-related costs.* Cost such as insurance, depreciation, and maintenance of physical facilities may be allocated on the basis of the relative square footage (or cubic footage) of the cost object.

   e. *Energy-related costs.* Costs such as electricity and steam may be allocated on the basis of the relative amount of installed horsepower or other measure of utility consumption of the cost object.

16. In deciding on the number of cost pools, the benefit of a more detailed calculation should be compared with the record-keeping cost of such detail. At one extreme, a single overhead rate may provide an adequate measure. At the other extreme, a large number of cost pools may be warranted.

17. If costs initially are allocated on the basis of a standard cost and the result does not approximate actual cost, variances between standard and actual cost should be allocated to the responsible cost center.

18. If cost allocation methods are prescribed by a regulatory body or by the terms of a contract, these requirements take precedence over any of the statements made above. For full costing guidance, firms should consider the promulgations of the Cost Accounting Standards Board (CASB) on allocation methodology, where appropriate. The CASB Standards provide a systematic approach of particular value for the full costing objective. (See Appendix A for a summary of relevant CASB Standards.)

Responsibility Costs

19. Responsibility costs are cost constructions designed to motivate the managers of responsibility centers to act in the best interests of the company. The comparison of actual costs incurred with budgeted or planned costs provides the mechanism to accomplish this purpose.

20. For responsibility costing, service and administrative costs should be allocated to a responsibility center only if (a) they can be influenced, perhaps only indirectly, by actions of the center's manager, (b) they are believed to

be helpful in indicating the amount of resources that headquarters provides as support to the responsibility center, (c) they improve the comparability of the performance of a responsibility center with that of an independent company that incurs these costs directly, and/or (d) they are used in product pricing decisions.

21. In order to encourage the use of certain staff services, such as consulting, audit, or legal services, the costs of these services often are not charged to responsibility centers or are charged at less than full cost even though they can be traced to responsibility centers.

22. In general, noncontrollable elements of service and administrative costs should be reported separately from elements of cost that the manager can control. Thus standard predetermined rates should be used where applicable.

Differential Costs

23. Differential costs are elements of cost that are expected to be different if one course of action is adopted as compared with the costs of an alternative course of action and are used in the decision-making arena. The alternatives range in magnitude from a proposal to accept a lower-than-normal price on an individual order to a proposal to enter a new type of business involving the construction of new plants and the development of production and marketing organizations.

24. Differential costs always result from estimates of what costs would be in the future. Historical costs, therefore, are irrelevant except as they help indicate what future costs will be.

25. Differential costs always relate to the specific alternatives being considered. Therefore, no general statements can be made about which, if any, elements of service and administrative costs are differential in the analysis of a given proposal.

26. In general, the larger the differences among the alternatives being considered, the more elements of service and administrative costs are likely to be different. Also, the longer the time period involved, the more elements of service and administrative costs are likely to be different.

Allocation Criteria

27. Four criteria are used in selecting a specific allocation base: (1) benefit, (2) cause, (3) fairness, and (4) ability to bear the costs. These criteria serve as the theoretical underpinning for allocation practices.

28. Of the four, the two most commonly employed are benefit and cause. For example, the "benefits" criterion can be applied to corporate administrative costs because it is felt that cost objects benefit from these costs and should share responsibility for them. Additionally, the "cause" criterion can be applied to corporate service costs when the user cost objects precipitate the costs involved. There is a good deal of ambiguity regarding the use of terms "benefit" and "cause"; often they are used interchangeably.

    Fairness is an often-discussed criterion, but it is difficult to use operationally because it is so broad.

Ability to bear the costs generally is tied to an allocation based on profit and is used in the context of an embryonic division or product line. This criterion is of limited use because of its dysfunctional effect on management behavior.

In order to demonstrate the criteria for selecting allocation bases, an analogy may be drawn between these criteria and taxation policy (allocation of tax burden). Table 1 illustrates this point. This table is provided solely for instructional purposes. Many managers perceive allocation of central costs as a charge against cost object earnings.

Table 2 provides a list of sample allocation bases and their related criteria.

29. Use of different allocation bases varies widely in practice. Some companies use one allocation base for all central service and administrative costs and for all purposes. Most frequently used is a broad measure of activity or size or a combination of these factors, including sales, operating revenue, net assets, and total direct expense. In a multidivisional setting, some firms use sales as the allocation base for simplicity as well as for consistency.

30. Other firms use a single allocation base for all expenses for a single purpose. The bases used in this context are also broad and include net assets, net sales, and number of employees.

31. Some firms use a single allocation base for one expense type for all purposes. Table 3 provides examples of shared service and administrative costs and related allocation bases. The bases are listed sequentially by frequency of use in industry.

32. Table 4 summarizes the three allocation objectives and the reasons for allocating or not allocating to achieve each objective.

TABLE 1

CRITERIA FOR SELECTING ALLOCATION BASES AS ILLUSTRATED BY VARIOUS TAXATION POLICIES (SEE PARAGRAPH 28 FOR CORRESPONDING TEXT)

Criterion	Taxation Allocation Method
Benefits	Tax rate is the same for all citizens, and taxes increase in proportion to wealth—for example, real estate tax. Increased property translates directly into increased need for police, fire, defense, and other services.
Cause	Original gasoline tax which funded highway construction and maintenance; tax increases in relation to use.
Fairness	Flat tax; all citizens are equal, so tax is the same for all, such as a poll tax.
Ability to bear	Progressive tax—for example, income-based tax; individuals with higher income are taxed at a higher rate (redistribution of income—not benefit related).

TABLE 2

SAMPLE ALLOCATION BASES REFLECTIVE OF THE CRITERIA OF TABLE 1 (SEE PARAGRAPH 28 FOR CORRESPONDING TEXT)

Criterion	Allocation Bases
	Net assets
	Employment data, such as number of employees for personnel department functions
Benefit	Algorithm for corporate executives' compensation
	Estimated time or usage for legal and governmental affairs department
	Sales
Cause	Estimated time or usage for accounting functions
	Number of purchase orders for purchasing functions

TABLE 3

EXAMPLES OF SERVICE AND ADMINISTRATIVE COSTS AND RELATED ALLOCATION BASES FREQUENTLY USED IN INDUSTRY (SEE PARAGRAPH 31 FOR CORRESPONDING TEXT).

Service and Administrative Costs	Acceptable Allocation Bases
Research and Development	Estimated time or usage; sales; assets employed; new products developed
Personnel department functions	Number of employees; payroll; number of new hires
Accounting functions	Estimated time or usage; sales; assets employed; employment data
Public relations and corporate promotion	Sales
Purchasing function	Dollar value of purchase orders; number of purchase orders; estimated time or usage; percentage of material cost of purchases
Corporate executives' salaries	Sales; assets employed; pre-tax operating income
Treasurer's functions	Sales; estimated time or usage; assets or liabilities employed
Legal and governmental affairs	Estimated time or usage; sales; assets employed
Tax department	Estimated time or usage; sales; assets employed
Income taxes	Net income
Property taxes	Square feet; real estate valuation

TABLE 4

REASONS FOR ALLOCATING AND NOT ALLOCATING PER THE THREE ALLOCATION OBJECTIVES (SEE PARAGRAPH 32 FOR CORRESPONDING TEXT)

Allocation objective: To compute income and asset valuation and to obtain a mutually agreeable price. (Full cost)

Reasons for allocating

a. Recover fair share of shared corporate costs.
b. Sensitize managers to the existence of shared corporate costs, which must be covered.
c. Allocation methods fairly reflect each cost object's share of necessary common costs.
d. When prices are governed by regulation, the allocation of service and administrative costs is required by those regulations.

Reasons for not allocating

a. Prices are determined by forces beyond management's control. Allocation methods will not affect them.
b. Allocations are arbitrary, and the resultant "full costs" are not reliable bases for pricing in certain strategic or tactical decision frameworks.
c. Product line managers are free to establish their own prices, and their profit margins are adequate to cover all costs.
d. The pricing policy is designed to provide a contribution margin from each product sufficiently high to cover all shared costs.

Allocation objective: To motivate managers. (Responsibility cost)

Reasons for allocating

a. Remind business unit managers that shared costs exist and that business unit profit must be sufficient to cover some portion of those costs.
b. Relate business unit profit to total company profits.
c. The method of allocation fairly reflects each business unit's usage of essential common services.
d. Stimulate business unit managers to participate in the control of shared costs.
e. Encourage the use of shared services.

Reasons for not allocating

a. Service and administrative costs are not related to individual business units, so allocations are arbitrary and tend to distort divisional profits.
b. Business unit managers object to charges for costs that are not within their control.
c. The allocation of service and administrative costs would not materially affect reported business unit profit.
d. There is a lack of agreement among business unit managers regarding an appropriate allocation method.
e. The cost of making allocations exceeds the potential benefits derived.

Table 4 *(continued)*

Allocation objective: To predict the economic effects of planning decisions. (Differential cost)

Reasons for allocating

a. Shared costs are relevant in determining the effect of the proposed decision on the company as a whole.

b. An allocation of service and administrative costs provides the best available approximation of expected changes in these costs.

Reasons for not allocating

a. Shared costs are not expected to be affected by the planning decisions made.

b. The allocation of service and administrative costs is arbitrary and presents a distorted view of prospective cash flows or profit resulting from a decision.

Summary of IMA Recommendations

33. Service and administrative cost allocations may or may not be appropriate for management accounting purposes depending on (a) the objective of the decision to be made and (2) the reasons that apply to each case. Management accountants therefore should determine which rationale, on balance, best fits the circumstances depending on the principal objectives of the prospective allocation.

34. In order to provide objective measurements of economic performance, allocation criteria should reflect cause or benefit.

35. For full costing purposes, costs should be allocated based upon a hierarchy of alternatives. Firms should consider the guidance provided by the CASB in this matter.

36. For the purposes of responsibility accounting:

    a. Allocation should be applied where appropriate with the use of predetermined or standard rates or amounts because business unit managers should not be held responsible for variances in certain shared service and administrative costs not traceable to their actions.

    b. Allocated corporate expense should be separated from nonallocated expense in order to focus the cost object manager's attention on the expense that he or she can control directly.

37. For differential costing purposes, the only relevant costs are those future costs that relate to the specific alternatives being considered.

APPENDIX A
CASB Standards

1. When market prices are not appropriate or available, an alternate method of obtaining a "fair" price is used. Cost Accounting Standards promulgated by the Cost Accounting Standards Board (CASB) outline acceptable methods of cost allocation with a view toward arriving at a "fair" price for government

contracts. For example, an aircraft manufacturer produces both commercial and military products. The price of a new military product for the United States government will include an allocation of service and administrative costs within the constraints of CASB rulings. CASB standards continue to have the force of law, and these standards, originally intended for use by defense contractors, now are required by virtually all nondefense contracts with the federal government in excess of $100,000. CASB Standards concerning the allocation of central corporate costs therefore provide guidance as to the methodologies that may be applied in situations not involving government contracts. References from relevant standards follow.

2. *No 403—Allocation of Home Office Expenses to Segments*
   This standard establishes criteria for allocating home office expenses to cost objects based upon the beneficial or causal relationship between such expenses and the cost objects. Three steps are delineated for this purpose:

   a. *Direct Allocation:* Expenses are identified for direct allocation to the maximum extent possible. For example, legal services are allocated based on the time devoted to a specific cost object's affairs.

   b. *Indirect Allocation:* Expenses that are not directly allocable but that are material in amount in relation to total home office expense should be pooled into logical and homogeneous groups and allocated on bases that reflect the relationship of expenses to the segment. For example, marketing policy costs may be allocated based on sales or segmental marketing costs.

   c. *Residual Expenses:* Expenses that remain unallocated by direct or indirect allocation should be allocated based on overall activity. For example, the expenses of top corporate officers are difficult to allocate based upon the criteria of a beneficial relationship. Sales or the Massachusetts formula are used to allocate these expenses because they represent overall activity of a segment.

   The Standard stresses the importance of minimizing the amount of residual expenses.

3. *No. 410—Allocation of Business Unit General and Administrative Expenses to Cost Objectives*
   This Standard provides criteria for allocating business unit general and administrative expenses and home office expenses to business unit final cost objects based on their beneficial or causal relationship.

   Business unit general and administrative expenses should be included in a separate indirect cost pool and allocated only to final cost objects. The bases for allocation are total cost, value-added input, or a single cost element such as direct labor hours.

4. *No. 418—Allocation of Indirect Cost Pools*
   This Standard provides criteria for the inclusion of indirect costs in cost pools, including service centers, and offers suggestions for the selection of allocation bases. Indirect costs are included in homogeneous groups based

upon the similarity of beneficial or causal relationships, but only if the resultant allocation would have been equivalent if individual items were allocated separately.

5. The preferred allocation basis is one that measures resource consumption, such as labor hours or machine hours. The second order of preference is measure of output, such as units produced or documents processed. If neither of the first two measures is usable, a surrogate measure of output or activity may be applied. Variances, material in amount and arising from the use of forecasted or standard costs, should be allocated to cost objects in proportion to the costs allocated previously using predetermined rates.

26-5 COMMENTS ON SELECTED "UNIQUE" EXPENSES

Before discussing the planning and control of G&A expenses, it may be helpful to comment on the expenses that are in some way unique to headquarters or central unit activities, and that are not found charged to most departments.

(a) CHARITABLE CONTRIBUTIONS

In most companies, charitable contributions are approved by the board of directors as a separate budget item. Therefore, this approved list, sometimes plus an approval allowance for contingencies, is the basis for planning and control. It presents no special problem. There will be instances where a specific contribution is for the benefit of a division or subsidiary, and may be charged (or allocated) to it.

(b) INCENTIVE PAY

Many companies have established incentive pay systems for the officers and top management, accruing the estimated expense in the G&A category (office of the chairman). Since the formula is known, the anticipated expenses can be planned and accrued on the basis of the expected relevant factors.

(c) AUDIT FEES

The cost of the annual audit by the independent accountants can be estimated, included in the planned expenses, and accrued. In many instances, the share attributable to the separate subordinate units of the entity can be charged to such organization and included in its budget.

(d) LEGAL FEES

In this litigious society, lawsuits are common. If certain litigation is underway or imminent, the cost can be estimated and accrued. Based on past history, if other litigation is likely, a contingency provision might be made. Again, if the legal costs relate to a particular organization unit (and not the corporate entity as a whole) then the provision for the accrual and budget may be made in that unit.

(e) INTEREST EXPENSE, INCOME TAXES

Interest expense, being directly related to borrowed funds, is kept within limits through the control of business indebtedness. Control of interest-bearing obligations affects control of interest expense. When the financial budget of the company has been established, the amount if interest expense can be calculated on the basis of predicted borrowings, payments, and similar facts. For this expense, as for any other, responsibility for control should be place in one executive, either the treasurer or controller. The reason for excess costs over budget should be explained. Aside from budgetary control, the primary problem is one of securing loans on the most advantageous terms.

There are very few control problems in connection with income taxes. The first requirement is to establish a proper tax plan to minimize tax payments, to estimate monthly the amount due, and to make the proper accruals in accordance with generally accepted accounting practice. Usually the method used in accruing estimated income taxes payable should be used in *planning* the tax expense and liability—that is, the respective budgets.

Another function of the controller is to review carefully methods and transactions, securing tax counsel where necessary, to comply with all technicalities and thus secure the greatest tax advantage. Other than this, his or her responsibilities relate to keeping the required records and substantiating data to support tax claims, advising on capital gain and loss transactions, and arranging the capital structure, as well as the investments, to secure the maximum benefits under the tax laws. Quite aside from the tax problems of the individual company, the chief accounting officer can actively promote equitable tax laws directly or through associations.

(f) CORPORATE EXPENSES

For businesses organized as corporations there are numerous corporate expenses that must be assigned to particular executives for control purposes—for example, state and federal capital stock taxes, franchise taxes, fees of fiscal agents, stock transfer taxes, and fidelity bonds and insurance. There is no particular problem of control. The controller can assist in estimating the expenses for budget purposes, prepare the necessary reports, and make the required accruals.

(g) EXCESS FACILITY COSTS

Occasionally, some companies find themselves in possession of distribution or production facilities that appear to be permanently excessive. Usually, the facilities were built or acquired without a sound analysis of the potential demand for the company's products or because of other errors in executive judgment. Whatever the reason, it is unwise to burden the current manufacturing and distribution operations with the charge. The costs are often carried as a separate administrative expense until the property can be disposed of. The continuing expenses usually consist of only depreciation, taxes, insurance, and a certain minimum amount of maintenance. It is a relatively simple matter to estimate the cost and to establish a budget to cover it. Management generally should be alert either to dispose of the property on favorable terms or possibly to rent it.

(h) BAD DEBT LOSSES

Another item of expense particular to the financial group is bad debt loss. Quite obviously this loss is not the sole criterion of the efficiency of the credit department. Any bad debt losses could be eliminated either by making only cash sales or by restricting credit sales to only the financially strongest firms. Such a policy would drive business to competitors who are willing to take reasonable credit risks. Any discussion of bad debt losses must therefore assume that a company is competitive from the standpoint of extending credit. Under such circumstances there are some measuring sticks to be applied to loss experience over a period of time. These include the following:

1. Percentage of bad debt losses to total sales. This is to be used where the cash sales are relatively insignificant. Such a basis avoids the necessity of segregating cash and credit sales if solely for this purpose.

2. Percentage of bad debt losses to total net credit sales.

If warranted, these bases can be refined through a segregation by different classes of customers, methods or terms of sales, or by different territories.

For the purpose of setting budgets, the applicable percentage can be applied against budgeted sales. Control of the expense rests on effectively policing accounts receivable to discover evidence of slow pay.

(i) OTHER INCOME AND EXPENSE

Most business firms have various items of income and expense that are of a nonoperating nature. The income may include interest income, royalties, rental income, dividends received, and income from sales of scrap; the expenses include loss on the sale of fixed assets and sales discounts. Based on past experience and knowledge about projected changes, reasonable estimates of these elements of income and expense can be made. Otherwise, control of a limited nature is exercised through the judgment of the official to whom the accounts are assigned.

In general, for all unique G&A expenses, as for all such usual expense, common sense dictates a way of estimating the cost and providing for it in the actual accounting as well as the planning budget, and comparing actual with budget.

26-6 THE BUDGETARY PROCEDURE

In most companies, G&A expense is not budgeted as a percentage of sales, since it is relatively fixed and does not vary with sales. However, many G&A functions can be viewed as step costs. For example, accounts receivable volume will decline as sales drop; if there is a significant reduction in sales volume, then the budget for a receivables position would be eliminated. On the other hand, there are many fixed costs. For example, director expenses are fixed, since the same number of board meetings will occur, no matter how much sales volume may vary. Figure 26-1 splits G&A expenses into discretionary, variable, step, and fixed costs.

The figure shows that there are almost no variable costs to budget. However, there are many discretionary costs. Withholding expenditures on discretionary items

Figure 26-1   G&A Functions.

Cost Description	Discretionary	Variable	Step	Fixed
Salaries			XXX	
Fringe benefits			XXX	
Travel & entertainment	XXX			
Telecommunications			XXX	
Repairs & maintenance	XXX			
Rent			XXX	
Dues & subscriptions	XXX			
Utilities				XXX
Purchased services			XXX	
Depreciation				XXX
Insurance				XXX
Incentive pay	XXX			
Director fees & expenses				XXX
Outside legal fees	XXX			
Audit fees			XXX	
Charitable contributions	XXX			
Consultant fees	XXX			
Gain/Loss on sale of assets	XXX			
Cash discounts		XXX		
Provision for doubtful accounts		XXX		
Interest expense				XXX

can have a marked impact on profits, so a separate analysis of discretionary G&A costs should be made available to management, especially if profitability is expected to be a problem.

Areas where costs may verge on variable costs instead of step costs are the salaries of the payroll, cost accounting, cashier's, and internal audit departments.

The budget preparation procedure for G&A varies somewhat from the procedure used for production, since there is no budget for purchased materials, inventory, cost of goods sold, or direct labor. A typical G&A budget preparation procedure includes these steps:

1. The controller or budget director makes available to each functional executive and/or department head, in either worksheet form or computer accessible data:

   a. Actual year-to-date expenses and head count.

   b. Assumptions to be used for budgetary purposes: percent of pay raise, fringe benefit cost percent, inflation rate, etc., generally acceptable rate of expense increase, etc.

   c. Any relevant information on the business level, economic conditions, etc.

   d. Instructions on preparing the planning budget.

Figure 26-2 Departmental Budget Request.

CONTROLLER'S DEPARTMENT
PROPOSED BUDGET—PLAN YEAR 19XX
(dollars in thousands)

Item	Current Year			Proposed Budget for 19XX		
	Actual Nine Months	Estimated Three Months	Indicated Final	Request	Increase/(Decrease) from Prior Year	
					Amount	Percent
Head Count	27	27	27	29	2	7
Expenses						
Salaries and wages	$ 701.25	$233.75	$ 935.00	$1,047.00	$112.00	12
Fringe benefits (40%)	280.50	93.50	374.00	418.80	44.80	12
Subtotal	981.75	327.25	1,309.00	1,465.80	156.80	12
Travel and entertainment	22.25	3.75	26.00	28.60	2.60	10
Communications	19.00	6.50	25.50	28.05	2.55	9
Professional fees (audit)	270.00	—	270.00	283.50	13.50	5
Dues and subscriptions	16.75	5.00	21.75	23.93	2.18	10
Supplies	12.25	4.50	16.75	18.43	1.68	10
Occupancy	120.00	40.00	160.00	168.00	8.00	5
Computer services	90.00	30.00	120.00	132.00	12.00	10
Repair and maintenance	8.70	5.60	14.30	15.73	1.43	10
Depreciation	108.00	36.00	144.00	150.00	6.00	4
Miscellaneous	4.50	.50	5.00	5.50	.50	10
Total	$1,653.20	$459.10	$2,112.30	$2,319.54	$207.24	10

Figure 26-3 General and Administrative Expense Budget.

GENERAL AND ADMINISTRATIVE EXPENSE
GROUP SUMMARY
PROPOSED BUDGET—PLAN YEAR 19XX
(dollars in thousands)

Group	Current Year			Plan Year 19XX		
	Indicated Final	Budget	Over/under Budget	Request	Increase/(Decrease) over Prior Year Actual	
					Amount	Percent
Chief executive	$17,900	$18,000	$100	$20,585	$2,685	15
President	5,100	5,200	100	5,865	765	15
Legal	7,230	7,500	270	8,000	770	11
Corporate strategic planning	1,250	1,250	—	1,313	63	5
Finance	6,720	6,750	30	7,190	470	7
Marketing	4,970	5,110	140	5,716	746	15
Manufacturing	2,340	2,340	—	2,457	117	5
Administration and services	5,610	5,700	90	5,330	(280)	(5) (2)
Human relations	4,860	4,900	40	5,200	340	7
Public relations	3,100	3,150	50	3,150	50	2
Interdepartment transfers	(430)	(430)	—	(460)	(30)	(7) (3)
Total	$58,650	$59,470	$820	$64,346	$5,696	10
Percent of sales	4.00%			3.95%		

Notes:

(1) Salaries and wages on all departments reflect a 5% general increase.

(2) Security services were transferred to Division "K."

(3) Represents computer service transfers.

2. The department head completes the budget proposal and sends it to his supervisor for approval, who then forwards it to the budget director. This format may be illustrated in Figure 26-2.

3. The individual department budget requests are reviewed by the budget director, checked for reasonableness and completeness, and, when acceptable, summarized for the central office by responsibility, perhaps in the format of Figure 26-3.

   When the aggregate G&A budget is accepted, it becomes part of the annual business plan. (See Chapter 16.)

4. Monthly, the departmental expenses—actual and budget—are compared for the department head, as in Figure 26-4, who takes corrective action where appropriate. This report explains the "why" or any significant over- or under-run. Budget performance could also be reported on a graphic basis. The entire G&A category may be summarized and actual can be compared with plan as in Figure 26-5. This report also explains significant over-runs. The monthly trend of

Figure 26-4 Departmental Budget Control Report.

CONTROLLER'S DEPARTMENT
BUDGET CONTROL REPORT
MONTH OF March 19XX
(dollars in thousands)

Expense	Month			Year-to-Date			
	Actual	Budget	Over/under Budget	Actual	Budget	Over/under Budget	
Salaries and wages	$ 85.25	$ 87.25	$2.00	$255.75	$261.75	$ 6.00	(a)
Fringe benefits (40%) . . .	34.10	34.90	.80	102.30	104.70	2.40	(a)
Subtotal	119.35	122.15	2.80	358.05	366.45	8.40	
Travel and entertainment	4.50	2.38	(2.12)	8.50	7.15	(1.35)	(b)
Communications	2.30	2.34	.04	6.90	7.00	.10	
Professional fees	251.00	260.00	9.00	251.00	260.00	9.00	
Dues and subscriptions . .	1.90	2.00	.10	5.60	6.00	.40	
Supplies	1.90	1.70	(.20)	4.30	4.60	.30	
Occupancy	14.00	14.00	—	42.00	42.00	—	
Computer services	11.30	11.50	.20	32.00	33.00	1.00	
Repairs and maintenance	2.61	1.31	(1.30)	5.73	3.93	(1.80)	(c)
Depreciation	12.50	12.50	—	37.50	37.50	—	
Miscellaneous	.20	.46	.26	1.00	1.38	.38	
Total	$421.56	$430.34	$8.78	$752.58	$769.01	$16.43	

Notes:

(a) Accounts receivable assistant not yet hired.

(b) Toronto trip not scheduled in budget.

(c) Computer outage.

Figure 26-5 General and Administrative Expense—Group Summary Budget Performance.

GENERAL AND ADMINISTRATIVE EXPENSES
GROUP SUMMARY—BUDGET PERFORMANCE
MONTH OF March 19XX
(dollars in thousands)

Group	Month			Year to Date		
	Actual	Budget	Over/ under Budget	Actual	Budget	Over/ under Budget
Chief executive ...	$1,700.00	$1,715.42	$15.42	$ 5,100.00	$ 5,146.25	$ 46.25
President	480.00	488.75	8.75	1,460.00	1,466.25	6.25
Legal	700.00	666.67	(33.33)	2,100.00	2,000.00	(100.00) (a)
Corporate strategic planning	109.00	109.42	.42	328.00	328.75	.75
Finance	680.00	700.00	20.00	1,890.00	1,890.00	—
Marketing	475.00	476.33	1.33	1,437.10	1,429.00	(8.10)
Manufacturing ...	200.00	200.00	—	612.00	615.00	3.00
Administration and services	410.00	440.00	30.00	1,416.50	1,332.50	(84.00) (b)
Human relations ..	433.33	433.33	—	1,300.00	1,300.00	—
Public relations ...	310.00	300.00	(10.00)	760.00	800.00	40.00
Interdepartment transfers	(38.33)	(38.33)	—	(115.00)	(115.00)	—
Total	$5,349.00	$5,491.59	$32.59	$16,288.60	$16,192.75	$(95.85)
Percent of sales ...	4.60%			4.10%	3.95%	

Notes:
(a) Norton litigation not anticipated this early.
(b) Higher demand for computer services on weekends.

performance, by group and in total, could be displayed in vertical bar chart or line graph. The entire group performance could be summarized as to budget and actual expense by natural expense category (salaries and wages, travel and entertainment, etc.).

26-7 CONTROL OF ACCOUNTING COSTS THROUGH THE USE OF STANDARDS

Budgetary control may be used to assist in keeping accounting expense, as well as some other expense, within the limits of business income. A second tool to be used in controlling accounting costs is standards of performance and cost. These standards can be applied to many office functions just as they have been applied to manufacturing and sales functions. They are not applicable to all accounting activities, nor can the same degree of accuracy be secured as in the factory. But in many offices, the possible cost savings for certain clerical activities are sufficient to justify the effort of establishing the standards.

Although the general method of setting standards was discussed in Chapter 19, the application to the measurement of clerical work is outlined as follows:

1. *Preliminary Observation and Analysis.* This step is fundamental in securing the necessary overall understanding of the problem and in selecting those areas of activity that may lend themselves to standardization. Also, it assists in eliminating any obviously major weakness in routine.

2. *Selection of Functions on Which Standards Are to Be Set.* Standards should be set only on those activities sufficient in volume to justify standards.

3. *Determination of the Unit of Work.* A unit must be selected in which the standard may be expressed. This will depend on the degree of specialization and the volume of work.

4. *Determination of the Best Method and Setting of the Standard.* Time and motion study can be applied to office work, with sufficient allowance being given for fatigue and personal needs.

5. *Testing of the Standard.* After the standard has been set, it should be tested to see that it is practical.

6. *Final Application.* This involves using the standard and preparing simple reports that the supervisor and the individual worker can see. It also requires a full explanation to the employee.

Illustrative accounting and clerical functions that lend themselves to standardization and the units of work which may be used to measure performance are these:

Function	Unit of Standard Measurement
Order handling	Number of orders handled
Mail handling	Number of pieces handled
Billing	Number of invoice lines
Check writing	Number of checks written
Posting	Number of postings
Filing	Number of pieces filed
Typing	Number of lines typed
Customer statements	Number of statements
Order writing	Number of order lines

In addition to performance standards, unit cost standards can be applied to measure an individual function or overall activity. Thus applying cost standards to credit and collection functions may involve these functions and units of measurement depending on the extent of mechanization:

Functional Activity	Unit Cost Standard
Credit investigation and approval	Cost per sales order
	Cost per account sold
	Cost per credit sales transaction
Credit correspondence records and files	Cost per sales order
	Cost per letter
	Cost per account sold
Preparing invoices	Cost per invoice line
	Cost per item
	Cost per invoice
	Cost per order line
	Cost per order
Entire accounts receivable records, including posting of charges and credits and preparation of customers' statements	Cost per account
	Cost per sales order
	Cost per sales transaction
Posting charges	Cost per invoice
	Cost per shipment
Preparing customers' statements	Cost per statement
	Cost per account sold
Posting credits	Cost per remittance
	Cost per account sold
Calculating commissions on cash collected	Cost per remittance
Making street collections	Cost per customer
	Cost per dollar collected
Window collections	Cost per collection

26-8 OTHER MEANS OF G&A COST CONTROL

The potential savings that may be realized through the reduction of G&A expenses are usually not as great as those in the factory or sales operations. This is natural because the major expenses of a business are concentrated in the two functions of production and distribution. However, depending on the size of the gross margin percentage, it is far more effective to reduce costs to increase profits than to increase revenues to increase profits. In the example that follows, we show the revenues required to cover the cost of a person with a $40,000 salary:

Salary Level	Gross Margin	Revenue Required
$40,000	90%	$ 44,444
$40,000	80%	$ 50,000
$40,000	70%	$ 57,143
$40,000	60%	$ 66,667
$40,000	50%	$ 80,000
$40,000	40%	$100,000
$40,000	30%	$133,333
$40,000	20%	$200,000
$40,000	10%	$400,000

This table shows that it is very much in the interests of a low-margin company to work hard to reduce G&A expenses to a bare minimum.

The previous section described various standards that can be used to measure performance in G&A areas. Standards tell the controller about the current level of efficiency, but do nothing to suggest improvements. The controller must explore many methods for cost control, methods quite independent of budgets and standards. Illustrative areas or specific points by which administrative or office expenses may be reduced through observation and analysis include:

1. *Clean Up the Area.* The first step in finding waste is being able to see it. Therefore, clean up all G&A areas by moving old files to storage and instituting a clean desk policy.

2. *Eliminate Duplicate Documents.* Review stored documents and eliminate duplicate items. For example, if an invoice is being stored alphabetically, numerically, and by customer code, then eliminate all but one. This step cuts filing costs.

3. *Eliminate Reports.* Reports are frequently created to meet a one-time need, but are then continually produced because no one ever notified the sender. Consequently, report users should be contacted periodically to see if they still need reports. Also, the information contained in ongoing reports can sometimes be combined into one report.

4. *Consolidate Forms.* Most companies have too many forms. Some forms can be combined, thereby reducing the number of approvals and paperwork required to complete transactions.

5. *Eliminate Multiple Approvals.* The time and effort required to get multiple approvals for anything usually exceeds the benefit obtained by the additional approvals.

6. *Eliminate Duplicate Tasks.* Tasks are frequently cross-checked by supervisors; this is a duplication of tasks, and should be eliminated. The reason for the cross-checking is usually because supervisors are looking for and correcting errors. The way to eliminate the need for cross-checking is to make the process mistake-proof. For example, staff can receive better training, and tasks can be either fully or partially automated.

7. *Apply Automation.* As technological advances reach the marketplace, utilize them to reduce the need for staffing. For example, the advent of voice mail systems reduces the need for a receptionist. Computerized word processing systems allow managers to write their own memos and reports, and reduces the need for secretaries. Computerized time clocks reduce the need for manual tracking of pay hours by payroll clerks.

8. *Reduce Cycle Time.* Cycle time is the total time required to complete a process. Analysis of most processes reveals that the bulk of the cycle time is the wait time between tasks, versus time spent adding value to the process. Flowchart key processes and itemize the time required to perform each process. Then work to remove the "dead time" from each process. As cycle times shrink, the need for staffing is reduced. For example, one company has elected to pay suppliers as soon as bills are received. It compared the cost of money from paying bills early to the cost of reprocessing paperwork for a month until the bills were due for payment. It concluded that it was cheaper to pay immediately.

9. *Rearrange Work Space.* After the closing process has been cleaned up and the paper flow made more efficient, the controller should review the work space. If the work space can be rearranged to reduce paper movement to a minimum and cut the level of nearby traffic (thereby reducing interruptions), then moving the staff is justified.

10. *Review Reproduction Costs and Locations.* Most firms have a small number of large copiers. A review of the situation usually reveals that most advanced copier functions are not needed. Instead, consider having a minimal number of high-end copiers in central locations for "power" users, and then buy a large number of inexpensive tabletop copiers to spread throughout the building. The benefits will be reduced capital costs and vastly reduced walking time by the staff to reach the nearest copier. Also, all copiers should be purchased from the same manufacturer in order to reduce the number of supplier contacts and the complexity of copier contract administration.

11. *Install LAN Fax Card.* If your company has a local area network (LAN), then consider purchasing a LAN fax card, so that employees can send and receive documents without ever leaving their computer workstations. However, noncomputer documents are also sent from time to time, so either a document scanner or a low-end fax machine should be retained for such items.

12. *Train the Staff.* One of the best ways to reduce errors is to train the staff. At a minimum, training must involve detailed instruction in current company procedures. Too often, management issues a procedure modification in a memo, and assumes that the staff will follow the change. Such procedural changes usually fail because follow-up training did not occur. If the controller wants to avoid costly errors, then training must take place. Also, one can upgrade low-level personnel into more demanding tasks by using additional training.

13. *Staff for Low or Average Work Loads.* Reduce staff levels to the point where they are always busy at normal or low transaction volumes. If the work load increases, then use either overtime or temporary help. However, staff efficiency tends to decrease if overtime exceeds 10% for extended periods.

14. *Outsource Functions.* Outsourcing G&A functions is becoming more popular. Some functions where this has proved effective are:

    - Payroll.
    - Cashiering (on site, but by bank or ATM).
    - Messenger service.
    - Travel arrangements.

15. *Shut Down Office to Match Factory.* If the production facility is closed, such as during the holiday season, then it may be possible to shut down the G&A area as well.

16. *Call in the Internal Auditors.* Have the internal audit staff review G&A functions and suggest process improvements to reduce costs. An additional audit task is to periodically review telephone records for private phone calls, and to recommend procedures to control this problem.

17. *Reduce per-Minute Phone Costs.* The elimination of the long-distance phone monopoly has sparked a great deal of competition. Some companies buy large blocks of phone time from the primary phone companies and resell it at considerably reduced prices. Contact a local phone time reseller for a comparison of rates. Also, "800" line service can now be moved among the phone companies without having to change the "800" number, so the controller can also do comparison shopping in this area.

18. *Institute Direct Purchasing of Office Supplies.* The cost to requisition an item, source a supplier, create a purchase order, and receive the item has been estimated at about $150. For office supplies, this is not a cost effective process. Instead, employees can order their own supplies with a pre-printed ordering form (containing pre-approved items) that is faxed to a predetermined supplier.

19. *Benchmark G&A.* After all of the above recommendations have been implemented and management is running out of cost reduction ideas, try comparing the company's G&A costs against those of other companies. Sometimes a consultant must be brought in to manage the benchmarking effort as a neutral third party. Be sure to contact firms that are outside of the company's industry, since the best performers may be located elsewhere.

Although some of these points may seem minor in reducing costs, savings can be quite sizable in the aggregate.

As reductions are implemented, the argument may arise that the talent needed to perform the essential functions must be retained at a minimum level. It cannot be terminated for a temporary downturn or transferred to low-skill positions. However, as departments shrink to apparently minimum levels, one can combine departments and cross-train staff to achieve an additional level of staff reduction.

Finally, the controller should review G&A costs on the balance sheet. The two primary items are office equipment and working capital. Careful attention to these areas will result in lower capital needs, lower depreciation and insurance costs, and a higher return on investment:

1. *Office Equipment.* The mix of copier equipment can be changed to favor low-end equipment, and fax machines can be replaced by a LAN fax card. Also, obsolete phone, copier, and fax equipment should be immediately removed from the fixed asset register in order to keep the company's insurable and taxable asset valuation as low as possible. Finally, office space should heavily favor cubicles over offices, because cubicle furnishings are cheaper and more staff can be contained in a smaller work space, thereby reducing occupancy costs.

2. *Working Capital.* The working capital a company needs is the value of its inventory and accounts receivable, less the amount of its accounts payable. There is a growing trend in businesses to strive for zero working capital or even negative working capital (see Selected References). The main item under partial control of G&A is accounts receivable. The controller can work to reduce the days of receivables by closely reviewing the billing process to ensure that products are billed immediately following shipment. Also, the Controller should send the collections staff to training classes offered by numerous credit collections firms such as Dun & Bradstreet.

Finally, close management of the collections function will ensure that overdue accounts are tightly monitored.

26-9 SELECTED REFERENCES

Tully, Shawn, "Raiding a Company's Hidden Cash," *Fortune,* Aug. 22, 1994, pp. 82–89.

PART FOUR

PLANNING AND ACCOUNTING CONTROL OF ASSETS, LIABILITIES, AND EQUITY INTERESTS

CHAPTER 27

Planning and Control of Cash and Short-Term Investments

27-1 INTRODUCTION

Most business executives have long been aware of the need for cash. Supplier bills must be paid by cash. Payrolls must be met with cash. But recently the ability of an entity to generate adequate cash has assumed more importance. Witness the attention given cash flow in leveraged buyouts (LBOs) or other proposed mergers or acquisitions. Or consider the standard issued by the Financial Accounting Standards Board (FASB) for cash flow reporting—FAS No. 95, Statement of Cash Flows.

In any event, sound cash management is a basic financial function. While it is usually the responsibility of the senior financial officer, the controller has an important role to play. This chapter reviews the phases that the controller either handles or has a direct interest in:

- Cash planning with emphasis on the annual plan.
- Some aspects of cash control, including internal control.
- Limited comments on temporary investments, given their close relationship to cash.

27-2 OBJECTIVES OF CASH PLANNING AND CONTROL

Cash is a particularly vulnerable asset because, without proper controls, it is easily concealed and readily negotiable. But it is something every business needs. From an overall viewpoint, cash management would have these objectives:

1. Provision of adequate cash for operations—both short and long term.
2. Effective utilization of company funds at all times.
3. Establishment of accountability for cash receipts and provision of adequate safeguards until the funds are placed in the company depository.
4. Establishment of controls to assure that disbursements are made only for approved and legitimate purposes.
5. Maintenance of adequate bank balances, where appropriate, to support proper commercial bank relations.
6. Maintenance of adequate cash records.

27-3 DUTIES OF THE CONTROLLER VS. THE TREASURER

With respect to cash management, a cooperative relationship should exist between the controller and treasurer. Duties and responsibilities will vary, depending on the type and size of the business firm. Under ordinary circumstances, the treasury staff has custody of cash funds and administers the bank accounts. Usually, it is the treasurer who is responsible for maintaining good relations with banks and other investors, providing the timely interest and principal payments on borrowed debt, and investing the excess cash. He usually would have primary responsibility for cash receipts and disbursement procedures.

The controller may have these responsibilities in companies large enough for separate treasury and controllership functions:

1. Development of some, or all, of the cash forecasts.
2. Review of the internal control system with respect to both receipts and disbursements to assure its adequacy and effectiveness.

3. Reconciliation of bank accounts—as part of a sound internal control system (and not to be done by members of the treasurer's department who have access to funds or by accounting personnel who record the transactions).

4. As may be deemed appropriate, preparation of selected cash reports.

27-4 THE CASH FORECAST

(a) PURPOSES OF CASH FORECASTING

A *cash forecast,* or cash plan, or cash budget, is a projection of the anticipated cash receipts and disbursements and the resulting cash balance within a specified period. This is a necessary function in any well-managed plan of cash administration.

The operation of any business must be planned within the limits of available funds, and, conversely, the necessary funds must be provided to carry out the planned business operations.

In these days of increasing sales and earnings, and taxes, business management is rediscovering that profits are not the same as cash in the bank. The company may show a small profit, or even a loss, and have a very sizable cash balance. Particularly in those industries requiring heavy capital investment, the cash generation by the operations, the "cash flow," may be very heavy and yet result in mediocre profits. For reasons such as these, cash forecasting is being recognized as a vital management function.

The basic purpose behind the preparation of the cash budget is to plan so that the business will have the necessary cash—whether from the short-term or long-term viewpoint. Further, when excess cash is to be available, budget preparation offers a means of anticipating an opportunity for effective utilization. Aside from these general purposes, some specific uses to which a cash budget may be put are the following:

1. To point out peaks or seasonal fluctuations in business activity that necessitate larger investments in inventories and receivables.

2. To indicate the time and extent of funds needed to meet maturing obligations, tax payments, and dividend or interest payments.

3. To assist in planning for growth, including the required funds for plant expansion and working capital.

4. To indicate well in advance of needs the extent and duration of funds required from outside sources and thus permit the securing of more advantageous loans.

5. To assist in securing credit from banks and improve the general credit position of the business.

6. To determine the extent and probable duration of funds available for investment.

7. To plan the reduction of bonded indebtedness or other loans.

8. To coordinate the financial needs of the subsidiaries and divisions of the company.

9. To permit the company to take advantage of cash discounts and forward purchasing, thereby increasing its earnings.

(b) CASH FORECASTING METHODS

At least two methods are in widespread use for developing a cash forecast. Although the end product is the estimated cash balance, the methods differ chiefly in terms of the starting point of the forecast and the detail made available. These techniques are described as follows:

1. *Direct Estimate of Cash Receipts and Disbursements.* This is a detailed forecast of each cost element or function involving cash. It is essentially a projection of the cash records. Such a method is the one most commonly used in business and is quite essential to giving a complete picture of the swings or gyrations in both receipts and disbursements. It is particularly applicable to those concerns subject to wide variations in activity. Moreover, it is very useful for controlling cash flow by comparing actual and forecasted performance. A cash forecast prepared on this basis is shown in Figure 27-1. The individual line items will depend on what items are significant, and/or on those in which the management is especially interested—presuming the actual data are also readily available from the cash records for comparing budget with actual results. The cash inflows and outflows from operations are shown; thus, management can easily see the cash flow generated by operations, and the cash flows from investing activities and financing activities are readily determinable.

   If changes in the annual plan (e.g., sales) cause adjustments in cash flow, the use of the computer for this detailed cash planning makes such modifications rather easy.

2. *Adjusted Net Income (or Indirect or Reconciliation) Method.* As the name implies, the starting point for this procedure is the estimated income and expense statement. This projected net income is adjusted for all noncash transactions to arrive at the cash income or loss and is further adjusted for cash transactions that arise because of nonoperating balance sheet changes. A worksheet showing the general method is illustrated in Figure 27-2.

   Since net income is used, the true extent of the gross cash receipts or disbursements is not known. Where a company must work on rather close cash margins, this method probably will not meet the needs. It is applicable chiefly where sales volume is relatively stable and the out-of-pocket costs are fairly constant in relation to sales.

   This format identifies the cash flows according to source—from operating activities, from investing activities, or from financing activities. This segregation is that suggested by the FASB for inclusion in published financial statements. It may or may not be used for internal planning purposes. If this style is utilized, it permits management to readily see the relative size of each estimated cash flow source approximately as it will appear in the annual report to shareholders.

(c) ESTIMATING CASH RECEIPTS

The sources of cash receipts for the typical industrial or commercial firm are well known: collections on account, cash sales, royalties, rent, dividends, sale of capital items, sale of investments, and new financing. These items can be predicted with reasonable accuracy. Usually, the most important recurring sources are collections on

The Manufacturing Company
STATEMENT OF ESTIMATED CASH RECEIPTS AND DISBURSEMENTS
FOR PLAN YEAR 19XX
(dollars in thousands)

Item	January	February	March	First Quarter Total	December	Fourth Quarter Total	Year Total
Cash and cash equivalents at beginning of period	$1,330	$ 756	$ 842	$ 1,330	$ 2,339	$ 7,245	$ 1,330
Cash Receipts							
From operations:							
Collections on account	2,985	3,255	3,975	10,215	4,087	12,413	47,946
Cash sales	70	40	110	220	200	710	1,730
Interest receivable	20	20	15	55	20	50	205
Insurance proceeds	—	—	360	360	—	—	360
Miscellaneous	20	20	20	60	20	20	240
Total from operations	3,095	3,335	4,480	10,910	4,327	13,233	50,481
From other activities:							
Common stock issue	—	—	2,000	2,000	—	—	2,000
Short-term borrowings	—	—	500	500	3,725	3,725	4,725
Long-term debt issue	—	—	1,000	1,000	—	—	1,000
Total from other activities	—	—	3,500	3,500	3,725	3,725	7,725
Total cash receipts	3,095	3,335	7,980	14,410	8,052	16,958	58,206
Total cash available	4,425	4,091	8,822	15,740	10,391	24,203	59,536
Cash Disbursements							
For operations:							
Accounts payable and accrued items	1,972	2,117	2,300	6,389	1,865	5,806	24,089
Payrolls	1,096	1,067	1,240	3,403	1,380	4,610	13,700
Interest	—	—	150	150	600	710	2,170
Federal and state income taxes	185	—	—	185	3,100	3,100	7,185
Total from operations	3,253	3,184	3,690	10,127	6,945	14,226	47,144
For other activities:							
Repayment on long-term debt	416	65	500	981	—	1,081	3,496
Dividends	—	—	650	650	650	2,600	2,600
Capital expenditures	—	—	2,000	2,000	—	3,500	3,500
Total for other activities	416	65	3,150	3,631	650	7,181	9,596
Total cash disbursements	$3,669	3,249	6,840	13,758	7,595	21,407	$56,740
Cash and cash equivalents at end of period	$ 756	$ 842	$1,982	$ 1,982	$ 2,796	$ 2,796	$ 2,796

Figure 27-2 Statement of Estimated Cash Flows (Indirect Method).

The Random Company
STATEMENT OF ESTIMATED CASH FLOWS
FOR PLAN YEAR 19XX
(dollars in thousands)

Item	January	February	March	First Quarter Total	December	Fourth Quarter Total	Year Total
Cash Flows from Operating Activities							
Net income	$ 500	$ 450	$ 600	$1,500	$ 800	$2,100	$7,000
Adjustments (all related to operations)							
Depreciation and amortization	20	20	20	60	25	75	265
Provision for losses on accounts receivable	10	8	12	30	15	40	125
Increase in receivables	(12)	(14)	(14)	(40)	(5)	(10)	(90)
Decrease in inventories	20	10	30	60	10	20	110
Decrease in accounts payable and accrued items	(70)	(10)	(20)	(100)	(20)	(40)	(220)
Increase in income taxes payable	10	10	10	30	10	30	120
Increase in other liabilities	5	5	5	15	—	5	30
Total adjustments	(17)	29	43	55	35	120	340
Net cash provided by operating activities	483	479	643	1,605	835	2,220	7,340
Cash Flows from Investing Activities							
Purchases of Companies M and P, net of cash acquired	—	—	(700)	(700)	—	—	(2,575)
Capital expenditures	(100)	(300)	(2,100)	(2,500)	(200)	(400)	(3,300)
Proceeds—sale of facility	70	—	—	70	—	—	70
Net cash used in investing activities	(30)	(300)	(2,800)	(3,130)	(200)	(400)	(5,805)
Cash Flows from Financing Activities							
Proceeds for long-term debt	—	—	1,000	1,000	—	—	1,000
Proceeds from stock issue	—	—	2,000	2,000	—	—	1,000
Dividends paid	—	—	(600)	(600)	(650)	(650)	(2,550)
Net cash flows provided by financing activities	—	—	2,400	2,400	(650)	(650)	(550)
Net change in cash and equivalents	453	179	243	875	(15)	1,170	(550)
Cash and cash equivalents at beginning of period	1,400	1,853	2,032	1,400	2,400	1,215	1,400
Estimated cash and cash equivalents at end of period	$1,853	$2,032	$2,275	$2,275	$2,385	$2,385	$2,385

account and cash sales. Experience and a knowledge of trends will indicate what share of total sales probably will be for cash. From the sales forecast, then, the total cash sales value can be determined. In a somewhat similar fashion, information can be gleaned from the records to enable the controller to make a careful estimate of collections.

Once the experience has been analyzed, the results can be adjusted for trends and applied to the credit sales portrayed in the sales forecast.

An example illustrates the technique. Assume that an analysis of collection experience for June sales revealed the following collection data:

Description	% of Total Credit Sales
Collected in June	2.1
July	85.3
August	8.9
September	2.8
October	.3
Cash discounts	.5
Bad debt losses	.1
Total	100.0

If next year's sales in June could be expected to fall into the same pattern, then application of the percentages to estimated June credit sales would determine the probable monthly distribution of collections. The same analysis applied to each month of the year would result in a reasonably reliable basis for collection forecasting. The worksheet (June column) for cash collections might look somewhat as follows:

	Description		
Month of Sale	% Total	Sales Net	June Collections
February	.4	$149,500	$ 598
March	1.9	160,300	3,045
April	7.7	290,100	22,338
May	88.3	305,400	269,668
June	2.1	320,000	6,720
Total collections			302,369
Cash discounts (May)	.5	305,400	(1,527)
Losses	.1		(320)
Total			$300,522

Anticipated discounts must be calculated, since they enter into the profit forecast.

These experience factors must be modified, not only by trends developed over a period of time but also by the estimate of general business conditions as reflected in collections, as well as contemplated changes in terms of sale or other credit policies. Refinements in the approach can be made if experience varies widely between geographical territories, types of customers, or channels of distribution. The analysis of collections need not be made every month; it is sufficient if the distribution is checked occasionally.

Figure 27-3 is an example of a typical statement of estimated cash receipts by customer type. In this instance receipts from particular contracts are set out, in addition to the usual collections from customer sales.

(d) ESTIMATING CASH DISBURSEMENTS

If a complete operating budget is available, the controller should have little difficulty assembling the data into an estimate of cash disbursements. The usual cash disbursements in the typical industrial or commercial firm consist of salaried and hourly payrolls, materials, taxes, dividends, traveling expense, other operating expenses, interest, purchase of equipment, and retirement of stock.

From the labor budget, the manufacturing expense budget, and the commercial expense budget, the total anticipated expense for salaries and wages can be secured. Once this figure is available, the period of cash disbursement can be determined easily, for payrolls must be met on certain dates, closely following the time when earned. Reference to a calendar will establish the pay dates. Separate consideration should be given to the tax deductions from the gross pay, since these are not payable at the same time the net payroll is disbursed—unless special bank accounts are established for the tax deductions.

The material budget will set out the material requirements each month. The more important elements probably should be treated individually—power units or engines, for example. Other items will be grouped together. Only in a few instances is material purchased for cash. However, reference to required inventories and to delivery dates as well as assistance from the purchasing department will establish the time allowed for payments. If 30 days are required, then usage of one month can be moved forward for the purpose of estimating cash payments. The effect of cash discounts should be considered in arriving at the estimated disbursements.

The various manufacturing and operating expenses should be considered individually because they are by no means all the same. Some are prepayments or accruals, paid annually, such as property taxes and insurance. Some are noncash items, such as depreciation expense or bad debts. For a large number of individually small items, such as supplies, telephone and telegraph, and traveling expense, an average time lag may be used.

Cash requirements for capital additions should be determined from the plant budget or other known plans. No particular difficulty presents itself because the needs are relatively fixed and are established by the board of directors or other authority.

Usual practice requires the determination of cash receipts and disbursements exclusive of transactions involving voluntary debt retirements, purchase of treasury stock, or funds from bank loans. Decisions relative to these means of securing or disbursing cash are reached when the cash position is known and policy formulated accordingly. When branch plants are involved, all such outlying activities must be consolidated to get the overall picture.

A typical cash disbursements budget is illustrated in Figure 27-4, with a format found practical for estimating purposes. The treatment of payments on other than a monthly basis is shown.

Figure 27-3 Statement of Estimated Cash Receipts by Source.

Consolidated Electronics Corporation
STATEMENT OF ESTIMATED CASH RECEIPTS
FOR THE PERIOD JANUARY 1, 19XX THROUGH MARCH 31, 19XX

Description	January	February	March	Total
ELECTRONICS				
Fixed Price Contracts				
U. S. Government				
Progress payments	$ 625,000	$ 820,000	$1,150,000	$2,595,000
Collections on delivery	333,500	470,200	695,000	1,498,700
Total	958,500	1,290,200	1,845,000	4,093,700
Foreign Governments				
Advances	21,500	—	10,000	31,500
Collections on delivery	32,500	21,000	8,500	62,000
Miscellaneous	8,000	6,000	5,200	19,200
Total	62,000	27,000	23,700	112,700
Total Receipts—FP Contracts	1,020,500	1,317,200	1,868,700	4,206,400
Incentive—Commercial				
Refinery				
Advances from customers	20,000	—	—	20,000
Collections on account	35,900	39,500	28,000	103,400
Cash sales	4,300	4,000	4,500	12,800
Total	60,200	43,500	32,500	136,200
Automotive				
Advances from customers	890,000	410,000	300,000	1,600,000
Collections on delivery	245,000	390,000	250,000	885,000
Total	1,135,000	800,000	550,000	2,485,000
Total Collections—Electronics	2,215,700	2,160,700	2,451,200	6,827,600
HEAVY MACHINE TOOLS				
Petroleum				
Deposits	5,500	—	2,000	7,500
Collections on account	8,300	9,200	6,400	23,900
Cash sales	2,000	2,000	2,000	6,000
Total	15,800	11,200	10,400	37,400
Chemical				
Collections on account	12,500	11,300	8,100	31,900
Deposits	500	200	300	1,000
Cash sales	1,000	750	500	2,250
Total	14,000	12,250	8,900	35,150
Total Machine Tools Collections	29,800	23,450	19,300	72,550
Miscellaneous	1,000	1,000	1,000	3,000
Total Cash Receipts	$2,246,500	$2,185,150	$2,471,500	$6,903,150

Figure 27-4 Statement of Estimated Cash Disbursements.

Consolidated Spacecraft Corporation
STATEMENT OF ESTIMATED CASH DISBURSEMENTS
FOR THE PERIOD JANUARY 1 THROUGH DECEMBER 31, 19XX

Description	January	February	March	November	December	Total
INVENTORY ITEMS						
Raw Material and Purchased Parts						
Project 615						
Power units	$1,350,000	$1,325,000	$1,375,000	$1,300,000	$1,300,000	$15,840,000
Landing gears	325,000	325,000	320,000	325,000	415,000	3,900,000
Radios	115,000	117,500	117,500	110,000	115,000	1,380,000
Tires and tubes	120,000	110,000	110,000	110,000	122,500	1,320,000
Other	35,000	30,000	35,000	30,000	25,000	360,000
Total	1,945,000	1,907,500	1,957,500	1,880,000	1,977,500	22,800,000
Project 616						
Power units	80,000	76,000	84,000	160,000	168,000	1,200,000
Radios	10,000	10,000	12,000	24,000	30,000	132,000
Other	4,000	3,500	5,000	10,000	12,000	72,000
Total	94,000	89,500	101,000	194,000	210,000	1,404,000
Total Raw Materials and Purchased Parts	2,039,000	1,997,000	2,058,500	2,074,000	2,187,500	24,204,000
Subcontracted Production						
Project 615	420,000	510,000	480,000	105,000	120,000	3,600,000
Project 616	20,000	10,000	10,000	–	23,000	150,000
Total Subcontracted Production	440,000	520,000	490,000	105,000	143,000	3,750,000
Expenses						
Salaries and wages—direct	560,000	458,000	562,000	657,000	665,000	7,380,000
Salaries and wages—indirect	36,500	36,000	36,500	36,000	37,000	432,000
Total salaries and wages	596,500	494,000	598,500	693,000	702,000	7,812,000
Payroll taxes, etc.	35,900	31,300	37,800	24,900	18,400	373,000
Property taxes	–	–	122,000	–	–	122,000
Property insurance	–	72,500	–	–	–	122,500
Supplies	2,000	1,800	2,100	2,000	2,000	72,500
Other	11,000	11,000	11,000	11,000	11,000	132,000
Total Expenses	645,400	610,600	771,400	730,900	733,400	8,534,300
Total Inventory Items	3,124,400	3,127,600	3,319,900	2,909,900	3,063,900	36,488,300
OTHER CASH DISBURSEMENTS						
Administrative expense	12,000	12,000	17,000	15,500	12,000	168,000
Selling and advertising	17,000	12,000	45,000	11,500	22,500	310,000
Advances to vendors	20,500	–	–	–	–	20,500
Additions to fixed assets	101,000	51,000	19,500	–	17,000	397,500
Other	2,000	2,000	3,000	3,000	2,000	30,000
Total	152,500	77,000	84,500	30,000	53,500	926,000
Total Cash Disbursements	$3,276,900	$3,204,600	$3,404,400	$2,939,900	$3,117,400	$37,414,300

(e) FASB STATEMENT OF FINANCIAL ACCOUNTING STANDARDS NO. 95—STATEMENT OF CASH FLOWS

Having discussed the two methods in general use for estimating cash flows, it may be appropriate to review the new standard issued by the FASB relating to statements of cash flow. It could be relevant to the cash forecasting process if management desires that the internal estimating procedure closely parallel the format to be used in reporting cash flow to the investor or security analysts and others.

The cash reporting procedure prior to this standard in many instances suffered from these weaknesses:

- *No Common Definition of Cash.* Should it include cash equivalents, compensating balances, postdated checks, etc.?

- *No Common Format.* The format for the issuance of a cash flow statement was not distinguished from the statement of changes in financial condition.

- In many instances it was difficult to identify the cash flows from normal operating activity. (They were combined with other cash producing/generating activities.) Thus, the potential investor was at a disadvantage in gauging the cash generating potential of the normal everyday activities.

The complete FASB Statement of Financial Accounting Standards No. 95—Statement of Cash Flows should be reviewed in its entirety by the controller. Though lengthy, the standard should be useful for many reasons, including these:

- It provides examples of the cash flow formats that meet the standard for general purpose external financial accounting and reporting. (See Chapter 35.) Examples of typical statements of cash flows included in the annual report to shareholders is discussed in Chapter 37.

- It includes the many helpful definitions regarding cash flows from the three basic sources: operating, investing, and financing activities.

- It contains useful background data on cash flow statements and the basis of the FASB for reaching the conclusions it did.

- In addition to examples of statements of cash flow for a domestic manufacturing company, it provides an example of a statement of cash flows under the direct method for a domestic manufacturing company with foreign operations.

Some examples of current reporting practices are provided later in this chapter.

(f) RELATION OF CASH BUDGET TO OTHER BUDGETS

From the preceding discussion, it is readily apparent that preparation of the cash budget is generally dependent on other budgets—the sales forecast, the statement of estimated income and expense, the various operating budgets, the capital budget, and the long-range strategic plan. It is in reality part of a coordinated program of sales and costs correlated with business sheet changes and expected revenues and expenditures.

It can be appreciated, also, that the cash budget is a check on the entire budgetary program. If the operating budget goals are achieved, the results will be reflected in the cash position. Failure to achieve budgeted performance may result in the treasurer seeking additional sources of cash.

Depending on the financial position of the company, the cash forecast may have a high priority. Many executives prefer to review the cash forecast ahead of other projected statements, and it may, therefore, take the number one spot in the complete report on expected operations.

(g) LENGTH OF CASH BUDGET PERIOD

The length of the budget period depends on several factors, including the purpose the budget is to serve, the financial condition of the company, and the opinion of the executives about the practicality and accuracy of estimating. For illustration, a short-term forecast would be used in determining cash requirements—perhaps for one to three months in advance. But if the cash margin is low, an estimate of cash receipts and disbursements may be necessary on a weekly basis or even daily. On the other hand, a firm with ample cash may develop a cash forecast, by months, for six months or a year in advance. For the determination of general financial policy a longer term budget is necessary. Some companies feel that estimating beyond three months is inaccurate and restrict the cash budget to this period. Other companies maintain a running budget for three or more months in advance, always adding one month and dropping off the present month. A controller will have to adapt his forecasting to the conditions he finds. He may prepare a short-term cash budget for cash requirements purposes and also a long-term forecast for use in financial policy decisions.

(h) PUTTING THE CASH BUDGET TO WORK

The controller can prepare the cash budget in the usual manner, indicating the extent of additional cash funds needed, if any, and the probable duration of such need. However, the responsibility for securing these funds on the most advantageous basis rests with the treasurer or chief financial officer. He, and not the chief accounting officer, would usually negotiate with banks for loans, or would invest surplus funds. Yet the part played by the controller is not always as routine as might appear. In times of adversity, he must be prepared to furnish extra information. Thus the treasurer may need to know the exact cash needs of the following week. This can be furnished by manually adding the bills payable at that time, as well as the payrolls. If the accounts payable are in the computer file, the requirements can be readily determined by tabulating the applicable due date file. The same procedure can be used in determining the funds, if any, to be transferred to each branch for the weekly period.

Cash requirements must be planned just as other operations are planned. It simply is not satisfactory to assume that a high volume of sales will automatically result in a sound financial position or that with a satisfactory budgeted profit and loss statement finances will take care of themselves. The controller can be an effective voice in establishing the necessity for a well-developed financial program.

27-5 CASH COLLECTIONS

(a) ADMINISTRATION OF CASH RECEIPTS

One of the primary objectives of financial management is the conservation and effective utilization of cash. From the cash collection viewpoint, there are two phases of control: (1) the acceleration of collections, and (2) proper internal control of collections.

(b) ACCELERATION OF CASH RECEIPTS

Two methods are commonly used to speed up the collection of receivables—the lock-box system and area concentration banking. The lock-box system involves the establishment of depository accounts in the various geographical areas of significant cash collections so that remittances from customers will take less time in transit—preferably not more than one day. Customers mail remittances to the company at a locked post office box in the region served by the bank. The bank collects the remittances and deposits the proceeds to the account of the company. Funds in excess of those required to cover costs are periodically transferred to company headquarters. Supporting documents accompanying remittances are mailed by the bank to the company. Collections are thus accelerated through reduction in transit time with resultant lower credit exposure. Arrangements must be made, however, for proper control of credit information.

Under the system of area concentration banking, local company units collect remittances and deposit them in the local bank. From the local bank, usually by wire transfers, expeditious movement of funds is made to a few area or regional concentration banks. Funds in excess of compensating balances are automatically transferred by wire to the company's banking headquarters. By this technique in-transit time is reduced.

The controller is expected to be aware of these and other devices for accelerating collections, and to assist the treasurer, should that be necessary.

While checks are the predominant means of collecting accounts receivable, an increasing amount of business is handled through electronic fund transfer (EFT). Moreover, there are various combinations of methods and instruments that speed collections. The controller may wish to review some of the Selected References dealing with aspects of these different collection methods:

- Lockbox.
- Depository transfer check (DTC).
- Preauthorized draft (PAD).
- ACH transfer (from one bank to another through the ACH system).
- Wire transfer.

Section 27-8 includes limited comments on the employment of the new technology in use and services that might be expected from the company's banking institutions.

(c) INTERNAL CONTROL OF CASH RECEIPTS

In most business organizations, the usual routine cash transactions are numerous. The following sources are typical: (1) mail receipts, (2) over-the-counter cash sales, (3) sales or collections made by salesmen, solicitors, etc., and (4) over-the-counter collections on account. Naturally, all businesses have other cash transactions of a less routine nature, such as receipts from the sale of fixed assets, that may be handled by the officers or require special procedures. Most of the cash problems will be found to center on the transactions just listed, because the more unusual or less voluminous cash receipts are readily susceptible to a simple check.

Regardless of the source of cash, the very basis for the prevention of errors or fraud is the principle of internal check. Such a system involves the separation of the actual handling of cash from the records relating to cash. It requires that the work of one employee be supplemented by the work of another. Certain results must always agree. For example, the daily cash deposit must be the same as the charge to the cash control account. This automatic checking of the work of one employee by another clearly discourages fraud and locates errors. Under such conditions, any peculations are generally restricted to cases of carelessness or collusion.

The system of internal control must be designed on the groundwork of the individual organization. However, there are some general suggestions that will be helpful to the controller in reviewing the situation in his own company:

1. All receipts of cash through the mails should be recorded in advance of transfer to the cashier. Periodically, these records should be traced to the deposit slip.

2. All receipts should be deposited intact daily. This procedure might also require a duplicate deposit slip to be sent by the bank or person making the deposit (other than the cashier) to an independent department—for use in subsequent check or audit.

3. Responsibility for handling of cash should be clearly defined and definitely fixed.

4. Usually, the functions of receiving cash and disbursing cash should be kept entirely separate (except in financial institutions).

5. The actual handling of cash should be entirely separate from the maintenance of records, and the cashiers should not have access to these records.

6. Tellers, agents, and field representatives should be required to give receipts, retaining a duplicate, of course.

7. Bank reconciliations should be made by those not handling cash or keeping the records. Similarly, the mailing of statements to customers, including the check-off against the ledger accounts, should be done by a third party. The summarizing of cash records also may be handled by a third party.

8. All employees handling cash or cash records should be required to take a periodic vacation, and someone else should handle the job during such absence. Also, at unannounced times, employees should be shifted in jobs to detect or prevent collusion.

9. All employees handling cash or cash records should be adequately bonded.

10. Mechanical and other protective devices should be used where applicable to give added means of check—cash registers, the tape being read by a third party; duplicate sales slips; daily cash blotters.

11. Where practical, cash sales should be verified by means of inventory records and periodic physical inventories.

(d) ILLUSTRATIVE CASH RECEIPTS PROCEDURE

A simple and effective cash receipts procedure can be executed that embodies some of the controls mentioned in the preceding section and that is adaptable by most industrial firms receiving cash by mail. All incoming mail not addressed to a specific individual is opened in the mail room. Any mail containing remittances is listed on a daily remittance sheet prepared in triplicate. The name, check number, date, and amount are detailed on the record (Figure 27-5). One copy is forwarded, with the envelopes and remittance slips, to the cashier; a second goes to the auditor, treasurer, or controller; and the third copy is retained by the mail room. The cashier records the cash received

Figure 27-5   Mail Room Remittance Sheet.

The Blank Company
MAIL ROOM REMITTANCE SHEET
Receipts of ___July 19, 19XX___

Check No., etc.	Source if Not Check	Sender	City and State	Amount
1602		The Rush Airplane Company	Scranton, Pa.	$ 126.12
195692	P.M.O.	Rentaul Air Service	Stamford, Conn.	19.50
2402		Automatic Service Company	Los Angeles, Calif.	316.00
1613		Voe Parts Dealer	Toledo, Ohio	2.90
9865		Brush Electric Company	Chicago, Ill.	25.50
2915		Ajax Manufacturing Company	Cleveland, Ohio	1,002.60
8512		Apex Machine Tool Co.	New York City	18.60

Total... $1,511.22

Prepared by ___J. J. B.___
Date ___7/19/XX___

Original: Cashier

via the mail room on his daily cash sheet or computer recording (Figure 27-6), indicating the nature of the receipt, along with any other receipts from other sources. This cash record is subsequently sent to the accounting department for posting, details as well as summary, after the cashier has made a summary entry in his records. The deposit slip is prepared in quadruplicate. The cashier retains one copy. Three copies go to the bank for receipting, one of which is retained by the bank; another is returned to the cashier as evidence the bank received the funds; and a third is sent to the auditing department or controller's office. This is then compared in total, and occasionally in detail, with the daily cash register. The remittance sheet is also test-checked against the deposit slip. The cashier, of course, does not have access to the accounts receivable records or general ledger, nor does he handle disbursements.

These basic methods may be adapted, in large degree, to personal computer systems.

(e) COMMON METHODS OF MISAPPROPRIATING CASH

An enumeration of some of the more common methods of misappropriating company funds may be a guide to the controller in recognizing points to guard against:

1. Mail receipts.
   a. Lapping—diverting cash and reporting it some time after it has been collected; usually, funds received from one account are credited against another account from which cash has been diverted earlier.
   b. Borrowing funds temporarily, without falsifying any records, or simply not recording all cash received.
   c. Falsifying totals in the cashbook.
   d. Overstating discounts and allowances.
   e. Charging off a customer's account as a bad debt and pocketing the cash.
   f. Withholding of miscellaneous income, such as insurance refunds.
2. Over-the-counter sales.
   a. Failing to report all sales and pocketing the cash.
   b. Underadding the sales slip and pocketing the difference.
   c. Falsely representing refunds or expenditures.
   d. Registering a smaller amount than the true amount of sale.
   e. Pocketing cash overages.
3. Collections by salesmen.
   a. Conversion of checks made payable to "cash."
   b. Failure to report sales.
   c. Overstating amount of trade-ins.

Where adequate internal control is used, most of these practices cannot be carried on without collusion.

Figure 27-6 Daily Cash Sheet.

DAILY CASH SHEET

Date April 20, 19XX

Check No.	Description	Debit Cash (101)	Trade Accounts Receivable (108)	Deposits (104)	CREDIT Cash Sales (501)	Employees Accounts Receivable (106)	OTHER Account	OTHER Description	OTHER Amount
1242	Jones Chemical Co.	$ 622.50	$	$	$ 622.50	$			$
846	Witmer Candy Co.	9,875.00	9,875.00						
101	Prescott Molding Co.	4,322.50	4,322.50						
10	Rush Mfg. Co.	12,500.00		12,500.00					
322	Monsanto Cyanamid Co.	16,321.50	16,321.50						
464	Laughlin Stamping Co.	421.12			421.12				
422	Aero Company	3,820.00	3,820.00						
	Marjorie Jones	16.00				16.00			
	Adela Castle	1.20				1.20			
	Pierre's Restaurant	19.70					662	Vending Machine Income	19.70
	Total	$47,919.52	$34,339.00	$12,500.00	$1,043.62	$17.20			$19.70

745

(f) OTHER MEANS OF DETECTING FRAUD

In addition to the segregation of duties that has been described, certain other practices may be adopted to further deter any would-be peculator or embezzler. One of these tools is surprise audits by the internal auditor as well as by the public accountants. Another is the prompt follow-up of past-due accounts. Proper instructions to customers about where checks should be mailed, and a specific request that they be made payable to the company, and not to any individual, also will help. Bonding of all employees, with a detailed check of references, is a measure of protection. Special checking of unusual receipts of a miscellaneous nature will tend to discourage irregularities.

For additional comments on internal control and fraud prevention, see Chapter 9.

27-6 CASH DISBURSEMENTS

(a) CONTROL OF CASH DISBURSEMENTS

In this area of cash administration, also, there are two aspects of control: (1) the timing of payments, and (2) the system of internal control.

Experience indicates the value of maintaining careful controls over the timing of disbursements to insure that bills are paid only as they are due and not before. In such a manner, cash can be conserved for temporary investment.

Another consideration in payment scheduling is the conscious use of cash "float." By recognizing in-transit items and the fact that ordinarily bank balances are greater than book balances because of checks not cleared, book balances of cash may be planned at lower levels. The incoming float may be balanced against the outgoing payments.

The relationship between the time a check is released to the payee and the time it clears the bank, the disbursement float, is made up of three elements:

1. The time needed for the check to travel by mail or other delivery from the issuer to the payee.
2. The time required by the payee to process the check.
3. The period required by the banking system to clear the check, i.e., the time from deposit by the payee to the time the item is charged to the issuer's account.

In controlling this "float," it often is helpful to trace the time interval of large checks to estimate the proper allowance for the period required for checks to clear. The controller should take measures to assure there is no abuse of float (e.g., writing of checks on banks in some remote location far from the recipient's address, so as to secure an additional three or four days of float).

(b) ADMINISTRATIVE BANK ACCOUNTS

In the control of disbursements, particularly where subsidiary or field office divisional transactions are involved, several special purpose bank accounts may be used (e.g., imprest accounts, zero balance accounts, and automatic balance accounts).

Under an imprest system, the unit operates with a fixed maximum balance. Periodically, such as weekly, or when the fund is below a minimum level, receipted bills are submitted for reimbursement.

With a zero balance account system, the clearing account for the organizational segment is kept at a zero balance. When checks are presented for payment, arrangements are such that the bank is authorized to transfer funds from the corporate general account to cover the items. Payment may be made by draft. Comparable arrangements can be made for the treasurer to make wire transfers to the zero bank account on notification of the items being presented for payment. Zero bank balance arrangements can facilitate control of payments through one or a limited number of accounts. The system may facilitate a quick check of the corporate cash position.

Automatic balance accounts use the same account for receipts and disbursements. When the account is above a specified maximum level, the excess funds are transferred to the central bank account; conversely, when the balance drops below a minimum level, the bank may call for replenishment.

27-7 INTERNAL CONTROL

(a) IMPORTANCE OF INTERNAL CONTROL

Once the cash has been deposited in the bank, it would seem that the major problem of safeguarding the cash has been solved. Control of cash disbursements is a relatively simple matter—if a few rules are followed. After the vendor's invoice has been approved for payment, the next step usually is the preparation of the check for executive signature. If all disbursements are subject to this top review, how can any problem exist? Yet it is at precisely this point that the greatest danger is met. Any controller who has had to sign numerous checks knows that it is indeed an irksome task—the review to ascertain that receiving reports are attached, the checking of payee against the invoice, and the comparison of amounts. Because it is such a monotonous chore, it is often done in a most perfunctory manner. Yet this operation, carefully done, is essential to the control of disbursements. Where two signatures are required, both signatures need not make the detailed review, but certainly one should. The other can review on a spot-check basis only. There are too many instances where false documents and vouchers used a second time have been the means of securing executive signatures. Prevention of this practice demands careful review before signing checks, as well as other safeguards. It cannot be taken for granted that everything is all right. Those who sign the checks must adopt a questioning attitude on every transaction that appears doubtful or is not fully understood. Indeed, the review of documents attached to checks will often bring to light foolish expenditures and weaknesses in other procedures.

(b) SOME PRINCIPLES OF INTERNAL CONTROL

The opportunities for improper or incorrect use of funds are so great that a controller cannot unduly emphasize the need for proper safeguards in the cash disbursement function. Vigilance and sound audit procedures are necessary. Although the system of internal control must be tailored to fit the needs of the organization, some general suggestions may be helpful:

1. Except for petty cash transactions, all disbursements should be made by check.

2. All checks should be prenumbered, and all numbers accounted for as either used or voided.

3. All general disbursement checks for amounts in excess of $x, e.g., $5000 should require two signatures.

4. Responsibility for cash receipts should be divorced from responsibility for cash disbursements.

5. All persons signing checks or approving disbursements should be adequately bonded.

6. Bank reconciliations should be made by those who do not sign checks or approve payments.

7. The keeping of cash records should be entirely separate from the handling of cash disbursements.

8. Properly approved invoices and other required supporting documents should be a prerequisite to making every disbursement.

9. Checks for reimbursement of imprest funds and payrolls should be made payable to the individual and not to the company or bearer.

10. After payment has been made, all supporting documents should be perforated or otherwise mutilated or marked "paid" to prevent reuse.

11. Mechanical devices should be used to the extent practical—check writers, safety paper, etc.

12. Annual vacations or shifts in jobs should be enforced for those handling disbursements.

13. Approval of vouchers for payment usually should be done by those not responsible for disbursing.

14. Special authorizations for interbank transfers should be required, and a clearing account, perhaps called Bank Transfers, should be maintained.

15. All petty cash vouchers should be written in ink or typewritten.

16. It may be desirable to periodically and independently verify the bona fide existence of the regularly used suppliers of recurring services, e.g., consultants, lawyers.

Additional aspects of internal control are addressed in Chapter 9.

(c) METHODS OF MISAPPROPRIATING FUNDS

The safeguards just listed are some of those developed on the basis of experience by many firms. Some common means of perpetrating fraud are these:

1. Preparing false vouchers or presenting vouchers twice for payment.

2. "Kiting," or unauthorized borrowing by not recording the disbursement, but recording the deposit, in the case of bank transfers.

3. Falsifying footing in cash records.

4. Raising the amount on checks after they have been signed.

5. Understating cash discounts.

6. Cashing unclaimed payroll or divided checks.

7. Altering petty cash vouchers.

8. Forging checks and destroying them when received from the bank—substituting other canceled checks or charge slips.

(d) BANK RECONCILIATIONS

An important phase of internal control is the reconciling of the balance per bank statement with the balance per books. This is particularly true with respect to general bank accounts as distinguished from accounts solely for disbursing paychecks. If properly done, the task is much more than a listing of outstanding checks, deposits in transit, and unrecorded bank charges. For example, the deposits and disbursements as shown on the bank statement should be reconciled with those on the books. A convenient form to handle this is illustrated in Figure 27-7. Then, too, it is desirable to compare endorsements with the payee and to check the payee against the record.

It has been mentioned previously that bank reconciliations should be handled by someone independent of any cash receipts or disbursements activities. The job can be handled by the controller or may be performed by the bank itself. Particular attention should be paid to outstanding checks of the preceding period and to deposits at the end of the month to detect kiting.

(e) PETTY CASH FUNDS

Most businesses must make some small disbursements. To meet these needs, petty cash funds are established that operate on an imprest fund basis, that is, the balances are fixed. At any time the cash, plus the unreimbursed vouchers, should equal the amount of the fund. Numerous funds of this type may be necessary in the branch offices or at each plant. A uniform receipt and uniform procedure should be provided, including limits on individual disbursements through this channel, proper approvals, etc. If it is practicable, the person handling cash receipts or disbursements should not handle petty cash. Other safeguards would include surprise cash counts, immediate cancellation of all petty cash slips after payment, and careful scrutiny of reimbursements. Although the fund may be small, very considerable sums can be expended. The controller should not neglect checking this activity.

(f) PAYROLLS

In most concerns, payroll disbursements represent a very sizable proportion of all cash payments. Proper safeguards for this disbursement are particularly desirable. The use of a special payroll account is a very common procedure. A check in the exact amount of the total net payroll is deposited in the payroll account against which the individual checks are drawn. This has advantages from an internal control standpoint, and it may facilitate the reconciling of bank accounts.

The preparation of the payroll, of course, should be separate from the actual handling of cash. Special payroll audits are advisable—by the internal audit staff—to review procedures, verify rates, check clerical accuracy, and witness the payoff.

Figure 27-7   Bank Reconciliation.

The Jones Company

BANK RECONCILIATION

Bank _____National Trust Co._____

Account _____General_____

As of _____December 31, 19XX_____

	Balance 11/30/XX	Receipts	Disburse-ments	Balance 12/31/XX
Per Bank...............	$126,312.50	$92,420.00	$85,119.00	$133,613.50
Add:				
Deposits in Transit				
Date per Bank Per Book				
12/1 11/30	5,600.00	(5,600.00)		
1/2 12/31		12,500.00		12,500.00
Deduct:				
Outstanding Checks				
Nov................	4,320.00		(4,115.00)	205.00
(Per List Attached)				
Dec................			6,110.00	6,110.00
Other Items:				
Bank Charges Not Re-corded.............			(5.01)	5.01
Per Books..............	$127,592.50	$99,320.00	$87,108.99	$139,803.51

Prepared by ___R. S.___

Date ___1/12/XX___

27-8 REPORTS ON CASH

(a) CASH REPORTS FOR INTERNAL USE

The cash reports used in most businesses are rather simple in nature but still provide important information. Reports on estimated cash requirements and balances or receipts or disbursements are illustrated in Figures 27-1 through 27-4.

For information purposes, a simple daily cash report is prepared in some companies for the chief executive and treasurer. It merely summarizes the cash receipts and cash disbursements, as well as balances of major banks. An example is shown in Figure 27-8. Such a report may be issued daily, weekly or monthly, depending on needs. A detailed statement of cash receipts is illustrated in Figure 27-9.

From the control viewpoint, it is desirable to know how collections and disbursements compare with estimates. Such information is shown in Figure 27-10, as well as the expected cash balance at month-end.

Figure 27-8   Daily Cash Report.

The Day Company	
DAILY CASH REPORT	
AS OF THE CLOSE OF BUSINESS, JUNE 16, 19XX	
Balance, June 15, 19XX	$135,300
Receipts	10,200
Total	145,500
Disbursements	15,300
Balance, June 16, 19XX	$130,200
Bank Balances, etc	
National City Bank—General	$ 65,900
Commerce National Bank—General	22,100
Ohio Trust Company—General	30,500
Total	118,500
Petty Cash and Payroll Funds	11,700
Total	$130,200

In addition to comparing actual and forecasted cash activity, it is also useful to periodically compare book balances with those required to meet service charges of the banks and compensating balances. Such a report compares the "objective" balance with actual book and actual bank balances. This type of report provides a periodic check on effective cash utilization by recording (1) the absence of excessive balances,

Figure 27-9   Statement of Daily Cash Receipts.

The X Y Z Company		
STATEMENT OF DAILY CASH RECEIPTS		
Date _____		

	Account	Amount
No.	**Name**	
201–1	Accounts Receivable—Aircraft	$
201–2	Accounts Receivable—Parts	
201–3	Accounts Receivable—Employees	
201–5	Accounts Receivable—Intercompany	
201–6	Accounts Receivable—Miscellaneous	
303	Claims Receivable	
801	Deposits on Account	
1001–1	Cash Sales—Aircraft	
1001–2	Cash Sales—Parts	
1001–3	Cash Sales—Scrap	
1001–4	Cash Sales—Miscellaneous	
6001	Revenue—Vending Machines	
6005	Royalty Income	
6010	Miscellaneous Income and Expense	
Total		$

Figure 27-10   Comparison of Actual and Estimated Cash Activity.

The Roth Company
WEEKLY CASH REPORT
FOR THE WEEK ENDED NOVEMBER 16, 19XX
(thousands of dollars)

Description	Actual Week Ended 11/16/XX	Month to Date Actual	Month to Date Estimated
Beginning Cash Balance	$17,890	$ 32,511	$ 32,510
CASH RECEIPTS			
Government	10,810	18,310	18,000
Wholesale	19,620	67,730	65,500
Retail	8,330	21,100	23,400
Total	38,760	107,140	106,900
CASH DISBURSEMENTS			
Accounts Payable—Expenses	12,330	12,860	12,300
Payrolls	12,660	37,010	36,900
Material Purchases	1,890	19,340	14,300
Federal Taxes	2,790	8,640	8,920
Capital Expenditures	13,370	39,990	40,190
Other	1,060	2,030	2,000
Total	44,100	119,870	114,610
Ending Cash Balance	$12,550	$ 19,781	$ 24,800
Estimated Month-End Balance			$ 30,000

and (2) progress in keeping bank balances adequate to fairly compensate the financial institution. A cash management report is shown in Figure 27-11.

There are any number of variations in cash reports, including some that are greatly detailed about daily cash receipts, etc. The suggested reports are merely examples; many may be adapted to computer applications.

(b) CASH FLOW ANALYSIS FOR INVESTMENT PURPOSES

Cash flow as a broad measure of company performance is discussed in Chapter 7. Reference also is made to "free cash flow," a further refinement of cash flow in that from "cash flow" is subtracted a provision for required capital expenditures and, in some calculations, the dividend payments. In this latter case, the subtrahend is the equivalent of "discretionary funds," and it represents sums that can be spent on acquisitions, stock buybacks, inventory, and many other items.

Where reported earnings are heavily reduced by depreciation, cash flow in some industries is an analytical yardstick of choice. It is useful to investors in spotting companies with ample resources to make them rewarding acquisitions. Additionally, corporate raiders are attracted to high cash flow situations because the cash stream may be used to pay down heavy debt incurred in a takeover. Periodically, listings appear

Figure 27-11   Actual and Objective Bank Balances.

The Steven Company
QUARTERLY REPORT ON BANK BALANCES
AS AT JUNE 30, 19XX
(thousands of dollars)

Bank	Actual per Books	Objective	(Over) Under Objective	Balance per Bank Statement
First National City . . .	$ 19,870	$ 20,200	$ 330	$ 23,070
Chase Manhattan	17,440	17,800	360	19,120
Morgan Guaranty	16,850	16,500	(350)	17,180
Bank of America	14,310	15,700	1,390	15,810
Chemical Bank	10,870	10,250	(620)	12,300
First Interstate	6,430	5,900	(530)	7,110
American Trust	5,510	5,800	290	5,840
Anglo-American	4,380	4,500	120	4,760
National Bank of Commerce . . .	2,890	3,000	110	3,020
Other Local	490	—	(490)	520
Total Cash in Banks—U. S. . . .	99,040	99,650	610	108,730
Subsidiaries—Foreign . . .	8,190	7,000	(1,190)	8,600
Cash Funds	760	750	(10)	
Total Cash	$107,990	$107,400	$ (590)	$117,330

comparing stock prices in terms of cash flow. For example, *Barron's* published a list of 50 companies selling at low multiples of cash flow, including:[1]

Company	Stock Price	Price/ Free Cash Flow	Price Cash Flow	P/E Ratio	LT Debt as % of Capital
Cleveland-Cliffs	$ 29.0	4.4	5.4	6.2	29.9%
Copperweld	13.8	5.7	4.0	7.6	25.2
Dow Chemical	100.3	8.8	5.5	6.7	30.0
Arco Chemical	37.1	9.5	5.8	7.3	16.3

The controller should be aware that cash flow may rank high in judging the investment worth of a company. It is a feature that usually deserves comment in any analytical effort.

27-9 CASH FLOW RATIO ANALYSIS

The requirement by the FASB for companies to provide shareholders (with access to the public and to potential investors) with a statement of cash flows—which identifies

---

[1] Jay Palmer, "Beyond P/E's, A List of Stocks Selling at Low Multiples of Cash Flow," *Barron's*, Aug. 21, 1989, p. 16.

cash flows from operating activities, as well as that from investing activities and financing activities—has facilitated and encouraged the use of certain cash flow ratios These ratios are useful in the planning and control of cash in that they may provide benchmarks or standards to measure the cash performance of a given company against other entities. Such comparisons may be helpful in evaluating financial performance of an acquisition target or other investments. Equally valuable, the ratios may be used to judge trends in the controller's own company and as compared with competitors or other selected best-in-their class entities.

The cash flow ratios are of two types. The *sufficiency* ratios directly measure the ability of a company to generate enough cash flow to meet the needs of the entity, such as the ability to pay long-term debt, provide for needed plant and equipment, and pay dividends to the owners. The *efficiency* ratios indicate how well a company generates cash from selected measures, such as sales, income from continuing operations, and from total assets (or total assets employed).

Some *sufficiency* ratios and their derivatives are as follows:

Ratio	Derivation
Cash flow adequacy	$= \dfrac{\text{Cash from operations}}{\text{Long-term debt paid} + \text{Funds for assets purchased} + \text{Dividends paid}}$
Long-term debt repayment	$= \dfrac{\text{Long-term debt payments}}{\text{Cash from operations}}$
Dividend payout	$= \dfrac{\text{Dividends}}{\text{Cash from operations}}$
Reinvestment	$= \dfrac{\text{Purchase of assets}}{\text{Cash from operations}}$
Debt coverage	$= \dfrac{\text{Total debt}}{\text{Cash from operations}}$
Depreciation − Amortization relationship	$= \dfrac{\text{Depreciation} + \text{Amortization}}{\text{Cash from operations}}$

Some *efficiency* cash flow ratios are:

Ratio	Derivation
Cash flow to sales	$\dfrac{\text{Cash flow from operations}}{\text{Sales}}$
Operations index	$\dfrac{\text{Cash flow from operations}}{\text{Income from continuing operations}}$
Cash flow return on assets	$\dfrac{\text{Cash flow from operations}}{\text{Total assets (or total assets employed)}}$

The cash efficiency ratios reflect the effectiveness or efficiency by which cash is generated from either operations or assets. Specifically:

1. The cash flow to sales ratio reflects the percentage of each sales dollar realized as cash.
2. The operations index reflects the ratio of cash generated to the income from continuing operations.
3. The cash flow from assets reflects the relative amount of cash which the assets (or assets employed) are able to generate.

These ratios will assist in the analysis of financial statements. However, there is still a need for a consensus as to what are useful cash flow ratios, and the development of norms or standards for companies and industries. (See Chapter 8 for additional comments about these and other financial and operating ratios.)

27-10 IMPACT OF NEW INFORMATION TECHNOLOGY AND ORGANIZATIONAL STRUCTURES

The vast majority of the basic cash management functions described earlier in this chapter have been performed for years and will continue to be accomplished. But *how* they will be done, and what organization structure will do them (*who*) is subject to change. The pressures or influences that are causing or accelerating adjustments are many and include:

- The substantial improvements in information technology, or computer technology.
- Growth in the global nature of business.
- Economic pressures that are causing entities to integrate horizontally, to reduce staff size (such as treasury or controllership functions), to focus on the principal business, and to do more subcontracting or outsourcing.
- Closer electronic integration with supplier, customer, or other third parties (such as banks).

The personal computer and the related software greatly aid in the analysis of data required for a cash forecast, as well as the actual preparation of the cash plan. As corporations and banks electronically integrate, there are many possibilities that should be of interest to the controller (for internal control and other purposes) including:

- Using an EDI file, a customer can supply selling company's bank directly with invoice data and arrange payment. The bank will then update the payee's account.
- Where banks handle the lockbox operations, they can book images of remittance documents in a computer file and avoid enormous sorting and reassociation of check copies, etc. Less paperwork means less cost.
- Arrangements can be made with a company's bank for automatic payment of taxes and/or other designated items. This reduces float and provides greater control over the payment.

- Companies can arrange a system for electronic payment of selected supplier in-voices thus reducing paperwork.
- For faster information, arrangements can be made for electronic account analysis.
- Banks can provide an automated check reconcilement through data transmission
- Other systems have been developed by banks, using modern technology at the time of check presentments to reduce fraud.

Aside from the technology involved, companies can select banks to perform du-ties regularly handled by their own internal departments, such as portfolio management; cash collections, cash disbursements; payroll check preparation, retirement funds custody, accounting, and disbursements. Outsourcing of some financial activities is no longer a dirty word. Hopefully, the treasurer will have close contact with the company's banks in order to keep abreast of what services can be proved (more cheaply) on an outsourcing basis.

27-11 INVESTMENT OF SHORT-TERM FUNDS

In many companies, surplus or excess funds not needed for either operating purposes or compensating bank balances are available for investment—even over weekends. Prudent use of otherwise idle funds can add to income. Although the financial officer ordinarily will direct the investment of these funds, the controller may be concerned with adequate reporting and control and generally should be somewhat knowledgeable about the subject.

(a) CRITERIA FOR SELECTING INVESTMENTS

Given the opportunity for earning additional income from temporary excess funds, what are some of the criteria to be considered in selecting the investment vehicle? There probably are five—and all somewhat related:

1. *Safety of Principal.* A primary objective should be to avoid instruments that might risk loss of the investment.
2. *Price Stability.* If the company is suddenly called on to liquidate the security to acquire funds, price stability would be important in avoiding a significant loss.
3. *Marketability.* The money manager must consider whether the security can be sold, if required, rather easily and quite quickly.
4. *Maturity.* Funds may be invested until the demand for cash arises—perhaps as reflected in the cash forecast. Hence maturities should relate to prospective cash needs. Temporary investments usually involve maturities of a day or two to as much as a year.
5. *Yield.* The financial officer of course is interested in optimizing the earnings or securing at least a competitive return on the investment and is thus interested in the yield. This is not necessarily the most important criterion, because low-risk, high-liquidity investments will not provide the highest yield.

The importance attached to each of these factors will depend on the management philosophy, condition of the market, and inclinations of the investing person. Is he conservatively inclined or not? Restrictions placed on the operation will influence the weighting of each.

(b) INVESTMENT RESTRICTIONS

Sometimes the board of directors will place restrictions on just how short-term funds may be invested. In other instances, the senior financial officer will provide such guidelines. Subjects covered would include the following:

1. Maximum maturity.
2. Credit rating of issuer.
3. Maximum investment in selected types of securities.
    By user.

    By type of instrument.

    By country.

    By currency.

Instruments for investment vary widely, and market conditions may dictate the most desirable at any particular time. Typical money market instruments include these:

U.S. Treasury bills.

U.S. Treasury notes and bonds.

Negotiable certificates of deposit.

Banker's acceptances.

Selected foreign government issues.

Federal agency issues.

Repurchase agreements.

Prime commercial paper.

Finance company paper.

Short-term tax exempts.

An illustration of the guidelines of an aerospace company for use in making temporary investments is shown in Figure 27-12.

(c) INVESTMENT CONTROLS

Many securities that companies purchase as short-term investments are negotiable. Additionally, these investments often are paid for through bank wire transfers. Given the nature and frequency of transactions, the control system should be adequate.

Many corporations contract with a major commercial bank to serve as custodian of the securities, to make payment on incoming delivery, and to receive funds on out-going delivery. The form of contract should provide maximum safeguards to the company.

Because opportunities for fraud exist, given telephonic transactions and wire transfer of funds, care must be exercised in the form and nature of confirmation secured and the internal controls used in authorizing payment.

Figure 27-12   Guidelines for Short-Term Investments.

The Aerospace Service Corporation
INTERNAL GUIDELINES
FOR TOTAL SHORT-TERM INVESTMENTS
EFFECTIVE NOVEMBER 1, 19XX

Objective

To invest excess cash in only top-quality–short-term investments, for optimum total return, commensurate with corporate liquidity requirements.

Liquidity

Liquidity shall be provided by minimum and maximum limits as follows:

1. At least $80 million shall be invested in overnight investments and in negotiable marketable obligations of major U.S. issuers.
2. No more than 50% of the total portfolio shall be invested in time deposits or other investments with a lack of liquidity such as commercial paper for which only the dealer and issuer make a market.

Diversification

Diversification shall be provided through a limit on each nongovernment issuer as listed next. These are general limits, and in each case quality review may result in elimination or a lower limit for an issuer. Overnight or repurchase investments must meet quality criteria but are not subject to limits on the amount invested.

1. U.S. Government and agencies—no limit.
2. Domestic bank certificates of deposit, time deposits and banker's acceptances —$30-million limit for banks with capital accounts in excess of $800 million (top 10 banks); $20 million for banks with capital accounts of $350 to $800 million (second 11 banks); $5 million for all other banks with capital accounts in excess of $250 million (11 banks).
3. U.S. dollar (or fully hedged foreign currency) obligations of foreign banks, each with capital accounts exceeding $500 million—limited to $15 million each for Canadian banks and $10 million each for other foreign banks, subject to an aggregate limit of $75 million for non-Canadian foreign banks.
4. Domestic commercial paper with P-1/A-1 rating only—$20-million limit for issuers with long-term senior debt rating of Aa or better; $10 million for issuers with debt rating of A; and $10 million for commercial bank-holding companies with capital accounts in excess of $500 million, within the overall limit of the flagship bank described in 2 above.
5. Foreign commercial paper unconditionally guaranteed by a prime U.S. issuer and fully hedged, subject to the guarantor's issuer limit described in 4 above.
6. Obligations of savings and loan associations, each with capital accounts exceeding $250 million—limited to $10 million each.

Operating Procedure

Payment shall be made only against delivery of a security to a custodian bank. Securities shall be delivered from custody only against payment.

Figure 27-12   *(continued)*

Due bills issued by a bank will be accepted for delivery only under exceptional conditions. No due bills issued by a dealer will be accepted.

Maturity Limits

The average maturity of the entire fund shall be limited to an average of two years.

The maximum maturity for each category is as follows:

U.S. government	5 years
Municipal obligations	2 years
Bank CDs, and BAs	1 year
Bank TDs	90 days
Commercial paper	270 days

(d) REPORTS TO MANAGEMENT

Periodic reports to top management, including the board of directors, will depend in part on this group's interest and the size of the investment portfolio. However, it is suggested, as a minimum, that where investments are significant, information should be conveyed regarding the type of investment and yield. Suggested report content would include the following:

1. Detail of individual securities, grouped by type and/or maturity.
2. Summary by type.
3. Summary by maturity.
4. Summary by yield.
5. Overall portfolio yield, by maturity.
6. Comparison of yield with selected index or by money manager, if appropriate.

An illustrative report comparing in-house performance with an outside money manager is shown in Figures 27-13 and 27-14.

27-12 SELECTED REFERENCES

Bort, Richard, *Corporate Cash Management Handbook.* Boston: Warren, Gorham & Lamont, 1989.

Carslaw, Charles A., and John R. Mills, "Developing Ratios for Effective Cash Flow Statement Analysis," *Journal of Accountancy,* Nov. 1991, pp. 63–70.

Drexel, Steven R., "Kelly's Automated Lockbox Network," *Management Accounting,* July, 1993, pp. 28–31.

Epstein, Marc. J., and Moses L. Pava, "How Useful Is the Statement of Cash Flows?" *Management Accounting,* July, 1992, pp. 52–55.

Fischer, Michael J., "Electronic Funds Transfers: Controlling the Risks," *Journal of Accountancy,* June 1988, pp. 130–132.

Figure 27-13 Report to Management, by Issuer, on Short-Term Investments.

THE CORPORATION SHORT TERM FUNDS

DISTRIBUTION BY ISSUER

AUGUST 31, 19XX
(DOLLARS IN MILLIONS)

	INTERNAL	MANAGER	TOTAL
U.S. GOVERNMENT			
COLLATERAL FOR RESALES	—	4	4
U.S. BANK OBLIGATIONS			
BANK OF AMERICA			
BANK OF NEW YORK			
BANKERS TRUST			
CHASE			
CHEMICAL			
CITIBANK			
CONTINENTAL ILLINOIS			
FIRST INTERSTATE			
FIRST NATIONAL CHICAGO			
HOME SAVINGS & LOAN			
MANUFACTURERS HANOVER			
MARINE MIDLAND			
MORGAN GUARANTY			
REPUBLIC NATIONAL NEW YORK			
SECURITY PACIFIC			
WELLS FARGO			

THE CORPORATION SHORT TERM FUNDS

DISTRIBUTION BY ISSUER (CONTINUED)

AUGUST 31, 19XX
(DOLLARS IN MILLIONS)

	INTERNAL	MANAGER	TOTAL
FOREIGN BANK OBLIGATIONS			
ALGEMENE	10	—	10
BANK OF MONTREAL	—	5	5
BNP	11	—	11
BANK OF NOVA SCOTIA	—	5	5
BARCLAYS	5	—	5
CREDIT LYONNAIS	—	5	5
DAI-CHI KANGYO	5	—	5
NATIONAL WESTMINSTER	—	5	5
SWISS BANK CORP	—	5	5
TORONTO DOMINION	3	5	8
INDUSTRIAL			
SPERRY RAND	5	—	5
TAX EXEMPTS			
NEW YORK STATE	5	—	5
GRAND TOTAL	216	104	320

Figure 27-14 Report to Management on Short-Term Investments by Maturity and Type of Obligation.

THE CORPORATION SHORT TERM FUNDS
DISTRIBUTION BY MATURITY - AVERAGE YIELDS
AUGUST 31, 19XX

	INTERNAL		MANAGER		TOTAL	
	$ MILL	%	$ MILL	%	$ MILL	%
UNDER 1 MONTH	47	22	94	90	141	44
1 – 3 MONTHS	71	33	10	10	81	25
3 – 6 MONTHS	98	45	—	—	98	31
	$216	100%	$104	100%	$320	100%

AVERAGE MATURITY, MONTHS: 3.2

AVERAGE YIELD, 4 MONTHS MAY – AUGUST
MARK TO MARKET: 8.19%
BOOK ACCOUNTING: 8.28%

MARKET PRICES, SEPTEMBER 1 FOR PRIME CD'S:
1 MONTH: 8.15%
3 MONTHS: 8.38%
6 MONTHS: 8.80%

THE CORPORATION SHORT TERM FUNDS
DISTRIBUTION BY TYPE OF OBLIGATION
AUGUST 31, 19XX

	INTERNAL		MANAGER		TOTAL	
	$ MILL	%	$ MILL	%	$ MILL	%
RESALES AND OVERNIGHT TIME DEPOSITS	8.0	3.7	7.7	7.4	15.7	4.9
U.S. BANKS – U.S. DOLLAR CD'S AND BA'S	128.5	59.4	18.0	17.4	146.5	45.8
CANADIAN BANKS – U.S. DOLLAR TIME DEPOSITS	—	—	15.0	14.5	15.0	4.7
FOREIGN BANKS – U.S. DOLLAR CD'S AND BA'S	30.9	14.3	10.0	9.7	40.9	12.8
U.S. BANKS – EURODOLLAR TIME DEPOSITS	35.0	16.2	25.0	24.1	60.0	18.7
COMMERCIAL PAPER	9.0	4.1	27.9	26.9	36.9	11.5
TAX EXEMPTS	5.0	2.3	—	—	5.0	1.6
TOTALS	$216.4	100.0%	$103.6	100.0%	$320.0	100.0%

Harding, Wayne and Chuck Kremer, "Using your Microcomputer for Cash Flow Statements," *Journal of Accountancy,* Feb. 1989, pp. 106–108.

LeTourneau, Harry D., "What to Expect from Your Bank," *Financial Executive,* May/June, 1992, pp. 23–26.

Lipis, Allen H. et al., *Electronic Banking,* New York: John Wiley & Sons, 1985.

Mahoney, John J., Mark V. Sever, and John A. Theis, "Cash Flow: FASB Opens the Floodgates," *Journal of Accountancy,* May 1988, pp. 27–31, 34, 38.

Randall, Andrew E., "Who Will Man the Treasury?" *Financial Executive,* March/April, 1994, pp. 27–30.

Stancill, James McNeill, "When is There Cash in Cash Flow?" *Harvard Business Review,* March–April 1987, pp. 38–49.

Sweeny, H. W. Allen, and Robert Rachlin (eds.), *Handbook of Budgeting.* New York: John Wiley & Sons, 1981, Chap. 16.

Willson, James D., *Budgeting and Profit Planning Manual* (2nd ed.). Boston: Warren, Gorham & Lamont, 1989, Chaps. 23, 24, and 25.

CHAPTER 28

Planning and Control of Receivables

28-1 INTRODUCTION

Customers' accounts receivable are an important item in the balance sheets of most business concerns. Proper procedures and adequate safeguards on these accounts are essential not only to the continued success of the enterprise but also to satisfactory customer relationships. Receivables extend beyond customers' receivables to amounts due from employees, notes receivable, freight claims receivable, insurance claims receivable, balances due from creditors, amounts due from affiliated companies, and so on. But customers' accounts receivable are usually the most important in aggregate value.

The planning function will take into account the amount to be invested in accounts receivable and measure this against an acceptable relationship to sales, as discussed subsequently in this chapter.

Control of accounts receivable begins, in reality, before the agreement to ship the merchandise, continues through the preparation and issuance of the billing, and ends with the collection of all sums due. The procedure is closely related to cash receipts control on one hand and to inventory control on the other. The receivable is the link between the two.

From the preventive management approach, there are three general control areas—points at which action can be taken to realize control of accounts receivable. These are as follows:

1. *Granting of Credit.* Credit policies and terms of sale must neither discourage sales to financially sound customers nor incur serious losses because of excessive bad debts.

2. *Making Collections.* Once credit is granted, every effort must be made to secure payment in accordance with the terms of sale and within a reasonable time.

3. *Installation and Maintenance of Proper Internal Control.* Even though credit and collection procedures are well administered or properly effected, this does not assure control of receivables. It does not guarantee, or even make reasonably certain, that all shipments are invoiced, or properly invoiced, to customers and that the payment finds its way into the company's bank account. An adequate system of internal control must be in operation.

An important subsidiary control area is to use information from collection calls to improve the quality of your company's products and services. Late payment may be caused by a customer's displeasure with services or products provided by your company. Customer complaints can be an invaluable source of information for future improvements.

Although reference is made primarily to accounts receivable from customers, the general principles are applicable to any receivables.

28-2 RESPONSIBILITIES OF THE CONTROLLER

The size of the firm, the kind of business, the type of organization, the capabilities of the controller—all these factors and others will determine the duties and responsibilities of the chief accounting officer in regard to accounts receivable. In many small- and medium-sized firms, the functions of the treasurer or controller are one and the same. In larger companies, the credit and collection functions are usually under the control of the treasurer. But even where the controller is not directly responsible for accounts receivable, he has certain real responsibilities. These may be outlined as follows:

1. In the context of planning, the determination, by appropriate time period, of the expected investment in accounts receivable.

2. Maintenance of the accounts receivable records in a satisfactory condition to meet the needs of the treasurer, credit manager, and controller.

3. Installation and maintenance of the necessary internal control safeguards.

4. Preparation of the required reports for management, the credit department, and others about the condition of the receivables and related matters.

5. Proper valuation of receivables on the balance sheet, including establishment of the necessary reserves.

In all these matters, the controller and the treasurer must work closely together.

28-3 PLANNING THE INVESTMENT IN RECEIVABLES

The *planning* function of the controller as related to accounts receivable largely has to do with the preparation of the annual business plan, and perhaps plans for a shorter time span. Working closely with the treasurer and/or credit manager, the controller's responsibilities include these:

1. Determining, within suitable interim time periods, the amount to be invested in accounts receivable for the planning horizon—the accounts receivable budget. Typically this is the month-end balance for each month of annual plan.

2. Testing the receivable balances to determine that the planned turnover rate or daily investment is acceptable or within the standard.

3. Based on past experience, or other criteria, estimating the amount required for a reasonable reserve for doubtful accounts.

4. Consolidating the accounts receivable budget with other related budgets to determine that the entity has adequate funds to meet the needed receivables investment.

The determination of the monthly investment in accounts receivable would produce a plan for the next business year substantially similar to that shown in Figure 28-1.

Additions to the monthly customer accounts receivable balance would be based on the sales plan. Collections would be determined as described in the preceding chapter on cash planning. Essentially the same "entries" would be made using the estimated

Figure 28-1 Planned Investment in Accounts Receivables.

The Johnston Company					
CUSTOMER ACCOUNTS RECEIVABLE BUDGET					
FOR THE YEAR ENDING DECEMBER 31, 19XX					
(dollars in thousands)					
Month	**Beginning Balance**	**Sales**	**Cash Collections**	**Adjustments Dr. (Cr.)**	**Ending Balance**
January	$15,620	$ 10,340	$ 9,760	$ —	$16,200
February	16,200	11,110	9,890	—	17,420
March	17,420	12,370	10,100	(80)	19,610
April	19,610	11,480	11,200	—	19,890
May	19,890	10,270	12,430	—	17,730
June	17,730	9,420	10,300	(60)	16,790
July	16,790	9,240	9,850	—	16,180
August	16,180	9,450	9,610	—	16,020
September	16,020	9,140	9,330	—	15,830
October	15,830	9,090	9,180	—	15,740
November	15,740	9,860	9,010	(110)	16,480
December	16,480	10,430	9,720	(120)	17,070
Total or balance	$15,620	$122,200	$120,380	$(370)*	$17,070

* Represents accounts written off.

data as are made for the actual monthly activity. The same process used in calculating the receivables balance for the annual plan may be used for the long-range plan—although only annual (not monthly) estimates need be used. Computer software programs are available to determine the receivable balance and to age the accounts.

While the illustration reflects the customer accounts receivable activity, a comparable procedure would be used to estimate the "other miscellaneous receivable" balances for such typically small transactions as:

- Amounts due from officers and employees.
- Claims receivables.
- Accounts receivable—special transactions.
- Notes receivable—miscellaneous.

28-4 TESTING THE REASONABLENESS OF THE RECEIVABLES BALANCE

When the receivables balances have been estimated, based on the expected sales and estimated cash collections based on the experienced collection pattern, it is prudent to test the balance for reasonableness. This may be done on a quarterly or annual basis.

(a) DAYS' SALES OUTSTANDING (DSO)

One test of accounts receivables is the number of days' sales outstanding (DSO). This standard may be used to check actual experience as well as the plan. The formula is:

$$\text{average number of days' sales outstanding} = \frac{\text{average receivables}}{\text{annual sales on credit}} \times 365$$

Applying this test to the data contained in Figure 28-1 produces this result (cash sales were only $98,400):

$$\frac{\text{average receivables}}{\text{annual credit sales}} = \frac{\$204,510,000/12}{\$122,220,000 - \$98,400} \times 365$$

$$= \frac{\$17,042.50}{\$121,236,000} \times 365$$

$$= 0.1405729 \times 365$$

$$= 36.5 \text{ days}$$

The average days' sales outstanding equates to 36.5 days. If the usual terms are net 30 days, then the average appears reasonable; however, if the terms are net 20 days, then the calculations in the formula and of the collection experience should be examined. Each month-end balance of the accounts receivable was used to obtain a weighted average.

The DSO concept illustrated is an *average* concept, measuring the average collections time, using as it does, the average receivables balance. A further refinement in measuring the age of receivables involves an analysis of each invoice (or group of invoices billed in a given day) and a calculation of the actual days each invoice is outstanding. The days for each age period (current, 30 days past due, 60 days past due, etc.) are determined by checking all outstanding invoices and weighting them according to the days outstanding. An illustrated example is shown in Figure 28-2 for the current month's billing. It reflects the late billing practice of Company B as compared to Company A.

If terms are net 30, it would be expected that the days outstanding would approximate 15 days, with some close to 30 days outstanding and the more recent 1 day outstanding. In the example, Company B is rather late in billing the sales. As a result, the actual days outstanding approximates only 10. Company A, by contrast, invoices rather quickly, and, with heavy sales in the early part of the month, the weighted days outstanding total almost 22. A comparable analysis for a given entity could compare invoices by actual day billed vs. when they could have been prepared.

A well-managed collection operation should maintain a days' sales outstanding figure that is about one-third beyond the terms of sale. For example, if invoices are due in 30 days, then an acceptable days' sales outstanding figure would be 40 days. If the ratio indicates poor collection performance, then the following items should be reviewed:

- *Review Prospects in Advance.* Work with the sales department to create a list of prospects and review the financial condition of those firms before contacting them regarding a sale. Not only does this avoid future collection problems, but it also makes more efficient use of salespeople's time. Without this up-front effort, sales made to marginal customers may lengthen the days' sales outstanding.

- *Bill Promptly.* Bill as soon as you ship! Review the billing paper flow at least once a year. If you do not find that invoices are being issued to customers within one day of shipment, then change the work flow to achieve this goal. Slow billing leads to excessive days' sales outstanding.

- *Track Overdue Accounts Closely.* Create a log of contacts with overdue customers and update it religiously. If a customer tells you that a check will be mailed by the fifteenth of the month and you do not receive it, call the customer on the twentieth to follow up—don't wait too long! If a customer realizes that you will badger the account until payment is received, you will have a much better chance of receiving the cash. Quick-paying customers reduce the days' sales outstanding.

- *Review Actual Terms of Sale.* Periodically review the actual sale terms granted to customers. You may find that special deals are being offered, possibly because prospective customers were not reviewed in advance (see first item). When sales are made to marginal accounts, extended terms are sometimes used in order to secure the sale. Long payment terms increase the days' sales outstanding.

- *Remove Other Receivables from the Receivables Account.* The days' sales outstanding account is typically based on the accounts receivable account (as opposed to the aging report total). If the account includes officer notes or taxes receivable, the days' sales outstanding figure will be skewed, showing excessive days' sales outstanding.

Figure 28-2 Calculation of Weighted Days Outstanding.

The Illustrative Company
CALCULATION OF WEIGHTED DAYS' SALES OUTSTANDING
CURRENT MONTH RECEIVABLES
(dollars in thousands)

	Company A				Company B		
Billed Amounts by Billing Date (1)	Actual Days Outstanding (2)	Weighted Days Amount (3)	Weighted Days Outstanding (4)	Billed Amounts by Billing Date (1)	Actual Days Outstanding (2)	Weighted Days Amount (3)	Weighted Days Outstanding (4)
$ 360.5	29	$10,454.5		$ 115.4	21	$ 2,423.4	
412.3	27	11,132.1		130.5	19	2,479.5	
140.7	24	3,376.8		89.7	17	1,524.8	
60.4	20	1,208.0		260.1	14	3,641.4	
110.2	19	2,093.8		12.6	13	163.8	
75.8	13	985.4		105.4	10	1,054.0	
41.2	10	412.0		303.2	6	1,819.2	
116.3	8	930.4		214.0	4	856.0	
81.9	2	163.8		168.4	1	168.4	
$1,399.3		$30,756.8		$1,399.3		$14,130.5	

Sales for month: $1,399,300

Terms: net 30

Average daily sales: $ 46,643

$$DSO = \frac{receivables}{average\ daily\ sales}$$

$$= \frac{\$1,399,300}{\$\ 46,643}$$

$$= 30$$

Weighted days amount ÷ billed amount (3) ÷ (1)   21.98   10.10

(b) RECEIVABLES TURNOVER RATIO

Another traditional method of measuring receivable performance is the receivables turnover ratio. This is calculated as:

$$\frac{\text{net sales}}{\text{customer receivables}} = \frac{\$122,200,000}{17,070,000} = 7.16 \text{ times}$$

The calculation shows that receivables have been collected, or "turned over," 7.16 times during the year. This turnover rate might be compared with that of the industry. Too low a number of turns could be the result of (a) too lenient a credit policy, (b) too lax a collection procedure, or (c) a combination of both.

This ratio is only a rough indicator of receivable quality. It is helpful when a consistent sales period is used and when the trend is followed, as in annual planning. It is inaccurate in that the receivable balance divisor may not relate to the sales dividend. Thus, to relate one month's sales to the ending receivables balance may not fairly reflect the uncollected balance from sales of, say, two months ago. Or, if all receivables relating to sales over six months ago have been collected, then relating sales of a year period may provide a distortion. Thus, as a control device, perhaps the DSO or weighted DSO method may be more revealing.

In summary, if the average receivables appear too high or too low, after consultation with the treasurer or credit manager if appropriate, an adjustment in the planned receivable balance should be made.

28-5 THE RESERVE FOR DOUBTFUL ACCOUNTS

Planning the accounts receivable investment includes providing a reserve for estimated doubtful accounts. This may be accomplished in one of two ways when actual sales are made: (1) Based on past experience, a percentage of monthly sales (or credit sales) may be set aside as a reserve, or (2) periodically the aging of accounts receivable (see Figure 28-3) may be reviewed and any probable uncollectibles may be reserved for. When dealing with the annual or long-term business plan, the estimated percent of sales is the method most commonly employed.

28-6 THE MEASUREMENT OR CONTROL FUNCTION— AN AGE ANALYSIS

Under the principle of separation of functions for good internal control (see Chapter 9), the accounting department would maintain the accounts receivable records—not the credit manager and not the treasurer. But the controller has a responsibility of preparing data for the use of the treasurer or credit manager. One of the most useful reports is an age analysis of accounts receivable—which may be readily prepared on the computer (Figure 28-3). This report indicates recent collection activity. Another summary (territorial) aging report reflects by organization segment the status of the receivables, as illustrated in Figure 28-4. This report also identifies different control objectives (expressed as DSO) for the various territories and channels of distribution.

The percentage of past-due receivables may be graphed monthly—a straight line chart—and compared with an objective such as 10% past due (Figure 28-5).

Figure 28-3 Aged Accounts Receivable Schedule.

The Illustrative Company
AGED ACCOUNTS RECEIVABLE
AS OF MARCH 31, 19XX

Customer	Total	Current	Past Due				Collections Effort in Past Month
			Total	30 Days	60 Days	90 Days	
Abbott Electrical Co.	$ 2,412	$ 2,110	$ 302	$ 302	$ —	$ —	—
Acme Computer Distributor	3,689	1,547	2,142	1,012	1,130	—	Terms lengthened net 45; $1,130 now paid.
Allied Maintenance Co. . .	1,010	—	1,010	160	830	20	$20 now paid.
Best Copper Co.	964	964	—	—	—	—	
Brighton Service Company	8,431	4,620	3,811	2,016	994	801	Note received for $1,795.
Case Applied Electronics .	2,562	1,922	640	640	—	—	
Welch Appliance Co. . . . :	828	430	398	398			
Williams Electronics . . . :	5,890	4,340	1,550	1,243	307		$307 promised on 4/15.
ZZ Best Radio Co. . . . . . :	12,406	6,851	5,555	2,310	2,016	1,229	Chapter 11 filed.
Total	$189,314	$147,210	$42,104	$21,825	$13,252	$7,027	
Percent	100	78	22	11	7	4	

Figure 28-4 Summary of Aged Accounts Receivable by Responsibility.

The Square Concern, Inc.
AGED SUMMARY OF CONSOLIDATED ACCOUNTS RECEIVABLE
AS OF JULY 31, 19XX
(dollars in thousands)

Region/Channel	Balance	Current	Total	Past Due 30 Days	60 Days	90 Days	DSO	Control Objectives
Wholesale								
North East	$ 41,814	$ 28,224	$13,590	$ 7,527	$ 4,554	$1,509	35	32 DSO
Percent		67.5	32.5	18.0	11.0	3.5		70% Current
Middle Atlantic	37,800	26,951	10,849	5,670	3,667	1,512	37	34 DSO
Percent		71.3	28.7	15.0	2.7	4.0		70% Current
South East	21,917	14,180	7,737	4,822	1,534	1,381	38	35 DSO
Percent		64.7	35.3	22.0	7.0	6.3		68% Current
Middle West	56,612	41,383	15,229	9,341	3,623	2,265	33	31 DSO
Percent		73.1	26.9	16.5	6.4	4.0		74% Current
Total—amount	158,143	110,738	47,405	27,360	13,378	6,667		
Percent	100	70	30	17	8	5		
Retail								
Boston	12,306	9,353	2,953	2,461	369	123	62	60 DSO
Percent		76	24	20	3	1		77% Current
New York	18,490	13,313	5,177	2,774	1,664	739	65	61 DSO
Percent		72	28	15	9	4		73% Current
Chicago	16,314	11,257	5,057	3,263	1,468	326	63	60 DSO
Percent		69	31	20	9	2		70% Current
Total—amount	47,110	33,923	13,187	8,498	3,501	1,188		
Percent	100	72	28	18	7	3		
Grand total—amount	$205,253	$144,661	$60,592	$35,858	$16,879	$7,855		
Percent	100	70	30	17	8	5		

Figure 28-5   Chart of Past-Due Accounts.

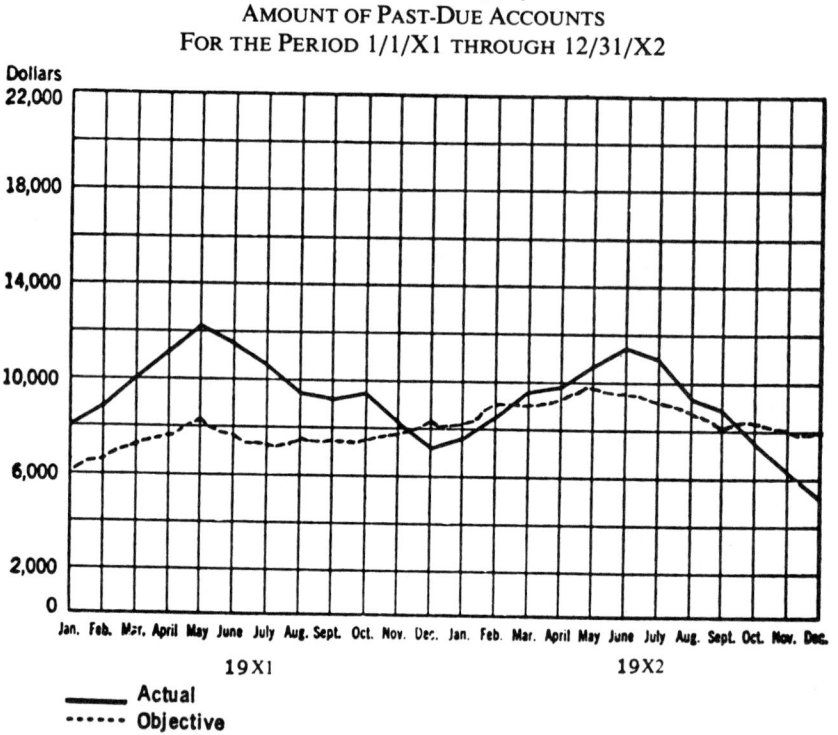

The Jones Company
AMOUNT OF PAST-DUE ACCOUNTS
FOR THE PERIOD 1/1/X1 THROUGH 12/31/X2

——— Actual
------ Objective

28-7 OTHER MEASURES AND REPORTS ON CREDIT ACTIVITY

The two principal measures of credit activity have been discussed: the number of days' sales outstanding (DSO) and the percentage of receivables that is past due. Typically these reports are prepared monthly by the accounting department.

Other indexes or means of judging the credit function and understanding the condition of accounts receivable include the following reports—some of which may be prepared by the credit department or by the accounting department:

- *Percent of Bad Debt Losses to Credit Sales.* This condition may be analyzed by type of customer, terms of sale, or other significant classifications for selected time periods, such as a quarter or a year. Too high a ratio might indicate excessively lenient credit terms or lax credit reviews.

- *Relationship of Credit Sales to Total Sales.* In some businesses this ratio might be significant—an indicator of the importance of credit terms.

- *Detail of Accounts Written off and Reasons Why.* Occasionally clues for desirable changes in credit-granting practices may be found in studying this report.

- *Details of Collections on Accounts Written Off.* Such a periodic report may provide useful information on the method of deciding what accounts should be written off, with effectiveness of the collection agency.

- *Comparison of Actual and Planned Receivables Balance.* An analysis of the reasons for the differences between the actual receivables balance at selected month-end periods vs. the planned balances may provide clues for improving the planning and/or control phases of the receivables balance.

A study of the credit and collection activity for a specific company may suggest other useful reports or measures.

28-8 ACCELERATING COLLECTIONS

Basic ingredients in keeping the company's investment in accounts receivable at an acceptable level is a sound procedure for granting credit and general adherence to terms of sale that are customary in a particular industry and/or region and that encourage a customer to remit payments on a timely basis. A wide-awake financial management usually is also interested in accelerating collections. The cash manager is interested in getting the cash payments into the company bank accounts as quickly as possible. On the other hand, the credit manager and the accounting department require transaction data that permit application of the payment to the proper account and invoice. Hence, cash acceleration procedures must address both of these concerns.

Various depository systems are used to transfer funds from the buyer's to the seller's bank account. Systems for companies in the retail business differ from those in nonretail activities by reason of volume, type of remittance, amount of individual remittances, and geographical dispersion, among other factors. Our comments relate principally to the nonretail applications.

Several methods are generally used to accelerate collections, and a few limited comments are made on each:

1. *Lockbox.* A lockbox is a post office box opened in the name of the seller (the depositor) but accessed and serviced by a remittance processor. Banks and others who process the remittances usually do so in a manner and at a time of day so that funds are more readily available to the depositor.

   Packaged software systems, used in conjunction with computers, are available to aid companies in selecting the location of the lockboxes. Those who wish to adopt or use lock box systems should talk to their (or other) bankers and/or others familiar with the many ramifications and considerations. Briefly, however, such systems usually offer these advantages over processing deposits at the premises of the seller:

   - Faster availability of the funds.
   - Greater security over the remittance.
   - Reduced processing costs.
   - Greater reliability in deposit processing.
   - Greater reliability in capturing necessary remittance data.

   As to the latter point, image processing has to do with capturing the image of the check and temporarily storing it in digital form. This enables the bank to immediately dispatch the check for clearing, while the image is used to complete work required by the bank. There are two methods of image processing: image lift and image capture. Those interested should examine both types as to cost and acceptability.

2. *Wire Transfer.* This is simply a series of telegraphic messages between two banks, usually through a Federal Reserve bank wherein the sending bank instructs the Federal Reserve bank to (a) charge the account of the sending bank and credit the account of the receiving bank, and (b) advise the receiving bank of the transfer.

3. *ACH Transfer.* This system, operating under the auspices of the National Automatic Clearing House Association (NACHA), is a method for the commercial banks to exchange electronic payments without the high cost of Federal wires. In most instances the payor initiates a payment for credit to the bank account of the payee.

4. *Depository Transfer Check (DTC).* Under this system, a bank prepares a DTC check on behalf of its customer against the customer's depository account in another bank. It is a means of more quickly getting funds from depository accounts into concentration accounts.

5. *Preauthorized Draft (PAD).* This is a draft drawn by the payee against the bank account of the payor. The method often is used by insurance companies or other lenders where the payment is fixed and repetitive. Of course the payor must authorize its bank to honor the draft—either an electronic transfer or a paper one.

Effective fund transfers have many ramifications and those interested in collection acceleration are urged to examine the possibilities and costs.

28-9 SHORTENING THE RECEIVABLES CYCLE

Accelerating the cash collections is one means of reducing the receivables. In fact, if sales personnel are involved in collections, an incentive based on customer payment habits might be considered. But the amount of funds tied up in receivables may result in part from antiquated or slow procedures in the order and billing process and not in the collection cycle. A detailed review of the procedures from receipt of the customer order, through shipment, to cash collection might be fruitful in spotting areas for improvement.

For example, in a typical manufacturing company, each step in the procedures from receipt of the customer order until final collection should be studied for means of expediting. Thus these events ought to be analyzed for means of speeding up the process:

1. Processing the customer order from receipt in the mail room or order department to the sales department.

2. Order processing steps in the sales department—separation of stock orders from custom orders, etc.

3. Steps in credit approval—segregation of orders to be expedited, separation of orders for certain known creditworthy customers.

4. Procedure in processing orders from credit department to shipping department.

5. Shipping department procedures.

6. Movement of documents from shipping department to invoicing department.

7. Invoice preparation and mailing.

8. Means of expediting invoice payment.

In this connection, given the advent of the microcomputer and the development of related software that integrates the financial system, the advantage of a simple computerized system should be considered. Some of the advantages might include:

- Billings may be sent out more promptly. Usually the more quickly the invoices are sent out, the more quickly they get paid. Those on the top of the pile of bills might be paid first. It is helpful to get invoices mailed within one or two days of the shipment date.

- Month-end statements may be sent out more quickly. With the data stored in the system, the statements may be prepared earlier. A timely end-of-the-month statement may encourage the customer to take the discount and make the payment.

- Up-to-date records makes management information more accurate. For example, it avoids such problems as dunning the customer for payment, only to learn that the funds were already received.

- Send Invoices by Electronic Data Interchange (EDI). Invoices no longer need to be sent to customers by mail. Instead, they may be sent by electronic data interchange (EDI). There are several ways to transmit invoices by EDI, but the most common one is for your company to send an invoice to a central computer clearinghouse, where the invoice is electronically stored. Your customer will access the clearinghouse regularly by modem, and will receive your electronic invoice at that time. The process is as follows:

    1. Obtain an EDI software kit. Call any of the major long-distance telephone companies for information on EDI software, or review a copy of the EDI Yellow Pages, which is a listing of EDI service and hardware providers. To obtain a copy of the Yellow Pages, call or write to EDI, Spread the Word!, 13805 Wooded Creek Drive, Dallas, Texas, (214) 243-3456.

    2. Load the software into a PC that is connected to a phone line by a modem. Dial the computer clearinghouse to verify that you are properly set up on the system.

    3. Contact your customers to inform them of your computer clearinghouse identification number, so that they can use it to send information to you through the clearinghouse.

    4. Enter an invoice into your PC's EDI software, and send it to the clearinghouse, having listed on it the identification number of the customer for whom it is intended.

    5. Once the customer receives the invoice, an acknowledgment will be sent back to you through the clearinghouse that the customer received the invoice. A good EDI software package will track the acknowledgment automatically, and tell you if the acknowledgment has not been received; if not, then call your customer to verify receipt of the electronic invoice.

Look for the following EDI features when purchasing software and selecting a computer clearinghouse:

1. *Unattended Operation.* The software should be able to automatically call the clearinghouse at least once a day for messages without any operator intervention.

2. *Inter-Clearinghouse Message Swapping.* The computer clearinghouse must be able to swap messages with other clearinghouse services. Since your customers may use different clearinghouses, this function is crucial.

3. *Interchange Control Numbers.* The EDI software should be able to number each exchanged document in sequence, so that missing or duplicate documents are flagged; when the system misses a number or receives two of a number from a trading partner, it notifies you with a message.

The following groups can provide additional information about EDI:

Secretariat
ASC X12 Data Interchange Standards Association, Inc.
1800 Diagonal Road–Suite 355
Alexandria, VA 22314
(703) 548-7005

Uniform Code Council, Inc.
8163 Old Yankee Road, Suite J
Dayton, OH 45458
(513) 435-3870

Electronic Data Interchange Association
1101 Seventh Street, N.W.
Washington, D.C. 20036-04775
(703) 838-8042

28-10 FUNCTIONS OF THE CREDIT DEPARTMENT

Having discussed the planning and control aspects of accounts receivable, it may be helpful to briefly comment on the functions of the credit department. This department is key to adequate control of the investment in accounts receivable. Very often in small-to medium-sized companies, the controller has responsibility for the credit-granting function. Moreover the relationship between the accounting department, which usually maintains the receivables records, and the credit department is and should be close. In the event of excessive levels of receivables, the controller should have some sense of the credit department functions.

In a broad sense, the credit manager should assist in stimulating business through a wise extension of credit, and also keep bad debt losses at a reasonably low level. In another sense, the credit manager should grant credit after due inquiry, if warranted, and collect the accounts receivable. A more detailed statement of the task is this:

1. *The Establishment of Credit Policies.* This involves such questions as these: what class of risk shall be accepted, how rigidly shall credit terms be enforced, what adjustment policies shall be followed?

2. *Credit Investigation.* This requires a continuous procedure for securing and analyzing information concerning the responsibility of present and prospective customers. The following sources can be used to collect customer information:

- Commercial credit reporting agencies, such as Dun & Bradstreet.
- Trade references supplied by the customer.
- Banks that hold a customer's loans, investment, and checking accounts.
- Collection agencies.
- The Securities and Exchange Commission stores detailed information on any companies that issue stock or bonds to the public.
- Stock exchanges store annual reports on those companies they list for trade.

The credit analyst typically will make a credit decision with the assistance of customer financial statements. If so, here are a few items to look for:

- *Ratios.* These ratios show where cash is being tied up in a customer's organization, thereby not allowing cash availability for payment of debts:

  1. *Days' Sales Outstanding.* If the customer's DSO is greater than its days of selling terms plus a third, too much of its cash is tied up in receivables.

  2. *Quick Ratio.* If the customer's quick ratio falls below 2:1, its ability to pay may be hindered.

  3. *Inventory Turnover.* If the customer's inventory turns are worse than the industry norm, too much cash is being tied up in inventory. The presence of *obsolete* inventory is sometimes indicated by low inventory turns accompanied by a good current ratio (since the excessive inventory appears in the numerator of the current ratio calculation). Alternatively, if a company has good inventory turns but a poor current ratio, the company may have too little working capital to support the level of business being transacted (called *over-trading*); if so, look for high debt levels or call the customer's bank for loan information. This type of company is a dangerous trading partner, for its heavy debt load may cause it to crash quickly if its level of business drops.

  4. *Debt Ratio.* If the customer's total liabilities are greater than 100% of equity, the equity cushion available for payments to creditors is too small.

- *Seasonality.* A company's books are typically closed during the slowest time of the year, when inventories are at their lowest, receivables have been collected, and debt has been paid down. If a company chooses to have its year-end in a different month than other companies in its industry, then its key ratios may vary dramatically from industry norms, even though it may operate in a similar manner.

- *Trends.* If possible, obtain the last three annual financial statements from your key customers, and look for the following danger signs that indicate where cash is being used, and is therefore not available for payments:

  1. Decrease in inventory turnover.
  2. Increase in the collection period.
  3. Increase in the ratio of total liabilities to equity.

4. Increase in the rate of working capital turnover. This is when sales increase, but the amount of working capital remains the same. Debt is usually substituted for the needed working capital, which increases fixed costs and therefore the risk to the creditor.

3. *Credit Approval.* This requires a procedure by which the credit department definitely approves new customers and the continuance of old ones.

4. *Establishment of Credit Limits.* Usually, approval is limited to a certain amount, and a plan must be designed to check the extension of credit at this point or, at least, to notify the proper authority when the limit is reached. In addition, there will be cases when credit terms should not be granted, but the sale can still be made. In these cases, one can either sell for cash or have backup guarantees by either an individual, a second corporation, or a stand-by letter of credit.

5. *Enforcement of Discount Terms.* Discounts offered for prompt payment are frequently taken by customers after the time allowed. A policy must be established and a procedure designed for the enforcement of the discount terms.

6. *Collection Methods.* Definite collection steps must be arranged for slow and delinquent accounts. This involves schedules of collection letters, follow-up procedure, and suspension of accounts from approved lists. In addition, the collections staff should be updated regularly on special collection techniques (such as attention-grabbing telegrams) and sent to trade association meetings to swap information with collection personnel from other companies.

7. *Credit Adjustments.* This involves settlement of accounts, participation in creditors' committees, and representation in receivership and bankruptcy proceedings.

8. *Approval of Writing off Bad Accounts.* Responsibility for writing off bad accounts must initiate with the credit departments, although final approval may be required from the treasurer or controller, in the interest of sound internal accounting control.

9. *Credit Records.* In the performance of the foregoing task, certain credit records must be maintained in addition to the general accounting records. These consist of files, reports, and ratings.

10. *Management of the Collection Process.* The following items contribute to a tightly managed collections process:

    • *Rapid Billings.* Quick billings lead to shorter days' receivables outstanding, whereas extremely delayed billings may be difficult to collect.

    • *Rapid Cash Application.* The job of the collections clerk is greatly improved when cash receipt information is quickly updated and forwarded to the collections staff. This avoids unnecessary calls on supposedly delinquent accounts that have actually already been paid.

    • *Tickler File.* This file informs the collections clerk of the need to call customers on specific dates.

    • *Confirmation Letters.* When a collection agreement is complicated, it is best to immediately summarize the agreement terms in a letter and send it to the customer, so there will be no confusion regarding payment.

11. *Measurement of the Collection Process.* Gain an understanding of the collection department's performance through quantitative measures such as days' sales

outstanding and the percentage of overdue invoices. In addition, a review of bad debt write-offs will indicate other problems, such as the reasons why credit was granted to customers who later defaulted. If these problems are tracked and corrected, then the volume of collection items will decline, thereby enhancing the quantitative performance measures.

An in-depth knowledge of the business may reveal reasons for large receivables balances that have nothing to do with high-risk customer accounts. For example, the days' sales outstanding can be skewed by one very large invoice, or by a large cluster of billings that occur at one time, such as at month-end. Also, a factoring arrangement may cause an abnormally low DSO.

28-11 ADEQUATE INTERNAL CONTROL

As the one last subject to be reviewed, the controller generally is responsible for adequate internal control in the enterprise. Internal control is discussed in Chapter 9, but because accounts receivable are closely linked to cash transactions, some special comments are appropriate on the internal control system as it affects the receivables.

The vast number of shipments to customers from most business concerns gives rise to an ever-present danger that all such goods are not properly charged to customers' accounts receivable. Further, even though an invoice is prepared, the customer may be billed for an incorrect amount because of differences in the quantity shipped, price, or extensions. Such happenings can be due to bookkeeping errors or fraud. Unfortunately, most customers do not complain about undercharges. Under the circumstances, the controller must assure himself that proper procedures are instituted to reduce such risks to a minimum.

Several practices have been found useful in combating discrepancies. Some of the more common are as follows:

1. Invoices to customers are compared to shipping memos by an independent party. This comparison includes both quantity and description of goods shipped.

2. All goods leaving the plant must have a shipping memo. Preferably these are prenumbered, and the independent party ascertains that all numbers are accounted for.

3. Prices appearing on invoices are independently checked against established price lists, and all extensions and footings are checked.

4. Periodically, the detail of the accounts receivable is checked against the control and reconciled, preferably by an internal auditor or other independent party.

5. Surprise mailings of monthly statements and confirmation requests should be made by third parties.

6. All handling of cash should be segregated from the maintenance of receivable records.

7. All special adjustments for discounts, returns, or allowances should have special approval.

8. A special record should be kept of all bad debts written off, and a definite follow-up should be made on these items to minimize the danger of collections being received and not recorded.

    9. On a test-check basis, remittance sheets can be compared with accounts receivable and shipping reports.

   10. Invoices may be mailed to customers by a separate unit.

28-12 SELECTED REFERENCES

Bort, Richard, *Corporate Cash Management Handbook*. Boston: Warren, Gorham & Lamont, 1989, Chap. 5.

Dun & Bradstreet Business Education Services, *Collecting Past-Due Accounts,* New York: The Dun & Bradstreet Corporation Foundation Business Education Services, 1993.

Dun & Bradstreet Business Education Services, *Credit and Financial Analysis,* New York: The Dun & Bradstreet Corporation Foundation Business Education Services, 1993.

Gangloff, John J., "Providing Real-World Financial Support to Sales," *Management Accounting,* Jan. 1989, pp. 41–44.

CHAPTER 29

Planning and Control of Inventories

29-1 INVENTORY MANAGEMENT

An effective material operation includes an inventory management function to plan and control inventories at optimum levels. It is necessary to determine the proper inventory quantities to satisfy the needs of the manufacturing requirements on a scheduled basis and customer orders. Broadly speaking, it encompasses the proper flow and handling of materials from receipt through warehousing and storage, into work in process and finished goods, and on to the customer. *Inventory planning* relates to determining what the composition should be, timing or scheduling, and location to meet the projected needs of the business. *Inventory control* is the controlling of the quantities and amounts within planned limits and the physical protection of the material on hand. There are many considerations of inventory management; however, we concentrate mostly on those aspects relating to the financial function and the role of the controller.

To some, "inventory management" might connote solely the management of inventory levels. To be sure, we will emphasize this end result. But inventory levels will depend in part on the nature and efficiency of these closely related functions:

- Purchasing.
- Receiving.
- Engineering.
- Manufacturing process.
- Inspection.
- Transportation.
- Warehousing and storage methods.

A chief objective of good inventory management is to find the least-cost method of satisfactorily meeting the customers' needs. Inventories serve as the link between purchasing and manufacturing on the one hand, and between manufacturing and delivery to the customer on the other. Hence, inventory management is a balancing act between production requirements, marketing needs, and the financial strength of the entity.

Just-in-time (JIT) production concepts are having a considerable impact on inventory management. Proponents of JIT point to the nonvalue-added costs of maintaining inventory and are using this to redefine the purchasing function into management of small numbers of suppliers who frequently deliver small quantities of parts. In addition, JIT concepts eliminate parts inspections and drastically shrink (if not eliminate) all warehouse space, as well as shrink work-in-process inventories by converting assembly line production facilities into manufacturing cells. Finally, JIT requires the inventory manager to closely coordinate activities with an additional department—engineering. The engineering department is responsible for creating accurate bills of material (BOMs). BOMs are needed by the purchasing department, for, when used in conjunction with the master production schedule, they tell buyers exactly how many units of an item to purchase.

Inventory levels will be dependent on the goods-handling processes and on the costs of alternate choices.

29-2 IMPORTANCE OF INVENTORY MANAGEMENT

A review of the annual reports of most industrial companies will reveal that the largest item included in current assets on the balance sheets is inventories. Inventories are listed on the balance sheet as an asset, but can be looked upon as a liability because the following expenses are associated with it:

1. The cost of insurance to protect inventory against loss.
2. The cost of obsolete inventory.
3. The cost of warehouse space to hold inventory.
4. The cost of moving inventory.
5. The cost of tracking inventory.
6. The cost of securing the inventory from pilferage.
7. The cost of converting from old, in-stock parts to new parts in a product design.
8. The cost of year-end inventory counting and costing.

A company's inventory must not be allowed to grow so large that the costs associated with it will erode the firm's profit margins. The controller must analyze inventories and costs associated with inventories, and provide management with adequate reports so that deficient conditions can be corrected in a timely manner. Many business failures occur because of excessive investments in inventories and slow management responses to the problem, resulting in cash shortages due to excessive working capital needs.

29-3 COST OF CARRYING INVENTORIES

The cost of carrying inventories is significant. This is particularly true in times of high interest rates and in many cases is not recognized by management. The interest cost is easily calculated when money is borrowed to obtain inventory or working capital—the interest on the loan. Interest may also be imputed by using a rate commensurate with the return on investment in other alternatives. As noted above, there are other inventory costs that must also be recognized such as insurance; taxes; warehousing, storage, and handling; pilferage; spoilage; shrinkage; obsolescence; etc. The total of these costs, including interest, could easily range from 25% to 40% of the inventory value on an annual basis. Therefore, the controller has an opportunity to reduce costs by improving inventory management. Increased inventory turnover alone would achieve considerable cost reductions. Management must be made aware of the large investments in inventory and the costs involved in maintaining high inventory levels relative to sales. The following examples indicate the extent of the problem:

1. *Bulk Purchasing.* The purchasing department is offered a great deal on wheels, $1 off the regular price if it buys 2,000 of them right now. The purchasing department buys the wheels, and records a $2,000 favorable purchase price variance. The purchasing manager receives a bonus for finding such a good deal. Meanwhile, the warehouse manager has no room for the inventory, and must lease warehouse space nearby at a cost of $1,000 per year. The company now has

a three-year supply of wheels, and will spend $3,000 over three years to store them. Also, the total cost of the wheels was $60,000. This amount is now tied up in working capital, instead of being available for other uses.

2. *Alternative Uses for Working Capital.* The company president wanted to buy a competing company for $5 million, but found that the company's credit lines were fully utilized. Upon further investigation, the president found that the vice president of sales had authorized a buildup of finished goods that forced the company to borrow $5 million to fund the increased stocking level.

3. *Change Control.* The company president enforces a policy of shipping all custom orders within four weeks of order receipt. To do so, the engineering department must order parts before the custom design is finalized and approved by the customer. As a result, parts are ordered that are never used, and additional materials staff must be hired to return excess parts to suppliers—at a discount, plus a restocking fee. Consequently, the added costs eliminate the company's net profit for the year.

29-4 ADVANTAGES OF INVENTORY MANAGEMENT

There are benefits to be gained from proper inventory planning and control. Proper inventory management has some significant advantages, among them these:

1. Keeps at a minimum the capital invested in inventories.
2. Eliminates or reduces waste and costs resulting from excess handling, spoilage, storage, obsolescence, and taxes and insurance on inventories.
3. Reduces risk from fraud or theft of inventories.
4. Avoids production delays by having necessary materials on hand—with resulting on-time shipments.
5. Permits more satisfactory service to customers by having the materials or goods on hand.
6. May reduce investment in storage facilities and equipment.
7. Permits the leveling out of production through fluctuating inventories and thus contributes to stability of employment.
8. Avoids or reduces losses resulting from price declines.
9. Reduces the cost of taking the annual physical inventory.
10. Through proper control and the information available on the inventories, permits purchasing of only the quantities needed for production.
11. Reduces sales and related clerical costs through better customer service.

Inventory management is recognized as an important facet of the management process of operating a business and affects every function: sales, production, purchasing, accounting, and administration. Good inventory management is increasingly viewed as the continual reduction of inventory. However, in some cases it is not necessarily maintenance of low inventories. All factors must be considered and properly balanced. The optimum inventory levels should be developed, recognizing all requirements of production, scheduling, costs, and customer needs.

29-5 KEY SEGMENTS OF AN EFFECTIVE INVENTORY MANAGEMENT SYSTEM

As in any function, certain key conditions are necessary for an effective inventory management system. While each will be shaped in part by the environment of a particular entity, these segments are essential:

1. Proper organization structure, and clearly defined authority and responsibility for the different types of inventory.
2. Well-defined inventory policies and objectives.
3. Capable personnel.
4. Adequate storage and handling facilities.
5. Adequate systems and procedures, among which are these:
   a. Proper classification and identification of inventories.
   b. A good system of standardization and simplification of inventory parts.
   c. Adequate inventory records.
   d. Acceptable procedures for *planning* the inventories.
   e. Adequate procedures for *control* of the inventory, including proper
      i.   reorder points,
      ii. order quantities,
      iii. turnover rates, and
      iv. timely and responsive reporting system.

Reorder points and order quantities apply only to specific situations, such as maintenance and repair items, low-cost parts, and selected retailing environments. Many manufacturing companies have abandoned reorder points and order quantities, especially for high-cost items, in favor of just-in-time purchasing of small quantities from local suppliers.

This listing constitutes a good checklist for controllers. Even though they may not have direct responsibility for many of the items, some knowledge provides a useful background.

29-6 RESPONSIBILITY FOR INVENTORY MANAGEMENT

As most readers know, organizational structure and assignment of responsibility and authority often depend on the personality and competence, as well as interests, of particular executives. However, aside from these personal factors, the specific structure may depend in part on the industry, the type of business, and the characteristics of the materials or products being handled. Certainly the organization structure and placement of responsibility, together with the requisite authority, must fit the needs of the entity.

But these generalizations probably are valid:

1. *Manufacturing-Related Inventories.* Responsibility for those inventories relating to manufacturing—raw materials, purchased parts, manufacturing supplies and

work-in-process—ordinarily rest with the chief manufacturing executive. By such an arrangement, he has complete command over the materials he needs to manufacture the finished product.

In some instances, when market conditions or supply factors are critical to procurement, the raw materials and purchased parts might be the responsibility of the purchasing executive—who may or may not report to the manufacturing executive.

2. *Sales-Related Inventories.* Responsibility for goods held for sale is sometimes placed with the sales executive, who may have an inventory manager plan and control the inventory for him. The thinking is that if the sales executive is responsible for the finished goods inventory, a better job of estimating sales requirements will result. Moreover, greater attention will be paid by the sales manager to disposing of obsolete or slow-moving items.

On occasion, since the principle task of the sales executive is to secure sales, he may be given responsibility only for field warehouse inventories—while those at the manufacturing facility will be managed by others.

3. *Specific Assignments.* Regardless of who is assigned the responsibility, it is certain that the assignment must be clear. It is amazing that some companies do not assign responsibility for the inventories, or do not make the assignment specific, until problems develop.

4. *Coordination Essential.* Regardless of where inventory responsibility is placed, there must be full and complete coordination between the purchasing function and the production function, as well as between production requirements and sales demand.

5. *Peripheral Duties.* While a particular executive will be assigned direct responsibility for a specific inventory, others will have related duties that will require coordination with the person responsible for the inventory. Thus:

  • The controller may be responsible for internal control matters related to inventories, perhaps also for the system of records, and for inventory valuation methods.

  • The facilities manager will be responsible for providing the physical warehousing and storage facilities, and the maintenance thereof.

  • The chief of plant protection will have responsibilities relating to prevention of theft, etc.

The functional outline or job description of each executive should spell out his responsibility and authority, if any, regarding inventories.

29-7 RESPONSIBILITY OF THE CONTROLLER

This raises the question about the function of the chief accounting official with respect to inventory management. Being a staff executive, he should not direct the day-to-day activities of operating control. That is the responsibility of the line executive. The controller, however, is in an excellent position to contribute a very real service on inventory planning and control. Regardless of where responsibility for inventory management is placed, the problem is secondary to the main function, whether it be sales, production, or purchasing. So the controller must be the coordinator, analyzing the conflicting needs and preparing a solution. He coordinates, assists, and suggests answers to the various problems. A general outline of the controller's more specific duties relating to inventories is as follows:

1. As a member of management or as a representative of the chief executive, assist in overall inventory policy determination.

2. As coordinator of the business plan, or forecast, or budget, ascertain that realistic inventory levels and investments are developed and changed as required; this function will include not only the overall budget but also related data such as the turnover objective.

3. Maintain usable inventory records.

4. Prepare and install required control procedures.

5. Prepare and issue regular periodic control reports on the inventory position for the guidance of line executives.

6. Install necessary internal controls for the protection of property from fraud and theft.

7. Supervise special audits or analyses as required.

8. Supervise the annual physical inventory unless it has been replaced by a perpetual inventory system.

9. Determine the method of costing inventories and related material flow.

10. Develop acceptable procedures and cost bases (interest rates, etc.) for determining the economics of carrying inventories.

11. Secure necessary compliance with instructions of regulatory bodies as regards the treatment of inventory and disclosure of valuations, etc.

12. Alter the procedures used to track inventory when a just-in-time production concept is deployed, since less paperwork is required in high-turnover JIT environments.

(a) INVENTORY MANAGEMENT OBJECTIVES AND POLICIES

Those responsible for carrying out the wishes of management in regard to inventories must clearly understand the rules of action by which they are to be guided. Nothing is quite so destructive of morale, and nothing creates so much confusion as being assigned a job and not knowing what is expected.

The general policies that will govern inventory accumulation, as well as the related functions in the various divisions of the business, should be made at the top-management level. Some of the matters to be covered as the following:

1. *Maximum Capital to Be Invested in Inventories.* What funds are available for investment in inventories? These limitations must be known.

2. *Extent of Speculative Purchasing Permissible.* To what extent can advantage be taken of forward buying? Should purchasing cover only the immediate needs of the production plans?

3. *Changes in Models, Customer Service, or Selling Effort.* The time and extent of such changes and their probable effect on sales should be known. Are credit terms to be eased? What policy will be followed with respect to customer delivery, i.e., must goods be shipped within 24 hours? Are any plans afoot for new products that will change the demand for present goods?

4. *Change to the Just-in-Time Operating Philosophy.* Adopting JIT has a startling impact on inventory management. By using reduced setup times and cellular manufacturing, production runs are shortened and work-in-process inventory shrinks dramatically. Because of the shorter production runs, parts do not have to be supplied in bulk, so raw material stocks shrink as well. Consequently, any contemplated change to JIT must be communicated to those responsible for managing the inventory.

(b) IMPORTANCE OF COMPETENT PERSONNEL

Inventory management is not attained by adherence to procedures, accurate maintenance of inventory records, or complex computer programs. It is secured through the action of experienced people, and there is no substitute for human intelligence and judgment. The records may show an item to be slow moving or may reveal an excess inventory, but the record can neither dispose of the item nor reduce the inventory. Someone must be responsible, at a minimum, for the following actions:

1. Manage a materials review board (MRB) that decides on the disposition of excess or obsolete parts in inventory.

2. Dispose of parts through restocking arrangements, scrap, donations, or other means.

3. Work with engineers to design excess parts into existing products, if necessary.

4. Track the level of inventory accuracy, and correct deviations from unacceptable levels.

5. Mediate between engineers, buyers, and the master scheduler to ensure that the correct parts are purchased in the correct quantities, and arrive on-site at the correct time.

This position should be filled by an experienced person with enough responsibility and authority to manage effectively. Training for this position should include the Certificate in Production and Inventory Management (see Chapter 12).

(c) ADEQUATE STORAGE AND HANDLING FACILITIES

A third essential factor in inventory control is adequate storage and handling facilities. No procedure, regardless of how well planned, can succeed in a disorganized, or ill-equipped warehouse or storage area. Because items cannot be located, excess or really unnecessary materials will be purchased. Shipping memos calling for one lot of material will be filled with another—at the risk of customer ill-will—without proper reporting. Losses from obsolescence and damage will run high. Such conditions will make perpetual records meaningless. Under such a handicap, good inventory control is virtually impossible. On the other hand, the facilities should not be so elaborate that they incur unnecessary handling and storage costs. For information about cleaning up a warehouse and starting a perpetual inventory system, see Chapter 59, Physical Inventory Procedures.

(d) CLASSIFICATION OF INVENTORIES

The usual inventory of a manufacturing firm includes the following classifications:

1. Raw materials.
2. Supplies.
3. Work in process.
4. Finished goods.

Each of these major categories may have further breakdowns, depending on the type of business. A commodity code structure may be used as a sub-breakdown to enhance control—such as the following:

1. Raw stock.
2. Standard parts.
3. Fabricated parts.
4. Hydraulic components.
5. Electric parts.
6. Electronic parts.
7. Nonmetallic raw material.
8. Castings.
9. Forgings.
10. Subassemblies.
11. Major components or high-value machined parts.

Other categories may include such identification as returnable containers, goods on loan, goods on consignment, material at vendors, or material in transit. These classifications should be recognized in setting up the budgets and controls and making sure that they are properly recorded.

Within each major classification, very often thousands of items must be accurately identified if the movement of material is to be reported correctly. Improperly identified material can cause production delays or at least unnecessary effort if the wrong item is brought to the production line. On the other hand, accounting control becomes quite useless if one item is requisitioned but reported as another. Proper classification and identification of material are necessary to an effective inventory control system.

Do not use excessive detail if there is not a good reason for recording the additional information. For example, glass parts can be recorded as a separate commodity, but the controller needs a good reason to extend the subclassification into different sizes of glass; since glass can be cut into an infinite number of configurations, the number of subclassifications can be endless. The work required to maintain such classification schemes may exceed the benefit from having the additional information.

(e) STANDARDIZATION AND SIMPLIFICATION OF INVENTORIES

Another important consideration in establishing sound inventory management is the standardization of materials and products and the simplification of the line. Simplification is merely the elimination of excess types and sizes. The elimination of those items that do not sell readily can contribute greatly to reducing the inventory which must be carried. Simplification is labor-intensive once inventory has been received, for considerable effort is needed to sell off excess inventory and ship it out of the warehouse. Less work is required if simplification is treated as a key step in designing new products, so that existing parts are used, rather than stocking new parts that may become obsolete.

Standardization is a more general term having to do with the establishment of standards. In the application to inventories, it has reference to the reduction of a line to fixed types, sizes, and characteristics that are considered to be standard. The object is to reduce the number of items, to establish interchangeability of manufactured parts and products, and to establish standards of quality in materials. With a reduction in the possible number of inventory items to be carried, the control problem is facilitated. Standardization extends even to such insignificant items as fasteners. If similar products can be designed to be assembled with a single bolt instead of ten slight variations on the same bolt size and material, then nine items can be eliminated, and no longer have to be tracked. Every time an item is removed from inventory, cost is reduced in the areas of cycle counting, obsolescence reserves, insurance, material moves, kitting, and receiving.

(f) ADEQUATE RECORDS AND REPORTS

Inventory planning and control presuppose a knowledge of the facts, and availability of the facts requires adequate inventory records and reports. Inventory records should contain the information to meet the needs of the purchasing, production, sales, and financial staffs. Typical information that may be required of any class of inventory is the following:

Quantities required for specific contracts.

Quantities required for a given manufacturing cycle.

Quantities on order.

Quantities in transit.

Quantities on hand.

Quantities set aside for specific contracts, customers, and production orders.

Historical experience.

Unit cost.

Minimum and maximum quantities.

Standard ordering quantities.

Reorder point.

Scheduling data.

Delivery times.

These are examples of the information required in developing an inventory control system. With the proper use of computers, a large amount of data is available at a minimum cost, allowing the controller to make economic analyses of inventory costs. The objective is proper inventory management, and it necessitates having adequate records and reports.

29-8 JUST-IN-TIME (JIT) INVENTORY/MANUFACTURING METHODS

Many of the basic factors involved in good inventory management have been briefly reviewed, but a key one yet to be discussed is the inventory and production system the management has chosen to use. None has drawn more attention recently than the just-in-time inventory system. The controllers may have little voice in which system is selected by the manufacturing executives. But they should be generally aware of the central philosophy—which basically is that all inventories are undesirable and should be eliminated or minimized—and the impact on purchasing and delivery systems, as well as the manufacturing system itself.

Adopting the just-in-time system requires major changes in purchasing and manufacturing strategies. In purchasing, the JIT system requires the manufacturers to select a few reliable suppliers who deliver, when needed, dependable materials and component parts with zero defects. The JIT manufacturing function is characterized by smaller lot sizes than traditional manufacturing, fixed production schedules for shorter periods, possible machine and process reconfiguration, as well as automation and a more flexible or multifunction workforce.

The objective of a JIT system is to produce and deliver:

- Finished goods just in time to be sold.
- Subassemblies just in time to be assembled into finished goods.
- Fabricated parts just in time to be made into subassemblies.
- Raw materials and purchased parts just in time to be converted to fabricated parts.

JIT has been described as a "pull" system of production control wherein the final assembly line production schedule triggers the withdrawal of materials or required parts at the needed time from the work centers that precede them in the manufacturing process. It may be graphically illustrated as in Figure 29-1. Workers secure the right quantity of parts to complete an order. Sequentially, each work center supplies parts to the next manufacturing operation and then manufactures parts to replace them. Thus, there is no stockpiling of work-in-process to offset lead times or to meet safety stock levels or the economic order quantities of subsequent production functions. (See the later discussion.) The results of this system are these:

- Lower inventories and lower carrying costs.
- Reduced rework and scrap.
- Improved quality control.
- Shorter production time and lead time, which assists the next result.
- Increased productivity.

Figure 29-1   The Just-in-Time "Pull System."

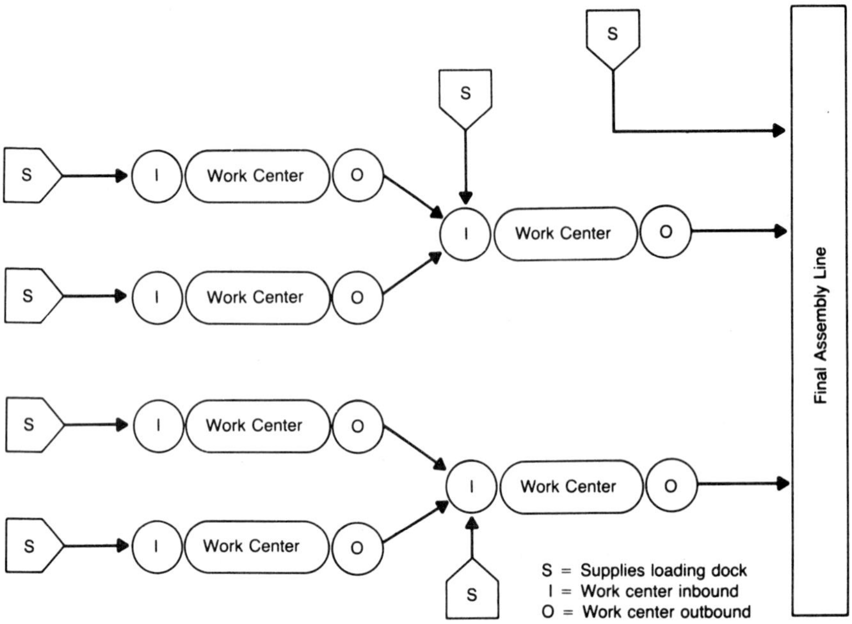

Source: Arjan T. Sadhevani et al., "Just-in-Time: An Inventory System Whose Time Has Come," *Management Accounting,* Dec. 1985, p. 42. Reprinted with permission.

(a) JIT PURCHASING

A successful JIT system depends, in the first instance, on a few reliable and depend-able suppliers who maintain a very close buyer-vendor relationship. JIT manufacturers enter into long-term contracts with fewer suppliers. Moreover, the suppliers handle smaller lot sizes, and use statistical quality control techniques to improve the quality of their products (rather than after-the-fact inspection). The suppliers essentially be-come specialized makers to the manufacturers, with facilities close to the JIT manu-facturers' plant, so as to make easier delivery of their products; and they are involved with the manufacturer in the product design and manufacturing process from the very outset.

The controller should be involved in the following special issues regarding JIT purchasing:

   1. *Target Costing.* The controller must include projected product costs in the bud-geting process. Under the JIT concept, there is more opportunity to influence product costs during the design process than later, in the manufacturing process. Thus, the controller should be involved in setting a target product cost and as-signing targeted subsidiary part costs to suppliers. Based on this targeted cost in-formation, the controller can prepare the material cost budget.

   2. *Collusion with Suppliers.* Another accounting issue involving JIT purchasing is the possibility of collusion between buyers and suppliers. Since JIT precludes competitive bidding, it may be possible for buyers to select suppliers who will kickback profits to the buyers in exchange for the business. This problem is real,

but is mitigated somewhat by the amount of interaction between company employees and the supplier. The product design function under JIT purchasing requires that the company's design engineers work closely with suppliers, so these people should recognize a sham supplier. A control that the controller can use is to compare supplier prices against those of the market on a spot basis. If prices seem excessive, then the controller should investigate further. Also, the controller can investigate whether or not previously agreed part price changes (usually downwards, for JIT suppliers) have taken place.

3. *Purchasing Paperwork.* JIT purchases tend to occur frequently and involve small part quantities. Under a traditional accounting system, this would present an increased paperwork problem, for there would be more receiving documentation to match to more invoices, and more checks to cut. Consequently, the controller should consider recording receipts based on the number of parts used in production (based on bills of material), plus parts that were damaged at the fault of the buyer. This system would require very accurate bills of material.

4. *Supplier Rating Systems.* Before JIT, suppliers ratings were based on the average unit price of parts sold to the company. Under the JIT philosophy, suppliers ratings should include ability to attain part cost targets, percentage of parts arriving on time ("on time" also means "not arriving too early," for such materials must be moved and stored, creating problems for the buying company), part defect rates, and the percentage of shipments containing the exact amounts ordered. The controller should be involved not only in the design of these information gathering systems, but also in the auditing of them for accuracy.

5. *Buyer Measurement Systems.* Before JIT, buyer ratings were based on the cost savings achieved from a standard cost for a part. JIT purchasing requires buyers to be facilitators rather than clerks, so that their new jobs require coordinating design teams from the two companies, assisting in qualifying suppliers, and shrinking the supplier base. Under JIT, continuing to judge a buyer based on the purchase price variance would be dysfunctional, since the buyer would be forced to put parts out to bid for the lowest price instead of working with one supplier to achieve a targeted cost. The controller should point out such dysfunctional performance measures to management, and recommend that they be eliminated. New performance measures for buyers are difficult to derive for individual buyers. Instead, the controller should consider formulating performance measures for groups, such as new product design teams that include buyers. A typical performance measure under this scenario would be achieving a product's cost that was originally targeted by management.

(b) JIT DELIVERY

JIT manufacturers closely link their production schedules to the suppliers' delivery schedules. Hence, suppliers and manufacturers are not only relocating, they are also eliminating storage areas and loading docks where delivered material can accumulate. Suppliers may feed materials and parts directly to the assembly lines.

(c) JIT MANUFACTURING

As would be expected, with the emphasis on small rather than large lot sizes, changes in manufacturing processes and machine arrangements usually are necessary. Under the typical U.S. production line, similar machines performing similar tasks are grouped together. This supposedly increases labor efficiency as well as the economy of large lot size production. Under the JIT system, "group technology" is used so that the small lot work moves rapidly through a common routing over several different types of machines, as illustrated in Figure 29-2. Hence there is little need for work-in-process inventory.

Moreover, rather than performing the task on only one machine, the worker is trained to operate all the machines of the work center. This leads to less boredom and assists in reducing defects, which, in the process, can be identified rather quickly.

For group technology to work, employees must be heavily cross-trained in the use of several pieces of equipment, since one employee will typically operate several machines. Also, since the company must invest in employee training, the cost of losing an employee is higher than would be the case in an assembly line environment, where less training is required. Finally, the employees must be willing to take responsibility for the quality of products produced; since an entire product can be produced by one

Figure 29-2   Just-in-Time Machine Arrangement.

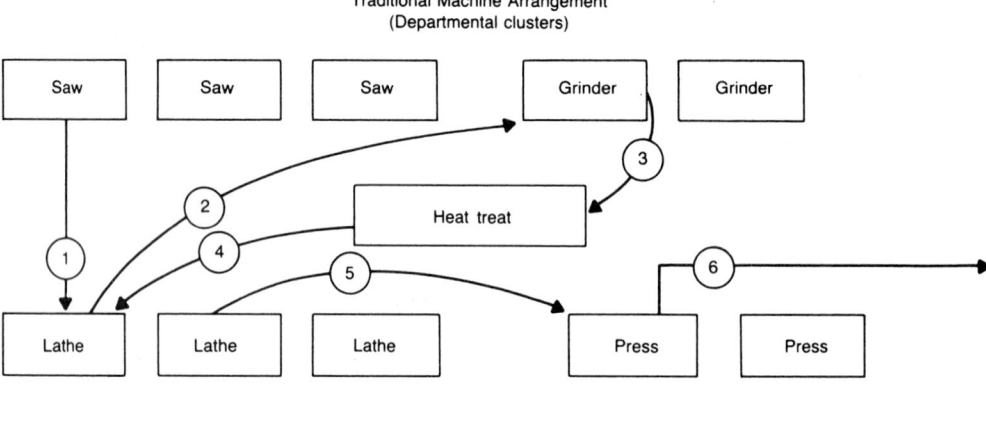

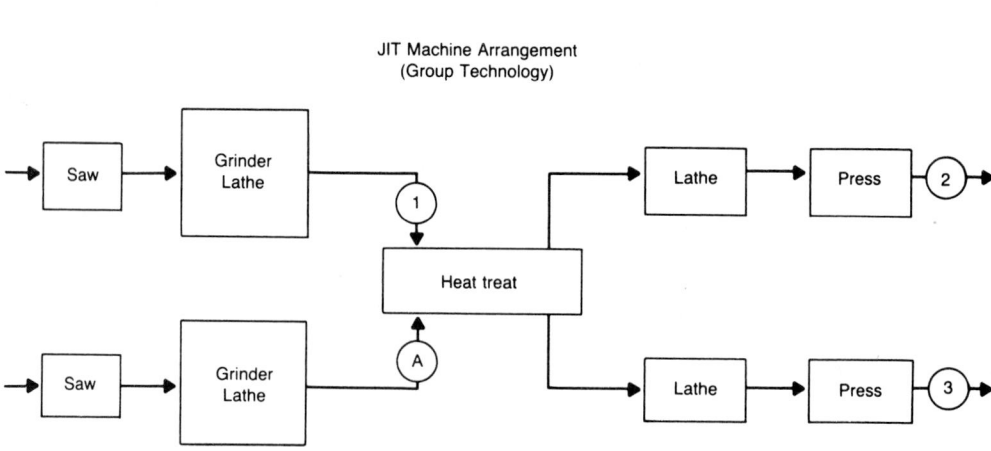

Source: Arjan T. Sadhevani et al., "Just-in-Time: An Inventory System Whose Time Has Come," *Management Accounting,* Dec. 1985, p. 43. Reprinted with permission.

employee or work group using group technology, part defects can be directly traced to individuals.

It is beyond the scope of this volume to discuss in detail the many operational aspects of just-in-time inventory planning and control. However, a review of one company's experience relative to purchased assemblies will give a good example of the pervasive impact that a JIT system can have on traditional financial controls. In this illustration, a high-cost subassembly is purchased from a single supplier with a longtime association and under a long-term contract. There is one such assembly in each finished product. Each day all assemblies needed for that day's production are delivered at 8:00 A.M. A routine was established between the supplier and the manufacturer whereby the supplier was paid weekly based on the number of finished products shipped by the *manufacturer* that week.

This procedure eliminated the preparation and handling of purchase orders, receiving reports, inventory details (receipts and disbursements), and invoices—the new control being that if a product were manufactured, tested, and shipped, then the subassembly must have been delivered. This is a very different process from the usual matching of purchase orders, receiving report, and invoice in order to effect payment.

Just-in-time concepts strongly impact several accounting processes, reports, and performance measures. The controller should be aware of the following items:

1. *Product Cost Tracking.* Under traditional assembly line production techniques, there were many opportunities to reduce product costs by closely examining the production process. However, with JIT, the glaring cost issues (e.g., excessive scrap and inventory levels) are eliminated from the production process. The controller may find that cost tracking systems on the production floor are not revealing cost savings. In fact, the tracking systems may cost more than the savings they generate. Consequently, the controller should consider cutting back on cost tracking systems on the shop floor and turn more attention to how well in-house and supplier design teams are achieving targeted cost goals when creating new products.

2. *Direct Labor Cost Tracking.* Traditionally, accountants have closely tracked all direct labor variances with the help of extensive shop floor labor reporting. However, in many companies, direct labor now accounts for less than 20% of a product's cost, so the cost expended to track direct labor may not be worth the benefit gained by reviewing labor variance reports. Therefore, the controller should consider eliminating direct labor reporting.

3. *Accounting Reports.* Most accounting reports are issued after the end of the month. Line managers review them and take action sometime well into the following month. With JIT operations, there is no work-in-process buffer to hide manufacturing problems, so line managers can spot most problems within minutes or hours of their occurrence. In short, JIT manufacturing personnel do not need monthly accounting reports as much as they used to. As JIT is implemented, the controller should periodically meet with line manager to ascertain their need for the information. The likely result will be fewer reports.

4. *Operational Auditing.* Under assembly line systems, operational audits focused on sources of waste from the system, such as pilferage, obsolete inventory, and scrap. With the greatly reduced inventory levels used by a JIT system, auditors

must now shift their focus to issues that will slow down JIT, such as problems with setup time reductions, process flow and workstation designs, and product designs.

5. *JIT Performance Measures.* Under assembly line systems, performance measures related to variances for direct labor and materials. With the assumptions under a JIT system that direct labor and materials costs are fixed and will have few variances, performance measures should shift to attaining targeted output and quality goals, the number of employee suggestions received, and the percentage implemented.

6. *Cost Generators.* Under assembly line systems, cost generators were viewed as direct labor and materials. With the assumptions under a JIT system that direct labor and materials costs are fixed, the controller should target other items. For example, close attention should be paid to:

- *Engineering change orders,* which can slow the product release process
- *Space utilization,* since excess space should be sublet for additional revenues
- *Inventory levels,* since less inventory leads to less space requirements, fewer obsolete items, less inventory tracking time, and reduced insurance costs
- *Equipment down time,* since product ship dates cannot be achieved if production facilities are not functioning

The reader is referred to the Selected References for more information on the system, as well as to other good books on the subject. The intent of these remarks is to make controllers aware of a recent development in inventory management. Of course, controllers must do their part in determining the financial impact of inventory levels based on the system existing within the entity, until such times as they can provide convincing evidence to the manufacturing management that there is a better system—all costs considered.

29-9 MATERIAL REQUIREMENTS PLANNING (MRP)

The JIT system of inventory planning and manufacturing is one method of reducing or eliminating raw materials and other inventories by keying materials and parts requirements to finished goods requirements. However, for years manufacturing companies with repetitive operations have used a materials requirement planning system (MRP) in production planning and scheduling and inventory control. Basically, with the use of a computer, a bill of materials and a master production schedule can be exploded or translated into the time-phased gross materials and purchased parts requirements. In theory, an MRP system should provide the necessary data indicating what items are required for the finished goods, and the related production runs, in the proper sequence and with minimum lead times. However, one writer indicates that the entire schedule process is geared to translating the needs into MRP economic order quantities.[1] Emphasis is thus on the order size—large lot sizes—so as to reduce the average set-up

---

[1] Robert W. Hall, *Productivity Machine: Production Planning and Control in Japan.* A Research Report. Falls Church, VA, 1981.

costs and the fixed inventory carrying costs. This may not lead to the lowest inventory level, although it permits rather precise inventory planning.

How does one compare the two systems? Both require high levels of inventory accuracy and bill of material accuracy. However, there are more differences than similarities, as shown below:

Result of System	Just-in-time	MRP
Reduces setup times	Yes	No
Reduces scrap	Yes	No
Reduces raw material inventory	Yes	Yes
Reduces work-in-process inventory	Yes	No
Emphasizes zero-defect production	Yes	No

The table shows that MRP is deficient in a number of areas as compared to JIT. However, MRP is an excellent methodology that can be used to establish accurate materials information (i.e., inventories, bills of material, and labor routings) that can then be used to implement a JIT system. Also, a company may wish to edge into JIT by keeping its MRP system and slowly adding JIT features like cellular manufacturing groups and reduced setup times. These items can be added to MRP without impairing the MRP system's performance.

29-10 SYSTEMS FOR THE PLANNING AND CONTROL OF INVENTORIES

The objectives of inventory management, in a general sense, include these:

- Having the finished product available to satisfactorily meet customer demand.
- Having access to raw materials and purchased parts, as needed, to manufacture the desired finished goods.
- Avoiding excess investments in inventories of any type.

No one system of planning and control is necessarily the best for a company, or even an industry. Perhaps for different circumstances a combination of methods may be most appropriate. Factors that may influence the selection of the system include these, among others:

- Nature of the product or products.
- Nature and location of the business.
- Competitive status.
- Industry practice.
- Type of marketing and delivery system.
- Number and distribution of warehouse or storage locations.
- Customer delivery and service requirements.
- Management complacence with the existing system.

Given the many variable factors that influence inventory management systems, there are a number of techniques or processes or devices in use, such as these:

1. Budgetary control.
2. Just-in-time system (JIT).
3. Material requirements planning (MRP).
4. Inventory turnover rates.
5. ABC method of inventory analysis.
6. Reorder point systems, including
   a. Minimum-maximum points,
   b. Reserve stock method,
   c. Reservation system,
   d. Visual check system, and
   e. Economical order quantity (EOQ).
7. Days' cost of sales in inventory.

Any one or several of these systems may be used in a company. Or one method may be predominant, with other devices employed as a checking or testing aid. In any event, the various methods often are closely interrelated. Limited comments on these follow.

29-11 BUDGETARY CONTROL

In most companies of any size, the management has learned the value of planning business operations—for at least a year in advance. So a prevalent method of planning and controlling inventories is through the budgetary route, in which inventory levels are closely planned to match expected operations. This technique involves (1) *planning* the proper inventory level for raw materials and purchased parts, for work-in-process, and for finished goods; and (2) *controlling* the amount in inventory by means of turnover rates, minimum-maximums, etc., to assure that the planned level is attained.

Budgetary control is discussed in some detail in the next several sections.[2] It should be understood that raw material inventory budgeting is closely related to the material purchases budget and the material usage budget. (See Chapter 22.)

29-12 BUDGETING THE RAW MATERIALS INVENTORY

There are basically two methods of developing the inventory budget of raw materials, purchased parts, and supplies:

1. Budget each important item separately based on the production program.
2. Budget materials as a whole or classes of materials, based on selected production factors.

---

[2] Adapted in part from J. Brooks Heckert and James D. Willson, *Business Budgeting and Control*, 2nd ed. (New York: Ronald Press Company, 1955), pp. 146–156.

Practically all concerns must employ both methods to some extent, although one or the other predominates. The former method is always preferable to the extent that it is practicable, since it allows quantities to be budgeted more precisely.

(a) BUDGETING INDIVIDUAL ITEMS OF MATERIAL

The following steps should be taken in budgeting the major individual items of materials and supplies:

1. Determine the physical units of material required for each item of goods to be produced during the budget period.

2. Accumulate these into total physical units of each material item required for the entire production program.

3. Determine for each item of material the quantity that should be on hand periodically to provide for the production program with a reasonable margin of safety.

4. Deduct material inventories that are expected will be on hand at the beginning of the budget period to ascertain the total quantities to be purchased.

5. Develop a purchasing program which will insure that the quantities will be on hand at the time they are needed. The purchase program must give effect to such factors as economically sized orders, economy of transportation, and margin of safety against delays.

6. Test the resulting budgeted inventories by standard turnover rates.

7. Translate the inventory and purchase requirements into dollars by applying the expected prices of materials to budgeted quantities.

In many instances, it is the controller's staff that translates the *unit* requirements and balances into values, based on the data received from production control or purchasing, and so on. In some cooperative efforts, the accounting staff may undertake the entire task of determining quantities and values, based on computer programs agreed to by the manufacturing arm (the explosion of finished goods requirements into the raw material components, etc.).

In practice, many difficulties arise in executing the foregoing plan. In fact, it is practicable to apply the plan only to important items of material that are used regularly and in relatively large quantities. Most manufacturing concerns find that they must carry hundreds or even thousands of different items of materials and supplies to which this plan cannot be practically applied. Moreover, some concerns cannot express their production programs in units of specific products. This is true, for example, where goods are partially or entirely made to customers' specifications. In such cases, it is necessary to look to past experience to ascertain the rate and the regularity of movement of individual material items and to determine maximum and minimum quantities between which the quantities must be held. This necessitates a program of continuous review of material records as a basis for purchasing and frequent revision of maximum and minimum limits to keep the quantities adjusted to current needs.

(b) BUDGET BASED ON PRODUCTION FACTORS

For those items of materials and supplies that cannot be budgeted individually, the budget must be based on general factors of expected production activity, such as total budgeted labor hours, productive hours, standard allowed hours, cost of materials consumed, or cost of goods manufactured. To illustrate, assume that the cost of materials consumed (other than basic materials which are budgeted individually) is budgeted at $1,000,000 and that past experience demonstrates that these materials and supplies should be held to a rate of turnover of five times per year; then an average inventory of $200,000 should be budgeted. This would mean that individual items of material could be held in stock approximately 73 days ($\frac{1}{5}$ of 365 days). This could probably be accomplished by instructing the executives in charge to keep on hand an average of 60 days' supply. Although such a plan cannot be applied rigidly to each item, it serves as a useful guide in the control of individual items and prevents the accumulation of excessive inventories.

In the application of this plan, other factors must also be considered. The relationship between the inventory and the selected factor of production activity will vary with the degree of production activity. Thus a turnover of five times may be satisfactory when materials consumed are at the $1,000,000 level, but it may be necessary to reduce this to four times when the level goes to $750,000. Conversely, it may be desirable to hold it to six times when the level rises to $1,250,000. Moreover, some latitude may be necessitated by the seasonal factor, since it may be necessary to increase the quantities of materials and supplies in certain months in anticipation of seasonal demands. The ratio of inventory to selected production factors at various levels of production activity and in different seasons should be plotted and studied until standard relationships can be established. The entire process can be refined somewhat by establishing different standards for different sections of the materials and supplies inventory.

The plan, once in operation, must be closely checked by monthly comparisons of actual and standard ratios. When the rate of inventory movement falls below the standard, the records of individual items must be studied to detect the slow moving items.

(c) MATERIALS PURCHASING BUDGET ILLUSTRATED

Some of the problems and methods of determining the total amount of expected purchases may be better understood by illustration. Assume, for example, that this information is made available regarding production requirements after a review of the production budget:

	Class			
	Units			Amount
Period	W	X	Y	Z
January	400	500		
February	300	600		
March	500	400		
Subtotal	1,200	1,500		
2nd quarter	1,500	1,200		
3rd quarter	1,200	1,500		
4th quarter	1,000	1,700		
Total	4,900	5,900	10,000	$20,000

Solely for illustrative purposes, the following four groups of products have been assumed:

Class W   Material of high unit value, for which a definite quantity and time program is established in advance—such as for stock items. Also, the material is controlled on a minimum-maximum inventory basis for budget purposes.

Class X   Similar to item W, except that, for budget purposes, minimum-maximum limits are not used.

Class Y   Material items for which definite quantities are established for the budget period but for which no definite time program is established—such as special orders on hand.

Class Z   Miscellaneous material items grouped together and budgeted only in terms of total dollar purchases for the budget period.

In actual practice, of course, decisions about production time must be made regarding items using Y and Z classifications. However, the bases described later in this chapter are applicable in planning the production level.

(i) Class W. Where the items are budgeted on a minimum-maximum basis, it usually is necessary to determine the range within which purchases must fall to (1) meet production needs and (2) stay within inventory limits. A method of making such a calculation is shown next:

	Units	
	For Minimum Inventory	For Maximum Inventory
January production requirements	400	400
Inventory limit	50	400
Total	450	800
Beginning inventory	200	200
Limit of receipts (purchases)	250	600

Within these limits, the quantity to be purchased will be influenced by such factors as unit transportation and handling costs, price considerations, storage space, availability of material, capital requirements, etc.

A similar determination would be made for each month for each such raw material, and a schedule of receipts and inventory might then be prepared, somewhat in this fashion:

Period	Units Beginning Inventory	Receipts	Usage	Ending Inventory	Unit Value	Purchases Budget
January	200	400	400	200	$200	$ 80,000
February	200	400	300	300		80,000
March	300	400	500	200		80,000
Subtotal ...		1,200	1,200			240,000
2nd quarter	200	1,350	1,500	50		270,000
3rd quarter	50	1,200	1,200	50		240,000
4th quarter	50	1,200	1,000	250		240,000
Total		4,950	4,900			$990,000

(ii) Class X.   It is assumed that the class X materials can be purchased as needed. Since other controls are practical on this type of item and since other procurement problems exist, purchases are determined by the production requirements. A simple extension is all that is required to determine the dollar value of expected purchases:

Period	Quantity	Unit Price	Total
January	500	$10	$ 5,000
February	600		6,000
March	400		4,000
Subtotal	1,500		15,000
2nd quarter	1,200		12,000
3rd quarter	1,500		15,000
4th quarter	1,700		17,000
Total	5,900		$59,000

(iii) Class Y.   The breakdown of the class Y items may be assumed to be as follows:

Item	Quantity	Unit Price	Cost
Y-1	1,000	$1.00	$ 1,000
Y-2	2,000	1.10	2,200
Y-3	3,000	1.20	3,600
Y-4	4,000	1.30	5,200
Total	10,000		$12,000

A determination about the time of purchase must be made, even though no definite delivery schedules, etc., have been set by the customer. In this instance, the distribution of the cost and units might be made on the basis of past experience or budgeted production factors, such as budgeted machine hours. The allocation to periods could be made on past experience, as follows:

Period	Past Experience Regarding Similar Units Manufactured	Units					Values (Purchases Budget)
		Y-1	Y-2	Y-3	Y-4	Total	
January	10%	100	200	300	400	1,000	$ 1,200
February	15	150	300	450	600	1,500	1,800
March	10	100	200	300	400	1,000	1,200
Subtotal ...	35	350	700	1,050	1,400	3,500	4,200
2nd quarter	30	300	600	900	1,200	3,000	3,600
3rd quarter	20	200	400	600	800	2,000	2,400
4th quarter	15	150	300	450	600	1,500	1,800
Total	100%	1,000	2,000	3,000	4,000	10,000	$12,000

The breakdown of units is for the benefit of the purchasing department only, inasmuch as the percentages can be applied against the total cost and need not apply to individual units. In practice, if the units are numerous regarding types and are of small value, the quantities of each might not be determined in connection with the forecast.

(iv) Class Z. Where the materials are grouped, past experience again may be the means of determining estimated expenditures by the period of time. Based on production hours, the distribution of class Z items may be assumed to be as follows (cost of such materials assumed to be $2 per production hour):

Period	Productive Hours	Amount
January	870	$ 1,740
Feburary	830	1,660
March	870	1,740
Subtotal	2,570	5,140
2nd quarter	2,600	5,200
3rd quarter	2,230	4,460
4th quarter	2,600	5,200
Total	10,000	$20,000

When all materials have been grouped and the requirements have been determined and translated to cost, the materials budget may be summarized, principally for the financial forecast, as follows:

			Class		

The Blank Company
PURCHASES BUDGET
FOR THE YEAR 19XX

Period	W	X	Y	Z	Total
January	$ 80,000	$ 5,000	$ 1,200	$ 1,740	$ 87,940
February	80,000	6,000	1,800	1,660	89,460
March	80,000	4,000	1,200	1,740	86,940
Subtotal	240,000	15,000	4,200	5,140	264,340
2nd quarter	270,000	12,000	3,600	5,200	290,800
3rd quarter	240,000	15,000	2,400	4,460	261,860
4th quarter	240,000	17,000	1,800	5,200	264,000
Total	$990,000	$59,000	$12,000	$20,000	$1,081,000

The foregoing illustration relates to raw materials. A similar approach would be taken with respect to manufacturing supplies. A few major items might be budgeted as the class W or X items just cited, but the bulk probably would be handled as Z items.

Once the requirements as measured by delivery dates have been made firm, it is necessary for the financial department to translate such data into cash disbursement needs through average lag time, etc.

29-13 THE RAW MATERIALS AND PURCHASED PARTS BUDGET ILLUSTRATED

When the quantities of raw materials and purchased parts have been translated into costs, as to both purchases and usage, then the inventory budget can be finalized, quite often in a format illustrated in Figure 29-3.

29-14 BUDGETING WORK IN PROCESS

The inventory of goods actually in process of production between stocking points can be best estimated by applying standard turnover rates to budgeted production. This may be expressed either in units of production or dollars and may be calculated for individual processes and departments or for the factory as a whole. The former is more accurate. To illustrate this procedure, assume the following inventory and production data for a particular process or department:

Process inventory estimated for January 1	500 units	(a)
Production budgeted for month of January	1200 units	(b)
Standard rate of turnover (per month)	4 times	(c)
Average value per unit of goods in this process	$10	

With a standard turnover rate of four times per month, the average inventory should be 300 units (1200 ÷ 4). To produce an average inventory of 300 units, the ending inventory should be 100 units:

$$\frac{500 + 100}{2} = 300$$

Using the symbol X to denote the quantity to be budgeted as ending inventory, the following formula can be applied:

$$X = \frac{2b}{c} - a = \frac{2\,(1200)}{4} - 500 = 100 \text{ units}$$

Value of ending inventory is $1000 (100 \times $10).

Where the formula produces a minus quantity (as it will if beginning inventory is excessive), the case should be studied as an individual problem and a specific estimate made for the process or department in question.

Control over the work-in-process inventories can be exercised by a continuous check of turnover rates. Where the individual processes, departments, or plants are revealed to be excessive they should then be subjected to individual investigation.

The control of work-in-process inventories has been sorely neglected in many concerns. The time between which material enters the factory and emerges as the

Figure 29-3 Budget—Raw Materials and Purchased Parts Inventory.

The Illustrative Company
BUDGET FOR RAW MATERIALS AND PURCHASED PARTS INVENTORY
FOR THE PLAN YEAR 19XX
(dollars in thousands)

Month	Beginning Inventory	Purchases	Usage	Ending Inventory
January	$186,400	$ 120,000	$ 110,000	$196,400
February	196,400	105,000	120,000	181,400
March	181,400	147,000	145,000	183,400
Subtotal	186,400	372,000	375,000	183,400
April	183,400	142,000	143,000	182,400
May	182,400	146,000	149,000	179,400
June	179,400	137,000	140,000	176,400
Subtotal	183,400	425,000	432,000	176,400
July	176,400	120,000	126,000	170,400
August	170,400	110,000	115,000	165,400
September	165,400	116,000	112,000	169,400
Subtotal	176,400	346,000	353,000	169,400
October	169,400	120,000	110,000	179,400
November	179,400	110,000	107,000	182,400
December	182,400	128,000	110,000	200,400
Subtotal	169,400	358,000	327,000	200,400
Grand total .	$186,400	$1,501,000	$1,487,000	$200,400

finished product is frequently much longer than necessary for efficient production. An extensive study of the automobile tire industry revealed an amazing spread of time between five leading manufacturers, one company having an inventory float six times that of another. This study indicated also, by an analysis of the causes of the float time, that substantial reductions could be made in all five of the companies without interference with production efficiency.

Although it is desirable to reduce the investment in goods actually being processed to a minimum consistent with efficient production, it is frequently desirable to maintain substantial inventories of parts and partially finished goods as a means of reducing finished inventories.

Parts, partial assemblies, processed stock, or any type of work in process that is stocked at certain points should be budgeted and controlled in the same manner as materials. That is, inventory quantities should be set for each individual item, based on the production program; or inventory limits should be set that will conform to standard rates of turnover. In the former case, control must be exercised through the enforcement of the production program; in the latter case, maximum and minimum quantities must be established and enforced for each individual item.

With the planned cost input to work-in-process known from the materials usage budget, the direct labor budget, and the manufacturing expense budget (see Chapters 22 and 23), and the quantities of planned completed goods furnished by manufacturing, the controller may develop the planned work-in-process, time-phased (condensed), as shown in Figure 29-4. The reasonableness of the budgeted inventory level should be tested by one of the several methods suggested in this chapter (turnover, etc.).

29-15 BUDGETING FINISHED GOODS INVENTORY

The budget of finished goods inventory (or merchandise in the case of trading concerns) must be based on the sales budget. If, for example, it is expected that 500 units of item A will be sold during the budget period, it must be ascertained what number of units must be kept in stock to support such a sales program. It is seldom possible to predetermine the exact quantity that will be demanded by customers day by day. Some margin of safety must be maintained by means of the finished goods inventory so that satisfactory deliveries can be made. With this margin established, it is possible to develop a program of production or purchases whereby the stock will be replenished as needed.

(a) BUDGETING FINISHED GOODS BY INDIVIDUAL ITEMS

Two general methods may be employed in budgeting the finished goods inventory. Under the first method, a budget is established for each item separately. This is done by studying the past sales record and the sales program of each item and determining the quantity that should be on hand at various dates (usually, the close of each month) throughout the budget period. The detailed production or purchase program can then be developed to provide such quantities over and above current sales requirements. The total budget is merely the sum of the budgets of individual items. This total budget can then be tested by the rate of turnover desired as proof that a satisfactory relationship will be maintained between inventory and sales and that it harmonizes with the general

Figure 29-4 Budget for Work-in-Process.

The Illustrative Company
BUDGET FOR WORK-IN-PROCESS
FOR THE PLAN YEAR 19XX
(dollars in hundreds)

Month/Quarter	Beginning Inventory	Charges to Work-in-Process				Transfers to Finished Goods	Ending Inventory
		Direct Material	Direct Labor	Manufacturing Expense	Total		
January	$264,800	$ 110,000	$ 84,700	$ 105,900	$ 300,600	$ 307,100	$258,300
February	258,300	120,000	92,400	115,500	327,900	314,400	271,800
March	271,800	145,000	110,200	137,750	392,950	402,800	261,950
Total—Quarter 1	264,800	375,000	287,300	359,150	1,021,450	1,024,300	261,950
Quarter 2	261,950	432,000	332,640	415,800	1,180,440	1,186,210	256,180
Quarter 3	256,180	353,000	271,800	338,700	963,500	969,100	250,580
Quarter 4	250,580	327,000	250,800	314,600	892,400	880,300	262,680
Grand total	$264,800	$1,487,000	$1,142,540	$1,428,250	$4,057,790	$4,059,910	$262,680

financial program. If it fails in either respect, revision must be made in the program of sales, production, or finance until a proper coordination is effected.

Under this plan, control over the inventory is effected by means of enforcement of the sales and production programs. If either varies to any important degree from the budget, the other must be revised to a compensating degree and the inventory budget revised accordingly.

Where the sales and production programs can be enforced with reasonable certainty, this is the preferable method. It is particularly suitable for those concerns that manufacture a comparatively small number of items in large quantities. The application is similar in principle to that illustrated in connection with raw materials controlled budget-wise by minimums and maximums.

(b) BUDGETING TOTAL FINISHED QUANTITIES AND VALUES

Where the sales of individual items fluctuate considerably and where such fluctuations must be watched for hundreds or even thousands of items, a second plan is preferable. Here basic policies are adopted relative to the relationship that must be maintained between finished inventory and sales. This may be done by establishing standard rates of turnover for the inventory as a whole or for different sections of the inventory. For example, it may be decided that a unit turnover rate of three times per year should be maintained for a certain class of goods or that the dollar inventory or another class must not average more than one-fourth of the annual dollar cost of sales. The budget is then based on such relationships, and the proper executives are charged with the responsibility of controlling the quantities of individual items in such a manner that the resulting total inventories will conform to the basic standards of turnover.

With such standard turnover rates as basic guides, those in charge of inventory control must then examine each item in the inventory; collect information about its past rate of movement, irregularity of demand, expected future demand, and economical production quantity; and establish maximum and minimum quantities, and quantities to order. Once the governing quantities are established, they must be closely watched and frequently revised if the inventory is to be properly controlled.

The establishment and use of maximum, minimum, and order quantities can never be resolved into a purely clerical routine if it is to be effective as an inventory control device. A certain element of executive judgment is necessary in the application of the plan. If, for example, the quantities are based on past sales, they must be revised as the current sales trend indicates a change in sales demand. Moreover, allowance must be made for seasonal demands. This is sometimes accomplished by setting different limits for different seasons.

The most frequent cause of the failure of such inventory control plans is the assignment of unqualified personnel to the task of operating the plan and the failure to maintain a continuous review of sales experience relative to individual items. The tendency in far too many cases is to resolve the matter into a purely clerical routine and assign to it clerks capable only of routine execution. The danger is particularly great in concerns carrying thousands of items in finished stock, with the result that many quantities are excessive and many obsolete and slow-moving items accumulate in stock. The successful execution of an inventory control plan requires continuous study and research, meticulous records of individual items and their movement, and a considerable amount of individual judgment.

The plan, once in operation, should be continually tested by comparing the actual rates of turnover with those prescribed by the general budget program. If this test is applied to individual sections of the finished inventory, it will reveal the particular divisions that fail to meet the prescribed rates of movement. The work of correction can then be localized to these divisions.

Whenever possible, the plan of finished inventory control should be exercised in terms of units. When this is not practicable, it must be based on dollar amounts.

In the context of preparing the annual business plan in monetary terms, and based on the quantities of finished goods (furnished by the cognizant executive) deemed necessary for an adequate inventory, the controller can develop the budget for the finished goods inventory, much as is shown in condensed form in Figure 29-5. When the total of the inventory segments is known, the total inventory budget for the company can be summarized as in Figure 29-6. Such a summary can be useful in discussing inventory levels with management. Any pertinent ratios can be included. Again, in testing the reasonableness of the annual business plan, the inventory—by segments, or perhaps in total—should be tested by turnover rate or another device suggested for control (or planning) purposes.

29-16 OTHER AIDS IN MANAGING INVENTORIES

Budgetary planning and control of inventories, as well as JIT methods and MRP systems, have been reviewed. There are some other techniques that will be briefly discussed, which may supplement the preceding systems or which may be used as a means of testing planning inventory levels or to periodically measure actual levels.

Figure 29-5   Budget for Finished Goods Inventory.

| | | Transfers | | | |
| | Beginning | from | Purchased | Cost of | Ending |
Month/Quarter	Inventory	Work-in-Process	Parts (a)	Goods Sold	Inventory
		The Illustrative Company			
		FINISHED GOODS INVENTORY BUDGET			
		FOR THE PLAN YEAR 19XX			
		(dollars in hundreds)			
January	$329,600	$ 307,100	$ 71,000	$ 365,400	$342,300
February	342,300	314,400	72,000	419,100	309,600
March	309,600	402,800	80,000	472,500	319,900
Total—Quarter 1 ...	329,600	1,024,300	223,000	1,257,000	319,900
Quarter 2 ...	319,900	1,186,210	64,500	1,243,700	326,910
Quarter 3 ...	326,910	969,100	41,400	1,017,500	319,910
Quarter 4 ...	319,910	880,300	49,600	932,900	316,910
Grand total	$329,600	$4,059,910	$378,500	$4,451,100	$316,910

Note: (a) Certain purchased parts are acquired for sale to customers, and do not enter work-in-process.

Figure 29-6   Summary of Budgeted Inventories.

The Illustrative Company
SUMMARY OF BUDGETED INVENTORIES
FOR THE PLAN YEAR 19XX
(dollars in thousands)

Item	Raw Materials and Purchased Parts	Work-in-Process	Finished Goods	Total
Beginning inventory	$ 186,400	$ 264,800	$ 329,600	$780,800
Quarter ending inventory				
March	183,400	261,950	319,900	765,250
June	176,400	256,180	326,910	759,490
September	169,400	250,580	319,910	739,890
Year ending inventory	$ 200,400	262,680	316,910	$779,990
Total annual usage—estimated	$1,487,000	$4,059,910	$4,451,100	
Daily average (255 days)	$ 5,831	$ 15,921	$ 17,455	
Number of days usage on hand—year end	34.4	16.5	18.2	

29-17 CONTROL THROUGH TURNOVER

Another means by which some companies control inventories is through turnover rate. Standard turnover rates may be established for an entire inventory or for different sections. The executives responsible for the inventories must keep within the limits. A variation of the same principle is the establishment of a limit on the funds that may be invested in the inventory. Department stores operate on a turnover basis, and each buyer is expected to secure the required rate. Thus if an inventory turnover of four times per year is required and if anticipated sales (cost) are $2,800,000, then the average inventory cannot be greater than $700,000. Such a method is feasible under rather stable conditions and when materials can be readily secured.

Turnover is obtained by dividing the usage factor by the average inventory. For example, the turnover of various inventories would be determined as follows:

Finished goods—cost of goods sold/average inventory of finished goods.

Work in process—cost of goods completed/average inventory of work in process.

Raw materials—materials placed into process/average inventory of raw materials.

Supplies—cost of supplies used/average supply inventory.

The result is the number of turns. Common practice is to express rate in the number of turnovers per year, although average length of time per turnover is often used. A turnover rate of four times per year would be expressed as a three-month turnover.

Such standards can be used as a guide, but their usefulness should not be overstated. A slow turnover can be an indication of overinvestment in inventories. On the other hand, a very high turnover can be secured by keeping an unduly small inventory and resulting lost sales or higher costs through fractional buying because of incomplete stocks. The objective of business is profit, not just turnover. Turnover can be secured through increased sales or usage, which also brings profit, and not merely by reducing inventories.

Turnover rates have a definite place in judging efficiency, but improvement in turnover should not be sought as an end in itself. They should by no means be an automatic control, arbitrarily imposed. An intelligent appraisal of the situation is always necessary.

29-18   VALUE ANALYSIS

Proper inventory planning and control begin with an analysis of the individual elements of the inventory. Each class or type of material has its own characteristics that may determine the technique applicable. It has been found in manufacturing companies that inventories may be segregated into three categories based on unit dollar value and usage: A, B, and C (also known as "ABC analysis" or proportional parts system). The experienced usage and cost relationship, based on a study of many companies, for each of the three groups is approximately as follows:

	Category			
	A	B	C	Total
Number of parts used	15%	35%	50%	100%
Annual dollar value	65	20	15	100

In other words, by carefully controlling only 15% of the parts, 65% of the inventory investment can be controlled. Further, when control is extended through the B parts, about 85% of the inventory value is covered.

The category of material may be the basis for establishing the inventory policy and procedure. Different policies are required for these three differing groups. The goal of this segregation or "fractionation" is to minimize the cost of inventory investment on high usage-value items, to minimize the cost of running out of stock, and to reduce to a minimum the acquisition cost of the low usage-value items.

Generally speaking, A items, or high-value items, are usually ordered, either externally or internally, on the basis of the more or less exact quantity needed to meet customer and manufacturing requirements. There may be a daily, weekly, or monthly review of requirements, and a consequent rather continuous scheduling of receipts. The budgetary control approach, discussed later, probably will be used. Changes in sales forecasts or trends must be quickly reflected in increases or decreases in quantities to be ordered and receipts to be scheduled. Because of the high-usage and high-value criteria, those fixed costs of order writing, follow-up, setup, record keeping, and material handling are a small proportion of the total cost.

B items, or middle-value items, very often are ordered in quantities that may vary from actual need for economic reasons. For example, they may be ordered a minimum of two times per year or a maximum of three times. By ordering a larger quantity currently needed, the unit cost per item may be reduced significantly. Size of facilities, setup cost, and so on will influence the amount purchased. These items may not be stocked in generally unlimited quantity by reason of carrying costs or the original cost of the item.

A mathematical formula has been devised that takes into account such things as usage, setup cost, carrying charges, and unit cost (material, labor, and overhead cost) of the item. The formula determines the economical order quantity for an item. For example, as setup cost rises, the quantity rises; and as carrying charges increase, the quantity declines. The formula is as follows:

$$Q = \sqrt{\frac{2 \times (\text{annual usage}) \times (\text{setup or order cost})}{(\% \text{ carrying charge}) \times (\text{unit cost})}}$$

C items, or low-value items, may be ordered also on the basis of economic order quantities or on a maximum and minimum basis as previously discussed. This method is generally used for low unit-cost items consumed in volume and at a steady rate. The maximums, minimums, and reorder point should be reviewed and analyzed periodically and adjusted as conditions change.

In applying the principle of value analysis, it is merely necessary to list each component in descending order of annual usage value, as in Figure 29-7. On such a basis, the controller can group the various items in accordance with the method of control he proposes to use. The desired turnover, optimum quantity to be stocked, etc., may then be applied to each item or group as may be applicable.

29-19 MAXIMUMS AND MINIMUMS

Another means available for inventory planning and control is the use of maximum and minimum stock quantities. A determination should be made about the suitability of that type of control in a specific business. It might apply to one class of inventory but not another. For example, it may be applicable to the supply inventory but not to the raw materials or finished goods. As a general rule, the use of maximums and minimums is

Figure 29-7   Sequential Listing for Use in Value Analysis of Inventory.

		VALUE ANALYSIS OF INVENTORY			
Part Number	Unit Cost	Estimated Annual Usage (Quantity)	Annual Usage Value	Cumulative Annual Usage	Sequence Number
4201	$2,000.00	200	$400,000.00	$ 400,000.00	1
9867	1.00	320,000	320,000.00	720,000.00	2
3026	312.00	1.000	312,000.00	1,032.000.00	3
5095	.10	2,600.000	260,000.00	1,292,000.00	4
8766	.25	1,000,000	250,000.00	1,542,000.00	5
3221	4.00	50,000	200,000.00	1,742,000.00	6
12415	190.00	1,000	190,000.00	1,932,000.00	7
3901	.05	200	10.00	9,999,997.00	8,762
8666	.03	100	3.00	10,000,000.00	8,763

practical where the rate of sale or use of the products is fairly stable and not subject to wide fluctuations or sporadic movements and where the order time is fairly short.

In establishing maximum and minimum inventory points, the following factors must be considered:

1. *The Rate of Usage or Shipment.* This can be secured from an analysis of past experience, although current production and sales plans must be considered. The rate of usage must recognize not merely the average rate but also the *range* of usage, i.e., the highest rate and lowest rate of consumption.

2. *The Time Requirement for Either Purchase or Manufacture.* This should be the time from the placing of the order until delivery, including a reasonable "safety" factor for delays. Past experience and a knowledge of current conditions are both important in making this determination.

3. *The Economical Quantities to Order.* Discount brackets, setup time in a machine shop, and similar considerations can be factors in determining the economical amount to purchase or manufacture.

4. *Storage Facilities Available.* The cost of outside storage and added handling may make this factor decisive.

5. *Working Capital Available.*

6. *Cost of Carrying the Inventory.* Rent, taxes, insurance, interest on investment, etc.

7. *Possibility of Deterioration or Obsolescence of Materials Stored.*

8. *General Market Conditions and Extent of Speculation.*

9. *Effect on Labor Turnover.* It may be desirable to fluctuate inventories to stabilize employment or retain basic personnel.

With this information the maximum and minimum stock points can be set. An explanation of the relationship of various quantities may be helpful. The minimum is the lower limit of the desirable inventory on a particular item. It represents a "cushion" or margin of safety to be used only in an emergency. Somewhat above the minimum point is the reorder point, which represents the minimum inventory, plus the quantity required for use between the ordering and delivery period. The maximum is the upper limit of the desirable inventory and usually is the minimum quantity, plus the standard ordering quantity.

Once the minimums and maximums have been set, the inventory should be reviewed periodically by an inventory manager to detect any need for changes. Further, it should be a responsibility of the controller to have the inventory detail reviewed periodically to ascertain that the limits are being observed and that the limits are reasonable. As business levels change, the upper and lower limits of the permissible inventory will require adjustment.

29-20 REORDER POINTS

Aside from the basic elements of a good inventory management system, the preceding discussion has centered on *what* the inventory levels should be. This is of concern to financial management as to (a) the amount of funds needed for investment in inventory, and (b) the risks and costs of carrying such inventory. The quantity to be ordered was touched upon in the review of the economical order quantity (EOQ), and in discussion of turnover rate, maximum-minimum levels, and value analysis. One other subject controllers should be sensitive to, even though they are concerned only to the extent of the efficiency of the system, relates to *when* specific materials or products should be ordered.

Suffice it to say that, when there are known requirements, the MRP, JIT, or similar methods will indicate when materials need to be ordered, and inventories can be planned accordingly. Where there is greater uncertainty, as in job-lot work, estimates of the volume level must be made, and a provision for error, through the use of safety stock may be used. The basic formula is represented in this fashion:

reorder point (ROP) = LCD plus safety stock

wherein:

L = anticipated lead time (in weeks)

D = estimated demand in units per week

At the time the stock level reaches the reorder point, a requisition is issued for additional inventory. Some of the more widely used means of signaling the time to reorder include these:

- *Minimum-Maximum System.* This method often is used in connection with the inventory record. The minimum quantity level is the reorder point; the maximum level might be the minimum quantity plus the economical order size.
- *Reserve Stock Method.* Under this system, the stock is divided into two parts: one for immediate use, and one as reserve. When use of the reserve is commenced, additional stock is reordered. This system may involve two bins (one with the reserve stock) or one bin with the reserve stock identified, e.g., in a separate bay, etc.
- *Visual Check System.* This is the old-fashioned way for the small business. When the owner or manager checks the stock level, with direct knowledge of the business activity, he or she can judge when to reorder.
- *Reservation Method.* This method recognizes the available stock as well as the physical stock. Available stock is defined as stock on order, plus physical stock, less the unfilled requirement. The reorder point is based on the available stock rather than the physical stock.

To reiterate, controllers are not directly involved in determining the reorder point. Their interest is a matter of background, and in knowing that the system is sufficient or efficient in the company.

29-21 INVENTORY MANAGEMENT SYSTEMS

The technological advances made in processing data by computers permit more sophisticated techniques than formerly. There are many computer programs available that are easily adopted to the peculiar requirements of a given business. Also, computer software packages have been developed for inventory systems of specific industries.

At a minimum, the set of data and functions needed for an inventory management system should include:

1. *Inventory.* Part numbers, descriptions, quantities on hand, quantities ordered, quantities reserved, storage location, unit of measure, and transaction history, as well as costed inventory reports sorted by location.

2. *Bills of Material.* Part numbers, units of measure, and quantities used in a part, as well as subassemblies and scheduled dates to swap old parts with new parts.

3. *Purchasing.* Reorder points for standard parts, multiple line items for purchase orders, supplier part number equivalents for company part numbers, comment fields, on-line reviews of available inventory, and open purchase order reports.

4. *Receiving.* Ability to call up the purchase order on-line and cancel individual line items as they are received, and cancel line items if amounts received are slightly high or low.

5. *Scheduling.* Ability to call up pick lists (based on bills of material) for items to be produced.

A good materials system is really a tightly interlinked set of modules that cover production planning, purchasing, payables, receiving, warehousing, and kitting. Thus, the effective inventory manager should have accurate systems running in all these areas to achieve optimum inventory levels at the lowest cost to the company.

This book has not attempted to describe in detail all computer processing techniques. The reader is advised to obtain pertinent available literature covering specific computer applications. Most computer manuals present descriptions of systems from a user's point of view. The data are presented in a manner usable by first-line supervision and management personnel. The computer systems descriptions usually include display type data, database descriptions, and an insight into the processing techniques. Although the descriptions are general in nature, they can be applied to a wide range of problems.

(a) INTERNAL CONTROL AND INVENTORIES

Accounting control of inventories is one of the most difficult problems faced by the controller. To obtain maximum effectiveness of the system, the records must be accurate and complete. In addition, the accounting department must coordinate activities with various levels of plant personnel.

Inventory adjustments result from obsolescence, shrinkage, theft, spoilage, and improper accounting. It is necessary to have more than general statements available when a major inventory shortage at year-end is reflected in the accounting records. Some adjustments result from poor accounting, but many adjustments arise from poor physical control of the materials.

If the total control system for inventories is to function properly, access to the material must be limited to authorized personnel. In most instances, this involves placing the inventory items in a secure area. Responsibility must be assigned for these areas, and materials must be issued in accordance with approved management procedures. As material is transferred from one location to another in the manufacturing process, adequate controls must be established. The controls should not result in inefficient manufacturing operations; however, departures from the controls should be minimal. Many inventory problems develop when controls are relaxed to expedite the manufacturing process. It is necessary that the records reflect the movement of material from receipt until shipped from finished goods. It is a matter not only of inaccurate inventory records but also of unrecorded losses because of manufacturing inefficiencies and excess usage of material.

To preclude shortages and inventory adjustments from poor physical control or a weakness in the internal control system, the following general suggestions are made.

1. Maintain secure areas for material. All items of high unit value should receive special attention, such as a bonded area.

2. Transfer of material from one location to another should be in accordance with management authorization. Issue items on the basis of approved requisitions only.

3. Segregate duties so that those who keep the records are not responsible for actual physical receipt or shipment.

4. Make rotational counts of items and reconcile to the inventory records.

5. Have the internal audit function make a thorough review of the inventory control system, including test counts.

6. Review and analyze the inventory records to determine any weaknesses that may exist.

7. Evaluate the personnel concerned with the inventory and make background checks if necessary.

8. Make periodic surveys of the security over the inventory and eliminate opportunities for any misappropriation.

9. Cross-check additional items that are requested from stock during a job's production, or returned to stock following a job's production. These transactions strongly indicate that a product's bill of material is incorrect. Since the controller bases year-end inventory projections on product costs that in turn are based on bills of material, correcting the bills may eliminate the annoyance of large year-end inventory variances.

The controller appreciates the value of good internal controls and therefore should work closely with manufacturing to develop strict procedures to reduce losses and minimize inventory adjustments.

(b) PHYSICAL INVENTORY

Inventory control management systems provide for a periodic determination of the physical quantities of material on hand. These inventory counts are usually annually— all at one time or on a rotational basis. Such counts are reconciled to the inventory records and discrepancies analyzed and adjusted. This annual physical inventory should be directed and supervised by the controller and any adjustments to the accounting records properly approved. For an alternative inventory tracking method, see Chapter 58.

(c) INVENTORY RECORDS

The exact type of inventory records to be maintained is a decision to be made by the controller in cooperation with the individual responsible for managing the inventory function. The needs of the operating departments, the type of business, and the organization must be considered. It is not within the scope of this book to discuss the design of specific inventory systems; however, some general observations can be made.

Certain information is required regardless of how the records are maintained. In those cases, when computer systems are not available, the controller must make sure that the records are simple and easy to use. The records must be kept on a current basis, and the transactions must be properly recorded on the stock or inventory record.

A simple stock record may include the following:

1. Item description.
2. Size.
3. Unit.
4. Code number.
5. Location—area, bin.
6. Minimum quantity.
7. Maximum quantity.
8. Quantity ordered.
   Date.
   Purchase order number.
9. Quantity received.
   Date.
   Purchase order or receiving number.
   Unit cost.
10. Quantity issued.
    Date.
    Requisition number.
    Unit cost.
11. Quantity on hand.
    Unit cost.

(d) INVENTORY REPORTS

The success of any inventory management system depends on how the information and data are communicated and used. The information must be useful to those receiving it, easily understood, and timely. With the advent of computers and peripheral equipment, many inventory reports are no longer required to be produced. The inventory data are stored in the computer, retrieved, and displayed on a screen or tube at a work station. This allows those responsible for making inventory decisions to have real time data available. This technological progress will improve the management and control of inventories and assist the controller in maximizing the return on assets.

The controller should keep management advised of the effectiveness of inventory planning and control. The reports should compare actual results to planned results, provided an analysis of variances and explain corrective actions being taken. Areas of concern or simplification should be pointed out for discussion. Inventory is the major asset of many businesses, and the controller should be creative in analyzing and reporting the facts to assist those charged with the responsibility for control. The following are indicative of the great variety of reports that may be useful:

1. Summary of inventory by category.
2. Comparison of the planned or budgeted inventory to the actual inventory by responsibility and classification.
3. Turnover analysis.
4. Summary of inventory activity—requirements, usage, balances by part, category, classification.
5. Movement of inventory—aging, indicating slow moving, obsolete, excess.
6. Report on overages and shortages.
7. Value analysis reports.
8. Inventory on hand vs. forecast or commitments.
9. Summary of physical counts and adjustments.
10. Special reports on high unit-value items.
11. Inventory sorted by location, to be used for cycle counting.

The controller should determine what information is most usable to each member of the inventory management team. As in most reports, it is suggested that information be summarized by responsibility as well as measured against predetermined objectives. Inventory data are normally voluminous, so it is best to summarize the information and in most cases use exception reporting. To improve the usefulness, charts or graphs are helpful, particularly to show deviations from a norm and trends.

(e) OBSOLETE INVENTORY

As was discussed, controls should be established to preclude the acquisition of material in excess of requirements. However, in most cases a certain amount of obsolete material is accumulated. This may result from product changes, market weakness, or errors in the control process. Inventories should be reviewed periodically with sales, production, and accounting representatives (frequently called the Materials Review Board or MRB) to determine the extent of any obsolete or excess inventory. Procedures should be developed for the orderly disposition of any such material. From the controller's viewpoint, provision should be made in the accounting records so that the inventory values are properly stated. Management should be advised of the magnitude of excess inventory and recommendations made for corrective action to avoid any further losses.

29-22 SELECTED REFERENCES

Aggarwal, Sumer C., "MRP, JIT, OPT, FMS? Making Sense of Production Operations Systems," *Harvard Business Review,* Sept.–Oct. 1985, pp. 8–16.

Ashton, James E., and Frank X. Cook, Jr., "Time to Reform Job Shop Manufacturing," *Harvard Business Review,* March–April 1989, pp. 106–111.

Barefield, Russell M., and S. Mark Young, *Internal Auditing in a Just-in-time Manufacturing Environment,* 1988. Altamonte Springs, FL: The Institute of Internal Auditors Research Foundation.

Foster, George, and Charles T. Horngren, "JIT: Cost Accounting and Cost Management Issues," *Management Accounting,* June 1987, pp. 19–25.

Karmarker, Uday, "Getting Control of Just-in-Time," *Harvard Business Review,* Sept.–Oct. 1989, pp. 122–131.

Klein, Janice A., "The Human Costs of Manufacturing Reform," *Harvard Business Review,* March–April 1989, pp. 60–66.

Robinson, Michale A., and John E. Timmerman, "How Vendor Analysis Supports JIT Manufacturing," *Management Accounting,* Dec. 1987, pp. 20–24.

Sadhwani, Arjan T., M. H. Sarhan, and Doyal Kiringoda, "Just-in-Time: An Inventory System Whose Time Has Come," *Management Accounting,* Dec. 1985, pp. 36–44.

Sadhwani, A. T., and M. H. Sarhan, "The Impact of Just-in-Time Inventory Systems on Small Businesses," *Journal of Accountancy,* Jan. 1987, pp. 118–130.

Schonberger, Richard J., *Japanese Manufacturing Techniques.* New York: The Free Press, 1982.

Swalley, Richard W., "Managing Your Inventory: New Use for an Old Tool," *Management Accounting,* May 1984, pp. 52–56.

Swann, Don M., "Where Did the Inventory Go?" *Management Accounting,* May 1986, pp. 26–29.

CHAPTER 30

Valuation of Inventories

30-1 SIGNIFICANCE OF PROPER INVENTORY VALUATION

The selection of the principle or method to value the inventory has a significant impact on the reported earnings and the financial condition of the particular company. Since the inventories are usually the most significant item in the current assets, the method of valuing inventories is a very important factor in determining the results from operations and the financial condition.

One of the objectives of accounting for inventories, including valuation, is to determine income properly by matching the applicable costs against the revenues of the firm. In the normal course of business, goods are purchased or manufactured and then sold; other merchandise is secured for additional sales. In this process of selling and either buying or making other goods for sale, it can be seen that the inventory is the "residual value"—the value remaining after costs have been applied to sales or the amount chargeable against future sales. A demonstration of the effect of inventory valuation by using different methods is simple. For example, suppose a dealer purchased an airplane for $250,000 and sold it for $300,000. Suppose further that he also had purchased another identical airplane for resale at a cost of $270,000. What is his profit? On one basis—first-in, first-out (FIFO), it is $50,000. By another method of valuation—last-in, first-out (LIFO), his profit is $30,000 ($300,000 less $270,000). Which is correct? The method of valuing inventories has a dramatic effect on the statement of income and expense. The controller has the responsibility for determining which method or basis of valuation more clearly reflects the results from operations—income.

Another objective of inventory valuation is to state correctly the financial position—the financial condition of a going concern, not one going out of business or in liquidation. The objective may be less important than income determination, since the actual value of inventory cannot be determined until sales are made in the normal course of future business. However, there are no conflicts between the two objectives about the selection of a valuation method.

The subject of inventory valuation includes not only a selection of the proper basis and method of valuation but also a determination about what costs are to be included. For example, should the expenses the purchasing or accounting departments incur be included? Is freight-in a proper cost to include in inventory? What about handling and storage costs? These kinds of questions can have a great significance in valuing inventories, and some are discussed later in the chapter.

30-2 CONTROLLER'S RESPONSIBILITY FOR INVENTORY VALUATION

There are many alternatives available to the accountant in valuing inventories; this means that the subject must be researched and analyses made to determine the most appropriate method. Thus inventory valuation is not an easy task and is not readily understood by many executives or managers. The controller must develop an awareness on the part of management about the effect different methods of valuation have on profits. To do this, several different methods should be applied and the results analyzed and interpreted for management's consideration. The controller must take the initiative in developing inventory valuation methods. Some of the duties and responsibilities to be assumed are as follows:

1. Select the basis of valuation that will most satisfactorily reflect income. The board of directors or chief executive actually may approve or select the method. However, the controller should prepare the case and guide or influence the decision. He should be the member of the management team most familiar with the ramifications.

2. Where necessary or desirable, prepare supplementary data about the effect on income of different bases, or changes in bases, of valuation, including standard cost changes and inflation.

3. Provide for a continuous review of procedures and records to assure that inventories are being properly valued. This will include procedures for notification when materials become unsalable and for keeping abreast of market conditions. It will involve constant vigilance about the effect of manufacturing developments on inventory balance and value.

   The controller is not the most qualified person to determine material obsolescence. Instead, a Materials Review Board (MRB) should be created to periodically review the inventory. The MRB has representatives on it from the Accounting, Quality Control, Engineering, Sales, and Materials departments. The combined expertise of this group can be relied upon to identify unsalable materials.

4. Study the effect of tax legislation on inventory valuation and records and make any necessary changes in the accounting procedures so as to economically have available the required tax basis data. Act in the best interests of the company in dealing with the representatives of the IRS and other taxing authorities.

30-3 EMPHASIS ON THE COST BASIS

Most of the methods of valuing inventories involve "cost." Our entire system of accounting is based on cost, and this same concept is applied to inventories. As related to inventory, *cost* may be defined as the sum of all applicable expenditures and charges directly or indirectly incurred in bringing an article to its existing condition and location.

Just what are "applicable" expenditures and charges? The cost principle is easy to state but difficult to apply. Judgment must be exercised in determining what costs ought to be included, and a consistent policy must be followed. It is generally accepted practice to exclude from inventory costs that share of general and administrative expense not clearly related to production. However, exclusion of all overhead charges from inventory costs would not constitute acceptable accounting practice. Then, too, abnormal costs of various types may be of such magnitude that they require omission. Some examples are excess spoilage, rehandling costs, and idle facility expense.

Product costing generally has followed the absorption costing concept as stipulated by generally accepted accounting principles (GAAP). On this basis, product costs have been defined in this manner:

Those costs of raw materials, direct labor, and other costs that are directly or indirectly involved in the production of goods and services for sale to customers. Indirect costs include such items as factory depreciation, equipment maintenance, factory utilities, and wages for facilitating services in the plants.[1]

It may be that the Tax Reform Act (TRA) of 1986 changes in inventory accounting for income tax purposes may cause some companies, for convenience reasons, to modify their definition of some indirect costs so as to avoid additional record keeping. (See the discussion later in this chapter.)

30-4 INVENTORY CHARACTERISTICS AND EFFECT OF THE VALUATION BASE

In a stable price economy fewer questions of inventory valuation policy normally arise. It is in periods of rapid price change that the valuation base selected may have a significant influence on income determination. The effect of price changes is not uniform in every industry or in every company. Certain features or characteristics of the inventory determine the effect of price changes on an individual business concern. Among these are the following:

---

[1] National Association of Accountants, "Management Accounting Terminology," *Statement on Management Accounting No. 2* NAA, 1983, p. 83.

1. Degree of selling price responsiveness to cost changes.
2. Relative share of investment in inventories.
3. Possibility of price hedge.
4. Rate of turnover.
5. Rate of inflation.

The heart of the problem is the responsiveness of selling price changes to costs. If prices bear little immediate relationship to costs, then the selling price to be realized on the disposition of the present inventory will not impair its value. There will be no problem of write-down.

Relative size or importance of the inventory is a factor, for the larger the inventory, the greater the risk and the more significant the write-down if values decline greatly. Certainly, a firm whose major investment is in inventory is considerably more vulnerable to market changes than one that requires a heavy investment in plant and equipment to engage in business. Under these latter circumstances the effect of price changes may be considerably diluted.

There are more costs associated with large inventories than just the risk of loss due to price changes. The following list should also be considered:

*   Cost of maintaining labor routings for those items in stock at period-end.
*   Cost of maintaining bills of material for those items in stock at period-end.
*   Cost of raw material cost accumulations for those items in stock at period-end.
*   Cost of obsolescence.
*   Cost of property taxes.
*   Cost of insurance (for warehouse facilities as well as the inventory in the warehouse).
*   Cost of inventory tracking (such as cycle counting and periodic audits).
*   Cost of inventory handling.
*   Cost of labor required to track old parts to be used up from stock before a newly engineered design replaces those parts.
*   Cost of money tied up in the inventory.

The reduction in risk when hedging operations are possible is known to those who use the process. Losses on the stock inventory are offset by gains on the futures. A similar hedge on finished goods inventory, of course, is accomplished by firm sales contracts.

Finally, inventory turnover is important. If the turnover is rapid, a shorter time will lapse between the sale of the goods and purchase of items for additional sales. Consequently, in periods of upswing or downswing the fluctuations will not be as violent, even when a traditional method of inventory costing, such as the FIFO, is used.

30-5 SELECTION OF THE COST BASE

The primary objective in choosing a cost basis for valuing inventories is to select that method which, under the circumstances, will most satisfactorily reflect the income of the period. In many instances, the units sold are not identifiable with the specific cost of the item, or at least such an application is impractical. For this reason, a variety of cost applications have been developed that recognize differences in the relationship of costs to selling prices under various conditions. For example, the LIFO method may be applicable where sales prices are promptly affected by changes in reproduction costs. In another situation, the conventional FIFO method may apply. Circumstances of the individual company or industry must govern, but uniform methods within the industry will permit useful comparisons.

A very brief description of the more common inventory valuation methods based on costs follows:

1. *Identified or Specific Costs.* Under this method, purchases are not commingled but are kept separate. The issue or sale is priced at the exact cost of the specific item. Such a system is not widely adopted because it requires too much physical attention as well as accounting detail. It is sometimes used in costing perishable stock or nonstandard units that have been purchased for a specific job.

2. *First-In, First-Out (FIFO).* This means is often known as the original cost method. It assumes that items first received are first issued.

   To illustrate the operation, assume an opening inventory of 50 units at $10 each, receipts on January 11 of 10 units at a cost of $15, and issues on January 3 and 12 of 40 each. The issue on January 3 would be costed at $10 per unit, leaving a balance of 10 units at $10 each. The issue of January 12 would be priced:

10 units at $10 each	$100
30 units at $15 each	450
Total	$550

The requisition must be priced on two bases since two different acquisitions were issued.

3. *Simple Arithmetic Average Cost.* The average is computed by dividing the total unit prices for the inventory on hand by the number of such prices, without regard to the quantities to which the prices relate. It is mathematically unsound.

4. *Weighted Average Cost.* This procedure involves the determination after each receipt of the total quantity and value on hand. The total units are divided into the total value to secure an average unit cost. All issues are priced at this average cost until the next receipt, when the new average is computed. The unit price must be carried out to sufficient decimal places to retain accuracy.

   Disadvantages of this method include the detail calculations necessary and the length of time taken to reflect recent purchases in the average. It has the advantage of stabilizing costs when prices fluctuate.

5. *Moving Average Cost.* This method uses an average price of a convenient period of time, such as three or six months. It is a variation of the weighted average method. The effect of price fluctuations is minimized.

6. *Monthly Average Cost.* The total beginning inventory and the receipts for the month are divided into the aggregate cost to determine an average. This average is then applied to the issues for the period. The method has the advantage of

eliminating some clerical work. But the disadvantage is that the requisitions cannot be costed for the month until the new average cost is determined. Sometimes this disadvantage is avoided by using the previous monthly average.

The period of time over which the receipts are accumulated need not necessarily be a month, nor need the end of the period coincide with the monthly closing.

7. *Standard Cost.* As the name implies, a predetermined or standard cost is used. The price variance on raw materials may be recognized when the material is received or when it is issued into process.

Use of standard costs eliminates much clerical effort. No cost columns are needed on the ledger cards, and the repeated calculation of unit costs is avoided.

8. *Last-In, First-Out Cost (LIFO).* The use of this method assumes that the last unit purchased is the first to be requisitioned. The mechanics used are very similar to the FIFO method, except that requisitions are priced at the cost of the most recent purchase. For example, assume that 100 units are purchased at $4 each and that later 50 units are purchased at $6 each. A requisition for 75 units would be priced as follows:

50 units at $6	$300
25 units at $4	100
75 Total	$400

The purpose of the LIFO method is to state, as closely as possible, the cost of goods sold at the current market cost. This method reduces unrealized inventory profits to a minimum. The following problems with LIFO must be considered:

- Record keeping is more extensive than that required for other valuation methods. If the oldest inventory costing layers are never used, the company can have costing layers that go back many decades.

- If inventory levels drop to zero at period-end, the profit impact could be enormous, for the oldest cost layers may stretch back many years to times when product costs were significantly different. For example, Product A currently costs $10 to build. If the oldest Product A cost layer is only $1 and all of the inventory is used, then the gross margin on sales of the oldest cost layer will increase by $9, yielding a startling improvement in the gross margin percentage.

9. *Replacement Cost.* By this method, the inventory is priced at the cost that would be incurred to replace it at current prices and in its current condition.

It can be seen that the method is not the same as LIFO, for the latter uses the latest price on the books, which is not necessarily replacement cost.

The method has many practical difficulties, is not approved by the IRS, and is not considered a GAAP. If used for internal purposes, it must be adjusted for external reporting.

10. *Retail Inventory Method.* This method is used largely in department stores, where the inventories are marked item by item at selling price rather than cost. The average margin or markup is determined for the period, and this is applied against the ending inventory at retail to ascertain cost. It is a type of average costing.

For details on each of these costing methods, the reader is referred to the many excellent accounting texts on the subject.

30-6 DEPARTURE FROM THE COST BASE

Under ordinary circumstances inventories should be valued at cost. There are occasions, though, where cost is not a proper measure of the charge against the revenues of future periods. In such instances, a departure from the cost basis is necessary if the utility of the goods disposed of in the ordinary course of business is less than cost. Loss in value can occur by reason of damage, deterioration, obsolescence, changes in the price level, and other causes. Such loss should be recognized as a charge against the period in which it occurs. In these instances, the goods should be valued at "market," which will be lower than cost.

How, then, is "market" defined? As used in the phrase "lower of cost or market" the term signifies current replacement cost by either purchase or manufacture, whichever is applicable. However, there are definite limits to the application of this rule. Market should not exceed the estimated selling price, less the costs of completion and disposal. On the other extreme, it should not be less than the estimated net realizable value, minus an allowance for the normal profit margin.

The explanation of the phrase "lower of cost or market" may be stated as follows:

9. The rule "cost or market, whichever is lower" is intended to provide a means of measuring the residual usefulness of an inventory expenditure. The term "market" is therefore to be interpreted as indicating utility on the inventory date and may be thought of in terms of the equivalent expenditure which would have to be made in the ordinary course at that date to procure corresponding utility. As a general guide, utility is indicated primarily by the current cost of replacement of the goods as they would be obtained by purchase or reproduction. In applying the rule, however, judgment must always be exercised and no loss should be recognized unless the evidence indicates clearly that a loss has been sustained. There are therefore exceptions to such a standard. Replacement or reproduction prices would not be appropriate as a measure of utility when the estimated sales value, reduced by the costs of completion and disposal, is lower, in which case the realizable value so determined more appropriately measures utility. Furthermore, where the evidence indicates that cost will be recovered with an approximately normal profit upon sale in the ordinary course of business, no loss should be recognized even though replacement or reproduction costs are lower. This might be true, for example, in the case of production under firm sales contracts at fixed prices, or when a reasonable volume of future orders is assured at stable selling prices.

10. Because of the many variations of circumstances encountered in inventory pricing, Statement 6 [which is a definition of the phrase "lower of cost or market"] is intended as a guide rather than a literal rule. It should be applied realistically in the light of the objectives expressed in this bulletin and with due regard to the form, content and compositions of the inventory. The committee considers, for example, that the retail inventory method, if adequate markdowns are currently taken, accomplishes the objectives herein. It also recognizes that, if a business is

expected to lose money for a sustained period, the inventory should not be written down to offset a loss inherent in the subsequent operations.[2]

In applying the rule of cost or market, whichever is lower, the question arises about whether the test should be applied directly to each item of the inventory or to the total inventory or major categories. Since the purpose is properly to reflect income of the period, the method that achieves this objective should be used. In practice, most companies apply the rule to each item in the inventory. There are instances, however, when application of the total inventory would have the greatest significance. Thus one component may be less than cost, and another component to the same article may have a market value equally higher than cost. If a balanced inventory condition exists, no adjustment might be necessary.

30-7 CONSISTENCY IN VALUATION

Irrespective of the method of pricing the inventory, an essential requirement is consistency from period to period. Over the long run, the basis of valuing inventories will not affect the total profit or loss from operations. However, from quarter to quarter or year to year the effect on profit can be significant if the basis or method is changed. If circumstances require a change, the reason for the change and the effect on profit should be fully disclosed in the financial statements presented to management and the shareholders. In addition, advance approval should be obtained from appropriate governmental agencies, if required.

The following items can cause inconsistent valuations:

- Changes to an inaccurate bill of material (BOM) from a previous period.
- Changes to an inaccurate labor routing from a previous period.
- Changes to BOMs and labor routings that affect items that are still in stock from the previous period.
- Changes in run sizes that impact labor routings from a previous period.
- Changes in labor dollars that impact overhead, since overhead is usually calculated as a percentage of labor.

30-8 FEDERAL INCOME TAX CONSIDERATIONS IN VALUING INVENTORIES

The valuation of inventory is obviously required to determine taxable income. We have considered the general principles of inventory valuation from the standpoint of good business practices, and, presumably, such methods would be acceptable for determination of taxable income. However, the Internal Revenue Code (IRC) and the Treasury regulations provide specific criteria that must be followed. Section 1.471-2 of the Treasury regulations provides two tests to which each inventory must conform:

---

[2] American Institute of Certified Public Accountants, Inc., "Restatement and Revision of Accounting Research Bulletins," Accounting Research Bulletin No. 43, pp. 31–32.

1. It must conform as nearly as possible to the best accounting practice in the trade or business.

2. It must clearly reflect the income.

Section 1.471-2 of the Treasury regulations further provides that to clearly reflect income, the inventory practice should be consistent from year to year, and greater weight is given to consistency than to any particular inventory method or basis of valuation. For those companies using the LIFO valuation method and who are pursuing just-in-time production techniques, note that the cost of goods sold percentage will vary drastically while the inventory is being reduced, since old cost layers with possibly very different costs will be used up; this change may draw an inquiry from the Internal Revenue Service, so ensure that your documentation of cost changes is accurate and complete. The bases of valuation most commonly used by business concerns and that meet the requirements of the Treasury regulations are (1) cost and (2) cost or market,[3] whichever is lower.

Under Section 1.472-1 the taxpayer is permitted to use the LIFO inventory method, provided the election of the method is approved by the commissioner and is consistently used. To more fully understand the transition to this method it is recommended that the full section of the Treasury regulation be studied in detail.

The Treasury regulations relating to the valuation of inventories are extensive, and many provisions are applicable to certain industries. The controller should thoroughly understand the applicable regulations and consult tax counsel to develop inventory valuation methods that will maximize a favorable tax position for the company.

(a) INVENTORY CAPITALIZATION CHANGES UNDER THE TAX REFORM ACT (TRA) OF 1986

The Tax Reform Act of 1986 may have a significant impact on some companies in that there are now some new uniform capitalization rules for inventories. To provide uniformity in the capitalization rules, the TRA added section 263A to the Internal Revenue Code.

Basically, for income tax purposes, pre-TRA regulations required the capitalization of all direct production costs and certain indirect production costs. Indirect production costs were grouped into three categories as shown in Figure 30-1.

1. Category 1 costs were required to be capitalized in inventory.

2. Category 2 costs were not required to be included in inventory.

3. Category 3 costs were to be included in inventory if they were included in inventory costs for financial statement purposes.

It is to be noted that the accounting treatment of many indirect production costs under GAAP and the pre-TRA regulations were the same, as for example, all

---

[3] Sections 1.471.3 and 1.471.4 of the Treasury regulations.

Figure 30-1   Treatment of Indirect Product Costs.

Costs (1)	Pre-Tax Reform Act (2)	Tax Reform Act (3)	GAAP (4)
Category 1 Costs			
Repair expenses	Capitalize	Capitalize	Capitalize
Maintenance	Capitalize	Capitalize	Capitalize
Utilities, e.g. heat, power, light	Capitalize	Capitalize	Capitalize
Rent	Capitalize	Capitalize	Capitalize
Indirect labor and production supervisory wages	Capitalize	Capitalize	Capitalize
Indirect materials and supplies	Capitalize	Capitalize	Capitalize
Tools and equipment not capitalized	Capitalize	Capitalize	Capitalize
Quality control and inspection	Capitalize	Capitalize	Capitalize
Category 2 Costs			
Marketing expenses	Expense	Expense	Expense
Advertising expenses	Expense	Expense	Expense
Selling expenses	Expense	Expense	Expense
Other distribution expenses	Expense	Expense	Expense
Interest	Expense	Expense	Expense
Research and experimental expenses	Expense	Expense	Expense
Losses under section 165	Expense	Expense	Expense
Percentage depletion in excess of cost ...	Expense	Capitalize	N/A
Depreciation and amortization in excess of that reported in financial statements .	Expense	Capitalize	N/A
Income taxes	Expense	Expense	Expense
Pension contribution related to past service costs	Expense	Expense	Expense
General and administrative expenses related to overall operations	Expense	Expense	Expense
Salaries of officers related to overall operations	Expense	Expense	Expense
Category 3 Costs			
Taxes other than income taxes related to production assets	Optional	Capitalize	Capitalize
Depreciation and cost depletion	Optional	Capitalize	Capitalize
Production employee's benefits	Optional	Capitalize	Capitalize
Costs of strikes	Optional	Expense	Expense
Rework labor, scrap, and spoilage	Optional	Capitalize	Capitalize or expense
Factory administration expenses	Optional	Capitalize	Capitalize
Officers' salaries related to production services	Optional	Capitalize	Capitalize

Source: Adapted from *Analysis: Tax Reform Act of 1986,* Coopers & Lybrand, New York, 1986, p. 176.

Category 1 costs.[4] Pre-TRA, Category 2 costs were expensed, but the TRA requires capitalization of:

- Percentage depletion in excess of cost, and
- Depreciation and amortization in excess of that reported in financial statements.

Formerly Category 3 cost treatment was optional, but post-TRA requires capitalization, except for costs of strikes, which may be expensed.

The purpose of these comments is not to discuss specific tax treatment, but only to (a) indicate some of the changes in the tax law, and (b) illustrate the detail of the category expenses that must be accumulated and separated for proper tax treatment.

If mixed-service costs exist, they must be allocated between a manufacturer's production and nonproduction activities by applying either (a) the regular service method or (b) a simplified service cost method. The regular production method may be more complicated than the simplified method, but the controller should consider not only the relative costs of implementing the inventory costing methods, but also the impact on current and future taxes. The simplified method may not be the lowest cost alternative over the longer period. The controller has a responsibility to (a) see that the accounting system of the manufacturer is capable of, and does, generate the data necessary to comply with the new inventory costing rules, (b) be familiar with the costing methods available under the new regulations, and (c) select those methods most beneficial to the company.

(b) IMPACT OF LIFO INVENTORY LIQUIDATION

Another federal income tax matter affecting inventory valuation that may need to be considered is the liquidation of a LIFO pool.

With inflation in the United States seemingly running at a rate of 5% or 6% per year, the advantage of using LIFO to defer income taxes is understandable. The improved cash flow that results can be significant over several years in that it either reduces borrowings and interest expense, or it makes the cash savings available for other uses. Moreover, the LIFO base can be said to relate current costs more closely with revenue.

In connection with inventory planning for the year, if it appears some of the LIFO layers might be reduced temporarily until the next tax year, it might be prudent to compare the short-term carrying cost of acquiring inventory, more than needed for operations, with the value of deferring the income tax otherwise payable.

In essence, a financial analysis should be made comparing the tax savings with the temporary cost of increasing the inventory to avoid liquidating the pool.

Basically, the (temporarily) higher inventory carrying costs of the following should be weighed against the lower tax expense:

- Physical storage.
- Insurance.

---

[4] From Harold P. Roth, "New Rules for Inventory Costing," *Management Accounting,* March 1987, pp. 33–45.

- Property taxes.

- Investment financing.

Assume these facts in an illustrative case:

Probable inventory liquidation amount	$50,000,000
Duration of otherwise lower inventory period—6 months	0.5 year
Funds borrowed to carry inventory at per annum rate	10%
Applicable income tax rate	40%
Storage costs per annum	16%
Insurance per annum	2%
Property tax rate on year end amount	2%

Then a comparison of income tax expense saved vs. the carrying costs for the temporary period would be as follows:

Income taxes payable on liquidation amount
(0.40 × $50,000,000) $20,000,000

	Before Income Taxes	Net of Taxes (60%)
Carrying costs		
Cost of borrowing funds		
(0.5 × 0.10 × $50,000,000)	$2,500,000	$1,500,000
Storage costs		
(0.5 × 0.16 × $50,000,000)	4,000,000	2,400,000
Insurance		
(0.5 × 0.02 × $50,000,000)	500,000	300,000
Property taxes		
(0.02 × $500,000,000)	$1,000,000	$ 600,000
Total carrying cost (net)		$ 4,800,000
Net advantage of temporarily replenishing inventory		$15,200,000

So, for the *temporary* reduction in inventory, it is economically advantageous to replenish the LIFO inventory.

30-9 INTERIM STATEMENTS

The method of valuing inventories poses no particular problems in connection with the preparation of interim statements. Under certain conditions, however, adjustments may be required, depending on the method used, such as LIFO. Generally, the controller must study the situation and determine the best practice under the circumstances for preparing interim reports.

Many companies issue interim financial reports that do not incorporate accurate perpetual inventory figures. Instead, they estimate the cost of goods sold based on the previous year's actual gross margin. This method can subject the company to year-end surprises if product costs have changed from the previous year. For more information on setting up a perpetual inventory system, see Chapter 59.

30-10 OTHER INVENTORY VALUATION PROBLEMS

The inclusion or exclusion of certain costs in inventory is a task that takes a considerable amount of study and effort. Normally, we think of inventory valuation as applicable to direct labor and material, although other components of inventory should be considered.

- *Storage and Handling Costs.* One debatable point is whether storage and handling charges should be included in raw material inventories. Many companies do not write up the raw materials to include such costs. Instead, they consider them part of the general manufacturing overhead and prorate the charges to work in process and finished goods.

  Such a practice is satisfactory unless there is a great variation or irregularity between receipts and consumption of the material. Under such circumstances, it may be permissible to include normal storage and handling costs in the raw material valuation.

- *Purchasing Department Expense.* A similar question is raised with respect to purchasing department overhead as well as the clerical costs of the accounting department that are related to raw materials. The costs of these departments generally would continue the same from one period to another regardless of receipts. Thus they are more attributable to the accounting period than to batches of material, and it is not desirable to increase raw material inventory value by these expenses. They may be treated more properly as manufacturing overhead.

- *Inbound Transportation Costs.* Where the cost of getting the goods to the factory site is identifiable with particular material or lots, the cost may properly be added to the raw material. If such allocation is impractical, it may be considered part of the manufacturing overhead.

- *Overhead and Burden.* In most cases, some indirect costs will be included in inventory values. For example, fringe benefit costs may be included as part of the labor rate applied to direct factory hours. In other instances only variable overhead costs are included, and fixed overhead costs are considered as period costs. Some practices consider all factory costs as part of production and thus included in the inventory value. General and administrative costs are normally not part of inventory and are period costed.

The proper treatment of these costs must be considered in the light of GAAP and the applicable tax regulations. Also, the overall discussion of overhead issues will become less important as more companies adopt just-in-time inventory systems. As inventories shrink, the impact of changes in the overhead structure will have a smaller impact on the financial statements, for the amount of overhead in the period-end inventory will shrink dramatically.

30-11 INVENTORY RESERVES

Inventory reserves are sometimes used to properly value the inventory. It may be well to emphasize here that controllers should take every precaution to report income as it is and not develop unsound reasons for reserves to report predetermined income. Extreme care should be exercised in creating any inventory reserves by charges to current operations that are not fully substantiated and documented.

As previously discussed in section 30-2, the Materials Review Board (MRB) is the ideal group to identify unsalable materials. The identification and resulting documentation of these materials by the MRB should be the basis for calculation of an inventory reserve.

The FASB[5] has determined that an accrual of an estimated loss charged to income must meet both of the following conditions:

1. Information available prior to issuance of the financial statements indicates that it is probable that an asset had been impaired or a liability had been incurred at the date of the financial statements. It is implicit in this condition that it must be probable that one or more future events will occur confirming the fact of the loss.

2. The amount of loss can be reasonably estimated.

The reserves under consideration here are those for which the provision is charged against the operations, the reserve itself being deducted from the inventory in the balance sheet, in accordance with generally accepted accounting principles. If such a practice is followed, any charges made against the reserve should be approved by the controller and separately reported to management, indicating the reasons for the charge. These charges should be analyzed and strictly controlled to preclude burying of losses and suppressing visibility by management.

30-12 SELECTED REFERENCES

Bohan, Michael P., and Steven Rubin, "LIFO/FIFO: How Would It Work?" *Journal of Accountancy,* Sept. 1986, pp. 106–110.

Roth, Harold P., "Guiding Manufacturers Through the Inventory Capitalization Maze," *Journal of Accountancy,* July 1988, pp. 60–70.

Roth, Harold P., "New Rules for Inventory Costing," *Management Accounting,* March 1986, pp. 32–45.

---

[5] Statement of Financial Accounting Standards No. 5, "Accounting for Contingencies."

CHAPTER 31

Accounting and Reporting for Selected Investments and Employee Benefit Plans

31-1 INTRODUCTION

In a broad sense, business management may be regarded as the management of investments—investments in cash, receivables, inventories, plant and equipment, and other objects. The planning and control of each of these investments has been discussed. However, they are reviewed individually and not necessarily as compared with alternatives. In deciding on a given investment, techniques of evaluation were discussed: relative return on assets, internal rate of return, discounted cash flow, and so on. Some of the more sophisticated methods are reviewed as applied to plant and equipment (Chapter 32), or acquisitions and mergers (Chapter 53). The return on identified programs or projects was discussed, for example, programs for research and development (Chapter 24). The same technique applies to manufacturing projects—such as building a particular aircraft. It also applies to selected products when considering the setting of sales prices (Chapters 20 and 21).

One broad area of investment has not been reviewed—debt and equity securities. This is a field that is growing in importance and complexity as businesses increase in size, and as they develop from national enterprises into multinational or global companies. Not only are the investment opportunities (and risks) becoming more numerous, but also the instruments themselves are becoming more complex. In addition to stocks and bonds, there are options, warrants, mortgage-based securities, derivatives, and a host of others. A review of the balance sheets of business entities reveals a larger number of asset classifications and related footnotes than several years ago, for example, investments in equity securities, investments in debt securities, "other investments," employee benefit plan assets (and liabilities). Given this diversity and complexity, it is desirable to briefly comment on the controller's viewpoint in the more complicated investment management environment and the impact of financial accounting standards.

31-2 IMPROVING THE INVESTMENT DECISION PROCESS

When the investment decisions are relatively few and simple, they can be viewed individually, without regard to other potential alternatives or needs. Each often is considered solely on its own. After the investment is made, the monitoring process stops.

In today's competitive environment, a broader view of the process must be taken by the controller. The need is greater as the business becomes larger, enmeshed in a complex organizational structure, and as the complexity of the decisions increases. When the business is small, the owner is involved in most phases and makes most of the decisions, but as the business grows, this personal contact becomes diluted.

Most experienced financial executives know that the amount of thinking and analysis involved in an investment decision varies greatly depending on the nature of the investment. For example, the effort devoted to deciding where to invest temporary surplus cash is much less than that related to making a sizable investment in plant and equipment, or acquisition of a new company. However, most investment decisions should form a consistent pattern and fit a matrix that moves the entity towards its mission. For example, an investment in a minority position in a business in Thailand, and another acquiring a subsidiary in Mexico should in some way be related to the overall strategy of the entity. Otherwise the pieces will not finally fit together.

When making a significant investment decision, the action must be part of an investment management program that should involve these related, key processes:

1. *Strategic Planning* (see Chapter 14).
   (a) Identifying the company mission or purpose.
   (b) Establishing related goals and objectives (including the annual plan to meet the long-term objective).
   (c) Establishing check points and performance targets to measure progress.
2. *Identification of alternative approaches to meeting the objective.* Example: acquisition, merger, divestment, or self growth of capability.
   (a) Includes identifying costs (and true cost drivers) of the option.
3. *Assessing, analyzing, and evaluating the alternative investments, including the risks.*

4. *Implementing the action.* Included would be (a) assigning the responsibility for execution, (b) integrating the investment object into the entity, and (c) establishing a monitoring or tracking system.

5. *Monitoring investment performance vs. the plan.*

These processes, though most obvious when using resources to purchase plant and equipment or acquisitions, can and should apply to most significant investments. The complexity of the process increases with the size of the company, the size of the project, and the levels of management involved. But the process should not be overlooked even in making investments in minority positions, equities, and other securities.

31-3 RELEVANT FINANCIAL ACCOUNTING STANDARDS (FAS)

Certain classes of investments—securities, as distinguished from working capital (cash, accounts receivable, inventories, and current liabilities) or plant and equipment—require special considerations.

The growth in multinational companies and global companies has increased the need, opportunities, and risks in making certain investments. Moreover, the explosion in the types of investments possible, and the need for appropriate disclosure, has raised serious questions about the adequacy of the accounting and reporting guidelines for these investments. This, in turn, has caused the Financial Accounting Standards Board (FASB) to address these matters, and to issue numerous statements. The controller must assume responsibility for application of the proper accounting treatment and meeting disclosure requirements as to the entity which employs him. The many SFASs are a topic for a specialized book, however, one guideline of widespread application deserves comment—the Statement of Financial Accounting Standards No. 115—Accounting for Certain Investments in Debt and Equity Securities, issued in September, 1993.

The controller should read and understand this SFAS in its entirety. However, this summary briefly discusses some major aspects which may impact the general accounting and required disclosures, and may influence the internal management reporting.

SFAS No. 115 addresses the accounting and reporting for investments in equity securities that have readily determinable fair values, and for all investments in debt securities. These investments are to be classified in three categories and accounted for as follows:

- Debt securities that the enterprise has the positive intent and ability to hold to maturity are to be classified as *held-to-maturity* securities and to be reported at amortized cost.

- Debt and equity securities that are bought and held principally for the purpose of selling them in the near term are to be classified as *trading securities,* and are to be reported at fair value, with the unrealized gains and losses to be included in earnings.

- Debt and equity securities not classified as either held-to-maturity securities or trading securities are to be classified as *available-for-sale* securities, and are to be reported at fair value, with unrealized gains and losses excluded from earnings and reported in a separate component of shareholders' equity.

The SFAS contains many exceptions and limitations. It should be mentioned that (a) the FASB chose to use the term *fair value* rather than market value (intending the term to be applicable whether the market for an item is active or inactive, primary or secondary) (paragraph 10a and b). There are, as expected, exceptions taken to the Statement in that fair value is not applied to all debt securities, and the standard does not solve the income manipulation problem (through the reclassification of the security into the trading category). Nevertheless, on balance most accountants at least agree the issuance of the Statement is a step in the right direction.

31-4 ROLE OF THE CONTROLLER

The controller normally would not be the executive managing any one of the three types of investments just discussed, or any related ones. Rather, this function usually would fall under the responsibilities of the chief financial officer, or treasurer and the relevant staff. The role of the controller regarding the categories of investments under discussion includes:

1. Ascertaining that the proper accounting standards or principles are applied in the classification and valuation of the assets, and related liabilities, if any.
2. Assuring that the proper supporting or "detail" records are maintained on a current basis to provide proper accountability and description of the assets and the related financial facts.
3. Determining that proper reports are issued to provide the financial information needed to properly oversee the management of the assets. This will include, as deemed appropriate, reports to the board of directors, executive management, trustees, if any, and fund managers.
4. As applicable, assuring that proper, timely, and adequate disclosure is made to the IRS, SEC, DOL (Department of Labor) and other appropriate government agencies, and to participants in defined benefit plans, or defined contribution plans (such as a 401(k) savings plan).
5. Performing any necessary reviews or audits to ascertain that an adequate internal control system exists and is operating properly.
6. As deemed appropriate, periodically taking, or causing to be taken, a physical inventory of the assets.
7. In those instances where financial know-how or analysis may be helpful and is requested by fund trustees, managers, or independent accountants, providing appropriate assistance.

The next sections elaborate on some of these functions.

31-5 ACCOUNTING RECORDS FOR SELECTED INVESTMENTS

For many reasons, a business entity may invest in equity securities or debt instruments. While the number of issues may not be great, it is highly desirable that a systematic manner be used to record information relative to the purchase, including the objective, and sale, adjustments made to the carrying value, income received, and relevant legal or tax information. In addition to the data required for proper valuations, detailed records are necessary to provide the information needed to manage the portfolio, as well as to establish and support gain or loss for tax purposes.

The file of invoices or statements from the broker may be thought sufficient in some cases. Indeed, these documents are the source of much information. Generally, however, it is necessary to establish a control account or accounts for investments in securities and to support this with a securities ledger or register. Such a record may be a simple loose-leaf book or a formal ledger (which may be a computer printout) as illustrated in Figures 31-1 and 31-2.

Often such records, with substantial related detail and much abbreviation, are maintained in computer files, with printouts available when required.

The basic information to be included in the securities ledgers consists of the following:

For Stocks

Description of issue—name, type, par value, certificate numbers.

Dividend dates.

Record of purchase—date, number of shares, price, commission, tax, total cost, broker.

Date and amount of dividends received.

Record of sale or disposition—date, broker, number of shares, sale or call price, commission, net proceeds.

Dividends in arrears.

Loss or gain.

For Bonds

Description of issue—name, interest rate, maturity date, interest dates, serial numbers, tax position.

Record of purchase—date, broker, price, accrued interest, commission, tax, total cost, maturity value.

Date and amount of interest received.

Amortization of premium or discount.

Record of disposition—date, broker, redemption or sale price, accrued interest, commission, net proceeds.

Loss or gain.

The ledger may be kept alphabetically by issuer. Where a large number of transactions are involved, computers are useful.

31-6 FINANCIAL REPORTS ON SELECTED INVESTMENTS

The activity in investments for most industrial firms normally will be quite limited and few reports need be prepared. Periodic reports to management to show the details

Figure 31-1 Stock Ledger Sheet.

ISSUED BY _____ ABC Corporation

CLASS ____ Common ____ PAR VALUE ____ $100

BOUGHT				SOLD				Profit or Loss	BALANCE		
Date	No. of Shares	Price	*Cost	Date	No. of Shares	Price	*Total Received		No. of Shares	Average Price	Cost
19XX				19XX							
Jan. 30	100	$30	$3,020						100	$30.20	$3,020
				Sep. 30	25	$36	$890	$135.00	75	30.20	2,265
Oct. 3	50	35	1,770						125	32.28	4,035
				Nov. 15	25	38	940	133.00	100	32.28	3,228

* Gives effect to commission and tax.

Figure 31-2 Bond Ledger Sheet.

NAME OF BOND	Asher Company, First Mortgage: Sinking Fund 1990
	NOMINAL RATE 10%
PURCHASED THROUGH	ABC Marks and Co. ACTUAL RATE 9.3%

DESCRIPTION:

NUMBERS	B1676, B1677	PRICE	10%
DENOMINATION	$5,000	COST	$10,750.00
WHERE PAYABLE	First Trust Co., Detroit	ACCRUED INTEREST ..	250.00
TRUSTEE	First Trust Co., Detroit		
DATED	Jan. 1, 1990	REMARKS	$5,000
WHEN DUE	Dec. 31, 2010		FACE AMOUNT
INTEREST PAYABLE .	Jun. 30–Dec. 31		
REDEEMABLE	No		

Date	Pieces	Memo	Price	Debit	Credit	Balance	Profit or Loss	Due	Interest Amount	Paid
19X0										
Apr. 1	2	Marks & Co.	107 ½	10,750				1990 6/30		1990 6/30
Jun. 30		Premium			50.00	10,750			500.00	
Dec. 31		Premium			100.00	10,700		12/31 1990	500.00	12/31 1990
19X1										
Jun. 30		Premium			100.00	10,600		6/30	500.00	6/30
Jul. 1	1	Can. Natl. Bk.	107		100.00	10,500	100.00			
					5,200.00	5,250				

840

Figure 31-3   Report on Investment Position.

				Total Dividends
Security	Number of Shares	Market Value	Purchase Price	Rate of Return*	for Year to Date
1. ABC Corporation ..	500	$ 37,000	$ 31,000	5.2%	$ 800
2. Atlas Construction .	100	2,400	2,400	6.3	75
3. National Co.	1,000	30,000	31,000	6.5	1,000
4. USA Corporation ..	1,000	65,500	64,000	7.8	2,000
5. JPC Corporation ...	100	1,900	1,875	7.5	70
6. Security Co.	500	42,000	38,000	5.3	1,000
Total or average ...		$178,800	$168,275	6.5%	$4,945

The Illustrative Company
INVESTMENT POSITION
AS OF JULY 31, 19XX

* Based on payments for past twelve months, or current rate if believed more applicable.

of the investment would appear desirable. These may be simple reports containing the following information and any other data considered relevant (see Figure 31-3):

For Each Security

> Name of security.
>
> Cost.
>
> Market value.
>
> Effective yield (rate).
>
> Dividend or interest received to date.

For All Investments

> Overall rate of return.
>
> Cost and market value.

Where significant movement takes place, it is desirable to advise management of the purchase or sale, together with the gain or loss in case of disposition.

31-7 ACCOUNTING AND DISCLOSURE REQUIREMENTS AND PRACTICES FOR EMPLOYEE BENEFIT PLANS

The accounting and reporting requirements or practices for certain equity investments or debt instruments, previously commented upon, are *relatively* simple. However, when the subject changes to comparable requirements and practices for employee retirement or benefit plans, the map becomes complex, with many exceptions, and a great many rules. For this reason, and because funded plan assets most often are held in restricted trusts or foundations that are segregated from the assets of the company, discussion of employee benefit accounting and reporting is discussed separately from other investments.

First, there are guidelines published by the Financial Accounting Standards Board (FASB), among which are these:

- FASB Statement No. 87, Employees' Accounting for Pensions.
- FASB Statement No. 88, Employers' Accounting for Settlements and Curtailments of Defined Benefit Pension Plans and for Termination Benefits.
- Statement of Financial Accounting Standards (SFAS) No. 106—Employers Accounting for Postretirement Benefits Other Than Pensions.
- SFAS No. 112—Employers' Accounting for Postemployment Benefits.

The controller should be aware of the requirements of these Statements, together with any amendments.

Additionally, employee pension benefit plans or qualified retirement plans are governed by both ERISA (Employee Retirement Income Security Act of 1974) and the Internal Revenue Code, as well as other related regulations. The rules relate to defined benefit plans of various types, and defined contribution plans, including profit sharing plans, money purchase pension plans, 401(k) savings plans, thrift or savings plans, and stock bonus plans. Moreover, there are qualification requirements, fiduciary responsibilities, reporting requirements, audit requirements, and disclosures to participants requirements of which the controller should have a general knowledge.

Aside from the requirements imposed by external forces, the controller must consider what further communications or reports are desirable to properly inform the board of directors, executive management, and plan participants.

Given the extensive investment needs of most employee benefit plans, the extreme importance of meeting the accounting, reporting, legal, and tax requirements, some selected topics are briefly discussed in the next section.

(a) INVESTMENT POLICY

Statements of investment policy are guidelines to be used in the earning of investment income. Usually, they are expressed in broad terms and reflect the views of management, including the investment committee, about how funds should be invested. Even where outside money managers are employed—and although the "prudent man" rule is followed—it is usually desirable to specifically indicate the matters listed next and, as appropriate, include the terms in the contract with the fund manager:

1. The general policy.
2. The performance objectives.
3. The extent of risk acceptable.
4. General constraints.
5. Specific restrictions.
6. Reporting and accountability.

With time and experience, these guidelines will change, and, of course, they must be tailored to basic changes in the marketplace and the needs of the company. An illustration of the policies and objectives for the retirement funds of an aerospace company is quoted next.

STATEMENT OF POLICIES AND OBJECTIVES
FOR
INVESTMENTS OF THE COMPANY'S RETIREMENT FUNDS

A. Policy

It is the policy of the _____ Corporation to invest the assets of the pension funds for total return over a period of several years, and not emphasize the return on any single segment of assets, i.e., equity securities, etc.

We seek the maximum return consistent with the fiduciary character of the funds, and in recognition of the importance of the preservation of capital and the needs of annuitants for timely payment of benefits.

B. Performance Objectives

Equity securities in the funds in the aggregate should earn not less than 10% compounded annually over a period of three to five years. It is expected that this rate of return will be achieved over a complete security market cycle.

While this rate of return is basic, a supplemental guide shall be to outperform the Standard & Poor's 500 Index by 10%. Thus, if the S&P Index increases by 10% on an annual basis, the funds' appreciation is expected to be an appreciation of 11%. Conversely, if the S&P 500 represents a depreciation of 10%, the company funds should depreciate by only 9%.

The target of an absolute rate of return of 10% is considered more important than the relative goal.

Consistency of investment yield is significant. If two equity funds earn the same over a 3–5 year period, we would express preference with that one with interim results less volatile.

Fixed income securities are expected to earn on an average over a 3–5 year period at least 9%, and should be 10% better than the Salomon Brothers High Grade Corporate Bond Performance Index, or any comparable Index.

Real estate investments should earn a rate roughly comparable to the common stock index.

C. Risks

To the extent that risk is measurable, these guidelines are applicable:

1. The risk inherent in a 15–25% potential annual appreciation is acceptable; but the risk factor involved in seeking substantially greater appreciation than this is considered too aggressive.

2. The risk inherent in assuring a 9% or less potential annual appreciation in equity securities would be considered as too conservative.

D. General Guidelines

Subject to the following guidelines, portfolio managers have full discretion in making investment decisions:

1. *Company Securities*—The retirement funds shall not invest in securities of the Corporation, or its subsidiaries, or its affiliates.

2. *Diversification*—No more than 10% of the funds, on a cost basis, should be invested in any one security and, preferably, no more than 5%.

    No more than 15% of the cost value of the funds should be invested in a single industry classification.

    While subject to change, based on the economic outlook, the investment in equity and fixed income securities should be generally limited to this share of the total funding, on a market basis:

	Fixed Fund	Equity Fund
Equities	20%	80%
Fixed income securities	70	10
Real estate (direct investments)	5	5
Cash equivalents	5	5
Total	100%	100%

The cash equivalent fund is subject to adjustment upward or downward depending on the trustees' estimate of the immediate term outlook in the equity or bond markets.

3. *Marketable Securities*—Generally, equities should be invested in marketable securities, which may include convertibles. Any exceptions, such as letter stock or restricted stock, should be cleared with the company. It is recognized that, to the extent that some of the equity funds are invested in a venture type capital, these funds will be less marketable.

E. Restrictions

It is contemplated that the trustees will be governed by the Prudent Man rule. Operating within this rule, the Investment Board believes that these types of financial activities should be prohibited:

1. Purchases of foreign issues unless registered on the New York Stock Exchange.
2. Short sales.
3. Puts, calls, straddles, or hedges.
4. Margin purchases or other uses of borrowed funds.
5. Purchase of securities of the investment manager's organizations.
6. Purchase of more than 5% of the total cost value of the funds in over-the-counter securities, unless express permission is given.

F. Reporting and Accountability

The investment manager will be requested to meet and review with the Investment Board, as required, the following items:

1. Current and expected performance of the equity and bond markets.
2. The economic outlook.
3. Current plan for investments in specific types of securities (aggressive growth, moderate growth, etc.).
4. Performance for the latest 3 month period, and the last 12 months, and since the inception of the fund.

5. A quarterly report for the Investment Board, containing at a minimum the following information:

   a) *Fund activity report:*

   Market value—beginning of year

   Net contributions

   Investment income

   Realized gain (or loss)

   Unrealized gain

   Market value—end of year

   Cumulative net contribution to date

   Cumulative investment return

   b) Statement of all property on hand showing cost, market, and unrealized gain or loss. Percentage of total funds invested should be shown for each security and each industry.

   c) Sales during period showing cost, market, and realized gain or loss.

   d) Purchases during period.

   e) Performance figures on a total fund basis—

       i. For the quarter, year to date, and each of the prior two years.

       ii. Compound rate of return from inception to date, three years to date, 12 months to date, and year to date.

       iii. Comparable performance figures for S&P 500, Dow Jones Industrial Average (DJIA), and any other indices you consider appropriate.

   f) Short (1–2 pages) report by the fund manager covering investment outlook, changes if any in investment philosophy and comments on performance of the fund during the past quarter.

In addition to meeting with the Investment Board, there will be more frequent meetings, as circumstances require, with the chief financial officer of the company and the administrator of the retirement plans.

G. Miscellaneous

1. While the need to change securities in the portfolio is understood, the Investment Board will periodically review the turnover of securities to see that it is not excessive.

2. In recognition of the right of the trustees to secure on a most advantageous basis the necessary research services, etc., the Investment Board will not direct any share of the brokerage business.

(b) SELECTION OF FUND MANAGERS

Most medium-sized to large enterprises sponsor trusteed pension plans. In creating and operating the plans, the company must decide the degree to which it wishes to be involved in the investment process. It may administer the trust itself, with company officers acting as trustees, and a bank acting as custodian of the securities. On the other hand, it may manage none or only a small portion, with most of the direct investment responsibility placed on outside money managers. Whether the fund will be internally administered will depend, among other things, on the availability of competent people, the relative costs, and the degree of responsibility the company or the management wishes to assume—given the presence of ERISA requirements.

Many corporate managements believe that the investment of retirement funds is a highly specialized activity best handled by those who devote full time to such activity.

Usually, the financial vice-president, or treasurer, perhaps with the advice of the controller, selects the manager or stable of several managers. Factors to be considered in selecting the particular firm include the following:

1. A proven track record (although this does not assure future top performance).
2. A compatible investment philosophy.
3. An organization structured and manned to be able to adequately serve the client company. The organization would be capable of providing a research staff, efficient execution of trades, and good communication and reports.

Some companies hire several money managers, each with different "styles" of investment in some cases and each with differing strengths to achieve a type of diversification. Some investment companies may do well managing equity investments, and others perform better in the fixed income field.

In any event, once managers are selected, the performance should be monitored. And, to reiterate, the management contract should spell out the terms and restrictions, etc.

(c) SELECTION OF THE PLAN(S) TRUSTEES

Although the money managers make the investments, that is, buy and sell the specific securities based on their expertise, usually a bank is hired as trustee and custodian of the assets. Securities are handled by the custodian. The custodian must have the ability to properly account for the securities and related income and provide the necessary detailed reports. In selecting the custodian, examination of the computer capabilities and a review with other customers may be desirable. Often, a master trust is established with one custodian for all types of pension or employee benefit plans that involve the holding of stocks or bonds.

(d) INTERFACE WITH THE ACTUARY

Once or twice a year the controller may interface with the actuary. *Actuaries* are the independent professionals who make the pension cost estimates. Through the discounting process, the present value of expected, future benefit payments are established. From this and related information the annual plan contribution is determined. The controller should be familiar, in a general way, with the process and results. Aside from indicating the amount to be paid into the funds, the actuarial report is the basis for the footnote to the financial statements. See Disclosure Requirements in later paragraph.

(e) QUALIFICATION WITH THE IRS

The controller is interested in seeing that pension plan contributions by the company are tax deductible in the year in which made and that the fund earnings are tax free. In order to qualify for the privileged tax treatment, all conditions set out by the IRS must be fulfilled. The objective is to insure that the trust funds are used exclusively for the benefit of the employees or their beneficiaries. A trust may lose its qualified status by engaging in certain prohibited transactions, including lending assets to the sponsor without adequate security; providing the means by which the plans discriminate in favor of special groups of employees, such as corporate officers; or diverting corpus or income to the employer. The controller, usually being responsible for tax administration and accounting, should make certain the company does all things necessary to qualify under the IRS directives.

The rules set up by the U.S. Treasury (which are subject to change) include these items:

1. The plan must be in writing and must be communicated to the employees for whose benefit the plan is operated.

2. The plan must offer deferred compensation; it must be funded; and, on plan termination, the employees' interest must vest to the extent of the assets.

3. The plan must be permanent, and the trust must be valid under state laws and must operate for the exclusive benefit of the employees and their beneficiaries; and, finally, it must qualify as exempt from federal income tax.

4. As previously stated, it must not discriminate in favor of owners, officers, or high-salaried employees.

(f) FINANCIAL AND OTHER DISCLOSURE REQUIREMENTS

ERISA greatly increased the reporting and disclosure requirements for pension benefit and welfare benefit plans. Various reports must be prepared and filed with the IRS, some with copies to the Department of Labor (DOL) as well as the Pension Benefit Guaranty Corporation. Initially, the plan administrator is required to file a summary plan description with the DOL, and to supplement it with amended descriptions, as necessary.

The most significant report is probably the annual report (Form 5500). For plans with 100 or more participants, the annual report, with certain exceptions must contain these data:

1. The financial statements, including:
   (a) Current value of plan assets and liabilities, at the beginning and end of the plan year.
   (b) Plan income, expenses, and changes in net assets for the plan year, with payments to/from insurance carriers.
   (c) These supporting schedules:
       (1) Schedule A—Insurance Information.
       (2) Schedule B—Actuarial Information.
       (3) Schedule C—Service Providers and Trustee Information (for each plan or fund).
   (d) Footnotes required for a full and fair presentation.
2. The report of the Independent Public Accountant.

(g) EVALUATING FUND AND MANAGER PERFORMANCE

One of the more difficult financial management tasks is that of evaluating pension fund performance. A firm with an exceptional record in a "down" market may perform relatively poorly in a "bull" market. What might constitute acceptable performance in the eyes of one corporate management might be deemed unacceptable by another. Then, too, performance over a few quarters of a year or two probably is not indicative. What must be judged is performance over several years, perhaps through a complete market cycle. Although quarterly or annual review is desirable, it is long-term performance that should govern. The rate of return, relative as well as absolute, over a period of years, probably is the only fair measure.

Rates of return should be calculated for each fund manager. These may be compared with appropriate measures such as the following:

For Equities

The Standard and Poor's Index of 500 stocks.

The Becker Data Bank.

For Fixed Income Securities

The Salomon Brothers Index.

For each manager, comparisons can be made against other managers of similar funds used by the enterprise and to any number of published fund results.

Measurement of a manager must involve the changes in market values from period to period and the manner in which consideration is given to the timing of cash flows into and out of the fund. Risk also must be weighted in the evaluation. Two statistical measures commonly used are (*a*) the internal rate of return (discounted cash flow), and (*b*) the time-weighted rate of return. Measurement of risk is attempted through variability in the rates of return and volatility comparisons.

The controller may work with the treasurer in developing acceptable measuring devices, reports, and other analyses.

An example of a comparative report of equity managers' performance with each other, with the composite of all, and with two indexes is shown in Figure 31-4. Any number of analyses may be prepared, depending on what the financial executive performing surveillance of the money managers feels will be helpful and the available data provided through the computer program. A tabulation to identify each individual investment, market value, percent of total portfolio, P/E ratio, and the gain or loss is illustrated in Figure 31-5.

(h) OTHER REPORTS TO MANAGEMENT AND/OR PLAN PARTICIPANTS

The ERISA reports discussed earlier represent mandatory reporting. Additionally, the annual report to shareholders usually provides summarized information concerning accumulated benefit obligations of a business entity vs. the plan assets at fair value, together with limited data on assumed long-term rates of return on pension assets, and so on. But what other financial data should be presented to the board of directors

Figure 31-4 Equity Fund Performance—by Manager.

EQUITY FUND
COMPARATIVE PERFORMANCE SUMMARY
(time weighted, total return)

Year Ended			Year to Date 9-30-X4
12-31-X1	12-31-X2	12-31-X3	(Unannualized)
S&P 500 — 23.8%	Manager B — -4.7%	Manager B — 11.1%	Manager E — 31.8%
Manager A — 18.3	Manager D — -4.8	Manager C — 9.5	Manager B — 20.6
Manager B — 1.5	Composite — -5.3	Composite — 9.5	Manager A — 19.6
Becker Median — 16.6	Becker Median — -5.5	Manager D — 8.7	Composite — 19.4
Manager C — 15.7	Manager A — -5.6	Manager A — 8.5	S&P 500 — 18.4
Composite — 15.5	Manager C — -6.3	Becker Median — 7.2	Manager D — 17.2
Manager D — 10.5	S&P 500 — -7.2	S&P 500 — 6.6	Manager C — 16.3
			Becker Median — 15.8

Figure 31-5   Investment Portfolio Summary—Manager C.

	MANAGER C—EQUITY PERIOD (ENDED SEPTEMBER 30, 19XX)			
Security Name	Market Value	Percentage of Assets	P/E Ratio	Dollar Gain (Loss)
ABC Company	$ 2,688,125	4.91	9.29	$ 340,480
DEF Corporation	2,261,350	4.13	7.33	240,038
GHI Corporation	2,033,775	3.71	15.66	237,127
JKL Ltd.	1,955,000	3.57	19.23	284,090
MNO Company	1,842,675	3.37	6.92	245,733
UUU Corporation	592,500	1.08	7.18	93,619
VVV Company	556,250	1.02	7.02	15,755
WWW Company	554,200	1.01	34.00	98,538
XXX Industries	356,103	0.65	12.32	−14,313
YYY Ltd.	343,838	0.63	7.67	−93,706
ZZZ Corporation	7,650	0.01	NA	7,650
Total	$54,755,683	100.00%	12.00	$7,757,733

or executive management to provide a sense of relative fund performance and significant financial aspects, or risks? Readily understandable financial facts should also be provided to plan participants.

Depending on the interest of the board of directors and executive management and the considered opinion of the financial executives as to the truly important aspects of the investment performance, and so on, about which these officials should be informed, some suggested topics for presentation are:

- Comparative asset allocation of funds (see Figure 31-6).
- Comparative rates of return on asset sectors over several years (see Figure 31-7).

Figure 31-6   Retirement Plan—Fund Allocation.

	THE DOUGLAS COMPANY Retirement Plan—Fund Allocation Percentage			
	Year			
Fund	1995	1994	1993	1992
U.S. Equity	50.25%	48.60%	47.75%	46.70%
Fixed Income	38.50	37.00	35.40	36.10
International Equity	4.15	6.30	7.25	8.00
Fund R	7.10	8.10	9.60	9.20
Total	100.00%	100.00%	100.00%	100.00%

Figure 31-7 Retirement Plan—Comparative Rates of Return.

THE DOUGLAS COMPANY
Retirement Plan
Comparative Rates of Return
1992–1995

Sector	1995	1994	1993	1992
Equities	15.10%	14.70%	14.50%	14.30%
Fixed Income	9.50	9.00	8.70	7.90
Real Estate	8.80	9.00	10.60	12.70
Total	11.70%	12.10%	12.00%	11.73%

- Historical comparison of retirement plan assets vs. projected benefit obligations (see Figure 31-8).
- Projection of estimated retirement plan assets vs. projected benefit obligations.
- For an equity fund—the top 25 holdings by company.

To fully comprehend the extent of the detail required, the reader probably should scan a copy of Form 5500 and the supporting schedules.

In addition to providing reports to the agencies of the federal government, ERISA requires that a Summary Annual Report (SAR) be provided to plan participants

Figure 31-8 Retirement Plan—Funded Status.

THE MCDONALD CORPORATION
Retirement Plan—Funded Status
(DOLLARS IN MILLIONS)
As of December 31

Description	1995	1994	1993	1992
Actuarial Present Value of Benefit Obligations				
Vested Benefits	$2,310	$2,051	$1,901	$1,700
Nonvested Benefits	182	160	140	120
Accumulated Benefit Obligations	2,492	2,211	2,041	1,820
Effect of Assumed Wage Increases	501	450	417	362
Projected Benefit Obligations	2,993	2,661	2,458	2,182
Less: Fair Value of Plan Assets	3,740	3,304	3,116	2,916
Excess of Assets over Projected Benefit Obligations	(751)	(643)	(658)	(734)
Unrecognized Items:				
Prior Service Costs	(90)	(112)	(102)	(90)
Net Gain	307	234	314	401
Accrued Pension Asset Included in Statement of Financial Position	$ (77)	$ (521)	$ (446)	$ (423)

Figure 31-9   Savings Plan—Financial Summary.

HIGH TECHNOLOGY, INC. Savings Plan Financial Summary (DOLLARS IN MILLIONS) As of June 30, 199x	
Fund	
Stock Fund	$ 549.3
Bond Fund	158.6
Money Market Fund	243.7
Hi-Tech. Inc. Fund (ESOP)	216.4
Total	$1,168.0

(for each relevant plan). Additionally, the plan participants have the right to request and receive a copy of the full annual report (usually for a fee).

Financial information for plan participants should be limited in quantity so as not to confuse, and should be summarized in nature and limited to historical data (not projected results). As an example, one high-technology company provides semi-annual data on the savings plan as follows:

- Financial summary by fund segment (see Figure 31-9).
- Investment performance by fund segment (see Figure 31-10).
- A summary of the categories of financial instruments in each fund (see Figures 31-11 through 31-13).
- A summary of the stock fund by industry investment (see Figure 31-14).
- The top 25 equity investments in the stock fund (see Figure 31-15).

Some discussion with participants will let you know other subjects of interest to them.

Figure 31-10   Savings Plan—Fund Performance.

HIGH TECHNOLOGY, INC. Savings Plan Investment Performance For Period Ended June 30, 199x				
	Latest	Preceding		
	Six		5	10
Fund	Months	Year	Years	Years
Stock	3.20%	4.70%	72.30%	291.10%
Bond	1.15	5.00	51.60	215.30
Money Market	.97	3.75	22.15	100.50
Hi-Tech (ESOP)	.30%	−1.10%	38.34%	41.00%

Figure 31-11 Savings Plan—Bond Fund Portfolio Structure.

HIGH TECHNOLOGY, INC.
Savings Plan
Bond Fund—Portfolio Structure
As of June 30, 199x

Instrument	% of Fund
Federal Agency Obligations	29.37%
U.S. Treasury Notes	25.61
Banking and Financial—Various	14.22
Wells Fargo Fund—Temporary Cash	12.20
Industrials	9.10
U.S. Treasury Bonds	3.46
Government Obligations	2.70
Other U.S. Government Securities	1.91
Other Corporate Obligations	1.43
Total	100.00%

In summary, the various management groups (board of directors, Investment Committee, executive management) should be advised of the important aspects (financial and otherwise) of the benefit plans so that they are reasonably informed, and can reach informed conclusions. The plan participants should have made available to them all legally required data, and any further information to make the general aspects of the plan financial status understandable to them.

Figure 31-12 Savings Plan—Money Market Fund—Portfolio Structure.

HIGH TECHNOLOGY, INC.
Savings Plan
Money Market Fund—Portfolio Structure
As of June 30, 199x

Instrument	% of Fund
U.S. Treasuries	43.52%
Wells Fargo Fund—Temporary Cash	20.40
Medium Term Notes	17.00
Certificates of Deposit	6.98
Asset Backed Securities	4.05
Repurchase Agreements	2.68
Government Agencies	2.40
Deposit Notes	1.48
Commercial Paper	1.49
Total	100.00%

Figure 31-13   Savings Plan—Company Stock.

HIGH TECHNOLOGY, INC.
Savings Plan
Hi-Tech, Inc. Fund (ESOP)
(DOLLARS IN MILLIONS)
As of June 30, 199x

	Market Value
High Technology, Inc.	
Shares held—5,436,201, or	
10.1% of outstanding stock,	
at $37.56 per share	$204.2
Dividends	10.2
Cash	2.0
Total	$216.4

Figure 31-14   Savings Plan—Stock Fund—Industry Structure.

HIGH TECHNOLOGY, INC.
Savings Plan
Stock Fund—Structure by Industry
As of June 30, 199x

Industry	% of Fund
Office Equipment & Electronics	7.94%
Consumer	7.00
Retailing	6.20
Pharmaceuticals	4.97
Medical Supplies	4.59
Utility—Telephone	4.01
Banks	4.00
Oil—Domestic	3.70
Oil—International	2.91
Transportation—Railroads	2.04
Leisure and Recreation	2.00
Automotive	1.92
Chemical	1.87
Forest Products	1.65
Paper Products	1.62
Electrical Equipment	1.59
Oil Service	1.50
Beverage	1.46
Machinery	1.39
Food	1.23
Utility—Electric	.70
All Others	35.72
Total	100.00%

Figure 31-15   Savings Plan—Highest Equity Instruments.

HIGH TECHNOLOGY, INC.
Savings Plan
Stock Fund—Top 25 Equities (All Common)
As of June 30, 199x

Security	% of Fund
Pfizer, Inc.	1.31%
Royal Dutch Petroleum	1.06
Johnson & Johnson	1.00
Atlantic Richfield Co. (ARCO)	.98
Chrysler Corp.	.86
Hewlett-Packard Co.	.85
Dayton-Hudson Co.	.72
CSX Corp.	.66
Merck & Co.	.66
Procter & Gamble	.57
Abbott Laboratories	.56
Colgate-Palmolive	.55
Schumberger, Ltd.	.54
Ford Motor Co.	.53
AT&T	.53
Minnesota, Mining & Mfg. Co.	.49
CPC International	.47
Kimberly-Clark	.46
Coca Cola	.46
General Electric Company	.44
Chevron	.41
Weyerhaeuser Co.	.38
Disney Co. (Walt)	.36
Monsanto Co.	.35
Citicorp	.35

(i) OTHER ADMINISTRATIVE MATTERS

Aside from the subjects covered earlier in this chapter, there is a multitude of administrative matters that typically are delegated to the financial executives most closely associated with pension plan management. The controller should be aware of the actions required, some of which may be his responsibility. Some are outlined here:

1. Proper internal procedures to readily identify retirement benefit payments due to the retirees and other employees.
2. Proper cost allocation procedures for each profit center, etc., if applicable.
3. Adequate internal control procedures relating to the following:

   • Investments (purchases, sales, and income proceeds).

   • Operating expenses.

- Benefit payments.

- Withdrawals.

Included should be periodic audits by the internal auditors.

4. Independent audits by a public accounting firm.

31-8 SELECTED REFERENCES

Akresh, Murray S., Harold Danker, and Judith E. Latta, "How to Handle FASB 112," *Journal of Accountancy,* Dec. 1993, pp. 71–73.

Beams, Floyd A., *Advanced Accounting.* Englewood Cliffs, NJ: Prentice-Hall, 1985.

Carrol, John B., and Stork Wayne, "Are Performance Fees Justified?" *Financial Executive,* May–June 1989, p. 26.

Herdman, Robert K., and Robert D. Neary, "How Will Full Adoption of Statement 87 Affect Your Liability Disclosure?" *Financial Executive,* March–April 1989, p. 12.

Jarnagin, Bill D., and Tsai Yen Chung, "Understanding the Accounting for Defined Benefit Pension Plans," *Management Accounting,* Sept. 1988, p. 34.

Jayson, Susan, "Pension Update: An Interview with Consultant Larry B. Wiltse," *Management Accounting,* Sept. 1988, p. 20.

Munter, Paul, and Stephen D. Willitts, "Understanding the New Pension Math," *Management Accounting,* Dec. 1986.

Samuelson, John L., "Simplified Employee Pensions," *Management Accounting,* Sept. 1988, p. 29.

Steinberg, Richard M., Murray S. Akresh, and Keith F. Jensen, "Auditing Postretirement Benefits: How to Deal with FASB 106," *Journal of Accountancy,* Aug. 1992, pp. 74–78.

Swenson, Dan W., and Thomas E. Buttross, "A Return to the Past: Disclosing Market Values of Financial Instruments," *Journal of Accountancy,* Jan. 1993, pp. 71–77.

Walker, David M. "Statements 87 and 88: The ERISA Implications," *Financial Executive,* Sept.–Oct. 1988, p. 10.

Zarowin, Stanley, "How Business Is Dealing with FASB 106," *Journal of Accountancy,* March 1992, pp. 67–69.

CHAPTER 32

Planning and Control of Plant and Equipment or Capital Assets

32-1 IMPACT OF CAPITAL EXPENDITURES

Capital expenditure planning and control are critical to the long-term financial health of any company operating in the private enterprise system. Generally, expenditures for fixed assets require significant financial resources, decisions are difficult to reverse, and the investment affects financial performance over a long period of time. The statement "Today's decisions determine tomorrow's profits" is pertinent to the planning and control of fixed assets.

Investment in capital assets has other ramifications or possible consequences not found in the typical day-to-day expenditures of a business. First, once funds have been used for the purchase of plant and equipment, it may be a long time before they are recovered. Unwise expenditures of this nature are difficult to retrieve without serious loss to the investor. Needless to say, imprudent long-term commitments can result in bankruptcy or other financial embarrassment.

Second, a substantial increase in capital investment is likely to cause a much higher break-even point for the business. Large outlays for plant, machinery, and equipment carry with them higher depreciation charges, heavier insurance costs, greater property taxes, and possibly an expanded maintenance expense. All these tend to raise the sales volume at which the business will begin to earn a profit.

In today's highly competitive environment, it is mandatory that companies make significant investments in fixed assets to improve productivity and take advantage of the technological gains being experienced in manufacturing equipment. The sophisticated manufacturing and processing techniques available make investment decisions more important; however, the sizable amounts invested allow for greater rewards in increased productivity and higher return on investment. This opportunity carries with it additional risks relative to the increasing costs of a plant and equipment.

These conditions make it imperative that wisdom and prudent judgment be exercised in making investments in capital assets. Management decisions must be made utilizing analytical approaches. There are numerous mathematical techniques to assist in eliminating uneconomic investments and systematically establish priorities. Since these investment decisions have a long-term impact on the business, it requires an intelligent approach to the problem.

32-2 THE CONTROLLER'S RESPONSIBILITY

What part should the controller play in the planning and control of capital commitments and expenditures? The board of directors and the CEO usually rely on first-level management to analyze the capital asset requirements and determine, on a priority basis, which investments are in the best long-term interests of the company. The controller has a key role to play in making the determinations. All the functional departments, like sales or manufacturing, will have valid reasons for expansion or cost savings through the purchase of new plant and equipment. In addition, each operating unit will have a real need to increase the capital asset expenditures to meet its goals and objectives. The controller, with his financial knowledge of all company operations, should be able to apply objectivity by making a thorough analysis of the proposed expenditures. In many cases, heavy losses have been incurred because the decision was made with an optimistic outlook but without adequate financial analysis. The responsibility is placed on the controller's staff to make an objective appraisal of the potential savings and return on investment. The board of directors and the CEO must have a proper evaluation of proposed expenditures if they are to carry out their responsibilities effectively.

After the decisions have been made to make the investments, the controller must establish proper accountability, measure performance, and institute recording and reporting procedures for control.

The following is a list of various functions that relate in some way to the planning and control of fixed assets and that typically come within the purview of the controller:

1. Establish a practical and satisfactory procedure for the planning and control of fixed assets.

2. Establish suitable standards or guides, also called hurdle rates, as to what constitutes an acceptable minimum rate of return on the types of fixed assets under consideration.

3. Review all requests for capital expenditures, which are based on economic justification, to verify the probable rate of return.

4. In the context of the business plans—whether short-term or long-range—ascertain that the plant and equipment expenditures required to meet the manufacturing and sales plans (or plans for R&D or any other function) are included in such plan, and that the funds are available.

5. As required, establish controls to assure that capital expenditures are kept within authorized limits.

6. As requested, or upon his or her own initiative, review and consider suitable economic alternatives to asset purchases, such as leasing or renting, or buying the manufactured item from others—a part of the "make-or-buy" decision.

7. Establish an adequate reporting system that advises the proper segment of management on matters related to fixed assets. Included could be these:
   • Maintenance costs by classes of equipment.
   • Idle time of equipment.
   • Relative productivity by types or age of equipment, etc.
   • Actual costs vs. budgeted or estimated costs (as in the construction or purchase of plant and machinery, etc.).

8. Design and maintain property records, and related physical requirements (numbering, etc.) to accomplish the following:
   • Identify the asset.
   • Describe its location, age, etc.
   • Track transfers.
   • Properly account for depreciation, retirement, and sale.

9. Develop and maintain an appropriate depreciation policy for each type of equipment—for book and tax purposes, each separate, if advisable.

10. Develop and maintain the appropriate accounting basis for the assets, including proper reserves.

11. Ascertain that proper insurance coverage is maintained.

12. See that asset acquisition and disposition is handled in the most appropriate fashion taxwise.

13. Ascertain that proper internal control procedures apply to the machinery and equipment or any other fixed asset.

While the controller and staff have certain accounting, evaluation, auditing, and reporting requirements to meet, it should be understood that the line executives have the major responsibility for the acquisition, maintenance, and protection of the fixed assets.

32-3 THE CAPITAL BUDGETING PROCESS

Having mentioned the responsibilities related to fixed assets that are typically assigned to the controller, we devote the principal part of this chapter to the capital budgeting process. Most of the accounting and reporting duties are known to the average controller, but more involvement in the budget procedure needs to be encouraged. Given the relative inflexibility that exists once capital commitments are made, it is desirable that the CEO and other high functional executives be provided a suitable framework and basis for selecting the essential or economically justified projects from among the many proposals—even though their intuitive judgment may be a key factor. And when the undertaking begins, the expenditures must be held within the authorized limits. Moreover, for the larger projects at least, management is entitled, once the asset begins to operate, to be periodically informed how the actual economics compare with the anticipated earnings or savings.

The sequential steps in a well-conceived capital budgeting process are outlined below. It should be understood that these steps are not all performed by the controller, but rather by the appropriate line executive. (In separate sections, some of the more analytical facets are explored.)

1. For the planning period of the short-term budget, which may be a year or two, *determine* the outer *limit* or a permissible range for capital commitments or expenditures for the company as a whole, and for each major division or function. This is desirable so that the cognizant executive has some guidance as to how much he can spend in the planning period. (There must be a starting point, and this is as good a one as any.) Depending on the circumstances, this may be an iterative procedure.

2. Through the appropriate organizational channels, *encourage* the presentation of worthy capital investment projects. For major projects, the target rate of return should be provided, and any other useful guidelines should be furnished (corporate objectives, plans for expansion, etc.).

3. When the proposals are received (and presumably there are many) make a preliminary screening to eliminate those that do not support the strategic plan, or that are obviously not economically or politically supportable.

4. After this preliminary screening:
   a. Classify all projects as to urgency of need.
   b. Also, calculate the supposed economic benefits. Those performing this task must be given guidance as to (1) the method of determining the rate of return and (2) the underlying data required to support the proposal.

5. When the data on proposed projects are submitted for top management approval, the financial staff should review and check the material as to:

   a. Adequacy and validity of nontechnical data.

   b. Rate of return and the related calculations.

   c. Compatibility with

      (i)   Other capital budget criteria,

      (ii) Financial resources available, and

      (iii) Financial constraints of the total or divisional budget, etc.

6. When the proposals have been reviewed and analyzed, and approved by top management, the data must be presented to the board of directors and approval secured *in principle.*

7. When the time approaches for starting a major project, the *specific* authorization should be reviewed and approved by the appropriate members of management. This process may require a recheck of underlying data to be sure no fundamentals have changed.

8. As a control device, when a project has started, periodic reports should be prepared to indicate costs incurred to date, and estimated cost to complete—among other information deemed critical.

9. At stipulated times, and for a stated period, after a major project has been completed, a post-audit should be made comparing actual and estimated cash flow.

As can be deduced, the role of the controller and staff as to capital budgeting relates to the financial planning, the establishment and monitoring of the capital budgeting procedure, the economic analyses, and the control reports during and after completion.

Now some explanatory comments are made on some financial or economic phases of the capital budgeting process.

32-4 ESTABLISHING THE LIMIT OF THE CAPITAL BUDGET

A common beginning point in the annual planning process is to set a maximum amount that may be spent on capital expenditures. There will be occasions when the "normal" limit is set aside because of an unusual investment opportunity or other extraordinary circumstances. Normally, however, top management will set a capital budget amount, based on its judgment and considering such factors as these:

- Estimated internal cash generation (net income plus depreciation and changes in receivables and inventory investment, etc.).
- Availability and cost of external funds.
- Present capital structure of the company (too much debt? etc.).
- Strategic plans, and corporate goals and objectives.
- Stage of the business cycle.
- Near- and medium-term growth prospects of the company and the industry.
- Present and anticipated inflation rates.

- Expected rate of return on capital projects as compared with cost of capital or other hurdle rates.
- Age and condition of present plant and equipment.
- New technological developments and need to remain competitive.
- Anticipated competitor actions.
- Relative investment in plant and equipment as compared to industry or selected competitors.

At different times, each of these factors will seem more compelling than others. As an additional rule of thumb for "normal" capital expenditures, some managements determine the limit based on the (a) amount of depreciation, plus (b) one-third of the net income. The remaining two-thirds of net income are used equally: one-half for dividend payout to shareholders, and the other one-half for working capital.

In considering the company investment in plant and equipment vs. the industry these two ratios may provide some guidance (see Chapter 8):

- *Ratio of Fixed Assets to Net Worth.* This ratio, when compared with those of competitors, indicates how much of the net worth is used to finance plant and equipment vs. working capital.
- *Turnover of Plant and Equipment.* The ratio of net sales to plant and equipment, when compared to industry data, to specific companies, or to published ratios such as those issued by Dun & Bradstreet, shows whether too much is invested in fixed assets for the sales volume being achieved.

32-5 INFORMATION SUPPORTING CAPITAL EXPENDITURE PROPOSALS

An important element in a sound capital budgeting procedure is securing adequate and accurate information about the proposal. In this connection, the reason for the expenditure is a relevant factor in just what data are needed.

In a sense, a capital expenditure may call for a *replacement* decision, that is, an existing piece of equipment is to be replaced. For such a decision the information necessary would include:

- The investment and installation cost of the new piece of equipment.
- The salvage value of the old machinery.
- The economic life of the new equipment.
- The operating cost of the new item over its life.

Presumably the economic decision would relate directly to the lower cost of production with the new piece of equipment, and possibly the opportunity to produce a greater quantity of output.

In contrast, consider an *expansion* type of decision. Assume a company wants to produce a new product to be sold in a new market. Then, not only must the economic data on the acquisition and operation of the new equipment be available, but also marketing information is required, such as estimates of:

- The market potential for the new product.
- The probable sales quantity and value of the output for X years.
- The marketing or distribution cost.

Such a capital investment obviously will involve more risk than a replacement decision.

One other comment may be germane to securing good ideas and adequate information about new capital items. First, those who would use the equipment and are knowledgeable should be consulted. Too often management does not listen to this valuable source of information. Secondly, management should encourage the flow of ideas about capital expenditures—especially new processes and perhaps new products. It is far better to have too many good ideas than not enough. And ideas should be sought from many elements of the organization and compared. What is most desirable is a balanced agenda, rather than a limiting of ideas to any one department or single source.

As is discussed later, economic data on proposals normally should include all relevant cash flow information—cash outgo—the complete installation costs and operating expense, and cash inflow—the expected net sales revenues less related marketing expense, etc. Any relevant economic data should be made available, such as tax data, inflation outlook, economic life of the project, other equipment needed, capacity data, cost information, and salvage value.

Here is an expanded list of the reasons that capital expenditures are made, all of which have a bearing on input data:

- To enable continued operation of the business.
- To meet pollution control requirements.
- To meet safety needs.
- To reduce manufacturing or marketing (distribution) costs through more efficient use of labor, material, or overhead.
- To improve the quality of the product.
- To meet product delivery requirements.
- To increase sales volume of existing or new products.
- To diversify operations.
- To expand overseas, etc.

32-6 METHODS OF EVALUATING PROJECTS

In an effort to invest funds wisely in capital projects, companies have developed several evaluation techniques. It is these expenditures that provide the foundation for the firm's growth, efficiency, and competitive strength. Since most companies do not have sufficient funds to undertake all projects, some means must be found to evaluate the alternate courses of action. Such decisions are not merely the application of a formula. The evaluation of quantitative information must be blended with good judgment, and perhaps good fortune, to produce that aggregate wisdom in capital expenditures that will largely determine the company's future earning power.

As will be seen, some entities have rather simple procedures while some of the more capital intensive managements feel a need for more sophisticated methods. Those companies using the more analytical tools find these three elements essential:

1. An estimate of the expected capital outlay, as well as the amount and timing of the estimated future benefits—the cash flow.
2. A technique for relating the expected future benefits to a measure of cost—perhaps the cost of capital, or other "hurdle rates."
3. A means of evaluating the risk—which relates to (a) the probability of attaining the estimated rate of return, and (b) a sense of how changes in the assumptions can affect the calculated return.

The more important valuation methods in use, which are quantitative in nature, consist of the following or some variation thereof:

1. *Payback Method.* This is the simple calculation of the number of years required for the proceeds of the project to recoup the original investment.
2. *Rate of Return Methods.* Among them are these:
   a. The "operators' method," so called because it is often used to measure operating efficiency in a plant or division. It may be defined as the relationship of annual cash return, plus depreciation, to the original investment.
   b. The "accountants' method," perhaps so named because the accounting concept of average book value and earnings (or book profit) is employed. This method is merely the relationship of profit after depreciation to average annual outstanding investment.
   c. The "investors' method" or discounted cash flow method. This rate of return concept recognizes the time value of money. It involves a calculation of the present worth of a flow of funds.

Some comments on these methods follow.

32-7   THE PAYBACK METHOD

Assume that project A calls for an investment of $1,000,000 and that the average annual income before depreciation is expected to be $300,000. Then the payback in years would be 3.3 years, calculated thus:

$$\text{payback time in years} = \frac{\text{investment}}{\text{yearly net income} + \text{depreciation}}$$

$$= \frac{\$1,000,000}{\$200,000 + \$100,000}$$

$$= 3.3 \text{ years}$$

In circumstances where the net income and depreciation are not approximately level each year, then the method may be refined to reflect cash flow each year to arrive at the payback time—instead of the *average* earnings. For example, assume an increasing stream of cash inflow followed by a decrease, then a matrix as in Figure 32-1, can be completed. In this illustration, the payback is completed in 5½ years (5 years plus a $900,000/$1,800,000 fractional year).

Figure 32-1   Payback Period—Uneven Cash Flow.

Year	Cash Outflow	Cash Inflow	Net Investment (Recovery)
0	$10,000,000	—	$10,000,000
1	—	$1,200,000	8,800,000
2	—	1,500,000	7,300,000
3	—	1,700,000	5,600,000
4	—	2,500,000	3,100,000
5	—	2,200,000	900,000
6	—	1,800,000	(900,000)

Briefly stated, the payback method offers these advantages:

1. It may be useful in those instances where a business firm is on rather lean rations cash-wise and must accept proposals that appear to promise a payback, for example, in two years or less.
2. Payback can be helpful in appraising very risky investments where the threat of expropriation or capital wastage is high and difficult to predict. It weighs near-year earnings heavily.
3. It is a simple manner of computation and easily understood.
4. It may serve as a rough indicator of profitability to reject obviously undesirable proposals.

There are, however, some very basic disadvantages to the payback method:

1. *Failure to Consider the Earnings after the Initial Outlay Has Been Recouped.* Yet the cash flow *after payback* is the real factor in determining profitability. In effect, the method confuses recovery of capital with profitability. In the foregoing example, if the economic life of the project is only 3.3 years, there is zero profit. If on the other hand, the capital life is 10 years, the rate of return will differ significantly from that produced by a 4-year life.
2. *Undue Emphasis on Liquidity.* Restriction of fund investment to short payback may cause rejection of a highly profitable source of earnings. Liquidity assumes importance only under conditions of tight money.
3. *Capital Obsolescence or Wastage Is Not Recognized.* The gradual loss of economic value is ignored—the economic life is not considered. This deficiency is closely related to item 1. Similarly, the usual (average) method of computation does not reflect irregularity in the earning pattern.

32-8 THE OPERATORS' METHOD

A manner of figuring return on investment, using the figures of the payback method, is as follows:

$$\text{return on investment} = \frac{\text{annual earnings} + \text{depreciation}}{\text{original investment}}$$

$$= \frac{\$200,000 + \$100,000}{\$1,000,000}$$

$$= 30\%$$

The technique may be varied to include total required investment, including working capital.

The operators' method has these advantages:

1. It is simple to understand and calculate.
2. In contrast with the payout method, it gives some weight to length of life and overall profitability.
3. It facilitates comparison with other companies or divisions or projects, especially where the life spans are roughly comparable.

The basic disadvantage is that it does not recognize the time value of cash flow. Competing projects may have equal returns, but the distribution of earnings, plus depreciation, may vary significantly between them year by year and/or the total period over which equal annual returns are received may vary between projects.

32-9 THE ACCOUNTANTS' METHOD

This technique relates earnings to the average outstanding investment rather than the initial investment or assets employed. It is based on the underlying premise that capital recovered as depreciation is therefore available for use in other projects and should not be considered a charge against the original project.

There are variations in this method, also, in that the return may be figured before or after income tax, and differing depreciation bases may be employed.

The rate of return using the accountants' method and assuming a 10-year life and straight-line depreciation on project A is shown in Figure 32-2.

This basic procedure has two chief shortcomings. First, it is heavily influenced by the depreciation basis used. Double-declining balance depreciation will, of course, reduce the average investment outstanding and increase the rate of return. Second, it fails to reflect the time value of funds. In the example, if the average investment was the same but income was accelerated in the early years and decelerated in later years (with no change in total amount) the rate of return would be identical. Such conditions are reflected in Figure 32-3. By many measures, the cash flow shown in this illustration is more desirable than that reflected in Figure 32-2, because a greater share of the profit is secured earlier in the project life, and is thus available for other investment.

Most projects do vary in income pattern, and the evaluation procedure probably should reflect this difference.

The accountants' method offers the advantage of simplicity over the discounted cash flow approach.

32-10 DISCOUNTED CASH FLOW METHODS

Given the importance of capital expenditures to business, especially the capital intensive enterprises such as steel or chemicals, much thought has been directed to ways and

Figure 32-2 Return on Investment—Accountants' Method.

RETURN ON INVESTMENT—THE ACCOUNTANTS' METHOD
AVERAGE BOOK INVESTMENT AND AVERAGE PROFIT
PROJECT A

Year	Net Earnings Before Depreciation	Depreciation	Net Profit	Average Investment Outstanding
1	$ 300,000	$ 100,000	$ 200,000	$ 950,000
2	300,000	100,000	200,000	850,000
3	300,000	100,000	200,000	750,000
4	300,000	100,000	200,000	650,000
:	:	:	:	:
:	:	:	:	:
9	300,000	100,000	200,000	150,000
10	300,000	100,000	200,000	50,000
Total	$3,000,000	$1,000,000	$2,000.000	$5,000.000

$$\text{Rate of return} = \frac{\text{Profit after depreciation}}{\text{Average outstanding investment}}$$

$$= \frac{\$2,000,000}{\$5,000,000}$$

$$= 40\%$$

Figure 32-3 Return on Investment—Decreasing Profit Condition.

RETURN ON INVESTMENT—THE ACCOUNTANTS' METHOD
DECREASING PROFIT
PROJECT A

Year	Net Earnings Before Depreciation	Depreciation	Net Profit	Average Investment Outstanding
1	$ 400,000	$ 100,000	$ 300,000	$ 950,000
2	400,000	100,000	300,000	850,000
3	400,000	100,000	300,000	750,000
4	400,000	100,000	300,000	650,000
5	400,000	100,000	300,000	550,000
6	200,000	100,000	100,000	450,000
7	200,000	100,000	100,000	350,000
8	200,000	100,000	100,000	250,000
9	200,000	100,000	100,000	150,000
10	200,000	100,000	100,000	50,000
Total	$3,000,000	$1,000,000	$2,000,000	$5,000,000

$$\text{Rate of return} = \frac{\text{Profit after depreciation}}{\text{Average outstanding investment}}$$

$$= \frac{\$2,000,000}{\$5,000,000}$$

$$= 40\%$$

means of comparing investment opportunities. It becomes very difficult to compare one project with another, particularly when the cash flow patterns vary or are quite different. *When* cash is received becomes very important in that cash receipts may be invested and earn something. The sooner the funds are in hand, the more quickly they can be put to work.

Accordingly, the discounted cash flow principle has been adopted as a far superior tool in ranking and judging the profitability of the investments. The principle may be applied in two forms:

1. The investors' method, also known as the internal rate of return (IRR).
2. The net present value (NPV).

The first one actually involves the determination of what rate of return is estimated. The second method applies a predetermined rate, or hurdle, to the estimated stream of cash to ascertain the present value of the proposed investment.

Comments on each procedure follow.

(a) THE INVESTORS' METHOD—INTERNAL RATE OF RETURN (IRR)

Technically, the rate of return on any project is that rate at which the sum of the stream of after-tax (cash) earnings, discounted yearly according to present worth, equals the cost of the project. Stating it another way, the rate of return is the maximum constant rate of return that a project could earn throughout the life of the outstanding investment and just break even.

The method may be simply described by an example. Assume that an investment of $1000 may be made and, over a five-year period, cash flow of $250 may be secured. What is the rate of return? By a cut-and-try method, and the use of present value tables, we arrive at 8%. The application of the 8% factor to the cash flow results in a present value of approximately $1000 is as follows:

Year	8% Annual Cash Flow (a)	Discount Factor (b)	Present Value (a) × (b)
1	$250	.926	$232
2	250	.857	214
3	250	.794	198
4	250	.735	184
5	250	.681	170
	Total present value		$998

The proof of the computation is the determination of an 8% annual charge with the balance applicable to principal, just as bankers calculate rates of return.

Year	Cash Flow (a)	Return at 8% of Investment Outstanding at Beginning of Year (b)	Balance Applicable to Investment (c) = (a − b)	Outstanding Investment at Year-End (d)
0	$ —	$ —	$ —	$1,000
1	250	80	170	830
2	250	66	184	646
3	250	52	198	448
4	250	36	214	234
5	250	19	231	3*

* Due to rounding.

By trial and error, application of the proper discount factor can be explored until the proper one is found. Using a 10% discount factor and a 40% discount factor, the $1,000,000 assumed investment, discussed in connection with other evaluation methods, to be recouped over 10 years, results in a 36% rate of return, as shown in Figure 32-4.

Figure 32-4   Trial and Error—Computation of Internal Rate of Return. n.

INTERNAL RATE OF RETURN
PRESENT VALUE OF STREAM OF CASH

Years from Start of Operation	(Expenditure) or Income	10% Discount Rate Discount Factor	10% Discount Rate Amount—M	40% Discount Rate Discount Factor	40% Discount Rate Amount—M
0	$(1,000,000)		$(1,000.0)		$(1,000.0)
0 to 1	300,000	.953	285.9	.844	253.2
2	300,000	.866	259.8	.603	180.9
3	300,000	.788	236.4	.431	129.3
4	300,000	.716	214.8	.308	92.4
5	300,000	.651	195.3	.220	66.0
6	300,000	.592	177.6	.157	47.1
7	300,000	.538	161.4	.112	33.6
8	300,000	.489	146.7	.080	24.0
9	300,000	.444	133.2	.060	18.0
10	300,000	.404	121.2	.041	12.3
Total Cash Flow	$ 3,000,000				
Discounted Cash Flow			$ 1,932.3		$ 856.8

Discounted Rate of Return:

$$10\% + 30\% \left[\frac{1,932 - 1,000}{1,932 - 857} \right] = 36\%$$

The steps in application of the method may be described as follows:

1. Determine the amount and year of the investment.
2. Determine, by years, the cash flow after income taxes by reason of the investment.
3. Extend such cash flow by two discount factors to arrive at present worth.
4. Apply various discount factors until the calculation of one comes close to the original investment and interpolate, if necessary, to arrive at a more accurate figure.

The disadvantages of the discounted cash flow method are as follows:

1. It is somewhat more complex than other methods; this apparent handicap is minor in that those who must apply the technique grasp it rather readily after a couple of trials.
2. It requires more time for calculation. However, the availability of handheld computers, or tabletop computers, with a software package or built-in programs, makes the calculations rather painless.
3. An implicit or inherent assumption is that reinvestment will be at the same rate as the calculated rate of return.

These disadvantages are more than offset by the benefits—among them, these:

1. Proper weighting is given to the time value of investments and cash flow.
2. The use of cash flow minimizes the effect of arbitrary decisions about capital vs. expenses, depreciation, etc.
3. Is comparable with the cost-of-capital concept.
4. Is a valuable tool for the financial analyst in evaluating alternatives.
5. Brings out explicit reasoning for selecting one project over another.

(b) THE NET PRESENT VALUE (NPV) TECHNIQUE

The NPV technique of evaluating capital expenditures (or acquisitions) also considers the time value of money and uses the discounting method. The difference as compared with the IRR is that a preselected rate is used—the rate that the company considers the minimum rate of return for taking the risk of the capital investment. As discussed later, this rate usually is higher than the cost of capital. If the sum of the present values of the stream of cash exceeds the cost of the proposed investment, then the rate of return exceeds the target and meets the earnings requirement. If the NPV is negative, then the proposal fails to meet the required earnings rate, and the project presumably should be rejected.

An example is given in Figure 32-5. The net present value is in excess of the cost of the investment. As illustrated in the figure, a profitability index may be calculated, relating the present value of the investment to the cost of the investment. Capital projects may be ranked by the internal rate of return or profitability index.

Figure 32-5   Net Present Value Calculation.

CAPITAL INVESTMENT PROPOSAL NO. 16
CALCULATION OF NET PRESENT VALUE

Year	Estimated Cash Flow	Discounting Factor 22%	Present Worth
0	$(800,000)	1.000	$(800,000)
1	370,000	.820	303,400
2	350,000	.672	235,200
3	301,000	.551	165,851
4	215,000	.451	96,965
5	170,000	.370	62,900
6	110,000	.303	33,330
7	40,000	.249	9,960
8	10,000	.204	2,040

Present value at 22% factor $ 909,646

$$\text{Net present value index} = \frac{\$ 909,646}{\$ 800,000}$$

$$= 1.14$$

32-11 HURDLE RATES

A hurdle rate is the minimum rate of return that a capital project should earn if it is to be judged acceptable. In reviewing this subject, on which there are a variety of opinions, perhaps these aspects are the more important ones:

- Value of using any hurdle rate.
- Value of using a single hurdle rate.
- Value of using multiple hurdle rates.

(a) VALUE OF HURDLE RATES

Many companies do not establish hurdle rates, for a variety of alleged reasons, including these:

- There is a large element of subjectivity in capital investments, and management wishes to review all proposals. It does not want to eliminate any from consideration simply because of the rate of return.
- When new business areas are to be considered, it is difficult to set a suitable hurdle rate.
- Many projects must be undertaken regardless of economic reasons: pollution abatement, safety equipment, etc.

- If hurdle rates are used, then data will be manipulated so that the minimum profit rate will seem attainable.

If management wishes to maintain flexibility in its capital budgeting process, it seems this can still be done with proper instructions or guidelines, despite the existence of hurdle rates. Thus, provision can be made for some expenditures that do not relate directly to a given profit rate. Moreover, sound analytical procedures, including dismissal, can minimize any efforts to fabricate justification data. Additionally, if a for-profit business is an economic institution, and the authors think it is, and if the management task is to enhance shareholder value, then it seems guidelines must include profit rates which by and large do not dilute the shareholders' equity.

(b) A SINGLE HURDLE RATE?

A great many companies that employ the hurdle rate concept use a single rate, as distinguished from different rates for various kinds of expenditures. The reasoning in the application of one hurdle rate is basically this:

- The cost of capital, a good point of departure, is about the same for all segments of the company (divisions, subsidiaries, product lines, etc.).
- The additional risk in attempting to earn an acceptable return on equity is essentially the same for all parts of the company.
- Given the elements of error in estimating the rate of return on the capital project, the future cost of capital, and the subjective nature of the decision, it isn't worth the effort to establish several hurdle rates.

One of the common single hurdle rates employed is closely associated with the cost of capital (discussed in the next section and in Chapter 34). Some projects do not earn the cost of capital, so a factor must be added as the goal of other projects so that, on average, the proper earnings level is maintained.

A single hurdle rate might be established thus:

Cost of capital	17%
Allowance to offset sublevel projects	5
Profit goal for capital projects	22%

32-12 COST OF CAPITAL—A HURDLE RATE

Technically, the cost of capital is the rate of return the long-term debt holders and shareholders require to persuade them to furnish the required capital. Thus, assume that:

1. A company capital structure target objective is $500,000,000 composed of 25% debt and 75% equity.
2. In the current market environment long-term bondholders require a 10% return (6% cost to the company after income taxes); a 17% return on equity is the going earnings rate.

Then the cost of capital would be calculated as follows:

Structure	Capitalization	Required Rate of Return (After Income Taxes)	Required Amount of Return
Senior debt	$125,000,000	6.0%	$ 7,500,000
Common stock	375,000,000	17.0%	63,750,000
Total	$500,000,000		$71,250,000

$$\text{Cost of capital} = \frac{\$\,71,250,000}{500,000,000}$$

$$= 14\%$$

It could be argued that if the company is to attract the capital required to stay in business, then, on average, all its capital investments should earn at least 14% after taxes. If this does not occur, then the shareholder return would be diluted. Of course, it would be well to consult with the investment bankers as to the bondholder and shareholder expectations on earnings of the company and industry for the next several years. Depending on their views, a cost of future capital might be determined based on the relation of expected earnings to expected market value of the stock, plus the yield the bondholders might require. In this manner, the minimum return for capital projects could be estimated.

This calculation represents the average cost of capital and seems a fair basis for capital investment decisions viewed on the thesis that the true cost of capital is calculated on a pool basis. However, there might be some circumstances where the marginal or incremental cost of capital basis may be calculated for informational use. This is the cost of capital for the most recent capital transaction considered, such as the opportunity cost of not repurchasing common stock, or of not repaying debt. However, this application would be viewed as the cost of a specific source of capital. It seems to the authors that the pool concept of capital is the more appropriate basis for evaluating capital expenditures.

In any event, cost of capital, or cost of capital adjusted for some subnormal rates of return on some projects, might be a suitable hurdle rate.

(a) MULTIPLE HURDLE RATES

In these days of multinational companies, and conglomerates operating in many business sectors, a case could be made for using multiple hurdle rates. The use of multiple hurdle rates could be justified for different segments of a business where:

- Different business risk exists (threat of expropriation, adverse business environment, etc.).
- Rates of return expectations are markedly different (as in some non-U.S. geographical areas).
- Experienced earnings rates are much different.

- Differing business strategies may apply and require different hurdle rates for a time.

However, whether different hurdle rates should be determined, or whether management should make mental adjustments to a single hurdle rate, depends on management inclinations. Intuitive judgment still plays an important role in capital expenditure decisions.

32-13 RISK ANALYSIS

Probably the discounted cash flow approach to judging the profitability of capital investments gives the investor a better measure of true return in that it recognizes the time value of money. The calculated rate of return is deemed to be the most probable rate of return. But it would be helpful to the decision maker to know not only the expected, or most likely, rate of return, but also the probability of receiving that rate, as well as the range of returns possible, together with the likelihood or probability of each occurring. The augmented investors' method applies a probability distribution to the DCF calculation. And packaged computer programs make possible the calculation of frequency distributions to represent the proposed alternative investments, as in Figure 32-6. It might be concluded that the probabilities favor Investment A as the preferred project.

32-14 SENSITIVITY ANALYSIS

Sensitivity analysis is a mathematical technique wherein changes may be made in each or any of the input factors, and the consequent movement in the result observed. Those making estimates of return on investments know that the answers depend greatly on the assumptions. It is important to test how much an error in an assumption can sway the result. Such knowledge can permit the analysts to concentrate their attention on the more important variables. The technique can provide considerable insight into the capital budget proposal. Perhaps several scenarios are necessary—not just the "worst case" and "most probable." If several key assumptions are involved, how much do results change?

Large capital investments may mean large risks. Management should be exposed to enough information and alternatives to understand the risk exposure.

32-15 INFLATION

Those involved in analyzing capital investments may ponder how inflation should be handled. Even so-called "modest" inflation rates of 5% or 6% can significantly influence results. In the budgetary process, these questions should be considered:

- Should adjustments be made for inflation in the cash flows?
- Should one inflation rate be applied to the entire period, or should year-to-date adjustments be made?
- If available, should specific estimated inflation rates be used on each factor, i.e., wages, material costs, product prices?
- Should the hurdle rate be adjusted to provide for inflation?

Figure 32-6   Probabilities of Rate of Return.

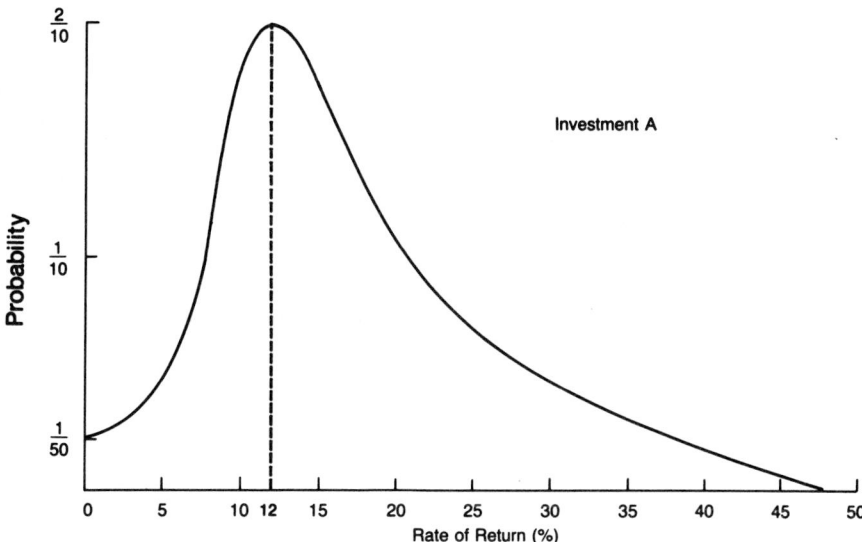

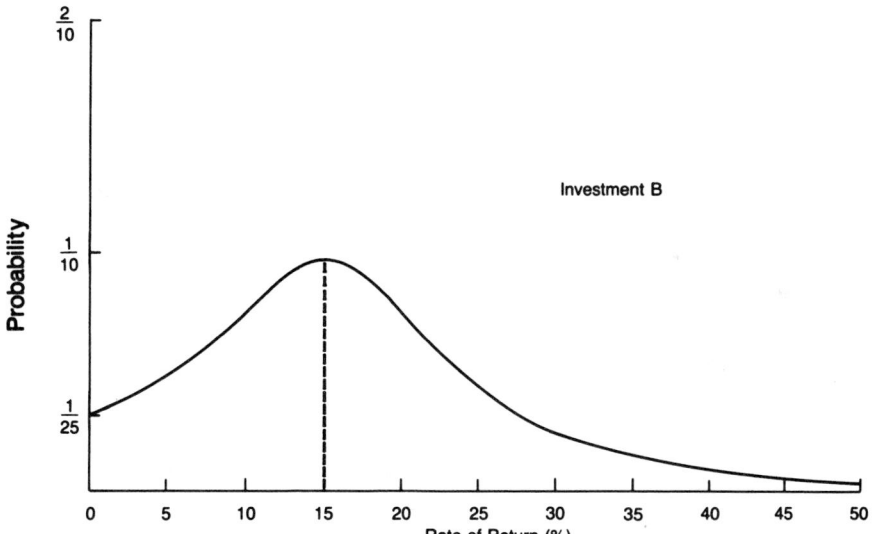

Comments on these questions are as follows:

1. In the experience of the authors, many companies do not adjust for inflation. The reasons for not recognizing inflation range from the pragmatic—that product prices and revenues changes probably will at least match cost movements—to the recognition of the difficulty in getting a reliable rate estimate.

  However, those more analytical souls, and those using DCF techniques and the computer, are more likely to adjust for inflation.

2. Many analysts engaged in long-range planning use an average inflation rate because of the difficulty of getting more realistic data. On the other hand, if estimates of inflation by near-term years are available, perhaps these should be used, with an average "guess" for the later years.

3. Specific price indices exist for some materials, or groups of materials, and for wages in particular industries.

   With the availability of computers, if the company believes there will be wide variations of inflation in segments of the business, it might be well to test the results of applying specific inflation indexes.

4. If cash flows are adjusted for inflation, then the hurdle rate also probably should be adjusted for estimated inflation. However, if constant dollars are used in projections, then obviously the hurdle rate should not be adjusted for estimated inflation.

In reaching conclusions on any of these points the analysts probably should secure estimates of inflation, and experiment on the computer with the impact on the answer.

32-16 FOREIGN INVESTMENTS

Investments by the multinationals in countries with hyperinflation rates must separately consider the effect of these conditions on the real rate of return—and the desirability of making any capital investments at all.

When a discounted cash flow method (or, indeed, any method) is used to evaluate investments in another country, it is to be emphasized that the significant test is the cash flow to the *parent*—not to the foreign subsidiary or entity. Among the impediments to cash flow to the parent, which must be considered (for each year) and factored into the decision, are such items as:

- Currency restrictions.
- Fluctuations in the foreign exchange rate.
- Political risk.
- Withholding taxes.
- Inflation (as mentioned).

Limited discussion of these topics is contained in Chapter 11.

32-17 IMPACT OF THE NEW MANUFACTURING ENVIRONMENT

Investments are made in capital assets with the expectation that the return will be sufficiently high not only to recoup the cost but also to pass the hurdle rate for such an expenditure. But the nature of the investment is changing, as are the attendant risks, in the new manufacturing environment.

The nature of this net setting is reflected in these characteristics:

- While automation is viewed as a primary source of additional income, this often is preceded by redesigning and simplifying the manufacturing process, before automation is considered. Many companies have achieved significant savings simply by rearranging the plant floor, establishing more streamlined procedures, and eliminating the nonvalue-adding functions such as material storage and handling. After this rearrangement is accomplished, then automation might be considered.

- Investments are becoming more significant in themselves. While a stand-alone grinder may cost $1 million, an automated factory can cost $50 million or $100 million. Moreover, much of the cost may be in engineering, software development, and implementation.

- The equipment involved often is more complex than formerly, and the benefits can be more indirect and perhaps more intangible. If there are basic improvements in quality, in delivery schedules, and in customer satisfaction (which seems to be the emphasis today), then methods can be found to measure these benefits. (These gains may lie in improvements or lower costs in the support functions—such as purchasing, inventory control—and greater sales volume.)

- Because of the high investment cost, the period required to earn the desired return on investment is longer. This longer-term horizon, together with the intangibles to be considered and the greater uncertainty, require the controller, budget officer, or management accountant to be more discerning in his evaluation. Usually the indirect savings and intangible benefits need to be recognized and included in the investment analysis. (The *direct* benefits may be insufficient to justify the investment.)

Some of the Selected References detail the complexities of the investment decision in the light of the new technologies.

32-18 IMPACT OF ACTIVITY-BASED COSTING

Chapter 6 discusses some of the changes required in the typical cost system as the result of activity-based costing. However, it should be mentioned here that one output of the cost system may be used to determine the real net cash flow from the capital investment—and that is the sales revenues less the variable costs or direct cash costs of the specific products to be manufactured. Often, the allocation methods and the depreciation system do not reflect the realities of the manufacturing process. Hence, the relevant cost of sales may be substantially incorrect, leading to an improper cash flow calculation. Alternatively, the technology costs related to the product may be in error and, the larger the technology costs, the greater the impact of misallocation of product costs. Accordingly, the controller as well as the financial analyst developing, or reviewing, the capital investment justification should ascertain that the costing system accurately mirrors the resources needed in the relevant decision.

32-19 CLASSIFYING AND RANKING PROPOSED CAPITAL PROJECTS

When the reviews and analyses have been completed, it is necessary to bring order out of chaos, and to classify and rank the projects in some order of priority for discussion purposes. This is a necessary procedure because usually there are many more proposed capital expenditures than would normally be undertaken within the bounds of financial capability. Projects are ranked for discussion with top management (and the board of directors) on the basis of perceived need. While *profitability* may be a ranking factor for some categories, it does not follow that it is the only basis.

A practical grouping that would be understood by management and operation executives alike might be in some such order as this:

1. Absolutely Essential.
   a. Installation of equipment required by government agencies, such as
      (i) Safety devices.
      (ii) Pollution abatement vehicles without which the business would be shut down.
   b. Replacement of inoperable facilities without which the company could not remain in business.
2. Highly Necessary.
   a. State-of-the-art quality control devices.
   b. New flame-retardant painting facilities.
   c. High-intensity laser drills.
3. Economically Justified Projects.
   a. New facilities in Vancouver, Canada.
   b. Robot assembly line for casings.
   c. Warehouse in Denver, Colorado.
4. All Other.
   a. Community center in Delaware, Maryland (public relations).
   b. New lighting facilities in parking area (two shifts will be starting).
   c. Outdoor cafeteria facilities for employees.

For projects based on the economic return, usually these projects may be ranked by rate of return. An example is shown in Figure 32-7. It will be noted that a profitability index also is provided. As explained under the "mutually exclusive projects" section, on some occasions the proposal with the highest rate of return may not be the one with the highest profitability index.

While a ranked list of economically desirable projects may be provided—which keeps the total capital budget request within the guideline amount—sometimes a "contingent capital budget project" listing also is prepared in the event management or the board of directors decides to appropriate more funds than originally contemplated. These projects would rank just below the formal proposals as to rates of return.

32-20 BOARD OF DIRECTORS' APPROVAL

Under normal circumstances, when management has decided what capital budget projects should be undertaken and be included in the annual business plan, approval of the board of directors is sought. Usually either the chief operating officer of the vice president in charge of facilities makes the presentation, perhaps with a visual aid much like that shown in Figure 32-8. The data are presented in some logical form and

Figure 32-7   Proposed Capital Projects by Economic Ranking.

The Money Company
PROPOSED CAPITAL PROJECTS
RANKED BY INTERNAL RATE OF RETURN
FOR THE 19XX CAPITAL BUDGET

Priority Ranking	Description and Location	Internal Rate of Return	Profit-ability Index	Cost
1	Electronics Assembly Plant—Wayne, Michigan	37.90%	1.62	$ 7,980,000
2	Robot Assembly Line, —Hawthorne, Calif.	29.75	1.40	6,300,000
3	Computer Assisted Design Facility—Hawthorne, Calif.	28.00	1.25	4,500,000
4	Spray Equipment—Boston, Mass.	25.00	1.20	2,500,000
5	Material Handling System —San Francisco, Calif.	25.00	1.24	4,610,000
6	Composite Materials Equipment —Pomona, Calif.	22.00	1.10	5,100,000
	Total			$30,990,000

display the significant facts. The objective is to make the board aware of the reason for, benefits of, and risks attached to, each project. The information included in the proposal as reflected in Figure 32-8 contains the following:

- An identification of each project.
- Priority and category of each project.
- Reason for the proposed item.
- Total anticipated cost.
- Rate of return (where this is the basis of selection).
- Timing of the expenditures.
- A contingency fund in the event of cost overruns.

Any cost estimates, the rate of return, and availability of funds, etc., should be checked, or calculated, by the controller's office before submission to the board (or management).

In securing the approval of the board of directors, there is one other aspect that often should be brought to the attention of the board and that has to do with GAAP.

(a) IMPACT OF GENERALLY ACCEPTED ACCOUNTING PRINCIPLES (GAAP)

Just as the discussion of activity-based costing has stimulated management accountants to recheck the cost drivers and allocation methods of the cost systems used in

Figure 32-8 Annual Capital Budget Request.

The California Company
ANNUAL CAPITAL BUDGET REQUEST—19X4
(dollars in thousands)

Project Description	Appropriation						Return on Investments (DCF)	Expenditures				
	Prior Years	New 1st Quarter	New 2nd Quarter	New Last Half	Total 19X4	Total Commitments		Prior Years	19X4	19X5	Later Years	Total
Replacements and Substitutions												
Absolutely essential												
Safety equipment—Plant 5	$—	$512	$460	$128	$1,100	$1,100		$—	$1,100	$—	$—	$1,100
Solvent disposal—Chicago	—	—	—	500	500	500		—	250	250	—	500
Cadmium grinders—Toronto	—	—	400	350	750	750		—	750	—	—	750
Total	—	512	860	978	2,350	2,350		—	2,100	250	—	2,350
Competitive necessity												
Quality control upgrading—all plants	200	50	100	300	450	650		100	510	40	—	650
Delivery equipment—Denver	—	—	375	—	375	375		—	375	—	—	375
Total	200	50	475	300	825	1,025		100	885	40	—	1,025
Total replacements, etc.	200	562	1,335	1,278	3,175	3,375		100	2,985	290	—	3,375
Expansion												
Manufacturing facility, Cleveland	850	1,800	2,300	700	4,800	5,650	26.50%	750	4,900	—	—	5,650
Warehouse, Toronto	—	400	600	2,000	3,000	3,000	17.50	—	2,400	600	—	3,00
Pneumatic loading system, Chicago	—	—	—	1,400	1,400	1,400	14.00	—	1,000	400	—	1,400
Total expansion	850	2,200	2,900	4,100	9,200	10,050		750	8,300	1,000	—	10,050
Other												
Community facilities, Cleveland	—	—	140	—	140	140		—	140	—	—	140
Landscaping, Plant 5	—	—	—	75	75	75		—	75	—	—	75
Total	—	—	140	75	215	215		—	215	—	—	215
Contingency	—				630	630			630			630
Grand total	$1,050	$2,762	$4,375	$5,453	$13,220	$14,270		$850	$12,130	$1,290	—	$14,270

their companies, so also recent articles about the tendency of GAAP applications to discourage needed investment in new equipment such as computer integrated technology, is causing some thought about the accounting methodology in use in certain circumstances. Some of the alleged difficulty arises because of the practice of expensing, and not capitalizing, the start-up costs of the new project, or perhaps the tendency to focus on short-term earnings, or the failure to recognize life-cycle accounting. The impact of a capital expenditure on earnings may cause the small company to reflect a loss in the initial years after the investment, even though the ultimate rate of return is excellent. But, allegedly a prospective loss might deter some banks from making a loan. (A diligent bank will carefully examine the cause of any expected loss.) This brings us to a consideration of what information should be provided to the board of directors and top management about the impact of new product development or major capital expenditures on the *earnings* of the company. It has nothing to do directly with the rate of return or project justification; these are separate considerations. It does relate to making the decision-makers aware of the profit impact of capital investments and the related costs.

Perhaps these three supplemental forecast earnings statements may be useful to an informed management when considering any *major* expenditure (as well as for the purpose of obtaining necessary financing):

1. A statement of estimated income and expense without the new investment—for a number of years in the future.

2. A statement of estimated income and expense, with the new investment, using GAAP (with emphasis on start-up expenses and depreciation)—if that is a point to emphasize.

3. A statement of estimated income and expense, with the new investment, with a modified or alternative capitalization and depreciation practice.

These are illustrated in Figures 32-9 through 32-11.

Figure 32-9 shows the anticipated decline in the operating profit of the Electronics Division without the investment under consideration (new manufacturing equipment also having additional capacity).

Figure 32-10 reflects the tremendous increase in operating profit, after the first two years, by making the investment in Project X. It also shows the effect of the write-off, in the years of incurrence of the start-up costs, and the depreciation of the capital asset cost of $1,500,000 over a 5-year life (straight line depreciation, with a one-half year of depreciation in 19XX). The use of a generally accepted accounting practice involving immediate write-off of start-up costs in the years of occurrence, and commencement as early as possible of depreciation charges on a straight line 5-year basis (not on a per unit of output), causes an operating loss in 19XX and a severe reduction in operating profit in 19X1.

Figure 32-11 shows the impact of a less conservative accounting practice—the immediate capitalization of the start-up costs, with the subsequent amortization of the charge over a 2-year period of operation, and the deferment of immediate depreciation of the capital assets, also for a 2-year period, and a subsequent write-off over a 5-year period. Such a practice avoids an operating loss in the first year of operations and avoids a large reduction in the operating profit of the second year of operation—

Figure 32-9   Statement of Estimated Income and Expense Without Project X Investment.

The Johnson Company
Electronics Division
STATEMENT OF ESTIMATED INCOME AND EXPENSES
WITHOUT PROJECT X INVESTMENT
19XX THROUGH 19X6
($ IN THOUSANDS)

Item	19XX	19X1	19X2	19X3	19X4	19X5	19X6
				Year			
Net sales	$2,500	$2,400	$2,100	$1,900	$1,700	$1,500	$1,200
Cost of sales	1,500	1,440	1,300	1,200	1,100	1,050	1,000
Gross profit	1,000	960	800	700	600	450	200
Selling expense	200	200	200	200	200	200	200
General and adm. expense	100	100	90	90	90	90	80
Operating profit or (loss)	$ 700	$ 660	$ 510	$ 410	$ 310	$ 160	$ (80)

Figure 32-10   Statement of Estimated Income and Expense with Project X Investment Using Current Accounting Practices (GAAP).

The Johnson Company
Electronics Division
STATEMENT OF ESTIMATED INCOME AND EXPENSE
WITH PROJECT X INVESTMENT
USING CURRENT ACCOUNTING PRACTICES (GAAP)
19XX THROUGH 19X6
($ IN THOUSANDS)

Item	19XX	19X1	19X2	19X3	19X4	19X5	19X6
				Year			
Net sales	$2,500	$2,700	$3,200	$4,000	$5,000	$6,000	$7,000
"Cost of sales"	1,500	1,620	1,920	2,400	2,500	3,000	3,500
"Gross profit"	1,000	1,080	1,280	1,600	2,500	3,000	3,500
Selling expense	200	200	200	200	200	200	250
General and administrative expense	100	100	100	100	100	100	100
Operating profit before start-up expenses and additional depreciation	700	780	980	1,300	2,200	2,700	3,150
Start-up expenses	500	100	—	—	—	—	—
Additional depreciation	150	300	300	300	300	150	—
Operating profit	$ (50)	$ 380	$ 680	$1,000	$1,900	$2,550	$3,150

Figure 32-11 Statement of Estimated Income and Expense with Project X Investment and with Modified Accounting Practices.

The Johnson Company
Electronics Division
STATEMENT OF INCOME AND EXPENSE
WITH PROJECT X INVESTMENT AND WITH
MODIFIED CAPITALIZATION AND DEPRECIATION PRACTICE
19XX THROUGH 19X6
($ IN THOUSANDS)

Item	19XX	19X1	19X2	19X3	19X4	19X5	19X6
				Year			
Net sales	$2,500	$2,700	$3,200	$4,000	$5,000	$6,000	$7,000
"Cost of sales"	1,500	1,620	1,920	2,400	2,500	3,000	3,500
"Gross profit"	1,000	1,080	1,280	1,600	2,500	3,000	3,500
Selling expense	200	200	200	200	200	200	250
General and administrative expense	100	100	100	100	100	100	100
Operating profit before start-up expenses and additional depreciation	700	780	980	1,300	2,200	2,700	3,150
Start-up cost capitalized	500*	100*					
Additional depreciation capitalized	150*	300*					
Amortization of start-up costs (1)			300	300			
Amortization of capitalized depreciation (2)			225	225			
Additional depreciation	—	—	300	300	300	150	—
Operating profit	$ 700	$ 780	$ 155	$ 475	$1,900	$2,550	$3,150

*See related write-offs (1) and (2).

with the heavier additional costs being deferred until there is a significant pick-up in sales and operating profit (before such additional charges).

Providing such data to the board of directors advises them of the impact on expected operating profit of the proposed investment on two different accounting bases. This information would be in addition to that listed earlier. It rounds out the financial picture and perhaps avoids later questions. The annual plan and strategic plan should incorporate the effect of the expenditures on the statement of income and expense, the statement of financial position, and the statement of cash flows. This same data should be made available to the commercial banks, or other financial sources, who are asked to provide the financing. The authors suggest full disclosure of the financial statements of the annual plan and long-range plan to the financing institution, including the schedule for complete payment of the obligation.

When and if the board approves the project, the cognizant officer is notified. This constitutes an approval *in principle*. Specific project approval, as discussed in the next section, is required before the project may proceed.

32-21 PROJECT AUTHORIZATION

Under most circumstances, the analysis and review done in connection with securing project approval by the board of directors should be sufficient to complete a detailed authorization request. However, circumstances do change, and a period of six months might pass between the gathering and analysis of data for the board review. So sometimes this re-review is worthwhile. Also, it causes the project sponsors to commit in writing to the project. An illustrative form is shown in Figure 32-12.

It should be mentioned that authority required to commence a project depends on the amount of the request. While approval of the president for all projects might be needed in a small firm, in larger ones there might be an ascending scale of required approvals, perhaps as follows:

Amount	Required Approval
Less than $10,000	Plant Manager
$10,000–99,999	General Manager
$100,000–499,999	Chief Operating Officer
Over $500,000	Chief Executive Officer

The sample form provides for comments and recommendations by the controller as well as the line approval (depending on the amount).

32-22 ACCOUNTING CONTROL OF THE PROJECT

When the work authorization has been properly approved, then the task of the controller is to keep tabs on both commitments and expenditures as well as expected costs to complete the project, and periodically report the data to the cognizant executive. Typically these figures are reported by project or work order:

- Amount authorized.
- Actual commitments to date.
- Actual costs incurred to date.
- Estimated cost to complete.
- Indicated total cost.
- Indicated overrun or underrun compared to the project budget.

An illustrated report, prepared monthly and in which control is by appropriation number, is shown in Figure 32-13.

For large and complicated projects a computer application may be appropriate.

32-23 POST-PROJECT APPRAISALS OR AUDITS

In many companies adequate analyses are made as to the apparent economic desirability of a project, and acquisition costs are held within estimate. Yet the project may not achieve the estimated rate of return. A sad truth is that some managements are unaware of such a condition because there is no follow-up on performance.

Figure 32-12   Request for Equipment and Facility Authorization.

REQUEST FOR EQUIPMENT AND FACILITY AUTHORIZATION

A.F.E. No. _____

Date: _____

Division	Plant

This request for authorization of a capital commitment and expenditure is made necessary by:

☐ Normal replacement   ☐ New product

☐ Change in manufacturing process   ☒ Increased volume

☒ Cost reduction   ☐ Styling changes

☐ Environmental regulations

Title: Pneumatic bagging equipment

Description and Justification: The present conveyor and manual handling system is too slow. It is anticipated that the state-of-the-art equipment will permit a volume of 1,500,000 2-lb. bags per year, with a reduction of 5 operators.

Use added pages if necessary.

- -

Estimated Cost:

		Return on Investment	
Machinery and equipment	$105,700	(DCF method)	43%
Installation	25,000		
Total	130,700	Payback period	2.1 yrs.
Contingency 5%	6,535	Estimated useful life	8 yrs.
Total	$137,235	Salvage value	$2,000

- -

Controller Comments and Recommendations:

Cash flow appears conservative

	Accounting Dept.	
	Acct. No.	Amount
Return is above hurdle rate of 20%	Capital M&E 21–310	$131,235
for this type of investment		
	Expense—sales tax 21-407	6,000
Approval recommended	Total	$137,235

_____

Controller

- -

Approval and Authorization:

Date _____

Requested by _____

	Approved	Rejected
Approved by _____		
Department head _____	_____	_____
Plant manager _____	_____	_____
Division manager _____	_____	_____
Executive Committee _____	_____	_____

Reason for Rejection:

885

Figure 32-13 Capital Appropriations and Expenditures.

Magraudy Manufacturing Co.
CAPITAL APPROPRIATION AND EXPENDITURE STATUS REPORT
FOR THE PERIOD ENDED APRIL 30, 19XX
(dollars in thousands)

Appro-priation No.	Description	Work Order No.	Amount Appro-priated	Actual Completion Date	Original Estimate	Outstanding Commitments	Actual Expenditures to Date	Estimated Cost to Complete	Indicated Total Cost	Amount (Over)/Under Appro-priation	Amount (Over)/Under Original Estimate
42	*Northridge Plant*		$2,500								
	Site clearance	460		2/20/19XX	$ 125	$ —	$ 107	$ —	$ 107		$ 18
	Buildings	461		9/01/19XX*	1,475	740	394	316	1,450		25
	Machinery and equipment	462		10/31/19XX*	850	500	—	360	860		(10)
	Total appropriation 42				2,450	1,240	501	676	2,417	$ 83	33
46	*Delivery Fleet*		950								
	4 ton	495		6/30/19XX*	360	300	40	10	350		10
	1 ton	496		6/30/19XX*	180	75	30	60	165		15
	½ ton pick-up	497		6/30/19XX*	400	140	260	—	400		—
	Total appropriation 46				940	515	330	70	915	35	25
50	*Miscellaneous*		1,750								
	Robot assemblers	525		5/19/19XX*	350	100	214	20	334		16
	Security system—plant 5	529		3/31/19XX	100	—	97	—	97		3
	Profiler—plant 6	533		6/30/19XX*	90	10	80	10	100		(10)
	Fleet communications	534		7/01/19XX*	75	30	50	5	85		(10)
	Lab pilot plant	542		11/30/19XX*	290	40	160	55	255		35
	Pallets	549		4/30/19XX	50	—	52	5	52		(2)
	Forklift trucks	550		9/30/19XX*	150	75	70	5	150		—
	New gates—employee parking	562		8/31/19XX*	75	—	5	67	72		3
	All others—complete				500	—	515	—	515		(15)
	Total appropriation 50				1,680	255	1,243	162	1,660	90	20
	Grand total		$5,200		$5,070	$2,010	$2,074	$908	$4,992	$208	$78

* Estimated

For large projects, especially, after a limited or reasonable period beyond completion—perhaps two years on a very large capital investment—when all the "bugs" are worked out, it is suggested that a post-audit be made. The review might be undertaken by the internal audit group, or perhaps a management team consisting of line managers involved with the project (but not among the original justification group) and some members of the controller's staff. The objective, of course, is to compare actual earnings or savings with the plan, ascertain why the deviation occurred, and what steps should be taken to improve capital investment planning and control. The scope might range from the strategic planning aspects (should the company be in the business?) through to the detailed control procedures.

The following advantages may accrue from an intelligently planned post-audit:

1. It may detect weaknesses in strategic planning that lead to poor decisions, which in turn impact the capital budget procedures.
2. Environmental factors that influence the business but were not recognized might be detected.
3. Experience can focus attention on basic weaknesses in overall plans, policies, or procedures as related to capital expenditures.
4. Strengths or weaknesses in individual performance can be detected and corrected—such as a tendency to have overly optimistic estimates.
5. It may enable corrections in other current projects prior to completion of commitments or expenditures.
6. It affords a training opportunity for the operating and planning staff through the review of the entire capital budgeting procedure.
7. Prior knowledge of the follow-up encourages reasonable caution in making projections or preparing the justification.
8. It may detect evidence of manufactured input data.

The scope and postcompletion period of the review will depend on circumstances. Some companies limit the audit only to major projects over $1,000,000 and only until the payback period is completed.

A simple form of graphic report quickly summarizing actual and expected performance is illustrated in Figure 32-14. The post-audit report commentary, of course, can touch on (a) estimated cash flow to date of the audit as compared with actual cash flow, (b) old vs. new break-even points, and (c) operating expenses, planned vs. actual, as well as other pertinent observations.

32-24 OTHER ASPECTS OF CAPITAL EXPENDITURES

(a) WORKING CAPITAL

This chapter, up to this point, has dealt with capital expenditures per se in the strictest sense. In many cases this is proper in that, when a capital expenditure other than cash outflow is made, there is no impact on working capital. Yet, many instances, such as growth or expansion in the business, will require additional investment in inventory and receivables as well as the plant and equipment needs. Suffice it to say that if additional working capital is necessary, then it should be reflected in the investment

Figure 32-14   Capital Expenditure Performance Report.

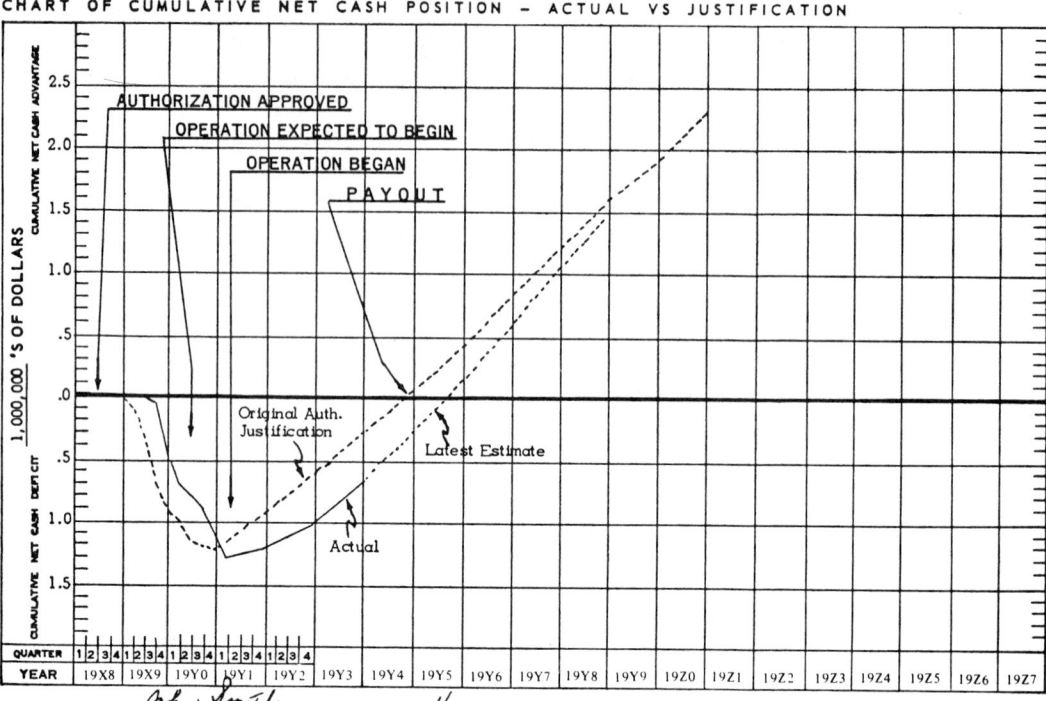

requirement and in the rate of return calculation. It is partially offset by the salvage value recovery when the business ceases.

(b) LEASE VS. BUY DECISIONS

Technically speaking, the acquisition of a long-term asset, whether purchased or leased, should be included in the capital budget. However, the rental of the asset or leasing it on a short-term basis would not warrant this treatment.

The discounted cash flow technique may be useful in reaching a decision whether to lease or buy, and several good reference sources are available on the subject. The best method to be used is either IRR or NPV, and treatment of some of the variables is controversial. The authors suggest the NPV method is perhaps easy to apply. If the marginal financing (net of taxes) cost of funds to purchase the asset is known, the same discount rate can be applied to the stream of lease payments to arrive at the net present value. Usually the alternative with the lower NPV, and the higher savings, should be the one selected. The comparative net present values of lease vs. purchase (with no investment tax credit) are shown in Figure 32-15. This application assumes a 15% interest borrowing rate, less a 40% tax rate, or a net cost of 9%. The net savings through purchase may be calculated as follows:

Present value of purchase	$1,000,000
Less: Present value of related tax savings	311,120
Net purchase cost	$ 688,880
Savings (NPV) by purchase over lease:	
Present value of lease cost	$ 733,632
Net purchase cost (above)	688,880
Net savings	$ 44,752

Figure 32-15 NPV Calculation—Lease vs. Buy.

NPV CALCULATION
LEASE VS. BUY
A. Purchase Basis

Year	Accelerated Cost Recovery	Income Tax Savings (40% Rate)	Discount Factor (9%)	Present Value
1	$ 200,000	$ 80,000	.917	$ 73,360
2	200,000	80,000	.842	67,360
3	200,000	80,000	.772	61,760
4	200,000	80,000	.708	56,640
5	200,000	80,000	.650	52,000
6	—	—		—
7	—	—		—
8	—	—		—
9	—	—		—
Total	$1,000,000	$400,000		$311,120

NPV CALCULATION
LEASE VS. BUY
B. Long-Term Lease Basis

Year	Pretax Lease Rental	Tax Savings at 40% Rate	After-Tax Lease Cost	Discount Factor (9%)	Net Present Value
1	$ 280,000	$112,000	$ 168,000	.917	$154,056
2	280,000	112,000	168,000	.842	141,456
3	270,000	108,000	162,000	.772	125,064
4	270,000	108,000	162,000	.708	114,696
5	120,000	48,000	72,000	.650	46,800
6	120,000	48,000	72,000	.596	42,912
7	120,000	48,000	72,000	.547	39,384
8	120,000	48,000	72,000	.502	36,144
9	120,000	48,000	72,000	.460	33,120
Total	$1,700,000	$680,000	$1,020,000		$733,632

(c) MUTUALLY EXCLUSIVE CAPITAL PROPOSALS

In the capital budgeting process there may be instances when the estimated rate of return on any two projects is the same, but funds are available for only one. The two projects, by definition, are mutually exclusive. How should a decision be made as to which proposal to accept? One complicating factor is that the IRR method may rank projects somewhat differently than the NPV approach. Such a condition can arise because the IRR method assumes that funds generated are reinvested at the discounted rate calculated for the initial investment. The NPV method assumes funds are reinvested at the rate used for discounting, which is often the cost of capital. Other reasons for differing evaluations relate to different project lines and different initial investments. When the projects are mutually exclusive, one way of making a decision is to (a) calculate the differences in cash flow, and (b) apply the opportunity cost rate, or cost of capital rate, to these cash flow differences.

Assuming the incremental or opportunity cost rate is higher than the capital budget cut-off rate, then the proposal with the higher value should be selected. As reflected in Figure 32-16, project B should be accepted.

(d) PLANT AND EQUIPMENT RECORDS

Adequate plant and equipment records are a necessary adjunct to effective control. They provide a convenient source of information for planning and control purposes as well as for insurance and tax purposes. Some of the advantages may be enumerated as follows:

1. Provide necessary detailed information about the original cost (and depreciation reserves) of fixed assets by type of equipment or location.

Figure 32-16   Incremental Investment—Mutually Exclusive Projects.

MUTUALLY EXCLUSIVE PROJECTS
COMPARATIVE CASH FLOWS
(dollars in thousands)

	Cash Flows			Present Value at 20% (a)	
Year	A	B	B – A Difference	Factor	Amount
0	$(50,000)	$(90,000)	$(40,000)	1.00	$(40,000)
1	12,000	30,000	18,000	.833	14,994
2	14,000	35,000	21,000	.694	14,574
3	15,000	35,000	20,000	.579	11,580
4	15,000	35,000	20,000	.482	9,640
5	15,000	34,000	19,000	.402	7,638
6	15,000	30,000	15,000	.335	5,025
7	10,000	21,000	11,000	.279	3,069
Total	$ 46,000	$ 130,000	$ 84,000		$ 26,520

(a) Incremental rate of 20% exceeds cut-off rate of 17%.

2. Make available comparative data for purchase of new equipment or replacements.

3. Provide basic information to determine proper depreciation charges by department or cost center and serve as a basis for the distribution of other fixed charges such as property taxes and insurance.

4. Establish the basis for property accountability.

5. Provide detailed information on assets and depreciation for income tax purposes.

6. Are a source of basic information in checking claims and supporting the company position relative to personal and real property tax returns.

7. Serve as evidence and a source of information for insurance coverage and claims.

8. Provide the basis for determining gain or loss on the disposition of fixed assets.

9. Provide basic data for control reports by individual units of equipment.

Property records include the plant ledgers and detailed equipment cards. The ledgers will follow the basic property classifications of the company. Detailed records must be designed to suit the individual needs of the company. Information in a data bank, preferably stored in a computer, should include the following:

Name of asset.
Type of equipment.
Control number.
Description.
Size.
Model.
Style.
Serial number.
Motor number.
Purchased new or used.
Date purchased.
Vendor.
Invoice number.
Purchase order number.
Location.
    Plant.
    Building.
    Floor.
    Department.
Account number.
Transfer information.
Original cost information.
    Purchase cost.
    Freight.

Tax.

Installation cost.

Material.

Labor.

Overhead.

Additions to.

Date retired.

Sold to.

Scrapped.

Cost recovered.

Depreciation data.

Estimated life.

Annual depreciation.

Basis.

Additional information may be required in particular companies. However, a database should be complete so that appropriate reports can be prepared.

There are numerous software packages available that permit the generation of most conceivable needs as regards reports or fixed assets. One such system is that of Global Software, Inc. of Raleigh, North Carolina. Its "Fixed Assets System" can provide data relating to:

- Project control for significant investments not yet in service.
- Book and tax depreciation data, including general depreciation methods and accelerated cost recovery system (ACRS) data.
- Lease accounting information.
- FASB 33 compliance data.
- Physical and accounting location data.
- Maintenance data.

(e) INTERNAL CONTROL AND ACCOUNTING REQUIREMENTS

Once the property has been acquired, the matter of proper accounting and control arises. Usually, such duties become the responsibility of the controller. The problem is essentially very simple, but a few suggestions may prove helpful:

1. All fixed assets should be identified, preferably at the time of receipt; a serial number may be assigned and should be affixed to the item. Use of metal tags or electrical engraving is a common method of marking the equipment.

2. Machinery and equipment assigned to a particular department should not be transferred without the written approval of the department head responsible for the physical control of the property. This procedure is essential to know the location for insurance purposes and to correctly charge depreciation, etc.

3. No item of equipment should be permitted to leave the plant without a property pass signed by the proper authority.

4. Periodically, a physical inventory should be taken of all fixed assets.

5. Detailed records should be maintained on each piece of equipment or similar groups.

6. Purchase requisitions and requests for appropriations should be reviewed to assure that piecemeal acquisitions are not made to avoid the approval of higher authority. Thus if all expenditures over $100 require the signature of the general manager, individual requisitions may be submitted for each table or each chair to avoid securing such approval.

7. Retirement of fixed assets by sale or scrapping should require certain approvals to guard against the disposal of equipment that could be used in other departments.

8. If possible, bids should be secured on any sizable acquisitions.

9. Provision should be made for proper insurance coverage during construction as well as on completion.

10. Expenses should be carefully checked to decrease the possibility that portions of capital expenditures are treated as expenses to avoid budget overruns.

(f) IDLE EQUIPMENT

Another phase of control over fixed assets relates to unused facilities, whether only of short duration or for more extended periods. In every business, it can reasonably be expected that some loss will be sustained because of idle facilities and/or idle workers. The objective is to inform management of these losses and place responsibility in an attempt to eliminate the avoidable and unnecessary costs. But aside from stimulating action to eliminate the causes of short-term idleness, such information may be a guide in determining whether additional facilities are necessary. Also, such knowledge may encourage disposal of any permanently excess equipment, giving consideration to the medium-term plans.

Losses resulting from unused plant facilities are not limited to the fixed charges of depreciation, property taxes, and insurance. Very often idle equipment also results in lost labor, power, and light, as well as other continuing overhead expenses, to say nothing of start-up time and lost income from lost sales.

Causes of idle time may be threefold:

1. *Those Controllable by the Production Staff.* These may result from the following:

    a. Poor planning by the foreman or other production department staff member.

    b. Lack of material.

    c. Lack of tools or other equipment.

    d. Lack of power.

    e. Machine breakdown.

    f. Improper supervision or instructions, etc.

2. *Those Resulting from Administrative Decisions.* For example, a decision to build an addition may force the temporary shutdown of other facilities. Again,

management may decide to add equipment for later use. Here certain idle plant costs may be incurred until the expected demand develops.

3. *Those Arising from Economic Causes.* Included are the causes beyond the control of management, such as cyclical or seasonal demand. In somewhat the same class is idle time resulting from excess capacity in the industry. The effect of such conditions may be partially offset by efficient sales planning and aggressive sales effort.

The cause of idle time is important in determining the proper accounting treatment. Where idle facilities result from economic causes or are otherwise highly abnormal—such as a prolonged strike—it may be desirable for the controller to have such costs segregated and handled as a separate charge in the statement of income and expense. Such expenses should not be included in inventory or cost of sales.

Some companies isolate in the manufacturing expenses the cost of idle time that is controllable by the production staff. In other cases, a simple reporting of the hours is all that is necessary. Where it is desirable to charge the costs of idle time to a separate account the segregation is simple through a comparison of normal and actual hours and the use of standard rates.

(g) VALUATION OF FIXED ASSETS

For most businesses, there is no significant problem pertaining to the basis for recording and valuing fixed assets. Normally, such accounting is at cost, less applicable allowance for depreciation, depletion, or amortization. There may be instances where the basis will be higher or lower than actual cost. The true value of capital assets is measured by the earning power.

The controller should be aware of any promulgations by the rule setters (see Chapter 4) regarding calculation and disclosure of replacement costs (SFASs or ASRs).

(h) DEPRECIATION ACCOUNTING

Depreciation has been defined in many ways, such as a dictionary definition, "decline in value of an asset due to such causes as wear and tear, action of the elements, obsolescence and inadequacy." The accounting profession has considered several definition, and after long consideration the AICPA Committee on Terminology formulated the following definition:

> *Depreciation accounting* is a system of accounting which aims to distribute the cost or other basic value of tangible capital assets, less salvage (if any), over the estimated useful life of the unit (which may be a group of assets) in a systematic and rational manner. It is a process of allocation, not of valuation. *Depreciation for the year* is the portion of the total charge under such a system that is allocated to the year. Although the allocation may properly take into account occurrences during the year, it is not intended to be a measurement of the effect of all such occurrences.[1]

---

[1] Paul Grady, Inventory of Generally Accepted Accounting Principles for Business Enterprises.

In arriving at the applicable charges for depreciation, there are at least three related objectives of proper accounting: (1) to state earnings correctly; (2) to protect the investment of owners and creditors by maintaining the integrity of the fixed capital accounts (a write-off of plant and equipment over the useful life, by charges against income, tends to avoid the payment of dividends out of capital); and (3) to secure useful costs through proper depreciation allocations to cost centers. Another objective might be to maximize tax deductions (depreciation) under the applicable IRS code.

The accomplishment of these objectives must lie largely in the controller's hands. The determination of the useful life of the plant and equipment is largely an engineering problem. However, the ramifications and implications of depreciation policy—such matters as treatment of obsolescence, accounting for retirements, determination of allocation methods, and selection of individual or group rates—are best understood by the accountant. For these reasons, the controller should be the primary force in recommending to management, as may be necessary, the policies to be followed.

(i) OBSOLESCENCE

Obsolescence, sometimes called "functional depreciation" as distinguished from physical depreciation, can be a highly significant factor in determining useful economic life. More often than not, the usefulness of facilities is likely to be limited by obsolescence, so that it may outweigh the depreciation factor. Such a condition can occur as a result of two causes. The product manufactured may be replaced by another, so that the need no longer exists for the facility. Or a new type of asset—one that produces at a much lower cost—may be developed to supersede present manufacturing equipment. Sometimes the need for expanded capacity has the effect of rendering obsolete or inadequate the existing asset.

Obsolescence may be of two kinds—normal or special. The former is the normal loss in value and can be anticipated in the same degree as other depreciation factors. It should be included in the estimate of useful life. Extraordinary or special obsolescence, on the other hand, can rarely be foreseen. The controller's responsibility generally should extend to a review of past experience and trends to determine whether obsolescence is an important consideration in his industry. If so, then it should be duly recognized in the useful life estimates.

In accounting for obsolescence, the question must be settled about whether a distinction should be made in the accounts between charges for obsolescence and depreciation. In practice, the normal obsolescence will be combined with depreciation in both the provision and the reserve. A highly abnormal and significant obsolescence loss probably should be segregated in the income and expense statement. Aside from this, circumstances may indicate the desirability of segregating a reserve for obsolescence. It may not be possible to identify obsolescence with a particular asset, although experience will indicate the approximate amount. This can be handled as a general provision without regard to the individual piece of equipment.

(j) FULLY DEPRECIATED ASSETS

In properly stating on the balance sheet the value of fixed assets and in making the proper charge to manufacturing costs for the use of the plant and equipment, the question is raised about the correct accounting treatment of fully depreciated assets. If the facilities are no longer of use, they should be retired and the amount removed from both the asset and the reserve. If the item is fully depreciated but still in use, then the depreciation charge to the earnings statement must be discontinued—unless a composite useful life estimate or a composite depreciation rate is being used. The controller should consider these conditions, as well as increased maintenance costs, in evaluating operating performance and in preparing useful reports for management.

(k) APPRAISALS AND APPRAISAL RECORDS

Management may request appraisals of property for any one of several reasons: for the purchase or sale of property, for reorganization or liquidations, for financing when the property is collateral, for insurance purposes, for taxation purposes, and for control purposes when the records do not indicate investment by process or cost center.

The basis of valuing fixed assets has already been reviewed, and the desirability of stating such property at original cost has been emphasized. However, occasions arise when management directs the valuation of property on another basis—perhaps to remove extremely high depreciation charges. When appraisals are recorded, the original cost and depreciation on original cost should continue to be reflected in the detail records, along with the appraised value and depreciation thereon.

(l) LOSS OR GAIN ON THE SALE OF FIXED ASSETS

The matter of accounting for the loss or gain on the sale or other disposition of fixed assets is primarily one of accounting theory. Some have supported the proposition that losses resulting from premature retirement or technological advances are properly capitalized and charged against future operations. Most authorities do not concur in this view. The sound value—or asset value, less accumulated depreciation—for all assets retired is a loss that should be charged off as incurred. It is in the nature of a correction of prior profits. Usual practice is to carry such gain or loss, if important, in the nonoperating section of the statement of income and expense.

(m) FUNDS FOR PLANT REPLACEMENT AND EXPANSION

Unfortunately, a great deal of confusion has arisen among laymen about the distinction between a reserve and a fund. Some think that the creation of a depreciation reserve also establishes a fund to replace the property. Accountants know that a reserve may exist independent of a fund and that a fund can exist without a reserve. The depreciation reserve does not represent a fund of cash or other assets that have been set aside. It only expresses the usage of the asset. If the operation has been profitable, and if dividends have not been paid in excess of the net income after recognizing depreciation, then values of some sort are available to offset the charge for use of the plant and equipment.

Most companies do not establish funds for property expansion or replacement but use the general funds instead. However, such funds can be created, and some exponents believe that public utilities and wasting asset industries, such as mining, should establish such funds. Such funds are not necessarily to be measured by the depreciation reserve, because replacement costs may be quite different. The depreciation reserve is a measure of expired *past* value, not *future* requirements for replacement.

(n) PLANT AND EQUIPMENT IN RELATION TO TAXES

Many local communities and states levy real and personal property taxes or enforce payment of franchise taxes based on property values. Maintenance of adequate records can be a means of satisfying the taxing authorities on problems of valuation.

Plant and property values, through the resulting depreciation charges, are important from the federal income tax viewpoint. As mentioned previously, the depreciation allowance for tax purposes, if significantly different from depreciation for book purposes, can distort the profit before taxes and the tax charge. Where the estimate of useful life and the base for tax and book purposes are not greatly different, an effort should be made to bring the two in line. It may save the maintenance of a separate set of records. In any event, the burden of proof about the correctness of the depreciation claimed is placed on the taxpayer, who must keep the necessary records and other data to support his claim.

(o) PLANT AND EQUIPMENT—SEC REQUIREMENTS

The increasing number of federal regulatory bodies gives added emphasis to the need for adequate records and reports. Many controllers are required to prepare data for filing under Regulation S-X of the SEC. The requirements of the SEC with respect to schedules on property, plant, and equipment and the related reserves should be reviewed in considering the type of records to be maintained.

32-25 SELECTED REFERENCES

Arnold, Jasper H. III, "Assessing Capital Risk: You Can't Be too Conservative," *Harvard Business Review,* Sept.–Oct. 1986, pp. 113–121.

Bennett, Robert E., and James A. Hendricks, "Justifying the Acquisition of Automated Equipment," *Management Accounting,* July 1987, pp. 39–46.

Brimson, James A., *Activity Accounting: An Activity-Based Costing Approach,* New York: John Wiley, 1991.

"Capital Investment Decisions," reprints from *Harvard Business Review.*

Copeland, Tom, Tim Koller, and Jack Murrin, *Valuation: Measuring and Managing the Value of Companies,* New York: John Wiley, 1990, Chapter 10.

Dmuchowski, Norman F., and William J. Regan, "Development for Capital Budgeting Framework Using Risk Adjusted Discount Rates at a Diversified Company," *Managerial Planning,* Nov.–Dec. 1981, pp. 14–20.

Glahn, Gerald L., Kent T. Fields, and Jerry E. Trapnell, "Capital Budgeting for Mixed Risk Projects," *Managerial Planning,* July–Aug. 1984, pp. 21–27, 31.

Gulliver, Frank R. "Post-Project Appraisals Pay," *Harvard Business Review,* March–April 1987, pp. 128–132.

Hergert, Michael, "Strategic Resource Allocation Using Divisional Hurdle Rates," *Planning Review,* Jan.–Feb. 1987, pp. 28–32.

Howell, Robert A., and Stephen R. Soucy, "Capital Investment Analysis in the New Manufacturing Environment," *Managerial Accounting,* Nov. 1987, pp. 26–32.

Hubbard, Charles L., and A. Davant Bullard, "The Anatomy of a Hurdle Rate for Capital Budget Decisions," *Managerial Planning,* Sept.–Oct. 1982, pp. 39–44.

Kester, W. Carl, and Robert A. Taggert, Jr., "Capital Allocation—Hurdle Rates, Budgets, or Both?" *Sloan Management Review,* Spring 1989, pp. 83–90.

King, Alfred M., "Asset Impairment Is Current Value Accounting Sneaking in the Back Door?" *Management Accounting,* March 1994, pp. 36–39.

King, Alfred M., "Let's Make America Competitive," *Management Accounting,* May 1992, pp. 24–27.

McKee, Tim C., and Raymond G. Laverdiere, "Maximizing Depreciation Benefits," *Management Accounting,* June 1987, pp. 35–38.

Meredith, J. R., and M. M. Hill, "Justifying New Manufacturing Systems: A Managerial Approach," *Sloan Management Review,* Summer 1987, pp. 49–61.

Parker, Thornton, and Theodore Lettes, "Is Accounting Standing in the Way of Flexible Computer-Integrated Manufacturing?" *Management Accounting,* Jan. 1991, pp. 34–38.

CHAPTER 33

Management of Liabilities

33-1 INTRODUCTION

It often has been said that the management, or planning and control, of the assets (excepting cash and temporary investments) of an enterprise rests largely in the hands of the operating executives but that management, or planning and control, of the liabilities and equity of the company is primarily the responsibility of the financial executives. In a certain sense this is true—up to a point—and the financial officers must exercise control over the liabilities of the entity to preserve its economic health.

The comments in this chapter relate to the practical or pragmatic considerations regarding liability planning and control, of which the controller must be intimately familiar. Remarks will relate to the traditional types of liabilities as well as new developments and concerns in this field of management.

33-2 LIABILITIES DEFINED

Although it is not the purpose of the chapter to deal at length with the accounting niceties regarding the recording of the liabilities of a company, the subject is defined for our purposes as follows:

> Liabilities are the economic obligations of an enterprise that are recognized and measured in conformity with generally accepted accounting principles. Liabilities also include certain deferred credits that are not obligations (such as, for example, deferred credits from income tax allocations) but that are recognized and measured in conformity with generally accepted accounting principles.

Liabilities are measured at amounts established in the exchanges involved, usually the amounts to be paid but sometimes at discounted rates.

33-3 OBJECTIVES OF LIABILITY MANAGEMENT

In the basic sense, the purpose of liability management is to assure that the enterprise has "cash adequacy"—the ability to meet cash requirements for any purpose significant to the short- or long-term financial health of the company. Thus it is not merely to avoid insolvency or bankruptcy. From the standpoint of the controller, the more specific objectives of liability management might include these:

1. The recording and disclosure in accordance with generally accepted accounting principles of the financial obligations of the company.
2. The reporting in proper form, as required by indentures or credit agreements, of the corporate liabilities.
3. Through effective planning and control, the maintenance of a sound financial structure, including the proper relationship of debt to equity capital.
4. Continuance of the ability to secure necessary borrowed funds in a timely manner and at a cost that is competitive.
5. To institute and maintain controls that restrict commitments within well-defined limits so that they do not result ultimately in excessive and burdensome liabilities.
6. To enable the company to be so well regarded in the financial marketplace that its common (and preferred) stock will command respect far into the future with an acceptable price-earnings ratio, and that the stock will reflect a gradual increase in earnings per share and consequent long-term appreciation for the benefit of the owners.
7. To permit the company to maintain a prudent dividend policy.

All of these objectives of liability management are interrelated.

33-4 DIRECT LIABILITIES

In an attempt to categorize the types of liabilities and to indicate some of the matters to be considered by the controller, a brief commentary follows.

(a) CURRENT LIABILITIES

Generally, liabilities classified as current are those due to be paid within the operating cycle—that ordinarily is within a period of one year. The importance of the proper segregation of current liabilities from other liabilities rests in the role played by various financial ratios, such as the current ratio, when funds are borrowed.

By another related definition, current liabilities include those obligations whose liquidation reasonably is expected to require the use of existing current assets or the creation of new current liabilities. Included in current liabilities are these classifications:

1. *Notes Payable.* Represent the obligations of the company under legal instruments in which there exists an explicit promise to pay a specified amount at a specified time.

2. *Accounts Payable.* Accounts payable usually are largely trade accounts payable and represent the obligations of the firm to its suppliers. Since these liabilities are recorded at the time the title passes to the goods or the services are received, the financial officers should be satisfied that clean cutoffs on the obligations exist. This is especially true in those instances where the working capital or current ratio requirement is critical in a credit agreement or the company is nearing the limits specified.

    Additionally, credit balances in various asset accounts, such as accounts receivable, usually are reclassified to the accounts payable category—especially at year-end—or when financial statements are published.

2. *Accrued Expenses.* When an obligation exists by reason of the benefits having been received but is not yet due and payable, it normally would be recorded as an accrued expense. Included would be such items as accruals for wages, salaries, commissions, rents, royalties, pension costs, and income and other taxes.

4. *Accrued Income Taxes.* Special mention is made of this liability, since often it is composed of two segments. The normal tax due within a year would be recorded under current liabilities as "currently payable." However, using the principle of matching costs with related revenues, yet recognizing that the tax laws permit the reporting of income in a different fiscal period than generally accepted accounting principles would either permit or require, there may be includable under current liabilities a "deferred" income tax obligation.

    There are rather continuously numerous official releases by the FASB, which provide new standards concerning income tax accounting. For example, in May 1992, the body issued Statement of Financial Accounting Standards No. 109—Accounting for Income Taxes. It supersedes FASB Statement No. 96, Accounting for Income Taxes and amends or supersedes a number of other accounting pronouncements. Statement No. 109 establishes financial accounting and reporting standards for the effects of income taxes that result from an enterprise's activities during the current and preceding years. It requires an asset and liability approach for financial accounting and reporting for income taxes. As the Standard says, "The objectives of accounting for income taxes are to recognize (a) the amount of taxes payable or refundable for the current year, and (b) deferred tax liabilities and assets for future tax consequences of events that have been recognized in an enterprise's financial statements or tax returns."

It is assumed the controller will keep abreast of tax reporting requirements and will see that the tax liability is properly recognized. (See also Chapter 18.)

This distinction becomes important in calculating cash flows and when considering acceptable terms in indentures or credit agreements.

(b) LONG-TERM LIABILITIES

Long-term liabilities, by definition, represent those obligations due in more than one year or those to be paid out of noncurrent assets. Only a few limited comments need be made.

1. *Long-Term Leases.* Under present-day accounting, if at its inception a lease meets one or more of the following criteria, it shall be classified as a capital lease by the lessee and placed on the balance sheet. Otherwise, it would be treated as an operating lease, with appropriate disclosure. The criteria for capitalization include these:

   a. The lease transfers ownership of the property to the lessee by the end of the lease term.

   b. The lease contains a bargain purchase option.

   c. The lease term is equal to 75% or more of the estimated economic life of the leased property (with certain exceptions).

   d. The present value at the beginning of the lease term of the minimum lease payments—excluding certain costs—equals or exceeds 90% of the fair market value of the property over the related investment tax credit retained or expected to be used by the lessor.

   For the specific criteria and the exceptions, reference should be made to the literature of the AICPA.

2. *Bonds.* Bonds are essentially long-term corporate notes issued under a formal legal procedure and secured either by the pledge of specific properties, or revenues, or the general credit of the issuer. Bonds differ from individual notes in that each represents a fractional interest of participation in a group contract, usually with a trustee acting as intermediary. The terms of the contract are set forth in the trust indenture.

3. *Other Long-Term Obligations, etc.* Depending on circumstances, there may exist other obligations and like items that are classified either as long-term obligations or items carried in the long-term section of the balance sheet above the shareholders' equity. These may include such items as the following:

   Deferred income taxes.

   Deferred compensation.

Accrued product warranty.

Employees pension, indemnity, retirement, and related provision.

Negative goodwill.

Minority interests.

The reader is referred to the various publications of the AICPA about the generally accepted principles that govern the recording of the item.

33-5 ILLUSTRATIVE PROVISIONS OF CREDIT AGREEMENTS

To be sure, within limits, indentures or credit agreements will be tailored to fit the desires of both the lender and the borrower. However, a great number of standard provisions apply to many loan agreements. Before further discussing the recording of the liabilities and, indeed, before considering the planning of indebtedness, it may be helpful to be aware of some of these usual provisions that relate to indebtedness limits and certain uses of cash. Excerpts from the note agreement for a 10-year private placement loan from an insurance company to a manufacturing concern include these clauses:

6A.   Current Ratio Requirement.   The Company covenants that it will not permit Consolidated Current Assets at any time to be less than an amount equal to 150% of Consolidated Current Liabilities.

6B.   Dividend Limitation.   The Company covenants that it will not pay or declare any dividend on any class of its stock or make any other distribution on account of any class of its stock, or redeem, purchase or otherwise acquire, directly or indirectly, any shares of its stock (all of the foregoing being herein called "Restricted Payments") except out of Consolidated Net Earnings Available For Restricted Payments; provided, however, that notwithstanding the foregoing limitations, the Company may make sinking fund and dividend payments on its outstanding preferred stock not in excess of $3,300,000 in the aggregate in any year, but provided further, that the amount of any such sinking fund payments and the amount of any such dividends paid or declared shall be included in any subsequent computation pursuant to this paragraph 6B. "Consolidated Net Earnings" shall mean consolidated gross revenues of the Company and its Subsidiaries less all operating and non-operating expenses of the Company and its Subsidiaries including all charges of a proper character (including current and deferred taxes on income, provision for taxes on unremitted foreign earnings which are included in gross revenues and current additions to reserves), but not including in gross revenues any gains (net of expenses and taxes applicable thereto) in excess of losses resulting from the sale, conversion or other disposition of capital assets (i.e., assets other than current assets), any gains resulting from the write-up of assets, any equity of the Company or any Subsidiary in the undistributed earnings of any corporation which is not a Subsidiary, any earnings of any corporation acquired by the Company or any Subsidiary through purchase, merger or consolidation or otherwise for any year prior to the year of acquisition, or any deferred credits representing the excess of the equity in any Subsidiary at the date of acquisition over the cost of the investment in such Subsidiary; all determined in accordance with generally accepted accounting principles including the making of appropriate deductions for minority interests in Subsidiaries. "Consolidated Net Earnings Available For Restricted Payments" shall mean an amount equal to (1) the sum of $10,000,000 plus 90% (or minus 100% in case of a deficit) of Consolidated Net Earnings for the period (taken as one accounting period) commencing on August 1, 19XX, and terminating at the end of the last fiscal quarter preceding the date of any proposed Restricted Payment, less (2) the sum of (*a*) the aggregate amount of all dividends and other distributions paid or declared by the Company on any class of its stock after July 31, 19XX, and (*b*) the excess of the aggregate amount expended, directly or indirectly, after July 31, 19XX, for the redemption, purchase or other acquisition of any shares of its stock, over the aggregate amount received after July 31, 19XX as the net cash proceeds of the sale of any shares of its stock. In the event that any shares of stock of the Company are issued upon conversion of convertible notes, bonds or debentures of the Company, the proceeds of the shares of stock so issued shall be deemed to be an amount equal to the principal amount of the obligations so converted. There shall not be included in Restricted Payments or in any computation of Consolidated Net Earnings Available For Restricted Payments: (x) dividends paid, or distributions made, in stock of the Company; or (y) exchanges of stock of one or more classes of the Company, except to the extent that cash or other value is involved in such exchange. The term "stock" as used in this paragraph 6B shall include warrants or options to purchase stock.

The company will not:

6C(2)   Debt—Create, incur, assume, guarantee or in any way become liable for any Funded Debt in addition to the Funded Debt referred to in paragraph 8D, or create, incur, assume or suffer to exist any Current Debt, except

(i)   Funded Debt of the Company or any Subsidiary provided that, after giving effect thereto and to the concurrent repayment of any other Funded Debt, Consolidated Net Tangible Assets shall be not less than an amount equal to (*a*) 250% of Consolidated Senior Funded Debt, and (*b*) 150% of Consolidated Funded Debt, and further provided that no Subsidiary shall create, incur, assume, guarantee or in any way become liable for any Funded Debt permitted by this clause (i) unless such Funded Debt shall be secured by a Lien on its property permitted by clauses (v), (vii) or (viii) of paragraph 6C(1), shall be of the type referred to in clause (iii) of paragraph 10G or shall constitute Funded Debt payable to the Company or another Subsidiary, and

(ii)   Current Debt of the Company or any Subsidiary, provided that the aggregate Current Debt of the Company and its Subsidiaries permitted by this clause (ii) shall not be in excess of the Permitted Amount on any day after December 31, 19XX unless, during the fifteen months' period immediately preceding such day, the aggregate Current Debt of the Company and its Subsidiaries permitted by this clause (ii) shall not have been in excess of the Permitted Amount for at least 60 consecutive days, and further provided that no Subsidiary shall create, incur, assume or suffer to exist any Current Debt permitted by this clause (ii) unless such Current Debt shall be secured by a Lien on its property permitted by clauses (v), (vii) or (viii) of paragraph 6C(1) or shall constitute Current Debt payable to the Company or another Subsidiary;

6E. Subordinated Debt. The Company covenants that it will not (i) pay, prepay, redeem, purchase or otherwise acquire for value any Subordinated Debt except as required by the original provisions of the instruments evidencing Subordinated Debt or pursuant to which Subordinated Debt shall have been issued, (ii) amend the instruments evidencing Subordinated Debt or pursuant to which Subordinated Debt may have been issued in such manner as to terminate, impair or have adverse effect upon the subordination of the Subordinated Debt, or any part thereof, to the indebtedness evidenced by the Notes; or (iii) take or attempt to take any action whereby the subordination of the Subordinated Debt, or any part thereof, to the indebtedness evidenced by the Notes might be terminated, impaired or adversely affected. The term "Subordinated Debt" as used in this paragraph 6E shall mean any Funded Debt of the Company or any Subsidiary which does not constitute Senior Funded Debt.

Thus it can be seen that overall debt constraints are included in this agreement and usually are a part of most credit agreements.

With respect to securing short-term credit, certain other types of restrictions may apply. Excerpts from a loan and credit agreement for short-term borrowings under a revolving line of credit between a manufacturer and a group of commercial banks contain clauses that, under specified conditions, do the following:

a. Restrict certain payments (such as cash dividends or purchases of company stock).

b. Restrict the sale or lease of assets.

c. Require the maintenance of a given ratio of shareholders' equity to senior indebtedness and a minimum amount of shareholders' equity.

d. Place restraints on specific contingent liabilities.

e. Place limitations on acquisitions of other companies.

f. Place limitations both on certain specific debts and on overall consolidated indebtedness.

The specific wording of some of the clauses relating to covenants or restrictions may be of interest:

Minimum Working Capital. Maintain Consolidated Working Capital at a level whereby consolidated current assets are at least 175% of consolidated current liabilities of the Company and all Consolidated Subsidiaries and, in any event, of at least $200,000,000. In any calculation of Consolidated Working Capital, an amount equal to Covered Customer Advances shall be excluded from both consolidated current assets and consolidated current liabilities and deferred income taxes reported by the Company as a current liability in its consolidated balance sheet shall be excluded from consolidated current liabilities.

Negative Covenants. So long as credit shall remain available to the Company hereunder and until the payment in full of all Notes outstanding hereunder and the performance of all other obligations of the Company hereunder, the Company will not, and will not permit any Consolidated Subsidiary to, without the prior written consent of Banks holding at least 66⅔% in aggregate unpaid principal amount of the Notes, or, if no Notes are then outstanding, Banks having at least 66⅔% of the aggregate commitments to make loans hereunder:

Restrictive Payments.   Declare, pay or authorize any Restricted Payment if (a) any such Restricted Payment is not paid out of Consolidated Net Earnings Available For Restricted Payments and (b) at the time of, and immediately after, the making of any such Restricted Payment (or the declaration of any such dividend except a stock dividend) no Event of Default specified in § 8 and no event which with notice or lapse of time or both would become such an Event of Default has occurred and (c) the making of any such Restricted Payment would reduce Consolidated Tangible Shareholders' Equity below $225,000,000.

Sale, Lease, etc.   Sell, lease, assign, transfer or otherwise dispose of any of its assets, tangible and intangible (other than investments permitted by § 7B(7) and obsolete or worn-out property or real estate not used or useful in its business), whether now owned or hereafter acquired, excluding from the operation of this clause sales, leases, assignments, transfers and other dispositions (a) in the ordinary and normal operation of its business and for a full and adequate consideration, (b) between the Company and any Consolidated Subsidiary, and between Consolidated Subsidiaries and (c) by the Company not in the ordinary and normal operation of its business provided the value on the Company's books of assets so transferred shall not exceed 10% of Consolidated Tangible Shareholders' Equity in the aggregate in any calendar year.

Maintenance of Shareholder's Equity.   Permit the amount of Consolidated Tangible Shareholders' Equity at any time to be less than 100% of the then aggregate outstanding amount of Consolidated Senior Indebtedness or less than $225,000,000.

Contingent Liabilities.   Assume, guarantee (which for purposes of this clause (4) shall include agreements to purchase or to provide funds for the payment of obligations of, to maintain the net worth or working capital or other financial test of, or otherwise become liable upon the obligations of, any person, firm or corporation) or endorse any obligation of any other person, firm or corporation (except the Company or a Consolidated Subsidiary, or any captive insurance subsidiary, as the case may be, as permitted by this clause (4)) or permit to exist any assumption, guarantee or endorsement, excluding from the operation of this clause, (a) assumptions, guaranties and endorsements in the ordinary and normal operation of its business as presently conducted, it being understood that performance guaranty bonds, bank guaranties for foreign work, advance payment bonds, direct guarantees for performance, or other surety bonds will be so considered; (b) guarantees by the Company or any Consolidated Subsidiary or direct obligations of the Company or any Consolidated Subsidiary for the payment of money, whether domestic or foreign, so long as an amount equal to the aggregate amount of such guaranteed obligations is deemed to be (without duplication). Indebtedness and/or Consolidated Senior Indebtedness, as the case may be, for purposes of §§ 7b(8) and 7B(9); (c) guarantees of the Company or any Consolidated Subsidiary issued, or obligations assumed, in connection with acquisitions of assets permitted under § 7B(5), *provided* that obligations for borrowed money (whether guaranteed or assumed) shall be treated as provided in the next preceding clause (b); and (d) guaranties by the

Company or any Consolidated Subsidiary of direct obligations of third parties for the payment of money, *provided,* that if the then aggregate amount of such obligations shall exceed an amount equal to 15% of Consolidated Tangible Shareholders' Equity, the amount of such excess shall be deemed Consolidated Senior Indebtedness for purposes of this Agreement.

Acquisition of Assets.   Acquire any assets of any other person through merger, consolidation or otherwise (including acquisition of capital stock of any other person if such acquisition is analogous in either purpose or effect to a consolidated or merger) except in the ordinary course of business, unless after giving effect to such acquisition (a) the Company shall be the surviving corporation, and (b) no Event of Default specified in § 8 or event which with notice or lapse of time or both would become such an Event of Default shall have occurred.

Other Debt.   Incur or have outstanding any Indebtedness or become or be liable with respect to any Indebtedness or sell any obligations of the Company or any Consolidated Subsidiary, excluding from the operation of this covenant,

(a) the Notes:

(b) indebtedness, other than for borrowed money, incurred in the ordinary course of business of the Company or a Consolidated Subsidiary, *provided* such indebtedness is not prohibited under § *7B(4)* or *7B(5);*

(c) liabilities in connection with capitalized leases;

(d) loans by the Company to Consolidated Subsidiaries, and loans by Consolidated Subsidiaries to the Company and other Consolidated Subsidiaries;

(e) indebtedness of the Company to Prudential, not exceeding $13,500,000, incurred pursuant to the Prudential Loan Agreement;

(f) commercial paper of the Company having a maturity of not more than nine months from its date, in amounts which in the aggregate do not exceed at any time outstanding the lesser of $75,000,000 or the sum of the unused Revolving Credit Commitments plus Bank lines of credit;

(g) existing indebtedness of Consolidated Subsidiaries not in excess of $2,075,000, *provided* that as said debt is paid or reduced it shall not be increased;

(h) a loan to X Company from a foreign bank in the amount of $2,075,000 (or the lira equivalent thereof), *provided* that as said debt is paid or reduced it shall not be increased;

(i) secured indebtedness permitted by § *7B(6)(g)* in an aggregate amount not to exceed the $100,000,000 original principal amount, *provided* that as said debt is paid or reduced it shall not be increased;

(j) other Consolidated Senior Indebtedness of the Company and Consolidated Subsidiaries which does not exceed $30,000,000 in the aggregate at any time, *provided* that the maturity of all such indebtedness in excess of an aggregate of $5,000,000 has been consented to in writing by Banks holding at least 66⅔% in aggregate unpaid principal amount of the Notes, or, if no Notes are then outstanding, Banks having at least 66⅔% of the aggregate commitments to make loans hereunder;

(k) borrowings from foreign sources in amounts not exceeding the equivalent of $50,000,000, *provided* the maturity and terms of all such indebtedness in excess of an aggregate of $5,000,000 has been consented to in writing by Banks holding at least 66⅔% in aggregate unpaid principal amount of the Notes, or, if no Notes are then outstanding, Banks having at least 66⅔% of the aggregate commitments to make loans hereunder;

(l) Subordinated Debt of the Company; and

(m) other Consolidated Senior Indebtedness of the Company (but not of any Consolidated Subsidiary), whether domestic or foreign, so long as after incurrence thereof (i) the then aggregate outstanding amount of Consolidated Senior Indebtedness of the Company and all Consolidated Subsidiaries would not exceed 100% of Consolidated Tangible Shareholders' Equity and (ii) neither the Company nor any Consolidated Subsidiary would be in default under this Agreement.

Limitation on Consolidated Indebtedness. Permit the Consolidated Indebtedness of the Company and all Consolidated Subsidiaries at any time to be more than 200% of Consolidated Tangible Shareholders' Equity.

In the day-to-day administration of loan agreements, it is obvious that the controller should be aware of the terms and should report the financial condition and financial data as required in the contract. Of equal or more importance, however, should be the controller's review of proposed financial actions to determine whether they would violate any present agreements and then to take appropriate action.

Aside from the reporting requirements, the controller should be aware of management's obligation not only to the shareholders, but also to the suppliers of debt capital. The indenture agreement may still be the best way of protecting the interests of the senior long-term lender. However, given some recent experiences wherein investment-grade bonds have been converted essentially into junk bonds in a very short period, the credit agreement may require more restrictive measures, taking into account the creativity of some lawyers, and the use of technical devices to circumvent some protective clauses. Many entities are now demanding the "poison put" provision discussed in the section on developments in the fixed income market.

33-6 PLANNING THE CURRENT LIABILITIES

Having discussed in a general way the different types of liabilities, it is now in order to review the planning process first for the current liabilities and later for long-term debt.

Planning of any specificity for current liabilities for most concerns relates to the annual business plan, for the next year or so, or to an even shorter time span. Basically, the short-term planning involves these steps:

1. Determining, based on the operating requirements for each month and each month end, the level of each type of obligation expected, e.g., accounts payable, accrued expenses, accrued salaries and wages, accrued income taxes, notes payable, dividends payable.

2. Ascertaining from the cash forecast (see Chapter 27) whether any borrowings are necessary to meet the payment requirements, and incorporating this need and the payments into the plan.

3. Testing the consolidated plan at selected intervals, such as every reporting period or every quarter, to see if the terms of any or all credit agreements are being met—or if the indebtedness is within company norms or standards—and taking appropriate action if not (securing bank waivers, deferral of purchases, securing of special terms from suppliers, acceleration of cash receipts, etc.).

It may be observed that the level of most current liabilities, other than notes payable, will be the result of other operating segments of the annual plan. Thus, accounts payable will relate to purchases for inventory or obligations for current operating expenses; accrued salaries and wages will relate to the planned payrolls for the continuing operations, and so on. Any required short-term borrowings will derive from the cash planning.

In planning any element of current payables, it is practical to accumulate the segment based on the normal grouping of costs and expenses needed for each type of transaction. Thus, as reflected in Figure 33-1, the aggregate liability for purchases of raw materials and purchased parts (probably one entry in planning material purchases) is recorded for each month. Perhaps all other current purchases of an expense nature are journalized for each month. Any significant "other transaction" is recorded separately for the plan, just as would be done for the actual expense. Payments would be estimated based on an average lag time as described in Chapter 27.

Figure 33-1   Accounts Payable Plan.

The Illustrative Company
ACCOUNTS PAYABLE BUDGET
FOR THE PLAN YEAR ENDING DECEMBER 31, 19XX
(dollars in thousands)

Item	January	February	March	1st Quarter	Annual Total
Balance, beginning of month .	$82,360	$88,530	$79,560	$ 82,360	$ 82,360
Add:					
Purchases—raw material . .	71,200	65,840	67,430	204,470	832,880
Purchases—capital assets .	3,450	1,070	860	5,380	14,970
Manufacturing expenses . .	4,810	4,650	4,850	14,310	58,210
Marketing expenses	3,270	2,970	3,110	9,350	39,620
R&D expense	1,920	1,840	1,870	5,630	24,940
Administrative expenses . .	2,470	2,560	2,500	7,530	33,160
All other	80	40	100	220	860
Total additions	87,200	78,970	80,720	246,890	1,004,640
Deduct: Payments					
Raw material	69,800	72,010	65,840	207,650	840,120
Capital assets	520	3,450	1,070	5,040	13,810
Operating expenses	10,610	12,400	12,020	35,030	144,950
All others	100	80	40	220	860
Total deductions	81,030	87,940	78,970	247,940	999,740
Balance, end of month	$88,530	$79,560	$81,310	$ 81,310	$ 87,260

Figure 33-2   Accrued Salaries and Wages Budget.

The Illustrative Company
ACCRUED SALARIES AND WAGES BUDGET
FOR THE PLAN YEAR ENDING DECEMBER 31, 19XX
(dollars in thousands)

Item	January	February	March	1st Quarter	Annual Total
Balance, beginning of month	$ 26,310	$ 30,850	$ 34,710	$ 26,310	$ 26,310
Add: Gross payrolls					
Manufacturing	85,030	82,100	85,620	252,750	1,060,400
Marketing	31,810	30,720	31,940	94,470	375,100
R&D	1,420	1,380	1,430	4,230	16,920
Administrative	20,640	20,600	20,650	61,890	247,560
Total additions	138,900	134,800	139,640	413,340	1,699,980
Deduct: Payments					
Salaries	41,800	42,300	42,300	126,400	506,600
Wages	92,560	88,640	107,710	288,910	1,155,640
Total payments	134,360	130,940	150,010	415,310	1,662,240
Balance, end of month	$ 30,850	$ 34,710	$ 24,340	$ 24,340	$ 37,740

Figure 33-3   Notes Payable Borrowing Plan.

The Illustrative Company
NOTES PAYABLE BUDGET
FOR THE PLAN YEAR ENDING DECEMBER 31, 19XX
(dollars in thousands)

Month	Beginning Balance	Borrowings	Repayments	Ending Balance
January	$ —	$2,500	$ —	$2,500
February	2,500	—	—	2,500
March	2,500	2,500	—	5,000
April	5,000	—	—	5,000
May	5,000	—	1,000	4,000
June	4,000	—	500	3,500
July	3,500	—	500	3,000
August	3,000	—	1,000	2,000
September	2,000	—	—	2,000
October	2,000	—	1,000	1,000
November	1,000	—	—	1,000
December	1,000	—	1,000	—
Total	$ —	$5,000	$5,000	$ —

The estimate of accrued salaries and wags is shown in Figure 33-2. The additions to the accrual would be in those groupings used to determine manufacturing costs (inventory) or other logical accumulations.

Based on the required borrowings and repayments as determined in the cash forecast, the plan for notes payable could be developed as in Figure 33-3.

The same procedure would be followed for each liability grouping deemed necessary and practical in the current liability planning cycle.

When all the current liabilities balances have been determined, they should be summarized as in Figure 33-4. As explained in the next section, the planned balances, as well as actual balances, should be measured against acceptable standards, as well as credit agreement requirements, and so on.

The above discussion of planning the current liabilities has been covered in the context of the annual business plan or any other short-term plan. The same principles would apply with respect to strategic planning or long-range planning (see Chapters 14 and 15), except that the time span usually can be by year and need not be by quarter or month. Moreover, the estimates may be arrived at on a ratio basis, and much less preciseness and detail usually are satisfactory.

Figure 33-4   Summary of Current Liabilities Plan.

The Illustrative Company
SUMMARY OF CURRENT LIABILITIES PLAN
FOR THE PLAN YEAR ENDING DECEMBER 31, 19XX

Item	Estimated Balance Current Year	Plan Year Ending 12/31/XX Quarter 1	2	3	4
Notes payable	$ —	$ 5,000	$ 3,500	$ 2,000	$ —
Current maturities of long-term debt	2,500	—	—	—	2,500
Accounts payable	82,360	81,310	83,240	85,190	87,260
Dividends payable	870	910	910	910	910
Accrued salaries and wages	26,310	24,340	28,920	34,870	37,740
Accrued income taxes	1,450	1,500	1,500	1,500	1,500
Other accrued items	90	100	100	120	120
Total	$113,580	$113,160	$118,170	$124,590	$130,030
Selected Ratios					
Current ratio	2.0:1	2.0:1	2.1:1	2.1:1	2.2:1
Quick ratio	0.39:1	0.40:1	0.41:1	0.41:1	0.42:1
Net working capital	113,580	113,160	129,987	137,049	156,036
Current liabilities to net worth	0.25:1	0.25:1	0.26:1	0.27:1	0.28:1
Number of days purchases in payables	23.6	21.4	22.5	22.9	23.6

33-7 STANDARDS TO MEASURE AND CONTROL CURRENT LIABILITIES

The planning task of the controller does not consist merely of determining what the level of current liabilities will be at stipulated times, based on operating plans or capital budgets or other financial plans. Additionally, these planned levels should be tested for acceptability. The standards by which such acceptability is judged should include (a) any legal requirements, such as those in bank lending agreements or in bond indentures, etc., (b) those developed by the company (probably by the financial officers) as deemed prudent to avoid undue financial exposure, or (c) those acceptable to knowledgeable persons in the industry. Dun & Bradstreet, for example, periodically issues selected ratios on each industry, showing the median and upper and lower quartile for certain operating ratios and financial conditions. The company could measure itself against these industry ratios or against performance of selected competitors or against standards developed or used by commercial bankers, investment bankers, or financial analysts. If these tests reveal unacceptable conditions, then corrective action should be taken, as discussed in the next section.

Some suggested ratios used to measure the acceptability of current liabilities include these:

- Current ratio.
- Quick ratio.
- Minimum net working capital.
- Current debt to net worth.
- Current debt to inventory.
- Number of days' payables on hand (accounts payable turnover).

Brief comments on each are as follows:

(a) CURRENT RATIO

The current ratio is discussed in Chapter 8. However, some brief comments are added here.

The current ratio is calculated by dividing the current assets by the current liabilities. It measures the protection the creditors have, even if the current assets prove to be less valuable than anticipated. Years ago, a ratio deemed satisfactory was 2 to 1. However, with the advent of the computer and improved receivables and inventory control, a ratio of between 1 to 1 and 2 to 1 is usually acceptable.

(b) QUICK RATIO

The quick ratio, also discussed in Chapter 8, measures the relationship of the highly liquid assets—cash, temporary investments, and accounts receivable—to current liabilities. This ratio, also known as the liquidity ratio or acid test, is an indicator of what very liquid assets are available to meet the demands of the short-term creditors.

(c) MINIMUM NET WORKING CAPITAL

This is an absolute amount—the difference between current assets and current liabilities. Some loan and credit agreements, including the one illustrated earlier, require a minimum amount of working capital at all times. The net amount indicates the extent to which the current assets could shrink and yet be sufficient to meet the current liabilities.

(d) CURRENT DEBT TO NET WORTH

To the extent that assets are financed by the owners, there is more protection (more assets) for the creditors. A low current debt (or total debt) to net worth ratio is some measure of how the owners are supplying more relative funds.

(e) CURRENT DEBT TO INVENTORY

A high ratio of current debt as related to inventory would suggest that goods are purchased, processed, and sold without payments being made to suppliers. Depending on the relative ratio, as compared to the industry and trade practice, a high relationship would indicate inadequate financing.

(f) DAYS' PAYABLES ON HAND

The number of days' payables on hand is determined by dividing the accounts payable balance by the amount of purchases, and multiplying by the days in the period. For example, in Figure 33-1:

1. The quarterly accounts payable balance planned is $81,310,000.
2. Purchases for the period were planned at $246,890,000.
3. Business days in the period are 65.

$$\text{Number of days' payables on hand} = \$81,310,000 \div \$246,890,000$$
$$= .3293369 \times 65 \text{ days}$$
$$= 21.41 \text{ days}$$

Such a result should be checked against industry standards, if available.

33-8 CORRECTIVE ACTION

If the annual plan reflects an unsatisfactory condition regarding current liabilities, or if actual results are not acceptable, what action can be taken? The controller might examine these alternatives with the appropriate line executive:

- Possibility of reducing inventory levels through different purchasing terms, inventory handling methods, or inventory control, e.g., JIT inventories.

- Reducing accounts receivable by granting special terms or cash discounts, etc.
- Making special arrangements with suppliers to receive goods on consignment or special payment terms.
- As a last resort, if the conditions appear temporary, ask the lenders to waive or relax the restrictive terms for a limited period.

If the condition appears more permanent, perhaps additional equity capital or long-term debt may be desirable. Or maybe less ambitious business plans may be considered for a time—less capital expenditures, lower sales volume, etc.

If actual unsatisfactory conditions emerge, then some of these same planning alternatives may need to be reviewed.

33-9 SATISFACTORY ACCOUNTING SYSTEMS

In these days of the minicomputer and microcomputer, along with flexible, adaptable software programs, as every controller knows, better accounting control can be maintained over accounts payable or payrolls, etc. For example, software systems have been developed which, with audit trails and balancing controls, etc., can write checks when payment is due, take discounts according to vendor terms, select who can process invoices, who can select vendors, create vendor files, etc. So proper control of current liabilities may mean reviewing the accounting system in use.

33-10 LONG-TERM DEBT

Having reviewed the planning and control of current liabilities, most of the remaining commentary in this chapter will relate to the management of long-term debt. But background information on just how much debt should be assumed will first be discussed.

33-11 RISKS OF TOO MUCH DEBT

The subject of long-term debt is closely related to the capital structure of the entity—meaning the combination of shareholders' equity and long-term debt that should be used to provide for the financing needs over the span of several years.[1] In considering this subject, the goal of the financial executive should be to so arrange the financing that the owners of the business will receive the maximum economic benefit over the longer run—through the increase in the share price and constantly rising dividend income.

It can be demonstrated over a period of time, assuming normal profitability and the deductibility of interest expense for tax purposes, that prudent borrowing will increase the return to the shareholder. Given this potential of gain, there exists a powerful deterrent that discourages using long-term debt to the maximum of its availability. That deterrent is the risk associated with servicing the debt. For debts and debt service must be paid when due regardless of the financial condition of the company to avoid unwelcome restraints or, worse, the loss of the enterprise.

---

[1] See Chapter 34 for a discussion of capital structure.

In the 1988–1990 period, the matter of excess debt was a particularly germane subject. In the spring of 1989, when leveraged buyouts were occurring with some frequency, some investors became concerned about a recession and the ability of some high-risk, high-yield bonds, known as junk bonds, to survive the storm. Prices were depressed and yields rose. Although no recession arrived, the average yield on junk bonds in September 1989 was 13.5%, which is 5.3 percentage points more than 10-year Treasury notes.[2] Moody's downgraded the credit rating of 104 speculative companies in the first eight months of 1988. The company's senior economist cited some basic business problems arising because of high debt:[3]

- Such companies were inviting targets for cash-rich competitors who will attempt to wrest market share through aggressive price cutting.
- In some instances, the heavy debt was causing a company to fall behind technically because the required funds were not being spent on research and development.

It is not merely the highly speculative companies that have succumbed to the high-debt philosophy. Some blue chip companies, out of takeover fear, became converts to the new-debt philosophy: Untapped borrowing power was just as wasteful as an idle factory.[4]

The debt binge of the 1980s did trigger various modes of behavior in different companies. Some did, indeed, become "lean and mean," and more competitive. In others, the threat of bankruptcy undoubtedly constrained management. But, according to some, the financial markets are now telling business management and financiers to pull back from the extremes of leverage.[5]

So a prudent financial executive should ask, "What are prudent debt limits?" It may be that mounting losses in junk bonds represent a watershed event.[6]

33-12 SOME BENEFITS FROM DEBT INCURRENCE

While the prudent financial executive should be aware of the risks of excessive debt, he or she should also recognize some of the advantages of a reasonable debt load. Here are a few:

- *Debt Reduces Tax Payments.* Since most interest cost is income tax deductible, tax payments are lower. This assists in reducing the cost of capital used in the business.

---

[2] Constance Mitchell, "Junk Bonds Fail to Recover from Recession Scare," *The Wall Street Journal,* Sept. 11, 1989, p. C-1.

[3] Ibid.

[4] Tim Bower, "The Bills Are Coming Due," *Business Week,* Sept. 11, 1989, p. 85.

[5] Christopher Farrell, "Why Junk in the First Place? Skimpy Savings," *Business Week,* Sept. 11, 1989, p. 92.

[6] Mathew Winkler et al., "The Party's Over. Mounting Losses Are Watershed Event for Era of Junk Bonds," *The Wall Street Journal,* Sept. 18, 1989, pp. A1, A9.

- *Prudent Borrowings Can Increase the Return on Capital to the Owners.* If the earnings from this borrowed capital exceed the cost net of taxes, then the return to the shareholder is higher. (See section 33-16 on leverage.)

- *Debt Imposes a Discipline on Management as to Normal Operations.* Investors know that too much cash can encourage wasteful spending practices. They tend to watch performance more carefully if sizable debt exists. Additionally, the management is more sensitive to the need for frugality to repay the debt. So more careful spending results.

- *Debt Motivates Managers and Owners.* Lowering the equity base with borrowed funds probably makes it easier for the management group to acquire a significant stake.

- *Debt Causes a More Appropriate Review of Proposed Capital Expenditures and Acquisitions.* Rigid repayment schedules probably cause a closer look at the economics of proposed expenditures as well as those units that don't produce sufficient earnings.

In summary, as one executive stated, "Debt is a just-in-time financial system."

33-13 SOURCES OF INFORMATION ON DEBT CAPACITY

For long-range financial planning, as well as judging the proposed terms or rating of contemplated new debt, what sources are available to secure guidance? In the final analysis, it must be management judgment that decides on acceptable limits for debt capacity. Some guidance in arriving at a decision may come from these sources:

1. *Institutional Lenders or Intermediaries.* Lenders, or commercial bankers, or investment bankers negotiate long-term loans at rather frequent intervals in contrast to the financial officer of an industrial enterprise. Consequently, they will be more familiar with the terms of recent agreements. Presumably, also, they are conservative and will tend to err in the conservative direction. They should be able to judge if proposed standards will be acceptable in the marketplace.

2. *Action of Competitors.* Ordinarily, the financial statements and loan agreements of comparable companies in the same industry are available. From such public information individual companies and group norms can be obtained—together with ranges.

3. *Analysis of Past Practice.* Finally, historical analysis of debt and income behavior in the particular company in times of adversity and normal conditions may provide some guide.

33-14 STANDARDS FOR DEBT CAPACITY

Conventionally, there are two types of standards by which to judge long-term debt capacity: (*a*) a capitalization standard and (*b*) an earnings coverage standard. In arriving at a debt policy for a particular company, each should be considered and interrelated. In working with internally generated data, the controller can make refinements ordinarily not possible with public data of other companies. He can thus guide his management about an acceptable relationship.

A widely used standard, often employed as a constraint in credit agreements, is the long-term-debt-to-equity ratio. Thus long-term debt should not be more than, say, 25% of equity capital. It can also be expressed as a percent of total capitalization.

In using such a standard, several determinatives should be calculated, showing the impact, for example, of a 20% debt ratio versus a 25% ratio to judge the risk involved. Then, too, recognition must be given to the often wide variation between the principal of the debt and the annual debt service charge of interest and debt repayment. A loan may be paid off in 5 or 30 years. Whereas the ratio of debt to equity may be the same in each case in a given year, the debt service burden is substantially different. Conversely, whereas the debt ratio could improve dramatically with a shorter-term loan, the debt service drain remains the same until complete repayment.

The "earnings coverage standard" measures the total annual amount required for debt service to the net earnings available for servicing the debt. By relating the annual cash outflow for debt service (and perhaps other items) to the net earnings available for this purpose, it seeks to assure that even in times of adversity there are sufficient funds to meet the obligation. Obviously, the greater the probable change in cash flow, the higher the desired times-coverage ratio. The observed times coverage varies greatly by industry and by company. Typical well-financed companies may have a coverage of 15 times or more.

In making analyses of his own company, the controller can apply a great deal of sophistication in changing anticipated cash outflows to judge the impact. Thus it may be desirable to measure not only times coverage of net income to debt service but also other cash requirements that should not be disturbed, i.e., dividends for shareholders, or certain research and development expenditures, or expected inventory build-up, or minimum capital expenditures. Each major cash outflow should be considered and reasonable sums provided even in times of adversity. An example of an analysis that might be made is shown in Figure 33-5. In this illustration, actual and planned cash sources and uses are satisfactory in the planning period. The debt coverage ratios are very good. However, with a major drop in sales, even planned cutbacks in receivables, inventory, and capital expenditures result in coverage ratios that although adequate are substantially below the levels the financial management considers desirable in a cyclical type of business. The need for a new debt issue in 19X5 should be reexamined in terms of the probability or danger of a sales decline. However, a long-term debt has been continually declining from 16% of capitalization in 19XX to 11% in 19X4; and even with the planned $70 million new debt issue in 19X5 it reaches only 17%. Hence, the critical point in this example is earnings coverage, not capitalization.

The magnitude of the *probable* downturn in earnings and changes in various cash outflows under such circumstances should be considered. A range of the *most probable* contraction in sales volume and, therefore, in net income should be determined and resulting times coverage determined.

In the final analysis, debt policy or appropriate capital structure can be determined only by an examination of the factors in the company and in the industry that influence the ability to repay debt. It is a matter of judgment and foresight regarding likely conditions, conservatively arrived at—and not mathematics.

33-15 BOND RATINGS

There exists a significant difference in interest cost, depending on the quality rating assigned to debt securities by the three rating agencies, and this is an important

Figure 33-5 Analysis of Cash Availability and Selected Debt Coverage.

The Aerospace Company
SOURCES AND USES OF CASH AND DEBT COVERAGE
(dollars in thousands)

	Actual				Planned		19X5 with Sales Decline	
	19XX	19X1	19X2	19X3	19X4	19X5	20%	30%
Sources of Cash								
Net income	$ 76,000	$ 82,000	$ 90,000	$ 93,000	$ 97,000	$100,000	$ 70,000	$ 50,000
Depreciation and amortization	42,000	45,000	47,000	48,000	51,000	52,000	52,000	52,000
Deferred income taxes	40,000	10,000	(40,000)	(10,000)	10,000	20,000	(20,000)	(20,000)
Total internal generation	158,000	137,000	97,000	131,000	158,000	172,000	102,000	82,000
Anticipated 19X5 debt offering	—	—	—	—	—	70,000	70,000	70,000
Loan and credit agreement—revolving	10,000	10,000	(20,000)	20,000	30,000	40,000	20,000	10,000
Common stock—under options	1,000	1,000	1,500	2,000	2,000	1,000	—	—
Sale of fixed assets	4,000	—	—	3,000	—	—	—	—
Total sources	173,000	148,000	78,500	156,000	190,000	283,000	192,000	162,000
Uses of Funds								
Accounts payable	10,000	5,000	1,000	—	5,000	20,000	10,000	5,000
Inventories	40,000	20,000	(20,000)	(10,000)	25,000	40,000	30,000	10,000
Accounts receivable	30,000	10,000	2,000	—	7,000	10,000	(20,000)	(30,000)
Income taxes (current)	50,000	31,000	37,000	41,000	43,000	44,600	44,600	44,600
Dividends	22,000	25,000	27,000	28,000	30,000	32,000	32,000	32,000
Capital expenditures	50,000	40,000	45,000	30,000	60,000	65,000	25,000	25,000
Debt repayment	4,000	4,000	5,000	7,500	7,500	7,500	7,500	7,500
Total uses	206,000	135,000	97,000	96,500	177,500	269,100	129,000	94,100
Increase (decrease) in cash	$(33,000)	$ 13,000	$(18,500)	$ 59,500	$ 12,500	$ 13,900	$ 63,000	$ 67,900
Other Data—Coverage								
Pre-tax income and interest/interest	7.6	7.9	8.6	8.8	9.1	7.2	5.3	4.1
Net income before interest/interest	4.5	4.7	5.1	5.3	5.4	4.3	3.3	2.7
Pre-tax income before rent and interest/rent and interest	3.8	3.9	4.1	4.1	4.3	3.9	3.1	2.5
Long-term debt as percent of capitalization	16	15	13	12	11	17		

consideration in selecting aggregate debt limits. Standard and Poor's Corporation, Moody's Investor Service, and Fitch Investor's Service—the three debt rating agencies—assign ratings that characterize judgment about the quality or inherent risk in any given security. The rating will depend, among many other factors, on the debt coverage relationship.

The symbols Moody's uses for the highest four ratings may be summarized or characterized as follows:

Aaa	The best quality; smallest degree of investment risk and generally considered "gilt edge."
Aa	Judged to be of high quality by all standards.
A	Higher medium grade obligations, with some elements that may be present to suggest a susceptibility to impairment at some time in the future.
Baa	Lower medium grade. Lack outstanding investment characteristics and, in fact, have speculative characteristics as well.

The objective of many well-financed companies is to secure at least an Aa rating for its bonds.

Presentations to secure the bond ratings should be carefully prepared, because poor ratings are not easily overcome.

In determining a debt rating, the agencies need adequate financial data, such as the following:

1. Consolidated balance sheets. Perhaps five historical years and five projected years.
2. Consolidated statements of income and retained earnings for five years historical and five years projected. Included would be dividends paid and per share data, including the following:
   Earnings.
   Dividends.
   Book value.
3. Consolidated statement of cash flows. Again five historical years and five prospective years.
4. Product group statements for historical and projected data regarding sales, operating margin, and margin rate.

The ratio analysis, including the coverage ratios, found helpful to the rating agencies is shown in Figure 33-6.

33-16 LEVERAGE

In considering capital structure, the financial officers necessarily must recognize and study the impact of leverage. Essentially, leverage consists of financing an enterprise with senior obligations to increase the rate of return on the common equity. The action is known also as "trading on the equity."

Figure 33-6 Ratio Analysis for Use by Rating Agency.

Aerospace Corporation
RATIO ANALYSIS

	Years Ended December 31,					Projected Years Ended December 31,				
19XX	19X1	19X2	19X3	19X4	19X5	19X6	19X7	19X8	19X9
Senior Total	Senior Total	Senior Total	Senior Total	Senior Total	Senior Total	Senior Total	Senior Total	Senior Total	Senior Total

Financial Ratios
Net current assets/long-term debt *
Net property/long-term debt
Net property and investments/long-term debt
Net tangible assets †/long-term debt
Long-term debt as percent of total
   capitalization

Coverage Ratios
Profit before rents, interest, income taxes,
   and non-cash charges/rents and interest
Profit before rents, interest, and income
   taxes/rents and interest
Profit before interest and income taxes/
   interest
Net income and interest/interest
Net income, rents, and interest/rents and
   interest
Long-term debt and capitalized rents ‡/net·
   income and noncash charges

Operating and Other Ratios
Current assets/current liabilities
Current assets/total assets
Net sales/net current assets
Net sales/net property
Pretax profit as percent of net sales
Net income as percent of net sales
Net income as percent of net worth
Accounts receivable as percent of sales
Inventory as percent of sales

* Long-term debt includes in all cases current maturities.
† Net tangible assets are defined as total assets less Current Liabilities, Intangible Assets, Other Deferred Liabilities, plus Current Maturities of Long-Term Debt.
‡ Annual rentals paid capitalized at ten times.

An application of leverage is shown in Figure 33-7. Assume that the management has been earning, before income taxes, 37% on capitalization; that it believes it can continue to achieve this same return; and that the company can borrow at an 11% rate. If it borrows 20% of equity and continues the rate of return on assets, the earnings per share, with favorable leverage, increase from $5.00 to $5.70 and the return on equity rises from 19.98 to 22.79%.

However, if, under unfavorable leverage conditions, management were too optimistic and the earnings rate less than the bond interest rate, the results can be unsatisfactory—as illustrated in Figure 33-8. Here, the rate of return on capitalization was less than the bond interest rate.

From an investor standpoint, in good times, the leverage increases the EPS and the price of the stock. However, in adverse times, the reverse condition exists, and the stock of a leveraged company becomes less attractive.

33-17 CONTINGENCIES

To this point in this chapter, the discussion has been related to *direct* liabilities of the enterprise. However, the management of liabilities must extend to contingent liabilities, including proper accounting for the items and proper disclosure. Aside from the matters covered herein, the controller should recognize that contingent liabilities of

Figure 33-7 Favorable Leverage.

ILLUSTRATION OF LEVERAGE
UNDER FAVORABLE CONDITIONS

	100% Common Stock	Common Stock, plus Bond Capitalization
Capitalization		
Bonds (11%)	$ —	$ 20,000,000
Common stock	100,000,000	100,000,000
Total	$100,000,000	$120,000,000
Number of common shares	4,000,000	4,000,000
Income		
Income before taxes and interest	$ 37,000,000	$ 44,400,000
Bond interest	—	2,200,000
Income before taxes	$ 37,000,000	$ 42,200,000
Income taxes (46%)	17,020,000	19,412,000
Net income for common	$ 19,980,000	22,788,000
Return on equity	19.98%	22.79%
Earnings per common share	$5.00	$5.70
Dividend (40% payout)	$2.00	$2.28

Figure 33-8   Unfavorable Leverage.

ILLUSTRATION OF LEVERAGE
UNDER UNFAVORABLE CONDITIONS

	100% Common Stock	Common Stock, plus Bond Capitalization
Capitalization		
Bonds (11%)	$ —	$ 20,000,000
Common stock	100,000,000	100,000,000
Total	100,000,000	120,000,000
Number of common shares	4,000,000	4,000,000
Income		
Income before interest and taxes	$ 10,000,000	$ 10,000,000
Bond interest	—	2,200,000
Income before taxes	10,000,000	7,800,000
Income taxes (46%)	4,600,000	3,588,000
Net income for common	$ 4,400,000	$ 4,212,000
Return on equity	4.4%	4.21%
Earnings per common share	$1.10	$1.05
Dividend (40% payout)	$ .44	$ .42

certain types may be weighted by a lending institution in agreeing to amounts and terms and conditions in a proposed loan agreement.

Moreover, in planning for the direct liabilities of the enterprise, the controller may find it necessary to estimate the timing and amount of contingent liabilities that should be treated as direct debt on a probability basis.

33-18 TREATMENT OF LONG-TERM LIABILITIES IN THE ANNUAL BUSINESS PLAN

Planning the long-term debt status for the coming year is one segment of the annual business plan. This phase of the business may be reported only as presented in the statement of financial position, with the beginning-of-the-year status and the end-of-the-year status indicated. However, if the items are numerous enough, or if the attention of the management and the board of directors should be directed to this matter, then the plan for long-term debt may be summarized and presented on an exhibit as in Figure 33-9. It should be noted that the proposed transactions are disclosed, as well as key ratios. In all published financial statements, the controller has the responsibility to properly value and properly disclose the significant long-term obligations in accordance with GAAP. It is suggested that in most instances the same basis be used in the planning statements. Obligations and contingent obligations that are covered by footnote in the annual report to shareholders can be disclosed by oral or

Figure 33-9 Summary of Planned Long-Term Debt.

The Magraudy Company No. 2
LONG-TERM DEBT
FOR PLAN YEAR ENDING DECEMBER 31, 19XX
(dollars in thousands)

Issue	Maturity Date	Interest Rate	Estimated Beginning Balance	New Indebtedness	Payments on Debt	Planned Ending Balance
Long-term Debt						
Bank term loans	9/30/98	Floating Prime + 1 1/2%	$ 49,200	$ —	$ 4,200	$ 45,000
	12/31/99	14%	50,000	—	5,000	45,000
Loan from insurance company ...	6/30/03	13%	—	75,000	—	75,000
Proposed mortgage loan	12/31/94	10%–15%	5,850	2,000	2,850	5,000
Other notes payable	12/31/97	11%	35,000	—	4,000	31,000
Subordinated debentures						
Total			140,050	77,000	16,050	201,000
Other Long-term Obligations						
Capital lease obligations			29,400	5,600	4,000	31,000
Accrued warranty costs			37,800	12,100	7,100	42,800
Other miscellaneous			2,760	—	760	2,000
Total			69,960	17,700	11,860	75,800
Total Long-term Obligations			$210,010	$94,700	$27,910	$276,800
Selected Ratios						
Long-term debt as percent of total capitalization			22			24
Debt to equity ratio			63			60
Times interest charges covered ...			12.2			9.6

written commentary in reviewing the annual plan (or long-range plan) with management or the board of directors.

33-19 THE LONG-RANGE FINANCIAL PLAN

As mentioned in Chapter 15, the strategic plans and long-range financial plans are much less detailed than the annual business plan. Accordingly, summarized data, much as presented in Figure 15-14, may be the only information formulated and provided to the management and the board of directors—unless, of course, they desire more detail, or if, because of great risks, etc., it is imperative these groups fully understand the debt status. In arriving at the planned indebtedness levels for the long-range plan, the process is much as implied in Figure 33-5; that is, the plans are summarized year by year in sequence. If more capital is required (a) to meet cash outflow or (b) to correct an unsatisfactory current debt picture, then long-term capital is planned. If it appears the marketplace will accept indebtedness under suitable terms, then borrowings can be assumed. If the long-term debt percentage would be too high or if service coverage would be insufficient, then the sale of equity may be the route necessary. Again, the objective of the financial officers should be to maintain the company in such good financial health that, under most circumstances (good times or poor), it should be able to secure any needed capital under reasonably acceptable terms.

An illustration of the process of allocating long-term fund needs as between long-term debt and shareholders' equity is presented in Chapter 34 on long-term equity planning.

33-20 MANAGING LIABILITIES—SOME PRACTICAL STEPS

We have reviewed the objectives of liability management, planning the liabilities, and, among other things, provided some of the standards to measure the amount of current debt as well as long-term debt. While the concerns of the controller and other financial executives have been addressed, perhaps it will be helpful to summarize some of the desirable steps in properly managing liabilities. Because of the differing nature of the various types of liabilities, it is practical in the accounting, planning, and control activities to treat each group separately. Here, then, are some suggestions as to what the controller might do to assist, in properly managing the liabilities:

Current Liabilities

1. *Plan* the liabilities by month or quarter or year as may be applicable (as in the annual business plan or longer term strategic plan). This can be accomplished after the various assets levels (cash, receivables, inventories, plant, and equipment) are planned and when the operational plans (sales, manufacturing expenses, direct labor, direct material, selling expense, G&A) are completed.

   It is practical to group the current liabilities according to the categories to be identified in the Statement of Estimated Financial Position, such as accounts payable, accrued salaries and wages, accrued expenses, accrued income taxes, notes payable.

   The accounts payable plan or budget, when finalized, for the annual plan might appear as in Figure 33-10. The budget or plan for all current liabilities, by

Figure 33-10 Accounts Payable Budget.

The New York Company
ACCOUNTS PAYABLE BUDGET
FOR THE YEAR ENDING 12/31/XX
(DOLLARS IN MILLIONS)

| Item | 1st Quarter | | | | Year |
	Jan.	Feb.	March	Total	19XX
Balance, beginning of month	$21,600	29,800	19,500	21,600	$ 21,600
Add:					
Purchases—Raw Materials and Parts	14,300	12,400	13,600	40,300	149,800
Purchases—Capital Items	9,500	1,500	1,000	12,000	20,000
Subtotal	23,800	13,900	14,600	52,300	169,800
Expenses—					
Manufacturing	4,800	4,300	4,500	13,600	52,400
Selling	2,100	2,000	2,300	6,400	25,900
R&D	1,200	1,400	1,500	4,100	15,000
General and Administration	1,900	1,900	1,900	5,700	22,800
All Others	100	200	100	400	1,400
Total Additions	33,900	23,700	24,900	82,500	287,300
Deduct:					
Payments—Raw Materials and Purchased Parts	13,600	14,400	12,900	40,900	161,700
—Capital Items	1,500	9,500	1,500	12,500	20,000
—Operating Expenses	10,600	10,100	11,200	31,900	124,200
Total Deductions	25,700	34,000	25,600	85,300	305,900
Balance, End of Month	$29,800	19,500	18,800	18,800	$ 3,000

quarter, for the annual plan could be somewhat as in Figure 33-11. Note that certain pertinent ratios are shown.

2. *Test* the plan for compliance with credit agreements or other internally developed standards such as current ratio, inventory turns, net working capital, and industry average or competitor performance. If necessary, modify the plan.

3. *Analyze* each line item for ways to reduce the obligation, for example, use of JIT inventories to reduce accounts payable or notes payable. "What if" analyses of actions on other assets (terms of sale, etc.) or liabilities can be made to improve the status, if warranted. Take any appropriate action.

4. *Monitor* the monthly or quarterly balances for any unfavorable developing trends, and take appropriate action.

5. *Issue* the appropriate control or informational reports, such as to the supervisor of accounts payable, board of directors, or creditors. This might include updating the projected debt status to the year end.

6. When appropriate, as in major developments, *revise* the financial plan.

Long-Term Liabilities

1. *Plan* the long-term debt, by appropriate category, as in Figure 33-9, for the annual plan, or strategic plan, based on the commentary or factors reviewed in the chapter.

2. *Test* the plan, before finalizing, against credit agreement requirements, or standards for debt capacity, including that which might exist under the least favorable business conditions which are likely to prevail in the planning period. Adjust the plan, if required.

3. *Monitor* actual performance or condition periodically during the plan term for unfavorable developments, and take appropriate action.

4. *Report* on the financial condition and outlook to the appropriate interests (bankers, bondholders, board of directors, etc.).

As to All Indebtedness Items

1. Review the accounting to ascertain that GAAPs are followed, to the extent practical.

2. Periodically have the internal controls checked to assure the system is functioning properly. (See also Chapter 9.)

3. Keep reasonably informed on the status and probable trend of the debt market, and the new debt instruments, both short- and long-term. If appropriate, this includes foreign markets. Such information may be gained from informal discussions with commercial bankers as well as investment bankers. Perusal of financial and business literature or periodicals also may be helpful.

Additionally, the controller and other financial executives should be sensitive as to the impact of new debt issues on the holders of existing debt.

By following these few common-sense practices, there should be no unpleasant surprises regarding the management of liabilities.

Figure 33-11 Summary—Current Liability Plan.

The New York Company
SUMMARY—CURRENT LIABILITY BUDGET
FOR THE PLAN YEAR ENDING 12/31/XX
(DOLLARS IN MILLIONS)

Item	Estimated Balance 12/31/XX-1	Plan Year Ending 12/31/XX Quarter			
		1	2	3	4
Notes Payable—Banks	$ 4,700	4,100	3,600	3,000	$ 2,000
Current Maturities—Long-Term Debt	1,500	1,400	1,300	1,200	1,200
Accounts Payable	21,600	18,800	17,400	10,600	3,000
Accrual Salaries and Wages	5,800	5,200	6,400	6,900	7,400
Accrual Income Taxes	1,400	2,300	2,500	2,500	1,500
Other Accrued Items	800	700	600	600	500
Total	$35,800	32,500	31,800	24,800	15,600
Selected Ratios/Balances					
Current Ratio	1.9 to 1	2.2 to 1	2.4 to 1	2.4 to 1	2.5 to 1
Quick Ratio	.50 to 1	.70 to 1	.70 to 1	.80 to 1	1.1 to 1
Net Working Capital	$68,020	71,500	76,320	59,520	$39,000

33-21 ACCOUNTING REPORTS ON LIABILITIES

Reports with respect to the status and management of liabilities will depend on the business needs. A limited number are necessary for monitoring the actual status and to disclose the results of short- and long-term planning. A suggested list includes these:

1. Usual monthly statement of financial condition perhaps by organization segment, comparing actual and planned status.
2. Monthly or quarterly comparison of actual liabilities with amounts, by detailed category, as compared with permitted amounts under credit agreements.
3. Planning reports comparing required indebtedness as compared to credit agreements and debt capacity.
4. Periodic analysis of special liabilities, whether actual or contingent:
   a. Long-term leases.
   b. Unfunded pension plan liabilities.
   c. Exposures of various health care plan trusts, etc.
   d. Foreign currency exposure.
5. Aging of payables.
6. Comparison of actual and budgeted obligations.
7. Detailed liability reports as required by credit agreements.
8. Periodic summaries of contingent liabilities and likely actual liability.

The controller should prepare those reports for financial management, or general management, as appropriate, to guide the business, with suitable oral or written commentary.

33-22 INTERNAL CONTROLS

Internal control of liabilities runs the gamut from routine accounts payable and payroll disbursements to the periodic payment of notes payable under the various indenture terms, etc.

A fundamentally sound routine for the recording of liabilities is basic to a well-founded disbursements procedure. The essence of the problem is to make certain that no improper liabilities are placed in line for payment. Routines must be instituted to see that all liabilities are properly certified or approved by designated authority. The proper comparison of receiving reports, purchase orders, and invoices by those handling the detail disbursement procedure eliminates many duties by the officers; but the liabilities not covered by these channels must have the necessary review. The controller or treasurer, for example, must approve the payrolls before payment. The chief purchasing agent, or chief engineer, or treasurer, or some official must approve invoices for services, because no receiving report is issued. Certain special transactions may require the approval of the president. Again, invoices for such items should be checked against the voucher file for duplicate payments. In summary, the controller should consider the system of recording payables somewhat independently of the disbursements procedure to give added assurance that the necessary controls exist.

Additional commentary on internal controls is presented in Chapter 9. Moreover, if computers play a large part in processing liabilities, much acceptable software is available. However, the existence and extent of internal controls should be checked.

33-23 SELECTED REFERENCES

Farrell, Christopher, "Learning to Live with Leverage," *Business Week,* Nov. 7, 1988, pp. 138–143.

Hackett, Lee P., and Scott E. Frederick, "You Can Be Your Own White Knight," *Financial Executive,* Sept.–Oct. 1989, pp. 48–53.

Hector, Gary, "The Bondholders' Cold New World," *Fortune,* Feb. 27, 1989, pp. 83–86.

Hector, Gary, "Junk After Milken," *Fortune,* Nov. 6, 1989, pp. 121–128.

Kitching, John, "Early Returns on LBOs," *Harvard Business Review,* Nov.–Dec. 1989, pp. 74–81.

Light, Larry, Leah Nathans Spiro, and Wendy Zellner, "A Stampede for Cheaper Money," *Business Week,* Jan. 20, 1992, pp. 26–27.

Martino, Rocco Z., "Back to Basics," *Financial Executive,* Jan./Feb. 1992, pp. 56–58.

Rollins, Theresa, et al., "The New Financial Instruments," *Management Accounting,* March 1990, pp. 35–41.

Ruhl, Jack M., and Scott S. Cowen, "How an In-house System Can Create Shareholder Value," *Financial Executive,* Jan.–Feb. 1990, pp. 53–57.

Sloan, Allan, "The Rape of the Bondholder," *Forbes,* Jan. 23, 1989, pp. 67–69.

CHAPTER 34

Management of Shareholders' Equity

34-1 INTRODUCTION

Shareholders' equity is the interest of the shareholders, or owners, in the assets of a company, and at any time is the cumulative net result of past transactions affecting this segment of the balance sheet. This equity is created initially by the owners' investment in the entity, and may be increased from time to time by additional investments, as well as by net earnings. It is reduced by distributions of the equity to the owners (usually as dividends). Further, it may also decrease if the enterprise is unprofitable. When all liabilities are satisfied, the balance—the residual—belongs to the owners.

Basic accounting concepts govern the accounting for shareholders' equity as a whole, for each class of shareholder, and for the various segments of the equity interest—such as capital stock, contributed capital, or earned capital. This chapter does not deal with the accounting niceties regarding the ownership interest. It is assumed the controller is well grounded in such proper treatment, or will become so. Our concerns relate to the shareholders' interest as a total and not any special accounting segments.

34-2 IMPORTANCE OF SHAREHOLDERS' EQUITY

As previously stated, capital structure is comprised of all long-term obligations and shareholders' equity—in a sense, the "permanent" capital. Some would describe the capital structure of the enterprise as the cornerstone of financial policy. Such policy must be so planned that it will command respect from investors far into the future. But of the two basic elements, it is the shareholders' equity that is critical. This equity must provide a margin of safety to protect the senior obligations. Stated another way, in most instances, without the shareholders' equity, no senior obligations could be issued. It is for this reason, among others, that proper management of the equity is of paramount importance. In a sense, the controller, together with other members of financial management, must safeguard the long-term financial interests of not only the shareholders but also the providers of long-term credit, to say nothing of the sources of short-term capital—such as commercial banks and suppliers. And this is accomplished, in part, by properly planning and controlling the equity base of the enterprise.

34-3 ROLE OF THE CONTROLLER

Given the importance of shareholders' equity and the need to manage it prudently, what should be the role of the controller? In a general sense, as one of the principal financial officers of the corporation, the controller must properly account for the shareholders' equity, providing those analyses and recommending those actions that are consistent with enhancing shareholder value over the long term. The task would require attention to these specific actions:

1. Properly accounting for the shareholders' equity in accordance with GAAP. This includes the historical analysis of the source of the equity and the segregation of the cumulative equity by class of shareholder.

2. Preparing the appropriate reports on the status and changes in shareholders' equity as required by agencies of the U.S. government (e.g., SEC), by management, and by credit agreements and other contracts.

3. Making the necessary analyses to assist in planning the most appropriate source (debt or shareholders' equity) of new funds, and the timing and amount required of each.

4. As appropriate, maintaining in proper and economical form the capital stock records of the individual shareholders, with the related meaningful analysis (by nature of owner—individual, institution, etc.—by geographical area, by size of holding, etc.) or assuring that it is done. (In larger firms, a separate department or an outside service might perform these functions.)

5. Periodically making the required analysis, reporting on, and making recommendations or observations on such matters as:
   - Dividend policy.
   - Dividend reinvestment plans.
   - Stock splits or dividends.
   - Stock repurchase.
   - Capital structure.

- Trend and outlook for earnings per share.
- Cost of capital for the company and industry.
- Tax legislation as it affects shareholders.
- Price action of the market price of the stock, and influences on it.

Plainly, there is a grassland of financial subjects on which the controller can graze and in due course make useful suggestions.

Before a discussion of specifics about the planning phases regarding shareholders' equity, some interesting relationships should be understood by our readers:

- Rate of growth in equity as related to the return on equity.
- Growth in earnings per share as related to return on equity.
- Cost of capital.
- Dividend payout ratio.
- Relation of long-term debt to equity.

34-4 GROWTH OF EQUITY AS A SOURCE OF CAPITAL

As a company grows, it usually requires additional funds to finance working capital and plant and equipment, as well as for other purposes. Of course, it could issue additional shares of stock, but this might dilute earnings per share for a time or perhaps raise questions of control. Another alternative is to borrow long-term funds. Some managements may wish to do neither. As a result, the remaining source of long-term capital (excluding some assets sales, etc.) is the growth in retained earnings. But such a method is typically a slow way to gain additional capital. The rate of growth of equity is germane to establishing target rates of return on equity, selecting sources of capital, and monitoring dividend policy.

The annual growth in shareholders' equity from internal sources may be defined as the rate of return earned on such equity multiplied by the percentage of the earnings retained. It may be represented by this formula:

$$G = R (1 - P)$$

where

G = annual percentage growth in shareholders' equity.
R = annual net rate of return on shareholders' equity.
P = the payout ratio or share of earnings annually paid out as dividends.

As an example, if a company can earn about 23% each year on its equity, and the payout ratio is 40%, then shareholders' equity will grow at 14% per year, calculated as follows:

$$G = 0.23 (1 - 0.40)$$
$$= 0.23 (0.60)$$
$$= 0.14$$
$$= 14\%$$

Under these circumstances, if the management thinks the company can grow in sales and earnings at about 30% per year, if additional funds will be needed at about this same rate, and if the dividend payout is to remain at 40%, then management will require some outside capital for the growth potential to be realized.

34-5 RETURN ON EQUITY AS RELATED TO GROWTH IN EPS

Another facet of the shareholders' equity role is the relationship of the return on equity to the rate of annual increase in earnings per share. This connection is often not understood even by some financial executives. Basically, the rate of return on shareholders' equity, when adjusted for the payout ratio, produces the rate of growth per year in EPS. It may be expressed in this formula:

$$\text{growth per year in EPS} = \text{ROE} \times \text{retention ratio}$$

This relationship is illustrated in Figure 34-1. Thus, assuming a constant return on equity of 20% and a constant dividend payout ratio of 25%, the EPS growth rate is calculated by means of the same formula as for the growth of shareholders' equity:

$$G = R\,(1 - P)$$
$$= 0.20\,(1 - 0.25)$$
$$= 0.20\,(0.75)$$
$$= 0.15$$
$$= 15\%$$

For illustrative purposes to management or the board of directors, these same factors can be translated into book value per share, earnings per share, and dividends per share, as shown in Figure 34-2. In such terms, explanations about the shareholders' interest often are more easily understood. It is to be noted in Figure 34-2 that, with a constant dividend payout ratio, the annual dividend rate of increase is the same as the annual growth rate in earnings per share.

34-6 GROWTH IN EARNINGS PER SHARE

Prudent financial planning will consider the impact of decisions on earnings per share. Management is concerned with the growth in EPS since one of its tasks is to enhance shareholder value. And continual increases in EPS each year will raise shareholder value through its recognition in a higher P/E ratio and usually a rising dividend payment. Moreover, the growth in EPS is one of the measures of management as viewed by the financial community, including financial analysts.

Given the importance of EPS, financial officers should bear in mind that the earnings per share will increase as a result of any one of these actions:

- The plow-back of some share of earnings, even as long as the rate of return on equity remains just constant—as illustrated by the calculations in Figures 34-1 and 34-2. (A growth in EPS does not necessarily mean that the management is achieving a higher rate of return on equity.)

Figure 34-1 Constant Return on Equity vs. EPS Growth.

The Electronic Company

RETURN ON EQUITY VS. EPS GROWTH

(dollars in thousands except per share)

Year	Beginning Shareholders' Equity	Net Income	Dividends Paid	Ending Shareholders' Equity	Rate of Return on Beginning Equity	Dividend Payout Percentage	EPS	Growth in EPS(%)
19X1	$250,000	$ 50,000	$12,500	$287,500	20%	25%	$ 5.00	—
19X2	287,500	57,500	14,375	330,625	20	25	5.75	15%
19X3	330,625	66,125	16,531	380,219	20	25	6.61	15
19X4	380,219	76,044	19,011	437,252	20	25	7.60	15
19X5	437,252	87,450	21,863	502,839	20	25	8.75	15
19X6	502,839	100,568	25,142	578,265	20	25	10.06	15
19X7	578,265	115,653	28,913	665,005	20	25	11.57	15

934

Figure 34-2   Per Share—ROE vs. Growth Rate.

PER SHARE DATA
RETURN ON EQUITY VS. EPS GROWTH

Year	1	2	3	4	5	6	7
Book value, beginning	$25.00	$28.75	$33.06	$38.02	$43.72	$50.28	$57.82
Earnings (a)	5.00	5.75	6.61	7.60	8.75	10.06	11.57
Dividends (b)	1.25	1.44	1.65	1.90	2.19	2.52	2.89
Retained earnings ...	3.75	4.31	4.96	5.70	6.56	7.54	8.68
Book value, ending ...	$28.75	$33.06	$38.02	$43.72	$50.28	$57.82	$66.50
Increase in EPS:							
Amount		$ .75	.86	.99	1.15	1.31	$ 1.51
Percent		15%	15	15	15	15	15%
Increase in dividends:							
Amount		$ .19	.21	.25	.29	.33	$ .37
Percent		15%	15	15	15	15	15%

(a) At 20% on beginning equity
(b) At 25% payout rate

- An actual increase in the rate of return earned on shareholders' equity.
- Repurchase of common shares as long as the rate of return on equity does not decrease.
- Use of prudent borrowing—financial leverage. (See Chapter 33.)
- Acquisition of a company whose stock is selling at a lower P/E than the acquiring company. (See Chapter 53.)
- Sale of shares of common stock above the book value of existing shares—assuming the ROE is maintained.

Financial planning should keep all the alternatives in mind. But of all these actions, the one most likely sustainable and translatable into a healthy growth in EPS is a constant, or increasing, return on shareholders' equity.

34-7 COST OF CAPITAL

Investors are willing to place funds at risk in the expectation of recovering such capital and making a reasonable return. Some individuals or companies might prefer to invest in a practically risk-free security, such as U.S. government bonds; others will assume greater risks but expect a correspondingly higher rate of return. Cost of capital, then, may be defined as the rate of return that must be paid to investors to induce them to supply the necessary funds (through the particular instrument under discussion). Thus, the cost of a bond would be represented by the interest payments plus the recovery of the bond purchase price, perhaps plus some capital gains. The cost of common shares issued would be represented by the dividend paid plus the appreciation of the stock. Capital will flow to those markets where investors expect to receive a rate of return consistent with their assessment of the financial and other risks, and a rate that is competitive with alternative investments.

Knowledge of the cost of capital is important for two reasons:

- The financial manager must know what the cost of capital is and offer securities that provide a competitive rate, in order to be able to attract the required funds to the business.
- In making investment decisions, such as for plant and equipment, he must secure a return that is, on average, at least as high as the cost of capital. Otherwise, there is no reason to make an investment that yields only the cost or less. He is expected to gain something for the shareholder. Hence, the cost of capital theoretically sets the floor as the minimum rate of return before any investment should even be considered.

Prudent management of the shareholders' equity, then, involves:

- Attempting to finance the company so as to achieve the optimum capital structure, and, hence, a reasonable cost of capital.
- Properly determining the cost of capital, and employing such knowledge in relevant investment decisions.

34-8 DETERMINING THE COST OF CAPITAL

Determining the cost of capital in a particular company is relatively easy in concept, although in actual practice a great deal of judgment may be involved. The steps in the process are these:

- Select the appropriate capital structure for the enterprise—the relative proportion of long-term debt and shareholders' equity.
- Determine for each segment of the capital structure the appropriate rate of return to the investor and the after-tax rate (cost) to the entity.
- Calculate the cost of capital by applying the appropriate rate to each weighted segment.

The example in Figure 34-3 illustrates the process. The capitalization may be summarized in this manner:

| Segment | Capitalization | | Cost | |
	Amount	Percent	Amount	Percent
Senior debt	$100,000,000	24.40	$ 8,970,000	8.97
Equity capital	310,000,000	75.60	46,800,000	28.00
Total	$410,000,000	100.00	$55,770,000	
Weighted rate				18.00%

Figure 34-3   Computation of Cost of Capital.

Type of Segment and/or Instrument	Principal Amount (Capitalization)	Investor Required Rate (Before Taxes)	After-Tax Rate to Company*	Company Cost of Capital
Senior Obligations				
Term notes	$ 50,000,000	15%	9.00%	$ 4,500,000
Mortgage bonds	25,000,000	12	7.00	1,800,000
Debentures	15,000,000	11	6.60	1,650,000
Capitalized leases	10,000,000	17	10.20	1,020,000
Total	$100,000,000			$ 8,970,000
Cost of senior capital—rate				8.97%
Shareholders' Equity				
Preferred stock	40,000,000	15%	15.00%	6,000,000
Convertible preferred	20,000,000	24	24.00	4,800,000
Common stock				
Present shares	100,000,000	24	24.00	24,000,000
Future issue	50,000,000	24	24.00	12,000,000
Total	$210,000,000			46,800,000
Cost of equity capital—rate ...				22.00%
Grand total	$310,000 000			$55,770,000
Combined cost of capital—rate				18.00%

* Assumed total of federal and state income tax is 40%.

These comments may be helpful:

- With the new equity to be issued, the actual capital structure, as well as the desired structure, will be 24.4% senior debt and 75.6% shareholders' equity.
- Based on the rates of each existing type of senior debt (or the estimate by investment bankers, if new issues are involved), the capital cost of this segment is easy to calculate. (For simplicity purposes, financing costs were ignored.) If the rate of each issue in a segment is approximately the same, then a single rate for senior debt may be used.
- The principal element in calculating the cost of equity capital is the market price of the stock in relation to earnings. In the example of Figure 34-3, the expected earnings as perceived by the market place was $5.50 per share and the price was $22.95 (net). Therefore, the cost of equity capital was:

$$\frac{\$5.50}{\$22.95} = 24\%$$

This rate was applied to all common stock or its equivalent (the convertible preferred). The cost of the existing (nonconvertible) preferred was known.

(a) TIME FRAME FOR RATE CALCULATION

Rates of return for senior securities and common stock may be calculated on several bases. Thus the cost of senior securities can be determined by checking the interest rates and noting the proceeds obtained for each past issue or those presently existing on the balance sheet. But historical rates may not be significant, given high inflation and other changes in the marketplace. Historical costs for equity capital would involve consideration of retained earnings, etc. Or costs might be calculated based on today's market. In summary, since management concern must be with *future* capital costs, more or less related to the period over which the investment must be recovered, the probable future costs, estimated over perhaps five years, should be the ones applied. This will involve financial judgment. The rates for senior securities can be determined from new issues and adjusted for probable trends. The advice of investment bankers should be helpful.

A great deal of judgment is involved in determining the cost of equity capital. It is to be noted that neither the historical earnings level nor the management estimate of future earnings was used—although some managements might employ such a base. Historical earnings, modified by the recent trend, are not necessarily an indicator of future earnings. And, of course, managements's earnings estimate is not generally known, so presumably it is not a factor. In any event, the controller can explore the historical P/E ratios and the EPS growth rate of the company in arriving at the cost of equity. Comparisons can be made with competitor ratios.

It is worth mentioning that the capital used by the company is that evidenced by the book value of the shares, not market value. Hence, the perceived cost of equity capital was applied to the book value—whether represented by the issue price less costs or the retained earnings.

The capital asset pricing model (CAPM) is an idealized picture of how financial markets price securities, giving weight to the perceived risk. While a detailed explanation of this model is beyond the scope of this chapter, the financial executive might wish to experiment with the application as to the estimated cost of capital in his company. (See the Selected References.)

34-9 DIVIDEND POLICY

Dividend policy is a factor to be considered in the management of shareholders' equity in that:

- Cash dividends paid are the largest recurring charge against retained earnings for most U.S. corporations.
- The amount of dividends paid—which reduces the amount of equity remaining— will have an impact on the amount of long-term debt that can be prudently issued in view of the long-term debt to equity ratio that usually governs financing.
- Dividend payout is an influence on the reception of new stock issues.

- Dividend policy is an element in most loan and credit agreements—with restrictions on how much may be paid.

(a) TO PAY OR NOT TO PAY CASH DIVIDENDS?

If a company has discontinued cash dividends, for whatever reason, or if a corporation has never paid a cash dividend, then most readers would appreciate the desirability of discussing whether cash dividends should be paid. However, even if cash dividends are now being disbursed, the question should be considered.

Some companies do not pay cash dividends on the basis that it can earn a higher rate of return on reinvested earnings than can a shareholder by directly investing in new purchases of stock. This may or may not be true. It should be recognized that one purpose of sound financial management is to maximize the return to the shareholder over the longer period. Therefore, this is the criterion: in the company involved, will it serve to increase the long-term return to the shareholder by paying a dividend? This question is asked in the context that the return to the common shareholder consists of two parts: (1) the dividend and (2) the appreciation in the price of the security. The financial management of the firm should consider the type of investor attracted to the stock and the expectation of the investors. The examination of the actions of other companies and the opinion of knowledgeable investment bankers may be helpful. In general, the ability to invest all the earnings at an acceptable rate of return is not a convincing reason to pay no dividend. After all, a dividend is here and now, and future growth is more problematical. Probably, other than in the case of a highly speculative situation or a company in severe financial difficulty, some case dividend should be paid. This decision, however, is judgmental.

Dividend payments are determined by a number of influences including:

- Need for additional capital for expansion or other reasons.
- Cash flow of the enterprise.
- Industry practice.
- Shareholders' expectations.

The amount to be paid may be calculated in one of two ways: (1) by the dividend payout ratio or (2) as a percentage of beginning net worth each year.

The most common practice is to measure dividends as a percentage of earnings. This payout ratio is determined as follows:

$$\text{payout ratio} = \frac{\text{annual dividends paid to common shareholders}}{\text{annual earnings available for common shareholders}}$$
$$\text{(after preferred dividends)}$$

And in this example the payout ratio of 25% is calculated in this fashion:

$$\text{payout ratio} = \frac{\$12,500,000}{\$50,000,000}$$
$$= .25 = 25\%$$

Another way of calculating dividends, although less common than the payout method, is as a percentage of beginning net worth (book value attributable to common shares). The procedure is as follows:

$$\text{dividend payment ratio} = \frac{\text{annual dividends paid to common shareholders}}{\text{beginning common shareholder book value}}$$
$$\text{(or retained earnings)}$$
$$= \frac{\$12,500,000}{\$156,250,000}$$
$$= 0.08 = 8\%$$

In an earlier chapter, it was suggested that a primary profit goal of an enterprise should be a specified rate of return on shareholders' equity. If this be accepted as a primary planning tool, then there is a certain logic that could justify using this same base (shareholders' equity) for the calculation of dividend payments—at least for internal planning purposes. Moreover, because earnings do fluctuate there is an added stabilizing influence if dividends are based on book value. Also, as long as shareholders' equity is increasing and dividends are a constant rate of beginning net worth, then dividends would increase, the dividend payout ratio would drop, and the retention share of earnings would increase.

Dividend-paying practices send a message to the financial community, and investors and analysts accept the pattern as an indication of future payments. Hence, when a dividend payment rate is set, a dividend reduction should be avoided if at all possible.

Dividend payment patterns may follow any one of several, such as:

* A constant or regular quarterly payment.
* A constant pattern with regularly recurring increases—perhaps the same quarter each year.
* A constant pattern with irregular increases.
* A constant pattern with period extras so as to avoid committing to regular increases.

In planning, any erratic pattern should be avoided.

34-10 LONG-TERM DEBT RATIOS

The subject of debt capacity is discussed in Chapter 33. However, the management of shareholders' equity usually must always keep debt relationships in mind when planning future financing—whether they be debt or equity.

There are two principal ratios used by rating agencies and the financial marketplace in judging the debt worthiness (or the value of equity) of an enterprise:

* Ratio of long-term debt to equity.
* Ratio of long-term debt to total capitalization.

The first ratio is calculated as:

$$\text{long-term debt to equity} = \frac{\text{long-term debt}}{\text{shareholders' equity}}$$

It compares the investment of the long-term creditors to that of the owners. Generally, a ratio of greater than 1 is an indication of excessive debt. However, a company ratio should be compared to others in the industry (the leaders) or to industry averages, such as those published by Dun & Bradstreet, Inc.

The second ratio is calculated in this fashion:

$$\text{long-term debt to total capitalization} = \frac{\text{long-term debt}}{\substack{\text{total capitalization} \\ \text{(including long-term debt)}}}$$

Again, a ratio of greater than 50%, as a rule of thumb, reflects excessive use of debt. Comparisons should be made with selected industry members (judged to be prudent businessmen) and industry averages.

34-11 OTHER TRANSACTIONS AFFECTING SHAREHOLDERS' EQUITY

In the management of shareholders' equity, any actions that are expected to impact this element of the financial statements should be reflected in the plans—the annual plan or the long-range plan, as may be appropriate. While earnings and dividends have been discussed, there are a host of other transactions that might be involved. These include:

- Repurchase of common shares.
- Conversion of preferred shares or convertible debentures.
- Dividend reinvestment programs.
- Exercise of stock options.
- New issues of shares.
- Special write-offs or adjustments.

Before approving any such actions or agreements on such matters, the management should consider their impact on debt capacity—especially where debt ratios already are high.

34-12 LONG-TERM EQUITY PLANNING

For those entities with a practical financial planning system, the long-term planning sequence might be something like this:

- The company financial management has determined, or determines, what is an acceptable capital structure and gets the agreement of management and the board of directors.

- As a step in the long-range financial planning, the amount of funds required in excess of those available is determined by year, in an approximate amount.
- Based on the needs over several years, the desired capital structure, the relative cost of each segment of capital (debt or equity), the cost of each debt issue, and any constraints imposed by credit agreements, or the judgment of management, the long-term fund requirements are allocated between long-term debt and equity.
- For the annual business plan, any actions deemed necessary in the first year of the long-range plan are incorporated with the other usual annual transactions to form the equity budget for the year.

This is another way of saying that, ordinarily, the needs of additional equity capital are known some time in advance. They can be planned to take advantage of propitious market conditions, under generally acceptable terms, with the result that the cost of capital is usually competitive.

Normally, good planning will let management know well in advance the amount and timing of the requirements; it is not a sudden discovery. And the company continues to move toward its desired optimum capital structure.

(a) ALLOCATING LONG-TERM FUNDS BETWEEN DEBT AND EQUITY

Now, let us provide some illustrations of these points. And let us assume that the company management has agreed with the recommendation of the CFO, concurred in by the controller, and that the capital structure should be as follows:

Segment	Preferred Structure	Minimally Acceptable Structure
Long-term debt	20.0%	25.0%
Shareholders' equity	80.0	75.0
Total	100.0%	100.0%

Moreover, at the end of the current year (19XX) the capital structure is expected to be (unacceptable):

Long-term debt	31.5%
Shareholders' equity	68.5
Total	100.0%

In the process of completing the strategic planning cycle and the related long-range financial plan, the required long-term funds, without designation as to type or source, are estimated to be $67 million in three years, as reflected in Figure 34-4, for

Figure 34-4 Long-Term Fund Requirements.

The Johnson Company
FUND REQUIREMENTS
LONG-RANGE PLAN
(dollars in millions)

Item	Current Year (Estimated)	Plan Year 1	2	3	4	5	Total
Funds Required							
Working capital	$25	$30	$36	$ 42	$ 55	$ 30	$193
Long-term debt repayment	12	12	12	12	12	15	63
Fixed assets	15	14	40	50	15	40	159
Dividends	8	9	10	12	14	15	60
Total	$60	$65	$98	$116	$ 96	$100	$475
Internally Generated Funds							
Net income	$40	$45	$50	$ 60	$ 70	$ 75	$300
Depreciation	10	12	20	25	28	31	116
Total	$50	$57	$70	$ 85	$ 98	$106	$416
Funds required (excess)	$10	$ 8	$28	$ 31	$ (2)	$ (6)	$ 59
Cumulative funds required (net)	$10	$ 8	$36	$ 67	$ 65	$ 59	

a program of substantial growth. Furthermore, after a slight hesitation in plan years 4 and 5, management thinks the cycle is to repeat again.

Now, here, are some comments looking to the year by year review for allocation purposes between long-term debt and equity:

- *General.* Since the cost of equity capital is highest, and issuance of new equity tends to dilute earnings, equity capital should generally be used sparingly—only to maintain the borrowing base and to reach and remain at the desired capital structure.
- *Current Year.* At the end of the current year, equity will provide only 68.5% of capital (Figure 34-5)—as compared to management's target of 80% and a minimally acceptable level of 75%. Obviously, the debt share of capitalization is too high.
- *Plan Year 19X1.* Given the start of an acceleration in annual earnings, management decides to hold the dividend payout ratio to 20%, and to borrow the needed $8 million under the term loan agreement (interest rate of 15%). The equity share of capitalization, even so, will increase from 68.5% to 72%.
- *Plan Year 19X2.* With $28 million in new funds required, the company decides, in view of the heavy investment in fixed assets and a lower borrowing rate available (12%), to issue a new mortgage bond. Some of the funds will be "taken down" or received this plan year and the balance in the next year. Despite the high level of borrowing, the equity share remains at 72%. The management

Figure 34-5   Long-Term Fund Allocation.

The Johnson Company
ALLOCATION OF LONG-TERM FUNDS
BETWEEN DEBT AND EQUITY
FOR THE PLAN YEARS 19X1 THROUGH 19X5, AND CONTINGENCY YEARS 19X6 AND 19X7
(dollars in millions)

Year/Item	Beginning Balance	Net Income	Dividends	New Equity Offering	Ending Balance	Year-end Percentage of Capitalization
Shareholders' Equity						
Current year ...	$260	$40	$ 8	$—	$292	68.5%
Plan years						
19X1	292	45	9	—	328	72.0
19X2	328	50	10	—	368	72.0
19X3	368	60	12	—	416	72.0
19X4	416	70	14	—	472	76.0
19X5	472	75	15	50	582	81.0
Contingency years						
19X6	582	80	16	—	646	80.0
19X7	646	85	17	—	714	83.0

	Beginning Balance	Debt Repayments	New Funds	Ending Balance	
Long-term Debt					
Current year—estimate					
Term loan	$100	$10	$—	$ 90	
Mortgage bonds—present .	46	2	—	44	
	146	12	—	134	31.5
Plan Years					
19X1					
Term loan	90	10	8	88	
Mortgage bond—present	44	2	—	42	
	134	12	8	130	28.0
19X2					
Term loan	88	10	—	78	
Mortgage bond—present	42	2		40	
Mortgage bond—new ..	—	—	28	28	
	130	12	28	146	28.0
19X3					
Term loan	78	10	—	68	
Mortgage bond—present	40	2	—	38	
Mortgage bond—new ..	28		31	59	
	146	12	31	165	28.0
19X4					
Term loan	68	68		—	
Mortgage bond—present	38	2		36	
Mortgage bond—new ..	59	—	58	117	
	165	70	58	153	24.0

Figure 34-5   (continued)

	Beginning Balance	Debt Repayments	New Funds	Ending Balance	
19X5					
Mortgage bond—present	36	13	—	23	
Mortgage bond—new ..	117	2	—	115	
	153	15	—	138	19.0
Contingency Years					
19X6					
Mortgage bond—present	23	13	—	10	
Mortgage bond—new ..	115	10	—	105	
Debenture—new			50	50	
	138	23	$50	165	20.0
19X7					
Mortgage bond—present	10	10		—	
Mortgage bond—new ..	105	10		95	
Debenture	50	—		50	
	$165	$20		$145	17.0

Note: The sum of the equity capitalization share at year end and that of long-term debt equals 100%.

decides it can "live with" such a level—for a temporary period, given the high level of income.

- *Plan Year 19X3.* The balance of the new mortgage bond proceeds covers the requirements with no reduction in the equity share of capitalization.

- *Plan Year 19X4.* With the net income now at a level of $70 million, and a proposal by an insurance company to provide new funds through a new mortgage bond, management decides to (a) accept this new loan of $58 million and (b) pay off the more expensive term loan. Given the continued high level of earnings, equity capital at year end will provide 76% of the capitalization. This is within the minimally acceptable standard used by the company.

- *Plan Year 19X5.* In this last year of the 5-year long-range plan, management believes the growth cycle is ready to start again. Without going through the complete long-range planning cycle again, it asks the financial vice president to estimate fund requirements for two more years—the "contingency" years. This quick review discloses that another $50 million will be needed in 19X6, with *possibly* a limited amount required also in 19X7. Accordingly, to raise the equity capitalization to the desired 80% level (19X6 borrowings considered) and to provide the needed equity base for the 19X6 borrowings and expansion in future years, it plans for an issue of $50 million in equity funds.

The management and board of directors feel comfortable with the increased equity base both in the event of a downturn in business for a limited period, or should it need to borrow additional funds.

The summary of the planned debt reduction, new indebtedness to be incurred, shareholders' equity, and capitalization percentages is given in Figure 34-6. These planned capitalization changes also will be reflected in the statements of planned financial position for the years ended December 31, 19X1 through 19X5.

(b) OTHER SUGGESTIONS IN MANAGING THE CAPITAL STRUCTURE

Section 34-12 provides guidance in allocating required funds annually between debt and equity. The disposition depends on the urgency of attaining a given preferred capital structure, or meeting debt indenture constraints, or other limitations. But managing the capital structure involves more than allocating the new capital needs between debt and equity. It also includes watching for signals that funding problems are slowly (or faster) developing, as well as providing safeguards against unwarranted action by the suppliers of funds.

A few of the steps that might be taken by financial management to avoid being caught off guard could include these:

- *Be sensitive to those product lines which provide the highest return on capital as compared to those that consume or require relatively heavy amounts of capital, and produce a low rate of return.*

   Thus, if a small share of the products requires, say, 70% of the new capital needs, and provides at least 70% of the return on capital, then the situation seems satisfactory. If, however, the products consuming 70% of the capital supply but a small return, then the matter requires careful monitoring. Perhaps a hurdle rate is needed by product line, or geographical area, or other factor. Then, careful estimates of requirements, by year, and expected return, by year, are made. Finally, actual performance then should be monitored to see if the expected increasing yields are forthcoming. Conservatism is required in predicting the capital requirements as well as the yield.

- *Continuously monitor the equity markets in an effort to judge when new equity should be acquired.*

   There are several stock market indicators to be followed which provide clues on the strength of the market, whether the market is overvalued, and whether new capital stock may be sold without diluting earnings. Included are these:

   —The S&P 500 price earnings ratio, as well as the price/earnings ratio of the company stock.

   —The S&P 500 dividend yield and the yield of the company security.

   —Price-to-book ratio. Typically the price of a stock is considerably higher than its book value. One major reason is inflation, since book value understates the replacement cost of the underlying assets. Since about 1950, the S&P Industrials index has moved in a wide band defined in market bottoms as one times book value, and 2.5 times book value near market tops.

   So, this ratio may be a signal as to whether the market is overvalued. This price-to-book measure sometimes is less significant than others due to the influence of large stock buy-back programs, corporate restructuring, or merger frenzy.

Figure 34-6 Summary of Planned Changes in Capital Structure.

The Johnson Company
PLANNED CHANGES IN CAPITAL STRUCTURE
PLAN YEARS 19X1 THROUGH 19X5
(dollars in millions)

Item	Interest Rate	Beginning Balance 1/1/X1 Amount	Percent	Increase (Decrease) 19X1	19X2	19X3	19X4	19X5	Ending Balance 12/31/X5 Amount	Percent
Long-term Debt										
Term loan (existing)	15%	$ 90		$(10) { 8	$(10)	$(10)	$(68)		$ —	—
Mortgage bond (existing)	14%	44		(2)	(2)	(2)	(2)	$(13)	23(a)	
Mortgage bond (new)	12%	—		—	28			(2)	26	
Mortgage bond (new)	11.5%	—		—		31	58		89	
Total		134	31.5%	(4)	16	19	(12)	(15)	138	19.0%
Shareholders' Equity										
Beginning balance		292							292	
Net income		—		45	50	60	70	75	300	
Dividends		—		(9)	(10)	(12)	(14)	(15)	(60)	
Net issue		—		—	—	—	—	50	50	
Subtotal		292	68.5%	36	40	48	56	110	582	81.0%
Total		$426	100.0%	$32	$56	$67	$44	$95	$720	100.0%

Note: (a) To be paid off in 19X6—$13 million; 19X7—$10 million.

—The market breadth. Changes in the Dow Jones average vs. the S&P 500 or the Nasdaq index.

—The relative trading volume. A high volume of, say, more than 200 million shares traded is said to be the sign of a strong market. Such factors, as well as the advice of investment bankers, may aid management in deciding on the approximate timing of a new stock issue.

- *Be careful in the search for the lowest cost sources of capital.*

  Not only must the cost be competitive, but the method and terms should be acceptable. Thus, in a private placement, perhaps the provisions should include a buy-back option to avoid the creation of a major voting block. Or maybe the acquisition of a cash-heavy source (existing cash balances and high cash flow) may be feasible.

- *Periodically check the cost of carrying current assets vs. the return.*

  Must a switch be made from asset intensive activities to low-cost service type business?

- *Analyze existing investment in assets for sales candidates or improved utilization possibilities.*

  Strategic planning implies more than calculating the changes in each asset category each year, based on expected operations and existing turnover rates. It requires an analysis of turnover to see where improvements can be made (e.g., use of JIT inventory methods) or idle assets, such as land which may be sold.

- *Relate predictable seasonal asset investment patterns, or cyclical ones, to incentives so as to reduce capital requirements.*

  Customers can be given special terms for early orders or early payment. Or, if an economic upturn is anticipated, this knowledge can be used to advantage in inducing earlier-than-usual orders.

Proper strategic planning should look beyond operational expectations to wise asset usage (and prudent use of supplier credits).

34-13 THE SHORT-TERM PLAN FOR SHAREHOLDERS' EQUITY

In terms of management of shareholders' equity, the emphasis should be on planning— especially long-term planning so as to achieve the proper capital structure and use it as the basis for prudent borrowing. Additionally, the many other aspects already discussed need to be reviewed, and policies and practices developed or continued that will enhance the shareholders' value.

Having said this, the annual business plan for the next year or two should reflect all anticipated near-term actions that impinge on the equity section or on the financial statements. When completed, that section of the plan relating to shareholders' equity may be summarized as in Figure 34-7.

34-14 OTHER CONSIDERATIONS

(a) DIVIDEND REINVESTMENT PROGRAMS

A supplementary facet of dividend policy is the question of offering a dividend reinvestment plan to investors. Under such a plan, shareholders may invest their cash

Figure 34-7 Budget for Shareholders' Equity.

The Jones Company
STATEMENT OF PLANNED CHANGES IN SHAREHOLDERS' EQUITY
FOR THE PLAN YEAR 19XX
(dollars in thousands)

Month	Beginning Balance	Estimated Net Income	Dividend Payments	Purchase of Treasury Shares(a)	Estimated Dividend Reinvestments	Estimated Options Exercised	Ending Balance
January	$158,500	$ 2,650		$1,000			$160,150
February	160,150	2,410		1,000		$ 500	162,060
March	162,060	2,790	$1,720		$ 80		163,210
April	163,210	2,840					166,050
May	166,050	2,620		1,200		500	167,970
June	167,970	2,530	1,620		100		168,980
July	168,980	2,600		1,000			170,580
August	170,580	2,860				500	173,940
September	173,940	2,820	1,620		100		175,240
October	175,240	2,770		1,000			177,010
November	177,010	2,710				700	180,420
December	180,420	2,800	1,520		100		181,800
Total	$158,500	$32,400	$6,480	$5,200	$380	$2,200	$181,800

Note: (a) Board to be asked to authorize 130,000 shares at average price of $40 per share.

dividends in the common stock of the company—sometimes at market price, usually with no brokerage fee, and sometimes at a discount, that is, 5% of the market price. Many dividend investment marketing plans utilize shares purchased in the open market. Others permit the issue of original shares directly by the company.

Dividend investment plans have now been expanded to permit the purchase of additional shares over and above the dividend amount with cash payments—sometimes with a ceiling on such quarterly or annual purchases, say, of $5,000,000. Also, some companies permit the preferred shareholders or bond holders to purchase common shares with the quarterly or semiannual dividend or interest payments.

Financial officers should consider such a practice. The costs of operating the program vs. the probable level of participation (based on industry experience, etc.) should be weighed. Trustees who handle such plans for other corporations—competitors or otherwise—may be helpful sources of information.

(b) STOCK DIVIDENDS AND STOCK SPLITS

This chapter is not intended to be a treatise on the types of stocks that may be issued or their advantages or disadvantages, and the many related subjects. However, the controller should be aware of the accounting treatment of stock dividends as well as stock splits and the arguments for and against the issuance of such designated shares.

Basically, the New York Stock Exchange has ruled that the issuance of 25% or less of stock is a stock dividend and that the issuance of more than 25% is a stock split. Both are essentially paper transactions that do not change the total equity of the company but do increase the number of pieces or shares. However, depending on state law, the accounting treatment may differ. Thus a stock split may not change retained earnings; only the par or stated value is changed. A stock dividend may cause the paid-in-capital accounts and retained earnings to be modified (but not the *total* equity).

The controller should be aware of the pros and cons, the expense involved, and the procedure for issuance of dividends, or splits, or reverse splits.

(c) REPURCHASE OF COMMON SHARES

Another subject to be considered by the financial management is the repurchase of common shares. Conceptually, a company is enfranchised to invest capital in the production of goods or services. Hence it should not knowingly invest in projects that will not provide a sufficiently high rate of return to adequately compensate the investors for the risk assumed. In other words, the enterprise should not invest simply because funds or capital are available. Business management should identify sufficiently profitable projects that are consistent with corporate strategy, determine the capital required, and make the investment. Hence shareholders might interpret the purchase of common stock as the lack of available investment opportunities. To some, the purchase of company stock is not an "investment" but a return of capital. It is "disfinancing."

Some legitimate reasons for the purchase of common stock are listed here:

1. Shares may be needed for stock options or employee stock purchase plans, but the management does not wish to increase the total shares outstanding.
2. Shares are required in the exercise of outstanding warrants or for the conversion of outstanding convertibles, without issuing "new" shares.
3. Shares are needed for a corporate acquisition.

Some guidelines to be heeded in considering a decision to repurchase shares are these:

1. If a company is excessively leveraged, it might do well to use cash to pay down existing long-term debt to reach the capital structure goal it envisages and not repurchase common shares.

2. The management should examine its cash requirements for a reasonable time into the future, including fixed asset requirements, project financing (working capital) needs, and other investment options, before it concludes that excess cash is available and that the equity capital genuinely is in excess of the apparent long-term demands.

3. The cash dividend policy should be examined to see that it helps increase the market price of the stock.

4. Only after such a review, should the conclusion be reached to dispose of "excess equity" through the purchase of the company stock.

Given these conditions, timing may be important. Thus if the market price of the stock is below book value, the purchase of shares in fact increases the book value of the remaining shares. It might be prudent to purchase shares below book value rather than at a price that dilutes the shareholder equity.

(d) CAPITAL STOCK RECORDS

An administrative concern in the management of shareholders' equity relates to the maintenance of necessary capital stock records. In the larger companies, the stock ledgers and transfer records are kept by the transfer agent. The information relative to payment of dividends on outstanding shares, for example, is secured from this source. Quite often the data base is contained on computer files, and any number of sortings can produce relevant data regarding ownership:

- Geographical dispersion.
- Nature of owners (individual, institution, etc.).
- History and timing of purchases.
- Market price activity.
- Volume of sales, etc.

Under these circumstances a ledger control account for each class of stock is all that is maintained by the company.

If a corporation conducts its own transfer department, then a separate account must be maintained for each stockholder regarding each class of stock. An illustrative simple form is shown in Figure 34-8. The ledger might contain the following information:

1. Name and address of holder with provision for address change.

2. Date of changes in holdings.

3. Certificate numbers issued and surrendered.

4. Number of shares in each transaction.

5. Total number of shares held.

Figure 34-8 Capital Stock Ledger Sheet.

Name and Address	John C. Doe 4161 Maxwell St. Toledo, Ohio 43612						
Common							

Old Balance	Date	Page	Certificate No.		No. of Shares		New Balance
			Dr.	Cr.	Dr.	Cr.	
	Dec. 12, 19XX	20		C 122		100	100
100	Jan. 16, 19X1	31		C 196		50	150
150	Nov. 17, 19X1	110	C 321		100		50

Optional information might include a record of dividend payments and the data mentioned above for the computer files.

The stock ledgers should be supported by registration and transfer records that give the details of each transaction. Transfer journals are not required in all states. In circumstances that justify it economically, computer applications may be desirable.

Finally, of course, sufficient records must be maintained to satisfy the reporting needs of the federal and state government—foreign holdings, large holdings, etc.

The management, of course, has an interest in monitoring, perhaps monthly, large holdings and the changes therein. Such a review may provide signals about possible take-over attempts, etc. For this purpose, as well as soliciting proxies, the services of outside consultants, such as Georgeson & Co., that specialize in such matters, may be used.

34-15 SELECTED REFERENCES

Childs, John F., *Encyclopedia of Long-Term Financing and Capital Management.* Englewood Cliffs, NJ: Prentice-Hall, 1976.

Day, George S., and Liam Fahey, "Putting Strategy into Shareholder Value Analysis," *Harvard Business Review,* March–April 1990, pp. 156–162.

Mullins, David W., Jr., "Does the Capital Asset Pricing Model Work?" *Harvard Business Review,* Jan.–Feb. 1982, pp. 105–113.

Porter, Michael E., "Capital Disadvantage: America's Failing Capital Investment System," *Harvard Business Review,* Sept./Oct. 1992, pp. 65–82.

Weston, J. Fred, and Eugene F. Brigham, *Managerial Finance* (4th ed.). New York: Holt, Rinehart & Winston, Inc., 1972.

PART FIVE

FINANCIAL AND RELATED REPORTS

CHAPTER 35

Improving External Financial Reporting

35-1 INTRODUCTION

Part Five, "Financial and Related Reports," deals with the format and practices regarding the various major groupings of reports prepared largely under the supervision of the company controller. The purpose is to illustrate some of the currently more acceptable or required formats and to discuss some of the better reporting practices. The suggestions that are made are conservative and serve as proven, successful communication devices—especially in the management arena.

In the external financial reporting area, there is considerable discussion about the need for major changes. The exchanges of ideas by various interested parties has not yet resulted in any recommendations to or by the American Institute of CPAs, but this should happen as attempts at implementation commence. Since the result of such efforts may produce major changes in public reporting practices (and impact some internal reporting), this broad movement is discussed before reviewing specific U.S. reporting practices in later chapters. To be effective, the controller must keep up-to-date on these developments.

35-2 SOME RELEVANT BACKGROUND

The field of accounting may be classified in these categories: management accounting, financial accounting (and reporting), tax accounting, not-for-profit accounting, international accounting, certain specialized areas of accounting (e.g., oil and gas), and national income accounting. These categories are discussed in Chapter 4.

While the controller as the chief accounting official of a company is often concerned with all these types of accounting, his or her attention probably is devoted much of the time to two groupings:

> *Management Accounting.* Management accounting is internal accounting specifically designed to meet the informational needs of managers. It consists of data used in making business decisions, and in the planning and control of operations at various administrative levels of a business enterprise or a not-for-profit organization. This is the type of information emphasized in this volume of *Controllership,* encompassing as it does, the activities of the management accountant. Such data is much more detailed than is considered appropriate or necessary for much external financial reporting—even though the same system often accumulates and processes the same accounting information for both management and external purposes.

> *Financial Accounting (and Reporting).* A more precise but cumbersome title for this category would be *general purpose external financial accounting and reporting.* This branch of accounting is concerned with general purpose financial statements of both business enterprises and not-for-profit organizations. The data are identified as general purpose external financial statements because several groups have common interests and common informational needs. These entities include investors, creditors, and other resource providers. These groups generally lack the power to compel the entity to supply the accounting data they think they need. They must rely on information made available by the entity.

The controller is largely responsible for seeing that (a) management has the accounting data needed for making business decisions in planning and control; and (b) for the timely issuance of accurate and reliable financial data to the public.

Yet, though the data may emanate from the same data bank, there are some key differences. This is a time of extensive change; and with changes come increased business risks. Business is characterized by increased globalization, technological innovations, differences in the capital markets, new types of financial instruments, new products and new markets, among other things. With such complexities, the information needs of investors and creditors are evolving. The timeliness of information also has been redefined. Advances in information technology, combined with the impact of new products in new markets, with new competitors, have increased the speed and volume of business transactions and the need for customers, investors, creditors, and others to know, on a timely basis, the impact of important changes on the entity. Significant delay can have serious consequences.

The evolving nature of accounting and financial reporting and attempts to improve the process is covered in the following sections.

35-3 EVOLUTION OF ACCOUNTING PRINCIPLES AND PRACTICES

In the management accounting area, the controller and other accounting executives operate in an environment where sufficient leeway or flexibility exists so that financial data can be analyzed, classified, and presented to meet the needs of the management. For example, in evaluating capital expenditures, the impact on net income might be reflected as in Figure 32-10, using "generally accepted accounting principles." Yet, if such a presentation did not make clear the complete story deemed essential, the controller might have prepared an income statement, similar to Figure 32-11, using other modified accounting. Communicating certain opinions usually is quite easy. But communicating to the general public or others who need general purpose financial statements often presents problems of comparability and standards. Most such statements refer to being prepared "in accordance with generally accepted accounting principles."

Yet the term "accounting principles" for a long period was somewhat elusive. Accordingly, different organizations or individuals—all accounting oriented—developed their version of what was variously called principles, standards, postulates, conventions, or concepts. During an extensive period, beginning in the 1937–1942 era, much public discussion took place as to the nature of accounting principles.

But even as late as the 1970s, none of the statements had come to be accepted or relied upon as the definitive statement of accounting's basic principles. There were essentially two schools: One group believed that accounting principles were generalized or drawn from practice without reference to a systematic or theoretical foundation. Another school was of the opinion that accounting principles are based on a few fundamental premises that, together with the principles, provide a framework for solving the accounting problems encountered in practice. It has been largely through the efforts of the Financial Accounting Standards Board (FASB) that a conceptual framework for financial accounting and reporting was developed. Since this initial effort in 1976, there has been continued improvement and development of other FASB statements.[1]

In the late 1980s and into the 1990s, there have been renewed calls for improvement in financial statements and reporting.

35-4   RECENT EFFORTS TO IMPROVE FINANCIAL ACCOUNTING AND REPORTING

The Concepts Statement No. 1 "Objectives of Financial Reporting by Business Enterprises" issued by the FASB in November 1978 states:

> Financial accounting and reporting is not an end in itself but is intended to provide information that is useful to present and potential investors, creditors, other resource providers, and other users outside an entity in making rational investment, credit, and similar decisions about it.

A good reporting system makes possible the efficient allocation of capital that in turn fuels economic growth under the private enterprise system. Capital markets depend on reliable financial information to operate properly. Moreover, to carry the process a step further, the financial decision makers depend upon the independent auditor for assistance that the information is indeed reliable. For the above-stated objective of financial accounting and reporting to be effective, the user must believe the process is

---

[1] See *Accountant's Handbook, Seventh Edition,* D. R. Carmichael, Steven B. Lilien, and Martin Mellman (eds.), Chapter 1, (New York: John Wiley & Sons, 1991) for a comprehensive discussion of the evolution.

sound. Highly publicized business failures raised questions not only about financial statements themselves but also about the effectiveness of the independent audit function, as well as the integrity, objectivity, and competence of independent auditors and the self-regulatory system under which the system exists. Hence, the American Institute of CPAs was wise, in its undertaking in 1993 an effort to review and improve financial reporting, to take a broad viewpoint and consider these five aspects of the process:[2]

1. Improving the prevention and detection of fraud.
2. Enhancing the utility of financial reporting to those who rely on it.
3. Assuring the independence and objectivity of the independent auditor.
4. Discouraging unwarranted litigation that inhibits innovation and undermines the profession's ability to meet evolving financial reporting needs.
5. Strengthening the accounting profession's disciplinary system.

From the standpoint of the controllership function, the remainder of this chapter relates to the more recent effort of improving the usefulness of external financial reporting.

35-5 FINANCIAL REPORTING: THE UNITED KINGDOM EXPERIENCE

In the United States during the early 1990s, but especially in 1993 and 1994, there were several articles published dealing with the efforts of the American Institute of CPAs, the FASB, the SEC practitioners, and others, to strengthen financial reporting in this country. One article dealt with the same concern by practitioners and others in the United Kingdom.[3] The article examined some relevant research about historical accounting vs. current value accounting.

In 1987, a research committee of the Institute of Chartered Accountants of Scotland (RCICAS) set out to find an alternative to historical cost accounting. For the United Kingdom, the committee called for a *revolution* in reporting practices which was rather different from a *gradual evolution* allegedly supported in the United States by the SEC and the AICPA. In 1988, the research committee reported its initial proposals for a financial reporting system in *Making Corporate Reports Valuable* (MCRV).

A number of conclusions and recommendations were made in the initial report, *some* of which are:

- *Financial statements.* Existing financial statements are unsatisfactory in that they (are) overly concerned with (a) form over substance, (b) the past rather than the future, (c) cost rather than value, and (d) income rather than wealth.

---

[2] Board of Directors of the American Institute of CPAs, "Meeting the Financial Reporting Needs of the Future: A Public Commitment from the Public Accounting Profession," *Journal of Accountancy*, Aug. 1993, p. 17.

[3] See the article by Tom Lee in the Selected References.

The balance sheet is an inconsistent hodgepodge of costs and values. The income statement excludes certain relevant wealth changes such as unrealized gains.

Some reporting practices are incompatible with a normal understanding of financial affairs and are almost incomprehensive to anyone other than their preparers.

- *Economic reality.* Financial statements need to reflect economic reality as well as provide to the users the same type of data required by the management to make business decisions.

The report suggested that information be provided the users on:

—Entity objectives.

—Wealth and wealth changes.

—Future expected status, performance, and resources of the entity.

—Present and future business climate.

—Ownership, control, and management status.

- *Substance over form.* It should be possible to report the economic substance of transactions rather than their legal form. Reported values could be added to identify the current state of assets and liabilities. The preferred valuation basis for assets should be net realized value.

- *Other desired disclosures.* These include segmented information, related party transactions, recent marketing or production innovations, three-year financial plans, etc.

While the initial report seemed to be couched in general terms, some subsequent studies have become specific. Practitioners on both sides of the Atlantic are in substantial agreement as to the type of data that should be made available in financial reports, and the need to make radical changes, and emphasize the need of the users.

35-6 THE JENKINS COMMITTEE: THE SPECIAL COMMITTEE ON FINANCIAL REPORTING

In 1991, the board of directors of the AICPA appointed a Special Committee on Financial Reporting, also known as the Jenkins Committee, to take a fresh look at financial reporting. The Board charged the Committee as follows:[4]

The special Committee should recommend (1) the nature and extent of information that should be made available to others by management and (2) the extent to which auditors should report on the various elements of that information. In developing its recommendations, the Special Committee should (1) determine the understanding of the information currently provided by financial statements and

---

[4] Gaylen N. Larson, "A Crisis of Confidence in Financial Reporting," *Management Accounting,* Feb. 1994, p. 52.

the perception of assurances provided by auditors and (2) evaluate the full range of information and assurances that should be made available.

The Jenkins Committee consists of 11 senior representatives from various accounting firms, 2 senior representatives from industry, and a well-known academic. To assist the effort, the FASB, the AICPA, and some of the large accounting firms have provided staff support. Moreover, representatives of the FASB and the SEC attend many of the Committee meetings.

That there is general support for the objectives of the Jenkins Committee is reflected in many widespread comments from various committees, study groups and individuals concerning financial statement deficiencies. Perhaps these piecemeal short statements are indicative:

- In their present form, financial statements are seriously incomplete.
- It is time to commit to enhancing the relevancy, usefulness, and credibility of corporate reporting.
- There is a growing irrelevance of conventional financial reporting in this new information age.
- Historically, financial statements have focused on how management has used the resources provided to it, but for the most part, financial statements do not disclose plans or forecasts—or risks and uncertainties facing the business.

In developing its recommendations, the Committee is following a practice of seeking out the view of various users, including equity investors and their advisors, creditors and their advisors, and groups representing these interests. Documents written by investors and creditors have been studied and analyzed.

The issues being considered by the Jenkins Committee vary greatly in nature. Some relate to nonfinancial information, forward-looking information, possible new accounting bases, segmented data, graphic displays, comparison of actual versus planned performance, and disclosures in footnote form.

Some of the areas being examined regarding adequate disclosure include these:[5]

- *Nonfinancial Information*

  Mission of the company

  Company objectives and strategies

  Key nonfinancial statistics used by management to run the business, e.g., average compensation per employee, prices of products or services

  Description of industry structure

- *Segment Information*

  Financial and nonfinancial information for each business segment

  Ditto for each material geographic region that presents significantly different uncertainties, risks, etc.

---

[5] For a more extensive listing of issues under consideration, *see Ibid.* pp. 53–54.

- *Leading indicators*

  Identity and future effect on key trends

  Factors or conditions management considers critical to achieving the broad company objectives

- *Accounting Issues*

  Should material noncancellable leases currently classified as operating leases by lessees be recognized as assets?

  Should nonoperating assets and liabilities be measured at current market value?

- *Issues of Display*

  Should the three categories of earnings—core earnings, net income and comprehensive income—be displayed in the income statement?

  If income statement should display core earnings, should the statement of cash flows display data such as cash flows?

- *Issues of Interim Reporting*

  Should segment information be presented quarterly?

  Should quarterly statements be a part of regular financial reporting?

  Should interim financial statements consist of a complete set of statements, including condensed notes?

Comments on current reporting practices to shareholders, before the impact of any Jenkins Committee recommendations, are made in Chapter 37.

35-7 AS AN EX-CONTROLLER SEES IT

To reiterate a statement made earlier regarding the controllership function, the chief accounting officer is involved with most of the types of accounting which are outlined. However, a great deal of time typically is directed to (a) management accounting and (b) general purpose external financial accounting and reporting. The growing professionalism of most controllers, coupled with the demands on them from management for relevant and timely financial data is reflected in sophisticated financial analyses and vastly improved presentations for internal purposes.

In the area of general purpose financial statements, the roadway is not as clear. Most of us have experienced situations in which financial statements "prepared in conformity with generally accepted accounting principles" didn't reflect what the user wanted to know. Or didn't disclose the extent of non-operating facilities or their impaired value. And we have recognized that in some situations the cost basis accounting was simply inadequate. Many controllers of public companies recognize the need for improvement in public reporting.

There is continuing progress in the nature of financial data being disclosed and in the quality of its presentation. A perusal of some 1993 annual reports to shareholders indicates further steps in making known data concerning some of the subjects under review by the Jenkins Committee. For example, the Hewlett-Packard 1993 Annual Report, in addition to many of the usual topics reviewed, has excellent commentary on: Factors that may affect future results; risk of off-balance sheet financing;

concentrations of credit risks; and estimated fair value vs. carrying value of certain financial instruments.

It is understood that some of the initial findings of the special committee have been formulated.[6] If this report or an early draft of the report of the Jenkins Committee is made available, it is hoped some of the more aggressive controllers as well as other members of the accounting profession will let their views be heard before the recommendations of the Committee are submitted to the AICPA board of directors late this spring. Continued improvement in the financial reporting process is in the best interest of all concerned—the users and the preparers.

We recognize that any additional disclosure must carefully consider:

- Competitive harm to the company.
- Litigation exposure (because the entity did not achieve plan, etc.).
- The need for clearly defined safe harbors, as well as possible tort reform.
- The cost vs. benefit trade-off of providing more data.

35-8 SELECTED REFERENCES

Jenkins, Edmund L., "An Information Highway in Need of Capital Improvements," *Journal of Accountancy,* May 1994, pp. 77–82.

King, Alfred M., "Asset Impairment. Is Current Value Accounting Sneaking in the Back Door?" *Management Accounting,* March 1994, pp. 36–39.

Larson, Gaylen N., "A Crisis of Confidence in Financial Reporting," *Management Accounting,* Feb. 1994, pp. 52–54.

Lee, Tom, "Mark to Market: The U.K. Experience," *Journal of Accountancy,* Sept. 1994, pp. 84–88.

Miller, Stephen H., "AICPA Announces Major Initiative to Strengthen Financial Reporting and Further Tort Reform Prospects," *Journal of Accountancy,* Aug. 1993, pp. 15–19.

White, Gerald I., "Financial Reporting in the Year 2000: Who Will Call the Shots?" *Financial Executive,* Jan./Feb. 1994, pp. 34–39.

---

[6] Paul H. Rosenfield, "Progress Report—AICPA Issues Report on Information Needs of Investors and Creditors," *Journal of Accountancy,* Jan. 1994, p. 21.

CHAPTER 36

Internal Management Reports

36-1 SOME BASIC PRINCIPLES

(a) MAKING THE INFORMATION EFFECTIVE

It may seem unnecessary to discuss at any length the importance of statement or report presentation. Yet costs will not be controlled, sales efforts will not be directed into the proper channels, and profit planning will not be effective unless the facts are presented to executives and supervisors in such a manner that they can understand them and will act on them. Merely to present the facts is not enough. These facts must be understood; their significance must be realized by the management team. Yes, the management must be motivated.

It is in this field, perhaps, that the accountant has performed less successfully than in others. A great deal of the reporting has been unsatisfactory. Facts have been poorly presented. There has been a tendency to submit mere tabulations or schedules.

Little or no attempt has been made to summarize or digest the data. The information must be refined and highlighted to provide the basis for executive action. If this is not done, the loss is double. The cost of preparing the data is wasted, and the corrective action is not taken for lack of necessary information.

The controller has at his or her disposal the financial data base. The staff has compiled the data and therefore understands what it means and how to use it. In turning the data into information, the controller must anticipate the needs of executives and as well as respond to their requests. In order to do this effectively, the financial staff professionals must have excellent analytic skills, be able to understand and use personal computers and computerized information, and express themselves intelligently.

Too often the controller may feel that the department managers should come to him if they want information. He would be superhuman if he could anticipate all needs. But he should take the initiative, to the extent practicable, in providing information that he feels is pertinent. Very often, he will be able to suggest a report better in scope and content than those requesting the data might have in mind. Certainly, he should possess this capability, since reporting techniques is one of his specialties. The successful controller cannot sit in an office and wait for others to ask for information. He cannot consider his work done when the figures are recorded in the books and the statements are issued. This is only the beginning.

(b) REPETITIVE AND SPECIAL REPORTS

Reports prepared in the controller's department can be classified as repetitive or special.

The repetitive report is one that is issued on a regular schedule. It should be in a consistent format that has been specially developed. Its purpose is well-known to the recipients as is the nature and meaning of the information being presented. Examples of repetitive reports are the monthly statements of income and expense and financial position and the daily or weekly reports of sales, cash, and manufacturing costs.

All reports should have an introduction. In the case of repetitive reports, the introduction is usually a brief overview of the information contained in the report.

Special reports are those prepared to identify a specific issue, for example, a cost item growing much faster than planned, or to make a major capital investment decision. Unlike repetitive reports, the format of a special report is whatever is pertinent to the contents. The introduction will clearly state the issue being addressed and, if necessary, may even include an index that outlines the decision process. All recipients should have an understanding of how the issue will be addressed. Special reports should also have a conclusion and recommendations. Alternatives to the recommendations should also be presented and the reason for their dismissal indicated.

Figure 36-1 outlines some suggested factors and steps to be considered in preparing repetitive reports as contrasted with special purpose or nonroutine reports.

(c) FIVE BASIC PRINCIPLES OF REPORT PREPARATION

In preparing effective reports for internal management purposes, the controller should observe certain general principles. Some of these principles are basic to sound management reporting; others may be regarded as subsidiary or supplemental. There are five basic and overriding guidelines.

Figure 36-1 Steps in Report Preparation.

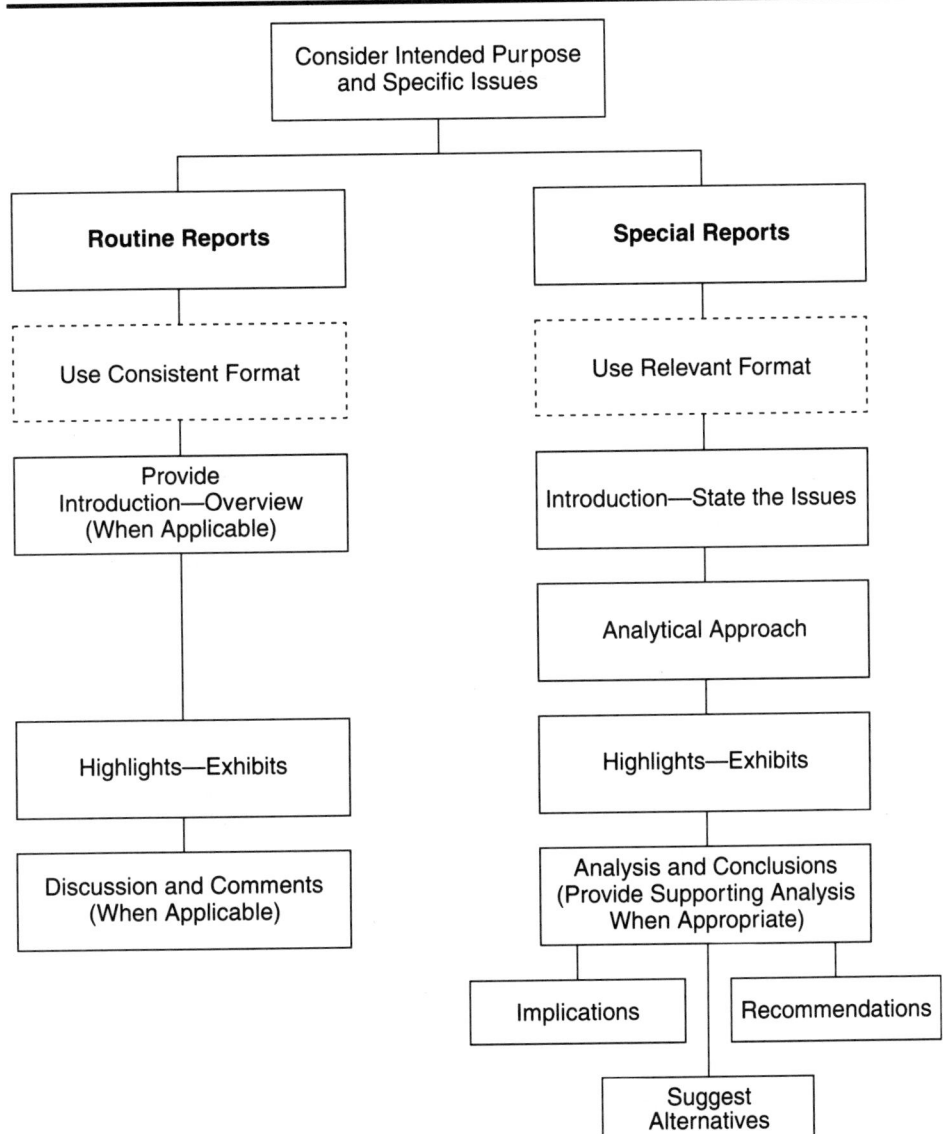

1. *The "Responsibility" Concept Should Be Employed.* Under responsibility reporting, the dissemination of facts and figures concerning revenues and costs relates to the segment of the organization being reported on. The communication concerns costs and/or revenues that can be controlled by the person being reported on or which are attributable to his efforts. Such a system avoids allocation of costs for *control* purposes to any organizational unit that does not control them and cannot be held accountable for them.

The principle is illustrated in Figure 36-2, relative to a simplified *expense* structure wherein the reporting follows the organizational chart. Since the

Figure 36-2 Responsibility Reporting—Flow of Information.

The Manufacturing Company Flow of Responsibility Reporting

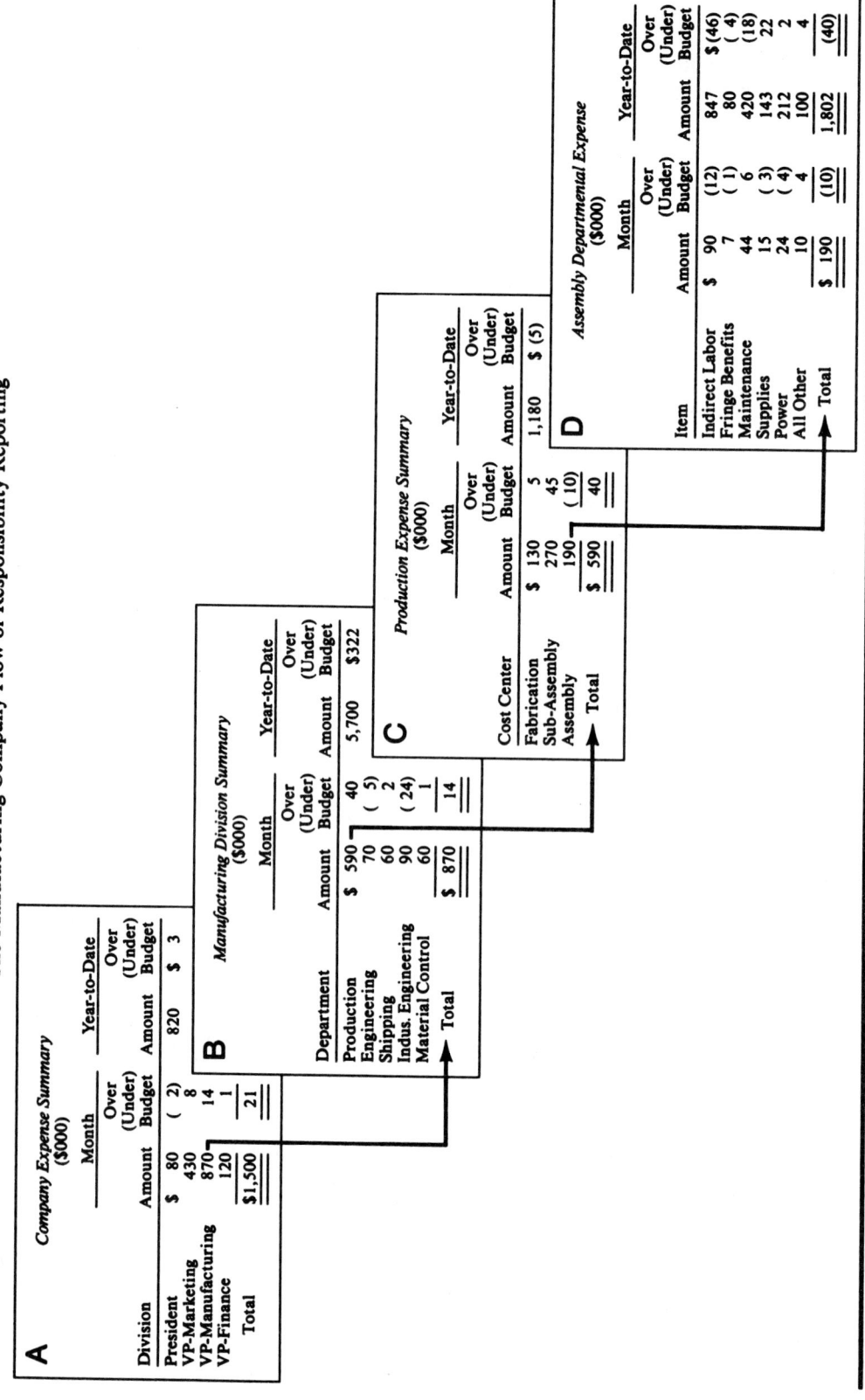

A *Company Expense Summary ($000)*

	Month		Year-to-Date	
Division	Amount	Over (Under) Budget	Amount	Over (Under) Budget
President			820	$ 3
VP-Marketing	$ 80	(2)		
VP-Manufacturing	430	8		
VP-Finance	870	14		
	120	1		
Total	$1,500	21		

B *Manufacturing Division Summary ($000)*

	Month		Year-to-Date	
Department	Amount	Over (Under) Budget	Amount	Over (Under) Budget
Production	$ 590	40	5,700	$322
Engineering	70	(5)		
Shipping	60	2		
Indus. Engineering	90	(24)		
Material Control	60	1		
Total	$ 870	14		

C *Production Expense Summary ($000)*

	Month		Year-to-Date	
Cost Center	Amount	Over (Under) Budget	Amount	Over (Under) Budget
Fabrication	$ 130	5	1,180	$ (5)
Sub-Assembly	270	45		
Assembly	190	(10)		
Total	$ 590	40		

D *Assembly Departmental Expense ($000)*

	Month		Year-to-Date	
Item	Amount	Over (Under) Budget	Amount	Over (Under) Budget
Indirect Labor	$ 90	(12)	847	$ (46)
Fringe Benefits	7	(1)	80	(4)
Maintenance	44	6	420	(18)
Supplies	15	(3)	143	22
Power	24	(4)	212	2
All Other	10	4	100	4
Total	$ 190	(10)	1,802	(40)

president is accountable for the *entire* business, he would receive an expense summary segregated by the functions incurring such expenses and assignable to the individual whom he holds responsible—item A in the illustration. In this case, the president's own departmental expenses are compared with budget, as are those of each vice-president who reports to him.

The vice-president for manufacturing receives a summary of expense performance for each organizational segment reporting to him—shown as item B in Figure 36-2. In turn, the production superintendent receives a summary on the three cost centers—item C—for which he is accountable. Finally, the departmental foreman is informed on his cost performance in detail by type of expense as reflected in item D.

Each manager may secure such further detailed reports as he desires on each area for which he is assigned responsibility, authority, or accountability.

2. *The "Exception" Principle Should Be Applied as Much as Possible.* Generally speaking, for control purposes, the out-of-the-ordinary operations should be emphasized. As the scope of a function expands, the responsible executive cannot oversee, check, or follow up on every detail. Therefore, the reporting must distinguish between those things that are progressing satisfactorily and those that need attention—the "exceptions." On such a basis, normal or routine situations do not receive prominence, and the executive need not waste time plowing through the detail of operations that are "on course." As an example, perhaps performance that exceeds budget by more than 5% should be reported on and not every deviation.

3. *In General, Figures Should Be Comparative.* Actual performance data alone usually are of little significance. Rather actual must be compared with a target or reasonable yardstick. Comparison with budget, standards, or past performance is necessary.

   As a corollary, significant trends and relationships should be revealed. Signals about what should be done or what requires attention are desirable. For example, it is one thing to report that warehouse labor costs were $10,000 for the month and quite another to indicate that such total labor cost has steadily increased despite a decline in the physical volume handled.

4. *To the Extent Practical, Data Should Be Increasingly in Summary Form for Each Successively Higher Level of Management.* It is perhaps obvious that the kind of information needed by a salesman differs from that to be furnished the sales manager. With a broad area of responsibility, the sales manager cannot look at every detail on each territory. As a general rule, reports should tend to a minimum of information rather than a maximum. Further, the communication should be long enough to get the story across—and no longer. It might be advantageous to commence each report with a summary and allow the remainder to be supporting detail that need not be read in its entirety.

5. *Reports Generally Should Include Interpretative Commentary or Be Self-Explanatory.* The primary purpose of a report is to *communicate* ideas. Anyone in the accounting profession soon learns the significance of the figures, but this is not true for many other functions. Consequently, it is usually desirable that commentary direct the attention of the reader to the important happenings and help him understand the data presented. Interpretative remarks explain the

"why" of the situation and very often indicate action taken or to be taken to correct an out-of-line condition.

(d) SOME SUPPLEMENTARY CONSIDERATIONS

These five principles are rather fundamental to a good financial reporting system. In addition, there are some other factors that will assist in getting an improved reception from the reader. These include the points described next.

1. *Reports Should Be Timely.* The frequency of issuance should be determined with care, and once a decision is reached, the reporting should be prompt. A late report is almost as useless as no report at all. Regular reports should be presented on a definite schedule. Often it will be found desirable to issue "flash" reports rather than wait for the final and exact figures. Controllers should perhaps consider first the preparation of the control reports and then the completion of the accounting process.

2. *Reports Should Be Simple and Clear.* They should be so designed that the reader will be able to secure all the essential facts with a minimum of effort. Technical accounting language should be avoided. Complicated statements should be omitted. Simplicity and clarity are requisites of all useful reports.

3. *Reports Should Be Expressed in Language and Terms Familiar to the Executive Who Will Use Them.* For example, tons, man-hours, and machine operating hours are likely to be more expressive terms to production executives than dollar costs of manufacturing. A statement that raw materials remain in the storerooms on an average of 90 days after time of receipt is likely to be more expressive than a turnover figure.

4. *Information Should Be Presented in Logical Sequence.* Just as displays attempt to show articles in natural surroundings or in use, so also a logical pattern should be followed in report presentation. Perhaps the sequence of operations should be followed in a labor report. Again, a statement of changes in financial position should indicate, first, what the significant changes are, and, next, the cause.

5. *Reports Must Be Accurate.* The information must be dependable and sufficiently accurate to satisfy the purpose of the report. Errors on reports result in a lack of confidence in them—and in the accounting department.

6. *The Form of Presentation Should Be Suited to the Executive Who Will Use It.* Statistical, graphical, or narrative or a combination of these may be used, depending on the desires and aptitudes of those who will use the report.

7. *Reports Should Be Standardized Wherever Possible.* To the extent consistent with the other rules of reporting, the style, design, and size of the report should be standardized. It is desirable, for example, that all plants of a company use a similar labor report. Further, when a report has been standardized, it is desirable to make changes only infrequently. The operating people become accustomed to a certain style, and a change may cause confusion for a time.

8. *The Report Design Should Reflect the Viewpoint of the Executive.* This requirement is quite inclusive. To begin with, the extent of responsibility and level of

supervision must be considered. Those supervisors far away from the scene of operations may require quite different information from those on the spot. The general executives are interested in general movements; the departmental executives, in the departmental performance; and the lower echelon of supervision, in the performance of individuals. In all cases, the information should be presented through the eyes of the executive and not the accountant.

9. *Reports Must Be Useful.* That a report should be useful to the executive for whom it is prepared may seem self-evident. Yet there is a tendency in some quarters to insist on "accepted form and in accordance with accepted accounting practice." For external reports, for final audited statements for creditors, stockholders, and governmental divisions this is desirable. But there should be no hesitancy in disregarding such methods in the preparation of periodic reports for managerial purposes when it is apparent that other means will provide more useful managerial data.

10. *The Cost of Report Preparation Should Be Considered.* Under ordinary circumstances the preparation of reports should be a natural process or step in the regular accounting and statistical work. But the cost of special reports should not be overlooked. Where such reports are interesting but have no particular value, the cost of preparation should be weighed in relation to the benefit. Again, when simple sketches will do the trick equally effectively, expensive artwork is to be avoided.

11. *The Care Taken in Preparing a Report Should Be Commensurate with Its Use.* Although *all* reports should be accurate and dependable, the more important a report, the greater the degree of care that should be exercised. Reports going to top executives should be double-checked, since important policy decisions may be made on the basis of information contained therein.

36-2 TYPES OF INTERNAL MANAGEMENT REPORTS

Consider the types of internal management reports a controller may be called on to prepare before discussing some of the detailed phases of report preparation. Although reports can be grouped in any one of several classifications, a very practical basis is according to their function or purpose. From experience, every controller knows that reports may fall into three groups: (1) planning reports, (2) control reports, and (3) informational reports. Planning reports deal with anticipated programs for future operations or the financial condition. As the name implies, control reports are intended to assist in the control of operations or the business by indicating areas that need corrective action. Informational reports are of a broader scope and use in that they are intended to present and interpret facts for management to use in planning and policy determination.

The distinction among these three kinds of reports is not a mere academic nicety. By recognizing the difference in purpose, the controller can plan a better system of reports. Differences in purpose result in differences in content, timing, and design. Stated more positively, the controller must know the purpose of the report before preparing it. One purpose may require one kind of cost, for example, out-of-pocket costs; another purpose may need another type of cost. It is difficult for one trained in accounting to realize how easy it is for some executives with other backgrounds to draw unwarranted or incorrect conclusions from a very routine accounting statement. By recognizing the differences in planning, control, and informational reports, the controller will be more careful in his or her interpretations and in limiting the use to which reports will be put—to the extent possible.

A brief outline of possible subdivisions of this threefold report classification follows.

(a) PLANNING REPORTS

1. *Short-Range Corporate-Wide or Division-Wide Forecasts.* Projections or programs, prepared on a regular time schedule, that deal with relatively broad sections of the company, either the entire operation or a major segment, and project results and conditions for a relatively short period of time—usually one year or less. Examples of such short-range planning reports include:

   a. Statement of estimated income and expense.

   b. Statement of estimated cash flows.

   c. Statement of budgeted capital expenditures.

   d. Statement of estimated financial condition.

2. *Special Short-Range Planning Studies of Particular Segments of the Business.* This grouping is intended to include those special studies of particularly troublesome or substandard segments on which planning attention must be focused to arrive at a suitable program. It encompasses all special studies that deal with only limited functions or geographical areas of the business. Such analyses as these might fit into this category:

   a. Product distribution in Y territory.

   b. Compensation of salesmen.

   c. Warehouse handling expense—Cleveland, Ohio.

   d. Expansion in the naphthalene market.

   e. Computer applications for credit cards.

   f. Plant location study for Los Angeles.

3. *Long-Range Forecasts.* Such studies must be rather general or "broad brush" in nature. They would include five or even ten or more years' projections of the company's activities overall or in particular areas or fields. Such studies very often are the result of joint effort with either the company's sales department or economic research groups. The controller's department forecasts the effect of proposed plans on future capital investment, cash availability, and operating results. For the company or major divisions, or even smaller segments, the reports, although less detailed, would be somewhat similar in nature to those included in the short-range planning reports.

Illustrations relating to the long-range financial plan are presented in Chapter 15.

Chapter 16 has many illustrations of annual plan or budget reports for the overall business and each function of the entity.

(b) CONTROL REPORTS

1. *Summary Control Reports.* These reports summarize the performance over a period of time, usually a month, and serve at least two useful functions: They inform higher management of the general effectiveness of performance, and they act as a check against the current control reports. Generally speaking, the current control reports should be reconciled with the summary control reports that "tie into" the financial statements. Since timeliness is a factor, some small differences are expected. Examples of summary control reports include:

   a. Statement of actual and budgeted income and expense.

   b. Statement of income and expense by products.

   c. Comparison of actual and budgeted sales by territory.

   d. Divisional or departmental summary cost reports.

   e. Summary of excess manufacturing costs by responsibility.

   f. Monthly statement of inventories.

   g. Monthly aging of accounts receivable.

2. *Current Control Reports.* These are reports, issued hourly, daily, or weekly, that point out deviations from planned or standard performance. The objective is prompt corrective action before large losses develop. Examples of this type of report include:

   a. Daily or weekly reports on sales by product, compared to quota or forecast.

   b. Daily or weekly reports on scrap or excess material usage.

   c. Real time inventory reports.

   d. Hourly, daily, or weekly reports comparing actual and standard man-hours.

   e. Monthly (or semimonthly) departmental expense statements of actual and budgeted expenses.

   f. Real time or weekly reports on cash receipts, disbursements, and balances compared to objective.

(c) INFORMATIONAL REPORTS

1. *Trend Reports.* These reports compare the results of an activity or a condition over a period of months or years to point out changes in growth or composition. They may be expressed as ratios (see Chapter 8) or in units. Trend reports cover a wide area and may relate to any income or cost items as well as assets, liabilities, and net worth in the balance sheet; or they may present relationships over a period of time, such as the percentage of selling expense to net sales.

2. *Analytical Reports.* For want of a better term, the other broad category of informational presentations is referred to as analytical reports. Essentially, analytical reports deal not especially with successive periods of time as do trend reports but more particularly with a limited time period and with reference to the composition or makeup of an item. Some illustrations of analytical reports include:

   a. Analysis of changes in gross profit or contribution margin.

   b. Analysis of sales by customer or product.

    c. Analysis of excess manufacturing costs.

    d. Analysis of changes in financial condition.

    e. Determination of break-even points.

    f. Determination of marginal income by products.

Other classifications of reports can be made, but the most important distinction for a controller to make is between reports for control purposes and those for policy and planning purposes. Quite often both types will be used in arriving at decisions.

36-3 CONTENTS OF REPORTS

The contents of an accounting report will depend on the needs of the situation. It may be a routine weekly report, or it may be a special report dealing with a particular phase of the business. The purpose of the report, the personalities of those who receive it, the subject—all these factors permit a great deal of latitude in content. Although a statement of principles may be somewhat repetitious, it would seem that the content should do the following:

1. Be restricted to the essential facts.
2. Indicate comparisons or trends and relationships.
3. Indicate areas where improvements or changes should be made.

A primary requirement, of course, is to report matters that need reporting. A vast amount of information is accumulated in the accounting records. The clerk in the corner of the factory, for example, may be busily recording facts that show the company is grossly overstocked with a certain kind of paint or that certain items in the inventory are slow moving. Although this information is in the records, if it does not get into an effective report, it might as well never have been recorded. Reports must bring to the attention of management conditions that need correction.

36-4 FREQUENCY OF REPORTS

The frequency with which reports should be issued also depends on the needs. If the situation is particularly critical or unsatisfactory, then reports would be issued more frequently than otherwise. The level of responsibility of the executive is a factor, too. Major executives, on the one hand, require monthly reports, with quarterly and yearly summaries. Some minor executives, on the other hand, such as foremen, may require hourly or daily reports of the performance of their employees. In general, the higher the level of responsibility, the less frequently the report is required.

36-5 FORM OF ACCOUNTING REPORTS

As previously observed, the form of the accounting report is to some extent determined by the content. Another primary consideration is the preference of the executives who use the reports. Some prefer more statistical detail than others; some prefer graphic presentation. In many cases, the controller may have to experiment to find the best method.

The chief accounting official and all of the financial-accounting management have available a rather wide selection of communication media in presenting the financial facts and figures of the business. The following summary outline indicates the principal forms that accounting reports might take:

1. Written.
   a. Tabular.
      1. Formal accounting statements.
      2. Statistical.
   b. Expository or narrative.
   c. Pictorial—graphic.
   d. A combination of all or some of these.
2. Oral.
   a. Formal group presentations; these may include the use of visual aids.
   b. Individual conferences.
3. Electronic.
   Which uses the form of written reports but delivers it via a computer network and terminals.

Before reviewing reporting principles or examples for each of the various levels of management, some remarks on nontabular techniques may be helpful.

(a) GRAPHIC PRESENTATIONS

The use of graphs is becoming widespread in presenting financial information. The principal advantage of graphic presentation for numerical data is the ease with which trends and relationships between figures may be visualized. Charts and similar devices minimize the time management must spend to grasp significant relationships or trouble spots. On the other hand, graphs do not readily permit the determination of a precise amount. Where the exact figure is desired, therefore, it is often desirable to accompany the charts with the related statistical tables. (See Figure 36-3.)

There are any number of methods for presenting statistical data in visual form, and there are many excellent texts on the subject. In summary, however, graphs may be divided into the following groups:

1. *Line or Curve Charts.* Variations in the data are indicated by means of a line or curve. The scale may be arithmetic, semilogarithmic, or logarithmic ruling. Straight lines (as in Figure 36-4) or bands (as in Figure 36-19) may be employed.
2. *Bar Charts.* The absolute bar charts contrast quantities by comparison of bars of varying length but uniform width. Simple percentage bar charts are constructed in a similar fashion, except that the length of the bar represents a percentage. Component bar charts may be used, wherein the bars are of the same width and length representing 100%, and the size of each segment indicates the percent of the total figure (as in Figure 36-5).
3. *Area Diagrams.* This technique contrasts quantities by comparing figures with varying areas. The most popular type is the pie chart, illustrated in Figure 36-6.

Figure 36-3   Graphs Supported by Related Statistics.

The Airconditioning Company
OPERATING RESULTS

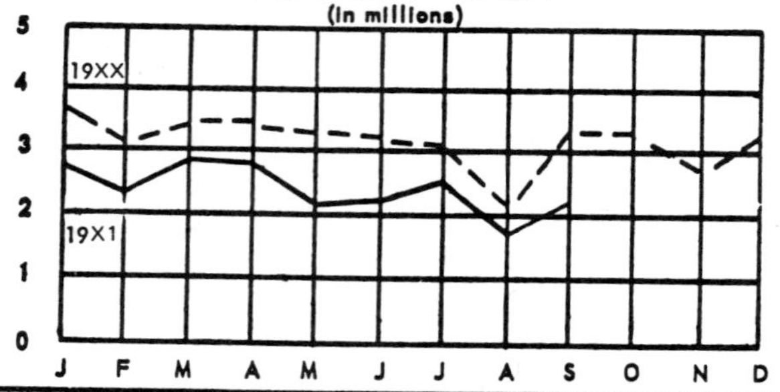

SALES BILLED – TOTAL (In millions)

MO.	MONTHLY (000) 19XX	19X1	CUMULATIVE (000) 19XX	19X1
J	3727	2791	3727	2791
F	3013	2336	6741	5127
M	3497	2800	10338	7927
A	3591	2750	13929	10677
M	3393	2133	17923	12810
J	3274	2240	20597	15050
J	3071	2533	23668	17583
A	2238	1766	25906	19350
S	3342	2300	29248	21649
O	3303		32551	
N	2740		35292	
D	3262		38553	

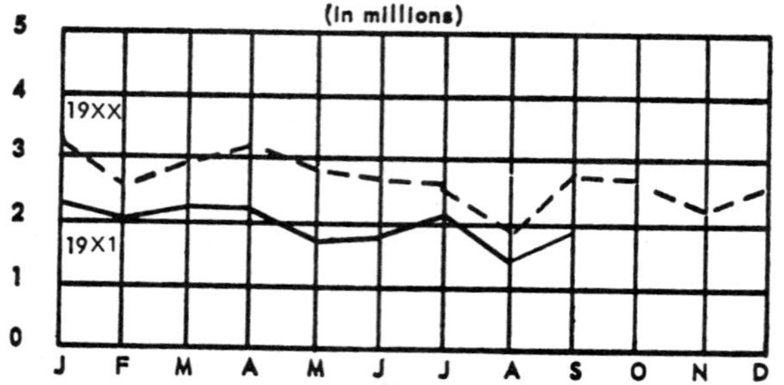

SALES BILLED – NATIONAL BRAND (In millions)

MO.	MONTHLY (000) 19XX	19X1	CUMULATIVE (000) 19XX	19X1
J	3104	2397	3104	2397
F	2512	2030	5615	4427
M	2911	2332	8526	6759
A	3158	2306	11684	9065
M	2901	1735	14585	10800
J	2741	1871	17326	12671
J	2712	2106	20038	14777
A	1911	1450	21948	16228
S	2745	1954	24694	18182
O	2739		27433	
N	2219		29652	
D	2627		32279	

SALES BILLED – PRIVATE BRAND

| | MONTHLY (000) | | | CUMULATIVE (000) | |
MO.	19XX	19X1	MO.	19XX	19X1
J	624	394	J	624	394
F	501	306	F	1125	700
M	687	467	M	1812	1168
A	433	444	A	2245	1612
M	492	398	M	2737	2010
J	533	370	J	3271	2380
J	360	426	J	3631	2806
A	327	316	A	3958	3122
S	596	345	S	4554	3467
O	564		O	5118	
N	521		N	5639	
D	635		D	6274	

SALES BILLED – PRIVATE BRAND
(In hundred thousands)

PROFIT AFTER TAXES

| | MONTHLY (000) | | | CUMULATIVE (000) | |
MO.	19XX	19X1	MO.	19XX	19X1
J	209	122	J	209	122
F	35	(29)	F	244	93
M	176	21	M	420	114
A	172	41	A	593	155
M	225	(7)	M	818	148
J	91	(68)	J	908	80
J	81	40	J	989	120
A	(94)	(101)	A	895	20
S	112	78	S	1007	98
O	121		O	1128	
N	5		N	1134	
D	216		D	1350	

PROFIT AFTER TAXES
(In hundred thousands)

Figure 36-4   Line Charts Used in Cost Presentation.

Costs and Expenses as Percent of Sales

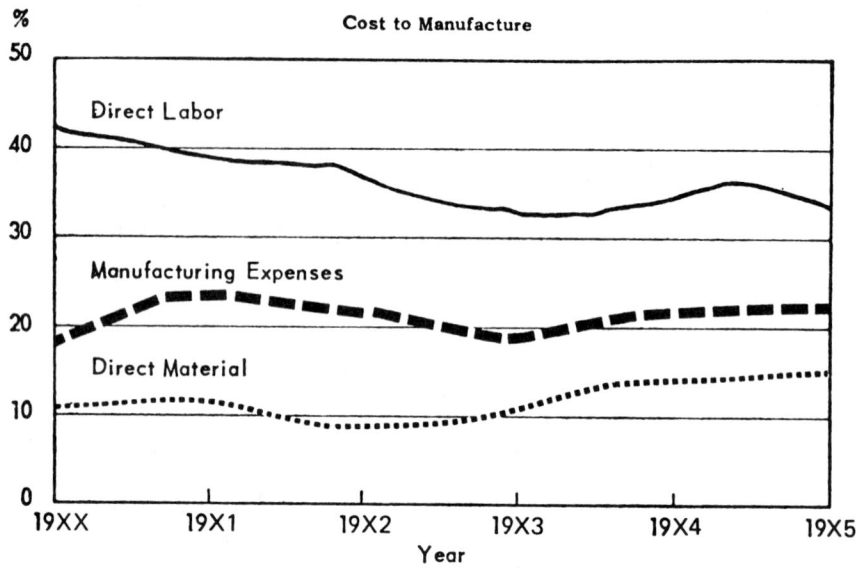

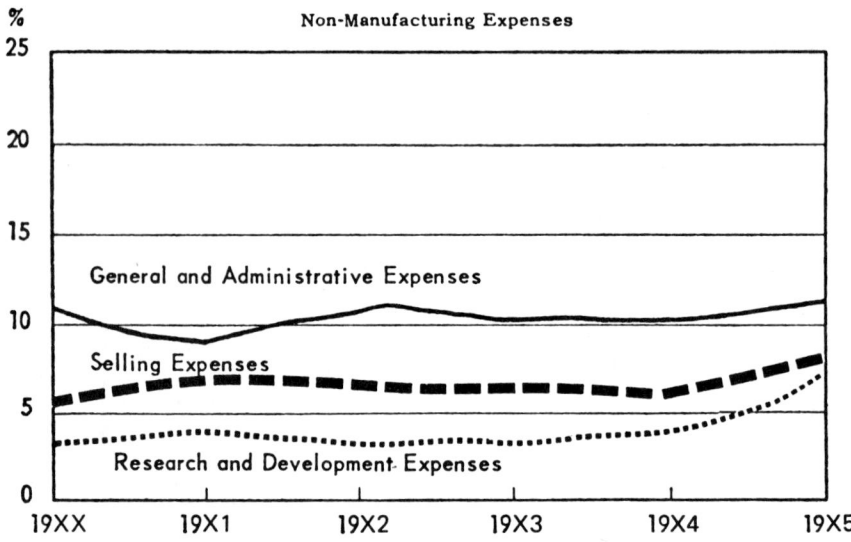

4. *Solid Diagrams.* These diagrams consist of geometric forms (cubes, spheres, cylinders, etc.) used to illustrate comparison of magnitudes through a comparison of volumes of the figures—and not the height or length of the figures. Accurate comparisons are therefore difficult to make.

5. *Map Graphs.* This method presents in pictorial form the facts in a geographic distribution.

Figure 36-5   Percentage Bar Chart Illustrating Status of Accounts Receivable.

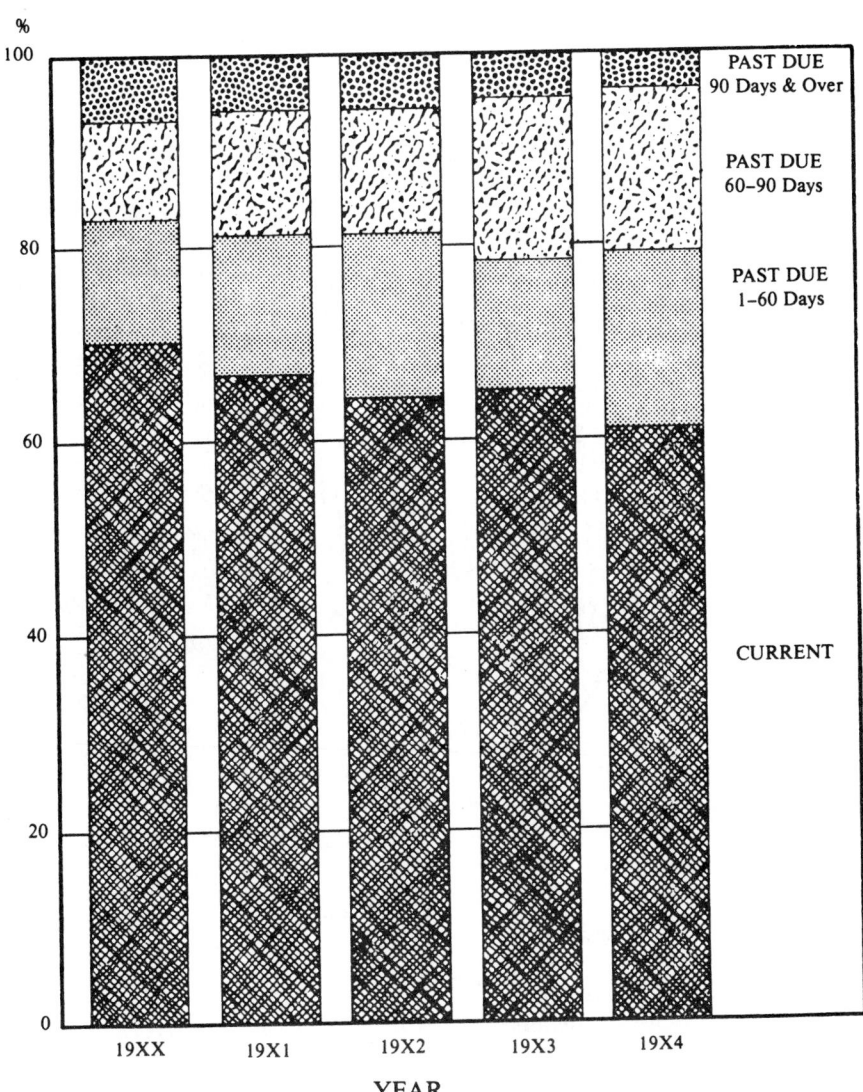

STATUS OF ACCOUNTS RECEIVABLE

The most simple and common types of graphic presentations for use with financial data are the line and bar charts. Figure 36-4 readily indicates the trend of the selected cost elements in relationship to sales. A component bar chart is used in Figure 36-7 to reveal the trend of sales, costs, and income. The relative composition of accounts receivable is well illustrated by the use of a percentage bar chart in Figure 36-5.

Charts are effective as an aid in oral presentation. Some companies follow a plan wherein a book of charts is maintained for either the entire top-management echelon or for each executive in the group. A more common practice, perhaps, is for each individual executive to maintain those particular charts he or she finds most useful.

Figure 36-6 Pie Chart Illustrating Analysis of Gross Profit.

GROSS PROFIT BY PRODUCT LINE
FOR THE TWELVE MONTHS ENDED NOVEMBER 30, 19XX

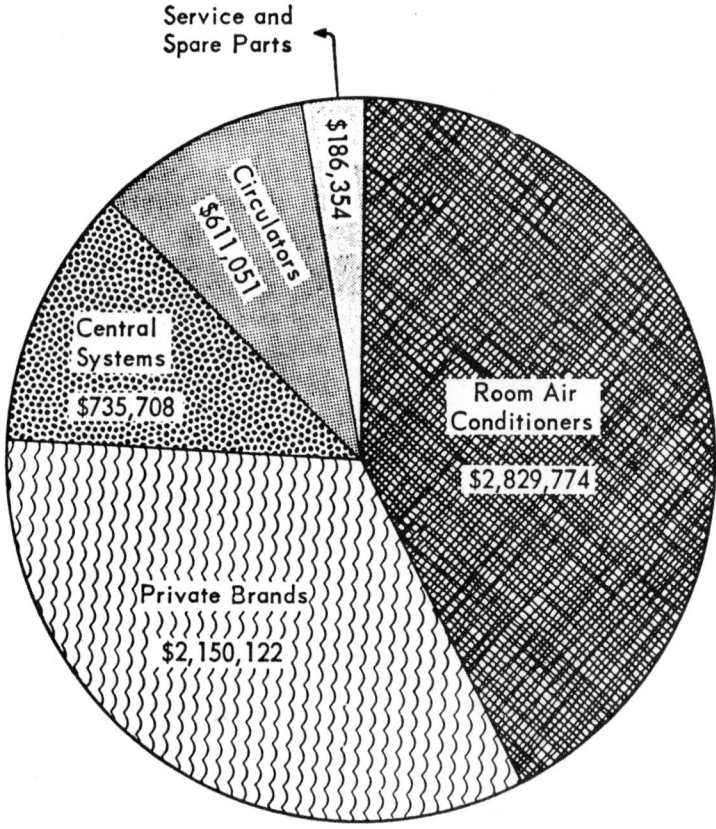

Product	% of Total
Room air conditioners	43.7
Private brand	33.2
Central systems	11.4
Air circulators	9.4
Service and spare parts	2.9
	100.0

With the rapid advancement in computer-generated graphics capabilities, all of the examples of charts and graphs that were just reviewed can be obtained as direct output of a computer. Such output is available as quickly as tabular printouts and can be modified or updated easily. Color is also available to enhance the effectiveness of graphs and charts. A computer with the necessary peripherals and software can produce:

- Traditional hard copy reports.
- Foils for use in oral reporting.
- Electronic reports via internal computer network.

Figure 36-7   Vertical Bar Chart Used to Depict Operating Results.

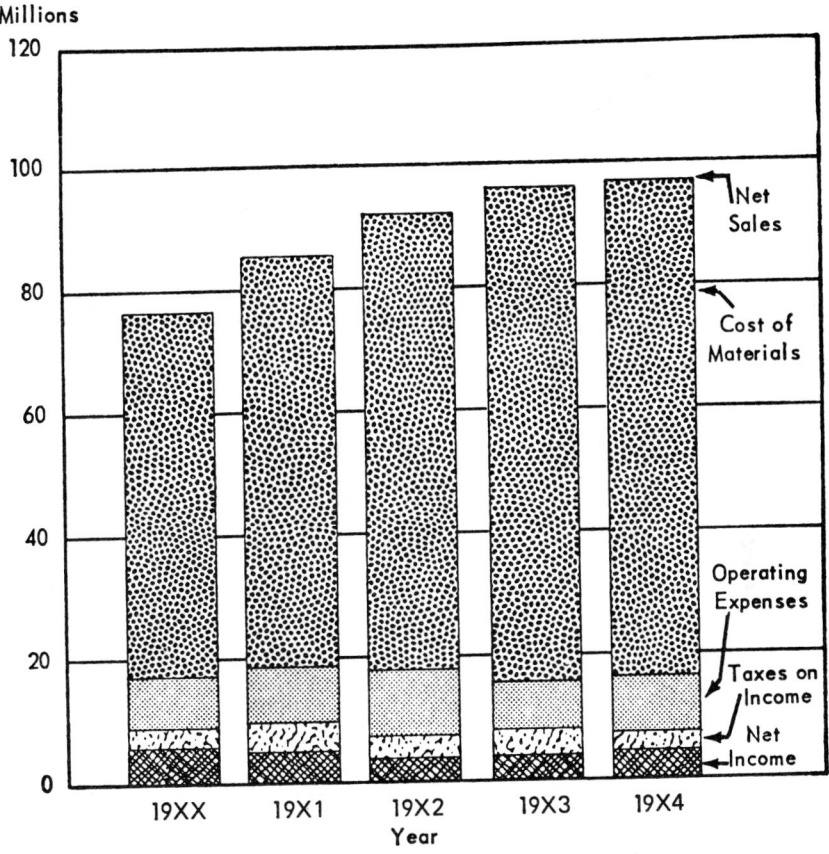

(b) "FLASH" REPORTS

Timeliness is often very important in the usefulness of financial figures. It is, therefore, found desirable in many instances to provide information that is largely, but not entirely, complete so that appropriate action may be taken. The dissemination of such data may mean a sacrificing of accuracy and the use of estimates instead of actual results, where such estimates will not impair the utility of the data. Such reports often are called "flash" reports and may be employed in a variety of circumstances. The monthly operating results in summary form—when sales volume, standard costs, and perhaps major variances are known—is an example of a quick report to meet the needs of top management. A handwritten report, in lieu of a typewritten one, may suffice. An electronic report is the quickest of all, if the recipients utilize a computer or terminal tied into a computer network. A "flash" income statement indicating the *reason* for the results is illustrated in Figure 36-8.

Illustrated in Figure 36-9 is another flash report for top management that summarizes company performance on the four important business factors—acquisitions (new orders), sales, net income, and EPS—and indicates the expected results for the fiscal year. As the year progresses, it often becomes important to predict year-end results or, in a "rolling forecast," to indicate results expected for the next 12 months.

Figure 36-8   "Flash" Report of Consolidated Net Income.

General Oil Company
FLASH REPORT - PRELIMINARY NET INCOME

H. O. Corp. Acctg.   *October, 19XX*   Confidential

November 4, 19XX

(Thousands of Dollars)	Prior Month	Current Month Actual	Current Month Better/(Worse) Than Forecast	Current Month Better/(Worse) Than Last Year	Year-to-Date Actual 1962	Year-to-Date Better/(Worse) Than 1961
1. Western Division	(2,475)	(2,200)	(1,748)	(1,012)	(9,648)	402
2. Southern Division	2,938	3,100	(100)	88	35,860	2,833
European Division	1,549	1,700	(247)	(333)	11,728	(12,272)
Arabian Oil Company	17	10	(83)	33	(881)	(724)
French African Division	(22)	(15)	(15)	(15)	(166)	(166)
3. Total European Operations	1,543	1,695	(345)	(315)	10,681	(13,172)
4. Foreign Expl. & Prod. Div.	(1,143)	(240)	119	131	(4,354)	(746)
5. Tanker Operations	(170)	(516)	(278)	(118)	(2,594)	(279)
6. Export Operations	82	146	(26)	(12)	1,331	(100)
7. Home Office	(982)	(1,039)	(42)	(284)	(10,257)	(2,994)
8. Other Subsidiaries	38	21	211	(90)	1,109	(589)
9. Consolidated Net Income	(769)	967	(2,209)	(1,612)	22,728	(14,635)
10. Preferred Dividend	311	309	—	(72)	3,444	(792)
11. Consol. Net Income applicable to Common	(480)	658	(2,209)	(1,684)	19,284	(15,427)
Per Share	$(.40)	$.05	$(.16)	$(.11)	$1.41	$(.99)

Consolidated Net Income - October - $967,000 - equal to $.05 per share after preferred
dividend. October results below current forecasted income by $2,209,000. Net income
- 10 months' operations - $22,728,000 - equal to $1.41 per common share.

Western Division - October loss - $2,200,000 - result of crude unit shutdown and further
weakening of gasoline prices to a new low for the year.

Southern Division - income for October - $3,100,000 - under estimate by $100,000.
Producing days in Texas were 8 (forecast - 9) with resulting lower crude and liquids
production.

European Division Income - $1,700,000 - up slightly over prior month - below forecast by
$247,000 - increased book depreciation charges due to revision of reserves.

Tanker Operations - loss for October - $516,000 - above forecasted loss by $278,000 -
due primarily to revised schedule for deliveries.

Supporting schedules accompany the summary and indicate for each of acquisitions, sales and net income detail the actual, planned, and expected year-end performance for each operating center. It is important to label flash reports as being "estimated" so that there is no confusion when final actual reports are available and may reflect slightly different amounts.

Computer technology can be helpful, indeed sometimes mandatory, in transmitting timely data quickly to the reader. (See Part VI on Computer Systems and Related Technology.)

(c) ORAL REPORTS

Oral communication is a very important phase of the reporting function. It can be appreciated that such personal contact permits a great saving of management time by the opportunity afforded to point out significant trends and relationships. Moreover, very

Figure 36-9 Flash Report with Updated Fiscal Year Estimate.

Company Private
ESTIMATED FLASH REPORT
FOR THE THREE MONTHS ENDED MARCH 31, 19XX
(dollars in millions, except per share)

	March 31			19XX	
	Year to Date	Year to Date Over (Under) Plan	Prior Year Actual	Indicated Final	Over (Under) Plan
New Orders	81.4	(66.3)	92.2	1,570.0	220
Sales	112.3	12.5	117.8	1,350.0	103
Net income	5.1	1.4	7.3	63.5	(6.1)
EPS	.36	.10	.51	4.46	.43

Interpretive Comments

New orders are under plan, primarily in the Electronics Division, by reason of a deferment for one month of the expected order form Raytheon. The indicated new orders for the year are expected to exceed plan because of increased orders from the United States Air Force for additional counter-measure equipment.

Sales: Sales are better than plan by 12.5 percent, principally in the Aircraft Division. An increase in the estimated sales for the year results from expected higher spares' sales.

Net income: Although net income is higher than plan for the three months, the continued invest-ment of the company funds in the RRE research project beyond that expected should result in net earnings about 8.7 percent or $6.1 million less than plan.

often it assures proper interpretation of the numerical data. The use of visual aids in either graphic or tabular form can be of substantial assistance and, in fact, may be essential to the effectiveness of oral reports. Just as short concise sentences are important in a written report, attributes important to the success of an oral report include:

1. *Visual Aids.* Must be neat and easy to read, have no errors in spelling or grammar and use color to highlight.

2. *Presenter.* Should have a professional appearance, be comfortable and relaxed but enthusiastic, know the material; encourage questions, vary voice and pace, and use smooth gestures.

3. *Presentation.* Be well rehearsed, have a smooth, not shaky, start, have a logical sequence, contain good examples, and have a conclusion and recommendation. Be as brief as possible while covering all relevant points.

Typical occasions for the use of oral reports by the controller are the review of monthly operating results or the annual review of the forecast for the next year. Members of the controller's staff also may discuss monthly cost and profit results at various departmental meetings or may be present at such conferences to answer questions concerning costs.

Aside from group conferences, a discussion between the controller and individual executives should prove beneficial to a better understanding of the facts and figures. And in the field of oral communications, mere *availability* of the chief accounting official and staff is an important consideration in the effective exercise of the controllership function.

(d) ELECTRONIC REPORTS

With the continuing installation and use of electronic data processing and the proliferation of terminals and personal computers, more and more reports are being made available electronically. The use of electronic reports has several benefits.

- Reports are available sooner because they don't have to be printed, reproduced, and distributed. The time saved increases if reports are sent to recipients who are geographically dispersed.
- There is a savings in the costs of materials and handling since the reports no longer require paper, printing, handling, and mailing.
- The reports no longer have to be filed or bound by the recipients since they can remain available on the system for subsequent viewing and use.

All of the considerations mentioned earlier in the chapter in connection with report preparation including the use of graphics apply to electronic reports, with some qualifications. Electronic reporting seems to be effective for control and informational reports that are repetitive and have a standardized format. Perhaps the best example of a report that is suited to electronic transmission is a department budget statement. This is usually sent to each department manager on a monthly basis and typically shows the current month and year-to-date expenses compared to the budgeted amounts along with the full year approved budget. By transmitting it electronically, the manager can review it earlier, at his or her leisure and can recall it or print it as specific items are analyzed.

Other reports that have been made available on an internal computer network are:

- Flash reports.
- Other control reports.
- Trend reports (especially when graphics are available).
- Analytical reports (that are repetitive).

See examples of these three types of reports given earlier in the chapter.

Data Security.   Data security is especially important when transmitting reports on a computer network, especially from two aspects: Who gets the report and who can affect the information?

There has to be a security system that permits only authorized people to view the reports available on the system. Usually the distribution lists of high level reports are limited and therefore it is relatively easy to control access to them. However, when every manager has access to the system it is important that a security system restrict individuals to reports to which they have a "need to know." For example, in the case of monthly department budget statements, every manager must be able to obtain a report for his or her department but not for anyone else's department. Higher level managers should be able to access such reports for all managers who report to them, and ideally have consolidated summaries also available through the system. These higher level executives may also have authorization to view other reports that the managers reporting to them do not have access to. The more extensive the organization, the more complex is the security problem.

While there will be a large number of managers receiving electronic reports, none should have the ability to edit (add, change, or delete) data. The recipients should have "read only" capability. The reports are usually compiled using the accounting/budget data base and the traditional input/output accounting controls must be observed. Changes to reports will result from changes to the accounting general ledger and budget systems and those will only be changed through journal entries or authorized budget changes.

(e) TELEPROCESSING

The use of teleprocessing in transmitting data and distributing reports cannot be over emphasized. It offers speed, control, and cost savings to report preparers and is a tool that controllers especially must understand and determine how best to use. In considering its applications, a controller should remember that not only can data be transmitted from distant offices to a central processing center but also that information can be rapidly returned to all locations in the form of current reports. It is invaluable in the handling and reporting of orders, shipments, and expenditures.

Even when used within a small geographic area teleprocessing allows on-line input and real-time feedback on important operating matters like material usage, labor hours, and cost levels of inventory. The computer, combined with teleprocessing, forms the most powerful tool that a controller can have in preparing reports to management.

36-6 APPLICATIONS OF INTERNAL MANAGEMENT REPORTS

(a) REPORTS FOR THE BOARD OF DIRECTORS

There is a great deal of variation between companies about the information presented to the board of directors. This may stem in large part from (1) differences in the composition of the board, (2) differences in the management philosophy, or (3) differences in the sophistication or experience in report preparation by the controller or in report reading by the recipients. If the board membership consists largely of successful businesspeople who must manage their own companies and who have no significant financial interest in the corporation, then the tendency is for less detailed reports. Moreover, some managements desire little assistance in the nature of direction of the company's affairs, and less data may be made available. At the other extreme is the board consisting largely of those with heavy investments in the business and a professional management that wishes to keep its board informed to a high degree in order to secure a maximum of assistance. Under such circumstances, a great deal of financial operating data is furnished.

Generally speaking, the board of directors is interested in broad policy matters, general trends of sales and earnings, competitive performance, and especially plans for the immediate and longer term. Under such circumstances, the reports of a financial nature to the board by either the president, chief financial officer, or controller (but usually prepared by the latter) should include and interpret such matters as:

1. Company-wide and major divisions monthly (or quarterly) and year-to-date operating results.
2. Statement of financial condition or pertinent excerpts therefrom.
3. Statement of cash flows.

All of the above is usually compared to plan.

4. Quarterly and annual forecasts by significant breakdown.
5. Status of capital expenditures.
6. Significant trends and relationships—special studies.

An example of a simple two-page report containing all vital financial information for board discussion purposes is shown in Figures 36-10 and 36-11. This concise report is accompanied by written remarks and usually by further oral comments of the CEO and chief financial officer relating to important underlying causes, trends, and so on.

An example of a somewhat more detailed income statement that includes comparison with both the plan and the prior year is illustrated in Figure 36-12. Such a report may be prepared for each division and for the entire company. Comparable financial data, indicating both the forecasted position and the actual condition at the end of the previous year, may be presented as shown in Figure 36-13 and incorporates the important measurements.

Very often the use of a graph or chart in the director's package will better highlight key information. For example, a graph showing revenue and profit by month for the current and prior year can be updated for each meeting and may help the director recall discussions at prior meetings.

(b) REPORTS FOR SENIOR EXECUTIVES

The interests of the senior executives encompass the entire business enterprise. Those executives in charge of a division are also concerned with the overall or composite picture. The vice-president in charge of sales, for example, is interested in production efficiency and volume, the research program, general business conditions, the price level, and a host of other matters. The vice-president's major concern is slanted toward his or her special function, but the vice-president is also concerned with the overall health and strength of the company as a whole.

Accordingly the regular reports for the senior executives usually present information such as the following:

1. Summary statement of financial condition.
2. Analysis of significant changes in financial condition.
3. Statement of cash position.

Figure 36-10 Summarized Report to the Board of Directors.

The Appliance Corporation
REPORT TO BOARD OF DIRECTORS
MARCH AND YEAR-TO-DATE 19XX

Item	Actual	Plan	% of Plan
OPERATIONS			
Net Sales			
Month	$ 3,044,907	$ 2,554,197	119.2
Year-to-Date	29,217,348	32,443,942	90.1
Income Before Taxes			
Month	401,852	221,987	181.0
Year-to-Date	3,412,776	3,236,330	105.5
% of Sales	11.7%	10.0%	
Net Income			
Month	193,713	97,746	198.2
Year-to-Date	1,746,623 [1]	1,387,958	125.8
Earnings Per Share of Common			
Month	.136	.069	198.2
Year-to-Date	1.233 [1]	.980	125.8
OTHER SELECTED DATA			
Cash	$ 2,447,777	$ 1,415,695	
Receivables (Net)	5,351,463	3,904,747	
Inventories	6,866,954	6,314,933	
Other Current Assets	252,903	381,500	
Total Current Assets	14,919,097	12,016,875	
Current Liabilities	4,929,618	4,506,056	
Working Capital	$ 9,989,479	$ 7,510,819	
Current Ratio	3.0 to 1	2.7 to 1	
Capital Expenditures	$ 465,717	$ 1,696,933	
Return on Capital Employed	9.0%	7.2%	
Return on Stockholders' Equity	11.2%	9.6%	
Book Value Per Common Share	$13.78	$12.38	

[1]All extraordinary gains on subsidiary dissolution have been excluded.

4. Condensed statement of income and expense.

5. Statement of income and expense by product lines or divisions of the business.

6. Statement accounting for changes in net profit.

7. Summary of sales by geographical area.

8. Summary of orders received, unfilled orders, sales, and production.

9. Financial and operating ratios, relationships, and trends.

10. General measurements of operating efficiency, by major division.

Figure 36-11   Report to the Board of Directors—by Responsibility.

The Appliance Corporation
SUMMARY OF DIVISION PERFORMANCE
MARCH AND YEAR-TO-DATE 19XX

Item	Actual	Plan	% of Plan
NET SALES			
Western Division			
Month	$ 1,676,566	$ 1,354,138	123.8
Year-to-Date	16,223,374	18,844,877	86.1
Eastern Division			
Month	947,390	788,377	120.2
Year-to-Date	9,398,478	9,918,521	94.8
South Central Division			
Month	271,818	295,483	92.0
Year-to-Date	2,672,630	2,330,649	114.7
Canadian Operations			
Month	175,073	53,389	327.9
Year-to-Date	1,103,441	745,034	148.1
General Electronics, Inc.			
Month	—	67,865	—
Year-to-Date	—	692,775	—
Consolidated			
Month	3,044,907	2,554,197	119.2
Year-to-Date	$29,217,348	$32,443,942	90.1

INCOME BEFORE TAXES—% OF SALES	Mo.	Y/D	
Western Division	12.7	10.8	
Eastern Division	13.0	14.4	
South Central Division	28.7	27.1	
Canadian Operations	(8.4)	(34.2)	

NET INCOME (OR LOSS)	Actual	Plan	% of Plan
Western Division			
Month	$ 102,541	$ 79,696	128.7
Year-to-Date	855,430	962,341	88.9
Eastern Division			
Month	59,230	(7,533)	—
Year-to-Date	766,963	289,810	264.6
South Central Division			
Month	37,401	41,469	90.2
Year-to-Date	349,642	244,538	143.0
Canadian Operations			
Month	(7,103)	(8,118)	—
Year-to-Date	(181,093)	(36,661)	—
General Electronics, Inc.			
Month	—	1,571	—
Year-to-Date	—	19,643	—
Consolidated			
Month	193,713	97,746	198.2
Year-to-Date	$ 1,746,623	$ 1,387,958	125.8

Figure 36-12 Comparative Income Statement—for Top Management.

The Appliance Corporation and Subsidiaries

CONSOLIDATED STATEMENT OF INCOME AND EXPENSE

For the Month, and _____ Months Ended _____

	Month		Year-to-Date	
	Amount	% Net Sales	Amount	% Net Sales
NET SALES—Regular—This Year				
Plan				
Last Year				
Less: Cost of Sales (excluding overhead)				
Gross Profit—This Year				
Plan				
Last Year				
LESS EXPENSES:				
Operating				
Manufacturing				
Selling and Advertising				
Administrative				
Total Expense—This Year				
Budget				
Last Year				
Operating Profit (Loss)				
OTHER INCOME				
OTHER EXPENSE				
LESS: Contribution to Pension Fund:				
Net Income before				
Federal and State				
Taxes on Income—This Year				
Objective				
Last Year				
Federal and States Taxes on Income (estimated)				
Net Income before				
Amortization of Goodwill				
LESS: Amortization of Goodwill				
NET INCOME—This Year				
Objective				
Last Year				
Amount applicable to Minority Interest in Gain or (Loss) of Subsidiaries				
Controlling Interest in Consolidated Net Income				

Figure 36-13 Highlights for Board of Directors.

Aerospace Corporation and Subsidiaries
HIGHLIGHTS—OPERATIONS
(dollars in millions, except per share)

Item	Year to Date			Year Projected			Year to Date March 19XX
	Actual	Over (Under) Plan	Prior Year	Indicated Final	Over (Under) Plan	Prior Year Total	Percent Over (Under) Prior Year
New orders	85.1	(62.6)	92.2	1,570.0	0	2,486.4	(36.9)
Sales backlog	2,070.3	(77.3)	1,170.2	2,319.7	0	2,099.7	10.5
Net sales	114.5	14.7	117.8	1,350.0	0	1,582.5	(14.7)
Operating margin	5.5	.6	9.1	86.6	(.2)	132.9	(34.8)
Operating margin—% of sales	4.82	(.08)	7.76	6.41	(.01)	8.40	(23.7)
Net income	4.8	1.1	7.3	63.5	0	90.3	(29.7)
Net income—% of sales	4.21	.53	6.19	4.70	0	5.71	(17.7)
Average assets employed	993.5	(4.4)	930.3	1,077.2	(22.4)	960.7	12.1
Turnover on average assets	1.38	.18	1.52	1.25	(.03)	1.65	(24.2)
Return on average assets—%	5.82	1.41	9.41	5.89	(.13)	9.40	(38.3)
Return on average equity—%	13.66	3.24	24.32	14.44	0	23.26	(37.9)
EPS	.34	.08	.51	4.46	0	6.35	(29.8)
Average shares outstanding (000)	14,226	0	14,218	14,248	0	14,219	.2
Book value per share	29.91	.08	25.55	32.20	0	29.58	8.9

11. Comparison of actual operations with the program.

12. Comparison of operations with general indexes of business conditions.

13. Forecast of the following period.

Such information is usually presented monthly to the general executives with suitable comparisons and explanatory comment and, although general, is in more detail than for the board of directors. The foregoing reports are only suggested examples and may be varied as circumstances warrant. For example, an aging of the accounts receivable or a report on inventory activity may be included. In any event, at this executive level the emphasis is on the *summary* or *overall* aspects and not departmental performance or other details.

Whereas the general contents of such reports is probably known to the reader, some illustrative material may be useful.

Figure 36-14 represents a page from the general summary comments on operations and financial condition, together with related graphs of comparative performance. This interpretation is supported by a company-wide income statement, shown in Figure 36-15 that compares actual performance with the plan or forecast and with standard. The "block" technique is used to identify the more important areas of variance from the plan or standard. The overall company statement is supported with summaries by division—the responsibility reporting principle. The condensed statement of financial condition (Figure 36-16) compares results with plan and the preceding year-end.

By means of a combination organization chart and operating profit performance data, the operating profit showing the *total* revenue or costs, and the share representing the favorable or unfavorable variance from budget or plan, *for which each major executive is responsible,* can be depicted graphically as shown in Figure 36-17. Alternatively, comparable performance may be communicated in the organization chart format reflecting only the departures from plan or budget as illustrated in Figure 36-18. To that calculation may be added the impact of alternative scenarios, as reflected, for example, in footnote 2 of Figure 36-18.

Again, for the use of the senior executives, the graph in Figure 36-19 gives a clear indication of the trend in costs and net profit.

A three-way comparison of the current year's sales, budgeted sales, and past year's sales is graphically presented in Figure 36-20. For the information of the general executive as well as the sales executive, sales performance by geographic area or by product lines may be summarized on a responsibility basis.

A summary of overall performance of the manufacturing division of a company is illustrated in Figure 36-21. An overall summary of the excess costs for all divisions, by responsibility, is illustrated in Figure 36-22.

A simple statement accounting for a change in operating profit is illustrated in Figure 36-23.

The chief executives are interested very often in simple, highly condensed reports that indicate the daily performance or condition. An example of a daily financial report for the president of a medium-sized corporation that provides information on the critical areas—sales, manufacturing efficiency, and working capital elements (for a company rather short in cash)—is that in Figure 36-24. The use of estimates is

Figure 36-14   Comments and Summary of Operations for Senior Executives.

Los Angeles, California
April 13, 19XX

REPORT ON OPERATIONS AND FINANCIAL CONDITION
March 31, 19XX

OPERATIONS—GENERAL SUMMARY

Consolidated net income for the first quarter of 19XX was $5,932,000, the equivalent of $.38 per common share after provision for preferred dividend. This is a decrease of $4,531,000 from the 19XX first quarter earnings of $10,463,-000, or $.70 per share. In comparing profit performance with this prior year period, it will be seen that all divisions and the subsidiaries, collectively, except the Eastern, produced $2,493,000 more profit. Income (loss) of the Eastern Division, reflecting service price weakness and the catalytic cracker shutdown in January, was $7,024,000 less favorable (more loss) than in the corresponding X-1 period.

Some of the price problems and excess costs were anticipated, in that the $5,932,000 net income represents a 95.8% achievement of the annual forecast first quarter earnings of $6,193,000. In this important comparison of actual performance with objectives, we find better than expected performance in the Southern and Foreign Divisions as well as the subsidiaries; but Western Division missed target by $1,256,000 (21.3%), and Eastern Division failed to meet the goal by $917,000 (15.8%). The better than forecast performance in the two divisions and subsidiaries, and a favorable LIFO inventory adjustment of $900,000 almost offset the Eastern-Western deficiency, and brought overall performance close to forecast.

Operating results were somewhat close to forecast because such projections, being realistic, did not assume standard performance. The review of the consolidated income statement for the first quarter reveals unfavorable sales price deviations from standard to the extent of $6,496,000, and controllable costs and expenses over standard aggregating $7,331,000. These are areas either of potential profit improvement or factors to be considered in long term planning.

FINANCIAL CONDITION

Consolidated *working capital* of $77,366,000, while adequate, has declined $12,341,000 since the first of the year as a consequence of recording the liability for the offshore acreage award of $14,907,000 during the first quarter 19XX.

Cash and equivalents of $39,683,000 is $1,600,000 lower than anticipated, entirely due to the decrease in earnings from that forecast. Despite this decrease in cash availability, the company has been able to absorb the payment in April of the aforementioned offshore acreage purchase ($14.9 million) with only a short term borrowing of $8 million. High cash generation during the month of April enabled us to repay one-half of this temporary borrowing on April 29.

Figure 36-14   *(continued)*

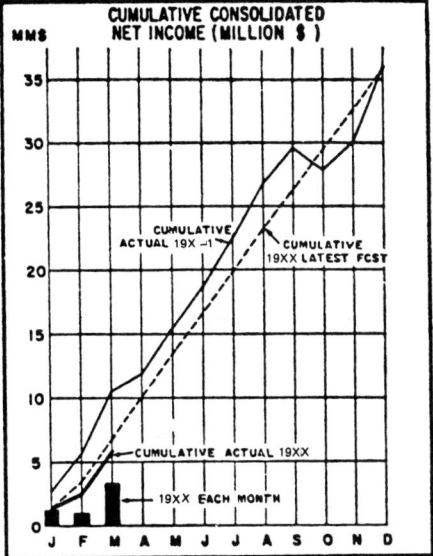

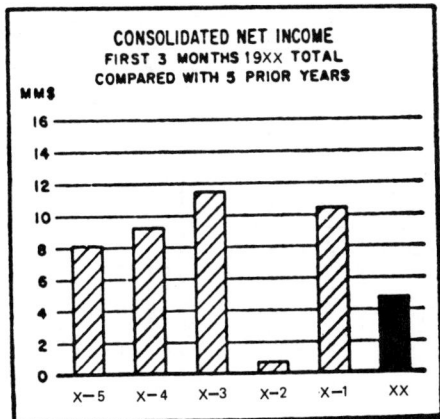

to be noted. Some companies extend the use of estimates to preparing a daily income statement.

Daily reports would, of course, apply to each major function as well as to the overall operation. Figure 36-25 pictures a daily statistical report on manufacturing costs. A graph of daily production as related to standard is illustrated in Figure 36-26.

It will be observed that some of the reports listed or illustrated are of the control type. Timeliness is important in their issuance. Where the reports are of an informational nature, for policy making and planning, the time factor is not quite as dominant. Nevertheless, a definite schedule should be prepared and adhered to, indicating the day or even the hour when the executive report is to be presented.

The controller should exercise care in the design of the form and physical characteristics of these regular executive reports. They should be neatly prepared, easy to read, and, insofar as possible, self-explanatory. They could be attractively bound in

Figure 36-15 Consolidated Income Statement for Senior Executives.

Description	Month of March 19XX	Month of March Better or (Worse) than Forecast	3 Months Year-to-Date 19XX	3 Months Year-to-Date Current Views	3 Months Year-to-Date Better or (Worse) than Original Forecast
REVENUES					
Gross revenues at standard	55,880	2,027	150,024	(1,872)	(400)
Sales price variance - (favorable) or unfavorable	3,113	(722)	6,496	(2,106)	(3,893)
Total revenues	52,767	1,305	143,528	(3,978)	(4,293)
CONTROLLABLE ITEMS					
Less:					
Controllable standard cost of goods sold (incl. raw material, purch. products and production costs)	26,383	(39)	70,512	3,097	1,949
Over or (under) standard	1,511	(1,144)	3,265	(445)	(291)
Gross margin before expenses	24,873	(322)	69,751	(1,326)	(2,635)
Less:					
Controllable standard manufacturing costs	4,162	(483)	12,061	1,241	(550)
Over or (under) standard	497	266	2,462	(420)	1,129
Controllable margin before mktg. and prod. transp. costs	20,214	(339)	55,228	(505)	(2,056)
Less:					
Controllable standard product transportation costs	1,330	157	3,868	94	(50)
Controllable standard marketing costs	4,549	(47)	12,701	(327)	327
Standard advertising expense	387	19	1,162	58	(47)
Mktg., transp. and adv. over or (under) standard	403	(6)	1,456	(1,077)	(152)
Less:					
Controllable exploration costs	1,055	153	3,090	183	168
Over or (under) standard	-	-	-	43	58
Less:					
Controllable standard General & Administrative costs	987	49	3,123	79	160
Over or (under) standard	54	16	148	48	69
Dividends and miscellaneous (income)	150	5	172	15	15
Margin before non-controllable costs	11,599	7	29,852	(1,389)	(1,508)
NON-CONTROLLABLE COSTS					
Depreciation, taxes and insurance	6,546	79	20,038	464	1,175
Interest expense	1,015	23	3,046	57	57
Other non-controllable costs	80	1	200	15	15
Total non-controllable costs	7,641	103	23,284	536	1,247
Income before taxes based on income	3,958	110	6,568	(853)	(261)
Taxes based on income	451	-	636	-	-
CONSOLIDATED NET INCOME	3,507	110	5,932	(853)	(261)
Preferred dividends accrued	241	-	734	-	-
Consolidated net income applicable to common shares	3,266	110	5,198	(853)	(261)
Per share	$ 0.24	($ 0.01)	$ 0.38	($0.06)	($0.02)

General Oil Company

CONSOLIDATED STATEMENT OF FINANCIAL POSITION AT JUNE 30, 19XX
(in M$ except per share)

Description	Actual June 30, 19XX	Better/(Worse) than Original 19XX Plan	Better (Worse) than	
			Actual 12/31/X-1	Actual 6/30/X-1
CURRENT ASSETS				
Cash and equivalents	$ 39,683	$(1,617)	$ 3,110	$(9,828)
Receivables	72,900	2,800	(1,660)	9,571
Inventories	53,370	(430)	(8,248)	(3,011)
Other current assets	13,946	3,846	3,991	2,678
Total Current Assets	179,899	4,599	(2,807)	(590)
CURRENT LIABILITIES				
Current portion of long-term debt	26,077	23	(104)	(15,029)
Accounts payable	76,456	(5,756)	(9,430)	(15,522)
Total Current Liabilities	102,533	(5,733)	(9,534)	(30,551)
NET WORKING CAPITAL	77,366	(1,134)	(12,341)	(31,141)
INVESTMENTS AND ADVANCES	14,944	(56)	(532)	754
Property and equipment				
At original cost	1,197,014	(1,886)	22,365	82,502
Less accumulated depreciation	(524,293)	707	(7,875)	(35,372)
LONG-TERM DEBT	281,945	55	2,806	7,376
Total Net Worth	483,086	(2,314)	4,423	24,119
NET WORTH				
Preferred stock outstanding at par	60,768	32	(845)	(1,625)
Common stock outstanding at par	138,529	(29)	—	7,631
Reinvested earnings and capital in excess of par value	283,789	2,311	5,268	18,113
Total Net Worth	483,086	2,314	4,423	24,119
Book Value of Common Shares	$ 30.49	$(0.06)	$ .38	$ 1.86

Figure 36-17 Operating Profit Control Chart.

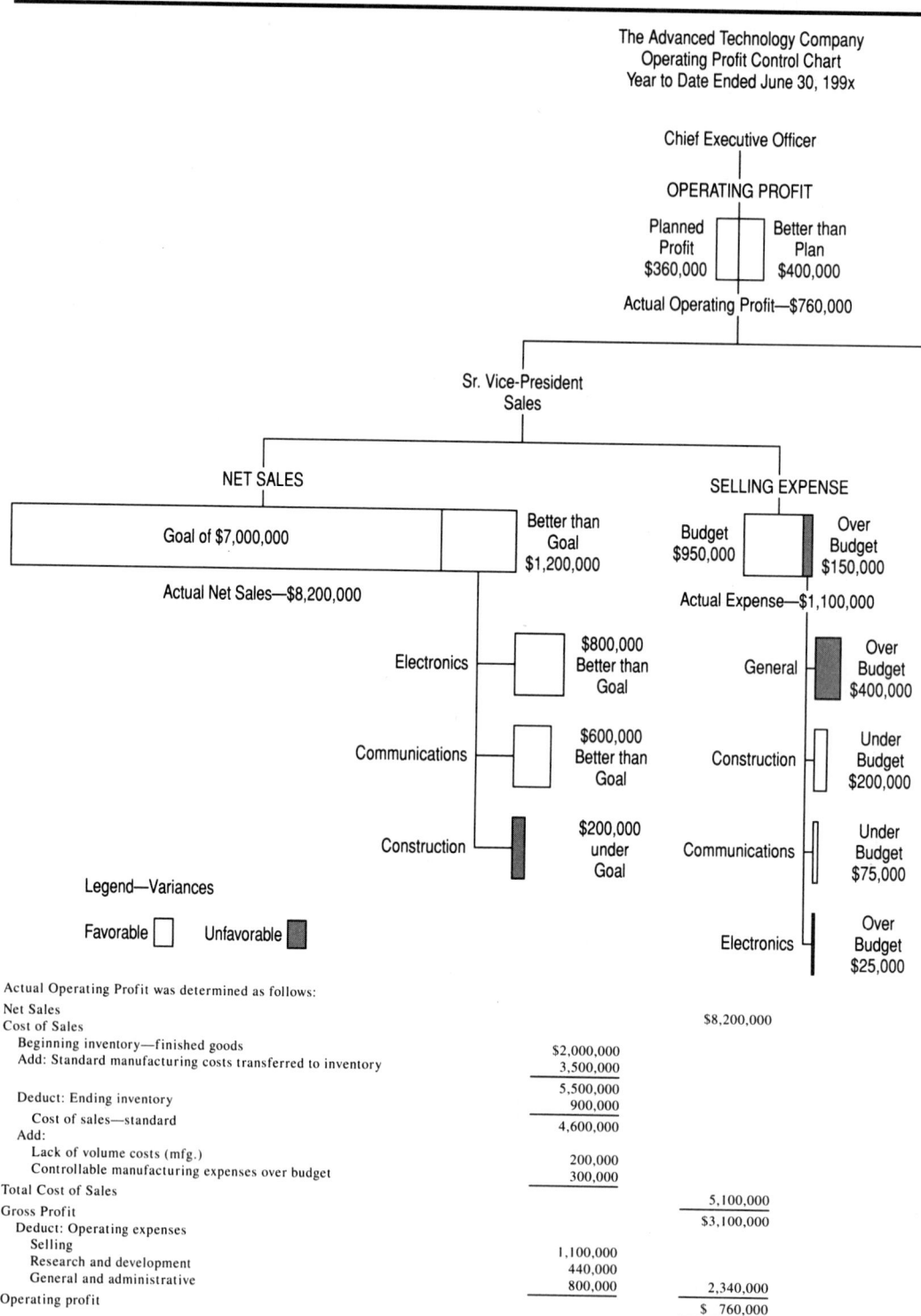

The Advanced Technology Company
Operating Profit Control Chart
Year to Date Ended June 30, 199x

Chief Executive Officer

OPERATING PROFIT

| Planned Profit $360,000 | | Better than Plan $400,000 |

Actual Operating Profit—$760,000

Sr. Vice-President Sales

NET SALES

| Goal of $7,000,000 | | Better than Goal $1,200,000 |

Actual Net Sales—$8,200,000

SELLING EXPENSE

| Budget $950,000 | | Over Budget $150,000 |

Actual Expense—$1,100,000

Electronics — $800,000 Better than Goal

Communications — $600,000 Better than Goal

Construction — $200,000 under Goal

General — Over Budget $400,000

Construction — Under Budget $200,000

Communications — Under Budget $75,000

Electronics — Over Budget $25,000

Legend—Variances

Favorable ☐   Unfavorable ■

Actual Operating Profit was determined as follows:

Net Sales		$8,200,000
Cost of Sales		
Beginning inventory—finished goods	$2,000,000	
Add: Standard manufacturing costs transferred to inventory	3,500,000	
	5,500,000	
Deduct: Ending inventory	900,000	
Cost of sales—standard	4,600,000	
Add:		
Lack of volume costs (mfg.)	200,000	
Controllable manufacturing expenses over budget	300,000	
Total Cost of Sales		5,100,000
Gross Profit		$3,100,000
Deduct: Operating expenses		
Selling	1,100,000	
Research and development	440,000	
General and administrative	800,000	2,340,000
Operating profit		$ 760,000

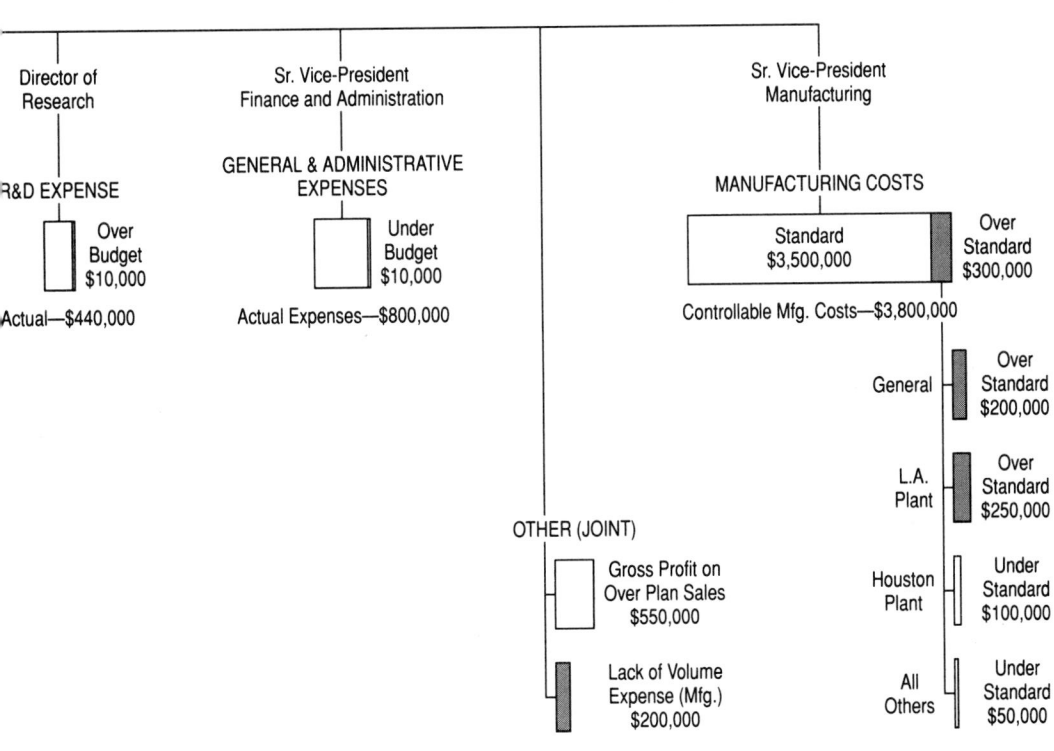

Director of
Research

R&D EXPENSE

Over
Budget
$10,000

Actual—$440,000

Sr. Vice-President
Finance and Administration

GENERAL & ADMINISTRATIVE
EXPENSES

Under
Budget
$10,000

Actual Expenses—$800,000

Sr. Vice-President
Manufacturing

MANUFACTURING COSTS

Standard
$3,500,000

Over
Standard
$300,000

Controllable Mfg. Costs—$3,800,000

General

Over
Standard
$200,000

L.A.
Plant

Over
Standard
$250,000

Houston
Plant

Under
Standard
$100,000

All
Others

Under
Standard
$50,000

OTHER (JOINT)

Gross Profit on
Over Plan Sales
$550,000

Lack of Volume
Expense (Mfg.)
$200,000

Figure 36-18   Operating Profit Control Chart—Variances Only.

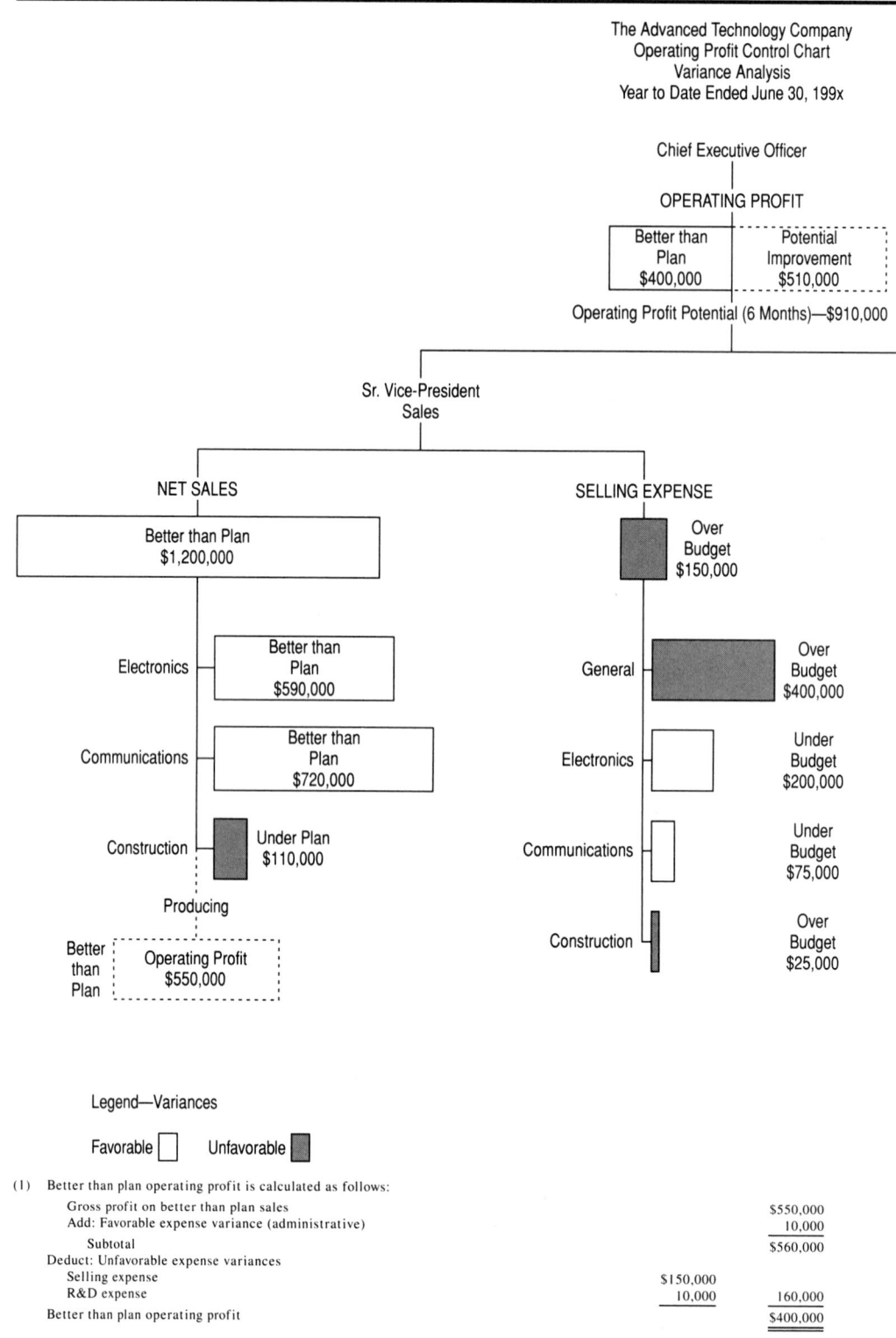

The Advanced Technology Company
Operating Profit Control Chart
Variance Analysis
Year to Date Ended June 30, 199x

Chief Executive Officer

OPERATING PROFIT

| Better than Plan $400,000 | Potential Improvement $510,000 |

Operating Profit Potential (6 Months)—$910,000

Sr. Vice-President Sales

NET SALES

Better than Plan $1,200,000

SELLING EXPENSE

Over Budget $150,000

Electronics — Better than Plan $590,000

General — Over Budget $400,000

Communications — Better than Plan $720,000

Electronics — Under Budget $200,000

Construction — Under Plan $110,000

Communications — Under Budget $75,000

Producing

Construction — Over Budget $25,000

Better than Plan — Operating Profit $550,000

Legend—Variances

Favorable ☐   Unfavorable ▣

(1)   Better than plan operating profit is calculated as follows:

Gross profit on better than plan sales		$550,000
Add: Favorable expense variance (administrative)		10,000
Subtotal		$560,000
Deduct: Unfavorable expense variances		
Selling expense	$150,000	
R&D expense	10,000	160,000
Better than plan operating profit		$400,000

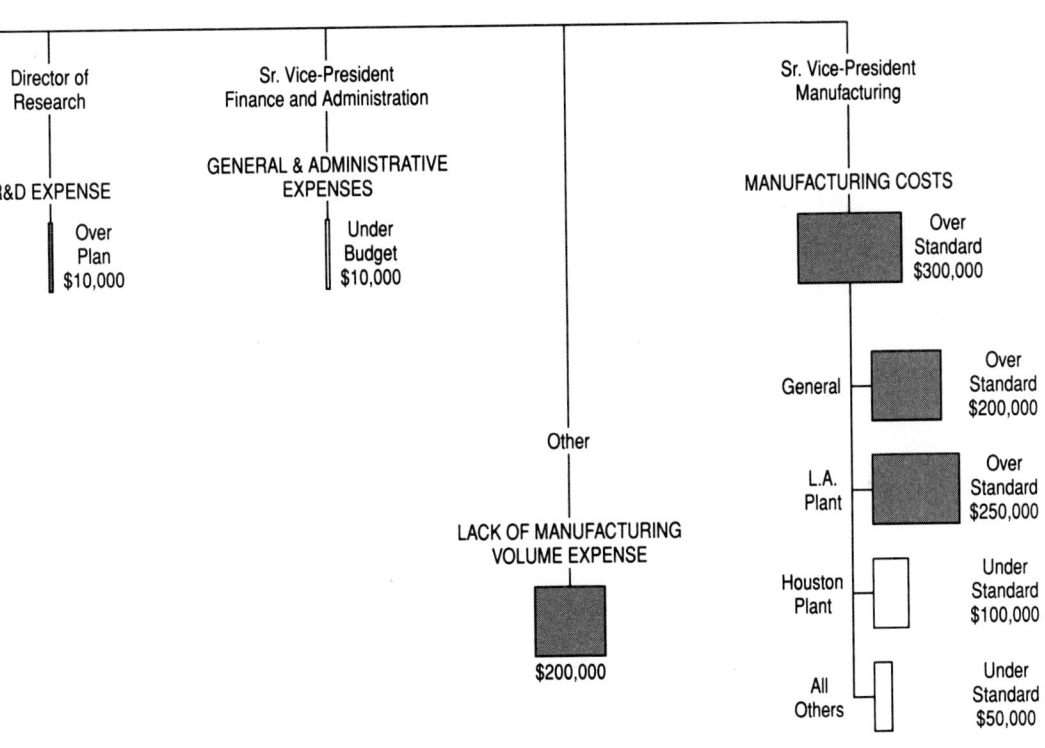

(2)   Calculation of operating profit potential for 6 months. (It is assumed that the better than
plan sales, which were made from inventory, can be replaced by a higher manufacturing level)

Operating profit better than plan	$400,000
Add:	
Elimination of lack of volume manufacturing expense	200,000
Elimination of over standard manufacturing expense (controllable)	300,000
Elimination of R&D over budget expenses	10,000
Potential operating profit above plan	$910,000

Figure 36-19 Trends in Costs and Profits.

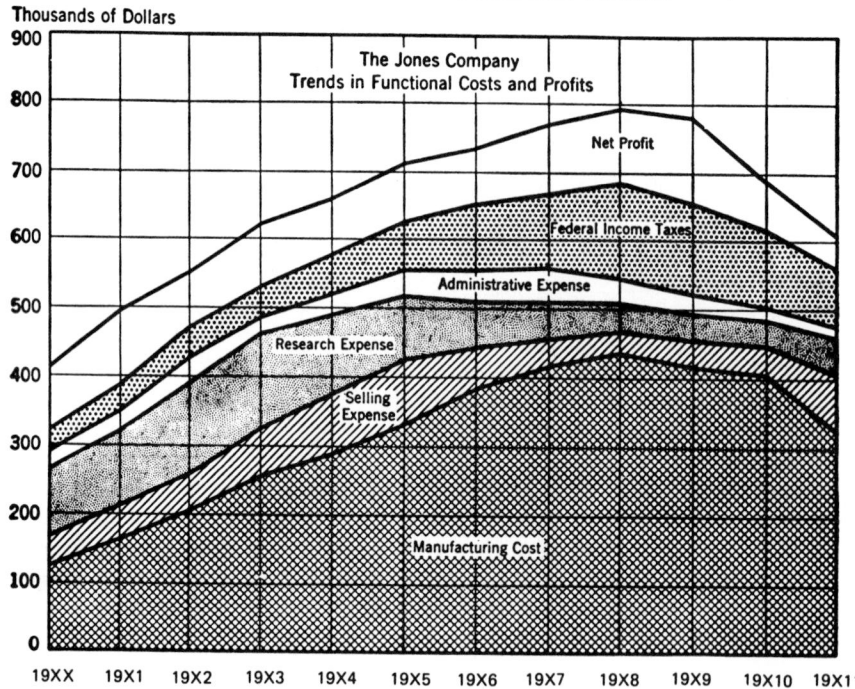

The Jones Company
TRENDS IN FUNCTIONAL COSTS AND PROFITS

Figure 36-20 Comparative Sales Chart.

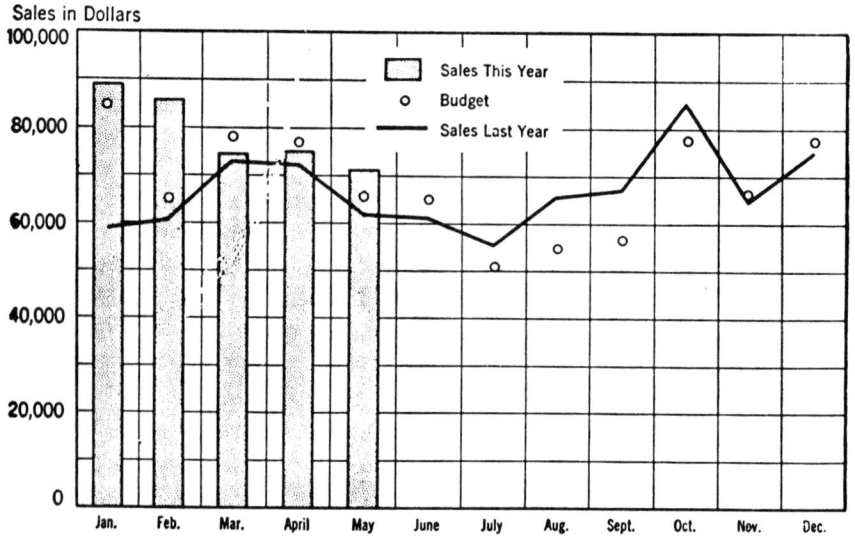

The Ball Manufacturing Company
COMPARATIVE SALES
This Year, Last Year, and Budget

Figure 36-21   Summary of Manufacturing Division Budget Performance.

CLEVELAND STEEL AND CHEMICAL CO.		BUDGET REPORT					
MONTH February		DEPT HEAD J.A. Jones DEPARTMENT Manufacturing Division NO _____ SUMMARY					
DESCRIPTION	CURRENT MONTH			YEAR TO DATE			
	BUDGET	ACTUAL	(OVER)/UNDER	BUDGET	ACTUAL	(OVER)/UNDER	
PLANTS							
Lorain Ave. Steel	$ 384,909	$ 396,433	$(11,524)	$ 684,639	$ 794,232	$(109,593)	
Coke Works	44,631	44,579	52	91,735	96,293	(4,558)	
Sharon Recovery	75,839	78,265	(2,426)	147,230	154,067	(6,837)	
Stout Chemical	322,699	336,196	(13,497)	613,955	644,565	(30,610)	
Bainbridge Chemical	227,354	239,805	(12,451)	491,422	522,480	(31,058)	
GENERAL MANUFACTURING OVERHEAD							
Works Administration	5,237	5,499	(262)	11,814	13,231	(1,417)	
Product Engineering	8,030	7,363	667	22,069	20,967	1,102	
Engineering	5,515	4,689	826	10,703	9,709	994	
Personnel	9,390	9,703	(313)	19,544	19,235	309	
Purchasing	2,755	2,798	(43)	5,520	5,719	(199)	
Stores	1,351	1,437	(86)	2,649	2,473	176	
Traffic	1,166	1,103	63	2,367	2,161	206	
Small Lot System	4,476	4,698	(222)	9,284	10,415	(1,131)	
Pilot Development Line	4,164	4,164	-	6,218	6,218	-	
Heat Treat Pilot Plant	2,470	2,470	-	4,716	4,716	-	
Industrial Engineering	1,950	1,991	(41)	1,950	1,991	(41)	
Operations Administration	1,743	1,597	146	1,743	1,597	146	
Process Water	3,488	4,502	(1,014)	6,896	7,763	(867)	
Boiler-G	16,077	17,719	(1,642)	31,358	32,780	(1,422)	
" -S	5,327	5,494	(167)	11,007	11,404	(397)	
Maintenance	28,158	31,422	(3,264)	54,681	61,458	(6,777)	
Yard	2,683	2,742	(59)	5,744	5,297	447	
OTHER							
Material Price	3,695	-	3,695	26,278	-	26,278	
Material Freight	79	-	79	2,489	-	2,489	
Lost Hrs.-Mat'l Shortages	(5,863)	-	(5,863)	(5,863)	-	(5,863)	
TOTAL DEPARTMENT PERFORMANCE	$1,157,323	$1,204,669	$(47,346)	$2,260,148	$2,428,771	$(168,623)	
PER CENT (OVER)/UNDER BUDGET			(4.09%)			(7.46%)	

This is the initial report summarizing the performance of the operations division. For detail, refer to monthly budget reports, the summary of excess costs by responsibility and the Profit and Loss Statement.

ISSUED BY THE ACCOUNTING DEPT. March 19

appropriate covers bearing the name of the executive to whom they are given. If preferred, the executives may be given loose-leaf report books, with dividing tabs for months or subjects, in which the reports may be filed as received.

(c) SPECIAL REPORTS TO TOP MANAGEMENT

In every business, special circumstances arise that require separate analysis and study. For example, continuing decline in the profitability of a territory may warrant special investigation. The possibility of acquiring a new plant in potentially profitable areas

Figure 36-22 Summary of Manufacturing Costs Over (or Under) Standard—by Responsibility.

The Appliance Corporation
SUMMARY OF MANUFACTURING COSTS OVER OR (UNDER) STANDARD BY RESPONSIBILITY
Month of February, 19XX

Description	Total All Products	PLANT Refrig- erators	Stoves	Small Appli- ances
CONTROLLABLE COSTS				
Manufacturing Division—				
Plant Superintendent's Level				
Direct Labor—Per Budget Report.	$17,277	$ 8,540	$ 6,322	$2,415
Direct Material—Per Budget Report.	9,795	7,980	1,310	505
Variable Manufacturing Expense— Per Budget Report.	7,883	4,395	2,478	1,010
Total Plant Superintendent's Responsibility.	34,955	20,915	10,110	3,930
General Manufacturing Expense Over or (Under) Budget.	5,260	3,110	2,070	80
Total Manufacturing Division..	40,215	24,025	12,180	4,010
Purchasing Division—				
Prices Paid for Raw Materials.	1,020	2,390	(910)	(460)
Sales Division—				
Idle Time—No orders (5-day cap.)..	12,307	9,100	3,207	–
Special Handling.	2,190	870	1,320	–
Total Sales Division.	14,497	9,970	4,527	–
Financial Division—				
Cost Department Over or (Under) Budget.	160	110	40	10
Payroll Department Over or (Under) Budget.	(70)	(30)	(30)	(10)
Total Financial Division.	90	80	10	–
TOTAL CONTROLLABLE COSTS.	55,822	36,465	15,807	3,550
NONCONTROLLABLE COSTS AND STANDARD APPLICATIONS, ETC.				
Fixed Expenses—Depreciation, Taxes, Insurance.	7,900	4,390	2,760	750
Fixed Expenses—General Manufacturing, etc.	4,640	3,110	890	640
Standard Applications.	935	125	770	40
Interplant Transfers.	1,020	670	340	10
Total Noncontrollable Costs and Standard Applications, etc.	14,495	8,295	4,760	1,440
Total Excess Costs per Income and Expense Statement.	$70,317	$44,760	$20,567	$4,990

Issued by Accounting Department—March 5

Figure 36-23 Statement Accounting for Change in Operating Profit.

The Ajax Corporation

STATEMENT ACCOUNTING FOR CHANGE IN OPERATING PROFIT
February, 19XX

OPERATING PROFIT

February, 19XX	$198,500
January, 19XX	67,300
Increase—February over January	131,200

Accounted for as follows:

Factors of Increase

Higher sales volume	$ 76,312
Reduced manufacturing expenses over standard	44,800
Reduced excess material usage	26,110
Reduced development expense	12,916
Total elements causing increase in operating profit	160,138

Factors of Decrease

Lower average profit margin	$ 8,602	
Increased selling expenses	12,420	
Higher raw material prices	4,125	
Increased extraordinary deductions	3,791	
Total elements causing decrease in operating profit		28,938
Net Change in Operating Profit, as above		$131,200

---

would need a review. Some such studies may be initiated by the controller. In many cases, they will be made at the request of the board of directors, the executive committee, or the chief executive. The method of presentation can be varied, for the field is broad. Certainly, the narrative portion of such reports is extremely important. An illustrative special report to the Executive Committee is presented later in this section. (The data are purely hypothetical and are used for illustrative purposes only.)

SPECIAL REPORT TO EXECUTIVE COMMITTEE

December 29, 19XX

BOARD OF DIRECTORS

The following confidential report briefly summarizes our operations for the past six years, indicating certain significant trends, and sets forth an estimate of what our Net Loss will be during the first three months of 19X1. It also sets forth a general estimate of our Net Loss for the entire year of 19X1. This will naturally be subject to revision from month to month and I shall make this revision in special reports from month to month.

Figure 36-24 Daily Conditions Report for Major Executives.

The Appliance Corporation, Inc. and Wholly Owned Subsidiaries

DAILY CONDITIONS REPORT

Date: January 29, 19XX

Working Days This Month ————— 22

Worked to Date ————— 20

SALES

	Today	Month to Date	Last Month to Date	Forecast to Date	Same Period Last Year
Parent	$ 173,401	$7,009,835	$ 866,716	$ 7,576,148	$4,968,717
Subsidiary	6,781	308,603	234,887	1,007,900	194,022
Consolidated Net	$ 180,182	$7,318,438	$1,101,603	$ 8,584,048	$5,162,739

PRODUCTION

Through 8:00 A.M.

Standard Hours	119,018
Actual Hours	130,203
% Efficiency	90.7%

WORKING CAPITAL

CASH

	Beg. Balance	Additions	Deductions	Ending Bal
Fourth Nat'l Bank—Los Angeles	$ 645,898	$ 466	$ 151,025	$ 495,339
First Nat'l Bank—Chicago	234,142	—	—	234,142
Other Accounts	88,307	—	—	88,307
Total Cash	968,347	466	151,025	817,788

				Past Due
ACCOUNTS RECEIVABLE				
Current—House Brand	1,125,162	(1,078)	(35,657)	1,159,741	$ 580,925
Private Brands	1,271,114	91,884	—	1,362,998	57,387
Deferred—House Brand	2,929,366	85,046	—	3,014,412	—
Subsidiary Distributing Co.	1,597,427	7,156	—	1,604,583	509,296
Total Receivables	6,923,069	183,008	(35,657)	7,141,734	1,147,608
INVENTORIES					
Raw Material & WIP	4,395,714	215,000	156,821	4,453,893	
Finished Goods	5,406,720	151,821	149,004	5,409,537	
Total Inventories	9,802,434	366,821	305,825	9,863,430	
OTHER CURRENT ASSETS	359,956	—	—	359,956	
Total Current Assets	18,053,806	550,295	421,193	18,182,908	
CURRENT LIABILITIES					
Notes Payable	7,350,000	—	—	7,350,000	
Accounts Payable	2,772,969	170,344	115,368	2,827,945	
Payrolls—Estimate	175,213	50,000	—	225,213	
Other Accruals—Estimate	1,578,396	6,108	—	1,584,504	
Total Current Liabilities	11,876,578	226,452	115,368	11,987,662	
WORKING CAPITAL	$ 6,177,228	$ 323,843	$ 305,825	$ 6,195,246	

Figure 36-25   Daily Plant Report.

GENERAL
MANUFACTURING CORPORATION

__Owosso___ Plant   **DAILY PLANT REPORT**   Date __February 13,__ 19 __

	TODAY					MONTH TO DATE					VARIABLE RATE	
	TOTAL BURDEN	DEDUCT FIXED	ACTUAL VARIABLE	STANDARD VARIABLE	SAVINGS	TOTAL BURDEN	DEDUCT FIXED	ACTUAL VARIABLE	STANDARD VARIABLE	SAVINGS	ACTUAL	STANDARD
INDIRECT LABOR	1,820	65	1,755	2,241	486	56,805	1,365	55,440	49,062	6,378	45.2	40.0
O. T. PREMIUM AND N. S. BONUS	730	–	730	810	80	13,124	–	13,124	12,265	859	10.7	10.0
OPERATING SUPPLIES	94	23	71	982	911	17,041	483	16,558	14,718	1,840	13.5	12.0
TOOLS	105	–	105	810	705	14,842	–	14,842	12,265	2,577	12.1	10.0
POWER	90	5	85	324	239	5,870	105	5,765	4,906	859	4.7	4.0
MAINTENANCE	1,002	–	1,002	2,661	1,659	26,739	–	26,739	25,144	1,595	21.8	20.5`
LOSSES	188	–	188	446	258	8,218	–	8,218	6,746	1,472	6.7	5.5
DEPRECIATION	812	135	677	810	133	15,959	2,835	13,124	12,265	859	10.7	10.0
INSURANCE AND TAXES	483	77	406	810	404	14,987	1,617	13,370	12,265	1,105	10.9	10.0
OTHER OVER-HEAD EXPENSES	921	–	921	1,044	123	16,801	–	16,801	15,947	854	13.7	13.0
CREDITS	–	–	–	–	–	–	–	–	–	–	–	–
TOTALS	6,245	305	5,940	10,938	4,998	190,386	6,405	183,981	165,583	18,398	150.0	135.0

	TODAY	MONTH TO DATE	YEAR TO DATE		TODAY	MONTH TO DATE	REMARKS:
ACTUAL PROD. LABOR	7,648	122,155	1,853,243	SCHEDULED SHIPMENTS	87,600	1,767,500	
STANDARD PROD. LABOR	8,102	122,654	1,843,570	ACTUAL SHIPMENTS	84,260	1,927,634	
SAVINGS LABOR	454	499	(10,327)	OVER/UNDER SCHEDULE	(3,340)	160,134	
SAVINGS BURDEN	4,998	38,477	10,425	RETURNS & CREDITS		6,119	
TOTAL SAVINGS	5,452	38,976	98				

DISTRIBUTION:

DATE ISSUED: 2–14–

(REVERSE SIDE FOR ADDITIONAL REMARKS)   DIVISION CONTROLLER

Figure 36-26   Graphic Trend of Daily Production.

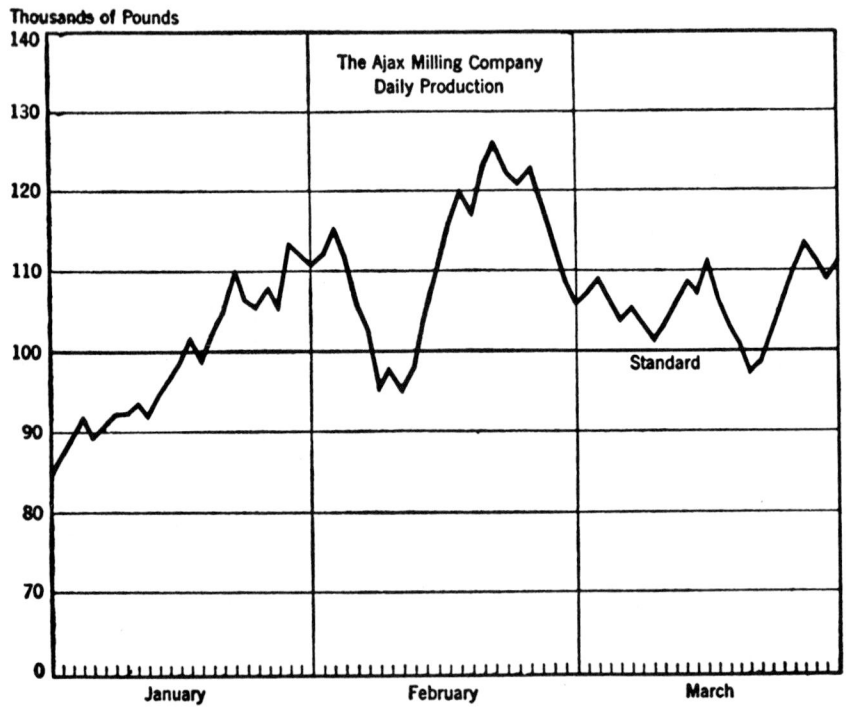

To save you time in reading a long report I have summarized the significant facts of this report in the first few pages and you need not refer to the remaining pages except as you wish additional information.

Throughout this report the figures for 19XX have been taken as a full year. To do this it has been necessary to estimate the results for the last two weeks of December; however any error in such estimate will be so small as to have no effect on the general situation.

SUMMARY

On January 1, 19X5, we had Assets of $4,241,000, Debts of $572,000, and a Net Worth of $3,669,000. In the six years to December 31, 19XX, we have operated at a Net Loss of $63,000 and during this time we have paid out in Dividends, $1,198,750; hence our Net Worth has been reduced during the six years by $1,261,750. This has greatly weakened our financial condition until now it appears as follows:

Assets	$3,316,000
Debts	909,000
Net Worth	$2,407,000

Our creditors now have an equity of 27.4% of the business which is entirely too much for a concern of this type in which the indebtedness is all current. The banks would be entirely justified in calling loans against such a condition.

The conclusion naturally is that we do not dare suffer any further inroads on our financial strength by either dividends or losses unless new capital is to be called into the business. Our operations from January 1, 19X1, must carry themselves or we shall have to secure new capital elsewhere.

For the year 19XX we shall have Net Sales of $3,119,000 and our Net Loss for the year will be $260,000.

It is impossible, of course, to accurately predict our volume for 19X1 but there are very serious reasons to question whether it will equal the volume for 19XX. These reasons are:

1. Business in the early months of 19X1 will certainly be at a lower level than in the early months of 19XX. That is, we shall start the year from a much lower level. December volume a year ago was $386,057; this year it will be $210,000.

2. Statistical services generally speaking do not see any improvement in the early months of 19X1.

3. Our level of prices will average lower in 19X1 than 19XX.

4. Our special-order volume may be smaller in 19X1 than 19XX.

5. The industries which constitute our main customers will be forced to curtail expenditures.

There are, of course, offsetting factors; we have two additional men in the sales division; the decline in business generally has leveled-out somewhat since July and there appear to be prospects of some special business which we did not get in 19XX.

It appears, however, that we cannot count on a volume of more than $3,000,000 to $3,250,000 in 19X1.

Our Cost of Goods Sold has run quite uniform. It will average about 62% of the Sales. This leaves us 38% to cover the Cost of Doing Business. This Cost of Doing Business is more or less a fixed cost except as it is arbitrarily changed by the management. Just now it amounts to $120,000 per month and consists of the following items:

Selling Cost	$ 62,600
Receiving and Shipping	6,150
Office	8,100
Administrative, Legal, and General	43,300
	$120,150

If our sales amount to $3,000,000 or an average of $250,000 per month, we shall lose $25,000 a month.

To carry our present overhead of $120,000 a month, without loss, would require sales of $315,700 per month or a total of $3,788,000 for the year.

To operate without a loss on the basis of sales of $250,000 per month will require that the overhead be cut from $120,000 to $95,000 per month, a cut of 20.8%.

It is recommended that we review every item of overhead expense in detail and make reductions effective at once which will reduce the overhead to a figure not to exceed $100,000 per month, and further that this amount be budgeted in detail to the various departments with responsibility for holding the figures to their respective allowances.

Barring such immediate reductions, I would estimate the operating results of the next three months to be as follows:

ESTIMATED NET LOSS FOR FIRST THREE MONTHS OF 19X1			
	January	February	March
Sales	$272,250	$228,250	$316,250
Gross Profit	106,200	89,000	123,000
Cost of Doing Business	120,000	120,000	130,000
Net Loss	$ 13,800	$ 31,000	$ 7,000

The foregoing figures are based on an expected $3,000,000 sales volume. The sales of these particular months give effect to the usual seasonal variations.

A preliminary estimate for the year 19X1 follows, on the assumption that overhead is not to be changed.

ESTIMATED NET LOSS FOR 19X1

With estimated sales for the year of $3,000,000 our operations should result as follows:

Sales	$3,000,000
Cost of Goods Sold	1,840,600
Gross Profit	1,159,400
Cost of Doing Business	
Selling Expense $751,200	
Receiving and Shipping 73,800	
Office Expense 97,200	
Administrative, Legal, and General Expense . . . 517,800	
Total	1,440,000
Net Loss	$ 280,600

Controller

As mentioned earlier in this chapter, special reports will take a form that is pertinent to the contents of the report. However, all reports should begin by clearly stating the issue and end with conclusions, and recommendations including, where appropriate, implementation and feedback responsibility. If the report is lengthy, an "executive summary" of no more than a few pages should also be included as a help to the reader.

(d) REPORTS FOR DEPARTMENT MANAGERS AND SUPERINTENDENTS

The duties and responsibilities of department managers and superintendents are more restricted than those of the general executives and are related to particular departments and cost centers. These executives have two major functions: (1) the supervision of the minor executives responsible to them and (2) the coordination of the departments over which they have authority so as to have a unified operation. Consequently, this echelon of executives should have reports on departmental performance. Although trend or planning reports are of use, the major emphasis is on current control.

A typical executive at the departmental level is the superintendent of a group of assembly departments. He needs to keep the material flowing to the cost center; he must keep the production of parts in balance within his groups, and he must keep expenses within budget. Since he has foremen responsible for the cost centers or sections, this executive's interest lies in the performance of the cost centers as units and not the individual workmen.

An outline of reports that would be useful to such an executive includes:

1. Daily report of labor performance by cost center.
2. Weekly report on labor performance by cost center.
3. Weekly report on material losses over standard (Figure 36-27).
4. Weekly report on idle machine time (Figure 36-28).
5. Monthly report on expenses by cost center.
6. Monthly summary of performance (Figure 36-29).

Figure 36-27 Weekly Report of Material Losses over Standard.

	The Illustrative Manufacturing Company REPORT OF MATERIAL LOSSES OVER STANDARD FOR WEEK ENDING SEPTEMBER 30, 19XX			
Department: Fabrication			Superintendent: A. Brown	
Material Used	Material Used		Quantity Variance	Comments
	Actual	Standard		
A	1,240	1,200	40	Poor workmanship
B	1,250	1,225	25	Poor material quality
C	2,404	2,400	4	
D	2,600	2,500	100	Machine failure
E	1,000	1,000	—	

Graphic presentation of performance can be effective at this level. Typical applications are the average percent of standard efficiency in Figure 36-30, and trend of material usage in Figure 36-31.

Each major division within the business has executives at this same level. The district sales manager might be at a comparable supervisory level. The chief concern of this executive would be the sales and expense performance by branch. A typical report is shown in Figure 36-32, summarizing the sales and selling expense performance.

(e) REPORTS FOR FIRST LINE SUPERVISORS

The executives at the lowest echelon of supervision are on the firing line. They deal with the individual performer—the salesperson, the operator or mechanic, the clerk, the laboratory technician. This is where controls commence, where the money is really spent, and where savings can be made. These supervisors are constantly engaged in suggesting how the sales of particular products may be increased, how material losses can be reduced, how the operation should be performed, how the machine should be used. These supervisors finally carry out the policies of the company. They are the ones who build morale among the workers, who pass on or create spirit and enthusiasm among the individual performers.

In some companies, the major executives believe that this lower level of supervision does not need reports. They feel that any good supervisor, for example, should be able to see what is happening, observe when performance is not satisfactory, and know exactly what steps should be taken to increase efficiency, lower costs, or improve quality. Whether reports are needed depends on the organization—the process, the concept of supervision at this level, the personality and training of the individual. In general, a good answer to the question is that, even with the best supervision, and keen and experienced observation, reports are of assistance in permitting review and comparison with past performance, standards, or budgets. The reports facilitate a review of progress and also record efficiency or inefficiency. They are a record of the degree to which the supervisory responsibility is being carried out. Moreover, the reports can contribute to the building of morale by showing who are the best performers. Again,

Figure 36-28 Summary of Idle Machine Hours.

The Chicago Chemical Company
SUMMARY OF IDLE MACHINE HOURS
For Week Ended October 19, 19XX

Department	Available Hours	Operating Hours	Lost Hours	% Available Hours Utilized	REASON FOR LOST HOURS				COST OF IDLE TIME			
					Lack of Material	Lack of Orders	Operating Down Time	Other Unacct. For	Out of Pocket	Total Dept. Cost	Lost Pounds	Lost Profit
PHENOLIC SYSTEM												
51 Mixing	304	304	-	100.0	-	-	-	-	$ -	$ -	-	$ -
52 Milling	456	456	-	100.0	-	-	-	-	-	-	-	-
53 Grinding	1,872	1,870	2	99.9	-	-	2	-	5	12	624	115
54 Granulating—1	48	45	3	93.7	-	-	3	-	16	43	1,437	376
55 Screening	864	864	-	100.0	-	-	-	-	-	-	-	-
56 Granulating—2	144	144	-	100.0	-	-	-	-	-	-	-	-
Total or Average	3,688	3,683	5	99.9	-	-	5	-	$ 21	$ 55	-	$ 491
MELAMINE RESIN SYSTEM												
21 Mixing	240	120	120	50.0	-	120	-	-	$ -	$ 738	135,451	12,466
22 Milling—5	120	46	74	38.3	-	-	-	74	548	1,907	191,257	16,352
23 Milling—7	240	164	76	68.3	-	-	-	76	293	521	53,387	4,565
24 Grinding	120	115	5	95.8	-	-	-	5	19	45	5,647	523
27 Granulating—3	120	96	24	80.0	-	-	-	24	56	118	6,228	532
31 Granulating—4	120	118	2	98.3	-	-	2	-	35	100	2,381	204
Total or Average	960	659	301	68.6	-	120	3	179	$ 951	$3,429	-	$34,642
INDUSTRIAL RESINS SYSTEM												
106 Drying	120	111	9	92.5	-	-	9	-	$ 72	$ 257	6,390	353
111 Blending	240	111	129	46.3	-	129	-	-	260	1,486	124,227	6,870
112 Liquid Resins	120	119	1	99.2	-	-	1	-	2	12	766	14
114 "200" Series	120	111	9	92.5	-	9	-	-	55	118	3,402	154
Total or Average	600	452	148	75.3	-	138	10	-	$ 389	$1,873	-	$ 7,391
Grand Total	5,248	4,794	454	91.3	-	258	17	179	$1,361	$5,357	-	$42,524

Issued by Accounting Department—October 22

Figure 36-29 Summary of Monthly Performance by Department.

The General Manufacturing Corporation
Wayne Avenue Plant

MONTHLY COST SUMMARY—SMALL PARTS SECTION
For the Month Ended January 31, 19XX

General Foreman _____ R. Jones

Cost Center	DIRECT LABOR			DIRECT MATERIAL			MANUFACTURING EXPENSE			TOTAL			
	Budget	Actual	(Over) or Under Budget	Budget	Actual	(Over) or Under Budget	Budget	Actual	(Over) or Under Budget	Budget	Actual	(Over) or Under Budget	Per Cent (Over) or Under Budget
Fabrication........	$17,755	$17,732	$ 23	$ 27,340	$ 29,983	$(2,643)	$ 4,376	$ 4,799	$(423)	$ 49,471	$ 52,514	$(3,043)	(6.15)
Subassembly.......	11,603	11,091	512	16,803	17,083	(280)	6,310	6,873	(563)	34,716	35,047	(331)	(.95)
Processing........	14,199	14,572	(373)	12,911	12,431	480	4,523	4,312	211	31,633	31,315	318	1.01
Machine Shop.....	6,631	6,709	(78)	6,430	6,479	(49)	1,432	1,471	(39)	14,493	14,659	(166)	(1.15)
Paint.............	9,080	8,078	1,002	29,310	29,987	(677)	3,684	3,627	57	42,074	41,692	382	.91
Final Assembly....	10,646	10,874	(228)	49,691	50,312	(621)	6,397	6,214	183	66,734	67,400	(666)	(1.00)
Total..........	$69,914	$69,056	$ 858	$142,485	$146,275	$(3,790)	$26,722	$27,296	$(574)	$239,121	$242,627	$(3,506)	(1.47)
Per Cent (Over) or Under Budget........			1.23			(2.66)			(2.15)				(1.47)

Issued by Cost Department—February 6

Figure 36-30   Trend of Direct Labor Efficiency.

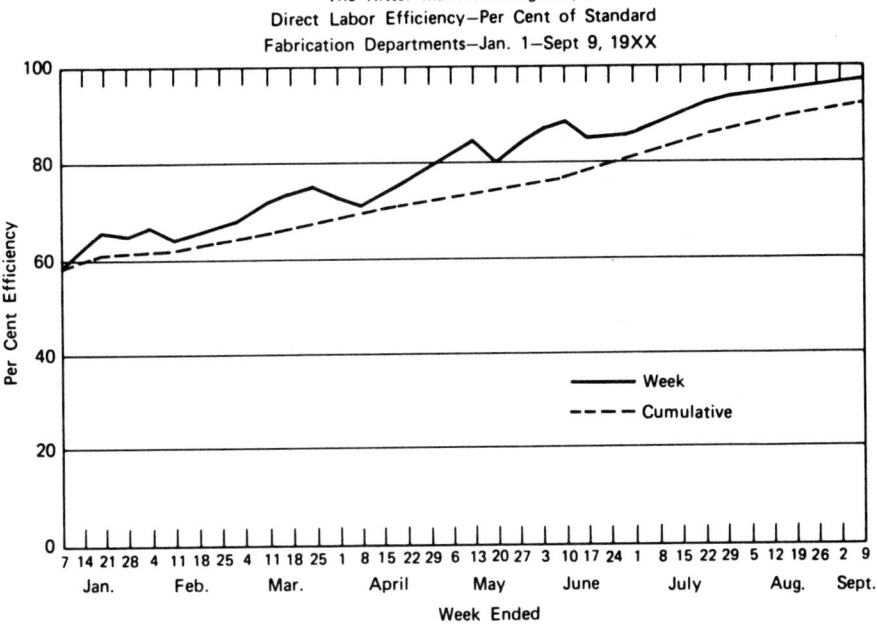

The Ritter Manufacturing Co., Inc.
Direct Labor Efficiency—Per Cent of Standard
Fabrication Departments—Jan. 1—Sept 9, 19XX

Figure 36-31   Trend of Material Usage.

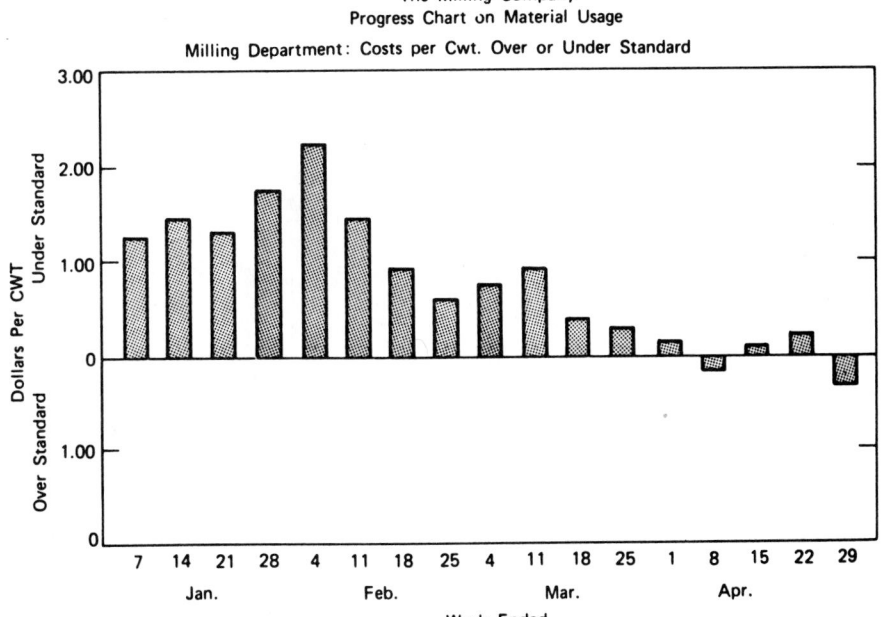

The Milling Company
Progress Chart on Material Usage

Milling Department: Costs per Cwt. Over or Under Standard

Figure 36-32 Report on Sales District Performance.

The Illustrative Company
DISTRICT SALES REPORT
For the Month of June, 19XX

Michigan   Manager _____ Cummcrow

Branch	Sales			Direct Selling Expenses					Remarks
	Actual	Budget	Over or (Under) Budget	Actual	Budget	(Over) or Under Budget	% of Net Sales Actual	% of Net Sales Budget	
SUBSTANDARD SALES PERFORMANCE:									
Ypsilanti	$14,610	$21,000	$(6,390)	$2,050	$2,100	$50	14.0	10.0	Account lost to competition
Ann Arbor	29,520	30,000	(480)	2,990	3,000	10	10.1	10.0	
Wayne	13,810	17,000	(3,190)	1,470	1,700	230	10.6	10.0	Plant closing down
Muskegon	6,400	12,000	(5,600)	640	1,200	560	10.0	10.0	Strike at X factory
Total	64,340	80,000	(15,660)	7,150	8,000	850	11.1	10.0	
STANDARD OR BETTER SALES PERFORMANCE:									
Detroit	241,620	215,000	26,620	15,870	16,000	130	6.6	7.4	5 new accounts
Monroe	74,100	73,000	1,100	6,020	6,000	(20)	8.1	8.2	
Pontiac	30,100	29,000	1,100	3,000	2,900	(100)	10.0	10.0	
Flint	12,090	12,000	90	1,270	1,200	(70)	10.5	10.0	
Green Bay	5,670	5,000	670	580	500	(80)	10.2	10.0	
Grand Rapids	47,770	46,000	1,770	3,470	3,500	30	7.3	7.6	
Lansing	25,050	25,000	50	2,000	2,000	-	8.0	8.0	
Total	436,400	405,000	31,400	32,210	32,100	(110)	7.4	7.9	
Grand Total	$500,740	$485,000	$15,740	$39,360	$40,100	$740	7.9	8.3	

they can be helpful in showing why a worker failed to earn the maximum bonus or what can be done to earn even more.

Since the minor supervisors are concerned with the performance of the individual worker, salesperson, etc., the reports should show individual performance. Although cost may be used, the emphasis should be on units of output and not necessarily on dollars. Some illustrative reports for the foreman are shown on Figures 36-33 through 36-35. Figure 36-33 is a daily report prepared on the computer showing actual hours by worker and the standard hours earned on each type of item produced. In Figure 36-34 the weekly spoilage of the operators is summarized. Figure 36-35 presents the actual labor cost, the standard allowance, and the reason for off-standard conditions. For the branch sales manager, or equivalent, reports on the activity of the individual salespersons are helpful. Figure 36-36 illustrates a weekly sales summary. Another weekly report giving information on the gross profit, direct expense, and number of calls is shown in Figure 36-37. A monthly report summarizing sales performance similar to Figure 36-38 is used extensively. A summary of budget performance of the individual salespersons, as in Figure 36-39, can be supported by a more detailed report given to the individual.

36-7 REPORTS ON NONFINANCIAL MATTERS

The vast majority of reports discussed in this chapter are of an internal financial nature—that is where the interest of the controller is focused. Yet, as explained in

Figure 36-33 Daily Labor Report—Computer.

THE ELECTRIC COMPANY

DAILY LABOR REPORT

DAY ENDED___5.P.M.___11/27/

CLOCK NO.	PART NO.	OPERATION NO.	QUANTITY	SHIFT	DEPT.	ACTUAL HRS.	STD. HRS.	ACTUAL HRS. VS. STD. HRS. UNDER	OVER
615	A51935	449	225 225	2	2	5 5	6 6		1 1
1069	A51935	455	270	1	2	32	31	1	
1162	A51935	455	288	2	2	38	31	7	
280	A51935	455	171	3	2	22	31		9
1069	A51935	455	27	1	2	2	31		29
1162	A51935	455	234	2	2	38	31	7	
1162	A51935	455	225	2	2	31	31		
280	A51935	455	180	3	2	30	31		1
			1395			193	217	15	39
807	A51935	459	300	2	2	20	10	10	
615	A51935	459	90	2	2	3	10		7
692	A51935	459	130	1	2	5	10		5
807	A51935	459	200	2	2	10	10		
692	A51935	459	200	1	2	10	10		
615	A51935	459	225	2	2	5	10		5
			1145			53	60	10	17
567	A51935	501	293 293	2	2	54 54	54 54		
331	A52338	302	1575	1	2	7	25		18
331	A52338	302	7735	1	2	25	25		
331	A52338	302	9675	1	2	30	25	5	18
			18985			62	75	5	
			113736			1677	1271	1907	1501

Figure 36-34 Weekly Spoilage Report.

The Manufacturing Company
WEEKLY SPOILAGE REPORT
WEEK ENDED NOVEMBER 30, 19XX

Cost Center___Polishing___   Foreman___R. Jones___

Operator	Total Production	Passed	Spoiled	Per Cent of Spoilage	Cost of Spoilage
1	356	324	32	8.99	$ 161.92
2	259	255	4	1.54	20.24
3	324	300	24	.74	121.44
4	292	281	11	3.77	55.66
5	302	276	26	8.61	131.56
6	313	298	15	4.79	75.90
7	290	267	23	7.93	116.38
8	327	302	25	7.65	126.50
9	184	164	20	10.87	101.20
10	288	277	11	3.82	55.66
11	318	296	22	6.92	111.32
12	299	278	21	7.02	106.26
Total.....	3,552	3,318	234	6.59	$1,184.04

Remarks:

sections 19-8 and 19-9, business managers know that many times measures of other types are needed. Thus, satisfied customers are a key to a successful business; innovation may be essential to survival; and comparisons of some activities with the industry, or specific competitors, or best-in-its-class entities may be useful. Hence, sometimes the controller's department, with the assistance of the functional manager, may gather nonfinancial data, and report on it, for such activities as these:

- *Customer Viewpoint.*
  (1) Number of new customers per month.
  (2) Number of customer complaints.
  (3) Number of on-time deliveries.
  (4) Share of key account purchases.
  (5) Percent of sales from new products.
  (6) Response time to customer questions.

- *Innovation.*
  (1) Time required to develop new products (vs. competitors).
  (2) Time to develop new processes.
  (3) Number of times ahead of competitor in new product introduction.

Figure 36-35   Daily Labor Report—Exception Reporting.

The Assembly Corporation
DAILY LABOR REPORT

Date __November 19, 19XX__

Cost Center ____Polishing____
Foreman ____Smith____

No.	Name	Actual	Standard	Over or (Under) Standard	Reasons for Off-Standard Costs
Operators		**Labor Cost**			
Off Standard					
1620	Smith..........	$ 14.81	$ 9.10	$ 5.71	Operator inefficiency
1697	Jones..........	13.98	12.00	1.98	Faulty tools
1722	Loy..........	12.14	11.72	.42	Fatigue
1732	Carl..........	15.62	12.99	2.63	Operator inefficiency
1781	Black..........	16.21	10.84	5.37	Nonstandard material
1798	Symanski......	13.87	12.07	1.80	Lack of materials
1801	Deal..........	19.87	14.77	5.10	Machine breakdown—overtime ($3.10)
	Total..........	106.50	83.49	23.01	
On Standard......		822.04	824.19	(2.15)	
	Total..........	$928.54	$907.68	$ 20.86	

Average Per Cent of Standard.................. 102.3%

Average Per Cent of Standard—Last Week.................. 103.4%

Figure 36-36 Weekly Branch Sales Summary Report.

The Sales Corporation
WEEKLY SALES SUMMARY
For Week Ended November 30, 19XX

Branch _____   Branch Manager _____

Salesperson	Pounds Sold		Sales by Product Line				
	Last Week	This Week	3100	3200	3300	Odd Lot	Other
Abrams........	16,100	21,500	10,100	3,000	8,300	–	100
Black.........	8,400	16,700	4,000	–	12,700	–	–
Coldwell......	9,100	9,100	–	6,100	3,000	–	–
Ernst.........	42,000	29,800	800	–	20,000	9,000	–
Gould.........	11,300	7,200	2,000	2,200	3,000	–	–
Horvath.......	1,900	1,300	–	–	1,300	–	–
Jones.........	8,100	10,500	–	–	5,500	–	5,000
Keeler........	3,400	2,200	–	200	2,000	–	–
Vaach.........	8,000	13,800	6,800	2,000	5,000	–	–
Total........	108,300	112,100	23,700	13,500	60,800	9,000	5,100

Standard Gross Margin........ $10,800

Remarks:

Special promotion on 3300

Figure 36-37 Weekly Report on Sales District Performance.

The Jones Company

WEEKLY SALES REPORT

DETROIT DISTRICT

Week Ended November 30, 19XX

Salesperson	Net Sales	Gross Profit		Direct Expense		Margin After Direct Expense	No. of Calls Made	New Customers
		Amount	%	Amount	% of Net Sales			
Walker........	$ 3,600	$1,656	46.0	$125	3.47	$1,531	23	1
Smead........	3,100	982	31.7	110	3.55	872	21	1
Piceu........	3,061	1,184	38.7	134	4.38	1,050	29	—
Taylor........	2,640	789	29.9	155	5.87	634	17	—
Brown........	2,200	972	44.2	105	4.77	867	20	3
Joll........	1,650	790	47.9	125	7.58	665	12	2
Total or Average..	$16,251	$6,373	39.2	$754	4.64	$5,619	20.3	7

Figure 36-38 Report on Quota Sales Performance.

Wayne Lathe Corporation
SALES INCENTIVE PLAN
ACTUAL VS. QUOTA SALES

Salesperson or Agent	For the Month of March, 19XX				For the Period October, 19X–1, Through March, 19XX			
	Quota	Actual	Over or (Under) Quota	% of Quota Attained	Quota	Actual	Over or (Under) Quota	% of Quota Attained
NEW UNITS								
Burdinhaw, R. W.	$ 180,000	$ 353,905	$ 173,905	196.6	$1,080,000	$1,603,226	$ 523,226	148.4
Farth, C. J.	155,000	122,747	(32,253)	(79.2)	930,000	550,252	(379,748)	(59.2)
Raymore, H. A., Jr.	–	54,951	54,951	–	–	257,170	257,170	–
Walker, C. E.	145,000	121,833	(23,167)	(84.0)	870,000	839,779	(30,221)	(96.5)
Saryan, H. J.	190,000	260,830	70,830	137.3	1,140,000	962,294	(177,706)	(84.4)
Sho, D. M.	180,000	201,685	21,685	112.0	1,080,000	1,069,694	(10,306)	(99.0)
Salesman Total	850,000	1,115,951	265,951	131.3	5,100,000	5,282,415	182,415	103.6
General Sales Corp.	300,000	403,800	103,800	134.6	1,800,000	3,106,700	1,306,700	172.6
Agents and Export	33,600	4,150	(29,450)	(12.4)	201,600	20,241	(181,359)	(10.0)
Total Sales	1,183,600	1,523,901	340,301	128.8	7,101,600	8,409,356	1,307,756	118.4
REPLACEMENT PARTS								
Burdinhaw, R. W.	30,000	–	(30,000)	–	180,000	12,000	(168,000)	(6.7)
Farth, C. J.	25,000	40,080	15,080	160.3	150,000	161,967	11,967	108.0
Raymore, H. A., Jr.	150,000	57,184	(92,816)	(38.1)	900,000	528,786	(371,214)	(58.8)
Walker, C. E.	25,000	1,854	(23,146)	(7.4)	150,000	43,372	(106,628)	(28.9)
Saryan, H. J.	25,000	–	(25,000)	–	150,000	11,288	(138,712)	(7.5)
Sho, D. M.	25,000	–	(25,000)	–	150,000	17,360	(132,640)	(11.6)
Salesman Total	$ 280,000	$ 99,118	$(180,882)	(35.4)	$1,680,000	$ 774,773	$(905,227)	(46.1)

NOTE: ( ) indicates unfavorable.

Issued by Accounting Department—April 12

Figure 36-39 Branch Report on Actual and Budgeted Selling Expense.

BUDGET REPORT

MONTH __Mar ch__

DEPT. HEAD. _____
DEPARTMENT. __New York Office__ NO. _____
__Selling Expense__

DESCRIPTION	CURRENT MONTH			YEAR TO DATE		
	BUDGET	ACTUAL	(OVER)/UNDER	BUDGET	ACTUAL	(OVER)/UNDER
SALESMAN						
Abbott	$1,234	$ 1,128	$ 106	$ 3,448	$ 3,628	$ (180)
Garrol	906	1,066	(160)	2,812	3,024	(212)
Higgins	1,489	1,230	259	3,678	3,855	(177)
Jones	1,189	1,625	(436)	3,720	4,200	(480)
Lambert	1,066	1,008	58	3,132	3,258	(126)
Orin	1,076	1,136	(60)	3,152	3,192	(40)
Prescott	1,770	1,719	60	4,790	5,100	(310)
Welsh	1,006	1,166	(160)	3,000	2,700	300
Total	$9,736	$10,069	$(333)	$27,732	$28,957	$(1,225)

TOTAL DEPARTMENT PERFORMANCE						
% of Net Sales	2.4	2.6		2.5	2.7	

ISSUED BY THE ACCOUNTING DEPT. __4/12/__

- *Other Internal Measures.*
  (1) Number of inventory outages.
  (2) Unit cost cycle vs. competitor.
  (3) Actual vs. planned time for process change.
- *Other External Measures.*
  (1) Share of the market.
  (2) Relative R&D expenditures vs. competitors, or industry.
  (3) Inventory turnover vs. competitor, or industry.

The chief point to be made is that some nonfinancial measures may be highly desirable in the scheme of management reporting.

36-8 A BALANCED REPORT PROGRAM

As a business firm becomes increasingly cost conscious or profit conscious, there is likely to be a growing and continued demand for accounting and statistical reports. More and more information is developed for the use of the executives. Coupled with this tendency is the dynamic character of most businesses, with their ever-changing needs and the availability of inexpensive computer power to handle, store, manipulate and retrieve data. Under such circumstances it is relatively easy, over a period of time, to continue the issuance of a mass of reports that do not necessarily serve a useful purpose. Old reports are continued because no one suggests that they be stopped, and new ones are added.

With such possibilities in mind, it is highly desirable that the controller attempt to keep the report program or structure in balance with the needs of the organization. When a request is received for a new report, he may find it advisable to inquire into the reason for the request and the purpose the information is designed to meet. Quite often another report already being prepared can be modified slightly and fill the requirement. Such a review also prevents a special or one-time report from becoming a routine report.

Besides this audit of report requests, the controller might profitably conduct a periodic survey of the report situation as follows:

1. Review with each executive the reports being issued to ascertain if the need still exists, if the information is in the desired form, and if other data are needed but are not being secured.

2. Analyze the reports and objectives in an attempt to suggest new and better ways of presenting the information.

3. Review the operations to find what monthly data can be conveniently summarized for useful informational reports and to see if any weak spots are developing that need emphasis for a time.

4. Cross-reference and reconcile all reports to make sure that the information is correct within the practical needs of the situation. Such a review will serve as a check on current control reports and may reveal any erroneous or otherwise unauthorized changes in the method of compiling the data.

Some companies have a report committee that passes on the need for additional reports and periodically reviews existing reports to determine the necessity of such. The objective is to provide the management team with sufficient and useful information without a duplication of reporting. After all, reports cost money.

A suggested report the controller might add to the list is an annual internal report for the top executives. It might consist of two sections: one including the comments and exhibits by each operating executive relating to his or her own division or function; the other, a section where the controller puts together financial facts and figures in an overall analysis.

36-9 A CONTROLLER'S CONTRIBUTION

The mere issuance of a report does not complete the controller's job by any means. The controller must know the company and its policies and methods. Through continuous contact with the functional and divisional executives, he must learn to see through the eyes of these executives. He must know their difficulties and be sympathetic with their problems. In some respects the controller is the contact person between central management and operating executives right down the line. He must not assume the role of chief executive, but he should attempt to interpret the policies and program of the company as the chief executive would like them to be known and followed. Conversely, he is in a position to present to central management many of the problems of the people at the front. The controller who can intelligently represent management in developing and enforcing the company program and who is accepted by operating heads as a welcome counselor will reach an extremely high level of usefulness to his company. This is but an expression of the fact that the controller, although objective in the approach to problems, cannot be an automaton, as financial people are so often pictured. He must be a human engineer who bridges the gap between a mass of meaningless figures and their translation into purposeful activity. Intelligent relations with employees are just as essential in the controller's department as they are elsewhere.

In all these matters, reports are but an aid to management and not a substitute for it.

36-10 SELECTED REFERENCES

Anderson, Anker V., *Graphing Financial Information, How Accountants Can Use Graphs to Communicate*, New York: National Association of Accountants, 1988.

deMare, George, *Communicating at the Top*, New York: John Wiley & Sons, 1979.

Douglas, Patricia P., and Theresa K. Beed, *Presenting Accounting Information to Managers*, New York: National Association of Accountants, 1986.

DuPree, Jean M., Al H. Hartgraves, and William H. Thralls, "How Management Accountants Can Communicate Better," *Management Accounting*, Feb. 1987 (pp. 40–43).

Kaplan, Robert S., and David P. Norton, "The Balanced Scorecard—Measures that Drive Performance," *Harvard Business Review*, Jan./Feb. 1992, pp. 71–79.

Meyer, N. Dean, and Mary E. Boone, *The Information Edge*, New York: McGraw Hill, 1987.

Peoples, David A., *Presentations Plus*, New York: John Wiley & Sons, 1988.

CHAPTER 37

Reports to Shareholders

37-1 INTRODUCTION

Chapter 36 on internal management reports focuses on providing all management levels with information to assist in running the business. That audience already possesses an intimate knowledge of those segments of the entity to which they direct their attention. But there is another large group that also has an interest in the business, but has somewhat limited knowledge of many aspects. It, too, needs reports providing essential information. This group is the shareholders or potential shareholders, and perhaps customers and the general public. Then, there are creditors, government agencies, stock exchanges, and others who would like information about the company. Reporting to each group poses separate problems and has been addressed in separate chapters.

The primary means of communicating with this group of owners or potential owners includes:

- The annual report (along with the Form 10-K and the proxy statement).
- The published quarterly report.
- Other written materials issued by the company.

- Other investor relations activities, including periodic meetings, special announcements.

These matters, with emphasis on annual reports and quarterly reports to shareholders, are reviewed in some detail, and format examples of excellent present practices are provided for convenience. (It is suggested that the controller peruse available reports to shareholders when reading this chapter.)

But there are questions being raised about the extent of financial disclosure—a subject with which the controller should be concerned. Accordingly, given a changing environment, some observations, suggestions, and criticisms from various professionals are briefly provided in the latter part of this chapter for the thoughtful consideration of the reader.

37-2 PURPOSE OF THE ANNUAL REPORT TO SHAREHOLDERS

The annual report to shareholders serves several purposes. It is an accounting of stewardship to owners and an assessment by management of the financial condition and potential of the company. It is also a compliance with SEC reporting requirements. It is, or should be, a means of permitting a discerning reader to analyze the operations and form a considered opinion of the current and possible future worth of the securities. An important related purpose of the annual report is to secure and hold venture capital. It is a selling device in attracting this capital from prospective shareholders.

There are other purposes to be served and should be considered during the preparation. Employees and prospective employees have a keen interest in the financial affairs of the company and the future. Customers generally desire to have an insight into the company. If the annual report is well done it can be used to improve civic relations and build goodwill with the general public.

37-3 THE CONTROLLER AND THE ANNUAL REPORT

Preparation of the annual report calls for the cooperation of several executives or departments. The financial staff must furnish the financial information and supervise its use. Those handling public relations or advertising must see that the report is attractive, understandable, and consistent with published utterances. The industrial relations department may contribute data regarding labor matters. Legal counsel should check the report for legal aspects. The chief executive and top management will give the report a general review and make certain policy decisions. Each of these groups, and others, can and should make a contribution to the corporate annual report.

However, the foundation of the annual report is the financial statements and the interpretation thereof. This basic information must come from the controller's office—from the accounting and statistical records of the business. For this reason, and because its managerial and accounting aspects are too important or too technical to be satisfactorily handled by others, the report should be the product of the controller's office in close cooperation with the operating and management staff. It should not be turned over to the advertising or public relations department. Although capable advertising people can do an outstanding job in many ways, there is often a tendency for them to make the annual report a somewhat blatant and obvious sales or advertising tool. As a result, the document's real purpose as a report of stewardship is somewhat obscured. Under the circumstances, it is believed the talents of these departments should be put to work for the controller and not the controller put to work for them.

Another question arises about the responsibility and liability of the controller to the shareholders, the directors, and the public. Although such matters have not always been clearly defined, there has developed an increased sense of responsibility by controllers for the published reports of their company. As a member of management the controller cannot escape a share of responsibility for those actions that come within his sphere of activity. Quite naturally, final responsibility for adequate disclosure must rest with the directors and officers of the company. But it is nevertheless the duty of the controller to make the facts known to management and to press for sufficient disclosure of information. If he finds that the wishes of management and the board of directors are substantially adverse to his sense of professional ethics, and the subject is material, then he probably will have to resign.

37-4 GENERAL CONTENTS OF THE ANNUAL REPORT

In considering the content and form of annual reports, the controller should be cognizant of the specific requirements of the SEC, the FASB, the New York Stock Exchange, state legal requirements, and other federal regulations. For example, Rule 14c-3 states that annual reports furnished to shareholders in connection with the annual shareholder meeting should include the following information:

Audited Financial Statements

- Balance sheets as of the 2 most recent fiscal years.
- Income statements for each of the 3 most recent years.
- Statement of cash flows for each of the 3 most recent years.

Rule 14c-3 also requires that the following financial information as specified in Regulations S-K be included in the annual report:

- Selected quarterly financial data.
- Selected financial data for the last 5 years.
- Segment information.
- Management discussion and analysis of financial conditions and results of operations.
- Disagreements with accountants on accounting and financial disclosure.
- Listing of company directors and executive officers.
- Market price of company's common stock for each quarterly period within the two most recent years.

It is apparent that in structuring the report, recognition should be given to all the requirements. Also, if more than one report is prepared, the controller should insure that they are conformed.

The kind and amount of information to be presented will depend on the type of industry and the specific company. A manufacturing company may find it appropriate to discuss new products or increasing productivity. A high-technology company will include comments on the applications of new technologies. A section of the report should be devoted to telling the reader about the industry, products, and type of business. Management should include those facts that will inform the shareholders and provide them with an understanding of the business. The annual report is an opportunity to create a broader and more fundamental understanding of the company. Discussion of the future, new ventures, R&D, foreign business, growth prospects, and management principles are topics of interest to the shareholder.

A review of many annual reports will indicate that most companies' reports do not change much from year to year. Changes are generally brought about by new reporting requirements or by recommendations from innovative financial or other management personnel. The operating departments should be contacted for ideas and suggestions for improvement. Consultants should also be considered and used, particularly for ideas to improve the readership of the report. The controller can also contribute new ideas by researching new techniques and applications. After the general theme, content, and format have been established, top management should review and approve.

A well-balanced report provides meaningful information to the shareholder and sufficient facts to meet the needs of the professional reader. One means to accomplish this is to provide highlight or condensed information with brief analytical comments. In another section of the report, detailed facts and figures can be presented that are used by financial analysts to formulate an investment opinion.

An outline of some of the more basic contents of an effective, easy-to-read annual report follows:

1. *Highlights or Summary Page.* Usually, a presentation of fundamental and comparative data on financial results. Examples are as follows:

   Sales.

   Net income.

   Earnings per share.

   Cash dividends paid per share.

   Investments in property, plant, and equipment.

   Long-term debt.

   Book value per share.

   Number of stockholders.

   Number of employees.

   Return on shareholders' equity.

2. *Letter to the Shareholders.* An opportunity for the chairman of the board or president or both to provide their comments on the company with regard to challenges, strengths, overview of operations, and goals and plans for the future. Generally, in this letter facts and figures are not included but are presented elsewhere in the report.

3. *Review of Operations.* This section of the report describes the business and can be considered a corporate review. The product lines are normally described and

illustrated by the use of photographs, charts, and graphs. Included in the commentary are the markets, customers, productivity, new products, and the future.

4. *Managements' Discussion and Analysis of the Summary of Operations and Financial Condition.* As required by the SEC to be included in the annual report, management should analyze and discuss the reasons for basic changes between the current year and the previous year. Also, the prior year should be compared to its previous year. The information presented should not be boiler plate or mechanistic. Data disclosed should be useful, meaningful, complete, and accurate so that the shareholder can make an informed investment judgment. The MD&A has become a focal point of the financial section of the annual report.

5. *Financial Statements.* Comparative financial statements, including appropriate footnotes and the independent accountants' reports.

6. *Report of Managements Responsibilities.* A report of management's responsibilities for financial statements and the system of internal control must be included in the annual report. It also provides management's assessment of the current effectiveness of the internal control system. Finally it includes management's response to significant recommendations made by its auditors, both internal and independent, concerning the controls.

7. *Supplemental Information.* There are other annual report requirements for data, such as unaudited quarterly information—sales, operating margin, net income, EPS, dividends per share, and the high and low stock prices.

   Each year new disclosure requirements may be added or old ones eliminated. The controller must be aware of such changes and incorporate them into the annual report. Recent examples of additions are disclosures on income taxes, consolidated financing companies, pension plans, and other post-retirement benefits, while the requirement for disclosing the effects of general inflation was dropped. The independent public accountants should be a useful resource to identify or confirm changing requirements.

8. *Other Data.* Certain additional information is useful to the shareholders in evaluating and keeping informed on the company. Such information includes the following:

   Members of the board of directors and their affiliations.

   Corporate officers.

   Board committees and members.

   Functions of board committees.

   Division and subsidiary officers.

   Registrars.

   Transfer agents.

   Outside counsel.

   Independent accountants.

   Stock exchanges where stock is listed and traded.

   Locations of principal offices and operating units.

   Statement of management responsibility.

Summary of significant accounting policies.

Notice of annual meeting of shareholders.

Table of contents for reference.

Historical statistical data.

The controller, as the chief accounting officer, is encouraged to review annual reports of the industry and of leading companies in other industries to be aware of trends in financial reporting. An excellent source of information is *Accounting Trends & Techniques,* published each year by the AICPA. It includes a compilation of data obtained be surveying annual reports to shareholders. It points out significant accounting trends, and the techniques discussed are illustrated by excerpts from the annual reports. Another source of ideas about financial reporting is the *Corporate Information Committee Report,* published each year by the Financial Analysts Federation. It has subcommittees, composed of experts in various industries, evaluate and rank the financial reporting practices of the companies in the industry. The strengths and weaknesses of each company are described in the hope that the preparers will have a better understanding of what investors want to know and why. The controller is also advised to keep informed on the various dates annual reports are required to be filed with concerned agencies and provided to the shareholders.

(a) HIGHLIGHTS OR SUMMARY PAGE

In presenting financial information to the shareholders, as well as to professional analysts, it is useful to provide a quick review of salient facts concerning operations. Usually, the first page or inside front cover of the annual report is a convenient place to present the highlights.

Although the amount of information provided will vary, depending on the company, an effective presentation by The Dow Chemical Company for a recent year is shown in Figure 37-1.

A company should consider what information is most useful to the shareholder in a highlight form. Normally, it should be comparative and presented graphically as well as in tabulated form.

(b) MANAGEMENT ANALYSIS OF OPERATIONS AND FINANCIAL CONDITION

Management's discussion and analysis (MD&A) of the results of operations and the liquidity and financial condition of the business has become one of the most important parts of the financial section of the annual report. Several years ago there were perhaps one or two pages used to present management's explanation and clarification of what the financial statements, primarily the income statement, reflected. A review of annual reports will reveal that some companies are using up to 20 pages to provide the readers with comprehensive explanations, of each of the financial statements. The average number of pages for the MD&As of large companies probably range between five and ten. While there is no set rule for how long this section should be, it clearly must be sufficient to enable investors to appraise the quality of earnings and to evaluate the fiscal soundness and financial potential of the company. It is an opportunity

Figure 37-1   Financial Highlights Page from 1993 Annual Report of The Dow Chemical Company.

In millions, except as noted	*1993*	*1992*	*% Change*
Net Sales	**$18,060**	$18,971	−5
Operating Income	**1,440**[1]	1,290[1]	+12
Income before Cumulative Effect of Accounting Change	**644**	276	+133
Research and Development Expenses	**1,256**	1,289	−3
Capital Expenditures	**1,397**	1,595	−12
Depreciation	**1,343**	1,342	−
Total Taxes	**1,219**	916	+33
Wages, Salaries and Benefits	**4,258**	4,201	+1
Employees *(in thousands)*	**55.4**	61.4	−10
Net Stockholders' Equity *(at year-end)*	**8,034**	8,064	−
Return on Average Stockholders' Equity	**7.9%**	3.1%[2]	+4.8 points
Average Common Shares Outstanding	**273.6**	271.6	+1
Earnings per Share before Cumulative Effect of Accounting Change *(in dollars)*	**2.33**	0.99	+135
Dividends Paid per Share *(in dollars)*	**2.60**	2.60	−

[1] *Includes special charges of $180 in 1993 and $433 in 1992. See Note A to the Financial Statements.*
[2] *Before cumulative effect of accounting change.*

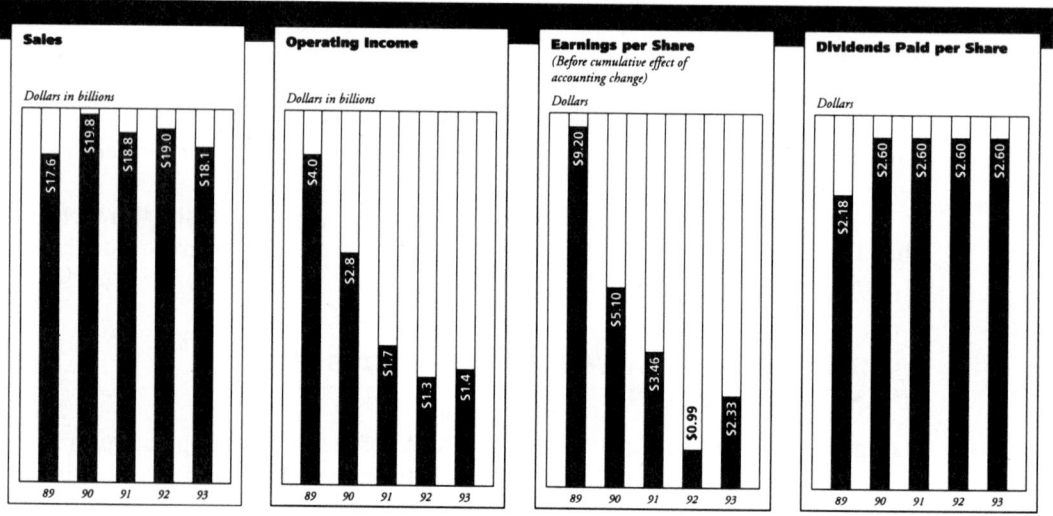

Source: Used with permission of The Dow Chemical Company.

for management to clarify ambiguities and spell out subtleties. Each company will have to decide how much explanation is needed for their readers to have enough information to make informed decisions.

An example of a concise MD&A is shown in Figure 37-2. This brief discussion by Kellogg Company for a recent year reviews strategic and financial objectives, global marketplace results of operations (two years), liquidity and capital resources, the future outlook.

(c) FINANCIAL STATEMENTS

The financial statements are the primary section of an annual report to shareholders. Obviously, the requirements of the stock exchanges and SEC and generally accepted accounting principles must be satisfied. Annual reports contain the following:

1. Statement of earnings.
2. Statement of financial position.
3. Statement of cash flows.
4. Statement of shareholders' equity.

The Statement of Financial Position is shown for the past two years; the other three statements present a three-year comparison.

In addition to these statements, a five-year summary of selected financial data is also shown. Some companies expand that presentation and show ten or more years as a convenient source for investors and analysts or to keep the information and/or certain trends from being misleading. As mentioned earlier, selected quarterly data for the most recent two years is also included in the annual report.

The controller should insure that the statements presented are consistent and in accordance with the terminology and requirements of the rule-making bodies of accounting.

(i) Statement of Earnings. The accounting profession has made considerable progress in the simplification of statements of earnings or the income statement. A very readable Consolidated Income Statement for Kimberly-Clark Corporation and Subsidiaries for a recent year is illustrated in Figure 37-3.

(ii) Statement of Financial Position. The titles used for this statement are usually Statement of Financial Position, Balance Sheet, or Statement of Financial Condition. The most commonly used title is Balance Sheet.

Formats will vary, but the account form of assets on the left-hand side equal to the sum of liabilities and stockholders' equity on the right-hand side is commonly used.

The Consolidated Balance Sheet of Kimberly-Clark Corporation for a recent year is shown in Figure 37-4.

(iii) Statement of Cash Flows. Statement of Financial Accounting Standard No. 95, Statement of Cash Flows superseded APB Opinion No. 19, Reporting Changes in Financial Position and requires a statement of cash flows classifying cash receipts and payments as to whether they result from operating, investing, or financing activities.

Figure 37-2 Management's Discussion and Analysis from Kellogg Company 1993 Annual Report.

Strategic and financial objectives

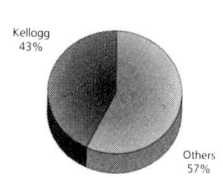

1993 Global Market Share
(volume)

Management's primary objective is to increase shareholder value over time. To achieve this objective, the Company has implemented a long-term business strategy which focuses on continuing aggressive investment in new cereal markets, increasing returns on existing investments, maximizing cash flows, and minimizing the cost of capital through appropriate financial policies. The success of this strategy is reflected in the Company's superior earnings, return on equity, total return to shareholders, and its overall strong financial condition.

Global marketplace

Because of its strong global market share leadership, the Company is uniquely positioned to benefit from the continued increase in cereal consumption around the world. As of December 31, 1993, our market share was 43% globally, 38% in North America, 47% in Asia-Pacific, 50% in Europe, and 78% in Latin America. This favorable positioning in existing markets is accompanied by leadership in entering new markets with substantial long-term potential. Kellogg opened a new cereal plant in Latvia in 1993 and has plants scheduled to begin production in India in 1994 and in China in 1995. We plan to make our products available to a billion new consumers by early in the next century, more than doubling our present reach.

Lifestyle and demographic changes in major markets around the world favor a continued increase in consumption of ready-to-eat cereal, our core product line. Two particularly important trends are ever-increasing recognition by consumers around the world of the nutritional value of cereal and the accelerating move of the "baby boom" generation from young adulthood, where cereal consumption is relatively low, to middle age,

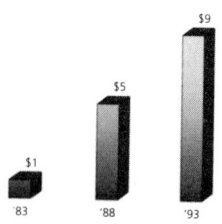

1993 Geographic Net Sales

**10-Year Growth of a
Dollar Invested in
Kellogg Company Stock**
(dividends reinvested quarterly)

where cereal consumption grows steadily. The Company believes it has developed the worldwide infrastructure and financial resources needed to continue its leadership of category growth.

Results of operations

1993 compared to 1992

Revenues

Kellogg revenues are obtained primarily from the sale of ready-to-eat cereals in more than 150 countries. Kellogg has been marketing cereals since 1906 and is the global market share leader by nearly a three-to-one advantage. Increased revenues are obtained by reaching consumers in both new and developed markets with products that are both nutritious and superior in quality. The introduction of new products is vital to the Company's long-term financial strength. For 1993, the Company introduced 24 new products worldwide.

Despite intense competition, continued recessions in several major markets, and unfavorable currency movements, worldwide revenues increased by 2% for 1993, marking the 49th consecutive annual increase. The increase was achieved through higher selling prices and a 2% increase in cereal volume, being negatively impacted by foreign currency movements. Forty percent of all revenues are derived from outside the United States and are subject to foreign currency fluctuations. Excluding the negative effects of currency movements, 1993 sales would have increased 6%. During 1993, sales within the United States rose by 6% from increased selling prices and volume for both cereal and convenience foods.

Source: Used with permission of Kellogg Company.

Figure 37-2 *(continued)*

1993 European sales, which were significantly affected by unfavorable foreign currency fluctuations, were down 8%. If the effects of foreign currency are excluded, European sales would have risen 4%. Sales for other areas grew by 2% from increased volume and higher selling prices, being partially offset by the negative impact of currency fluctuations. Excluding the effects of negative currency movements, other area sales would have increased 6%.

Other revenue for 1993 includes a total pre-tax gain of $65.9 million ($.20 per share) from the sale of the Company's British carton-container division ($.10 per share) and its Argentine snack food business ($.10 per share). In recent years the Company has divested units that do not fit with its long-term strategic plan. Other deductions for 1993 includes pre-tax charges of $64.3 million ($.18 per share) from the write-down of certain assets in Europe and North America.

Expenses and profit margins
Cost of goods sold as a percent of sales was 47% for the year, the lowest in the last decade. Higher selling prices, increased volume, and worldwide productivity gains in factory operations are among the factors that contributed to this lower ratio.

Intense global competition requires heavy investment in value-added marketing. Selling and administrative expense represented 36% of each sales dollar in 1993. The Company is committed to building strong, long-term brand franchises through effective advertising.

Gross interest expense, prior to amounts capitalized, increased to $40.4 million for 1993, compared to $33.6 million for 1992. Higher debt levels caused the increase. The Company expects average borrowing levels and related interest expense to be slightly higher during 1994.

The Company's effective tax rate was 34.2% for the year, compared to 36.2% for 1992. The tax rate declined for a number of reasons. Decreased statutory rates in countries such as Germany, Australia, Canada, and South Africa more than offset the United States tax rate increase of 1993. The Company's 1994 effective tax rate is expected to be approximately 38%.

For 1993, earnings per share were $2.94 and earnings were $680.7 million, compared to 1992's earnings per share of $1.81 and earnings of $431.2 million. Excluding all one-time events for both years, earnings per share were $2.92, up 6% over $2.75 in 1992; and net earnings were $675.5 million, up 3%. Without the negative impact of foreign currency fluctuations, earnings per share would have been up 10% and net earnings up 6%.

Geographically, earnings before the cumulative effect of an accounting change were lower by 1% for the United States and by 1% for Europe, and up 7% for other areas. Excluding all one-time events for both years, the United States would have been up 7%, Europe down 9%, and other areas up 2%. Without the negative impact of foreign currency movements, Europe would have been up 4% rather than down 9%.

Statement of Financial Accounting Standards 112, "Employers' Accounting for Postemployment Benefits," was issued in November 1992. This statement had no material effect on the Company's financial condition or results of operations.

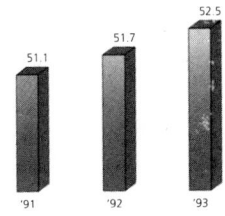

Gross Profit Percentage

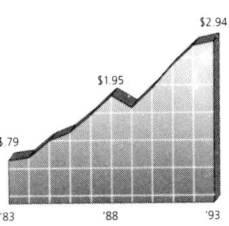

Earnings Per Share
(before accounting change)

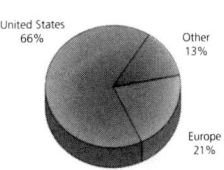

1993 Geographic Earnings
(before accounting change)

Figure 37-2 *(continued)*

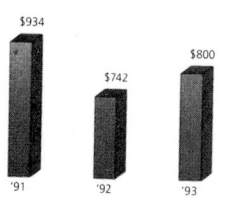

Cash Flow From Operations
(millions)

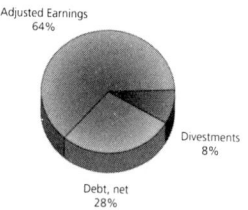

1993 Sources of Cash

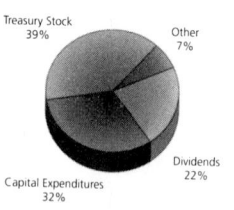

1993 Uses of Cash

1992 compared to 1991

Worldwide revenues for 1992 increased 7% to $6.2 billion on the strength of a 5% gain in cereal volume and higher selling prices. During January 1992, the Company sold Fearn International Inc., a U.S. food-service subsidiary. Excluding 1991 sales by Fearn, 1992 sales would have increased by 9% instead of 7%. Foreign currency fluctuations had a minimal impact on 1992 worldwide revenues.

Sales within the United States increased by 5%; however, excluding Fearn sales from 1991, the increase was 8%. This increase resulted from increased volume coupled with higher selling prices. European sales were up a solid 14% for the year due to a volume gain of 6% coupled with higher selling prices and the positive impact of foreign currency fluctuations. Sales for other areas grew by 6% from improved volume and selling prices, partially offset by negative foreign currency movements.

Other revenue includes a total pre-tax gain of $58.5 million ($.16 per share) from the sale of Fearn International Inc. Other deductions includes a pre-tax charge of $22.4 million ($.05 per share) from the disposition of convenience foods operations in Canada and other North America assets.

Cost of goods sold as a percent of sales was 48%, compared to 49% in 1991. Factors such as improved volume, positive inventory management, and improved factory productivity contributed to the decline. Selling and administrative expense represented 35% of each sales dollar in 1992, compared to 33% in 1991.

Gross interest expense, prior to amounts capitalized, decreased to $33.6 million, compared to $60.7 million in 1991. Lower interest rates and debt levels led to the decline. The Company's effective tax rate was 36.2%,

compared to 38.4% for 1991. The decline in the rate resulted from lower effective tax rates in certain international locations.

For 1992, earnings per share were $1.81 and earnings were $431.2 million, compared to earnings per share of $2.51 and earnings of $606 million in 1991. Excluding all one-time events and the accounting change, earnings per share were $2.75, up 10%, and earnings were $657.1 million, up 8%.

Effective January 1, 1992, the Company adopted Statement of Financial Accounting Standards (FAS) 106, "Employers' Accounting for Postretirement Benefits Other Than Pensions." This standard requires that the estimated cost of postretirement benefits, principally health care, be accrued over the period earned rather than expensed as incurred. The transition effect of adopting FAS 106 on the immediate recognition basis, as of January 1, 1992, resulted in an after-tax charge of $251.6 million or $1.05 per share.

Geographically, earnings before the cumulative effect of the accounting change were up 18% for the United States, up 9% for Europe, and down 6% for other areas. Excluding the sale of Fearn and the one-time asset writeoffs, United States earnings would have been up 9% and other areas up 5%.

Liquidity and capital resources

The financial condition of the Company remained strong during 1993. Company operations have historically provided a strong, positive cash flow which, along with the program of issuing commercial paper and maintaining worldwide credit facilities, provides adequate liquidity to meet the Company's operational needs. Cash and

Figure 37-2 *(continued)*

cash equivalents totaled $98 million at December 31, 1993, compared to $126 million at December 31, 1992.

Cash provided by operating activities amounted to $800 million in 1993, compared to $742 million in 1992 and $934 million in 1991. The Company's current ratio (current assets over current liabilities) was 1.0:1.0 for 1993 and 1.2:1.0 for 1992.

The Company maintains credit facilities with banking institutions in the United States and other countries where it conducts business. At year-end, the Company had $613 million of short-term lines of credit, of which $569 million were available.

Funds expended for capital improvements in 1993 totaled $450 million, compared to $474 million in 1992 and $333 million in 1991. In 1994, capital expenditures are expected to be approximately $400 million as the Company continues to invest globally in expansion and modernization of its facilities. The capital program remains focused on producing the highest quality product at the lowest possible cost.

The Company's debt to total capital ratio was 35% at December 31, 1993, compared to 21% in 1992. The Company's increased share repurchase program led to higher debt levels resulting in the higher ratio. The Company continues to enjoy the highest available debt ratings on both its commercial paper and long-term debt.

At December 31, 1993, the Company had on file a "shelf registration" of $200 million with the Securities and Exchange Commission to provide for the issuance of debt in the United States. The net proceeds from any offering under the "shelf" would be added to the Company's working capital and be available for general corporate purposes.

In October of 1993, the Company issued $265 million Canadian Eurodollar 5-year Notes with a 6.25% interest rate.

During 1992, $300 million 5-year notes were issued with a 5.9% interest rate. The first two years of both notes were swapped into variable rate debt. In March 1992, the Company's $200 million 9.5% Eurodollar Notes matured.

Notes payable are comprised principally of floating interest rate obligations that had an average interest rate of 4% in 1993, compared to 6% during 1992.

Dividends paid per share of common stock rose 10% in 1993, marking the 37th consecutive year of increase. The trend of increased dividends is expected to continue in 1994.

During 1993, the Company purchased 9,487,508 shares of its common stock at an average cost of $58 per share. In 1992, a total of 3,497,000 shares were purchased at an average cost of $63 per share. Treasury stock purchases were made under plans authorized by the Company's Board of Directors. At December 31, 1993, an additional $353 million of stock could be purchased through December 1994 under current Board authorization.

Looking forward

Management is not aware of any adverse trends that would materially affect the Company's strong financial position. Should suitable investment opportunities or working capital needs arise that would require additional financing, management believes that the Company's triple A credit rating, strong balance sheet, and history of exceptional earnings provides a solid base for obtaining additional financial resources at competitive rates and terms.

Kellogg is a global market leader backed with a solid financial infrastructure that provides a competitive advantage. The Company is committed to long-term earnings per share growth with above average return on equity.

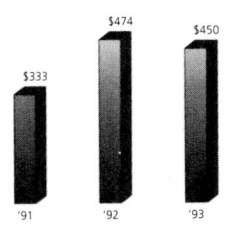

Capital Expenditures
(millions)

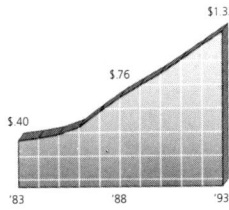

Dividends Per Share

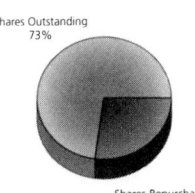

Shares Outstanding
73%

Shares Repurchased
27%

**Stock Repurchased
Since 1984**
(based on shares
outstanding at 12/31/83)

Figure 37-3   Consolidated Income Statement for Kimberly-Clark Corporation and Subsidiaries 1993 Annual Report.

(Millions of dollars except per share amounts)	Year Ended December 31		
	1993	1992	1991
Net Sales	**$6,972.9**	$7,091.1	$6,776.9
Cost of products sold	**4,581.4**	4,534.5	4,332.4
Gross Profit	**2,391.5**	2,556.6	2,444.5
Advertising, promotion and selling expenses	**1,068.3**	1,255.6	1,202.5
Research expense	**158.5**	156.1	148.8
General expense	**371.2**	351.8	351.4
Restructuring charge	**–**	250.0	–
Operating Profit	**793.5**	543.1	741.8
Interest expense	**(112.6)**	(99.4)	(102.1)
Other income (expense), net	**32.1**	18.2	44.6
Income Before Income Taxes	**713.0**	461.9	684.3
Provision for income taxes	**284.4**	186.3	236.1
Income Before Equity Interests	**428.6**	275.6	448.2
Share of net income of equity companies	**98.0**	82.9	72.8
Minority owners' share of subsidiaries' net income	**(15.7)**	(13.5)	(12.7)
Income Before Cumulative Effects of Accounting Changes	**510.9**	345.0	508.3
Cumulative effects of accounting changes:			
Other postretirement benefits, net of income taxes	**–**	(245.0)	–
Income taxes	**–**	35.0	–
Net Income	**$ 510.9**	$ 135.0	$ 508.3
Per Share Basis			
Income before cumulative effects of accounting changes	**$ 3.18**	$ 2.15	$ 3.18
Cumulative effects of accounting changes:			
Other postretirement benefits, net of income taxes	**–**	(1.53)	–
Income taxes	**–**	.22	–
Net income	**$ 3.18**	$ .84	$ 3.18

Source: Used with permission of the Kimberly-Clark Corporation.

       The Consolidated Cash Flow Statement of Kimberly-Clark Corporation and Subsidiaries for a recent year, commencing with the net income shown in Figure 37-3 is reflected in Figure 37-5.

(iv) Statement of Shareholders' Equity.   This statement presents an analysis of the changes in each caption of the shareholders' equity presented in the balance sheet. It is in the form of a reconciliation of the beginning balance to the ending balance for each period for which an income statement is presented. The amount of dividends paid for each share and the aggregate for each class of shares is also stated.

Figure 37-4 Consolidated Balance Sheet of Kimberly-Clark Corporation and Subsidiaries from 1993 Annual Report.

		December 31	
(Millions of dollars)	ASSETS	*1993*	*1992*
Current Assets			
Cash and cash equivalents		$ **34.8**	$ 41.1
Accounts receivable		**738.7**	775.1
Inventories		**775.9**	719.7
Deferred income tax benefits		**93.7**	81.8
Prepaid expenses		**32.1**	64.9
Total Current Assets		**1,675.2**	1,682.6
Property			
Land and timberlands		**121.0**	93.6
Buildings		**1,004.5**	935.5
Machinery and equipment		**5,034.6**	4,609.1
Construction in progress		**212.7**	335.9
		6,372.8	5,974.1
Less accumulated depreciation		**2,330.0**	2,199.3
Net Property		**4,042.8**	3,774.8
Investments in Equity Companies		**398.3**	349.7
Deferred Charges and Other Assets		**264.4**	222.0
		$6,380.7	$6,029.1

Source: Used by permission of Kimberly-Clark Corporation.

It is presented in differing formats. Figure 37-6 for a recent year for Colgate-Palmolive Company provides the data in two segments: A Consolidated Statement of Retained Earnings and a Consolidated Statement of Changes in Capital Accounts to identify the changes in the other shareholders equity accounts.

37-5 REPORT OF MANAGEMENT'S RESPONSIBILITIES

This report by management is required by the SEC. It states that the integrity of the financial statements and information included in the Annual Report is management's responsibility. It further describes the accounting control system on which the statements are based and the audit activities used to test and verify compliance with procedures and adequacy of policies. It highlights the role and makeup of the audit committee of the board of directors, addresses significant audit recommendations made during the year and evaluates the effectiveness of the overall accounting control system at the end of the year. An illustrative statement of management's responsibilities for the financial statements, covering a recent year, for Eastman Chemical Company, together with the related Report of Independent Accountants, is shown in Figure 37-7.

Figure 37-4 *(continued)*

LIABILITIES AND STOCKHOLDERS' EQUITY	December 31	
	1993	1992
Current Liabilities		
Debt payable within one year	$ 684.8	$ 445.3
Trade accounts payable	322.0	372.9
Other payables	116.1	99.6
Accrued expenses	594.6	674.8
Accrued income taxes	121.8	95.2
Dividends payable	69.2	135.0
Total Current Liabilities	1,908.5	1,822.8
Long-Term Debt	933.1	994.6
Noncurrent Employee Benefit Obligations	430.0	409.3
Deferred Income Taxes	585.0	554.6
Minority Owners' Interests in Subsidiaries	66.9	56.7
Stockholders' Equity		
Common stock – $1.25 par value – authorized 300.0 million shares; issued 161.9 million	202.4	202.4
Additional paid-in capital	27.1	27.6
Common stock held in treasury, at cost – 1.0 million and 1.1 million shares at December 31, 1993 and 1992, respectively	(32.9)	(38.9)
Unrealized currency translation adjustments	(240.6)	(197.9)
Retained earnings	2,501.2	2,197.9
Total Stockholders' Equity	2,457.2	2,191.1
	$6,380.7	$6,029.1

A key factor in evaluating the financial performance of a company is the accounting policies that were followed. APB Opinion No. 22, "Disclosure of Accounting Policies," concludes that information about the accounting policies adopted by a reporting entity is essential for financial statement users and should be included as an integral part of the financial statements. The disclosure should identify and describe the accounting principles followed and the methods of applying those principles that materially affect the determination of financial position, changes in financial position, or results of operations.

Paragraph 13 of APB No. 22 states:

Examples of disclosures by a business entity commonly required with respect to accounting policies would include, among others, those relating to basis of consolidation, depreciation methods, amortization of intangibles, inventory pricing, accounting for research and development costs (including basis for amortization), translation of foreign currencies, recognition of profit on long-term construction-type contracts and recognition of revenue from franchising and leasing operations. This list of examples is not all-inclusive.

With regard to format and location, there is flexibility as long as the disclosure is an integral part of the financial statements. In most cases the disclosure is a separate

Figure 37-5 Consolidated Cash Flow Statement of Kimberly-Clark Corporation and Subsidiaries from 1993 Annual Report.

	Year Ended December 31		
(Millions of dollars)	1993	1992	1991
Operations			
Net income	**$510.9**	$135.0	$508.3
Depreciation	**295.9**	289.0	265.5
Restructuring charge	–	250.0	–
Cumulative effects of accounting changes	–	210.0	–
Deferred income tax provision (benefit)	**23.6**	(3.4)	7.0
Equity companies' earnings in excess of dividends paid	**(49.0)**	(35.6)	(20.9)
Minority owners' share of subsidiaries' net income	**15.7**	13.5	12.7
Changes in operating working capital	**(71.7)**	(92.7)	(53.0)
Other	**21.3**	(11.8)	(14.7)
Cash Provided by Operations	**746.7**	754.0	704.9
Investing			
Capital spending	**(654.5)**	(690.5)	(537.0)
Other	**(11.1)**	(79.0)	(8.1)
Cash Used for Investing	**(665.6)**	(769.5)	(545.1)
Financing			
Cash dividends paid	**(273.4)**	(262.8)	(231.9)
Changes in debt payable within one year	**239.5**	138.7	(103.3)
Increases in long-term debt	**83.9**	237.4	233.0
Decreases in long-term debt	**(145.4)**	(117.5)	(86.8)
Other	**8.0**	18.0	11.8
Cash (Used for) Provided by Financing	**(87.4)**	13.8	(177.2)
Decrease in Cash and Cash Equivalents	**$ (6.3)**	$ (1.7)	$ (17.4)

Source: Used with permission of Kimberly-Clark Corporation.

summary of significant accounting policies preceding the notes to financial statements or as the initial note.

(i) Other Disclosures. The matter of how much information should be included in the report to shareholders is a combination of required disclosures (SEC regulations, FASB Standards, etc.), and management judgment. Much of the supplemental information now included in notes to the financial statements is mandated, for example, disclosures in connection with leases, segments, pensions, consolidations, and taxes, in addition to previously mentioned accounting practices, quarterly data, and selected five-year data. These requirements are added to, reduced, and/or modified on an ongoing basis and the controller must be aware of developments in this area. New disclosures often require a lot of preparation, for example, new accounts, in order to be able to comply with them. Insofar as other disclosures are concerned, the authors believe that the annual report should bring to the owners and investors attention any significant trends or developments that affect their equities. Matters like interest rates, labor problems, sales trends, inventory levels, industry uncertainties, stock repurchase plans, mergers, and

Figure 37-6   Consolidated Statement of Retained Earnings and Consolidated Statement of Changes in Capital Accounts for Colgate-Palmolive Company from 1993 Annual Report.

Consolidated Statement of Retained Earnings

COLGATE-PALMOLIVE COMPANY

Dollars in Millions	1993	1992	1991
Balance, January 1	$2,204.9	$1,928.6	$1,960.8
Add:			
Net income	189.9	477.0	124.9
	2,394.8	2,405.6	2,085.7
Deduct:			
Dividends declared:			
Series B Convertible Preference Stock, net of income taxes	21.1	20.2	20.3
Preferred stock	.5	.5	.5
Common stock	209.8	180.0	136.3
	231.4	200.7	157.1
Balance, December 31	$2,163.4	$2,204.9	$1,928.6

Consolidated Statement of Changes in Capital Accounts

Dollars in Millions	Common Stock Shares	Common Stock Amount	Additional Paid-In Capital	Treasury Stock Shares	Treasury Stock Amount
Balance, January 1, 1991	133,207,216	$171.1	$ 123.6	37,940,242	$ 706.5
Shares issued through public offering	11,500,000	–	230.9	(11,500,000)	(214.6)
Shares issued in connection with acquisitions	1,571,730	–	33.3	(1,571,730)	(29.3)
Shares issued for stock options	1,238,377	.4	14.6	(827,203)	(15.4)
Treasury stock acquired	(188,245)	–	–	188,245	.2
Other	14,258	–	9.0	(14,258)	.3
Balance, December 31, 1991	147,343,336	171.5	411.4	24,215,296	447.7
Shares issued in connection with acquisition	11,648,693	11.7	532.4	–	–
Shares issued for stock options	2,441,044	–	9.5	(2,441,044)	(46.6)
Treasury stock acquired	(976,983)	–	–	976,983	54.0
Other	(215,686)	–	32.0	221,656	12.2
Balance, December 31, 1992	160,240,404	183.2	985.3	22,972,891	467.3
Shares issued for stock options	1,408,105	–	9.6	(1,408,105)	(34.7)
Treasury stock acquired	(12,610,423)	–	–	12,610,423	698.1
Other	218,517	–	6.0	(218,517)	(6.7)
Balance, December 31, 1993	149,256,603	$183.2	$1,000.9	33,956,692	$1,124.0

Source: Used with permission of the Colgate-Palmolive Company.

capital planning are all of potential interest. Again, the primary objective is to state the facts so clearly that the chance of misconception is reduced to a minimum.

As with the growth in the size and importance of the MD&A, the notes to the financial statements have also continually increased and now take up 10 to 20 pages of most annual reports. There are innumerable financial factors that should be considered for inclusion in the annual report. It takes innovative thinking and sound judgment to develop and present in an understandable manner the financial information that is relevant to a thorough evaluation of the company.

Figure 37-7 Statement on Management's Responsibility for Financial Statements, and report of Independent Accountants, from Eastman Chemical Company 1993 Annual Report.

Report of Independent Accountants

To the Board of Directors and Shareowners of Eastman Chemical Company

In our opinion, the accompanying financial statements appearing on pages 31 through 44 present fairly, in all material respects, the consolidated financial position of Eastman Chemical Company and subsidiaries at December 31, 1993 and their combined financial position at December 31, 1992, and the results of their combined operations and their combined cash flows for each of the three years in the period ended December 31, 1993, in conformity with generally accepted accounting principles. These financial statements are the responsibility of the Company's management; our responsibility is to express an opinion on these financial statements based on our audits. We conducted our audits of these statements in accordance with generally accepted auditing standards which require that we plan and perform the audit to obtain reasonable assurance about whether the financial statements are free of material misstatement. An audit includes examining, on a test basis, evidence supporting the amounts and disclosures in the financial statements, assessing the accounting principles used and significant estimates made by management, and evaluating the overall financial statement presentation. We believe that our audits provide a reasonable basis for the opinion expressed above.

As discussed in Notes 16 and 12, respectively, the Company changed its methods of accounting for postemployment benefits other than pensions in 1993 and income taxes in 1992.

Management's Responsibility for Financial Statements

Management is responsible for the preparation and integrity of the accompanying consolidated financial statements of Eastman Chemical Company and subsidiaries appearing on pages 31 through 44. These consolidated financial statements have been prepared in accordance with generally accepted accounting principles and of necessity include some amounts that are based on management's best estimates and judgments.

The Company's accounting systems include extensive internal controls designed to provide reasonable assurance of the reliability of its financial records and the proper safeguarding and use of its assets. Such controls are based on established policies and procedures, are implemented by trained, skilled personnel with an appropriate segregation of duties, and are monitored through a comprehensive internal audit program. The Company's policies and procedures prescribe that the Company and all employees are to maintain the highest ethical standards and that its business practices throughout the world are to be conducted in a manner that is above reproach.

The consolidated financial statements have been audited by Price Waterhouse, independent accountants, who were responsible for conducting their audits in accordance with generally accepted auditing standards. Their report is included herein.

The Board of Directors exercises its responsibility for these financial statements through its Audit Committee, which consists entirely of nonmanagement Board members. The independent accountants and internal auditors have full and free access to the Audit Committee. The Audit Committee meets periodically with the independent accountants and the Director of Corporate Auditing of the Company, both privately and with management present, to discuss accounting, auditing, and financial reporting matters.

Source: Used with permission of Eastman Chemical Company.

(a) SUMMARY ANNUAL REPORTS

In the last few years, there has been an adverse reaction by some management to the large amount of required supplemental information. They have instead chosen to issue a condensed or summary annual report. In this approach, the full financial disclosure is detailed in the 10K and proxy statement while the annual report presents only certain limited information. Generally, the companies who have prepared summary annual reports have eliminated almost all the footnotes and much of the MD&A. While it varies, most summary reports still present the primary financial statements and refer the reader to 10K/proxy for full disclosure. As a result, the financial section of the annual report has been substantially reduced. It should be noted that the SEC's guidance on preparing summary annual reports requires that the proxy be sent at the same time as, or before, the summary annual report. Therefore, the preparation of all financial information must be completed in about the same time frame as before, but now a new set of statements must also be prepared for the summary report. The extra work along with concerns about shareholder perception and confusion seems to be deterring companies from trying this summary approach. So far, only a handful of corporations are using it. It is an available option however and each controller should evaluate if it is right for his or her company.

37-6 THE IMPORTANCE OF FORM

The annual report should effectively explain the financial statements and provide any additional data or analyses that will clarify any significant item, trend, or issue. It is up to the accountants and the accounting profession to develop financial reporting principles that keep the shareholder fully informed.

The data that is included in the annual report is certainly important, but how it is presented has much to do with getting the message understood. Summarized next are some comments on various aspects of the physical form of the report that, if heeded, may assist in getting the document read:

1. *Language.* Short sentences and a simple and brief conversational style have been found most effective. Appeal to the reader level; avoid legalistic phrases.

2. *Arrangement.* A summary presented at the beginning is helpful. Distinctive headings and subtitles make reading easier. A division of the report into technical and nontechnical sections can be helpful.

3. *Illustrations.* An increasing use of photography or illustrations is being made to get and hold attention. These devices relieve the monotony of a page, and they may be excellent for illustrating the use of the product.

4. *Graphs.* Graphs can be important time-savers and are an easy means of illustrating trends. Supporting tables are desirable.

5. *Cover.* The cover preferably should identify the company and indicate the contents to be the annual report. The name of the corporation should be easily readable and perhaps placed against an effectively colored background. Application or uses of the company's product may be effectively illustrated.

6. *Repetitions.* Avoid giving the same information several times in the report.

7. *Information.* Tell readers what they do not know, not what they already know. Be careful about the extent of promotional material as compared to answers.

8. *Size.* Most annual reports are $8\frac{1}{2} \times 11$ inches, and it is more convenient if all the reports are the same size.

37-7 STANDARDIZATION IN ANNUAL REPORTS

It is evident that the annual report should be clearly identified with the company and its products. This requires independent thinking and an individual approach to the preparation of the annual report. New ideas are refreshing and will create an interest in the company. There are, however, certain areas that can be standardized. The accounting rules that have been promulgated have to a great extent standardized financial reporting requirements. This will tend to promote a better understanding of the financial data. As the financial accounting and reporting principles are more refined and standardized, it will be easier for the shareholder to compare the results of different companies and make informed judgments about them.

37-8 OTHER REPORTS TO SHAREHOLDERS

Providing the owners of the business with adequate information requires some consideration of frequency. The annual report issued only once a year, and perhaps several months after the fiscal period has ended, can hardly be said to inform the shareholders on current operations. There are several means of contact with the shareholders. Some of the more commonly used devices include these:

1. Quarterly report to shareholders.
2. A letter of welcome to new shareholders.
3. Minutes of the annual shareholders' meeting.
4. News releases.
5. Communications included with the dividend check.
6. Special occasion material, such as an anniversary.
7. Advertising in periodicals and newspapers.
8. Reprints of speeches by executives.

Obviously, the most common is the quarterly report to shareholders, since it has been a financial reporting requirement of the New York Stock Exchange and the SEC.

The quarterly report is simple and not as elaborate as the annual report; however, in recent years it has become more valuable in keeping shareholders and analysts informed on a current basis. Some of the information typically included in quarterly reports to shareholders follows:

Financial highlights (Figure 37-8).

Letter to shareholders.

Consolidated condensed statements of income.

Other financial data.

Management's discussion and analysis of operations and financial condition.

Selected industry segment information.

Consolidated condensed statements of financial position.

Consolidated condensed statements of cash flows.

Consolidated condensed statements of shareholders' equity.

Notes to consolidated condensed financial statements.

Given the information technology changes, the cost of mailing quarterly statements, and the need to provide information to the shareholders on a timely basis, some companies are changing the way they communicate to their shareholders. There is a

Figure 37-8   Financial Highlights from Kimberly-Clark Second Quarter 1994 Report to Shareholders.

(Millions of dollars except per share amounts)	1994	% Change vs. 1993	% of Sales 1994	% of Sales 1993
THREE MONTHS ENDED JUNE 30				
Net Sales	$1,830.1	+ 6.0	100.0	100.0
Gross Profit	620.2	+ 2.7	33.9	35.0
Operating Profit	216.1	+12.8	11.8	11.1
Income Before Income Taxes	190.4	+10.4	10.4	10.0
Income Before Equity Interests	115.2	+ 7.8	6.3	6.2
Net Income	151.5	+13.7	8.3	7.7
Net Income Per Share	.94	+13.3		
SIX MONTHS ENDED JUNE 30				
Net Sales	$3,606.6	+ 5.2	100.0	100.0
Gross Profit	1,225.6	+ 1.6	34.0	35.2
Operating Profit	428.3	+10.5	11.9	11.3
Income Before Income Taxes	374.0	+ 7.7	10.4	10.1
Income Before Equity Interests	230.0	+ 6.9	6.4	6.3
Net Income	287.7	+11.5	8.0	7.5
Net Income Per Share	1.79	+11.2		

	1994	1993
Capital Spending	$201.9	$339.0
Depreciation	162.4	141.4

TWELVE MONTHS ENDED JUNE 30

	1994	1993
Net Income Return on Average Stockholders' Equity	21.8%	14.1%[a]
Operating Profit Return on Average Assets	13.8%	9.1%[b]
Ratio of Total Debt to Capital	38.9%	39.9%
Closing Price: KMB Common Stock Per Share	$52⅞	$49½

[a] Includes the impact of deducting a restructuring charge in the fourth quarter of 1992 ($172.0 million after-tax). Excluding this effect from net income, net income return on average stockholders equity for the 12 months ended June 30, 1993 was 21.2 percent.

[b] Includes the impact of deducting a restructuring charge from operating profit in the fourth quarter of 1992 ($250.0 million pretax). Excluding this effect, operating profit return on average assets for the 12 months ended June 30, 1993 was 13.5 percent.

Unaudited

Source: Used with permission of Kimberly-Clark Corporation.

trend to either a substantial reduction in the size of the quarterly statement or an attempt to replace the routine mailings entirely. ARCO of Los Angeles, California has evaluated the best ways to make current information available quickly and economically to all shareholders. Instead of mailing quarterly shareholders reports either directly or with the dividend checks, these investor information telephone services have been initiated:

- *Fax Requests.* To request quarterly results and other current news directly to a facsimile machine, a free of charge, 24-hours-a-day, seven-days-a-week, Fax number is provided. Earnings information is to be available on the day it is announced.
- *Mail Requests.* Quarterly earnings, as well as the quarterly and annual results filed with the SEC (Forms 10-Q and 10-K) will be mailed on request.

Additionally, to keep shareholders up-to-date on the progress of important projects, the company sends to the owners an abbreviated mid-year report that will supplement the annual report received with the proxy each Spring.

37-9 INFORMATION FOR SECURITY ANALYSTS AND INVESTMENT ADVISERS

Much of the preceding commentary has related to, or emphasized, simplified reporting to the owners of the business. Yet the fact remains that the material must usually serve also as a contact document with the security analysts and investment advisers. And ordinarily such professionals desire a great deal more information than the shareholder wishes or is capable of understanding. One means of solving the problem is to provide, on request, a financial and statistical supplement for this group. It could contain more analyses of the type requested by these professionals.

In addition, a knowledgeable financial executive should be designated as a contact point for the financial analysts; someone they can call for answers to questions they may have.The analytic information to be given to this professional group should be disseminated equally and fairly. Top management, the CEO, and CFO, working with the controller should choose what data will be released. Examples of supplemental information that may be made available are:

1. *Sales Analyses.* Perhaps for several years to show trends as follows:
   a. By product.
   b. By division.
   c. By major program.
   d. By industry segment.
2. *Income Analyses.*
   a. By product.
   b. By division.
   c. By major program.
   d. By industry segment.

3. *Expense Analyses.*

    a. By type in relationship to sales.

    b. Identified types of expenses, such as employee benefits, pension costs, advertising, R&D.

    c. Industry comparisons.

4. *Selected Ratios.* Many can be calculated from available data in the annual report.

    a. Return on capital employed.

    b. Return on common shareholders' equity.

    c. Profit margin, before and after taxes, as a percent of sales.

    d. Percent of net income paid in dividends and retained in business.

    e. Current ratio.

    f. Turnover of working capital.

    g. Turnover of receivables.

    h. Turnover of inventories.

    i. Special statistics applicable to an individual industry.

For analysts to arrive at investment decisions, they usually need more information than what is included in the interim and annual reports. Their interests are more detailed and concern other areas such as market share, technological changes, program production schedules, political and economic environment, backlog analyses, and industry statistics. The controller can provide a valuable service to the financial analysts, shareholders, and the company by being innovative in developing the information needed about the company to make informed investment decisions. Chapter 13 has some suggestions about the role of the controller in investor relations.

37-10 CONTEMPORARY OPINIONS AND SUGGESTIONS ON ANNUAL REPORTS AND FINANCIAL ACCOUNTING

Around the time the AICPA appointed the Special Committee on Financial Reporting, commentary in the press and elsewhere substantially increased concerning needed improvements in financial reporting. As might be expected, many of the issues have two sides. Some of the observations and/or suggestions gleaned from various sources are highlighted below:

- The sheer quantity of financial information in its present form is so great that the readers are overwhelmed.

The chairman of the accounting firm of Ernst & Young, Mr. Ray J. Groves, has made these observations and suggestions.[1]

Full and fair financial disclosure statements are a major reason why the U.S. capital markets are the best in the world. However, important financial information is getting lost in the forest because the existing system does not distinguish between

---

[1] "Here's the Annual Report. Got a Few Hours?" *Wall Street Journal,* Aug. 4, 1994, p. A14.

information critical to decision making and that which is not. Among other reasons, each disclosure requirement from such groups as the FASB, the SEC, and the AICPA is a stand-alone document. Each of these groups focuses on its own requirement of the time and no one looks at the totality.

He makes two suggestions:

1. A two-tier approach could be applied to disclosures. This results in packaging the information differently, but does not reduce the total.

Tier I would be the annual report to shareholders with its wide distribution. It would contain much less information but still conform to GAAP and include an auditor's opinion. Tier II would be a separate, supplemental report with much more disclosure (for a much more limited audience). It would be available on request to shareholders, analysts, bankers, and others who have a real need for it. This approach substantially follows the British practice.

2. The second suggested approach to the apparent excessive disclosure requirements would be a mandatory review every five years authorized by each disclosure-requiring group. It should reexamine the requirements and ascertain as a totality what is then considered essential.

- The Management Discussion and Analysis (MD&A) section of the annual report needs considerable improvement.

The 1980 mandate of the SEC was that the annual report of public companies include an analysis section that assesses the enterprises' liquidity, capital resources, and operations—in a manner that investors can understand.

One of the objectives was to make available public information about predictable future events that may affect future operations of the business. The SEC wanted company specific and industry specific trends affecting net income. It concluded in the late 1980s that while most companies did a good job describing historical events, very few provided useful information about the future. Further, when predictions were made, the managements did a much better job of forecasting good news than bad news. Moreover, in the public document, at least, management was more successful in predicting company-specific events than either industry-specific or economy-specific ones.

- More information is wanted on the various business segments of the entity.

Most companies provide only the information mandated by FAS No. 14, Financial Reporting for Segments of a Business Enterprise, and FAS No. 30, Disclosure of Information about Major Customers. Progress has been made in this area, but more data is wanted on the condition of the segments as well as the operating results—but only if it will not cause a competitive problem for the company.

- Depending on the amount of discussion in the media, and as circumstances seem to make them relevant, more disclosure is wanted on some specific financial/accounting matters:

(1) Impact of current value accounting.

(2) Pending litigation or threatened law suits that could have a material impact on the company.

(3) Disclosure of unasserted potentially material claims that management knows about.

(4) Significant financial irregularities.

• Finally, some shareholders want the outside auditors to verify or audit certain management representations:

(1) MD&A commentary.

(2) System of internal control.

(3) Pending litigation or lawsuits.

(4) Quality of management audits.

It should be stated that directives of the SEC, among others, has resulted in more complete information (usually in the proxy statement) on such subjects as:

• Executive compensation.

• Stock options and appreciation rights.

• Pension and other retirement benefits.

37-11 IMPACT OF JENKINS COMMITTEE REPORT

Some extensive comments about the efforts of the Jenkins Committee of the AICPA are made in Chapter 35. While it will be some time before the final recommendations are made public and action has been taken by the AICPA, some of the probable conclusions are leaking into the press,[2] including:

• Eliminate the standard auditor's statement in the annual report (which is mainly boilerplate unless a company has a major financial problem) and instead recount in some detail any problems or potential for problems at the company.

• Require companies to report "core" and comprehensive earnings instead of merely stating companywide profit.

• Require financial statements to include so-called "soft" information such as estimates of potential competitors able to enter the industry.

• Require larger companies to issue much more financial data than smaller entities.

• Demand that companies break down financial data into more segments than at present so that investors and financial analysts could know more about the individual business segments.

---

[2] Lee Berton, "Accounting Group Is Expected to Call for Increase in Data in Annual Reports," *Wall Street Journal,* Aug. 26, 1993, p. A3.

And, as reported in the *Journal of Accountancy:*[3]

1. Management should not report information that would harm the company's business.

2. Management should not report information about other companies.

3. Management should not be required to provide projected financial or nonfinancial measures, but should provide information that help users make projections for themselves.

4. Management should be under no obligation to search for nonfinancial information it does not have or need to manage the business.

5. Management should not be expected to disclose forward-looking information carrying a high risk of subsequent litigation.

It is also reported that the committee plans to develop a prototype financial reporting model to illustrate the application of its ideas. However, final recommendations will be made only after a survey of users is completed as to the responsiveness of the model to their needs.

37-12 SELECTED REFERENCES

Accounting Trends & Techniques, Annual Publication of the AICPA.

The Corporate Information Committee Report, including an Evaluation of Corporate Financial Reporting, Annual Publication of the Financial Analysts Federation.

Epstein, Marc J., and Moses L. Pava, "Profile of an Annual Report," *Financial Executive,* Jan./Feb. 1994, pp. 41–43.

Fraser, Lyn M., *Understanding Financial Statements, Through the Magic of a Corporate Annual Report,* Reston, VA: Reston 1985.

Gibson, Charles H., and Nicholas Schroeder, "How 21 Companies Handled Their Summary Annual Reports," *Financial Executive,* Nov./Dec. 1989, pp. 45–48.

Groves, Ray J., "Financial Disclosure: When More Is Not Better," *Financial Executive,* May/June 1994, pp. 11–14.

Hamilton, Jim, "Summary Annual Report," *Management Accounting,* Jan. 1990, pp. 38–40.

Hawkins, David F., *Corporate Financial Reporting and Analysis,* Homewood, IL: Dow Jones-Irwin, 1986.

Helfert, Erich A., *Techniques of Financial Analysis,* Homewood, IL: Dow Jones-Irwin, 1987.

Munter, Paul, and Thomas A. Ratcliffe, *A Guide to Financial Statement Disclosures,* New York: Quorum Books, 1986.

O'Glove, Thornton L., *Quality of Earnings: The Investor's Guide to How Much Money a Company Is Really Making,* New York: The Free Press, 1987.

Pava, Moses L., and Marc J. Epstein, "How Good Is MD&A as an Investment Tool?" *Journal of Accountancy,* March 1993, pp. 51–53.

---

[3] "Special Committee on Financial Reporting," *Journal of Accountancy,* Dec. 1993, pp. 76–77.

Pavlock, Ernest J., Frank S. Sato, and James A. Yardley, "Accountability Standards for Corporate Reporting," *Journal of Accountancy,* May 1990, pp. 94–100.

Sever, Mark V., and Ronald E. Boisclair, "Financial Reporting in the 1990s," *Journal of Accountancy,* Jan. 1990, pp. 36–41.

Steckmest, Francis W., *Corporate Performance: The Key to Public Trust,* New York: McGraw-Hill, 1982.

CHAPTER 38

Reports to Employees and to the General Public

38-1 REPORTS TO EMPLOYEES

(a) THE EMPLOYEE AND HIS RELATIONSHIP TO THE BUSINESS

There is some thought that the principle concerns of the employee regarding the business enterprise are for higher wages, shorter hours, a financially sound retirement plan, adequate provision for health care, and improved working conditions. This may be true to a certain extent for many. Yet, for the more thoughtful employee, there is mutuality of interest far beyond this.

From the business viewpoint, competent and productive employees are essential to progress and maintenance of a satisfactory competitive position. And from the employee vantage point—whether he or she is a recent acquisition or one who already has devoted numerous years to the firm—there are two essential ingredients to the success of the private enterprise system: (1) a recognition by management of its obligation to the employees, including the responsibility to manage wisely; and (2) a recognition by the wage earners that increased earnings and reasonable job security are highly dependent on a competent management. The sharing of information with the employees can assist in a better understanding of this mutuality of interests.

(b) OBJECTIVES OF REPORTS TO EMPLOYEES

It is recognized that the employee is entitled to information about the company's operations. The employee's job and wages ultimately depend on earnings, just as much as do the shareholders' dividends. The fact that an employee has not been interested in the operations may be due in part to a failure to recognize his stake in the progress of the company. Such understanding can be enhanced by providing the necessary facts.

The problem with which management is faced appears to have four aspects:

1. To convey to the employees and the general public an appreciation of the relationship among the shareholders, employees, management, and the customers.

2. To bring about a clear understanding of the company's progress during the year, including its income and its expenses, and its outlook for the coming year or years.

3. To outline some of the economic problems that shareholders, employees, and management must face together in the future.

4. To frequently update the employees about key nonfinancial performance measures that indicate change in corporate efficiencies.

Giving information to employees to meet these objectives does not mean giving them a mass of confusing figures, but it does mean giving facts that employees would comprehend because of their natural interest. It does imply giving facts that will take employees beyond the machines and daily routine to a better understanding of the business. Employees need to understand the relationship and interdependence between their own work, those who furnish the tools of production, and those who manage them.

(c) SPECIAL REPORTS TO EMPLOYEES

Reports to employees may be of an infinite variety. However, this discussion is concerned with two areas:

1. *Financial Reports.* Preparing special annual reports on operations for employees. Employees may need a special report, for they are interested in subjects that are of little or no interest to shareholders. Also, whenever the feeling may be prevalent among employees that facts are distorted or withheld, a compromise solution is the preparation of special reports that emphasize the interests of each group; both reports should then be available to shareholders and employees.

The report to employees provides an opportunity to discuss the business environment, special problems, or issues facing the corporation, and to present the results of operations for the period or year. Some corporations now list selected quarterly data in advertisements.

Company management may include the year's financial results in a section of the house magazine, or provide an abbreviated communication to the employees, with an invitation to secure a copy of the annual report to shareholders.

Figure 38-1 is a newspaper ad used by the Dial Corporation to report to employees and shareholders on 1994 results.

In preparing financial communications to fellow wage earners, these guidelines may be helpful:

- Move away from the increasingly complicated annual report to shareholders to a format more attractive to the employee.
- Expend as many resources on the annual report to employees as on the annual report to shareholders.
- Do not patronize when summarizing financial results in reports to employees.

2. *Nonfinancial Reports.* Preparing frequent non-financial reports to employees regarding progress toward attainment of company efficiency goals. Total quality techniques dictate that the company update employees on key performance statistics as frequently as each day. This information is necessary, for total quality is based on the principle that employees provide many of the ideas that improve efficiency. Therefore, if employees are not informed, they will not produce as well.

(d) THE CONTROLLER'S ROLE

As the executive who has the responsibility to establish and maintain financial data bases and prepare meaningful statements and reports, the controller must be deeply involved in any special reporting to employees. In addition to contributing to the format and description of the reports, the controller working with other executives should determine what information will be included in the employee report and then ensure that there is adequate data to develop the information. Sometimes, the company schedule of accounts may have to be expanded in order to accommodate this data gathering. The controller must be willing to do so, when cost justified. Finally, the controller should consider having the public accountants review all financial data and provide a statement of assurance to the employees that the report is a fair and reasonable representation of the facts.

Nonfinancial data collection and presentation presents special problems for the controller. Nonfinancial data is not collected through the usual information channels used by the controller (e.g., receivables and payables) and the results may need to be presented more frequently than monthly (e.g., production results for the last shift). For example, the results of weekly inventory or bill of material accuracy audits should be presented to employees immediately, so they can correct their behavior right away if the reported results do not meet expectations. As another example, the controller must collect information about the number of parts received versus the number ordered, as well as the time and date received in order to track the accurate, on-time delivery of parts by suppliers. This information collection channel is quite outside of the controller's normal data collection process.

(e) INFORMATION PRESENTED TO EMPLOYEES

The job of a daily wage-earner is an important influence in his life. When the wage-earner reads about company operations, he relates the facts and figures to his own job. He is interested in how much income the company received and what happened to it, the past history of the company and its prospects for the future, the use and importance of

Figure 38-1 Newspaper Advertisement—Special Report to Shareholders and Employees (Used by Permission of The Dial Corp).

In the second quarter, The Dial Corp achieved a 32 percent increase in income per share from continuing operations and a 9 percent increase in net income, compared to the second quarter of 1993. For the first six months, income from continuing operations was up 37 percent, and net income per share was 11 percent higher than the same period in the prior year.

The fine results of the second quarter, building on the first quarter's strong revenue and income increases, reflect the success of the company's restructuring and the focus on growing our consumer products and service businesses.

Focus Brings Results

Results were strong in almost all areas and include the positive effects of recent acquisitions. We are also reaping the benefits of focusing on our core businesses, where a combination of competitive advantage, major market share and high return on investment all point toward continued success.

**Two-for-One Split,
Strong Gains**

A two-for-one stock split was paid on July 1, 1994, to shareholders of record as of June 1, 1994, and the following share data reflect this.

Overall, second-quarter revenue increased 20 percent to $931.9 million, up from $774 million in the same 1993 quarter. Income from continuing operations for the second quarter was $43.4 million or $.50 per share, compared to $33.4 million or $.38 per share in last year's quarter.

Revenue for the first half of 1994 were $1.7 billion, up 22 percent over 1993's $1.4 billion for the same period.

Dial's consumer products group continued its strong performance, posting the 29th consecutive quarter of increased operating income over the year-earlier quarter. Operating income increased 15 percent on a 6 percent revenue boost. Total revenue from the service sector increased 35 percent, while operating income was up 26 percent in the quarter.

Product and Service Success

Our growth in the consumer area includes strong showings by the laundry division and its Purex liquid detergents, as well as by Renuzit, the air freshener business acquired in 1993.

The impressive gains in service revenues were aided by the impact of acquisitions of convention services businesses and the United Airlines flight kitchens.

Convention services revenues increased 66 percent, and operating income more than doubled in 1994's second quarter. This dramatic improvement is due primarily to the United Exposition and Andrews, Bartlett acquisitions of 1993, as planned operating efficiencies are being realized for the merged operations.

Airline catering and other food revenues increased 55 percent, and operating income was up 48 percent over the previous year's quarter. The planned phase-in of the United Airlines flight kitchens is proceeding smoothly and on schedule, thanks to extensive planning and an excellent team effort by both Dobbs and United employees. Dobbs is now the largest domestic airline caterer, serving 100 million meals annually.

Confidence in Growth

The excellent second-quarter results continue to prove our ability to deliver predictable sales and earnings growth. This gives us great confidence that we will continue to enhance shareholder value in the future.

[signature]

John W. Teets
Chairman, President and
Chief Executive Officer,
The Dial Corp

The Dial Corp
Profit Through Leadership

If you'd like to know more, please write us at Department PR,
The Dial Corp, Dial Tower, Phoenix, AZ 85077-2452 or call 602/207-5600.

*The Consumer Products Group
has recorded 29 consecutive quarters
of increased earnings.*

*Travelers Express sells
more money orders than the
U.S. Postal Service.*

*GES is now number one in the
fast-growing trade show and
exposition industry.*

*Dobbs ranks as the leading domestic in-flight caterer,
serving 100 million meals annually.*

*Purex achieves strong sales in the
growing price/value segment
of the detergent market.*

*Renuzit contributes
to strong results in
household products.*

*New Dial Plus™ soap
for women bolsters the
line of regular Dial soap
and Liquid Dial.*

"Either You Shape The Future, Or The Future Shapes You."

the products manufactured, the wage rate for his job as compared with the wage rate for like jobs in other companies, and the benefits the employees of other companies receive. There are any number of questions of this nature the employee raises. If management's reports are to be useful to the employee and if the employee is to read the reports, then they must provide many of the answers.

No single list of topics will serve all companies in terms of what information should be given to employees. Current trends also are an influence. What one company may find desirable, another will consider inadvisable.

Furthermore, the more detailed the listing, the greater the area of disagreement. For example, many will agree that the employee should be provided with financial information about the operations. Yet one firm would include information on executive salaries, whereas another would not. Some topics on which there is general agreement, however, include the following:

Company finances, including understandable financial statements	Productivity
	Company products and their uses
Company personnel and organization	Expansion plans
Company history	Sales and order prospects
Employment and payrolls	R&D activities
Labor policies	Industry outlook
Company position in its own industry and competitive activity	Taxation
	Educational activities

Many of these are proper subjects for discussion in the annual report.

The emphasis here relates more particularly to the financial aspects of the reports, where a great many topics can be used to bring about a better understanding of the company and the economy. Basically, the employee is interested in his share of the total reward, and the financial statements should set this out in clearly understandable language. If every corporation would make certain that its employees have a full knowledge of the earnings and the disposition of these earnings, employee relations would be greatly improved. As has been mentioned, the employee should understand the relationship between those who provide the tools and those who use them.

A more specific indication of financial subjects that may be covered in employee reports is suggested in the following outline:

1. Investment.
   a. Explanation of statement of financial condition.
   b. Nature of properties.
   c. Source of capital.
   d. Need for shareholders.
   e. Investment per employee.
2. Operations.
   a. Total gross income (and disposition).
      1. Relative share for wages, material, etc.

    b. Comparative or analytical net income information.
       1. With other years.
       2. Net Income per employee.
       3. Net Income per dollar invested.
       4. Net Income per dollar of sales.
       5. Net Income per unit of product sold.
    c. Salaries and wages.
       1. Total.
       2. Salaries of executives.
       3. Average weekly or hourly wage.
       4. Comparisons with other industries, cost of living, etc.
    d. Taxes.
       1. Per employee.
       2. In relation to wages.
       3. Per share of stock.
       4. In relation to dividends.
       5. In relation to net income.
    e. Dividends.
       1. Total amount.
       2. In relation to wages.
       3. Per shareholder and per employee.
       4. As a percent of investment.
    f. Depreciation.
       1. Total amount.
       2. Nature and value to employee.
    g. General.
       1. Nature and importance of the break-even point.
       2. Trends in industry.
       3. Effect of expansion on job opportunities, etc.
       4. Appraisal of future outlook.
       5. Discussion of achievements in production, sales, or safety.
       6. Explanation of how the company benefits the community and the nation.
       7. Explanation of changes in pension, welfare, or other such plans or policies.
       8. New contracts.
       9. New plants.
     10. New products.
     11. Number of employees.

Similarly, frequent reporting of nonfinancial operating data helps the employee to understand the day-to-day trend of process efficiencies in the production facility. If efficiencies are trending upwards, this helps to improve employee morale. If it is trending downward, employees know they must improve efficiencies, and thereby improve the company's financial results.

(f) FINANCIAL STATEMENTS FOR EMPLOYEES

There is no consistent pattern about the practice of giving financial statements to employees. Some managements give the same statements to both employees and shareholders, whereas others restate the data in what is considered to be a more understandable form. Other managements do not make financial statements generally available to employees but rather present extracts from statements, together with explanatory comments. Still other companies feel it desirable to avoid statements in any form and use other devices to get the picture of company operations across to the employees.

If statements are to be made available, there is general agreement that such statements should be in simple, nontechnical language without any attempt to "write down" to employees. The same general principles applicable to simplified statements for shareholders, as discussed in the preceding chapter, can be applied to employee statements. Such an approach may develop along any one of three lines or a combination. Employees may be given the following:

1. The modified or "single-step" earnings statement and modified statement of owner capital given to shareholders. There is, of course, a certain value in presenting the same type of statement to employees as to shareholders. Some companies provide every employee with a copy of the annual report whether they are shareholders or not.

2. A simplified type of statement characterized by departure from conventional accounting form and terminology.

3. A "per-employee" statement or statements that translate the financial data into terms of a single employee.

(g) SIMPLIFIED STATEMENTS

Another possibility for employee statement presentation is a somewhat more simplified statement. Perhaps the only difference between this classification and the modified shareholder-employee statements is the degree to which conventional accounting terminology has been abandoned.

Since the emphasis in an employees' report is directed more toward the salaries and wages, the shareholder-employee operating statement may be rearranged to a "first-cost" statement. Basically, this merely involves deducting all costs and expenses from income to arrive at the balance distributed to employees and shareholders or retained in the business. An example of such a presentation, together with the inclusion of "per-employee" data, is illustrated in Figure 38-2. No particular additional comments are necessary regarding this approach to the problem, except to point out the desirability of showing all other employee benefit expenditures in addition to salaries and wages and to suggest that there may be good reason for setting out executive compensation to reveal the relative cost as compared to the payments to other employees. Such information is usually available to shareholders, so why not give it to the employees?

Figure 38-2   Illustrative Statement of Income and Expense for Employees.

The Parent Company
STATEMENT OF INCOME AND EXPENSE
For the Year Ended December 31, 19XX

	Total Amount	Amount per Employee	Cents per Dollar of Receipts
The Company Received:			
From customers for goods and services purchased............................	$12,490,500	$11,783	97.8
Dividends from subsidiaries...............	265,000	250	2.1
Interest on receivables, miscellaneous income, etc...........................	12,300	12	.1
Total Company Received.............	12,767,800	12,045	100.0
The Company's Expenses Were:			
For materials, supplies, and other expenses...	7,392,450	6,974	57.9
For wear and tear on buildings, machinery, and equipment (depreciation).............	267,800	253	2.1
For taxes—federal, state, and local, but excluding social security..................	248,900	235	1.9
Making a total of....................	7,909,150	7,462	61.9
Which left for wages, salaries, dividends, and reinvestment in the business.............	4,858,650	4,583	38.1
This Was Divided as Follows:			
Paid to employees (excluding officers) as wages and salaries	3,621,430	3,416	28.4
Paid for employee benefits, including social security taxes, contributions to pension fund, group life insurance, etc.............	365,400	345	2.9
Total..............................	3,986,830	3,761	31.3
Paid to officers as compensation............	119,800	113	.9
Paid to stockholders as dividends for the use of buildings, machinery, and equipment and working capital provided by their investment.................................	405,300	382	3.2
Reinvested in the business to cover the growing needs of the company...............	346,720	327	2.7
Total division......................	$ 4,858,650	$ 4,583	38.1

(h) THE "PER-EMPLOYEE" STATEMENT

"Per-employee" figures are determined by dividing the dollar value of each item in the statement by the number of employees in an effort to indicate the relationship of each such item to the individual employee. It is an attempt to convey to the employee what the investment of the shareholder, as well as the items of expense, means to each one individually. There are at least three general methods of presenting the per-employee statement:

1. *Use of the Modified Statement.* Accounting terminology is discarded, and ordinary language is used to itemize the elements (see Figure 38-2). While total figures as well as per-employee figures are usually included, some companies present only individualized data.

2. *Use of Parallel Columns.* In one column appear the data employed in the statement to stockholders, usually with a detailed explanation of the item. In the other column is presented the per-employee information with further explanation.

3. *Use of Conventional Statement.* This method presents both the total amount and per-employee amount in usual accounting form. The description, however, is followed by an explanation of each item in everyday language.

The limitations of the per-employee data should be recognized. Accompanying explanations should attempt to clarify as much as possible. Thus it is not to be implied that a lower tax expense per employee would result in higher pay. Moreover, the investment per employee should not be construed as the *value* of the company. It may be more or less than this sum. Be that as it may, if it is correctly used, the per-employee data can serve a useful purpose in explaining facts to company personnel.

The emphasis to this point has been on understandable and readable reports on employees. Where the management has done a good job in employee communications—where the employees have been educated to the basic facts of business—then it is easier to secure an understanding of the problems faced by the business.

(i) FORMAT OF REPORTS

Whether the employee reads the reports will depend greatly on the form. The same comments made previously regarding shareholders' reports are applicable here and need not be repeated. Simple, frank statements; the effective use of graphs, charts, or illustrations; and employment of color will assist in telling the business story. Moreover, the report should have a certain dignity. It may be found desirable to mail it to the employee's home.

(j) CRITICISMS OF EMPLOYEE REPORTS

With a trend toward special communications to employees concerning the financial results and condition of the company, criticism naturally has appeared. A summary of present-day (limited) adverse comments is as follows without any attempt at evaluation:

1. Those reports that attempt to appeal to both shareholder and employee usually fail to "get through" to the employee.

2. Reports tend to be too skimpy, including only bare essentials.

3. Many needlessly extol the free enterprise system without adequately telling the story of the company itself—that is, how it fared.

4. Some reports are burdened with special gimmicks in an attempt to secure attention, thus burying the story of the company's progress.

With a knowledge of the risks and dangers, ways can be found to present the company story intelligently.

This chapter has been concerned with the provision of information by company management to employees as a communication device. It has not been concerned with the desire of organized labor for further information for purposes of collective bargaining.

(k) OTHER AVAILABLE MEDIA

Several other channels, in addition to the special or separate annual report, are available for getting information to the employee, be it financial or otherwise. These means, with brief comments, are outlined as follows:

1. *House Organ.* This means, which may be addressed to customers as well as employees, is often used as a device to present the salient parts of the annual report or periodic financial information. It is a way of building esprit de corps and presenting timely subjects in the employee's language.

2. *Letters or Leaflets (Direct Mail).* Such means usually generate interest at home and can be effective in that area.

3. *Bulletin Boards.* This is a useful means for getting a brief message to all employees.

4. *Payroll Inserts.* Generally, this method should be used only for items directly affecting an employee's pay.

5. *Advertisements.* This medium reaches the employees and the public at the same time.

6. *Handbook.* This means is useful primarily to acquaint new employees with company policies, and so on.

7. *Personal Contact.* Regular meetings between employees and their managers or supervisors is the best way to get information to employees. It may mean preparing information packages to be given to managers to help them run such meetings, but the effort is worth it. Other means of personal contact include employee mass meetings or civic group meetings where facts can be presented by members of management.

8. *Films and video cassettes.* This means has been developed as a way of getting visual and auditory contact with employees.

9. *Closed Circuit Television.* This means is another recent development that permits top executives to communicate directly with all the employees in a "live" way that is usually precluded by distance and numbers of people.

10. *Electronic Mail.* When companies have an electronic mail system, messages including financial reports, can be transmitted to each phone or workstation.

38-2 NONFINANCIAL STATEMENTS FOR EMPLOYEES

Nonfinancial reports typically contain information such as accuracy percentages for inventory, bills of material, and labor routings, or actual production quantities versus scheduled amounts. This information can be presented as trend lines, showing improvements or declines versus a target figure. In Figures 38–3 through 38–5, we

Figure 38-3   Inventory Accuracy.

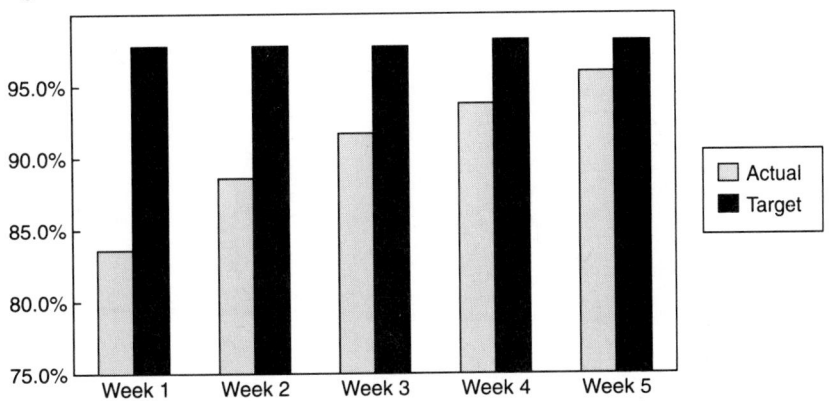

present nonfinancial reports to employees for inventory accuracy, days to produce financial statements, and average overtime percentage.

38-3 REPORTS TO THE GENERAL PUBLIC

(a) THE OBJECTIVE

A large number of people think that business makes unwarranted profits, that corporations are owned by a few wealthy individuals, that large companies are not to be trusted, that business is responsible for rising prices on the one hand and depressions on the other, and that business always profiteers out of any war or defense effort. To answer those who spread such misinformation, it is not enough to reply with broad unsupported generalities. The public needs to know the *facts* about business, since it is they who ultimately will determine the kind of economic order that will predominate. The basic objective is to convey to the general public facts about business in a way it

Figure 38-4   Days to Produce Financials.

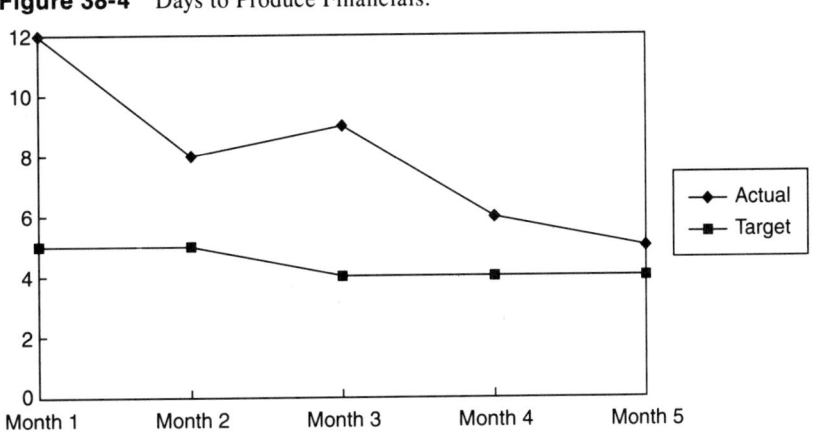

Figure 38-5   Average Overtime Percentage.

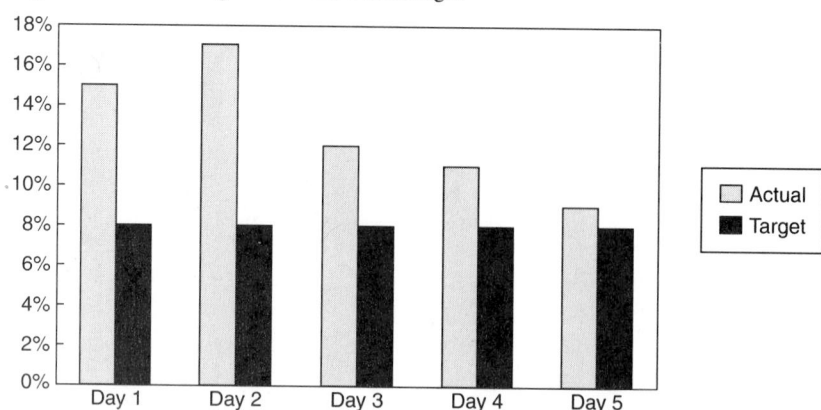

will comprehend. The individual business wants to create a "good impression" concerning itself, and business generally needs to explain the advantages and gains of the private enterprise system to the community at large. Similarly, it may be desirable to tell the business story to appropriate political interests in Congress.

(b) THE CONTROLLER'S ROLE

Although the problem may be attacked from several avenues, the fact remains that accounting information must play a major role. It is largely from a misunderstanding by the public of the financial statements or misunderstanding by those who "tell" the public that many of the misconceptions have arisen. Clear, simple, and understandable financial statements are among the best tools available to correct these distortions and half-truths.

Since the proper interpretation of the financial operations is a main support in the solution of the problem, a certain responsibility must fall on the accountant—and that means the controller. The controller will require the active help and support of those who are experts in persuasion—the public relations director, the advertising manager, and so on. However, as the chief problem is the proper presentation and interpretation of accounting data, he must assume a major responsibility. Whether the public continues to believe the distortions of those who for selfish reasons do not provide all the facts and whether, indeed, private enterprise will be strengthened and the public will realize the tangible benefits of this system depend in no small part on the accounting profession. The presentation of complete, unbiased, and clearly interpreted financial information can contribute much to the confidence of the general public in our economic system.

(c) WEAKNESSES IN PRESENT-DAY REPORTS

With reference particularly to the financial statements and annual reports, there are certain definite weaknesses that have prevented business from getting its story understood by the public. Although some of these were reviewed in the preceding sections, they are summarized in the following discussion.

(i) Common Everyday Words Are Used in a Special Technical Sense. A most commonly misunderstood term is "reserve." Although the word has several connotations to an accountant, to the layman it is something set aside for future use. Such terms as these must be eliminated when presenting information to the public if there is to be a clear understanding.

(ii) The Form and Designation of Financial Statements Are Misleading. Traditional financial statements are logical and complete to those who understand the system. To those who do not, which is most people, they are incomplete and even misleading. For example, a traditional Balance Sheet is presented with assets on the left and liabilities and net worth on the right. A layman will raise the question: If assets are equal to liabilities, how can a company be prosperous? While the title Profit and Loss Statement has been replaced by Statement of Income (or Earnings) there still remains many "profit" lines, for example, Gross Profit, Operating Profit, which are confusing. Only a few companies have addressed the definition of profit. For most people, profit is what is left over after all operations are finished and bills paid. Many think it is cash available for management's personal use. The Income Statement format even encourages this view by ending with the line "Net Earnings." While there has been improvement in the format and descriptions of the financial statements for example, the Statement of Cash Flows, much remains to be done in clarifying what is being reported.

(iii) Inadequate Information Is Given. Nothing breeds distrust as much as half truths or a feeling that information is being withheld. Not everything of importance can be disclosed. No one expects a company to reveal information that will injure it by providing competitors with confidential information. On the other hand, unusual nonrecurring activities or changes in accounting or tax rates should be disclosed and discussed when they affect earnings by even 1 percent (usually there is no disclosure if an item is "immaterial," often defined by the professionals as less than 3% or 4% of sales). Even if the traditional report formats do not highlight a particular situation, it can be brought out in the MD&A or even in the CEO's letter to shareholders at the beginning of the annual report. There is nothing more damaging to the overall image of Corporate America than to read an annual report that is upbeat and encouraging and find that six months later the company declares bankruptcy.

(iv) Presentations Aid Misinterpretation. Some attempts to lead to misinterpretation are deliberate and fall into the propaganda classification, but in many instances the misunderstanding results from a poor presentation. Examples of what may be described as poor judgment in report presentation include (1) a comment on return on investment, calculated on total capital invested under circumstances when a comment about return on shareholder equity might have been more appropriate; (2) an attempt at conveying the impression that the employees received most of the sales dollar when this is not borne out by the facts; (3) emphasis on the high level of taxes, with the implication that this condition prevented higher wages, when such may not be the case.

(d) PRESENTING FACTS TO THE PUBLIC

The same principles discussed in previous chapters are applicable in presenting financial information to the general public. The report should contain all the pertinent facts on the subject, presented in an understandable manner. The mass of information should be ignored and the really vital aspects covered. Moreover, in many cases it will be advisable to give figures for several years. Then, too, the use of clear, simple language; color; photography; and charts can be effective.

It is desirable that the subject matter be directed to the audience. Items of particular interest or concern to the public should be emphasized. Some suggested topics that may be a part of an annual report or of data released at the same or other times include the following:

1. The place of free, private enterprise in our economy.
2. Unsound legislation.
3. Unsound governmental policy.
4. Taxation.
5. Interrelationship of industries; of labor, agriculture, and industry.
6. Cooperation between government and industry.
7. The relationship of the industry to the community.
8. The extent of research.
9. The creation of new markets.
10. Financial data of many sorts:
    a. Relationship of sales volume and profits.
    b. Profit as a percentage of net sales.
    c. Reasons for increased profit.
    d. Comparison of profits with other periods.
    e. The cost of management.
    f. The distribution of corporate ownership.
    g. Reasons for price increases.
    h. Distribution of the sales dollar.
11. Relationship with labor.
12. The outlook.

The consumer, employee, and shareholder and investor will all have an interest in many of these subjects.

(e) FORMS OF STATEMENTS FOR THE PUBLIC

A question arises about the necessity of preparing any special forms of financial statements for the public. As previously mentioned, the public as well as the shareholders and employees often do not understand the conventional statements. However, the simplified forms or summary data are as well suited to the needs of the public as to the owners or employees. No special construction is considered necessary.

(f) METHODS OF REPORTING TO THE PUBLIC

Several media are available to convey the business story to the public:

1. *Shareholders' Reports.* Many companies make a wide distribution of the annual report to the general public. A related practice is to make such reports available to certain special groups that may be interested.

2. *Institutional Advertising.* Some of the corporations purchase newspaper or magazine space to summarize the results of operations, to present the company's position on some particular topic, or to explain why certain action was taken. Perhaps it might be regarded as a duty of a particular company, rather than merely a right, to inform the public how it serves. To be sure, there are times when an industry or a company is faced with special problems or misconceptions, and efforts must be exerted to provide some facts. In Figure 38-6, Mobil lists its investments in refineries in the Asia Pacific region, informing the public about where the company is making capital investments. In Figure 38-7, TRW Corporation outlines the growth in its key market segments. In Figure 38-8, General Electric Corporation notes record quarterly earnings in an advertisement.

3. *Press Releases.* Information may be released to the press on specific points, such as earnings, employee benefits, and new products.

4. *Radio and Television Broadcasts.* This medium can be used effectively to explain particular subjects—financial or otherwise.

5. *Special Letters, Booklets, and Pamphlets.* Reprints from magazines can be made available to visitors or to the public as requested.

Each medium has its particular purpose and can be used to present the facts about business. Several media may be employed to get the proper coverage.

38-4 SELECTED REFERENCES

Dickson, Douglas N., *Business and Its Public,* New York: John Wiley & Sons, 1984.

O'Glove, Thornton L., *Quality of Earnings: The Investors Guide to How Much Money a Company Is Really Making,* New York: The Free Press, 1987.

Purcell, W. R., Jr., *Understanding a Company's Finances,* Boston: Houghton Mifflin, 1981.

Figure 38-6   Marketing and Refining Opportunities.

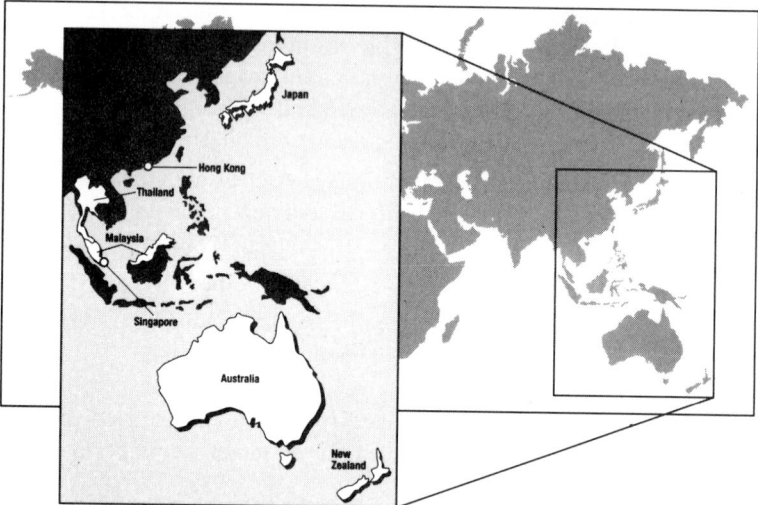

Mobil, a world of opportunities:

Marketing & Refining in the Asia Pacific region

To capture more of the growing appetite for premium petroleum products and chemicals in the fastest-growing part of the world, Mobil is investing more than a billion dollars to improve our Asia Pacific refineries.

With nearly a third of our refining capacity in this region — a higher proportion than any major competitor — we aim to maintain our profitable position. These upgradings will allow us to use lower-cost heavier crudes, convert more crude oil into premium products and deliver fuels that can meet a range of environmental standards. Here's what we're doing in the region:

■ In Singapore, we've just streamed a $700 million refining and petrochemical complex. It includes an aromatics plant that supplies building blocks for making polyester, nylon and other synthetic fibers. Another unit, a catalytic reformer, produces feedstock for the aromatics plant and raises unleaded gasoline capacity by 17,000 barrels a day. The third unit turns out low-sulfur diesel. Most of these products will be marketed throughout Southeast Asia.

■ At the Chiba refinery in Japan, Mobil and its partners are investing nearly $300 million. One unit, which makes low-sulfur diesel to comply with more stringent air-quality regulations, is already operating. Under construction is a specialized cracking unit that will enable us to increase the gasoline and distillate yields from heavy feedstocks.

■ In Australia, where we acquired additional refining and marketing assets several years ago, we'll add a new catalytic cracker at our Altona refinery. This upgrade, which should be operating by 1997, will reduce the cost of making unleaded gasoline and boost our capacity to make high-octane fuel.

Upgrading core assets in growing markets — one of Mobil's strategies for building shareholder value.

building shareholder value

©1994 Mobil Corporation

Source: Used by Permission, © Mobil Corporation.

Figure 38-7   Growth in Key Market Segments (Used by Permission, © TRW Corporation).

Figure 38-8   In This Advertisement, General Electric Publicizes Record Growth with a
Broad Thank You.

To all our customers and employees, thanks a million.

(Make that 1.52 Billion.)

It's impossible to describe the hard work and dedication of every GE employee
or the support and confidence of our customers. But you can demonstrate results.
We posted the **best** second-quarter results in our 116-year history, with record orders, sales and earnings.
As we look forward to next quarter, only two words come to mind.

Thank you.

We bring good things to life.

CHAPTER 39

Interface with the SEC:
Reports to Governmental Agencies
and Stock Exchanges

American business remains highly regulated and subject to numerous financial reporting requirements. Although there may have been a reduction in operating regulations during the recent decade, there has been an increase in the amount of financial reporting and disclosure required by government agencies. In some cases, the regulations are quite clear and specific; in others, they are ill-defined and subject to wide interpretation. Unfortunately, it is not uncommon to have conflicting reporting rules issued by the multitude of government agencies interested in or regulating business.

39-1 GOVERNMENTAL REGULATORY AGENCIES

Governmental regulation is effected by means of statutory direct control, charter, franchise, or other methods. However, legislation primarily effects regulation by creating

This chapter was revised by Terry Palmer, Partner, Ernst & Young LLP, Denver.

administrative agencies and delegating to them certain powers and duties. It is the responsibility of the controller to determine the financial reporting requirements of the governmental agencies concerned. Most companies are affected by such rule-making bodies as the SEC, FTC, Interstate Commerce Commission (ICC), Federal Power Commission, Federal Communications Commission (FCC), Treasury, Department of Commerce, ERISA, along with other specialized agencies or commissions. A company that must file periodic reports will find that each of the reports must meet certain standard specifications. Some of the required reports cover information or statistical data and are not necessarily prepared from the accounting records. In any case, responsibility for reporting to the government must be clearly assigned and procedures established to insure appropriate review and approval prior to filing. In addition, it is important to develop a schedule of all reports filed with the respective government agencies. Such a schedule should include the name of the report, form number, frequency, who prepares, period covered, who files, where filed, source of data, and who approves. Documentation for each report included on the schedule should be maintained as shown in Figure 39-1. A simple schedule of a partial list of government reports is set forth in Figure 39-2.

Numerous government agencies impose reporting obligations on business. In some cases, an industry is regulated, such as utilities, and the accounting procedures may be prescribed. Other federal agencies, as well as many state commissions, have reporting requirements for particular types of businesses in which the public is deemed to have a special interest. The prescribed reports and records may vary greatly in nature and extent. The range includes the following:

1. A complete and detailed uniform system of accounts that sets forth the data to be maintained in each account and the accounting principles to be applied thereto.

2. Extensive instructions about the forms and contents of reports and records to be maintained but not a prescribed chart of accounts.

Figure 39-1   Government Reports Data.

Agency:
Report Name:
Form Number: (sample form attached)
Date to be filed:
Where filed: (complete address)
Prepared by:
Source of data:
Supporting data filed: (location)
Copy of report and documentation retained: (destruction date)
Period covered:
Reviewed by:
Approved by:

Figure 39-2   Schedule of Government Reports.

Report Identification	Due Date (After Closing Period)
MONTHLY	
DEPARTMENT OF CENSUS (FORM M-3) Manufacturers Shipments, Inventories and Orders	20 Days
DEPARTMENT OF LABOR PRODUCERS PRICE INDEX	15 Days
DEPARTMENT OF TREASURY (Form CM) Dollar Deposit and Certificate of Deposit Claims on Banks Abroad	30 Days
DEPARTMENT OF TREASURY (Form FC-3) Report of Assets, Liabilities and Positions in Specified Foreign Currencies of Firms in the U.S.	30 Days
QUARTERLY	
DEPARTMENT OF TREASURY (Form FC-4) Consolidated Report of Assets, Liabilities and Positions in Specified Currencies of Foreign Branches and Subsidiaries of Firms in the U.S.	60 Days
DEPARTMENT OF COMMERCE (BE-577 Report) Direct Transactions of U.S. Reporter with Foreign Affiliate	30 Days
DEPARTMENT OF TREASURY (Form CQ-1) Financial Liabilities to Unaffiliated Foreigners & Financial Claims on Unaffiliated Foreigners	30 Days
DEPARTMENT OF TREASURY (Form CQ-2) Commercial Liabilities to Unaffiliated Foreigners and Commercial Claims on Unaffiliated Foreigners	45 Days
DEPARTMENT OF COMMERCE (Form QFR101) MANUFACTURING, MINING AND WHOLESALE TRADE FINANCIAL REPORT	45 Days
DEPARTMENT OF COMMERCE FORM (PE-X) STRUCTURES AND EQUIPMENT EXPENDITURES	45 Days
DEPARTMENT OF LABOR, BUREAU OF LABOR STATISTICS Price Indexes	5 Days
SEMI-ANNUAL	
DEPARTMENT OF COMMERCE (Form BE-133 B/C) Schedule of Expenditures for Property, Plant and Equipment of U.S. Direct Investments Abroad (June & December)	June 1 & Dec. 1
ANNUAL	
DEPARTMENT OF COMMERCE (Form BE-11) Annual Survey of U.S. Direct Investment Abroad	May 31
DEPARTMENT OF COMMERCE (Form BE-22) Annual Survey of Selected Services	90 Days After Fiscal Year End
DEPARTMENT OF COMMERCE / BUREAU OF CENSUS REPORTS	
Form MA-35R Shipments/Computers & Office and Accounting Machines	30 Days After Receipt
Form MA-36P Communications Equipment (Including Telephone) Machines	30 Days After Receipt
Form MA-36Q Semiconductors, Printed Circuit Boards & Other Electronic Components	30 Days After Receipt
RD-1 Research and Development Costs	60 Days After Receipt

(continued)

Figure 39-2 *(continued)*

Report Identification	Due Date (After Closing Period)
Form NC-9901 Report of Organization—Headcount & Payroll data for HQ & Field Locations	30 Days After Receipt
COMMONWEALTH OF VIRGINIA Survey of Manufacturers/Shipments, Payroll, Headcount	30 Days After Receipt
MISCELLANEOUS . . . (on request, 5-year intervals etc.)	
DEPARTMENT OF COMMERCE / BUREAU OF CENSUS REPORTS	
Form BE-10 Benchmark Survey of U.S. Direct Investment Abroad	5-Year Intervals
Form MA-175 Shipments/Federal Government Agencies	On Request
Form MA-200 Pollution Abatement Cost	On Request
Form MQ-C1 Plant Capacity Utilization	On Request
Form MA-1000 Survey of Manufacturing / Shipments, Payroll & Inventory	On Request
Form 38-B Selected Instruments & Related Products	On Request
Form B-507 Annual Survey of Service Revenue	On Request
Form TC 9402 Transportation Survey By Type of Transportation	On Request
Form MC-5001 Survey of Water Use in Manufacturing	On Request
Form CB-5081 Field Locations Revenue, Expenses, Payroll & Headcount	On Request
Form CB-5063 Field Locations Revenue, Expenses, Payroll & Headcount	On Request
Form ES-9200 Regions, HQ & Districts Payroll, Capital Expenditures, Inventories	On Request
Form OA-98XX Miscellaneous Foreign Locations Revenue, Expenses, Payroll & Headcount	On Request
Form MC3520 Purchases and Shipments of Office and Computing Machines	On Request
Form MC3613 Purchase and Shipments of Electronic Components and Accessories	On Request
Form B3805 Purchase and Shipments of Photographic Equipment and Supplies	On Request
Form B500S Asset and Expenditure Survey	On Request
Form B500T Service Annual Survey	On Request
Form CB7306 Computer and DP Processing	On Request
Form ES9100 Enterprise Summary Report—Payroll, Benefits, Inventories, Assets, Etc.	On Request
Form MC9601 Summary of Sales by Class of Customer	On Request

   3. Very limited record requirements having little effect on the form of how the information is maintained and referring to information that probably would be retained despite the government requirements.

39-2 THE SECURITIES AND EXCHANGE COMMISSION (SEC)

As the principal accounting officers of industrial corporations, controllers are directly involved in complying with the requirements of the SEC. It is an independent regulatory agency of the federal government. The function of the SEC is primarily administrative, relating to the Securities Act of 1933 and the Securities Exchange Act of 1934. Of course, it also has other responsibilities relating to other regulations, such as the Trust Indenture Act of 1939 and the Investment Company Act of 1940. The Securities Act of 1933 may be described as a disclosure statute requiring full and fair disclosure of all material facts concerning the company issuing securities so that the potential investor can make an informed judgment. Such a disclosure is effected by filing a registration statement with the SEC. The statement includes a prospectus that contains:

- Description of the registrants properties and business.
- Description of the significant provisions of other security being offered for sale and its relationship to other capital securities of the company.
- Information about the company's management.
- Financial statements certified by an independent CPA.

The Securities Exchange Act of 1934 is concerned primarily with trading in issued or outstanding securities. It requires the dissemination of updated financial information through the issuance of periodic reports and provides for regulation of the securities market.

The effect of the various acts is to give the SEC extensive powers with respect to the accounting and financial reporting by all corporations with publicly traded securities. The statutes do not give any authority to interfere with the actual operations or internal management of operating businesses, except regarding financial matters relating to public-utility-holding companies and companies emerging from reorganization. Moreover, the acts do not authorize the SEC to pass on the investment merits of securities.

39-3 THE SEC AND FINANCIAL REPORTING

The SEC has extensively exercised its rule-making authority. It has adopted general rules and regulations relating to all securities acts administered by it. The powers of the SEC are exercised through several means:

1. *Regulation S-X.* The Securities Act and Securities Exchange Act granted broad power regarding accounting matters but left the prescribing of detail accounting requirements as an administrative matter for the Commission. Pursuant to such authority, Regulation S-X governs the form, content, and timing of most of the financial statements filed with the SEC under the acts of 1933, 1934, and 1940. The table of contents of Regulation S-X is shown in Figure 39-3.

2. Regulation S-K states the requirements applicable to the content of the nonfinancial statements required to be filed with the SEC. The table of contents of Regulation S-K is shown in Figure 39-4.

During the 1980s, the SEC took steps to integrate and simplify the reporting requirements for public companies. Regulation S-K was reorganized and expanded and now covers all nonfinancial information required in Form 10-K, Registration Statement and other SEC statements. Regulation S-X was also modified to be used in conjunction with Regulation S-K.

Figure 39-3   Contents of Regulation S-X.

TABLE OF CONTENTS

Figure 39-3   *(continued)*

(continued)

Figure 39-3   *(continued)*

17 CFR	Subject
210.12–08	Guarantees of securities of other issuers ....
210.12–09	Valuation and qualifying accounts ....
210.12–10	Short-term borrowings ....
210.12–11	Supplementary income statement information ....
210.12–12	Investments in securities of unaffiliated issuers ....
210.12–12A	Investments—securities sold short ....
210.12–12B	Open options contract written ....
210.12–13	Investments other than securities ....
210.12–14	Investments in and advances to affiliates ....
210.12–15	Summary of investments—other than investments in related parties ....
210.12–16	Supplementary insurance information ....
210.12–17	Reinsurance ....
210.12–18	Supplemental information (for property-casualty insurance underwriters) ....
210.12–21	Investments in securities of unaffiliated issuers ....
210.12–22	Investment in and advances to affiliates and income thereon ....
210.12–23	Mortgage loans on real estate and interest earned on mortgages ....
210.12–24	Real estate owned and rental income ....
210.12–25	Supplementary profit and loss information ....
210.12–26	Certificate reserves ....
210.12–27	Qualified assets on deposit ....
210.12–28	Real estate and accumulated depreciation ....
210.12–29	Mortgage loans on real estate ....

3. Releases are issued by the SEC to supplement Regulations S-X and S-K. They announce or codify rules and regulations of the commissions on accounting and reporting matters. From 1937 to 1982 Accounting Series Releases (ASRs) were issued. In 1982, ASRs were stopped and two new series of releases were initiated:

- Financial Reporting Releases (FRRs) cover financial accounting and reporting matters.

- Accounting and Auditing Enforcement Releases (AAERs) cover enforcement actions.

All of the old ASRs that were still in effect when the new series began, were transferred by topic to FRR. Figure 39-5 is a list of the Financial Reporting Releases. The first AAER includes an index to SEC views on enforcement matters related to ASRs.

4. Staff Accounting Bulletins (SABs) inform the financial community of the commission's views on certain accounting and disclosure matters.

  They are not rules or interpretations of the commission nor do they bear official commission approval, but they represent interpretations and practices followed by the Division of Corporation Finance and the Office of the Chief Accountant.

Figure 39-4   Contents of Regulation S-K.

TABLE OF CONTENTS

Subject

Figure 39-5   Financial Reporting Releases.

List of Financial Reporting Releases

No.   **Subject**
1. Codification of Financial Reporting Policies
2. Rules for Pro Forma Financial Information Presentation
3. (Rescinded)
4. Interpretation: Public Availability of Correspondence about Accountant's Independence
5. Accountants' Liability for Reports on Unaudited Supplementary Financial Information
6. Interpretive Release about Disclosure Considerations Relating to Foreign Operations and Foreign Currency Translation Effects
7. Adoption of Foreign Issuer Integrated Disclosure System
8. Financial Statement Requirements for Registered Investment Companies
9. Supplemental Disclosure of Oil and Gas Producing Activities
10. Qualifications and Reports of Accountants; Amendment of Rules Regarding Accountants' Independence
11. Revision of Financial Statement Requirements and Industry Guide Disclosure for Bank Holding Companies
12. Accounting for Costs of Internally Developed Computer Software for Sale or Lease to Others
13. Revision of Industry Guide Disclosures for Bank Holding Companies
14. Oil and Gas Producers—Full Cost Accounting Practices; Amendment of Rules
15. Interpretive Release Relating to Accounting for Extinguishment of Debt
16. Rescission of Interpretation Relating to Certification of Financial Statements
17. Oil and Gas Producers—Full Cost Accounting Practice
18. Business Combination Transactions—Adoption of Registration Form S-4
19. Business Combination Transactions—Adoption of Registration Form F-4— Foreign Registrants
20. Interpretive Release on Disclosures of Reserves for Unpaid Claims and Claim Adjustment Expenses of Property-Casualty Underwriters
21. Technical Amendments to Regulation S-X and to Rules and Forms under the Securities and Exchange Acts Relating to Financial Statements Requirements
22. Technical Amendments to Rules and Forms
23. Interpretive Release on the Significance of Oral Guarantees to the Financial Reporting Process
24. Disclosures Relating to Use of Repurchase and Reverse Repurchase Agreements
25. Consolidated Financial Statements of the Registrant and Its Subsidiaries
26. Disclosure of the Effects of the Tax Reform Act of 1986
27. Amendments to Industry Guide Disclosures by Bank Holding Companies
28. Accounting for Loan Losses by Registrants Engaged in Lending Activities
29. Accounting for Distribution Expenses
30. Disclosure of the Effects of Inflation and Other Changes in Prices
31. Disclosure Amendments to Regulation S-K, Form 8-K and Schedule 14A Regarding Changes in Accountants and Potential Opinion Shopping Situations
32. Statement of the Commission Regarding Disclosure Obligations of Companies Affected by the Government's Defense Contract Procurement Inquiry and Related Issues
33. Public Availability of Correspondence About Accountants' Independence
34. Acceleration of the Timing for Filing Forms 8-K Relating to Changes in Accountants and Resignations of Directors; Amendments to Regulation S-K Regarding Changes in Accountants
35. Reporting Requirements for Issuer's Change of Fiscal Year; Financial Reporting Changes; Period To Be Covered by First Quarterly Report After Effective Date of Initial Registration Statement

Figure 39-5 *(continued)*

36. Management's Discussion and Analysis of Financial Condition and Results of Operations; Certain Investment Company Disclosures
37. Acceptability in Financial Statements of an Accounting Standard Permitting the Return of a Nonaccrual Loan to Accrual Status after a Partial Charge-off
38. Roll-up Transactions
39. Integrated Disclosure System for Small Business Issuers
40. Amendments to Rules and Forms to Conform to Recently Adopted Accounting Standards

(a) ACCOUNTING MATTERS

Decisions, rules, or policies of the SEC may be said to relate to three main phases of accounting activity:

1. *Matters of Accounting Principles or Practice.* These pertain to the recording of financial transactions and the presentation of financial statements. The SEC has recognized the Financial Accounting Standards Board as the authorized accounting standards setter for the United States. (Previously the American Institute of Certified Public Accountants [AICPA] had the authority to establish U.S. accounting principles.) Accordingly, all SEC registrants must adhere to the Financial Accounting Standards promulgated by the FASB in their accounting and financial reporting activities. This relationship is discussed further in Chapter 4 of this book.

2. *Matters of Auditing.* Such comments relate to the procedures by which accountants review and report on financial statements prepared by corporate management.

3. *Matters of Professional Conduct.* These relate to the standards of professional conduct of those public accountants who certify financial statements, such as the matter of the independence of auditors.

A comment is in order about the procedure of the SEC. After financial statements have been filed, they are reviewed by the SEC staff. If such statements have not been prepared in accordance with generally accepted accounting principles or if they otherwise fail to meet the requirements of the SEC in any significant respect, a so-called deficiency letter or letter of comment is prepared and sent to the registrant. These letters serve as the basis of correspondence or conferences with the corporations, whereby accounting questions usually are expeditiously resolved without time-consuming and expensive formal hearings. Of course, if the matters are not satisfactorily resolved or if the company fails to modify the statements as requested, then proceedings are instituted to determine whether the statements are in fact materially inadequate or misleading. The SEC has the authority to issue stop orders, whereby the securities of the company may not be offered to the public.

39-4 NATURE OF DEFICIENCIES REPORTED BY THE SEC

The controller should be aware of the types of deficiencies that have been found prevalent as an aid in avoiding them. With respect to deficiencies in financial statements, a majority of the deficient items are the result of the failure to comply with specific rules contained, for the most part, in Regulation S-X.

A review of the specific types of items that have been the subject of deficiency letters issued by the SEC will indicate that they cover all areas. In the past several years, particular attention has been focused on the adequacy of the Management Discussion and Analysis (MD&A) of Financial Condition and Results of Operations. A large majority of those MD&As reviewed were deemed to be deficient by the SEC staff. Another recent focus item has been the timing of revenue recognition, with many disclosures that firms were recognizing revenue too early, or with insufficient evidence of performance and a lack of accounting controls. Some other common issues raised are statement captions, inadequate description or disclosure, contingency reserves (including environmental), methods of pricing inventories, classification of assets, and footnotes relating to pension plans and stock options. Many of the subjects of the deficiency letters are covered by FFR's, SAB's, and statements of the FASB. The controller should be familiar with all aspects of the issues and respond to any deficiency notices in a positive and complete manner.

The statutes administered by the SEC recognize the necessity of independence. The regulations specifically require that certain prescribed financial statements be certified by independent public accountants. Thus Rule 2-01(b) and (c) of Regulation S-X prohibits the accountant from having any interest in the registrant. The Commission will not recognize any certified public accountant who is not in fact independent. This means that all partners of the firm and all professional employees participating in the audit cannot have any direct or material indirect financial interest in the registrant, its subsidiaries or other affiliates. In determining whether an accountant may in fact not be independent, the SEC will give consideration to all relevant circumstances, including evidence bearing on all relationships between the accountant and the registrant.

In another related matter, SEC regulations specifically prohibit directors and officers from making false or misleading statements to the outside auditors relative to the examination of the company's financial statements.

The SEC continually issues releases that announce proposed changes to existing rules and regulations. For example, during the 1980s, the SEC, in order to reduce the amount of financial reporting required of registrants, integrated much of the annual report to shareholders and the annual reporting to the commission. Certain information reportable in the Form 10-K became required in the company's annual report. However, the annual report could then be incorporated by reference into the 10-K thereby reducing the need to produce two different sets of financial reports. Recently, there has been some criticism of the amount of financial detail now included in the annual report. The concern being expressed that such a large amount of space was required by the compliance schedules that it took away from the rest of the report as the primary communication vehicle between management and their shareholders and the general public. The SEC was sympathetic to this complaint and agreed to permit Summary Financial Reporting to be included in the annual as long as complete reports were sent to shareholders with enough time before the annual meeting to review and understand them. This would usually mean in the proxy statement. However, after several years, only a handful of companies have opted for a Summary Annual Report, so it remains to be seen if the idea is here to stay. In such a dynamic environment, it is obvious that a controller must keep current on all SEC developments. Any materially inaccurate or incomplete information in Form 10-K can expose a company and its officers and directors to liability under the Securities Acts.

39-5 REPORTING FORMS TO THE SEC

A corporation subject to the securities laws has a responsibility to keep the public informed on significant corporate matters. Reporting requirements were adopted to insure that investors had sufficient information available to make an informed judgment about the value of the securities. There are numerous reports required on an annual, quarterly, or interim basis. Not all companies are required to file all reports.

The report form prescribed by the SEC must be used. The SEC has certain rules which establish the requirements that reports must satisfy regarding format and technical matters. For example, if an item requires information in a particular form, such as a tabulation, the information must be provided in the form specified. In addition, the definitions that have been provided and apply to the reports must be followed.

By regulation, the SEC has established the requirements about the number of copies of reports to be filed:

- Annual Report Form 10-K—Three complete copies, including exhibits and other documents filed, plus five additional copies that may exclude exhibits.
- Quarterly Report Form 10-Q—Same as 10-K.
- Current Report Form 8-K—Three complete copies, including exhibits, plus five additional copies that may exclude exhibits.

A minimum of one copy of each report filed must be manually signed as prescribed by the appropriate form. Annual Form 10-K must be signed by the Chief Executive Officer, the Chief Financial Officer, the Chief Accounting Officer, and a majority of the Board of Directors. Other copies not manually signed must have the typed or printed signatures. Quarterly reports on Form 10-Q must be signed by a duly authorized officer as well as the principal financial officer or chief accounting officer.

As previously indicated, numerous reports are to be filed, and the controller should determine which reports are applicable and obtain appropriate forms from the SEC. The Annual Report Form 10-K and the Quarterly Report Form 10-Q are of primary concern to the controller.

Both number of copies and signature requirements change with electronic filing (EDGAR).

(a) EDGAR

EDGAR (Electronic Data Gathering, Analysis and Retrieval System) was authorized as part of the Securities and Exchange Commission Authorization Act of 1987. This program will require companies to make all required filings electronically using one of the following media:

Direct transmission

Diskette

Magnetic tape

On April 26, 1993, mandated electronic filing commenced for certain companies. Phase-in of all domestic registrants is expected to be completed by mid-1996. (See Figure 39-6, EDGAR Filer Phase-in Schedule.)

Electronic submissions are governed principally by Regulation S-T, which contains rules prescribing requirements and procedures relating to electronic submissions. In addition, the SEC has published the EDGAR Filer Manual, which provides details on technical formatting requirements for electronic submissions. The rules provide that, with specified exemptions, all Commission filings by or with respect to phased-in registrants must be in electronic format. Circumstances involving both paper and electronic filers, such as business combinations, are specifically addressed.

Electronic filers that obtain an exemption from the provisions of Regulation S-T for specified submissions and filers that are not phased in will file in paper format in accordance with existing rules and regulations. In addition, there are transitional rules governing how amendments or exhibits that are filed electronically will be incorporated into previous documents that were filed in paper format. Regulation S-T and the EDGAR Filer Manual provide details of the mechanics of filing, including the hours the Commission will be available for receipt of documents and documentation of required signatures. The rules require all electronic filers to submit copies of electronic filings to the Commission in paper format for a one-year period after the commencement of electronic filing.

Rules requiring electronic registrants to submit "Financial Data Schedules" have been adopted with a deferred effective date in order to permit adequate time for system programming. The Schedules included specified financial data extracted from the financial statements, schedules and disclosures pursuant to industry guides, placed in formatted schedules and identified with special tags to facilitate retrieval of the information by EDGAR. This will enable the EDGAR system to perform numerous functions with the data automatically, such as the calculation of financial ratios or the identification of companies with certain financial characteristics.

Figure 39-6   EDGAR Filer Phase-in Schedule.

Domestic registrants will be brought onto the EDGAR system pursuant to the schedule listed below. The identity of the companies in Groups CF-01 through CF-10 is contained in Appendix B to the April 26, 1993 EDGAR Release.

July 15, 1992	— Voluntary Pilot filers commenced filing.
April 26, 1993	— Remaining Pilot filers and approved volunteers (Group CF-01) commence mandated electronic filing.
July 19, 1993	— Registrants listed in Group CF-02 (approximately 700) commence filing.
October 4, 1993	— Registrants listed in Group CF-03 (approximately 700) commence filing.
December 6, 1993	— Registrants listed in Group CF-04 (approximately 900) commence filing. This is the last of the "significant test group."
August, 1994	— Registrants listed in Group CF-05 commence filing.
November, 1994	— Registrants listed in Group CF-06 commence filing.
May, 1995	— Registrants listed in Group CF-07 commence filing.
August, 1995	— Registrants listed in Group CF-08 commence filing.
November, 1995	— Registrants listed in Group CF-09 commence filing.
May, 1996	— Registrants listed in CF-10 plus any other parties submitting materials to the SEC and not previously named in Appendix B commence filing.

The benefits of EDGAR are expected to be shared by all participants in the financial reporting process:

Registrants who will no longer have to prepare, deliver, and store hard-copy reports and who in the future may meet the filing requirements of stock exchanges, states, and other regulators, by their having access to the EDGAR data base.

The SEC staff who will be able to accept, process, and analyze filings more effectively using computer workstations.

Security analysts, investors, and the general public who will have immediate access to corporate data via computer screens.

The controller of any company required to file with the SEC must become aware of the EDGAR capabilities and requirements and make an informed decision as to how he can best serve his company in this regard.[1]

39-6 ANNUAL REPORT FORM 10-K

The SEC's Form 10-K is not to be used as a blank form to be filled in, but only as a guide in preparing the report. The report should be filed within 90 days after the end of the fiscal year covered by the report. The report must contain the item numbers and captions as listed here:

Part I

(Part I may be incorporated by reference to the Annual Report to Shareholders)

Item 1   Business

- A discussion of the development of the business since the beginning of the current fiscal year (and earlier if it is material to an understanding of the year).
- Financial information about *industry* segments including a three-year summary of sales, operating profit or loss, and assets for each segment.
- Description of the business and major segments including principal products, services, market areas, and competition, major customers, sources of raw materials, working capital, order backlog, research, and other pertinent information.
- Financial information about *geographic* segments including a three-year summary of sales, operating profit or loss, and assets.

---

[1] Questions or comments can be directed to: The Office of EDGAR Management, Securities Exchange Commission, 450 Fifth Street, N.W., Washington, D.C. 20549:
- SEC Filer Support   (202) 942-8900
- EDGAR News Subscription   (202) 942-8600
- EDGAR Phase-In   (202) 942-2940
- EDGAR Rules   (202) 942-8920

Item 2   Property

Information on the location and nature of principle plants, offices, and other important physical property. Identify the industry segment(s) related to the property and describe the adequacy, capacity, and utilization of the facilities.

Item 3   Legal Proceedings

Briefly describe pending litigation where the corporation or any subsidiary may be a party and any proceedings terminated during the period.

Item 4   Matters Submitted to a Vote of Security Holders

Briefly describe any matters submitted to a vote of security holders during the 4th Quarter including their disposition or settlement.

Part II

(Part II may be incorporated by reference to the Annual Report to Stockholders)

Item 5   Market for Registrants Common Equity and Related Shareholder Matters

Describe the securities and identify the markets where stocks are traded and pertinent market price information. Set forth the number of holders of each class of stock. Report the amount of dividends declared and their frequency and future probability.

Item 6   Selected Financial Data
  • Provide a five-year financial summary including sales, operating income, income per share, total assets, long-term obligations, and redeemable preferred stock and cash dividends per common share.

Item 7   Management Discussion and Analysis of Financial Conditions and Results of Operations

Discuss the financial condition, results of operations and changes in financial condition liquidity, significant trends, and events that are expected to occur in sufficient detail to provide an understanding of the business and/or significant segments of it with special emphasis on liquidity.

Item 8   Financial Statements and Supplementary Data

File Consolidated Balance Sheets for the two most recent years and Statements of Income and Cash Flow and Changes in Stockholder's Equity for the three most recent years. The detailed instructions for these and other supplementary data are included in Regulation S-X.

Item 9   Changes in and Disagreements with Accountants on Accounting and Financial Disclosure

Identify changes in independent accountants during the previous two years along with reasons for the change.

Part III

(Part III is required to be incorporated by reference from the proxy statement unless it is not filed within 120 days after the end of the year)

Item 10   Directors and Executive Officers

Provide a list of officers and directors of the company and pertinent information about them.

Item 11   Executive Compensation

Furnish the amount of compensation earned by the CEO and each of the four other most highly compensated executives (no disclosure is required of the other four executives if total compensation for the individual does not exceed $100,000) and report earnings of all other officers as a group. The compensation and pension plans of officers must be described.

Item 12   Security Ownership of Certain Beneficial Owners and Management

Provide information about ownership of voting securities for directors and certain other owners.

Item 13   Certain Relationships and Related Transactions

Describe briefly transactions and relationships between the company and certain officers, directors, and other specific parties as defined in the S-K Regulations.

Part IV

Item 14   Exhibits, Financial Statements, Schedules, and Reports on Form 8-K

List documents filed as part of the report including financial statements, supplemental disclosures, and reference to Form 8-K, if filed. Where any statement or exhibit is incorporated by reference the incorporation should be indicated on the listing.

Certain information is not required to be provided if it has been filed previously. Information may also be incorporated that has been filed separately. The controller must be intimately familiar with all aspects of the Form 10-K and be prepared to discuss it in detail with the SEC. The previous listing and condensed description of the items to be included in the 10-K filing is provided only as a general outline of the subject. SEC Regulations S-K and S-X must be used in the actual preparation of a

Form 10-K Report. The regulations are complex and require the cooperation of corporate officers, attorneys, and independent auditors.

39-7 QUARTERLY REPORT FORM 10-Q

Quarterly reports are required by the SEC for the first three fiscal quarters of each year. The information provided represents the company's obligation to disclose all material information to the public on a current basis. It is a condensed, unaudited interim financial report. The report must be filed within 45 days after the end of each of the first three quarters. No report is filed for the fourth quarter of the fiscal year.

Quarterly Reports to security holders may be combined with the information required of Form 10-Q and be suitable for filing with the SEC.

The Form 10-Q requires the following information, like Form 10-K, it is not a blank form to be filled in but a guide in preparing the report:

Part I

Item 1   Financial Statements
- A summary Balance Sheet as of the end of the most recent quarter and the end of the prior fiscal year.
- A summary Income Statement for the current quarter year-to-date, and the corresponding periods of the prior years.
- A summary Statement of Cash Flows for the same periods as the Income Statement.

Item 2   Management's Discussion and Analysis of Financial Conditions and Results of Operations

Provide information similar to that described in Form 10-K requirements.

Part II

Items 3 to 6   Specific information relative to legal proceedings, changes in securities, defaults, matters submitted for a vote of stockholders and any information not previously reported on Form 8-K.

Again, this is a condensed list and description of Form 10-Q requirements provided to the reader only as an outline. Regulations S-K and S-X must be used to understand and prepare the actual filing.

39-8 SMALL BUSINESS ISSUERS

The SEC continually has been challenged to reduce the regulatory burden placed on smaller registrants and to provide smaller businesses the same access to capital markets as larger enterprises by reducing the initial cost of registration and ongoing expenses of being a public company. In August 1992, the SEC completed the initial phase of Regulation S-B for small business issuers. Regulation S-B simplifies the registration and reporting process by reducing the financial and non-financial disclosure requirements. The guidance relaxed the requirements for audited financial statements, including audited financial statements for acquired businesses. The SEC has stated they will continue to work with state securities administrators on reducing the regulatory burdens placed on small business issuers.

To take advantage of the reduced requirements under S-B, the issuer must be a U.S. or Canadian company with revenue of less than $25 million in its last fiscal year and voting stock that does not have a public float of $25 million or more. The public float of a company making an initial public offering of securities is determined based on the number of shares held by non-affiliates prior to the offering and the estimated public offering price of the securities. Once eligible, a company may continue reporting under the small business integrated disclosure system until it exceeds $25 million in revenue for two consecutive fiscal years or $25 million in public float for two consecutive years. Similarly, once a company exceeds these limits and thus becomes not eligible to file under Regulation S-B, the company must meet the definition of a small business issuer for two consecutive years before it will be eligible to file under Regulation S-B. Continued eligibility to use the small business reporting system will be determined at the beginning of each fiscal year.

With respect to the financial statement requirements, Regulation S-B requires one less year of audited financial statements than does Regulation S-X. Specifically, Regulation S-B requires an audited balance sheet as of the end of the most recent fiscal year and audited statements of income, cash flows, and changes in shareholders' equity for each of the two years preceding such audited balance sheet. These financial statements must be prepared in accordance with generally accepted accounting principles (GAAP) and do not need to provide the additional disclosures called for in Regulation S-X. The rules for audited financial statements for businesses acquired were also relaxed to limit the requirement to no more than two years of audited financial statements of the business acquired, depending on the significance of the acquired business to the registrant. Additionally, where audited financial statements of the acquired business are not readily available, they are automatically waived where the significance of the acquisition does not exceed 20%.

Certain nonfinancial statement disclosure requirements covered in Regulation S-K, such as executive compensation and description of business, have been simplified and other disclosures, such as selected financial data and supplementary financial information, are no longer required. Management's Discussion and Analysis is required for small business issuers that have had revenue in each of their last two fiscal years; other small business issuers would provide business plan information. Executive compensation disclosure rules issued by the SEC in October 1992 are not applicable to, or are phased in for, small business issuers eligible to use Regulation S-B.

There are three forms for use in registering securities under Regulation S-B, as follows:

SB-1   This form is used to register up to $10 million of securities to be sold for cash provided the issuer had not registered under the Securities Act more than a total of $10 million of securities in the last 12-month period. Disclosure requirements are somewhat less than those under Form SB-2.

SB-2   This form is to be used by those Small Business Issuers to register securities under the Securities Act who do not qualify to use Form SB-1.

10-SB   This form is used to register securities under the Securities Exchange Act and accomplishes the same objectives of larger filers who register currently outstanding shares using Form 10.

With respect to annual and quarterly reports, Regulation S-B created Form 10-KSB as an annual report form and Form 10-QSB as a quarterly report form. Form 10-KSB provides for reduced financial and nonfinancial statement disclosures from those required in Form 10-K. The financial statement requirements are reduced by one year to provide for one balance sheet as of the end of the most recent fiscal year and two years of statements of income, cash flows, and shareholders' equity. The quarterly report on Form 10-QSB requires essentially the same disclosure as the Form 10-Q; however, one difference is that Form 10-QSB does not require a balance sheet as of the preceding fiscal year end.

Controllers of companies who might qualify to use Regulation S-B should become familiar with the requirements as use of this process will likely result in reduced legal, accounting, and auditing costs to access the public markets.

39-9 SIMPLIFIED REPORTING AND THE SEC

In discussing the matter of reports to shareholders, employees, and the public, the authors have stressed the need for simplified financial statements that would *inform* the users and readers. Although the conventional statements have their uses, information should be provided in nontechnical accounting language so that the public can be better informed. Much the same problem presents itself concerning the requirements of the SEC; the data must be easily understood to satisfy the requirements of the investor.

The SEC has made considerable progress in improving disclosure of information available to the public. Generally, it has tried to make reports, statements, and data more readable and understandable, as well as getting timely information to the investor. Although the financial statements have remained the traditional ones, there has been a continuous effort to require more interpretative analysis of the financial information.

For example, Management's Discussion and Analysis, which at one time focused on operations now has expanded to cover separately liquidity, financial position, and prospective information. More attention is also being paid in MD&A's to segment information, both business and geographic, and to the five-year comparison of selected data. There is probably no better way for a company to disclose important financial information than through the MD&A. When done right, it turns data into information that helps readers understand the business.

As the SEC continues to develop new proposals it will seek comments on them, controllers should provide constructive comments consistent with the accounting profession and the public's requirements.

39-10 THE SECURITIES EXCHANGES

The Securities Exchange Act of 1934 was passed by Congress to regulate the various stock markets. Most of the control was delegated to the newly created SEC, although some power was conferred on the Federal Reserve Board. The SEC was given considerable latitude for the exercise of administrative discretion and, in turn, has adopted a policy of securing voluntary cooperation of the exchanges, including the encouragement of the adoption of adequate self-regulations or exchange rules.

The foundation of federal regulation is the requirement that all national securities exchanges must register unless specifically exempted by the SEC by reason of limited volume, among other things. Any exchange may be registered by filing a statement of agreement to comply with and enforce on members any rules and regulations made under the Act and by filing also certain other data, including a copy of its constitution, bylaws, and rules of procedure.

The following exchanges are registered with the SEC:

New York Stock Exchange.

American Stock Exchange.

Boston Stock Exchange.

Chicago Board Options Exchange, Inc.

Midwest Stock Exchange.

Philadelphia Stock Exchange.

Pacific Stock Exchange.

Cincinnati Stock Exchange.

Spokane Stock Exchange.

Intermountain Stock Exchange.

(a) OUTSIDE THE UNITED STATES

With the growing importance of international trade and worldwide capital formation, the use of securities exchanges outside the United States is rapidly expanding. The most important of these exchanges are in: Austria, Belgium, Canada, England, France, Germany, Japan, Switzerland, and the Netherlands.

39-11 LISTING REQUIREMENTS—NEW YORK STOCK EXCHANGE

The listing and reporting requirements of the national securities exchanges have been influenced by the Securities Exchange Act of 1934. Before securities may be admitted to trading on the exchanges, they must be approved for listing by the exchange and also must be registered with the SEC. Listing on the exchange is effected by the submission to, and approval by, the exchange of an application prepared and signed by the issuer in conformity with the rules of the exchange. Under the Securities Exchange Act, a filing of a registration statement must be made with both the SEC and the exchange that conforms to the rules of the SEC. The listing process is described in the following write up from the New York Stock Exchange Company Manual.

Section 1
The Listing Process

Table of Contents

Section 1
The Listing Process

101.00   Introduction

A listing on the New York Stock Exchange is internationally recognized as signi-
fying that a publicly owned corporation has achieved maturity and front-rank
status in its industry—in terms of assets, earnings, and shareholder interest and
acceptance. Indeed, the Exchange's listing standards are designed to assure that
every domestic or non-U.S. company whose shares are admitted to trading in the
Exchange market merit that recognition.

The Exchange welcomes inquiries from corporate officials who wish to explore the advantages of listing with Exchange representatives. Discussions can be
held at company headquarters, at the Exchange, or over the telephone.

Prospective applicants for listing are invited to take advantage of the Exchange's free confidential review process to learn whether or not the company is
eligible for listing and what additional conditions, if any, might first have to be
satisfied. A company requesting such a review incurs no obligation whatever.

A company that has qualified for listing can normally expect its shares to be
admitted to trading within four to six weeks after filing its original listing application. (See Section 7 of this Manual for detail concerning listing applications.)
Refer to the New York Stock Exchange Company Manual for additional details.

39-12 REPORTING REQUIREMENTS OF THE NEW YORK STOCK EXCHANGE

When stocks are listed on the New York Stock Exchange, such listing application contains an agreement relative to the publishing of certain annual reports and periodic interim statements. In this connection it is of interest that the financial statements
contained in the annual reports of the corporation to its shareholders must be in the
same form as the statements contained in the listing application.

The current disclosure requirements of the New York Stock Exchange[2] cover the
following topics:

---

[2] *New York Stock Exchange Company Manual.*

Section 2
Disclosure and Reporting Material Information

39-13 CONCLUSION

Governmental regulatory agencies continue to have a significant affect on businesses. It is the responsibility of the corporate controller to determine and understand the record keeping and financial reporting requirements of these agencies. For companies with public reporting responsibilities, the Securities and Exchange Commission will have the most influence over a company's accounting and financial reporting obligations. The controller of a privately held company should also understand the SEC regulations due to the significant influence the SEC has in establishing generally accepted accounting principles.

The SEC is continually working to reduce the regulatory burden placed on registrants and has simplified the registration and reporting process for smaller businesses by reducing the financial and non-financial disclosure requirements. For larger companies, the SEC requirements continue to be significant with increased attention being given to the adequacy of financial statement disclosures and Management's Discussion and Analysis.

The SEC's filing requirements are becoming increasingly automated, through the introduction of EDGAR (Electronic Data Gathering, Analysis and Retrieval System). All companies will be filing their reports using EDGAR no later than mid-1996. This program will allow efficient analysis of financial data by security analysts, investors, and the general public by allowing immediate access to corporate data via computer screens.

For today's corporate controller, up-to-date knowledge of the requirements of the various governmental agencies is a must.

39-14 SELECTED REFERENCES

Ernst & Young LLP, "Deciding to Go Public—Understanding the Process and the Alternatives," Denver: Ernst & Young LLP, 1993.

Karmel, Roberta S., *Regulation by Prosecution: The Securities and Exchange Commission vs. Corporate America,* New York: Simon and Schuster, 1982.

O'Flaherty, Joseph S., *Going Public, The Entrepreneur's Guide,* New York: John Wiley & Sons, 1984.

Phillips, Susan M., and J. Richard Zecher, *The SEC and the Public Interest,* Cambridge, MA: The MIT Press, 1981.

Skousen, Fred K., *An Introduction to the SEC,* Cincinnati, OH: South-Western Publishing Co., 1987.

Stevens, John M., Steven L. Wartick, and John W. Bagby, *Business-Government Relations and Interdependence,* New York: Quorom Books, 1988.

CHAPTER 40

Reports to Creditors

40-1 CREDITORS' REPORTS AND THE CONTROLLER

For discussion purposes, reports to creditors have been categorized as follows:

1. Reports and financial statements to secure trade credit.
2. Reports to creditors, usually on a periodic basis, to inform credit grantors about the financial condition of the company and to provide certain requested information.
3. Reports to prospective creditors to secure new funds.

Reports to trade creditors, commercial banks, bond holders, and other lenders make up an important segment of necessary financial information. Usually, the responsibility for the preparation of such information falls to the controller. It is the controller's task to determine that the statements reflect the true facts with regard to the financial condition and results of operations and that the other financial data presented are correct.

Another phase of creditors' reports relates to the review of prospective customers' financial statements in considering an extension of credit. Very often this function is handled by the credit manager or treasurer, but the controller is frequently consulted and called on to review the reports and make recommendations or comments.

40-2 THE USE OF FINANCIAL STATEMENTS FOR CREDIT

The proper understanding and interpretation of financial statements are essential to the successful operation of the business from both the credit-granting and borrowing viewpoints as well as the internal management aspects. But even for credit purposes financial statements are only one of the requisites to sound decisions. The financial information is not the only type of information needed, whether to judge a credit risk or to secure a satisfactory line of credit. The data needed for the extension of credit may be classified somewhat arbitrarily into these three categories:

1. Financial information.
2. Antecedent information.
3. Investigational facts.

Financial information relates to all available financial facts. These may be extremely detailed financial statements with supporting data, on the one hand, or mere rumors concerning financial strength, on the other. Oral statements from salesmen, creditors, or lawyers may be the sole source.

Antecedent information includes the following pertinent data about the people who manage or own the business, whichever is applicable: their experience and ability; their record of failures or fires; previous employment and position; married or single status. It is intended to shed light on the *character* and experience of the management team.

Investigational facts include the following data secured from banks, trade creditors, and insurance companies that aid in appraising the financial information: payment habits, such as discounting, prompt, or slow; size of bank balances; borrowings and nature of collateral.

The information provided in the financial statements is only a part of the whole data that creditors attempt to secure and analyze in judging the soundness of a credit risk.

40-3 TRADE CREDIT INFORMATION

Credit information must be made available to the trade or mercantile creditor. There are many sources that may provide such data to the business needing it. Among them are the following:

1. The mercantile agencies—both general and special.
2. The credit risk (i.e., the company seeking credit).

3. Credit bureaus, which exchange ledger experience.

4. Other creditors, through direct exchange of experience.

5. Other general sources, such as trade and financial publications and corporation manuals.

6. Special representatives who are familiar with the credit risk: banks, attorneys, salesmen of the creditor.

In the usual circumstances, where the company is furnishing financial information to creditors, a copy of the annual report to shareholders or the interim published statement may suffice. Regarding the mercantile agencies, perhaps the most important source of credit data, a special report may be required. Mercantile agencies, fundamentally, are companies organized primarily for the purpose of gathering credit information on businesses and making such data available to their subscribers. The best-known general mercantile agency is Dun & Bradstreet, Inc. There are, in addition, special agencies that serve only a single trade, or area, or line of business. Some examples are the National Credit Office, Inc., the Iron and Steel Board of Trade, Lyons, and local credit bureaus.

These agencies generally have their own standard forms for the gathering of financial data. Every company should provide Dun & Bradstreet, the National Credit Office, and other mercantile agencies with complete and accurate financial statements in a format acceptable to them (some use available statements, others want their own form used).

Supplemental information should also be provided as requested or if deemed important by the company itself. The reason for such cooperation is simple, if the information is not furnished by the company, it will be obtained elsewhere. The "usually reliable sources" used range from estimates made by fairly knowledgeable bankers to conversations with competitors' salesmen. Any information so gathered can be inaccurate and misleading. It is therefore important for the controller to ascertain that the information collected on his company is accurate and current and, if it is not, then to have it corrected.

The following information is typically gathered in connection with credit reports and should be affirmed by the controller:

I. *Company Background and Operations*
- Company name and address.
- Owners, directors, and managers and their background.
- Line of business; what the company produces or sells, to whom, and any unusual aspects about it.
- Year the business started or came under present control.
- History of operations and current sales and profit trends.
- Conditions of the business.
- Financing arrangements (capital and debt).
- Net Worth.
- Number of employees.

II. *Payment History*

Reflects information obtained outside the company from suppliers about how the company pays its bills, and from banks about loan experience including a repayment record.

III. *Financial Quality*

Includes current detailed Balance Sheets, Income Statements, and Statements of Cash Flows, with supplemental information on liquidity, major leases, insurance coverage, bank balances, and so on.

As an interesting additional service, NCO offers to deliver to the suppliers and banks of a company's choice photostatic copies of that company's latest financial statements. The reasons why a corporation should provide a financial statement to NCO for dissemination are listed next:

1. Every day NCO receives more than 1,000 requests for information from its subscribers. Without exception, the first question they ask about a company is "What is the date of their latest statement?"

2. Credit needs are rapidly increasing—if your financial responsibility has not been clearly established, raw materials could prove difficult to get in an emergency.

3. New suppliers are usually more impressed with a favorable credit report than a favorable reputation.

4. Many suppliers use only NCO for credit references. As specialists in an industry, their analysts are extremely knowledgeable.

5. NCO photographs your statement for use by its analysts, so there is never any danger of an erroneous report due to an error in transcribing.

6. If anything in your statement is confidential, NCO will use the figures only as a basis for a credit recommendation, and will not reveal the actual information.

7. Even though some concerns give statements to state authorities, they are not usually available to suppliers until long after they are released. NCO will supply credit information in 48 hours or less.

8. NCO will provide you with as many copies of your statements as you need—or will send copies to any bank or supplier you designate.

9. Full disclosure, even in a relatively poor year, is less likely to cause credit curtailment than not releasing your statement. It avoids exaggerated conjectures on the part of suppliers.

10. NCO's Analysts are able to recommend credit for over 80% of the concerns who send us their financial statements.

11. In these days of personnel shortages—why not lighten the burden on your staff by eliminating the need to answer credit inquiries about your company. We'll do it for you.

12. Many look to NCO reports for investment purposes—be it private or corporate. And prime government contractors are constantly using NCO reports to determine financial stability of their suppliers.

Ability to supply the necessary credit information, of course, assists the NCO.

40-4 REVIEWING A CREDIT REPORT

Although the company financial officers are responsible to see that proper information is provided to credit agencies, such as Dun & Bradstreet, Inc., their interest probably should go beyond this. Someone in the financial organization should monitor credit reports issued about the company. If financial information has been wrongly interpreted, the matter should be clarified. If unsatisfactory conditions are disclosed, such as slow pay, efforts should be taken to correct the matter and reinstate the desired credit rating and history, etc. In any period, but especially in periods of material shortages, high inflation, or tight credit conditions, the financial officers of the company, whether the treasurer, controller, or others, should see to it that the trade credit reports reflect the facts and they are acceptable trade credit practices.

40-5 DATA FOR CREDIT RATING AGENCIES

When a company intends to be, or is, active as a borrower in the capital market it will have contacts with rating agencies. The two major credit rating agencies are Moody's Investor Service and Standard & Poor's. Both of them rank securities in order of the perceived probability of default, and then publish ratings as letter grades. Thus Moody's rates bonds from Aaa, the best quality and smallest degree of risk, to C, the lowest quality, with poor prospects of attaining real investment standing. Standard & Poor's comparable ratings range from AAA, the best, to C or D.

The primary determinant of the credit rating is an analysis of the creditworthiness of the borrower; and the basic procedure for the analysis is the same whether the security to be rated is a long-term debt issue or a short-term obligation.

Suffice it to say that, as far as the author can tell, the capacity of an industrial borrower to make timely payment of principal and interest seems to relate to these nine criteria:

- Industry risk.
- Issuer's industry/market position.
- Issuer's industry position and operating efficiency.
- Management evaluation.
- Accounting quality.
- Earnings history and prospects.
- Leverage and asset protection.
- Cash flow adequacy.
- Financial flexibility.

It is to be noted that four of the categories relate to the overall business analysis and the last five are financial in nature.

A company's credit rating is important because it is a factor in securing access to the capital markets and to specific suppliers. Hence, it is suggested that the controller or the CFO communicate effectively with the more important rating agencies. There should be ongoing dialogue with the sharing of information, the avoidance of negative "surprises," and a communicated effort to maintain an excellent or good credit rating.

Moreover, it might be added that because of the assessment of management, it may be well occasionally to have some rating agency contacts between other members of management—not just the financial side.

40-6 REPORTS TO COMMERCIAL BANKS AND LONG-TERM CREDITORS

Usually, the financial statements and related financial data to be provided commercial banks under credit agreements or to long-term lenders, or bond holders are prepared by the controller's staff. What specific financial information a creditor bank needs is determined in part by bank preference and negotiation.

(a) REVOLVING CREDIT AGREEMENT

The clauses of a revolving credit agreement (for short-term credit and term loans) of a major industrial company relative to furnishing financial statements are that the company will do the following:

Furnish Financial Statements. Furnish to each Bank and to the Agent:

(a) within 90 days after the end of each fiscal year of the Company, a consolidated balance sheet of the Company and the Consolidated Subsidiaries as at the close of such fiscal year and consolidated statements of income and shareholders' equity of the Company and the Consolidated Subsidiaries for such year, certified by _____ or by other independent public accountants selected by the Company and satisfactory to the Agent;

(b) within 30 days after the end of each calendar quarter when loans are not outstanding under this Agreement, and within 30 days after the end of each month (except December and January, for which months the deadline shall be March 31) of each fiscal year of the Company when loans are outstanding under this Agreement, a consolidated and consolidating balance sheet of the Company and the Consolidated Subsidiaries as at the end of such quarter or month, as the case may be, and consolidated and consolidating statements of income and shareholders' equity of the Company and the Consolidated Subsidiaries for such quarter or month and for the period from the beginning of the fiscal year to the end of such quarter or month, certified by an authorized financial or accounting officer of the Company;

(c) within 30 days after the end of each quarter, a list (in reasonable detail) of the guarantees referred to in § 7B(4)(d), as of the end of such quarter, certified by an authorized officer of the Company or authorized employee of the Company who is satisfactory to the Agent, except that individual guarantees in an amount of less than $5,000,000 need not be reported in detail;

(d) promptly upon becoming available, copies of all financial statements, reports, notices, proxy statements, and final prospectuses sent by the Company to shareholders or the Securities and Exchange Commission or any governmental agency successor to any or all of the functions of said Commission;

(e) subject to governmental restrictions, such other certificate or certificates, statement or statements of the position and affairs of the Company and of Consolidate Subsidiaries and the status of their contracts, open accounts and budgets or forecasts, and other financial information, as may be reasonably requested by the Agent;

(f) with each of the financial statements called for by subclause (a), a certificate by the independent public accountants certifying such statements to the effect that they are familiar with the provisions of this Agreement and that in preparing the financial statements which they certified, they acquired knowledge of no Event of Default specified in § 8 nor any event which, with the giving of notice or the lapse of time or both, would become such an Event of Default or, if the contrary is the case, specifying the nature of such Event of Default or event; and

(g) within 30 days after the end of each quarter of each fiscal year of the Company, a statement by an authorized financial or accounting officer of the Company to the effect that no Event of Default specified in § 8 has occurred and no event has occurred which, with the giving of notice or the lapse of time or both, would become such an Event of Default or if any such Event of Default or event has occurred, describing it and the action taken or proposed to be taken by the Company in respect thereof.

(b) COVENANTS ON LONG-TERM DEBT

Because much more money is involved, there are usually more financial stipulations required of the borrower than in line-of-credit agreements. These agreements or covenants are both affirmative and negative. Affirmative covenants are fairly common to all long-term borrowings and require the borrower to agree to:

- Provide specific financial statements in accordance with a stated schedule.
- Pay interest and principal on time.
- Maintain the corporate existence including keeping all properties in good working order, having adequate insurance, paying taxes and other claims when due, etc.
- Have an office or agency where the securities may be transferred or exchanged.
- Submit periodic certification of compliance with the loan agreement.

Negative covenants are negotiated. Borrowers want the least number of restrictions on them. Lenders want restrictions that protect their investment; usually as many as possible. It is a difficult task for the borrower to ascertain the right balance between more restrictions and lower interest rates and fewer restrictions with higher interest rates. With lots of experience in the field, investment brokers provide this service to their clients. There are many different kinds of negative or restrictive covenants; some examples are:

- Limit on the absolute dollar amount that can be outstanding at any given time, for example, $10,000,000.

- Limit of debt based on ratios or coverage, for example, debt may be no more than X percentage of total net worth or working capital or debt may be no more than X percentage of property, plant, and equipment.
- Earnings must be at a specified level before additional debt can be incurred and/or must be "X" times (e.g., 3) the interest charges.
- Limitations on dividend payments (e.g., X percentage of net income after taxes) and stock repurchases.

In this era of leveraged buyouts, junk bonds, corporate raiders, and so on, there seems to be a lack of concern for debt investors and so there may be even stricter negative covenants associated with placing future long-term debt. Most every restrictive covenant requires the controller to consider the restrictions as he assembles the annual and strategic plans. He must ensure that all covenants are being and will be met. Accordingly, he must also be part of any covenant negotiation team to provide much of the financial input needed for the process.

(c) OTHER CONSIDERATIONS

The financial information to be provided major creditors will depend on the agreement or contract reached. Generally, when the relationship has been established for some time and a favorable record developed, the requirements will be less stringent. Financial statements prepared in accordance with generally accepted accounting principles and an annual review of the one-year plan usually will be sufficient. Often is will be found helpful to visit the lending institutions quarterly and review the financial statements and, for example, discuss any departure from plan and the outlook for the remainder of the year.

For those whose experience with banks and other financial institutions is somewhat limited, or relationships are new, the following comments may provide some insight.

The amount of information a banker needs varies with the situation. The size and term of the loan are important. Naturally, a small loan does not require the information that a large loan does; the risk to the bank is not as great, and the need for a detailed analysis is correspondingly less. If a longer-term loan is under consideration, the important factor is future income. The risks are correspondingly greater in terms of economic developments, such as the business cycle and general economic conditions; and the management factor, such as the chances for losses by reason of unsound management decision. In sharp contrast is a short-term loan, where normally the liquidation of current assets is the primary consideration.

The size of the borrower very frequently is a matter that affects the form of reporting. Strange as it may seem, a large well-managed enterprise may be required to furnish fewer details than a smaller company with mediocre management. A large firm may be viewed in general, although the opportunity for management errors in the smaller company may require more frequent and detailed reporting.

The approach of credit analysts, including bankers, might be described as one of proportions. Statements often are analyzed in terms of relationships.[1] The ratios on

---

[1] See Chapter 8.

which emphasis is placed depend, among other things, on the type of loan. For a short-term loan, the working capital and liquidity are of greater importance than the fixed assets.

Typical of the ratios in which a bank might be particularly interested are these:

1. *Current Assets to Current Liabilities.* The short-term lender is concerned with liquidity as measured by this current ratio. In many cases, the financing institution will want to see the projected improvement.

2. *Average Number of Days' Sales Outstanding.* Comparison with industry average, or specific competitors, might be made to determine if receivable turnover is adequate.

3. *Number of Inventory Turns per Year.* If investments in inventory are relatively large, an inability to operate on a conservatively low stock-to-sales ratio might cause detailed questioning on this phase of the business.

4. *Fixed Asset Turnover.* A low ratio of sales to fixed assets could raise questions about the prospects of increasing sales to a point where facility utilization is adequate.

5. *Ratio of Equity Capital to Total Debt.* As the tendency to rather higher borrowings grows, this ratio is being used to check the required margin of safety.

6. *Number of Times Debt Service and Long-Term Rental Obligations Are Earned.* This ratio measures the margin that earnings before debt service and lease obligation bear to such annual call on cash. As a rule of thumb, some banks want a coverage of at least two times.

7. *Percent Return on Total Capital Employed or on Shareholders' Equity.* Lenders are interested in the leverage through the use of borrowed funds as well as comparative earning power.

8. *Cash Flow.* These may relate to cash flow sufficiency or cash flow efficiency. (See Chapter 27.)

40-7 PRESENT FINANCIAL CONDITION AND OPERATING RESULTS

As a general statement, the creditor bank wants assurances that the assets and liabilities as well as the income and expense are properly stated. The certificate of independent public accountants is relied on in this respect. It will bear mentioning, however, that experience with the differing abilities of accountants has led many banks to request the long form of auditor's report as some added assurance of an examination of sufficient scope.

To generalize, the matters on which a bank usually is particularly interested are essentially the same as those with which an effective management is concerned and include the following (especially for small businesses and new accounts).

(a) ACCOUNTING PRACTICES

Any change in accounting methods should be indicated and the effect on the current statement made known.

(b) CASH

The amount of cash on hand, if material, should be segregated from cash in banks. Often, the amount of cash in each depository must be identified. Funds that are in any way restricted or earmarked for any specific purpose should be designated. A statement of cash flows for the most recent several years and a current year plan, is of particular interest to creditors.

(c) ACCOUNTS AND NOTES RECEIVABLE

Accounts receivable should be segregated from notes receivable. Receivables should be aged to permit an appraisal of the *quality* and comparison with standard sales terms, as well as a determination of the adequacy of the reserve for doubtful accounts.

Trends in collections and bad debt losses should be made known. The relationship of bad debts to sales for several years should be indicated.

Receivables from other than trade customers should be segregated if material—such as loans to officers, and so on.

Any marked concentration of receivables in a relatively few customers, together with their financial ratings, might be a useful disclosure.

(d) INVENTORIES

Inventories, when appropriate, should be segregated by the stage of manufacture. The basis of valuation should be indicated. Aside from the overall inventory, if any one major item is excessive, it might be advisable to list the quantities on hand and indicate, based on present plans, the number of weeks of sales or manufacturing represented. Comment should also be made about the accounting treatment of any obsolete stock, as well as the date of the last physical inventory and percent of loss or shrinkage normally experienced.

(e) CASH SURRENDER VALUE OF LIFE INSURANCE

The beneficiary, amount, names, and positions of the insureds and cash surrender value of each policy should be disclosed. Also, policies assigned to secure indebtedness should be identified.

(f) PROPERTY, PLANT, AND EQUIPMENT

Schedules similar to those used for 10-K purposes would ordinarily meet any information needs of bankers.

For each major classification of property, and its related reserve, data regarding (1) beginning balance, (2) additions during the period, (3) reductions during the period, and (4) ending balance are desirable.

The basis of valuation and depreciation methods will be helpful in appraising the adequacy of allowances for depreciation and depletion. Any liens or encumbrances should be designated.

(g) CURRENT LIABILITIES

Liabilities should be segregated between current (due within one year) and long term. Notes payable should be identified as those due to banks, principal suppliers, owners, affiliates, and others. Endorsed or guaranteed obligations or those on a secured basis should be disclosed.

It may be helpful to segregate and describe any accounts payable to other than trade creditors. Trade accounts payable should be summarized by date of origin and related to customary trade terms. The names of important suppliers and the annual purchases from them should be identified, since the bank may wish to contact them. A reasonable detail of all other current accruals, and so on, should be given.

(h) INCOME TAX LIABILITY

A full disclosure of the status of this tax liability should be made, including the most recent date through which federal income returns have been examined. Disclosure should be made of any significant findings, or assessments, and the company position in regard to the expected liability.

(i) LONG-TERM LIABILITIES

Such information as this is desirable: a schedule showing the repayment due dates and amounts; the matter of compliance with the indenture or other agreements, and pertinent credit features of such agreements—rates of interest, maturity acceleration, collateral security, and so on.

(j) LEASE OBLIGATIONS

The extent of any major long-term lease obligations segregated as to operating and capital leases should be indicated. Usually, the bank desires a schedule of the annual lease rental obligations. The terms, including penalties for early termination, preferably should be summarized.

(k) CONTINGENT LIABILITIES

Any significant current or future commitment ought to be explained in terms of the purpose, nature, and amount. Included in this category would be purchase and sales contracts, pending lawsuits, repurchase agreements, and unsettled claims. *Unfavorable* sales contracts should be disclosed.

(l) EQUITY INTERESTS

Disclosure in this area would include the analysis of changes in the capital accounts and such information as this:

1. Identification of the principal owners.
2. Summary of rights for each class of stock.

3. Dividend (or other) payments made to shareholders in recent years, including the share of earnings paid out.

4. Explanation of any adjustments to retained earnings.

(m) INSURANCE COVERAGE

A summary schedule of insurance coverage, and related book value and market value, as applicable.

(n) INCOME AND EXPENSES

The analysis of significant trends and relationships is suggested, including these:

1. Trend of sales by major product line over past several years.

2. Identification of changes in the sales levels due to volume, prices, and abnormal situations, including strikes or "windfalls."

3. Either profit by product line or contribution to fixed costs and profit by product line.

4. Identification of trends in each significant cost category of labor, material, and expense in relationship to sales (by type of cost and not by responsibility or department).

5. Comparative costs, if available, as related to industry or competitors; very often the banks have such data.

6. Disclosure of special or nonrecurring income or expense.

(o) OTHER

Any other conditions or developments a prudent management would consider significant, such as the following:

1. The planning and control system.

2. The system of internal accounting control.

3. The management team.

In this latter case, the lender will be most interested in the ability and experience of all major management and not merely the chief executive and financial officer. Very often the loan officer will evaluate the management, giving consideration to company size, industry, etc., on a score sheet somewhat as follows:[2]

---

[2] From Research Institute of America, Inc., Report to Management, File 31, "Your Business through a Lender's Eyes," Oct. 29, 1958.

Good	Av'ge	Bad		Good	Av'ge	Bad	
☐	☐	☐	Organization, including depth of management.	☐	☐	☐	Condition of buildings and equipment.
☐	☐	☐	Training and development programs.	☐	☐	☐	Condition of inventory; inventory control.
☐	☐	☐	Knowledge of industry and competitors.	☐	☐	☐	Efficiency of credit and collection operations.
☐	☐	☐	Familiarity with markets, distribution channels, sales methods.	☐	☐	☐	Quantity and quality of advertising and sales promotion.
☐	☐	☐	Planning for the future.	☐	☐	☐	Customer service, handling of complaints, claims.
☐	☐	☐	Personnel policies, employee relations.				
☐	☐	☐	Knowledge of costs, cost control.	☐	☐	☐	Supplier relations (prompt payment, proper claims, etc.).
☐	☐	☐	Use of financial and other controls.	☐	☐	☐	Management balance among sales, production, finance, etc.
☐	☐	☐	Efficiency and attitude of labor force.				
☐	☐	☐	Housekeeping.	☐	☐	☐	Community relations.
☐	☐	☐	Plant layout.	☐	☐	☐	Alertness to new ideas, procedures, techniques.

The key point in the foregoing is *disclosure,* and the preparation of financial statements in accordance with generally accepted accounting principles consistently applied. Moreover, much of the information outlined is that included in the "long-form" audit report of the knowledge independent public accountant—particularly when he or she is informed that the statement will be provided to banks and may be used for credit purposes.

40-8 BUDGETS AND FORECASTS

Preceding comments have related primarily to the historical financial statements. Yet most lenders are concerned with the primary question, "Will the loan be repaid at maturity?" Emphasis is on the *future.* Hence, in negotiating or securing a loan, prudent company officials give particular attention to prospects. The business plans, instead of being in someone's head, will be translated into financial statements.

It is believed the request for short-term or long-term loans should be supported by *realistic* and *conservative* estimates of the future. Almost anyone can prepare optimistic projections that never materialize, and never were based on sound business judgment—which ultimately work against the best interests of the company. It is suggested that, with appropriate commentary, the future plans of the company be supported by the following:

1. A statement of estimated income and expense, for the current forecast period—usually one year.

2. A statement of estimated cash flow for the sort term, indicating the source and disposition of funds.

3. The statement of estimated financial position at the end of the forecast period.

4. The projected income and expense statement, and cash flow, to the end of the loan period.

In many instances, it is the practice of the management (the CFO or controller) to make a graphic presentation to the board of directors on the essential elements of the annual business plan (and/or long-range plan). It is suggested the same presentation, at least the major elements, might be made at the start of the business year to the major commercial banks granting the revolving credit and/or term loans. This permits the financial officer to communicate the important financial (or other) plans to this important group of creditors. Also, it is an excellent forum for responding to questions.

Some suggested visual aids for the annual business plan could include these topics:

1. Major Assumptions
2. Plan Highlights (compared with prior year performance)
   - New orders
   - Sales
   - Net Income
     —amount
     —% of sales
     —% return on equity
   - Earnings per Share
   - Cash flow from operations, investments, and financing
   - Capital expenditures
3. Sale Graph by Divisions or Organizational Group
4. Comparative Summary of Income and Expense
5. Net Income by Product or Organizational Group
6. Summarized Quarterly Results (Sales and Net Income)
7. Statement of Cash Flows
8. Statement of Consolidated Financial Position
9. Other Selected Graphs
   (a) Sales—Comparative growth rate (several years)
   (b) Net Income for past five years
   (c) Earnings per share—five years
   (d) Return on assets—several years
   (e) Return on equity—several years

As a general word of caution, experience indicates the wisdom of *periodically* reviewing financial prospects with the company's principal bankers. Keeping these financial institutions informed, irrespective of the immediacy of the need for a loan, will do much to maintain sound banking relationships and tend to insure that necessary funds will be made available when needed.

40-9 A REGISTRATION STATEMENT

When a management decides to issue new securities, company counsel, of course, will handle the legal aspects, but the controller will be heavily involved in the prospectus and registration statement. Needless to say, the specific instructions of the SEC must be interpreted and adhered to. Securities regulations change, and the controller should be up to date on requirements. The basic registration statement consists of two principal parts.

Part 1 is the prospectus (the legal offering or "selling" document) which must be furnished to all prospective purchasers. It is a printed document that contains the essential facts regarding the company's business operations, financial condition, and management.

Part 2 contains supplemental information that will be available at the SEC for inspection by the public.

The basic registration form is Form S-1. It requires a company to disclose among other things:

- A description of the business.
- Its properties.
- Material transactions between the company and its officers and directors.
- Competition.
- Identification of officers and directors and their remuneration.
- Certain pending legal proceedings.
- The plan for distributing the securities.
- The intended use of the proceeds.

It is not prepared as a fill-in-the-blank form, but is similar to a brochure with information provided in a narrative format. There are also detailed requirements concerning financial statements, including the requirement that such statements be audited by an independent certified public accountant.

In addition to the information expressly required by the form, the company must also provide any other information necessary to make the statements complete and not misleading. If sufficient adverse or risk factors exist concerning the offering and/or the issues, they must also be set forth prominently in the prospectus, usually in the beginning. Examples of such factors are:

- Lack of business operating history.
- Adverse economic conditions in the industry or any segment.
- Lack of a market for the securities offered.
- Dependence on key personnel.

(a) SIMPLIFIED REGISTRATION FORMS

Under certain conditions, the comprehensive and extensive registration requirements of Form S-1 can be replaced by more simplified alternate forms. The more common ones are:

- Form S-18—This is available for registering securities the aggregate offering price of which does not exceed $7.5 million, *providing* that the issuer is not subject to the SEC's continuous reporting requirements under the exchange act. Continuous reporting requirements include filing annual and other periodic reports to update information contained in the original filing.
- Forms S-2 and S-3—These forms are available to those companies that have filed statements with the SEC under the Securities Acts for the last three years, in a timely and complete way, and who have had no material changes in their fiscal affairs since that last filing. All information contained in previous 10-Ks, annual reports, proxy statements, and so on, are incorporated by reference and little or no new reporting is needed.
- Form S-3 is used by companies who have either $150,000,000 in aggregate market value of voting stock issued and held by nonaffiliates, or $100,000,000 in aggregate market value held by nonaffiliates and trading volume of 3,000,000 shares annually.
- Form S-2 is used by most others.

There are other simplified forms available for use in special circumstances, for example, S-4 for certain foreign registrants, S-8 for employee plans, and S-11 for Real Estate Investment Trusts. The requirements for all the registration statements should be determined by reviewing the SEC literature.

40-10 SUMMARY

In issuing financial statements and related data for creditor use, the controller is responsible for presenting the information fairly and accurately. The more the controller understands the needs and analytical procedures of the users of such information, the more he can provide useful data to facilitate the intelligent granting of credit.

Finally, it is suggested that the controller keep in mind the possible changing information needs of creditors (as well as investors) resulting from the technology revolution, the globalization of many businesses, the changing capital market, the changes in financial instruments, and the generally increased risks arising from new products and new competitors. (See Chapter 35.) This may revise his/her techniques as to the method and time frame in communicating.

40-11 SELECTED REFERENCES

Cole, Robert H., *Consumer and Commercial Credit Management,* Homewood, IL: Richard D. Irwin, 1980.

Kallberg, Jarl G., and Kenneth Parkinson, *Current Asset Management; Cash, Credit and Inventory,* New York: John Wiley & Sons, 1984.

Rubin, Richard L., and Philip Goldberg, *The Small Business Guide to Borrowing Money,* New York: McGraw-Hill Book Company, 1980.

Wilson, Bruce, "The Rating Agency Dance," *Financial Executive,* May/June, 1992, pp. 28–31.

Wilson, Richard S., *Corporate Senior Securities, Analysis and Evaluation of Bonds, Convertibles and Preferreds,* Chicago, IL: Probus Publishing Co., 1987.

PART SIX

COMPUTER SYSTEMS AND RELATED TECHNOLOGY

CHAPTER 41

Role of the Computer in Accounting and Financial Analysis

41-1 OVERVIEW

Management has long recognized the ability of the computer to handle routine clerical tasks and to store and retrieve data. Forward-looking companies have extended the role of the computer into the area of decision making. Good management has always been a combination of hunch and analysis, or of the qualitative and the quantitative. Using the computer to assemble, correlate, and analyze great masses of data, a manager can establish and alter assumptions and check computer-generated results against experience and intuition in a series of controlled iterations. The rapid strides in the development of user-friendly computer software and ready access to a computer have given managers the ability to make better strategic and tactical decisions and to reap the rewards of applying information intelligently and aggressively.

In this chapter, we discuss the possible uses of new computer technology in accounting and financial analysis (e.g., strategic planning, annual business planning, sensitivity analysis) and provide an overview of some of the methodology. In addition, we briefly describe the controller's role in using computers for day-to-day accounting tasks.

This chapter covers the use of computers in those areas of the controller's primary responsibility. Subsequent chapters cover several computer-related topics that are important to the controller, but which have wider applicability than just the accounting department, such as selecting software, implementing disaster recovery planning, electronic data interchange, and information systems security.

41-2 ROLE OF THE CONTROLLER

The controller is responsible for effective financial systems. For this purpose, we deal with the application of the computer to financial problems or procedures, irrespective of the organizational placement of the general information services. The controller should perform the following tasks:

1. Be responsible for the effective utilization of computer applications in the traditional accounting and financial functions, such as:

   - Formal financial records—trial balances and ledgers and subsidiary ledgers.
   - Accounts payable.
   - Payroll.
   - Cash disbursements.
   - Fixed assets.
   - Inventory.
   - Accounts receivable.
   - Cash receipts.

2. Gain knowledge of computer-based systems for other departments that can enhance the controller's performance by providing more accurate information more quickly, allowing the controller to close periods rapidly or to control costs and key operational measures in real-time. Examples of such systems are:

   - On-line inventory tracking systems.
   - Bar-coded time clock systems.
   - Material requirements planning systems.

3. Direct the use of new computer techniques in financial planning and modeling.

4. Gain knowledge of the newest computer hardware.

5. Be aware of developments in software, especially those that relate to application products useful in financial or business processes. As manufacturing and materials systems become more tightly integrated due to the advent of Material Requirements Planning (MRP) and Just-in-Time (JIT) systems, software packages are appearing that also integrate the accounting function into those systems.

6. Review actual computer system installation costs versus budgeted costs, and follow up on significant variances.

7. Create audit trails for new computer systems to assist both internal and external auditors. In particular, swapping information such as invoices and purchase orders with trading partners via electronic data interchange will require close attention by the controller to ensure that adequate controls are in place.

8. Review new computer systems to ensure that sufficient security and confidentiality safeguards are in place and operating as planned.

9. Finally, use new computer technology to enhance the efficiency and effectiveness of accounting functions. A few examples are:

- Electronic funds transfer.
- Modem access to account balances at servicing banks.
- Electronic data interchange.
- Document storage on optical disc.

The controller's goal in using information systems technology is to provide improved user access to information, enable a faster closing cycle, and improve the cost-effectiveness of the accounting department. Also, if the controller has an information systems group that is devoted to creating, installing, and maintaining financial applications, the following benefits can be realized:

1. *Enhance Productivity:*
   - Provide expert consultation to increase productivity and control.
   - Foster partnerships with other business processes, such as manufacturing and materials.
   - Provide education to the accounting staff to assure that they maintain current relevant systems knowledge.
   - Decrease the time and cost of developing and implementing new financial systems and software releases.
   - Investigate new technologies and their applicability to the accounting function.
   - Research appropriate make/buy decisions for the department's hardware and software.

2. *Provide Systems That Meet User Requirements:*
   - Deliver systems that provide increased user functionality.
   - Deliver "bug-free" systems that match user needs.

3. *Support and Enhance Ongoing Operations:*
   - Develop system enhancements as required.
   - Install and support new software releases through documentation and training.
   - Provide a liaison with those data processing personnel that do not report to the controller.
   - Ensure continuous accounting operations during system installations, upgrades, and relocations.
   - Ensure that disaster recovery and security requirements are met.

41-3 USES FOR THE COMPUTER: CONTROLLER APPLICATIONS

The following applications are related to the controller's responsibilities that can be totally or partially converted to electronic spreadsheets or databases on a computer. This list is not complete, for new applications arise each year. The controller should peruse magazines such as *Computerworld, Journal of Accountancy,* and *Management Accounting* for information about leading-edge applications.

1. *Accounting Applications:*

   - *General Ledger.* Convert the database to a commercial or custom package.
   - *Subsidiary Ledgers.* Convert the database to a commercial or custom package.
   - *Fixed Assets.* Convert the database to a commercial or custom package, and provide bar codes for fixed assets for periodic audits.
   - *Payroll.* Convert the database to a commercial or custom package, or use a service bureau; also, collect time card data with a time clock that recognizes either bar-coded or magnetized employee badges.
   - *Accounts Receivable.* Convert the database to a commercial or custom package; also, use electronic data interchange to receive payments directly into the company's bank account.
   - *Accounts Payable.* Convert the database to a commercial or custom package; also, use electronic data interchange to pay suppliers. This function frequently requires interfaces to the purchasing and receiving functions to ensure that parts have been legitimately ordered and received before the supplier is paid.
   - *Product Costing.* Convert manual bill of material records to an automated system, so the cost accountant can easily access the data. Also, implement a FIFO or LIFO cost layering system as part of the accounts payable function, so products can be costed based on actual received part costs.
   - *Cash Receipts and Disbursements.* Install one or more lock boxes in conjunction with the company's bank, and then use modem access to verify daily check clearings, thereby increasing the amount of cash available for investment.
   - *Bank Reconciliations.* Create an electronic spreadsheet that will itemize all variances and automatically recalculate totals.
   - *Inventory Tracking.* Convert the database to a commercial or custom package; in addition, bar code all inventory locations and install wireless terminals that update the database in real time as transactions occur. Voice-activated systems are also becoming available that fulfill the same function.

2. *Taxation Applications:*

   - *Forecasted Tax Returns.* Create an electronic spreadsheet that requires the input of specific data, and returns an estimated tax payment or refund.
   - *Tax Return Preparation.* Use a commercially available package to complete the tax return; such packages automatically roll up totals from subsidiary schedules and recalculate totals as additional information is entered.
   - *Tax Accruals and Distribution.* Use an electronic spreadsheet to calculate and distribute this information.

3. *Planning Applications:*

   - *Strategic Planning.* This topic encompasses pro forma financials for cash flows, income, and financial condition. Use electronic spreadsheets to create the financials.

- *Intercompany Transfer Pricing.* Use an electronic spreadsheet to calculate transfer prices. In more complicated pricing situations, some companies design their own systems that extract the relevant information from the databases of the shipping and receiving companies.
- *Capital Investment Decision.* This encompasses selecting alternative investments. Use an electronic spreadsheet to calculate the internal rate of return and net present value of various capital investments.
- *Manpower Planning.* Convert the labor routing database to a commercial or custom system, and multiply the labor routings by anticipated production requirements to derive manpower projections.
- *Merger and Acquisition (M&A) Analysis.* Use electronic spreadsheets for numerous M&A analyses.

4. *Control Applications:*
   - *Annual Budget or Business Plan.* This encompasses comparing actual results to the business plan and analyzing variances. Many commercial accounting packages perform this function, or do so with a report writer add-on package. Alternatively, the comparisons can be made with an electronic spreadsheet.
   - *Departmental Budget Performance.* Many commercial accounting packages perform this function, or do so with a report writer add-on package. Alternatively, the performance analysis can be done with an electronic spreadsheet.

5. *Cash Management Applications:*
   - *Schedule Short-Term Cash Needs and Surpluses.* Use an electronic spreadsheet for forecasting, using inputs from the receivable and payables systems, as well as the bank's database that shows daily check clearings.
   - *Develop Short-Term Portfolio Strategy.* Use an electronic spreadsheet to analyze the rates of return of various investments.

6. *Employee Benefits Applications:*
   - *Determine Individual Benefits.* Use an electronic spreadsheet to calculate employee benefits and costs under various scenarios.
   - *Design Benefit Plans.* This encompasses calculating spendable income after retirement versus before. Use an electronic spreadsheet to present various payout options to employees under varying scenarios.

7. *Insurance Applications:*
   - *Analyze Insurance Alternatives.* Use an electronic spreadsheet to compare alternative insurance proposals in terms of varying risks, costs, options, and other features.
   - *Analyze Prepayments and Accruals.* Use an electronic spreadsheet to review these items.
   - *Analyze Claims.* Use an electronic spreadsheet to review these items.

8. *Reporting Applications:*
   - *Create Financial Statements.* Use a commercial or custom accounting package with an attached report writer to create financial statements. Report

writers are usually sold separately, but are useful in designing custom report layouts.

- *Create Financial Ratios.* Use an electronic spreadsheet to create and update both financial and operating ratios. The spreadsheet should have a graphics capability, so the ratios can be presented in that manner.

- *Create Flexible Budget Reports.* Use the budget module of a commercially available accounting package or an electronic spreadsheet to create budget reports.

- *Create Charts and Graphs.* Use an electronic spreadsheet with a built-in graphics capability or a graphics software package to create charts and graphs. Most packages now allow color charts and graphs.

9. *Finance Applications:*

- *Evaluate Financing Alternatives.* Use an electronic spreadsheet to review financing alternatives, including comparisons of time periods, interest rates, buyout provisions, and downpayments.

- *Evaluate Investment Decisions.* Use an electronic spreadsheet to review investment alternatives, including comparisons of investment liquidity, interest rates, impact of exchange rates, minimum investment periods, and other factors.

10. *Other Applications:*

- *Automate Internal Audit Workpapers.* Use an electronic spreadsheet to reduce the totaling and crossfooting work of manual audit workpapers.

- *Record Retention Schedules.* Use an electronic spreadsheet to update record retention information. A word processor can also be used for this function.

Large companies have skilled information systems professionals who are knowledgeable about the many software packages available for business use. The following summary will help controllers of smaller businesses establish a software library that will handle their financial needs:

Application	Software Package
1. Essential Functions	
• Database Management Used for collecting all business information, both financial and nonfinancial	Microsoft Access, Paradox, Dbase IV
• General Accounting Used for general ledger and subledger recording	Peachtree, ACCPAC Plus/BPI, Access to Platinum/Platinum Series, Cima, Great Plains, MAS/90, Macola, Solomon
• Graphics Used to prepare statements and reports from data files	Powerpoint, Harvard Graphics, Aldus, Charisma, Freelance Graphics, Delta Graph Professional

Application	Software Package
2. *Other Basic Functions*	
• Word Processing Used to prepare correspondence, reports, etc.	Ami Pro, Microsoft Word, WordPerfect
• Spreadsheet Used to prepare analysis and summaries of numerical data	Quattro Pro, Lotus 1-2-3, Microsoft Excel
3. *Other Business Functions*	
• Project Management Used to collect and report information by project	Project Scheduler 5, Microsoft Project, ABT Project Workbench
• Time Management Used to manage calendar, collect time spent by client, etc.	Instant Recall, Calendar Creator Plus, Timeslips
• Taxation Used to assemble tax returns	Tax Partner, Tax Cut, Turbo Tax
• Data Utilities Used to access data files residing outside the company	America On-line, Prodigy, Compuserve

41-4 THE ANATOMY OF A FINANCIAL MODEL

A financial model provides answers to specific questions posed by the user. The underlying formulas vary considerably by model. For example, a company in an expanding industry may want a model that shows cash requirements if the company expands due to an increase in the size of the market or its share in the market. On the other hand, a company in a mature industry may assume that the market size or market share will not change drastically, and instead will focus its model on answering questions about the impact of cost reductions or changes in the income tax rate. The questions that models answer can vary considerably by type of market, company, or a host of other variables.

However, the basic structure of a financial model does not change. The typical model consists of five parts:

1. *Documentation.* As in any financial decision, the assumptions are critical to the solution and should be recorded. In particular, the more complex formulas within the model should be documented. This permits audit or other reviews and a reference as may be necessary.

2. *Input Assumptions.* Input data may be actual (i.e., historical) or judgmental (i.e., estimated). The source of the data should be documented. Also, the model should have a date and time formula that is automatically updated; since the input assumptions are frequently changed, management must know the date of the printed output.

3. *Managerial Ratios.* Ratios usually form an integral part of the financial model. Many ratios are inputted as part of the assumptions and outputted as part of the projections. Some common ratios would be these:

- Net sales to receivables.
- Inventory to cost of sales.
- Net income to sales.
- Current ratio.
- Accounts payable to inventory.

   Such relationships are used to examine the reasonableness of the answers, provide signals about wrong assumptions, and even to test the reasonableness of the question. For example, the model's current ratio may suddenly drop from 2:1 to 1:1. Upon further review, the controller may find that the receivables calculation formula wrongly assumes that days of receivables will decrease from 60 days to 30 days, thereby dropping the receivables amount and worsening the current ratio.

4. *Projections.* The printed output over the planning horizon is known as the projection. The format may be tabular or graphic, but it must be understandable to the user. Since it is a communication device, it should not be highly technical, but should be oriented to the financial presentations the readers understand. Some models now put the output graphics at the front of the model, followed by key assumptions, with the actual model at the back of the presentation; this approach starts with high-level summarizations and provides more details later on if that information is required.

5. *Base Case.* The base case is the initial set of the model's assumptions and may include unacceptable or unrealistic data and, through an iterative process, finally is considered a plan or case. With the advent of interactive models on personal computers, the controller can now alter the model during a management meeting, so that the outcome of suggested changes can be determined instantly and shown to the management team on a large computer screen or an overhead projector.

Finally, the model should be periodically checked for missing or incorrect information, formulas, or assumptions. Models are constantly updated with additional variables and supplementary sets of detailed information, and formulas within the model may not be altered to account for these additions, yielding erroneous results.

41-5 STRATEGIC PLANNING MODELS

The computer is useful in the strategic planning process, but we must first establish who should use the computer in this role. Senior executives could use it, but their expertise is in exercising their judgment, not in manipulating information. Thus, the most appropriate users are the staff reporting to those responsible for strategic planning.

   A strategic model is defined as a financial model with a long-range planning horizon (e.g., 5 to 15 years) to be used in establishing the goals and objectives of the enterprise. It may deal with outside factors such as the gross national product, the size of the product market, or the inflation rate, as well as internal data. Often it deals with items on a "broad band" basis and is not too detailed. A typical strategic model could

Figure 41-1   Summary of Financial Information.

ABC TOY COMPANY
5-Year Strategic Plan
Summary of Financial Information

Key Measure	1995	1996	1997	1998	1999
Acquisitions	1,100	6,809	2,836	2,835	3,562
Sales Backlog	1,258	6,377	7,382	8,030	8,956
Net Sales	1,700	1,691	1,831	2,188	2,637
Operating Margin %	8%	7%	8%	9%	10%
Net Income %	5%	5%	5%	5%	6%
Average Assets	840	979	1,048	1,158	1,329
Turns on Ave. Assets	2.02	1.73	1.75	1.89	1.98
% Return on Ave. Assets	10%	9%	8%	10%	11%
% Return on Ave. Equity	27%	22%	19%	22%	25%
Earnings per Share	6.07	5.85	5.89	7.78	10.43

produce the computerized summary statement shown in Figure 41-1. This model would typically be supported by subsidiary schedules that provide more detailed information. The advantage of a computerized model is that any change to the detailed information automatically updates the summary information.

A computerized model not only reduces the clerical work involved in maintaining a strategic plan, but also can highlight key relationships to assist in management decisions. For example, a *key ratios output* page can be part of the model. This page groups ratios together that change as a result of specific inputs. Changing the days of inventory assumption will alter the working capital requirement, which in turn alters the interest income/expense, which in turn alters net income. A portion of the key ratios output page is shown in Figure 41-2.

41-6 ANNUAL BUSINESS PLANNING MODELS

The annual business plan model is defined as a model with a 1-year planning horizon, to be used to model a company's key success factors. It is *not* the company's annual budget. The model is much shorter than the budget, and the model only presents information on a summary level. Key success factors are identified by the company's management and incorporated into the model. The key success factors are then used as the

Figure 41-2   Key Ratios Output Page.

	1995	1996	1997	1998	1999
Input—Days of Inventory	90	80	70	60	50
Output—Working Capital	800	750	700	650	600
Output—Interest Expense	56	53	49	46	42
Output—Net Income	100	102	104	106	109

primary variables in determining possible financial results for the year. For example, management feels that improving the sales per salesperson is critical to improving net profits. This measure must then be included into the model, so that changes in the sales per salesperson will cause a change in net profits.

In addition to the key success factors section, the model should include a short, summary-level income statement that reacts to changes in the critical success factors. The balance sheet can either be shown in a summary version or only key items may be listed, such as the total amount of working capital, debt, or key debt covenants, such as current ratios.

An annual model gives management a rough cut review of financial projections for the upcoming year. The management team can use the model to rapidly input changes to key variables and review the outcome immediately. The management team then agrees upon how it wants to change its key variables in the upcoming year in order to obtain the desired financial result, and creates a budget targeted at achieving those changes.

A computer is indispensable for annual plan modeling. A computer allows the user to input changes in key variables and instantly obtain information about how the company's income or assets will change as a result. The computer can be brought into management meetings, so that the results of suggested changes can be fed back to the team in real time, for further discussion.

The structure of an annual business planning model will vary not only by company, but even from year to year for the same company, as critical success factors change. However, a typical model should be able to answer any of the following questions:

- What sales level is required to achieve an income level of XXX dollars?
- What profit level is required to achieve earnings per share of XXX dollars?
- What unit volume is required to offset a unit price decrease of XXX dollars?
- What is the break-even level in units sold?

A simplified business planning model is shown in Figure 41-3. In this model, the management of the ABC Toy Company has become concerned about the amount of working capital being used by the company, so the model's key variables include days of inventory, payables, and receivables. The management team can then vary the days of each item and forecast working capital needs as a result.

41-7 SENSITIVITY ANALYSIS

When developing strategic and annual plans, management frequently experiments with key variables to determine how changes will impact the models' results. This technique is called "sensitivity analysis." Using it, management can vary each component of a decision to see the possible extent of variation in outcomes.

Using the key variables shown in Figure 41-3, we list typical sensitivity analyses in Figure 41-4 in a tabular format and in Figure 41-5 in a graphical format. These analyses only deal with the extent of changes in net profit as key variables are altered. Another form of sensitivity analysis is to determine the greatest risk to the company. For example, if a new product appears on the market and takes 25% of the ABC Toy Company's market share, what will happen to earnings? Alternatively, what if a price

Figure 41-3 A Simplified Planning Model.

	Quarter 1	Quarter 2	Quarter 3	Quarter 4	Totals
ABC Toy Company Budget—1996 Assumptions					
Input Ratios:					
Gross margin percentage	40%	40%	40%	40%	
Unit price	$40	$45	$55	$45	
Market size (number of units)	1,000,000	1,000,000	1,000,000	1,000,000	
Market share %	25%	23%	23%	24%	
Sales per salesperson	125,000	125,000	135,000	125,000	
Total cost per salesperson	16,250	16,250	16,250	16,250	
Days of inventory	90	85	80	75	
Days of receivables	60	50	45	43	
Days of payables	35	34	33	32	
Tax rate	38%	38%	38%	39%	
Output Ratios:					
Break-even level (units sold)	210,450	209,861	179,758	213,111	
Working capital to sales %	31.9%	28.1%	25.6%	23.9%	
Inventory to sales %	25.0%	23.6%	22.2%	20.8%	
A/R to sales %	16.7%	13.9%	12.5%	11.9%	
A/R to sales %	9.7%	9.4%	9.2%	8.9%	
Revenues	10,000,000	10,350,000	12,650,000	10,800,000	43,800,000
Less:					
Cost of Goods Sold	6,000,000	6,210,000	7,590,000	6,480,000	26,280,000
Gross Margin	4,000,000	4,140,000	5,060,000	4,320,000	17,520,000
Gross Margin %	40%	40%	40%	40%	40%
Less:					
Sales Expense	1,300,000	1,345,500	1,522,685	1,404,000	5,572,185
General & Administrative	2,067,200	2,432,000	2,432,000	2,432,000	9,363,200
Pre-tax Profit	632,800	362,500	1,105,315	484,000	2,584,615
Less:					
Tax	392,336	224,750	685,295	295,240	1,597,621
Net Profit	240,464	137,750	420,020	188,760	986,994
Net Profit %	2.4%	1.3%	3.3%	1.7%	2.3%

war develops, and the product price sinks by a maximum of $10? Modeling these kinds of questions allows the company to project best-case and worst-case scenarios.

41-8 SUMMARY

This chapter highlighted areas of controller responsibility that can be improved with computer technology, such as accounting software, automated inventory tracking systems, and bar-coded timeclock systems. In addition, we listed a number of commercially available software packages that the controller can use for accounting functions

Figure 41-4 Sensitivity Analysis in a Tabular Format.

Sensitivity Analysis:	Qtr 1	Qtr 2	Qtr 3	Qtr 4
Price % Change	0.0%	5.0%	10.0%	15.0%
Net Profit %	1.0%	1.5%	1.9%	2.2%
Gross Margin % Change	0.0%	5.0%	10.0%	15.0%
Net Profit %	1.0%	1.8%	2.5%	3.3%
G&A % Change	0.0%	5.0%	10.0%	15.0%
Net Profit %	1.0%	1.5%	1.9%	2.4%
Sales/Salesperson % Change	0.0%	5.0%	10.0%	15.0%
Net Profit %	1.0%	1.3%	1.5%	1.7%

Figure 41-5 Sensitivity Analysis in a Graphical Format.

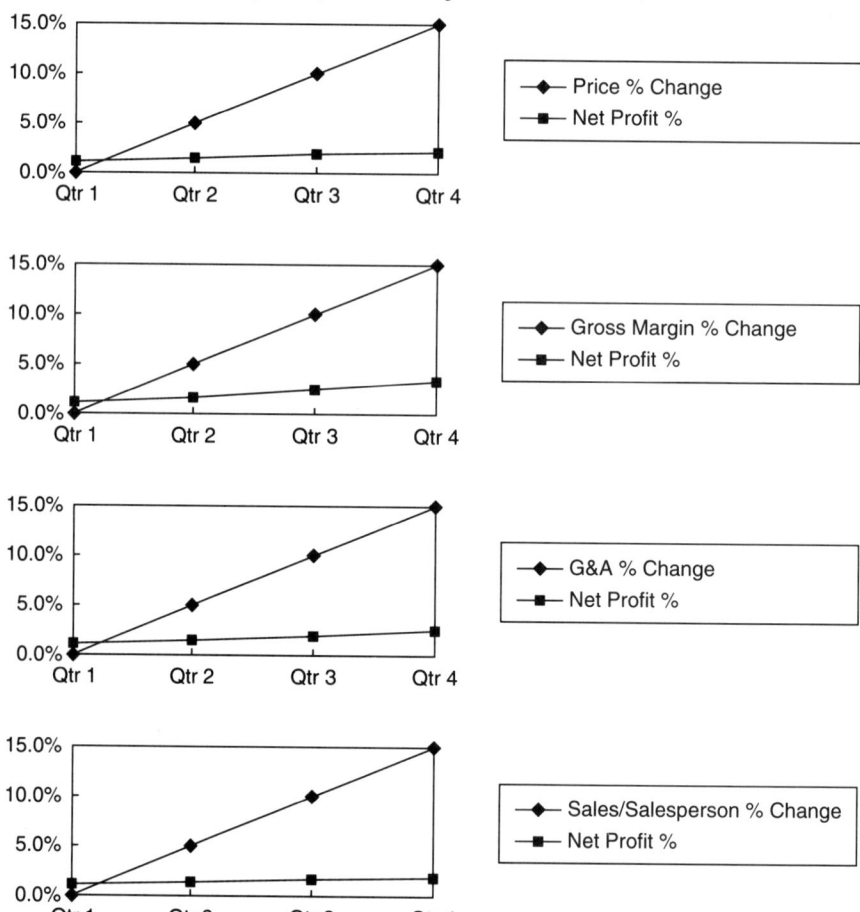

and financial modeling. Finally, we discussed the uses of computers in financial modeling, in the areas of strategic and annual planning, and for sensitivity analysis.

Computers take away much of the drudgery of recording accounting transactions and recomputing multiple iterations of financial models. This allows the controller to allocate resources away from these areas and into more value-added activities such as studying possible cost reductions and working with design teams to plan costs for new products.

41-9 SELECTED REFERENCES

Christie, Linda Gail, *Managing Today and Tomorrow with On-Line Information.* Homewood, IL: Dow Jones-Irwin, 1986.

Harding, Wayne, and Chuck Kramer, "Using Your Computer for Cash Flow Statements," *Journal of Accountancy,* Feb. 1989, pp. 106–108.

Mazhin, Roza, "A Spreadsheet Template for the Statement of Cash Flows," *Journal of Accountancy,* March 1989, pp. 110–123.

Victor, Ralph E., and C. Douglas Poe, "Statistical Sampling Software of Auditing," *Journal of Accountancy,* May 1989, pp. 143–150.

Willson, James D., *Budgeting and Profit-Planning Manual* (1994 ed.). New York: Warren, Gorham & Lamont, Chapters G1 thru G5.

CHAPTER 42

Computer Hardware Trends

42-1 INTRODUCTION

Business managers must perform many jobs in order to effectively manage their organizations. Unfortunately, the manager cannot be a specialist in all functional areas of the organization. Accounting personnel cannot and should not be expected to be information technology specialists; however, some knowledge of the current trends in computer hardware technology is recommended. This chapter provides a summary overview of the current computer hardware trends and capabilities relevant to finance and accounting professionals.

42-2 PC-BASED SYSTEMS

(a) MICROPROCESSORS

The core of any computer system is its central processing unit or CPU. It is the capability of the CPU that ultimately determines the overall usefulness of the total computer system. The CPU is the "engine" of the system. The development of the microprocessor can be illustrated through these personal computers developed by IBM. The micro-

The author of this chapter is David M. Bassett, Consultant, Ernst & Young, Denver.

processors used in personal computers are predominately supplied by Intel and a handful of other manufacturers supporting the Intel standards. When referring to processor types, it is common to use an Intel-based numerical reference (e.g., 286, 386, 486) which refers to the model number of the microprocessor. Intel's newest processor has broken this trend by using a tradename for its 586 (Pentium).

A CPU runs at a *clock speed* that greatly affects the operating speed of the unit; clock speeds are referred to in Megahertz (Mhz), millions of machine cycles per second. An alternative measure of a processor's speed is millions of instructions executed per second or MIPS. The original IBM personal computer introduced in 1982 used an Intel 8088 running at 4.77 Mhz. Today processor speeds of greater than 60 Mhz are common. While clock speed is important, the CPU architecture is also a determining factor in processing throughout.

(b) INTEL 486 AND PENTIUM

Intel introduced the 80486 microprocessor in the early 1990s. The 80486 has a small but effective memory cache built into the microprocessor. It is currently available in many versions. The DX version has a built in math coprocessor that can greatly reduce processing time in certain numeric-intensive applications, the SX version does not have the math coprocessor. While running at compatible speeds to the 80386 series, the 80486 realizes more processing throughput for a given speed in Mhz. Another very important feature built into the 80486 processor is the option of installing a "clock-doubling" processor chip. Tests have shown the resulting improvement from this option in system performance is around 70 percent. A fully configured 486-based system can be purchased for about $1,000. Single-user systems using the 486 processor with a speed of 60 Mhz should be considered the absolute minimum requirement for new business system applications. Intel released the next generation of the 80×86 compatible microprocessor in 1993. The processor, called Pentium, is capable of running over 100 million instructions per second (MIPS) or roughly twice as many as the fastest 80486 66-Mhz computer. The Pentium-based systems have replaced the 486 as the minimum business workstation-engine at many organizations.

(c) STORAGE DEVICES

Nearly every system has at least one removable media storage device. Frequently, these are hard disk drives. There has been an increasing standardization on the 3.5-inch disk system that holds roughly 1.44 million characters of information. The 5.25-inch floppy drive has lost popularity. Fixed or hard disk drives are increasing in speed and storage capacity while decreasing in physical size. In years past, there were several interface options available; however, there is a movement to the integrated drive controller (IDE) on the hard disk that provides greater speed and standardization. Although the reliability of today's fixed disks as measured by the mean time between failures (MTBF) is very good, it is still necessary to make backup copies of important data. One way this can be accomplished easily is with a magnetic tape drive. Tape storage is good for reading and writing large amounts of sequential data. The drawback is in retrieval. The entire tape must be loaded to locate any data. Optical disks are increasing in popularity as storage devices to overcome this drawback.

(d) PORTABLES

One of the segments of the PC market that is experiencing significant growth is the portable or laptop PC market. A new benchmark system for laptop PCs would include a 486 microprocessor and a hard disk with a capacity of about 50 million characters (megabytes), and a fax/modem for communications over telephone lines. As of mid-1995, such systems cost about $1,500. Upcoming trends recently introduced and likely to gain popularity include the proliferation of color displays, integrated modem and Local Area Network (LAN) connections on the system board of the unit and cellular modems for communications from virtually any location. Most units also have built-in pointing devices analogous to a desktop "mouse."

42-3 PERIPHERALS

The term *peripherals* refers to the accessory devices connected to a CPU for a specific task. Peripherals generally fall into the categories of input devices and output devices; however, some are both input and output devices.

(a) PRINTERS

The laser printer is the standard for the majority of businesses. While impact printing is still necessary in some business applications, laser printers are the choice because of their output quality, flexibility, and quietness. Resolutions of 300 dots per inch (dpi) is standard with some manufactures reaching beyond 600 dpi. Greater resolution in dots per inch requires more printer memory; to print 300 dpi full-page graphics requires 1.5 million characters of printer memory.

One major printer manufacturer has developed technology that changes the sizes of the individual dots to give the illusion of higher effective resolution. Many laser printers now support an industry standard method of communicating typefaces and sizes called Post Script. Post Script-compatible output is available across different computer systems including the Apple Macintosh. While output quality is generally superior, Post Script compatible lasers carry a $500 to $1,000 premium over basic models. Post Script is highly desirable in graphically intensive applications such as desktop publishing.

Color printing similar to laser output has existed for several years. Recently, prices for color capable lasers has dropped below $5,000. While the laser printer has gained tremendous acceptance, impact printing is still necessary for certain applications such as multiple part form printing.

(b) VIDEO DISPLAY MONITORS

Video display technology is also rapidly advancing. The recent Enhanced Graphics Array (EGA) standard of the late 1980s has given way to the newer Video Graphics Array (VGA) technology. The primary difference between the EGA displays and VGA is that EGA used digital signals to achieve a maximum of 16 onscreen colors at one time. Displays using VGA technology operate using analog signals similar to a standard television; therefore, each of the primary colors can be blended in an almost infinite combination to achieve up to 256 simultaneous onscreen colors. Standard VGA resolution is 480 screen pixels (points) by 800 pixels. Most VGA video display interfaces and many software applications also support a Super-VGA mode of 800×600 pixels that enables more data to be seen onscreen at one time. Similar to laser printers, increased display resolution requires more memory. To support basic (640×480) resolution with 16 colors usually requires 256 million characters of video memory; the same resolution with 256 colors requires 512 million characters of video memory. Systems using 1024×768 resolution have begun to gain market acceptance and are likely to be the new standard in the mid-1990s as applications which use Graphical Users Interfaces (GUIs) such as Microsoft's Windows and IBM's Operating System/2 proliferate. Newer technology includes putting the video system on the same processing system as the microprocessor. Called Local Bus Video (LBV), improves display speeds for new graphics-intensive applications such as teleconferencing, multimedia, and so on. Some of the speed benefits of LBV can be achieved by add-in video accelerator boards available from a variety of manufacturers.

(c) CD ROM

Compact Disc Read-Only Memory (CD ROM) is a technology that has existed since the mid-1980s but has now gained mainstream acceptance. Prices have fallen from the thousands of dollars at introduction to below $200 and sales of the units are increasing at 30 to 40 percent per year. A CD ROM operates on the same principles as an audio compact disc. Tiny pits in an encoded disc are read and translated into the digital language of computers, streams of 0s and 1s or bits. Also similar to an audio compact disc, the information is read-only and therefore cannot be rerecorded. Whereas a floppy disk can hold the equivalent of approximately 1,000 pages of information, one CD ROM can hold 350,000 pages. CD ROM technology is promoting the development of multimedia software that utilizes the integration of interactive video, sound, and language. Many more companies are using CD ROM in more traditional applications such as reducing the costs of distributing and receiving large volumes of data and increasing the timeliness of data access.

(d) MODEMS

The growing need for connectivity and networking frequently requires computers at different locations to be connected. A modem is a device that takes digital computer signals and translates them into analog signals for transmission over telephone lines. Modems are rated by the speed at which they communicate data in bits per second (bps). Most currently installed modems provide a speed of at least 2,400 bps. Some manufacturers have introduced various data compression techniques into their hardware that can effectively double a modem's speed if communication conditions are favorable. More and more businesses are switching to the newer 9,600 and 14,400 bps modems. Recently, the ITV standards organization has defined the V.34 modem standard providing uncompressed data transmission rates of 28,800 bps. With data compression, it is theoretically possible to achieve transmission rates of 115,200 bps on regular dial-up telephone lines. Businesses should consider upgrading to faster modems that can quickly pay for themselves with reduced long distance bills. In the long term, all modems may become obsolete as analog telephone connections are replaced by the Integrated Services Digital Network (ISDN), an integrated digital telephone and communications network. Users will eventually be able to plug their systems directly into a high-speed network outlet, thus bypassing the need for a modem altogether.

(e) CONNECTIVITY AND INTEROPERABILITY

One recent trend is the movement toward connecting systems via a network. There are two classifications of networks. Local area networks (LANs) tie systems together within small geographic regions such as a work group, department, or building. Wide area networks (WANs) link systems or individual LANs over greater geographic areas. There are many types of networks in common use but most make use of a common "server" machine that provides storage, communication, and printing services for the various "client" computers connected to it via telephone, coaxial, or fiber optic cable. Each unit connected to a network requires a specific adapter. The most prevalent networking cabling and signaling scheme for small systems today is the Ethernet system which is supported by the leading industry networking system provider, Novell, and many others. Ethernet systems utilize a shared one-way "electronic roadway" with "collision avoidance" software to access the server. Another common signaling scheme found in many business networks is the IBM Token-Ring system. Token-Ring networks look to the machine ahead of them for a "token" or authorization to access the network. The "token" is continuously passed around the "ring" of machines. The more expensive Token-Ring system is commonly found where connection to a mainframe or minicomputer is required because it treats mainframes and PCs as peers on the same network. Through the use of devices called bridges, routers, and gateways, networks have dissimilar signaling schemes can be linked. For example, an Macintosh AppleTalk network can be routed to an Ethernet PC network which is bridged to a mainframe in a Token-Ring network.

(f) DOWNSIZING AND CLIENT/SERVER COMPUTING

The advent of widespread networking has generated significant interest in mainframe downsizing. Downsizing refers to taking an application, such as a database or general ledger system, from a mainframe and running it on smaller systems. Many full-featured accounting software packages capable of running a medium-size organization run very well in a LAN environment. Another upcoming trend is toward "client/server" computing (see Figure 42-1). With client/server technology, data may remain on the client host system or on the server. The server becomes a "mini-mainframe" serving many clients. Once heralded as distributed processing systems where processing would be shared between the client and server, in reality, much of the processing work is still taking place on either the client or server individually.

   Currently, client/server systems are primarily limited to database queries and decision support systems. Fully implemented client/server applications such as accounting and personnel management are readily available; however, businesses's attitudes to client/server technology are mixed. One reason involves the "hidden" costs of

Figure 42-1 Client/Server Architecture.

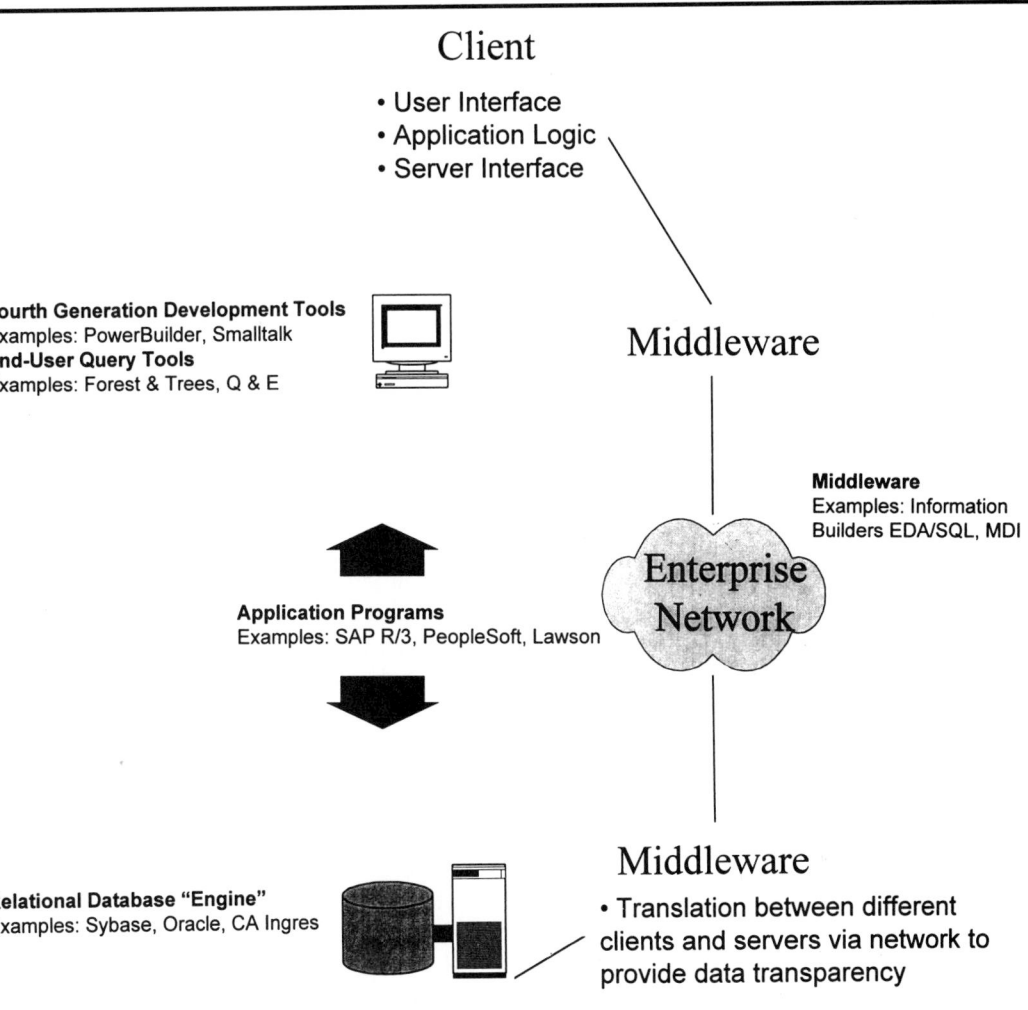

Client

- User Interface
- Application Logic
- Server Interface

Fourth Generation Development Tools
Examples: PowerBuilder, Smalltalk
End-User Query Tools
Examples: Forest & Trees, Q & E

Middleware

Middleware
Examples: Information
Builders EDA/SQL, MDI

Enterprise
Network

Application Programs
Examples: SAP R/3, PeopleSoft, Lawson

Middleware

- Translation between different clients and servers via network to provide data transparency

Relational Database "Engine"
Examples: Sybase, Oracle, CA Ingres

Server

- Data Storage
- Data Retrieval
- Application Logic

training and support. Another concern involves data security and recovery in a distributed database environment.

42-4 ALTERNATIVE SYSTEMS

(a) SINGLE-USER SYSTEMS

While the IBM-compatible PC has gained the most support of business users, it is estimated that 25 percent of all businesses have Macintosh systems as well. A single-user
system refers to a small computer system where the CPU is typically utilized by one
user.

The Macintosh was designed with a Graphical User Interface (GUI) in mind. In
a GUI interface, applications and data files are represented on screen as icons which
are graphic depictions of their functions; applications run within visual windows
which can be re-sized. Users manipulate icons and windows through the use of a pointing device such as a mouse. Since the Macintosh was designed with a GUI in mind it is
particularly well suited to graphical applications. The latest Macintosh models can
read and write PC files directly thus eliminating file-sharing problems for businesses
that support both standards.

Another system available is the workstation. A workstation is based on a different type of microprocessor called a RISC (Reduced Instruction Set Chip). More powerful than even the fastest PC or Macintosh, these systems are most suitable for
engineering design and scientific use where speed and superior graphics are a necessity. Workstations usually operate on the UNIX operating system; therefore, business
application software availability for workstations is significantly less than for the PC
or Macintosh.

(b) MINIS AND MAINFRAMES

Single user systems continue to attract a significant amount of attention in business circles. Single user systems have put sizable computing power on the desks of the end users
at a fraction of the cost of larger systems. Users have seized the opportunity to circumvent long lead times associated with requests from information technology departments.
While the trend is to downsizing, minicomputers and mainframes will continue to fill a
niche in business computing. Mainframes and minicomputers remain the best systems
for wide-scale online access, heavy file processing, or large numbers of end users. An
emerging role for mainframe systems is that of a "super" server for data warehousing applications. How the various pieces of hardware fit together is shown in Figure 42-2.

42-5 CONCLUSION

It is axiomatic to state that Information Technology is continually advancing. While
finance and accounting professionals do not need to be information technologists
aware of every development, a top-level overview of current computer trends and capabilities is strongly recommended. Such knowledge can enhance the quality of a professional's planning, control, and decision-making process by enabling recognition of new
opportunities and effectively evaluating technology alternatives.

Figure 42-2   Schematic Showing How Hardware Fits into a System.

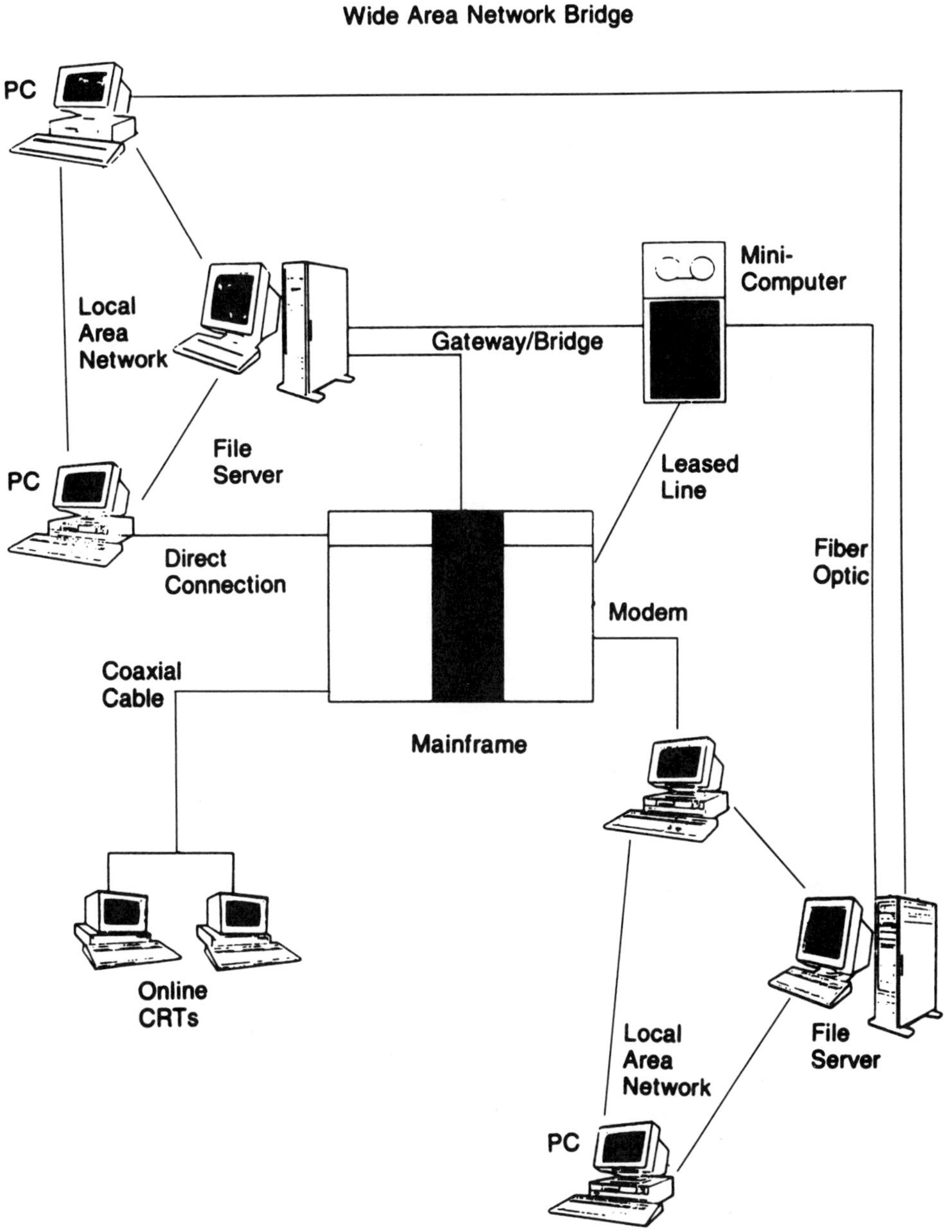

Wide Area Network Bridge

PC

Local
Area
Network

Gateway/Bridge

Mini-
Computer

File
Server

PC

Direct
Connection

Leased
Line

Fiber
Optic

Modem

Coaxial
Cable

Mainframe

Online
CRTs

Local
Area
Network

File
Server

PC

42-6 SELECTED REFERENCES

(a) MAGAZINES

Computerworld

Information Systems Management

Information Week

Journal of Systems Management

LAN Magazine

LAN Technology

Network Computing

PC Week

PC Magazine

CHAPTER 43

Client/Server Computing

43-1 INTRODUCTION

A radical change is unfolding within the information technology arena: client/server computing. Alternatively touted as a panacea or a Pandora's Box, client/server is here and gaining momentum. The impact of client/server computing on the hardware and software acquisition and development strategies utilized by a corporation cannot be underestimated. Therefore, it is extremely important for controllers to have knowledge of client/server-related concepts and trends and the effect they may have on the organization's information technology (IT) budget and strategies.

43-2 THE PAST: THE TERMINAL-HOST ARCHITECTURE

Terminal-host computer systems are centralized and rely on the memory and processor of a single computer such as a large IBM mainframe or DEC minicomputer. Database processing, logic processing, and terminal display management are handled by

---

This chapter was written by David Bassett, Senior Consultant, Ernst & Young, Denver, Colorado.

the single host computer. "Dumb" terminals, tied in via local or wide area networks, serve only as input/output devices. Typically, many transaction processing activities on host-based systems are run in "batch mode" (i.e., off-line while the computer is "down"). Terminal-host systems are particularly effective in processing large volumes of transactions. For example, these systems frequently are used to run airline reservation systems and automated teller machine networks and process insurance claims. However, terminal-host systems tend to be expensive to maintain and update.

43-3 THE FUTURE: CLIENT/SERVER ARCHITECTURE

One of the most ambiguous terms in the computing industry is client/server technology. It has been heralded as everything from "the flavor of the month" to the "cure all" that will be the enabler of a new "paradigm" for computing. An exhaustive definition of what is and is not client/server and the various configuration topologies is beyond the scope of this chapter. However, briefly, a client/server system is different from host-based systems in that it is actually two computers processing related information concurrently and independently. The top ten elements of client/server computing are listed in Figure 43-1.

Perhaps one of the easiest ways to conceptualize the client/server concept is to view computing as a spectrum of processing options. At one end of the spectrum, an individual user runs programs (e.g., Lotus 1-2-3, WordPerfect, and Harvard Graphics) on a stand-alone basis. At the other end, many users log on to a mainframe (i.e., terminal-host) system or they execute large, batch-oriented programs, see Figure 43-2.

Figure 43-1   Top Ten Elements of Client/Server Computing.

1. A client/server architecture consists of a client process and a server process that are distinct, yet interact seamlessly.

2. The client portion and the server portions can, and typically do, operate on separate computer platforms.

3. Either the client platform of the server platform can be upgraded without having to upgrade the other platform. ·

4. The server can service multiple clients concurrently. In some client/server systems, clients can access multiple servers.

5. The client/server system includes some sort of networking capability.

6. The application logic is split in different proportions between the client and the server, sometimes all running on the client.

7. Action is usually initiated by the client, not by the server. However, database servers can "take action" based on "triggers" (i.e., specific events), business rules and stored procedures.

8. A user-friendly Graphical User Interface (GUI) typically resides on the client.

9. Most client/server systems possess a structured query language (SQL) capability.

10. The database server provides data protection and security.

Source: Reprinted with the permission of Software Magazine, Jan. 1993, Sentry Publishing Company Inc., 1900 West Park Drive, Westborough, MA 01581, U.S.A.

Figure 43-2

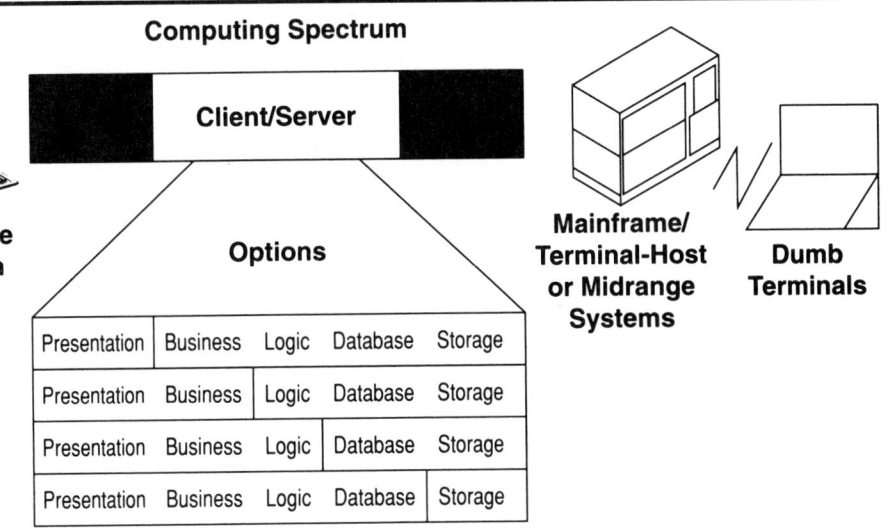

Computing Spectrum

Presentation	Business	Logic	Database	Storage
Presentation	Business	Logic	Database	Storage
Presentation	Business	Logic	Database	Storage
Presentation	Business	Logic	Database	Storage

Data processing applications may run solely on personal computers or on mainframes or midrange computers. However, a growing number of applications *execute* parts of their programs on both kinds of machines; this is considered a client/server environment.

A C/S environment consists of two participating programs, one requesting service and one providing service. The one that "speaks" first is the client. Client/Server means more than running multiple programs; there must be some kind of request/ service relationship between them.

One of the key reasons client/server computing is so popular is it enables "right-sizing" of midrange to large mainframe corporate systems to a potentially more cost effective computing platform. Processing data at both the client and server locations reduces the amount of information that must be bidirectionally sent over the data network. In a client/server arrangement, only required data is sent to the client. The server manages the data requested by the client. A key advantage of client/server is data can be accessed throughout the organization. Data in a relational database management system (RDBMS) can be designed to be application independent so users can access the data with a simple query tool or develop sophisticated departmental applications that access the common data. Top RDBMSs that are currently being used for client/server applications include Oracle, Sybase, Informix, Ingres, Microsoft SQL Server, and IBM's DB2.

43-4 INTEROPERABILITY AND SYSTEMS INTEGRATION

Interoperability refers to the capability of systems to work together. Most terminal-host based systems were designed around proprietary hardware and software architectures that complicated attempts to integrate multiple systems. There is currently a movement to "open systems" architectures where hardware, network topology, and

system software provided by any vendor is interoperable with another vendo
Client/server technology frequently is implemented where there are a variety of ve
dors. The movement to open systems is likely to bolster significant growth
client/server implementations as companies attempt greater systems integration.

43-5 GRAPHICAL USER INTERFACE

A primary characteristic of current client/server front ends is the graphical user inte
face (GUI) (i.e., a mouse-driven or "point & click" interface). The proliferation
GUIs is redefining end-user expectations for ease of use. A GUI requires less traini
and potentially can yield substantial productivity benefits, particularly in low transa
tion volume environments.

43-6 MOVEMENT TO CLIENT/SERVER

According to a Computerworld survey of "Premier 100" information systems exec
tives, client/server technology and open systems are considered critical for compet
tive success in the next five years. The same survey also noted, however, the tin
frame for implementing these initiatives is at least two to four years. The surve
highlighted an immediate demand for new applications and budgetary control as t
highest immediate-term priorities. A summary of the ranking of various critic.
competitive technologies is shown in Figure 43-3.

43-7 CLIENT/SERVER AND THE RE-ENGINEERING OF
WORK PROCESSES

According to Clive Ingham of Unisys, "Some organizations are moving to client/serv
computing to lower costs, but those whose motivation is to re-engineer the busine
will realize far greater benefits. CEOs and CIOs need to understand the value
client/server technology as an enabler for business process re-engineering." It is no
becoming apparent that client/server technology can be an important component
changing business processes.

Figure 43-3   IS Organization's Ranking of Critical Technology for Competition in Next
Five Years.

Client/Server Technology	45%
Open Systems	20%
Electronic Data Interchange (EDI)	17%
Object-Oriented Programming	13%
Distributed RDBMS	8%

Source: Copyright 1993 by Computerworld, Inc., Framingham, MA 01701—Reprinted with permissio
from Computerworld.

One of the key enablers of process re-engineering is systems integration through the use of client/server technology. Tom Davenport commented about the capabilities of information technology in general:

> We have had sophisticated commercial computers and data communications at our disposal for approximately 35 years. In terms of price and functionality these technologies have become incredibly useful and usable. It is time to capitalize on them fully by employing them as enablers for business process innovation.[1]

Accounting systems, particularly client/server based systems, can contribute to business process re-engineering by bringing information closer to where it has the greatest effect.

43-8 EXECUTIVE INFORMATION SYSTEMS

A specialized application of systems integration and client/server technology is an Executive Information System (EIS). An EIS is an easy-to-use senior management tool designed to present information from a variety of sources (e.g., internal financial information and external databases) in a variety of formats (e.g., pie charts and bar graphs). These systems are generally based on some variety of a graphical user interface (GUI) and are designed to let the user select the level of detail displayed. For example, a controller could "drill-down" through the divisions and centers to find the source of a budget variance. The EIS may have interfaces to production, shipping, and other dynamic non-accounting data. An EIS generally incorporates many information sources; therefore, a high degree of systems integration must be in place to effectively implement an EIS.

43-9 IMPLEMENTATION ISSUES

(a) PROPRIETARY ARCHITECTURES AND OPEN SYSTEMS

Implementation of a client/server system has moved from the "bleeding edge" of technology into the mainstream. One of the primary advantages of client/server can be its "open systems" independence from proprietary software and hardware. (This is both good news and bad news!) Under proprietary systems, it was assumed that an organization's network, software, and hardware would work reasonably well together. If there were problems, the single vendor would likely be able to identify the problem and recommend a solution within a reasonable timeframe. Troubleshooting in the relatively "uncharted waters" of client/server and open systems environment is not quite as easy. It is critical for IT management to build a client/server system on products that have been thoroughly tested and proven to integrate well. Other steps to a successful migration to client/server are listed in Figure 43-4.

---

[1] Reprinted with permission, Davenport, Thomas H., *Process Innovation: Reengineering Work through Information Technology,* p. 40. Copyright 1993.

Figure 43-4   Steps to Developing a Strategy for Client/Server Migration.

1. Establish business guideposts for a migration strategy to client/server and justify reasons for migration.
2. Win corporate support by demonstrating cost-effective viability and bottom-line benefits.
3. Define migration paths first with a pilot program then move to more mission-critical applications.
4. Train staff in the new architecture.
5. Choose proven products that integrate well.
6. Avoid running parallel systems wherever possible.

Source: Adapted from Corporate Computing.

(b) CAUTIONS

Contrary to earlier predictions, migration to client/server technology does not always immediately produce cost savings. Therefore reducing costs should not be the only consideration when contemplating migration to a client/server. For example, migrating to client/server environment can lead to an increased need for systems support, service, and administration personnel. These functions are largely centralized in a host-based system but can grow incrementally in a distributed client/server architecture. Other factors such as increased data access, improved ease of use, enhanced systems integration, and facilitated business process re-engineering efforts need to be factored into the migration decision.

(c) SECURITY AND INTEGRITY ISSUES

With host-based systems operating on mainframes and minicomputers, data security and integrity measures are relatively easy to implement and administer. Commercially available access control software (ACS) such as IBM's RACF and Computer Associates' Top Secret and ACF2 have existed for some time and are mature, robust, and effective products. In a client/server environment, security can be more difficult to monitor and increased opportunities for data loss and corruption can exist. To date, there has been limited development of enterprise-wide security systems for client/server. However, this should be changing in the near future.

43-10 CLIENT/SERVER ACCOUNTING

Many of the major mainframe and PC-based accounting software vendors originally had taken a wait-and-see strategy regarding client/server application development. Since the technology has matured, these vendors have stepped up their client/server development efforts. For example, key mainframe or proprietary system software vendors such as Dun & Bradstreet, American Management Systems, Ross, and Lawson have recently released client/server-based versions of their products. These systems will compete with such vendors as Oracle and PeopleSoft in the increasingly cut-throat client/server accounting software marketplace.

Some of the potential benefits of client/server-based accounting systems compared to mainframe/terminal-host systems can include:

- Easier to learn because of the GUI component.
- Quicker and easier to modify due to the underlying RDBMS data architecture.
- Scalability. Generally, the client/server software can run on a variety of hardware platforms.
- Less expensive, in some cases, to operate due to the decreased system "overhead" associated with client/server environment.

Client/server based accounting packages are not a panacea. However, they have evolved to a stage where they can now be considered a viable alternative to mainframe- or PC-based software. (See Chapter 45 for a structured approach to defining system requirements and selecting software.)

43-11 SUMMARY

Client/server computing is a viable strategy for meeting an organization's information processing and reporting needs. In many cases, it can offer a viable alternative to the mainframe/terminal-host environment. However, as with any relatively new technology, the buyer needs to "beware" prior to adopting it. It is critical for organizations to carefully assess the financial- and human-related costs and benefits of migrating to a new computing environment. Additionally, once a decision has been made to move to a client/server environment, both the technical and human aspects of the change must be carefully monitored and managed.

43-12 SELECTED REFERENCES

"Client/Server Architecture," *Journal of Object Oriented Programming,* Feb. 1992, p. 40.

"Client/Server Computing: The Strategic Edge for a Changing Landscape," *Information Week Special Supplement,* Spring 1993.

Davenport, Thomas, *Process Innovation: Reengineering Work through Information Technology,* 1993.

"Defining Client/Server Computing: Make It a Custom Definition," *Software Magazine Client/Server Special Edition,* Jan. 1993, p. 68.

"Justifying the Cost of Client/Server Applications," Gartner Group: Software Management Strategies (File K-017-1093), Dec. 31, 1991.

"Macola Details Client/Server Product Strategy," *Accounting Today,* Nov. 15, 1993, p. 30.

"Packaged Applications: When to Move to Client/Server?" Gartner Group: Software Management Strategies (File K-003-1097), Dec. 31, 1991.

"PC-Based SQL: Time to Commit?" *PC Magazine,* Oct. 12, 1993.

"Planning Client/Server Architecture: The Next Two Years," Gartner Group: Office Information Systems (File E-231-945), Dec. 13, 1991.

"RFP: Migrating Accounting to a Global Client/Server Network," *Corporate Computing,* April 1993, p. 112.

Schwartz, David, "Oracle Applications Client/Server Overview," Proprietary ORACLE White Paper (Part No. A10545), March 1993.

"Tempting Fate: Exclusive Security Survey," *Information Week,* Oct. 4, 1993, p. 42.

CHAPTER 44

Automated Financial Accounting Systems

44-1 OVERVIEW

Automated financial accounting systems perform everyday accounting tasks faster and with fewer errors than humans. Today's systems allow immediate input and display immediate results.

Although the most popular financial accounting systems in use by organizations are represented by packaged software, in-house developed systems can provide unique functionality not found in marketplace software. Another system option available to organizations is *outsourcing* financial applications. Outsourcing is an emerging trend supported by complex functionality, like payroll processing, or extenuating circumstances, like a short implementation time frame.

This chapter was written by Sandra Borchardt, Senior Manager, Ernst & Young, Boston.

This chapter provides an overview of automated financial accounting systems, discusses the role these systems play in the organization, and identifies the features and functionality supported by these systems. The intent of this chapter is to:

- Indicate the benefits and disadvantages of automation.
- Show the impact of the financial system on an organization and its functions.
- Provide a sense of how some key financial applications function.

44-2 ORGANIZATIONAL IMPACT

Almost all organizations, whether for-profit or not-for-profit, have some form of accounting system. Many organizations automate their accounting system to take advantage of features and capabilities not available in a manual accounting system. Automated financial accounting systems range from spreadsheets, to off-the-shelf software, to custom-built systems. These systems operate on a variety of platforms ranging from microcomputers to mainframes. In all of these cases, however, the purpose of the accounting system remains the same: to track, measure, and report the financial events of the organization.

(a) THE ROLE OF THE FINANCIAL ACCOUNTING SYSTEM IN AN ORGANIZATION

One role of automated financial accounting systems is that of processing the routine financial transactions that comprise the day-to-day operations of the organization. In a retail business, these transactions include cash and credit sales; in a bank, deposits and withdrawals; and in a government agency, pre-encumbrance and encumbrance accounting. In this capacity, the automated accounting system supports the accounting function within the organization.

The automated accounting system also plays a key role in measuring the overall financial performance of the organization. Financial reporting allows senior management to evaluate the organization's performance against plan or budget, and against market indicators and the performance of competitors. Management reporting supports a measurement of the profitability of products or services offered by the organization and the effectiveness of management performance. Management reporting also enables profit center managers to reflect on past performance while supporting their day-to-day operational decision making.

Communication of a range of information, from financial results to transaction status, is another role supported by the automated financial accounting system. Investors, creditors, and employees all have a stake in the financial stability of the organization; quarterly and annual reports, produced by the financial accounting system, communicate the financial results of the organization. Automated financial accounting systems also support the communication of the status of a transaction (e.g., whether or not a purchase order has been completed or an invoice paid).

It is important to note several key characteristics of automated financial accounting systems. Accounting systems do not supply all of the information about the organization, only about financial events. Thus, nonfinancial information must be secured from some other source. Accounting systems are not only applicable to businesses but also to individuals and other organizations such as hospitals, churches, and universities. Finally, during the life of any organization there may be many individuals or groups desiring information on the financial position and activities of the organization. Thus accounting systems must be flexible and capable of serving many different users of financial information.

(b) TYPES OF FINANCIAL ACCOUNTING INFORMATION

There are two categories of users who utilize accounting information as a basis for making decisions, those external to the organization and those internal (management), as depicted in Figure 44-1. The automated financial accounting system must be capable of serving both categories of users.

Typically, the types of information desired by external users include an overall picture of where the business stands at a point in time, the assets the organization possesses, the obligations it faces, and whether or not the organization has been successful in its profit-making activities since the last financial report. These information needs are met by the publication of general purpose financial statements, such as the balance sheet and income statement.

In some cases, more specific information is required by external users. Customers require a receipt for a cash sale or a bill for a credit sale. In many cases, customers require a quote or estimate prior to committing to the transaction. Suppliers frequently require routine documents such as purchase orders and payment transaction documents. Further, if an order is not accepted, information regarding the return must be provided to the supplier.

Stockholders receive annual and quarterly reports and possibly dividend checks and related dividend information for tax purposes at the end of the year. Organizations must provide benefit deduction information and, at the end of the year, W-2 forms to

Figure 44-1 Users of Financial Information.

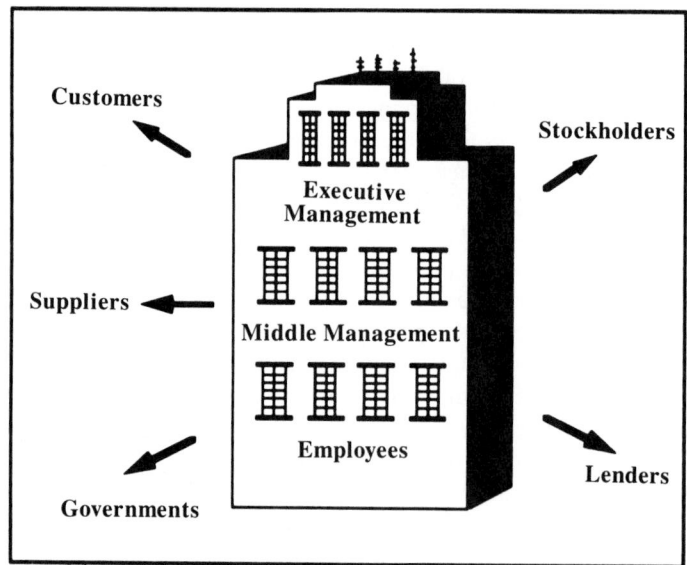

employees. Lenders require financial statements and budgets before establishing a line of credit or extending a loan. Governments require information about the organization's profits, the amount of taxes owed, sales taxes collected, and employee taxes withheld.

Internal users require a variety of information usually based on the level of user and how the information will be used. Executive management uses financial information along with other internal and external information to monitor and change the direction of the company and to evaluate the performance of middle management and the products/services offered. Middle management uses financial information to identify and correct situations highlighted by a significant variance and to assist in daily operations management such as pricing and purchasing decision making.

Whether the user is external or internal, the automated financial accounting system must be capable of quickly adapting to changes in regulatory or government requirements or management/organizational needs. If insufficient information is received, if the information is not timely, or if the information is not accurate, external users may levy sanctions in the form of fines or additional taxes and internal users may perform less effectively. Thus, the automated financial accounting system plays an important role in the effectiveness of the organization.

(c) PROCESSING ALTERNATIVES

Several processing options are available with today's automated financial accounting systems. Most systems support two types of transaction input—batch input and on-line input—and two types of transaction processing—batch processing and real-time processing. Historically, automated financial accounting systems supported only batch input of financial transactions. In this scenario, a batch file of transactions, created as an output file by an interfacing system (either an interfacing financial system or some type of keystroke data capture system), is processed by the automated financial accounting system, updating the financial records. Minimal if any editing of these transactions is conducted prior to processing by the accounting system. The majority of transaction edits take place during the update of the financial records.

On-line input capabilities allow financial transactions to be entered immediately through an interactive design that utilizes a terminal to capture the transaction keystrokes. In most systems, immediate editing features are utilized by the system to communicate keystroke errors or invalid values at the time of input; the transactions must be corrected before the system will recognize the transactions and update the financial records. Therefore, a transaction edited on-line has a better chance of updating the financial records without error than a minimally edited batch of transactions.

Updating the financial records with on-line input can occur in batch or real-time. Today, batch processing is supported by most systems for the majority of financial accounting applications. Typically, the batch processing cycle is run at night, when the on-line system is not in use. In a batch cycle, the transactions input during the day update financial records during the nightly cycle. Other system maintenance activities are processed by the batch cycle including additional input edits, updates of accounting totals for reporting purposes, system date changes, and so forth.

Real-time processing updates the financial records immediately and makes the updates available immediately through on-line screen inquiry or reporting. Because of the additional system maintenance required to update financial records, frequently real-time systems do not perform all the updates until the nightly batch cycle. Therefore, it is important to understand which reports and inquiries will reflect the real-time transactions and which will be updated during the nightly cycle.

(d) SYSTEM ALTERNATIVES

Automated financial accounting systems can be developed in-house, purchased as off-the-shelf software or outsourced to a company that processes the transactions on their system and provides the necessary financial reports and documentation back to the organization.

Most companies purchase package software rather than undertaking an in-house development effort for automated financial accounting systems. With the prevalence, variety, and capabilities of package financial accounting software, it is often less efficient, both in terms of time and effort, to develop an in-house application. Package software has the advantage of being tested in the marketplace, and thus most of the software problems have been identified and corrected. Also, the costs of commercially developed software are spread across the marketplace, leading to an individual site cost that is often lower than what would be expended in an in-house development effort. Because of maintenance agreements and a desire to service their client base, software companies usually offer timely software updates which meet changes in external regulatory or governmental requirements (e.g., a payroll software vendor will offer a software update to reflect changes in tax laws). Similarly, software vendors add enhancements to their software based on customer requests and competitor features, frequently at no cost if the customer is covered by a maintenance agreement, or at a minimal upgrade cost.

A third system option is becoming more popular today: outsourcing of financial applications. In this scenario, the organization contracts with a second organization to process their accounting transactions. A well-known example of this is the use of an external organization for payroll processing. Considerations for outsourcing include:

- *Risk.* Outsource companies focus on particular applications and have developed and proven procedures, controls, and software. Implementation can be accomplished quickly and is supported by the company's previous implementation experience, so that tasks are not forgotten and deadlines are realistic.

- *Control.* Outsourced applications are under the control of the outsource company. An organization is absolved of all responsibility of the application per the outsource contract. Thus the organization does not have to worry about the accomplishment of that processing. However, outsource companies have many clients and may not be as responsive to special requests as in-house staff. Special one-time or additional services not included in the initial contract may be costly. Organizations may be at the mercy of the outsource company when it comes time to renew the contract.

- *Costs.* In some cases, purchasing packaged software will be more cost effective than outsourcing, but consideration must be given to the reduction/elimination of internal staff to implement and support the application. Outsourcing may be beneficial in start-up situations where operation deadlines do not lend themselves to even the shortest package software implementation. Manually intensive or highly specialized applications (e.g., payroll processing including payroll tax filing, W-2 processing, and direct deposit handling) may be more cost effective if outsourced.

Outsourced contracts can be written in a manner that is beneficial to the organization, for instance, by basing fees on production in start-up situations or on a percentage of profits in more mature applications and establishing a payback for schedules missed by the outsource company. Finally, outsourced applications may reach a break-even point where the application has grown to a size that can be brought in-house at less cost. Figure 44-2 summarizes the relative advantages and disadvantages of custom built applications, packaged software and outsource contracting.

(e) STANDARD FEATURES

Common features supported by most automated financial accounting systems include:

- *On-line help.* A function that is immediately accessible by the user from a terminal and supplies the user with additional information on how the software works. On-line help can be screen-specific or field-specific. Many automated systems support both.

  Screen-Specific: On-line help pertaining to the information currently appearing on a display screen. It allows the on-line user to press a "help" key at any

Figure 44-2 Evaluation of System Alternatives.

	Alternatives		
	Custom Built Application	Package Software	Outsource Contract
Time to implement	− −	−	+
Control	+ +	+	−
Marketplace tested	−	+	+
Software cost	+	−	+
Hardware cost	+	−	+
Monthly contract fee	+	+	−
Ongoing maintenance cost	−	−	+
Programming cost	−	+	+
Operations cost	−	−	+
User training cost	−	−	+

+ Advantage   − Disadvantage

screen to invoke the help function. The help session will display on the user screen presenting all functions and field-specific information necessary to complete the screen from which help was invoked. Frequently, this type of on-line help resembles pages out of the user documentation.

Field-Specific: On-line help pertaining to a single piece of information (i.e., a field) currently appearing on a display screen. Field-specific help can be invoked by placing the cursor on the field where help is desired and pressing the key that commences the help session. Field-specific help usually limits its discussion to the field from which the help session was invoked.

- *User-defined help screens* allow the user to identify acceptable field values for the organization, enter these values into a "help" portion of the system and enable users to access this user-defined help as well as the system-defined help function through the use of different function keys.

- *Menu options across the top of the screen* and *function key references across the bottom* inform the user of functions/menu choices available at the screen. Moreover, some systems display all acceptable values for a field through the use of a function key.

- *On-line inquiry* allows users to access information either by pressing a function key from the current screen or via a stand-alone menu or command option. The ability to make a database query while performing a function in the system is quite valuable. For example, during on-line input of a journal transaction, on-line inquiry can be used to verify an account in the chart of accounts database.

  If on-line inquiry is not accessible from any screen, the user must exit the current screen, access the area in the software where on-line inquiry is available, perform the inquiry, and then access the original screen and resume the activity in progress. This can mean entering and exiting several screens to accomplish a single inquiry. On its own, however, stand-alone inquiry is valuable for specific research and maintenance purposes and should be available in all systems whether or not screen-accessible inquiry is available.

(i) Reporting.   Reporting capabilities of various types may be available in automated financial systems. Some of the more common features include:

- *Standard Reports.* Most automated financial systems support a set of pre-designed and pre-coded financial reports. These reports include daily transaction-type reports such as trial balances, posted batch lists, and ledgers; maintenance-type reports such as lists of database additions, deletions, revisions and audit trail reports; and financial reports such as a balance sheet, income statement, and consolidated reports. These reports usually come as is and cannot be modified by the user to reflect user-desired formats or sort sequences.

- *Report Writing Capabilities.* Most automated financial accounting systems support some type of report writing capability (i.e., custom) that supplements the standard reports. Using this capability, reports can be constructed to meet the unique reporting requirements of the organization. Report writing facilities may require programming skills to develop the reports or may be quite simple to use. Frequently, a simpler report writer sacrifices the ability to customize quite complex reports. Thus, in many systems, more than one report writer facility is available, one for the everyday user and one for more complex, specialized report designs.

- *Ad Hoc Reporting.* These are similar to the report writing capability discussed above from the standpoint of providing the ability to customize a report. Ad hoc capabilities differ from a report writer because ad hoc reports are considered one-time requests or infrequent requests for information. Ad hoc reporting usually supports simple selection, sorting and totaling capabilities and is usually used for database printing (e.g., print out all the expense accounts used by a cost center in the last three months).

- *Downloads.* Many systems support downloading (the process of transferring data to a smaller platform) of information into a file that is readable by microcomputer spreadsheets or other microcomputer software. This feature provides additional reporting capabilities by allowing information to be formatted and reported by the spreadsheet. Control is an issue in this instance, in that values can be changed via the spreadsheet program and thus totals represented on the spreadsheet many not equal totals in the automated financial accounting system.

(ii) Security. The description of security presented in this section is a short summary related specifically to software access security. Chapter 51 presents a more extensive discussion of security. Most automated financial systems have security features which allow access to be defined by one or more of the following elements:

- *Terminal/System.* This type of security allows for the definition of the devices that can access the financial system. For example, a certain terminal/printer set-up may be defined as the only system that can access the check printing facility of an accounts payable system.

- *User.* User security identifies a user sign-on and password. Automated audit trails can then be used to track application accesses by specific users, including access attempts to secured areas. In more sophisticated systems, user access records can also be used to track performance such as number of collection transactions handled by a user in a day, and so forth.

- *Application.* Application security allows access to be defined at the application level, (e.g., a user may have access to the general ledger but not to the accounts receivable application).

- *Organizational Unit.* This type of security allows access to be defined by the organizational unit to which the user belongs (e.g., a user can only access financial information for his/her department).

- *Function.* Security by function specifies particular types of access, such as read only, read and input but no update capabilities, update only capabilities, and so forth.

- *Screen.* Screen security allows access to specific screens (e.g., only certain users should have access to the security definition screens in the system).

- *Field.* Field-level access allows for certain fields to be accessible for input (e.g., account descriptions may not be accessible for maintenance in the journal posting screen). Specific users may be identified to maintain the chart of accounts and descriptions via another system facility.

(iii) Edits.   In automated financial accounting systems, an "edit" is an error message or diagnostic message generated by the software program. Most on-line financial accounting systems will support a number of edits for on-line input. These edits vary from field format edits to valid value edits.

Field format edits include edits for fields that should be all numeric (e.g., dollar amount fields), or input in a certain format (e.g., a date field format of mm/dd/yy means that January 1, 1993, should be input as 01/01/93 not as 1/1/93). Valid value edits include edits for incorrect dates (e.g., 13/34/92 would be an incorrect date) or for a predesignated set of values (e.g., the account must be defined in the chart of accounts database). On-line edits reduce the number of erroneous transactions that enter the system by forcing errors to be corrected before the system will accept the transaction and update the financial records.

Additional input edits are performed in the batch cycle. A transaction may pass all the on-line edits but may still be forced to an error correction list/file based on these batch edits. Batch edits frequently repeat the on-line edits due to transactions that enter the system in batch (i.e., from interfacing systems).

(iv) Maintenance.   All automated financial accounting systems support some type of maintenance facility. Single-input facilities are required to build a general ledger chart of accounts or establish an accounts payable vendor record. High volume maintenance is a feature allowing multiple records to be updated at once. High volume maintenance features are particularly valuable, for example, when establishing a new center by copying an already established center or when defining a new account for use by each center.

(v) Navigation.   Navigation features (movement from screen to screen or function to function within software) differ from system to system and typically fall under one of the following formats:

- *Menus.* Lists of options appearing on a display screen that allow the user to select which part of the software to interact with. Menus assist first-time or infrequent users by displaying all available choices and allowing the user to select the choice desired. Menus can become cumbersome for the more frequent, sophisticated users, because several choices across several menus may be required in order to access a desired screen.

- *Commands.* Instructions supplied by the user which access the part of the software with which the user intends to interact. These allow more sophisticated users to type in specific characters or word sequences, which, when executed, invoke the specific screen represented by the command.

(vi) Documentation, Support, Training, and Enhancements.   Other software features include:

- *Documentation* including user manuals, installation guides, operations guides, and so forth.

- *Support* including client services representatives, on-site support, assistance with installation, 800 hotline support, local maintenance support, maintenance agreements, enhancement agreements, custom development services, and so forth. Support can be offered as part of the software package or for an additional fee.

- *Training* including on-site, classroom, classroom based training (CBT), and tutorials.
- *Enhancements* including software upgrades for regulated changes, user-group-sponsored changes, and so forth. User Groups are independent social organizations that meet to discuss the use and implementation of the particular package and share ideas and strategies to meet unique processing requirements. User groups also sponsor enhancements that are often acted on by the vendors.

44-3 TYPICAL APPLICATIONS AND GENERAL FEATURES

This section provides a general overview of the features and functionality of financial accounting software currently available in the marketplace. Although the list of financial accounting applications is lengthy, the following discussion has been limited to four applications:

- General ledger.
- Accounts receivable.
- Accounts payable.
- Payroll.

These applications were chosen because they are frequently the core financial applications employed by an organization.

(a) GENERAL LEDGER

A general ledger collects summary financial information from detailed subsidiary ledgers (e.g., accounts receivable, accounts payable, payroll) and based on this summary financial information, produces financial and management reports (Figure 44-3). In most organizations, the general ledger is the source of period-end financial reporting, management responsibility reporting, and external regulatory, government, and financial statement reporting.

Typically, financial information enters the general ledger in the form of a journal transaction, which may originate from many sources including an automated interface from a subsidiary system, a batch of transactions which are manually entered and subsequently update the financial accounts, a real-time transaction which is manually entered and immediately updates the financial accounts, or through the use of special automated journal features such as recurring, shell, and reversing journal transactions.

Once the financial accounts are updated, usually the result of a posting cycle, transaction reports are produced. These reports document the journal transactions input in the system and identify transactions that are incomplete, not balanced or otherwise in error.

At the end of a reporting period, usually monthly or quarterly, period-end reports are produced and certain maintenance activities are completed to ready the system to begin collecting the next period of financial transactions. At the end of the

Figure 44-3   General Ledger System Diagram.

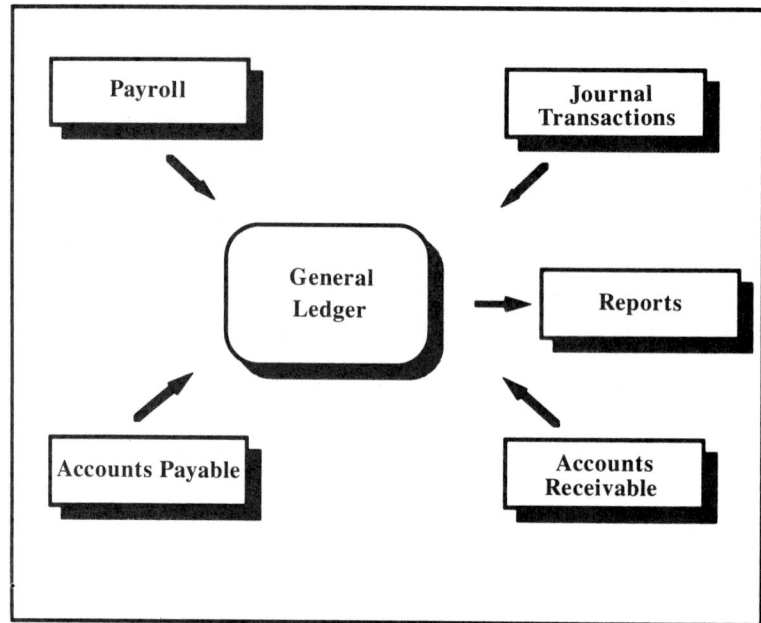

fiscal year, additional maintenance activities are performed including rolling the ending balance sheet account balances to the beginning balances for the new fiscal year, zeroing out income and expense accounts, updating the system fiscal year, and so forth.

(i) Account Key.   The account key is the basis for the structure of the records in the general ledger. In most automated general ledger systems, the account key is made up of entries containing at least three user definable elements: an element which identifies the company or legal entity, an element which identifies an organizational unit (e.g., department, center, division), and an element which identifies the accounting element or account. Due to additional reporting needs especially in the financial services industry (e.g., insurance and banking), many systems provide additional elements available for definition.

Defining the account key is an important process. The reporting requirements of the general ledger must be carefully considered. If the level of detail required by the reports is not collected by the general ledger through the use of the account key, the reports cannot be produced. Thus, it is important to design the account key to capture the lowest level of information required by the reports.

When deciding on the lowest level of information required by the general ledger, consideration must be given to the question of what information the general ledger should capture and report. It is easy to allow the general ledger to be the catch-all application. Careful thought must be given to satisfying a reporting requirement using other subsidiary systems or realizing that a reporting requirement cannot easily be met by the general ledger and must be accomplished elsewhere.

Consideration must also be given to the effort involved in capturing the lowest level of detail. Undue burden on the accounting department in the organization to gather and input this level of detail may offset the benefits of the information produced by the general ledger.

In most automated financial systems, detail can be summarized at different levels through the report writing facility. For example, if the center is the lowest reporting level of the organization and if centers combine to make departments, which combine to form divisions, then there is no need to capture general ledger input at the department and division levels. The reporting facility of the general ledger should allow for these levels to be reported by simply combining centers.

(ii) Journal Transactions.   Several journal transaction (i.e., journal) features are available in today's automated general ledgers. These include:

- *Standard journals* are the typical entries made in the general ledger. Standard journals may record an asset purchase or adjust an error. Standard journals can be received via a file from an interfacing system and processed in batch, or input on-line, and updated real-time or via the batch processing cycle. On-line features include the ability to input, edit, and balance the journal. Security features include the ability to restrict the user to input-only and another to post-only privileges.

- *Shell journals* are established for those transactions that use the same accounts but different dollar amounts each period. Utility expense and certain other month-end transactions fall into this category. A shell journal is created with the corresponding accounts. Prior to posting, the dollar amounts are input to complete the entry.

- *Recurring journals* are for those transactions that use the same accounts and the same amounts each period. Rent, loan and lease payments may fall into this category of journal transactions. As with shell journals, recurring journals are set up ahead of time with their corresponding accounts and amounts and, in many systems, can be scheduled for automatic release to the posting cycle.

- *Reversing journals*—in many automated general ledgers, standard, shell and/or recurring journals can be defined as reversing journals. For example, if the shell journal feature is set up for a monthly accrual transaction, this transaction can also be defined as a reversing journal and thus will be reversed at the start of the new period. In some systems, specific reversing dates or periods can be defined for the reversing transaction.

- *Error handling* can be accomplished in several ways. On-line edits, discussed in the previous section, identify input errors for immediate correction. Erroneous journal transactions identified during the batch cycle can be handled via a suspense account, through an error file, or dropped out of the cycle. Suspense posting posts the erroneous transaction to a user-defined account, an error suspense account. Then whenever this account shows a balance, the erroneous transaction is researched and a subsequent transaction is input to reverse the suspended balance and post the balance to the proper account.

  Use of an error file suspends the transaction prior to posting to allow the user to correct the transaction on-line. Each posting cycle will then read the error file and post all corrected transactions. Transactions not yet corrected will remain in the error file. The third type of error handling in a batch cycle is to report the transaction in error and require re-input of the entire journal.

Both the suspense and error file methods eliminate the need to re-enter the journal and do not cause the entire batch of journals to be rejected, only the erroneous transactions. The difference is that the suspense account method posts as much of the transaction correctly as possible, thus correctly stating total balances. The error file method holds the transaction in a prior-to-posting state, thus system balances do not reflect the erroneous transaction.

(iii) Budgeting or Planning.   Most automated general ledgers allow for budget input and reporting, usually at the account level. Additional budgeting features available in some but not all systems include: prior and future year(s) budget reporting and comparisons; storage and reporting of original, approved, revised and other versions of the budget; and budget preparation features including what-if processing, use of last year's actuals or budget as the basis for this year's budget, increasing/decreasing of budget amounts by multiplying by a factor, and so forth.

(iv) Allocations.   Another feature of many automated general ledgers is an allocation facility. Allocations involve the distribution of costs and/or revenues from one organization unit to another organization unit or to corresponding products or services. Allocation features can be as simple as automatically allocating an input transaction (e.g., rent) to organizational units based on a predetermined fixed percentage (e.g., percent of total square footage) through the use of a journal transaction feature. Or allocations can be as complex as requiring statistical amounts (either input or calculated), and originating and destination organizational units and accounts.

The more complex the allocation process, the more complex and time-consuming the set-up, and thus the more prone to error the process will be. Complex allocations can also consume large amounts of system processing time and resources and the results can constitute a large number of records. It is sometimes useful to store allocation results in another portion of the database, merging the results for reporting purposes via the report writing capabilities of the system.

Other allocation features include the ability to allocate actual, budget, statistical, or previously allocated amounts; the ability to allocate based on a fixed or variable percentage; the ability to round allocations so that the final destination is given the remaining amount (i.e., so that rounding features do not result in less than or greater than 100% allocations); the ability to perform allocations on monthly, quarterly, or annual amounts; and the ability to generate allocation reports documenting which amounts were allocated from which organizational units or products/services, to which organizational units or products/services.

(v) Consolidations.   Many automated general ledger systems offer consolidation features which combine separate entities (e.g., corporations, divisions, subsidiaries) for organization-wide consolidated reporting. Consolidation features include automatically generating elimination entries, allowing for consolidation of corporations with similar charts of accounts, or allowing for consolidation of corporations with different charts of accounts.

(b) ACCOUNTS RECEIVABLE

The accounts receivable system is the primary cash receipts system in organizations that do not require immediate payment upon delivery of goods or services. The accounts receivable application is designed to monitor cash inflows from sales and collections and provide information that will assist in managing the collection of cash held as receivables.

The accounts receivable system interfaces with the general ledger by passing summary transactions that update the accounts affected by sales and payments on account. Many organizations interface an order processing system with the accounts receivable system. The accounts receivable system passes customer credit limits and other customer demographics to the order processing system and in turn receives billing information and orders shipped from the order processing system. The accounts receivable system may also interface with a billing system if the accounts receivable system does not support the production of customer bills or statements. Lastly, an accounts receivable system may interface with accounts payables, passing customer refund information for payment by the accounts payable system. Figure 44-4 illustrates the system flows to and from the accounts receivable system.

Common features of an automated accounts receivables system include:

- *Cash Application.* Most accounts receivable systems support several options governing how received funds are applied to outstanding receivables. The choice among such options is called cash application.

    Cash application based on check Magnetic Ink Character Recognition (MICR) numbers (characters printed with a special magnetic ink, like those at the bottom of personal checks, used primarily in banking, public utilities and

Figure 44-4   Accounts Receivable System Diagram.

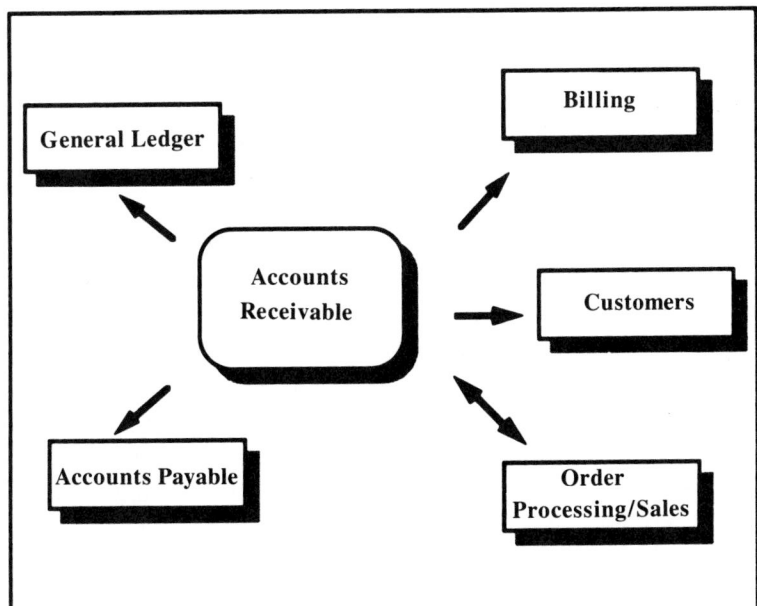

credit card industries), amount, invoice number, oldest document, document range or customer name, are common automatic cash application features. For those accounts that cannot be supported by an automatic cash application feature, a more manual, research capability is available. Lockbox features are often available including bank tape lockbox processing using the automatic cash application features of the system. Several other payment posting options may be available including acceptance of a single payment for multiple invoices, a single payment for multiple customers, partial payments, prepayments, and deposits.

- *On-Line Inquiry.* Many systems support on-line inquiry into the accounts receivable system including all open items, open amounts within a specific range, all debit memos, all credit memos, last payment entered, or all information on a specific invoice.

- *Aging Reports.* Most systems support user-defined aging formats and aging period definition for reporting. Formats include customer summary, invoice summary, or organizational summaries by company, department, division, or sales representative.

- *Collection Features.* Most accounts receivable systems support a variety of collection features including:

    On-Line Comments/Notes: Allows the collector to keep track of customer calls, disagreements, commitments and follow-up actions.

    On-Line Tickler File: Provides a reminder of commitments made by the collector and customer for follow-up and a reminder of follow-up dates based on dunning severity, notifies the collector of new invoices past due, and assists in prioritizing collection duties. Some systems also use this feature to track sales leads or, for example, to remind a user to request a current financial statement from customers.

    Credit and Service Hold: Provides the ability to place a problem customer on credit hold and/or service hold (as a motivator to pay) and to set credit limits by customer. Some systems support this feature automatically based on user-defined rules.

    Small Balance Write-Offs: Provides the ability to write off small balance amounts within tolerance limits to ensure that collectors are concentrating on the most critical accounts.

    Collector Statistics: Measures and reports collectors' effectiveness using automated rules or in some cases user-defined rules.

    Collections Reporting: Provides the ability to review collection call notes, follow-up dates, customer promises and call history.

    Dunning Letters: Allows for the definition of content, addressee, outstanding invoices, dunning severity levels and frequency of mailing. Many systems support numerous different types and levels of dunning letters.

- *Customer Statements.* Most systems allow for printing of customer statements. In some systems, statement formats are user definable. Further, some systems allow for statements to be generated for all customers, customer ranges or only those customers over a certain age limit.

- *Customer History.* Most accounts receivable systems support the maintenance of complete customer history. This feature makes it easy to investigate discrepancies and disputes by having all past customer activity available to determine the correct response and action. Also, many systems maintain statistics on customers' paying habits and past performance, including, for example, a monitoring of past accounts receivable balances and average days to pay.

- *Other Features.* Other payment features often supported by accounts receivable systems include: discounts, finance charges, adjustments, other receipts (e.g., investment income, refunds), insufficient funds and prepayment handling. Reporting features such as: payment reporting, accounts receivable and collections productivity reporting, and cash forecasting features are frequently available. Other features include linkages to rating bureaus for customer credit information.

(c) ACCOUNTS PAYABLE

An accounts payable system is one important cash disbursement system of the organization, payroll being the other. In its role of supporting the organized and controlled disbursement of funds to external organizations, the accounts payable system monitors the amounts due to suppliers for goods and services, issues disbursement checks and provides information for cash management purposes. Additionally, the accounts payable system should control disbursements so that cash outflows do not occur any sooner than necessary. In many organizations, the accounts payable system is also used for other cash disbursement activities such as processing customer refunds, tax liability payments, employee advances, and employee payables.

The accounts payable system can interface with a variety of systems in the organization. Some of these interfaces include:

- *General Ledger.* The accounts payable system interfaces with the general ledger by passing summary entries on purchases, payments and adjustments which affect the cash, accounts payable, assets, purchases, and miscellaneous expense accounts.

- *Sales/Purchasing.* The accounts payable system interfaces with the sales/purchasing system by receiving data relating to purchases and by passing vendor analysis information to the sales/purchasing system which can be used in future purchase decisions.

- *Receiving.* The accounts payable system interfaces with the receiving system by accepting documentation confirming the receipt of goods which is then matched to the purchase documentation and scheduled for payment.

- *Accounts Receivable.* The accounts payable system interfaces with the accounts receivable system by accepting documentation regarding customer refunds.

- *Fixed Assets.* The accounts payable system interfaces with the fixed asset system by providing asset invoice and other information for the establishment of a new fixed asset record.

- *Project Costing.* The accounts payable system provides project-related expense information to the project costing system.

Other interfaces include inventory for inventory costing or cost accounting purposes and work order costing for work orders that include processing by an outside vendor. Figure 44-5 illustrates the system flows to and from the accounts payable system.

Common features of an automated accounts payable system include:

- *Invoice Processing.* Automated features include using defaults from the vendor file for easy invoice processing with input of minimal information such as vendor, invoice number, date and amount. Many systems support a variety of invoice types including regular invoices, credit and debit memos, prepaid, recurring, employee travel advance and employee expense invoices. When processing an invoice, many systems allow for allocation of expenses to multiple organizational units (e.g., divisions, departments, centers).

- *Check Writing.* Features include supporting multiple check forms, multiple bank accounts, multiple currencies, multiple payment methods (e.g., automatic and manual checks, electronic funds transfers, wire transfers, etc.), separate remittance advice, and payment voiding. Check printing features include printing checks in any sequence—by vendor number for easy filing or by ZIP code for low-cost mailings. Check stock control features include recording the checks used and issuing a warning prior to running out.

- *Reconciliation.* Features include bank tape processing or cleared check input. Reporting features include calculation of average float days per vendor so that payments can be adjusted to optimize cash management.

Figure 44-5 Accounts Payable System Diagram.

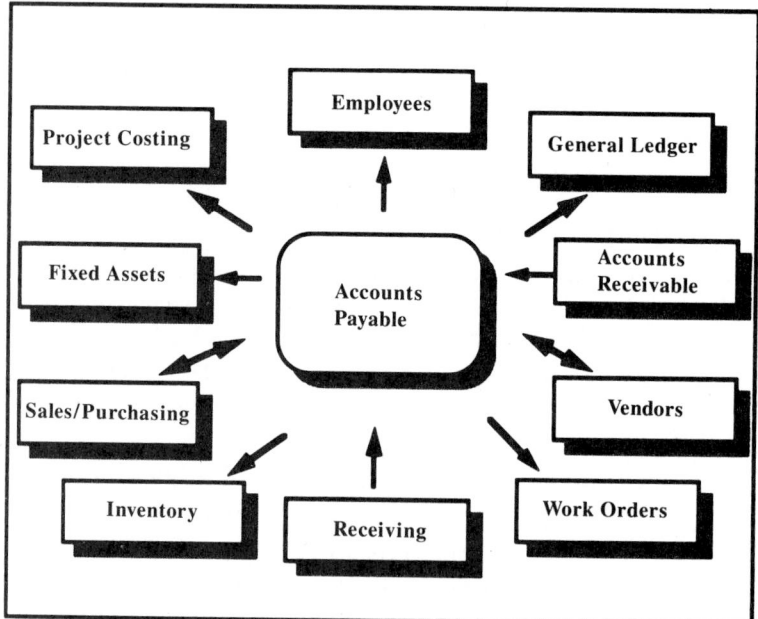

- *Cash Management.* Features include determining how much to pay and when to pay. Forecasting features include identifying cash needs. Reporting features include cash management, aged payables, and other reports.

- *Payment Optimization.* Allows for identification of open invoices due for payment and the ability to hold payments, create partial payments, or allow everything to be paid. Other payment optimization features include automatic calculation of the discount amount and determination of when and if a discount should be taken.

- *IRS 1099 Reporting.* Features include complete tracking and reporting of 1099 expenditures and all return/amount types the federal government requires, and provisions for flexible IRS 1099 generation and reporting allowing compliance with federal reporting requirements.

- *Vendor Analysis.* Includes the maintenance of statistics on all vendor and payable activity such as invoice amounts by period, invoice volumes, discounts taken or lost, and number of exception invoices. These features can frequently assist in negotiating better discounts and prices, and resolving problems efficiently.

- *Other Features.* Includes the ability to order from one-time vendors without storing that vendor's information permanently; supports the tracking of unlimited vendor addresses and contacts (e.g., order address, payment address, inquiry address); produces vendor lists, labels, and customized form letters; and supports invoice matching (e.g., four-way matching requires purchase order, invoice, receipt and requestor acceptance documentation before payment is scheduled; three-way matching requires purchase order, invoice, and receipt documentation before payment is scheduled). Other features include automatic tax liability calculation and tracking of sales taxes paid to vendors.

(d) PAYROLL

The payroll system in the organization is very important because good employee relations require payroll disbursements to be reliable and timely. However, today's payroll function is quite complex resulting from multiple classes of employees, the proliferation of deductions, special employee arrangements, governmental reporting requirements, and management's need for cost information. Further, because the payroll function is a major cash disbursement function in the organization, cash management and control are important to the payroll process. Thus, it is no wonder that payroll departments find that they need a sophisticated, automated system capable of recording, processing, and reporting on large volumes of complex transactions.

Payroll systems are designed to streamline the employee payment process, to reduce the costs associated with payroll administration, and to provide organizations with maximum flexibility to define their unique payroll processing requirements. Inputs to the payroll system include:

- *Time Records.* Documents that record an employee's time. This information is used in the calculation and preparation of the paycheck. Sick days, vacation days, and overtime hours are captured on the time documents as well.

- *Payroll Adjustments.* Includes additions, deletions, and adjustments of various kinds to employee payroll records. Examples include salary or wage rate changes, terminations, new employee additions, address changes, departmental transfers, tax exemption changes, and deduction authorization changes.

Outputs of the payroll system include employee paychecks (or direct deposits to employee bank accounts), employee earnings statements, various reports required by governmental authorities, and various reports useful to payroll, personnel or management staff.

The payroll system interfaces to the general ledger by passing summary earnings and deduction transactions to the general ledger. Other information required by the payroll system may be interfaced from another system (e.g., sales activity, the basis of compensating a sales staff, is passed to payroll from the sales system). In turn, the payroll system may provide information to an employee benefits system or labor distribution system. Figure 44-6 illustrates the system flows to and from the payroll system.

The basic features and capabilities of an automated payroll system include the following:

- *Hours Worked.* Input of hours worked can be accomplished via an interface from a time and attendance system, via on-line input or in aggregate for the entire pay period, by day or by job.

- *Earnings.* Features include managing salaried, hourly, and daily earnings as well as jury duty, personal leave, vacation, sick leave, holidays, overtime, bonuses, and downtime. Also many payroll systems support distributions to different pay groups on different schedules.

Figure 44-6   Payroll System Diagram.

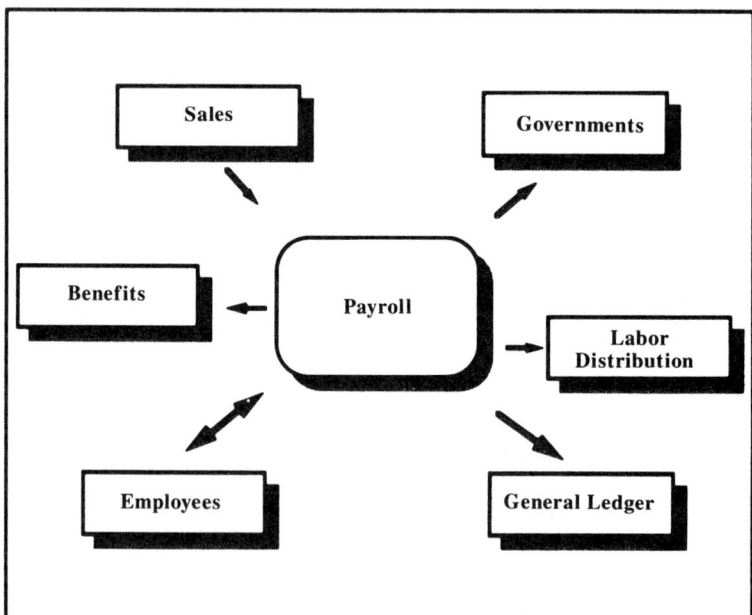

- *Deductions.* Control features include limit amounts, start dates and stop dates for each deduction. Other features include identification of employer-paid, employee-voluntary, or employee-involuntary deduction categories and taxable, tax-exempt, or FICA-exempt categories.
- *Taxes.* Features include withholding calculations for all United States (at the very least) federal, state, county, and local taxes, providing updates for these calculations per regulatory changes, and providing tax reporting on magnetic media where required. Both employee and employer tax calculations should be supported.
- *Payroll Processing.* Features include control of organizations to be paid, the pay and deductions to be calculated, the dates, the labor distribution, and the month-end accruals. Pay frequencies supported include on-demand, daily, weekly, bi-weekly, monthly, and quarterly.
- *Check Writing.* Features include supporting multiple check forms, multiple bank accounts, multiple currencies, multiple payment methods, (e.g., automatic and manual checks, direct deposit, electronic funds transfers, and wire transfers), separate remittance advice, and payment voiding. Check stock control features include recording the checks used and issuing a warning prior to running out.
- *Other Features.* These include tracking of labor costs, distribution of labor costs to one or multiple organization units, automatic reversal of voided checks, historical retention of check and adjustment data, automatic bank tape processing for check reconciliation, and automatic W-2 preparation.

44-4 THE 1990s—FUNCTIONALITY AND NEW FEATURES

Companies selling automated financial accounting software have added so many features and so much functionality to their systems that it is difficult to determine the precise advantages of different vendors' systems. Thus, when selecting automated financial accounting software, an organization should first assess their unique needs and match these needs with the corresponding features and functionality provided by available software packages.

For example, modules desired by an organization may include general ledger, accounts payable, fixed assets, and capital projects. Many software packages may not offer a capital projects module. Thus the organization should first look to packages which provide software for all these modules then evaluate whether each module can support the organization's unique needs. Similarly, if the organization has a need for encumbrance accounting, multi-currency functionality or support for the accounting standards of a foreign operation, software systems that meet these needs should be evaluated first.

It should be noted that automated interfaces between modules such as general ledger and accounts payable are usually standard in packaged software purchased from a single vendor. However, if the functionality of a module of the system does not meet the organization's needs, the value of the standard interface diminishes extensively. Although purchasing software from one vendor streamlines training, installation and maintenance, an organization should not be hesitant to purchase modules from multiple vendors if these modules best meet the organization's needs. However, custom interfaces will have to be built to automatically link the modules. (Many software systems have facilities that assist in interfacing to "foreign" modules.)

Some of the newer features include:

- *Platform-Independent Software.* For larger organizations, there is a growing need for software that runs on multiple platforms existing in different locations of the organization. For a smaller organization, the ability to update a platform, grow to a larger platform or select platform-specific software is also important. In the past, software was selected first, then the platform was selected based on the options available for the selected software. Today's vendors recognize the need for platform-independent software and are working to that end.

- *Graphical User Interface.* "User-friendly" has taken on a new meaning in the 1990s with the advent of GUI ("gooey") interfaces. Steven R. Anderson, in an article in the *Hewlett-Packard Journal* [1990], discusses the three basic principles of these interfaces: (1) Selecting from a list of alternatives (e.g., a menu) is easier than remembering all of the alternatives; (2) Choosing alternatives by direct manipulation, such as pushing a button on a mouse or dragging an icon, is often preferred over typing in text commands; and (3) Using metaphors from the real world (e.g., a trash can) can ease understanding. Tools important to GUI interfaces include the mouse, menus, graphical icons, and overlapping windows.

- *Client/Server Architecture.* Although consensus on the definition of client/server architecture may not be easy to come by, this phrase relates to a networking capability where the "server" is the central facility that services all the nodes or workstations (i.e., "clients"). The server and client can exist on the same or different platforms with the server issuing the host commands, commands which are invisible to the client. For example, the server may coordinate the use of software among several users or clients. (See Chapter 42 for a further discussion of computer hardware trends.)

In the 1980s, vendors of automated financial accounting systems made great strides to match the features and functionality of their competitors. Therefore, the 1990s present an opportunity for striking new features, features forced by the need to distinguish one software vendor from another.

44-5 SELECTED REFERENCES

Anderson, Steven R., "Creating an Effective User Interface of HP IVIBuild," *Hewlett-Packard Journal 41*:5, 1990, p. 39.

Bochenski, Barbara, "Client/Server Products: Every Which Way But Easy," *Computerworld,* Dec. 17, 1990, p. 53.

For additional references on the subject of Automated Financial Accounting systems, see the following magazines or journals:

Computers in Accounting

Management Accounting

Journal of Accountancy

Corporate Controller
Datamation
Financial Accounting Systems
Information Systems Management
Information Week
IBM Systems Journal
Macworld
PC Magazine
PC World

Specialized Industry Magazine or Journal References:

Banking

ABA Banking Journal
Bankers Magazine
Banking Software Review

Healthcare

Computers in Healthcare
Healthcare Computing and Communications

Insurance

Best's Review Life/Health
Best's Review Property/Casualty
Insurance and Technology

(a) SOFTWARE DIRECTORIES

ICP Software Directory
Data Sources
DataPro
Dataworld

(b) AVAILABLE ON CD-ROM

Computer Select (with a listing of journal/magazine articles and data sources software directory)

(c) PUBLICATIONS

Filed in libraries under the library call number: HF5679

CHAPTER 45

Selecting a Financial Information System

45-1 INTRODUCTION

The controller is primarily responsible for seeing that the financial information system meets the needs of those who receive and use its output—management, shareholders, creditors, suppliers, customers, government agencies, and stock exchanges as well as the general public.

This chapter contains a proven approach to selecting and implementing an automated financial information system (FIS). It includes an overview of reasons why financial system software should be purchased instead of developed in-house, how to thoroughly define systems requirements, an approach to preparing a Request for Proposal (RFP), and ways to evaluate software, hardware, and the associated vendors. (Chapter 46 contains a detailed discussion of how to implement an FIS.) Selection and implementation of an FIS are extremely important to an organization's financial operation. As a result, the organization must be willing to devote a substantial amount of time and effort to these activities, or hire outside consultants to assist in the process.

For the purposes of this chapter, it is assumed that the selection process includes both computer hardware and software. Many selecting organizations already have computer hardware in place. However, where possible, it is recommended that an organization select software that best meets its needs without being constrained by the hardware currently in place.

45-2 REASONS TO PURCHASE SOFTWARE

In general, it is recommended that software packages be purchased, instead of developed in-house, to meet the needs of an organization's financial operations. The reasons include:

- *Implementation Speed.* Packaged software generally can be implemented much quicker than software developed in-house because the software is readily available and the process of designing and coding the systems is not necessary.

- *Fewer Software Problems.* Packaged software normally has already been thoroughly tested and "debugged" before it is sold.

- *Lower Overall Cost.* The total cost of packaged software tends to be significantly less than the cost of software developed in-house. Software developed in-house normally requires a very significant investment of time and human resources.

- *Software Vendor Assistance.* Most software vendors, especially those in the midrange (i.e., minicomputer) and mainframe market, provide ongoing support and maintenance for their software. This means that the support required from in-house information systems (IS) staff can be minimized.

- *Package Enhancements.* To maintain market position and sales, software vendors generally provide enhanced functionality and new modules.

- *Documentation.* Most software packages come with a variety of manuals including user, technical, and operations. Therefore, the acquiring organization does not have to invest in developing this type of documentation.

- *Training.* The vast majority of software vendors provide a variety of training classes for user and technical personnel.

- *Research and Development.* Software vendors are in the business of selling system solutions. To maintain (and improve) a competitive market position, they must invest a substantial amount of money in research and development. (Most organizations can't afford to invest substantial sums in improving existing in-house-developed financial systems.)

- *Information Systems Support.* In general, it is much easier to locate personnel who are familiar with packaged software and can support it than with in-house systems. Also, with in-house developed software, employee turnover presents greater problems.

- *Prevalence of Software Problems.* Software vendors normally thoroughly test their products before allowing them to be sold. In addition, packaged software is generally used by numerous users in a wide variety of ways. Therefore, software problems (i.e., "bugs") are likely to appear relatively early in a package's life cycle. To survive in the long run, the software vendor must correct these bugs as rapidly as possible. This is not necessarily so for systems developed in-house, which are generally used only by the developing organizations. As a result, it may take years before a bug is uncovered. Also, once the bug is found, considerable time may pass before it is corrected.

- *The User Group.* Packaged software vendors tend to support and encourage user groups. Participation in these groups can be an effective means of identifying ways in which to more efficiently use the system. Also, it tends to be an effective way of encouraging the vendor to improve its software.

45-3 WAYS TO DEFINE SYSTEMS REQUIREMENTS

Before software is selected, the specific requirements need to be precisely defined. The application areas typically included in an FIS are:

- Budgeting.
- Purchasing.
- Accounts payable and check reconciliation.
- General ledger.
- Accounts receivable and revenue accounting.
- Fixed assets.
- Cost accounting.
- Inventory.
- Order entry and billing.
- Cost accounting.

If application requirements are not thoroughly defined and documented, the software selected probably will not meet the organization's needs. It will be useful to a Systems Requirements Definition (SRD) document that:

- Serves as the basis for the Request for Proposal (RFP).
- Communicates the organization's requirements to the vendors.
- Helps the selected software meet the organization's current and future needs
- Enhances the organization's understanding of each application area (e.g., accounts payable and accounts receivable) and how automation can assist in improving access to information in that area.
- Prioritizes the application areas to be automated.
- Matches requirements against the software's capabilities to determine where it is deficient, and where modifications must be developed.

There are a number of approaches that may be used to develop FIS requirements. These approaches include questionnaires, executive interviews, document reviews, and outside sources.

(a) QUESTIONNAIRES

Questionnaires may be used to develop a general understanding of an organization, its objectives, and the environment in which it operates. They may also be used to define major financially-oriented tasks, analyze transactions, determine major systems interfaces, and assist with the development of FIS requirements.

Prior to developing a questionnaire, the individuals preparing it (normally an FIS steering committee or some other such group) need to make sure that they have top management's support for the selection project. Without this support, it is doubtful that the questionnaire will be returned in a timely manner with complete and accurate responses.

The questionnaire should not be so long that it discourages completion. Alternatively, it should not be so brief that it does not identify specific requirements. Figure 45-1 illustrates the types of questions that can appear in the questionnaire. Note that a cover letter should be attached to the questionnaire, clearly defining its purpose, the date it is to be returned, and the importance of complete and accurate responses. Also, the cover letter should be signed by someone with authority, such as the Chief Financial Officer, Controller, or the Director of Information Systems.

(b) EXECUTIVE INTERVIEWS

The purposes of conducting executive interviews include:

- Developing an overall understanding of the organization—its environment and objectives.
- Defining executives information needs.
- Determining the executives opinions on the current system.
- Identifying the organization's goals, objectives, and critical success factors.
- Identifying executives system expectations.
- Predicting growth areas or new needs that must be planned for by IS.
- Improving executives "buy in" to the selection process.

Executive interviews should not be designed to elicit detailed information on systems specifications. Rather, they should help elicit general information needs and strategic goals and objectives of the organization.

It is important that the information and reporting needs of executives be emphasized and identified early in the selection process. Too frequently, only the needs of staff and middle management are incorporated. The resulting FIS frequently does not provide executives with the necessary reports for effectively managing the application areas.

(c) DOCUMENT REVIEWS

Another way to develop systems requirements is to review input forms and reports. Doing so provides the organization with a listing of its current data elements and helps to define the minimum reporting requirements of the proposed FIS.

Figure 45-1   Sample Questionnaire for Defining Application Requirements.

QUESTIONNAIRE TO DEFINE FIS APPLICATION REQUIREMENTS

1.   For what functions are you responsible?

_____

_____

2.   What are the primary goals of your job?

_____

_____

3.   With what other departments do you interface?

_____

_____

4.   What major tasks do you perform?

_____

_____

5.   What reports do you prepare? (Please attached a sample of each report.)

_____

_____

6.   What forms do you use? (Please attach a sample of each form.)

_____

_____

7.   Where do these forms originate?

_____

_____

8.   Where do these forms go when you complete them?

_____

_____

9.   What financial information do you receive from other departments?

_____

_____

10.   What changes do you predict will occur in your job over the next one to three years?

_____

_____

11.   What additional information could you use?

_____

_____

12.   What automated system do you currently utilize?

_____

_____

Audit work papers often contain information that may be useful for developing system requirements. The flow charts contained in the work papers frequently provide an overview of how an accounting "system" operates. Also, the work papers often contain volume estimates, such as the number of A/P checks issued and the number of customers in the accounts receivable file.

(d) OUTSIDE SOURCES

A final source of requirements that should be included in an SRD is the environment in which the financial organization exists. Economic trends, changes in laws and practices, and revisions to governmental regulations may all affect the reporting requirements of an FIS and, therefore, should be reviewed.

There is a cost involved in collecting systems requirements. As a result, an organization should not spend an excessive amount of time documenting them, because it may never get to the point of selecting software.

45-4 EXISTING SYSTEM DOCUMENTATION

After the questionnaires and executive interviews have been completed and the other sources of information reviewed, it is critical the existing manual and/or automated financial systems be documented. Included in this documentation should be the following factors:

- The key objectives of the system (e.g., maintain the general ledger and produce financial reports).
- Who supports the system.
- The major system inputs, edits, controls, and outputs (i.e., reports).
- All system interfaces and special features.
- The volume of transactions processed by the system.
- The approximate costs of operating the system.

In addition, if the system is automated, it is important to note the hardware platform on which it operates, the language in which it is written, its age, and the approximate amount invested in the system.

The main objectives of documenting existing manual and automated systems include:

- Ensure the SRD contains, at a minimum, the features currently available, if desired.
- Identify specific weaknesses in the current system.
- Determine what is currently available and what is missing from the existing systems.
- Document required and unnecessary reports.
- Highlight procedures that are poorly defined.

45-5 JOINT SESSIONS

An effective and efficient means of ensuring a thorough system requirements survey is by conducting "joint sessions" with the employees who will be utilizing and supporting the system. The benefits of conducting joint sessions include development of a more complete SRD and an improved user "buy in." The steps required to conduct a joint session include:

- Prepare "straw man" requirements for each application (e.g., accounts payable). These requirements generally are based on research previously conducted by the organization, information obtained from software vendors or computer-related literature, or IS consultants.
- Distribute the requirements document to the employees interested in or affected by the specific application. (For example, the accounts payable (A/P) requirements should be distributed to the A/P supervisor and clerks and other interested accounting personnel.)
- Conduct a joint session for each application area. During these sessions, which generally are facilitated by a selection team member or a consultant, the participants are asked to:
  —Prioritize each requirement (i.e., state whether the requirement is required, desired optional, or not applicable).
  —Identify additional requirements.

After the current financial systems are documented and the joint sessions conducted, it is then time to finalize the SRD. The purpose of the SRD, which will become part of the RFP, is to communicate to software vendors the organization's systems requirements and allow the vendors to identify software products that can meet those requirements.

The SRD should be divided by application area (e.g., general ledger and accounts payable). The application area should be further divided into the following topics:

- General systems narrative.
- Processing requirements.
- Inquiry requirements.
- Reporting requirements.
- Data requirements.

The requirements should be stated as a single sentence. Figure 45-2 gives a very abbreviated example of these factors for an accounts receivable system. System requirements documents may be from 5 to well over 100 pages per application, depending on the number and the level of detail desired. Be careful not to overdefine the requirements or make the SRD so general that it allows all software packages to meet its needs.

After completing the SRD, the prioritization of the applications should be performed. It is vital for an organization to clearly define each application in the order of importance, to help it evaluate the completed RFP and identify the factors upon which

Figure 45-2 Accounts Receivable System Requirements.

ACCOUNTS RECEIVABLE SYSTEM NARRATIVE

The accounts receivable system should be designed to handle all of the organization's receivable and collection requirements. The system must interface with both the order entry system, to obtain billing information, and the general ledger system, to post billings, cash receipts, and bad-debt journal entries.

Processing Requirements
The accounts receivable system should be able to perform the following functions:

☐ Post to different revenue accounts depending on the type of service performed.

☐ Enter non-accounting data to the master file on-line.

☐ Disallow the deletion of data with an account balance greater than zero.

☐ Interface with the order entry/billing system.

Inquiry Requirements
The accounts receivable system should include the following inquiry features and capabilities:

☐ On-line review of billing and payment history

☐ Inquiry as to the status of a bill using a variety of data elements including:

- Customer name
- Customer number
- Invoice number

Reporting Requirements
The accounts receivable system should produce the following reports:

☐ *Accounts receivable aging report*—a report indicating the amount of time an accounts receivable balance has been outstanding.
Frequency: weekly and on demand

☐ *Cash receipts register*—a register containing information on:

- Date of receipt
- Check number
- Customer name and number
- Dollar amount
- Invoice number applied to
- General ledger account posted to

Frequency: daily and on demand

Data Requirements
The Customer Master File should contain the following data elements:

- Customer Name—60 alpha/numeric characters
- Customer Number—20 alpha/numeric characters

(continued)

Figure 45-2   *(continued)*

- Customer Address 1
    —Street—60 alpha/numeric characters
    —City—20 alpha characters
    —State—2 alpha characters
- Customer Address 2
    —Street—60 alpha/numeric characters
    —City—20 alpha/numeric characters
    —State—2 alpha characters
- Customer Contact 1
    —Name—40 alpha/numeric characters
    —Phone number—9 numeric characters
    —Street—60 alpha/numeric characters
    —City—20 alpha characters
    —State—2 alpha characters

---

the software selection will be decided. Factors to consider when assigning priorities to applications to be automated include:

- *The impact of the system on the organization and its customers.* How many employees will come into contact with the system? Will the system affect relations with customers (as would a billing system)? How will the system benefit the selecting organization?

- *The costs and benefits of the system.* Will the system affect the organization's financial position? Can the system influence the organization's productivity? What are the total direct and indirect costs of the system?

- *The demand for the system.* Are accounting employees requesting a new system? Does senior management support the system? How long will it take to get the system implemented?

- *The dependence of the system on other systems.* Will the implementation of the accounts receivable system, for example, have to be delayed until the billing system is on-line?

45-6 PREPARING THE REQUEST FOR PROPOSAL (RFP)

An RFP is used to effectively communicate the FIS's requirements to software and/or hardware vendors. It is prepared after the SRD and serves the following purposes:

- Communicates the organization's systems requirements to vendors and facilitates a uniform response to those requirements.
- Requests specific commitments from vendors, such as the system's functionality, the level of support and documentation provided, the costs, and contractual arrangements.

- Serves as a tool for effectively comparing vendors. The RFP should be designed in a way that allows the selecting government organization to easily compare the proposals of various vendors.

Depending on the organization's situation, RFPs may be prepared for software, hardware, or both. However, no matter what the organization selects, the RFP must be well-structured and precise in order to elicit a clear and concise response from vendors. A vague and poorly organized RFP is likely to result in proposals that are too general and difficult to compare and are lacking details in many areas. Figure 45-3 shows a typical Contents page for an RFP.

(a) COVER LETTER

The cover letter notifies the hardware and/or software vendor that the organization is requesting a proposal for specific applications and/or hardware. In addition, the cover letter should contain the following information: important deadlines (such as the date of the bidders conference and when the proposal is due) and the projected installation and implementation dates; the overall objective of the RFP; the individual within the organization to contact with questions; and the format and content of the RFP.

(b) GENERAL INFORMATION/PROPOSAL GUIDELINES

The general information/proposal guidelines section contains information on how the proposal is to be completed, how the selection process will be conducted, and the importance of a concise and timely response. Also included in this section is whether site visits will be made by the organization, a statement that the cost of preparing the proposal is entirely the vendor's responsibility, that the organization reserves the right to reject any and all proposals, and that the confidentiality of the material contained in the RFP.

(c) BACKGROUND MATERIAL

The background material includes information about the organization that is of interest to the vendor. Generally included in this section is a description of the organization's different business functions currently being performed and by which

Figure 45-3 RFP Table of Contents.

REQUEST FOR PROPOSAL
TABLE OF CONTENTS

I. Cover Letter
II. General Information/Proposal Guidelines
III. Background Material
IV. Vendor Questionnaire
V. Vendor Cost Summary
VI. System Requirements

departments; volume statistics (e.g., the number of payroll and accounts payable checks issued per month and the number of general ledger transactions); the current hardware, financial system software and modules, and operating system, if any; and the hours of operation. This information is very useful for vendors when preparing their proposals.

(d) VENDOR QUESTIONNAIRE

The vendor questionnaire asks a variety of questions on the vendor's background, clients, training, and growth; systems reliability, security, and performance; how modifications are handled; how reports are produced; acceptance testing and implementation schedule; data control; staffing; R&D expenditures; documentation; and hardware proposed, if any. The answers to these questions will assist the organization with determining the final vendor. This section must be extremely well-constructed and the questions concisely formulated. (See Appendix 1 for examples of vendor evaluation criteria.)

(e) VENDOR COST SUMMARY

In the vendor cost summary, the vendor is requested to complete a cost schedule specifying the costs of the proposed FIS. Each vendor generally is asked to provide information on recurring and nonrecurring costs over a five-year period and supplemental schedules to explain the derivation of all costs and what is included in such items as installation and maintenance fees. An example of a vendor cost summary schedule is shown in Figure 45-4.

(f) SYSTEM REQUIREMENTS

The system requirements section sets forth the processing, inquiry, reporting, and data requirements developed during the systems requirement definition process. Each vendor is asked to complete a matrix that contains all application requirements.

The vendor is asked to respond to the following categories for *each* requirement:

- Whether the current system can satisfy the requirement. The only acceptable responses are yes or no.
- Cross Reference (X-REF)—Where in the vendor's documentation is the requirement described.
- Comments—Any comments the vendor may have regarding the specific requirement.

Figure 45-5 reproduces a page from an accounts payable information requirements section, together with a possible vendor response.

45-7 DISTRIBUTION OF THE RFP

Once the RFP is completed, the organization must determine the vendors to whom it will be sent. With over 50,000 software packages available, narrowing the field can be a difficult task. However, there are some basic factors to consider.

Figure 45-4   Vendor Cost Summary.

VENDOR COST SUMMARY						
			Year			
	1	2	3	4	5	Total
Recurring costs						
Hardware						
CPU lease	$___	$___	$___	$___	$___	$___
Terminal lease	___	___	___	___	___	___
Printer lease	___	___	___	___	___	___
Other lease	___	___	___	___	___	___
CPU maintenance	___	___	___	___	___	___
Terminal maintenance	___	___	___	___	___	___
Printer maintenance	___	___	___	___	___	___
Other maintenance	___	___	___	___	___	___
Software						
Software license	___	___	___	___	___	___
Software support	___	___	___	___	___	___
Other fees	___	___	___	___	___	___
Supplies						
Disks, tapes	___	___	___	___	___	___
Ribbons, paper	___	___	___	___	___	___
Other	___	___	___	___	___	___
Total	$___	$___	$___	$___	$___	$___
Nonrecurring costs						
Hardware						
CPU purchase	$___	$___	$___	$___	$___	$___
Terminal purchase	___	___	___	___	___	___
Printer purchase	___	___	___	___	___	___
Other purchase	___	___	___	___	___	___
Software						
Software purchase	___	___	___	___	___	___
Installation						
Freight	___	___	___	___	___	___
Cabling	___	___	___	___	___	___
Site preparation	___	___	___	___	___	___
Training	___	___	___	___	___	___
Customization	___	___	___	___	___	___
System initializing	___	___	___	___	___	___
Installation	___	___	___	___	___	___
Other	___	___	___	___	___	___
Total	$___	$___	$___	$___	$___	$___
TOTAL	$___	$___	$___	$___	$___	$___

Figure 45-5   Completed Accounts Payable System Requirements.

Requirement	Response Yes	No	X-REF	Comments
1. Enter invoices on-line.	X		User Manual Pg.5-22	
2. Enter vendor credit memoranda future payments.	X		User Manual Pg. 6-21	$5,000 additional fee
3. Write checks automatically based on invoice date and a predefined pay period (e.g., 30 days from invoice date).	X		User Manual Pg.3-22	
4. Automatically process recurring payments.		X	User Manual Pg.2-10	
5. Process and post manual checks to correct vendor and general ledger account.	X		User Manual Pg.3-12	
6. Automatically interface with general ledger system.	X		User Manual Pg.7-12	
7. Edit for duplicate invoice numbers to the same vendor.	X		User Manual Pg.6-10	$3,000 additional fee
8. Allow for standard discount terms (e.g., 1/10 net 30).	X		User Manual Pg.3-20	

- *Geographic location.* The ability to receive timely support is extremely critical. Since many software vendors may not have offices located near the organization, this factor can be used to eliminate many vendors.
- *Hardware considerations.* Many software programs run only on certain hardware configurations (e.g., IBM or Hewlett Packard hardware only). Therefore, if the organization owns hardware or has a preference for a certain manufacturer, the software options are significantly reduced.
- *Organization size.* The size of the organization influences the size of the computer system that must be acquired. Software is generally designed to run on either microcomputers, midrange systems, or mainframes. As a result, the software vendors to which the organization may send the RFP are limited.
- *Organizational preference.* Some organizations prefer to deal with firms that only develop software. Other organizations prefer to deal with turnkey vendors that supply both a hardware and software solution. The organization's decision in this area will influence the number of vendors to which the RFP can be sent.
- *Vendor characteristics.* It is frequently possible to prescreen vendors to determine if it is appropriate to send them an RFP. This can be accomplished by calling a vendor representative, reviewing vendor literature, looking at one of the many software reference manuals such as *Datapro* or *Data Decisions*, or discussing vendors with organizations similar to yours. When prescreening a

vendor, look at factors such as the vendor's stability and related experience, list prices, and flexibility.

Other means of identifying vendors that should receive the RFP include engaging a consultant experienced in hardware and software selections, reviewing computer-oriented magazines, contacting hardware vendors for lists of potential software suppliers, and networking with other organizations.

In general, the RFP should be sent to between five and ten vendors; any more than that, and the process becomes cumbersome; any fewer, and the choices become too limited. The vendor should be given sufficient time—3 to 6 weeks—to complete the RFP accurately and thoroughly.

45-8 REVIEW OF THE VENDOR'S COMPLETED PROPOSAL

When the proposals are returned, they should be given an initial brief review. This brief review will most likely eliminate the proposals that do not meet the organization's minimum critical needs.

In general, systems decisions should be more heavily influenced by the software, not the hardware. Therefore, the organization should first review the software proposed by the vendors. The goal of this review is to determine the two or three finalists. (The field should be narrowed to two or three, because any more makes the final selection cumbersome; any fewer leaves the organization in a risky situation. For example, if only one finalist vendor is selected and it goes out of business, the organization will have to begin the selection process again.)

There are two types of software the organization needs to evaluate: application and systems. Application software is the software that performs the functions needed by the end-user, such as generating paying invoices, preparing financial statements, and recording cash receipts. It is used to perform specific processing or computational tasks. Examples of application software include accounts payable, accounts receivable, and general ledger systems. Systems software makes it possible to utilize the application software. Included in this broad category are operating systems, database management systems, report writers, database compilers, and debugging aids.

The system requirements section of the RFP is used to review the vendor's application software. As previously mentioned, each vendor is asked to respond to each requirement. The selecting organization should tabulate these responses to determine how well the vendor's software meets the organization's needs. Use the following guidelines:

1. Prepare a spreadsheet listing all of the requirements. The spreadsheet should look exactly like the information systems requirement section displayed in Figure 45-5.
2. Determine the number of points a response is worth. For example, a "Yes" response to a "Required" requirement may be worth 10 points, but only 6 points on a desired feature. (A sample scoring scheme follows.)
3. Tally the vendor's responses.
4. Total the score by application area.
5. Determine the vendor's total score.

Response	Required	Desired	Optional
Yes	10	6	4
No	0	0	0

The spreadsheet should look exactly like the information systems requirement displayed in Figure 45-5.

The rating sheet in Figure 45-6 can be effective in evaluating the vendor responses. In addition, the organization should review the following characteristics of each vendor's application software:

- *Flexibility.* Is the software easy to modify? Will it handle the organization's needs five years from installation? Is it easy to debug? Flexibility is also an important factor to consider when reviewing systems software and hardware.

- *Documentation.* Is it easy to use? Is it accurate and thorough? Is it regularly updated? Does it describe all error messages? Are all screen formats presented? Does it clearly describe recovery procedures? Are terms defined? Who maintains it?

- *Controls.* Is a clear audit trail of all transactions available? Are data validated before files are updated? Does password security exist? Are all errors flagged? Is a listing of log-on attempts provided? Are different authorization levels available? Can check digits be used? Are batch totals available?

Figure 45-6   Application Software Rating Sheet.

Requirement	Required or Desired	Response Yes	Response No	Comments
1. Enter invoices on-line.	R			
2. Enter vendor credit memoranda on-line and apply credits to future payments.	R			
3. Write checks automatically based on invoice date and a predefined pay period (e.g., 30 days from invoice date).	R			
4. Automatically process recurring payments.	D			
5. Process and post manual checks to correct vendor and general ledger account.	R			
6. Automatically interface with general ledger system.	R			
7. Edit for duplicate invoice numbers.	R			
8. Allow for standard discount terms (e.g., 2/10 net 30).	D			

Analyzing systems software can be more difficult than analyzing application software, because it is harder to quantify. However, the following guidelines can be useful:

1. *Determine the systems software factors to be evaluated.* For example, it is likely that the selecting organization will want to review the following:

   • The operating and database management system.

   • Multiuser capabilities.

   • Programming language utilized.

   • Compilation speeds.

   • Systems utilities such as file maintenance programs, backup and restore programs, and sorting and text editors.

   • Systems support software such as file management processors, password protection, screen formatters, report writers, and print spoolers.

   • Compatibility of the system with other software products.

   • Interactive and communications capabilities.

   • Ease of operation.

2. *Once the factors have been determined, prioritize and assign numeric values to them.* For example, the selecting organization may need a certain type of operating system. Therefore, this would receive a high priority.

3. *Review the vendor's proposal and assign a score to each factor.* Assigning scores is a somewhat subjective process. However, it is important that it be performed.

4. *Total the vendor's score in this section.* Figure 45-7 provides an example of how systems software can be prioritized and scored.

As previously mentioned, the software decision usually takes precedence over the hardware decision. However, a thorough review of the proposed hardware is extremely important to ensure that the FIS will meet the organization's needs.

Figure 45-7   Scoring for Systems Software.

SYSTEMS SOFTWARE		
Factor	Points Assigned	Vendor A Score
1. Operating system	18	16
2. DBMS	12	12
3. Multiuser capabilities	10	6
4. Programming language	6	6
5. Compilation speed	6	2
6. Systems utilities	8	6
7. Systems support software	10	7
8. Compatibility	8	8
9. Interactive and communications capabilities	10	9
10. Ease of operations	12	8
Total Points	100	80

The size of the proposed hardware system depends on a number of factors:

1. The volume statistics listed in the background section of the RFP.
2. The organization's projected growth rates.
3. The vendor's experience with similar clients.

Acquiring a system that meets the organization's current and future needs is extremely important. Either an in-house IS specialist or an experienced IS consultant must review the capabilities and flexibility of the proposed hardware configuration. Other hardware factors to review include:

- Central processing unit.
- Peripheral devices (such as disk and tape drives).
- Remote devices (such as communications support equipment).
- Environmental considerations.
- Flexibility and expandability.
- Systems reliability.

Once the hardware evaluation factors have been identified, they should be prioritized and assigned a numeric value. (This is similar to the method recommended for reviewing systems software.) Then, each vendor's proposal should be reviewed and assigned a score on each factor. The total score on hardware is then determined.

After the hardware and software have been evaluated, the next step is to evaluate the vendor(s). Depending on the system desired, this may involve reviewing a software vendor and a hardware vendor. The primary factors to consider when evaluating a vendor are:

- Product support.
- Reputation and financial stability.
- Experience.
- Product availability and enhancements.
- Documentation.
- Training.

Once the software, hardware, and vendor have been thoroughly evaluated, the selection of the finalist vendors can occur. The finalists are then analyzed further by means of reference calls, attendance at vendor demonstrations, and site visits. Because substantial amounts of time and money are invested in reviewing the finalist vendors, it is vital that the selecting organization choose vendors who can actually provide it with an FIS that meets its needs.

45-9 REFERENCE CALLS

One of the most important aspects of the systems selection process is making reference calls to existing systems users. Reference calls are a means by which an organization can find out what a vendor may not want them to know. For example, the organization may discover that a vendor's documentation and support are not as good as its sales literature claims.

Reference calls should be made for all finalist vendors. The calls should be directed to users with similar hardware and software configurations to get the most relevant information. Software does not run equally effectively on all hardware platforms.

The questions asked during a reference call should be both fact- and opinion-oriented. The users should be asked to list the software implemented and their overall opinion of the software. Topics to cover when making a reference call include:

- Type of Organization.
- Volume Statistics.
- Software Packages Purchased.
- Software Packages Implemented.
- Ease of Installation.
- Operating System.
- Data Base Management System.
- Hardware Installed.
- Hardware Dependability.
- Systems Security.
- Response Time.
- Quality of Reports.
- Approach to System Selection.
- Why Vendor(s) Were Chosen.
- Ease of Operation.
- Quality of Training.
- Quality of Documentation.
- Modifications Made.
- Quality of Support.
- Vendor Dependability.
- Unforeseen Costs.
- User Group Membership/Satisfaction.
- Overall Satisfaction.
- Names of Other Users.

The names of other systems users are important because vendors frequently provide only the names of satisfied users. Asking a user for names of other users may lead to one who is not pleased with the system.

45-10 DEMONSTRATION

After the reference calls have been completed, the organization should consider attending vendor demonstrations to:

- Obtain additional information on the software and vendor.
- See how the software operates.
- Review the "look and feel" of the system, its ease of use, and the level of complexity.

Prior to attending the vendor demonstration, the organization should:

- Prepare an agenda for the vendor to follow.
- Develop a feedback form for the attendees to rate various aspects of the software and the vendor (e.g., screen layout and ease of use).
- Prepare a list of questions and sample transactions for the vendor to enter into the system (e.g., matching a purchase order and invoice).

It is important to remember that the vendors obviously will be presenting their software in its "best light." You must be in a position to evaluate this information.

45-11 SITE VISITS

After the reference calls have been made and demonstrations attended, the organization should arrange to see the system at a working installation, not at the vendor's headquarters. The purpose of the site visits includes:

- Viewing the system in a "real-life" environment.
- Answering questions that may have arisen during the selection process.
- Assisting the organization in deciding whether the system will meet its current and future needs.

The site visit should take place at a user's place of business and should be on a "live," not "demo," system so that the vendor has no opportunity to manipulate the demonstration to its advantage. Although the majority of vendors are ethical, manipulation of potential customers is not unheard of.

The individuals present at the demonstration should include in-house IS personnel; potential system users, such as the accounts payable supervisor; and the IS consultant, if one is being used. The visit should take no more than a day to complete. The selecting team representatives should come prepared with a set of questions to ask the other organization and a feedback form on which to record ratings of the vendor.

If possible, the organization should arrange to make site visits within a two-week period to more easily compare the systems.

45-12 COST OF THE SYSTEM

The costs of purchasing hardware, software, and implementation support can be a very critical factor in a selection process and should be carefully analyzed.

The vendor cost summary portion of the RFP may be used to compare the costs of proposed systems. However, other cost factors need to be clarified before comparing the total costs of the proposed systems. Consider:

- What will the proposed enhancements cost?
- How will the cost of future enhancements be determined?
- Is there an additional fee for installation?
- Is there an additional fee for training?
- How much does maintenance cost?
- Is there an additional fee for twenty-four-hour support?
- Is there a charge for system updates?
- Will the organization receive a discount if it purchases other applications?
- Does the software license allow for the use of the software at multiple sites? If not, what is the charge for the other sites?

- How much does the warranty cost and how long is it in effect?
- When does the warranty go into effect? (Ideally, the warranty should go into effect on the date the system is accepted, not on the date the system is installed.)
- Does the vendor guarantee in writing a full refund if the software does not perform as promised?
- Is the price of documentation included in the total price?
- Can the organization duplicate the documentation, or must it pay for additional copies? If so, what is the cost for additional copies?
- Is the source code (i.e., copy of the programs) included in the system's price? If not, what is the charge for the source code?

45-13 FINAL SELECTION

Once the software, hardware, and vendor have been thoroughly reviewed and the reference calls, demonstrations, and site visits completed, the organization is in a position to select the system. If the organization has completed the steps outlined in this chapter, it should find itself with an FIS that meets current and future needs. Once the final selection has been made, the organization is in a position to begin contract negotiations.

45-14 CONTRACT NEGOTIATIONS

After the software and hardware have been selected, preparation for contract negotiations between the organization and the vendor(s) should ensue. The objectives of contract negotiations are:

- Define the organization's expectations clearly to avoid misunderstandings.
- Define precisely what remedies are available if the vendor fails to perform as promised.
- Protect the organization against unexpected occurrences, such as the bankruptcy of the vendor.
- Ensure the best terms possible for the organization.

Negotiating a contract can be a long and costly process. When negotiating, there are several points to remember:

1. *Do not accept the vendor's standard contract.* These contracts tend to be one-sided in favor of the vendor and to disclaim all responsibility for performance and support.
2. *Negotiate with someone with the authority to bind the vendor.* Negotiating with a vendor representative who has no power is useless, because the promises they make may be overturned by their superiors.
3. *Never accept oral promises.*
4. *Do not make unreasonable demands.*

5. *Obtain advice from a professional experienced in contract negotiations.* The organization should not assume it can negotiate a mutually beneficial contract without the help of a professional (e.g., a lawyer specializing in contract law).

Four specific steps are essential for effectively negotiating a mutually beneficial contract:

1. Select a negotiating team to represent the selecting organization, including an IS specialist, an individual who will be using the system, an attorney or consultant with significant computer-related contract experience, and a purchasing department representative.

2. Determine the specific objectives of the negotiations and prepare a plan of action to take if the negotiations fail.

3. Review the standard contract terms offered by the vendor and identify problem areas and points that are missing.

4. Meet with the vendor to negotiate the contract.

The contract should clearly specify the costs for hardware, software, maintenance, installation support, modifications testing, and upgrades. The organization should attempt to ensure it is protected from any price increases without its written consent. The contract should also clearly identify the terms of payment. The organization should hold back a substantial portion of the purchase price (e.g., 10 to 30 percent) until the system is fully operational for a specified period of time and has passed all acceptance tests.

45-15 SELECTED REFERENCES

(a) PERIODICALS

Computerworld

Computers in Accounting

Information World

(b) PRODUCT REVIEW/INFORMATION

Datapro

Data Sources

Gartner Group

ICP Software Directory

(c) BOOKS

Willson, James D., and Jack F. Duston, *Financial Information Systems,* 2nd ed., New York: Warren, Gorham & Lamont, 1986.

Eliason, Alan L., and Kent D. Kitts, *Business Computer Systems and Applications,* Chicago: SRA 1979.

APPENDIX: VENDOR EVALUATION CRITERIA

Key factors to consider when evaluating vendors:

PRODUCT SUPPORT

- Location of nearest sales and support office.
- Size of the support staff at nearest service office and their qualifications.
- Availability of remote diagnostics.
- Availability of twenty-four hour support and associated cost.
- Guaranteed response time for system problems.
- Preventive maintenance approach and policies.
- Problem resolution procedures.
- Availability of installation and implementation support.
- Existence of and level of support of a user group.
- Existence of complete user and technical documentation.
- Frequency of documentation and system updates.

REPUTATION AND STABILITY

- Number of years in the computer industry.
- Number of similar installations of the particular system still operating.
- Sales growth rate of applications being reviewed.
- Financial condition of the vendor and/or its parent company.
- Research and development budget and number of staff.

CHAPTER 46

Software Package Integration

46-1 INTRODUCTION

Software package integration projects (e.g., the implementation of an accounting or human resources system) differ from custom-built projects in that the application to be integrated is already coded, operational, and, in most cases, marketplace-tested. Once the software package is selected, only the steps to integrate it into the organization remain. The execution of these steps can result in a successful project or in a project that fails miserably.

    Many organizations find it difficult to structure, plan, and budget for an integration project and then meet these estimates with a successfully executed integration

---

Written by Sandra Borchardt, Senior Manager, Ernst Young LLP, Boston, MA.

effort (i.e., one that results in an application system that meets user and organizational requirements). System implementation projects typically do not fail because of technical problems; rather, they fail because of a lack of management. Controllers and chief financial officers (CFOs) frequently are responsible for the successful implementation of a variety of systems, therefore it is particularly important for them to make certain that the appropriate techniques are used and the appropriate steps are taken to better ensure the success of the project.

The focus of this chapter is twofold. Presented first are four management techniques that if employed early on and throughout an integration project, will help to better insure the success of the project. Following these techniques, the specific steps of an integration project are outlined. Note that each project is different and thus calls for an individual evaluation and subsequent identification of the management techniques and integration steps best suited to handle the unique characteristics and issues of the project. If done, however, the project will have a greater probability of absorbing surprises during the integration and concluding in a manner that results in a cost-effective system that meets the goals and requirements that justified the project in the first place.

(a) MANAGEMENT TECHNIQUES FOR SOFTWARE PACKAGE INTEGRATION

Integrating software into an organization successfully depends on many factors including effective project leadership, a clear understanding of the project, and organizational commitment and adaptability. In addition to these factors, certain project management techniques can be used to increase the chance of success of the project by overcoming common project stumbling blocks. Four specific management techniques are presented on the following pages: project management, risk management, change management, and quality management (see Figure 46-1).

46-2 PROJECT MANAGEMENT

Project management is the process by which a project is planned, executed, and completed. The objective of project management is to conduct the project in a systematic and organized fashion in order to reduce uncertainty and encourage productivity.

Project management is made difficult by the very nature of projects. The communication process is at best inexact, causing potential misunderstandings of the project scope, requirements, and expectations. Changes in the regulatory environment or in the business itself may change the goals of the project or even render the project unnecessary. A project estimate is just that—a best guess at how long it will take to complete the project; how many resources, when, and with what skill set, will be needed; and what costs will be incurred. Quality deliverables may take more time than expected to complete. To obtain high productivity, project team members must be led, motivated, counseled, and apprised of their performance. To combat these difficulties, however, certain project management techniques can be used. Project planning, although an estimate at best, can provide the initial focus and step-by-step guide for the project. Project tracking can then be used to monitor actual progress against plan, identifying exceptions early and allowing for replanning based on these experiences.

Figure 46-1   Management Techniques for Software
Integration.

(a) MANAGING PROJECTS

Project management begins at the start of a project and continues throughout the proj
ect until its completion. Project management techniques are project-tested and hav
been used successfully to integrate software packages into organizations. Some com
mon project management techniques include the following:

- *Planning.* The planning process begins by identifying and confirming the busi
  ness problem to be solved. How to overcome the problem becomes the initial def
  inition of the project. The project scope is then defined, deliverables ar
  identified, and high-level estimates of time frames, required effort, and costs ar
  developed.

- *Estimating.* The estimating process builds on the information developed durin
  the planning process. Plans are detailed to achieve the project objectives withi
  the terms defined in the project scope; for example, a detailed work plan woul
  clearly define what work needs to be done, how long it will take, who will do i
  and when it will be completed. Risk, change, and quality management plans ar
  incorporated in the detailed work plan.

- *Defining Deliverables.* After the planning process has outlined the types of de
  liverables required by the project, this process customizes these deliverables fo
  the project situation. Deliverable definitions clearly identify exactly what wor
  will and will not be done during the project. These definitions serve as a com
  munication tool to help ensure that project members have the same expectation
  for the project.

- *Monitoring.* The monitoring process is an ongoing process that measures actual progress against planned progress and identifies those areas requiring corrective action or adjustments to the plan. Results of this process feed subsequent estimating processes.

- *Managing Risk.* The risk management process consists of early identification and control of project risks through the use of tools and techniques for identifying project risks, assessing their criticality, and developing and implementing strategies to manage these project risks. (Risk management will be discussed in more detail later in this chapter.)

- *Managing Change.* In the context of project management, change management has two important meanings:

  1. *A technique that targets the human factor affected by the project*—This type of change management identifies resistance to the changes brought on by the project, works to understand the nature of the resistance, and implements change management strategies to overcome the resistance. (The change management concept will be discussed later in this chapter.)

  2. *A mechanism through which project changes can be requested, tracked, investigated, and rejected or approved*—A change of this nature is an addition to, deletion from, or modification of a system during its design, development, or implementation. Although these types of changes are normal occurrences during a project, they can have a serious impact on a project's scope, cost, or schedule. The change management process for this type of change works to identify changes that are good for the project and those that, in the overall analysis, may not benefit the project or may cost more than the benefits to be gained.

- *Managing Quality.* The quality management process consists of the use of tools and techniques to build quality into a project. Through the use of quality management techniques that focus on preventative-based strategies, projects should better meet expectations, requirements, budget estimates, and planned time frames. (Quality management will be discussed in more detail later in this chapter.)

Project management tools support project management techniques throughout the life of the project. Some of the more common project management tools include:

- *Scope Document.* The project scope document identifies what will be accomplished by the project and what will not. It contains the definition of the project, its boundaries, and its completion criteria. Other information about the project, such as the budget, time frames, and resource requirements, may be included in the scope document.

- *Work Plan.* The project work plan is a detailed, step-by-step plan that clearly defines what work needs to be done, how long it will take, who will do it, and when it will be completed. The project work plan provides a tool against which actual progress can be measured. Figure 46-2 provides a sample page of a detailed project plan. Figure 46-3 presents a high level plan in a PERT chart format.

- *Status Reports.* Status reports identify accomplishments, work-in-progress, issues, and tasks that, when compared to the project plan, are overdue. Status

Figure 46-2 A Page of a Detailed Work Plan.

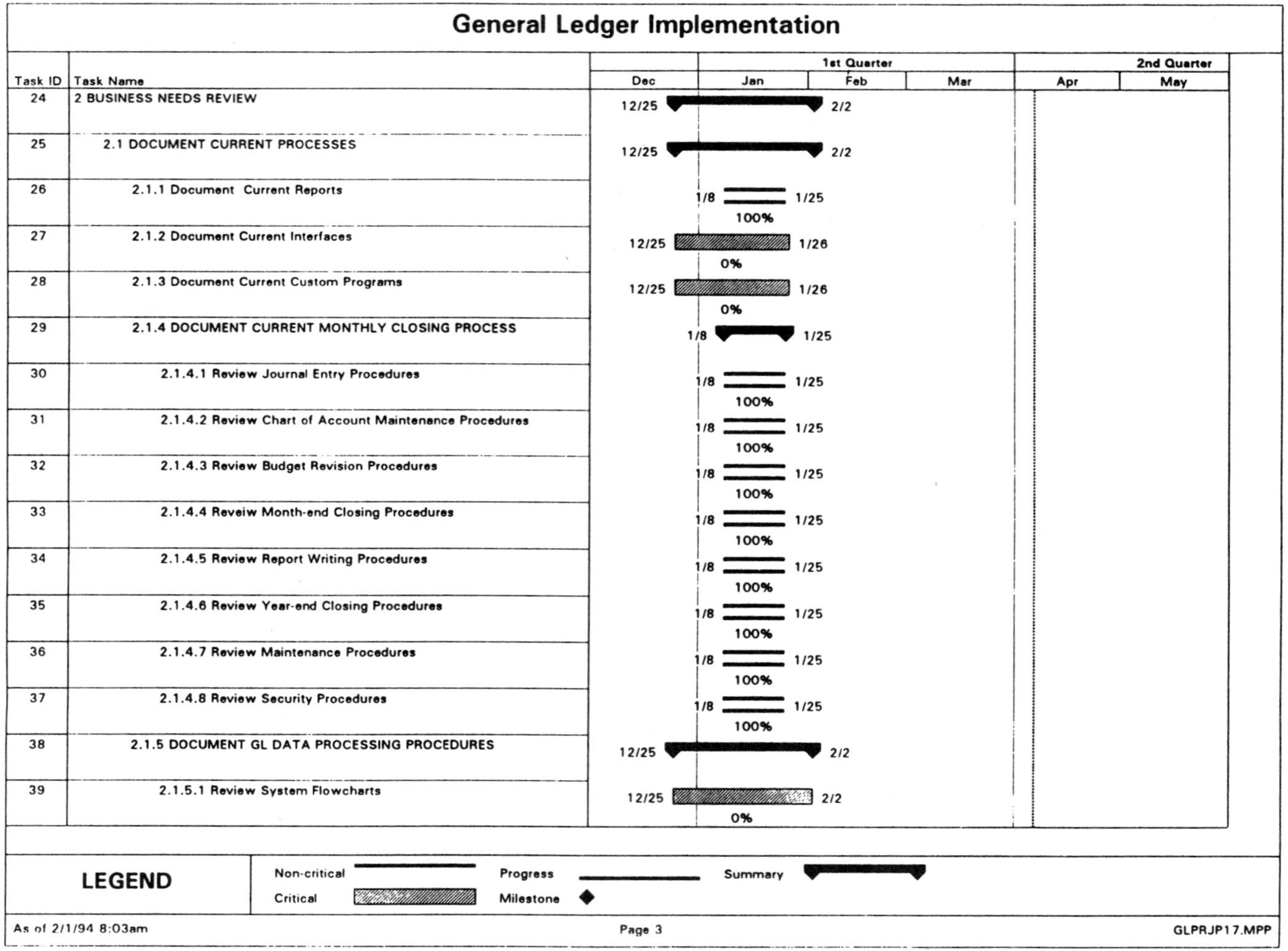

General Ledger Implementation

Task ID	Task Name	Dec	Jan	Feb	Mar	Apr	May
				1st Quarter			2nd Quarter
24	2 BUSINESS NEEDS REVIEW	12/25		2/2			
25	2.1 DOCUMENT CURRENT PROCESSES	12/25		2/2			
26	2.1.1 Document Current Reports		1/8 — 1/25				
27	2.1.2 Document Current Interfaces	12/25	100% 1/26				
28	2.1.3 Document Current Custom Programs	12/25	0% 1/26				
29	2.1.4 DOCUMENT CURRENT MONTHLY CLOSING PROCESS		0% 1/8 1/25				
30	2.1.4.1 Review Journal Entry Procedures		1/8 — 1/25				
31	2.1.4.2 Review Chart of Account Maintenance Procedures		100% 1/8 — 1/25				
32	2.1.4.3 Review Budget Revision Procedures		100% 1/8 — 1/25				
33	2.1.4.4 Reveiw Month-end Closing Procedures		100% 1/8 — 1/25				
34	2.1.4.5 Review Report Writing Procedures		100% 1/8 — 1/25				
35	2.1.4.6 Review Year-end Closing Procedures		100% 1/8 — 1/25				
36	2.1.4.7 Review Maintenance Procedures		100% 1/8 — 1/25				
37	2.1.4.8 Review Security Procedures		100% 1/8 — 1/25				
38	2.1.5 DOCUMENT GL DATA PROCESSING PROCEDURES	12/25	100% 2/2				
39	2.1.5.1 Review System Flowcharts	12/25	0% 2/2				

LEGEND

Non-critical		Progress		Summary
Critical		Milestone ◆		

As of 2/1/94 8:03am

Page 3

GLPRJP17.MPP

1188

Figure 46-3 A Pert Chart Representation of a Project Work Plan.

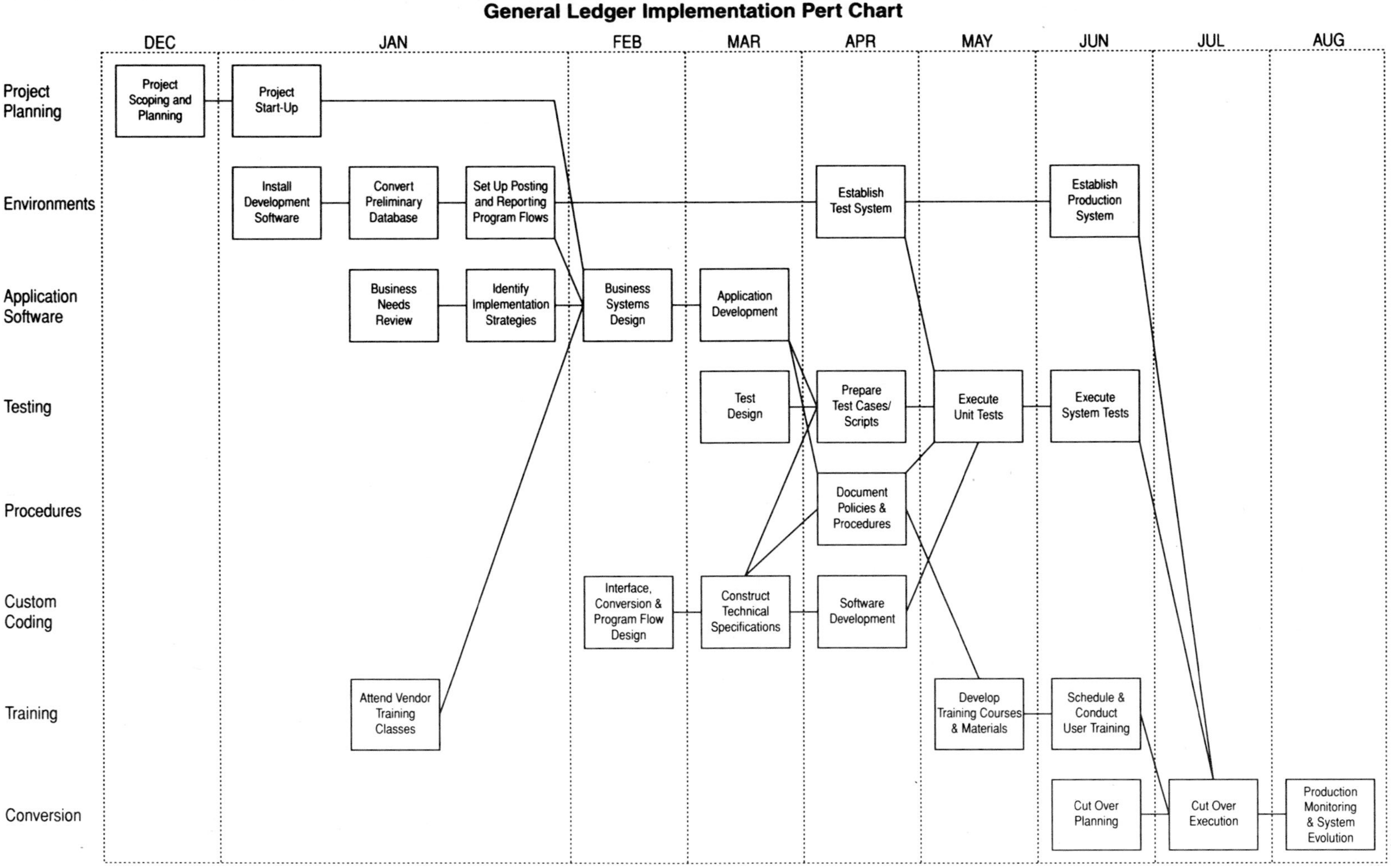

General Ledger Implementation Pert Chart

	DEC	JAN	FEB	MAR	APR	MAY	JUN	JUL	AUG
Project Planning	Project Scoping and Planning	Project Start-Up							
Environments		Install Development Software	Convert Preliminary Database	Set Up Posting and Reporting Program Flows		Establish Production System			
Application Software			Business Needs Review	Identify Implementation Strategies	Business Systems Design	Application Development			
Testing					Test Design	Prepare Test Cases/ Scripts	Execute Unit Tests	Execute System Tests	
Procedures						Document Policies & Procedures			
Custom Coding				Interface, Conversion & Program Flow Design	Construct Technical Specifications	Software Development			
Training			Attend Vendor Training Classes			Develop Training Courses & Materials	Schedule & Conduct User Training		
Conversion							Cut Over Planning	Cut Over Execution	Production Monitoring & System Evolution

1189

reports should be frequently and regularly produced by project team members. These reports communicate progress against plan and outstanding issues.

- *Issue Log.* Issues identified during the project (e.g., on status reports) are captured, reported, and tracked using an issue log. Issues are matters that require decisions to be made by project team members or other organizational representatives. Issues may impact project progress and must be analyzed in a timely manner.

- *Project Meetings.* Frequent and regular project meetings with project team members, and separate meetings with project sponsors, provide a forum for discussing progress to date, outstanding issues, and follow-up items. Responsibilities and deadlines can be assigned to issues and follow-up items during these meetings; in subsequent meetings, reports of progress on these assignments can be discussed. Presentations of status reports and issue logs can be used to guide these meetings. Project meetings are an excellent communication tool and also serve to evaluate progress against plan.

- *Change Requests.* Change requests are the formal documentation of an addition to, deletion from, or modification of a system during its design, development, or implementation. Change requests allow for the proper tracking of changes and their resulting rejection or approval.

- *Project Documentation.* Project documentation organizes the project management information used to manage the project. Project documentation contains the project scope, project organization, detailed project plans, standards and procedures, project deliverables, and all project authorizations and related correspondence.

46-3 RISK MANAGEMENT

Risk in a software integration project is the probability that the project will not finish on time or within budget, or, upon completion, that the system will not function as expected. Other risks include the possibility that the application will not integrate with the hardware or other applications systems, or will not meet technical performance expectations, or will fail to provide the expected benefits. Risk management is the early identification and control of these and other project risks through the use of tools and techniques for identifying project risks, assessing their criticality, and developing and implementing strategies to manage these project risks (see Figure 46-4).

(a) IDENTIFYING RISKS

The risk identification process should begin early in an implementation project and be reviewed and adjusted throughout the project. Early identification allows for a broader choice of options to deal with the risk. Detailed questionnaires of typical project risks are often used to perform the initial and follow-up risk identification. These questionnaires cover topics ranging from project size to project structure and technology.

Examples of risks related to the size of the project include: the number of hours estimated to complete the project, the project time frame (estimated over calendar months or years), the size of the project team, the number of interfacing systems, and the number of entities within the organization involved in the project. The greater the magnitude of any of these project size indicators, the greater the risk of the project.

Figure 46-4 The Risk Management Process.

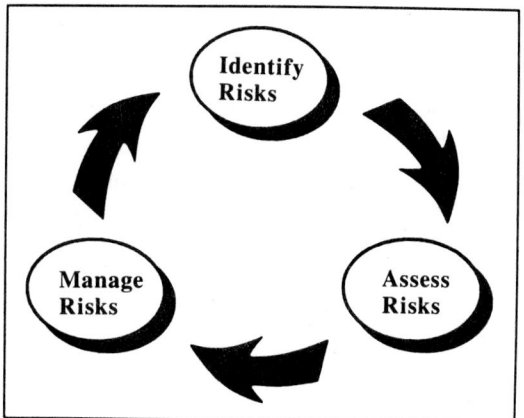

Risks related to project structure include:

- How well defined are the scope, deliverables, benefits, and requirements of the project?
- Does the project team include knowledgeable application, technology, and business area specialists?
- Does the project have an organizational sponsor and the support of management and users?
- How extensively will the system change current work flows, policies, procedures, and organizational structure?

A well-defined project, when staffed with a knowledgeable project team, supported by the organization, and expected to have little impact on current operations, is a much less risky project than any of the alternatives.

Technology risks include those risks related to the need for new hardware or systems software, the number of technologies required by the new system, and the project team's knowledge of the package to be installed. A project that requires no new hardware or software and only minimal additional technologies and that is supported by a knowledgeable project team will be less risky than a project that requires new hardware and systems software, supports multiple technologies, and lacks a knowledgeable project team.

(b) ASSESSING RISKS

Once potential project risks have been identified, these risks must be assessed as to their criticality. Different projects may identify similar risks; however, the magnitude of these risks is project-specific. For example, the risks identified for the following two projects were:

Project I   Implementation of an automated system to replace manual processes.
Project II Implementation of additional automated features to enhance already automated processes.

The types of risks these two projects may encounter include:

- *Timing.* Can the new automated processes accomplish the tasks as fast as or faster than the current processes without additional staffing? Will the new auto mated processes cause bottlenecks? How will the new processes work if the sys tem experiences downtime?
- *User Acceptance.* Can the user community be trained adequately to understand the new system's functionality, the changes in work flow, and the changes in their job descriptions, in order to successfully operate the new system once it i in place?

In this example, Project I is much riskier than Project II. Timing is less of an issue in Project II, because changes to processes would be less drastic than in Project I. Fur ther, contingency plans would more likely be in place and experienced in Project II a a result of the current automation, whereas these would need to be developed as part o the integration of the new system in Project I.

User acceptance would also be less of a risk in Project II because the users are ex perienced and comfortable with automation; thus, changes in their current processes work flows, and job descriptions would most likely be less severe.

Risk identification and assessment should involve all levels of the project team including the project sponsor, project management, and user and technical representa tives. Reconciling these different perceptions of risk will enable all parties to come to the same understanding of the risks of the project. With this basis, these project repre sentatives can then reduce risk by revising the assumptions on which the project i based, or accept risk by agreeing that the result is in line with the organization's goals

(c) MANAGING RISKS

Although most of the recommended approaches to risk management focus on specific aspects of the project (e.g., size, structure, or technology), there are some genera strategies to manage a project's overall risk, as follows:

- Understand and document expectations and what will be done during the project
- Assign appropriately trained staffed to the project, including industry, applica tion, and technology specialists.
- Partition the work into manageable segments.
- Reduce the dependency of the project on other development efforts.
- Involve users in the project.
- Prepare the organization for changes that will occur as the result of the system' implementation.

Specific risk management strategies relate to the specific risks identified. For exam ple, risks associated with a lengthy implementation time frame include the following:

- Team members may leave the project and other personnel inexperienced in the specifics of the project may be assigned to replace them.

- Team members' motivation and sense of urgency are hard to maintain on a long project, and a potential result may be lower levels of productivity.
- A change in the organization's business could cause a change in user requirements.
- A change in the organization's executive levels could lead to revised priorities.

Strategies for managing these risks include:

- Partition work into subprojects that build on one another and show results frequently.
- Identify clear milestones and deliverables throughout the project.
- Recognize individual needs of team members and provide work variety accordingly.
- Use application development tools (e.g., Computer-Aided Software Engineering (CASE) tools) to enhance productivity, thereby reducing the time needed to complete specific tasks. Note that this strategy may mean introducing new technology, which may increase risk in that area.
- Reduce project scope to reduce the amount of work to be done, which in turn will reduce the overall project time frame.

When developing strategies to manage risk, examine the relationships and dependencies among risk factors. In some cases, a strategy to reduce risk in one area actually increases risk in another. For example, a decision to reduce the risk of a lengthy project by increasing team size may increase the risk of ineffective team coordination and communication.

46-4 CHANGE MANAGEMENT

Change management in a software integration project is a technique that targets the human factor affected by the project. A software application project may be successfully integrated, but if the new system and surrounding changes to work flows, policies, and procedures are not accepted by the users, the entire project could fail.

In one example, patient billing software was successfully integrated into a multiphysician clinic. Less than three months later, piles of patient charges had yet to be entered and several hundred thousand dollars' worth of insurance claims remained unbilled. Upon closer investigation, it was discovered that the office manager was threatened by the new system and prevented the billing department from completing its work by prioritizing other tasks over system tasks.

The human factor is one of the most powerful determinants of the success or failure of any new system. An application system that exceeds all user expectations might sit idly on a desk if the users do not want to use it, do not know how to use it, are frightened of changing their ways, or are worried that their jobs might be threatened. Before bringing in a new application, the organization must try to determine the attitudes and responses of the people who will actually use the application. If the organization suspects these attitudes are negative, then the organization must determine how to change them.

(a) IDENTIFYING RESISTANCE

A person's tendency to resist change is the result of many factors. Some personalities are more apt to accept and even look forward to change; others prefer stability and constancy. Certain personalities are sure change will mean a loss of status, power, or even their jobs; others expect to move ahead with the change. It is often difficult to determine people's true feelings, because these feelings are securely masked or even unknown.

Organizational culture may breed innovation or encourage routine. An organization that is tradition-bound and committed to time-tested systems and procedures will probably be less likely to accept new systems and new procedures than an organization with a more flexible attitude.

Resistance to change is inevitable. Thus, the success of a project hinges on the ability of management to understand change from the perspective of the user. Once the true reason for resistance is identified, management can begin to implement strategies to reduce the cause. Most importantly, once the users can feel secure that the project will have a positive effect on their role in the organization, then and only then will they begin to accept the change.

(b) MANAGING CHANGE

Managing change begins with an understanding of the concerns of the organization, as illustrated in Figure 46-5. Once these concerns are identified, the following basic strategies can be employed to reduce resistance:

- *User Involvement.* Involving the people who will actually use the application in the project will provide them with a better understanding of the change and, thus, will help in "demystifying" the change. Making these users responsible for aspects of the project, such as planning and design, will encourage acceptance of the change because they will be accepting their own decisions. Further, involved users will serve as role models, encouraging other peer users to understand and accept the change.

  Many projects that are less than successful have been conducted with minimal user involvement. When turned over to the users, these projects have been saddled with problems such as: a poor understanding of the system design; a system design that did not meet user requirements or expectations; an inability of the users to quickly take over ownership of the system, resulting in a dependence on the system designers; or an inability of the users to understand the system and use it properly.

- *Communication.* Often, the fear of change is the fear of the unknown, and, too frequently, the unknown becomes false information or rumors. Disseminating true information as soon as possible to all employees affected by the change will demystify the change and reduce rumors. One technique to communicate change is holding regular forums to provide information to and elicit feedback from employees. Other techniques include circulating newsletters or posters to communicate information, and using contests or social and information events to encourage employee learning and participation.

Figure 46-5   The Change Management Process.

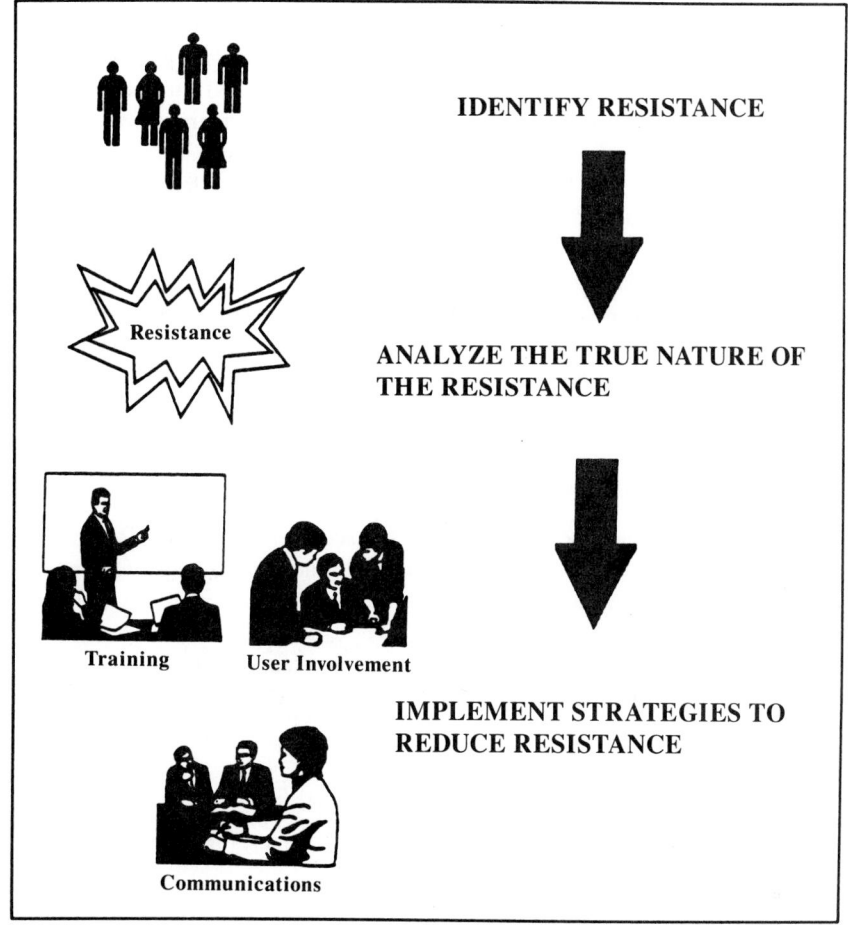

- *Training.* For users to be able to use the new application, they must be trained. Training includes not only classroom training, but also training events, occurring throughout the project, that provide information about the overall project, and training assistance during the initial days or months of using the new system. Follow-up classroom training, once the system is operational, will enforce current understanding while providing retraining on functionality not absorbed in the initial session. Training content should include not only application functionality but also policies, procedures, and work flows.

- *Timing.* Resistance to change cannot be conquered overnight. Change that occurs over time will have a better chance of overcoming resistance than immediate change. Involving users early, maintaining effective communication throughout the project, and continuously "training" users on the change will allow users to slowly but more comfortably overcome their resistance.

46-5 QUALITY MANAGEMENT

Quality management is the use of tools and techniques to build quality into a project. Through the use of quality management techniques, projects should better meet expectations, requirements, budget estimates, and planned time frames.

Quality assurance is the set of actions performed to bring about quality in a project. Quality control checks for, and corrects, exceptions in completed work products or projects. The difference between the two is that quality assurance techniques are preventative measures whereas quality control techniques are after-the-fact quality measures.

It has been proven that preventative measures are much more cost-effective than inspection-based measures. However, it is important to note that quality control can be used to monitor the quality assurance program, indicating how closely the project is meeting expectations and requirements, and in what areas improvements are needed to provide a better quality product.

(a) MANAGING QUALITY

The quality management process is based on building quality strategies into the project, beginning at the start of the project. Each of the quality management strategies illustrated in Figure 46-6 is discussed below:

- *Exceed Expectations.* Every project team member—in fact, the project as a whole—should strive to exceed the expectations of the organization, project

Figure 46-6   Quality Management Strategies.

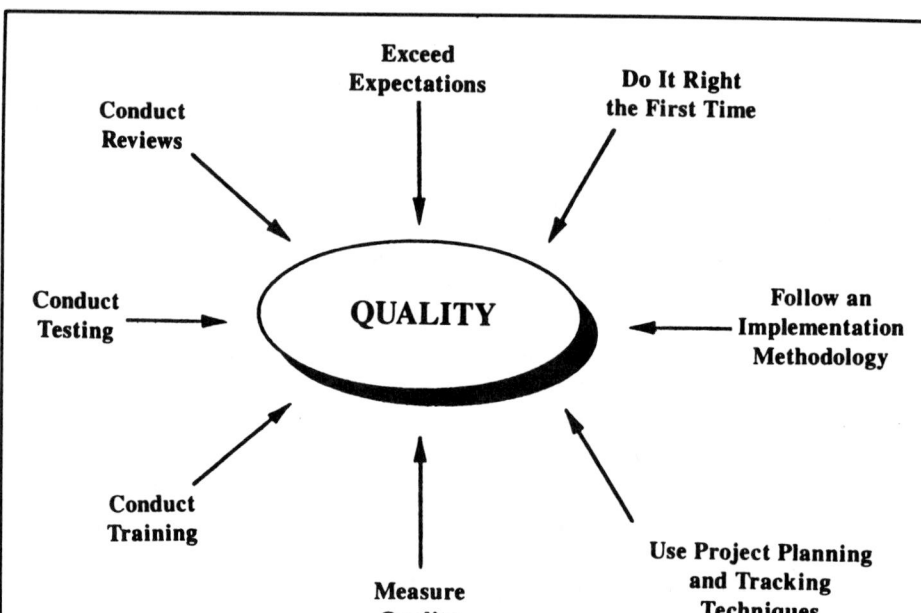

management, and users. Expectations can be exceeded through advanced delivery of quality deliverables and by completing tasks under budget.

- *Do It Right the First Time.* Careful project planning and monitoring, along with knowledgeable and experienced project management, will help ensure that the correct tasks have been identified and that the project team is executing the tasks properly.

- *Follow an Implementation Methodology.* A quality project will, more likely than not, result from following a proven implementation methodology. Project management should be experienced with the methodology, and the methodology should be project-tested and should include steps for building quality into the project.

- *Use Project Planning and Tracking Techniques.* A detailed plan constructed by knowledgeable and experienced project management will clearly define what work needs to be done, how long it will take, who will do it, and when it will be completed. Tracking actual results to the detailed plan will allow for revision of estimates, early identification of bottlenecks and potential problems, and actual experience that can be used in the next planning effort.

- *Measure Quality.* Although many quality indicators are not easily measured, certain indicators, such as project costs, time frames, and results, can be measured against initial cost and time-frame estimates and user requirements, respectively. Quality measurements can also point out weaknesses in the software integration process so that improvements can be made to the implementation methodology prior to initiating the next project.

- *Conduct Training.* Training project team members is essential for a quality project, especially if team members have never before been involved in a software integration project. The types of training needed by project team members include understanding of the project scope; user requirements; implementation methodology; project technology; project plan, including work steps, budgets, and time frames; project tracking and documentation tools; and key deliverables.

- *Conduct Testing.* A formal, rigorous test of the system prior to placing the system into production is essential to the quality of the project for several reasons. Testing new custom programs ensures that the code executes without error and meets all requirements documented in the technical specifications. Unit testing the software modules ensures that each module executes as expected, without error. Integration testing of the entire system ensures that all modules interact with each other as expected and without error. Acceptance testing ensures that the system accomplishes the user requirements in a manner acceptable by the user community.

  All tests should be documented and expected results identified prior to executing the test, thus providing for an objective and formal test. Once the tests are executed, actual results should be documented and compared to expected results, and all inconsistencies should be noted, researched, and resolved. Representatives throughout the organization—including programming, operations, users, and even the software vendor—must be involved with testing. Not only will these representatives assist in the execution and documentation of the tests, but they will be responsible for the research and resolution of any inconsistencies.

- *Conduct Reviews.* The earlier an exception from expected results is identified, the broader the options for handling the exception. Quality review points throughout the project will assist in the identification of any exception. Among the several types of reviews recommended for integration projects are:

  1. *Project Team Review.* Project management reviews work products to ensure consistency across the project, to ensure completeness of individual pieces of the project, and to provide the final, comprehensive review of a deliverable before it goes to the organization for approval.

  2. *Organizational Review.* Organization management and users review the work products to ensure that expectations and requirements are met, to allow for feedback of concerns or suggestions, to communicate project information and status, and to involve responsible executives in the major organizational and operational decisions related to the project.

  Reviews can be executed by reading the deliverable and meeting with appropriate project team members to question points and provide feedback. Reviews can also be executed through the use of formal presentations, where the project team member(s) responsible for the deliverable presents the ideas and conclusions to an audience of reviewers. This type of structured presentation provides immediate feedback and a forum for working through revisions to the deliverable.

  In all cases, reviews should be strategically placed throughout the project to ensure a quality project through early identification of inconsistencies. The need and placement of review points will vary from project to project. For example, identification of a high-risk situation in a project may call for additional reviews to monitor and control the risk. Review points also communicate project information and status to the organization, which aids the change management process.

46-6 INTEGRATION STEPS

This section deals with the specific steps necessary to integrate software. In some cases, certain steps may not apply. For example, one integration step pertains to hardware/software installation. If in fact the software to be integrated will operate on hardware already installed and operational in the organization, the step of hardware installation is not applicable to this particular integration project. Thus, when beginning an integration project, all integration steps should be reviewed and elaborated as to their specific role in the project under consideration.

(a) PROJECT ORGANIZATION

Project organization is a critical aspect of the project planning process. Before the project can get underway, it is necessary to identify the major project roles and the responsibilities that accompany those roles. Individuals must then be selected to fill the roles, based on their skills and experience in solving similar problems.

The organization for a specific project depends on the nature of the project: the software package being installed, the particular project responsibilities of the organization, the vendor, and other project characteristics. However, certain roles are common to every project. The following paragraphs discuss these roles and Figure 46-7 shows how they fit into a sample project organization.

Figure 46-7   Sample Project Organization.

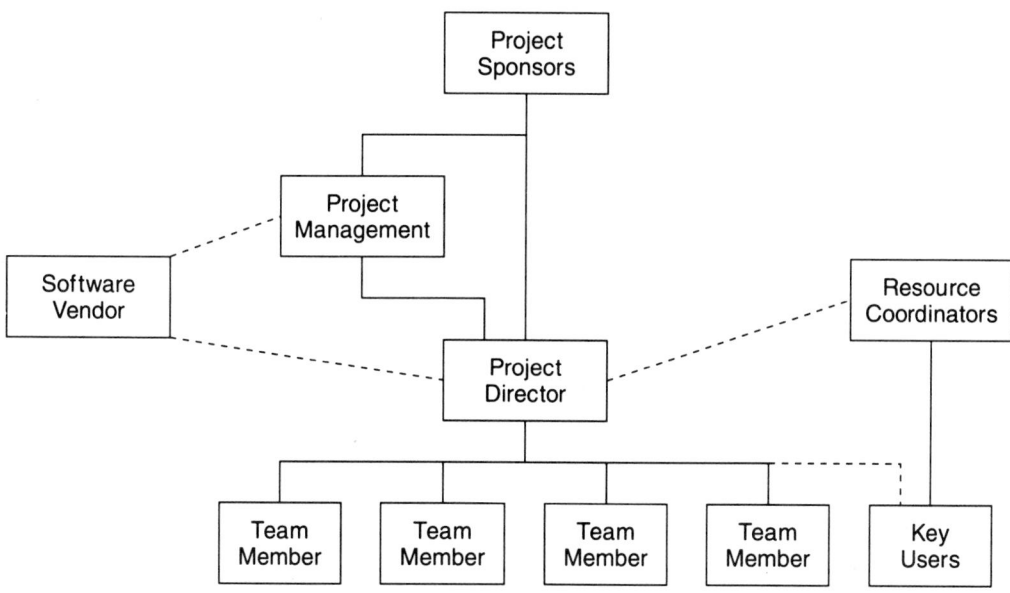

- *Project Sponsors.* Project sponsors have the ultimate authority over and responsibility for the project. The sponsors are executives who have a vested interest in the results of the project, fund the project, resolve conflict over policy or objectives, and provide high-level direction. Project sponsors are also responsible for approving changes to the software package during the integration process, for providing the additional funding required to implement those changes, and for accepting the new system at the end of the project. The project sponsors do not need to have systems development experience or knowledge of information systems, since their role is primarily that of a business decisionmaker for the project.

- *Resource Coordinators.* Hold management level roles in the organization and are in some way, shape, or form affected by the project. Resource coordinators provide support to the project by providing staffing for project tasks and subject matter expertise for the organizational functions for which they are responsible. Resource coordinators themselves may not be members of the project team; their staff may. The resource coordinators must commit resources and take responsibility for their commitment. Resource coordinators in turn should be kept up to date on project status and informed well in advance of the resources needed from their area.

- *Project Managers.* Executives within the organization who have a direct responsibility or stake in the results of the project. Project management is not only responsible for approving the work of the project team throughout the entire project but also ensuring that the information system that results from the project will meet the requirements and be properly integrated into the organization. Other responsibilities include inspecting project deliverables and making the decision regarding final acceptance of the system.

- *Project Director.* Has primary management responsibility for the entire project, including administration, planning and scheduling, issue resolution, and technical leadership. This person works closely with Project Management in addressing the needs of the organization and in coordinating joint implementation efforts within the organization. The Project Director's role is further defined in the *Project Management* step below.

- *Project Team.* Is made up of various individuals with various skill sets which in combination provides the overall talent necessary to successfully integrate the application into the organization. System analysts, designers, programmers, documentation specialists, and trainers all comprise the types of roles of the project team. Project Team members may represent all areas of the organization affected by the integration effort, including user and technical organizations. Although a core project team will support the integration effort from start to finish, other project team members may be brought in (e.g., for system acceptance testing) as specialized talent is needed.

- *Key Users.* May not support the project directly as project team members but are important to involve in the integration project for two reasons. User involvement is essential to ensure that the new application is designed and integrated in a manner that satisfies user requirements and that the transition to the new system is straightforward (because the users have been involved and have a stake in the effort). Key users can supplement the project team on an as-needed basis to assist with the design of the application as well as any decisionmaking regarding functionality. Key users should be kept informed throughout the project as to project status and key decisions and be involved in the project as much as their schedules permit.

- *Software Package Vendor.* The software vendor is primarily responsible for the delivery and installation of the base software package. In addition, the software vendor or an independent consultant may participate in validation and system testing, provide user and operations training, and assist in conversion activities. Software vendors are frequently responsible for customizing the software packages. The exact nature of the vendor's and consultant's responsibilities on an engagement should be clearly defined in a contract. A more comprehensive list of services most often provided by vendors or independent consultants can be found in Figure 46-8.

(b) PROJECT MANAGEMENT

As discussed earlier in this chapter, the objective of project management is to plan and control the integration project from initiation to conclusion with high levels of productivity and quality and low levels of uncertainty. And again, project management begins at the start of a project and continues throughout the project until its completion.

The role of a Project Director is one of a leader and a process manager. As a leader, the Project Director is responsible for managing and communicating a clear vision of the project objectives, and motivating the project team to achieve them. As a process manager, the Project Director must ensure that the right timing, resources, and sequencing of work efforts are applied to create the project deliverables within a given timeframe and budget.

Figure 46-8 A List of Vendor/Consultant Integration Services.

Characteristics of a good Project Director generally include previous system integration and/or company experience, flexibility, sound interpersonal skills, and the ability to say "no"! Project sponsors as well as project team members will be more apt to follow direction from an experienced Project Director; simply put, an experienced Project Director is more credible. Projects, even with carefully and completely documented scopes, are rarely static; thus, a Project Director must be flexible. For example, discovery of additional tasks not originally documented in the scope, identification of required functionality thought not necessary at the start of the project, and the loss of seasoned project team members or the addition of new team members all require the Project Director to incorporate these new tasks and resources into the project plan. A Project Director must have the interpersonal skills necessary to lead and motivate the project team, manage the project sponsorship relationship, create a highly productive and synergistic project environment, and be able to say "no" to additions not originally planned for if the cost of these additions outweigh their expected benefits.

Project management activities can be grouped into six major processes as depicted in Figure 46-9.

- *Structuring the Project.* The focus of this project management process is to document the objectives of the project, secure project sponsorship, define the project approach, and estimate the project in terms of effort, duration, and cost. These tasks are conducted initially at the start of the project but are also revisited throughout the project as the project evolves and changes.

- *Planning the Project.* Tasks in the planning process include developing a detailed work plan including a budget and resource assignments; defining a plan

Figure 46-9   Project Management Processes.

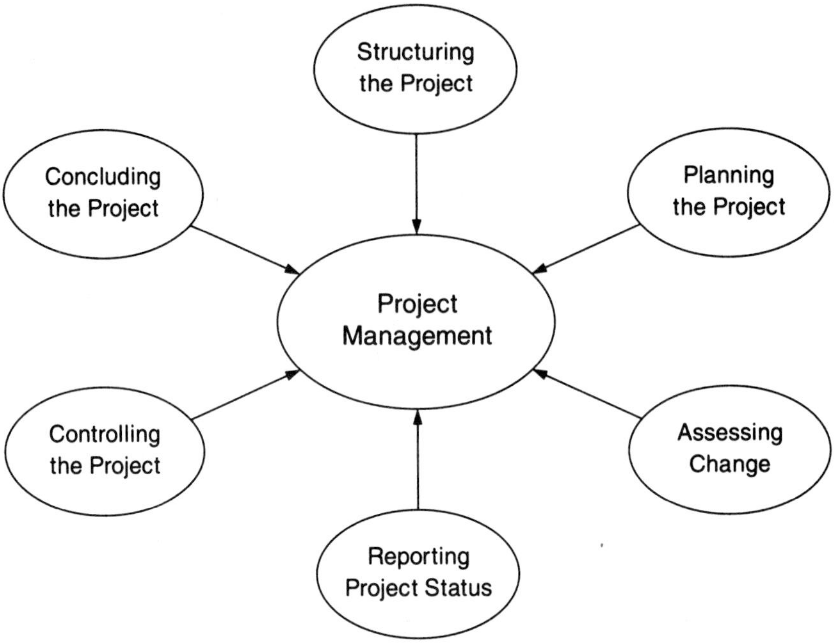

to manage risk, quality, issues, and scope; and gaining approval from project sponsors and executive management on the project plans. Again, these tasks are conducted initially at the start of the project but are also revisited throughout the project as the project evolves and changes.

- *Assessing Change.* In the context of project management, change management has two important meanings:

  1. A technique that targets the human factors affected by the project, and

  2. A mechanism through which project changes can be requested, tracked, investigated, and rejected or approved.

  It is the second meaning that is the focus of this project management process. This project management process occurs throughout the project.

- *Reporting Project Status.* These reports identify the status of a project or a part of a project at a certain point in time. Status reports should be frequently (e.g., weekly) communicated to project management, project sponsors, the user community, and other interested parties. This project management process occurs on a regular basis throughout the project.

- *Controlling the Project.* During the execution of the project, it is the responsibility of the Project Director to compare actual progress to planned progress, evaluate the results of this comparison to determine project status, and recommend or take appropriate actions based on the results of the evaluation. This process occurs on a regular basis throughout the project.

- *Concluding the Project.* This process normally occurs in the final stage of a project. It takes place once project management and sponsorship have agreed that the project has satisfied its completion criteria as defined at the start of the project. However, this process may be invoked for a project which has yet to satisfy its completion criteria (i.e., a project that the organization has decided to stop midway through the project, for whatever reason). In either case, concluding the project is the process by which the project is formally ended and the project history and its resources evaluated.

(c) PROJECT PLANNING

Project planning is one of the first steps of any integration project. Tasks included in project planning are: documenting the scope of the effort, assessing project risks, evaluating change management challenges, identifying a quality management program, and constructing a detailed work plan. Each of these deliverables were discussed in earlier sections of this chapter.

(d) PROJECT START-UP

Tasks in the project start-up step include: identifying the project team members who will satisfy the resource requirements identified in the plan; establishing the project environment (e.g., desks, telephones, supplies, computer equipment, system access); briefing the project team, user community, and other interested parties on the project goals, approach, and schedule; and establishing the project control system (e.g., documentation standards, issue capture and control mechanisms, time reporting, filing). Often, application and technical training are considered parts of this task. Initial application and technical training are conducted for all project team members (usually by the vendor or independent consultant), to establish an initial basis of understanding regarding the design and functionality of the application to be integrated.

(e) PROJECT MEETINGS

Although at first glance, this step would appear to be more logically associated as a task of another step in the integration project instead of its own step, it is broken out due to the number of hours associated with preparing for, attending, and documenting project meetings. The project meetings covered under this step include:

- *Project Team Meetings.* Conducted by the Project Director on a frequent basis (usually weekly), these meetings facilitate communication regarding progress to date on assigned tasks, outstanding issues, and follow-up items. Assignments and deadlines are often distributed during these meetings as well as responsibility for follow-up on issues and other items. In subsequent meetings, reports of progress on the assignments can be discussed. Project meetings are an excellent communication tool and also serve to evaluate progress against plan.

- *Project Management Meetings.* Conducted by the Project Director, these meetings can occur less frequently than team meetings. They serve to keep project management up to date on the project status and major project issues. As project management is comprised of executives with a stake in the project, these meetings serve as a communication tool for project activities and as a forum to outline strategies and action steps to resolve major project issues like resource shortfalls, critical design issues, and application/technical direction. At these meetings, project management in turn serves in a support role to the Project Director while addressing project approach and execution issues.

- *Senior Executive Meetings.* Conducted on a more infrequent basis or on an as-needed basis, these meetings serve as a communication tool for appropriate senior executives in the organization. The first Senior Executive Meeting is usually conducted once the project scope and plan are finalized to communicate and gain agreement on the overall project objectives, scope, approach, schedule, and budget. Subsequent meetings focus on project status or on recommendations resulting in major changes to the original project objectives, scope, approach, schedule, or budget. These meetings are conducted by the Project Director or a member of the project management team.

- *Resource Coordinator Meetings.* As noted previously, resource coordinators are organizational representatives affected by the integration project but do not participate directly on the project team. Resource coordinators usually support the project team in one of two ways: by providing additional resources to assist in accomplishing project tasks, and/or by supplementing project team knowledge with their expertise of their organizational function. Usually the Project Director works closely with resource coordinators, confirming resource availability and commitment and securing resource coordinator review and approval of project deliverables.

- *User Meetings.* Users who are not part of the project team must be kept up to date regarding the project. This communication begins at the start of the project often via a formal meeting at which the project objectives, approach, and schedule are presented. Throughout the project, user involvement is critical not only in designing and integrating an application that meets their needs, but also in facilitating the change process so that once the application is available for everyday use, the users feel comfortable and confident with the new application. Involving the users can take many forms: design interviews, deliverable reviews, update meetings, and even special programs such as newsletters, poster campaigns, and informal social outings.

- *Organizational Meetings.* Any major integration project will be of interest to the organization as a whole. Communication via a formal meeting to organizational representatives (or the entire organization) will provide the organization with real information regarding the project rather than allowing informal communication, which could misstate elements of the project, to satisfy curiosity. At the very least, an organizational meeting at the start of the project will present project objectives, approach, schedule, and team members, and a second meeting prior to going live on the application will confirm the objectives, expected results, and final timetables of the integration project. These sessions should encourage questions from the audience so that, to the extent possible, all unanswered questions and concerns regarding the project are satisfied.

(f) BUSINESS NEEDS REVIEW

The results of the Business Needs Review step form the foundation for the new application. It is critical to the success of the integration project to review the business requirements to confirm or redefine the application needs. To accomplish this, key members of the project team gather and finalize data about the information requirements of the business areas with appropriate business managers and staff. As the result of these interviews, project team members document, at a high level, current business inputs and outputs, processes, manual workflows, and controls. These interviews will also provide the project team with the necessary information to develop high-level information models. Additionally, high-level specifications for key interfaces as well as data, operational, and technical requirements will be reviewed. Lastly, a current systems reports and forms binder is constructed as part of this step.

The deliverables of this step include a requirements document and documentation of the current processes. Figure 46-10 provides an example of documentation for one of the current system processes: a high-level interface chart.

(g) HARDWARE/SOFTWARE INSTALLATION

At the very least, a software integration project requires that the software to be integrated must be installed on the organization's information systems. It is often the case, however, that new hardware and/or system software (i.e., software necessary to operate the hardware and application software together) is required and must be installed as well. This step of the project represents these installations as well as testing of the installation to ensure that the new software and hardware are operational. Information systems representatives usually participate in the hardware and software installation, but information systems and user representatives both should participate in the execution of the installation test scripts. Testing the installation not only helps ensure a proper and complete installation of the software and hardware but also provides additional training for information systems personnel and the users regarding application functionality as well as system construction and operation.

Hardware and software vendors usually provide additional assistance during this step of the integration project. Vendors may provide on-site assistance with the installation as well as supply and help execute test scripts to ensure a complete installation. Alternatively, instead of providing on-site assistance, software vendors may provide a tape with instructions for loading the software and executing test scripts. Installation support is also available via a "1-800" phone number which accesses the vendor's help desks. It is important to understand exactly what type of installation assistance will be provided by the vendor's contract terms prior to signing the contract for the purchase/lease of hardware and software. Prior to executing the contract, compare the installation services offered with the capabilities and comfort of your own information systems staff and construct an installation support agreement that is satisfactory to all parties.

Additional software and hardware may need to be installed in order to allow user access from their desks. This is often referred to as remote hardware installation and includes the installation of the wiring, hubs, emulation and/or network software, desktop terminals/personal computers, printers, and so on that are needed for users to access the new software and operate the application from their desks in the business unit.

Figure 46-10   Interface Chart.

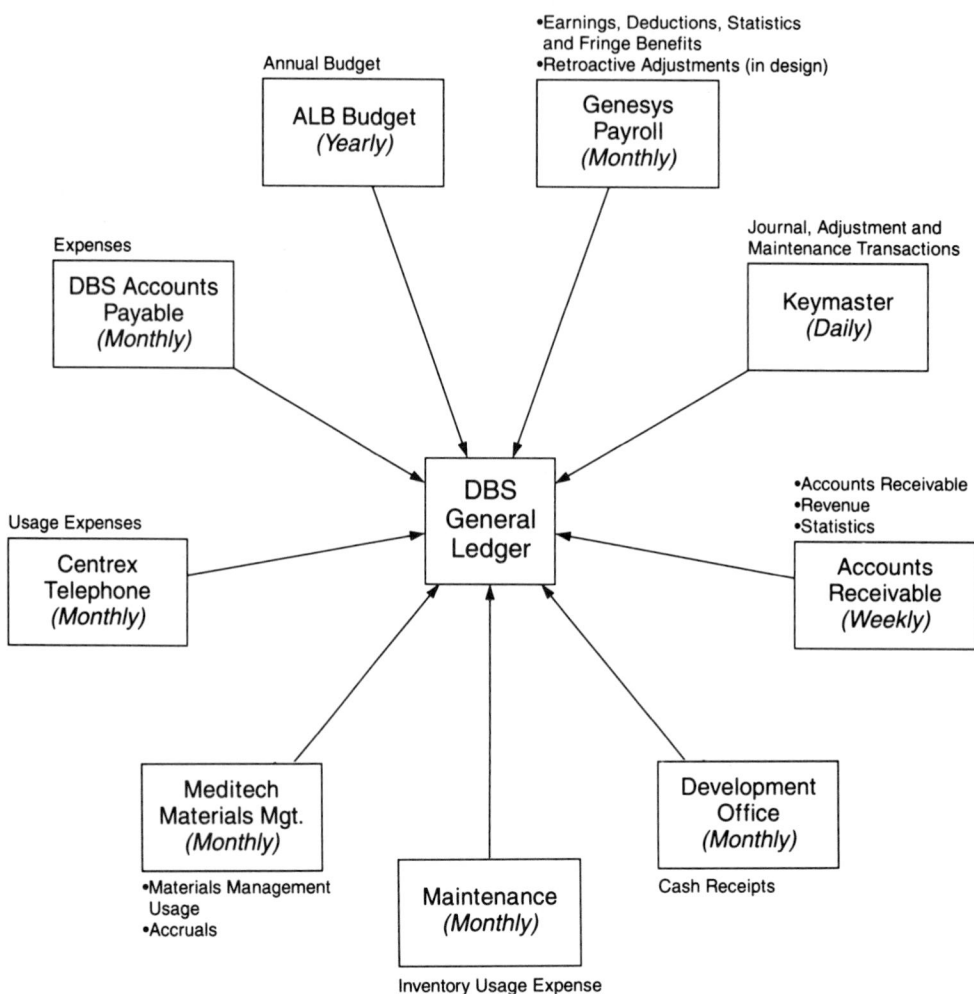

General Ledger Input Interfaces

(h) BUSINESS SYSTEMS DESIGN

In this step, the application is designed from the end user's perspective. Project team analysts design application parameters, tables, and files as well as the policies and procedures necessary to support the business. Reports and forms for each module of the application are also designed.

At this point in the project, project team members should have a fairly good understanding of the new system functionality based on the vendor training provided in the *Project Start-Up* step. Matching the new application's functionality to the requirements identified in the *Business Needs Review* step will often highlight deficiencies in functionality that must be addressed. Decisions as to how to handle these gaps must be made. Several alternatives for handling gaps are available and are discussed below.

- *Customize the Application.* This alternative requires design, implementation, and testing of application customizations that will overcome gaps in required application functionality. In many cases, the vendor will code these customizations based on a design (or functional specification) provided by the organization. Further, if known at the start of the project, customizations can be included in the vendor contract. However, it should be noted that customizations increase the complexity and length of the project, usually significantly. Additionally, customizations can invalidate the software warranty and make the application of upgrades extremely difficult. Therefore, any customizations should be carefully reviewed and every attempt made to avoid customizations for this very reason.

- *Create a Work-Around.* Instead of specifying a customization to the application, this alternative suggests the development of a process in or around the application that will handle the requirement. In many cases, the cost of customizing the application to meet the requirement far outweighs the benefit of the functionality. In this situation, other application functionality or manual processes should be considered for handling the requirement.

- *Reject the Requirement.* In many cases the requirement driving the gap in functionality is a desire but not critical to the application's success in solving the business need. In these cases, it is recommended to integrate the application as is, operate the application at least six months, and then determine if the functionality is required. If the functionality is determined necessary, then the organization can begin the process of specifying the functionality design and contracting with the vendor to customize the application to include the functionality.

No matter which alternative is determined to be the most optimal for handling each gap in functionality, the results of this task must be incorporated into the project work plan.

Another task included in this step is process assessment and redesign. In the past, organizations have integrated new applications to solve their business needs with little or no attention paid to the processes existing before and after the integration of the new application. This particular task suggests that the current business processes should be reviewed and non-value or redundant processes eliminated. Then, based on the functionality of the new application, the current processes should be redesigned to take advantage of the new application. The deliverable for this particular step is a design of new workflows which maximizes the benefits of the new application.

Last, strategies for future steps in the integration project are defined at a high level. Strategy statements for data conversion, testing, training, and operations are developed as part of this step. For example, a strategy statement for data conversion would include a high-level discussion of the following aspects of conversion: the scope and pace of the effort; data conversion techniques; the approach for data reconciliation, maintenance, and synchronization; the plan for data security; and a contingency strategy for production cut-over.

Deliverables for this step include:

- A brief description of what data will be loaded in the parameters, tables, and files of the new application; where the data will come from; resource requirements; and timeframe necessary to complete the data loading.

- An outline of the procedure manuals proposed for the project, a design of the structure of these manuals, identification of the resource requirements, and the timeframe necessary to complete the documentation effort.
- A design of new reports and forms required by the new application.
- A gap analysis report with recommendations of how functionality gaps will be handled by the project.
- A design of the processes surrounding the new application.
- High level strategy statements for key steps of the integration project: data conversion, testing, training, operations, etc. Figure 46-11 provides an example of one such strategy statement.

(i) INTERFACE AND PROGRAM FLOW DESIGN

This step defines a specific approach for developing automated interfaces to and/or from the new application. Also, as part of this step, technical design of program flows and the nightly batch processing are completed, if necessary. Each will be discussed separately.

When investigating which interfaces might be appropriate for the new application, apply the following tests:

- If the new application replaces a previously automated system, any established automated interfaces to/from the to-be-replaced application are prime candidates for replacement (and probably should be replaced).
- If data needed for input into the new application is available from a report generated by an automated system, an interface is quite feasible from the source system.
- If data needed for input into the new application is available on another automated system, an automated interface should be evaluated.
- If data which is expected to be in the new system is needed in a downstream system, an automated interface from the new application to the downstream system should be investigated.

Many system integration projects limit the number of interfaces to be implemented to only those that replace a previously automated interface. This is done for several reasons, but primarily to limit the scope of the project and by doing so, better ensure project success (by meeting aggressive deadlines and conservative budget estimates). Interfaces, because they usually result in custom coding, add significant time and resource needs to the integration project for design, coding, testing, and so on. Further, interfaces identified but not implemented during the initial integration of the application can always be implemented once the application is up and running.

Software vendors can assist with coding the side of the interface that will directly interact with their application, usually for a price. Thus, custom interface needs should be identified prior to contracting with the software vendor and included in the contract at an agreeable price. On the other hand, the organization is usually responsible for coding the side of the interface that directly interacts with a source or destination system (again the vendors of these systems can assist in designing, coding, and

Figure 46-11 Sample Training Strategy.

Two types of general ledger training efforts will be undertaken during this project: 1) training the implementation team and 2) training end users.

The implementation team consists of those users who will assist in the definition of how the upgraded software will be implemented for the organization and in the execution of this design. Depending on their role in the implementation, implementation team members will attend vendor training courses on the general ledger and/or both report writers. We will also provide internal training to project team members who did not attend the vendor sessions. We envision that this internal training will occur at various times during the implementation on an as needed basis.

End user training will be scheduled for late June/early July as we hope to time the training of users with their actual use of the system for the July close. At this point in the project we think that an off-site training session would be beneficial for end users for several reasons:

- Motivation—Getting away from the office for a day and spending the day in a nice training facility will have a motivational impact to learn the new features and functionality and focus on how to apply these features to their own environment.

- Positive PR for the upgrade—A day away from the office in a nice facility with professional trainers will definitely boost the goodwill towards the system.

- Focus—A day away from the office will allow the end users to focus entirely on the subject matter at hand: learning the new general ledger.

- Training Expertise—Professional trainers will set scripts and exercises that will not only cover the necessary material completely but will reinforce how to use the general ledger through exercises and question and answer periods.

Since we have developed internal training classes, we will need to evaluate whether or not the off-site training will be handled by the organization at its training center or by the vendor at their training location.

In either case, we envision end user training to consist of a one day session which will cover the following topics: basic journal processing, special journal processing, maintenance and error correction. We plan to include organization specific information into the training session, like how to number journal batches, how to use source code, how to code intercompany journals, etc.

We also plan to develop reporting and budget training courses for use initially to train implementation team members. These courses would be offered to a subset of end users; those users who will be actively involved with report writing and/or budgeting for the department.

Once live on the upgraded general ledger, each operating area will be responsible for training new employees or retraining current employees on the use of the general ledger.

testing the interface for a price). Note that interface requirements include the reports necessary to balance and reconcile the interfaces. These reports contain information such as records read and records written and dollar (or other totals) balancing. Interface reports are reconciled with source and destination system reports. These source and destination system reports should be identified prior to determining the design and format of the interface reports so that similar levels of detail can be generated on the interface reports to allow for easier balancing/reconciling.

As part of designing the interfaces, their relationship to how the application operates must also be determined. For example, if a daily interface from an accounts receivable package to a new general ledger application is proposed, and if the accounts receivable transactions are posted in the general ledger application once received, a potential program flow scenario might be to execute the interface (which loads the transactions into the general ledger) then execute the general ledger posting program. Each interface must be reviewed individually as to where it fits in relation to the new application's program flows, resulting in a new flow design.

Further, applications may provide for many different program scenarios which also must be designed in this step. For example, suppose that the expectations for the new general ledger application include nightly posting (five days per week), weekly reporting, and on the last working day of the month, posting of all allocations of overhead and monthly interfaces and the generation of the monthly reports. Thus, the program flow on Monday through Thursday (except at the end of the month) would include posting but would not include reporting, allocations, or interfaces. The program flow on Fridays (except at the end of the month) would include posting and weekly reporting but not allocations, interfaces, or monthly reporting. Saturday and Sunday cycles would not include posting, reporting, allocations, or interfaces. On the last day of the month, all monthly cycles would be executed (including posting of the allocations and interfaces). A monthly schedule for this example is illustrated in Figure 46-12. It

Figure 46-12 A Sample Monthly Processing Schedule.

\						\
\			**June**			\
SUNDAY	MONDAY	TUESDAY	WEDNESDAY	THURSDAY	FRIDAY	SATURDAY
			1	2	3	4
			Posting	Posting	Posting, Weekly Reporting	
5	6	7	8	9	10	11
	Posting	Posting	Posting	Posting	Posting, Weekly Reporting	
12	13	14	15	16	17	18
	Posting	Posting	Posting	Posting	Posting, Weekly Reporting	
19	20	21	22	23	24	25
	Posting	Posting	Posting	Posting	Posting, Weekly Reporting	
26	27	28	29	30		
	Posting	Posting	Posting	Allocations Overhead Posting Monthly Reports		

is easy to see that determining daily, weekly, monthly, etc., program flows is not straightforward and must be carefully planned. Also allow for a process to insert ad hoc programs into an established program flow as needed (for example, if the weekly reporting programs need to be executed midweek).

The deliverables for this step of the integration project include functional specifications for all automated interfaces, interface reports, and program flows.

(j) DATA CONVERSION DESIGN

This step defines a specific approach for converting necessary data from each to-be-replaced source system to the appropriate destination database. Two types of approaches are most often used in data conversions:

- Automated—This approach transfers data automatically from the source system to the new application's database(s) while providing an audit trail of the process.
- Manual—This approach is used when an automated approach is not practical and consists of manual procedures for loading the application database(s).

Most data conversions consist of both of these approaches. An automated approach is ideal for converting a source database that is very similar to a destination database. For example, most general ledgers store account balances. If a general ledger is being replaced and the chart of accounts for the most part remains the same, an automated program to convert the chart of accounts and account balances to the new application may be beneficial. When deciding on a data conversion approach, factors such as the amount of time it would take to manually convert a database versus the amount of time it would take to design, code, and test an automated conversion program must be weighed. Factors that can complicate automated conversions include combining data from multiple sources where data records are not a one-to-one match, where the data cannot be sorted in the same manner, or where data elements were used inconsistently between and within each system.

Manual conversions are usually recommended for converting data off of a manual system; for converting data from a source database that differs significantly from the destination database; for source databases that require a maximum of scouring to produce data that is accurate, complete, and timely; or for new applications where automated conversions are not recommended. One way to convert manually is to develop an input sheet that closely resembles the input screen of the new application. Each input sheet is then completed with the data to be input and then reviewed for completeness and accuracy. Data conversion, then, is accomplished by manually inputting the data off of the input sheet directly into the new system. (Data input can be accomplished by temporary help if available resources are limited.) Often, the manual conversion will be partially automated by creating the data input sheets automatically from the source system, including information available from the source system. The data automatically loaded on these sheets from the source system can then be reviewed and updated and new data items, not available on the source system, can be added.

Prior to conversion, using either approach, it is recommended that the organization make a concentrated effort to review, correct, or delete the information to be converted so that the database which is ultimately converted is accurate, complete, and timely. A software integration project is a perfect opportunity to clean up current information and establish an accurate, complete, and timely database on the new system.

A third conversion option exists: not to convert. Some situations warrant the completion of open transactions on the current system while executing all new transactions on the new system. For example, it might be more cost beneficial to complete the open purchase orders on the current accounts payable system rather than converting these to the new system. Reasons for doing this include the complexity of converting one system's transaction records to another system's format; many times this conversion is not straightforward. Also, the new system numbering scheme usually differs from that of the old system, yet all vendor correspondence regarding the old system's purchase order will include the old system's purchase order number. This approach, however, has its costs, including maintaining the old system and staff to operate it, sorting invoices and check requests between old system transactions and new system transactions, and responding to inquiries, some regarding old system transactions and some regarding new system transactions. At some point, it becomes more cost beneficial to convert the remaining transactions off of the old system and phase out the old system. Usually this conversion can be accomplished manually due to the small number of transactions remaining on the old system.

The deliverables of this step of the integration project include:

- An overall design document which discusses the approaches, strategies, resource requirements, timing, and contingency plans to be used to establish the databases in the new application system.

- A functional specification for each automated data conversion being considered, including the approach, strategy, and overall discussion of the particular data conversion; mapping of the source system file layout to the new application system file layout; timing considerations; resource requirements; security needs; reconciliation processes; contingency plans; and documentation strategy to satisfy internal/external audit requirements. This functional specification will be used by programmers to develop the conversion programs.

- A functional specification for each automated download being considered. Again, these automated downloads would consist of source system data formatted onto an input document representing the input screen of the new application. Included in this specification are the approach, strategy, and overall discussion of the file download; mapping of source system data records to positions on the input document; plans for reviewing, confirming, and completing the input documents; resource requirements; prioritization schemes; documentation control processes; contingency plans; and documentation strategy to satisfy internal/external audit requirements. This function specification will be used by programmers to develop the programs to create the input sheets.

(k) TEST DESIGN

During this step, high-level plans for unit, integration, and acceptance testing of the application software components are developed. Test plans defined the approach, controls, objectives, conditions, and test scripts for conducting software testing. The three primary objectives of testing are:

- Prove that the application system addresses the business problem and satisfies the user's requirements.
- Uncover application system defects.
- Help ensure quality throughout the project.

Several types of tests are planned for in this step and include:

- *Unit Tests.* The most basic level of testing to verify that the software code works according to its specifications and to validate program logic. Unit tests are independent tests of application functionality and include tests of the baseline software, interfaces, conversion programs, and any other customizations. The objective of these tests is to ensure that each function of the application independently operates as expected. Typically, the test team is responsible for executing unit tests.

- *Integration Tests.* The testing of combinations of individually unit-tested pieces of code as they are united into a complete unit, i.e., testing of the application as a whole. Whereas unit testing ensures that each application function can operate independently, integration testing ensures that all functions, interacting together in a simulated live environment, operate as expected. Often the information systems staff that will be responsible for the application once it is in production, will participate to simulate the true live environment. The test team, in this test, usually functions as the user would in the live environment.

- *System Tests.* Many types of tests can be conducted as part of system tests including: usability tests, final requirements tests, volume and stress tests, performance tests, security and control tests, recovery tests, documentation and procedures tests, and multi-site tests. Although all of these tests are important, a focus on volume, stress, and performance tests is critical to ensure that the application will function as expected under typical operating conditions.

- *Acceptance Tests.* Demonstrates that the application meets the original business objectives and satisfies user and information systems requirements. If the user is not involved in the execution of unit and/or integration tests, acceptance testing is a must. Acceptance tests are executed by the user so that the user can confirm (and feel comfortable) that the application will function as expected under normal operating conditions. Usually a subset of the integrated tests are used in the acceptance test with the focus on simulating a typical day, month-end, and year-end situation. At the end of these tests, users often sign-off on the results of the tests and their acceptance of the application. It is important to note that some training of the user must take place prior to their involvement in acceptance testing so that they know how to conduct the tests. Even with training, users participating in the acceptance test may need assistance executing the tests. It is also recommended that user application training occur prior to acceptance testing so that the user, with a minimum amount of training on how to conduct acceptance tests, is able to independently execute the tests.

- *Bench Tests.* Another type of test conducted as part of an integration project and is related to custom code development. Bench testing is the first of all tests conducted and is performed by the programmer to ensure that the custom code developed meets the requirements identified in the functional and technical specifications. Custom code is developed for interfaces and conversion programs, for example, and thus bench testing is an integral part of the development of that code. Bench testing will be discussed in more detail in the *Software Development* section of this chapter.

A test plan or design consists of several components: an overall test strategy; the test control system; and test objectives, conditions, and scripts. Each are discussed below:

- *Test Strategy.* Discusses the overall plan for accomplishing testing during the integration project. A test strategy identifies which tests will be conducted, by whom, and in what time frames. The strategy also defines the scope and approach for each of the tests to be executed. Other elements of the test strategy include specifications for the test environment (i.e., a controlled copy of the application that is only used for testing); requirements for security; the design of the initial database (some data may need to be loaded prior to conducting the first tests); backup and recovery considerations; documentation needs (including requirements necessary to satisfy internal/external auditors); and resource and responsibility assignments.

- *Test Control System.* The system developed to document and control when tests will be executed and by whom, what tests are complete, what tests have yet to be executed, and what tests did not complete as expected and require follow-up. Typical output of a test control system is a schedule of tests by day and responsibility, a log of all tests and their status, and a log of all tests needing follow-up (usually called an issues log). The issues log indicates the specific test that did not execute as expected, who was responsible for executing the test, who is responsible for following up and resolving the issue, priority of the issue, current status of the issue, resolution of the issue, and date resolved. The issue log is used to manage incomplete tests and their timely resolution.

- *Test Objectives, Conditions, and Scripts.* Once the test strategy is understood, the detailed tests can be documented. Detailed tests consist of three major elements: objectives, conditions, and scripts as presented in Figure 46-13. Test objectives are the overall statement as to the goal of the test. Test conditions break the objective into testable components. Test scripts document the input, predicted results, and execution conditions of a given test item. Test scripts in total provide tests for each objective and condition. For each test script, specific data is collected and anticipated results are predicted. In other words, test scripts provide the information for the tester of exactly how to test the condition(s) and includes an expected outcome for each of the tests. The expected outcome, during test execution, is compared to the actual outcome to verify that the test executed as expected. If the expected outcome does not match the actual outcome, the test is then logged on the issues log and investigated as to why it performed as such. Note that there is not necessarily a one-for-one relationship between a test script and condition. For example, multiple conditions may be tested by a single script, a single condition may be tested by a single script, or even a single condition may be tested several times in several scripts, scripts which also test other conditions, etc.

Figure 46-13 Sample Test Objective, Conditions, and Script.

Unit Test Script   **Case Number: AP01**

Accounts Payable—Invoice Entry

Test Objective: To unit test the invoice function using all invoice types of the organization.   **Forms/Reports Used:** Vendor Invoice

Test Cycle: 1   **Report(s) Produced:** Transaction Schedule,

Test Schedule Date: 6/4/94   Transaction Log

Condition #	Condition Description	Activities	Expected Results	Verified By	Date	Issue #
1. AP01.01	Complete Match: Invoice total matches P.O. and Receiver.	Process the invoices, using the Invoice Entry Procedure and the invoice(s) marked to be used for this condition.	Invoice is able to be entered in summary due to complete match.	B. Scott	6/4/94	None
1. AP01.03	Incomplete Match: Invoice total does not match P.O. and Receiver but within tolerance.	Process the invoices, using the Invoice Entry Procedure and the invoice(s) marked to be used for this condition.	Invoice is within tolerance and is able to be input in detail.	B. Scott	6/4/94	9
1. AP01.06	Enter an invoice a second time.	Process the invoices, using the Invoice Entry Procedure and the invoice(s) marked to be used for this condition.	System replies "already on file" for duplicate invoice.	B. Scott	6/4/94	None
1. AP01.57	Process a standing order invoice.	Process the invoices, using the Invoice Entry Procedure and the invoice(s) marked to be used for this condition.	Standing order invoice is able to be processed. Adjusted standing order balance correct.	B. Scott	6/4/94	11

(l) TRAINING DESIGN

During this step, detailed training programs for users and information systems support staff are developed. Included in the training material are participant training manuals, training presentation materials, and "hands-on" exercises. Prior to developing the training materials, the types of training classes necessary and their content must be identified. To do this, the training audience and their skill set must be evaluated. Often the vendor provides training and materials; however, vendor training is usually generic and not customized for the organization's needs. Customized training that reflects the system use expected on a day-to-day basis is much more beneficial and easier to understand by the user. It is more difficult to learn a system whose examples reflect a car dealership and translate that use into a manufacturing organization than it is to learn a new system using everyday examples of the transactions currently processed in the manufacturing organization. However, vendor training materials are a great basis for building training programs customized for the organization.

Identifying who will conduct the training is another task covered by this step in the integration project. Again, the vendor usually is able to supply a trainer for a cost (vendor training can be contracted for when the software is purchased/leased). However, it is important to develop trainers internally not only to provide ongoing training to new users or update classes for current users, but also to eliminate the dependency and cost of resorting to vendor training once the system is operational.

A train-the-trainer program can be used to train a number of employees to become trainers on the software functionality. A train-the-trainer program is one where a knowledgeable project team member or vendor representative trains a group of users, identified as potential trainers, on how to conduct training classes on software functionality. These new trainers then team teach with the vendor or project team trainer until they feel comfortable taking on the class themselves. The project team trainer or vendor then reviews and supports the trainers until the new trainers are experienced enough to handle classes on their own. Formal surveys of attendees can also diagnose trainer issues as well as content, format, and other issues and are recommended for all training classes.

Other tasks included in this step are identifying responsibility for and scheduling of the training sessions, preparing the appropriate hardware and facilities in which to conduct the training, identifying the database requirements necessary for execution of the training courses, and preparing the system database so that training exercises can be completed in class.

(m) SOFTWARE DEVELOPMENT

All custom software (i.e., interfaces, conversion programs, and application customizations) is coded and bench tested as part of this step. (Bench testing, as described in the *Test Design* step, is the testing conducted by the programmer to ensure that the program code executes without error and meets the requirements identified in the functional specification.) This step includes preparing a technical specification from the functional specification developed in the *Business Systems Design, Interface and Program Flow Design* and *Data Conversion Design* steps. A technical specification, usually developed by a technical analyst, is a more detailed specification as to how the program modules will be designed, coded, and linked to accomplish the functionality documented in the functional specification. Often a pseudo coding language is used in the technical specification; this language is easily translated into program code by a programmer. The technical specification also addresses requirements for the construction and bench test environment and the development and testing of common models and program skeletons. These components are then used to develop the specific software.

As previously discussed, the vendor can be used to develop much of the custom software components. Areas requiring the organization's involvement include programming to provide the vendor with interface or conversion data directly from the organization's source systems. The vendor then takes the data and restructures it into a format that is acceptable to the new application. The vendor can also provide an output interface in a format readable by the organization's destination systems, however the organization may need to develop programs that reformat the data into files that can be accepted by the destination system.

(n) APPLICATION DEVELOPMENT

This step of work includes loading the application software per the specifications developed during the *Business System Design* step. Tasks include loading set-up parameters, tables, files, screens, and reports. Note that in some cases, application files may be loaded automatically by the conversion programs designed in the *Data Conversion Design* step and constructed in the *Software Development* step.

If certain large files are not able to be loaded automatically, as discussed in the *Data Conversion Design* step, this step, *Application Development,* is where the data input sheets would be completed, reviewed, and manually keyed into the new system. Note that file building of this nature may not be trivial. For example, if the application to be integrated is a purchasing and/or accounts payable application, building the vendor file manually is not trivial, especially if the current vendor file maintains information on thousands of vendors (as most do). Be sure to plan plenty of time to gather and validate all the necessary file information as well as the time necessary to input the required number of files. If time constraints do exist, one approach can be used to build a very usable if not complete file. Using the vendor file as an example, sort all the vendors maintained in the current system in terms of purchase volume, current activity, and/or dollar volume. Use this ranking criteria to prioritize the vendors whose profiles are to be completed first. That way if only half of the vendor file is built by the time the system is operational, at least the half that is built may represent 80% or so of the purchases. Then as new vendors are needed, the remaining vendor files can be built as part of daily operations.

(o) PROCEDURE DEVELOPMENT

User manuals required to implement and operate the new application are completed in this step. These manuals are developed according to outlines generated and approved during the *Business Systems Design* step. Procedures cover areas such as user procedures, data center operations, help desk, data security and control, disaster recovery, and application maintenance.

The procedures documented in this step can range from abbreviated desktop user procedures (see Figure 46-14 for an example)—which focus only on how to operate

Figure 46-14   Sample Desktop Procedure.

H1.4   DELETING AN ENTIRE JOURNAL ENTRY

The DELETE JOURNALS (JRNLDEL) screen is used to delete both the header and detail lines from the system without having to delete each item individually. To delete both header and detail journal records from the system, select the DELETE JOURNALS screen as follows:

STEP 1: Place an X to the left of the JRNLDEL DELETE JOURNALS transaction on the JOURNAL MENU screen.
Press ENTER.
The Delete Journals screen (H1.4) will appear on the terminal.

```
OGLDDJRO                     FINANCIAL MANAGEMENT SYSTEM
JRNLDEL                          DELETE JOURNALS                      STEP

ORG ID:  ORG NAME:
JRNL ID: DESCRIPTION:

LN $ T/  EFFEC E/JOURNAL  D/C                            No        Reversal
NO # T   DATE H/SOURCE    G   CONTROL TOTAL   XLAT SJE  STA  ERR OOB  DATE
                                    000                           00/00/00




DELETE? (Y/N):              LINE NO:
NEXT FUNCTION: JRNLDEL    NEXT KEY:
DC800003 ORGANIZATION NOT DEFINED
```

STEP 2: Type in the journal key to identify the journal entry.
Press ENTER.
Remember, the journal key is made up of five items:
- ORG ID
- JRNL ID
- $/#
- T/T
- EFFEC DATE

The system will display the Expanded Journal Header information associated with the journal key. Detail line item information will not be displayed. Also notice a DELETE? (Y/N) promptly at the bottom of the screen. The cursor will appear to the right of the prompt. Verify that the appropriate journal is displayed.

STEP 3: If this is the journal to be deleted, replace the N with a Y at the DELETE? (Y/N) field.
Press ENTER.
The system will respond with the message RECORD DELETED.
If the wrong journal has been selected, do not replace the N at the DELETE? (Y/N) field and press ENTER.

STEP 4: To return to Journal Menu,
Press CLEAR.

the system—to full-blown policy and procedure manuals—which cover not only the procedures necessary to operate the system, but also the workflow procedures required in and around the system and the organizational policy statements regarding the particular transaction being documented. At the start of the project, a procedure strategy should be developed to identify the type, content, and scope of the procedures to be documented as part of the integration effort. This strategy can then guide the outlines developed in the *Business Systems Design* step as well as the final procedures documented in this step.

Whatever strategy is implemented for procedure documentation, two types of documents will assist in the development of procedures: vendor procedure manuals and current organizational policy and procedure manuals. Vendor documentation provides a sound basis for the development of the procedures of how to operate the system. Similar to the comments regarding the use vendor training only, system usage procedures should be customized using organizational examples. Again, trying to use a new car dealership example for how to use the system to process a certain transaction will not be as useful to the user as using a real-life example from the organization.

Current organizational policy and procedure manuals provide a sound basis for developing procedure manuals that cover not only system usage but the other workflow procedures to be used with the new system as well as company policy statements regarding the transactions involved. Note that organizational policy for certain transactions may not change as the result of integrating the new system, however, in many cases, workflows will. The current documentation can assist in the design and format of the new policy and procedure manual (or improvements to it) as well as provide a checklist to ensure that the new policy and procedure manual is complete (as compared with the topics discussed in the current manual).

(p) TEST EXECUTION

Project team members, users, and information systems representatives will execute the tests developed in the *Test Design* step to help ensure that the system meets its specified functional performance and service level objectives. Test execution consists of following the instructions contained in the test scripts and comparing actual results with expected results (also documented in the test scripts). If the actual result does not match the expected result, the outcome is documented on an issue log (see Figure 46-15 for a sample issue log).

Issues arising as a result of differences between actual results and the acceptance criteria will be analyzed and corrective action taken. Usually issues fall into one of four categories:

- *Software Bug.* Issues of this type are those where the software functions incorrectly. These issues are usually communicated to the vendor who in turn corrects the software and provides the correction to the organization. Correction of these types of issues may not be trivial and thus time must be planned for in this step to allow the vendor an opportunity to correct the application and test the correction prior to providing new code to the organization for retesting.

- *Expected Is Incorrect.* Issues of this type are those where the software does not act as expected. This does not mean that the software is functioning incorrectly;

Figure 46-15   Sample Issues Log.

Issue	Function	Test Cycle	Test Run	Test Case #	Test Cond. #	Tester Name	Software Function	Issue Description
1.	Purchasing	1	1	ACQ1-11	All	E. Smith	2.10.3.11.8	Detail Purchase Order not organization's form
2.	Purchasing	1	1	ACQ5 ACQ7	All	E. Smith	2.10.3.1	Cannot print summary purchase order
3.	Purchasing	1	1	ACQ2	All	E. Smith	None	Requisitions need to be modified to match actual test case
4.	Purchasing	1	1	ACQ7	All	E. Smith	None	Requisitions need to be modified to match actual test case
5.	Inventory	1	1	INV1-INV2	1.INV1.04 1.INV2.04	T. Jones	2.9.5.2	A/xxxxxx -Alternate Reference Number search not working in test environment.
6.	Purchasing	1	1	ACQ1-11	All	E. Smith	2.10.8.2	Message displayed "**Warning**" Primary vendor: (blank) when pulled up catalog item w/o vendor in catalog
7.	Inventory	1	1	INV1-INV5	All	T. Jones	None	Need a report that shows quantity on-hand, by location, by item number, but not by vendor
8.	Inventory	1	1	INV1-INV5	All	T. Jones	None	Need a report that shows vendor packaging units, and Location and Issue packaging units on same report
9.	Accounts Payable	1	1	APO1	.03 and .57	B. Scott	4.1.1.1	Vendor address differed from PO address
10.	Accounts Payable	1	1	APO1	44,52a,52b	B. Scott	2.10.3.1	Could not print a summary PO; see Issue #2 above
11.	Accounts Payable	1	1	APO1	57	B. Scott	None	The vendor was a discount vendor; another procedure would have been used.

Figure 46-15   *(continued)*

Issue Log Last Updated: 07/13/94   - Shaded Area = Closed Items

Date	Assigned	Date	Age	Status	Date Resolved	Resolution/Status
6/2/94	Vendor	6/4/94	41	Open		The custom forms have not yet been delivered. Target date: June 25, 1994. 07/02/94—custom forms delivered and loaded. Retest.
6/2/94	Vendor	6/4/94	41	Open		The custom forms have not yet been delivered. Target date: June 25, 1994. 07/02/94—custom forms delivered and loaded. Retest.
6/2/94	Test Coordinator	6/4/94	41	Open		Requisition will be retested.
6/2/94	Test Coordinator	6/4/94	41	Open		Requisition will be retested.
6/3/94	Vendor	6/4/94	40	Open		Update routine will be installed in test area by June 15, 1994. Please retest. Retested June 23, 1994. Still not working. 7/2/94—Vendor conducting further investigation.
6/2/94	Vendor	6/4/94	41	Open		Please indicate a sample item to allow for evaluation. Sample submitted to vendor 7/6/94.
6/4/94	Vendor	6/4/94	7	Closed	6/11/94	Please refer to software option 2.9.3.2.
6/4/94	Vendor	6/4/94	7	Closed	6/11/94	Please refer to software option 2.9.3.2.
6/4/94	Test Coordinator	6/8/94	21	Closed	6/25/94	The PO address instead of the Billing address was used on the paper invoice for .03 and a non PO/billing address was used on .57; Will retest.
6/4/94	Vendor	6/4/94	39	Open		The custom forms have not yet been delivered. Target date: June 25, 1994. 7/2/94—custom forms delivered and loaded. Retest
6/4/94	Test Coordinator	6/8/94	39	Open		Retest with a non-discount vendor.

in fact, it most probably is functioning as expected from the vendor point of view but maybe not how the organization expected it to function. For these types of issues, either the user corrects the expected result in the test script and executes the test again, or the user works with the vendor to identify another way to satisfy the test condition with the software (in the case of how the software functions is not acceptable to the user).

- *Script Is Incorrect.* Issues of this type result from errors in the test script. In other words, the actual results of the test were correct based on the way the test script was written. However, the expected results were based on how the test script was thought to be constructed, and thus the expected and actual results did not match. In these cases, the test script should be corrected to meet the condition(s) to be tested and executed again to validate the test.

- *Script Was Executed Incorrectly.* Issues of this type result from errors in executing the test script (i.e., incorrect keystroke). In other words, the actual results of the test were correct based on the way the test script was executed, but did not match the expected results because the test script was not executed as written. In these cases, the test script should be executed again to validate the test.

Note that in executing tests, unit tests should be executed and all issues resolved and retested prior to beginning the integration tests. In turn, the integration tests should be completed prior to conducting the systems tests, and the same for acceptance testing. Internal and external auditors should be notified at the start of test execution so that they can plan to observe the tests or review the documentation, if necessary, during the test effort. Test scripts, control documentation, and test results should be accumulated, filed, and stored in case internal or external auditors need to review the tests at a later date.

On completion of testing, user and management acceptance of the new application system will be obtained before proceeding with the integration project.

(q) TRAINING EXECUTION

This step consists of executing the training designed in the *Training Design* step. Training execution should be conducted early enough at the end of the integration project so that the training is complete prior to going live; however, training should not be conducted too early so users forget the training or so the training is not reinforced as the result of operating the new system.

Training courses may need to be held more than once for the same or a subset of a previously trained audience, to reinforce the concepts or to allow the audience to pick up additional knowledge not clearly understood the first time around. Providing a training database and requiring all trainees to spend a certain amount of self-study time to reinforce the concepts taught in a training session also provide another avenue for additional training. Note that training examples should be available in the training database to assist the trainees in their self-studies.

Lastly, training does not end when the system becomes operational. Probably within the first month or two on the new system, a refresher training course will help to fill in the gaps not understood in the pre-live training or not used/reinforced in day-to-day use of the system. Also training for new hires must be considered. Will it be the responsibility of the organizational area to train their new users? Or will the organization sponsor training courses organizational-wide on the new application at frequent intervals? If the organizational area is responsible, it is important that a trained trainer conduct the training for the area and that complete training materials are used. Similarly, a seasoned trainer who is knowledgeable of how the organization uses the new application should be used to provide the organizational-wide training. Finally, training materials must be reviewed and updated as the organization expands or revises its use of the application through live operations.

(r) CUT-OVER PLANNING

Cut-over planning includes the establishment of the production environment and development of the plan for the transition to the new user and information systems organizations. During this step, all procedure manuals and training programs are finalized to reflect any timing changes. The old system and its operating documentation is phased out and final system documentation is assembled and distributed (unless the old system is planned to continue to operate for some time after live; see the conversion discussion regarding the no-conversion approach in the *Data Conversion Design* step). In this step, the maintenance and testing environment will be established (so that new software releases or updates can be tested before installing them into the production environment) and a process for monitoring new system performance will be planned.

A detailed cut-over schedule is developed as part of this step. Included in the schedule are what activities regarding establishing operations on the new application will be executed each day during the cut-over period. For example, if the application to be integrated is an inventory application, activities such as conducting a final physical inventory and loading beginning inventory balances into the new system must be scheduled and staffed appropriately. Also, a plan is documented for how inventory transactions that need to continue during this "time-out" for physical inventory taking will be accomplished. Further, on what day all inventory receipts will begin to be input into the new system and how the purchase orders for these receipts will be converted to the new system must be planned for and scheduled.

A detailed schedule of at least the first month of operations is also constructed during this step and includes activities like what reports will be printed each day, what batch processing will occur each evening, when the application will be available to the user on weekdays and on weekends, etc. Tasks like how to handle employees that do not use the new forms must be identified, documented as to what response will be given, and responsibility for handling this situation assigned. Lastly, organizational-wide communication of the new system must be delivered to let the entire organization know what will be happening and when. This organizational-wide communication can be executed via a variety of means including meetings, newsletter articles, and memos.

(s) CUT-OVER EXECUTION AND PRODUCTION SUPPORT

This step covers the actual execution of the cut-over plan as well as production support and fine tuning during the initial months of the new system (especially the first period-end close). If the cut-over plan is well thought-out and documented, execution of the plan becomes straightforward. That is not to say that the cut-over does not have to be managed. In fact, it must be managed closely because many cut-over tasks are dependent on other tasks; failure to execute properly and completely any of the cut-over tasks may have severe ramifications to subsequent tasks and thus to the transition of operations to the new application. Further, not all events can be planned. In fact, most transitions to a new application do not go without a hitch. But those projects that develop a detailed, well thought-out cut-over plan are more likely to successfully mitigate any unplanned problems than those projects that cut-over without a plan.

The project is not over once the cut-over plan has been executed. Much is learned in the first few days and weeks of operating the new system. Procedures, workflows, and training must be reviewed and adjusted for aspects of the application not considered during the integration project. Further, system tuning (i.e., making the system operate more efficiently from a technical standpoint) is often conducted during the first few months of an operational application. Lastly, until the application system is put through its daily, weekly, monthly, quarterly, and year-end paces at least once, these initial period-end processes may be bumpy at best.

46-7 SUMMARY

Software integration projects, by their very nature, are not straightforward. Their complexity and probability of failure is affected by factors such as the number of organizational areas affected by the application, the organization's ability to change, and the number and scope of other integration projects underway in the organization. However, the potential for success of an integration project can be greatly enhanced by securing executive commitment and support, following sound project management techniques, procuring a team that satisfies resource estimates and required skill sets, and executing the project following a step-by-step process.

The focus of this chapter is to provide organizations with project management techniques and a step-by-step process to successfully integrate software into the organization. Again, realizing that no two integration projects are the same, each of the techniques and steps described in the chapter should be reviewed and tailored to better meet the particular project's requirements prior to beginning the integration effort. Once the tailoring is complete, project structuring and planning can begin using the tailored techniques and steps as input for the plan estimates.

Again, any integration project can be described on the outset as high risk. How the organization mitigates this risk via the management and structure of the project will either result in a successful project or one that was bound for failure from the start.

CHAPTER 47

Electronic Data Interchange (EDI)

47-1 INTRODUCTION

Electronic Data Interchange (EDI), has become one of the most talked about technologies. An increasing number of articles are being published in various magazines and newspapers exhorting the benefits of EDI. Corporate executives are hearing from many of their colleagues how EDI is helping to streamline corporate information and business processes. Many executives are exposed to EDI through initiatives of their suppliers or customers (or both). Yet, EDI is not new. What is new is the increasing acceptance of EDI as a standard way of doing business.

EDI, similar to Just-In-Time (JIT) manufacturing, Total Quality Management (TQM), Business Process Redesign (BPR) and many other *acronym-based* business strategies is becoming a way of life for competitive organizations. Successful firms are coupling these strategies to gain further competitive advantage and strength.

(a) WHAT EXECUTIVES SHOULD KNOW ABOUT EDI

Any corporate CEO, CFO, or high level executive should have a working knowledge of technologies or business strategies that will change the way business is conducted. EDI is one of the few technologies that is also a new strategic business approach. EDI crosses all corporate boundaries, requires profound organizational change and

---

This chapter was written by Jeffrey L. Sturrock, Sr. Manager, Ernst & Young, Dallas.

enhanced customer/supplier relationship management, and can change the traditional "paper-based" process flow. In some instances, EDI redefines legal transactions, eliminates historical data retention methods, and can change asset and liability boundaries. A corporate executive need not become an expert on EDI, but generic knowledge of capabilities, opportunities and issues is a prerequisite.

47-2 EDI DEFINED

Electronic Data Interchange (EDI) is the computer-to-computer exchange of information in a standardized format. There are three key parts to this definition:

* Computer-to-computer exchange, more precisely defined, is the application-to-application (i.e., purchasing application to order entry application) exchange of data with no manual intervention.

* Information is any data that is *necessary* to conduct business, and is typically interchanged in the form of a legal business transaction (i.e., a purchase order or an invoice).

* Finally, an important part of the EDI definition requires use of standardized and commonly accepted data formats for the structured definition of interchange data.

EDI is not FAX, nor Electronic Mail (E-Mail), nor Electronic Order Entry, nor distributed computing although each of these has an appropriate place in corporate MIS strategies. Information interchange techniques can be placed in roughly four categories (see Figure 47-1). Person-to-person interchange techniques, such as the telephone, facsimile, or paper mail are intended for interpersonal communications. Person-to-application interchange techniques such as electronic order entry or captive terminal applications are used for person-to-computer data entry. Application-to-

Figure 47-1   Interchange Matrix.

Person-to-Person	Person-to-Application
Telephone FAX Voice Mail Electronic Mail Paper Mail	Electronic Order Entry Captive Terminal CAD/CAM
Batch Reporting Automated Error Suspense Distributed Processing	Electronic Data Interchange (EDI)
Application-to- Person	**Application-to- Application**

person techniques such as batch reporting or automated error suspense notification are automated computer-to-person communications. EDI is one of the few application-to-application (computer-to-computer) communication techniques, offering automated, integrated information interchange without manual intervention.

Several recent surveys have indicated that although corporations have become computerized over time, there is still an enormous amount of manual processing performed. Estimates indicate that approximately 80 percent of all information traffic between corporate traders is printed from one computer and re-keyed into another computer for processing (see Figure 47-2).

EDI allows corporate traders to bypass this *print-send-enter* process that has traditionally caused delay, errors, and increased overhead costs. Simply stated, EDI allows companies the ability to conduct business in a paperless environment and manage the information flow in a much more effective manner (see Figure 47-3).

(a) EDI AS A CORPORATE STRATEGY

Although EDI appears to be an MIS technology, it is actually much more. EDI has a greater impact upon the underlying business departments and processes than it does upon the MIS department.

Today's global marketplace is increasingly more competitive in nature and calls for new corporate approaches. In a recent international quality survey conducted by Ernst & Young, three interesting factors should be noted:

- Technology is playing a much greater role in meeting customer needs.
- Global corporations are looking more to streamlining processes and providing information, rather than simple process automation.
- Cycle-time and other indirect indices are being used to measure success.

Figure 47-2   Flow of Information Between Corporate Leaders.

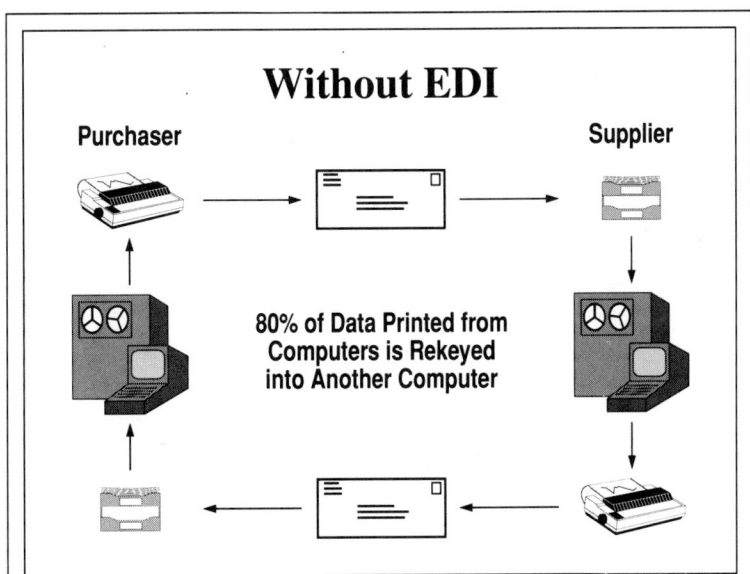

Figure 47-3   Conducting Business in a Paperless Environment through EDI.

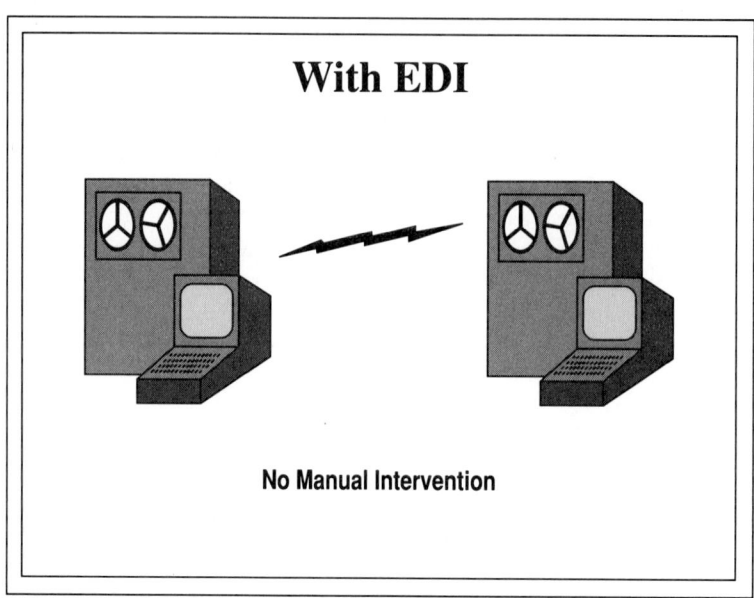

These findings indicate that today's corporations are taking a more strategic and leveraged approach to global competition, where information, cycle time, and value added processes are as important as yesterday's "bottom line" indicators. In each of the areas mentioned, the survey indicated that the Japanese employ these new approaches significantly more often than did the other respondents from Canada, Germany, and the United States.

The global market leaders (private and public) use EDI daily. The U.S. EDI market is predicted to double for the next five-to-ten years, while conservative international market predictions are even greater. While EDI is not the reason these companies are successful, each of these organizations realize that inter-enterprise information sharing is important. Much of this information is shared between various functional areas within a corporate structure. If EDI is properly integrated with corporate information systems and underlying business processes are re-engineered, then executive decision makers can make competent trading management conclusions.

EDI is just one of many tools that support corporate priorities. Coupling of EDI with other strategic tools such as bar coding, Just-In-Time (JIT) manufacturing, Computer Integrated Manufacturing (CIM), Computer-Aided Design (CAD), and Evaluated Receipt Settlements (ERS) offers the greatest benefits to the implementor.

47-3 A BRIEF HISTORY OF EDI

EDI actually has been in existence for over 20 years. The term EDI was coined in the mid 1970s. In EDI's early existence, data was exchanged between companies using mutually defined proprietary formats on media such as magnetic tape, punch cards, and so on. During the mid-to-late 1970s, several pioneering industry sectors began to mold EDI into a formal industry-wide strategy.

One of the first industries to take the lead in the area of EDI was the transportation sector. The rail and ocean mode carriers were being inundated with a large volume of paper necessary to move goods through the transport chain. Often, more than 15 or 20 different pieces of paper were required to move a single shipment from shipper, through the various transport points, to the ultimate consignees.

As the transport industry began to automate and computerize, they recognized that much of the data on each piece of paper was redundant. Accordingly, the transport industry formed a group called the Transportation Data Coordinating Committee (TDCC) that was responsible for developing an electronic data exchange format standard for the member transport companies. By the early 1980s, most of the transactions required to move goods through the transport chain had been modeled and electronic interchange data format standards had been developed. These format standards were call *transaction sets.*

Other industry groups in the United States and abroad were also developing industry specific standards for data interchange during this time. It became evident that cross-industry data exchange was a necessity. The definition of industry specific format standards would not allow different industry sectors to communicate effectively.

In 1979, the American National Standards Institute (ANSI) chartered the Accredited Standards Committee on EDI–X12 (ASC X12), to begin establishing cross industry, or *generic* EDI standards. Today there are over 100 ANSI standards that define a full range of data formats supporting the effective interchange of data throughout the entire business life cycle (see Figure 47-4). Essentially, initial request for quotation to final payment can now be performed electronically using the X12 EDI standards.

Likewise a set of international EDI standards called EDIFACT (EDI for Administration, Commerce, and Transport) is being developed for international trading needs. The EDIFACT standards are developed under the auspices of the United Nations and the International Standards Organization (ISO).

Figure 47-4   Electronic Information Life Cycle.

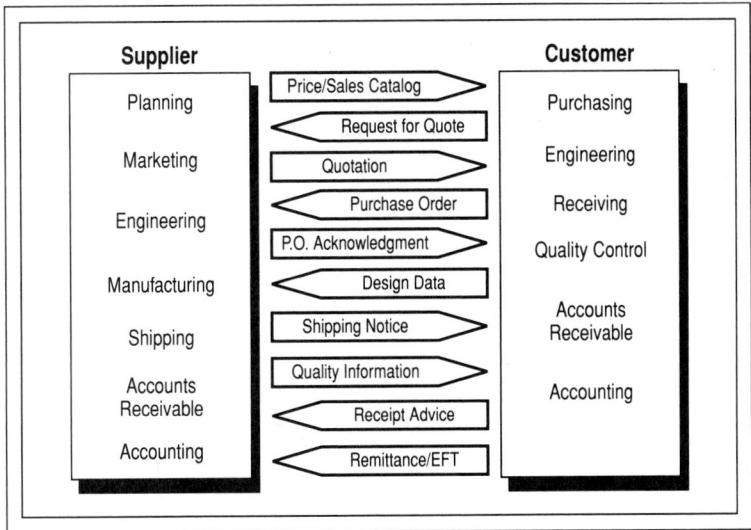

It is estimated that there are some 25,000 to 35,000 companies world wide using EDI to reduce costs and increase quality services to customers, and that this base is doubling each year.

47-4 THE BENEFITS OF EDI

Although there are immediate savings associated with the implementation of EDI, the greatest benefits can be gained through the integration of EDI into corporate information systems coupled with the redesign of underlying business process. Consequently, EDI changes the way companies do business. Some areas where EDI has helped provide the greatest level of benefits are:

- Decreased transcription and input errors.
- Increased ability to support manufacture-to-order through the electronic interchange of quote, design, and order data.
- Enhanced Just-In-Time (JIT) processes at both the supplier and customer interface points.
- Decreased overhead and indirect costs associated with paper processing.
- Enhanced cash flow through electronic cash management and Electronic Funds Transfer (EFT).
- Increased information availability without increased overhead costs.
- Increased competitive advantage through value-added information and technology services.

The ultimate savings and cost avoidance potential of each of these items is dependent upon the level and degree of EDI integration into corporate information systems and the redesign of underlying business processes. Simple emulation of paper-based business processes will only magnify inherent errors, while process re-engineering will truly offer added value and benefits. EDI "cost savings testimonials" of major companies are detailed weekly in major, popular publications.

While each of these "testimonials" are impressive, EDI was just one part of the solution that allowed each organization to achieve the stated benefits. Early EDI implementations that simply *emulated* manual paper processes showed little or no benefits. Sophisticated EDI users state clearly that strategic use of EDI with the redesign of underlying business processes changes the way they do business and offers the greatest benefits. In addition to changing base business processes, EDI is now being used in areas other than purchasing and invoicing. Some of the potential EDI business scenarios include:

- Planning data can be passed from customer to supplier to support Just-In-Time (JIT) processing.
- Request for Quote (RFQ) and Response to RFQ can be negotiated electronically.
- Invoices can be eliminated through the reconciliation of electronic purchase orders to electronic advanced ship notices and to physically received goods.
- Suppliers can manage customer replenishment levels through receipt of demand and consumption data.

- Computer Aided Design (CAD) data can be passed between customer and supplier via EDI during product design and development phases.
- Payments can be made through EDI and Electronic Funds Transfer (EFT) and can include remittance information for final supplier account reconciliation.
- Waybills, bills of lading, and freight bills can all be exchanged, reconciled and paid electronically.
- Price/sales catalogs, product information and product specifications can be exchanged via EDI.
- Quality reporting and parametric data can be exchanged electronically and automated into firm-wide quality programs.

These are just a few of the uses of EDI. Many executives contemplating the use of EDI, however, wonder what benefits are offered by implementing EDI. In a survey conducted by The American National Standards Institute, Accredited Standards Committee on EDI–X12, the top 500 EDI users in the United States cited *improved relations* and *competitive advantage* as the top two EDI benefits realized.

The majority of North American EDI users never performed a cost justification prior to EDI implementation. New EDI users, however, want to know what the "bottom line" benefits are from the use of EDI and business process redesign. Following are a few case studies where companies have implemented successful EDI programs in conjunction with business process redesign, other technology tools and organizational change.

(a) EDI BENEFIT CASE STUDIES

There are a number of case studies that support the claim that changing business through the use of EDI is beneficial. The majority of the Fortune 500 firms use EDI. All of the top 5 have been using EDI for some time. Many of the recent Malcolm Baldridge Quality Award recipients have used EDI for some time including Motorola, Federal Express, and General Motors (Cadillac Division). These case studies have been taken directly from press articles.

(i) Texas Instruments. Texas Instruments (TI) has one of the most successful EDI programs in the world. EDI is used throughout all of TI's operating divisions including semiconductor, defense and aerospace, and consumer products. TI uses EDI throughout the entire business cycle including purchasing, order entry, invoicing, and so on. Today, TI has over 1,700 EDI trading partners using 50 different EDI transactions around the world. TI's underlying strategy includes the use of EDI, redesign of business processes, integrated application systems and organizational change. Some of the benefits from TI's efforts include:

- One division bypasses the field sales office on 80 percent of incoming orders via EDI, offering TI sales and marketing representatives time to service the customer rather than shuffling paper.
- Through the use of EDI, bar code and warehouse automation, TI enjoys 98 percent on-time delivery in several product lines.

- Several operating areas report reduction of up to 80 percent in returns caused by administration errors.
- Order processing time has been reduced from 4 days to 1 day for many products.
- Entry and processing costs have been reduced by sending 70 percent of purchase orders (i.e., approximately 4,000 line items per day) via EDI.

(ii) Ford Motor Company.   Ford Motor Company has been an EDI user for over 10 years. In the past several years, Ford has employed EDI, bar code, JIT techniques, integrated systems design, and business process redesign to implement a number of successful business initiatives. Some of the areas of use and associated benefits are:

- The invoice has been eliminated in several areas through the use of EDI, all but eliminating historical accounts payable organizations. Payment is made to the supplier on receipt of goods after reconciliation with the original purchase order/release and the physical (bar coded) receipt record. This process reduced the matching process from 4-way to 2-way, reduced headcount requirements some 40% and substantially reduced billing/payment errors.
- Ford suppliers are also benefiting through improved cash availability and predictability, same day accounts receivable update and improved customer relations.

(iii) Hanes Hosiery.   Hanes Hosiery has implemented EDI in conjunction with bar code, automated package identification, systems integration and business process redesign in support of its "Quick Response" (QR) program. Hanes has EDI links with over 70 trading partners and has seen the following benefits:

- Reduction in customer lead time from 22 to 14 days.
- Reduction in order processing by at least 1 day.
- Decreased distribution center inventories by 14 percent.
- Total, end-to-end, manufacturing cycle reduction from 25 days to 10 days.
- Higher sales growth, better inventory management, increased return on investment, better customer service, and enhanced information.

(iv) Military Traffic Management Command (MTMC).   The U.S. Army's Military Traffic Management Command (MTMC) that is jointly staffed and industrially funded manages movement of 1.4 million freight shipments valued at $800 million per year. MTMC has established electronic bulletin boards to interface between MTMC, brokers, carriers and internal shippers to access rates, identify operations problems, issue traffic management advisories, and assist in rate filing. Some 2.3 million government bills of lading can be handled through this system. Through elimination and reduction in data entry, mail and processing, MTMC will save some $11.8 million per year in costs.

There are numerous other EDI success stories; however, all EDI successes hinge upon the use of EDI coupled with other technologies, business process redesign, integrated systems and organizational change. EDI users cite the intangible benefits of competitive advantage, enhanced customer service, enhanced quality and increased productivity as primary benefits, but as described above, the "bottom line" benefits are substantial.

47-5 THE MECHANICS OF AN EDI SYSTEM

Technically, EDI is not difficult. A simple EDI implementation can be performed with a microcomputer, software and a modem. Conceptually, there are five base components to any EDI system: Hardware, business application software (e.g., purchasing and accounts receivable systems), translation software, telecommunications facilities and EDI standards (see Figure 47-5). EDI can be performed on any type or size of hardware, from a PC or Macintosh, to mid-range computers, to large mainframe computers. Business application software, such as purchasing systems, are the author or recipient of the EDI business transactions (i.e., purchase order and purchase order acknowledgment). Translation software is used to format the business application proprietary data language into a common EDI business format language, understandable by the intended trading partner recipient. The standards, as mentioned above, offer a common electronic language easily comprehended by the worldwide business community.

A typical EDI transaction example might include the following steps (see Figure 47-6):

- A purchaser's buyer enters a purchase order into a purchasing system.

- Periodically, individual purchase orders (POs) are batched to the EDI translator software.

- The translation software reformats the PO data into a common EDI standard format and stages the data for communication to the supplier.

- Communications software sends the EDI standard data over the public telephone lines or via a Value Added Network's (VAN's) electronic store-and-forward mailbox facilities to the intended recipient.

- The recipient's (supplier's) translator software reformats the PO data from the EDI standard format into an internal proprietary format, and batches the PO data to the supplier's order entry system.

Figure 47-5   EDI System Components.

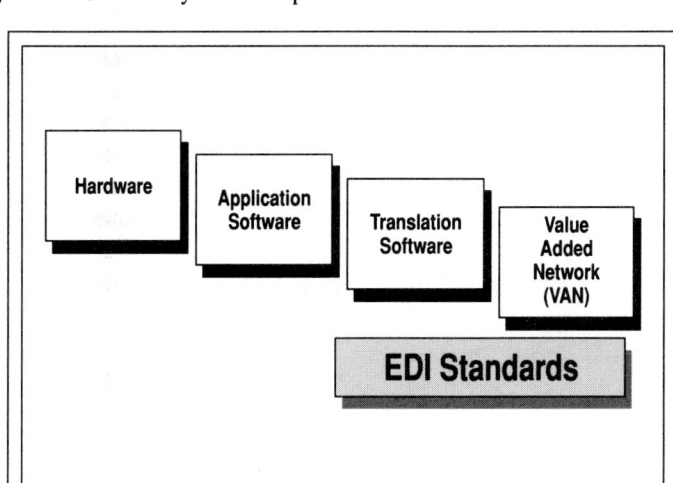

Figure 47-6   How EDI Works.

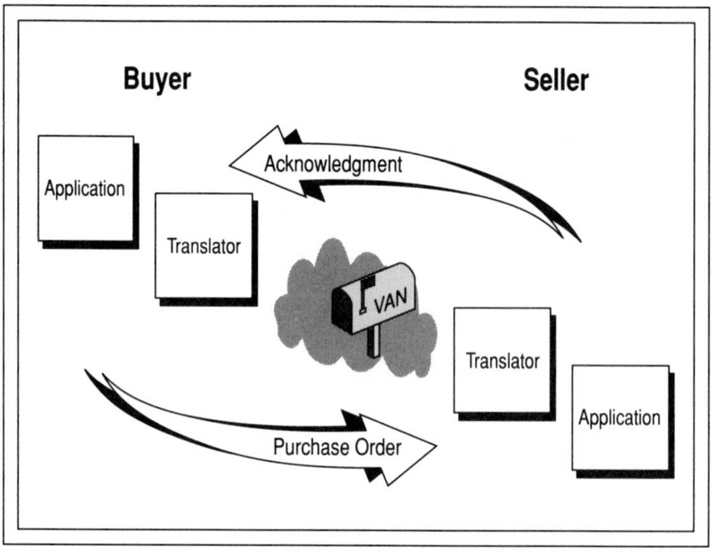

- The supplier's order entry system evaluates the PO data and generates an internal order on the order entry system.
- After evaluation, validation, and review, a sales representative confirms the conditions of the purchaser's order on the order entry system.
- The order entry system generates a PO acknowledgment which in turn starts an EDI reply to the original purchaser.

Although EDI is not technically difficult, the implementation of EDI can be logistically difficult. To enjoy the benefits described above, effective planning is necessary to fully integrate EDI into the corporate information systems structure. Some business and technical issues must be considered and addressed.

(a) TECHNICAL ISSUES AND CONSIDERATIONS

- Are the in-house applications capable of sending and receiving EDI transactions, or are application changes necessary to fully integrate EDI into the information processing flow?
- What hardware platform should support EDI processing?
- Should data interchange with the source application occur in a batch or transaction-based processing mode?
- Are software checkpoints in place to validate (and correct) incoming EDI data prior to application input?
- Has all data for each potential transaction been identified to support business data requirements both in-house and for the trading partners?
- Has all identified data been mapped correctly into the EDI standard format?

- Should translator software be developed in-house or purchased?
- Have all data flow management tools been implemented to support EDI operationally?
- Should data be communicated directly over switched telephone communications facilities or through third-party, Value Added Network's (VAN's) store-and-forward mail boxing facilities?
- Are hardware and software tools in place to support data communications requirements?
- Are operational fall-back, troubleshooting, and error recovery contingency plans in place?
- Are proper security measures implemented to protect internal systems?

(b) BUSINESS ISSUES AND CONSIDERATIONS

An EDI implementation typically requires some level of business process redesign and organizational change. EDI implementation planning requires representation from all functional areas of the corporate business environment. An effective EDI implementation is best directed by a corporate-level steering committee with representation from upper management in all functional areas (e.g., purchasing, planning, manufacturing, and accounts payable). It is essential that the chosen project leader have a good understanding of all functional areas, and have the delegated authority to carry out necessary changes in support of EDI.

Some business issues that must be considered during an EDI implementation include:

- Are all business processes executed in an efficient manner in support of functional business requirements?
- What data is necessary to complete a functional business event, and when and where is certain data needed?
- What functional business transactions are candidates for EDI?
- What other technological tools should be integrated with EDI?
- What trading partners are candidates for EDI?
- What organizational changes will be precipitated by EDI implementation?
- Is a realistic roll-out implementation plan in place?
- Have review processes been set up to evaluate the benefits and payback from the EDI implementation?
- Are all audit, legal, and security procedures in place to support a paperless EDI process?
- Have internal personnel and external trading partners been informed and educated concerning potential EDI implementation impacts?

These are just a few of the technical and business questions that must be considered prior to EDI implementation. Like any corporate program, strategic implementation planning can provide an excellent tool in addressing these issues. Actual EDI implementation can take from 4 to 60 weeks. The current industry average for EDI implementation is 32 weeks.

47-6 IMPLEMENTING EDI

The decision by corporate management to implement EDI can be a decision that affects all aspects of the corporate culture. EDI is not just another MIS *bells and whistles* technology; EDI is a premeditated business strategy utilizing technological tools to support the corporate business priorities.

There are several steps that can enhance the EDI implementation process.

- Learn more about how EDI can work for specific needs.
- Obtain executive management consensus and commitment.
- Organize for an EDI implementation.
- Develop an EDI strategic plan.
- Perform process and technology assessments and analysis.
- Design a corporate-wide EDI system and program.
- Develop a deployment strategy that includes trading partners.

47-7 SUMMARY

EDI is a tool that can be an enabler for strategic business objectives. While EDI is not technically difficult, it does require an understanding and a commitment by executive management. EDI by itself is not an answer; however, coupled with other strategic corporate initiatives, it can become a powerful enabling facilitator. Most leading U.S. and international industries are using EDI. Information and education is readily available.

47-8 SELECTED REFERENCES

The 1992 EDI Directory, Potomac: Phillips Publishing, 1992.

Barber, Norman F., *Organizational Aspects of EDI: A Project Manager's Guide,* Electronic Data Interchange Association.

Emmelhains, Dr. Margaret Ann, *EDI: A Total Manager's Guide,* New York: Van Nostrand Reinhold.

Kutten, L. J., Bernard D. Reams, Jr., and Allen E. Strahler, *Electronic Contracting Law, EDI and Business Transactions, 1992–1993 Edition,* New York: Clark Boardman Callaghan.

Powers, William J., *EDI Control and Audit Issues for Managers, Users and Auditors,* EDIA.

Shaw, Jack, and Mike Witter, *The EDI Project Planner,* EDI Executive Publications.

Wright, Benjamin, *The Law of Electronic Commerce—EDI, Fax, and E-Mail: Technology Proof, and Liability,* Boston: Little, Brown.

CHAPTER 48

Graphics in Business

48-1 INTRODUCTION

What comes to mind when someone mentions the word *graphics?* Do you envision pie charts and bar charts? Company logos or a drawing of some sort? All of these and much, much more encompass the term *graphics*. This chapter briefly explores the purpose of graphics, various graphics elements, and some of the current software tools that support graphics for the business world. The chapter may be viewed as a valuable complement to Chapter 36, indicating the capability of computer technology.

48-2 PURPOSE OF GRAPHICS

The creation of any business document involves three key elements:

1. *Objectives.* The document answers the question, "Why is this document being created?" The intent is to understand what is to be accomplished by the document (e.g., impart knowledge, persuade, or entertain).

2. *Audience.* The document answers the question, "Who is the intended audience of this document?" Not only are the specific recipients determined, but, more importantly, such information as their existing knowledge base, attitudes, position, and reasons for viewing the document contributes to its wording and presentation.

This chapter was written by Melissa W. Breeze, Manager, Ernst & Young, Denver.

3. *Environmental Constraints.* Two questions, "In what time frame does the document require creation?" and "What tools are available to support document creation?" are answered.

When these three elements are combined, decisions are made on the nature of the resulting document. Is a brief memorandum presenting the results of a process all that is required, or is a more substantial report detailing the process and its results necessary? Each set of document objectives, intended audience, and environmental constraints results in a different solution.

Why are graphics created? For two major reasons:

1. *Achieving effective information transfer.* Everyone has heard the old adage, "A picture is worth a thousand words." It's true! A simple graphic may instantly, clearly, and cleanly convey information that would otherwise require substantial text to describe (and may not be as clearly understood by the intended audience).

2. *Obtaining/Maintaining audience attention.* If a document's intended "audience" is a file drawer, forget the graphics. If, however, human beings make up all or part of the intended audience, you may want to utilize means that may improve the probability of their viewing the document and increasing their corresponding attention level. A document that is "pleasing to the eye" or "attractive" is much more likely to get and maintain its audience's attention.

When determining the extent to which graphic elements should be included as part of a business document, the document's objectives, intended audience, and environmental constraints must all be considered.

48-3 GRAPHICS ELEMENTS

Most people probably think of a "picture" of some sort when they think of graphics—a type of data chart (e.g., a pie chart or column chart), an organizational chart, or perhaps a cartoon. However, if you view graphics as all elements that can help effect information transfer and/or get and maintain audience attention, the possibilities expand. Graphics elements can then include:

- *Fonts.* When discussing fonts, we need to address three components:
  1. *Type*—the specific name of the font. For example:

     CG Times

     `Courier`

     Univers

  2. *Size*—the height and width of the font characters. Sizes for some fonts are described as "characters per inch" (cpi); others are described in "points" (the bigger the point number the larger the resulting character). For example:

     `Courier 10 cpi`

     `Courier 12 cpi`

     Univers 12 pt

     Univers 14 pt

3. *Appearance*—the style of the font characters. For example:

Underlined

Bold

Italicized

Shadowed

~~Strike Out~~

- *Character Symbols.* The • or "bullet" is probably the most universally used and recognized character symbol. However, most word processing software provides the user with a variety of other character symbols. For example, ✓ and ☐ may be used in place of a bullet. Other examples are:

◆   ❂   ι   ✎   →   ◀   ★

- *Frames/Borders.* Horizontal and vertical lines used alone or in combination can "frame" textual or pictorial material and thus draw attention to it. For example:

> A shaded "text" box allows you to bring attention to a specific message or piece of information. It can also be used to interrupt a document's visual flow and thus revive the audience's attention level.

"Tables" are another way of framing information so that it is more clearly presented, as shown in the following example.

Market Share*

The Top Three Presentation Graphics Products in
Three Categories, in Terms of U.S. Units Shipped

DOS	Macintosh	Windows
Software Publishing Corp.	Microsoft Corp.	Microsoft Corp.
Harvard Graphics	PowerPoint	PowerPoint
WordPerfect Corp.	Deltapoint, Inc.	Micrografx, Inc.
DrawPerfect	DeltaGraph	Charisma
Lotus Development Corp.	Aldus Corp.	Lotus Development Corp.
Freelance	Persuasion	Freelance for Windows

* "The CW Guide: Presentation Software," *Computerworld,* Jan. 25, 1993. Copyright 1993 by CW Publishing, Inc., Framingham, MA 01701. Reprinted from *Computer World.*

- *Shapes.* Using common shapes to present information pictorially is a frequently used business graphic technique. Organization charts and flow charts are examples of this graphic technique. Figure 48-1 is a sample organization chart.

Figure 48-1 Sample Organization Chart.

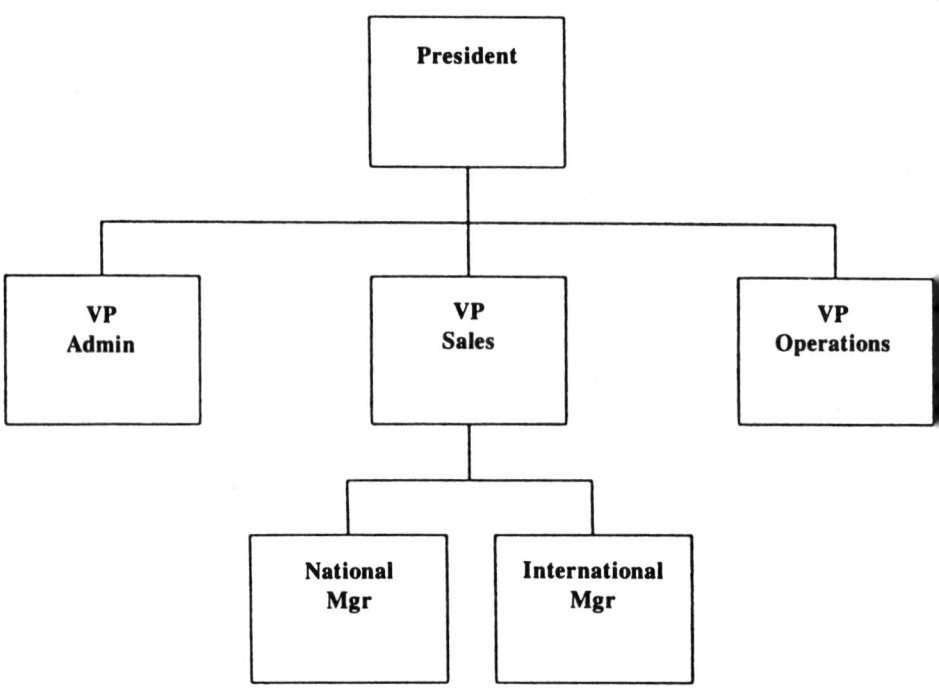

- *Data Charts*. Data charts can concisely and persuasively illustrate numeric data. Some of the more common types of data charts are described later in the chapter.

- *Illustrations*. These can range from elementary school variety stick figures to cartoons, professionally developed works of art, or objects and creatures "drawn" on the computer screen (see Figure 48-2). Sources of illustrations range from original work to commercially available "clip art" (see section 48-4).

Figure 48-2 Sample Clip Art.

- *Color.* The use of color has become widespread on the business scene during the very recent past. With the ever increasing cost-effectiveness of color printers and copiers, color is fast becoming an everyday component of business documents. As with other graphics elements, the use of color should be governed by a document's objectives, intended audience, and environmental constraints.

48-4 SOFTWARE TO SUPPORT YOUR BUSINESS GRAPHICS NEEDS

Creation of today's business documents may be accomplished by using a single type of tool (e.g., word processing software) or by combining output from multiple types of tools (e.g., word processing, spreadsheet, and presentation graphics software). The graphics contributions that various types of software tools can make are presented below. An emphasis is placed on presentation graphics software.[1]

(a) PRESENTATION GRAPHICS SOFTWARE

The following popular packages are primarily geared toward creation of data, text, and graphic (pictorial) slides for hard-copy output:

Aldus Persuasion	Freelance Graphics
Charisma	Harvard Graphics
DeltaGraph Professional	Microsoft PowerPoint
DrawPerfect	Softcraft Presenter

All these packages perform a similar core set of tasks and typically have the following capabilities:

- *Presentation Management.* These packages provide a central slide creation and organization scheme that supports achievement of a consistent look across a presentation. Templates or masters or both may be used. The use of common slide backgrounds is also usually supported.
- *Text Charts.* Direct or imported text entry for preformatted word/text charts is supported by these packages. Functionality usually includes automatic text wrap, text justification, freeform labels, and bullet charts with user-defined bullets. Many of the packages also provide a spelling checker. Examples of two common text charts—a title chart and a bullet chart—can be seen in Figures 48-3 and 48-4.
- *Data/Business Charts.* The following chart types are commonly supported (see Figure 48-5 for some examples and descriptions):

  Plain, stacked, overlapped, and clustered bar charts and column charts.

  Projected and shadowed 3-D bar charts and column charts.

---

[1] The "full featured" nature of today's software demands only a cursory examination here. Readers are encouraged to increase their graphics awareness by further investigating the graphics-related capabilities of their existing software tools and the many available product offerings.

Figure 48-3   Sample Title Chart.

> **Everything You
> Wanted to Know About**
>
> **Graphics and Business**
>
> **(But Were Afraid to Ask)**

Figure 48-3   Sample Bullet Chart.

> **Types of Text Charts**
>
> • **Title Charts**
> • **Simple Lists**
> • **Bullet Lists**
> • **Two Columns**
> • **Three Columns**
> • **Freeform**

2-D and 3-D pie charts.

Line and scatter plots.

Area charts (unstacked, stacked area total, and stacked 100 percent area).

High-low-open-close charts.

Figure 48-6 provides suggested data chart types, depending on what your data are intended to illustrate.

Additional data/business chart functionality usually includes semi-log and log-log scaling,[2] interactive chart editing, and WK1 (i.e., Lotus format) file importation.

- *Clip Art.* Importation of vector clip art is a common capability of presentation graphics software. In addition, these packages normally include a library of clip art images. Some examples of clip art are shown in Figure 48-7.

- *Annotation and Illustration.* Basic drawing tools support creation of lines, polylines, boxes, and circles for chart annotation and diagram creation. The ability to move an object to front and back or to resize it is also typical.

- *Electronic Presentation.* These packages normally support creation of "screen shows." In addition, most offer stand-alone runtime players that support "on the road" runtime versions.

- *Hard-Copy Presentation.* With these packages, you can print a single slide or an entire presentation. Many include communications software for transmitting to slide generation service bureaus.

- *Multimedia Capabilities.* Current presentation graphics software varies greatly in its ability to support multimedia functionality (e.g., sound, video, and animation). However, such capabilities are gradually becoming standard features.

---

[2] Logarithmic scaling can be used to show the relative change of large variation in data and to compare data expressed in different magnitudes. A log chart also shows a rate of change and compresses large variations within a series. Because of the independence of X and Y axes, you can chart either a semi-log graph (usually the Y axis is scaled) or a log-log graph (both the X and Y axes are scaled).

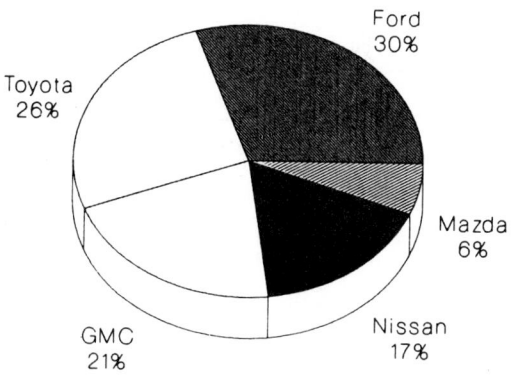

Pie charts are most often used to show parts relative to a whole. In this example, the total number of trucks sold is broken out by percentage of each type sold as represented by a piece of the pie.

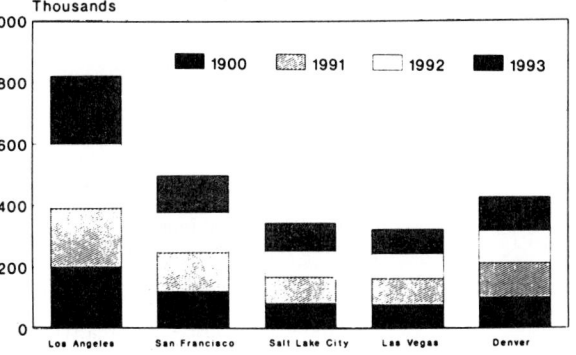

Column or bar charts are commonly used for comparing separate groupings. The above example charts the number of participants by city in an ongoing survey. Each year is represented by a different pattern (or color if available). Both the total and breakout by year can easily and simply be displayed.

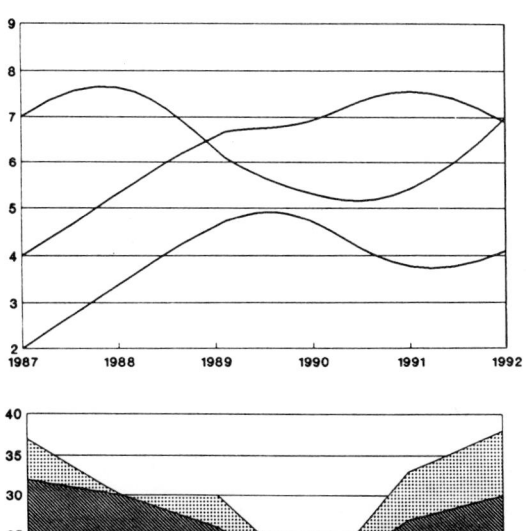

Line charts are quite useful if trend information is to be shown. With the capabilities of current charting software, straight-line values can be smoothed into curves, at option of the user.

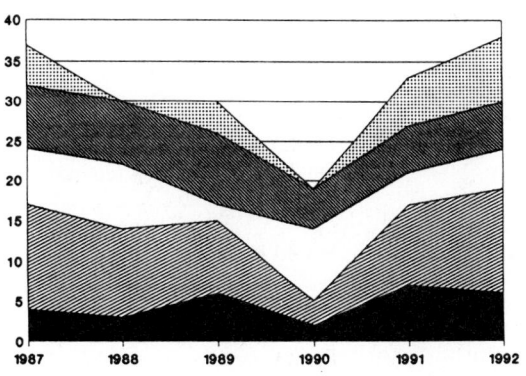

Area plot charts are often used to show the contribution which many items make to a total over a period of time. The above example could illustrate product category sales over time with each product category being represented by a different color line.

Figure 48-6   Suggested Common Data Chart Types by "What You Want to Show."

What You Want to Show	Suggested Chart Type*
Change in volume	Area/Area with 3-D overlap effect Line with 3-D overlap effect
Change over time	
Over a few time periods	Bar (horizontal or vertical) Bar/Line combination Line (zigzag or curve)
Over many time periods	Area Area/Line combination Line (zigzag or curve) Line with 3-D overlap effect High-Low-Close with area style
Emphasis	
On a part of a whole	Pie with cut slice
On volume	Area/Area with 3-D effect
On one of several series	Bar/Line combination Line (zigzag or curve)
On sum of one series in relation to another	Proportional pie
On continuity and fluctuation of minimum/maximum data	High-Low-Close with area style
Parts of a whole	
At a specific time	Pie/Column
At 2 different times	2 Pies/Columns 2 Stacked Bars
Over a few time periods	Stacked Bars 100% Bars
Over many time periods	Area Stacked Bars 100% Bars
Relationship between two series	
Over a few time periods	Bar (vertical or horizontal) Bar/Line combination
Over many time periods	Line (zigzag or curve)
Relationship between two (or more) series	
That differ widely in magnitude	Dual Y axis Dual Y axis with log scaling
That use different units of measure	Dual Y axis
Comparison of two series with the same X axis classification	Paired Bar
Correlation	Paired Bar Point Chart

Figure 48-6 *(continued)*

What You Want to Show	Suggested Chart Type*
Running totals	Area Bar Cumulative Line
Stock/bond prices	High-Low-Close
One series over another and frequency distribution	Histogram
Relative or percent of change	Logarithmic
Trends	
Statistical trends	Line (trend)
Over a few time periods	Line (zigzag, trend, or curve)
Over many time periods	Bar (vertical)

* Harvard Graphics® Reference Manual.

Figure 48-7 Clip Art Samples.

(b) WORD PROCESSING SOFTWARE

Many of today's word processing packages, while providing extremely full text-related functionality, also support an ever increasing graphics capability. Fully integrated graphics control and high-powered drawing tools are quite common. In many cases, individuals are using their word processing software to integrate the result of output created in other tools (e.g., spreadsheets, presentation graphic software, and business illustration software). Examples of popular word processing software include:

Ami Professional	WordPerfect
Microsoft Word	WordPerfect for Windows
Word for Windows	WordStar

Many current word processing packages users would be surprised at the graphics related capabilities their existing tool provides.

(c) SPREADSHEET SOFTWARE

Spreadsheets are designed to handle a variety of tasks, including: analysis and model building, consolidation and linking, charting, worksheet publishing, interoperability and applications development. Examples of popular spreadsheet packages include:

CA-Supercalc	Microsoft Excel
Lotus 1-2-3	Quattro Pro

These packages, and others, offer varying levels of charting capabilities. The types of charts offered, the existence (or nonexistence) of slide-show capability, and a user's ability to customize the charts with titles, notes, multiple typefaces (i.e., fonts), clip art, colors, and shading should be reviewed when assessing a spreadsheet's ability to meet all or some of your graphics needs.

(d) INTEGRATED SOFTWARE

Most integrated software packages include, at a minimum, word processing, database, and spreadsheet capabilities. Others also offer one or more of the following capabilities: business charting, vector drawing, graphics importing and editing, and telecommunications. Examples of the latter type of software include:

Eight-In-One for Windows	Microsoft Works
Framework XE	PFS:WindowWorks
Lotus Works	WordPerfect Works for DOS

On the plus side, these integrated software packages can offer affordability, all-in-one convenience, and easy data sharing. What you will tend to give up is an overall richness of features. The individual parts are unlikely to offer the same sophisticated and complex functionality as their counterpart stand-alone packages. However, depending on your requirements, including graphic-related ones, an integrated package might more than meet your needs.

(e) DESKTOP PUBLISHING SOFTWARE

These products are aimed at users who develop business publications. Their functionality includes: text formatting, graphics handling, layout creation, and printing. The sophistication and corresponding capabilities of desktop publishing packages vary greatly. Examples of current desktop publishing products include:

Avagio	PagePlus
Express Publisher	PageMaker
Microsoft Publisher	Ventura Publisher

These products, and others, will allow you to create complex layouts by automatically wrapping text around pictures, linking text frames, and jumping stories to noncontiguous pages.

A key component of this type of software is its ability to import text and graphics from other sources (e.g., word processing software and presentation graphics software). With such functionality, you can create newsletters, business forms, brochures, and a variety of other publications-related materials.

(f) BUSINESS ILLUSTRATION SOFTWARE

Unlike professional illustration software, business illustration software caters to nonartists. These packages typically offer routine vector drawing tools, simple image manipulations (e.g., rotate and flip), a few text effects, limited color handling, a library of clip art, a variety of font-related capabilities, and the ability to import and export files in a standard format(s) (e.g., .PCX). The following packages are examples of this type of software:

Arts & Letter Apprentice	KeyDraw! Plus
ComputerEasy Draw	Windows Draw 3.0 plus OLE

(g) MISCELLANEOUS

A discussion of graphics would not be complete without mentioning two types of hardware: scanners and printers. Scanners are hardware devices that allow preexisting graphic images (e.g., photographs and any printed matter) to be "read" into a computer system and then "placed" in an appropriate software tool (e.g., presentation graphics and desktop publishing software) where they can then be manipulated. Available devices run the gamut from gray-scale hand-held devices (do not attempt to use after too much coffee!) to gray-scale flatbed scanners to color flatbed scanners. Depending on your graphics needs, an appropriate scanning device can prove invaluable. Some potential uses for a scanner are:

- Your company's logo for use on reports, presentations, and similar documents.
- Preexisting art work for use in a presentation (e.g., product renderings, cartoons drawings).
- Proposals to potential clients.

Without a printer that supports your graphics output, your work may be for naught Fortunately, there is a full range of products from which to choose. Whether you re quire monochrome or color capability, there is a printer that will meet your needs.

48-5 CONCLUSION

A significant amount of business communication, including written documents, in volves persuasion. Graphics elements, when appropriately used (i.e., the document' objectives, intended audience, and associated environmental constraints are clearly defined), can help present information effectively and compellingly. With the graphic capabilities provided by today's software products, only your imagination (and perhaps your wallet) will limit your ability to create documents that transfer information effectively and obtain/maintain your audience's attention.

CHAPTER 49

Groupware

49-1 INTRODUCTION

Groupware is fast becoming one of the most talked about topics in management circles. However, although many people have heard the term, read a few articles, or been to a product demonstration, they are still left asking "What is it?" and "What will it do for me?"

The term groupware refers to *software designed to support the work of groups*—more specifically, software designed to facilitate the collaborative efforts of work teams. The goal of groupware applications is to improve the productivity of groups.

49-2 HISTORY

Computer systems have fallen into two main categories: (1) organizationwide systems that centrally process transactions and produce management information, and (2) personal systems with a wide array of tools designed to enhance individual productivity (e.g., office automation, word processors, spreadsheets, and database applications).

As defined in the chapter appendix, current trends in computing include: client-server applications, computer networking, distributed processing, downsizing/right-sizing, end user computing, electronic data interchange, PC workstations, graphical user interface, object-oriented technology, and open systems. All of these technologies share a few common characteristics: they are smaller, scalable, faster, user friendly, user accessible, and support information sharing.

This chapter was written by Hans Hultgren, President, Integrated Systems Group, Inc., Golden, Colorado.

Meanwhile, current trends in management philosophies suggest a focus on teamwork, flat organizational structures, participative management, employee empowerment, workgroup dynamics, decentralized global organizations, total quality management (TQM) teams, and increased communications. In particular, the teamwork concept appears to be growing rapidly where teams are created for a specific purpose (based on their expertise, not their classification or location) and for a finite period of time.

Groupware represents the logical response to these computing and management trends. It takes advantage of the technological trends to focus on the actual work of the team. Groupware is designed to capitalize on the growing local area network (LAN) environment through facilitating group information sharing and collaboration on team projects.

49-3 GROUPWARE DEFINED

Groupware is basically software designed for teams of people working together using shared information. Groupware is used to disseminate information, organize information, and support interactive or collaborative uses for information. It is modeled around, and supports, workflow processes.

The categories of groupware functionality are: mail capabilities, information sharing, document management (including interactive update), and group meeting support. (See Figure 49-1.)

(a) MAIL CAPABILITIES

In the first category, mail capabilities, documents are created by one person and then "mailed" to other persons on the same system. Electronic mail (E-mail) is very popular today and typically includes enhanced features such as one-to-many mailings, reports on opened and unopened mail, ability to link up with other systems, and mail management (archiving, purging, and reporting). With advanced groupware tools, the sender can attach other documents such as spreadsheets, graphs, diagrams, and reports.

Groupware frequently includes mail-enabled applications: the mail can be initiated from within the application itself. For example, while reviewing a financial statement in a spreadsheet application, you have a question for Sue on figures submitted from the East Coast branch. Without leaving your spreadsheet application, you select the portion of the statement related to your question, initiate the mail functionality, write a quick memo, and send both documents to Sue. A message appears on Sue's PC alerting her to the incoming mail. When she "opens" the mail, she will immediately see the spreadsheet attached.

A large auditing company is using groupware to access its top experts in tax law. A person with a specific question will write a memo, attach spreadsheets and any other background information, and send it to one of the experts. The expert can then read and review the file and related information on his/her schedule and respond electronically. The response is stored and can be accessed by other employees who may have a similar question.

Figure 49-1 Groupware Functionality.

GROUPWARE TYPE / FUNCTIONALITY MATRIX

GROUPWARE FUNCTIONALITY

GROUPWARE TYPE	LOCATION	TIME	GROUP DELIVERABLE	MEMBERS INTERACTIVE	SHARE APPLICATION	SHARE DOCUMENT
MAIL CAPABILITIES	ANYWHERE	ANYTIME	NO	NO	NO	YES
INFORMATION SHARING	ANYWHERE	ANYTIME	NO	MAYBE	MAYBE	YES
DOCUMENT MANAGEMENT	ANYWHERE	ANYTIME	MAYBE	MAYBE	MAYBE	YES
MEETING SUPPORT Different time	ANYWHERE	ANYTIME	MAYBE	MAYBE	YES	YES
MEETING SUPPORT Same time / Different place	ANYWHERE	SAME	YES	YES	YES	YES
MEETING SUPPORT Same time / Same place	SAME	SAME	YES	YES	YES	YES

(b) INFORMATION SHARING

The information sharing begins with the basic LAN capabilities for file sharing. Beyond the typical file-server concept, groupware can allow multiple individuals to share data simultaneously. This type of software is often known as group communication software. A LAN allows a user to retrieve and view the same document; within a groupware application, several people in the same application can use the same version of the document at the same time.

Each person has the ability to annotate the document by inserting notes, graphics, or spreadsheets at specific locations. This is especially useful for documentation review and peer review of draft reports or other documents. The team members can also edit the document while other team members are viewing it. An employee who is viewing his/her draft report can actually see the comments as they are attached or see the edits as they occur. Full interactive group communication is facilitated.

(c) DOCUMENT MANAGEMENT

The document management, includes tracking, version control, and support of the real-time viewing, annotating, and editing of documents. Additionally, the groupware application will track and log any updates and handle any data contention issues.

This functionality lends itself well to tracking systems. For example, a team member may be monitoring the status of several audits or other projects. Typically, these projects will center around an audit or project folder containing all the original data and related materials. Traditional tracking systems might keep track of where the folder is, whether it is on schedule, and any issues related to it. Groupware will accomplish these same functions; however, it can also maintain the entire folder online with all of its attachments. In this scenario, any team member could view the most current version of the audit, project plan, or software design at any time.

Groupware also coordinates a team's access to global data. For example, the team may be interested in market activity in Sweden. The groupware application could be designed to read a financial news wire, look for anything related to Sweden, and then ship that section of the news to a team member's attention.

(d) MEETING SUPPORT

The last category is *meeting support groupware*—software used to enhance the productivity of a meeting. This type of groupware focuses on transforming the typical meeting, where participants talk about work to be done, to one where work is actually completed. This is accomplished through the ability to solicit ideas from more than one person at a time, automatically capture all meeting information, and allow participants to voice opinions anonymously. Each person in the meeting has a PC, which is used for submitting recommendations, making comments, prioritizing, or any other type of communication.

There are inherent inefficiencies in the way meetings are typically run. These inefficiencies translate to large costs for a typical company where, on average, professionals may spend between 30 percent and 70 percent of their time in meetings. Many meetings do not allow for everyone to "get their say." The "20/80 rule" applies to meetings: 20% of the people do 80% of the talking. By allowing multiple people to comment at the same time, the people who do not normally participate in meetings are given the opportunity. Ideas and input from those who are afraid to speak in front of others can be captured by having them anonymously submit comments. Controversial ideas that normally would not be discussed can be communicated. Participants need not be embarrassed or worried that their ideas might be seen as ridiculous. (This is particularly noteworthy because most paradigm shifting ideas would probably fall into this category.)

Meeting support groupware reduces the frequency of "Groupthink," where all members of a group pocket their concerns with a particular idea in support of the perceived "group opinion." This is especially important when a team is faced with making a hard decision (a budget crunch, how to downsize, elimination of a division, etc.). Meeting support groupware makes the most of meetings by making them more productive, more flexible, and shorter.

Meeting support groupware applications vary, depending on which of the following types of meeting they are designed to support:

Same time-same place meetings, where people interact face-to-face.

Same time-different place meetings, where people meet through the groupware system from several locations.

Different time meetings, where, regardless of location, people carry on a meeting over a period of time but are not required to interact in real time.

In a same time-same place meeting, the subject matter has dictated that a face-to-face interactive meeting is required. In this case, the key focus is facilitating the meeting (not the technology). Many people find that, without the nonverbal cues and other interaction that occur in a face-to-face meeting with people applied to a specific task, people's attention will wander.

In a same time-different place meeting, several people may be at other locations. In this event, groupware strives to "emulate" a same place meeting as much as possible. Often, the concept of a "virtual meeting" is employed: video screens allow people in various places to interact as if they were face-to-face. This type of meeting calls for people to sit at PCs in front of large screens at different locations. The screens then create the illusion that all team members are in the same room.

With different time meetings, groupware concentrates on managing and tracking the meetings. An agenda may be created, specific people assigned, and deliverables identified. The groupware can then track the progress of the team and help to keep the meeting moving.

Typical uses of meeting support groupware include: group conferencing, status reporting, project management, group discussions, brainstorming, global brainstorming, document draft review and editing, candidate or request for proposal (RFP) review, strategic planning, organizational changes, auditing, and employee surveys.

For example, a person presents annual plans, a budget, a marketing plan, or some other document to a group of peers or team members who then simultaneously provide edits, ideas, comments, and constructive criticism. Comments are later reviewed in private by the presenter with no knowledge of who wrote them and no requirement to respond to or challenge the comments. All ideas have the same weight because no one knows who submitted them.

49-4 CURRENT INDUSTRY STATUS

Groupware products vary greatly, depending on the functions they are designed to support. Several products that support mail capabilities, including several word processing applications, are available.

Within the categories of information sharing and document management capabilities, Lotus Notes is a complete product that addresses these functions and more. Notes is also an application development tool that allows the user to create custom applications to suit specific needs.

There are three key competitors in the area of meeting support groupware: VisionQuest (Collaborative Technologies Corporation), GroupSystems V (Ventana Corporation), and TeamFocus (International Business Machines Corporation).

49-5 CONCLUSION

Groupware is a growing and viable new software direction that can translate into strong benefits for any organization. Specifically, organizations moving toward a workgroup structure should consider implementing groupware. A review of the shared data requirements, cooperative efforts, and document tracking tools will serve as a basis for analyzing the benefits of a move to groupware.

Operations that require frequent meetings to perform—ongoing planning, prioritizing, brainstorming, and other cooperative efforts—may find strong benefits from the meeting support groupware applications. A review of the time spent in meetings, the extent to which the meeting deliverables are produced through an iterative process, and the need for creative and free-flowing ideas will provide the information necessary to evaluate meeting support groupware applications.

Software tools are designed to automate some process. This automation can provide strong benefits if the process is strong; however, automating a bad process will usually result in a bad system. Organizations that do not support the team concept and the open sharing of information will not realize the benefits of groupware applications.

APPENDIX: DEFINITIONS

Client-server applications. Applications developed on a LAN server architecture for the support of specific workgroup activities. The processing can occur on an individual's personal computer/workstation or the server. Typically, the environment where applications are developed or customized by the people connected through the server is user friendly.

Computer networking. The linking of local area network (LAN) and geographically dispersed or wide area network (WAN) computers through direct or dedicated lines. Applications are typically stored on the server computer at the heart of the LAN/WAN. Designed to support the sharing of software and peripherals.

Distributed processing. The concept of moving portions of the actual computer processing from a centralized processor to local computers. Typically designed to maximize performance and minimize costs associated with processing and telecommunications.

Downsizing/Rightsizing. The process of moving software applications to the most efficient hardware platform. Typically involves conversion of applications from a large system to a smaller one. In many cases, the costs are quickly recovered and considerable savings are realized. Initially referred to as "downsizing" because most of the efforts centered on moving from a mainframe to a minicomputer (midrange) platform; currently referred to as rightsizing.

End user computing. The concept of moving the development of software applications to the employees actually using the systems. Typically involves end users' developing queries or custom reports on their own computer.

Electronic data interchange. The process of transferring business documents between two organizations that are geographically dispersed. Typically, EDI occurs with requisitions, purchase orders, and invoices sent between two companies that have a customer-supplier relationship. The two companies do not need to have the same type of systems or software. (See Chapter 47.)

PC workstation. Powerful personal computers used to run application software at the local level. Typically, their capacity includes specific applications that support a particular company function. The use of workstations has greatly grown as lower costs of these systems have made them accessible.

Graphical user interface (GUI). A type of user interface characterized by the use of graphics, icons, pop-up menus, and the mouse-driven "point-and-click" interface. There is typically consistency in the look and feel of all applications running under a specific GUI environment (MAC, Windows, OS/2, etc.).

Object-oriented technology. System software and application software developed to view all data elements, programs, screens, and reports as "objects." These objects are viewed in their relationship to each other, which organizes the software so that the time spent on maintenance and modifications is greatly reduced. For example, a change to a field length typically requires multiple changes to all programs, processors, screens, and reports. With object-oriented systems, the change is made one time and all objects (programs, processors, screens, and reports) that relate to that object (changed field) reflect the change.

Open systems. The extent to which differing hardware, systems software, and application software can work together. Open systems goes one step beyond data sharing to the universal compatibility level.

CHAPTER 50

Information Systems Security

50-1 INTRODUCTION

It is estimated that computer fraud costs American organizations between $300 million and $5 billion per year. To reduce your organization's susceptibility to fraud, a well-planned and implemented approach to information systems (IS) security is required.

Information systems security can be defined as the protection of information assets (e.g., the hardware, software, and associated data) from unauthorized or intentional disclosure, modification, or destruction. Also included under the IS security "umbrella" are the steps necessary to control access to system resources and ways in which to respond to unauthorized and/or unintentional access to systems. Information systems security should be designed to ensure the integrity, confidentiality, and accessibility, where authorized, to the organization's information assets.

50-2 TYPES OF SECURITY THREATS

There are a wide variety of threats to information systems security. Basically, these threats can be summarized into the following categories:

- *Intentional Mischief.* Caused by theft, intentional destruction of data and other IS assets, and "hackers" (i.e., individuals who obtain unauthorized access to a computer).

- *Lack of an Effective IS Security Policy.* Such as the failure to perform regular system back ups (i.e., saving your computer's software and data on tape or disk) or allowing system users to share their passwords.
- *Human Accidents and Errors.* Such as spilling coffee on a computer keyboard or tripping into a disk drive and causing loss of data. (Information systems security can't "cure" human accidents and errors. However, it can reduce the risk of and loss from them by limiting access to IS assets.)
- *Power Supply Threats.* Sudden lapses or surges of power that cause the loss or scrambling of data.
- *Natural Disasters.* Earthquakes, fires, floods, and tornadoes fall into this category.
- *Network Access.* Unauthorized access to your voice or data network.
- *Viruses.* Malicious (in general) programs that attack legitimate programs and destroy data or computer codes (e.g., the Michelangelo Virus).
- *Data "Diddling."* The unauthorized alteration of data as it is entered into a computer or the changing of data stored in the computer (e.g., changing students' grades, eliminating speeding tickets, reducing amounts owed the organization, and transferring money from one account to another).

What can an organization do to protect against these numerous threats? The next section discusses a number of proven measures that can be utilized to protect the organization's IS assets.

50-3 WAYS IN WHICH TO PROTECT INFORMATION SYSTEMS ASSETS

Given the large investment in and dependence on IS assets, it makes economic and business sense to protect those assets. Described below are some of the key means by which an organization can help ensure the integrity, assessability, and confidentiality of its IS resources.

(a) PHYSICAL SECURITY

There are a large number of physical measures an organization can implement to improve the security surrounding its systems:

- *Physical Access Controls.* By restricting access to IS assets, an organization can reduce the opportunity for unauthorized use and malicious harm to its computers. The computer room should be located away from public areas and protected by a security system (e.g., a key-card or combination lock).
- *Fire Suppression Control System.* The computer room should be protected by a fire suppression system (e.g., an automatic water or Halon system). Also, the room should have fire extinguishers and be kept as clean as possible to reduce the opportunity for fires to spread.
- *Water Detection and Control System.* Each year, a significant amount of water damage is incurred in computer rooms. The main causes of water damage includes

burst pipes, leaking air conditioning systems, and roof leaks. To reduce the opportunity for water damage, organizations should periodically review their plumbing, air conditioning systems, and roof. Also, the computer room should be equipped with a water detection system and plastic covers for the computer equipment in the event of a leak.

- *Power Supply Monitoring Systems.* To protect against power fluctuations and outages, organizations should strongly consider investing in an Uninterruptible Power Supply (UPS) system. UPS systems filter power supply fluctuations and ensure a constant power supply to computers. Also, in the event of a power outage or blackout, they can provide power for a limited period of time. This power can allow the organization to safely shut down its computers without the loss of data.

- *Offsite Storage of Backup Tapes and Disks.* One of the easiest ways in which an organization can protect its IS assets is to store copies of *all* of its software off-site in a protected environment. The software to be stored offsite should include copies of the operating system and other system software, application software (e.g., the general ledger), and all data, including master files and transaction details. The offsite storage facility should be located sufficiently far from the organization's data center to ensure it is not susceptible to the same natural disasters (e.g., tornadoes) the data center is. The organization needs to ensure it keeps a complete and accurate inventory of all tapes and/or disks located at the offsite facility.

(b) TECHNICAL SECURITY MEASURES

There are a number of technologically based security measures an organization can implement to improve the security surrounding its IS assets. These measures include:

- *Encryption.* The "scrambling" of data, based on a mathematical algorithm, that makes it unreadable to those without a "key." Encryption can be an effective security measure for organizations that transmit data between different locations.

- *Callback Devices (also known as Port Protection Devices).* A relatively effective means of controlling telephone access to an organization's computers. After calling into a system, a user must supply its identification code and password for authentication by the device. The device then disconnects the user and calls the user's preauthorized telephone number to verify the identify of the user.

- *Password.* A sequence of alphabetic and/or numeric characters which must be entered at the beginning of a computer session to verify the user's identity and obtain access to the system. Passwords can be an effective means of limiting access to a system, especially if they are frequently changed (e.g., every 60 days), random (e.g., not a person's last name or birthdate), and are not shared with others. Also, the longer the password, the harder it is to guess (e.g., a three digit password has 47,000 possible combinations, a 6-digit password has 2 billion possible combinations).

- *Access Control Software (ACS).* Mainly available for mainframe and large midrange (minicomputer) systems, can be a valuable security measure. ACS provides an additional "layer" of security on top of the application and operating system security. It also provides the ability to limit access to designated employees, monitor user violations (e.g., unauthorized attempts to access the payroll system), and report security breaches.

- *Biometric Devices.* Instruments that perform mathematical analysis of biological characteristics. Today, there are wide variety of these types of devices including:

  —Voice recognition and verification systems.

  —Signature dynamics verification systems.

  —Retinal pattern verification systems.

  —Hard print geometry verification systems.

  —Fingerprint Identification.

  Biometric systems have been in use for some time now. Before selecting one of these systems, the organization should consider (1) the cost versus the benefits of the systems. Biometric devices can be very expensive. (2) The error rate should be very low. This means the system must be able to spot "counterfeits" while making allowances for normal variations (e.g., a blister on one's hand or a cold). (3) The time required to enroll people into the system.

(c) END-USER COMPUTER SECURITY

Microcomputer and local area networks (LANS) are becoming increasingly popular. As their popularity grows, so do the associated security risks. Unfortunately, most organizations tend to focus on mainframe security and fail to recognize the importance of microcomputer and LAN security. To increase the security surrounding these systems, a number of steps can be taken:

- *Security Agreements.* Ensure that all personnel sign an agreement stating they will *not:*

  —Share their password.

  —Upload or download any software or data to the organization's computers unless instructed to do so.

  —"Pirate" (i.e., make illegal copies of) the organization's software.

- *Physical Security.* Verify that the organization's microcomputers and LANs are appropriately located (e.g., in a separate computer room) and protected from power fluctuations, fire and water damage.

- *Data Security.* Ensure that the software and the data on microcomputers and LANs are backed up on a frequent (e.g., daily) basis and the backup tapes or disks are stored offsite.

(d) EMPLOYEE SECURITY

There are a number of key measures an organization can take to limit its exposure to IS security risks. These measures include:

- *Performing Background Checks.* Prior to hiring an employee, an organization should perform a thorough background check of all prospective employees. The background check should include an analysis of the prospective employee's educational background and work history. Also, the organization should investigate whether the employee has a criminal record.

- *Analyzing Employees' Security Posture.* The security "posture" of all employees should be investigated on an annual basis. This investigation should determine whether the employees' legal or credit position has changed.

- *Obtaining Security Agreement Signatures.* All employees should be required to sign a security agreement.

- *Communicating with the Personnel Department.* The Personnel Department should immediately formally notify the IS Department of all personnel changes (e.g., employees that are leaving the organization or whose responsibilities have changed). Doing so can help guard against unauthorized access to the system by former or transferred employees.

(e) INSURANCE COVERAGE

Organizations should maintain sufficient insurance to reduce the exposure to losses from floor, fire, theft, and other types of disaster. The types of insurance coverage that should be maintained include:

- Computer equipment and facilities.
- Media reconstruction.
- Business interruption.
- Errors and omissions by employees.

(f) DISASTER RECOVERY PLANNING

Disaster Recovery Planning, also referred to as contingency planning or business resumption planning, is one of the most important aspects of IS security. A disaster recovery plan (DRP) is an organized and documented approach to responding to a disaster. A proven approach to developing and maintaining a DRP is outlined next:

- *Phase I—Assess the Situation.* During this phase, the organization determines the types of risks to which it is vulnerable (e.g., fires, tornadoes, or earthquakes) and the potential impact of these risks.

- *Phase II—Analyze Recovery Strategies.* The key steps to be completed during this phase include determining the IS resources currently in place and then analyzing the alternatives for recovery. These alternatives can include:

  —*Constructing a backup site.* This involves building a data center in a location sufficiently far from the main data center so it is not subject to the same disasters.

  —*Utilizing a service bureau.* This option involves using the computer resources of a third party immediately after the disaster.

—*Sharing computer facilities.* Under this option, the organization shares the computer systems and software of another organization for a limited period of time.

—*Obtaining hot or cold site facilities from a vendor.* This option involves contracting for the use of a computer facility while the organization's own data center is being restored. A cold site is a "computer-ready" 'room in which an organization can move its existing or replacement computer. A hot site is a fully operational facility with a computer and network already in place.

- *Phase III—Develop the DRP.* During this phase, the organization develops its DRP. The plan should include the following areas:

  —*An overview of the plan* (e.g., the purpose of the plan, recovery, and restoration strategies, key recovery activities, and how the plan will be maintained and tested).

  —*Emergency procedures.* The procedures to be taken to safeguard human life, limit damage to the data center, and minimize loss of data.

  —*Response action plan.* The steps needed to respond to a disaster (e.g., how to assess the damage, notification procedures, and recovery team members and responsibilities).

  —*Recovery operations.* A description of the major recovery tasks (e.g., the recovery logistics, off-site storage, and operating system, network, data, and personnel plans).

  —*Restoration plan.* An approach to restoring the data center (e.g., the construction and site preparation schedule, and hardware/software and telecommunication acquisition plans).

- *Plan Testing and Review Strategy.* An approach to ensuring the DRP is properly tested on a periodic basis.

- *DRP Maintenance.* An organized approach to maintaining, updating, and storing the plan.

- *Phase IV—Test and Maintain the DRP.* The objectives of this phase include:

  —Thoroughly testing the DRP to ensure that if a disaster were to occur, the organization could recover from it on a timely and efficient manner.

  —Developing an approach to maintaining the plan on a regular basis.

See Chapter 51 for a more complete discussion of disaster recovery planning.

50-4 THE CONTROLLER'S ROLE IN INFORMATION SYSTEMS SECURITY

The controller and/or chief financial officer should play a key role in implementing and ensuring employee adherence to security policies. These individuals should be leaders in implementing security policies and monitoring compliance to them. Specifically, they should:

- Communicate security policies to all employees within their span of control This can be achieved by developing a security awareness program, requiring employees to sign security agreements, and providing security training.
- Ensure employees understand security risks.
- Assess risk on a periodic basis.
- Verify that all IS assets are inventoried.
- Ensure that backups are regularly made and stored off-site.
- Review the disaster recovery plan on a regular (e.g., annual) basis and ensure it is annually tested.
- Verify that access authorizations are appropriate.
- Investigate security violations.
- Ensure dismissed or transferred employees are removed from the system.
- Communicate a positive attitude towards security.
- Instigate period independent audits or reviews of the organization's computer security.

The controller can delegate some of these functions to a security officer or other appropriate employee. However, they should ultimately be responsible for ensuring these tasks are completed.

50-5 CONCLUSION

As previously noted, IS security is an extremely important area. There are numerous threats to IS assets. However, there are numerous ways in which to protect those assets. It is up to the controller to play an active role in ensuring the organization's IS assets are protected and secure.

50-6 SELECTED REFERENCES

(a) PERIODICALS

Computerworld

Computers in Accounting

Information Week

Management Accounting

Disaster Recovery Journal

(b) PRODUCT REVIEWS/INFORMATION

Datapro

Data Sources

Gartner Group

ICP Software Directory

CHAPTER 51

Disaster Recovery Planning

51-1 INTRODUCTION

Management is becoming increasingly interested in the area of disaster recovery planning. Recent disasters, such as the Oklahoma Federal building bombing, Hurricane Andrew, and the Midwest flood, have contributed to this increased level of interest. As mentioned in Chapter 50, disaster recovery planning is one of the most important aspects of information security. This chapter explores a number of aspects related to disaster recovery planning, including trends related to it and a proven approach to developing and testing a disaster recovery plan.

51-2 DISASTER RECOVERY PLANNING TRENDS

Recent trends related to disaster recovery planning include:

- *Organizationwide Focus.* In the past, disaster recovery planning was viewed as strictly an information systems department issue; this is no longer the case. Now, senior management, as well as the board of directors, is keenly interested in the plans that are in place to ensure efficient and effective recovery from a natural or manmade disaster.
- *Legal Requirements for Disaster Recovery Planning.* Your organization may be required to have a disaster recovery plan for the following legal reasons:

1. *Industry.* For over ten years, banks have been required to have disaster recovery plans and to test and revise those plans periodically.

2. *IRS Audit.* In the unfortunate event that your organization is audited by the IRS, you may be required to produce financial and business records going back three years or more. If you cannot deliver these records to the IRS because they were destroyed in a disaster, good luck!

3. *Contractual.* Your organization may be contractually obligated to have a disaster recovery plan. Increasingly, companies are requiring their suppliers to have a current and tested disaster recovery plan in place, to ensure they will not be stranded without supplies for an unreasonable amount of time.

4. *Common Law.* Your organization may be required to have a disaster recovery plan in place under common law. Organizations may have fiduciary responsibilities and "duties of care" to their customers, shareholders, and/or bondholders. If an organization does not exercise "good business judgment" and develop, test, and maintain a disaster recovery plan, it may find itself in court in the event of a disaster from which it did not quickly recover and from which it suffered significant losses.

- *Nonmainframe Disaster Recovery Planning.* Organizations are becoming increasingly reliant on personal computers, local area networks (LANs), and midrange computers. Historically, these mainframe alternatives were not included in a disaster recovery plan. However, with the increased use of nonmainframe computing environments, organizations have begun to include them as an integral part of the overall recovery process.

- *Business Continuity Planning.* In the past, disaster recovery plans covered only the information systems (IS) portion of the business. This is no longer the case. Organizations must now plan how they will recover *all* of their operations, not just the IS portion, in the event of a disaster; hence the term business continuity planning (BCP). Business continuity plans are designed to provide an organization with an approach for recovering all aspects of its operations. (This chapter focuses on how to recover from a disaster in the IS area.)

Additional trends on the horizon include the need to have a global disaster recovery plan that addresses an organization's worldwide operations, alternatives to the traditional hot and cold sites, and increased user involvement in the development and testing of the disaster recovery plan.

51-3 AN APPROACH TO DEVELOPING A DISASTER RECOVERY PLAN

Described below, and depicted in Figure 51-1, is a proven approach to successfully developing a disaster recovery plan. It is divided into five phases:

Phase I—Assess the environment in which the organization operates.

Phase II—Analyze recovery strategies.

Phase III—Document components of the disaster recovery plan.

Figure 51-1   Approach to Developing a Disaster Recovery Plan.

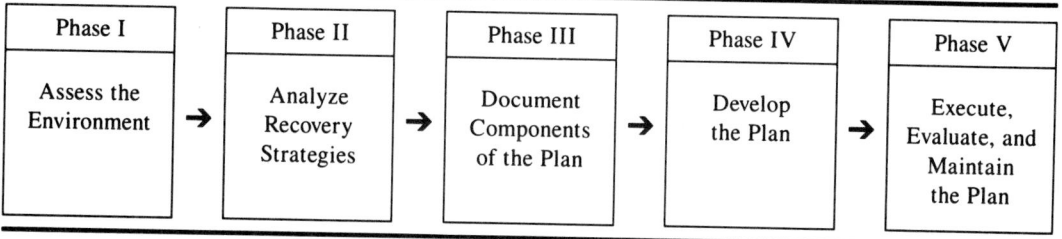

Phase IV—Develop the disaster recovery plan.

Phase V—Execute, evaluate, and maintain the disaster recovery plan.

(a) PHASE I—ASSESS THE ENVIRONMENT IN WHICH THE ORGANIZATION OPERATES

The objective of this phase is to determine the types of risks to which your organization is subject and the potential impact of those risks on your IS operations.

The key steps involved in this phase are:

1. Determine what risks the organization will most likely confront (e.g., fire, tornadoes, earthquakes, or terrorism).

2. Determine the potential impact on IS operations of the risks to which your organization is subject. To complete this step, the organization should accomplish the following tasks:

   Identify the functions performed by the organization.

   Determine which functions are critical to the success of the business.

   Estimate the impact on the business if it could not perform critical functions for one hour, one day, two days, one week, one month, and so on.

At the end of this phase, the organization should have a reasonably good assessment of the risks to which it is subject and the potential impact of those risks on the business.

(b) PHASE II—ANALYZE RECOVERY STRATEGIES

The key objectives of this phase are to define the IS resources currently in place, analyze recovery alternatives, and select an alternative that best meets your organization's goals.

The key steps that comprise this phase are:

1. *Define Your Organization's IS Resources.* These resources most likely will include a centralized computer, a variety of personal computers and LANs, application and system software (e.g., operating systems and database management systems), and the data center.

2. *Evaluate Recovery Alternatives.*

To accomplish the second step, the main activities are:

- *Define the Evaluation Criteria,* such as these listed in Figure 51-2. Some of the criteria on which to make a recovery selection decision include: cost, subscriber-to-site ratio (i.e., the number of hot site or cold site subscribers per facility), location of the hot or cold site, the level of security surrounding the site, the amount of data storage available at the hot or cold site, the communication capabilities at the site, the availability of professional consultants to assist your organization with planning for and recovering from a disaster, the amount of support personnel available to assist your organization in the event of a disaster, the availability of office space and supplies at the site, the financial stability of the site vendor, the number of hours per year your organization can use the site for testing its disaster recovery plan, the location of the nearest airport, the vendor's approach to protecting its site (e.g., whether the vendor has a fire control system and what flood or water damage control system is in place), and the type of backup system in place in the event of a disaster at the site.

- *Determine the Recovery Alternatives That Should Be Analyzed.* During this activity, the organization needs to determine which recovery alternatives it will analyze. The options may include hot sites, cold sites, warm sites, mobile sites (i.e., hot sites located in a mobile trailer), or a contingency agreement (i.e., an agreement between your organization and another to serve as a recovery site in the event of a disaster at one of the locations).

- *Assess the Alternatives.* The purpose of this activity is to assess the costs and benefits of each alternative. Using the evaluation criteria identified above, the organization completes a detailed assessment of each alternative.

- *Select an Alternative.* Based on the assessment performed in the previous step, the organization selects the recovery alternative that best meets its needs.

Prior to signing any contract for recovery-related services, it is important to complete a number of activities:

- Ensure the contract includes all oral promises made by the vendor.
- Avoid automatic renewal clauses.
- Ensure the contract provides your organization with sufficient time to test the recovery plan.

Figure 51-2   Key Recovery Site Evaluation Criteria.

• Cost	• Site communication capabilities
• Subscriber-to-site ratio	• Site vendor-consulting capabilities
• Site location	• Site support staff capabilities
• Site security	• Availability of site office space
• Site fire and water protection features	• Location of nearest airport
• Site data storage capacity	• Site backup systems
• Site vendor's financial stability	• Annual hours available for testing the plan

- Have an attorney and an IS consultant familiar with recovery-related services review the contract prior to signing it.

(c) PHASE III—DOCUMENT COMPONENTS OF THE DISASTER RECOVERY PLAN

During this phase, the disaster recovery plan components are clearly documented. The key steps of this phase are:

1. *Develop the Timeline for Recovery.* During this activity, the organization defines its recovery time targets for each major function (e.g., the mainframe must be recovered within 48 hours and personal computers must be replaced within one week).
2. *Develop Recovery "Scripts" (i.e., Action Plans) for Each Major Function.* The scripts should include: tasks to be completed, who specifically will be responsible for each task, the timing of the task, where the task will occur (e.g., at headquarters or the hot site), and how to complete the task.
3. *Develop the Recovery Schedule.* The objective of this task is to develop the precise schedule of events that will occur in the event of a disaster.

(d) PHASE IV—DEVELOP THE DISASTER RECOVERY PLAN

The objective of this phase is to prepare the disaster recovery plan. A sample recovery plan is shown in Figure 51-3.

The key components of this phase are:

1. An executive overview of the disaster recovery plan (i.e., an executive summary of the scope and objective of the plan, and a high-level presentation of the recovery strategies).
2. Emergency response procedures. An overview of the procedures that should take place in the event of a disaster (e.g., shutdown of the computers, fire suppression techniques, evacuation procedures, and notification procedures).
3. Action plan for responding to the disaster. Approaches for assessing the damage, notifying employees, and activating the disaster recovery plan.

Figure 51-3 Sample Disaster Recovery Plan—Table of Contents.

- Executive Overview
- Emergency Response Procedures
- Action Plan for Response
- Approach for Recovering Operations
- How Operations Will Be Restored
- How to Test and Maintain the Plan
- Appendices
- Glossary

4. The approach for recovering operations. Procedures for recovering the hardware, software, and network, and for ensuring that data entry operations are resumed in a timely manner.

5. How operations will be restored. An action plan for restoring operations at the disaster site or at an alternative site. The plan should contain an approach for constructing a new facility, acquiring new hardware and software (if appropriate), and testing the new system prior to implementation.

6. How to test and maintain the plan. A detailed approach to tests and maintenance of the plan.

7. Appendices. Relevant information on the inventory of hardware and software, employee contacts, insurance policies, software licensing agreements, network and hardware vendor support agreements, and the list of data stored offsite and instructions on how to obtain it.

8. Glossary. Definitions of technical terms used in the plan.

One final note: Be sure a copy of the plan is stored offsite in a fire and waterproof location. In the event of a disaster, it won't be destroyed if given proper protection.

(e) PHASE V—EXECUTE, EVALUATE, AND MAINTAIN THE DISASTER RECOVERY PLAN

The main objectives of this phase are to verify that the disaster recovery plan works as designed and that the plan is appropriately maintained. The scope of the testing should include hardware, system and application software, and the communication network.

The key steps in this phase, which are depicted in Figure 51-4, are:

1. Develop the disaster recovery plan test objectives and evaluation criteria. Specifically, the organization needs to define what it is trying to achieve by testing the disaster recovery plan, and how it will evaluate the success or failure of the test.

Figure 51-4   Approach to Executing, Evaluating, and Maintaining the Plan.

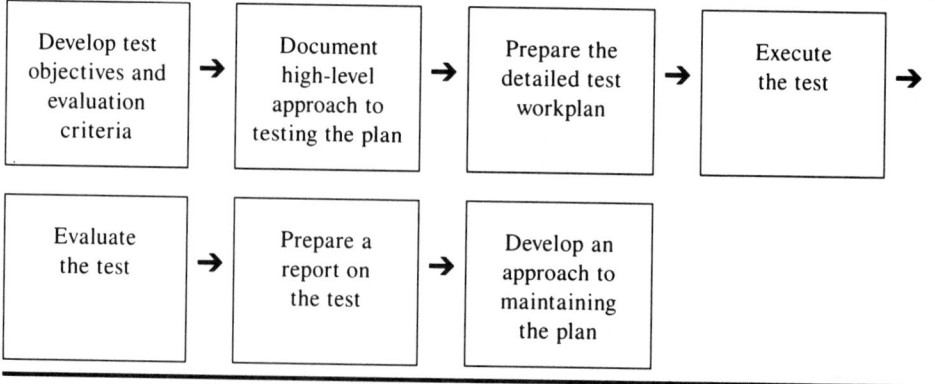

2. Document the high-level approach to testing the disaster recovery plan. During this activity, the organization needs to define clearly what is to be tested and how it will be tested.

3. Prepare the detailed test workplan. The purpose of this step is to identify and document the specific steps to be taken to test the disaster recovery plan. Who will perform the test? Where will they perform the test? When will they perform the test?

4. Execute the test. During this step, the test is conducted.

5. Evaluate the test. This is one of the most important steps of this phase. The organization needs to critically evaluate what went right and what went wrong during the testing process, and incorporate appropriate changes into the plan.

6. Prepare a written report on the test. In this step, the testing team documents the scope and objective of the test and its own approach to the test. The results of the test and the changes made to the disaster recovery plan after conducting the test should be included in this document. The report should be presented to senior management, as well as to internal and external auditors, for review and comments.

7. Develop an approach to maintaining the plan. During this step, an approach to storing the plan is documented. The frequency (e.g., quarterly) with which the plan needs to be reviewed and revised is formalized.

51-4 CONCLUSION

Disaster recovery planning is one of the most important areas on which an organization can focus. Without an effective disaster recovery plan, an entity is extremely susceptible to natural and/or manmade disasters. An organization that has no current and well-tested plan may find itself subject to a lawsuit or at a competitive disadvantage. It is the responsibility of all senior executives, not just the director of information systems, to ensure that an organization can quickly and effectively recover from a disaster.

CHAPTER 52

Change Management

52-1 INTRODUCTION

Most companies are undergoing significant change. Much of this change is dictated by business environments because companies must respond to competitors' improvements. The need to change has not escaped the Controller Division. It is now very common for the Controller Division to have several significant initiatives underway simultaneously, such as the implementation of a new financial system, a new chart of accounts, a new purchasing process, and the like. Information technology is an area in which organizations are making changes to enhance their competitive position in today's volatile business environment.

Frequently, companies are disappointed with the results of their projects. In fact, research has shown that the majority of projects fail to achieve their objectives on time and within budget. Some projects fail because they are abandoned before they can be installed. However, even if the project is completed, unless the original schedule and budget are achieved, the benefits expected from the project have eroded—perhaps seriously.

Why do major projects fail to achieve their full potential so frequently? Most of the time, the identified solution is adequate for addressing the problem or opportunity that exists. Consequently, a search for a "better solution" is not likely to improve implementation. Instead, most failures are directly attributable to the implementation of the solution.

This chapter was authored by Sara Moulton, Senior Manager, Ernst & Young LLP, Denver, CO.

Most major projects involve changes to technology and business processes. These changes will affect the way people do their work—what they will do and how they will do it. Implementing a new financial system, for example, may require people to use new equipment, understand and navigate new software packages, handle transactions in a different way, and use new types of information or report formats. In implementing a project such as this, careful consideration is typically given to the hardware platform, data and reporting requirements, interfaces, and the like. Although a high degree of care is devoted to this type of technical requirements, typically less than 5% of effort on projects is devoted to managing the effects the technical changes will have on the people.

Transition is uncomfortable; for organizations, it is also costly. One recent study shows that, during transition, productive time is consumed by a large increase in both social/gossip time and retraining requirements. This study showed that productive time can be as little as 25% of its regular levels during transition. The data clearly shows how important it is to manage transition issues so that regular productivity can be achieved as quickly as possible.

The practice of managing the human elements associated with projects is known as *change management*. Most companies struggle with change management; consequently, most projects fail to achieve their objectives on schedule and within the originally established budget. Although there may be some comfort in being part of the majority, a competitive opportunity exists for the companies that can increase their effectiveness in this difficult area.

52-2 DEFINING THE CHANGE MANAGEMENT CHALLENGE

Ernst & Young, LLP has identified several change management principles that have been shown to lead to successful project implementations. These principles have been developed through their experience managing numerous major implementation projects and through the contributions of companies such as ODR, Inc. These guiding principles can be used to increase the likelihood of success on any project implementation.

The most important initial step in successfully managing a project is to define the change management challenge. In other words, how much time and attention needs to be devoted to managing the difficult transition period so that people can reach full productivity under their new job requirements? Understanding the change management challenge is important to the development of a realistic schedule and budget for any project.

There are several factors that can help a management team to define the change management challenge. When a project sponsor, perhaps with the assistance of the next tier of management, carefully and candidly considers these areas, a picture of the likelihood of project success will begin to emerge. The most important thing is to consider these factors *very early* in the life of the project when there is time to devote attention to the human aspects of the project's implementation.

A complete list of change management factors is beyond the scope of this text. However, several important factors that can help an organization to define the change management challenge are:

- Implementation history.
- Competing projects.

- Degree of disruption.
- Cost of failure.
- Change management risks.

(a) IMPLEMENTATION HISTORY

Organizations, like people, tend to follow the patterns they have established in the past. Consequently, a careful review of a company's implementation history is valuable for understanding the challenges faced by the current project. The most applicable patterns emerge when the current project is compared to recent projects that involved the same types of changes and/or the same groups of people.

In considering the organization's implementation history, it is important to identify facets that were effective as well as facets that were ineffective toward achieving project success. After this, the reasons behind effective and ineffective results should be explored. Both pieces of information are valuable. Overcoming past weaknesses is frequently an important key to achieving success on the current project. In addition, each organization has its own reasons for success, and these strengths should be used to fullest advantage.

In considering implementation history, start by identifying the past projects that can provide valuable "lessons learned" for the current project. Then categorize these projects by the level of success achieved. The categories may include projects where:

- Objectives were achieved on schedule and within budget.
- Objectives were achieved, but somewhat off schedule and/or over budget.
- Objectives were achieved, but significantly off schedule and/or over budget.
- Objectives were not achieved, although the project was implemented.
- Project was scrapped before installation.

After categorizing the projects, look for patterns to emerge in the way the project's implementation effort was managed. Ask tough questions, such as:

How realistic were the implementation budgets and schedules?

What support, in addition to training, was given to the people who had to do their work differently as a result of the project?

How much notice was given before the change took place?

Were people given adequate time to learn their new activities while balancing regular work responsibilities?

How much communication was done, and what types of communication methods appear to have been the most effective?

In what ways were middle and lower level employees involved in the decision making process?

How were people held accountable for performing the new job requirements?

How were people rewarded for adequately performing the new job requirements?

How effectively were the projects managed?

How were unexpected events handled during implementation?

How well did the organization focus on the project when day-to-day problems competed for people's attention?

What are people's perceptions about the overall effectiveness of the organization's implementation history, and how could this perception positively or negatively affect the current project?

Although the exercise of considering past successes and failures can be difficult and humbling, it can give the management team insight into the specific actions that should be managed for the current project to be successful. If the organization has a troubled implementation history, it is important to recognize that this can be extremely difficult to overcome. However, overcoming a troubled history is possible when the organization devotes itself to the extraordinary effort and attention that will be necessary to overcome the deficiencies of the past.

In critically assessing their implementation histories, some companies discover that their employees have very long memories. Even problems that occurred many years ago can taint people's opinion as to their organization's ability to be effective. As it assessed its implementation history, one private utility company had to deal with employees surfacing problems from nearly a decade earlier. To put a positive light to these long memories, the president reached back to a time when the organization was held in high respect by its employees. Members of the project team received pins that portrayed the company's logo from that positive time in its history. These pins brought prestige to the project and the members of the team. However, much more important than this symbol, the "hands-off" president stayed actively involved in project activities. This demonstration of sponsorship and support was viewed very positively as a step toward overcoming some of its more recent troubled implementations.

(b) COMPETING PROJECTS

Many companies are pursuing a large number of initiatives at the same time. Aside from the resource drain and coordination problems that often exist, this agenda of initiatives frequently impacts the same groups of people with little, if any, relief between project implementations. Too much change too quickly can leave people feeling "shell shocked," which reduces productivity even beyond that normally expected during transition. People who feel overwhelmed are less productive, more prone to conflict, more likely to miss work, and the like. To make this concern even greater, it is important to remember that changes happening at work are only one type of change going on in a person's life at any given time. A person within the controller's division that is attempting to learn the new financial system may also be dealing with the birth of a child, an illness in the family, or a divorce.

To gain an appreciation for the total amount of change the organization is requiring of its people, it is important to take a full inventory of projects. It is not unusual for this exercise to produce an amazingly long list of projects. These projects may be analyzed from several perspectives:

- How well does each project support the strategic direction of the company and/or the long-term goals of the division or department?

- Are the strategic direction and long-term goals made clearer to the organization as these projects are rolled out?
- How well do the projects relate to and support each other?
- Do certain projects detract from other projects or from the goals of other departments or groups?
- Are there adequate connections between related projects?
- Are all impacted groups adequately represented in the project teams or management advisory groups?
- Who are the people to be impacted by each project and how significant will the impact be?
- What is the timing of the impact? Are there overlapping impacts and timeframes that should be managed or reconsidered?
- Who will perceive that they "win" something as a consequence of the project? Who will perceive that they "lose" something?

Armed with this information, the management team needs to make the following determinations:

- What are the project priorities?
- What projects can be delayed or scrapped?
- What are realistic time frames for implementation taking all projects and their overlapping impacts into consideration?

These are especially important questions. Often organizations consider each project to be of equal importance. This is neither realistic nor effective. One of the critical elements to focus the attention of the organization and effectively use scarce resources most advantageously is to look at each project and how it supports the overall strategy and goals of the organization. Also, note that business conditions are constantly changing, so project priorities may require periodic reassessment.

- How should projects with overlapping impacts or time frames be managed to help reduce the potential of overwhelming the people?
- How should project priorities and other important information such as strategic direction be communicated throughout the organization?

It is important to acknowledge that people have only a finite ability to accept change over a given period of time. When this ability is not adequately considered, the company will pay a price in lost productivity that exceeds what is necessary. One company chose to implement a fully integrated information system at the same time that its industry was deregulating and jobs were changing significantly to accommodate the industry changes. The system changes were significant, but when it was added to the simultaneous job and departmental changes, the near term effect was nearly disastrous. At one point, nearly half of the organization was involved in the Employee Assistance Program for problems such as severe stress, alcoholism, and the like. To assist with these problems, the company chose to employ change management activities in conjunction with documenting and confirming the processes required by the new system. Although the problems were smoothed out over time, the near-term situation could have been made less painful, and less costly, for the organization and its employees if change management assistance had been employed before, rather than after, the system implementation.

(c) DEGREE OF DISRUPTION

Most people are startled to discover that people actually *do not resist change.* Instead, people *resist the disruption* that change brings. This is an important distinction because people may resist projects that they believe in and want to see implemented because they fear change. Consequently, measuring the degree of disruption is the first way to start predicting the degree of resistance expected from the project.

Measuring the degree of disruption caused by a project is not especially easy, nor are there exact quantitative means to do it. However, there are several specific questions that help to define the degree of disruption:

- How significantly will the project affect the way that people do their work?
- How easy will it be for people to understand the project and accurately predict how it will effect them?
- How much of the necessary knowledge and skills do the people presently possess?
- How much will daily routines differ after the project is implemented?
- How will the project impact the organization's power and influence structures?
- How much change has been expected of the people in the past, and how willing have they been to embrace it?

In defining the degree of disruption, management frequently underestimates the degree of disruption a project will create in the lives of the people who are impacted. For this reason, it is valuable to ask the people that will be impacted for their answers to the same questions.

In defining disruption, two related considerations can be helpful. First, the organization's history with regard to change can help to define people's expectations about change. Some organizations have had to accommodate greater amounts of change due to industry factors, company growth, and the like. Companies that expect change on the basis of their history may find smaller amounts of change to be less disruptive. One fast-growing high technology organization described itself as "good at change." In assessing the challenge posed by a significant process reengineering effort, the organization admitted that the amount and types of revisions required by the project differed from its experience. For this reason, change management activities were used to support achievement of the reengineering project. Second, organizations that have workforces who feel a high degree of time pressure may find virtually any change to be disruptive. The reason for this is that the people understand the energy and effort it will take to make the change and may feel that there is simply no way to "fit it in." Frequently, these organizations need to carefully prioritize competing initiatives and make tradeoffs that allow people more time to cope with change.

(d) COST OF FAILURE

When a project fails, there are costs that will be paid by the organization. The most obvious ones include wasted time, money, and effort, and the fact that little or nothing was accomplished in addressing the problems and opportunities that launched the project. However, these costs actually may have less impact on the organization than the costs that may seem less obvious.

In addition to the financial costs associated with failure, there are costs that are harder to define in financial terms. These costs include the potential for decreased morale, especially for the people who worked on the project and those who were highly committed to the project goals. Also, people may begin to doubt the organization's leadership. Ultimately, the people may learn to ignore directives, believing that new projects will fail like ones in the past. These nonfinancial costs can have devastating effects on the ability to start and sustain projects.

The management team needs to carefully consider what would happen if the project were to fail to achieve its objectives on schedule and within budget. During this analysis, it is especially important to assess the nonfinancial costs because they can have the longest impact on the organization. Since some projects are much more important to the organization than others, this type of analysis can help determine the projects that warrant the greatest degree of care, especially in the area of managing the "people" risks.

Once the costs associated with failure are considered, a very important question needs to be asked: Can the organization afford the cost of failure?

- If so, there may be more important initiatives that warrant increased emphasis and attention.
- If not, it is important to ensure that realistic schedules and budgets are produced and that significant effort is devoted to managing the human aspects of the project.

In one organization undertaking a significant reengineering initiative, the 10 members of the executive staff were asked questions in the area of failure costs. Then each executive was asked whether or not the organization could afford to fail at the effort. The results indicated that six of the executives felt that the project was "mission critical" and that they could not afford to fail. The other four, while believing the project was very important, felt that the project was not critical to the organization. The "correct" answer was not as important as getting these key sponsors to agree as to the criticality of the project. In this instance, these differences of opinion had begun impacting the project schedule and quality. The executives who believed that the organization could afford to fail with the project were devoting resources that were inadequate to achieve the schedule and budget that had been approved. Surfacing these types of differences early in the project lifecycle allows for reconciliation so that there will be minimal impacts to project objectives, schedules, and budgets.

(e) CHANGE MANAGEMENT RISKS

There are a series of elements that can help to define a project's risk from a change management perspective. Research has shown that active management of these risks is very beneficial for achieving project objectives on schedule and within budget. Applying the practices known to be associated with successful projects, as well as avoiding the mistakes others have made, can greatly enhance the potential for success on any project. The full list of these risk elements is rather lengthy, but making an effort to manage the following factors can be of great benefit:

- Adequacy of sponsorship.
- Adequacy of the motivation.
- Vision clarity.
- Degree of resistance.

(i) Adequacy of Sponsorship. Sponsorship is the single most important change management risk factor. Without sponsorship that is *adequately demonstrated,* the project is virtually certain to fail to achieve its objectives on schedule and within budget. Most people within organizations know the importance of sponsorship, but it is difficult for many people to define whether or not it will be effective.

When considering a project's sponsor, most people think of a member of top management or, perhaps the person responsible for the day-to-day management of the project. In fact, to be successful, there needs to be a network of sponsors that moves down the entire management chain starting at the individual or group of people who have the organizational power to start and stop the project. Managers and supervisors of in-scope personnel must also sponsor the project because they have direct access to the people who need to change as a result of the project's requirements. Managers and supervisors can also send strong messages about the project's importance by using managerial decisions such as promotion/advancement, compensation, and rewards to motivate people toward achievement of the project objectives.

Although it is important to have a network of sponsors, sponsorship emanates from the top. The specific definition of "top" depends on the project and the departments that will be impacted by it. In determining who needs to be the ultimate sponsor of the project, it is often valuable to draw a picture of all the groups of people to be impacted, their management chain, and especially influential people within those groups. The purpose of this picture is to determine how the project will actually unfold in the organization so the formal and informal influence networks need to be added to the picture. Although it may be valuable to use an organization chart in beginning to draw this picture, the end result will not look like the organization chart if the informal network is adequately considered. For instance, there may be influences that cut beyond departmental boundaries due to historical or personal circumstances, as well as individuals with specific expertise that will apply to the project.

This picture should be drawn starting from the bottom of the organization. As the picture moves up through the organization, it is important to look for the first place that the in-scope groups come to a common manager. This may be the ultimate sponsor of the project. However, it is important to consider whether or not this manager has the authority to stop the project unilaterally. If not, considering this question may help to determine the ultimate sponsor(s). Most people in the organization know the people who have the specific authority to make these types of decisions for any given project and to believe that the project has the needed sponsorship to be successful, they must see that the project is truly the priority of these people.

The ultimate sponsor needs to work with his or her direct reports and other influential people within the organization to help them to understand the reasons for the project and its importance to the organization. Depending on the way the project was identified and launched, there may be the need to educate the ultimate sponsor in this important area. The ultimate sponsor also needs details about the vision. This is the first step in building the network of sponsors necessary to make the project successful.

A common misconception about sponsorship is that it can be delegated to others. Unless it is absolutely clear and believed, that the project "belongs to" the person or people who have the authority to start and stop it, it is possible for people to give the project less priority and support than it needs to be successful. For this reason, sponsorship cannot be a "spectator sport"; it must be demonstrated by the right people to be effective. The following are some characteristics of effective sponsors:

- Effective sponsors devote adequate time and attention to communications about the project, its importance, the objectives, and status. This time is spent both with groups and one-on-one with key people on specific issues. The more time that is devoted to the project by the key sponsors, the more credibility the project will enjoy.

- Effective sponsors make sacrifices to increase the likelihood of success for the project. These sacrifices may including postponing or slowing initiatives that compete for the same resources, devoting extra personal effort, or allowing near-term financial shortfalls for the sake of achieving the project objectives.

- Effective sponsors ensure that adequate resources are dedicated to the project and maintain these resources throughout the project. These resources include the time of specific key individuals from the organization, even if this choice impacts other priorities. Sponsors who devote resources that are available rather than the best resources are sending a signal to the organization that the project is not especially important. In addition to dedicating specific key individuals, effective sponsors ensure that the budgets and time frames are adequate for enabling the project to be successful.

- Effective sponsors are willing to make difficult staffing and personnel decisions, but only after they have empathetically considered the impact to the individuals and the organization. Frequently, sponsors must spend a great deal of time with specific individuals to help them to understand the importance of the project and what these individuals need to do—and *not* do—to make the project successful. Even the most resistant of people can frequently be brought around to support a project after the sponsor has devoted adequate time and attention to gaining their support. However, if the project is jeopardized by the resistance, or inappropriate actions of specific individuals, staffing and/or job changes may be required. These decisions can be especially tough because changes may be needed among key contributors to the organization's past successes. In making these decisions, it is valuable to weigh the trade off between making the difficult personnel decision versus accepting the risk that the project may fail to achieve its objectives on schedule and on budget if a personnel change is not made.

Finally, sponsors need to be aware that people "listen" to several things. First, they listen to what sponsors say and how they said it. Also, they "listen" to what the sponsors did *not* say. Finally, they "listen" to what the sponsors *do,* which has the strongest impact because it indicates the sponsor's true intent. In sponsoring a project, it is most important to carefully consider every action and make sure that people perceive these actions as consistent with achievement of the project objectives, schedule, and budget.

(ii) Adequacy of the Motivation. Transition is uncomfortable. In particular, transition attacks a person's feelings of confidence, competency, comfort, and control by replacing the known and familiar with the unknown and unfamiliar. It takes significant emotional and mental energy to learn new things and gain new habits. Consequently, people do not willingly initiate change if it does not appear necessary, or if the benefits do not outweigh the effort that will be required to make the transition. The more significant the transition will be, the more motivation a person will need to initiate and move through that transition.

Motivation is created by an understanding of problems that need to be addressed or opportunities that can be used advantageously. These problems or opportunities may either exist in the present or be expected in the future. For many people, problems create more motivation for change than opportunities. Also, existing conditions tend to be more motivational than anticipated conditions. However, adequate motivation can be created even for anticipated opportunities. The key to creating motivation is focusing on the reasons for making the change. In other words, what are the benefits to be gained by implementation of the project? Conversely, without implementation of the project, what would be lost? Frequently, communications about projects focus almost exclusively on details about the solution and neglect to build adequate motivation among the people to make the transition to that solution.

As unusual as it sounds, to motivate people to change, it is necessary to help them to feel dissatisfied or uncomfortable with the way things are today. If people are comfortable with the way things are, they have little or no motivation to go through the discomfort of transition. Creating adequate motivation is a matter of helping people to see and feel how unacceptable it would be to maintain the status quo.

Building adequate motivation starts by an understanding of what the organization perceives about its current state. If people are dissatisfied with the way things are today, the necessary motivation may already exist. If, however, there are some people who are resistant to the project, a good first step in dealing with that resistance is to test their level of motivation:

- Do people really understand what will happen if the project objectives are not achieved in a timely, cost effective manner? Do people understand how they might be impacted if the project were to be unsuccessful? Creating this level of understanding requires time, often one-on-one with people.

- For example, will current problems reach a level where the systems, processes, and work schedules will break down? Will the company lose market share, industry position, or its customer base? Will competition catch up or pull ahead of the company? Will employment and/or advancement opportunities be negatively effected?

- Do people really believe that the project will happen? What specifically can be done to overcome any skepticism that may exist?

- Are people getting consistent messages from all levels of management and from different departments about the importance of the project?

Some activities that organizations have used to raise the degree of motivation toward a project include:

- Establishment of a standing agenda item for staff meetings to discuss the project status and development of periodic update packages for managers to present during these staff meetings.
- Periodic executive/top management departmental visits for question and answer sessions.
- Distribution of regular project updates to management and employees through a variety of different media, such as newsletters, memos, phone messages, etc.
- Executive/top management one-on-one meetings with specific important, influential, and/or resistant individuals.

(iii) Vision Clarity.   Once people are adequately motivated to achieve a project's objectives, they need to see that the project's vision represents an answer to the problems or opportunities that make up their motivation. Feeling motivated to take action without knowing what to do gives people a hopeless or frustrated feeling. In essence, without a clear vision, people are being asked to move toward something that they do not understand nor believe will bring the relief they seek. In this situation, most people will do nothing, but some people will take action to relieve the anxiety they feel. However, without a vision to guide them, it is very unlikely that even the people who do move forward will arrive at the desired end.

Most people understand the need to provide a vision to their people. However, where most project visions fall short of their goal is in providing people with a clear picture of what the future will look and feel like. In other words, what will be each person's daily working conditions once that vision is fulfilled? Frequently, visions contain lofty concepts, platitudes, and "politically correct" language. Although few people would disagree with these types of visions, even fewer people know how to create and work toward them. Effective visions are built with an understanding that their purpose is to target people's actions. This requires visions to be clear and actionable.

Creating an effective vision requires time. It also must involve the sponsors of the project to a heavy extent to ensure that the visionaries behind the project are revealing their expectations and ideas about the future. The vision needs to answer several important questions, such as:

- What are the objectives this vision seeks to achieve?
- What are the detailed changes that will occur, and what is the timing/staging of these changes?
- What are the requirements to achieve the vision?
- What will be the daily working conditions for specific job categories after implementation of the vision? For example:

    —What equipment and procedures will people use?

    —What types of decisions will they make?

—How will they need to interact with others to perform their job requirements?

—How will their performance be evaluated, compensated and rewarded?

—How will the departments, groups, and teams be structured?

—What knowledge and skills will be necessary to perform the work?

Evaluating these questions in detail among the sponsors and project team is an important clarification step in any project. One project team discovered firsthand the importance of taking the time to clarify its vision in this manner. After presentation of the vision to the sponsors, the vision had been approved. The team carefully documented its approved vision, primarily to enable easy communication of the vision to groups that had not been involved in the vision's development. However, when presented in the new written format augmented with more details, the vision was found to differ from the expectations and understanding of the sponsors. This problem was discovered and corrected quickly, and the potential for wasted effort was avoided.

After the vision is documented, it needs to be communicated so that people understand it and its impact. One way that organizations have used to communicate their visions is to give their employees "day-in-the-life" information. In other words, describe what life will be like for certain departments or jobs using fictitious newspaper articles written for the future, role plays, prototype tools, and so on. Also, recognize that effectively communicating a vision requires repetition using multiple means because communication mechanisms are not equally effective, nor do they all reach the intended audience with the desired message.

One final note about communicating a vision: as people begin to understand the future, they will also begin to understand the disruption it will cause. Until a vision is fairly well understood, it is common for very little resistance to be felt from the organization. However, once the vision and its corresponding disruption is understood, the organization frequently displays resistance for the first time. This can leave the sponsors and project team wondering if there is something wrong because things may have seemed relatively smooth up to that point. This is an important time to carefully distinguish between real objections based on content versus the objections that represent resistance to the disruption and manage each accordingly.

(iv) Degree of Resistance. To repeat an important concept: People do not resist change; rather they resist the disruption caused by the change. This concept is important in explaining why people will resist a change that they view positively, and perhaps even initiated themselves. For this reason, resistance must be expected and planned for because it cannot be avoided. It is also important to note that resistance is not necessarily an indication that something is wrong. Instead, it is frequently an indication that the person understands what they are being asked to do to and correspondingly, what it will take for the project to be accomplished. From this perspective, resistance may be a good indication that effective communication has taken place.

Resistance has a variety of causes. Some of the most common ones are:

- Confusion about the project vision.
- Inadequate motivation.

- Unclear or inconsistent messages from sponsors and other key individuals about the importance of the project (e.g., changing or conflicting priorities).
- Poor implementation history.
- Lack of adequate time to respond to and absorb the changes.
- History of failing to deal adequately with people who ignore project directives.

It is important to create an environment that resistance can be expressed openly without fear of retribution. Suppressed resistance will still negatively affect the project's goals, but will be much more difficult to surface and manage.

Resistance is addressed by first identifying its source. One source of resistance is lack of knowledge and skills to perform to the new expectations. This contributes to the person's feelings of inadequacy and incompetence. Addressing this type of resistance is through education and training. A "just-in-time" philosophy to education and training is especially effective because it enables the person to use the knowledge and skills soon after learning them. The second source of resistance comes from a lack of willingness to perform the project's requirements. Addressing resistance from this source involves several steps:

- Does the person really understand the need for the change? (see *Adequacy of the Motivation*).
- Are there any inconsistencies that need to be corrected? (see *Adequacy of Sponsorship,* and *Vision Clarity*).
- Are there adequate rewards for performing to project requirements and consequences for neglecting or performing poorly against those same requirements?

The final step requires that specific measures to assess project progress and individual achievement of project expectations be developed. Then, achievement against those measures needs to be assessed periodically. This step also requires a commitment to following up with people on the results of those assessments—either by giving them rewards that are valuable to them or consequences that will be motivational toward improvements in the future. This type of program can be difficult to administer because it involves the distinct possibility of having to confront nonperformance, which most people find unsettling. However, if the project is truly important to the organization, allowing people to resist willingly and successfully invites a project's failure.

52-3 CONCLUSION

Change is going to be a way of life for organizations for the foreseeable future. Business conditions are dictating the need for projects across all areas of organizations, including the controller division. Unfortunately, research shows that the majority of these projects will fail to achieve their objectives on schedule and within budget.

The difference between successful and unsuccessful projects is most frequently the degree to which the human factors associated with the projects receive the appropriate level of attention. In defining the level of attention appropriate to a particular project, it is important to look at the organization's implementation history, competing initiatives, the degree of disruption the project will cause, and the costs that the organization would have to pay if the project were to fail. It is also important to know the degree of risk the project faces, particularly in the areas of sponsorship, motivation, vision, and resistance. It is most valuable to consider these factors early in the life of a project so that there is time to take action to increase the likelihood of success for the project.

Managing these change management factors takes time and effort. However, this time and effort pays off by enhancing the likelihood that the project will achieve its full benefits for the organization.

52-4 SELECTED REFERENCES

Bridges, William, *Surviving Corporate Transition,* Mill Valley, CA: William Bridges & Associates, 1993.

"Building Commitment to Organizational Change," Denver, CO: Ernst & Young LLP, and ODR, Inc., 1992.

"Change Inventory and Priority Assessment," Denver, CO: Ernst & Young LLP, 1994.

Conner, Daryl R., *Managing at the Speed of Change,* New York: Villard Books, 1993.

"Determinants of Successful Organizational Change," Denver, CO: Ernst & Young LLP, and ODR, Inc., 1992.

"The Emotional Cycle of Change," Denver, CO: Ernst & Young LLP, and ODR, Inc., 1992.

Ernst & Young U.S. LLP Performance Improvement Series: Organizational Change Management Methodology, Denver, CO: Ernst & Young LLP, 1992.

Hefner, Mark, and Dave Schrader, "Merging Effectively: Taking the Mystery Out of Managing Change," *Current Issues,* June 1994.

"How to Be an Effective Sponsor of Organizational Change," Denver, CO: Ernst & Young LLP, and ODR, Inc., 1992.

"Implementation History Assessment," Denver, CO: Ernst & Young LLP, and ODR, Inc., 1992.

Merlyn, Vaughan, "When Change Becomes Continuous," Denver, CO: Ernst & Young LLP, 1994.

Oakley, Ed, and Doug Krug, *Enlightened Leadership,* Denver, CO: StoneTree Publishing, 1992.

"Predicting the Impact of Change," Denver, CO: Ernst & Young LLP, 1993.

"Role Map Application Tool," Denver, CO: Ernst & Young LLP, and ODR, Inc., 1992.

"X-Factor Change Readiness Assessment Technique," Denver, CO: Ernst & Young LLP, 1994.

PART SEVEN

SOME ADMINISTRATIVE AND SPECIAL ASPECTS OF THE CONTROLLER'S DEPARTMENT

CHAPTER 53

Financial Planning and Analysis for Acquisitions, Mergers, and Divestments

53-1 HISTORY OF ACQUISITIONS AND MERGERS

A review of U.S. business history of the last three-quarters of a century will reveal recurring cycles of industrial combinations and acquisitions. The principal manner by which this may be accomplished may change periodically—for example, from a predominance of large, horizontal, multiform consolidations to conglomerate acquisitions of relatively smaller companies. Styles and types of consideration and amounts paid relative to market price of the stock may change, for example, from negotiated agreements to contested tender offers, from a package of securities to largely cash, from small premiums above stock market price of the acquired to substantial premiums. Given the decline in the value of the dollar, the rapid rate of inflation with consequent high facility replacement costs, and the greater potential stability in the United States, there has been more merger activity in the late 1980s than in some of the earlier periods. Greatly increased levels of activity tend to create a sellers' market and consequently to put added value on sound analysis. The number of acquisition candidates that are available at prices to permit the acquiror to earn a fair return on investment is limited; therefore, the buyer presumably will be more discerning than otherwise.

In the mid-1990s, there is an acceleration of acquisition activity. The characteristics of this current wave, which are discussed later in this chapter, include these features:

- Mergers of groups already large in their own right, which are measured in the billions of dollars.
- Many foreign-based entities are acquiring U.S. companies, induced in part by the depreciation of the dollar vs. foreign currencies.
- Exceedingly high initial bids as compared to market value of the stock of the target (or its book value).
- Securing a much stronger place in the highly competitive national or international market for companies that are already large.
- Achieving a better degree of vertical integration.
- A reduction in the number of highly leveraged buyouts wherein the cash flow of the target pays for the acquisition, and many divisions of the acquired group are sold to reduce the excessive or heavy debt.
- The current rise in acquisition, merger, and divestment activity involving fields such as health, aerospace, food, banking, media, transportation, and telecommunications, indicates that acquisition and merger activity reached approximately $340 billion in 1994.

This chapter reviews the reasons for acquisitions, as well as divestments, and discusses some sound acquisition procedures, including valuation techniques.

53-2 RELATION OF ACQUISITIONS TO CORPORATE OBJECTIVES

Corporate objectives may be achieved by several means, and effective planning must consider alternative routes available to any given company. Corporate goals of growth in earnings may be attained by internal means, but such growth may take many years and in fact may involve more cost and risk than acquiring a suitable existing company. Consequently, as discussed in Chapter 14, it is understandable that some firms will look to acquisitions or mergers to achieve some of the corporate objectives.

In any given time, there are several financial or operating reasons for which a corporation may wish to acquire another active business. Some of these are listed here:

1. Diversification for growth.
2. Diversification by market or customer to offset seasonal factors, to counteract a declining product market, etc.
3. Broadening, completing, or complementing product lines.
4. Acquiring needed research and development capabilities.
5. Creating or acquiring new product lines.
6. Integrating or otherwise securing an adequate supply of critical materials or parts.
7. Broadening markets, including previously untapped foreign markets.
8. Improving management by filling voids in talent or aging capabilities.
9. Acquiring modern manufacturing or research facilities.
10. Providing additional working capital or other funds.
11. Achieving the maximum permitted advantage of tax, or other, laws.
12. Investing idle capital.
13. Increasing the market value of the stock.
14. Providing customers with new services.
15. Improving the corporate image and reputation.

Financially speaking, these may be summarized in large part as meeting a long-range objective of increased earnings and higher market value of the stock, based on improved or superior service and/or products for the customer.

53-3 REASONS FOR DIVESTMENTS

Just as there are good reasons why the acquisition route may be used as the strategy of attaining a corporate objective, so also there are valid arguments for selling a business or parts thereof. For example, an entity may acquire a company and dispose of some segments in order to raise cash to reduce heavy indebtedness; or, especially, privately held entities may be sold for a variety of good reasons. Whatever the reason in a specific case, a number of causes for divesting a business include these:

- Need to reduce excess indebtedness.
- Need to diversity an estate.
- Management or owner dissension.
- Incomplete product line.
- Lack of required funds, or means of securing them, for necessary research and development, or market penetration.

- Lack of management succession.
- Declining or inadequate rate of profit.
- Inability of the management to cope with new technology, foreign competition, or other major market changes.
- Pending unfavorable legislation or regulations (air pollution, antitrust developments, etc.).
- Failure of management to understand foreign marketing, and presence of a buyer especially knowledgeable in this area.
- Probability of adverse income tax developments.

The amount and type of financial analysis desirable when disposing of a business is covered later in this chapter.

53-4 AN OVERVIEW OF THE ACQUISITION CYCLE

Having discussed the reasons for acquisitions, it may be helpful to get an overview of the acquisition cycle before considering in detail any of the steps.

A successful acquisition cycle is depicted in Figure 53-1. Finding a suitable acquisition candidate is not, or should not be, a haphazard event. It should be part of a carefully planned process. And, of course, determining that the acquisition route, rather than self-growth of the business, is the proper method of entering a business area, is a component of the strategic planning process discussed in Chapter 14.

Some brief comments on the acquisition steps in Figure 53-1 follow:

1. *Strategically Plan the Type of Acquisition Needed.* The acquisition cycle in fact commences when the strategic decision is made to pursue the acquisition route.

2. *Establish Suitable Criteria.* Initially it may appear that any number of acquisition candidates may meet the business need. However, certain aspects, such as insufficient present sales volume, may prove to be unsatisfactory. Therefore, to conserve management time and to assist in getting one of the most suitable candidates, it is helpful to establish certain acquisition criteria. These are discussed later in this chapter.

3. *Make a Diligent Search for Potential Candidates.* While members of top management, or the acquisition team, may have some logical candidates in mind, it is probably worth the special effort to develop a creditable and adequate list of potential candidates.

4. *Screen the Acquisition Candidates.* When the list of potential candidates is completed, each should be judged against the criteria established for the acquisition. Those appearing less suitable should be put aside.

5. *Make a Preliminary Analysis of the Candidates.* This review can be performed using public information, such as annual reports, 10K reports, industry data, etc., without the need of contacting the target. Such analysis probably will bring out facts that will eliminate some candidates from further discussion, or will identify the better ones.

Figure 53-1   Acquisition Cycle.

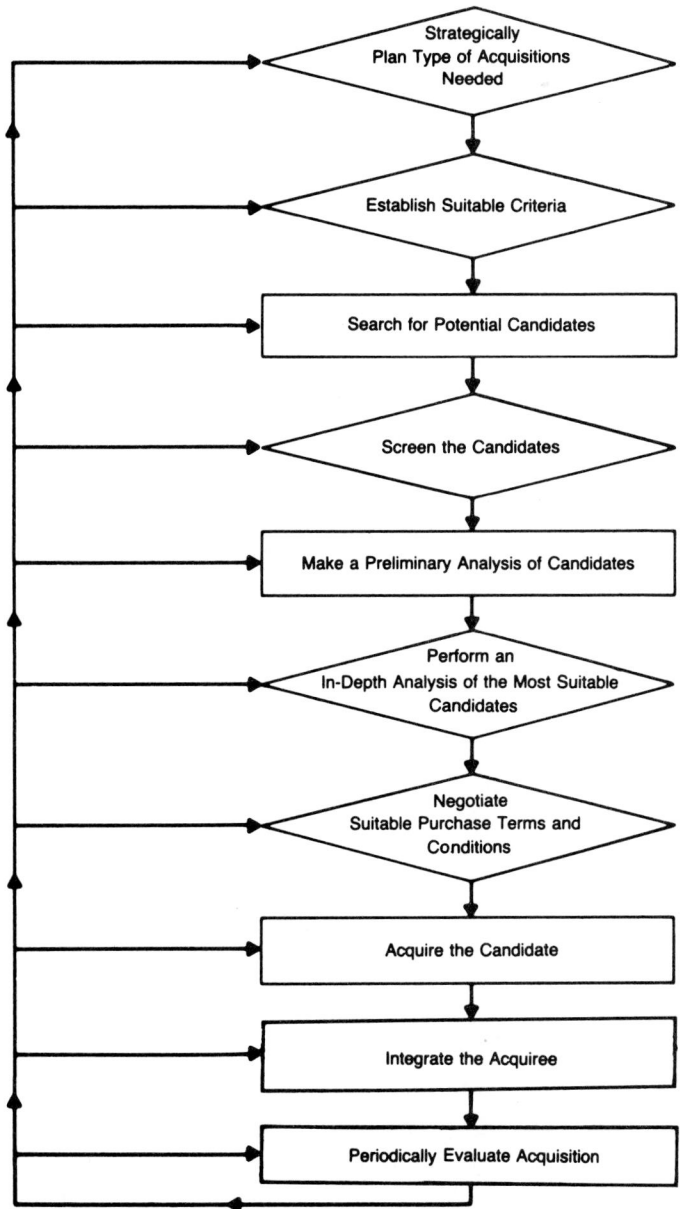

6. *Perform an In-Depth Analysis and Evaluation of the Apparently Most Suitable Candidate or Candidates.* This will necessitate contact with the potential acquiree and extensive in-depth reviews if the candidate is agreeable.

7. *Negotiate Suitable Purchase Agreement.* This will involve considering the wishes of the selling candidate and the most mutually acceptable method of structuring the acquisition.

8. *Consummate the Acquisition.* The terms of purchase and sale are carried out.

9. *Integrate the Acquiree.* Careful attention must be paid to *how* the candidate is integrated into the new group. Lack of follow-up and consideration of the viewpoint of the acquiree officers and employees often has caused an acquisition to be an economic disappointment.

10. *Finally, the Acquisition Should Be Periodically Evaluated.* How the acquiree performs vs. expectations should be reviewed. It usually cannot simply be left on its own. Guidance, and sometimes modification of operative conditions, etc., may be necessary.

Now, a few detailed comments on some of the acquisition steps made.

53-5 ACQUISITION CRITERIA

Usually it is prudent to set criteria for acquisitions and generally to adhere to them. Too many exceptions could lead to unsatisfactory combinations. Thus, management time is limited, and acquiring little companies could lead to excessive time demands by the smaller operations, usually to the detriment of more important matters. Hence, a minimum sales volume requirement could well be one of the criteria. Each industry has factors that are critical to success, as does each company. These matters may influence the criteria. Examples of some commonly used constraints in acquiring businesses include:

Type of Business

- Relation to a specific business need.
- Line of business (SIC codes).
- Ease of entry.
- Competitive posture.

Sales

- Sales volume.
- Share of market.
- Market growth rate.
- Share of foreign business.
- Share of U.S. government sales volume.

Financial/Economic

- Capital intensiveness.
- Capital structure (amount of debt).

Profitability

- Percent return on sales.
- Percent return on assets.

- Percent return on equity.
- Minimum absolute amount.

Other

- Quality of management.
- Specific management capabilities (e.g., sales manager).
- Physical location.
- Patent protection.
- Management compatibility.

In summary, proper guidelines or criteria can increase the chances of making a successful acquisition.

53-6 SOURCES OF ACQUISITION INFORMATION

Whether in the search for potential candidates, or for data in the preliminary analysis, or the in-depth review, there are a reasonable number of public information sources which may be helpful. These may relate to the economy, the industry, or specific competitors or companies. To be sure, some useful leads or data may be secured from such sources as trade meetings, informal social events, investment bankers, etc. But written data are available from a variety of sources (and there exist helpful retrieval systems on particular subjects):

1. *State of the Economy.*
   a. Annual *Statistical Abstract of the United States* provides information on a variety of economic factors, such as employment, prices, business, and income.
   b. The monthly *Survey of Current Business* is a source of statistical summaries about various business or economic matters.
   c. Periodic *Bureau of the Census* reports can be very helpful. Included are:
      - Census of Manufacturers.
      - Census of Wholesale Trade.
      - Census of Retail Trade.
      - Census of Selected Services.
   d. Business newspapers and magazines, such as the *Wall Street Journal, Business Week, Fortune, Forbes,* and *Barron's,* contain information on company and industry matters.
   e. Trade and industry associations usually publish informative industry data.
   f. Numerous other publications from the Superintendent of Documents, U.S. Government Printing Office, Washington, D.C., are a good source of documents.
   g. Summaries and other data from stock brokerage houses, firms of Certified Public Accountants, or consultants, or, for a fee, public data from firms specializing in providing data on selected topics can be helpful.

h. Dun & Bradstreet directories or other publications providing data based on SIC codes may be useful.

2. *Industry Data.*

a. The quarterly *Standard & Poor's Industry Surveys* provides industry and selected comparative information.

b. Some financial services such as *Value Line Investment Survey* provide industry summaries as well as data on specific companies.

c. The *Directory of Companies Required to File Annual Reports,* by the Securities and Exchange Commission (SEC), contains listing of companies required to file reports, arranged alphabetically and by industry groups.

d. The *Annual Statement Studies* by Robert Morris Associates provides financial statistics by companies and by industry.

e. *Almanac of Business and Financial Ratios,* also published by Robert Morris Associates, contains useful data.

3. *Competitors and/or Specific Companies.*

a. Annual Reports, or Form 10K, or 8K, usually can be obtained from the investor relations department or secretary of the company itself—or from firms who specialize in providing financial information.

b. *Moody's Manuals* and related updates and *Standard and Poor's Stock Reports* provide specific data on many businesses and industries.

c. The SEC can be a source of information about selected public companies. See the *Directory* mentioned above.

Usually personnel of libraries, such as public libraries or the Library of Congress or those of various schools of business, will be most helpful in locating data, or suggesting sources of information.

53-7 THE ACQUISITION TEAM

A knowledgeable in-depth analysis of a suitable acquisition candidate is a complex task. While the financial aspects certainly are important, the analytical process is not a matter of simply projecting earnings, cash flow, and financial condition. In fact, the authors would state that an acquisition ordinarily should not be made only for apparently sound financial reasons. Rather, the entire business must be carefully examined: the manufacturing operations and facilities; the marketing organization, and marketing policies and procedures; the research capabilities; the general management group; and so on, ad infinitum.

Because the in-depth analysis is so critical, and because correct conclusions often rest on the perception and intuition of the acquisition team, its composition and method of operation merit special attention. The acquisition team, sometimes also called the due diligence team, is assigned the responsibility for making the investigations. Its responsibilities may extend from the establishment of criteria, through the selection of potential candidates, the preliminary analysis, the in-depth review, and the negotiations, to the actual acquisition.

Some general observations that may be worth thinking about are these:

1. The person who will manage the target company after the acquisition should be considered for the position of team leader (although many times the team leader is a senior member of the acquiring company's financial management).

2. Team membership may extend from the executives and employees of the acquiror to such outside sources as CPAs, lawyers, specialized appraisers, or knowledgeable individuals (including investment bankers). Of course, some of these noncompany specialists may supply their expertise on an as-needed basis only.

3. In any event, the acquisition team should include members with appropriate expertise. (See the listing later in this section.)

4. Team members should be aware of the buyer's reason for the proposed acquisition—the need it is expected to fill.

5. Each team member should be aware of the key factors in his area of expertise that should be analyzed and understood in the appraisal of the function, or product, or relevant asset or liability.

6. Team members should be in communication with each other rather frequently, so that (a) any overlapping is eliminated, and (b) findings in one area that significantly impact the work effort or conclusions of another team member are made known to him.

7. Nonfinancial team members who gain important knowledge that will impact the financial results or conclusion should make such information available to the financial executive where it is relevant to his work effort and conclusions.

8. Each team member should be fully aware of what data or information must be reviewed as to his assigned area of responsibility so that proper conclusions may be drawn as to the activity or condition. The examination should be carefully planned, including the use of checklists, so that all relevant facets are examined and proper conclusion drawn.

So people knowledgeable in what areas should be represented on the team? That depends, of course, on the needs of the specific case: the present knowledge of the acquiror about the candidate, the suspected or known weaknesses of the potential acquiree, the reasons why the sellers are willing to sell, the success factors in the business generally and so on. Generally the investigation will relate to these fields:

1. Products.
2. Markets and marketing methods.
3. Manufacturing processes and facilities.
4. Research and development capabilities.
5. Quality control.
6. Human resources and organization structure—an inventory of skills.
7. Information resources—equipment, methods, and plans.
8. Method and style of general management.

9. Financial aspects, including:
   - Accounting principles and practices.
   - Taxation and tax laws.
   - Financial planning and control systems.
   - SEC reporting.
   - Antitrust reporting.
10. Legal matters, including:
   - Structure of acquisitions.
   - Antitrust law and considerations.
   - Pending and potential litigation.
   - SEC compliance.

Comments on what type of data may be reviewed are made later in this chapter.

53-8 EVALUATING THE PROSPECT: THE IN-DEPTH ANALYSIS

Evaluating a company is no easy task. The matching of values of two businesses to determine an equitable exchange of equities or other suitable consideration requires special and careful analysis. Although one firm may have a less favorable earnings history than another, certain franchises, or patents, or production facilities may be of special importance to the acquiring company. One corporation may own a modern plant and be well located with respect to raw materials and markets but may lack sales know-how. In contrast, another business may possess a superb nationwide sales organization and an excellent product but be burdened with obsolete manufacturing facilities. Still another company may have acquired an excellent research organization, and the question arises about how this is evaluated. Much judgment is required to weigh earnings against assets and organization. When this stage is reached, much analysis must be undertaken.

The kinds of information to be gathered will depend on the particular situation. Many labor-hours ordinarily will be spent in collecting and organizing all the pertinent facts that are considered necessary to arrive at a fair estimate of the value of the business. The company to be acquired may be seeking the same data with respect to the acquiring company.

To repeat, the primary areas of investigation ordinarily will include the following:

1. Management and personnel.
2. Market and product.
3. Manufacturing facilities and processes.
4. Research and patents, etc.
5. Finances.
6. Legal matters.
7. The information system.

Although each acquisition team should develop its own approach to an analysis of the business, the following checklist developed by a well-known aerospace company (and subject to change as laws or circumstances change) indicates the many aspects to a complete study:

A. *General*

1. Statement of proposed transaction and objectives.
2. History of business and general description.
3. List of officers and directors; affiliation.
4. Stock distribution—number, principal holders, etc.
5. Organization chart.
6. Policy manual.

B. *Financial*

1. Latest audited financial statements.
2. Last available financial statements.
3. Ten-year summary financial statements.
4. Projected operating and financial statements.
5. Full description of securities, indebtedness, investments, and other assets and liabilities other than normal day-to-day accounts.
6. Chart of accounts and/or description of accounting practices relative to inventories, fixed assets, etc.
7. List of bank accounts, average balances.
8. Credit reports from banks and Dun & Bradstreet.
9. Federal income tax status: i.e., any loss or unused tax credit carry forwards, latest year audited, any deficiency claims, etc.
10. Summary of state and local tax situation: i.e., applicable taxes, unemployment tax rate, any deficiency claims, etc.
11. Tax status of proposed transaction: recommendation for best method of acquisition.
12. Complete list of insurance policies, including description of coverage and cost; workmen's compensation rate.
13. Statement of responsible officer of business regarding unrecorded or contingent liabilities.
14. Nature of inventory.

C. *Sales*

1. A brief description and history (if any) of the product line.
2. A 10-year record of product sales performance.
3. A long-range forecast of growth or contraction trends for the industry of which the product line is a part.
4. A three- to five-year forecast of anticipated demand for the product.
5. An estimate of the industry's ability to supply present and anticipated demand.

6. A three- to five-year forecast of sales expectations for this company (share of the market).

7. An analysis of the effect of anticipated increased volume and/or cost reduction on the following:

   a. Product demand and share of the market.

   b. Market saturation and overcapacity.

8. An analysis of the effect of the geographic location of the new facility on the following:

   a. Product demand and share of the market.

   b. Distribution costs (freight savings, warehousing, etc.).

   c. Competitive position.

9. A review of present sales management, selling force, advertising and sales promotion policies for adaptability and adequacy in relation to new facility.

10. A review of present competitors and competitive practices, including these:

    a. Description of *competitive* products.

    b. Location.

    c. Estimated share of market.

    d. Pricing policies.

    e. Methods of distribution.

11. An analysis of present and/or probable pricing policies for the product line considering these factors:

    a. Competitive position.

    b. Cost pricing.

12. An analysis of present and potential domestic and export customers.

    a. Major types of customers and percent of sales to each.

    b. Geographical location.

    c. Buying habits.

D. *Manufacturing*

1. Description and layout of plant and property.

2. List of principal machine tools and computers—age and condition.

3. Opinion regarding maintenance and "housekeeping."

4. Utilities—availability, usage, rate.

5. Estimated total annual fixed cost.

6. Organization, departmentalization.

7. Transportation facilities.

8. Description of area, including climate, hazards from flood, etc.

9. Opinion regarding adequacy of auxiliary equipment—tools, patterns, material, handling equipment, etc.

10. Detail expense schedule.

11. Building codes, zoning laws, and restrictions.

E. *Purchasing*

1. Principal materials used.

2. Relation of material costs to sales.

3. Purchasing methods.

4. List of principal suppliers, items, location.

5. Inbound freight costs.

6. Work load—last 12 months.

    a. Number of purchase orders issued.

    b. Value—purchase orders issued.

    c. Value of outstanding commitments.

F. *Research and Engineering*

1. Description and condition of facilities.

    a. Drafting room and office.

    b. Experimental room.

    c. Laboratory.

    d. Special test equipment.

2. Engineering personnel—quality and quantity of technical talents—employed—unemployed.

3. Product designs—evaluation, condition of drawings.

4. Patents and trademarks—coverage, existing applications, litigation.

G. *Labor*

1. Analysis of characteristics and number—present employees.

2. Direct, indirect, administrative: number and cost.

3. Number of potential job applicants from surveys or census.

4. Determination of types of skills available in the area from state employment service and other sources, and critical skills in short supply.

5. Location and availability of students from high schools and technical schools.

6. Union—copy of contract.

7. Labor relations history.

8. Appraisal of working conditions.

9. Statistics on turnovers: reasons.

10. Description of incentive system: average rates incentive and hourly.

11. Employment and personnel policies.

12. Accident frequency.

13. Ratio of total labor cost to sales.

14. Pension and welfare plans.

15. Appraisal of transportation, community recreation facilities, housing.

16. Evaluation of labor situation in area.

17. Compliance with the applicable labor laws.

H. *The Information System*

1. Type of system (computer-based?).

2. Adequacy in meeting management needs.

3. Adequacy in serving the financial/accounting requirements.

4. Use of groupware.

5. Use of electronic data interchange.

6. System security.

7. Relation to major customer/supplier systems.

With the continual changes in the competitive marketplace, in tax law, in antitrust emphasis, etc., the checklist would need to be updated periodically. Additionally, it should be mentioned that some of the leading public accounting firms have excellent, and extensive, checklists that might be available.

53-9 OBJECTIVES OF FINANCIAL ANALYSIS

In a volume whose principal audience is likely to be financially oriented, discussion of the purpose of financial analysis would be expected.

A soundly conceived acquisition screening procedure will require extensive analysis by various disciplines. To be sure, the financial review is but part of the total analysis. But it is an important one in looking to the potential financial impact of the acquiree on the acquiror. An indication of the objectives of the financial analysis as part of the acquisition study may be gained from this listing:

1. Determination of existing financial condition of selling company and impact on the combined financial position.

2. Determination of present earning power, using the acquiring company accounting practices.

3. Identification of income-producing segments:
Product lines.
Geographical areas.
Customers.

4. Determination of major financial strengths and weaknesses:
Product sales trends.
Margin trends.
Commitments and contingent liabilities.
Nature and magnitude of investments.

5. Identification of potential synergisms of the two companies, when integrated.

6. Estimation of earning power and related cash flow from operations.

7. Estimating an acceptable price range.

8. Consideration of the *best* financial method of acquiring the company—tax impact considered.

9. Securing appraisal of the potential acquiree's financial staff.

10. Review of "control" aspects of the acquiree vs. the acquiror.

The chief purpose is to focus on all those financial matters that should be known by the management of the acquiror. Some of the forementioned items may require elaboration.

53-10 IMPACT OF DIFFERING ACCOUNTING POLICIES

Even given the use of generally accepted accounting principles, there can be significant differences in financial condition and earnings by reason of differences in accounting policies. It is presumed that an acquired company will report its financial results on the basis of the accounting of the acquiring corporation. Hence the financial statements of the company under examination should be restated on such a basis. Differences in accounting practices in terms of inventory valuation, depreciation, pension funding, fringe benefit accruals, etc., may cumulatively have a significant impact on reported earnings. A comparative analysis of the income statement is shown in Figure 53-2. The comparative data and reflections in market value of the stock are summarized here:

	Using Acquiror Policies	Using Present Accounting of Acquiree
Reported net income	$675,000	$1,335,000
Number of shares outstanding	550,000	550,000
EPS	$1.23	$2.43
Earnings decline due to accounting changes	$1.20	
Market value		
At P/E ratio of 10	$12.30	$24.30
At P/E ratio of 12	$14.76	$29.16
At P/E ratio of 15	$18.45	$36.45

Failure to bring these differences to the attention of management could result in disappointing future earnings.

When making estimates of future earnings, and the impact on the acquiror, it may be desirable to present three levels:

1. The candidate—with its present practices—both accounting and operating.

2. The candidate—with the acquiror accounting and operating practices (where applicable).

3. The candidate—with synergisms and acquiror practices.

Figure 53-2 Impact of Differing Accounting Practices on Net Income.

COMPARATIVE STATEMENT OF INCOME AND EXPENSE
WITH DIFFERING ACCOUNTING PRACTICES
(dollars in thousands)

	Y Company			
	Using Acquiror Company Accounting		Using Present Accounting	
	Amount	% Net Sales	Amount	% Net Sales
Net Sales	$10,000	100.0%	$10,000	100.0%
Comparable costs				
Cost of goods.sold	5,000	50.0	5,000	50.0
Selling, general, and administrative expenses	2,000	20.0	2,000	20.0
Subtotal	7,000	70.0	7,000	70.0
Accounting differences				
Inventory—last in, first out vs. first in, first out	400	4.0	—	
Depreciation, straight line vs. double declining balance	400	4.0	100	1.0
Moving expenses	150	1.5	70	.7
Research expenses	300	3.0	100	1.0
Pension costs	200	2.0	50	.5
Deferred compensation	200	2.0	10	.1
Total	1,650	16.5	330	3.3
Total costs	8,650	86.5	7,330	73.3
Income before taxes	1,350	13.5	2,670	26.7
Income taxes	675	6.8	1,335	13.4
Net income	$ 675	6.7%	$ 1,335	13.3%

53-11 VALUATION OF AN ACQUISITION

There is, of course, a direct relationship between the results of the financial analysis of a potential acquisition and the price to be paid, as well as the method by which the transaction will be accomplished.

A sound in-depth financial analysis should yield these results, as well as provide data on operating results, margins by product lines, and on specific assets and liabilities, etc.:

• Heighten management's awareness of the financial impact—both operating results and financial condition—of the acquisition on the financial statements of the acquiror.

- Identify the advantages and/or disadvantages of using differing means of affecting the acquisition—more debt or less debt, a taxable vs. a tax-free transaction, impact of using various packages of securities, etc.
- Clarify the tax impact of the proposed acquisition, and the preferred method, tax wise, of consummating the transaction.
- Alert management as to the areas of risk and the amount thereof, as well as the earning potential and cash flow of the candidate.
- Identify segments, if any, of the potential acquiree that should be considered for sale.
- Provide valuable information useful in strategic and short-term planning.
- Provide the basis of determining the fair market value of the enterprise.

The purchase price of the acquisition, including the stock exchange ratios, or package of securities used, etc., will be determined largely by negotiation. However, the financial analysis will provide data about (1) the impact on future earnings of changes in accounting policy, (2) future earnings potential, (3) different valuation bases, (4) the market value of assets, (5) the extent of actual and contingent liabilities, and other subjects that could serve as a starting point in setting a price.

Several methods are in use for determining the value of an enterprise. Some are simple and easily applied; others are more sophisticated and of greater worth in determining a possible price. A few applicable comments are made on these commonly used methods:

- Book value.
- Market value.
- Capitalized earnings (P/E multiples).
- Appraised value.
- Discounted cash flow.

(a) BOOK VALUE

To some owners, book value per share (common shareholders' equity divided by the number of shares outstanding) with or without adjustments arising from the financial analysis, is indicative of the relative worth of the company. For them, it is a measure of the reasonableness of the stock exchange ratio, or perhaps of the cash value of the acquiree. This measure may be used alone or in combination with other methods. Many of us are aware that book value relates to original costs and past earnings, and is not necessarily an indicator of future earning power or cash flow or market value of fixed assets, and so on.

(b) MARKET VALUE

For a publicly traded company stock, the market price, along with the related aggregate value, is a measure of worth. If a stock exchange is to be made, the market price (before the news leaks out about the possible merger or combination) may be an important determinant. In many instances the market price plus a substantial premium of, say, 25%, 50%, or even 100%, may be employed to entice the owner to sell. So market value, with or without adjustment, may be an indication of worth of the stock.

(c) CAPITALIZED EARNINGS (P/E MULTIPLES)

Another method of determining worth is to capitalize earnings, or its equivalent, the application of a P/E ratio to a stream of earnings, to arrive at a market value. This has validity in that acquiring a business entity is for the purpose of securing a stream of future earnings (or cash flow).

This technique has at least two variants: (1) to apply the P/E to a stream of *historical* earnings, either weighted or unweighted, for, let us say, a five-year period, or (2) to apply the P/E to projected earnings. More than a single year is used to avoid the risk of an abnormal year, or to give recognition to the trend of earnings. Figure 53-3 shows the applications on both a simple and a weighted basis, for a *historical* five-year period with a rate of return equal to 8.5% (a P/E of 12) for the limited risk. Recent years are given a greater weighting. The illustration reflects the influence of the earnings trend—with company A producing an increasing return per year, and company B showing a decreasing trend on identical total earnings. These earnings can be adjusted to reflect any accounting differences.

Application of the method to *projected* earnings is shown in Figure 53-4. In this illustration, the stream of earnings as estimated by the seller is adjusted by the buyer to reflect any relevant changes. In this example, the earnings of the candidate seller are adjusted for:

1. Use of differing accounting principles (depreciation and retirement plan provisions—five years instead of ten),
2. Expected cost level reductions to be initiated by the buyer, and
3. A difference in judgment of buyer and seller as to the 15% growth rate foreseen by the seller to a 10% rate anticipated by the buyer.

It should be noted that the compounding effect of a lower growth rate in earnings is substantial.

The P/E ratio employed by this capitalized earnings method may be one of several:

- A P/E representative of the industry.
- The current P/E at which the seller stock is being traded—if a public company.
- A P/E ratio representing the acquiring company's required rate of return. If, for example, the acquiror desires a 20% net after-tax rate of return, then an equivalent P/E of 5 is applicable.
- A rate mutually agreed upon between buyer and seller.

(d) APPRAISED VALUE

The appraised value is determined by an independent appraisal of the property by a knowledgeable person usually hired by the prospective buyer (perhaps with the consent of the seller). This method often is used when the transaction is to be a purchase of assets (not stock). An appraisal of each asset may be useful for tax purposes. This method assigns replacement cost or market value to every piece of property. It can be used in allocating the purchase price to each such asset and goodwill but may bear

Figure 53-3 Capitalized Earnings—Simple and Weighted.

CAPITALIZED EARNINGS (HISTORICAL)
ON BOTH A SIMPLE (EQUAL WEIGHTING) AND WEIGHTED BASIS
COMPANY A AND COMPANY B
(dollars in thousands)

Year	Weighting Factor	Company A		Company B	
		Earnings	Weighted Earnings	Earnings	Weighted Earnings
19X1	1	$10,200	$ 10,200	$17,100	$ 17,100
19X2	2	11,600	13,200	15,600	31,200
19X3	3	13,300	39,900	13,300	39,900
19X4	4	15,600	52,400	11,600	46,400
19X5	5	17,100	85,500	10,000	51,000
Total	15	$67,800	$201,200	$67,800	$185,600
Average earnings (÷ 5)		$13,560		$13,560	
Weighted average earnings (÷ 15)			$ 13,413		$ 12,373
Capitalized earnings (P/E of 12)			$160,960		$148,480

Figure 53-4 Capitalized Earnings Based on Projected Levels.

Jeffrey Company, Inc.
CALCULATION OF MAXIMUM PURCHASE PRICE
TO YIELD 20% NET BASED ON ADJUSTED PROJECTIONS
(dollars in thousands)

Year	Weighting Factor	Earnings Estimated by Seller	Adjustments				Earnings as Adjusted	Earnings	
			Accounting Differences	Cost Level Changes	Judgmental	Increase (Decrease) Total		Equal Weighting	Weighted
Actual									
1988	1	$ 18,600	($ 670)	—	—	($ 670)	$ 17,930	$ 17,930	$ 17,930
1989	2	21,390	(730)	—	—	(730)	20,660	20,660	41,320
1990	3	24,600	(750)	—	—	(750)	23,850	23,850	71,550
Subtotal		64,590	(2,150)	—	—	(2,150)	62,440		
Projected									
199A	4	28,290	(770)	$ 2,540	($ 1,230)	540	28,830	28,830	115,320
199B	5	32,535	(960)	2,920	(2,769)	(769)	31,766	31,766	158,830
199C	6	37,415	(980)	3,300	(4,673)	(2,353)	35,062	35,062	210,372
199D	7	43,030	(1,060)	3,450	(7,013)	(4,623)	38,407	38,407	268,849
199E	8	49,490	(1,090)	4,450	(9,872)	(6,512)	42,978	42,978	343,824
Subtotal		190,760	(4,820)	16,660	(25,557)	(13,717)	177,043		
Total	36	$255,350	($6,970)	$16,660	($25,557)	($15,867)	$239,483	$239,483	$1,227,995

Average earnings (÷ 8) $ 29,935
Weighted average earnings (÷ 36) $ 34,111
Capitalized earnings (P/E of 5) $ 170,555

little relationship to the productivity of the particular asset. This method is a check against other appraisal bases, and may be useful in assigning value to patents, or completed research, and so on.

(e) DISCOUNTED CASH FLOW (DCF)

Finally, a method widely used for years in evaluating capital expenditures,[1] that is, expenditures for plant and equipment now is being applied to acquisition or divestment transactions. It involves discounting a future stream of cash to the present time. The principle is employed in two ways: A specified interest rate (discount factor) is applied to the estimated cash stream to determine its *net present value* (NPV) or worth. In another application where a purchase price for a business is proposed or used, this outflow of cash, together with the future needs or sources of cash of the business, to arrive at the rate of return expected to be earned over the life of the project—the internal rate of return (IRR).

An application of each technique is discussed next.

(f) PRESENT VALUE OF FUTURE CASH FLOWS

Because the discounted cash flow method is technically correct in that it recognizes the time value of money, a somewhat more lengthy explanation of its use—both the NPV and IRR application—may be helpful. Since the price to be paid for an acquisition will be arrived at by negotiation, the present value amount is a point of reference. If the discount factor used is the minimum rate of return that a management must earn, then the NPV is the maximum price that the purchaser will pay and still attain its expected rate of return. If the discount factor is a rate greater than the minimum (thereby decreasing the amount to be paid) expected rate of return, then it may be regarded simply as a reference point.

The procedure to arrive at this present value of future cash flows (NPV), illustrated in Figure 53-5, is as follows:

1. Determine the probable income after taxes of the target operation for a given period into the future (say 5 to 10 years; column 1). Preferably this should be on the acquiror's basis of accounting—not that of the selling company.

2. Convert this net income to cash flow from operations by adjusting for the noncash items (columns 2 and 3). Usually the only noncash item is depreciation or amortization of fixed assets.

3. Further adjust the cash flow to recognize additional cash needs, if any (columns 4 and 5). Typically, as the business grows, additional funds will be required for working capital and plant and equipment. These adjustments should then produce year by year the net cash generation or need for the period of the projection (column 6).

4. Determine the going-concern value, or salvage value, of the business at the end of the planning period. Typically this is a multiple of earnings ($10 \times$ or $8 \times$, etc.)

---

[1] See Chapter 32.

Figure 53-5 Present Value of Future Cash Flows.

The Jeffrey Company
PRESENT VALUE OF FUTURE CASH FLOWS
BASED ON A 17% RATE OF RETURN
(dollars in thousands)

	Estimated Net Income (1)	Depreciation (2)	Operating Cash Flow (3)	Additional Investments		Net Cash Flow (6)	17% Interest Factor (7)	Percent Value (8)
				Working Capital (4)	Fixed Assets (5)			
0								
1	$ 16,300	$ 2,119	$ 18,419	—	—	$ 18,419	.855	$ 15,748
2	18,745	2,436	21,181	$ 980	$1,100	19,101	.731	13,962
3	21,557	2,802	24,359	1,960	1,400	20,999	.624	13,103
4	24,790	3,012	27,802	2,100	—	25,702	.534	13,725
5	28,509	3,610	32,119	2,000	2,230	27,889	.456	12,717
6	32,785	4,262	37,047	2,700	840	33,507	.390	13,068
7	37,703	4,312	42,015	3,000	—	39,015	.333	12,992
8	43,358	4,210	47,568	3,500	790	43,278	.285	12,334
9	49,862	4,440	54,300	4,600	—	49,702	.243	12,078
10	57,341	4,110	61,451	7,000	—	54,451	.208	11,326
	$330,950	$35,313	$366,263	$27,840	$6,360	$332,063		
Estimated going value (10X)						$573,410	.208	119,269
Total (NPV)								$250,322

if sold as a going concern, or the cash value if sold on a liquidating basis (receivables, inventory, and fixed assets; shown at the bottom of column 6).

5. Apply a discount factor taken from present worth discount tables (column 7) to arrive at the present value (column 8).

This represents the maximum amount that can be paid to purchase the future stream of cash and still earn the designated rate of return.

In the illustration, Figure 53-5, the sum of $250,322,000 can be paid for the Jeffrey Company and yield the desired 17% rate of return after taxes. This assumes that the premises as to earnings and cash flow are correct.

(g) INTERNAL RATE OF RETURN (IRR)

In some acquisition situations (a) the seller specifies a desired price and (b) the buyer has a minimum desired rate of return (the IRR). This may represent the return that may be earned on other projects, or it may be the cost of capital, adjusted for risk, etc. In any event, the task is to determine if the specified selling price will enable the buyer to earn the desired rate of return on the investment. The procedure is quite similar to that of determining the present value, in that the stream of future cash flow by years and the liquidating value must be estimated. But the discounted rate of return is the unknown. Reference to Figure 53-6 will help in understanding the process:

1. The requested price is treated as an outflow of cash in year 0—$12,000,000 in the illustration.
2. The future cash generation is determined as explained for Figure 53-4.
3. By trial and error and the use of present value tables, the rate of return is calculated.

Basically a "guess" is made as to the rate of return, and this tentative rate (discount factor) is applied to the stream of cash. When the sum equals zero, the discount rate at which this occurs is the IRR. If the sum is greater than zero, then the earning rate is more. Then a higher rate is used until a negative position results. The applicable rate between the two discount factors is arrived at by interpolation—shown at the bottom of the figure.

If the calculated rate of return is at least the minimum set by the buyer, then the quoted price is deemed acceptable, or is the basis for further negotiation.

This same technique may be used for alternative calculations. Thus, if borrowed funds are to be used in the acquisition, the impact of leverage on the buyer's investment may be determined. Figure 53-7 reflects the same transaction as Figure 53-6 except that the buyer uses borrowed funds of $9,600,000 for the initial investment (out of a gross price of $12,000,000) and, in later years, an additional $2,250,000 of interim borrowed funds to finance the purchase. The net result, after interest payments, is a return of 41.9% on the buyer's equity investment.

(h) MORE ABOUT DCF

These comments may be helpful in understanding some of the characteristics of the discounting process:

Figure 53-6 Determining the Discounted Cash Flow Rate of Return.

DISCOUNTED CASH FLOW
GROSS INVESTMENT
(*$000*)

Year	Investment: Permanent	Investment: Working Capital	Profit after Taxes and Depreciation	Depreciation (DDB)	Cash Flow	Cash Generation (Requirement)	Discounted Cash Flow: Discounted at 9%: Factor	Discounted at 9%: Amount	Discounted at 10%: Factor	Discounted at 10%: Amount
0	($12,000)	$	$	$	$	$(12,000)	1.000	$(12,000)	1.000	$(12,000)
1			460	490	950	950	.917	871	.909	864
2	(1,500)		890	610	1,500	—	.842	—	.826	—
3		(400)	1,340	540	1,880	1,480	.772	1,142	.751	1,111
4		(300)	1,460	470	1,930	1,630	.708	1,154	.683	1,113
5		(300)	1,510	420	1,930	1,630	.650	1,060	.620	1,011
6			1,670	400	2,070	2,070	.596	1,224	.564	1,167
Subtotal						(4,240)				
Sale of business (net of tax)						11,850	.596	7,063	.564	6,683
Total	($13,500)	($1,000)	$7,330	$2,930	$10,260	$ 7,610		$ 514		($ 51)

Discounted rate of return: $9\% + 1\% \left[\frac{514}{514 - (-51)}\right] = 9.9\%$

Figure 53-7 Adjusting the Discounted Cash Flow Rate of Return for Borrowed Funds.

DISCOUNTED CASH FLOW
INVESTMENT NET OF BORROWINGS
($000)

Year	Gross Investment	Profit after Taxes and Depreciation	Depreciation (DDB)	Cash Flow	Interest Expense (Net)	Gross Cash Generation (Requirement)	Borrowings	Net Cash Generation (Requirement)	Discounted at 41% Factor	Discounted at 41% Amount	Discounted at 42% Factor	Discounted at 42% Amount
0	$(12,000)	—	—	—		(12,000)	9,600	(2,400)	1.000	(2,400)	1.000	$(2,400)
1	—	460	490	950	(288)	662	—	662	.709	469	.704	466
2	(1,500)	890	610	1,500	(303)	(303)	1,350	1,047	.503	527	.496	519
3	(400)	1,340	540	1,880	(328)	1,152	360	1,512	.357	540	.349	528
4	(300)	1,460	470	1,930	(344)	1,286	270	1,556	.253	394	.246	383
5	(300)	1,510	420	1,930	(352)	1,278	270	1,548	.179	277	.173	268
6	—	1,670	400	2,070	(178)	1,892	—	1,892	.127	240	.122	231
Subtotal							11,850	5,817		47		(5)
Loan Repayment							(11,850)	(11,850)				
Sale of business (net)								11,850				
Total	$(14,500)	7,330	2,930	10,260	(1,793)	(6,033)		5,817		47		($ 5)

Discounted Rate of Return: $41\% + 1\% \left[\dfrac{47}{47-(-5)} \right] = 41.9\%$

- The importance of the discounted cash flow technique lies in the fact that it recognizes the time value of money, i.e., if cash is received earlier rather than later, it can be invested to produce more earnings.

- The discount factor, representing a given rate of return, to use in arriving at net present value (NPV) is already established in the discount tables. It merely needs to be applied to the stream of cash. This rate can be used as a starting point for the trial-and-error approach of calculating the actual or precise internal rate of return (IRR). The company may have a minimum IRR as a cut-off point for acquisition (or capital assets). Additionally, software packages are available to determine NPV or IRR using a personal computer.

- The interest factor—the discount rate—declines very rapidly so that events transpiring after five to eight years have very little impact because of the relatively low discount factor.

- Because the assets of the acquiree at the end of the planning period should have value, this salvage value or going-concern value should not be overlooked in the NPV or IRR calculation.

- The method implicitly assumes that the cash flows each years can be invested at the discount factor (interest rate).

53-12 COMPARING THE VALUES

When the value of a target company is determined by several methods, and they are all in the same general "ball park," this probably is an indication that the determination is realistic. Quite often it is desirable to summarize the results of the various measures of worth. Such a schedule, based on assumed values, is as follows:

COMPARATIVE FACTORS IN PROPOSED MERGER

Evidence of Value	Company A	Company B	Relationship Ratio/Share
Five-year average earnings/share	$ 3.60	$ 3.90	.92 to 1
Five-year average dividends/share ...	$ 1.80	$ 1.90	.95 to 1
Market price (recent before merger influence)	$54.00	$51.40	1.03 to 1
Present worth of future cash flows ...	$46.00	$42.80	1.07 to 1
Book value/share	$11.37	$17.89	.64 to 1
Net current assets/share	$ 8.96	$ 7.12	1.26 to 1

These are the factors usually taken into account in arriving at a stock exchange ratio. The weighting, a matter of judgment and bargaining power, depends on the opinion of both buyer and seller. In the foregoing example, if earnings, market price, and net current assets are the important factors in the eyes of both buyer and seller, there is a strong probability that one-for-one will be the stock exchange ratio.

In the process of valuation, several scenarios may be developed, using varying assumption about growth rates or target rates of return. While the management of the buyer may not be interested in the details, a sense of the impact of various assumptions or discount factors may be useful. Thus, in Figure 53-8, the rate of return estimated for

Figure 53-8   Rates of Return Based on Selected Offering Prices.

The Johnson Company
ESTIMATED RATES OF RETURN, NET OF TAXES,
FOR THE ELECTRONICS ARM, INC.
AT SELECTED OFFERING PRICES

Offering Price ($ Millions)	Scenario (%)		
	Most Likely	Conservative	Optimistic
100	14.75	13.35	16.25
95	15.50	14.25	17.00
90	16.75	15.50	18.25
85	18.00	17.00	19.10

some selected offering prices is presented. And Figure 53-9 provides the rate of return for several scenarios—most likely, conservative and optimistic—and at differing offer prices.

53-13 MULTINATIONAL BUSINESS VALUATION

With the trend to globalization, there is a need to understand some of the complications of considering a *foreign* acquisition. While the same basic principles and procedures used in evaluating a domestic entity are employed in appraising a foreign operation, there are these several additional factors to be considered:

• Translation of the foreign currency or currencies
• Restrictions on currency transfers

Figure 53-9   Maximum Cash Offering Price.

MAXIMUM CASH OFFERING PRICE
TO ACHIEVE INDICATED RATE OF RETURN
FOR THREE SCENARIOS

Scenario	Target Rate of Return		
	14%	16%	18%
A. Most likely			
Aggregate price ($ millions)	$276	$244	$212
Per share price	$138.00	$122.00	$106.00
B. Conservative			
Aggregate price ($ millions)	$252	$220	$195
Per share price	$126.00	$110.00	$147.50
C. Optimistic			
Aggregate price ($ millions)	$305	$265	$235
Per share price	$152.50	$132.50	$167.50

Figure 53-10   Cash Flow for a U.S. Company's Foreign Subsidiary.

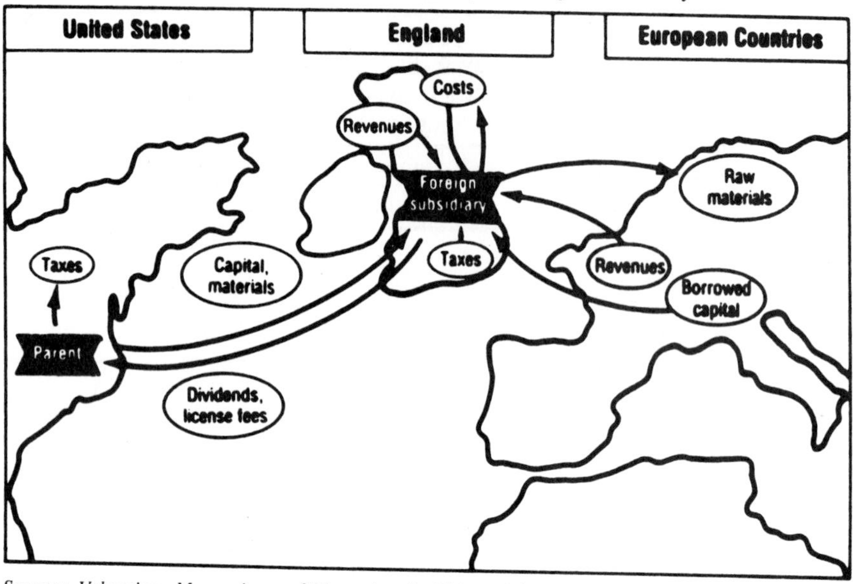

Source: Valuation: Measuring and Managing the Value of Companies, Thomas Copeland, Tim Koller, and Jack Murrin, © 1990, John Wiley & Sons, Inc. Reprinted by permission of John Wiley & Sons, Inc.

- Differences in foreign tax and accounting regulations or purchases
- Impact of transfer pricing on earnings and taxes
- Lack of adequate and relevant data about markets, competitive activity, and so on
- Need to evaluate political risk
- Impact of foreign exchange (FX) hedging on value
- Determining the appropriate cost of capital.

Some of these subjects are discussed in the following sections. It is assumed that the valuation basis is the discounted cash flow (DCF) method.

Representative cash flows of a U.S. domiciled parent, with a wholly owned subsidiary domiciled in England, is shown in Figure 53-10.[2] In this example, the English subsidiary receives revenues from both France and England, buys raw materials supplied from Denmark, incurs costs for labor and materials in England, and borrows funds from Switzerland as well as England. Further, it receives capital and raw materials from its U.S. parent, and provides cash flow to its parent in the form of both dividends and license fees. These many sources and uses of cash must be properly accounted for.

The steps in valuing a foreign subsidiary are reflected in Figure 53-11.[3] The starting point is to estimate or forecast the free cash flow in each foreign currency.

---

[2] From Tom Copeland, Tim Koller, and Jack Murrin, *Valuation: Measuring and Managing the Value of Companies* (New York: John Wiley, 1990), p. 282. Used by permission.

[3] *Ibid.,* p. 283. Used by permission.

Figure 53-11   Steps in Valuing a Foreign Subsidiary.

1. Forecast free cash flow in the foreign currency
   • Use nominal foreign currency cash flow
   • Make accounting adjustments for FX translation, foreign accounting standards, and for "hidden assets"
   • Use foreign inflation predictions
   • Estimate the effective tax rate
   • Use appropriate transfer prices

2. Use forward FX rates to convert cash flow to subsidiary's domestic currency
   • Predict forward FX rates
   • Translate foreign-denominated cash flow to subsidiary's domestic currency

3. Estimate the subsidiary's cost of capital
   • Estimate subsidiary's capital structure
   • Estimate cost of equity
   • Estimate after-tax cost of debt
   • Use the after-tax weighted average cost of capital to discount cash flows

4. Estimate the subsidiary value in your domestic currency
   • Discount the translated foreign currency free cash flow at the subsidiary's cost of capital
   • Translate the subsidiary value to your currency using the spot FX rate

Source: Valuation: Measuring and Managing the Value of Companies, Thomas Copeland, Tim Koller, and Jack Murrin, © 1990, John Wiley & Sons, Inc. Reprinted by permission of John Wiley & Sons, Inc.

English revenues are estimated in pound sterling and French revenues are estimated in French francs. Next the nonsterling cash flow is converted into pound sterling by using forward FX rates. When the estimated cash flows are converted to pounds, they are discounted at the English cost of capital This sterling value is then converted to U.S. dollars, the home currency, using the spot FX rate. In forecasting free cash flow, the political risks, convertibility restrictions, withholding taxes, proper transfer prices, and the estimated inflation rate must be considered. A key point in foreign acquisition analysis is to focus on the cash available to the *parent.* Impediments to cash flow from the subsidiary to the parent might be:

• Currency restrictions
• Exchange rate fluctuations
• Withholding taxes.

You may wish to review Chapter 10 of the reference in footnote 2 as well as section 11-8. Because of the changing tax regulations and political risks, it might be appropriate to seek the assistance of knowledgeable counsel when evaluating a specific foreign acquisition prospect.

53-14 LEVERAGED BUYOUTS (LBOs)

Other than briefly discussing the economic effect of differing cash/securities packages in evaluating a particular acquisition candidate, we have not attempted to explain the mechanics of *how* an acquisition should be accomplished. Thus, such matters as hostile tender offers or leveraged buyouts have been avoided. But the number of LBOs and their dollar value in the late 1980s and early 1990s have been so high—reaching $60 billion in 1988 alone—and the later heavy defaults and discounts on junk bonds have been so disastrous in some cases—that some general comments on this popular acquisition procedure are warranted. As the LBO method is also a study in managing liabilities (or not properly managing them) some facets of the subject are discussed in Chapter 33.

But first, let us review what the procedure is, and why it is so popular. The basic steps in a leveraged buyout are these:

1. A company with the desired characteristics (discussed later) is purchased (often by the management).

2. Most of the funds needed for the purchase are borrowed.

3. Unwanted assets are sold. The funds from such sales, plus the cash flow, are used to service the large debt and to pay down the indebtedness to reasonable levels as quickly as possible.

In a typical LBO, the transaction is financed with these securities:

Security	Share of Capitalization (%)
Secured senior debt	50–60
"Junk" bonds—unsecured, less-than-investment grade junior bonds—carrying a very high interest rate	30–40
Preferred stock and common stock	10

Why have LBOs been so popular? Among other reasons, if the candidate is well selected, properly managed, and successful, the return on the investment is very high. Additionally, the incentives paid to the investment bankers for corralling the funds is lucrative. And the rewards to a successful management are bountiful.

On the other hand, the risks to the equity holders (and junk bondholders) are great when the venture is ill-planned and/or ill-managed. In the event of an economic downturn, the results can be disastrous—restructuring or insolvency.

What are some of the desirable characteristics for a leveraged buyout? They include many of these attributes:

• A heavy and stable cash flow.

• Segments or businesses that can be sold without negatively impacting the remaining operations.

• A relatively low debt-to-equity ratio.

• Stable working capital requirements.

• Stable capital expenditure needs.

• Preferably, management continuity.

- A noncyclical business pattern.
- Sizeable cash dividends.

The essence of an LBO is the payment for the entity from its future earnings and from proceeds arising through the sale of assets.

A highly leveraged LBO forces the management to focus on effectively and efficiently running the business—or the management won't have a business to run. Some of the techniques or methods of achieving a successful operation include:

- *Emphasizing Cash Flow.* The need to reduce debt (and interest expense) causes a focus on increasing cash flow and cash availability. How can the investment in receivables be reduced? Through JIT techniques, can we lower inventories?
- *Relating Compensation to Cash Flow and/or Profitability of Operation.*
- *Motivating the Officers and Managers through Stock Ownership.* Heavy stock ownership can stimulate an entrepreneurship attitude—and more aggressive action.
- *Involving the Board of Directors.* The outside directors, frequently investors also, often have good ideas—which are listened to.
- *Communicating Effectively and Frequently with Employees.* The fact that they are "wired in" and kept informed motivates them. They feel they are "part of the team."
- *Focusing on the "Critical Success Factors"—the Essentials.* These elements, and the reasons for their importance are communicated to the managers. They thus know where their attention should be directed. Proper emphasis is given to matters such as:

  a. Customer satisfaction.

  b. Improved quality.

  c. The sales organization.

  d. Renegotiating contracts.

  e. Reducing nonvalue adding activities.

  f. Keeping research and development effective.

  g. Expanding product uses, etc.

- *Involving All of Management in the Annual Planning Process.* When the managers have a say in the annual plan, then it becomes "their" plan—not that of the CFO.

But high rewards can carry high risks. Some unpleasant LBO results are discussed in Chapter 33.

53-15 ACCOUNTING FOR A BUSINESS COMBINATION

The impact of differing accounting policies as between acquiror and acquiree has been discussed earlier. But there is another significant decision to be made, and that relates to which accounting method is to be used in recording the business combination.

When making an acquisition, the acquiring corporation can, if certain conditions are met, structure the transactions in one of two ways: the *purchase method* of accounting or the *pooling-of-interest* method. The method chosen can significantly affect the book income and financial position of the combination after the acquisition. Generally speaking, when the purchase price of an acquired company exceeds the historical book value, the purchase method will result in lower future earnings than if the pooling method is used. It behooves the controller to know the accounting rules applicable, and to prepare pro forma financial statements on both bases in order to illustrate the impact. The differing results may be a factor in how the transaction is structured.

The Accounting Principles Board (APB) has issued standards through APBs 16 and 17 (AC1091 and 5141) identifying when either the purchase method or the pooling-of-interests method may be applicable. Also, in December 1987 the Financial Accounting Standards Board issued Statement No. 96, Accounting for Income Taxes, which mandates the liability method instead of the net-of-tax method for business combinations accounted for as purchases in a tax-free exchange—which may change how the purchase price is allocated. If interested, the reader may wish to peruse all three documents (and any other changes).

Basically, as stated in APB No. 16, a business combination that meets specified conditions requires accounting by the pooling-of-interests method. A new basis of accounting is not permitted for a combination that meets the specified conditions, and the assets and liabilities of the uniting companies are combined at their recorded amounts. All other business combinations should be accounted for as an acquisition of one or more companies by a corporation.

The two techniques are defined as follows:

Purchase Method

11. The purchase method accounts for a business combination as the acquisition of one company by another. The acquiring corporation records at its cost the acquired assets less liabilities assumed. A difference between the cost of an acquired company and the sum of the fair values of tangible and identifiable intangible assets less liabilities is recorded as goodwill. The reported income of an acquiring corporation includes the operations of the acquired company after acquisition, based on the cost to the acquiring corporation.

Pooling of Interests Method

12. The pooling of interests method accounts for a business combination as the uniting of the ownership interests of two or more companies by change of equity securities. No acquisition is recognized because the combination is accomplished without disbursing resources of the constituents. Ownership interests continue and the former bases of accounting are retained. The recorded assets and liabilities of the constituents are carried forward to the combined corporation at their recorded amounts. Income of the combined corporation includes income of the constituents for the entire fiscal period in which the combination occurs. The reported income of the constituents for prior periods is combined and restated as income of the combined corporation.[4]

As a general statement, a business combination is classified as a purchase if the method of payment takes the form of cash or other security instruments, other than

---

[4]*Opinions of the Accounting Principles Board, No. 16, Business Combinations,* Aug. 1970, pp. 284–285.

the exchange of at least 90% of common stock for common stock. On the other hand, the combination is a purchase if the stockholder group of one of the combining companies emerges as the dominant controlling interest.

If a combination is accounted for as a purchase, market values, including goodwill where appropriate, are recorded in the preparation of the consolidated financial statements. The write-off of these increased values assigned to the income statement reduces consolidated income. In contrast, the pooling-of-interests method accounts for a combination as a change in ownership interests by recording only an exchange of equity securities. The basic assumption of a pooling of interests is that the transaction is merely an arrangement between shareholder groups. No new basis of valuing assets need arise. Each of the shareholder groups continues to maintain its relative ownership interests and the proportionate risk in the new entity.

Finally, an idea of the comparability of pooling and purchase accounting can be seen in this matrix of some of the effects:

Pooling	Purchase
Assets, liabilities, and shareholders' equity are based on book value.	Assets, liabilities, and shareholders' equity are based on market values.
No market values of assets and liabilities in excess of book values are recognized. Hence, no depreciation, amortization or other sums related to market values impact the income statement.	Market values of assets and liabilities in excess of book value are periodically assigned to the income statement after the date of acquisition. (However, it may be that under the TRA of 1986 a tax might be levied on any markup, and the tax benefit of depreciating the markup might be lost.)
No goodwill is recognized as arising from the combination. No amortization, therefore, is needed.	Goodwill, represented by the excess cost of net assets acquired over their market values is recognized, and may be amortized. (Any net operating loss may affect the amount of goodwill.)
Net income of the acquired entity becomes part of the consolidated net income in the year of acquisition.	Net income of the acquired entity becomes part of consolidated net income only as earned after the date of acquisition.
For the presentation of prior period income statements, the net income of the acquired entity is included in consolidated net income.	For the presentation of prior period income, no part of the net income of the acquired business is included in consolidated net income.
The direct incremental costs of the combination are expensed in the year incurred.	The direct incremental costs of the combination are treated as part of the cost of investment.
Retained earnings of the acquired entity at the date of acquisition ordinarily become part of consolidated retained earnings.	No share of the acquired business' retained earnings at the date of acquisition may become consolidated retained earnings.

Note: FASB 96 may influence the accounting for goodwill and depreciation. The appreciation of the statement should be reviewed with the particular facts in mind.

53-16 TAX CONSIDERATIONS IN ACQUISITIONS AND MERGERS

One corporation may acquire another through either a taxable or nontaxable transaction. Moreover, under either method a sale of assets or a sale of stock may be accomplished. It is quite obvious that the tax consequences may be of particular interest to either buyer or seller. It usually is an important factor in properly structuring the transaction, and, of course, on the price to be paid.

The controller should be generally aware of the tax aspects, and in any proposed purchase or sale, the tax consequences for the company (and sometimes as to the other side) should be calculated. This, of course, should be determined with knowledgeable assistance, whether from the tax manager or the firm of independent accountants or tax counsel or legal counsel.

Because tax law changes frequently, only a general background is provided herein. With a case in hand, the controller will want to be updated on the current laws.

Basically there are six ways of making an acquisition under U.S. law, and some have several variations. The primary methods are these:

1. An asset acquisition.
2. A Section 338 transaction.
3. A stock acquisition.
4. A Type A reorganization.
5. A Type B reorganization.
6. A Type C reorganization.

The first three usually are considered to be taxable. Type A, B, or C reorganizations generally are tax free, under IRC 368; they ordinarily should not have income tax consequences for the parties involved.

A few brief comments are made on each method.

(a) ASSET ACQUISITION

In this type of acquisition the acquiring party purchases all or a part of the assets of the target company for cash, stock, or other considerations. Payment is made by the acquiring entity to the target company and the latter remains in existence. The transaction is viewed by the IRS as a taxable sale of assets. However, if the target company, pursuant to a plan of liquidation distributes all of its assets, there is no tax payable by the selling entity. But the owners of the latter must recognize gain or loss upon distribution of the proceeds.

(b) SECTION 338 TRANSACTION

Under this type of acquisition, the acquiring company purchases the stock of the target company from its shareholders for cash, stock, other securities, or other consideration. Pursuant to IRC 338, by the 15th day of the ninth month after the month of acquisition, it elects to treat the transaction as if the target sold its assets for a price equal to their fair market value. Such a series of transactions is considered by the IRS as a taxable sale by the shareholders of the target.

(c) STOCK ACQUISITION

Under this type of acquisition, the acquiring company purchases the stock of the target for cash, stock, other securities, or other consideration. The transaction is regarded by the IRS as a taxable sale by the shareholders of the target.

(d) TYPE A REORGANIZATION

Under the general category there are four types of Type A reorganization: (1) Type A statutory mergers, (2) Type A statutory consolidations, (3) Type A subsidiary mergers, and (4) Type A reverse subsidiary mergers.

All are regarded as nontaxable. A brief explanation of each follows:

1. *Type A Statutory Merger.* This kind of reorganization occurs when two corporations, pursuant to a state statute, combine in such a manner that one company remains in existence and the other disappears. In the eyes of the IRS, the merged company is considered to have exchanged its assets for the stock of the surviving—the acquiring—company. The acquired company distributes the stock of the acquiring corporation to its shareholders in exchange for the stock of the target company. Thus, a nontaxable stock exchange takes place.

2. *Type A Statutory Consolidation.* A Type A statutory consolidation occurs when two or more corporations are combined into a new corporation. In the eyes of the tax law, the combined corporations are viewed as having exchanged their assets for the stock of the new corporation. These combined corporations, upon receiving the stock of the new corporation, distribute it to their shareholders in exchange for their shares in the combining company.

3. *Type A Subsidiary Merger.* A Type A subsidiary merger, also referred to as a standard triangular merger, occurs when the target company merges into a controlled subsidiary of the acquiring corporation in exchange for the stock of the acquiring company. The acquiring entity must acquire substantially all of the assets of the target company. Also, no stock of the subsidiary may be given to the shareholders of the target entity. The merged (target) company is considered to have exchanged its assets for stock. The target company then distributes its newly acquired stock to its shareholders in exchange for its stock held by them.

4. *Type A Reverse Subsidiary Merger.* In such a transaction, a controlled subsidiary of the acquiring company merges into the target corporation—by reason of a legal need for the target to remain in existence. The shareholders of the target company receive the stock of the acquiring corporation, and the acquiring entity receives the stock of the target. When this transaction is completed, the target corporation must hold (a) substantially all of the assets it held before the transaction, and (b) substantially all of the assets of the subsidiary merged into it.

(e) TYPE B REORGANIZATION

This type of reorganization usually may be accomplished in one of two ways: (1) stock of the parent is exchanged for stock of the target company, or (2) subsidiary stock is exchanged for stock of the target company. When the first of the two methods is undertaken, the acquiring company must exchange its voting stock for stock of the target in a sufficient amount to control the target (i.e., 80% of the combined voting power of all voting stock and at least 80% of all other categories of target stock). Thus, in effect, the target becomes a subsidiary of the acquiring corporation. In the second variation of a Type B reorganization, the acquiring entity may use its own stock or that of its subsidiary in an exchange—but not both. The acquiring company may pass its stock down to the subsidiary, which exchanges that stock for the stock of the target company. As an alternative, the subsidiary may issue its own stock in exchange for the stock of the target. Thus, in effect, the target becomes a subsidiary of the acquiring company's subsidiary.

These Type B reorganizations are nontaxable.

(f) TYPE C REORGANIZATION

This type of reorganization may be effected in one of two ways: (1) an exchange of parent stock for assets, or (2) an exchange of subsidiary stock for assets. In the first instance the acquiring corporation exchanges its voting stock for substantially all of the assets of the target. In the second case, the subsidiary (of the acquiring company) exchanges its own voting stock, or voting stock of its parent, for substantially all of the assets of the target.

In a Type C reorganization, the acquiring corporation or its subsidiary usually does not recognize any gain or loss. On the other hand, the target company and its shareholders recognize no gain or loss if only voting stock is received. However, when the target is liquidated, its owners takes a tax basis in the acquiring company common stock equal to that of their target company stock. If "boot" is part of the transaction and is distributed to the target company shareholders, it is taxable to them.

(g) TAXES—A SUMMARY

These further comments are helpful:

1. From the standpoint of the buyer, the objective is to select an acquisition method that represents the most advantageous or least-cost type that is negotiable.

2. To reiterate, tax laws and their interpretation change. So the financial officers of the acquiring company (or the acquired) must secure the best up-to-date tax advice possible before their company consummates a transaction.

3. This tax consideration discussion has focused on federal taxes. However, the impact of state and local taxes, which may be considerable, also should be carefully examined.

53-17 FINANCIAL IMPACT OF AN ACQUISITION

A great many factors must be weighed, and alternatives considered—both financial and nonfinancial—when a potential acquisition is under study and/or discussion. What these factors are depends on the circumstances, of course, and the particular interests of the management and board of directors of the acquiring entity. In the final analysis, a most important subject is the impact on earnings. Most readers may be aware of these influences, but we will briefly comment on three aspects:

- Earnings per share.
- Impact of product line growth rates.
- Influence of differing cash/securities packages as consideration.

These matters are in addition to subjects already discussed, including whether a taxable or tax-free transaction should be used in a particular transaction, and whether a pooling of interests or purchase accounting may be most advantageous.

(a) EARNINGS PER SHARE (EPS)

The financial community and many chief executives pay a great deal of attention to earnings per share, or more specifically to *growth* in EPS. An increase in this financial measure can be accomplished by several means (see Chapter 34), including buy-back of outstanding shares, more intensive use of debt instead of equity to finance growth, as well as a real increase in annual earnings. Of course, if an acquisition is made at a lower price-earnings (P/E) ratio than the acquirer has achieved, the EPS may increase. Aside from this relative P/E factor, usually management expects an acquisition to improve the EPS ultimately, if not immediately. Some acquisitions, however, do dilute earnings for a period of time. In any event, the financial executives should be sensitive to EPS and include commentary on this fact in the acquisition report. It may be a simple comparison, as shown in Figure 53-12.

Figure 53-12   Impact of Acquisition on EPS.

	The Johnson Company		
	ESTIMATED IMPACT ON PER SHARE EARNINGS OF		
	ACQUIRING SUPERTECHNOLOGY CORP., INC.		
	Johnson Company EPS Without the Acquisition	Supertechnology Earnings Expressed in Johnson EPS*	Adjusted EPS
199R	$6.40	(.82)	$5.58
199S	$7.02	1.02	$8.04
199T	$7.71	1.70	$9.41
199U	$8.60	2.40	$11.00
199V	$9.75	2.90	$12.65
199W	$10.80	3.78	$14.58
199X	$11.96	5.06	$17.02
199Y	$12.14	5.75	$17.89
199Z	$12.60	6.25	$18.85

* Allowance made for interest expense at 10.25% per annum on estimated borrowing of $40 million.

(b) IMPACT OF PRODUCT LINE GROWTH RATES

Another phenomenon that impacts earnings and EPS is the growth rate of any or all product lines. The impact on earnings of a different growth rate in the presumed sales, and therefore earnings, of a proposed acquisition was illustrated by the judgmental adjustment of projected earnings in Figure 53-4 for differences of opinion between buyer and seller. In any event, the impact on earnings for different assumptions as to growth rate (of an acquisition) might be graphically presented in the acquisition analysis as illustrated in Figure 53-13.

(c) IMPACT OF DIFFERING PACKAGES OF CASH/SECURITIES

One of the tasks of the financial officer of the acquiring company should be to explore the impact on earnings and earnings per share of differing combinations of the consideration, for example, varying amounts of cash and common stock and/or preferred stock. Again, a graph can effectively portray the impact of various packages, and might be included in the acquisition report. (See Figure 53-14.)

Figure 53-13 Impact of Product Line Growth Rates.

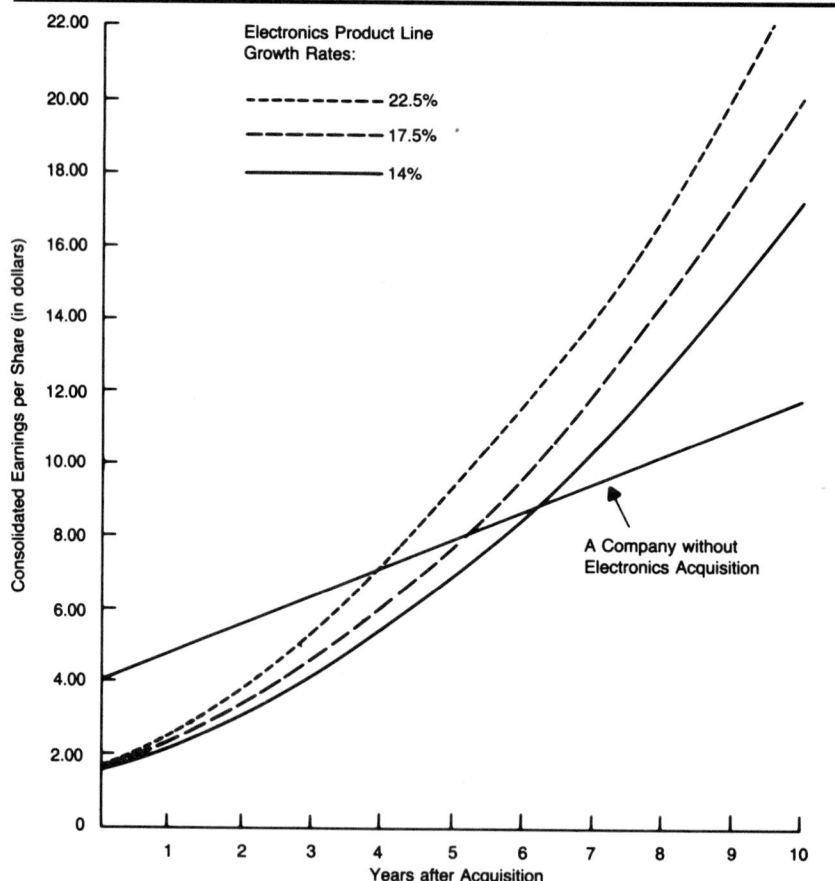

Figure 53-14   Impact of Differing Cash/Securities Packages.

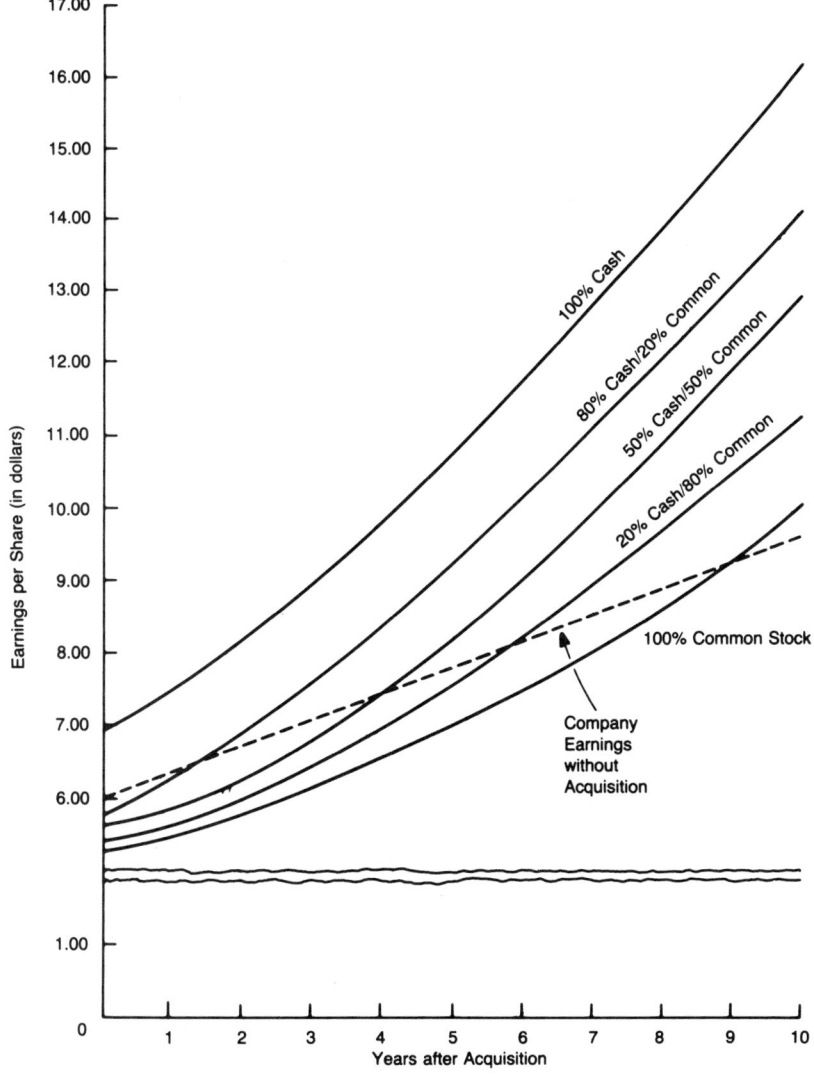

53-18 ACQUISITIONS BY FOREIGN BUYERS

Recently, most readers probably are aware of the high prices being paid for the purchase of U.S. companies by foreign buyers. And some may have experienced direct foreign competition in bidding on a prospective acquisition candidate. So the question might be asked, "How can a foreign bidder pay such high prices—perhaps a 100% premium over the market value of the stock?"

In summary, there are several reasons, or a combination of them which may explain the cause:

- Some foreign buyers assess a company on quite a different basis than do many U.S. buyers. Whereas sophisticated domestic buyers may use the present value of a stream of cash flow, or a multiple of cash flow, etc., foreign buyers tend to bypass such methods and concentrate on such long-term strategic factors as market penetration.

- The relatively weak U.S. dollar causes purchases based on foreign currency to seem quite high in terms of dollars.

- The cost of capital in many foreign countries is much less than in the United States. This factor would tend to decrease the expected rate of return on capital employed.

- U.S. companies may feel handicapped by some domestic accounting practices. Thus, in Japan, at this time, goodwill need not be recognized as such; and in some countries goodwill is taken as a deduction against shareholders' equity—not earnings.

- Finally, some foreign tax laws work to the advantage of a buyer.

There isn't much a U.S. company can do to counter premium prices, etc.—other than to examine prices and growth prospects quite carefully, and carefully weigh the long-term results. But the financial officer should understand some possible reasons for the foreign action.

53-19 THE FINANCIAL REPORT ON A POTENTIAL ACQUISITION

When the in-depth acquisition analysis is complete, when the nonfinancial executives and financial executives have reviewed, discussed, and generally agreed upon any operating matters that will have a significant financial impact (sales volumes, terms of sales, rates of growth, product margins, manufacturing costs, marketing expense levels, research and development, new facility requirements, to mention a few) and when these conclusions are reflected in the relevant sales volumes, costs and expense levels, and asset levels of the financial statements, together with financial type decisions as to sources of cash, etc., accounts receivable levels, etc.—then the financial segment of the acquisition report can be prepared.

The financial commentary and tabulations often comprise one segment—albeit an important one—of the acquisition report. As to this review, it is the responsibility of the financial officers, sometimes primarily the controller, to summarize and interpret the actual and projected financial statements for the benefit of all of top management, including the board of directors. The purpose should be to *communicate* all *significant* financial facts about the proposed acquisition and the financial impact on the acquiring company. An informed conclusion on these matters and the best manner, financially speaking, of consummating the acquisition—if it is to be acquired—should be reached by the financial officers and communicated to the management and the board of directors.

This group of presumably largely nonfinancial executives should not be inundated with excessive detail. While a certain amount of relevant detail may be included in an appendix, etc., the summarized financial data should simply and clearly explain and support the recommendation. Again, the exact format and content will depend in part on the interests of the audience and the important facts that must be communicated. Though an oral presentation (with graphs) may be highly desirable, some suggested written commentary and related tabulations to be part of the content are these:

Summary

Brief tabulation or graphs, perhaps extending over 5–10 years, as appropriate, showing:

- Basic assumptions.
- Net sales.
- Earnings and rate of growth.
- Earnings per share and impact of acquisition (dilution or accretion).
- Return on investment (DCF).
- Return on shareholders' equity.
- Cash flow from operations.
- Condensed financial condition, showing sources of funds, (necessary borrowings), and debt capacity.
- The proposed consideration (package of cash, stock, etc.).
- Financial risks of the acquisition.

The summary, if appropriate, could include some alternative scenarios such as most probable, pessimistic, and optimistic results or conditions. Depending on circumstances, certain supporting data might be presented (or be available):

Net Sales

- Growth by area or market.
- Competitor status and/or actions.
- Impact of alternative growth rates (see Figure 53-13).

Earnings

- Basic company planned earnings, acquiree earnings, and combined earnings.
- Inflation impact.
- Adjustments to seller data.
- Impact of accounting changes (acquiror vs. acquiree).
- Anticipated savings or synergisms.
- Growth rates.
- Earnings of target by significant segments.

Cash Sources and Uses

- Segregation as between target, basic company and combined.
- Significant new equity issues, if any.
- Significant borrowings.

- Dividend payments.
- Capital expenditures (basic company and target, each separate).

Financial Position

- Condensed statements (most likely) of both basic company, target, and consolidated (perhaps also the worst-case scenario when discussing risks).
- Key financial ratios, with target, and without, related to credit agreement requirements.
- Tax status of transaction.
- Contingent liabilities, basic company, target, and consolidated.
- Return on assets—with and without target.
- Analyses of shareholders' equity—showing earnings of target, and basic company; dividends status and growth; return on equity (with and without the acquisition).

Proposed Acquisition Package

- As recommended, including impact on EPS.
- Alternatives (see Figure 53-14).

Other

- Basic assumptions.
- Extent of financial risk—amount, and probability of occurrence, and period of greatest exposure.

In summary, the major financial points should be communicated. There should be available, if appropriate, further detailed results by year and perhaps by line of product. Naturally, the financial officers should be prepared to answer any and all financial questions directed to them. Hopefully, the presentation will have anticipated most questions.

An illustrative condensed financial report on selected phases of an acquisition is presented in Figure 53-15, largely in the form of a short narrative. It is designed to indicate that a meaningful financial presentation can be made without reams of detailed figures. If, on the other hand, management is highly analytical, and figure oriented, then supporting data to the commentary could be attached as an appendix, as shown in Figures 53-16, 53-17, and 53-18.

53-20 MISTAKES BY MANAGEMENT

In the past, there have been a high number of successful acquisitions. Yet, there also have been a significant share that have not achieved the results anticipated. While expectations may have been too high in some instances, in other cases some seemingly minor oversights led to disappointment by the new owners. A summarization of some causes of failure may be useful:

- *Failure to Respond to Customer Needs, or to Emphasize Quality.* Perhaps the emphasis was on costs or selling prices, while neglecting customer complaints.

Figure 53-15   Illustrative Condensed Acquisition Report.

TO: CEO
FROM: Controller
SUBJECT: Acquisition of Supertechnology, Inc.

You have asked for a concise report on the financial impact on our company of the proposed acquisition of Supertechnology, Inc., with information as to net sales, net income, earnings per share, and dividend-paying ability for the next five years. You have also requested a succinct statement on the proposed package to be issued in payment for the acquisition, and the resulting return on the company's gross investment in Supertechnology, Inc. The summarized data is presented below.

Net Sales

Based on discussions with the vice-president-marketing regarding the sales outlook, by detailed product lines, we are of the opinion the following sales pattern represents the most likely combined result for the next five years (dollars in thousands):

Year	Parent Company	Super-technology, Inc.	Combined
Historical			
Last year	$128,000	$ 35,000	$ 163,000
This year (est.)	131,500	40,250	171,750
Total	$259,500	$ 75,250	$ 334,750
Projected			
199R	$138,075	$ 46,290	$ 184,365
199S	144,980	53,235	198,215
199T	152,230	61,220	213,450
199U	159,840	70,405	230,245
199V	167,830	80,965	248,795
	$762,955	$312,115	$1,075,070

It is estimated that the parent company sales will continue to increase, but only at about 5% per year. On a most probable basis, the sales of Supertechnology, Inc., will increase about 15% per year to a level of $80,965,000 for the year 199V. Thus, by that year combined sales of the companies will approach $250 million.

A very conservative forecast would see Supertechnology, Inc., sales increase at about 10% to a level of $67,774,000 by 199V. In contrast, an optimistic sales estimate reflects a potential of 20% per year growth—or a level of $95,990,000 by 199V.

Net Income

Using the net income of our five-year plan, and income and expense levels estimated for Supertechnology, Inc., and agreed to by the functional managers of both companies, the most likely consolidated net income, in comparison with the past two-year actual or expected net income, is as follows (dollars in thousands):

(continued)

Figure 53-15   *(continued)*

Year	Parent Company	Super-technology, Inc.	Combined
Historical			
Last year	$ 7,680	$ 4,200	$11,880
This year (est.)	7,890	4,830	12,720
	$15,570	$ 9,030	$24,600
Projection			
199R	$ 8,285	$ 5,555	$13,840
199S	8,700	6,388	15,088
199T	9,134	7,346	16,480
199U	9,590	8,450	18,040
199V	10,070	9,715	19,785
	$45,779	$37,454	$83,233

The parent company earns 6% on net sales, whereas Supertechnology is expected to secure a 12% return on a most likely basis (even after making certain interest expense adjustments—discussed later). With this rate of return on sales, the parent company is expected to earn $10,070,000 in 199V, whereas, Supertechnology probably may achieve earnings of $9,715,000 in the same year—a combined total of $19,785,000. This compares with expected net income of the parent company only approximating $7,890,000 this year.

On even a pessimistic scenario, Supertechnology is estimated to earn $7,290,000 in 199V; and the optimistic forecast of net income for this potential subsidiary is $12,630,000 in this same year.

Earnings Per Share

Based on the above net income, the estimated earnings per share of common stock to be contributed by Supertechnology, Inc., and the combined results are as follows:

Year	Parent Company	Super-technology, Inc.	Combined*
Historical			
Last year	$3.840		
This year (est.)	3.945		
Projected			
199R	4.140	$2.780	$6.92
199S	4.350	3.194	7.54
199T	4.567	3.673	8.24
199U	4.795	4.225	9.02
199V	5.035	4.857	9.89

* After providing for interest on newly borrowed funds.

These earnings per share are based on 2 million shares of outstanding common shares. It is not expected that either additional common shares or any preferred shares will need to be issued for this acquisition.

Figure 53-15 *(continued)*

Dividends on Common Shares

At the present time the company follows a practice of paying out about 40% of the estimated sustainable earnings level. The dividend on the common stock presently is at the rate of $1.50 per share annually. Even after providing for the interest expense on some planned borrowings, if the board of directors approves, annual dividends per share *could* rise to the following level and still not exceed the 40% payout ratio:

Year	40% Payout
199R	$2.77
199S	3.02
199T	3.30
199U	3.61
199V	3.96

With a planned accelerated repayment of a term loan over the next five years, it is not recommended that the full 40% payout ratio be reached over this time period.

Purchase Price for Supertechnology, Inc.

The owners of Supertechnology, as a nonpublic company, initially quoted an asking price of $80,000,000 payable in 2,000,000 shares of our common stock or a new convertible preferred for 100% of the stock of their company. However, in examining (a) the impact of doubling the existing number of shares, and possibly raising problems of management control; (b) the seller's intention to dispose of most of the stock; (c) the seller's need for cash; (d) certain advantageous investments in municipal bonds for the aging sellers; (e) the tremendous impact on earnings per share of doing a cash transaction and avoiding dilution; and (f) the sizable amount of cash and temporary investments held by our company, your three principal officers convinced the sellers to immediately accept a cash counteroffer of $65,000,000. So, if you and the board of directors agree, the transaction will call for a payment of this sum, with no issuance of stock.

The impact of this transaction, if the estimated earnings and cash flow materialize, is a rate of return of 18.2% after taxes. This is somewhat higher than our internal target of 15% calculated on a discounted cash flow basis.

Impact on Financial Position

The current financial position of the company, as of September 30, 199Q, is summarized on Exhibit I, attached.

We propose to borrow $15,000,000 as a term bank loan, payable in 7 years, with interest at two percentages above the prime rate. At the present time, the interest rate would be 12.5% per annum. The company would be permitted to prepay any part of this loan at any time without penalty. Accordingly, a share of the earnings from the Supertechnology operations, after a provision for "dividends" (to 40% or less), would be applied to pay down the bank loan of $15,000,000. It is estimated that the term loan would be repaid in five years, from the Supertechnology earnings, as shown on Exhibit II, attached.

(continued)

Figure 53-15   *(continued)*

The chief financial officer of the company is of the opinion the cash available will be greater than this estimate in that (a) the earnings estimate is reasonably conservative because expense levels have been estimated on the high side; (b) the investment in receivables, inventory, and fixed assets for Supertechnology included above, amounting to $17,580,000 probably is 25% greater than actually needed; (c) probably the dividend payout ratio will be kept below 40% for perhaps three years to assure ourselves that the earnings level is attainable.

These further comments apply as to the company's financial position:

(1) As you know, we have been keeping funds available for a possible acquisition, so that the use of $50 million of the $54,400,000 still leaves ample cash for our operating needs.

(2) The company capitalization now, and with the term loan, would be as follows ($000):

	At Present		With Term Loan	
	Amount	Percent	Amount	Percent
Long-term liabilities	$30,000	32.00%	$ 45,000	41.00%
Shareholders' equity	64,200	68.00	64,200	59.00
Total	$94,200	100.00%	$109,200	100.00%

In the opinion of our investment bankers and commercial bankers, the long-term debt as a percentage of total capitalization, with the proposed borrowing, or the long-term debt to equity ratio is reasonably conservative in our industry—especially in view of the company's tract record. We believe the company has additional borrowing capacity—which we do not plan to use.

I hope these comments answer your questions. Please call me if you have any more.

J.J.J.
Controller

EXHIBIT I—to letter dated October 14, 199Q

Re: Acquisition of Supertechnology, Inc.
      Impact on Financial Position ($000)

Assets

Current Assets
Cash and temporary investments	$ 54,400
Other current assets	24,800
Total current assets	$ 79,200

Fixed Assets
Property, plant and equipment	44,000
Total assets	$123,200

Figure 53-15 *(continued)*

Liabilities and Shareholders' Equity

Current Liabilities

Accounts payable .... $ 13,600

Accrued items 15,400

Total current liabilities .... $ 29,000

Long-Term Liabilities (insurance loan) 30,000

Total liabilities 59,000

Shareholders' equity 64,200

Total liabilities and shareholders' equity $123,200

EXHIBIT II—to letter dated October 14, 199Q

Re: Acquisition of Supertechnology, Inc.
Impact on Financial Position ($000)

Year	Earnings (A)	Investment Net of Depreciation (B)	Net Cash Flow (C)	Less Applicable "Dividend" (D)	Available for Loan Payment (E)	Amount to Prepay (F)
199R	$ 5,555	$ 300	$ 5,855	$ 2,342	$ 3,513	$ 3,000
199S	6,388	(280)	6,108	2,443	3,665	3,000
199T	7,346	(1,070)	6,276	2,510	3,766	3,500
199U	8,450	(2,000)	6,450	2,580	3,870	3,500
199V	9,715	(2,530)	7,185	2,874	4,311	2,000
199W	11,172	(2,700)	8,472	3,389	5,083	—
Total	$48,626	($8,280)	$40,346	$16,138	$24,208	$15,000

A – B = C
D = 40% of net cash flow

Figure 53-16   Comparative Sales, Earnings, and Cash Flow Data for Merger Study—in Substantial Detail.

APPENDIX I   **Western Manufacturing Corporation and Southern Manufacturing Company**
SALES, EARNINGS, AND CASH FLOW
FOR THE YEARS 19X – 4 THROUGH 19X5
(dollars in thousands)

	Net Sales		Pretax Earnings		Net Income		Cash Flow *	
	Amount	% Increase Preceding Year	Amount	% Net Sales	Amount	% Net Sales	Amount	% Net Sales
WESTERN MANUFACTURING CORPORATION								
Actual								
19X–4	184,216	2.72	18,230	9.90	13,611	7.39	28,319	15.37
19X–3	189,817	3.10	18,493	9.74	13,809	7.27	29,877	15.74
19X–2	190,066	.10	17,894	9.41	12,202	6.42	28,067	14.77
19X–1	197,430	3.87	20,311	10.29	14,666	7.43	31,412	15.91
19X	204,684	3.67	22,430	10.96	16,427	8.03	33,660	16.44
Total	966,213	—	97,358	—	70,715	—	151,335	—
Average	193,243	2.64	19,472	10.08	14,143	7.32	30,267	15.66
Forecast								
19X1	208,310	1.77	20,831	10.00	15,415	7.40	32,288	15.50
19X2	216,990	4.17	22,784	10.50	16,057	7.40	33,633	15.50
19X3	226,300	4.29	23,762	10.50	16,746	7.40	35,077	15.50
19X4	239,800	5.97	26,378	11.00	17,745	7.40	37,169	15.50
19X5	253,670	5.78	27,904	11.00	18,772	7.40	39,319	15.50
Total	1,145,070	—	121,659	—	84,735	—	177,486	—
Average	229,014	4.28	24,332	10.62	16,947	7.40	35,497	15.50
SOUTHERN MANUFACTURING COMPANY								
Actual								
19X–4	107,660	1.96	8,612	8.00	4,218	3.92	6,318	5.87
19X–3	108,320	.61	9,430	8.71	4,706	4.34	6,988	6.45
19X–2	107,899	—	8,976	8.32	4,491	4.16	6,619	6.13

19X–1	113,660	5.34	10,866	9.56	5,403	4.75	7,562	6.65
19X	117,432	3.32	10,311	8.78	5,011	4.27	7,184	6.12
Total	554,971	—	48,195	—	23,829	—	34,671	—
Average	110,994	2.29	9,639	8.68	4,766	4.29	6,934	6.25
Forecast								
19X1	118,980	1.32	10,110	8.50	5,000	4.20	7,140	6.00
19X2	122,820	3.23	11,050	9.00	5,280	4.30	7,490	6.10
19X3	124,200	1.12	11,800	9.50	5,590	4.50	7,575	6.10
19X4	129,030	3.89	12,260	9.50	5,805	4.50	7,870	6.10
19X5	134,610	4.32	12,790	9.50	6,055	4.50	8,210	6.10
Total	629,640	—	58,010	—	27,730	—	38,285	—
Average	125,928	2.73	11,602	9.21	5,546	4.40	7,657	6.08
MERGED COMPANIES								
Historical 19X–4	291,876	2.50	26,842	9.20	17,829	6.11	34,637	11.87
19X–3	298,137	2.15	27,923	9.37	18,515	6.21	36,865	12.37
19X–2	297,965	—	26,870	9.02	16,693	5.60	34,686	11.64
19X–1	311,090	4.40	31,177	10.02	20,069	6.45	38,974	12.53
19X	322,116	3.54	32,741	10.16	21,438	6.66	40,844	12.68
Total	1,521,184	—	145,553	—	94,544	—	186,006	—
Average	304,237	2.51	29,111	9.57	18,909	6.22	37,201	12.23
Projection 19X1	327,290	1.61	30,941	9.45	20,415	6.24	39,428	12.05
19X2	339,810	3.52	33,834	9.96	21,337	6.28	41,123	12.10
19X3	350,500	3.15	35,562	10.15	22,336	6.37	42,652	12.17
19X4	368,830	5.23	38,638	10.49	23,550	6.39	45,039	12.21
19X5	388,280	5.27	40,694	10.48	24,827	6.39	47,529	12.24
Total	1,774,710	—	179,669	—	112,465	—	215,771	—
Average	354,942	3.67	35,934	10.12	22,493	6.34	43,154	12.16

* Net income, plus depreciation, depletion, and amortization, if applicable.

Figure 53-17   Selected Detailed Shareholder Data for Merger Discussions.

APPENDIX II   Western Manufacturing Corporation and Southern Manufacturing Company

SELECTED SHAREHOLDER DATA
19X – 4 THROUGH 19X5

	No. of Shares Issued† (000)	Common Equity at Year-End		Dividends		Earnings Applicable * to Common		Market Price Per Share	Price Earnings Ratio
		Amount ($M)	Per Share ($)	Amount ($M)	Per Share ($)	Amount ($M)	Per Share ($)		
WESTERN MANUFACTURING CORPORATION									
Actual 19X–4	2,000	220,000	110.00	6,000	3.00	13,611	6.81	54.48	8.0
19X–3	2,000	227,809	113.96	6,000	3.00	13,809	6.90	55.29	8.0
19X–2	2,000	234,011	117.00	6,000	3.00	12,202	6.10	45.75	8.5
19X–1	2,000	242,077	121.04	6,600	3.30	14,666	7.33	58.64	8.0
19X	2,000	251,904	125.95	6,600	3.30	16,427	8.22	69.87	8.5
Total	—	—	—	31,200	15.60	70,715	35.36	—	—
Average	2,000	235,160	117.59	6,240	3.12	14,143	7.07	—	—
Forecast 19X1	2,000	260,719	130.36	6,600	3.30	15,415	7.71	69.39	9.0
19X2	2,000	270,176	135.10	6,600	3.30	16,057	8.03	72.27	9.0
19X3	2,000	280,322	140.17	6,600	3.30	16,746	8.37	75.33	9.0
19X4	2,000	290,867	145.43	7,200	3.60	17,745	8.87	79.83	9.0
19X5	2,000	301,639	150.82	8,000	4.00	18,772	9.39	84.51	9.0
Total	—	—	—	35,000	17.50	84,735	42.41	—	—
Average	2,000	280,745	140.38	7,000	3.50	16,947	8.48	—	—
SOUTHERN MANUFACTURING COMPANY									
Actual 19X–4	1,000	90,000	90.00	2,000	2.00	4,218	4.22	31.65	7.5
19X–3	1,000	92,706	92.71	2,000	2.00	4,706	4.71	32.97	7.0
19X–2	1,000	95,197	95.20	2,000	2.00	4,491	4.49	29.18	6.5
19X–1	1,000	98,600	98.60	2,000	2.00	5,403	5.40	37.80	7.0

19X	1,000	101,111	101.11	2,500	2.50	5,011	5.01	35.07	7.0
Total	—	101,111	—	10,500	10.50	23,829	23.83	—	—
Average	1,000	95,523	95.52	2,100	2.10	4,766	4.77	—	—
Forecast									
19X1	1,000	103,611	103.61	2,500	2.50	5,000	5.00	37.50	7.5
19X2	1,000	106,391	106.39	2,500	2.50	5,280	5.28	39.60	7.5
19X3	1,000	109,481	109.48	2,500	2.50	5,590	5.59	44.72	8.0
19X4	1,000	112,786	112.79	2,500	2.50	5,805	5.81	46.48	8.0
19X5	1,000	115,841	115.84	3,000	3.00	6,055	6.06	48.48	8.0
Total	—	—	—	13,000	13.00	27,730	27.74	—	—
Average	1,000	109,642	109.64	2,600	2.60	5,546	5.55	—	—
MERGED COMPANIES									
Historical 19X−4	2,600	310,000	119.23	8,000	3.08	17,829	6.86		
19X−3	2,600	320,515	123.28	8,000	3.08	18,515	7.12		
19X−2	2,600	329,208	126.62	8,000	3.08	16,693	6.42		
19X−1	2,600	340,677	131.03	8,600	3.30	20,069	7.72		
19X	2,600	353,015	135.78	9,100	3.50	21,438	8.25		
Total	—	—	—	41,700	—	94,544	—		
Average	2,600	330,683	127.19	8,340	3.20	18,909	7.27		
Projected 19X1	2,600	364,330	140.13	9,100	3.50	20,415	7.85	74.58	9.5
19X2	2,600	376,567	144.83	9,100	3.50	21,337	8.21	78.00	9.5
19X3	2,600	389,803	149.92	9,100	3.50	22,336	8.59	85.90	10.0
19X4	2,600	403,653	155.25	9,700	3.73	23,550	9.06	90.06	10.0
19X5	2,600	417,480	160.55	11,000	4.22	24,827	9.55	95.50	10.0
Total	—	—	—	48,000	—	112,465	—	—	—
Average	2,600	390,367	150.14	9,600	3.70	22,493	8.65	—	—

* For simplicity, illustration assumes no preferred stock issued.
† Exchange ratio of .6 share of Western Manufacturing for each share of Southern Manufacturing.

Figure 53-18 Summary of Combined Operating Results with Additional Detail.

Year	Buying Company	Selling Company	Combined
ACQUIRING CORPORATION SUMMARY OF COMBINED RESULTS *(dollars in millions, except per share)*			
A. Net sales			
19X1	$ 390	$ 90	$ 480
19X2	430	120	550
19X3	450	150	600
19X1–X9	5,400	2,320	7,720
Average	$ 540	232	$ 772
B. Net income			
19X1	$ 23.4	$ 5.7	$ 29.1
19X2	26.7	7.7	34.4
19X3	28.4	9.7	38.1
19X1–X9	340.2	155.4	495.6
Average	$ 34.0	15.5	$ 49.5
C. Earnings per share			
Number of shares outstanding			10,000,000
19X1	$ 2.34	$ .57	$ 2.91
19X2	2.67	.77	3.44
19X3	2.84	.97	3.81
19X1–X9	34.02	15.54	49.56
Average	$ 3.40	$ 1.55	$ 4.95
D. Rate of return			
Discounted cash flow basis			
19X1–X9	17.6%	16.0%	17.1%
On assets employed			
19X1	9.8	9.6	9.7
19X2	10.3	9.7	10.1
19X3	10.4	9.8	10.3
19X1–X9	10.6	9.9	10.5
On shareholders' equity			
19X1	24.3		24.2
19X2	23.7		23.9
19X3	23.4		24.2
19X1–X9	23.2		25.1

- *Failure to Properly Integrate the Acquisition.* This aspect is discussed in the next section.

- *Undue Emphasis on Labor Costs.* Some acquirors have focused attention on labor costs, even though, with automation, such costs aggregate less than 15% of total costs. Perhaps more is to be gained by motivating the labor force instead of downsizing.

- *Focusing Attention on the High-Margin Products While Neglecting Low-Margin Items.* In some endeavors, such as the commodity business, attention to small but vital upgrades in the high volume products can produce significant profit improvement.

- *Failure to Recognize the Weaknesses of Portfolio Management.* Some acquiring managements treat each acquisition as a separate investment, emphasizing growth market share and growth rate. It hopes to move each investment into a more favorable cash generator sector.

  If the management of an acquired business regards itself as a stand-alone or salable business, barriers arise between the two managements, and the exchange of technology or management ideas becomes inhibited. Moreover it may become necessary to match the investment of less diversified competitors of each such separate businesses—reducing the anticipated rate of return.

- *Failure to Commercialize Innovation.* Often it is said the Americans invent the product but the Japanese successfully sell or commercialize it. Such mismatching can be reduced in many cases by closely linking R&D, and manufacturing and marketing. U.S. companies perhaps should consider the setting of goals for commercializing of innovation, measuring the development time, and making every effort to shorten it.

- *Failure to Take a Long-Term View of Discounted Cash Flow Analysis.* The DCF process gives great weight to the immediate years; but it may be necessary to consider the entire product life cycle. The near-term development years may reflect a low DCF rate of return which is more than offset by a very high rate of return in the later years. As someone allegedly has said, "If IBM had demanded as high a rate of return on its early computers as it earned on other products, it might still be making adding machines."

- *Acquiring a Business the New Management Did Not Really Understand.* This is discussed in the next section.

(a) DIVERSIFICATION AWAY FROM THE CORE BUSINESS

As mentioned in section 53-2, among the reasons for acquiring another business may be diversification for growth as well as diversification by customer or market to offset seasonal factors or a declining product market. These, indeed, may be legitimate reasons for diversification.

However, in connection with the environmental analysis desirable in strategic planning, a company management should be aware of the "success" factors, also called "critical success factors" that are responsible for a company's progress. (See Chapter 14.) It is equally true that in making an acquisition the acquiring company management should really understand the business of the acquiree. Many company managements assume that if they can successfully run one business, then they can run any other business. An implicit assumption in this thinking is that it can learn sufficient about the new business in a timely manner. But the numerous failed acquisitions attest to the fact that the acquiring management simply did not understand the critical success factors. So the generalization can be made that diversification into new, unrelated lines carries with it increased risk; and some provision should be made to at least partially compensate for these risks. But how? One well-known authority, in a thought-provoking article has these suggestions for improving the success rate of nonspecialized diversification.[5]

- *Choose the Right People.* Quite often, the people at the top corporate level are those who built the company. They may have strong ideas about changing the method of doing business. Therefore, if a present manager is unable or unwilling to accommodate rapid change, a reassignment of duties may be desirable before attempting to diversify.

- *Change the Environment.* Any major change in how business is done usually carries with it a major change in the corporate culture. It may be prudent, therefore, to relocate the company headquarters in an attempt to eliminate the old cultural trappings.

- *Choose the Proper Organization Structure.* In many old companies there exists strong central control—perhaps too strong. Yet, many successfully diversified companies are decentralized so as to allow the local business managers to make competitive decisions as to product prices and customers. But, top corporate management continues to plan the *general* course of the company and to *monitor* the subsidiary or division businesses it controls. Therefore, two levels of management, physically separated, may be necessary.

- *Choose the Right Strategies when Diversifying.* Quite often, when companies decide to diversify they select the wrong acquisition before considering these courses of action:

  1. Diversify gradually—since assimilation takes time. Don't attempt to digest too much too soon.

  2. Identify the acquiring company's distinctive capabilities to see if they can be used. These might include special manufacturing know-how, research and development expertise, a marketing organization, or organization strength.

  3. Eliminate the (old) industry-imposed restrictions that impede business decisions.

  4. Explicitly plan for change as distinct from business operational planning. This will include a two-tier planning organization as previously mentioned.

- *Choose the Right Timing.* As in many actions, the proper timing is important. For example, a growing company in a growing industry would seem to lack a compelling reason to diversify. If the potential acquiree is in decline, the best time to make the purchase may have passed.

-----

[5] Adapted from Milton Leontiades, "The Case for Nonspecialized Diversification," *Planning Review,* Jan.–Feb. 1990, pp. 28–32.

53-21 EFFECTIVE INTEGRATION

There are situations wherein the product line of the acquired company was superb, the marketing policies and strategies well founded, the manufacturing processes excellent, and the financial analysis for the acquisition unsurpassed. Yet the acquisition was basically a failure. Why? Because the target entity was not properly integrated into the acquiring company. The management of the acquired company was left largely alone. It was not guided or given assistance in solving some of its problems. Moreover, the acquiring company's procedures were forced on it. A successful integration of two cultures involves a mutual educational process. The management of the acquiring company, including the controller and other financial officers, should give thought to these conditions:

- The business of the acquired company must be so managed that market share, competitive position, and operating efficiency are not lost. To accomplish this may require management support and financial help from the acquiring company. (The required investment should have been provided for in the cash flow estimate.)
- The benefits or opportunities foreseen before the acquisition must be pursued so as to be realized. They cannot be left to chance.
- The policies and procedures of each company, acquiring and acquired, ought to be examined to see if changes should be made in either segment to benefit the new operations. It well may be that many of the acquired's practices should be continued and not changed to that of the acquiror.
- The organization structure, reporting relationships, and authority and responsibility of each manager should be examined for any desired changes. Each manager should know his status or position in the new scheme of things. He should be made to feel "comfortable" and a part of the organization.
- As developments dictate it, new strategies may need to be considered.
- Periodically, the actual results of the newly acquired operation should be compared with what was expected to see if any corrective action is required.

53-22 DIVESTMENTS

Up to this point, the discussions of this chapter have centered largely on acquisitions. Yet, for whatever reason, divestments often must be considered if the unsatisfactory operations or conditions cannot be corrected, or if the disposal is part of a "bust-up" acquisition.

In any event, when it is finally decided that divestment is the best course, then the controller or other appropriate financial officer must make an analysis of the divestment candidate so that its fair value is known. Technically, some of the same techniques reviewed earlier for establishing the value of an acquisition can be utilized to determine the value of a divestment candidate.

The financial analysis should seek to establish these judgments:

- The probable future earnings potential of the business segment.
- The probable future cash flows of the segment.

- An estimated fair market value.
- What return can be secured from an investment of the divestment proceeds.
- Whether or not any minority interest should be retained in the divested segment
- The impact on the owning company of the divestment—earnings and financia position, including contingent liabilities, possible tax consequences, retiremen fund liabilities, etc.

53-23 SUMMARY

An attempt has been made in this chapter to review those topics thought to be of par ticular importance to the controller or other financial executive. But acquisitions, mergers, and divestments are complicated subjects at best, so many facets simply can not easily be discussed in the limited space available in a volume on controllership. Fo example, no meaningful comments are made on such subjects as:

U.S. Department of Justice guidelines.

Federal Trade Commission requirements.

Meeting state statutory guidelines.

SEC requirements.

Need to schedule acquisition review cycle.

Compliance with various labor laws.

Sensitivity in timing acquisition events.

And, of course, there are other subjects that may be important in a particular case. Reference should be made to the many excellent current books on mergers and acquisi tions for more information.

53-24 SELECTED REFERENCES

Bibler, R., ed., *The Arthur Young Management Guide to Mergers and Acquisitions.* New York: John Wiley & Sons, Inc., 1984.

Copeland, Tom, Tim Koller, and Jack Murrin, *Valuation: Measuring and Managing the Value of Companies,* New York: John Wiley & Sons, 1990.

Gorman, Jerry, "M&A's: The CPA as Acquisition Adviser," *Journal of Accountancy,* Aug. 1988, pp. 36–42.

Hennessy, J. H., Jr., *Acquiring and Merging Businesses,* Englewood Cliffs, NJ: Prentice-Hall, 1966.

Kelly, Kevin, and Richard A. Melcher, "Merger Today, Trouble Tomorrow?" *Business Week,* Sept. 12, 1994.

Key, Stephen L., and Simon S. Strauss, "Allocating Purchase Price in an Acquisition: A Prac tical Guide," *Journal of Accountancy,* Nov. 1987, pp. 32–37.

Kissin, Warren, and Ronald Zulli, "Valuation of a Closely Held Business," *Journal of Accoun tancy,* June 1988, pp. 38–44.

Kitching, John, "Early Return on LBOs," *Harvard Business Review,* Nov.–Dec. 1989, pp. 74–81.

Leontiades, Milton, "The Case for Nonspecialized Diversification," *Planning Review,* Jan./Feb. 1990, pp. 26–32.

Loomis, Carol J., "The Biggest Looniest Deal Ever," *Fortune,* June 18, 1990, pp. 48–72.

McCarthy, George D., *Acquisitions and Mergers.* New York: The Ronald Press, 1963.

Morris J., *Acquisitions, Divestitures and Corporate Joint Ventures.* New York: John Wiley & Sons, Inc.

Ordway, Nicholas, and Jacqualyn A. Fouse, "New Rules for Allocating the Purchase Price of a Business," *Management Accounting,* May 1988, pp. 50–53.

Read, William J., and Robert Bartsch, "How to Account for Acquisitions Under FASB 96," *Journal of Accountancy,* May 1989, pp. 54–60.

Willens, Robert, "M&A's: The CPA as Tax Adviser," *Journal of Accountancy,* Aug. 1988, pp. 44–52.

CHAPTER 54

Productivity Improvement; Reengineering

54-1 INTRODUCTION

Whether judged by the number of articles in business books, periodicals, or newspapers, or the broad scope of the subjects reviewed, productivity improvement has been an important and popular subject for the past several decades. In this short chapter, we address some of the concerns, causes, and possible solutions to the problem. Moreover, we will review the role of the controller, as well as other members of management, in productivity improvement.

But, first, what is "productivity"? The Bureau of Labor Statistics defines productivity as the value of goods manufactured divided by the amount of labor input. In this chapter, the term is used in the same sense, although we will also discuss services as well as manufacturing.

In reviewing statistics on productivity, be aware of possible deficiencies in the measurement of productivity. Consider these factors:

- The productivity equation—output (value of goods produced) divided by input (labor)—doesn't take into account the many changes in output.

    For example, quality is now a more important value to the customer. But how can it be quantified?

- How are factors such as variety of product, timeliness, and customer service considered?

- Data the BLS uses to calculate productivity covers only about 42% of the service sector economy—thus leaving more than one-half of the economy uncounted.

- Pricing may cause productivity to be understated. For example, if a product is greatly improved and the price drops (perhaps due to competition), the price decrease may not fully reflect the value of the improvements.

- As evidenced by the periodically published figures, the data is volatile. Quite often the preliminary figures are revised when the full statistical data is in.

These factors cause many to believe that, over a period of time, productivity figures significantly understate the benefits achieved.

Despite these weaknesses, it should be remembered that productivity is an important factor in determining the nation's standard of living, and the competitiveness of its products in the global market.

54-2 THE PRODUCTIVITY CYCLE IN THE UNITED STATES

Productivity appears to change at differing rates over time, between manufacturing vs. services, and in different industries. In the last century, the average productivity growth rate in the United States was 2%. In the 15-year period ending in 1973, the average annual increase in the output of labor per hour was 2.7%. From 1973 until the 1990s, the increase in output was only 1%. Manufacturing productivity, which rose an average of 2.4% per year in the 1980s, substantially increased to 3.8% in the 1991–1995 period.

Productivity in service industries, which is difficult to measure, but is an increasingly dominant segment of the economy, declined in the late 1970s, remained flat during the 1980s, and has grown at a 1.5% annual rate during the 1990s. Some service industries have increased productivity much faster, for example, 5% in the telecommunication industry for 1991 and 1992.

Japanese and German productivity gains of 4% to 5% in 1988 and 1989, were reported—far higher than the United States. However, as one source states, "Whatever the absolute growth rate of U.S. productivity in both manufacturing and services, it has been sufficient to keep America No. 1 on this front, well ahead of Japan and Europe."[1]

The long-awaited increase from reorganizations to reflect the substantial use of computers, networks, and the related information technology tools is now beginning to be reflected in the U.S. national productivity figures. Some additional comments are in order about the service sector of the economy.

---

[1] Myron Magnet, "The Productivity Payoff Arrives," *Fortune,* June 27, 1994, p. 80.

(a) THE KNOWLEDGE AND SERVICE WORKERS

While some statistics may reflect a drop in the rate of gain in *average* productivity, it is not because productivity in manufacturing and moving goods has declined. These activities in the United States were still displaying a rising productivity level. The difficulty is that too few people are employed in making and moving goods for their increase in productivity to greatly influence the average rate of improvement for *all* workers. In most of the developed countries, workers in manufacturing constitute no more than 20% of the workforce, with about 80% of the workers being in other fields. As Peter F. Drucker says, "The single greatest challenge facing managers in the developed countries of the world is to raise the productivity of knowledge and service workers."[2] This category ranges from research scientists and cardiac surgeons to the workers in fast-food restaurants.[3] Another source has indicated that service productivity is no better than it was about a dozen years ago, but that the drop in output per hour has halted.[4]

Moreover, in the service area, greater productivity probably does not require heavy capital expenditures. Better operational practices could lead to a great improvement, and some of these are outlined in the next section. The primary purpose of this brief statement is to alert the controller to the basic problem area of low productivity—the knowledge and service segment of business, and not manufacturing per se. Those manufacturing companies faced with international competition may have to more closely examine the service segments of their businesses—where there are difficulties in measuring productivity.

54-3 METHODS USED TO INCREASE PRODUCTIVITY

Over the past several decades, even centuries, business managers often have found themselves under pressure to improve performance. A great many techniques have been developed, some much more effective than others. The problem is complicated by the fact that the same description is used (often erroneously) to identify what are really different methods. Moreover, the names often change with the passage of time. *Some* of the tools currently in use include:

Activity-based costing.	Cost reduction program.
Activity-based cost management.	Critical success factor review.
Benchmarking.	Cross-functional team analysis.
Continuous process improvement.	Customer satisfaction measurement.
Competitor profiling.	Cycle time reduction.
Continuous process improvement.	Downsizing.
Core competencies.	Dynamic simulation models.

---

[2] Peter F. Drucker, "The New Productivity Challenge," *Harvard Business Review*, Nov.–Dec. 1991, p. 69.

[3] *Ibid*, p. 71.

[4] Joseph Spiers, "Productivity Looks Promising," *Fortune*, Mar. 9, 1992, p. 21.

Groupware.

Horizontal organization.

Just-in-time techniques.

Information technology.

Mass customization.

Micromarketing.

Pay for performance.

Portfolio analysis.

Reengineering.

Restructuring.

Shareholder value analysis.

Strategic alliances.

Total quality management (TQM).

Virtual corporation.

Vision and mission rethinking.

The balance of this chapter will briefly discuss some general aspects of productivity improvement before reviewing in somewhat more detail two basic and popular methods: reengineering and continuous process improvement, also known as total quality management (TQM).

54-4 ONE BASIC ACTION TO INCREASE PRODUCTIVITY— RESTRUCTURING

Before discussing productivity improvement programs, it may be helpful to summarize how many American companies in recent years have sought to increase productivity. Beginning with the severe 1980–1982 recession, a period when U.S. business was in a weak competitive position as compared to some foreign entities, management commenced (and in 1996 is still engaged in) a massive restructuring that has involved assets, management procedures, and, to a lesser degree, finances.

As to restructuring that involves assets, the first category might be classified as *strategic* asset restructuring—a decision is made to dispose of the product line. It could result from a conclusion that the potential return on investment will be insufficient because of the relative cost of capital. Or, it might be concluded that the rate of return on the product line could never be as profitable as available alternatives. Other reasons for management's disposing of the line can result from a conclusion that the entity could never become the lowest-cost producer—a key requirement for survival—or that the company could never achieve a market leadership position, i.e., the number one or two marketeer—also regarded as a strategic requirement for growth and/or profitability. Examples of such strategic decisions include the sale by Pfizer of its Coty perfume business and the sale by General Electric of its small electrical appliances business to Black & Decker.

An example of a *tactical* sale of assets could be the disposition of outmoded manufacturing plants or warehouses and relocation to a modern and more suitable site.

An illustration of a restructuring that involves management practices and procedures would be a reorganization as a flatter type organization, eliminating layers of management in an environment that has become too slow and inefficient in reacting to negative conditions or in simply reaching business decisions. It may be decided that a new management could employ the principle of worker participation or cross-functional teams that motivate employees, reduce costs, improve quality, and respond more quickly to customer needs. Incidentally, such an environment could lead to reduced inventories through just-in-time manufacturing practices, or perhaps to a lessened need for new equipment.

The third type of restructuring that has taken place is of a financial nature and involves the balance sheet. In some cases, high-cost debt has been eliminated and replaced with equity, or the debt has been refinanced at a much lower interest cost, which has reduced the interest burden.

In some instances, these restructurings may have involved heavy one-time income charges related to personnel reduction. However, the final results often were a more competitive company, improved long-term profitability, improved productivity, and a financially stronger entity.

54-5 INCREASING PRODUCTIVITY— THE VIRTUAL CORPORATION

With the intense competition in the global marketplace, a new type of operation is emerging and becoming more prevalent—the virtual corporation. The virtual corporation is a temporary network of independent companies, linked by information technology, to share skills, costs, and access to each other's markets. It may be so named because of the dictionary definition of "virtual": "being such in essence or effect though not formally recognized or admitted," as in a virtual promise to do something.

This type of organization seems to have these six characteristics:

1. *Excellence.* Each partner commits its "core competence" to the effort. It follows that every process or function could be world-class—a condition that most entities would find hard to achieve.

2. *Opportunism and Temporary Status.* The associations are less permanent and less formal. They band together to meet a particular need and disband when the need no longer exists. Presumably, there is a benefit for each member.

3. *Technology Dependence.* The widely dispersed companies link up, communicate, and work together through information networks. The use of electronics speeds up exchange of ideas and information, and reduces the amount of legal work.

4. *Indeterminate Borders.* With the numerous contacts among customers, suppliers, and others, it is more difficult to define corporate boundaries.

5. *Co-Reliance.* The nature of the new relationships is such that each member of the group may become highly dependent on the other participants.

6. *Loss of Control.* Within this more flexible organization, one problem can be the possible loss of control over some operations.

The controller should be alert to this emerging form of organization. It gathers together competencies and offers the possibility of increased productivity and effectiveness.

54-6 FACTORS BEARING ON LOW PRODUCTIVITY

In undertaking studies of low productivity, sometimes the emphasis wrongly is on factory direct labor—even though direct labor now is often only 15% or less of total costs— or on the factory, even though other functions many times constitute a larger element of the total cost. Then, too, some study team members emphasize capital equipment and tend to downplay the need to properly motivate and train the employees despite a possible deterioration in the quality of future workers. Worker involvement is a key factor in productivity levels.

Before reviewing a productivity improvement program (PIP), we suggest these areas of possible study:

- *Capital Assets.*

  Extent of investment in modern equipment

  Proper maintenance of plant and equipment

  Proper training of employees in use of equipment (new and used)

  Use of proper criteria in reviewing economics of new equipment (DCF, etc.)

  Effective utilization of equipment

- *Inventories.*

  Use of "just-in-time" (JIT) techniques

  Use of consignment accounts

  Changes in lot sizes

  Fewer stocking points (hence, less handling)

  Improved vendor selection and/or scheduling

  Possibly increased standardization or simplification

- *Operational Changes.*

  Use of "just-in-time" (JIT) production techniques

  Increased subcontracting or out sourcing

  Improved quality control methods

  Changes in material types used

  Improved training and motivation of all employees

  Elimination of nonvalue-adding functions

  Improved attention as to the real "cost drivers"—those factors which increase costs—engineering changes, schedule changes, product design methods

- *Organizational Changes.*

  Elimination, or better grouping, of functions

  Reduced levels of organization

  Reducing service departments employees through transfer to direct departments

  Increased responsibility, or scope of operations, of individual workers

- *Changes in Information Technology and Cost Control Techniques.*

  Improved use of computers in providing real-time cost control information

  Use of local area networks (LANs) in tracking production and inventory status at various sites

Expanded use of computers and LANs for scheduling vendor deliveries and customer orders

From the above listing, it can be deduced that the emphasis on productivity improvement is in eliminating or reducing nonvalue-adding functions, not on simply working faster.

54-7 REENGINEERING: ITS RELATIONSHIP TO CONTINUOUS PROCESS IMPROVEMENT (CPI)

During the mid-1990s, in the context of productivity improvement, the "hottest" managing tool seemed to be reengineering. As one writer allegedly stated, "To get approval, whether buying new chairs or directing an across-the-board layoff, label it reengineering and approval is assured." Michael Hammer, the consultant who is often credited with coining the term "reengineering," says his brief definition of the word is, "The radical redesign of business processes to achieve dramatic improvements in performance."[5] As he further states, there are three key words to the concept. The first is "dramatic." It is a search for quantum leaps rather than incremental betterment. The second key word is "radical"—meaning that you don't just improve the process in existence. Rather, you go to the root of the process and start over. You begin with a blank sheet of paper. And the third word is "process." He states that the domain of reengineering is not organizations, not business—it's the process.

The reengineering concept is subject to continual evolution. While the emphasis is on the processes, there are instances where process changes resulted in reorganization, and even, with the study of the business objectives and strategies, the entity, in effect, became a new business.

In the 1980s, when a firm wanted to improve operational performance, it adopted continuous process improvement programs. (See section 54-8.) In the 1990s, some of these same entities began experimenting with reengineering. The two approaches are different, and each may be carried on by different functions or individuals in the same organization. There can be conflict between the two approaches in that one group would prefer to modify (improve) existing processes, while the other group prefers to start from scratch, unencumbered by the existing process. The recent tendency is to use the two approaches in a single program of operational change.

While the subject is too complex to deal with in any depth in this chapter, it may be helpful to outline in simple terms some of the similarities and differences in the two approaches. Further, it may be helpful if a model is illustrated and explained, which integrates the two processes. (The Selected References identifies some excellent articles on the subject.)

A brief comparison of reengineering and continuous process improvement is made in this tabulation:

---

[5] Robert M. Randall, "The Reengineer," *Planning Review,* May/June 1993, pp. 18–21.

Reengineering	Continuous Process Improvement

Similarities

- Both emphasize the process as the basic area of analysis.
- To be successful, both require a rigorous measurement of performance.
- Both need an environment that fosters change and an intent to improve operations.
- The above requisites in turn usually demand behavior (attitude) changes and organizational changes.
- Finally, both processes will usually require considerable time (and related costs) for training, and organizational adjustments, before significant improvement can be seen—perhaps a year or more.

Differences

Reengineering	Continuous Process Improvement
• Reengineering programs, by definition, attempt to cause radical changes for major improvements in cost, quality, and time.	• Continuous improvement programs strive for more modest improvements over a period of time.
• Reengineering begins with "a clean sheet of paper," i.e., no preconceived restrictions, and with persons who imagine what the process should be.	• Improvement programs begin with the existing process and chip away to make it better.
• The radical ideas are more likely to come from sources not (previously) closely associated with the process—sources outside or top side.	• Ideas for improvements are usually from those who have been working with the process.
• Top management involvement is more likely (through a steering committee) as the changes will be of great magnitude.	• Because of an incremental approach, there is less top management interface, interference, or concern.
• Innovative programs are more likely to involve external consultants in designing the program, in providing the methodology, and in training the teams.	• Improvement programs are much more likely to be more participative, and to use mostly company personnel.

Suffice it to say that if reengineering and continuous improvement programs are not fully integrated, there can be a waste of manpower, unnecessary costs, and a decline in morale among company personnel. Thus, without proper integration, employees might spend considerable time improving a process that is eliminated by the innovators.

Having made these general comments, it may be useful to outline and describe an integrated process reengineering model. It will be appreciated that the specific steps in each reengineering project will depend on the specific circumstances that exist.

Comments on each step in the procedure follow. Because successful process reengineering must be a team project, it is basic that the methodology be communicated to all team members, and that the responsibility of the teams be established.

Step 1: *Determine Customer Requirements and Set Goals for the Process.* Customers may be internal (e.g., sales department or manufacturing) or external. The needs or expectations of the customer needs to be understood, and the deficiencies identified. In this illustration, the process involves customer sales orders. The objectives were to:

(a) Reduce the order-receipt to shipping product cycle time.

(b) Eliminate order processing errors and the need to rework the order.

(c) Reduce the order handling cost.

Step 2. *Flowchart the Process and Measure Present Performance.* In this step, the objective is to understand the existing process before seeking solutions to defects. An accepted method is to map or flowchart the process, and determine the time, cost, efficiency, and so on, of each step. Some noted defects were:

(a) Excessive time from receipt by the sales representative until delivery to the warehouse.

(b) Excessive reworking of the erroneous orders.

(c) High order handling expenses.

Step 3. *Analysis of the Existing Process and Identification of Improvement Areas.* At some stage, many companies must decide whether to change the existing process, or to discard it and create an entirely new one. This may occur as steps 3 and 4 are underway or completed. Regardless of the decision, those using the process should be encouraged to form cross-functional teams and search for these items, among others:

(a) Ways to eliminate unnecessary steps.

(b) Ways of improving those steps which build customer value (improved quality and/or a speed for specific steps).

(c) Ways to apply concurrent steps instead of sequential ones.

Step 4. *Benchmarking the Operation.* This is a search for dramatic ways to improve the process. Continuous improvement programs may assist in better processes. But benchmarking of external operations (see Chapter 19) may provide some excellent ideas. While benchmarking may be performed by internal personnel, very often this is assigned to an external reengineering team.

Step 5: *Reengineer the Process.* If potential continuous improvements are located, and if benchmarking uncovers other major improvements, then the combination provides the impetus to reengineer the process.

Step 6. *Implement the New Process.* This could involve these steps:

(a) Provide time and budget for the new process.

(b) Perform trial runs of the process.

(c) Train or retrain the employees.

(d) Monitor the results.

Experience has demonstrated the need for such actions as:

(a) Securing top management support.

(b) Allocating *adequate* resources to the project.

(c) Avoiding simply automating the existing process (defects and all).

(d) Sharing information among the teams; increasing communication.

(e)   Rewarding the present owners (users) of the system and encourage their cooperation. Help them see that the change is a positive help to the function. Assure them that none will lose their jobs (and will be transferred to other functions if necessary).

The process and the relationship between continuous process improvement and reengineering is graphically illustrated in Figure 54-1. The relative impact of continuous improvement and benchmarking (Steps 3 and 4) is shown in Figure 54-2.

Figure 54-1   Steps in a Process Reengineering Project.

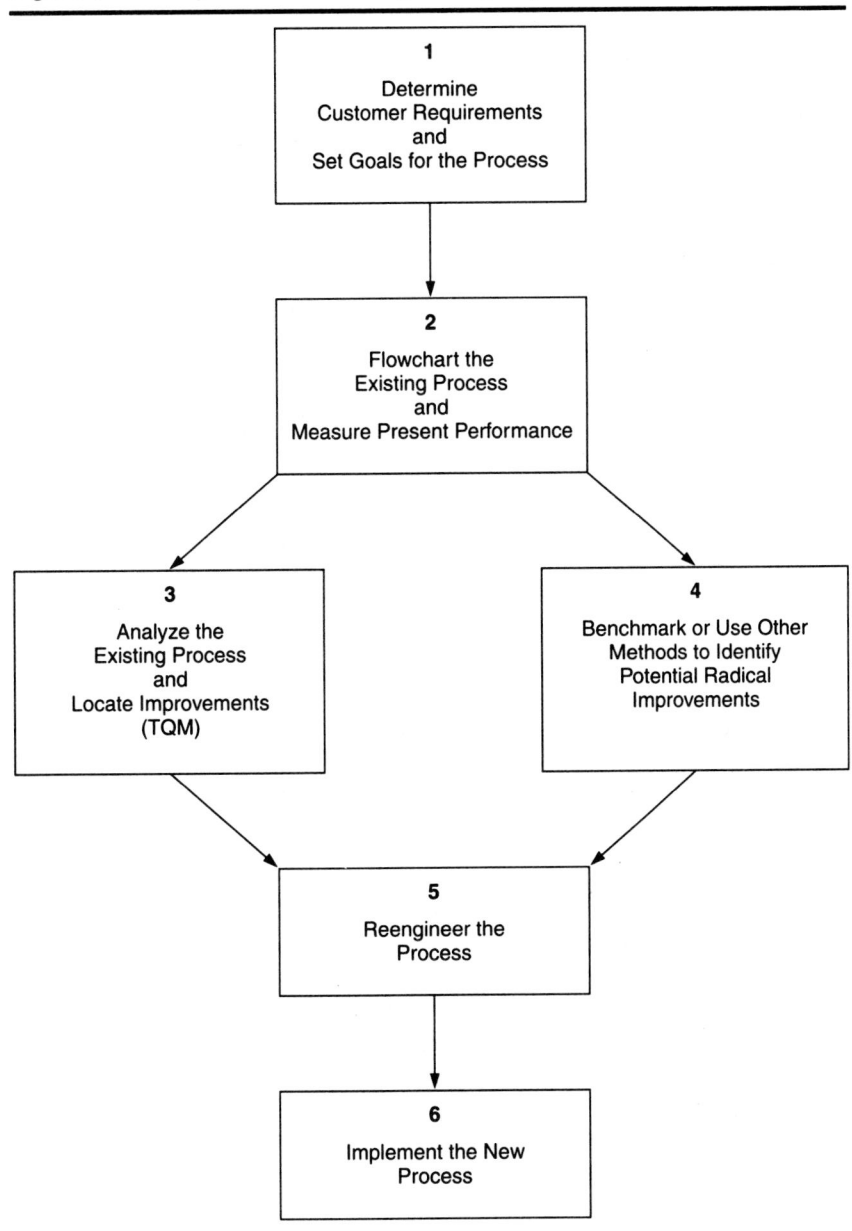

Figure 54-2   Continuous Improvement Combined with Reengineering Illustrated.

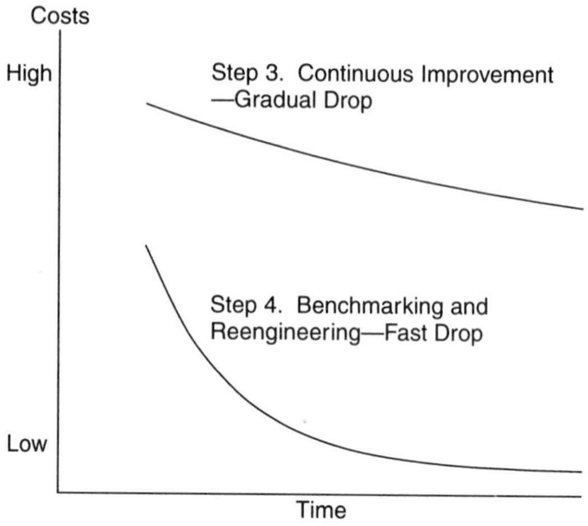

Having reviewed reengineering and continuous improvement, it may be helpful to illustrate an in-company productivity improvement typically employed.

54-8 THE NATURE AND ROLE OF A PRODUCTIVITY IMPROVEMENT PROGRAM (PIP)

A productivity improvement program may be described as an organized effort for reviewing internal operations with a view to securing increased efficiency and economy. The emphasis is on the internal operations—those which the entity can control—as distinguished from those external conditions which the company cannot control. This type of undertaking is sometimes called a *cost reduction effort*—although in fact the program can extend to price increases and margin improvement or a profit improvement program (PIP).

But if a company has a good product and an ostensibly sound planning and control system, why should another organized effort be required to improve productivity? There are at least two answers to this question. First, if a management is even just reasonably successful, over a period of time it tends to become somewhat lax and often simply ceases to look for more efficient methods. Second, the outside world keeps changing, and competition usually grows more intense. So an entity is forced to improve, or it may cease to exist. Some signs of a need for internal change include: severe reductions in sales volume, substantially reduced margins, major competitive product changes, new products for the same market, and growth of world class competitors. Consequently, in most companies there is a need for a continuing formal program to increase productivity.

54-9 STEPS IN A PRODUCTIVITY IMPROVEMENT PROGRAM

The exact nature of a productivity improvement effort in a particular company will depend on the local circumstances. Some of the factors that will influence both the vehicle or organization structure used and the intensity and duration of the activity include:

- Perceived extent of the problem.
- Company organization structure and style of management.
- General status of planning and control techniques.
- Availability of qualified internal personnel to participate in the study.
- Financial constraints.
- Complexity of the different functions or activities to be reviewed.

Under the usual circumstances, as discussed later, representatives of the controller's department, because of their knowledge of costs and the expense structure, participate in the studies. For like reasons, including his understanding of the cost-volume-profit relationships, cost trends, and a need for his appraisal of the financial impact of proposed actions, the controller himself is likely to be involved in certain phases. In some instances, although this is not necessarily recommended, he may be the leader or coordinator of the effort.

Here are some suggested steps in formulating and implementing a profit improvement program (to be conducted largely by in-house personnel and not by consultants):

1. Designate an executive of sufficient stature who will be held responsible for directing the program (at least initially) either overall, or in each major department.
2. Develop some productivity improvement objectives for the company, division, or profit center, taking into account some tentative objectives for each function or activity.
3. Identify those study areas that should have priority, based on the potential improvement thought possible, or the opportunity to show early results.
4. Tentatively schedule the reviews.
5. Select the study participants, using a team or task force approach.
6. Plan the audit or review in reasonable detail.
7. Conduct the study or audit.
8. Review with the appropriate level of management the tentative recommendations.
9. As necessary, conduct an in-depth analysis to ascertain the need for a further study by outside consultants or to verify the extent of cost savings, the practicality of the recommendations, the impact on the company, and the difficulties of implementing the suggested changes.
10. Implement the changes.
11. Monitor the progress towards the productivity improvement objectives.

An elaboration on some of these suggestions follows.

(a) ORGANIZATION STRUCTURE AND LEADERSHIP FOR THE PIP

The organization structure and leadership assignments for productivity improvement programs (PIPs) will depend largely on the management attitude about such studies and its style of management as well as the size of the company. In some situations, especially larger entities, PIPs will be included in strategic planning and the required organization would be more or less permanent. In other circumstances, perhaps the core manager and an assistant might be the only "permanent" staff, with a temporary staff for the periodic bursts of activity—perhaps every two or three years or more. In even smaller companies, the PIP staff would be entirely temporary with other duties being the principal activity of the participants.

The corporate leader of the PIP, and the leader for each large functional department should have specific duties. A position description for the coordinators (of the entire operation or a large department) is illustrated in Figure 54-3 for a large petroleum company. As can be seen, a team or task force approach (discussed later) is employed.

(b) SETTING PIP OBJECTIVES

In most companies, an analysis of historical data will reveal (1) the areas of highest costs; (2) those spots where cost growth has been the greatest in the past several years; (3) the nature of the costs, segregated as between fixed and variable; (4) comparisons of cost levels or productivity of the entity vs. competitors; and (5) relative profitability information, where applicable. Quite often such data can be provided and interpreted by the controller or his staff. The company and departmental PIP leader and coordinators should have such information available in setting the departmental and/or company PIP objectives.

Figure 54-3   Position Description—PIP Coordinator.

BASIC FUNCTION:
The PIP coordinator is primarily responsible for planning and supervising profit improvement studies within his department. In addition, he is responsible for guiding the implementation of study recommendations to ensure that identified savings opportunities are realized.

SPECIFIC DUTIES AND WORKING RELATIONSHIPS:
Within approved limits of authority and company policy, the PIP coordinator is responsible to the department manager for carrying out the duties and relationships set forth below:

1. Recommends studies to be undertaken based on an evaluation of savings potential, overall value to Chemicon and the ease with which savings can be achieved. Assigns priorities to studies using the stated criteria.
2. Works with the department manager to set ambitious savings goals for each study.
3. Selects and trains study team members, with particular emphasis on those who can contribute materially to the study effort, can help to implement the team's recommendations, and can benefit from the experience.
   a. Indoctrinates team members in the purpose and objectives of the PIP program and the specific study.
   b. Provides specific training in fact-finding, analysis, and other study techniques.
4. Assists the team in writing the preliminary study plan, ensuring that the plan is sound and that all relevant tasks are included.
   a. Ensures that the plan is targeted toward the study objectives and that a reasonable timetable has been established for conducting the study.

Figure 54-3 *(continued)*

---

    b. Reviews the plan with appropriate supervisory personnel to ensure its completeness and feasibility.

5. Monitors the fact-finding phase of all PIP studies to ensure that the team develops adequate, useful, and accurate information. Reviews sources of information to ensure that supervisors and other appropriate personnel are contacted.

6. Reviews the team's work planning and scheduling summary sheet to ensure that all ideas are being considered and that all savings opportunities have been identified. Helps the team to develop a sound analytical approach.

7. Reviews an outline of the team's report to ensure that it is accurate and complete.
    a. Analyzes recommendations to ensure that they are practical and that they will meet the savings objectives.
    b. Ensures that the report contains an action plan which includes specific responsibility assignments and time schedules.
    c. Ensures that recommendations are supported by adequate controls.

8. Assists the team in preparing a study abstract and an edited summary sheet to serve as an index for the working papers.

9. Reviews a final draft of the report with department management to secure concurrence with recommendations and action plan. Negotiates modifications as required.

10. Assists line supervisors in the implementation of recommendations.
    a. Checks periodically with responsible supervisors at all levels to be sure that implementation schedules are being met.
    b. Reviews implementation problems with appropriate managers to seek satisfactory solutions.
    c. Maintains a current file of working papers to assist in solving implementation problems.

11. Publishes periodic progress reports on all PIP study activities for appropriate management personnel.
    a. Issues a monthly savings summary to the department manager, comparing savings achieved against savings identified.
    b. Issues a program progress summary at the completion of each study.
    c. Releases a biannual report of the studies scheduled during the next 12 months.

12. Maintains close working relationships with team leaders and coordinates activities of various study teams within the department.

13. Provides liaison between department management and study teams. Participates in all observer sessions.

14. Maintains contact with his counterparts in other departments by exchanging project abstracts and other pertinent data.

(c) SELECTING PRIORITY STUDY AREAS

Most human efforts will be further spurred or encouraged when progress can be shown. For this reason, while most areas may be expected to provide some productivity improvement, and while not all functions necessarily can be studied at the same time, it is desirable to give priority for review to those departments that are expected to provide the maximum improvement in a minimum of time. Those knowledgeable about the operations and the cost levels normally will have some rather definite ideas about the best targets of opportunity. Consideration should be given to:

- Relative ease of accomplishment.
- Importance of the function.
- Magnitude of expected improvement.
- Transferability of the productivity improvement techniques to other functions or departments.

(d) THE PIP TASK FORCE

Most PIP efforts, whether as part of a long-term program, or a short-term "burst of activity," which are directed and handled mostly by an in-house staff, are structured as part of a team or task force effort. Aside from the executive leadership, the composition of this task force probably is the primary determinant of the success of the project.

The task force should include these elements:

- The *team leader* must train the team members and direct the review.
- The *program coordinators* (see Figure 54-2) often from both the corporate office and the division or subsidiary headquarters can provide ideas, secure some of the needed background data, summarize results, and monitor implementation.
- The *individual team members* in the proper mix or composition, including one from the department being studied; a skilled functional specialist; one from the financial department who has knowledge of the costs, their behavior, and significance of financial or accounting procedures; and one or more from other departments who are scheduled for review (to train them) or from functions that are in some way affected by the department under review.

The key to a successful study often is how effectively this diverse group or team can operate together in ferreting out an appropriate solution.

(e) OTHER STEPS IN THE PROGRAM

Only the basics of productivity improvement are commented upon in this chapter. Suffice it to say that the other steps in a PIP program mentioned earlier in this chapter should be pursued in a careful, analytical way. Many companies have manuals that discuss the steps from planning the reviews through monitoring progress. The American Productivity Center in Houston, Texas, may have relevant guides, or may otherwise be of assistance. The functions of planning the reviews, conducting the study,

Figure 54-4   Graph—Progress in Productivity Improvement Program.

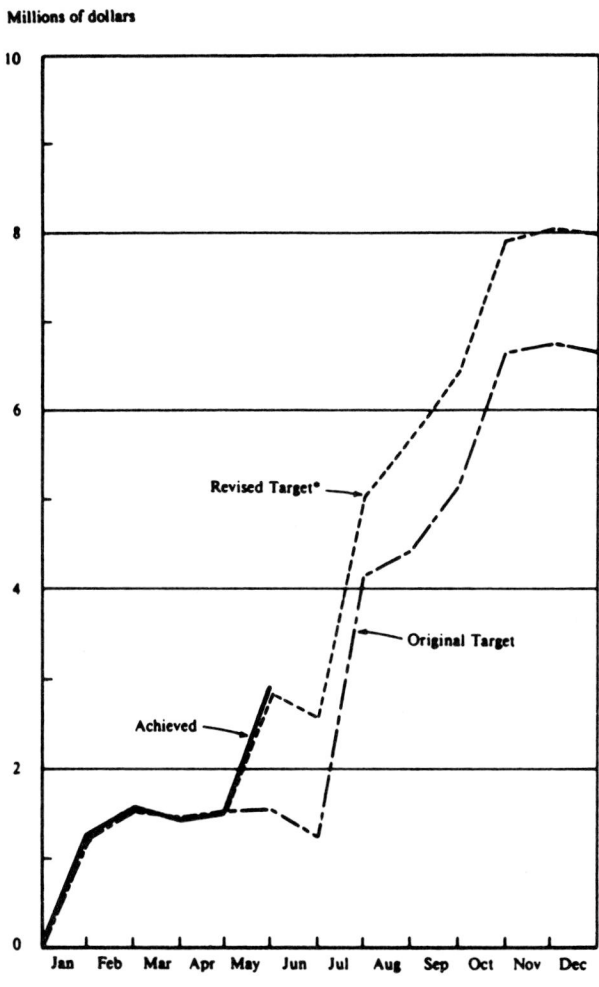

Millions of dollars

* In April more ambitious improvement goals were agreed upon. These goals are represented by the Revised Target.

implementing the recommendations, and monitoring progress normally would be conducted just as any other analytical review of costs or operations would be.

It is desirable to monitor progress, either by each departmental project, or as to the cumulative total accomplishment. A simple line graph comparing actual savings with the original target and a tougher, revised target is illustrated in Figure 54-4.

54-10 MANAGEMENT RESPONSIBILITIES

As with any important function, the success of a productivity improvement program is aided by the support of top management. And in these days of intense global competition, a fruitful productivity improvement activity may be the difference between growth and stagnation, as well as the key to survival. That being the case, what are the responsibilities of senior management as regards a PIP? These basic steps are suggested:

1. Advise the entire organization of the commitment by senior management and departmental leaders to productivity improvements.

2. Assign sufficient resources to the program.

3. Review the major planned objectives to assure that they are consistent with the organization's goals and strategies.

4. Determine that the PIP is properly integrated into the management process. This might include such actions as: (a) making productivity improvement an element of the evaluation (and compensation) process; (b) assuring that productivity improvement activity is one element of the job description; (c) possibly incorporating some productivity improvement factors in the planning and budgeting process for each department.

5. Periodically monitor progress of the program by comparing actual results with the goals set.

The controller may be one of the prime movers in encouraging a productivity improvement program. For many reasons, some psychological, it is probably desirable that a line executive head up the PIP activity. However, the controller as the chief accounting executive, and a skilled financial analyst, should accomplish these functions:

- Assure that the PIP executive and the coordinators receive in a practical and useful form the financial data they request (or that the controller can suggest tactfully would be helpful).

- Based on his or her knowledge of cost trends and behavior within the company, and on observations and talks with financial executives in other entities, suggest areas or functions for possible review.

- Review for business and financial impact or exposure (such as insurance and taxes) the major recommendations and convey his or her thoughts to the appropriate executive.

- Ascertain that productivity is measured in an acceptable manner.

- Assure that the results of any productivity improvement are reflected in the planning and control procedures, if appropriate.

- Assure that his or her staff makes a full effort on improvements in the accounting/financial departments.

54-11 WORKER PARTICIPATION

The primary focus in this chapter has been on a brief and intensive organized effort, largely or entirely by inhouse personnel, to secure increased efficiency. Some alternative studies may be longer in duration and involve the assistance of outside consultants.

In an effort to increase productivity and thus be competitive in a global economy, as most controllers would recognize, some of the emphasis in such studies has been on the need for capital expenditures or extended use of high technology. Yet such solutions take time and may require high investment. Studies in the 1990s are showing that increased productivity can result from workers participation in the decision-making process—and often at lower cost. Employee participation, when accompanied by appropriate forms of worker compensation (such as profit sharing), can be a quicker route to improved productivity. So the message is, "Listen to the workers."

(a) WHITE-COLLAR OVERHEAD

Encouraging worker participation is one means increasingly used in the 90s. Another area being screened is white-collar overhead. Excessive overheads are a second reason why there is so much cutting of white-collar forces and the delayering of management.[6]

A survey conducted by Boston University found that overhead equaled 26% of sales for U.S. manufacturers, vs. 21% for Western Europe and 18% for Japan.[7]

54-12 SELECTED REFERENCES

Byrne, John A., Richard Brandt, and Otis Port, "The Virtual Corporation," *Business Week,* Feb. 8, 1993, pp. 98–102.

Chew, W. Bruce, "No-Nonsense Guide to Measuring Productivity," *Harvard Business Review,* Jan.–Feb. 1988, pp. 110–118.

Davenport, Thomas H., "Need Radical Innovations and Continuous Improvement? Integrate Process Reengineering and TQM," *Planning Review,* May–June 1994, pp. 6–12.

Drucker, Peter F., "The New Productivity Challenge," *Harvard Business Review,* Nov.–Dec. 1991, pp. 69–79.

Dumaine, Brian, "Who Needs a Boss?" *Fortune,* May 7, 1990, pp. 52–60.

Frost, Halsey R., "Office Technology: Streamlining the Controller's Job," *Management Accounting,* Nov. 1989, pp. 46–49.

Furey, Timothy R., "A Six-Step Guide to Process Reengineering," *Planning Review,* March/April 1993, pp. 20–23.

Hall, Gene, Jim Rosenthal, and Judy Wade, "How to Make Reengineering *Really* Work," *Harvard Business Review,* Nov./Dec 1993, pp. 119–131.

Harrison, D. Brian, and Maurice D. Pratt, "A Methodology for Reengineering Businesses," *Planning Review,* March/April 1993, pp. 6–11.

Housel, Thomas J., Chris J. Morris, and Christopher Westland, "Business Process Reengineering at Pacific Bell," *Planning Review,* May/June 1993, pp. 28–33.

Katzenbach, Jon R., and Douglas K. Smith, "The Rules for Managing Cross-Functional Reengineering Teams," *Planning Review,* March/April 1993, pp. 12–13.

Klein, Lawrence, and Randy M. Jacques, "'Pillow Talk' for Productivity," *Management Accounting,* Feb. 1991, pp. 47–49.

Magnet, Myron, "The Truth About the American Worker," *Fortune,* May 4, 1992, pp. 48–65.

Randall, Robert M., "The Reengineer," *Planning Review,* May/June 1993, pp. 18–21.

Rigby, Darrell, "The Secret History of Process Reengineering," *Planning Review,* March/April 1993, pp. 24–27.

Stewart, Thomas A., "Reengineering: The Hot New Managing Tool," *Fortune,* Aug. 23, 1993, pp. 41–48.

---

[6] Thane Peterson, "Can Corporate America Get Out From Under Its Overhead?" *Business Week,* May 18, 1992, p. 102.

[7] *Ibid.*

CHAPTER 55

The Closing Procedures

55-1 MANAGEMENT INFORMATION REQUIREMENTS

It is essential that management be provided with summarized information for the various operating periods such as month, quarter, and year. Management decisions to a large extent are based on past performance, trends, and actual results relative to potential or plan. The more current the information is, the better are the chances for taking effective and prompt action. Management is normally interested in obtaining highlight information quickly after the end of an operating period with detailed analyses to follow. It has an interest in the following:

1. Sales volume related to plan, budget, or quota and compared to the previous period and same period last year.
2. Operating margin by major segments of the business and compared to plans.
3. Net profit by management responsibilities.
4. Summary of significant financial factors such as business booked, excessive manufacturing costs, capital expenditures, and important ratios.
5. Financial position.

The controller must consider the most expeditious methods of obtaining the information quickly and presenting it in a usable manner. Questions that must be considered in connection with periodic summarizing of data and closing procedures are these:

1. On what date should the fiscal year end?
2. What interim periods should be reported?
3. What comparisons should be made?
4. What actions can be taken to prepare periodic reports quickly to be of maximum use to management?

55-2 CONSIDERATIONS IN SELECTING THE FISCAL YEAR

Although the controller is not faced with the selection of a fiscal year very often, he should consider whether the present basis used is the most suitable. The most common accounting year in use is the calendar year, which ends on December 31 each year. The natural business year of a business is the period of 12 consecutive months that ends when the business activities have reached the lowest point in their annual cycle. Generally, at this time the inventories are the lowest, the peak volume of sales have passed, and the receivables are declining. For the same reason, borrowings and other liabilities are at a minimum or are being reduced.

Each business usually has a natural business year, and as a rule it does not coincide with the calendar year. From a practical viewpoint, the selection of a fiscal year ending other than December 31 may have certain distinct advantages. For years, the accounting and legal professions have advocated that companies adopt a natural business year. Many retail establishments are changing or have changed their fiscal year to January 31. The advantages of adopting the natural business year lie in facilitating certain operations essential to the conduct of the business. The following are indicative:

1. *Inventory Taking.* Physical inventories can be taken at a lower cost and with fewer interruptions in the normal activities. Smaller stocks mean that the count can be taken, checked, and summarized more easily. The smaller scope of the job perhaps signifies also a smaller margin of error in valuing the inventory. Further, with other activities at a lower ebb, regular employees are available to assist in the inventory taking. (Physical inventories need not be taken at the end of the fiscal year, but they must be taken near that time. The public accountants review all inventory transactions between the date of the annual inventory and the date of the statements being certified.)

2. *Preparation of More Accurate Financial Statements.* Financial statements are always a combination of facts and opinions. With smaller inventories and receivables, there are fewer estimates or arbitrary provisions. Valuation reserves are lower because of such lower values.

3. *Preparation of More Informative Statements for Planning and Control Purposes.* New policies and goals are often introduced at the beginning of the natural business year. Financial statements prepared at the end of such a period, reflecting as

they do a complete annual cycle of operations, provide management with a better check on the effectiveness of these new policies.

4. *Formulation of Policies.* Closely related to the foregoing is the general consideration of policies. When business is slack, the executives have more time to consider information and develop new programs and policies. Not only is the information available but also the time is more likely to be propitious.

5. *Securing Credit.* Bankers or other creditors prefer statements at the end of a natural year because they may better appraise the business. The statements contain more facts and fewer estimates, and a more accurate opinion may be formed about liquidity. It is usually to the advantage of the company if the financial statements show its most liquid condition.

6. *Annual Audit.* If the work of public accountants were spread more evenly throughout the year, through companies having different fiscal years, they could give more attention to the individual needs of each client.

55-3 DETERMINING THE NATURAL BUSINESS YEAR

It is a relatively simple matter to determine the natural business year of an entity. The controller is probably already familiar with the peaks and valleys of the business. However, one approach is to tabulate the monthly data to determine what month has the lowest activity or minimum investment in such matters as these:

> Value of production.
> Inventories.
>> Raw materials.
>> Work in process.
>> Finished goods.
> Sales
> Accounts Receivable.
> Accounts Payable.

This may be done by listing the dollar values for each item for each month of the year and in total. Conversion of the amounts to percentages of the total for each factor may more clearly indicate the fluctuation. The more important factors should be considered, and the trend over several years should be checked.

Once the natural business year is known, the question arises about how it should be adopted. Some businesses, convinced of the advantages, have hesitated to make the change because of possible complications in connection with the tax laws. However, procedures involved in adopting the natural business year are few and simple.

For existing corporations desiring to change their fiscal year, it is important to obtain approval from the IRS to effect the desired change. Normally, permission is granted when based on sound reasons. Similar permission may be required from state or other authorities, or, at a minimum, there may be required a notification of the change or special reporting as for example to the SEC. In establishing a new corporation, the desired fiscal year is simply written in the bylaws.

55-4 SELECTING THE INTERIM REPORTING PERIODS

(a) NORMAL CALENDAR MONTHS

Most concerns use the calendar month as a basis for summarizing and reporting operating results within the fiscal year. There are certain advantages that may be considered. Executives frequently think in terms of calendar months, and statistics relative to business generally are usually expressed for such periods. Many charges, such as salaries and wages, are based on the calendar month and are frequently set on a monthly basis, and billings to customers are usually made monthly. Relations with customers and vendors are likely to involve the calendar month as a basis of calculation.

There are, however, certain objections to the use of a calendar month as an accounting period, principally from the standpoint of comparability. Because the calendar month seldom contains the same number of respective days of the week as did the same month in the preceding year, or as did the preceding month, the sales or expense statements for a given month may not be comparable with these preceding periods. Yet comparison is a common practice; consequently, at least mental adjustments, if not detailed analyses, must be made for the total number of days in the month and also for the number of working days in the month. Where such variations significantly affect the value of comparisons, alternatives are available, such as a 13-month fixed calendar and a 13-period year.

Brief comments follow on each of the alternatives. It should be realized that the choice of an interim accounting period has no direct connection with the selection of the fiscal year. Each is a separate problem with different considerations.

(b) THE 13-MONTH FIXED CALENDAR

The 13-month calendar consists of 13 months of 28 days each, which accounts for 364 days. The extra day, called "year-day," is not in any month, and "leap day" is similarly treated. Each month within a year would start on the same day of the week, and each would so close. For example, the first day of every month might begin on Sunday and end on Saturday. The campaign to adopt this calendar has been going on for more than 40 years, and there is no particular indication that it will be accepted in the foreseeable future.

(c) THE 13-PERIOD YEAR

A plan adopted by some firms is to split the present calendar into 13 periods, each with 28 days. The extra day, or two in a leap year, may be treated in one of three ways:

1. Accumulate the extra day, and insert a week every five or six years. An advantage is that every period would begin on the same day of the week. The longer period would not be strictly comparable with the others.

2. Include the extra day or days in the thirteenth period. Most of the periods would be comparable.

3. Exclude January 1, which is a holiday, from the calendar. The leap day only is added.

The 13-period calendar gives the advantage of better period-to-period comparability, with the resulting greater usefulness of the data for control purposes. In some instances, because of the avoidance of partial week activities, accounting and clerical costs may be reduced. Also, the lapsed time between summary periods is shorter. However, the 13-period calendar poses several disadvantages or weaknesses:

1. It corrects only a part of the problem. Although adjustment is made for the total days in a period, it does not adjust for legal holidays or plantwide vacation periods; therefore the number of workdays will often differ from period to period.

2. It is adaptable for internal accounting purposes only. When monthly or period statements are prepared for stockholders or the government, adjustments must be made to conform to the calendar periods. This will usually require additional effort and cost.

3. It results in one added closing; instead of 12 there are 13.

4. Fixed charges will create a problem. Where contracts require payments on a calendar basis, or where salaries are paid monthly, some periods could receive an extra charge. This objection could be overcome, however, by revised contracts, depreciation, calculations, and other adjustments.

55-5 THE NEED FOR PROMPT REPORTING

No subject deserves more emphasis from the viewpoint of effective controllership than that of reporting information promptly. The reports of the controller are an impelling force in the guidance of business policy and in cost and revenue control. A careful analysis of the facts is expected from the accounting department, but, as stated previously, the data are valueless unless they are timely. If reports are tardy, not only is management left without the facts it needs and problems go unaddressed, but also the cost of preparing them is wasted.

(a) VALUE OF COMPUTERS

No tool can contribute as much to timely reporting as the computer. The ability of computers to handle huge volumes of data with great speed provides the controller with the way to ensure that information gets to operating management quickly and accurately. As discussed in Chapter 36, computer databases can be instantaneously made available to managers as soon as the processing is complete. Since input and processing of different information are completed at various stages of the closing cycle, the output of well-controlled subsystems can be made available long before the completion of the accounting closing.

Things that would normally be available early are these:

• Sales, volume, and amount.

• Inventory of parts and raw materials.

• Direct labor hours.

• Total disbursements (payroll and accounts payable).

(b) SUBSYSTEMS

It should be noted that, in order to have this reliable data early, there needs to be separate programs and databases for each of the major functions. Called subsystems, these have their own sets of input, processing, and output controls. Each of these subsystems also has its own closing schedule that, when completed, provides useful management information and serves as input to further processing. For example, a revenue subsystem will develop and accumulate information on company sales for the period. This data can be used to prepare flash reports for management. The output of the subsystem will also become input to the general ledger systems and to the accounts receivable subsystem. Figure 55-1 depicts a revenue subsystem in a manufacturing operation.

In this example procedures and controls would be established to ensure that all shipments were identified and billed or accrued in the correct period, that returns and adjustments were authorized and controlled, and that the resultant revenue was classified into categories and accounts useful for management reporting. Based on the sophistication of the database, the records could be accumulated, sorted, and analyzed in different categories and segments. This subsystem is usually closed on the last day of the period and the sales information is then available shortly thereafter (overnight or the next day). There is no need to wait for the rest of the accounting closing to be completed before reporting this data. There may be minor adjustments made as the data is analyzed but management should be aware of this and use it accordingly.

Other subsystems that can be managed and controlled in the same manner, thereby allowing early availability of key information, include these:

- Labor claiming (direct labor hours).
- Payroll.
- Vendor disbursements.

The output of these subsystems is used as input to the general ledger and to other subsystems that process the data into useful information. Some of these second-tier systems are:

- Cost accounting.
- Fixed assets.

Figure 55-1 A Manufacturing Operation Revenue Subsystem.

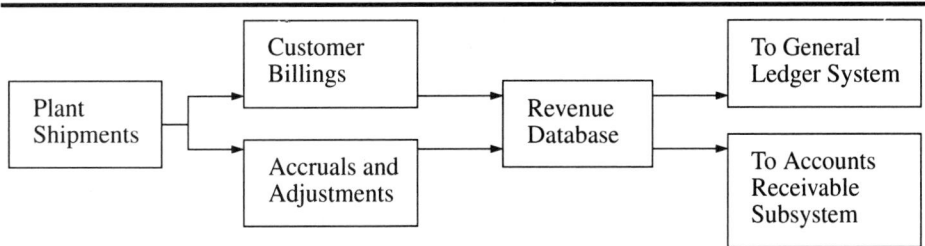

From this processing come important reports on cost accounting variances, depreciation, and cost of goods sold. The last step in the closing process is the preparation of the statements of income and expense and financial position, which will include the key data reported earlier.

(c) TELEPROCESSING AND DECENTRALIZATION

For companies with branches, plants, subsidiaries, divisions, etc., that are geographically distant from headquarters, the electronic transmission of data, rather than the delivery of hard copy reports, is used to speed up the closing.

For those companies with multiple reporting locations but without the funding for electronic reporting, a good "low tech" approach is to fax the information to corporate headquarters or to deliver the information on a diskette by overnight mail.

In a decentralized operation, each site is given the responsibility for a specific activity; very often the responsibility for accounting for the activity will also be delegated to the same site (or to a regional or divisional office when individual site activity is too small to warrant a separate accounting ledger). It is very important that the corporate controller has clearly assigned the accounting responsibility for every operation of the business. He must ensure that there are no gaps in recording and no duplications.

With the accounting delegation goes the responsibility for the accuracy and integrity of the data. The local chief financial executive, often a site controller, must develop controls and procedures to ensure an efficient and effective accounting operation. One of the procedures to be developed is a local accounting closing procedure. This must harmonize with and support the corporate closing schedule. When the local closing is completed, as with the subsystem's closings discussed earlier, the data must be reviewed and analyzed by the responsible management. They are then ready to be sent forward, on schedule, for consolidation with other decentralized accounting data in order to produce the financial statements and reports of the company (and/or major segments of it).

Once the data are ready to be sent on, three other elements must be in place:

1. The computers and transmission hardware needed.
2. The software to support the transmission.
3. The format to be used.

The format of the report includes a description of all the information that is to be reported—as well as the amounts to be used, i.e., full dollars, thousands, hundred thousands, millions, etc. The description of the information is directly related to the standard schedule of accounts issued by the corporate controller. Usually the report includes only a very high level of summarization of accounts. But its understandability is based on uniform account definitions that have been consistently implemented by the local accounting departments.

The use of high-speed communication technology that allows direct computer-to-computer interfacing has been available for several decades. This is a very competitive service area that results in lots of expert advice being available from the various vendors in the field. A controller should be familiar with the alternatives available, as well as with the strengths and weaknesses of the method the company uses.

Software to run and control a teleprocessing operation is commercially available. In addition, many large companies develop their own reporting systems. The key areas that a controller must ensure are addressed in connection with teleprocessing financial data are these:

1. Only authorized input is accepted for processing.
2. All data expected to be received are received.
3. The data received are what were sent.
4. Controls are in place to prevent tampering with data or intercepting confidential information.

There are many techniques for accomplishing these controls. Most companies in the 1990s have experience to some degree with teleprocessing and/or other forms of electronic data interchange. The controls needed for this media are most often the traditional ones modified to handle paperless transactions.

55-6 OTHER CONSIDERATIONS

However, even in companies without computers, much information can be reported promptly without a monthly closing, and much is. The daily labor report, the daily report on excess material requisitioned, weekly reports on labor costs, supplies, scrap, sales, or inventory are examples of reports quite independent of the monthly closing procedure. Moreover, even certain facts covering the entire month need not await the completion of the periodic closing. For example, the gross sales in units and value usually can be quickly summarized and checked as a part of the closing procedure, and the information can be reported.

Other information that is primarily of a profit nature ordinarily is determined only after the closing is completed. Yet possibly the accounting philosophy should be this: first, preparation of key reports and then completion of the formal closing. Perhaps the flow of information should be such that the reports themselves serve as the basis for the formal accounting statements.

The final test of an efficient accounting department is getting the financial data promptly into the hands of management, with a follow-up about interpretation, if necessary.

In addition to carrying out the controllership function properly, the controller will find incidental advantages accruing from a well-designed program that reports results promptly:

1. Operating executives become more cost conscious and profit motivated when data are provided promptly.
2. Usually, economies result because of the streamlining of the procedures and greater efficiency.
3. Improved overall control is made possible by timely action in almost all phases of the accounting control process.
4. Billings to customers are frequently advanced with a favorable effect on cash flow.

5. Management more readily understands the need for accounting information, communications improve, and more accounting guidance is sought.

6. The morale of accounting personnel is improved, since they feel part of the decision-making process and see that the accounting information is really utilized.

55-7 DEVELOPING CLOSING PROCEDURES

As we have seen, it is important that pertinent financial facts be reported to management on a timely basis. With computers, controllers have the capability to provide executives with the monthly reports on a real-time basis. In most companies, information can be available within the first few days after the end of the period. There are numerous computer software packages available that can be tailored to the needs of a particular user in order to achieve this goal. The controller must understand and avail himself of these modern techniques so that the reports are of real value in planning and policy determination. It is not the purpose of this book to delve into all the various computer applications available but rather to address the closing procedure itself. It is assumed that the latest processing techniques will be employed to achieve a timely reporting system.

Computers can speed up the process of delivering information to management, but the processes being automated are frequently in need of overhaul as well. In fact, without a careful review of the underlying systems, new computer automation may speed up a process that is not even needed. The next section contains a number of process improvement steps to follow in order to cull unnecessary items from the closing process and thereby make computer processing of the remaining steps more efficient.

(a) QUALITY AND THE FAST CLOSING

This section discusses the concept of quality and how it can be used to reduce the time required to close an accounting period.

Why should the controller consider quality in the closing process? Manufacturing operations have so far been the primary focus of quality improvement efforts. Recently, the same improvement techniques have been used by controllers to improve their operations and control their headcount. It has been estimated that a good "quality" program can reduce closing activities by 25% to 40%. That is the estimated amount of effort required by accountants to correct errors, eliminate roadblocks, and ensure the accuracy of their data.

A quality manufactured product is one that meets the customer's specifications and is delivered on-time and at the right price. How can that definition be applied to the accounting closing process? To answer that question, we must look at each part of the definition in detail:

- *Who is the customer?* The customer is whoever uses the output from the process. Therefore, the customer is the user of the financial statement, which is usually lenders, investors, and management.

- *What is the customer's product specification?* The specification of this set of customers is to receive financial information that is accurate. The definition of the word "accurate" is crucial, for perfect accuracy is expensive in manpower and time requirements. However, if "accuracy" is defined as "information that will not lead to incorrect decisions by the customer," then the controller can cut both the manpower and time required to issue the financials.

- *When is delivery required?* The optimum delivery time should be at midnight on the last day of the accounting period. This may seem impossible, but the goal should be set; if the current time requirement is 18 days, then work to shave a day off the process, and continue to close in on an instantaneous close as an ongoing process.

- *What is the right price?* Closing the period does not add any value to the product received by the company's final customer, so the effort going into it should be considered a non-value-added activity. Consequently, the goal should be to close the period at minimal cost, preferably using zero manpower and assets. Again, this goal may seem impossible, but the ongoing process of reducing costs must be established.

Thus, we now have a definition for a quality close of an accounting period:

> The product of the accounting close must provide information to lenders, investors, and management that will not lead to incorrect decisions by those users. The information must be provided immediately after the close of the accounting period at no cost to the company.

The definition sounds impossible. Let's look at ways to make it possible. The following set of sequential steps, when processed iteratively, will help the controller gradually reduce the time required to produce financial statements. We emphasize that this process should be repeated continually, for additional processing improvements can always be found; in addition, new technological developments will appear that will shrink the processing effort even further, and must be incorporated into the process as they are perfected. For example, using electronics data interchange for receiving accounts payable will eventually allow the controller to close the accounts payable subsystem immediately following the end of the accounting period, with no time lag whatsoever.

1. *Clear Out the Junk.* The process is similar to cleaning out your garage. The first step is throwing out the trash so you can have a better look at what is left. In this case, try the following:
   - Eliminate items that require multiple approvals; one should be enough.
   - Eliminate items that must be filed multiple times (e.g., alphabetically, numerically, by state); one should be enough.
   - Clean the accounting area; if it is inundated in paper, then either file the paper away or (even better) review its usefulness and then (hopefully) throw it away.

2. *Document the Process.* Do not implement solutions without first reviewing the process in detail. Here are several ways to document the process—you should use *all* of these techniques before continuing:
   - *Create a Flowchart.* This is a quick review of how the process flows. There are few symbols to remember; just list the process sequentially. In addition,

Figure 55-2   Flowchart.

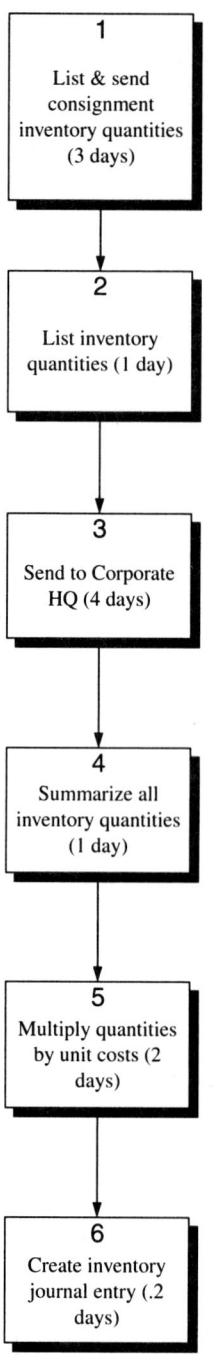

include the time required to perform each step, including the time required to go from step to step. A flowchart is shown in Figure 55-2.

- *Create a Functional Flowchart.* This shows how a process moves between departments or personnel within departments, and is very useful in pinpointing where time accrues during the process. A functional flowchart is shown in Figure 55-3.

- *Create a Geographic Flowchart.* This shows where paper travels during a process, and leads the controller to determine where wasteful travel occurs. A geographic flowchart is shown in Figure 55-4. The flowchart indicates that the controller should swap the locations of the receivables clerk and the cost accountant in order to reduce the receivables clerk's travel time to the fax, copier, and storage room.

Figure 55-3 Functional Flowchart.

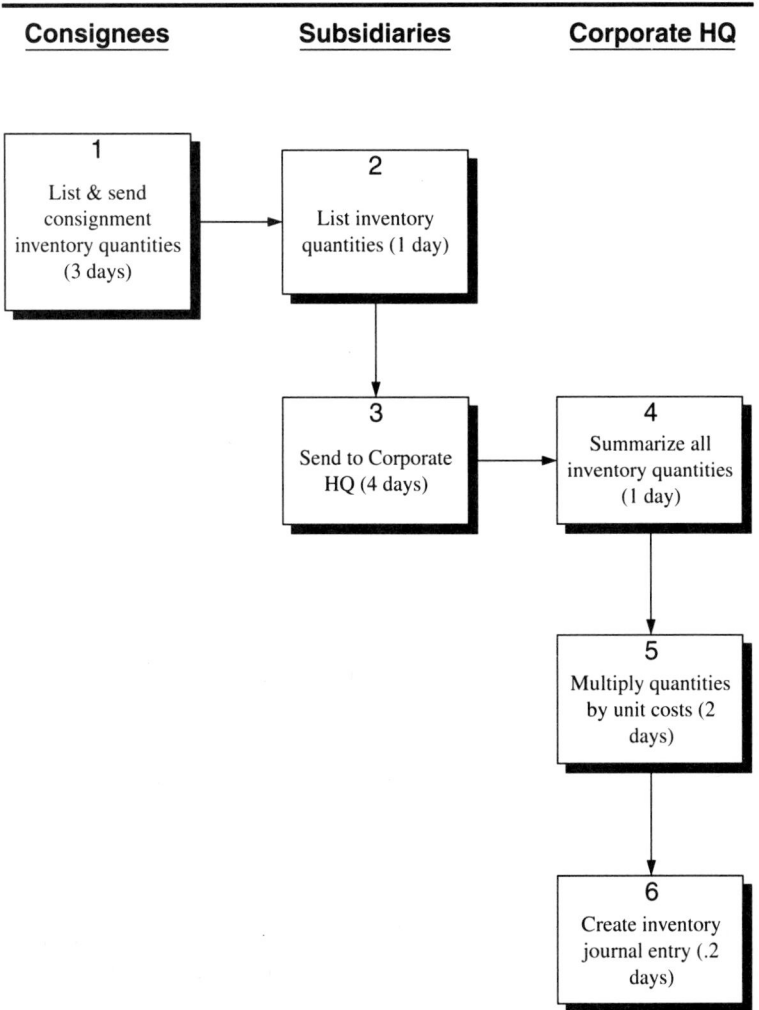

Figure 55-4 Geographic Flowchart.

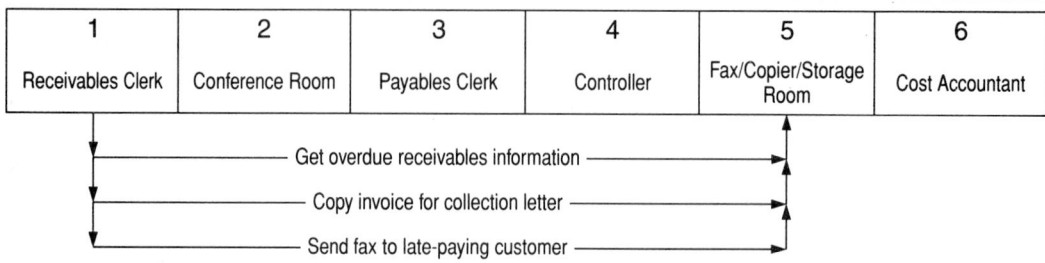

1	2	3	4	5	6
Receivables Clerk	Conference Room	Payables Clerk	Controller	Fax/Copier/Storage Room	Cost Accountant

Get overdue receivables information

Copy invoice for collection letter

Send fax to late-paying customer

3. *Eliminate Duplication.* Duplication typically occurs in two places during the closing process. First, information compiled at a subsidiary location is cross-checked at the consolidating location. Second, a subordinate's work is reviewed by a supervisor. Using the flowcharts developed during the preceding stage, highlight duplications and eliminate them. Elimination is not easy if the cross-checking is done to fix numerous mistakes. The process must first be made error-proof so that errors cannot be made. For example, staff can receive better training, and tasks can be either automated or simplified.

4. *Defer Routine Work.* Take note of those items being performed during the closing process that are unrelated to it and can be deferred until a later date. For example, performing account analysis on janitorial supplies is not crucial, and can wait until the financial statements have been issued.

5. *Automate Standard Items.* Prepare certain accounting entries on a standard basis and adjust periodically as in the case of depreciation and insurance. This is a common area for errors, because standard entries eventually change, and the changes are frequently missed. To avoid mistakes from occurring, the underlying documents that show change dates should be attached to the journal entry documents. For example, a lease payment amount changes once a year. Rather than file the change schedule separately, either attach it to the journal entry or conspicuously note the change date on the journal entry form, and cross-reference the source document.

6. *Set Investigation Levels.* If variances are minor, then their impact on the accuracy of the financials will be minimal. Investigation can safely be done after the financials have been issued, with any adjustments appearing in the financial statements for the following period.

7. *Move Activities into the Previous Month.* Many tasks associated with the closing can be performed prior to the end of the period. For example:

   • *Prepare Forms in Advance.* If journal entries or other reports are included in the closing process, then complete as much information as possible in advance, such as descriptions, account names, plan or budget data, and prior period figures.

   • *Anticipate Problems.* Be aware of areas where problems may develop and do as much analysis and reconciling as possible prior to closing. This could be the case where intercompany transactions are extensive and reconciliations may be difficult.

- *Develop Distributions.* Create as many needed factors as possible before the end of the period. Allocation bases and certain ratios for distribution of costs may be determined in advance.

8. *Reduce Cycle Time.* Cycle time is the total time required to complete a process. For example, the cycle time is the total time shown in Figure 55-2 to perform that process. The example shows that actual value-added time is minimal, whereas the wait time between steps constitutes the bulk of the process time. Target the longest wait times and take steps to reduce them.

9. *Automate Manual Processes.* After reviewing cycle times, select the manual processes that take large amounts of time, and automate them. For example, taking inventory and extending unit costs to derive a total inventory valuation is extremely time-consuming. However, with an on-line perpetual inventory (see Chapter 58) and automatic collection of unit costs through the accounts payable system, this activity can be reduced to a few keystrokes on a computer.

10. *Replace Serial Activities with Parallel Activities.* Based on the flowcharts developed earlier, identify steps that are currently performed in sequence, but which could be performed in parallel; and then convert to parallel processing. For example, when the information on a report is needed by three people in order to generate their closing reports, don't wait for them to pass it along from one person to the next. Instead, give copies to all three so that they can process the information in parallel.

11. *Rearrange Work Space.* After the closing process has been cleaned up and the paper flow made more efficient, the controller should review the work space. If the work space can be rearranged to reduce paper movement to a minimum and cut the level of nearby traffic (thereby reducing interruptions), then moving the staff is justified. This is also a good time to review the location of the nearest copies and fax machines to see if moving or adding such equipment would reduce unnecessary travel time. Copier and fax machine prices continue to drop, thereby possibly justifying the purchase of basic units to service small groups of staff.

12. *Train the Staff.* The accounting staff must be well trained in the closing procedures. Cross-training the staff will minimize the problem of peak loads, trouble spots, and absenteeism. The training should include indoctrination in the closing schedule. The schedule should include:

- Tasks to be accomplished.
- Responsibilities for recording, preparing, analyzing, or transmitting information.
- Exact times (day and hour) by which each task must be completed.
- Specific cutoff dates by subsystem.
- Periods to be reported.
- Number of weeks to be included in each month or quarter.
- The day of the week on which the period closes.

Reviews with all managers must be held before the schedule is finalized to ensure that everyone fully understands the closing process and can execute it. Any period-specific trouble spots (such as scheduled vacations) should be analyzed and solved at this time.

13. *Do It Again.* This improvement process must be repeated again and again in order to continually shrink the processing time. There are several reasons for this: first, bureaucracy tends to creep into a process via extra filing requirements, added steps, and additional approvals. Bureaucracy must be guarded against by constant review of the process. Second, the competition is always refining its processes. If the competition continues to cut its costs and cycle times while your company does not, then the competition will eventually gain an advantage through reduced overhead costs. Finally, staff morale is good whenever you attend to their needs. If the process review is always ongoing, then the staff will feel that they are important, and will both perform better and support the continuing improvements.

   In addition, interview your customers periodically to see if portions of their needed information can be sent to them prior to the issuance of completed financials, if there is additional information they need, or if there is information they no longer need. Finally, read the literature for ideas—there are many publications that help controllers interested in improving the quality of their closing procedures; several are included in the Selected References at the end of this chapter.

For a fast closing to be successful, it requires a well-coordinated organization, teamwork, and good leadership. The controller must lead the process of constantly reducing the time and effort required to achieve a quality closing.

(b) OTHER STEPS TO CONSIDER

In the development of a quick closing procedure there are many factors to be considered. Each company will have its priorities about what data are required first and the amount of detail needed. Consideration must be given to particular needs of the company; however, the following may provide areas to be evaluated in developing the closing procedures:

1. Develop a practical and uniform chart of accounts. This should include (a) the proper grouping of accounts and (b) significant control accounts that are meaningful when summarized in statement form. This will help ensure uniformity, both between the segments of the business and from period to period.

2. Establish a firm schedule of management report due dates from which to determine the cutoff of various types of transactions and recording of accruals if applicable. Normally, this schedule will be established based on the day of the month that the board of directors meet and therefore when the financial statements, reports, and accompanying analyses should be finished. It should be noted that the report due dates should be consistent with the need. For example, a flash report may be required on the second day after closing, highlights of operations on the fifth day, and a summary of intercompany transactions on the tenth day.

3. Make sure that the data for the period being reported are on a basis consistent with comparative data. For example, the actual results for a four-week period should be compared to the plan for the same four-week period. In some cases, early cutoffs will distort the information and indicate erroneous variances.

4. Control the release of information so that premature or incomplete reports are not given to management. Otherwise, an excessive amount of time may be required to correct information that may have been inaccurate. Also, management may make decisions based on inaccurate information.

5. To the extent feasible, use exception reporting to save management time as well as the costs of producing voluminous reports. Certain variance levels can be determined, below which there is no impact and therefore need not be reported. The reports will also be more usable and more easily understood.

6. Realistic cutoff dates must be established for branches, overseas operations, and remote locations. Use telephone or leased lines to transmit the data on a current basis. In most cases it will be transmitted directly to the central computer system, negating the need for sending hard copies.

55-8 SELECTED REFERENCES

Crosby, Philip B., *Quality without Tears—The Art of Hassle Free Management.* New York: McGraw-Hill, 1984.

Cushing, Barry E., and Marshall B. Romney, *Accounting Information Systems and Business Organizations* (4th ed.). Reading, MA: Addison-Wesley, 1987.

Harrington, H. James, *Business Process Improvement.* New York: McGraw-Hill, 1991.

Mann, Bruce M., "Closing the Books: On-line Editing Smooths the Way," *Management Accounting,* Sept. 1989, pp. 40–43.

Robinson, Leonard A., James R. Davis, and C. Wayne Alderman, *Accounting Information Systems, A Cycle Approach.* New York: Harper & Row, 1986.

CHAPTER 56

Preparation and Maintenance of Manuals

56-1 POLICIES AND PROCEDURES

Manuals contain policies and procedures. A *policy* is a statement by top management to be used as a general guide by the organization on how to deal with a situation. A *procedure* is a specific rule or series of steps to follow in accomplishing a task. Procedures can be developed at any level in the organization.

All entities have policies and procedures. However, many have only informal systems whereby policies and procedures are created and modified daily; these systems result in inconsistent treatment of similar activities with resulting inefficiencies and loss of uniformity. It is therefore important that the policies and procedures be written down and published in the form of a manual.

The manual helps supervisory personnel in the day-to-day handling of their jobs; it is an instrument of communication. It provides a common understanding of policy interpretations and clearly states the steps to be performed to complete tasks.

56-2 PURPOSE AND USE OF MANUALS

As a business expands, the responsibility and authority are delegated. Manuals then become more important, since they become the primary means by which management communicates its goals and controls the implementation of those goals. Also, manuals bind together dispersed but similar operations into a single entity. They are the device by which the company says, "This is how we do it."

Policy and procedure manuals are normally prepared for each of the functional units, such as engineering, personnel, materials, quality control, finance, and accounting.

In matrix organizations, manuals are also prepared for product lines that involve the activities of many functional areas.

Companies may create manuals to fulfill any of the following needs:

1. To communicate to all management levels and organizations the basic policies and procedures of the company.

2. To provide a common understanding of policy interpretations and to define and clarify policy or procedure issues that may arise.

3. To promote standardization and simplification. Preparation of a manual usually considers alternative courses of action or methods, resulting in the most appropriate being adopted.

4. To train employees assigned to new jobs. It is extremely beneficial to have a manual of instructions for the new employee that indicates how the specific job is to be accomplished.

5. To implement new procedures quickly and with a greater degree of understanding throughout the company.

6. To allow timely communication of changes in policies and procedures.

7. To create an internal control tool for management and form the basis for an audit of performance for compliance.

8. To provide a reference source for corporate-approved methods in resolving jurisdictional disputes.

9. To avoid duplication of effort and promote harmony among employees by clearly stating responsibilities. The manuals may include complete job descriptions for key positions.

10. To reduce the amount of management time in providing instructions and directions.

56-3 ORGANIZATION OF MANUALS

The procedure writing task may be assigned to either the department primarily concerned, or to a departmental unit organized and staffed primarily for such a purpose. The size of the company will probably dictate where the responsibility for procedure writing is placed. In smaller companies, the procedure function may be carried out by an individual under the direction of the controller. In larger companies, the procedures work may be a staff function to the president or general manager. There are several reasons for the controller to be involved regardless of where the responsibility is placed:

1. Internal control is an integral part of the management process, and trained accounting personnel are uniquely aware of these requirements.

2. Many interdepartmental procedures involve paper flow that is of concern to the accounting department.

3. An overall rather than departmental approach to procedures is necessary and the controller's organization normally is involved in transactions that cut across departmental lines.

4. Many procedures are directly related to accounting transactions, such as payroll, accounts payable, cash, fixed assets, and purchasing.

5. The controller's involvement insures that appropriate checks and balances are built into the procedures.

If the procedure writing task is assigned to the department primarily concerned, then there is a danger that different departments will create manuals that do not have consistent formats. Top management should distribute a standardized format to all departments, so that at least the following items are standardized:

1. *Page Numbering.* All procedure pages must be numbered. Otherwise, users will not know if steps are missing.

2. *Revision Dates.* Procedures are revised continually. Without revision dates on every page, users may follow outdated guidelines.

3. *Step Numbering.* Long procedure steps are difficult to follow. Guidelines should have examples of short steps with opening, explanatory, and closing sentences.

4. *Flowcharting Guidelines.* Flowchart symbols may mean different things in different departments. If a rectangle represents a document in one department and a process in another department, then external users will be confused.

The time needed to create policy and procedure manuals is significant, and it is imperative that responsibility for the manual be properly placed and that they be efficiently created to achieve maximum return on the investment.

56-4 STEPS IN PREPARING A MANUAL

Effective manual creation starts at the top of the organization. Management must determine which manuals should be created. Without this high-level decision, unnecessary manuals may be produced. Manuals are generally needed for all departments, but management can determine the priority in which manuals will be created.

The following general points should be considered when preparing a manual:

1. Determine who will use the manual and how it will be used.

2. Determine the manual's objectives, and its contents based on those objectives.

3. Prepare a rough outline of the manual.

4. Define problem areas for each procedure and note alternative decision points.

5. Collect all forms and reports related to each procedure.

6. Review procedure steps currently being used.

7. Prepare a draft of each proposed procedure.
   - Drafts should provide sufficient space for reviewers to make changes.
   - Titles should be used in lieu of personal names.

8. Secure comments on the draft from all interested departments.

9. Prepare a revised draft reconciling conflicting viewpoints and incorporating suggestions made to the extent practicable.

10. Establish and obtain the approvals required to publish the completed procedure. The following approvals are recommended:

Title	Area Requiring Approval
President or CEO	All statements of basic policies.
Division General Executive	All procedures implementing corporate policies relative to functions under the position's control.
Controller	All procedures that relate to accounting and control, including cash, cost transfers, and the recording of all economic events.
Procurement Executive	All procedures concerning the purchase of materials or services.
Industrial Relations Executive	All procedures relating to personnel, employee benefits, safety, labor relations, and compensation.
Research & Engineering Executive	All procedures relating to technical activities.

All basic policies must be approved by the CEO, those relating to specific functions by the functional head, and those of an operating unit by the manager of the unit.

11. Determine the distribution list.

12. Prepare and distribute the manual.

56-5 AN ACCOUNTING MANUAL

An accounting manual should set forth all the accounting policies and related procedures. The content and organization of such a manual will vary according to the size of the business unit, nature of the business, and organizational structure; however, the following index is illustrative of a format and the subjects to be covered:

1. *General*
   - Purpose and use of manual.
   - Methods for making and approving changes.
   - Organization charts—accounting and finance function as well as reference to the overall organization of the business unit and the company.
   - Functional outlines of all accounting units.
   - Job descriptions of accounting and finance positions.
2. *Financial Policies and Procedures*
   - All policies related to finance and accounting as well as detailed implementation procedures.

3. *Accounting Procedures*
   - Chart and text of accounts, including classification and a general description of each account.
   - Detailed implementation procedures.

4. *Accounting Closing and Reporting*
   - Closing procedures and schedules.
   - Internal and external reports prepared, stating designated responsibility, due date, and distribution.
   - Master schedule of reports required by and from the controller's organization.
   - SEC reports.

5. *Specialized Policies and Procedures*
   - Specialized reports such as cost determination and allowability on government contracts.
   - Property control.
   - Foreign exchange.
   - Payroll.
   - Inventory.
   - Government contracts.

6. *Accounting Documents*
   - Standard accounting forms such as payment authorizations, travel expense reimbursement, budget authorization, customer invoices, and intercompany invoices.
   - Standard report formats including Profit and Loss statements and department expense reports.
   - Standard letters (e.g., collection follow-ups in series, bank transfers).

7. *Records Retention Requirements*
   - See Chapter 57.

Figures 56-1 through 56-3 illustrate some styles and formats currently in use.

56-6 REVISION OF THE PROCEDURES MANUAL

Once a company has created a procedure manual, it is imperative that it be kept up to date and consistent with current policies. A periodic review of each manual should be made to ensure consistency, avoid duplication, and eliminate needless or outdated procedures. This review can be made by the procedures staff, functional heads, or, in some cases, the internal auditor.

Manuals should be reviewed for cost-effective procedures. When new technologies are available, procedures should be updated to reduce costs.

The responsibility for revisions to procedures should be placed with the same business units involved in the development and release of the manuals. Revisions follow the

Figure 56-1   A Corporate Policy Statement.

Subject: Organization Charts
Policy Number: 27-A
Page: 1 of 1
Date: May 5, 1995
Supersedes: 27

I. Policy

It is the policy of the Corporation that each element of the company include organization charts as part of its policy manual series.

II. Responsibilities

A. Charts shall be prepared in block form to reflect the organization structure at least to and including the third level of management. Each block shall include the name and title of the incumbent and the name and number of the organization.

B. When changes to the structure of an organization occur, revised charts shall be issued within thirty days. When personnel or title changes occur that do not affect organization structure, revised charts shall be issued within sixty days.

C. Corporate policies and procedures personnel shall be responsible for coordinating this directive with the operating elements and for revising and issuing corporate organization charts.

same steps as developing a new procedure, including the necessary approvals. The following suggestions are relative to revising an existing procedure:

1. Review procedures periodically for currency and effectiveness.
2. Revisions should be coordinated with all organizations.
3. The specific changes to an existing procedure should be highlighted in the draft.
4. The revision should indicate the effective date and indicate that it is a revision.
5. All procedures and revisions should be numbered using a system that clearly indicates to the users that they have the most current revision.
6. Documentation of the revision with review comments, issues, and purpose of the changes should be retained by the procedures unit for future reference.

56-7 DISTRIBUTION OF THE MANUAL

The individual or organization responsible for the manual should maintain an up-to-date distribution list of all manuals. The list should be reviewed periodically to determine that distribution is being made to those with a real need. To the extent a manual contains proprietary or classified material, controls should be established so that the manuals are only distributed to approved personnel and are not available to outsiders. Care must be exercised so that manuals are returned to the originator when employees no longer have a need or are terminated from the company.

Figure 56-2 A Typical Procedure Layout.

Subject: Processing of Cash Receipts
Procedure Number: 147-C
Page: 1 of 1
Date: January 12, 1995
Supersedes: 147-B

I. Purpose

This procedure describes the steps required to process cash receipts. The attached flow-chart shows the requirements for the system.

II. Procedure Steps

1. Prepare a remittance advice for each check received, if no remittance advice is included.
2. Log the checks on form GL-13, Cash Receipts Log.
3. Restrictively endorse and take checks to cashier for deposit.
4. Match each remittance advice with an open invoice.
5. File remittance advices in an active file for input into the database.
6. Prepare a deposit slip and deposit cash (deposit daily).
7. Collect all remittance advices from the active file.
8. Complete form GL-4, Journal Transactions, to record cash received.
9. Calculate the batch total of the cash receipt transactions to be entered.
10. Prepare form GL-3, Batch Control Slip, recording the number of the batch and the batch total.
11. Enter the batch total and all cash receipt transactions in screen 17.01, Journal Transactions.
12. Print report 01.63, Recurring/Unprocessed Journal List, to verify that all transactions were entered.
13. Compare the detail on the GL-4 form and the Recurring/Unprocessed Journal List to determine that all transactions are entered correctly.
14. Use the Journal Transactions screen to access the batch, make any necessary changes, and release the batch for posting.
15. Record your initials on the report to signify that the batch is in balance and ready for posting to the General Ledger.
16. Use screen 01.52, Post Transactions, to post the cash receipt transactions to the General Ledger.
17. Print report 01.62, Posted Transactions, to post the cash receipt transactions to the General Ledger.
18. File the remittance advices, GL-3 form, and GL-4 form with their corresponding Recurring/Unprocessed Journal list, and Posted Transaction List or Batch Control Reports.

Figure 56-3 A Typical Procedure Flowchart.

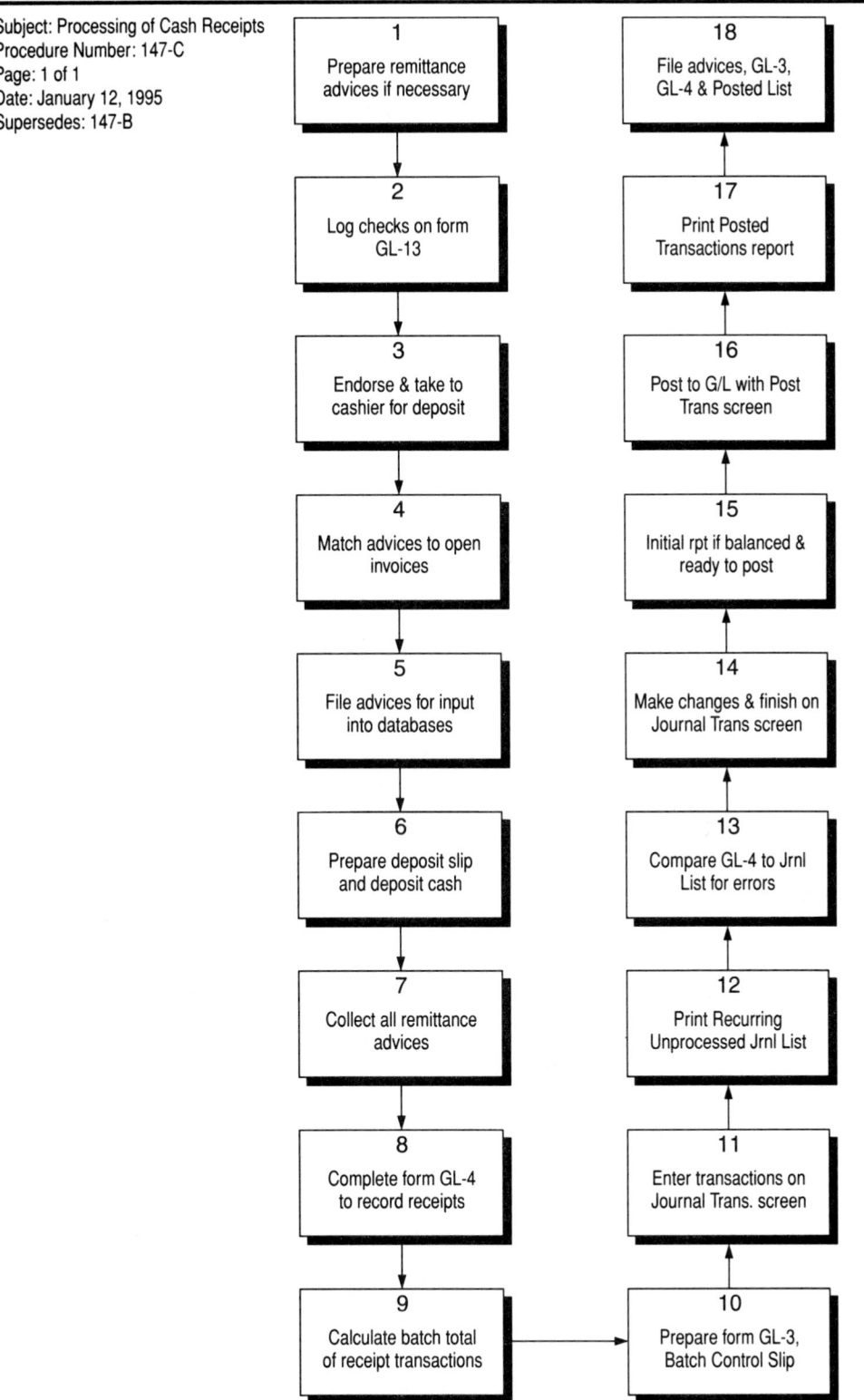

Subject: Processing of Cash Receipts
Procedure Number: 147-C
Page: 1 of 1
Date: January 12, 1995
Supersedes: 147-B

1	Prepare remittance advices if necessary
2	Log checks on form GL-13
3	Endorse & take to cashier for deposit
4	Match advices to open invoices
5	File advices for input into databases
6	Prepare deposit slip and deposit cash
7	Collect all remittance advices
8	Complete form GL-4 to record receipts
9	Calculate batch total of receipt transactions
10	Prepare form GL-3, Batch Control Slip
11	Enter transactions on Journal Trans. screen
12	Print Recurring Unprocessed Jrnl List
13	Compare GL-4 to Jrnl List for errors
14	Make changes & finish on Journal Trans screen
15	Initial rpt if balanced & ready to post
16	Post to G/L with Post Trans screen
17	Print Posted Transactions report
18	File advices, GL-3, GL-4 & Posted List

Manuals can also be published electronically. The manuals can either be stored in a central database, distributed by electronic mail, or stored and distributed on a compact disc. All the traditional steps used in developing and approving policies and procedures are followed except that there is no paper flowing between individuals. The elimination of the typing, retyping, printing, proofreading, binding, packaging, and shipping is a big cost saver and an even bigger morale boost to the personnel responsible for completing such tasks.

56-8 SUMMARY

The effectiveness of a company's manuals depends on these factors:

1. Qualified people to develop procedures.
2. The cooperation of all concerned, including the procedures staff and operating units, and the reconciliation of conflicting viewpoints.
3. The necessary management discipline to insure adherence to published manuals.
4. Continuing revision of manuals to insure consistency in operating decisions and understandability of results.
5. Periodic compliance audits to enforce adherence to the published policies and procedures.

56-9 SELECTED REFERENCES

Brown, Harry L., CPA, CDP, *Design and Maintenance of Accounting Manuals,* New York: John Wiley & Sons, 1988.

IFM Guide to the Preparation of a Company Policy Manual, Greenvale, NY: Institute for Management, Division of Panel Publishers, Inc., 1987.

CHAPTER 57

Maintenance and Destruction of Records

57-1 THE IMPORTANCE OF RECORDS MANAGEMENT

A special aspect of recordkeeping has to do with the retention and destruction of inactive records. Records are the memory, the history, and the story of the company and its transactions. They are important assets necessary to the ongoing operation of the business and generally cannot be replaced if lost or destroyed (although some may be reconstructable). The increasing size and the complexity of the business enterprise, as well as the significant growth of government regulations and control, have resulted in a need for maintaining more records and retaining certain records for a greater length of time.

Today, it is imperative that all companies establish and maintain a records management program to include the retention and destruction of inactive and obsolete records. A properly developed program of records inventory and retention schedules can sharply reduce the costs of recordkeeping. A policy of retaining all documents for an indefinite period of time would become very expensive. However, the arbitrary destruction of records would put the company in an untenable position with regulatory agencies and deprive them of information that may be critical to the success of the company. Thus premature destruction of records may result in the loss of essential data required for the effective defense or prosecution of lawsuits, settlement of federal income tax matters, resolution of contract disputes, or the favorable disposition of many corporate problems requiring documentary proof. In case of litigation, a record disposal program that has been consistently followed can demonstrate that a company is not trying to destroy records selectively in order to conceal evidence. The records management program must be cost effective, and all costs of maintaining records must be recognized and considered: storage and space costs, investment in special equipment and facilities, insurance, transportation, and administrative and clerical costs incident to operating a successful record retention system.

The task of determining which records must be retained is extremely difficult and requires a considerable amount of analysis and judgment. The future need and value of the record must be considered vs. the cost of storing and retaining such a record. To be effective, the record management program must be well thought out, and sound policies and procedures must be developed and properly communicated to all levels of the organization. There are three basic points to consider: (1) What records must be kept? (2) How long must they be retained? (3) How should they be stored?

57-2 RESPONSIBILITY FOR RECORDS RETENTION AND DISPOSITION

As with any cross-functional and cross-departmental operation, the clear support of top management is essential for a successful records management program. Once this is understood, the next important step is to assign responsibility for the program to a specific executive. The individual should be one who can take a broad company-wide view and who has an understanding of the business processes of the company. It will also have to be someone who is willing and able to evaluate recommendations and contend with other executives if he disagrees with their recommendations. Finally, it should be an executive who realizes the importance of essential records but who will not automatically "play it safe" when determining their disposition. The chief administrative executive is usually a good candidate for this responsibility since his or her normal responsibility usually includes service functions that cross department lines, such as telecommunications, mailroom, and secretarial pool. He may also already have skills on his staff relative to filing, indexing, and office equipment. An area where he may not have adequate knowledge and which is becoming a larger part of records storage and processing is in computers. This knowledge is the province of the Management Information Systems (MIS) executive. Perhaps he is a good candidate for records retention responsibility. If it is not assigned to MIS, a knowledgeable computer person should be part of the records management team so that the unique problems and capabilities of computers and computerized data are fully considered. The controller is also an executive with the right skills and training to manage a records control program.

Because of the complexities of business and the multitude of government regulations, the responsibility for a complete records management program that includes everything from form design to records disposition has been given to a new staff executive. It has been this executive's responsibility to hire or develop skilled records management people, to establish company-wide policies and procedures, to assemble an inventory of records, and to develop an appropriate approval and retention schedule by working with the organizations responsible for various records.

In any event, the controller has a key role to play regardless of where the responsibility is placed. He has the job of keeping the official accounting records of the company that properly reflect transactions; thus they create many of the documents and records involved. The controllers' knowledge of taxes, contract matters, and regulatory requirements make him a vital participant in any program. An error in judgment about the retention or destruction of a record could have grave consequences downstream. The law department or legal staff must also be involved in any program pertaining to the disposition of records. The legal positions and opinions should be carefully evaluated, however, to ensure that they have not been too conservative and want to retain all records "just in case." The controller usually can evaluate the requirements for retention and balance the cost of retention with the real need for it.

In summary, there are several ways to assign the responsibilities and accomplish the objectives; however, the controller is usually involved or charged jointly with other executives with the responsibility for determining the retention period of records and for authorizing their destruction. Because of the potential impact on the future of the company, it is imperative that all organizations be consulted and involved in making the determination about what records should be retained and for how long. Having a valid records retention schedule is like having an insurance policy, and the schedule needs to be in force before a lawsuit arises and critical records are no longer available.

(a) PROCEDURES

When the responsibility has been assigned and the organization created for records retention, appropriate policies must be established by management and applicable procedures developed. A comprehensive records management program, including the retention and disposition of inactive records, should include at a minimum:

1. The preparation of a complete inventory of all documents and records, together with sufficient supporting information to provide for an evaluation of the disposition.
2. Preparation of a schedule of retention and destruction of all records. The corporate legal staff should be consulted when determining destruction dates for selected documents.
3. Provision for the disposition of records not covered by the retention schedule.
4. Provision for retention schedule maintenance, updating, and revision as appropriate.
5. Establishment of an economical and efficient records storage center.
6. Procedures for the administrative process of transferring records (storage, retrieval, and destruction of obsolete documents).
7. Maintenance of adequate records concerning follow-up, transfer, and destruction.
8. Provision for a periodic audit to determine adherence to the program.

These procedures must be written and incorporated into the standard operating manuals of the company.

(b) FACTORS CONSIDERED IN THE RETENTION OF RECORDS

There are no standards about retention periods or procedures; however, there are some basic factors and considerations in determining which records must be retained and for how long. Some of these are as follows:

1. Statutes of limitation.
2. Governmental or regulatory requirements.
3. Nature and value of the record or document itself.
4. Type of business.
5. Contractual requirements.

Reference is commonly made to the statute of limitations in determining the retention period. There are many to be taken into account, and they must be carefully reviewed. Because these statutes fix or limit the period of legal action, related records must be retained until the statutory period has passed. The statutory period varies from state to state and for various types of actions and is subject to revision by legislative action.

Many governmental departments or regulatory agencies prescribe the length of time certain records must be kept for certain types of businesses. Under various laws, both federal and state requirements have been established for record retention that affect a significant share of the documents and records generated by a business. Some of the government agencies involved are IRS, FTC, SEC, Interstate Commerce Commission, Federal Power Commission, FCC, and numerous state regulatory bodies.

The nature of the record is an important factor in determining the record disposition or retention. For example, the certificate of incorporation is quite different from the triplicate copy of a vendor's invoice. Features that may influence the value of the record include the following:

1. The value of the document in terms of future company operations.
2. The availability of similar or identical copies.
3. The extent to which the data may be summarized or included in other available documents.
4. The extent to which the record is the original evidence of certain transactions— basic document.
5. The period of time the record will be used in day-to-day operations.

The type of business also may be a factor in record retention. Thus, if a product must be aged several years before use or sale, the lot sheets attending the process would probably be retained much longer than manufacturing lot sheets for the fabrication of a piston. Where quality control considerations are paramount, as in aircraft manufacture, such records may be retained for an indefinite period or until the aircraft is no longer in use. The type of business may also determine the type of governmental regulation concerning the records retention for, say, utilities.

Contractual requirements may dictate that certain records must be retained until after final payment on the contract or may subject the company to a particular law or regulation requiring even a longer retention. This may be the case where the customer has the contractual rights to audit the cost records for a given period of time after the completion of the contract.

(c) CLASSIFYING RECORDS FOR RETENTION

One of the first steps in the development of the records procedure is the classification of records according to those to be retained permanently; those to be retained for a period of time—perhaps microfilmed—and then destroyed; and those to be preserved for some time and then destroyed. Each type of record should be considered with respect to such probable future reference needs as the following:

Supports title to property.

Supports payments made to others.

Supports claims against outside parties.

Is required by regulatory commission or other public law.

Provides protection against future tax claims.

Provides essential operating statistics.

There are several means of classifying records, but a single one is suggested that recognizes five groups: (1) vital or essential, (2) valuable, (3) important, (4) useful, and (5) nonessential.

Essential records are irreplaceable or are not replaceable immediately and are needed for the company's continuance in operation. This group would include the following:

Certificates of incorporation	Securities
Charters or franchises	Powers of attorney
Capital stock records	Copyrights, patents, and trademark
Constitution, bylaws, and amendments	authorizations
	Formulas and product analyses
Deeds and leases	Blueprints, drawings, and sketches
Directors' minutes books	General journals
Stockholders' lists and proxies	General ledgers

Valuable records are those necessary to prevent financial loss or to recover money or property. Some examples are these:

Accounts receivable ledgers	Insurance policies
Fixed asset ledgers	Contracts
Claims files	Tax returns and reports
Inventory records	Audit reports

Important records are administrative tools that might be reconstructed after considerable effort or delay and would not adversely affect essential operations to any serious degree. The great bulk of cost studies and summary accounting records would fit into this category. Some examples are as follows:

Cost and profitability studies

Credit reports

Price records

Operating data

> Customer data records
>
> Personnel and payroll records (other than those required by law)
>
> Manuals and policy directives
>
> Canceled checks
>
> Government reports
>
> Shipping documents

Useful records are those that are not needed for current operations but are helpful for reference and similar purposes. Such records ordinarily would be destroyed when current usefulness ceases. Most special studies would fall into the "useful" category.

The nonessential records, for example, transmittal letters (and most intradepartment memos), are those that are available for destruction relatively soon and have no long-term value.

It is to be noted that the above classification is useful in considering the necessity for record duplication for protection against losses resulting from fire, war, or other catastrophe—quite distinct from the matter of record retention.

A classification of records on the foregoing suggested basis, when considered also in the light of governmental or other legal requirements, permits those who review the records to determine which documents are essential and must be preserved.

(d) THE RETENTION SCHEDULE

One of the most important phases of record maintenance is the preparation of a retention schedule. To prepare such a schedule, an inventory and analysis of the records must be made. Figure 57-1 may be used for such a purpose.

Each department head must be given an ample supply of the forms to cover all of his needs. It is particularly important to obtain the department manager's opinion about retention requirements. All required definitions should be provided with the form for consistency in application.

Those assigned the task of determining the retention period must give careful evaluation to the actual and potential value of all records. Each record must be considered in the light of the real needs of the particular business. Figure 57-2 is illustrative of what may be provided on a retention schedule.

In evaluating the need to retain any given record, an objective approach is suggested. Simple cost analyses may assist in determining that the costs of retention of certain records are not effective. Unless real need is demonstrated, records should not be retained for personal comfort or satisfaction. Since the decision is judgmental, retention periods for each record must be challenged.

57-3 COMPUTER RECORDS

Most of what has been discussed in this chapter has been in the context of hard copy paper documents. Almost everyone is familiar with and comfortable with this kind of record and so it is easier to talk about records retention that way. However, the pervasive use of computers in business has resulted in new kinds of records being produced, that is, magnetic media or computer processable data. This has in turn presented new records retention problems and opportunities that must be addressed. For example,

Figure 57-1   The Retention Schedule.

ABC Company
RECORDS RETENTION/DISPOSITION ANALYSIS
AND AUTHORIZATION

Date _____

Division _____

Department _____

Record or Document Title _____

Form No. (if applicable) _____ Originator _____

Description and Purpose _____

Remarks:	Retention Period:
(Legal requirements, reasons for retention, how filed, where filed, annual review, use while retained)	Active _____
	Inactive _____
	Retention Classification:
	☐ Vital ☐ Valuable
	☐ Important ☐ Useful
	Approvals:
	Department _____
	Controller _____
	Tax Counsel _____
	Legal _____
	Division _____

---

many accounting records are identified as active in the department for one year and then inactive in storage for four years: Customer invoices is a case in point. (See Figure 57-2.) In an automated environment, the record of each invoice has been transferred to computer tapes or magnetic disks. It is inexpensive to retain the record in computer memory for the period it will be used. It is also simple to search for and retrieve the data accurately and rapidly while it is in memory. At the end of a year, when the data will no longer be used, it can be transferred to off-line storage in one of several ways:

- Using magnetic tape.
- Using magnetic disk.
- Using computer output microfilm.

Computer tapes and disks can be retained in controlled environments for very long periods of time. The data is retrievable via computer as needed.

Retrieving information stored on magnetic media can be a considerable problem when information is stored using an operating system or application program that the company subsequently discards. The alternatives for retrieving such information are:

- Keep copies of the original operating systems and application programs on file. When old information must be retrieved, reload these programs onto a computer

Figure 57-2 Retention Schedule.

RECORDS RETENTION SCHEDULE

Type of Records	Retention Period (years)			Remarks
	Active (in Department)	Inactive (in Storage)	Total Retention	
Accounting and Finance				
1. Accounts payable				
Cash credits	1	4	5(T)	
Vendor invoice	1	4	5(T)	
Distribution or analysis	1	4	5(T)	
Voucher	1	4	5(T)	
Receiving record	1	4	5(T)	
Purchase order	1	4	5(T)	
Debit memos and credit memos	1	4	5(T)	
2. Accounts receivable				
Invoices	1	4	5(T)	
Credit memos and debit memos	1	4	5(T)	
Cash sheets	1	4	5(T)	
3. Audit reports				
Internal audit reports	5	5	10(T)	
Internal audit report working papers	2	2	4(T)	
Public accountant's report	5		Permanent	
4. Bank reconciliations				
Bank statements	1	5	6(T)	
Deposit slips	1	5	6	
Debit or credit slips	1	5	6	

5. Budgets			
Allocation of expense or cost	1	4	5
Standard rate sheet	2	—	2
Comparison of manufacturing expense to budget	1	4	5
Monthly reports	1	4	5
Annual cumulative reports	1	4	5
Working papers	1	4	5
6. Burden—rates	2	3	5(T)
7. Cash			
Daily cash report	2	—	2
Cash advance authorization	1	5	6
Petty cash voucher	1	5	6(T)
8. Checks			
Payroll canceled	1	2	3
Commercial canceled	1	5	6
Dividend canceled	1	5	6
9. Consolidated financial statements corporation and subsidiaries			Permanent
10. Cost estimates	1	4	5(T)
11. Credit			
Application for credit, approval forms, qualification reports	WA + 1	—	WA + 1
Correspondence—collection	2	—	2(T)
Customer financial statements	3	—	3
Guarantees and subordination agreements	WA	—	WA(T)
Security agreements and financing statements	WA	—	WA(T)
Trade clearances	3	—	3
Marginal accounts	WA	—	WA

(continued)

1395

Figure 57-2 (*continued*)

Type of Records	Retention Period (years)			Remarks
	Active (in Department)	Inactive (in Storage)	Total Retention	
Disputed accounts	WA	—	WA(T)	
Embarrassed debtors	WA	—	WA(T)	
12. Expense reports				
Department expense reports	1	4	5(T)	
Employee travel expense	WA	6	WA + 6(T)	
13. Export papers				
Custom and declaration papers	2	4	6(T)	
14. Financial statements and analytical reports				
Divisions	1	4	5(T)	
Subsidiaries			Permanent(T)	
Corporate office (consolidated statements)			Permanent(T)	
15. Forecasts	1	2	3	
16. Freight bills	1	3	4(T)	
17. General book of accounts				
Journal entries				
Cash distribution	1	9	10(T)	
Cash received	1	9	10(T)	
General				
Miscellaneous	1	9	10(T)	
Purchase	1	9	10(T)	
Sales	1	9	10(T)	
Ledgers				
Accounts payable	Current	10	10(T)	
Accounts receivable	Current	10	10(T)	
Cost	2	Permanent	Permanent	

Expense	Current	10	10(T) / Permanent(T)	
General and supporting information				
Notes payable	WA	15	WA + 15(T)	General Ledger original records must be retained—not microfilmed.
Notes receivable	WA	15	WA + 15(T)	Original records must be retained.
Subsidiary ledgers			Permanent(T)	
18. Insurance general				
Claims (other than employees)	WA	3	WA + 3(T)	
Policies (workmen's compensation and third-party liability)	WA	3	WA + 3(T)	
Policies (other)	WA	3	WA + 3(T)	
Bonds, surety	WA	3	WA + 3(T)	
Fire valuation data	WA	3	WA + 3(T)	
Fidelity bonds of employees	WA	3	WA + 3(T)	
Workmen's compensation cases	WA	3	WA + 3(T)	
19. Inventory and cost records				
Cost sheets	1	2	3(T)	
Physical inventory cards	1	2	3(T)	
Cost reports and statements	1	2	3(T)	
20. Material requisitions	1	2	3(T)	
Administrative—General and Legal				
Annual reports to shareholders	WA	* Permanent	Permanent	(Secretary's copy only)
Applications for patent	WA		* Permanent	* Ribbon copies only
Applications for copyrights and trademarks	WA	5	WA + 5	
Articles of incorporation	WA		Permanent	
Business licenses issued to company	WA + 1	4	WA + 5	
Contracts and agreements	WA + 1	5	WA+ 6(T)	
Deeds	WA	10	WA + 10	Retain as long as company owns property, plus 10 years—then retain permanent card file listing. Review before discard.

(continued)

Figure 57-2 (continued)

Type of Records	Retention Period (years)			Remarks
	Active (in Department)	Inactive (in Storage)	Total Retention	
Easements	WA	10	WA + 10	Same as "Deeds"
Formal documentation pertaining to acquisitions	—	—	Permanent	
Registration of securities				
In California	WA	5	RA5	
With SEC	WA	5	RA5	
Listing of securities	WA	5	RA5	
Historical data	3	7	10	
Leases	WA + 1	9	WA + 10	10AT—review before discard.
Litigation	WA	5	WA + 5	
Franchises	Franchise Term	3	Franchise Term + 3	
Minute books				
(a) Directors			Permanent	
(b) Shareholders			Permanent	
(c) Executive committees			Permanent	
Minute books of committees of the board of directors			Permanent	
Minute books of subsidiaries				
(a) Directors			Permanent	
(b) Shareholders			Permanent	
Mortgages and trust deeds	Mortgage Term	5	Mortgage Term + 5	(Cancellation to be recorded)
Notes Canceled				
Overhead technical authority	2	8	10	
Plans			10	

Record				Remarks
Progress reports	2	8	10	
Technical reports	2	8	10	
Policies of title insurance	WA	5	WA + 5	
Royalty records	5	—	5(T)	
Tax files, returns, briefs, and appeals	Governed by Accounting and Finance—Taxes			
Plans				
Annual business plans	2	3	5	
Long-range plans	2	3	5	
Patent licenses issued to or by company	WA	5	WA + 5(T)	
Shareholder records				
Canceled certificates			See Remarks	5 years from receipt of certificates from transfer agent.
Certificate correspondence	WA	Permanent	Permanent	
Proxies—routine elections	1	5	6	
special stockholder action	1	5	6	
Voting stockholder list	1	5	6	
Advertising				
Contracts with agencies, printers, etc.	WA	5	WA + 5(T)	
Agency invoices for ads and services	2	4	6(T)	
Tear sheets and proofs (major campaigns)	2	—	Permanent	
Research reports/conference reports			2	
Original artwork (returned by agency)			10	
Advertising budgets/schedules	3	—	3	
Media and market data	3	—	3	

Code

WA: while active.
ABI: after becoming inactive.
RA: review after.
AT: after termination.
(T): retain until settlement of tax year.

and use that computer to access the information. Since many operating systems and application programs are leased, the cost to keep these programs on-site may be prohibitive. Also, the time and computer storage space required to reload the programs may not make this a worthwhile alternative.

- Convert the data structure of the stored information to a computer-readable format. Some current application programs can read data that was stored in a different format. The company may have to pay a computer services firm to convert the data.

(a) COMPACT DISC

On-line record retention with compact disc jukeboxes is becoming more common. In this process, documents are scanned using a flat-bed scanner. The digitized image is then stored on a compact disk, which is itself stored with a number of other compact discs in what is called a jukebox. Each digital image is stored using at least one search key. For example, a purchase order could be accessed with the purchase order number, the item number ordered, or the supplier code. A few key issues regarding this new technology are:

- *Storage requirements.* A key decision when scanning documents is the dots per inch (DPI) to be used. A low DPI of 100 will vastly reduce storage requirements, but the image will be very grainy in comparison to a 600 DPI scan that requires ten times as much storage. We recommend a minimum DPI of 100; anything below that size may result in unreadable electronic documents. As the cost of storage decreases, high-DPI scans will become more cost-effective.

- *Modification of Scanned Images.* There is a legal concern that documents can be altered after they have been digitized. For example, a signature could be altered on a purchase order, making the company liable for a purchase that it never ordered. To answer this concern, WORM (Write Once, Read Many) drives are available. These drives only allow the initial scan to be recorded on a compact disc; no further changes to the record are possible. The legal standing of digitized documents are still being decided by the courts. In lieu of a definitive judgment by the legal community, it would be wisest to retain crucial original documents in storage, and to use digitized images for quick access to key information.

Compact disc technology may eventually allow the controller to retain all records on-line, and to eliminate off-site storage entirely. However, this mode of storage is still relatively expensive, and the legality of digitized images is still in question. The controller should periodically consult with qualified legal personnel to see if backup document retention may not be necessary at some future time.

(b) ELECTRONIC DATA INTERCHANGE RECORDS

From the perspective of records retention, electronic data interchange (EDI) presents a unique set of challenges because it has no "hard copy" records at all. EDI transactions can involve purchase orders, invoices, cash transfers, and nearly any other ongoing transaction in the firm. The most common transfer of EDI information is from the customer or supplier to a computer service firm's mainframe, and from there to the company (and vice versa). At no point during this interchange of electronic data is there a requirement for a paper record.

How does the company maintain an audit trail of its transactions? There are three sources of such information:

1. *Trading Partners.* Periodically confirm transactions with trading partners. (However, if they are fully converted to EDI, then they won't have records either!)

2. *Computer Service Firm.* Have the computer service firm store records of all transactions. However, this would seriously tax the storage capabilities of any service firm, since the transaction volume flowing between many trading partners is immense, and would entail significant additional fees to the company.

3. *Record Transactions Internally.* This option is the only one under the direct control of the company, and is therefore the one most capable of being implemented. Transactions received from or sent to the computer service firm must be offloaded to storage, and printed from there for record retention.

The company should retain any contracts it has regarding initiating EDI relationships with its trading partners, since those are the only EDI-related documents it will have that contain signatures.

The problem of EDI record retention is still in its infancy, and will become more of an issue as more companies convert a greater volume of their transactions to EDI.

(c) COMPUTER OUTPUT MICROFILM

The use of a computer to produce high-speed output directly onto microfilm (COM) is not as well known, but it is available and has proved to be valuable to controllers. COM bypasses the hard copy printouts and instead produces a microfilm record in a fraction of the time (10,000 lines per minute). It is especially useful where a high volume of detail is available that can be accessed via a terminal while in active computer memory and that is needed only very selectively while in inactive storage.

In establishing a records retention program in a computerized company, an objective should be to reduce the amount of hard copy records produced and instead to use and store electronic records only.

A computer-assisted retrieval (CAR) system is needed if computer generated storage records are used. Such a system will allow fast and accurate retrieval of such data.

57-4 GOVERNMENT REQUIREMENTS

In considering record retention, maintenance, and disposition, the varied requirements of many government agencies must be reviewed in detail to insure compliance. As the requirements become more complex and probably less definitive, businesses must exercise prudent judgment in developing their records management program.

Some of the regulations promulgated by agencies of the federal government are very specific and detailed, whereas others may merely stipulate the retention period and the general class of records to be maintained. Perhaps the best guide on government requirements is published by the Office of the Federal Register National Archives and Records Service, General Services Administration, as a special edition of the *Federal Register*. It is called the "Guide to Record Retention Requirements." This guide is in digest form to the provisions of federal laws and regulations relating to the keeping of records. It includes (1) what records must be kept, (2) who must keep them, and (3) how long they must be kept. The guide is published annually. Copies may be purchased from the Superintendent of Documents, U.S. Government Printing Office, Washington, DC.

The controller will probably find it appropriate to review the particular governmental regulations applicable to his business and consult with concerned legal counsel. For example, under the Internal Revenue Code it is advisable that supporting documentation is available until settlement of the tax year. Many of the acts specify the retention periods for payroll records, contracts with the government, union agreements, and other legal documents.

57-5 TRANSFERRING THE RECORDS

A brief comment is in order regarding the transfer of records to inactive storage. Some companies transfer their files once a year and set up the new files for the current year. The tendency is to send all the records to the storage vault, hoping to find time to dispose of useless ones later. However, the proper time to prepare the records is when they are current. Much material of a temporary nature gets into the files that should not have been filed in the first place. Examples are letters of transmittal, temporary reports or forms, and so on. Some companies have installed a very practical procedure that indicates the destruction dates on papers as they go into the file. Some have temporary use and may be placed in a 30- or 60-day file and then destroyed. If the records are commingled with permanent papers, the pulling and destruction may be done a little each day after the regular filing has been completed. As another suggestion, where several copies of reports are prepared, or copies of correspondence distributed within the company, consider one as permanent and set a short retention period for the others. The originating department is designated as the keeper of the permanent copy.

(a) DUPLICATION OF RECORDS

Many companies use microfilming as a means of reproducing their records. It is a useful means of recording, processing, storing, and retrieving data in a reduced manner. There are many advantages in using this technique, such as these:

1. Requires a minimum of storage space.
2. It is rapid and relatively inexpensive when used in a large volume.
3. Accuracy—actual image of document.
4. Relatively permanent.
5. Simplification of procedures.
6. Under some circumstances may be used as a substitute for the original document.

In recent years, significant progress has been made in the duplication of records by microfilming or a similar process. It is suggested that the advantages be explored and considered in developing the records management program. It should be integrated into the overall concept. Frequently, records are microfilmed, and the originals are then destroyed. Before such destruction, it may be well to consult with the legal function concerning the rules of evidence or future legal requirement for the original vs. microfilm copy. It is essential that the microfilm records be organized, sequenced, classified, and controlled.

57-6 THE STORAGE AREA

Most companies have a records center in which they store inactive records. These centers should be located to provide cheap storage but with fast retrieval of items requested. Unless there is unused space available on-site, these centers should be off-site and designed for the specific purpose of storing and retrieving records. The controller must carefully evaluate the alternatives of establishing a records center, including these:

- Should a facility be leased or bought?
- Should a commercial records center be used?

The considerations will include present and future storage needs, facilities required, and ongoing operational costs: typical make-or-buy conundrums.

A complete discussion of the details about the selecting and equipping of a permanent storage area is outside the scope of this book. However, based on the authors' practical experience, the following suggestions may prove helpful:

1. The area preferably should be of fireproof construction.
2. Ample provision should be made for future requirements.
3. The aisles in the storage area should be lettered or numbered to permit quick identification if the location is of any considerable size; also each rack or container must be numbered or lettered to facilitate further identification.
4. Each storage box or reel of tape, etc., should be labeled clearly to indicate the contents: name of record, period covered, department, etc.
5. Confidential records may need lock-equipped facilities.
6. Responsibility for custody of the material should be definitely assigned, and material should be procurable only with a properly approved requisition.
7. Enclosed containers are preferable; open bins and shelving ordinarily are not satisfactory.
8. Magnetic tape can stick together when exposed to excessive humidity and magnetic disks can be destroyed by proximity to strong magnetic fields; these factors should be considered when selecting a storage area.
9. Some archived corporate records can be extremely valuable, especially those that may be of use in a future lawsuit. Consequently, the storage area must be secure, and access to it must only be by authorized personnel.

An ideal depository is one conveniently located, fireproof, floodproof, temperature and humidity controlled, and equipped to fumigate the records before filing. The danger from rodents and vermin can present a serious problem.

57-7 INDEX OF INACTIVE RECORDS

Merely to store inactive records in a suitable manner is not enough. When these records are needed, they must be located quickly and easily. To facilitate this location of documents, a simple index may serve a twofold function: (1) a record of the location in the storage area and (2) a record showing the date of destruction. Generally, the following information should be included in an index system, whether manual or computerized:

Description of record	Destruction date
Location	Cross-reference
Retention period	Other pertinent remarks

Sometimes color coding facilitates identification of records, e.g., colors may be used for the records of different divisions.

57-8 FINAL DESTRUCTION OF THE RECORDS

The index file for inactive records may be used as a tickler file for the removal of records scheduled for destruction, in addition to being a record of destruction dates for material already disposed of. In many instances, it will be found practical to destroy records once a year.

By use of a schedule of retention, it seems a well-established procedure in many companies to destroy records more or less automatically after the retention period has expired. Of course, such a practice obviates the need for a periodic review and repeated authorizations for destruction. However, some companies prepare and execute a form similar to that shown in Figure 57-3, for authorization to destroy records. This permits a recheck of the decision to destroy, even if on the retention schedule. This might be necessary if the retention periods are changed by law or other circumstances arise.

Each record scheduled for destruction should be checked, because it is far too easy to destroy vital records through erroneous filing. In no event should a drawer of records be destroyed on the basis of the label; the contents should be reviewed.

There are many different ways that records can be destroyed. For paper, the cleanest and most efficient method is shredding, after which the paper can be baled and sold. An alternative is to pulverize and recycle, although this may be unacceptable for confidential material. Finally there is incineration, which is not good for the environment and often also leaves unburned pieces of paper. Whatever method is used, strict accountability as to what was done, when, and how successful it was is needed to ensure adequate control of the process. Some companies are required by federal statute to execute cremation certificates. Even without such a requirement, it seems desirable to have a destruction certificate prepared and filed. A suggested form of such a certificate is incorporated in the authorization for destruction of records (Figure 57-3).

Figure 57-3 Authorization Form for Destruction of Records and Cremation.

AUTHORIZATION FOR DESTRUCTION OF RECORDS AND CREMATION CERTIFICATE

No. ____________

Date ____________

To: (Controller)

Authority is requested for destruction of the following records:

Form Number	Filing Schedule Number	Description of Records	Date of Records		Recommended Retention Period	Minimum Age	
			From	To		Yr.	Mo.

Destruction Recommended by ____________

Destruction Approved by ____________

- -

Date ____________

I hereby certify that I have this day destroyed, by cremation, the accounts, records, and memoranda listed above, and further that no accounts, records, or memoranda other than those named were destroyed herewith.

____________ (witness) ____________ (signed)

____________ (location) ____________ (position)

57-9 SELECTED REFERENCES

Diamond, Susan Z., *Records Management—A Practical Guide.* New York: American Management Association, 1983.

The Institute of Internal Auditors, *Audit, Control, and Security of Paperless Systems.* Altamonte Springs, FL: The Institute of Internal Auditors Research Foundation, 1991.

Ruprecht, Mary M., and Kathleen P. Wagoner, *Managing Office Automation—A Complete Guide.* New York: John Wiley & Sons, 1984.

Smith, Milburn D., *Information and Records Management.* New York: Quorum Books, 1986.

Tweedy, Donald B., *Office Records Systems and Space Management.* New York: Quorum Books, 1986.

CHAPTER 58

Physical Inventory Procedure

58-1 NEED FOR PHYSICAL INVENTORY

One of the basic responsibilities of the controller is the preparation of accurate reports on the results of operations and the financial condition of the company. Of all the elements affecting these statements, none is generally more significant than the inventory. Moreover, it is usually a relatively more important influence on the income and expense statement than on the balance sheet. For example, an error of 3% in the inventory might double or half the profit but make no significant change in the current assets. It is evident that the accuracy of the financial statements depends on the value placed on the inventories, and this relates to two factors: (1) the quantities on hand and (2) the valuation placed on the reported quantities.

The value of the company's inventory may be determined by an annual physical inventory taken at or near the end of the fiscal year, maintenance of highly accurate perpetual inventory records, maintenance of perpetual inventory records supported by periodic physical counts and in some instances periodic counts of significant selected items. *A physical inventory* is defined as the periodic counting, weighing, measuring, and valuing of the goods and materials owned. Even though a perpetual inventory system is maintained, it is usually necessary to make periodic counts and reconcile any variances to verify the accuracy of the system. There may be additional reasons for taking a physical inventory:

1. Where inventory control procedures have been found weak by internal audit or noted shortages.
2. Where the type of material lends itself to shrinkage or loss when in storage.
3. When management policy specifically requires it as a matter of policy; significant value is involved with small units that are portable, readily disposed of, and subject to theft.
4. Where, for practical purposes, the units of receipt are different from units of disbursement, i.e., receipts in pounds and issues in units or gallons.
5. Where the nature of the operation or process makes it difficult to check against usage or production because of differences in moisture content, etc.

If perpetual inventory records are maintained with high accuracy, then no complete annual physical inventory (with a plant shutdown) need be conducted. An increasing number of companies are turning to this method for the following reasons:

1. *Avoid Wasted Time.* Staff time is not being efficiently utilized during the physical inventory process, because they could be involved in other activities. Also, the production facility is shut down, not allowing revenue-generating products to be manufactured.
2. *Improve Product Delivery Performance and Reduce Freight Costs.* High inventory record accuracy allows companies to promise shipments to customers with greater confidence, because products can be built without delays due to missing parts. Also, rush charges for missing parts are avoided.
3. *Achieve Higher Accuracy with Ongoing Counts.* Inventory counts should be done by the experts—the warehouse staff—and should be done at their leisure, which ensures higher count accuracy. If a complete plant-wide physical inventory is performed, then accuracy drops due to counts by less experienced nonwarehouse staff and the short timeline required to complete the count.
4. *Avoid Year-End Surprises.* Many companies have been unpleasantly surprised by unexpected changes in inventory levels at year-end. These surprises can be avoided by constantly monitoring inventory levels with a perpetual inventory system.
5. *Use Data to Reduce Inventory and Cut Costs.* The transaction history that is a byproduct of a perpetual inventory system allows the materials manager to make informed decisions regarding deletions of parts from stock. This is of value to the controller, since cash requirements for additional inventory are reduced, and can be enhanced as inventory is sold back to suppliers. As inventory is reduced, the staff needed to track it and the insurance needed to insure it can both be reduced, thereby improving the company's cash flow a second time.

The next part of this chapter describes the steps needed to implement an accurate perpetual inventory system that can replace a complete physical inventory and its associated plant shut-down.

58-2 IMPLEMENTING AN ACCURATE PERPETUAL INVENTORY SYSTEM

A complete annual physical inventory can be eliminated if accurate perpetual inventory records are available. Many steps are required to implement such a system, requiring considerable effort. The controller should evaluate the company's resources prior to embarking on this process, and adjust those resources accordingly in order to complete the project. In addition, the controller must realize that, once high accuracy levels are achieved, continued monitoring is needed to maintain those levels.

The steps needed to implement an accurate perpetual inventory system are:

1. *Select and Install Inventory Tracking Software.* The primary requirements for inventory tracking software are that it:
   - *Track Transactions.* One of the primary uses of a perpetual inventory system is the ability to list the frequency of product usage, which allows the materials manager to increase or reduce selected inventory quantities.
   - *Update Records Immediately.* The perpetual inventory data must always be up-to-date, because production planners must know what is in stock and because cycle counters must have access to accurate data. Batch updating of records is not acceptable.
   - *Report Inventory Records by Location.* Cycle counters need inventory records sorted by location in order to most efficiently count the inventory.

2. *Test Inventory Tracking Software.* Create a set of typical records in the new software, and perform a series of transactions to ensure that the software functions properly. In addition, create a large number of records and perform the transactions again, to see if the response time of the system drops significantly. If the software appears to function properly, continue to the next step. Otherwise, fix the problems with the software supplier's assistance, or acquire a different software package.

3. *Train the Warehouse Staff.* The warehouse staff should receive software training immediately prior to using the system, so that they do not forget how to operate the software. Enter a set of test records into the software, and have the staff simulate all common inventory transactions, such as receipts, picks, and cycle count adjustments.

4. *Revise Rack Layout.* It is much easier to move racks prior to installing a perpetual inventory system, because no inventory locations must be changed on the computer system. Create aisles that are wide enough for forklift operation, and cluster small parts racks together for easier parts picking.

5. *Create Rack Locations.* A typical rack location is, for example, A-01-B-01. The meaning of this location code is as follows:
   - A = Aisle A
   - 01 = Rack 1

- B = Level B (numbered from the bottom to the top)
- 01 = Partition 1 (optional—subsection of a rack)

As one progresses down an aisle, the rack numbers should progress in ascending sequence, with the odd rack numbers on the left and the even numbers on the right. This layout allows an inventory picker to move down the center of the aisle, efficiently pulling items based on sequential location codes.

6. *Lock the Warehouse.* One of the main causes of record inaccuracy is removal of items by staff from outside the warehouse. To stop such removal, all entrances to the warehouse must be locked. Only warehouse personnel should be allowed access to the warehouse. All other personnel entering the warehouse should be accompanied by a member of the warehouse staff to prevent the removal of inventory.

7. *Consolidate Parts.* To reduce the labor of counting the same item in multiple locations, group common parts in one location.

8. *Assign Part Numbers.* Have several experienced personnel verify all part numbers. A mislabeled part is no better than a missing part, since the computer database will not show that it exists. Mislabeled parts also affect the inventory cost; for example, a mislabeled engine is more expensive than the item represented by its incorrect part number, which identifies it as a spark plug.

9. *Verify Units of Measure.* Have several experienced personnel verify all units of measure. Unless the software allows multiple units of measure, the entire organization must adhere to one unit of measure for each item. For example, the warehouse may desire tape to be counted in rolls, but the engineering department had rather create bills of material with tape measured in inches instead of fractions of rolls.

10. *Pack the Parts.* Pack parts into containers, seal the containers, and label them with the part number, unit of measure, and total quantity stored inside. Leave a few parts free for ready use. Only open containers when additional stock is needed. This method allows cycle counters to rapidly verify inventory balances.

11. *Count Items.* Count items when there is no significant activity in the warehouse, such as during a weekend. Elaborate cross-checking of the counts, as would be done during a year-end physical inventory, is not necessary. It is more important to have the perpetual inventory operational before warehouse activity increases again; any errors in the data will quickly be detected during cycle counts and flushed out of the database. The counts must include the part number, location, and quantity.

12. *Enter Data into Computer.* Have an experienced data entry person input the location, part number, and quantity into the computer. Once the data is input, another person should cross-check the entered data against the original data for errors.

13. *Quick-Check the Data.* Scan the data for errors. If all part numbers have the same number of digits, then look for items that are too long or short. Review location codes to see if inventory is stored in nonexistent racks. Look for units of measure that match the part being described. For example, is it logical to have a pint of steel in stock? Also, if item costs are available, print a list of extended costs. Excessive costs typically point to incorrect units of measure. For example,

a cost of $1 per box of nails will become $500 in the inventory report if nails are listed in eaches.

14. *Initiate Cycle Counts.* Print out a portion of the inventory list, sorted by location. Using the report, have selected staff count blocks of the inventory on a continuous basis. They should look for accurate part numbers, units of measure, locations, and quantities. The counts can concentrate on high-value or high-use items, but the entire stock should be reviewed regularly. The most important part of this step is to examine why mistakes occur. If a cycle counter finds an error, the cause of the error must be investigated and then corrected, so that the mistake will not occur again.

15. *Initiate Inventory Audits.* The inventory should be audited frequently, perhaps as much as once a week. This allows the controller to track changes in the inventory accuracy level and initiate changes if the accuracy drops below acceptable levels. In addition, frequent audits are an indirect means of telling the staff that inventory accuracy is important, and must be maintained. The minimum acceptable accuracy level is 95%, with an error being a mistaken part number, unit of measure, quantity, or location. This accuracy level is needed to ensure accurate inventory costing, as well as to assist the materials department in planning future inventory purchases.

In addition, establish a tolerance level when calculating the inventory accuracy. For example, if the computer record of a box of screws yields a quantity of 100 and the actual count reveals a quantity of 105, then the record is accurate if the tolerance is 5%, but inaccurate if the tolerance is 1%. The maximum tolerance should be 5%, and this figure could be reduced for high-value or high-use items.

16. *Post Results.* Inventory accuracy is a team project, and the warehouse staff feels more involved if the audit results are posted against the results of previous audits.

17. *Reward Staff.* Accurate inventories save a company thousands of dollars in many ways. Therefore, it is cost-effective to incent the staff to maintain and improve the accuracy with periodic bonuses based on reaching higher levels of accuracy with tighter tolerances.

The previous section dealt with the basic steps needed to implement an accurate perpetual inventory system. However, there are several special cases that require additional steps. Some of the more common cases include:

1. *Customer-Owned Inventory.* Customer-owned inventory cannot be valued, since the company does not own it. There are different solutions for different companies. For example, one can avoid assigning a cost to the part, assign different part numbers to a part based on who owns it, or segregate the materials in an uncounted area. Be careful when assigning several part numbers to the same part, for engineering drawings and bills of material usually list only one part number for a part.

2. *Consignment Inventory.* One technique used by materials departments to improve the production process is to turn over some items to suppliers, who then have title to their own inventory in the production area. Because it is owned by suppliers, it should not be costed. To avoid incorrect costing, this consignment

inventory should be stored in clearly marked areas, and should not appear in the inventory database.

3. *Materials at Supplier Locations.* Company-owned materials are sometimes kept at supplier or customer locations. These items can constitute a large unseen part of the inventory, and can easily escape an otherwise rigorous inventory tracking system. It is the responsibility of the materials department to track this inventory. Track these items by using a special location code for the off-site location, and verify the item quantities with the customer or supplier as part of the cycle count and periodic audit process.

4. *Floor Stock.* Floor stock is defined as the fasteners kept on the shop floor to assemble product. These are typically kept in uncounted bins, and replenished from the warehouse as the bins empty. The easiest treatment of this material on the computer system is to avoid it. Floor stock is generally not expensive, and therefore has no significant impact on the accuracy of the financial statements if they are expensed instead of being capitalized into inventory. Also, the cost to count floor stock may not be worth the additional level of record accuracy in the perpetual inventory.

    Another approach to floor stock is to return as much of it as possible to the warehouse. A close review of floor stock turnover typically reveals that some of it turns slowly. If so, those items can be returned to stock and later requisitioned back to the shop floor as needed. This technique reduces the amount of uncounted floor stock.

5. *Work in Process.* Work in process (WIP) must be tracked in the perpetual inventory system, because it can be large enough to have a significant impact on the financial statements. The easiest approach to this problem is to utilize cell manufacturing to reduce the WIP in the manufacturing process—if it isn't there, you don't have to count it. However, because cell manufacturing is beyond the job scope of most controllers, the next approach may be more appropriate; encourage data collection at each job station on the assembly floor.

    Data collection outside of the warehouse is difficult, for the staff is usually less well trained in data entry methods. Several methods are possible, based on the controller's level of confidence in the staff's ability to enter data:

    • Each manufacturing station can log in those items entering its area, and log out those items leaving its area. This is a time-consuming process that can move faster with bar coding.

    • If bills of material are accurate, then one can track the progress of jobs through the shop by simply logging in the stage of completion of the job. If the inventory tracking software is sophisticated enough, the WIP cost is calculated by comparing the job's reported stage of completion to the bill of materials.

58-3 PLANNING THE PHYSICAL INVENTORY PROCEDURE

Most effort is more productive if intelligently planned, and this is certainly true in the case of taking a physical inventory. The time available to take the inventory is usually limited. It must be scheduled and accomplished over a weekend or requires a plant shutdown with the consequent loss in production. Second, the inventories must be accurate to be of any value, and each step in taking the inventory must be carefully planned. Because of time limitations, the employees used are generally untrained in inventory-taking procedures, and detailed planning is critical to overcome this handicap. The cost of taking a complete physical inventory is significant, and every effort should be made to reduce the cost and increase the accuracy of the results. Since it is another burden on the accounting staff, the inventory should be planned sufficiently in advance of the end of the year to minimize peak loads and allow time for analysis and adjustments.

Many factors influence the amount of planning and advance preparation that may be necessary, such as size and type of inventory, conditions under which stocks are maintained, number of locations, experience of the inventory-taking staff, time available to take the inventory, and sufficiency of the material control system and records.

Planning for the physical inventory must include both the aspects of dealing with the physical count and those relating to the accounting records. The plan must be well coordinated in advance of the actual counting, particularly with manufacturing, material warehousing, and accounting. A well-developed plan should include at a minimum the following:

1. Organization and staffing with assigned duties and responsibilities.
2. Detailed written instructions.
3. Schedule of critical dates—cutoff dates, dates for taking each segment of the inventory, plant shutdown dates, publishing dates for the various summaries, reports, and accounting entries.
4. Training—it is desirable to conduct training sessions in the methods of counting, completion of forms, and cutoff procedures.
5. Design, preparation, and distribution of forms and supplies to be used.
6. Detailed floor plan layouts of areas locating each type of inventory and control points.

58-4 ORGANIZATION FOR TAKING INVENTORY

A vital first step in planning the physical inventory procedure is the establishment of an appropriate organization indicating specific responsibilities. As the inventory taking is not a full-time job, it is mandatory that the authority, responsibilities, and duties be clearly stated and established. The responsibility may be assigned to production manufacturing executives or a committee; however, normally, the controller is charged with the total inventory responsibility, including a final management report. Figure 58-1 is a typical organization chart for taking an annual physical inventory.

In addition to the functions listed, a larger company may involve an advisory committee, including such functions as material control, warehousing, data processing, production control, and cost accounting.

Some of the specific responsibilities are outlined as follows:

1. *Controller.* Responsible for complete planning and execution of the physical inventory program.

Figure 58-1 Organization for Physical Inventory.

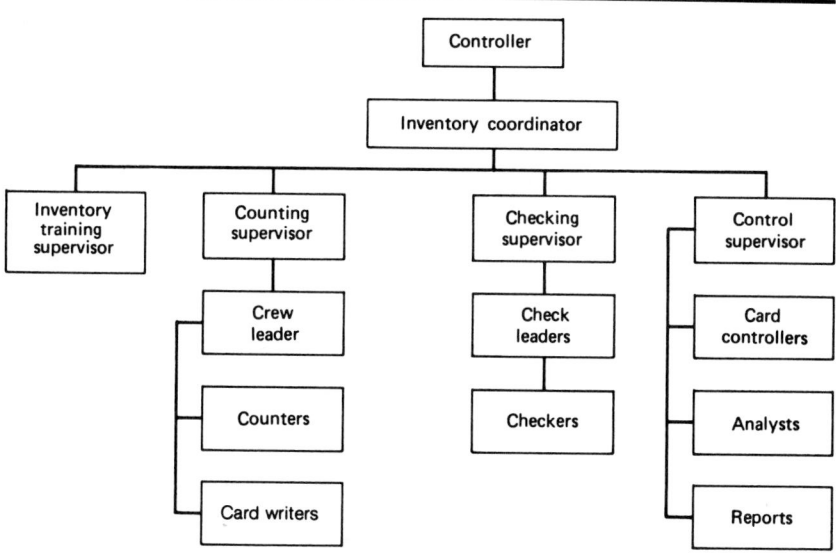

2. *Coordinator.* Insures complete coordination of all inventory activities with all functional heads.

3. *Training Supervisor.* Responsible to train everyone concerned with the inventory taking, including those preparing the areas and arranging stock; development of a training program and arranging for the proper selection of employees to participate.

4. *Counting Supervisor.* Responsible for proper identification and counting of all materials to be inventoried and making sure that inventory cards are properly prepared.

5. *Checking Supervisor.* Responsible for recounting and verifying the accuracy of the counts and insuring that all items have been counted and tagged.

6. *Control Supervisor.* Responsible for issuance and control of all inventory cards and tags, analysis of variances, and preparation and distribution of applicable reports.

Other plans of organization may be used such as along departmental lines with line supervisors responsible for carrying out certain duties in their departments. It should be pointed out that checks and balances should be built into the organization to provide for proper elements of internal control. The individual responsible for an inventory as his regular assignment should not be in charge of taking the physical count and reconciling it to the accounting records. The inventory plan and the organization should be well communicated to all levels of the company and everyone concerned motivated to accomplish the task in a minimum amount of time.

58-5 INVENTORY INSTRUCTIONS

Because the physical inventory is a major undertaking, the instructions should be prepared in writing so that the procedures may be more readily enforced. Since the physical custody and control of inventories are under an operating head, and not under the controller, the cooperation of both groups is necessary. Both have a stake in the accuracy of the physical inventory, and the two should work together. As an aid in accomplishing this, the inventory instructions should be prepared in draft form and routed to the supervisory staff of both the production and accounting groups for their criticism and approval. The instructions should be written in simple, clear language. Also, where circumstances require very detailed and lengthy procedures, it is preferable that they be prepared by sections so that each participant gets only the data relating to his responsibility rather than a long dissertation. Charts and sample forms are useful and may be incorporated in the manual.

The detailed physical inventory instructions should cover the following points:

1. Date and places of physical inventory.
2. Categories of inventories to be covered.
3. Detail of the duties of each person assisting in the inventory.
4. Special instructions in case of unforeseen trouble, difficulties, or problems.
5. Explanation of the method of control and distribution of cards, tags, and other forms.
6. Method of completing records and tags.
7. Method of identifying materials.
8. Required preparatory work in nature of cleanup, records, etc.
9. Listing and examples of items not to be counted.
10. Detail of counting method—use of scales, estimates, etc.
11. Description of checking methods.
12. Special instructions regarding the confirmation of warehouse stocks, goods in hands of customers, customers' property in company possession.
13. Instructions regarding the treatment of obsolete, spoiled, or slow-moving goods.
14. Instructions on the method of accounting for all card and tag numbers.
15. Instructions on pricing and valuation methods.
16. Procedure to be followed in cutoff—stamping paperwork "after inventory," etc.
17. Instructions relating to comparison with perpetual records.
18. Instructions on listing, extension, and summarizing methods.
19. Instructions about restrictions on the movement of goods between plants and departments.
20. Cooperation with the independent auditors and other observers.

(a) ILLUSTRATIONS

Each company will necessarily have its own issues and problems, and instructions must be prepared accordingly. The following are examples of specifics that may be included in physical inventory instructions or a manual.

(b) INVENTORY CARD

See Figure 58-2.

1. To insure legible cards, ballpoint pens and a clipboard should be used.

2. For clarity and uniformity, an "X" rather than a check (✓) will be placed on the card where this type of entry can be used.

3. Quantities that end in fractions will be rounded down to the nearest whole number.

4. Special care must be used in handling the cards to avoid folding, curling, and tearing, since they will be used in data processing equipment.

5. Inventory cards are to be attached to containers and material in such a way that they can be readily seen and are accessible.

6. Under no circumstances will erasures be allowed on any inventory cards. Corrections will be made by drawing a line through the incorrect entry and inserting the correct information either above or below. All corrections must be initialed by the person making the correction.

Figure 58-2   Inventory Card.

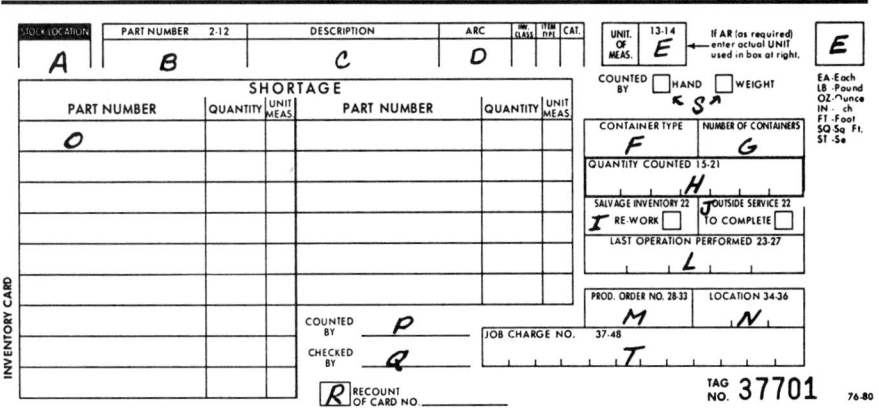

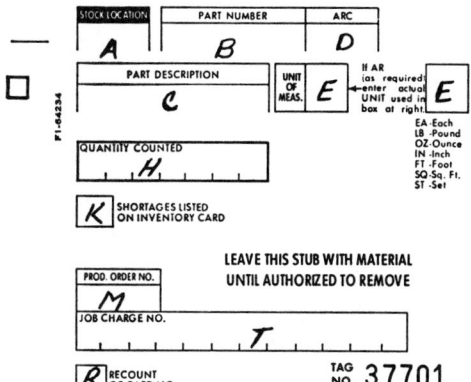

7. If it is necessary to void an inventory card, the department supervisor will indicate such action by printing the work "VOID" and his department across the face of the card. The reason for voiding should be written briefly on the card. Return the card to Inventory Control Headquarters, with issued lots.

8. The following steps should be taken to record the required information on the inventory cards (coded to Figure 58-2):

A.   Stock location number (preprinted or written).

B.   Part number (preprinted or written).

C.   Description of item (preprinted or written).

D.   Area of responsibility code (preprinted or written)—manufactured or purchased part (use master file).

E.   Unit of measure as shown on Stock Status (preprinted or written). (If an error is found in Stock Status, please notify accounting.)

F.   Container type—i.e., box, can, jar, etc.

G.   Number of containers.

H.   Total quantity counted. The part may be located in stock bins, on the shelves, or both. The material with the same part number in more than one container in close proximity shall be inventoried on one card with a "counted" card attached to additional containers. If the identical parts are not in close proximity, more than one inventory card will be used.

I.   Rework holding. Designated by tag stating "Rework Holding" and stamped rework holding.

J.   Outside service. Parts at outside vendor (Accounting and Purchasing).

K.   Shortage indicator—indicates shortages listed.

L.   Last operation performed (preprinted or written).

M.   Production order number (printed or written).

N.   Location where item is being counted.

O.   Shortage part numbers: quantities, unit of measure, work in process. (Do not list bulk issues or any item marked as required (A/R) on Manufacturing Routing Production order.)

PQ.   Counted by and checked by—write in employee's identification number.

R.   Recount card number—used for recount.

S.   Counting method—designate hand count or weight count.

T.   Job charge number (job charge number written—12 digits).

(c) INVENTORY CUTOFFS

1. *Receiving and Receiving Inspection*

   a. No paperwork or parts will be forwarded to the Central Stores area later than 11:00 AM, Friday, October 26, 19XX. This will allow paperwork to be processed and stock put away.

   b. Beginning October 15, 19XX, all receivers processed by Receiving Inspections must be stamped "Before Inventory."

2. *Central Stores*

a. Receipts: All paperwork on parts received from Receiving Inspection must be transferred to Data Processing before 4:30 PM, Friday, October 26, 19XX.

b. Issues: The paperwork on all issues to open orders and job in process must be completed and sent to Data Processing before 4:30 PM, Friday, October 26, 19XX. On issues for sales orders, the issue documents and parts must be in the staging area or shipping area *before* 3:30 PM, Friday October 26, 19XX.

3. *Finished Goods Area*

a. Staging Area: These are segregated parts by sales orders. If the parts are not shipped before 3:30 PM, Friday, October 26, 19XX, they will be retained as part of storeroom inventory.

b. Receipts into Finished Goods Area from Order or Job Number Completion must be received and the paperwork sent to Data Processing before 4:30 PM, Friday, October 26, 19XX. The Production Control assigned representative should make sure that all finished units are placed in stock and that the paperwork did go to Data Processing before the 11:00 AM cutoff.

c. Issues: (1) On issues for sales orders, the issue card and parts must be in staging or shipping area before 11:00 AM, Friday, October 26, 19XX. (2) Issues to orders and job numbers—all paperwork on issues to work in process must be in Data Processing before 4:30 PM, Friday, October 26, 19XX.

(d) INVENTORY RELEASE TEAM AND RESPONSIBILITIES

After the Section Supervisor and the Production Control Representative have signed the Preliminary Release Form, they will notify Inventory Headquarters for the Preliminary Inventory Release Team to come in and review the department and sign the Preliminary Release Form. The Preliminary Inventory Release Team will review the department to be sure all parts have been inventoried, spot-check inventory tags and cards for counts, completeness, and legibility to satisfy the requirements that the inventory has been taken in accordance with established procedures. The team should look for the following fraudulent schemes that may have occurred during or before the inventory count:

- Empty or mislabeled boxes.
- Incorrect units of measure.
- Diluted liquid inventory.
- Excessively advanced state of WIP completion.
- Including customer-owned stock in the inventory.

On completion of a satisfactory review, the Preliminary Inventory Release Inventory Team will sign the Preliminary Release Form that will authorize Inventory Cards to be pulled. The Preliminary Release Team will advise Inventory Headquarters of the results from each area inspected.

The Final Release teams will be composed of the Manager of Manufacturing and the Cost Control Manager. Final Release approval is the responsibility of the Cost Control Manager.

(e) APPROVAL

Inventory location _____ has been inspected for compliance with Inventory Procedures and has been approved to proceed with the pulling and sorting of inventory cards.

_____   _____
Manufacturing Representative   Accounting Representative

(f) INDEPENDENT AUDITORS

Representatives of _____ , independent auditors, will be present to observe the inventory-taking procedure and make test counts. If they request any recounts, personnel should make such counts and cooperate in every reasonable way.

(g) INVENTORY TO BE COUNTED

1. 100% Physical count
   a. Central stores and wire cut—basement building #1.
   b. Receiving inspection.
   c. Staging areas in buildings 1, 2, and 4.
   d. Finished goods area.
   e. Central stores areas—first floor—building 1.
   f. WIP in all area—buildings 1, 2, and 4.
   g. Raw stock—bar stock—sheet metal—building 2.
   h. Bulk storage—building 4.
   i. Kits and shipping—building 4.
   j. Outside storage parking lots—building 4.
   k. Rework holding—plant-wide.
   l. OSV—material.
   m. All material that does not have a production order but is being performed for manufacturing. Shop orders will be assigned at physical inventory time.
   n. Hardware (bulk issue) in production areas.
   o. Packaging materials—plant-wide.

(h) INVENTORY NOT TO BE COUNTED

1. All production aids and tools.
2. Capital equipment (including all test equipment).
3. Material handling equipment and containers.
4. Segregated unallocated inventory written off.
5. Maintenance equipment and supplies.
6. Office supplies and equipment.

7. All material that does not have a production order number and is being performed for Engineering or Special Products.

8. Departmental expense items such as glue, paint, solder, weld rods, solder wire, brazing supplies, tape, chemicals.

9. Customer service material in plant for rework or repair.

10. Material out to vendors on Return to Vendors (RTV's) form.

11. Items tagged with a "Do Not Inventory" form.

12. All consignment inventory.

The foregoing is not to be a complete and comprehensive manual but to indicate some specifics and the amount of detail required to insure that a complete and accurate inventory is taken.

58-6 CLASSIFICATION OF INVENTORIES

The various categories of items counted must be grouped to permit identification with the proper inventory account. Separate classes should be used, such as:

1. Raw materials.

2. Work in process.

3. Finished parts.

4. Finished goods.

5. Operating supplies.

6. Perishable tools.

7. Returnable containers.

8. Goods out on consignment.

9. Miscellaneous—e.g., property of others in our possession.

To avoid improper grouping, it may be helpful to use differently colored tags for each classification. In other instances the proper category must be checked on the inventory tag.

58-7 FORMS USED IN TAKING PHYSICAL INVENTORY

The two chief forms prepared in a physical inventory procedure are inventory tags and inventory sheets. Usually, the count is taken by using a tag to be affixed to each lot. The tags are numbered serially in advance; and since a portion of the tag is left on the stock, it serves as a means of assuring that all lots are counted. In the event of suspected errors, the remaining portion can be used for rechecking.

A form of inventory tag is shown in Figure 58-3. Space is provided on the reverse side for noting movements so that slow-moving items may be counted in advance of the regular count. This is a two-part tag, the lower section being collected for summarization. Where further precaution is considered necessary, a three-section tag can be utilized, in which the third section duplicates the second. A count is made and the third

Figure 58-3   Inventory Tag.

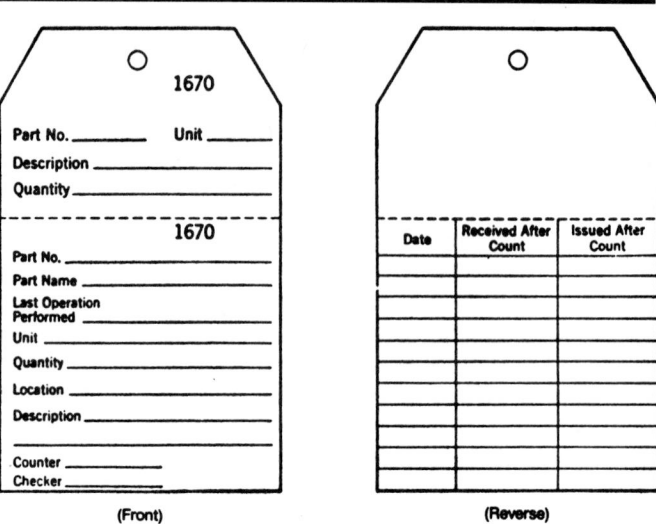

(Front)   (Reverse)

section is removed; then another count is taken and recorded on the second section. This second section is then removed and compared with the previous count. Instead of a perforated card, a cardboard back with attached paper forms may be used.

A list of representative information usually required on an inventory card or tag is as follows:

1. Part or assembly number.
2. Description and size of item.
3. General classification of item, viz., raw material, finished part, incomplete assembly, returnable container, etc.
4. Last operation completed.
5. Quantity on hand.
6. Unit of measure (pieces, pounds, feet, etc.).
7. Location of item.
8. Names or employee numbers and initials of counters and checkers, etc.

When the count is completed, all tags are gathered and all numbers are accounted for, perhaps with the use of check-off lists. The data are then listed on an inventory sheet. A standard printed form is illustrated in Figure 58-4.

It may be found, however, that the many reconciling factors to be considered will make a worksheet more desirable, as in Figure 58-5. In this instance it was not practical to make an inventory count on the last business day of the month, so adjustments were made to carry the physical count to the end of the period on which the books of account were kept.

Figure 58-4   Worksheet for Pricing of Physical Inventory.

Reference	Description	Unit	Quantity	Cost		Market		Lower of Cost or Market	
				Unit	Value	Unit	Value	Value	Remarks
1820	Batteries – 10 CL	ea.	24	$10.12	$242.88	$10.00	$240.00	$240.00	
1821	Lead clamps	doz.	3	1.80	5.40	1.80	5.40	5.40	
1822	Plastic caps	doz.	8	.25	2.00	.28	2.24	2.00	

Inventory Listing

Sheet No. __8__

Department __Final Assembly__

Written By __R. Jones__   Priced By __C. Comes__   Checked By __L. Austin__

58-8 PROCEDURE FOR PHYSICAL COUNT

The detailed procedure for securing an accurate physical count is evident from a re-view of the standard instructions in a preceding section. The importance of securing an accurate count should be emphasized. The quantity and necessary descriptive data for each pile, bin, or batch should be recorded on the inventory tag and attached to the bin or bag by tape, wire, or otherwise. As the count proceeds, it should be ascertained that all lots are properly tagged. If items are not to be counted, sometimes a "Do Not Count" tag is placed thereon in advance.

Usually, the count is done by stocktakers working in pairs, one person listing and one counting. It may be advantageous to use an accounting department member for list-ing and a production department member for counting. Those who list can from time to time make test checks of the count. When the counting has been completed, another group should remove the section of the tag, make test checks of the count, and verify that all lots have been tagged.

Usually, physical inventories are attended by the independent public auditors as well as the company's own internal auditors. These representatives make test counts, observe the procedure generally, and subsequently trace the counts to the inventory summary. The presence of the representative is another incentive for accurate counts.

Where inventories are located in warehouses, arrangements may be made to make counts or secure confirmation from the outside agencies regarding the quantities on hand. In any event, no inventory should be overlooked.

58-9 OTHER METHODS

With the advancement of computers and other technologies there are many methods available now to enhance the inventory-taking procedures. These modern methods may be readily applied and may materially shorten the time within which final results can be made available. Even the use of prepunched or "mark-sensing" cards can save a con-siderable amount of time as well as improve the accuracy.

Some companies use mark scanning, optical readers, or optical character recog-nition techniques. Several systems are available for adapting to the unique conditions

Figure 58-5 Worksheet for Physical Inventory Summary.

The Illustrative Company
ANNUAL PHYSICAL INVENTORY, OCTOBER 28, 19XX
INVENTORY SUMMARY

Description	Unit	Physical Inventory 10/28/XX	ADJUSTMENTS				Adjusted Physical Inventory	SUBSEQUENT TRANSACTIONS			Adjusted Inventory 10/31/XX	Unit Price	Value
			Unrecorded Liabilities	Process Back to Raw*	Other	Total		Production	Usage & Shipments	Other			
CHEMICALS:													
Glycerine U.S.P.	lbs.	10,000	–	–	–	–	10,000	–1,000	+5,000	–	14,000	$.25	$3,500
Castor oil	lbs.	44,600	–4,600	+2,000	–	–2,600	42,000	–5,000	+1,000	–	38,000	.33	12,540
Linseed oil	lbs.	13,900	–2,400	–	–	–2,400	11,500	–	–	–	11,500	.28	3,220
Phenol	lbs.	6,800	–	–	–	–	6,800	–	–	–	6,800	.26	1,768

*Unrecorded process batch sheets.

of a particular inventory system. For example, there are hand-held units that resemble a calculator; to use the units, the operator scans a bar-coded tag for the proper product identification number, then punches the quantity counted and the other data such as counter or checker number, location, etc. The data are then transmitted over telephone lines to the computer center. There is also extensive use of online terminals located adjacent to the stores' location. With the visual display available, inventory checkers are notified immediately if there are differences between the actual count and the inventory record. Recounts can be taken immediately, and it minimizes the reconciliation effort. Since there are numerous books and prepackaged systems available on inventory control, it is not the purpose here to discuss these systems in detail.

It is imperative for those companies with sophisticated computer capabilities to obtain peripheral equipment to fully utilize the computer in simplifying the inventory-taking procedure. No matter what the process is, however, it must be remembered that the basic elements of internal control must be included in the inventory procedures.

58-10 THE INVENTORY CUTOFF

Even if the counting is accurate and the summarizing and pricing are done with care, the inventory can be grossly misstated if the proper coordination is not secured between the physical count and the books of account. Thus the inclusion in the inventory of a single carload of merchandise, if the liability is not recorded, may be the cause of more difference than all the errors in counting. The controller should be quite certain that this aspect of physical inventory taking is handled properly.

To reduce errors from this source to an absolute minimum, the following precautions should be considered:

1. Generally, all receipts or shipments of goods should cease during the count.
2. Goods received or shipped after inventory should be so indicated on the receiving and shipping records as "Shipped After Inventory" or "Received After Inventory." Rubber stamps may be used.
3. Goods on the receiving and shipping docks at the time of the count may have stamped on the appropriate documents "Counted" or "Before Inventory."
4. The files of receiving reports should be checked for papers not yet matched with vendor invoices to account for unrecorded liabilities.

The controller should watch for the following fraudulent schemes that can occur when performing the inventory cutoff:

• Double-counting inventory that is in transit between two company-owned locations.
• Counting inventory for which payables have not been recorded.

58-11 COMPARISON WITH PERPETUAL INVENTORY RECORDS

Perpetual unit records may be maintained for material control or other purposes. When a physical inventory is taken, the results should be checked immediately against such information. The advantages are twofold: (1) it serves as a check against the physical count and may suggest items to be recounted, and (2) it permits quick adjustment of plant records so that up-to-date data are available when operations resume.

Any substantial differences between book records and the physical inventory should be investigated. This review can be accomplished in several ways but could include these steps:

1. Review inventory tags for possible errors in pricing or descriptions.
2. Compare present and previous inventory to locate seemingly unwarranted changes.
3. Review all large quantity or value items for errors in extensions and footings.
4. Where detail and control accounts are available, check the transactions for the period to reveal errors on purchases or usage.
5. Check similar materials for corresponding but opposite overages or shortages, indicating wrong postings and similar errors.
6. Have production people review the inventory to spot errors or secure explanations of shortages.

The object of the physical inventory is to count and price all individual items and prepare a summary that can be compared with the financial records of the company. The controller must be certain that all items counted are included in the summary and properly priced for extension. The summary may be a manual listing, or, as in most large companies, it will be provided by the integrated data processing system. In either case, certain points should be considered to obtain a timely and accurate summarization:

1. Management should decide on the method of pricing in advance as part of the overall plan.
2. Controls should be established to account for all inventory tags or cards.
3. A determination should be made about the various reports to be produced so that all relevant data can be recorded.
4. The inventory listings should be reviewed for reasonableness and test checks made for accuracy.
5. All variances should be resolved and approved by management personnel not directly responsible for the items.

58-12 INVENTORY VARIANCES

When the physical inventory has been completed and all discrepancies reviewed and approved, the records should be brought into agreement with the resulting physical inventory. In the case of perpetual inventory records, the cards should be marked "physical inventory," and the date and correct count should be indicated. Even if the count is in agreement with the record card it should be so noted to indicate the date of the inventory. Variances or differences should be summarized for a report to management. The report may also serve as a basis for making adjustments to the inventory control accounts.

In summarizing the results of the physical inventory, the controller should analyze the differences and determine the causes, such as obsolete items, market writedowns, unaccounted for losses, salvage, etc. No inventory adjustments should be made to the accounting records without proper documentation and approvals.

58-13   RETENTION OF PHYSICAL INVENTORY RECORDS

The forms, documents, and summaries used for taking a physical inventory and making adjustments should be considered in developing the records retention program (see Chapter 57). The records should be filed and retained as appropriate for further reference since they may be needed for tax purposes, support of contract adjustments, or future inventories.

58-14   INTERNAL AUDIT OF THE INVENTORIES

The purpose of the internal audit—for a company large enough to support such—should not only be to observe and check the annual physical inventory but also to perform a very useful function in making periodic checks of the records to (1) determine the correctness of the records, (2) evaluate the system of internal control, and (3) check to see that there is compliance with established procedures. Although this is in part a phase of inventory control, it is directly related to physical inventory problems. The results of the auditor's examinations may be used to good advantage in planning the yearly inventory. Also the audit recommendations are useful for improving the overall inventory system. To maximize the use of the internal audit function, those inventory-related efforts should be effectively planned and coordinated.

58-15   SELECTED REFERENCES

Hawkins, David F., *Corporate Financial Reporting and Analysis.* Homewood, IL: Dow Jones-Irwin, 1986.

Meigs, Walter B., and Robert F. Meigs, *Accounting: The Basis for Business Decisions* (5th ed.). New York: McGraw-Hill, 1981.

Shah, Pravin P., *Cost Control and Information Systems.* New York: McGraw-Hill, 1981.

Sullivan, Jerry D., Richard A. Gnospelius, Philip L. Defliese, and Henry R. Jaenicke, *Montgomery's Auditing* (10th ed.). New York: John Wiley & Sons, 1985.

CHAPTER 59

Tax Records and Procedures

59-1 INTRODUCTION

The reporting requirements of all governmental agencies has and will continue to increase significantly and become more complicated and complex. This is particularly true as the reporting requirements relate to federal, state, and local taxes. Federal budgetary pressures have increased demands for more thorough and efficient collection of revenues. These pressures have also caused the federal government to mandate more responsibilities to the states. Federal, state, and local pressures have led to increased demand for information from taxpayers. This translates to seemingly endless rules and regulations from numerous taxing authorities that taxpayers must comply with. Additionally, the United States probably has the most extensive audit procedures and enforcement capability of any country in the world. State and local taxing authorities are following the federal government's lead and enhancing their enforcement capabilities. It is mandatory that businesses develop and maintain adequate records to meet the

---

The author of this chapter is Marty Gold, Senior Manager, Ernst & Young LLP, Denver, CO.

requirements of these widely diverse patterns of federal, state, and local tax requirements. If the records and reporting system are not properly planned, a company could be subject to considerable financial exposure. Emphasis must be placed on the proper recording of financial transactions, accuracy in preparing data for tax reports, and timely reporting to concerned taxing authorities.

Many companies find it necessary to refer some or all federal, state, and local tax matters to tax consultants (both CPAs and attorneys). With the complexities of the various tax laws, this is the best approach. This does not, however, relieve the controller of overall responsibility for the tax products. No matter how well tax consultants know the company's business, the controller has a more intimate knowledge of the company. Additionally, the application of the tax laws must be considered in many of the day-to-day operating decisions. The controller has as a primary function the determination of the periodic and annual earnings, and the federal, state, and local tax laws are an important factor in such a determination. The controller has a fundamental responsibility to be fully informed on tax matters. A controller has not properly carried out his or her duties if every possible step to minimize overall tax liability has not been taken. It is his or her responsibility to see that the federal tax problems are handled competently.

In summary, the controller should have a working knowledge of the more important tax computations. The controller and key accounting staff should also have a basic understanding of the tax laws and should be sufficiently aware of tax implications to inquire into, and secure an answer to, the probable tax results of any given transaction. Finally, the controller should be able to arrive at intelligent conclusions regarding the management policies that will result in the most beneficial tax results.

59-2 THE TAX ORGANIZATION

The responsibility for the tax activities should be placed with a financial executive who understands the relationship of the accounting function to the tax compliance and planning function. Because the tax function affects cash flows and accounting determinations, it is generally considered to be a controller's function.

The increasing importance of taxes as a cost of doing business and the significant number of taxing authorities to be considered make it imperative that the administration of tax matters be regarded as a separate and distinct function in the organization. The plan of organization in most companies gives formal recognition to the tax function. In some companies with complex tax challenges and worldwide business interests, the tax function is headed by a vice-president of taxes. In other companies, a separate department is established, headed by a manager responsible for all facets of taxes. Depending on the complexity and challenging nature of the tax issues, the tax department may be organized according to the types of taxes:

- Federal income taxes.
- State income taxes.
- Sales and use taxes.
- Property taxes.
- Payroll taxes.

In other cases, companies use a functional breakdown such as:

- Tax compliance.
- Tax planning and research.
- Tax counsel.

A prime consideration in organizing and staffing a tax department is the degree of centralization concerning the administration of tax matters. This is particularly important when a company has several plants, branches, operating units, and international operations. A generic organizational chart of a home office tax department is illustrated in Figure 59-1.

59-3 CENTRALIZED TAX DEPARTMENT

For a tax department to be effective, it must relate to all geographic locations and departments of the business, including subsidiaries, divisions, branches, plants, and local offices. It also must be privy to key transactions of the company before they occur. A top policy decision must be made about the degree of centralization of the corporate tax function. Normally, a centralized tax organization will exercise control over all tax policies and procedures within the company. In addition, it will manage the home office tax organization and in some cases, direct the day-to-day activities of the decentralized tax people. However, in any event, functional control over the field tax organization should be vested in the corporate tax manager or executive.

Figure 59-1   Organization Chart for a Tax Department.

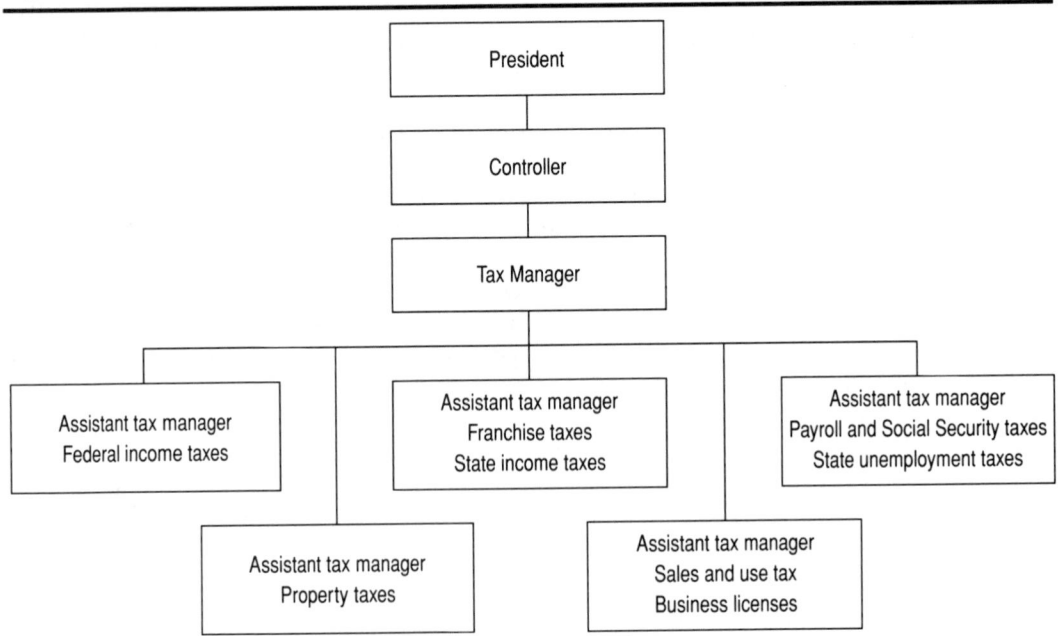

There are some advantages to having local personnel handle certain tax functions because of the relationships with the local taxing authorities as in the case of property taxes. The corporate tax manager should make periodic reviews in these instances.

The preparation of tax returns can be centralized or decentralized, depending on the circumstances and economics. If the data are in the local office, it may be advantageous to have the return prepared locally, with appropriate review by the tax manager's staff. Local preparation may have the advantage of greater familiarization with the applicable operations. With the availability of remote data processing capabilities, there may be advantages to centralized preparation. The records to be maintained and the format of the tax information work papers should be prescribed by the corporate tax department. Some companies, for example, have the payroll department of each entity prepare payroll tax returns, since the detail information is readily available from the payroll records. In this case, it would be prudent for the tax manager to review, sign, and file the returns.

Some of the advantages in centralization of the tax responsibilities include:

1. More economical.
2. Permits a higher degree of specialization.
3. More efficient use of tax resources—library, services, etc.
4. Promotes uniformity.
5. More flexibility in handling a workload.

In some circumstances, a centralized tax organization may be at a disadvantage because of lack of sufficient contact with local taxing authorities or the local operating entities. This can be overcome by proper planning and making the effort to achieve the proper relationships with the local taxing authorities and the local operating personnel. As in many other areas, good communication is a key ingredient in making the relationships work well.

In developing a tax organization, it is possible to decentralize some phases of the tax function, particularly when the various types of taxes and related records are considered. However, in these instances, guidance, instructions, and review must come from the central tax department. Unique and complex challenges associated with international tax operations are discussed in Chapter 18.

59-4 FUNCTIONS OF THE TAX MANAGER

The functions of the tax manager will vary with the organization. However, the following is an indication of the extent of responsibilities assigned to the tax department in a generic large company:

1. Develop, recommend, and implement approved plans for an effective tax management program applicable to all elements of the corporation. Insure that the company complies with all applicable laws, rules, and regulations related to all applicable taxes.

2. Select personnel, assign duties, and establish appropriate control over tax department activities.

3. Plan for the administration of local or branch office tax functions.

4. Maintain organized and adequate tax records, prepare forms and working papers, and establish an adequate filing system.

5. Prepare a complete tax manual establishing procedures and responsibilities.

6. Evaluate the effect of tax laws, regulations, rulings, and court cases on the company's tax liabilities and potential business activities.

7. Develop policies and procedures to minimize the company's overall tax liability.

8. Determine that the company has filed all tax returns, reports, and declarations required by law.

9. Review and recommend action concerning all tax adjustments proposed by the various taxing authorities or by the company's independent public accountants and represent the company, or cause the company to be represented, in all negotiations affecting the company's tax liabilities.

10. Initiate action, as directed, to obtain IRS approval, when required, with respect to changes in accounting methods, and procedures and matters pertaining to retirement or savings plans.

11. Prepare and prosecute in cooperation with tax accounts and/or attorneys as appropriate, or cause to be prepared and prosecuted, formal protests, claims, petitions, or court actions with respect to disputed tax matters involving the company, coordinating all such activities with other concerned functions, such as legal and accounting.

12. Initiate action when required, to obtain IRS rulings regarding the company's tax liability.

13. Analyze the tax implications of proposed acquisitions to determine present or potential problems and examine tax carry back or carry over possibilities.

14. Provide information concerning federal, state, local, and foreign tax matters, based on the advice of counsel. where necessary.

15. Analyze the tax effect of legal documents affecting the company and render advice regarding appropriate action to minimize the company's tax liabilities with respect thereto.

16. Review the annual and strategic plans to develop the tax liabilities for each period and incorporate the results into the approved plan.

17. Prepare, analyze, and review book accounting for income taxes.

59-5 TAX COMMUNICATIONS

It is imperative that the tax department communicate with *all* units of the organization. To be effective, the tax department should be involved in management decisions on business acquisitions, pension plans and fringe benefit programs, financing agreements, establishment of foreign entities, including their location and form, contract terms related to taxes, divestitures of business units or products, location of facilities (state, city, or county), various kinds of business arrangements such as joint ventures or consulting agreements, and any other activity that could possibly have a federal, foreign, state, or local tax impact. Tax planning includes making all levels of management aware of the significance of tax considerations in the decision-making process. An effective tax manager will create the opportunity to present sound and creative tax ideas to members of the management team on a regular basis.

The tax manager must have an intimate knowledge of the company and its products, services, and general business operations. To achieve this, he must be in touch with all concerned and develop a network of communications sensitive to situations having potential tax implications. Success is when the tax department is consulted before, during, and after the fact on transactions involving tax matters.

Another area for tax planning is involvement in the company's short- and long-term planning process. The legitimate deferral of taxes is a significant source of funds for many companies, and this fact should be recognized in the development of the company's business plans. a consistent "effective tax rate" also helps in the comparison of year-to-year earnings.

Much of the communication and coordination is with the accounting department, because tax returns are based on or reconciled to the accounting records.

59-6 TAX RECORDS IN GENERAL

The tax laws are so complex, so great in number, and of such variation that it is not practical to keep in mind all the provisions of the laws and all the facts of the business which have a direct bearing on taxability. Consequently, the company must have the necessary records if the desirable tax planning is to be consummated, if management is to have a clear view of the tax situation, or if any degree of administrative control is to be successful. The penalties for oversight or incompetence may be severe.

The nature of the records will be governed by the relative complexity of the tax issues. Broadly speaking, however, certain records are needed for administrative control purposes, to support the tax returns, and to meet the specific requirements of the law. Tax records may be grouped into four major classifications:

1. Tax calendar.
2. Information records.
3. Working paper files.
4. Supporting ledgers.

Although these will be reviewed briefly, it should be understood that in the final analysis, their suitability and timeliness depend on an alert staff. Records cannot be suggested that will meet all needs for all times. Flexibility must be provided in the organization. Thus, if sales are made in a new state and require the collection of a sales tax, the tax staff must take the initiative to get the necessary sales analysis by states or the necessary accounts established. There is no substitute for such initiative, and it should be recognized and rewarded to foster its presence in the organization.

59-7 TAX CALENDAR

An administrative tool needed in most companies is a tax calendar. It is a schedule that serves as a reminder to those responsible regarding the due dates of filing tax returns,

Figure 59-2 Tax Calendar.

Federal (Consolidated)

	Jan	Feb	Mar	Apr	May	Jun	Jul	Aug	Sep	Oct	Nov	Dec
Estimated Payments for Calendar Year 19__				15		15			15			15
Tax Return for YE 12/31/__			15*			15*			15 Final			
Mail Tax Packages to Subs and Divisions For YE 12/31/__	15											
Preliminary Analysis of Liability Account for Financial Statements	31	28										
Discuss Retirement, 5500 etc. Package To Be Completed												
Final Analysis of Liability Account for YE 12/31/__										X		
[1] Form 599-1099		28										
[2] Federal Use Tax—Highway Vehicles							31					
[2] Federal Use Tax—Commercial Aircraft							31					
[2] Federal Excise Quarterly Return	31			30			31			31		
[2] Federal Excise Monthly Prepayment (2nd)	31	28	31	30	31	30	31	31	30	31	30	31
[2] Federal Excise Monthly Prepayment (1st)	15	15	15	15	15	15	15	15	15	15	15	15

* May Extend—Not extension of time to pay total tax liability, only extension of time to file final return
[1] Tax organization will file Federal, New York, Mass., Washington, D.C. and North Dakota
[2] Whenever applicable during tax year

1432

preparation of various reports, payment of tax bills, hearing dates, audit dates, assessment dates, and any key tax event. The tax calendar may take several forms; however, the most common is illustrated in Figure 59-2.

When computerized, the value of such a schedule is enhanced because automatic reminders can be programmed into the system so that all levels of the staff are made aware of upcoming deadlines. Daily status reports are also available to help management plan and prioritize the work.

Such records may be perpetual records with revisions made as needed, or the calendar can be prepared in December of each year for the following year. Regardless of the form, the important point is the need to provide a systematic and dependable means of bringing the subject or tax event to the proper attention of those responsible in a timely manner. The advantages are clear—avoid penalties, interest, and embarrassment for filing late returns and late payments.

59-8 TAX INFORMATION RECORDS

Another basic type of record may be called a "tax information record" and represents a summary of the tax law and related matters as they affect the business. Such a record is used as a reference when preparing the tax return. The information may be stored in a computer or filed on cards, on loose-leaf sheets, or even as part of the tax manual. Information to be available concerning each tax are the following:

1. Name of tax.
2. Description of tax.
3. Basis.
4. Tax rates.
5. Exemptions from tax.
6. Time of filing return.
7. Return form number and name.
8. Approximate time required for preparation.
9. To whom return is sent and when.
10. Source of data for return preparation.
11. Why company is subject.
12. The tax accounting.
13. Procedure, including any special instructions.
14. Penalties for nonpayment.

A page from a tax information record is shown in Figure 59-3. Where such data are part of a tax manual, it may be helpful to include other information, such as exhibits of the forms, perhaps a simple form of a tax calendar, general comments, and the procedure for handling. If the manual is sufficiently large, a table of contents is desirable.

Since tax law is changing constantly, it is imperative that these information records be updated on a regular and frequent basis.

Figure 59-3   Tax Information Record.

Information Needed		Federal Income Tax	California Franchise Tax
Description and type		Income	Privilege of doing business Tax based on income
Locations covered		All except foreign legal entities, insurance co, etc.	All locations—domestic and foreign
Who must file		All domestic legal entities— consolidated	All legal entities, domestic and foreign—combined reporting
Where filed (address)		IRS Fresno, California	Franchise Tax Board Sacramento, California
Form number		1120, plus any other applicable forms	100, plus any other applicable forms
Period(s) covered		19__	19__
Due Dates		3/15/__ Extensions through 9/15/__	3/15/__ Extensions through 9/15/__
Rate or basis of tax		35%	9.3%
Approximate amount of tax		$5,000,000	$300,000
Information required		Information requested in package: Detailed income statement and balance sheet and a comprehensive analysis of differences between book income and taxable income. Calculation of alternative minimum taxable income (AMTI).	Information requested in package: 1. Apportionment data by state regarding property, payroll, and sales 2. Comprehensive analysis between federal and state taxable income
Source of data		Books and records of various profit centers	Books and records of various profit centers
Account charged		Number 260	Number 256
Contacts	(Company)	Chief financial officers at various profit centers	Same as federal
	(External)	1. Company outside counsel 2. Company independent auditors 3. Company tax consultants	Same as federal
File index		Federal file #3, drawer 2	California file #1, drawer #1
Comments		1. Insure compliance with "DISC" regulations 2. Revise scheduling for asset depreciation range and guideline depreciation 3. Consider tax law changes to be enacted for the next year	1. Insure appropriateness of certain companies included in combined report regarding the "completed contract method of accounting for tax purposes" 2. California does not allow "DISC" deferral

59-9 TAX WORKING PAPERS AND FILES

The two types of records just discussed are of a reference nature. The remaining records may be considered as the working files and contain the figures and facts incident to the year-to-year returns. These operating files are of an infinite variety and are comparable to the permanent files and working paper files in connection with an audit. The central theme is a complete and orderly record of how the amount of tax was determined each year, the payment dates, and so on. These files may include information such as:

1. Record of payments.
2. Record of assessments.
3. Reconciliations of tax data to the records.
4. Copies of the return.
5. Refund record, including basis.
6. Correspondence on the tax.
7. Research supporting the tax position or positions taken.

Such files must be prepared on the basis of the judgment of the tax manager based on the needs of the company.

59-10 THE INTERNAL REVENUE CODE AND RECORD REQUIREMENTS

Under any tax law, the challenge is to set up records that will provide the necessary data with the minimum cost and effort. In considering record keeping requirements under federal tax laws, the principal source of data is the Internal Revenue Code and corresponding regulations. The law is very general in regard to records, and Congress has specifically granted to the Commissioner of the Internal Revenue Service the power to prescribe records that are necessary to determine the liability of the tax or will properly reflect the taxable income of the business. There are, however, various specific record keeping requirements, especially where foreign owned companies are involved. Care should be taken to insure that these record keeping requirements are met.

59-11 DIFFERENCES BETWEEN INCOME TAX ACCOUNTING AND BOOK ACCOUNTING

The principal source of information required for federal income tax returns is, of course, the regular accounting records of the company. Although tax accounting and book accounting are more or less similar in many respects, there are three important respects in which these two differ:

1. Income and expenses specifically excluded for tax purposes. Examples include the tax-exempt income from government bonds, contributions in excess of the allowable maximum, and 50% of meals and entertainment expenses.

2. Differences resulting from the recognition of time when losses or income may be recognized. The reserve positions and related charge-offs are included in this group.

3. Differences in cost bases. This general category would include differences in depreciation rates and bases, treatment of maintenance and repair costs, and inventory valuation.

A vital schedule for the controller's review is the reconciliation of net income contained in the federal income tax return. This schedule reveals the major differing points between tax and book accounting.

(a) ALTERNATIVE MINIMUM TAX

The Tax Reform Act of 1986 (TRA) had as one of its objectives the elimination of situations in which Congress perceived that companies were reporting healthy earnings and paying little tax on them. Certain deductions were eliminated; for example, the investment tax credit was repealed. But also the alternative minimum tax (AMT) was significantly strengthened. It is a parallel system of taxation that has a broader income base than the regular tax system. It must be calculated in addition to the "regular" tax. If the AMT is larger, it is the tax to be paid; if the regular tax is larger, then that must be paid instead. As with the rest of TRA, AMT is a complex specialized area. (See Chapter 18 for a more detailed explanation.)

Controllers should be aware of the following:

1. The alternative minimum tax must be calculated each time a regular federal income tax calculation is made.

2. Adjustments have to be made in calculating AMT, the biggest of which is changes to less accelerated methods of depreciation than are allowed for regular tax purposes.

3. Further adjustments are necessary in bringing income more in line with a company's adjusted current earnings or ACE. These adjustments use an earnings and profits basis in calculating income and include a further depreciation adjustments for assets placed in service before 1994.

The effect of all this is that while before the TRA, the controller had to reconcile between book and tax net income. Now there is a third and fourth net income called AMTI (alternative minimum taxable income) and ACE (adjusted current earnings), that must also be developed and reconciled to the other two. These calculations are very important to monitor, since they can have a direct effect on how much tax a company pays.

(b) TREATMENT OF THESE DIFFERENCES IN THE RECORDS

The controller and tax manager are faced with the problem of how these differences should be treated in the records. It is necessary to maintain a running record of these differences and to reconcile book and tax figures if a company is to secure the maximum tax benefits. The maintenance of such records is essential to insure that the company will not overlook a tax deduction to which it could properly be entitled to in a subsequent year. However, it does not follow that a completely independent set of books need be maintained for tax purposes.

Some useful generalizations can be made, based on the three groups of differences listed in the preceding section. The first group of items presents no significant problem of carry over from year to year. Based on specific provisions of the IRC, they are excluded from income or expense. They appear on the reconciliation, and usually ends the matter, unless any excess of a limitation can be carried forward. Where such items are numerous, it may be found helpful to establish separate accounts, or groups of accounts, for such income or expenses. A good example of this is a separate for the tax limited meals and entertainment deduction.

The second group represents those items taken into the accounts earlier or later than is required or permitted under the statute or regulations. Thus, although a provision for a contract loss may be set up on the records of a company, for tax purposes, only actual costs may constitute allowable deductions. An analysis of the accounts that would probably be prepared for the independent auditors anyway, will provide much of the necessary temporary difference data for tax purposes. Supplementary worksheets generally are sufficient for this group, and separate ledgers will usually not be necessary.

The major challenges arise when different cost bases are used. In any business, an analysis is necessary to determine whether a separate series of supplementary accounts need be maintained. Where substantially different depreciation bases and rates are used, separate ledgers may be required. It is becoming more common for companies to maintain the depreciation records in a computerized data base downloaded from the company's fixed asset ledger.

Due to its complexity and varying methods of calculation, it is important to maintain detailed and accurate depreciation and fixed asset records. The burden of proof about the correctness of the depreciation charges is clearly on the taxpayer. Although no particular form of record is required, it is essential that permanent records be maintained to reconcile the book and tax depreciation amounts from year to year.

59-12 A PROPER CLASSIFICATION OF ACCOUNTS

When designing the accounting records and account structure or chart of accounts, the controller should be aware of and consider the accounting data required for the preparation of tax returns. If provision is made in the establishment of the accounting records, it can facilitate the tax work and protect the interests of the company from a tax viewpoint.

It is desirable to include in the account structure the capability for detailed analysis of various accounts. For example, repairs and maintenance should be structured so that it can be readily demonstrated that additions to a plant have not been expensed. Also, where practical, a segregation of nontaxable income and non allowable deductions should be made in the accounts. Such an account structure will save valuable time and increase the efficiency in preparing an accurate tax return.

59-13 OTHER TAXES

In addition to the federal income tax, there are many other taxes that the business enterprise is subject to, such as:

State income taxes	State franchise taxes
Excise taxes	Real property taxes
Sales taxes	Use taxes
Personal property taxes	Stamp taxes
Payroll Taxes	City taxes
Gross receipt taxes	Foreign income taxes
Gasoline taxes	Value added taxes

The tax manager must be alert in developing procedures to accumulate the required date in an economical, efficient, and timely manner. He or she must also be current on all changes in statutes and regulations. Provision must be made in the procedures so that applicable refunds are obtained and excessive overpayments not be made.

59-14 INCOME TAXES AND BUSINESS PLANNING

Management must consider the tax consequences in its business planning for the future. The tax manager should be involved in the detailed planning process so that business arrangements or contracts include the proper provisions to maximize the tax savings. This may be in the form of reduced taxes or deferred tax payments that can enhance considerably the cash flow for the company. Another area of planning consideration is the payment of foreign taxes; these taxes can generate a credit against the federal income tax liability. This area, however is very complex and care should be taken in foreign tax credit planning.

59-15 SPECIAL TAX REPORTS

The controller or tax manager has a responsibility to see that the significant tax burden placed on the company is communicated to all concerned. Generally speaking, most key people in the company are not always aware of the significant amounts paid out in the various forms of taxes assessed to the company. In some companies, the tax manager prepares an annual report for management detailing the amounts of all of the taxes paid during the year. It is also sometimes prudent to include in this report how much taxes have been saved through the use of planning ideas. These types of reports can be a useful communication tool to let others in the company know the true extent of the tax burden and what's being done about it.

In summary, the controller should continually evaluate the tax planning and tax compliance to insure that the company minimizes the overall tax burden through adequate knowledge of regulations, trends, decisions, and their application to the challenges facing the business.

59-16 GAAP FOR INCOME TAX ACCOUNTING

See Chapter 18 for a discussion on FASB Statement No. 109, which has superseded both APB 11 and FASB Statement No. 96. FASB Statement No. 109 represents a shift to the liability method of accounting for income taxes.

59-17 SELECTED REFERENCES

Blake, John Freeman, *Financial Planning After the Tax Reform Act of 1986.* Washington, DC: Bureau of National Affairs, 1988.

Implementing the New Rules on Accounting for Income Taxes, FASB Statement 109. Denver, CO: Ernst & Young LLP, 1992.

Internal Revenue Code. Chicago, IL: Commerce Clearing House, Inc. Version, 1993.

Sommerfeld, Ray M., Hershel M. Anderson, Horace R. Broch, Silvia A. Madeo, and Valarie Milliron, *An Introduction To Taxation.* New York: Harcourt, Brace, Jovanovich, 1988.

Strassels, Paul N., *The 1986 Tax Reform Act, Making It Work for You.* Homewood, IL: Dow Jones-Irwin, 1987.

CHAPTER 60

Insurance Records and Procedures

60-1 INTRODUCTION

A prime requirement of a well-managed business is that a sound and complete risk management program be developed and implemented. Some insurance coverage is compulsory, such as workers' compensation; some may be required for contractual reasons, such as fire insurance required under a bank loan agreement; and some is carried because of the risks inherent in the business. Management has the responsibility to protect the shareholders' and creditors' interests, and prudent judgment dictates that certain risks should be covered by insurance.

The responsibility for a well-defined insurance program should be assigned to a key financial executive so that it receives the proper attention and direction. Much of the information required for insurance purposes is found in the accounting records, so it is logical that the risk management function be assigned to a financial officer. In any event, the controller should be involved and understand the insurance requirements and procedures and provide appropriate information and guidance.

In most large companies, the insurance function will normally be assigned to a professional insurance and risk manager, reporting to the chief financial officer, treasurer, or controller. This executive will be charged with the responsibility of implementing procedures consistent with the corporate policy and objectives relative to insurance. The policy statement may be set forth by the board of directors or delegated to a member of senior management such as the chief financial officer for his action. The policy may include financial limits for risk assumption or retention, self-insurance parameters, uninsurable risks, captive insurance companies, and organization responsibilities.

The function of the risk manager is to develop a plan with implementing procedures to control the risks to which the company is exposed. He should work closely with other functional groups such as engineering, safety and health, personnel and industrial relations, production, plant security, legal, and accounting. It is imperative that he have a thorough knowledge of the company and its operations, products, and services so that he can evaluate the risks and exposures properly. The risk manager must be sure that the company is adequately protected against all significant losses.

The risk and insurance manager is responsible to provide qualified assistance and guidance to all elements of the company, including divisions, subsidiaries, and other operating units. The procedures must recognize the total corporate organization structure to control risks and insure an objective loss prevention program. Some of the specific functions to be performed include:

1. Ascertain and appraise the risks.
2. Estimate the probability of loss due to the risks.
3. Insure compliance with state, federal, and local requirements regarding insurance.
4. Select the optimum method of protecting against loss, e.g., insurance.
5. Work with insurance agents, brokers, consultants, and insurance company representatives.
6. Supervise a loss prevention program, including planning to minimize losses from anticipated crises.
7. Maintain appropriate records for all aspects of insurance administration.
8. Continually evaluate and keep current on all company operations and activities.
9. Keep abreast of new techniques being developed in the field of insurance.

In smaller companies where a full-time risk insurance manager cannot be economically justified, it may require that the financial executive responsible for insurance seek outside assistance. There are available many competent professional insurance people outside the company, such as these:

1. Insurance agents.
2. Brokers.
3. Underwriters.
4. Insurance company specialists.
5. Consultants.

(a) RISK CONTROL

A prudent risk manager will act in advance to reduce the risk of losses occurring. The following techniques can be used:

1. *Duplicate.* The company can retain multiple copies of records to guard against the destruction of critical information. In addition, key systems such as local area networks, telephone systems, and voice mail storage can be replicated at off-site locations to avoid a shutdown caused by damage to the primary site. For

example, airlines maintain elaborate backup systems for their seat reservation databases.

2. *Segregate.* The company can split up key assets such as inventory and distribute it to multiple locations (e.g., warehouses). For example, the military maintains alternate command centers in case of war.

3. *Prevent.* The company can institute programs to reduce the likelihood and severity of losses. For example, some companies invite OSHA to inspect their premises and report on unsafe conditions; the companies then correct the issues to reduce their risk of loss. If a company requires employees to wear hardhats in construction areas, then a falling brick may still cause an accident, but the hardhat will reduce the incident's severity. Examples of prevention techniques include improving lighting, installing protective devices on machinery, and enforcing safety rules.

60-2 THE INSURANCE PROCEDURE

To protect adequately the properties and financial position of a business, it is mandatory that a well-planned insurance procedure or program be developed covering all vital points. Whether starting new or reviewing the existing insurance coverage, the following procedure outlines the points that must be considered:

1. Determine the insurable hazards of the company through a complete review of the properties and operations. This would include a review not only of physical properties and processes but also of contractual obligations, leasehold requirements, and governmental regulations. The review can be performed with insurable hazard checklists that are provided by insurance companies, or with the aid of a consultant, or by reviewing historical loss data provided by the company's insurance firm. Also, the company's policies and procedures should be reviewed to identify any practices that may create exposure.

2. Match each hazard with a method of dealing with it. The possible options for each hazard are avoidance, reduction of the hazard, retaining the hazard (self-insurance), or transferring the risk to an insurance company. The selection of an option should occur after a cost-benefit analysis that weighs the cost of each hazard against the cost of avoiding it, factoring in the probability of the hazard's occurrence.

3. Select desirable underwriters and brokers.

4. Determine the types of policies and bases or valuations to be used.

5. Establish proper reporting procedures and the necessary records, including an insurance manual.

6. Introduce a program for control or reduction of hazards and rates.

7. Make provision for a periodic audit or review of coverage.

This outline covers the essential phases of an insurance program. However, the actions need not follow in the order enumerated. The selection of a broker or underwriter, for example, may precede other steps.

60-3 SELECTING THE INSURABLE HAZARDS TO BE COVERED

The groundwork for a sound insurance program lies in an intelligent analysis of the company's properties and operations to determine the extent and types of exposures. This analysis should not be superficial review; it is preferable and necessary that narrative write-ups, worksheets, and schedules be prepared showing all details. The more effort invested in this analysis at an early point will save time later on and will assist in determining the extent of required insurance coverage. Checklists available from outside sources, such as professional associations, state regulators, brokers, and underwriters, can be a substantial help in identifying the risks to be evaluated. There are several matters to be covered in the analysis and review:

1. *Buildings and Equipment.* The type of construction, the location, and the hazards to which exposed should be listed. Each structure and major piece of equipment should be listed separately. The current condition in terms of wear and tear should be determined and the replacement cost evaluated. Assistance may be required from other experts such as engineers, safety, and construction personnel.

2. *Other Assets.* The purpose of a sound insurance program is to protect all the properties of the company. A review should be made of the following:

   a. Cash and negotiable securities.

   b. Inventories—raw material, goods or work-in-process, and finished goods. In particular, raw materials that contain toxic substances should be segregated, and the related storage and handling procedures should be reviewed.

   c. All receivables.

   Exposure to all types of losses, whether by fire, flood, theft, or otherwise should be considered and evaluated for appropriate insurance coverage.

3. *Business Interruption.* It may be advisable to protect the company against loss of profits and continuing expenses during the time the business may be wholly or partially shut down as the result of a specified hazard or peril. Insurance covering business interruption (use and occupancy) should be considered and obtained when conditions warrant.

4. *Liability to Other Parties.* A review should be made of possible loss or damage to other parties and to their properties by reason of company products, services, or operations or acts of employees. This analysis should include a review of all contracts, sales orders, purchase orders, leases, and applicable laws to determine what commitments have been undertaken and what exposure exists.

Such an analysis will indicate the general nature of the risks, hazards, and exposures faced by the company. The next step is to obtain any additional facts required and formulate an insurance plan or program consistent with the company's policy on risk management and insurance. Decisions will need to be made relative to risk assumption, avoidance, or insurance for the following:

1. Is insurance coverage available and in what form for each type of hazard? Generally, most losses are insurable. The broker or insurance specialist can assist in this area.

2. What is the extent of the exposure? It is assumed that most of the information will be available from the detailed analysis made. It involves a consideration and evaluation of the probability of loss, the degree, and the frequency. For example, what is the greatest amount of cash to be transported to the bank daily or weekly? Or what are the maximum, minimum, and average inventories at particular locations and what is the length of time?

3. What is the cost of insurance protection against the hazard? What are the alternatives of reducing risks, risk retention, deductibles, or retrospective rating plans?

4. What would be the cost effectiveness of the company becoming a qualified self-insurer for one or more of the types of insurance?

The determination of whether to insure against a risk is a matter of weighing the probability of loss against the insurance premium cost. The probable maximum loss from a single occurrence and the annual cost of all such losses should be compared to the premium. If the difference is slight, it may not be economical to insure. Generally, most companies will insure against catastrophic losses that will have an adverse affect on the financial position of the company.

60-4 SELECTING THE BROKER AND UNDERWRITER

The methods of selecting an insurance broker have become more complex because of the range of services needed and the requirements involved. It is not as easy as selecting a broker based on the lowest bid. The broker can contribute a great deal in developing the strategy for an overall insurance program. The broker's viewpoint can be extremely important in adding expertise and dimension to the in-house insurance capability. In selecting a broker or an insurance company, the following factors should be given due consideration:

1. Comparative insurance rates.
2. Types of coverages.
3. Financial strength of the insurer.
4. Reputation and facilities for service—specialized expertise in such areas as engineering, safety, inspection programs, location of service compared to risks involved.
5. Availability of representatives to be responsive to the requirements in a timely manner.
6. The ability to grow with the company in new product areas and technologies.
7. Underwriting knowledge.
8. Postloss service.

There are several types of insurance companies, and the net insurance cost may vary considerably among them. Each may serve the needs very well, but it is desirable to investigate the areas of capabilities discussed in this chapter before placing the insurance contracts. The types of companies include the following:

1. *Mutuals.* Each policyholder is an owner, and earnings are distributed as dividends. If net losses result, policyholders may be subject to a levy of extra assessments. In most cases, however, nonassessable policies may be issued.

2. *Stock Companies.* Such corporations are similar to other corporations in that earnings not retained in the business are distributed to shareholders as dividends and not to policyholders.

3. *Lloyds of London.* This underwriter operates under special authority of the English Parliament and may write insurance coverage of a nature that other companies will not underwrite. This organization also provides the usual types of coverages.

4. *Reciprocal Organizations.* These are associations of insured operated by a manager. Advance deposits are made, against which are charged the proportionate cost of operations.

5. *Captive Insurance Companies.* A stock insurance company formed to underwrite risks of its parent company or in some cases a sponsoring group or association.

Another way to categorize insurance companies is by type of services offered. For example, a *monoline company* provides only one type of insurance coverage. A *multiple line company* provides more than one type of insurance. A *financial services company* provides not only insurance but also financial services to customers.

It is important that the financial condition of the insurance companies under consideration be assessed before a final choice is made. The insurance industry in the United States had losses in the mid-1980s, with some companies hurt more than others. There are several sources where information is available to help in this financial evaluation.

1. Published financial statements.

2. Comparative ratings as published by A. M. Best Company, and the Standard and Poors corporate ratings.

3. Financial ratios that have been provided to insurance regulators. These are available through the Insurance Regulatory Information Systems (IRIS). They are also summarized annually by the A. M. Best Company's "Best's Trend Report."

In addition to these financial analyses, information can be gathered (from trade journals, participation in professional associations, etc.), about signs of a company in trouble, such as high turnover of management and slow payment of claims.

A company can also use *self-insurance*—this is when the company deliberately plans to cover losses from its own resources rather than those of an insurer. It can be appropriate for cases of small losses where the administrative cost of using an insurer exceeds the amount of the actual loss, when the company has sufficient excess resources available to cover even the largest claim, when excessive premium payments are the only alternative, or when insurance is not available at any price. A form of *partial self-insurance* is to use large deductibles on insurance policies, so that the company pays for all but the very largest claims. Finally, the company can create *a captive insurer* that provides insurance to the parent company. Captive insurers can provide coverage that is tailored to the parent organization, and can provide less dependence on the vagaries of the commercial insurance market. A captive insurer variation is a *fronting program,* when a parent company buys insurance from an independent insurance company, which then reinsures the exposure with a captive of the parent company; this technique is used to avoid licensing the captive insurer in every state where the parent has business, though the captive insurer must still be authorized to accept reinsurance. Fronting also allows the parent company to obtain local service from the independent insurance company while shifting the exposure to the captive company. In whatever form the self-insurance may take, the controller should set aside funds as *loss reserves* to pay claims as they arise.

In some states, the company can become a self-insurer for workers' compensation. To do so, the company must qualify under state law as a self-insurer, purchase umbrella coverage for catastrophic claims, post a surety bond, and create a claims administration department to handle claims. The advantages of doing this are lower costs (by eliminating the insurer's profit) and better cash flow (since there are no up-front insurance payments). The disadvantages of doing this are extra administration costs and the cost of qualifying the company in each state in which the company operates.

60-5 TYPES OF INSURANCE

There is a great variety of types of insurance coverages, and a detailed discussion of each is beyond the scope of this book. It is suggested that an insurance broker be consulted and a handbook on insurance coverages be obtained. In general, most industrial firms require the following types of insurance coverages:

1. *Commercial Property Insurance.* The basic form of this insurance covers losses from fire, explosions, windstorms, hail, vandalism, and several other perils. The broad form includes everything covered by the basic form, plus falling objects, weight of snow, water damage, and some causes of building collapse. Optional coverages include an inflation escalator clause, replacement of destroyed structures at the actual replacement cost, and coverage of finished goods at their selling price instead of their cost.

2. *Comprehensive Crime.* This insurance covers property theft, robbery, safe burglary, premises burglary, and employee dishonesty; in the case of employee dishonesty, the company purchases a fidelity bond, which can either cover a named person, a specific position, or cover all employees. Some policies will also cover ransom payments.

3. *General Liability Insurance.* This insurance covers claims involving accidents on the company's premises,products, services, agents, or contractors. An *umbrella policy* usually applies to liability insurance, and provides coverage after primary coverage is exhausted. An umbrella policy normally has few exclusions.

4. *Workers' Compensation.* This insurance provides medical and disability coverage to workers who are injured while performing duties related to their jobs. The insurance is mandatory, the employer pays all costs, and no legal recourse is permitted against the employer. There are wide variations in each state's coverage of workers' compensation, including levels of compensation, types of occupations that are not covered, and the allowability of negligence lawsuits.

5. *Comprehensive Auto Liability.* This insurance coverage is usually mandatory and requires minimum coverage of bodily injury and property damage.

6. *Business Interruption.* This insurance allows the company to pay for its continuing expenses and in some cases will pay for all or part of its anticipated profits.

7. *Inland Marine Insurance.* This insurance covers company property that is being transported. Examples of covered items would be trade show displays and finished goods being shipped.

8. *Ocean Marine and Air Cargo Insurance.* This insurance covers the transporting vehicle (including loss of income due to loss of the vehicle), liability claims against the vehicle's owner or operator, and the cargo.

9. *Group Life, Health, and Disability Insurance.* There are several types of life insurance; *split-dollar life insurance* covers an employee and its cost is split between the company and the employee, *key person insurance* covers the financial loss to the company in case a necessary individual dies, and a *cross-purchase plan* allows the co-owners of a business to buy out the share of an owner who dies. Health insurance typically covers the areas of hospital, medical, surgical, and dental expenses. Disability insurance provides income to an individual who cannot work due to an injury or illness. The disability insurance category is generally subdivided into short-term disability (payments while recovering one's health following an injury or illness) and long-term disability (continuing payments with no anticipation of a return to work).

10. *Boiler and Machinery Insurance.* This insurance covers damage to the company's boilers and machinery, as well as payment for injuries caused by the equipment. Boiler and machinery insurance providers normally review the company's equipment and issue a report recommending safety improvements.

11. *Directors and Officers Insurance.* This insurance provides liability coverage to corporate managers with respect to actions taken while acting as an officer or director of the corporation.

The risk and insurance manager should review the various types of policies and understand the need and the value to determine that the company is properly covered. Care should be exercised in reading the terms and conditions of each policy to determine that the coverage is required. For example, an *all-risk agreement* will cover all losses except those specifically excluded, while a *named-perils agreement* will cover losses caused by a specific list of perils (e.g., earthquakes, meteorites, and tsunamis). Many insurance policies also have *exclusions,* which are losses not covered by the insurance policy. For example, a policy may exclude losses due to nuclear war. In addition, policies may exclude specific properties. For example, an insurance company may agree to insure a corporation's headquarters building, but not its warehouses located in another country.

60-6 INSURANCE RECORDS—GENERAL

Insurance recordkeeping is vital to ascertain that adequate insurance coverage has been obtained and is being administered properly. The exact types of records will vary and will be influenced by the kinds of insurances, size and nature of the operation, policy reporting requirements, and management needs. A well-designed system of insurance records will include the following:

1. *Policy Information.* For each insurance policy the following data should be listed:
   a. Type of insurance coverage.
   b. Insurer.
   c. Effective dates.
   d. Policy number.
   e. Broker.
   f. Abstract of coverage, including exclusion, if any (Figure 60-1).
   g. Policy register (Figure 60-2).
   h. Reporting requirements with due dates.
   i. Rates, premiums, refunds.
2. *Administrative Records.*
   a. Binder records—to indicate coverage, pending the issuance of the policy.
   b. Location records—outlining the insurable values at various company or plant locations.

Figure 60-1   Abstract of Insurance Coverage.

Policy No.: X01730778
Type of Coverage: Liability
Description of Coverage:
Comprehensive general liability insuring worldwide legal liability for bodily injury and property damage arising out of premises, automobiles, malpractice, contracts, nuclear energy, and nonaviation products
Limits:
$1,000,000 bodily injury per occurrence
$1,000,000 property damage per occurrence and aggregate
Excludes:
Automobile coverage
Jobs 5005 and 5006
Premium Payments:
Quarterly payment, annual audit
Claims:
Reported to broker—New York office
Claims desk—Joe Smith, telephone (XXX) XXX-9121
Broker:
J&H—Policy service—Ted Jones, telephone (XXX) XXX-9125
Insurer:
Aetna

Figure 60-2 Insurance Policy Register.

Policy No.	Insurer	Policy Period	Premium	Type of Coverage	Broker	File Reference
M3961816	Great American	2-24-X0 2-24-X3	$75,000	Marine Cargo	M&M	A 12.7
02-8311	American Home	8-25-X0 8-25-X1	$70,000	Fidelity Bond	J&J	D 1.3

c. Value report files—a summary of the insurable values when a reporting form of policy is used.

d. Transportation logs—location and trip records of all vehicles, including autos, trucks, and aircraft.

e. A sensitivity or tickler file to signal key events:

1. Expiration dates of policies.

2. Reporting dates.

3. Premium payment dates.

4. Notice of hearing, settlement, rebates.

5. Special accounting adjustments.

6. Binder follow-up for policies.

7. Inspections.

8. Operations reviews.

f. Property appraisals:

1. Actual cash value.

2. Replacement cost.

g. Expense distribution records. It is necessary to maintain detailed records indicating the payments, accruals, write-off to expense, allocation to operating units, refunds, and bases utilized for making charges or allocations.

h. Records of losses, settlements, and premiums. A historical record should be maintained of premium costs compared to losses and indicate any trends that may be developing. The records should be used to determine the necessity for insurance coverage and the need for changes in the loss control program.

i. Claims files. An effective claims guide and files should include the following:

1. Status of each claim—dates, hearings, etc.

2. Support and documentation for each claim filed.

3. Claims representatives.

4. Emergency plans.

5. Claims procedures.

6. History file on closed claims.

7. Reserves established.

j. Insurance manual. An administrative guide should be prepared setting forth the detailed procedures for handling all aspects of the insurance function. It should include instructions about the procurement of insurance coverage, reporting forms, claims procedures, specific instructions on accounting requirements, allocation methods and bases for charging out premiums to operating units, and historical data for reviewing insurance coverages. A flexible system should be used so that the manual can be updated easily and maintained on a current basis. In some cases it may be advisable to maintain separate manuals for various types of insurance—property insurance, group insurance, liability insurance.

60-7 CLAIMS ADMINISTRATION

It is essential that responsibility for maintaining adequate claim records and establishing claim procedures be clearly defined. Proper attention must be directed to establishing good controls to insure that losses are reported promptly and properly substantiated.

A claims procedure guide should be prepared, particularly in a complex or decentralized organizational structure. Such a guide will contain at the minimum:

1. Names of claims representatives for handling each line of insurance.
2. Outside adjusters to be used in specialized cases.
3. Key personnel to be notified.
4. Instructions for analyzing claims to determine remedial measures that need to be taken.
5. Establish guidelines for the accumulation of loss data and documentation of claims.
6. An audit program covering claims to insure the compliance with procedures, the adequacy of documentation, and the expertise with which claims have been settled.

Completed and well-organized loss records are essential to proper claims administration. It is necessary to know what kinds of losses are occurring, where they happen, what the causes are, and what their significance or extent is. Risk management personnel should make periodic reviews of all losses to determine trends and develop corrective action plans. Minimizing the losses is an economic objective of all risk managers. Loss records that contain the proper data, are kept in a simple form, and, when properly analyzed, can contribute to lower insurance premiums and increased profitability for the business.

Should a loss occur, provision should be made for such matters as these:

1. Segregation and safeguarding of damaged material from undamaged until the adjusters have completed their review.
2. Preparation of detailed lists of all losses—including book cutoffs to determine inventory values, estimates, appraisals, and replacement costs.

3. Development of accounting techniques to accumulate all costs incidental to the loss, such as claims preparation, security and property protection, cleanup, repair costs, property identification, and storage costs.

The claims records should provide for proper and timely follow-up of all aspects of a claim. If claims are not recorded in the formal accounting records, memo records should be established so that a control total of claims outstanding can be maintained to insure that each claim is resolved.

Some companies have found it to be cost-effective to have certain claims administered by outside service companies, quite often the insurance carrier itself. Usually high-volume, low-cost-per-unit items such as medical benefits claims are in this category. When outside services are used, the controller must establish with the provider the controls to be followed and the reports to be prepared. Very often the reports are similar to those prepared when claims are administered in-house. Periodic audits of the outside claims-processing operation should be made by the insuree to satisfy itself that things are being handled in a controlled and effective manner.

60-8 INSURANCE AUDITS AND REVIEWS

A well-developed insurance program needs to be reviewed periodically to determine the adequacy of insurance coverage relative to the current risks in the business. An examination should be made at least annually by the risk manager with other executives to insure that changed conditions have been considered in all policy renewals. It may also be appropriate from time to time to engage an outside independent consultant with expertise in auditing insurance programs, assessing risks, controlling insurance costs, and reviewing claims, and have a comprehensive report prepared.

60-9 ANNUAL INSURANCE REPORT

To keep management informed on risks and insurance coverages, it may be desirable to prepare an annual insurance report. It is suggested that the report be in summary form for easy reference and include such items as these:

1. Descriptions of insurance—a listing of the various types of insurances, with brief descriptions of the coverage.
2. Comparison of insurance costs—a listing of insurance coverages showing the limits of coverage and costs for each of the last five years.
3. Uninsured risks.
4. Analysis of reserves for self-insured risks.
5. Anticipated changes in the insurance program for the next year—rates, coverages, insurance markets, safety, increased exposures, and risks.
6. Loss and recovery analyses and if significant related to premiums.
7. General comments on overall adequacy of insurance program and appropriate recommendations for management's consideration.

60-10 OTHER CONSIDERATIONS

The recordkeeping functions of insurance management can be readily adapted to computers. There are several software computer programs available for purchase to prepare computerized loss reports, analyze claims, and allocate insurance costs. The utilization of such computer programs will allow the professional risk manager to more effectively use his time in technical insurance matters, make more timely decisions, and reduce insurance costs.

Inflation is a vital concern of business and must be considered in managing an insurance program. Underwriters have developed inflation-guarded endorsements that provide some protection; however, insurable values must also be considered in the light of continuing rates of inflation.

60-11 SELECTED REFERENCES

Greene, Mark R., *Risk and Insurance*. Cincinnati, OH: South-Western Publishing Co., 1977.

Hampton, John J., *Essentials of Risk Management and Insurance*. New York: American Management Association, 1993.

Head, George L., *The Risk Management Process*. New York: Risk and Insurance Management Society, 1978.

McIntyre, William S., IV, and Jack P. Gibson, *101 Ways to Cut Your Business Insurance Costs Without Sacrificing Protection*. New York: McGraw-Hill, 1988.

Williams, C. Arthur, Jr., and Richard M. Heins, *Risk Management and Insurance*. New York: McGraw-Hill, 1981.

INDEX